ABNORMAL PSYCHOLOGY

ADVISING EDITOR IN PSYCHOLOGY

Salvatore R. Maddi
The University of Chicago

ABNORMAL PSYCHOLOGY

Second Edition

Richard H. Price
University of Michigan

Steven Jay Lynn
Ohio University

The Dorsey Press

Chicago, Illinois   60604

ISBN 0-256-03248-3

Library of Congress Catalog Card No. 85–72826

Printed in the United States of America

1 2 3 4 5 6 7 8 9 0 MP 3 2 1 0 9 8 7 6

To Barbara Lynn, Harriette Lesser
and
Grace and the late Clarence Price

Preface

We have written *Abnormal Psychology* as a text for the first course in abnormal psychology. The book was written in the belief that the field of abnormal psychology is one in which the human, scientific, and clinical concerns of psychology converge. As a consequence, our book views human problems alternately from the point of view of the scientist, the clinician, and the human experience of the individual.

Because we believe a text in abnormal psychology can emphasize clinical insight, scientific rigor, and an appreciation of individual psychological experience, we have provided balanced coverage of clinical and scientific aspects of abnormal psychology. Clinical case examples or research examples introduce each chapter. They are offered to help the student appreciate the excitement of the study of abnormal behavior. We have offered detailed accounts of particular research programs or studies because we believe that learning about abnormal psychology involves in part telling the story of research. Telling the research story helps the student understand *how* we know *what* we know about abnormal psychology. We offer both clinical case histories to provide rich examples of the phenomenon of abnormal behavior, and scientific case histories that help the student to appreciate the excitement of scientific inquiry.

A number of major theoretical perspectives in the field of abnormal psychology continue to stimulate research and to provide conceptual frameworks for alternative modes of treatment. Our text presents coverage of each of these theoretical perspectives including biological, dynamic, learning, sociological, and humanistic points of view. We have introduced these perspectives early in the book, and they are later discussed in chapters concerned with specific disorders. We have also described new developments in some of these perspectives such as the emergence of object relations theory in the dynamic approach. We note the strengths and weaknesses of each perspective and show how they can illuminate our understanding of various disorders and also provide a conceptual rationale for different treatment strategies.

Features of the new edition. In writing the second edition of *Abnormal Psychology* we wanted to write a book that instructors would feel was solid and balanced but that students would find genuinely interesting and engaging. In fact, while the text is a revision, it should be thought of as virtually a new book. We have completely reorganized and revised the text and have added new chapters on stress, adjustment, and post traumatic stress disorders (Chapter 5), anxiety, somatoform, and dissociative disorders

(Chapter 7), disorders of childhood and adolescence (Chapter 10), disorders of the later years (Chapter 11), and organic disorders and mental retardation (Chapter 12).

Each chapter in the new edition begins with an engaging case study, and boxes have been appropriately placed in each chapter providing clinical examples of various disorders and special examples of important research programs. *Abnormal Psychology* also has new coverage on legal issues, cognitive approaches to understanding abnormal behavior, new developments in psychoanalytic theory, a discussion of eating disorders, and coverage of the role of stress and coping in abnormal behavior.

Psychology as a discipline has contributed much to our understanding of the treatment of abnormal behavior. We have also tried to reflect the extent and detail of this new understanding and the real achievements that have been made by providing extensive coverage of treatment methods. We have devoted four chapters to the treatment of abnormal behavior that link the student's understanding of various disorders to an understanding of their treatment.

Organization of the text. Abnormal Psychology is divided into six parts. The first part, *Approaches to Understanding Abnormal Behavior,* offers historical, theoretical, and scientific perspectives to the student. Abnormal psychology is seen in the light of important historical and cultural changes that have shaped the way we view those suffering from psychological disorders. The chapter on perspectives shows how biological, learning, sociological, dynamic, and humanistic perspectives shape our thinking and inspire scientific research. The strengths and weaknesses of each perspective are detailed, and how they shape the way we see abnormal behavior is illustrated. Chapters 3 and 4 on research, classification, and diagnosis provide the student with an understanding of how scientists attack the problem of definition and description and how they search for the causes of abnormal behavior.

Part 2, *Stress, Coping, and Disorders of Adaptation,* shows how new research on stress and coping help us understand abnormal behavior in the context of human adaptation. The chapter on psychophysiological disorders includes new coverage on the rapidly developing field of behavioral medicine. Part 2 concludes with a discussion of anxiety, somatoform, and dissociative disorders.

Part 3, *The Major Disorders,* examines the affective disorders and schizophrenia. Descriptive research, etiological research, and treatment approaches are described in detail. Both chapters provide clinical and research examples with particular emphasis on the new developments in biological research.

Part 4, *Abnormal Behavior through the Life Span,* introduces three entirely new chapters and moves from an examination of disorders of childhood and adolescence through disorders of the later years, and also describes organic disorders and mental retardation. This new section provides coverage of research and treatment at both the early and the later periods of the life span.

Part 5 focuses on *Personality Disorders and Social Deviation.* The chapter on personality disorders includes new material on a range of personality disorders including borderline personality. The chapters on unconventional sexual behavior and substance use disorders have been extensively updated to include new research in these rapidly developing, and sometimes controversial, fields of research.

Finally, in Part 6 on *Treatment,* we have sampled a broad spectrum of treatment strategies and the research that evaluates their effectiveness. Our survey begins with insight-oriented therapies and moves to behavioral and cognitive-behavioral approaches.

We then survey the more socially oriented group, family and community based approaches, and conclude with an updated survey of biological treatment of abnormal behavior.

In writing this book, we have incurred many debts, both intellectual and personal. In addition to the numerous reviewers, consultants, and colleagues who have shared their ideas and insights with us and who are listed below, we would like to thank Jennifer Lynn, Mary Price, Allan Harkness,

Kim Dudley, Judith Rhue, Jeffrey Gfeller, Donald Penzien, James Moore, Erroll Liebowitz, Michael Nash, David Frauman, John P. Garske, Barbara Lynn, David Zakin, Barbara Strane, Amy Fuhst, Patti Fuhst, and Danielle Hogston. Each has contributed in ways that make *Abnormal Psychology* a richer and more absorbing learning experience.

Richard H. Price
Steven Jay Lynn

REVIEWERS OF *ABNORMAL PSYCHOLOGY*

Thomas F. Cash, Ph.D.
Old Dominion University

Ira S. Cohen, Ph.D.
State University of New York

Carl J. Cooper, Ph.D.
Curry College

James C. Coyne, Ph.D.
University of Michigan

Charles Dicken, Ph.D.
San Diego State University

Kenneth France, Ph.D.
Shippensburg University of Pennsylvania

Donald K. Fromme, Ph.D.
Oklahoma State University

Bernard S. Gorman, Ph.D.
Nassau Community College

John M. Grossberg, Ph.D.
Marquette University

Richard T. Grow, Ph.D.
Weber State College

Nancy A. Gulanick, Ph.D.
University of Notre Dame

Scott B. Hamilton, Ph.D.
Colorado State University

George L. Hampton III, Ph.D.
University of Houston Downtown College

Yvonne Hardaway Osborne, Ph.D.
Louisiana State University

Gail F. Hicks, Ph.D.
Eastern Washington University

Alfred D. Kornfeld, Ph.D.
Eastern Connecticut State University

Patricia B. Lacks, Ph.D.
Washington University

Alan R. Lang, Ph.D.
Florida State University

Ben Lebovits, Ph.D.
Roosevelt University

Donald B. Leventhal, Ph.D.
Bowling Green State University

William K. Levy, Ph.D.
Manchester Community College

Andrea Lindstrom, Ph.D.
University of Wisconsin–Green Bay

Robert J. Leuger, Ph.D.
Marquette University

William R. Miller, Ph.D.
University of New Mexico

Michael T. Nietzel, Ph.D.
University of Kentucky

Katherine M. Noll, Ph.D.
Elmhurst College

Joseph Palladino, Ph.D.
Indiana State University

Richard Pomazal, Ph.D.
University of Pittsburgh at Bradford

William F. Sacco, Ph.D.
University of South Florida

Pamela Clift Scavio, Ph.D.
California State University

Norman A. Scott, Ph.D.
Iowa State University

Norman N. Silverman, Ph.D.
Loyola University of Chicago

Charlotte Simon, Ph.D.
Montgomery College

James D. Smrtic, Ph.D.
Mohawk Valley Community College

Felicia F. Thomas, Ph.D.
California State Polytechnic University

Contents

Part One
Approaches to Understanding Abnormal
Behavior

1. **Introduction and Historical Views of Abnormal Behavior**   2
   Introduction, 3
   Abnormal Behavior as a Scientific
      Problem, 4
         The Search for Scientific Definitions, 4
         The Role of Culture, 5
         Description, Measurement and
            Classification, 7
         The Scientific Search for Causes and
            Explanations, 7
   Abnormal Behavior as a Human
      Problem, 8
         Social and Human Cost, 8
         Abnormal Behavior as a Personal
            Problem, 8
   Abnormal Behavior in Historical
      Perspective, 9
         Prehistory: Spirit Possession and
            Exorcism, 10
         The Classical Period, 11
         The Middle Ages: Witches and Their
            Hunters, 13
         Beginnings of the Modern Era, 16

2. **Perspectives on Abnormal Behavior**   32
         What's Wrong with Me? 33

Perspectives in Conflict, 34
Models and Perspectives in Scientific
   Thinking, 34
The Biological Perspective, 35
      Biological Research: The Example of
         Schizophrenia, 36
      Biological Treatments, 37
The Biological Perspective and the
   Idea of Mental Illness, 38
The Dynamic Perspective, 39
      Overview of Psychoanalytic Theory, 40
      Fundamental Assumptions of the
         Dynamic Perspective, 40
      Mental Structures, Conflict, and
         Anxiety, 41
      Defense Mechanisms, 43
      Current Trends: Object Relations
         Theory, 44
      Dynamic Explanations, 45
The Learning Perspective, 46
      Classical Conditioning, 47
      Instrumental Conditioning, 48
      Social Learning and Modeling, 50
      Overview of the Learning Perspective, 52
The Sociological Perspective, 53
      Norms and Roles and the Career of a
         Mental Patient, 53
      Being Sane in Insane Places: An Example
         of the Sociological Perspective in
         Action, 54
      Reactions from the Medical Community to
         the Sociological Viewpoint, 56

Contributions of the Sociological
Perspective, 57

The Humanistic Perspective, 57

Carl Rogers' View of the Development of
Abnormal Behavior, 57

Maslow: Self-Actualization and
Psychological Help, 58

**Using Perspectives to Understand and
Treat Abnormal Behavior, 61**

3. **Research Strategies in the Study
of Abnormal Behavior**   **64**

Introduction, 65

**Thinking about the Causes of
Abnormal Behavior, 66**

Perspectives and Causes, 66

Types of Causes, 67

Research Methods, 68

Case Histories, 68

Correlational Approaches, 69

Experimental Methods, 74

Experimental Analogues, 74

Single-Subject Experimental
Strategies, 76

High-Risk Methods, 76

Meta-Analysis: Combining Results, 78

**Ethical Issues in the Study of
Abnormal Behavior, 80**

Ethical Research Principles of
Psychologists, 81

4. **Assessment and Diagnosis of
Abnormal Behavior**   **84**

Introduction, 85

Psychological Assessment, 86

Clinical Interview, 87

Psychological Tests, 88

Behavioral Observation, 94

Neuropsychological Assessment, 95

Computer-Assisted Assessment, 96

Problems in Assessment, 98

Test Results and Illusory Correlation, 99

Sex-Role Stereotypes, 100

Race Differences, 101

Diagnosis and Classification, 102

Uses of Diagnosis, 103

The Diagnostic and Statistical Manual of
the American Psychiatric Association:
(DSM III), 104

Strengths and Weaknesses of DSM
III, 105

Part Two
Stress, Coping, and Disorders of
Adaptation

5. **Stress, Adjustment Disorders,
and Posttraumatic Stress
Disorders**   **110**

Introduction, 111

**Theoretical Perspectives on Stress,
Coping, and Adjustment, 111**

Definitions of Stress: Stimulus, Response,
Transaction, and Appraisal, 113

**Clinical Reactions to Life
Stressors, 113**

Adjustment Disorders, 113

Posttraumatic Stress Disorder, 117

**Factors Affecting Vulnerability to
Stress, 122**

Hardiness: Challenge, Commitment, and
Control, 122

The Protective Effects of Social
Support, 123

Graded Exposure: Natural Healing
Process of the Mind, 124

**Treatment and Prevention of Stress-
Related Disorders, 126**

Stress Inoculation Training, 126

Treatment for Rape Victims, 127

6. **Psychophysiological Disorders
and Behavioral Medicine**   **130**

Introduction, 131

Behavioral Medicine and Health
Psychology, 132

Definition of Psychophysiological
Disorders, 133

Range of Psychophysiological
Disorders, 134
Distinguishing Features, 135
Headache, 136
Tension Headaches, 138
Migraine Headaches, 138
Overview of Treatment, 139
Essential Hypertension, 142
Factors Causing Hypertension, 142
Overview of Treatment, 143
Coronary Heart Disease and the Type
A Behavior Pattern, 145
The Type A Behavior Pattern, 145
Overview of Treatment, 146
Asthma, 147
Overview of Treatment, 149
Ulcers, 150
Overview of Treatment, 152
Chronic Pain, 152
Overview of Treatment, 154
Theories of Psychophysiological
Disorders, 155
Psychoanalytic Perspective: The Specific
Emotion Hypothesis, 157
Learning Perspective: Autonomic
Learning and the Vicious Circle, 157
Stress Perspective, 158
Social Perspective: Stressful Life
Events and Coping, 160

7. **Anxiety, Somatoform, and
Dissociative Disorders**   **164**
Introduction, 165
Neurosis and DSM III, 165
Anxiety Disorders, 166
Phobias, 166
Anxiety States, 170
Obsessive-Compulsive Disorders, 171
Somatoform Disorders, 172
Somatization Disorders, 173
Conversion Disorders, 174
Dissociative Disorders, 175
Psychogenic Amnesia, 177
Fugue, 177
Multiple Personality, 177

Treatment Strategies, 179
Psychodynamic Approach, 179
Learning and Behavioral Approaches, 180
Biological Approaches, 181

Part Three
The Major Disorders: Affective Disorders
and Schizophrenia

8. **Affective Disorders and
Suicide: Description,
Research, and Treatment**   **184**
Introduction, 185
Depression, 186
Clinical Picture, 186
Manic Episodes, 188
Clinical Picture, 188
Classification of Affective
Disorders, 191
Bipolar Disorders, 191
Major Depression, 192
Theories of Depression, 192
Psychoanalytic Theory, 193
Biological Theories, 196
Cognitive Theories, 198
An Interpersonal Perspective, 201
Treatment of Affective Disorders, 204
Biological Treatments, 205
Psychotherapy, 206
Suicide, 210
Factors Associated with Suicide Risk, 210
The Predictors of Suicide, 213
Suicidal Intention and Ideation, 215

9. **Schizophrenia: Description,
Research, and Treatment**   **218**
Introduction, 219
Description, 220
History, 221
Clinical Description, 222
Course over Time, 224
Diagnosis and Classification, 227
DSM III Diagnostic Criteria, 227
Alternative Approaches to
Classification, 228

Experimental Research on Schizophrenic
Behavior, 230

Schizophrenics Report on Their Own
Experiences, 231

Determinants of Schizophrenia, 232

The Biological Search for Causes, 234

Family and Society as Contexts for
Schizophrenia, 241

An Integration of Perspectives:
Vulnerability, 247

Treatment, 249

From Hospital to Community, 249

Drug Treatment, 250

Treatment Combinations, 252

Part Four
Abnormal Behavior through the Life Span

10. **Disorders of Childhood and
Adolescence**   **258**
Judith Rhue and Steven Jay Lynn

Introduction, 259

Behavioral and Emotional Disorders of
Childhood, 261

Reactive Attachment Disorder of
Infancy, 261

Childhood Depression and Suicide, 262

Childhood Fears and Phobias, 264

School Phobia/Separation Anxiety
Disorder, 266

Disorders of Elimination, 268

Functional Enuresis, 268

Functional Encopresis, 270

Attention Deficit Disorder, 271

Developmental Features, 271

Incidence and Clinical Picture, 272

Child Abuse, 273

Physical Abuse, 274

Specific Developmental Disorders, 275

Pervasive Developmental
Disorders, 279

Infantile Autism, 279

Childhood Onset Pervasive
Developmental Disorder, 283

Disorders of Later Childhood and
Adolescence, 286

Conduct Disorder, 286

Anorexia Nervosa, 288

Bulimia, 291

11. **Disorders of the Later Years**   **296**
Jean Drevenstedt and David Russell

Sara D.—A Confused Lady, 297

Thoughts about Aging, 299

The Elderly—Our Fastest Growing
Population, 299

Who is Old? 301

Concepts of Age, 301

Effects of Senescence versus Effects of
Disease, 303

Prevalence of Mental Disorders in
Older People, 304

Areas of Adaptation in Aging, 305

Frameworks for Understanding
Behavioral Changes with Aging, 305

A Response-to-Stress Framework, 306

A Learning Framework, 307

A Social-Breakdown Framework, 309

Special Concerns of the Elderly, 310

Retirement, 310

Housing, 311

Family Transitions, 311

Mobility, 311

Health, 312

Sensory Changes, 313

Bereavement, 313

Psychopathological Problems of a
Functional Nature, 314

Depression, 315

Pseudodementia, 318

Suicide, 318

Paranoia, 320

Hypochondriasis, 323

Substance Misuse and Abuse, 324

Anxiety, 326

Schizophrenia, 326

Psychological Assessment of the
Elderly: Issues and Problems, 327

Cognitive Assessment, 328
Interventions with the Elderly, 329
Psychotherapy with the Elderly, 330
Chemical and Biological Treatments, 332

12. **Organic Disorders and Mental
    Retardation   336**
    *Paul Sandberg, Judith Rhue, and
    Steven Jay Lynn*

Introduction, 337
The Brain, 339
Disorders Resulting from Trauma, 345
Dementia, 346
Cortical Dementing Disorders, 347
Subcortical Dementing Disorders, 350
Delirium, 357
Other Organic Syndromes, 357
Seizures, 358
Mental Retardation, 362
A Brief History, 362
Definition and Classification, 362
Explanations, 365
Chromosomal Abnormalities, 365
Abnormalities of Amino Acid
    Metabolism, 366
Infections and Toxic Agents, 367
Fetal Alcohol Syndrome, 367
Premature Birth, 368
Trauma, Injury, and Other Causal
    Factors, 369
Environmental and Cultural-Familial
    Retardation, 369
Approaches to Remediation, 369
Prevention, 369

Part Five
Personality Disorders and Social Deviation
13. **Personality Disorders   374**
    David Zakin and Richard Price

Overview of the Personality
    Disorders, 375
Compulsive Personality, 377
Clinical Picture, 377
Childhood Origins, 377

Histrionic Personality, 379
Clinical Picture, 379
Cognitive Style, 380
Childhood Origins, 380
The Antisocial Personality, 382
Clinical Picture, 382
Theory and Research, 384
Narcissistic Personality, 387
Clinical Picture, 387
Childhood Origins, 388
Paranoid Personality, 390
Clinical Picture, 390
Cognitive Style, 393
Childhood Origins, 393
The Paranoid and Society, 394
Borderline Personality, 395
Clinical Picture, 395
Childhood Origins, 397
Diagnostic Utility and Future Trends, 399
Treatment, 400

14. **Unconventional Sexual
    Behavior and Dysfunction   402**
Overview, 403
The Gender Identity Disorders and the
    Paraphilias, 405
Transsexualism: A Gender Identity
    Disorder, 405
Description, 405
The Etiology of Transsexualism: The
    Development of Atypical Gender
    Identity, 407
Unconventional Choice of Sexual
    Object or Activity: The
    Paraphilias, 410
Unconventional Choices of Sexual
    Object, 410
Unconventional Choices of Sexual
    Activity, 412
Psychoanalytic and Learning Theory
    Explanations and Treatment
    Implications, 417
Psychoanalytic Explanations, 417
Learning Theory Explanations, 418
Homosexuality, 420

Is Homosexuality a Psychological
Disorder? 420
The Kinsey Report, 421
The San Francisco Study, 422
Diversity of Experience, 425
Explanations, 426
Treatment of Ego-Dystonic
Homosexuality, 427

Psychosexual Dysfunction and Its
Treatment, 428
The Sexual Response Cycle, 428
Explanations and Assessment, 431

The Psychosexual Dysfunctions, 432
Inhibited Sexual Desire, 432
Inhibited Sexual Excitement, 432
Inhibited Orgasm, 432
Premature Ejaculation, 433
Functional Dyspareunia and Functional
Vaginismus, 433

Direct Therapy for Sexual
Dysfunction, 433
Mutual Responsibility, 434
Information and Education, 434
Attitude Change, 434
Eliminating Performance Anxiety, 435
Increasing Communication and
Effectiveness of Sexual Technique, 435
Changing Destructive Lifestyles and Sex
Roles, 435
Prescribing Changes in Behavior, 435

New Directions and Issues in Sexual
Dysfunctions and Their
Treatment, 436
Diversity of Applications, 436
Sexual Dysfunctions and
Homosexuals, 436
The Effectiveness of Sex Therapy, 437

15. **Substance Use Disorders**   440
Overview, 441
Common Factors in Drug Use, 443
Substance Abuse and Dependence, 445

The "Social Drugs", 447
Alcohol, 447
Treatment, 453
Tobacco, 458

The Illegal Drugs, 460
Marijuana, 460
Short-Term Effects of Marijuana, 461
Some Consequences of Marijuana Use, 462
The Opiate Narcotics: Heroin, 465
Cocaine, 470

The Prescription Drugs, 473
Amphetamine, 473
The Sedative-Hypnotics:
Barbiturates, 475

Explanations of Drug Use, 477
The Psychodynamic Perspective, 477
A Sociocultural View, 478
The Learning Perspective, 479
Genetic and Biological Evidence, 480

Part Six
Treatment

16. **The Insight Therapies**   486
Barbara Lynn and Steven Jay Lynn

Overview, 487
The Client, 489
The Therapist, 490
The Therapeutic Relationship, 490

Insight Therapies, 491
Dynamic Psychotherapy, 491
Psychoanalysis, 492

Developments in Psychoanalysis, 495
The Neo-Freudian Tradition, 495
Ego-Analytic Psychotherapy, 499

Humanistic-Existential
Psychotherapy, 501
Rogers' Client-Centered Therapy, 502
Gestalt Therapy, 505
Logotherapy, 508

Similarities and Differences, 509
Is Psychotherapy Effective? 511

17. **The Behavior and Cognitive
Behavioral Therapies**   514
Overview, 515
Techniques of Behavior Therapies, 517
Systematic Desensitization, 517
Confrontation Procedures, 521

Modeling, 523

Assertion Training, 524

The Token Economy: Achievement Place—A Treatment Program for Delinquent Adolescents, 526

Aversion Therapies, 529

Self-Control Procedures, 531

Cognitive Behavioral Therapies, 533

Issues in Contemporary Psychotherapy, 536

Insight versus Behavior Therapy: The Issue of Outcome, 536

Common Factors in Psychotherapy, 537

The Trend toward Eclecticism and Integration, 539

18. Group, Family, and Community-Based Treatment 542

Overview of Group Therapy, 543

Curative Factors in Group Therapy, 544

Psychodrama, 547

T-Groups, 548

Encounter Groups, 549

Marathon Groups, 552

Evaluation of Group Therapy, 552

Family Therapy, 554

Structured Family Therapy, 557

Evaluation of Family Therapy, 557

New Ways of Helping: Mental Health and the Community, 558

Community Mental Health Today, 559

From Mental Hospital to Community, 562

Crisis Intervention, 565

The Promise of Prevention, 566

Legal and Ethical Issues in the Treatment of Abnormal Behavior, 571

Ethical Problems in Identifying High-Risk Cases, 571

Ethics and Psychotherapy, 571

Involuntary Commitment, 573

Patients' Rights and Informed Consent, 574

The Insanity Defense, 576

19. The Biological Treatments 580

Introduction, 581

Antipsychotic Drugs, 582

Side Effects and Complications of Antipsychotic Drugs, 583

Prescribing Antipsychotic Medication: Treatment Considerations, 585

Antidepressant Drugs, 586

Lithium, 588

Antianxiety Drugs, 590

Some Concluding Comments on Chemotherapy, 590

Electroconvulsive Therapy, 593

Psychosurgery, 594

Glossary, 601

References, 617

Name Index, i

Subject Index, ix

List of Figures

2-1 Relationship among the Unconscious, Preconscious, and Conscious Domains of Psychological Life 41

2-2 Classical Conditioning Paradigm 47

2-3 The Development of Defensive Behavior 58

3-1 Three Possible Correlational Relationships between Previous Life Events Reflecting Loss and Rated Current Severity of Depression 70

3-2 Percent of Time Ann Spent in Social Interaction with Adults and with Peers during Approximately Two Hours of Each Morning Session 77

3-3 Design for a Study Using High-Risk Samples of 200 Children with Schizophrenic Mothers and 100 Low-Risk Control Subjects 78

3-4 The Results of the Smith and Glass Study of the Effectiveness of Psychotherapy 79

4-1 Six of the Bender-Gestalt Figures—Originals and Copies by a 62-Year-Old Brain-Damaged Man 97

5-1 Model of Factors Relevant to Victim Recovery 121

5-2 Mortality Varies Not Only with Age But with the Number of Connections in One's Social Network 124

5-3 Tonic Skin Conductance as a Function of Events Leading up to and Following a Jump for Novice and Experienced Parachutists 125

7-1 Example of Glove Anesthesia (a Conversion Disorder) and Pattern of Anesthesia That Would Occur If Actual Neurological Damage Were Involved 175

8-1 Catecholamine Activity in Neurotransmission 197

8-2 Interactional View of Depression 202

8-3 Modification of Depressive Behavior Using Reinforcement and Extinction Techniques Taught to Family Members 209

9-1 Course of Disorders over Time 225

9-2 Models of Causation in Schizophrenia 233

9-3 Lifetime Risks of Developing Schizophrenia Are Largely a Function of How Closely an Individual is Genetically Related to a Schizophrenic and Not a Function of How Much Their Environment Is Shared 237

9-4 Polygenic Threshold Model of Schizophrenic Causation 238

9-5 The Dopamine Hypothesis in Schizophrenia 239

9-6 Vulnerability Model of Schizophrenia 248

9-7 Percent Distributions of Inpatient and Outpatient Care Episodes in Mental Health Facilities, by Type of Facility: United States, 1955 and 1973 250

9-8 Relapse Rates of Total Group of 128 Schizophrenic Patients after Nine Months with Their Families 254

10-1 Relative Frequency of Various Fear Responses 265

10-2 Writing Sample from Dyslexic Child 278

10-3 Drawing Sample from Autistic Child, Age Three 281

11–1 Number of Persons Age 65 and Older Compared with Total Population, from 1900   300

11–2 Percent of the Total Population in the Older Ages: 1900 to 2040   301

11–3 Persons by Age and Sex: 1980 and 1970   302

11–4 Schematic Diagram Illustrating Relationships between Stressors and the Behavioral and Physiological Responses   307

11–5 Coping Resources   308

11–6 A Systems Representation of SBS as Applied to Old Age with Negative Inputs from the External Social System   310

11–7 Suicide Rates in the United States in Relation to Age and Race (1974)   319

12–1 Decision Tree for Organic Brain Syndromes   340

12–2 Chemical Messages Are Sent by Neurotransmitters That Are Secreted from the End of the Axon of the Sending Neuron onto the Dendrite of the Receiving Neuron at the Synapse   341

12–3 Comparison of the Brain Structures of Five Animals   342

12–4 The Three Layers of the Human Cerebral Cortex Are Evolutionarily Distinct and Incompletely Integrated   343

12–5 The Human Neocortex with Brain Areas Defined   344

14–1 Heterosexual-Homosexual Rating Scale   423

14–2 The Human Sexual Response   430

15–1 Effects of Different Amounts of Alcohol   451

15–2 The Speed Cycle   475

17–1 Mean Number of Snake-Approach Responses Performed by Subjects before and after Receiving Different Treatments   525

17–2 Weight Profile of Four Women Undergoing Behavior Therapy for Overeating   533

19–1 Number of Psychiatric Patients in VA Hospitals   583

List of Tables

2-1 Personal Structure According to the Psychoanalytic Perspective   42

2-2 Perspectives on Abnormal Behavior   60

4-1 Excerpts from a Mental Status Interview of a 29-Year-Old Male   88

4-2 Psychiatric Evaluation Form—Diagnostic Version   89

4-3 Personality Characteristics Associated with Elevations on the Basic MMPI Scales   90

4-4 Illustration of the Use of Patterson's (1969) System of Behavioral Observation: Thirty Seconds in the Life of a Boy Named Kevin   90

4-5 Major Diagnostic Headings in DSM III   105

5-1 Summary of Target Phobias for 25 Treatment Candidates   127

6-1 Comparison of Organic and Psychophysiological Disorders with Conversion Reactions and Hypochondriasis   136

6-2 Somatic Treatment of Psychophysiological Disorders   137

6-3 Social-Readjustment Rating Scale   160

8-1 DSM III Symptom Criteria for a Depressive Episode   187

8-2 Parallels between Learned Helplessness and Depression   200

9-1 DSM III Criteria for the Diagnosis of Schizophrenia   226

9-2 Schizophrenic Subtypes Identified in DSM III   227

9-3 Characteristics of Process and Reactive Schizophrenia   229

9-4 Illustration of Possible Outcomes of Twin Studies Indicating Different Degrees of Genetic Involvement in Schizophrenia   235

9-5 Analysis of Symptom Sensitivity to Phenothiazines   252

10-1 Differential Patterns of School Phobia Symptoms   268

10-2 A Comparison of the Characteristics of Early Infantile Autism with Childhood Onset Pervasive Developmental Disorder   284

10-3 Classifications and Descriptions of Conduct Disorders Based on DSM III Criteria   287

11-1 Signs and Symptoms of Depression in the Elderly   316

11-2 Development of Paranoid Disorders in Late Life   321

11-3 Goals of Assessment of the Aged   328

12-1 Diagnostic Criteria for Delirium   357

12-2 Seizure Classification   360

12-3 New Terms and Concepts in Common Use   363

12-4 DSM III Diagnostic Categories of Mental Retardation Based on IQ Score, Parallel Educational Terms, and Expected Level of Intellectual, Vocational, and Social Functioning   364

13-1 The DSM III Classification of Personality Disorders   377

14-1 Overall Results of the Masters and Johnson Treatment Program (1970)   433

15-1 Lifetime Prevalence and Recency of Use, by Age, in Percent   442

17-1 Behaviors and the Number of Points They Earn or Lose   529

18-1 Suggestions for Possible Primary Prevention Programs Applicable to Various Institutions and Agencies   569

19-1 The Spectrum of Antipsychotic
Side Effects   584

19-2 Generic and Brand Names of
Antidepressant Drugs   586

19-3 Factors Correlating with
Likelihood of Response to
Tricyclic Antidepressants   586

19-4 Rate of Recurrence of Mania or
Depression in Bipolar Manic-
Depressives with Lithium or
Placebo   589

Part One

Approaches to Understanding Abnormal Behavior

1

Introduction and Historical Views of Abnormal Behavior

Abnormal Behavior as a Scientific Problem
The Search for Scientific Definitions
The Role of Culture
Description, Measurement, and
Classification
The Scientific Search for Causes and
Explanations

Abnormal Behavior as a Human Problem
Social and Human Cost
Abnormal Behavior as a Personal
Problem

Abnormal Behavior in Historical Perspective
Prehistory: Spirit Possession and Exorcism
The Classical Period
The Middle Ages: Witches and Their
Hunters
Beginnings of the Modern Era

Summary

INTRODUCTION

At the age of 21 Alma is brought in by her parents for a psychological consultation. In the last few years she has shown excessive weight loss and experienced increasing difficulties with her family. Alma was raised in the Midwest by parents who tried to provide the best for her and her older sister. Her father was a successful businessman while the mother participated in many social activities. At first glance the parents' lives appeared to be trouble free. However, both parents were frustrated by careers that fell short of their original hopes and ambitions. The parents found solace in their daughters, whom they provided with the best educational opportunities. However, Alma's older sister did not live up to the parents' high expectations and was only average in her abilities. Disappointed, the parents turned to Alma for honor and accomplishment and expected great things of her. At first, Alma lived up to her parents' expectations and excelled in school, sports, and the arts; she was also very popular with her peers. Suddenly, at age 15, Alma rebelled and for the first time did not compliantly go along with her parents' plans for her. Listen to Bruch (1978) as she describes the case:

> At 15 Alma had been healthy and well-developed, had menstruated at age 12, was 5 feet 6 inches tall, and weighed 120 pounds. At

that time, her mother urged her to change to a school with higher academic standing, a change she resisted; her father suggested that she should watch her weight, an idea that she took up with great eagerness, and she began a rigid diet. She lost rapidly and her menses ceased. That she could be thin gave her a sense of pride, power, and accomplishment. She also began a frantic exercise program, would swim by the mile, play tennis for hours, or do calisthenics to the point of exhaustion. Whatever low point her weight reached, Alma feared that she might become "too fat" if she regained as little as an ounce. There were many efforts to make her gain weight, which she would lose immediately, and she had been below 70 pounds most of the time. There was also a marked change in her character and behavior. Formerly sweet, obedient, and considerate, she became more and more demanding, obstinate, irritable, and arrogant. There was constant arguing, not only about what she should eat but about all other activities as well.

When she came for consultation she looked like a walking skeleton, scantily dressed in shorts and a halter, with her legs sticking out like broomsticks, every rib showing, and her shoulder blades standing up like little wings. Her mother mentioned, "When I put my arms around her I feel nothing but bones, like a frightened little bird." Alma's arms and legs were covered with soft hair, her complexion had a yellowish tint, and her dry hair hung down in strings. Most striking was the face—hollow like that of a shriveled-up old woman with a wasting disease, sunken eyes, a sharply pointed nose on which the juncture between bone and cartilage was visible. When she spoke or smiled—and she was quite cheerful—one could see every movement of the muscles around her mouth and eyes, like an animated anatomical representation of the skull. Alma insisted that she looked fine and that there was nothing wrong with her being so skinny. "I enjoy having this disease and I want it. I cannot convince myself that I am sick and that there is anything from which I have to recover" (Bruch, 1978, pp. 2–3).

Alma suffers from *anorexia nervosa*, a psychological disorder characterized by the relentless pursuit of excessive thinness. Her preoccupation with being thin is so great that she is oblivious to the damage she is doing to her body, damage that can result in death even after normal weight is restored. How are we to understand why a healthy 15-year-old girl suddenly becomes so afraid of gaining weight that she allows herself to live in a constant state of semistarvation? Does the explanation lie in the family's excessive demands and expectations, Alma's unconscious wishes and fears, sociocultural pressures, or perhaps even in some underlying physiological disturbance? There is not necessarily just one correct answer that experts agree upon. Instead, the explanation depends upon the underlying conception of the causes and dynamics of abnormal behavior. In the pages that follow, you will encounter dozens of additional examples of behavior that appear odd, puzzling, or difficult to explain. Some will represent severe forms of abnormal behavior while others may be relatively commonplace. Describing what is known about such behaviors and their treatment is the purpose of this book.

Most of us would agree that the behavior described in the above example is in some ways abnormal. But it is often not that easy to distinguish between the normal and abnormal. Whether a behavior is considered normal or abnormal depends not only upon our definition of abnormality but also the context in which it occurs. Understanding abnormal behavior is therefore both a scientific and a human problem. In our discussion we will examine various forms of abnormal behavior from a scientific perspective. At the same time we will focus on the experience of the individual as he or she copes with the demands of living in a changing society. Let us first consider some of the scientific issues raised in the study of abnormal behavior.

ABNORMAL BEHAVIOR AS A SCIENTIFIC PROBLEM

The Search for Scientific Definitions

As we shall soon see, scientists from many different disciplines have attempted to understand the causes of abnormal behavior and have searched for effective methods of treatment. Biochemists, anthropologists, psychologists, and many other scientists have conducted scientific research and developed theories to explain various forms of abnormal behavior. Still, no single definition can encompass all the diverse forms of abnormal behavior we will examine. But three major approaches to defining abnormal behavior have been commonly used as a starting point.

One approach emphasizes subjective distress, a second, social disability, and a third, the violation of social norms. Each applies more readily to some forms of psychological disorders than to others.

Subjective distress refers to the internal psychological state of the person and usually

Behavior that violates social rules and norms is often seen as "abnormal." (Owen Franken/Stock, Boston, Inc.)

encompasses such emotions as fear, sadness, or feelings of loss of control. The criterion of subjective distress applies especially well to some of the mood-related disorders, such as depression, that we will discuss later in the book. On the other hand, other forms of abnormal behavior seem not to be accompanied by any clear sense of subjective distress. An example is antisocial personality disorder, which is discussed in Chapter 13.

A second criterion for defining abnormal behavior is that the person appears to be *psychologically or socially disabled*—that is, less able to cope with the demands and stresses of life. Many of the major psychological disorders, such as schizophrenia, can be extremely disabling. Yet other forms of abnormal behavior may produce almost no

social disability and may be tolerated by the person with little or no difficulty.

The third major defining criterion of abnormal behavior is that some forms clearly seem to be in *violation of accepted social rules and norms*. Consequently, the behavior pattern in question may be disturbing to others. But a moment's reflection may suggest to you that whether a certain pattern of behavior is disturbing to others or not depends very much on the situation in which it occurs and the cultural norms and rules of the local setting. Indeed, some social scientists have argued that an adequate definition of abnormal behavior must take into account the *culture* in which the behavior occurs.

Although the criteria of subjective distress, psychological disability, and the violation of social rules each contribute to the definition of abnormal behavior, we should recognize that none of them is adequate by itself. There is no clear line between what is considered "normal" and what is considered "abnormal," even though it is possible to find vivid examples of particular patterns of abnormal behavior.

The Role of Culture

What is the role of culture in understanding the nature of abnormal behavior? Anthropologists use the term *ethnocentrism* to refer to the tendency to view our own culture as somehow automatically better, more advanced, and superior to other cultures both within our own country and elsewhere in the world. This attitude can creep into our thinking without our being aware of it. We might be tempted to regard our own cultural practices as "natural," "good," and "right," while viewing those of other groups as "primitive" and "unnatural." It is important not to confuse that which is different with abnormality.

Another important idea relating the concept of abnormality to the idea of culture is *cultural relativism*. This idea, introduced by anthropologists early in this century, argues that there are no universal standards that can be applied to all cultures and societies. Each culture is unique, and the practices of each must be understood on its own terms. From this viewpoint the idea of "normality" depends greatly on the culture being examined (Strauss, 1979). Some advocates of cultural relativism have gone so far as to argue that there are no universal forms of abnormal behavior that can be found in all cultures. But are there forms of abnormal behavior that are universal, or are they entirely unique to each culture?

Evidence used to support the cultural relativistic view often involves some forms of abnormal behavior that are clearly unique to a particular cultural group. Examples include *susto*, a form of magic fright reportedly observed among Indian tribes in Central and South America and in the highlands of Peru and Bolivia. Susto usually affects young children and adolescents. Victims show a loss of strength, rapid heartbeat, weight loss, intense anxiety, and depression. Usually they are treated by having their bodies rubbed with various plants and animals.

Still another example of a culturally unique form of abnormal behavior is *pibloktoq* (Wallace, 1972). It occurs only among polar Eskimos in northern Greenland. It begins with the victim appearing mildly irritable and withdrawn. Suddenly, with little warning the victim becomes wildly excited, may tear off his or her clothing, shout obscenities, or throw objects. The person may place himself or herself in great danger by climbing on icebergs and leaping into snowdrifts. This period is usually followed by convulsive seizures and a deep sleep. After the sleep the victim seldom has any memory of the experience and behaves normally.

The fact that there are culturally unique forms of abnormal behavior does not suggest that all forms are culture bound. But these examples do help us to appreciate two ways in which culture can affect abnormal behavior. First, the *style* and *content* of abnormal behavior may be strongly affected by the culture in which it occurs. For example, *koro,* the fear that the penis will withdraw into the stomach, is related to sexual concerns of the affected cultural group in Southeast Asia. The content of intense beliefs and fears may often be determined by cultural preoccupations.

A second role of culture in abnormal behavior may be seen in *the way a person copes* with the fear of disabling aspects of a disorder. Wallace (1972) points out that in the case of pibloktoq, the Eskimo may try to withdraw from others rather than place them in physical danger. Wallace notes that this way of coping is consistent with the reluctance to endanger or burden others found in Eskimo culture.

Diet is a third source of disorders unique to a culture, but it is often overlooked. Nutritional patterns, eating habits, and ecologically common chemicals or foods may affect the biochemistry of particular groups. Toxic disorders that result in extreme and uncontrolled behavior may occur as a consequence. An excellent example of this is pibloktoq. Wallace notes that there is now much evidence to indicate that this disorder may be produced by a calcium deficiency. The deficiency produces a neuromuscular disorder that is often complicated by emotional and cognitive disorganization. Thus, a *culturally determined dietary and nutritional pattern* or the *physical ecology* of a particular culture may play a role in the development of disorders that are culturally unique.

Are there forms of abnormal behavior that are universal? Researchers have studied this question in great detail. Wallace (1972) summarizes the research literature by saying: "*Yes,* different cultures do encourage different styles of mental illness, *but* the major categories of mental illness (the organic psychoses, the functional psychoses, the neuroses, the situational reactions, etc.) seem to be universal human afflictions" (p. 1).

Thus, although culture exerts a variety of powerful influences on the expression of abnormal behavior, it is not the only determining factor. The fact that some common forms of abnormal behavior can be observed in widely different cultures suggests that other biological and psychological causes also play a powerful role.

Description, Measurement, and Classification

Even though we have not arrived at a final definition of abnormal behavior, scientists have devised a variety of methods to aid in the measurement and description of abnormal behavior. As we shall see in later chapters, these methods range from the case history, which provides a narrative description of the course of a particular pattern of abnormal behavior, to psychological tests, to sophisticated biochemical and genetic methods of measurement. Thus methods from all of the sciences are being brought to bear on the scientific description of abnormal behavior.

Scientists not only try to describe the phenomenon in which they are interested, they also attempt to find ways to classify it in order to bring order out of diversity. We will study a variety of types of abnormal behavior and consider several ways in which such behavior can be classified. We will take a close but critical look at the latest version of the *Diagnostic and Statistical Manual of the American Psychiatric Association* (1980), which we shall refer to as DSM III. It is now used as one means of classifying abnormal behavior.

This most recent edition of DSM III has captured the interest and attention of scientists and clinicians alike because of the sweeping changes it brought to the field. Perhaps the most important of these changes was the provision of specific criteria for deciding whether a particular pattern of abnormal behavior should receive a particular diagnosis. Even now, this descriptive system is to be revised again (Spitzer & Williams, 1983), and we can expect this new revision to shape the way scientists and clinicians think about and describe abnormal behavior.

The Scientific Search for Causes and Explanations

We have observed that many of the examples of abnormal behavior are puzzling in a variety of ways. We want to ask ourselves: What could lead a person to behave in that way? How can we make sense out of the behavior?

Several different theoretical approaches to explaining the nature and causes of abnormal behavior are currently in use (Price, 1978). One is the view that abnormal behavior is a form of illness or disease. Another argues that it is a result of attempts to deal with the inner conflict of motives. Still another view argues that the peculiar or puzzling behavior we observe is actually learned in the social environment. Another viewpoint stresses the importance of the reaction of others to abnormal behavior. Finally, some theories focus on the development of one's sense of self and the psychological experiences of the person as the most critical processes to consider.

Each of these perspectives sheds light on important aspects of the human experience. And ultimately, each will have to be considered in any comprehensive theory of abnormal behavior. Throughout the text we will consider the ways in which each of them helps us to understand a particular form of abnormal behavior.

Scientists not only try to provide a conceptual framework to explain the development of abnormal behavior, they also conduct research to isolate its causes. It is already clear that abnormal behavior is the product of *multiple determinants*. For example, people with severe depression or prolonged feelings of sadness may be responding to causal factors in the larger culture, the economy, their family, their learning history, their own biochemistry, or any combination of these. With such a diverse range of possible causes of abnormal behavior, the scientific challenge is great. In learning about the search for the causes of various forms of abnormal behavior, we will encounter scientific detective stories that can be, in their own way, as exciting as the conventional kind of detective story.

ABNORMAL BEHAVIOR AS A HUMAN PROBLEM

We are living in a time of rapid social and economic change. Changes are occurring in social norms and expectations about which behavior is acceptable and which is not. Changes in sex roles, in the structure of the nuclear family, in attitudes toward sexuality, and in our sense of economic security mean that each of us is coping and adapting in the face of uncertainty.

Social and Human Cost

The social and human cost of psychological disturbance is very great. Major studies in both urban and rural areas (Robins et al., 1984; Myers et al., 1984) have reported relatively high proportions of the population experiencing psychological impairment. These figures will vary greatly depending on the economic status, sex, geographic location, and other characteristics of the people under

study; but there is no question that a substantial part of our population will experience relatively severe degrees of psychological distress at some time in their lives.

According to extensive epidemiological surveys of both rural and urban communities (Regier et al., 1984), 19 percent of all Americans suffer from at least one psychological disorder. Anxiety disorders are the most common, involving 8 percent of the adult population. Drug or alcohol dependence affects 6 percent, as do mood disorders. More severe disorders such as schizophrenia affect approximately 1 percent of the population. Furthermore, an analysis by Rice, Feldman, & White (1977) has calculated that the cost of illness in a single year was approximately 146 billion dollars, 7 percent of which was due to mental disorders. Still another way to examine the social and human cost of mental disorder is to recognize that more long-term hospital care days are devoted to the care of mental disorders than to cardiovascular diseases, cancer, accidents, poisonings, and violence combined (Rice et al., 1977).

Because abnormal behavior is a major social and human problem, the development of new methods of treatment and prevention is a critical scientific priority. In the chapters that follow we will examine a variety of studies focused on the development of more effective treatments. Indeed, the last several chapters of this book are devoted to a description of various biological, behavioral, psychological, and social treatment approaches and the research that has both stimulated them and evaluated their effectiveness.

Abnormal Behavior as a Personal Problem

Many people take a course in abnormal psychology as a way of getting to know themselves better. This can be a helpful experi-

Everyone confronts problems in living from time to time, and this is a normal part of everyone's life.
(Cathy Cheney/EKM-Nepenthe)

ence, but for some it can also provide moments of worry and uncertainty. There may be times, for example, when you are reading a case history or a description in this book and suddenly feel as if you "recognize" something of yourself in it. Then you are likely to wonder, "Is my behavior abnormal?" Or, "Maybe my problems are more serious than I thought."

At times like this, it is useful to know of the pattern medical schools have noticed and call *medical students' syndrome*. As the students begin to become familiar with the symptoms of particular diseases, they may find themselves focusing more on their own bodily processes. Soon it is hard to stop wondering whether a slight twinge in the chest might not be an early warning of heart trouble or a headache might not be the first sign of a tumor.

Much the same thing can happen when you are learning about abnormal behavior. It is *natural* to "see yourself" in some patterns of behavior described in this book, partly because our behavior is so complex and multi-faceted that everyone will share some of the same impulses and fears from time to time.

It may be that now or at some time in your life you will find yourself with a problem or concern that is so disturbing and persistent that you will want to talk with someone about it. If so, there are several ways you can find out whom to talk with. Your school may have a counseling center or mental health clinic. There also may be a "hot line" or telephone referral service where you can get information about who will be able to discuss your problems with you. Your dormitory counselor may also be able to help. Finally, your instructor is likely to know of appropriate helping services and may be willing to give you some leads. If you are really concerned, don't hesitate to ask.

In our discussion of various forms of abnormal behavior, we have tried to keep always in mind that human beings are at the same time biological, psychological, and cultural creatures. Each of these qualities is an equally important facet of the human context in which abnormal behavior must be understood. A rigorous, yet humane, science of abnormal behavior requires no less.

Both the scientific and the human aspects of abnormal behavior and its treatment are mingled in history. How society has understood and dealt with abnormal behavior in the past provides us with an intellectual history of abnormality and is a fitting place for our discussion to begin. It is to this history that we now turn.

ABNORMAL BEHAVIOR IN HISTORICAL PERSPECTIVE

To write a history of abnormal behavior that conforms to the "march-of-progress" school of thought is tempting. This version of history sees each age as a step in the progress of human society and humane science. A history written from this point of view tends to focus on scientific breakthroughs in every age and to concentrate its attention on great men and women. This approach is tempting because it prompts us to look only for signs of progress in our thinking about abnormal behavior and our treatment of those who display unusual behavior. Indeed, there are signs of progress and change. But the progress approach to the history of abnormal behavior has some real drawbacks. First, such a history often has a self-justifying, self-congratulating tone. It tends to see the present as the best of all possible worlds. If we are not careful, it leads us to use history as a justification for current practices because they are the "latest developments."

Another drawback of the march-of-progress school of thought is that it fails to draw a crucial lesson from history. Not only can history help to tell us how we got where we are but, more important, it also reminds us that the cultural beliefs and the social context of earlier eras shaped the assumptions about what caused abnormal behavior, just as they shaped the assumptions of all emerging sciences. Likewise, our current social context and culture shape our beliefs about the causes and cures of abnormality. To look at the history of abnormal behavior as a string of chronologically ordered events, then, is to fail to fully understand ourselves today.

We can try, instead, to understand previous events in their social context. With this approach to history, we may begin by looking at the prevailing beliefs about the causes and cures of abnormal behavior. But in order to understand those beliefs, we must ask a number of other questions as well. For example, we might ask about the social institutions of the time. What were people's ideas of the good life? What did people believe about the nature of human beings? What were the economic and political issues of the day? Answers to these questions will help us to make sense of the events of that time. As

Riegel (1972) has pointed out, the economic and cultural conditions of society provide a basis for the direction and growth of the science, and that includes the science of abnormal psychology.

History, then, rightly understood, can give us a perspective on ourselves and perhaps make us more humble about our achievements. History abused becomes a justification for our current practices rather than an attempt to deeply and truly understand ourselves.

In this chapter we will examine a brief history of abnormal behavior from ancient times to the present. We will focus on people's explanations of abnormal behavior and their attempts to cope with those displaying the behavior. We will try to keep at least one eye fixed on the context of their beliefs so that when we finish our history, we will be ready to ask ourselves something about our own beliefs and practices today and, perhaps, even to make some guesses about tomorrow.

Prehistory: Spirit Possession and Exorcism

There is very little evidence of how abnormal behavior was thought of in ancient times. Some evidence can be derived from Biblical sources. For example, in the Old Testament King Saul is described as having killed himself, presumably because of a severe depression. Greek myths provide many descriptions of apparently abnormal or irrational behavior. Ajax apparently suffered from the delusion that some sheep were his enemies. He killed them and later killed himself in remorse. The Greeks attributed such odd behavior to a madness induced by vengeful gods.

Another sort of evidence is from archaeology. Human skulls have been found with holes cut in them, as a result of what we presume was a surgical procedure. This proce-

Drilling or cutting holes in the skull, called trephining, during the stone ages. (Courtesy of the American Museum of Natural History)

dure, called *trephining,* is believed to have been used to release evil spirits from the heads of people afflicted with some form of abnormal behavior. A number of people treated in this way apparently survived the operation since there are indications of healing around the skull openings. Selling (1940) believed that while the operation was done to allow evil spirits to escape, brain pressure was relieved in this way, thus confirming for early people the effectiveness of the treatment.

Imagine what the world of primitive people must have been like. They dealt daily with unseen, powerful, and frightening forces in nature. Earthquakes, storms, fires, and illness all occurred without known explanation. And yet to survive, we require an ability to predict and, in some degree, to control our environment. It is not hard to understand how positive, life-sustaining events in the environment would be thought of as possessing good spirits, while unpredictable and dangerous events would be seen as possessing evil spirits.

In this context the unusual or frightening behavior of a person could easily be explained as possession by evil spirits. The "cure" was *exorcism,* the attempt to drive the evil spirits out of the afflicted person.

Exorcism took a variety of forms, including starvation, flogging, or prayers.

These magical and religious beliefs and practices were clearly an attempt to cope with an overwhelming and powerful environment. And exorcism, after all, does provide a sense of mastery over mysterious events. Since it almost surely had an effect in some cases, the idea that abnormal behavior was due to spirit possession was probably strengthened.

The Classical Period

Classical Greece and, later, Rome were important early sources of ideas about the nature of abnormal behavior. During the period of the Hellenic enlightenment in Greece, curiosity, observation, and rationality were all highly valued. It was a time of rapid growth in understanding the nature of people and the world in which they lived. There were attempts to understand not only abnormal behavior but also physiology, architecture, political science, logic, and drama. Zax and Cowen (1972) suggest that the Greeks had the leisure to pursue intellectual problems partly because they were slave owners

Hippocrates. (National Library of Medicine)

and therefore had the time and energy to pursue the life of the mind.

Two views of madness prevailed in the classical period. On the one hand, irrational behavior was often thought to have supernatural origins, either as a punishment from the gods or as a "sacred disease" indicating special powers as a prophet. On the other hand, Greek medicine rejected supernatural explanations of abnormal behavior and believed it to be a physiological disease of natural origins.

Cleomenes, a Spartan king, illustrates this dual view of irrationality quite well. A vigorous and erratic person, he often struck his subjects in the face with his scepter for no apparent reason and committed acts of sacrilege. Finally, he was restrained by having his feet placed in stocks. Herodotus, the greatest historian of the time, recorded the explanations offered for the king's erratic behavior. Most informed Greeks saw Cleomenes' behavior as a punishment sent by the gods for his various sacrileges. Others, however, were convinced that his behavior was due to heavy drinking and chronic alcoholism. Thus sacred and naturalistic views of abnormal behavior competed for prominence (Rosen, 1968).

Hippocrates (460–377 B.C.), a Greek physician, was a product of this age. He was a keen observer of human behavior and a scientist interested in natural causes. He argued, among other things, that epilepsy was not a "sacred disease" inflicted by the gods but was a result of brain disease. He also believed that madness was due to an excess of bile in the body and that most peculiar or unusual behaviors could be explained by imbalances among the four humors—blood, black bile, yellow bile, and phlegm. For example, a person suffering from too much phlegm in his or her body would appear lazy, sluggish, or phlegmatic. Depression and other mood changes could be traced to other imbalances, it was believed.

Other beliefs about the nature and cause of abnormal behavior by the Greeks had a similar physiological flavor. For example, it was believed that hysteria, a physical disability with no apparent organic cause, was a disease that only afflicted women and was caused by the wandering of the uterus throughout the body.

Roman thought differed in some interesting ways from that of the Greeks. The Romans were practical and political creatures. They were less given to detailed and detached inquiry than the Greeks, and much of their thinking about abnormal behavior was influenced by Greek thought and Greek physicians. Their practical orientation led them to be particularly interested in clinical treatment. Asclepiades (ca. 124 B.C.), a Roman physician, is said to have focused much of his energy on treatment including various physical therapies and baths.

Galen (A.D. ca. 130–200), a physician writing toward the end of the classical era, summarized a great deal of Roman thought. He stated that abnormal behavior was a result of either brain disease or disease of some other bodily organ. In addition, he believed that various environmental events could play a role in the development of abnormal behavior. For example, economic losses, disappointments in love, fear, or shock could be instrumental in producing abnormal behavior.

Although early Greek views of madness invoked supernatural explanations, Greek and later Roman medicine had a profound influence as well. Perhaps the most important thing to remember about the conception of abnormal behavior during the classical period

is that the Greeks' and Romans' curiosity about the universe extended to the physiology of the person. Their later thinking about the nature of irrational behavior is best thought of as a natural extension of their interest in physiology and medicine. Thus the classical period marks the beginning of two important themes in the history of abnormal behavior. First, irrational behavior began to be seen as a natural phenomenon, and second, its causes were located chiefly in the physiology of the person.

The Middle Ages: Witches and Their Hunters

To appreciate how abnormal behavior was explained and dealt with in the Middle Ages,

Exorcism was often attempted in the medieval church as a cure for deviant behavior. (National Library of Medicine)

we must understand something about the role of the Western church. The church was not just a religious institution; it was also the intellectual establishment. Scholarship resided only within the church, and the church was the final authority on questions of human conduct and faith.

Until around the year 1000, the Western church and the society it structured and controlled had little reason to doubt themselves. The church continued to grow, and pagans in the north and east of Europe were beginning to accept Christianity as a world view and a code of conduct. Like many existing establishments, once the church had gained control, it was reluctant to respond to criticism with internal change. When groups within the church suggested reforms, they were accused of wishing to destroy the church. These suggested reforms soon became known as heresy, and by the 13th century the church developed a new judicial procedure for dealing with alleged heretics. As the church continued to defend its hard-won territory, a papal bull was issued in 1231 authorizing a new procedure for dealing with heresy. Anyone accused of heresy could not be found guilty unless he or she confessd, an apparently enlightened procedure. But torture was allowed in order to obtain a confession, and this ruling marked the beginning of the Inquisition.

Witches and warlocks were common in the Middle Ages—part of the neighborhood life of most villages. Few people thought of them as anything more than eccentric people whose danger, if any, was strictly a local affair. But with the coming of the Inquisition, witches came to be thought of as conspirators with the devil, threatening the authority of the church.

In 1484 Pope Innocent VIII issued a papal bull requesting all the clergy in Europe to begin to search out witches and extract confessions. Local witches—those who were in some ways bothersome or different—were promoted from village nuisances to enemies of society.

Two Dominican friars wrote a manual, *Malleus Maleficarum*—"The Witch Hammer"—that described how witches could be recognized—from patches on their skin and other "symptoms"—and how they could be examined to determine whether or not they were truly witches. Janeway (1975) describes the process in the following way:

> Intellectually, the process was convincing. Since what was known about a witch cult was what the Inquisitors racked out of the accused witches, it agreed with itself in a most impressive way. If one witch came up with a new wrinkle, the next was sure to be asked about it, and confirm it for the same reason that she had confessed in the first place. (Increasingly it was a she.) Had she rubbed a stool with black magical ointment and taken off by air to meet with her neighbors to worship a huge toad? Yes. Had she kissed the creature on arrival? Yes. Had she had intercourse with the Devil? Yes, and it was extremely unpleasant since his member was ice-cold. Had she murdered children? Yes, indeed, including her own. And so on and so forth (p. 82).

Although the church took advantage of people's fear of witches, it did not necessarily create this fear. We must remember that the Middle Ages were not only a time when the church dominated society but it was also a period of great tumults and catastrophes. The Black Plague, the Hundred Years' War, peasant uprisings, the kidnapping of a pope, and other events kept medieval society in a turmoil of fear and uncertainty. Often in times of great upheaval, people seek out *scapegoats* to blame for the misfortunes that occur. Scapegoating allows people to identify the cause of their suffering. Once the cause is known, life becomes less frightening because seemingly uncontrollable events now can be

EXPLANATIONS FOR BEHAVIOR IN THE SALEM WITCH TRIALS

One of the most fascinating and well-known episodes in the history of collective epidemics of abnormal behavior involved the Salem witch trials, which occurred at Salem, Massachusetts, in 1692. A number of residents of the village were accused of witchcraft by their neighbors and subsequently tried as witches. A striking aspect of the accusations was that the people accusing the witches appeared to go into convulsions and to behave in odd or abnormal ways. What was happening to the villagers who accused their neighbors in the Salem witch trials? Was it some form of mass hysteria or abnormal behavior? The answer to that question comes in the form of a scientific and historical detective story.

One scientist, Caporael (1976), has argued that the people who accused others of witchcraft in Salem were suffering from delusions and convulsions caused by poisoning as a result of eating a fungus called ergot. Under some conditions ergot can infest rye and other cereal grains. Caporael suggested that a pattern of abnormal behavior previously thought to have been generated by conditions in the social environment might actually have been due to organic origins.

Spanos and Gottlieb (1976) examined this explanation carefully, and the results of their study are both fascinating and important to our understanding of group outbreaks of abnormal behavior throughout history. In order to test Caporael's hypothesis, Spanos and Gottlieb catalogued the symptoms that commonly occur in ergot poisoning. Then they examined the detailed records of the Salem witch trials to see if the behavior of the accusers actually corresponded to the patterns of symptoms we might expect in ergot poisoning. They observed that "rather than ergot poisoning, these descriptions suggest that the afflicted girls were enacting the roles that would sustain their definition of themselves as bewitched and that would lead to the conviction of the accused" (p. 1391).

In other words, Spanos and Gottlieb argued that the convulsive behavior of the accusers was meant to make more credible their accusations that other members of their community were witches. Spanos and Gottlieb also noted that many large-scale witch crises occurred in the 16th and 17th centuries. Such events usually began with accusations against some socially deviant person in the community. These accusations escalated quickly, but sometimes when judges and other officials became skeptical, the epidemic or panic would end abruptly, suggesting that the behavior actually had social origins.

controlled. Witches made convenient scape-goats during the Middle Ages because their eccentric behavior set them apart from the rest of society. By blaming witches for their troubles and then punishing them, people in the Middle Ages were able to feel that they were doing something about their plight. Through the "Witch Hammer" manual the church not only sanctioned the scapegoating of witches but also used the prevalent mistrust of witches to its own advantage. Soon after the manual was written, a witch craze swept across Europe, and people unfortunate enough to behave peculiarly were often described in terms of the dogma on witchcraft.

It is too easy to dismiss the great witch craze as merely the product of a bygone age. The human mind, then as now, sought explanations. It searched for causes. Janeway points out that swarms of demons and evil witches could "explain" the misfortunes of the era. The witch provided a ready target for the fears and uncertainties that threatened social order in the Middle Ages.

Thus the great witch hunts of the Middle Ages can be seen not merely as a curious practice from an earlier time but as the reaction of the church, the major institution of society, to real and imaginary threats to its existence and authority. Many people were caught up in the net of the Inquisition. Few, if any, were a serious danger to the body politic or the church. Yet to assert itself, the church required something against which to react, and those who were different became the victims.

Beginnings of the Modern Era

Early in the 14th century, even as the great European witch craze ended, major changes began to occur in Western civilization. In order to appreciate how the dominant view of abnormal behavior shifted in this period, we must look at the larger historical and social context for a moment.

Perhaps the most basic change in society, beginning in the 15th century, was the shift in authority from the church to the modern nation-state. National armies began to appear late in the 15th century. Hospitals, once exclusively controlled by the church, were taken over by the state. The idea of cure became increasingly associated with secular and medical remedies rather than religious salvation. During the earlier medieval period it was believed that human passions could be

controlled only with great spiritual effort. The world was a mysterious and fearsome place in which to live. At the beginning of the modern era, a new optimism began to emerge. The Italian Renaissance was under way. Copernicus offered a new theory of astronomy. Shakespeare and Cervantes wrote their great works, and Galileo and Kepler launched a new physics. The world again opened itself to the inquiring mind. A new awareness of the social environment and a humanistic tradition began to emerge.

By the beginning of the 19th century, still other changes showed the shift in intellectual and political climate that had occurred. The early 19th century saw the rise of the factory system in England and the development of the Industrial Revolution. The Industrial Revolution did not just represent the coming of factories to our lives but ushered in a new conception of how people ought to be. Alongside the huge growth in technology and science came a change in society's standards of normal behavior. This new morality served the needs of the factory system. The work ethic emerged with a new set of virtues. Diligence and industry, it was thought, spelled success.

Thus the Industrial Revolution brought two changes that ultimately affected our conception of abnormal behavior. The first set of changes was scientific and technological, occurring from the end of the Middle Ages to the beginning of the 19th century. These changes laid the groundwork for rapid growth in science and medicine. At the same time, a new morality emerged, with a new set of assumptions about appropriate behavior. Work, diligence, and achievement were considered primary virtues, and this new morality served as a prescription for the emerging working class in Europe and, somewhat later, in America.

Still a third major change in the human and social context began to occur. At the beginning of the Victorian Age, the virtues of industry and diligence began to be supplemented by still other moral standards. A great tightening of moral norms and a shift in public morality marked the Victorian Age. Shakespeare was published in abridged editions with any suggestive content removed. Victorian women put curtains on the legs of their pianos to avoid offending people's moral sensibilities. Legs became "limbs." Great emphasis was placed on suppressing the passionate aspects of human behavior. The middle class came to dominate society, and its domination changed standards for appropriate and for abnormal behavior.

Against this background we will discuss three streams of thought about the nature of abnormal behavior that emerged in this period and remain with us today. The first focuses on the social environment both as the major cause and the source of "cure" of abnormal behavior. This tradition has its roots in the humanism of the Renaissance and the social and political awareness stimulated by the French and American revolutions.

The second major stream of thought emphasizes the organic and medical aspects. It focuses on physiology as the source of abnormal behavior and sees the solutions to problems of abnormal behavior in medicine. This

Hospital of St. Mary of Bethlehem (Bedlam) in London, shown in this Hogarth engraving, reflects the appalling conditions of the 18th century. (National Library of Medicine)

tradition draws on the steady scientific development that began in the 15th century and on the technological growth associated with the Industrial Revolution.

The third stream of thought is psychological. Not until the end of the 19th and the beginning of the 20th centuries does a truly psychological approach to human behavior develop. This view, most notably characterized by Freud's psychoanalysis, focuses on human sexual and aggressive impulses and is preoccupied with their control, as one might expect of the Victorian Age.

These patterns of thought have alternated, emerged, and reoccurred throughout history. In ancient times magicoreligious views predominated, while in classical Greece and Rome both religious and organic-physiological views were very important. During the Middle Ages the predominant view of abnormal behavior was again religious, but as the authority of the church began to be replaced by that of the state, conceptions of abnormality also changed. The development of nation-states can be thought of as a precursor of the environmental view. The Industrial Revolution saw the end of a long development leading to medical-organic views, and the Victorians, with their strong emphasis on suppressing the passions, laid the groundwork for the emergence of the psychological view of abnormal behavior.

The First Stream: The Social Environment as Cause and Cure.   We said earlier that one of the three streams of thought that emerged at the beginning of the modern era was the idea that the social environment was important in both the causation and the cure of abnormal behavior. This idea took slightly different forms in Europe and in America. For the past two centuries the insane, criminals, and debtors had been housed in large prisons and fortresses. This was a relatively new practice, stemming perhaps from the confining of lepers in leprosariums during the Mid-

dle Ages. Although leprosy practically disappeared from Europe at the end of the Middle Ages, as Foucault (1965) points out, the idea of separating the "undesirables" from the rest of society had been established.

In France the French Revolution had just ended; it was a time of reform. Phillippe Pinel (1745–1826), a French physician in charge of a large hospital for the insane in Paris, found himself staggered by the conditions he found there. A humanist and reformer, he believed that disturbed people ought to be treated with concern rather than chained in the hospital's dungeonlike atmosphere. As the hospital's superintendent, Pinel unchained the inmates and treated them with kindness. His example was followed by others; soon France had 10 new mental hospitals, all practicing benign environmental treatment.

Philippe Pinel. (National Library of Medicine)

William Tuke. (National Library of Medicine)

It was not long before the reform movement found its way to England. Among the reformers in England was William Tuke, who established a retreat where patients could live, work, and rest in a benign atmosphere. Of course, we cannot know how many cases of severely disturbed behavior actually were improved by these reforms. But it is clear that many people suffering serious abuses in the asylums of the day were able to lead relatively normal lives once the asylums' oppressive atmosphere was replaced by kindness, concern, and support.

Thus the reform movement in Europe exemplified by the work of Pinel in France and of Tuke in England was partly stimulated by a political and social climate of reform. The target of reform was the oppressive environment of the dungeons that had housed the insane and the afflicted. We will see that this same spirit of reform and focus on the social environment took a different form in the United States in the Jacksonian Era.

Europe's concern with the role of the environment had not developed alone. In America, too, the role of social and environmental factors began to gain attention and prominence. In colonial times, as David Rothman (1971) notes, it had not occurred to Americans to institutionalize severely disturbed people. They were cared for by the family, relatives, or neighbors and remained for the most part in the community. Suddenly, however, about 1820, prisons, asylums, almshouses, and retreats for children began to appear and swept across America in a great wave. This was, Rothman suggests, a great revolution in social practice. Before 1810, only a few states in the East had private institutions to care for the mentally ill, and only Virginia had a public asylum. But by 1860, only 50 years later, 28 of the 33 states had public institutions for the insane, and institutionalization of the insane had become standard practice. What caused this revolution in social practice? What were the beliefs in this period about the causes of abnormal behavior, and how did they affect therapeutic practices?

Rothman argues that Americans of the 1820s and 1830s strongly believed that the origins of deviant behavior and insanity lay in the chaotic community organization of the time and the rapid social change present in the Jacksonian Era. In fact, it was not just rapid social change, but other aspects of social life—politics, social mobility, inflation, and even ambition in business—that were seen as the causes of insanity. American physicians of the Jacksonian Era speculated on the causes of abnormal behavior. For example, Edward Jarvis, a prominent physician of the time, explained to a Massachusetts Medical Society meeting:

In this country . . . the ambition of some leads them to aim at that which they cannot reach, to strive for more than they can grasp. Their mental powers are strained to their utmost tension; they labor in agitation . . . their minds stagger under the disproportionate burden (quoted by Rothman, 1971).

Given these assumptions about the causes of abnormal behavior, it is much easier to understand the rationale underlying the rapid development of the asylum in the United States in the 1820s and 1830s. Rather than try to change American society, medical and scientific leaders of the time believed that they could create a distinctive environment that would eliminate the tensions and stresses of the social environment. At the same time, they hoped to create a model society that would show the advantages of an orderly, regular, and disciplined routine. It was to be a "demonstration project" to the larger society.

Moral Treatment.   It is important to realize that the asylum of the Jacksonian Era was not a last resort after all other treatment attempts had failed. Rather, the asylum was believed to be the most effective approach to the treatment of abnormal behavior. As Rothman notes, physicians believed that the American environment had become so treacherous that insanity struck American citizens with great regularity. "Create a different kind of environment, which methodically corrected the deficiencies of the community, and a cure for insanity was at hand. This, in essence, was the foundation of the asylum solution, and the program that came to be known as *moral treatment*" (p. 133).

The heart of moral treatment was disciplined routine. Asylums were placed in the countryside because it was believed that the peace and serenity of the country and removal from the rapid pace of city life were essential to cure. Each patient's day was carefully ordered and each activity had a specified time in the schedule and routine. Even the physical environment was arranged so that it was

symmetrical and well ordered. Thus the cure for abnormal behavior, 19th-century Americans believed, was a "well-ordered institution" to provide both a refuge from the chaos of the outside world and a model of what society should be like.

Reformers of the day, such as the famous Dorothea Dix, shared the same general idea. She promoted the mental hospitals in legislatures across the country from 1841 to 1881. She began by condemning the conditions for the insane in jails and poorhouses and then recommended in their place well-ordered asylums. As Rothman notes, "Her formula was simple as she repeated it everywhere: first assert the curability of insanity, link it directly to proper institutional care, and then quote prevailing medical opinion on rates of recovery" (p. 132).

Claims for recovery during this period of moral treatment were very optimistic. Often as much as 80 percent of patients were

Dorothea Dix. (National Library of Medicine)

A variety of treatment devices were used even after the Humanitarian Reform movement. Here we see a device for suspending patients to aid in their treatment. (Historical Pictures Service, Inc., Chicago)

THE RISE AND FALL OF TENT THERAPY IN THE 19th CENTURY

The enthusiasm for environmental explanations of the causes and cures of abnormal behavior took a variety of forms in 19th-century America. Ruth Caplan (1969) offers a striking example of this enthusiasm. When the threat of an epidemic of tuberculosis arose, the superintendent of Manhattan State Hospital decided to reduce overcrowding by erecting a tent for some of the patients on the hospital grounds. About 20 patients were moved into the tent. Great enthusiasm for and attention to the patients, excellent meals, and extreme sanitary precautions characterized the move. Physicians at the hospital began to note marked improvement in the behavior of a number of these patients.

When they were returned to the hospital, many of the patients suffered relapses.

Feeling that a new and effective treatment had been discovered, case histories and articles in learned journals were published attributing the therapeutic success to fresh air, environmental change, and healthy living conditions. Soon the experiment was repeated, and large numbers of patients were moved to tents to profit from the remarkable new treatment. Patients were allowed to participate in designing and decorating the tents. Soon tent therapy spread to other states, including California, Illinois, and Ohio.

Before long, however, these camps became crowded and the lifestyle became

Tent Therapy—This outdoor setting produces a dramatic change in the treatment environment and the change itself may have had beneficial, if temporary, effects. (National Library of Medicine)

routine and boring. Staff shortages became more apparent, and tent therapy was soon abandoned as ineffective.

Even today, our enthusiasm for new treatments encourages premature adoption of new approaches. An important chance to learn about what were probably the effective ingredients of tent therapy (the participation of patients in their own treatment, enthusiasm, and increased contact with other patients) was lost.

Unfortunately, new approaches to treatment are still too often hailed as "scientific break-throughs" and treated as cure-alls. "Wonder" drugs, new environmental therapies, group techniques, and other approaches to the treatment of abnormal behavior are often overpraised and undertested. Too often the result, like tent therapy, is a cycle of great hope and enthusiasm followed by disillusionment when the promised results diminish and fail to appear.

reported cured. For example, Samuel Woodward, superintendent of the Massachusetts Hospital at Worcester, claimed 82.25 percent of patients recovered, and a number of other superintendents flatly claimed 100 percent recoveries. Only recently have historians pointed out that sometimes a single patient who had been admitted, discharged, and readmitted several times was listed as having been "cured" each time, thus distorting statistics regarding the effectiveness of moral treatment.

In the early 20th century moral treatment gave way to asylums serving as internment centers for those unable to function in society. Little if any treatment took place in these large, impersonal institutions. Instead, the staff devoted much of their energy to keeping the inmates under control, using such devices as straitjackets and solitary confinement. Patients were crowded together in sparsely furnished rooms and often left to live in their own waste. Since little treatment was performed, those unfortunate enough to be committed to such an institution might well remain there the rest of their lives.

In the latter part of this century, there was great public outcry at the condition of many asylums. Efforts were made to improve the physical conditions of the asylums and to ensure that patients were offered

treatment. In addition, a movement began to empty the asylums of patients who could function in society if provided some minimal support. Halfway houses were created to help the transition back into society of patients who needed to relearn how to take care of their daily needs. Since the movement to return mental patients to the community began in the 1960s, the number of persons in mental institutions has dropped dramatically. However, Price and Smith (1983) have shown that in many cases patients returned to their communities have been badly neglected and have remained dependent. We will return to this problem in the final chapter.

Thus we see one of the main streams of thinking about the causes and cures of abnormal behavior—the social environmental view—beginning in Europe with the reforms of Pinel and extending to its logical extreme in the optimistic, environmentally oriented, moral treatment of the 1800s in America. As we will learn in later chapters, strongly held beliefs about the power of the social environment to affect behavior continue to pervade our thinking today.

The Second Stream: Emergence of the Organic and Medical Views. The new age of technology in Europe and England created by the Industrial Revolution strengthened

The well-ordered asylum in America during the early part of the 19th century. (Historical Pictures Service, Inc., Chicago)

the belief that science could solve the problems of human behavior. Not long before, Darwin had offered his theory of evolution, and Pasteur had shown that disease could be produced by germs. Medical science was looking for new worlds to conquer, and abnormal behavior had, as yet, been largely neglected as a subject of scientific study.

William Griesinger (1817–1868), a German physician, was a product of this belief. Early in his life he published a textbook that flatly asserted that abnormal behavior was due to brain disease. As Zax and Cowen (1972) point out, Griesinger made no distinction between psychiatry and neurology. For Griesinger there was only one form of abnormal behavior. He called it *insanity* and believed that its cause lay in the brain.

To understand Griesinger's assurance and optimism, we must remember that other scientists were making remarkable progress at the same time. Koch, for example, isolated the bacteria that caused anthrax in 1876. For the next 25 years various bacteria and other organisms were found to play important roles in a variety of diseases. There was every reason to believe that microorganisms could explain virtually everything that was wrong with people, even erratic behavior.

In addition, three of the most common diseases of the time, syphilis, tuberculosis, and typhoid, were better understood. Physicians noted with great interest that these diseases sometimes produced irrational thinking and behavior in those affected. Scientists and physicians reasoned that other forms of peculiar and apparently irrational behavior might also be caused by diseases.

Neurology, too, was becoming an important medical specialty. Areas of the brain were located that appeared to serve specific functions, such as centers of speech and vision. Earlier, in 1811, Sir Charles Bell had stimulated much of this progress by proposing that different psychological functions had different anatomical locations. He argued that the dorsal side of the spinal cord consisted of sensory nerves, and that motor nerves were located on the ventral side. It is not surprising, then, that a new medical specialty, psychiatry, developed and took as its territory the minds of the insane, who presumably also were suffering from diseases.

The final stamp of the organic and medical view of abnormal behavior was made on psychiatry by Emil Kraepelin (1856–1926). Kraepelin classified irrational behavior in great detail. As we shall see when we discuss schizophrenia, Kraepelin's thinking and influence persist today and provide a major basis for the way we classify schizophrenia. It is important to realize that Kraepelin did more than just classify abnormal behavior. By providing detailed descriptions and classifications, he made the study of abnormal behavior a truly legitimate medical discipline. Irrational behavior could now be described in terms of *disease entities* associated with *symptoms*.

Thus the victory over certain physical diseases that produced abnormal behavior, the rapid progress in medicine, especially neurology, and the scientific and technological optimism of the times all contributed to enthusiasm for the new medical discipline of psychiatry. Irrational behavior, once the domain of witch doctors and then of inquisitors during the Middle Ages and later the province of social critics and reformers, now came under the influence of medicine. And, like the social-environmental stream of thought we described earlier, the medical-organic view of abnormal behavior persists today as an influential approach to understanding abnormal behavior.

The Third Stream: The Psychological Viewpoint. Although the psychological view of human behavior did not reach its full influence until the end of the 19th and the beginning of the 20th centuries, it has some roots in the Greek tradition. The Greeks believed that reason could overcome irrational behavior. Later the humanism of Pinel and Tuke also stressed the psychological qualities of the person.

It was Anton Mesmer (1734–1815), sometimes called the father of hypnotism, who brought the psychological view into focus. Mesmer believed that people had magnetic fluids within them and could be influenced through redistributing these fluids. In 1779 he opened a clinic in Paris and claimed to be able to cure all sorts of diseases by using *animal magnetism.* His treatment involved various forms of suggestion and the use of elaborate rods and mechanical devices thought to affect the magnetic fluids. He was a dramatic figure and often appeared in flowing robes to attend his patients. A variety of complaints were relieved by Mesmer's efforts. Although Mesmer was often attacked as a fraud, he was also a critic of earlier practices such as exorcism, as Hilgard (1977) notes in this fascinating account:

Hypnosis and exorcism had a confrontation 200 years ago at a time when Father Johann Joseph Gassner (1717–99) was curing many of his parishioners, and others from afar after his fame spread, by using the Church's rituals of exorcism. He had cured himself by getting rid of "the Evil One" while he was a Catholic priest in a small village in Switzerland. There was much opposition to Gassner, because this was the Age of Enlightenment, and many wished to be rid of practices that they considered magical and irrational. The Prince-Elector Max Joseph of Bavaria appointed a commission of inquiry in 1775 and invited Franz Anton Mesmer (1734–1815), then an Austrian

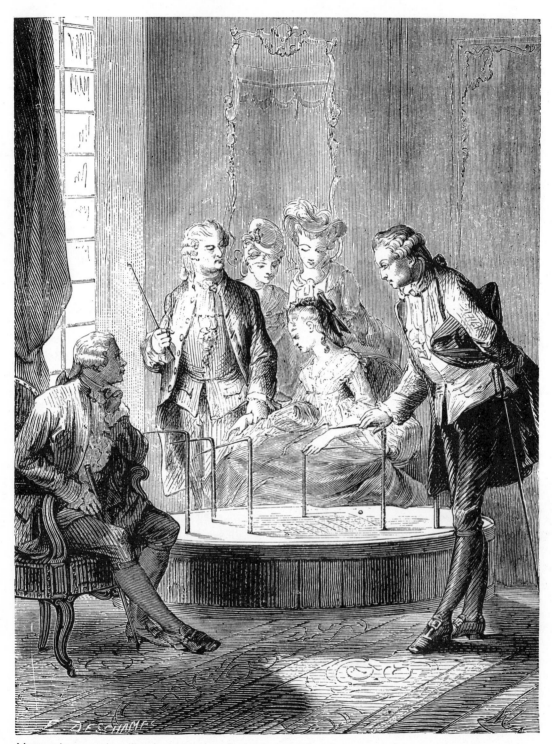

Mesmer in an early setting for hypnosis or "animal magnetism." (Historical Pictures Service, Inc., Chicago)

physician, to show that the results of exorcism could be obtained as well by his "naturalistic" method of animal magnetism, the precursor of hypnosis. Mesmer was able to produce the same effects that Gassner had produced—causing convulsions to occur and then curing them. Mesmer won the day, and Gassner was sent off as a priest to a small community. Pope Pius VI ordered his own investigation, from which he concluded that exorcism was to be performed only with discretion" (p. 19).

The age of animal magnetism in the beginning of the 19th century greatly speeded the development of the psychological approach to human behavior. It helped establish the ideas of conscious and unconscious thinking;

it opened up psychological exploration of mental events; and, most important, it revived the idea that one person could help another change his or her irrational behavior.

Psychology was not only the province of physicians and hypnotists. In literature Ibsen, Shaw, and Nietzsche wrote about human behavior in ways that revealed a growing awareness of human motivation and conflict. Dostoevski's descriptions of madness had a richness and complexity that was very different from the classification efforts of the psychiatry of the day. Thus the 19th century was fertile ground for the reemergence of the psychological approach to understanding human behavior.

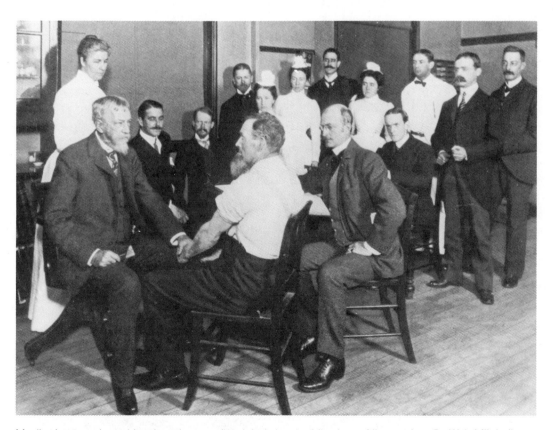

Medical research and treatment were often intertwined, at the turn of the century. Dr. Weir Mitchell (1829–1914) interviewing a patient and taking his pulse. (National Library of Medicine)

SOME CONTEMPORARY APPLICATIONS OF HYPNOSIS

Since the days of Mesmer, some of the world's most eminent scientists, such as Benjamin Franklin, Freud, Pavlov, and William James, have tried to find out just what hypnosis can and cannot do. Today hypnosis, as used in treatment, is a private affair between therapist and client; the client is usually given instructions to relax and to focus his or her attention on some aspect of the environment. Those subjects who possess a hypnotic ability will then eventually enter a deeply relaxed state during which suggestions by the therapist are vividly experienced and acted upon as if they were reality (e.g., the arm becomes numb, hearing is impaired, client vividly reexperiences past events, client smells odor that is not present).

While psychologists have long since abandoned Mesmer's claims of miraculous healings, hypnosis is still accepted as a treatment technique for a variety of psychological and psychosomatic disorders, provided qualified psychologists, psychiatrists, physicians, and dentists administer such treatment. Many individuals seek help in gaining control of unwanted habits like smoking and overeating, but hypnosis has many other applications.

Enhancement of Insight in Psychotherapy

Some experimental evidence (Nash, Johnson, & Tipton, 1979) suggests that the hypnotic subject has an enhanced ability to vividly reexperience past events and emotions associated with events. Some therapists believe that hypnosis enables their clients more easily to recognize and integrate previously repressed feelings or memories that might otherwise remain inaccessible. When used in this way, hypnosis is said to be an uncovering technique. In recent years hypnosis has taken its place alongside free association and dream interpretation as an important way of exploring memories and feelings that might be otherwise inaccessible.

Enhancement of Behavior Therapies

Hypnosis also has been used as a part of behavior therapies. Behavior therapy relies less on the attainment of insight into problems than on directly changing the problem behavior itself. Systematic desensitization, one such behavior therapy technique, involves helping the client cope with unrealistic fears by vividly imagining the feared object or situation while remaining deeply relaxed. Lazarus (1976), a noted behavior therapist, has suggested the use of hypnosis to help some clients more easily relax during desensitization. Hypnosis has also been used to increase the vividness of images in systematic desensitization. When used in this way, hypnosis is said to be a supportive technique.

Control of Pain

One of the most interesting and oldest applications of hypnosis is the control of acute and chronic pain. For acute pain, hypnosis has been successfully used as a substitute for drugs in major surgery, childbirth, amputations, and tumor extractions. Complicated operations such as the removal of breast tumors, hysterectomies, removal of genital tumors, plastic surgery, and oral surgery, have all been carried out painlessly with nondrugged, hypnotized patients (Kroger,

1977). Pain that is more lasting (headaches, cancer-induced pain, arthritic pain) can be minimized and sometimes even eliminated by some clients with hypnotic ability who are properly trained in techniques of self-hypnosis and pain control. Special hypnotic procedures have been successful in helping children with serious cancer cope with the pain and discomfort associated with the treatment of this disease.

Treating Physical Disorders

Dermatitis, warts, rashes, and many other skin disorders may be responsive to hypnotic suggestion. When Sinclair-Giebin and Chambers (1959) suggested to 14 hypnotized patients that their severe warts would clear from one side of their bodies, warts on the suggested side did indeed disappear; the warts on the other side did not. But better-controlled studies have not consistently documented skin changes in response to hypnotic suggestions (DePiano & Salzberg, 1979). If hypnosis plays some part in ridding the body of warts, the way in which it works is a mystery (Bowers, 1976). Stress-related disorders such as migraine, tension headaches, and asthma have been treated with hypnosis. Of the three disorders, asthma appears to be the most responsive to treatment by hypnosis (DePiano & Salzberg, 1979).

Treating Amnesia and Multiple Personality

Cases of amnesia and multiple personality have been identified and treated by hypnotic procedures. Persons with amnesia cannot recall important personal events in their past. In cases of multiple personality, two or more distinct "personalities" seem to coexist within the same person. Some of the most famous cases of multiple personalities (for example, Sybil and the three faces of Eve) were treated with hypnotherapy. In a classic case study, Prince (1906) used hypnosis to reintegrate the five personalities of Miss Beaucamp. Prince concluded that hypnosis enables the therapist to more easily communicate with the various personalities. (Prepared by Michael Nash)

In psychiatry changes were also beginning to take place toward the end of the 19th century. Jean Charcot, a neurologist in Paris, began to explore hypnosis and its relationship to certain disorders that seemed to have no organic basis.

These disorders, termed *hysterias*, involved impairment or loss of body functioning in a manner that did not correspond with the actual neurological connections of the body and appeared to be curable by hypnotic suggestion. Charcot insisted that these disorders had no organic basis. Pierre Janet, another major French physician in this period, asserted that neurotic behaviors were a result of fixed subconscious ideas. He claimed that these disorders could be treated by using "automatic talking" as therapy.

Yet it was a young Viennese physician, Sigmund Freud, who almost single-handedly framed and consolidated a uniquely psychological view of human action and abnormal behavior. Freud studied under Charcot in 1885 and was impressed by the power of hypnosis to affect certain forms of abnormal behavior. He returned to Vienna and worked with another physician, Joseph Breuer, who had developed a treatment called the *cathartic method*. This treatment, the talking cure, consisted of hypnotizing patients and allowing them to discuss their concerns while hypnotized. Often the patients' difficulties

Jean Charcot. (National Library of Medicine)

choanalysis, in more detail. But here it is important to see what became of Freud's thinking in the Victorian Age and late 19th century. Recall that it was an age of new and more restrictive morality. Freud believed that much of irrational or abnormal behavior was really the result of conflicts between sexual or aggressive impulses and the demands of conscience and reality. It is likely that in Vienna, in the late 19th century, moral constraints were so great that much of the content of his patients' discussions did, indeed, reflect conflicts between sexual impulses and strict, prudish social standards. As we shall see later, Freud's views of both the role of women and of sexuality are strongly flavored by 19th-century Victorian thinking.

Thus the psychological stream of thought, culminating in Freud's major contributions,

began to disappear as a result of the talking cure.

As Freud observed and considered the process by which these cures were achieved, he was struck by the fact that much of the content of the patients' discussions while hypnotized was not accessible when they were awake. These thoughts, said Freud, were "unconscious," and although not available to awareness by usual means, they still seemed to be very important determinants of behavior. Thus hypnosis, the talking cure, and Freud's acute ability to observe human behavior led him to suggest that abnormal behavior could actually be a result of purely psychological processes.

In the next chapter we will discuss Freud's perspective on human behavior, *psy-*

Sigmund Freud. (National Library of Medicine.)

was strongly influenced by the Victorian Age. With its restrictive standards of conduct, Victorian morality helped to produce many of the conflicts that would become central to Freud's view of the nature of abnormal behavior.

SUMMARY

In this chapter we have examined abnormal behavior from a scientific, humanistic, and historical perspective. We have noted that there is no single definition of abnormality. Instead, abnormal behavior is usually defined either in terms of subjective distress—social or psychological disability—or as the violation of social norms. From a cross-cultural perspective we observed that to some degree at least, whether a behavior is seen as abnormal or not will depend on the cultural context. Furthermore, certain forms of abnormal behavior appear to be expressed differently, depending on the cultural setting in which they occur.

The scientific study of abnormal behavior involves attempts to describe and measure various aspects of abnormality through the use of psychological tests, behavioral and biological measurements, and the use of diagnostic classification systems. The *Diagnostic and Statistical Manual of the American Psychiatric Association* (DSM III) is currently the most widely used classification system. We will frequently refer to DSM III in our discussion of various forms of abnormal behavior throughout the text.

Abnormal behavior can have great social and economic costs. We noted that a substantial portion of our population will experience a relatively severe form of psychological distress at some time in their lives. The social and economic costs of treatment and rehabilitation of psychological disorders rival those of other major medical disorders. Both to reduce human distress and because of the economic consequences of abnormal behavior, scientists continue to search for the causes of such behavior. Their search ranges across biological, behavioral, and social fields of inquiry. We will review much of the research designed to understand the causes of abnormal behavior in the pages that follow.

Our survey of the history of abnormal behavior has carried us from prehistoric times, when trephining was used to release evil spirits from possessed people's heads, to the 20th century, with its psychological, organic, and social environmental approaches to the understanding of abnormal behavior. But a history that does no more than teach us discrete facts is of little enduring value. Let us ask ourselves again a question with which we began this chapter. Are there things that the history of abnormal behavior can tell us about today's views and practices?

Perhaps the most important lesson we can learn from our survey is that the views of abnormal behavior that exist in any given period reflect the major cultural preoccupations of that time. Thus the prevailing ideas about abnormal behavior may tell us something about our own culture, our concerns, our fears, and our hopes for humanity. These ideas about abnormality serve as a kind of mirror. Instead of just accepting them as the "latest" ideas, we can view them as reflections of social and cultural influences to which we are all subject. In the next chapter we will examine several current perspectives on abnormal behavior. In these present-day views we will recognize the influence of the earlier organic, social, and psychological views we have just discussed.

2

Perspectives on Abnormal Behavior

What's Wrong with Me?

Perspectives in Conflict

Models and Perspectives in Scientific Thinking

The Biological Perspective
Biological Research: The Example of Schizophrenia
Biological Treatments
The Biological Perspective and the Idea of Mental Illness

The Dynamic Perspective
Overview of Psychoanalytic Theory
Fundamental Assumptions of the Dynamic Perspective
Mental Structures, Conflict, and Anxiety
Defense Mechanisms
Current Trends: Object Relations Theory
Dynamic Explanations

The Learning Perspective
Classical Conditioning
Instrumental Conditioning
Social Learning and Modeling
Overview of the Learning Perspective

The Sociological Perspective
Norms and Roles and the Career of a Mental Patient
Being Sane in Insane Places: An Example of the Sociological Perspective In Action

Reactions from the Medical Community
to the Sociological Viewpoint
Contributions of the Sociological
Perspective

The Humanistic Perspective
Carl Rogers' View of the Development of
Abnormal Behavior

Maslow: Self-Actualization and
Psychological Help

**Using Perspectives to Understand and Treat
Abnormal Behavior**

Summary

What's Wrong with Me?

I guess I first started to wonder about myself, seriously, I mean, when I was 13 years old. I was caught stealing some nylon stockings in a department store near where I lived. But the funny thing was, I really couldn't remember even walking into the store. My dad thought I was lying, and he beat me worse than he ever did. In a way I wish I had been lying, at least I could understand that. I was so afraid to tell him about it, because just before the incident he and Mom were fighting and I knew that he had been drinking. That really wasn't all that unusual, you understand; we were all pretty used to his blowing up for no good reason. I wasn't arrested or anything, but, looking back on it, the whole incident made me feel even more worthless, if that's possible. I always felt that I wasn't good enough, smart enough, pretty enough. All the time I was growing up, I felt nervous and awkward. Sometimes I felt

that nothing was real, like I was living my life in a dream or a movie. The kids in school stayed away from me. Somehow they sensed that I was "different." You know, I never really had a friend. But I did have my fantasies. One of my favorite ones was being waited on hand and foot by a handsome guy who looked like a prince. But my life sure hasn't turned out that way. Both of my marriages were total disasters. Before Tom took off, he said that he was sick of my "moods" and my constant complaining. During my marriages I did do some pretty strange things. Once I remember walking around the bus station in Cleveland; I had no idea how I got 200 miles from my house or exactly what I was doing there. Since Tom left two years ago, it's been all downhill. I'm afraid to leave the house now. I hate men. I have fantasies of hurting them that I can't seem to get out of my mind. I don't trust myself, and I'm afraid of just about everyone but my mother.

33

She brought me here, you know. When I told my doctor that I was afraid that I was going to "explode" and maybe kill someone, he asked me if I'd come into the hospital. My mother thinks I'm doing the right thing by coming in too. Dad doesn't really care one way or the other. What's wrong with me?

Faced with the question, "What is really wrong with this patient?" experts in the field would likely give a wide range of answers. "This person is suffering from an unresolved Oedipal complex." Or, "This person has nothing at all wrong with her, but is merely being labeled 'sick' because of some unusual behavior." Still another might argue, "A functional analysis of this person's living situation suggests that certain behaviors emitted by the patient are consistently receiving reinforcement."

In this chapter we are going to try to understand how those experts, all examining the same patient, could come up with such different explanations of that person's behavior. We are also going to look at some of the conceptions of abnormal behavior currently receiving much attention.

PERSPECTIVES IN CONFLICT

Disagreements are certainly not unique to the emerging science and study of abnormal behavior. In fact, a look at the evolution of nearly any science will suggest that at some time experts in that field disagreed about fundamental assumptions. Such disagreements mark times of great excitement and controversy in a science.

Thomas Kuhn (1962), a historian of science, has pointed out that most sciences go through periods of what he calls *paradigm clash*. At such times several points of view about the nature of a phenomenon under study compete with each other. These are also times when scientists advocating one point of view are unlikely to accept even the most fundamental assumptions of scientists advocating another.

But most sciences move through these times of paradigm clash into what Kuhn calls periods of *normal science*. During these normal periods one viewpoint predominates, and important work continues within this dominant framework. Most fields seem to move back and forth between periods of disagreement and periods of normal science, although younger disciplines tend to have more disagreements among fundamental points of view.

The field of abnormal psychology seems to be going through a period of paradigm clash. And so it is important to describe each of these competing views of abnormal behavior and to show what is compelling about each. Let us return to our first question. How can scientists look at the same case and explain it in such radically different ways?

MODELS AND PERSPECTIVES IN SCIENTIFIC THINKING

To answer the question of how scientists can disagree so fundamentally we must look at their thought processes. Price (1978) has suggested that scientists use *analogies* to provide a framework for understanding a puzzling new event.

The analogy applies a *concept* that organizes the puzzling event or phenomenon by treating it *as if* it were a more familiar one. The scientist says in effect, "In order to understand the brain I will treat it *as if* it were a computer." Then the scientist can use the computer as a *model* of the brain. This allows the scientist to *select* some events as relevant for study, to *represent* aspects of the puzzling events, and to *make hypotheses* about how the events are organized.

Because adopting a particular model or analogy for representing abnormal behavior exerts such a powerful influence on how we "see" or perceive the events in question, we have chosen the term *perspective* to characterize the approaches we will describe in this chapter.

In fact, we do make sense out of complex events by applying a framework that emphasizes some aspects of those events and deemphasizes others. And so we will see that the various views of abnormal behavior emphasize one aspect of a person's behavior rather than another.

For example, the *sociological* perspective emphasizes the effect of social forces acting on the person displaying the abnormal behavior. The *dynamic* view focuses much more on events in the subjective life of the person and how inner needs may conflict. The *learning* view stresses the role of rewards and punishments on our behavior while the *biological* perspective focuses on our biological nature. Finally, the *humanistic* perspective emphasizes the conditions needed for psychological growth. Each view focuses on different aspects of the life of the person and, in doing so, produces a coherent and yet in some ways incomplete picture. Let us now examine each perspective.

THE BIOLOGICAL PERSPECTIVE

You will recall that in Chapter 1 we said that the 19th century ushered in a new age of medical and biological understanding of the nature of infectious disease. Louis Pasteur showed that diseases could be produced by bacteria and that there was increasing evidence that a number of microorganisms could cause disease. Furthermore, evidence was developing that a number of common diseases such as typhus, tuberculosis, and syphilis could at times produce irrational behavior in victims. New medical specialties such as neurology, the study of the brain and nervous system, were becoming important,

and physicians like Paul Broca discovered the speech area of the brain and localized a variety of specific behavioral functions. Emil Kraepelin, a physician, engaged in elaborate attempts to classify various patterns of abnormal behavior so that they could be described in terms of symptoms and diseases. These developments led to the modern biological view of abnormal behavior.

The *biological perspective* assumes that abnormal behavior is a result of biological abnormalities that either affect behavior directly or do so in combination with stressful environmental influences. Biologically oriented researchers tend to look for evidence to support this view in at least two areas. First, they may attempt to demonstrate that people who develop abnormal behavior are more *genetically similar* to each other than people who do not develop disorders. If this can be shown, the case for genetic origins of abnormal behavior is strengthened. We will examine the strategies for genetic research in the biological perspective in what follows.

A second approach to discovering the biological origins of abnormal behavior is *biochemical*. Because any genetic disorder must express itself through biochemical pathways before developing into observable abnormal behavior, researchers may look for biochemical differences between normal and abnormal individuals. If in fact such differences can be observed, the case for a biological basis for abnormal behavior is strengthened. Furthermore, the biological perspective assumes that *biological treatments* are appropriate to treat abnormal behavior since the nature of the disorder itself is assumed to be hereditary, biochemical, or the result of an invading organism or disease of the nervous system. We will examine several forms of biological treatment for abnormal behavior later in this section.

Biological Research: The Example of Schizophrenia

Biologically oriented researchers have long pursued the hypothesis that a severe form of psychological disorder, *schizophrenia,* has a genetic basis. While we will consider research on the origins of schizophrenia in a later chapter in more detail, a brief examination of the biological research on the determinants of schizophrenia is instructive in illustrating the nature of the biological perspective.

There is considerable evidence that a child with one schizophrenic parent has a risk of developing schizophrenia himself or herself that is 10 times greater than someone selected at random from the general population. Furthermore, a child with two schizophrenic parents has a risk that is 40 times greater. Biologically oriented researchers see this as plausible evidence for the genetic basis of schizophrenia. Interestingly, as we shall see later in this chapter, researchers interested in social learning theories might argue that this is evidence for the impact of social learning in the family context on the behavior of children.

Since the evidence we have just described is open to alternative interpretations, genetic researchers have attempted to rule out the experience of living in a schizophrenic family as a possible cause of the disorder. The most common strategy for doing so is to study twins.

Twin Studies. The strategy behind twin studies depends on the fact that identical twins have developed from the same egg and are genetically identical while fraternal twins have developed from separate eggs and are no more genetically similar then other siblings. If the frequency of schizophrenia in pairs of identical and fraternal twins is compared, we can begin to estimate the effects of the environment and those of heredity. By identifying samples of identical and fraternal twins in which one member is schizophrenic and then examining the other twin for signs of disorder, rate of concordance in both groups can be compared. Rosenthal (1970) reviewed a large number of such twins studies that had been conducted over the previous 30 years. The results tend to show higher concordance rates in monozygotic than in dizygotic twin pairs. That is, the likelihood of both twins displaying the disorder was higher in monozygotic twin pairs.

Another strategy for engaging in research on the genetic origins of abnormal behavior involves studying children who are born to schizophrenic parents but who were put up for adoption early in life. If genetic factors are important in the disorder, children who have been adopted from schizophrenic parents ought to be more likely to develop abnormal behavior than would other adopted children who were not born to schizophrenic parents.

Rosenthal (1970) studied such adopted children in Denmark, where highly detailed birth records are available. By studying all of the children who had been adopted in Denmark over a 23-year period, Rosenthal was able to identify a group that had later become schizophrenic. The results of this study supported the genetic hypothesis. Children who had been adopted and who had been born of parents suffering from schizophrenia were more likely to develop schizophrenic symptoms themselves than were children who had been adopted but were born to biological parents with no history of psychological disorder. These and other studies of the genetic basis of schizophrenia have encouraged biologically oriented researchers to believe that there is likely to be a biological or genetic component in at least some severe forms of abnormal behavior.

But how a genetic component in a severe disorder expresses itself in terms of abnormal behavior has led researchers in another direction. Presumably the biochemistry of the brains of people suffering from severe forms of abnormal behavior would be different from persons not suffering from the disorder. This has led biologically oriented researchers on a search for biochemical differences.

Biochemical Research. Early biochemical research in the study of schizophrenia and other severe behavior disorders sought some biological factor that was unique to the group under investigation. It was believed that if the biological "X factor" in disorders such as schizophrenia or depression could be found, then the biological cause and cure would not be far behind.

Today, however, researchers are studying the chemistry of the brain rather than looking for a factor unique to each form of abnormal behavior. Biological researchers are attempting to understand the fundamental nature of the chemical function of the brain and assume that chemical balances or malfunctions lead to various forms of abnormal behavior.

The focus of research attention has recently been on the brain's *neurotransmitters*. These chemicals, which transmit electric impulses from one nerve cell to the next, have been implicated in the development of a number of disorders, including depression and schizophrenia. Nearly a dozen neurotransmitters have been identified and it is assumed that interference with their functioning by drugs or disease can dramatically affect behavior.

Dopamine is a neurotransmitter that has been implicated as a possible determinant of schizophrenia (Snyder, 1975). Some of the evidence for the role of dopamine as a neurotransmitter in schizophrenia is indirect. For example, some of the major tranquilizers used to treat schizophrenia have the effect of interfering with the action of dopamine.

These drugs inhibit transmission of nerve impulses by blocking the nerve cell receptor sites where dopamine normally has its effect.

Biological researchers have become interested in a variety of different chemicals that may affect the functioning of the brain. A portion of the brain, the hypothalamus, appears to be involved in the production of a group of regulators called the *neuropeptides*. These chemicals, sometimes called *endorphins*, were first found in the brain and were studied primarily for their opiatelike pain-reducing qualities.

The general action of these chemicals seems to be through their capacity to control the effects of neurotransmitters in the brain cell. Two of the best-known are the *beta endorphins*, which reduce physical response to pain, and the *enkephalins*, which also appear to have pain-relieving qualities. Other neuropeptides appear to affect learning and remembering new information, while still others appear to turn the sympathetic nervous system on or off.

Many researchers are convinced that the endorphins and enkephalins may play an important role in brain action involving mood, behavior, and emotion. Some researchers suggest that they may play a role in major disorders such as depression and schizophrenia as well as in alcohol and drug abuse. Thus we see that the biological perspective on the origins of abnormal behavior is being greatly strengthened by new research in brain biochemistry.

Biological Treatments

Just as biologically oriented researchers have pursued the causes of abnormal behavior through genetic and biochemical research, so have medical personnel, particularly in psychiatry, pursued a wide range of biological treatments for a range of disorders, including depression. The assumption seems straightforward. If abnormal behavior has a biological disorder as the underlying cause, then biological treatments should be most appropriate for their treatment. The primary biological treatments consist of *electroconvulsive therapy, psychosurgery,* and *psychoactive drugs.*

Today electroconvulsive treatment is used primarily in cases of severe depression that do not respond readily to other types of treatments. The patient is typically injected with an anesthetic, given a muscle relaxant, and strapped down to a bed to prevent bone fractures. Electrodes are placed on each side of the forehead. For approximately two seconds a current is sent through the brain to produce convulsions that look much like seizures.

Following treatment, patients are often confused and cannot remember the treatment itself or the events that occurred just before or afterward. New methods of treatment cause convulsions only on one side of the brain typically and produce less confusion and memory loss. Electroconvulsive therapy remains controversial as a form of biological treatment and no one understands the precise mechanisms by which it wcrks. Stephen Rose (1975) suggests that shock treatment is like "attempting to mend a faulty radio by kicking it." We will discuss electroconvulsive therapy in more detail in Chapter 19 on biological treatments.

Psychosurgery, widely used in the 1940s but now used only infrequently, is a second major biological treatment. During the 1950s psychosurgery was conducted on an extremely large number of mental patients. Although the technique did have a calming effect for some patients, it also had a variety of unintended side effects, including epileptic seizures, impaired intellect, and stupors. Newer techniques destroy much less brain tissue and produce fewer side effects. Valenstein (1973) has conducted an extensive re-

view of the research on psychosurgery and has concluded that a major problem with most techniques is the damage to other normal neural tissue.

The use of psychoactive drugs for the treatment of disordered behavior is a major outgrowth of the biological perspective and, at the same time, it reinforces the belief that abnormal behavior is primarily a biological phenomenon. Beginning in the 1950s the development of psychoactive drugs that alter psychological states for the treatment of abnormal behavior has grown rapidly and has had a dramatic impact on some types of disorders. Some psychoactive drugs appear to relieve many of the worst symptoms of depression and schizophrenia and have allowed many individuals to resume a more productive life. However, psychoactive drugs are far from a cure-all. Many produce undesirable side effects and some can lead to addiction. Furthermore, psychoactive drugs control rather than cure the symptoms of a psychological disorder; when the drug treatment regime is stopped, symptoms often will return.

Typically, psychoactive drugs are divided into four major groups: major tranquilizers for psychotic symptoms, minor tranquilizers designed to treat anxiety, various antidepressants, and stimulants. Each of these types of psychoactive drugs will be described in detail in Chapter 19 on biological treatments, but it is important to note here that the success of the use of psychoactive drugs has substantially reinforced the credibility of the biological perspective on abnormal behavior.

THE BIOLOGICAL PERSPECTIVE AND THE IDEA OF MENTAL ILLNESS

Thus far we have considered biologically based research on the causes of abnormal behavior as well as biologically based treatments to illustrate how biological assumptions direct our thinking about the causes and cures of abnormal behavior. However, we should also note that the biological perspective, especially as it is applied in the context of the medical speciality of psychiatry, tends to shape our thinking about the nature of abnormal behavior. Indeed, the term *mental illness* suggests that abnormal behavior is a form of illness, and much of the language of the biological perspective reflects this assumption.

The biological perspective and the social institution of medicine and psychiatry tend for the most part to accept this set of assumptions. Indeed, the assumption that some forms of deviant behavior are a result of illnesses can easily lead to the broader and erroneous conclusion that all forms of behavior that are somehow "different" are also the results of illness or disease.

The best-known attack on the notion that abnormal behavior is best understood as mental illness has been mounted by Thomas Szasz (1976). Although Szasz himself is a psychiatrist, he has been one of the most strident critics of the illness perspective on abnormal behavior. Szasz claims that mental illness is a myth. Instead, he believes the behavior we view as peculiar in others can be better thought of simply as "problems in living." According to Szasz, the concept of mental illness will not withstand logical analysis. Although mental illness is a medical term, it actually is defined by social standards. Szasz believes that we use the term *mental illness* to refer to people who communicate in ways that we find peculiar. Szasz may be correct that the application of biological assumptions to a wide range of forms of abnormal behavior sometimes occurs on the basis of very little evidence.

On the other hand, the biological perspective has already scored some important victories. Typically, once the organic basis for a disorder is found, it leaves the domain of psychiatry and abnormal psychology and is treated as just another biological disorder. A classic example of this shift in our view of a disorder is the apparently strange behavior that often accompanies pellagra, a nutritional disease. Once a vitamin deficiency was found to be the main cause and a simple effective treatment was found, pellagra was reclassified as an organic rather than a functional psychological disorder. Although there are rare cases in this country, it is not viewed as a psychological disorder even though bizarre behavior can, in some cases, still occur with it.

In later chapters we will see that the biological evidence for various disorders is far from uniform. Some disorders such as schizophrenia and some forms of mood disorders do appear to have important biological components. For other types of disorders, little or no solid biological evidence has yet been found. This of course raises the question of the degree to which the biological perspective or, for that matter, any perspective is equally applicable to all forms of abnormal behavior. We will be able to form opinions about that question at several points in later chapters.

We have seen that the biological perspective on abnormal behavior is widely accepted and has its own language and concepts. The view that some people may be biologically predisposed to certain disorders such as schizophrenia remains a viable one. We will review the evidence for this idea in later chapters. We should note, though, that the biological perspective, like all perspectives, gives an incomplete picture of abnormal behavior. It is a picture that minimizes the importance of social and interpersonal events in the life of the person.

THE DYNAMIC PERSPECTIVE

Sigmund Freud (1856–1939) has probably had the greatest impact of any person on the field of abnormal psychology. For more than

50 years he lectured and wrote scientific papers and books that have profoundly influenced how we think about human behavior. Freud has inspired historians, social critics, and entire schools of literature through his ideas. Even today his influence pervades our thinking and language.

Large segments of the mental health professions are devoted to the *psychodynamic* point of view originated by Freud. Psychoanalysis is taught as a primary way of understanding and treating abnormal behavior in a number of medical schools and clinical training programs throughout the country. Even though the dynamic viewpoint has had to compete with other approaches in recent years, it still must be counted as a major source of ideas in the field of abnormal psychology. Actually, a number of dynamic approaches have developed from Freud's original theories both as reactions to some of his propositions and as elaborations of his ideas. What all dynamic theories have in common is the view that abnormal behavior is the result of intrapsychic conflicts.

Overview of Psychoanalytic Theory

In the following discussion, we will dwell on the *psychological structure of the individual* in understanding the dynamic perspective on the development of abnormal behavior. Nevertheless, as Holzman (1970) has noted, psychoanalysis is not a single perspective; it is a group of perspectives focusing on three general areas. First, Freud wrote on the nature of *thinking and perception.* Second, psychoanalysis formulated a series of propositions and ideas on the *nature and course of human development.* Finally, part of Freudian thinking is devoted to the nature of *abnormal behavior and its treatment.* We will focus on this last aspect of psychoanalytic theory.

Fundamental Assumptions of the Dynamic Perspective

Holzman (1970) has offered an excellent summary of the basic assumptions about human behavior made by the psychoanalytic perspective.

Psychological Processes. These may operate outside our conscious awareness. Although Freud did not originate the concept of *unconscious psychological processes,* posthypnotic phenomena and the failure of many of his patients to recall crucial events in their lives convinced him that such processes must be occurring.

Indeed, Freud postulated the existence of unconscious, preconscious, and conscious mental activity. Conscious processes are those which are immediately within awareness at any given time. Preconscious processes are thoughts, ideas, and memories that may be outside of immediate awareness but readily available. The ability to recall a telephone number from preconscious processes is an example. Unconscious processes, on the other hand, represent a great reservoir of memories, hopes, fears, and fantasies that cannot easily be brought into awareness. Freud believed there was a "censoring" process that kept these unconscious thoughts from coming into awareness. A summary of this viewpoint process is shown in Figure 2–1.

Freud also believed that behavior was purposive, that is, motivated or caused. Within the psychoanalytic framework even symptoms are thought to serve a purpose. In fact, symptoms are thought to symbolize unconscious fantasies or wishes that are too threatening to be allowed to consciousness. For example, the little boy's forbidden sexual desires for his mother may be symbolically expressed in his imitation of the mother's behavior.

Developmental Determinants of Behavior. Psychoanalysts believe that early experiences have a profound effect on later adult

FIGURE 2-1
Relationship among the Unconscious, Preconscious, and Conscious Domains of Psychological Life

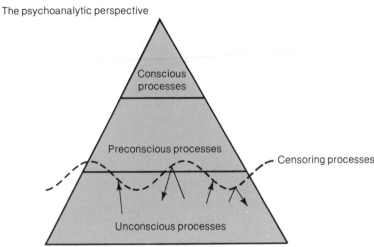

functioning. As Holzman (1970) phrases it, for each person the "past persists into the present." Freud described development in terms of psychosexual stages that all children must pass through. At each stage the child faces new conflicts and developmental tasks. Only by successfully meeting the developmental challenges of each stage can the individual attain mature adult functioning, which Freud sees as the ability to love and work. Failure to meet the challenges of a given stage may result in a fixation at that level of development. Fixation refers to the developmental arrest at a given psychosocial stage. Behaviors or motives that are fixated at infantile levels of development persist into adult life. For example, the infant whose mother is cold and unresponsive during breastfeeding may become a heavy smoker as an adult. Freud would explain this behavior as the individual's unconscious attempt to obtain the oral gratification that was denied him or her as a child.

Drives or Needs Can Differ in Their Intensity. This is often called the *quantitative* assump-

tion in dynamic thinking. According to this view, much of what we call abnormal behavior is abnormal in its degree or intensity rather than qualitatively different.

The Adaptive Nature of Behavior. Freud believed that human behavior should be understood as a response to the demands of the physical and social environment. Rapaport and Gill (1967) have called this the "adaptive point of view." It serves to emphasize that the psychoanalytic perspective recognized the impact on people of important interpersonal and social events and saw each person as continuously coping, shaping, and being shaped by the social environment and culture.

Mental Structures, Conflict, and Anxiety

Freud believed there were three major structures in the mental life of each person: the *id*, the *ego*, and the *superego* (see Table 2-1). Each of these structures operated in dynamic relation to the other two, and the final

TABLE 2-1
Personality Structure According to the Psychoanalytic Perspective

Structure	Functioning Principle	Mode of Operation
Id:	*Pleasure Principle*	*Primary Process*
The instincts; source of psychic energy; biological substratum of personality.	Seeks to gratify instinctual drives immediately.	Direct motor discharge of energy or drive, such as dreams, wish fulfillment.
Ego:	*Reality Principle*	*Secondary Process*
Developed from the id; reality oriented; judging; executive.	"Executive function," that is, moderates demands of instinctual impulses and demands of external reality.	Differentiates objective from subjective reality; relies on past experience; judges.
Superego:	*Moral Evaluation*	*Conscience*
Developed from the ego; represents introjection of parental moral standards and values.	Judges right and wrong, "good" and "bad."	Source of moral judgment.
		Ego Ideal
		Image of person child would like to become.

Source: From *Abnormal Behavior: Perspectives in Conflict,* Second Edition, by Richard H. Price. Copyright © 1978 by Holt, Rinehart and Winston. Copyright © 1972 by Holt, Rinehart and Winston, Inc. Reprinted by permission of Holt, Rinehart and Winston.

product of these relationships was the behavior of the person.

The *id* was thought by Freud to represent the primitive biological drives of the person. The id was thought to be in "chaos, a caldron of seething excitement" (Freud, 1933, pp. 103–4). The id's goal was to release this biological energy in aggressive or erotic ways; thus the id was described as operating according to the *pleasure principle.*

Freud called the second major structure in the person's mental life the *ego.* Whereas the id operates by the pleasure principle, the ego operates by the *reality principle.* That is, the ego takes into account the demands and constraints of the outside world in attempting to gratify the sexual and aggressive impulses of the id. One can think of the ego as a kind of executive branch that judges the feasibility, reality, and appropriateness of our actions.

Freud described the third major structure in the person's psychological life as the *su-perego.* As a child is reared, he or she usually learns that certain acts and even certain impulses are "good" and others are "bad."

The superego is the internal representation of the moral standards of society. It controls and judges our actions as we plan or fantasize about them, or as we carry them out. Actually, the superego is composed of two separate parts, the *conscience* and the *ego ideal.* The conscience represents the individual's sense of right and wrong while the ego ideal represents the individual's fantasized self, the ideal person he or she wishes to be.

It is the *conflict* between these three structures, Freud believed, that determines much of our behavior. For example, the instinctual demands of the id may conflict with either the reality-oriented concerns of the ego or the moral demands of the superego. When such conflicts occur and are not readily resolved, they are thought to produce tension or anxiety.

Seemingly irrational behavior can be understood as the ego's attempt to mediate between the demands of the id and the superego. The ego's attempt to satisfy the conflicting demands of both structures is illustrated in *bulimia*, an eating disorder characterized by binge eating followed by self-induced vomiting. Persons with this disorder are torn between a wish to gorge themselves and a preoccupation with maintaining an ideal weight. The ego first satisfies the id's demands for immediate gratification by allowing the unrestrained eating of previously shunned foods.

While the eating binge satisfies the demands of the id, it violates the superego's demands for discipline and living up to one's ideals. Again, the ego must intervene, this time on behalf of the superego. Through the act of self-induced vomiting the ego satisfies the superego's demands for self-punishment and restitution. Thus the binge eating and subsequent vomiting of the bulimic allows the gratification of both id impulses and superego prohibitions.

Freud thought that people felt different kinds of anxiety depending on which structures among the id, ego, and superego were in conflict. *Reality anxiety* was believed to be produced when the ego perceived some real physical threat in the outside world. *Moral anxiety*, as the name implies, was thought be a product of conflict between the id and the superego. Finally, *neurotic anxiety* was thought to occur when the id and the ego were in conflict.

In the last two cases, the person undergoes an inner struggle between conflicting impulses. This struggle can be so great, Freud believed, that the person finds the resulting anxiety intolerable.

Defense Mechanisms

Freud was, among other things, a brilliant and perceptive observer of human behavior. When he detected a patient's defensive reality-distorting strategies, he was especially curious and persistent in his inquiries. His years of trying to unravel the complexities of his patients' fantasies, dreams, and apparently irrational behavior patterns yielded the discovery of several distinctive *defense mechanisms*.

The ego, Freud believed, in the role of protector at times had to take irrational measures to shield itself from this conflict-produced anxiety. The means of protection are called *ego defense mechanisms*. They are psychological ways of distorting reality to reduce the anxiety caused by, for example, the id-ego conflict. The most important of them is called *repression*. Here the id impulse, in conflict with the ego or the superego, is totally dismissed from consciousness. That is, repression takes the impulse out of awareness and, by so doing, temporarily relieves us of id-ego conflict and its resultant anxiety.

Another important aspect of defense mechanisms is that they act *without our ever being aware of them*. Therefore, the energy from the original conflict still exists and may manifest itself in anxiety from time to time; but we may not know why we are anxious because the original causes of the conflict are repressed.

Freud thought that much of the behavior that seemed odd, irrational, or abnormal was evidence of defense mechanisms at work shielding the ego. These defenses might at first seem illogical, but actually they have an internal logic of their own. Furthermore, trying to understand a defense mechanism and how it works to protect the person could yield clues about the person's underlying conflict.

One of the most common defense mechanisms is *rationalization*. Simply put, rationalization involves finding excuses for undesirable feelings or happenings. Actually, there are two common types of rationalization—

"sweet lemon" and "sour grapes." Sweet lemon rationalization refers to our tendency to focus on the few positive aspects of an otherwise bleak situation. For example, the person turned down for a job may focus on the leisure time he or she can now enjoy. Sour grapes rationalization, on the other hand, refers to people's tendency to devalue what they cannot possess. For example, the person turned down for a job may focus on how little the job pays and how poor the working conditions would have been.

Projection is a mechanism in which an individual attributes his or her own unacceptable impulses to others. For example, a person who is frightened by his or her own sexual impulses might accuse others of thinking only about sex. By projecting the unacceptable impulses onto others, the individual finds an acceptable explanation for the presence of sexual thoughts and fantasies.

Reaction formation is a mechanism in which expressed conscious attitudes or behaviors are the opposite of an internal wish or impulse. The pursuit of activities appropriate to the forbidden wishes serves to convince the person that he or she does not possess those underlying impulses. For example, the man who has homosexual inclinations may convince himself that he is not a homosexual by leading a crusade to ban movies that depict homosexual relations. Notice that in this instance the man can safely obtain gratification of his wishes through exposure to forbidden material in the noble guise of acting as guardian of the public's morality.

Displacement refers to the mechanism in which an impulse directed at one person or object is shifted to another more acceptable substitute person or object. When a child strikes a younger brother instead of expressing anger toward a parent, displacement may be at work.

It is important to note that the use of defense mechanisms is not in itself pathological. In fact, all of us use different defense mechanisms every day. For example, many students who do poorly on an examination will rationalize their performance as due to their lack of effort or an unusually difficult test. In many such instances the use of defense mechanisms can protect us from experiencing the self-blame and doubt that often accompany failure. Defense mechanisms are a cause for concern only when employed to such an extent that the person loses touch with reality. For example, individuals who consistently blame all their troubles on external forces and deny any personal responsibility will encounter even more difficulties as their thoughts and behavior become increasingly inconsistent with the world around them.

Current Trends: Object Relations Theory

Recently, psychoanalytic theorists have moved away from describing personality in terms of instincts and drives. Instead of focusing on biological determinants, modern-day theorists emphasize the role of interpersonal relations in personality development. This new understanding of human development is known as *object relations theory.*

Object relations theory maintains that a child's early interactions with his or her mother are critical determinants of later adult functioning. The first five years are especially critical since during this period the child must successfully accomplish a number of important developmental tasks. A mother who is responsive to the child's changing needs is necessary for the successful resolution of developmental challenges and the formation of a healthy sense of identity. Disruptions in the early mother-child relationship are thought to explain later adult psychopathology.

Mahler, Pines, and Bergmann (1975) see *separation and individuation* from the mother as one of the child's most important tasks. In the process of establishing a separate identity from the mother the child passes through four different subphases. The first subphase, which extends from five to nine months of age, involves the child's development of a body image. During this period the child learns to distinguish between inner and outer experience and gains a sense of self as separate from the outside world. In the second subphase, age 10 to 14 months, the child first begins to disengage from the mother. The important task of this period is for the child to learn to be able to maintain a sense of self when the mother is not present, During the third subphase, age 14 to 24 months, the child first begins to move away from the mother and explore the outside world on his or her own. It is important that the mother respond appropriately to her child's attempts at separation and be neither too protective nor too detached. During the final subphase, age two to three years, the child overcomes his or her *separation anxiety* and is able to maintain a constant sense of self, independent of the mother. The child recognizes that his or her identity is constant, despite moment-to-moment changes in emotions.

Adult personality disturbances are said to result from disruptions in the process of separating from the mother. For example, the child's failure to maintain a constant sense of self, independent of the mother, underlies a characterological disorder known as narcissistic personality. The term *narcissistic personality* describes a person who is unable to maintain a constant self-image and who fluctuates between feelings of superiority and feelings of worthlessness. We will ex-

plore this disturbance in more detail later in Chapter 13, "Personality Disorders."

Dynamic Explanations

Freud has been credited with being one of the great original thinkers of this century. Sometimes his contributions are not clearly appreciated. But there is no doubt that his most important contribution is the idea of the *dynamic unconscious*. This idea implies that the explanations we offer for our own behavior cannot be taken at face value. Instead, the true meaning or purpose of a given behavior always remains hidden from our conscious awareness.

In addition to this idea, Freud and his followers developed a treatment technique

In psychoanalysis the patient is frequently asked to free-associate. (Nancy Bates/The Picture Cube)

based on the theory of psychoanalysis. In this treatment individuals and sometimes groups are helped to examine the symbolic meaning of their behavior in order to find the psychological causes of their difficulties or symptoms. The effectiveness of this treatment method is still in dispute; yet it remains one of the most sought-after treatments today.

Some features of Freud's sweeping and complex theories have been much criticized, especially by philosophers of science and empirically oriented scientists. Perhaps the most important of these criticisms is that Freud's concepts often do not meet the criterion of *falsifiability* described by Sidney Hook (1959). What do we mean by falsifiability? Concepts should be constructed so that we can gather evidence that will help us decide whether or not the concept is consistent with the evidence at hand. If we cannot do this, the concept has little scientific usefulness. This is a slippery but important point. Let us taken an example from Hook that illustrates it.

> For example, we hear that someone is "intelligent" or "friendly." Many types of behavior can be cited as evidence of the presence of "intelligence" or "friendliness." *But, unless we are also told what we would have to observe to conclude that an individual is not "intelligent" or "friendly," the terms could be applied to anyone in all situations* (pp. 214–15, italics added).

The important point here is that if a concept does not specify the conditions under which it *is* applicable or *is not* applicable, it is of very little use in science.

Ideas like repression and defense share this problem of falsifiability. For example, if a person expresses great love for his father, is he expressing genuine affection or is this evidence of a reaction formation? Likewise, if you characterize another person as "hostile," are you reporting an accurate impression or projecting your own hostile feelings,

or both? It is problems of evidence and the criteria for application of Freud's concepts like these that have led to criticism of his system. The responsibility of those who follow such a bold explorer is to refine his ideas and to test them against observation and evidence.

THE LEARNING PERSPECTIVE

Perhaps the fastest growing approach to the study and treatment of abnormal behavior is the learning viewpoint. Although American psychologists have long studied the learning process, it is only in the last 30 years or so that they have applied learning principles to the analysis and treatment of abnormal behavior.

Pioneers in this relatively new approach to understanding abnormal behavior were encouraged by the early work of B. F. Skinner. More than 20 years ago Skinner published a book called *Science and Human Behavior.* The book applied learning principles, in particular those of instrumental conditioning, to a variety of human behaviors ranging from gambling and fishing to learning a language.

Another group of pioneers developing the idea that abnormal behavior could be learned was Jules Masserman and his colleagues. These researchers followed the lead of Ivan Pavlov and began to do laboratory experiments with animals to see if it was possible to create conditions in which abnormal behavior could be learned. They called the behavior they were able to produce *experimental neurosis.* This research led to the optimistic hope that if we were able to produce abnormal behavior in the laboratory, we would soon understand the naturally occurring circumstances under which abnormal behavior is produced.

A variety of mechanisms have been proposed to explain how abnormal behavior is acquired, how it is maintained. and how it might be eliminated. We will examine (1) classical conditioning, (2) instrumental conditioning, (3) modeling and observational learning, and (4) cognitive processes in the learning perspective.

Classical Conditioning

The first of these processes is called *classical conditioning.* This process was first described by Ivan Pavlov and explains how an event in the environment that originally elicited no reaction can, by being systematically paired with other events, evoke *conditioned responses.* Figure 2–2 shows how this process takes place.

Perhaps the most famous demonstration of how classical conditioning could produce abnormal behavior was done by Watson and Rayner (1920). They chose as their subject an 11-month-old child named Albert who was very fond of animals. Their goal was to show that through classical conditioning fears that looked irrational and phobic could be learned. In the laboratory, they closely observed Albert's behavior.

Whenever he reached out for a white rat to which he was attracted (the white rat represents the *conditioned stimulus*), a loud noise was created. Not surprisingly, Albert was startled and began crying. (The boy's reaction is considered the *unconditioned*

Ivan Pavlov. (National Library of Medicine)

John B. Watson. (The Ferdinand Hamburger, Jr. Archives, The Johns Hopkins University)

FIGURE 2–2
Classical Conditioning Paradigm

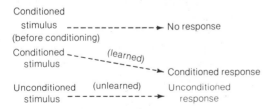

Source: Adapted from *Introduction to Psychology,* Third Edition by Ernest R. Hilgard, copyright © 1962 by Harcourt Brace Jovanovich, Inc. Reprinted by permission of the publisher.

response, and the loud noise is thought of as the *unconditioned stimulus*). After a number of such pairings of the white rat with the loud noise, Albert was terrified whenever the rat was presented to him. Furthermore, his reaction generalized to other furry objects as well. Watson and Rayner then argued that they had demonstrated that apparently irrational fears (phobias) can be learned through classical conditioning. That is, by pairing a previously neutral stimulus (the rat) with a stimulus that could evoke a strong response (the loud noise) it was possible to obtain a fear reaction to the rat when it was later presented by itself.

Instrumental Conditioning

The second major mechanism used to explain how abnormal behavior is acquired and maintained is called *instrumental conditioning.* With this process, the *consequences* of a particular behavior affect the likelihood that the behavior will occur again. This idea, developed by a number of psychologists including Thorndike and elaborated most by B. F. Skinner, suggests that *contingencies* are extremely important in understanding the development of abnormal behavior. In this approach events that immediately follow particular behaviors on a systematic basis are called *reinforcements.*

Instrumental Conditioning of Symptoms. Is it possible to reward a behavior using instrumental conditioning procedures so that, after a while, the very persistence and frequency of the behavior make it seem strange and abnormal? An example of the development of abnormal behavior using the instrumental conditioning process has been provided by Haughton and Ayllon (1965). They created "abnormal behavior" in a hospitalized 54-year-old woman and then eliminated it using principles of instrumental conditioning. After depriving the patient of her ciga-

rettes, the researchers proceeded to "shape" the behavior they had selected arbitrarily. They decided to demonstrate that it was possible to have this patient stand upright holding a broom. All that was needed to increase this behavior was to follow it quickly (contingent reinforcement) with a cigarette. A staff member approached the patient whenever she happened to be holding the broom, handed her a cigarette, and left with no explanation. As time went on, the broom-holding symptom became very pronounced and was accompanied by a number of other abnormal behaviors. For example, the patient became quite stereotyped in her broom-holding behavior; she resisted giving up the broom and remained in a circumscribed part of the hospital ward for long periods.

These researchers then took their demonstration a step further: they asked two psychiatrists holding a dynamic perspective to "explain" the behavior of the patient. Of course, they did not reveal how the patient had acquired the broom-holding behavior. The psychiatrists interpreted the behavior as a "magical act" in which the broom might represent either a "phallic symbol" or a "scepter of an omnipotent queen."

Even if it is possible to create artificial situations in which abnormal behavior can be produced, we might well ask, are these same mechanisms responsible for the production of abnormal behavior in natural settings? Certainly, Haughton and Ayllon have shown that instrumental conditioning mechanisms can produce behavior that is perceived as abnormal, particularly when the reinforcement contingencies are not known to the observer.

The Example of Depression: Seligman's Learned Helplessness Theory. One recent account of the development and maintenance of depressive behavior is offered by Seligman (1975), who argues that depression is a learned response to an uncontrollable environment. Seligman bases his argument on

SKINNER OFFERS A LEARNING INTERPRETATION

Consider a young man whose world has suddenly changed—he has graduated from college and is going to work, let us say, or has been inducted into the armed services. Most of the behavior he has acquired up to this point is useless in his new environment. We can describe the behavior he actually exhibits, and translate the description, as follows: he lacks assurance or feels insecure *(his behavior is weak and inappropriate)*; he is discouraged *(he is seldom reinforced, and as a result his behavior undergoes extinction)*; he is frustrated *(extinction is accompanied by emotional responses)*; he feels anxious *(his behavior frequently has unavoidable aversive consequences that have emotional effects)*; there is nothing he wants to do or enjoys doing well—he has no feeling of craftsmanship, no sense of accomplishment *(he is rarely reinforced for doing anything)*; he feels guilty or ashamed *(he has previously been punished for idleness or failure, which now evoke emotional responses)*; he is disgusted with himself *(he is no longer reinforced by the admiration of others, and the extinction that follows has emotional effects)*; he becomes hypochondriacal *(he concludes that he is ill)*; or neurotic *(he engages in a variety of ineffective modes of escape)*; and he experiences an identity crisis *(he does not recognize the person he once called "I")*.

The italicized paraphrases suggest the possibility of an alternative account, which alone suggests effective action. What the young man tells us about his feelings may permit us to make some informed guesses about what is wrong with the contingencies, but we must go directly to the contingencies if we want to be sure, *and it is the contingencies we must change if we are to change his behavior.*

From *Beyond Freedom and Dignity*, by B. F. Skinner. Copyright © 1971 by B. F. Skinner. Reprinted by permission of Alfred A. Knopf, Inc.

B. F. Skinner. (Courtesy of B. F. Skinner, photo by Christopher S. Johnson)

the results of animal studies and on observation of how people react under adverse conditions beyond their control.

An animal first confronted with a painful event, such as an electroshock, will attempt to avoid or escape the situation. For example, if a dog is shocked in a box separated from another box by a small barrier, it will immediately jump the barrier and escape the shock. However, if previously the dog was forced to endure inescapable electroshocks, when later placed in the same situation, it will not try to escape by jumping over the barrier. Instead, the dog passively endures the painful shocks. Seligman (1975) argues that the dog has learned that there is nothing it can do to influence its environment and therefore resigns itself to experiencing the painful event. The effect is so powerful that even when given the chance to escape, the dog will not take advantage of the opportunity. Seligman refers to this acquired state of passivity as *learned helplessness.*

Seligman believes that depression in humans can be explained in terms of learned helplessness. Over time some people may encounter so many uncontrollable events that they will begin to feel that they possess little control over their own lives. The result is a feeling of helplessness that causes the individual to withdraw or respond passively when faced with adverse life events.

Such reactions are dramatically illustrated when individuals confront catastrophic circumstances beyond their control. A good example of this phenomenon is found in Bettleheim's (1960) description of the reactions of inmates in Nazi concentration camps:

Prisoners who came to believe the repeated statements of the guards—that there was no hope for them, that they would never leave the camp except as a corpse—came to feel that their environment was one over which they could exercise no influence whatsoever. . . .

Once his own life and the environment were viewed as totally beyond his ability to influence them, the only logical conclusion was to pay no attention to them whatsoever (pp. 451–52).

The reactions of the concentration camp inmates in many ways resemble the symptoms found in clinical depression. Thus depression may be described as a state of learned helplessness that results from continued contact with an uncontrollable environment. We will explore the merits of this theory in more detail in Chapter 8.

Social Learning and Modeling

In addition to the mechanisms of classical and instrumental conditioning, observational learning and modeling represents a third possible mechanism that may play an important role in the development of abnormal behavior. In general, as Bandura (1966) has suggested, the observation and imitation of others may be an important factor in the development of new maladaptive behavior even when no direct classical or instrumental conditioning of responses has occurred.

Bandura and Rosenthal (1966) have demonstrated one of the most interesting examples of this process. This was in a study in which they were able to produce "vicarious conditioning" of phobic behavior. In the demonstration a person who was actually the researchers' accomplice was observed by experimental subjects while attached to an electrical apparatus that made it look as if the accomplice was about to get a shock. The apparent shock was accompanied by the sound of a buzzer. Later the observers showed dramatic increases in emotional response themselves to the sound of the buzzer, even though it had never been directly paired with the aversive event as would have been required with classical conditioning.

Albert Bandura. (Courtesy of Albert Bandura)

Perhaps the most famous illustrations of the power of observational learning in the development of abnormal behavior were done by Bandura and Walters (1963). They showed that small children will behave aggressively after observing an adult model behave aggressively. In the classic experiment, adult models attacked a Bobo doll while children looked on. Later, without any instructions, the children also displayed the same patterns of violently aggressive behavior.

Thus observational learning and vicarious conditioning are highly plausible ways in which abnormal behavior may be learned.

In recent years learning theorists have placed greater emphasis on the thoughts or cognitions people have about their environment. *Cognitive social learning theory* explores how a person's belief about a situation influences his or her subsequent performance. Instead of treating the environment as unchanging, cognitive social learning theory stresses the influence people have on the situations with which they interact. Actual behavior is seen as a product of the ever-changing person-situation interaction.

The cognitive social learning approach is illustrated by the different reactions people have to the same stimulus or event. For example, two college roommates are invited to a party where they will know few people. The first welcomes the opportunity to meet new people and anticipates having a pleasant evening. In contrast, the second roommate worries that he will have no one to talk to and anticipates feeling awkward and uncomfortable. When the two roommates arrive at the party, the first immediately strikes up a conversation with a stranger while the second heads straight for the food table and hides behind the pretzels and potato chips. Not surprisingly, the first roommate has an enjoyable time and stays late while the second roommate has a very unpleasant time and leaves early.

This example illustrates that not only do our existing beliefs affect how we perceive a given event, but that the beliefs we possess also influence the environments we choose. For instance, one would expect that in the future the second roommate will refuse to attend parties where he would know few other people. Thus, rather than being passively influenced by their environments, people are seen as actively interpreting and shaping the world around them.

The recent emphasis on the role of cognition in human behavior has resulted in a new approach to treating abnormal behavior known as *cognitive behavior therapy*. This approach is based on the notion that changing people's thoughts will result in changes in their feelings and behaviors (Meichenbaum,

This series of pictures shows an adult exhibiting aggressive behavior which is then modeled by children who have observed it. (Source: Albert Bandura, Dorothea Ross, and Sheila A. Ross, "Imitation of Film-mediated Aggressive Models." *Journal of Abnormal and Social Psychology*, 1963, *66*, 3–11. Copyright 1963 by the American Psychological Association. Reprinted by permission.)

1977; Chambless & Goldstein, 1979). One cognitive behavior therapy technique focuses on changing the statements people make to themselves before entering a given situation. It is assumed that by changing a person's negative expectations to positive expectations he or she will experience a favorable outcome. For instance, in the earlier example the roommate who experienced social fears might be taught to concentrate on more positive thoughts and expectations. Another technique involves teaching people better ways to solve problems in interpersonal situations by helping them formulate various alternatives. This approach assumes that many difficulties in interpersonal situations are caused by deficits in social skills. Chambless and Goldstein (1979) note that training people to think through problems

enables them to be their own therapists when facing new situations in the future.

Overview of the Learning Perspective

As we said earlier, the learning viewpoint has gained considerable support over the last several decades in American psychology. Yet one of the strongest objections to this view is raised because of the assumptions learning theorists make about human nature. Often objections have focused on B. F. Skinner's views, in particular those in his book *Beyond Freedom and Dignity* (1971). There he argues that our underlying assumptions that humans are autonomous have had a destructive effect on our society. Some of the by-products of these assumptions are overpopulation, pollution, and war. Traditional views about human freedom and dignity, Skinner argues, have stood in the way of meaningful change. Instead, we should see humans for what they are—behaving organisms controlled largely by the reinforcement contingencies in the environment. The task, as Skinner sees it, is to design a culture that squarely faces the responsibility to control human behavior for the collective benefit of all.

Skinner's critics argue that the learning perspective offers an overly mechanical view of humans and human behavior—it fails to take account of the individual's inner experience and subjective life. Most likely Skinner does overstate his case, perhaps for polemic reasons. We should recognize, however, that it is not necessary to deny the subjective experience of humans in order to assert that some or even all aspects of abnormal behavior are learned. In the nature of perspectives, however, both advocates and critics tend to take an "all-or-nothing" approach to understanding abnormal behavior.

The fact that the learning perspective has gained such support recently probably has little to do with the plausibility of the view that abnormal behavior is learned. Instead, strong support for the learning viewpoint comes mostly from the many impressive demonstrations that learning principles can be applied to the *treatment* of abnormal behavior. One of the most impressive aspects of the learning viewpoint is that it has closely tied assessment methods and behavior-change strategies.

A variety of techniques based on instrumental conditioning have been used to shape the behavior of children and hospitalized patients. These treatment methods have met with a fair amount of success, and one of the great merits of the learning perspective is that it has developed treatment techniques that can not only be applied systematically but whose results can also be effectively measured.

Some supporters of the learning perspective have argued that *because* we can treat abnormal behavior by using learning principles, the behaviors were learned in the first place. Tempting as this logical leap is, it does not follow from the evidence. Buchwald and Young (1969) make this point with the example of a person who has lost the ability to speak because of a brain injury. A person can sometimes be taught to speak again using learning principles. Yet this does not mean that the loss of speech was "learned" in the first place.

In sum, the learning perspective has in recent years greatly influenced our thinking about the nature and origins of abnormal behavior. The perspective has grown as a result of both creative insights and research on problems like observational learning and cognitive events and because of the development of learning-based treatment methods.

THE SOCIOLOGICAL PERSPECTIVE

Still another important perspective on abnormal behavior shifts our attention away from the behavior of the individual to that of people around the person and their reactions to his or her behavior. It argues that mental illness exists to a great degree in the eyes of those people who come in contact with the "labeled" person. This is a unique departure, one that calls attention to the social environment of the individual. It suggests that other approaches to abnormal behavior mistakenly remove the behavior of the person from the context in which it occurs.

Norms and Roles and the Career of a Mental Patient

Not surprisingly, many of the advocates of the sociological perspective, such as Erving

Goffman (1961) and Thomas Scheff (1975), were not trained in medicine or psychology but rather in sociology. Their sensitivity to the social context of the person adds a dimension to our understanding. They stress that people who are called "abnormal" often are viewed as such because they violate certain *social norms* or socially agreed-upon rules of conduct. They also suggest that being a patient in a mental hospital means that one is *cast into the social role of patient.* This role consists of a set of behaviors that are subtly rewarded by those around the patient. Finally, they point out that a great deal of mental patients' behavior can be explained by looking at the social institutions with which the patients have to interact instead of studying the patients' biochemistry, learning history, or childhood traumas.

How, then, do people become mental patients, according to this view? In general, both Goffman and Scheff agree that when a person behaves in a way that is puzzling or frightening to us, we are likely to seek an explanation. If an obvious one is not forthcoming, we may at last settle on the explanation that the person is "mentally ill" or "sick."

Once the person has been labeled, it is quite natural to begin to see different aspects of the person's behavior as consistent with the view that he is "crazy" or ill. The labeling itself, then, alters the way we behave toward the person. And the labeled person, in turn, seeing our change in attitude, may further change his or her behavior toward us. This cycle of events may continue until eventually the person is led through a series of interactions with social workers, ministers, or others who may recommend that the individual be hospitalized. Thus the sociological perspective suggests that the series of interactions that a person has with others may produce a "deviation amplifying system" that finally leads to hospitalization. This is often described as the *career* of a person on the path to patienthood.

Being Sane in Insane Places: An Example of the Sociological Perspective in Action

We have said that the sociological viewpoint stresses others' reactions to the person who is labeled mentally ill. This view also suggests that the person is cast in the role of mental patient by relatives, friends, and employers, and by medical personnel who accept the view that abnormal behavior is an illness.

One of the most dramatic and fascinating studies offered in support of the social perspective has been done by Rosenhan (1973). Rosenhan asked the question, "Can the sane be distinguished from the insane?" and decided to do a study he thought would help him find out. He began with a group of friends and collaborators. In the group were three psychologists, a psychiatrist, a pediatrician, a painter, and a housewife. These people were asked by Rosenhan to become "pseudopatients"—that is, they were each to report to a mental hospital and request admission. The only "symptom" they were allowed to report to the examining physicians during the intake interview was that they heard voices which were unclear but seemed to say "empty," "hollow," and "thud."

The pseudopatients also falsified their names and their work, but otherwise presented themselves as they really were. All of them were admitted to the hospital upon reporting their symptom, even though the symptom had never been recorded in the psychiatric literature as an indicator of severe psychiatric disorder. Furthermore, all but one of them were diagnosed as being schizophrenic. All were later discharged, most of them with a diagnosis of "schizophrenia in remission."

Rosenhan believes that the results of his study dramatically demonstrate that it is not possible to tell the "insane" from the "sane" in the psychiatric hospital. Perhaps more important for our purposes is that Rosenhan believes he has demonstrated the power of labels to affect our perceptions and behaviors. Once the person is labeled "schizophrenic," the hospital staff comes to expect that the person will continue to behave like a schizophrenic.

This shows how *patienthood* can be thought of as a social role. Once hospitalized and diagnosed as schizophrenic, these people found themselves cast in the role of patients and treated as if they were mentally ill. It is hard to resist being cast into this role; any protests denying one's status are likely to be seen as evidence that the individual does not yet have "insight" into his or her own behavior.

Let us look at some examples of how Rosenhan's pseudopatients were cast in the role of the mentally ill:

One tacit characteristic of psychiatric diagnosis is that it locates the sources of aberration within the individual and only rarely within the complex of stimuli that surrounds him.

Consequently, behaviors that are stimulated by the environment are commonly misattributed to the patient's disorder. For example, one kindly nurse found a pseudo-patient pacing the hospital corridors. "Nervous, Mr. X?" she asked.

"No, bored," he said (Rosenhan, 1973, pp. 250–58).

Or consider what happened to pseudopatients when they asked doctors when they would likely be discharged from the hospital:

The encounter frequently took the bizarre form. (Pseudo-patient) "Pardon me, Doctor X. Could you tell me when you are eligible for grounds privileges?" (Physician) "Good morning, Dave. How are you today?" (moves off without waiting for a response) (Rosenhan, 1973, p. 256).

We should not assume that nursing and psychiatric staff are the only people within the psychiatric setting who help convince the people that they are indeed ill. Consider this example Scheff gives (1966, p. 86).

The mental hospital environment can often subtly reward patients in the hospital for engaging in the role of patienthood. (Zalesky/Black Star)

New patient: I don't belong here. I don't like all these crazy people. When can I talk to the doctor? I've been here four days and I haven't seen the doctor. I'm not crazy.

Another patient: She says she's not crazy [laughter from patients].

Another patient: Honey, what I'd like to know is, if you're not crazy, how did you get your ass in this hospital?

New patient: It's complicated, but I can explain. My husband and I. . .

First patient: That's what they all say [general laughter].

So, we see that the reactions of others, including other mental patients, can help cast a person in the role of someone who is mentally ill. Ultimately, in these circumstances the person cast in such a role begins to accept the role as appropriate and realistic for himself or herself and to question his or her own stability.

We can conclude that the sociological perspective sees mental illness as a set of expectations, stereotypes, and labels that we apply to people whose behavior or motives are difficult for us to understand. Once applied to a person, these labels shape not only how we see that person, but how we interact with that person and how that person sees himself or herself.

Reactions from the Medical Community to the Sociological Viewpoint

Rosenhan's study is certainly not the first in which a social scientist had himself hospitalized in order to find out what it was really like inside a mental hospital. Predictably enough, though, the study has brought intense reaction from the medical community. Again we see advocates of other perspectives reacting strongly to evidence that they see as threatening the basic assumptions of their viewpoints. Let us look at a sampling of reactions published in letters to the journal *Science*, where Rosenhan's study was originally published.

I am deeply concerned about the state and fate of psychiatric care in this country. I am also deeply concerned about the destructive potential of such pseudo-studies as the one under discussion. Appearing in *Science*, it can only be productive of unwarranted fear and mistrust in those who need psychiatric help and make the work of those who are trying to deliver and teach about quality care that much harder (*Science*, Vol. 180, p. 358).

If complaints of isolated auditory hallucinations are believed by the doctor, they can require neurological investigations including lumbar puncture, skilled x-ray series, radio-isotope brainscans. None of these procedures is without risk to the patient, but the risk is less than leaving undiagnosed brain disorders that can give rise to isolated hallucinations. One wonders if the volunteers for this reckless experiment were informed of this risk (*Science*, Vol. 180, p. 360).

A much more impressive demonstration of his point could be made by Rosenhan if he were to take obviously insane persons and, by giving them a new name and releasing them to a new community where they were not known, successfully pass them off as sane (*Science*, Vol. 180, p. 361).

The attack on psychiatric nomenclature as some kind of pernicious labeling comes very close to a denial that any mental disorders characterized by objectively ascertainable symptoms, behaviors, and tests altogether exist. In the not so distant past, "tuberculosis" and "syphillis" were words shunned by polite society. Fortunately, this did not deter physicians and researchers diagnosing and treating these conditions (*Science*, Vol. 180, p. 364).

Contributions of the Sociological Perspective

Although this view of abnormal behavior has become very popular recently, it has received a great deal of criticism as well. Walter Gove (1975) has done a series of evaluations of studies of hospital admissions and of mental patients returning to the community. The sociological perspective would predict that hospital admissions would be very perfunctory, would seldom result in patient release, and would presume that ex-mental patients would suffer discrimination because of having been labeled. Gove's evidence, however, fails to support any of these predictions. There is little doubt that stereotypes and erroneous beliefs about the nature of mental illness affect our behavior and even that of mental health professionals and social policy decision makers. It is quite another thing, however, to argue that abnormal behavior is nothing but a labeling process.

Perhaps the greatest strength of the sociological perspective is its persistent focus on the *social context* of behavior as a crucial element in the development of a more complete understanding of abnormal behavior. Its greatest weakness, on the other hand, probably lies in its lack of attention to the initial causes of the person's abnormal behavior and subsequent career.

THE HUMANISTIC PERSPECTIVE

Advocates of the humanistic perspective have suggested that, in addition to behaviorism and psychoanalysis, there is a "third force" in American psychology, with a distinctly different orientation and emphasis. Actually, the humanistic movement in psychology reflects a number of different viewpoints including self-theories, existentialism, and a phenomenological view. In recent years it has been broadened further, and a new stress on psychological growth has emerged.

In this section we will examine some of the main themes of the humanistic perspective and see how the humanistic view of abnormal behavior is distinctive.

Carl Rogers' View of the Development of Abnormal Behavior

Rogers' viewpoint represents one of the most important intellectual traditions within the humanistic perspective. Deeply concerned about inner psychological experience and strongly focused on questions having to do with the conditions that promote psychological growth, Rogers' approach to the understanding of the development of abnormal behavior is a clear example of the humanistic perspective.

Rogers' viewpoint focuses on the concept of the *self*; it identifies the course of early development as crucial in whether the person develops defensive or disturbed behavior or continues on a path of psychological growth.

Rogers' view of the development of defensive behavior can be seen in Figure 2–3 below.

Rogers argues that unconditional positive regard is a state in which a person (e.g., a parent) values another (e.g., child) for himself, not for what the person wishes him to be. Rogers believes that this is essential for the child's psychological development. When this condition is missing, the child does not regard him or her self positively. Instead the child values himself in terms of certain external standards such as achievement or an attractive appearance. This produces what Rogers calls *conditions of worth* within the self.

When one experiences such conditions of worth, it is inevitable that one's sense of self and one's experience will not be congruent, as in Figure 2–3. If one then encounters a

FIGURE 2-3
The Development of Defensive Behavior

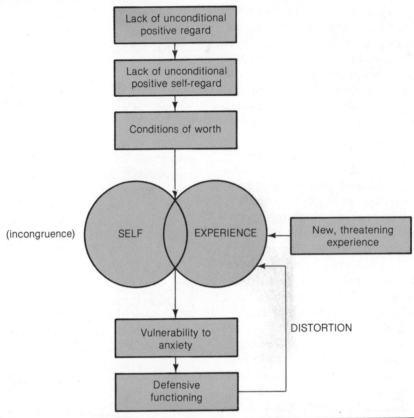

Source: Carl R. Rogers, *On Becoming a Person* (Boston, MA.: Houghton Mifflin, 1961). Copyright © 1961 by Houghton Mifflin Company. Reprinted by permission of the publishers.

new and threatening experience, the person, already vulnerable to anxiety, will begin to behave in a defensive way in order to protect his already fragile identity. This defensive functioning distorts experience and may lead to chronic interpersonal difficulties and a deep personal sense of inadequacy.

Maslow: Self-Actualization and Psychological Help

Another major proponent of the humanistic perspective is Abraham Maslow (1954), who saw the concept of *self-actualization* as a critical goal for personal development. He saw it as a kind of growth principle and an indication of positive psychological health.

Maslow has argued that what is essential for positive mental health is meeting a variety of basic human needs. These needs have been arranged in a hierarchy: (1) physiological needs, (2) a need for love or belongingness, (3) a need for the esteem of others, and (4) a need for self-actualization. Self-actualizers were people who had a need to be spontaneous, to be creative, and to show interest in others.

ROGERS DESCRIBES THE SEARCH FOR THE SELF

I have been astonished to find how accurately the Danish philosopher Søren Kierkegaard pictured the dilemma of the individual more than a century ago, with keen psychological insight. He points out that the most common despair is to be in despair at not choosing, or being willing, to be oneself; but that the deepest form of despair is to choose "to be another than" oneself. On the other hand "to will to be that self which one truly is, is indeed the opposite of despair," and this choice is the deepest responsibility of man. As I read some of his writings I almost feel that he must have listened in on the statements made by our clients as they search and explore for the reality of self—often a painful and troubling search. . . . A few statements from a person who had completed a series of psychotherapeutic interviews will illustrate this. She uses many metaphors as she tells how she struggled to get to the core of herself:

> As I look at it now, I was peeling off layer after layer of defenses. I'd build them up, try them, and then discard them when you [sic] remained the same. I didn't know what was at the bottom and I was very much afraid to find out, but I *had* to keep on trying. At first I felt there was nothing within me—just a great emptiness where I needed and wanted a solid core.

Then I began to feel that I was facing a solid brick wall, too high to get over and too thick to go through. One day the wall became translucent, rather than solid. After this, the wall seemed to disappear but beyond it I discovered a dam holding back violent, churning waters. I felt as if I were holding back the force of these waters and if I opened even a tiny hole I and all about me would be destroyed in the ensuing torrent of feelings represented by the water. Finally I could stand the strain no longer and I let go. All I did, actually, was to succumb to complete and utter self-pity, then hate, then love. After this experience, I felt as if I had leaped a brink and was safely on the other side, though still tottering a bit on the edge. I don't know what I was searching for or where I was going, but I felt then as I have always felt whenever I really lived, that I was moving forward.

I believe this represents rather well the feelings of many an individual that if the false front, the wall, the dam, is not maintained, then everything will be swept away in the violence of the feelings that he discovers pent up in his private world. Yet it also illustrates the compelling necessity which the individual feels to search for and become himself (Rogers, 1961, pp. 110–11).

TABLE 2-2
Perspectives on Abnormal Behavior

	Psychoanalytic	Biological	Learning	Social	Humanistic
Basic metaphor	Intrapsychic conflict	Biological disorder, disease	Learning	Deviance; norm violation	Actualization; growth
Subordinate concepts	Id, ego, superego, anxiety, defense	Etiology, symptom, syndrome, prognosis	Stimulus, response, reinforcement, classical and operant conditioning, modeling	Norms, rule-breaking, career, stigma	Experience, self-concept, incongruity, conditions of worth; consciousness expansion
Causal factors	Intrapsychic conflict	Organic, biochemical, genetic	Reinforcement; classical and operant conditioning	Diverse factors: Organic, psychological, social; labeling	Conditions of worth, deficiency needs; social demands
How abnormal behavior is described	Defense and anxiety	Symptoms, syndromes, disorders	Maladaptive behavior; helplessness	Behavior is deviant; audience reaction emphasized	Defensive and disorganized behavior; false outer self
Means of therapeutic intervention	Psychoanalysis	Medical treatment: drugs, shock treatment, surgical procedures	Behavior therapy, desensitization, shaping	Institutional reform; community mental health	Client-centered therapy; sensitivity training; Gestalt therapy; yoga; meditation
Major proponents	Freud	Kraepelin, Meehl, Snyder	Bandura, Eysenck, Krasner, Seligman, Skinner, Ullmann, Wolpe	Becker, Goffman, Sarbin, Scheff	Maslow, May, Ornstein, Rogers, Tart

Source: From *Abnormal Behavior: Perspectives in Conflict*, 2d ed. (p. 215) by R. H. Price, 1978, New York: Holt, Rinehart & Winston.

Abraham Maslow. (Courtesy of Bertha G. Maslow, photo by Marcia Roltner)

Maslow and Rogers both see external social events as having the potential to block the satisfaction of needs, or in the case of Rogers, producing conditions of worth. Thus, although the humanistic perspective is primarily concerned with psychological growth and development, it sees social events as playing an important role in enhancing or blocking that growth.

USING PERSPECTIVES TO UNDERSTAND AND TREAT ABNORMAL BEHAVIOR

Now that we have examined each of five major perspectives for understanding abnormal behavior, we can see how each of them makes sense of complex behavioral events. The biological, dynamic, learning, sociological, and humanistic perspectives all place some facts and phenomena in the foreground while deemphasizing other aspects of abnormal behavior. But does this only mean that each perspective has a somewhat different emphasis? While that is certainly true, there is a good deal more to the differences among perspectives.

One important difference among perspectives is that some types of abnormal behavior seem to be better explained by some perspectives than by others. For example, we have noted that there is a rapidly growing body of evidence for biochemical and neurological determinants of schizophrenia. We will examine that biological evidence in more detail in Chapter 9. On the other hand, some of the reactions to differences in sexual preference and practice described in Chapter 14 may be best understood from a sociological perspective. Since abnormal behavior has many different causes and manifests itself in many different ways, we should not be surprised that various perspectives differ in their capacity to help us understand different forms of abnormal behavior.

Some of the disorders that we will discuss in the chapters that follow will emphasize some perspectives much more heavily than others. For example, some fears and phobias have been examined extensively from the learning and dynamic points of view but the humanistic perspective has had much less to say about them. In other chapters we will see two or more perspectives competing to explain a particular form of abnormal behavior. Whenever these conflicts in perspectives emerge as, for example, between the learning and biological perspectives in the study of depression, we will explore that conflict. It is there that much of the scientific and theoretical excitement in the study of abnormal behavior becomes evident.

As Table 2-2 suggests, the perspectives we have described are also used to help design attempts to treat abnormal behavior. In fact, various psychological and biological treatments of abnormal behavior have the perspectives we have described in their rationale. In Chapter 16 we will discuss the insight therapies developed both from a dynamic and a humanistic point of view. In Chapter 17 we will discuss the behavior and cognitive behavior therapies that have emerged from the learning perspective. Chapter 18 considers the treatment of abnormal behavior in the community; here it is the sociological perspective that has been most influential. And, finally, in Chapter 19 we will describe biological treatments for abnormal behavior that have the biological perspective as their theoretical and research framework.

The perspectives discussed in this chapter frame the problem of abnormal behavior in distinctively different ways. Nevertheless, different forms of abnormal behavior appear to be more or less adequately explained by different perspectives. Attempts to treat abnormal behavior also draw upon different perspectives for their rationale, and we have organized our discussion of the treatment of abnormal behavior at the end of the book to reflect these differences in perspective.

SUMMARY

In this chapter we have surveyed the rich array of perspectives on the nature of abnormal behavior. Each conceptual approach begins with its own basic set of concepts to provide a framework for understanding the nature, causes, mechanisms, and description of abnormal behavior. A summary of these ideas is given in Table 2-2.

Depending on his or her theoretical orientation, the clinician will address different aspects of a presenting psychological problem. For the learning theorist, what is important are the observable symptoms and behaviors. In examining these behaviors, the learning theorist is interested in discovering how they are formed and maintained by environmental contingencies.

Whereas the learning perspective focuses on the individual's behavior and reinforcement contingencies, the sociological approach emphasizes the broader social context. The sociologically oriented clinician is most interested in the role the person plays in his or her family system and in the community. Specifically, the clinician might wonder whether the person was being cast into the social role of patient.

In contrast to the learning and sociological perspectives' emphasis on the environment, psychoanalytic theory emphasizes unconscious conflicts that are said to underlie the presenting problems. Instead of becoming the focus of treatment, the presenting problems are treated as symptoms of an underlying disturbance. In attempting to understand these conflicts, the psychoanalytic clinician focuses on the person's early history, especially his or her early relations with primary caretakers.

From the humanistic perspective, psychological difficulties represent frustration in reaching one's goals and potential. Consequently, the clinician with a humanistic orientation is interested in the person's desires and aspirations. Although inner psychological experience is stressed, the emphasis is on conscious motivation and not on the unconscious motivation that is the focus of the psychoanalytic approach.

Finally, the biological perspective conceptualizes psychological disorders in terms of disease and illness. The biologically oriented clinician is interested in the duration, intensity, and effects of the symptoms. Rather than searching for underlying psychological mechanisms, the clinician aims for an objective account of the person's physical and psychological functioning.

Thus we see that each of these perspectives exerts a powerful influence on how we perceive abnormal behavior, what elements seem most important to understand, and what research questions need to be asked. In later chapters we will meet each of these perspectives again as we consider the theory, research, and treatment approaches for specific disorders.

3

Research Strategies in the Study of Abnormal Behavior

Thinking about the Causes of Abnormal Behavior
    Perspectives and Causes
    Types of Causes

Research Methods
    Case Histories
    Correlational Approaches
    Experimental Methods
    Experimental Analogues
    Single-Subject Experimental Strategies
    High-Risk Methods
    Meta-Analysis: Combining Results

Ethical Issues in the Study of Abnormal Behavior
    Ethical Research Principles of
        Psychologists

Summary

Summary

INTRODUCTION

After a moderate dose of LSD "visual effects began. Objects of all sorts took on a new beauty and richness. Colors and textures and lines, even the pores in one's skin, began to stand out visually." The contours of objects may become distorted. Time-sense alters dramatically. A minute may seem like an hour or a day. The sense of distance also changes. "Flicking one's finger seems like hurling it across the room, and walking across the room is like traversing the corners of the universe"(Snyder, 1974, p. 43). Drugs such as LSD have been described as *hallucinogenic* (capable of producing hallucinations), and as *psychotomimetic* (capable of producing states that mimic psychotic states).

Reports of the LSD experience in the 1950s began to capture the imagination of the scientific community. It was not long before scientists began to wonder whether the chemistry and subjective states of the psychedelic experience might not provide some insight into the nature of one of the most puzzling forms of abnormal behavior, schizophrenia. The analogy between the LSD experience and schizophrenia was too compelling to be ignored. Scientists began to speculate on how the experience and biochemistry of LSD might inform their thinking about schizophrenia.

One hypothesis argued that it was possible that the bodies of schizophrenics might be producing some toxic substance resembling LSD. If this were the case, then, one should examine the body chemistry of schizophrenics to discover what was producing a chemical agent that in turn produced the schizophrenic symptoms.

In 1952 two British scientists, Osmond and Smythies, noted a striking chemical similarity between adrenalin and the mescaline molecules. Adrenalin is a chemical secretion of the adrenal gland that prepares the body for emergency action during periods of stress. Osmond and Smythies reasoned that, if the body were able to change adrenalin into some chemical resembling mescaline, this might be the toxin they were seeking that produced schizophrenia.

Soon afterward, Dr. Abram Hoffer reported an apparently exciting breakthrough that seemed to confirm this idea. His research strategy appeared to be deceptively simple. Hoffer had found a derivative of adrenalin called *adrenochrome* in blood and urine samples of schizophrenics but not in those of nonschizophrenics. Adrenochrome is a pink-colored chemical that results when oxygen combines with adrenalin, as is the case when adrenalin is exposed to air. Thus Hoffer felt he had isolated a chemical substance, adrenochrome, in the blood of schizophrenics that might be related to their illness. To test this possibility, he administered this substance to normal subjects. He reported that they experienced psychedelic effects similar to those of LSD.

A great wave of excitement swept through the scientific community. Scientists all over the world attempted to repeat Hoffer's experiments. These attempts almost universally failed, and careful measurement indicated that adrenochrome did not appear to a greater degree in the blood of either schizophrenics or nonschizophrenics. Apparently Hoffer had allowed the blood samples of schizophrenics to remain in the open air longer than those of nonschizophrenics, thus producing the pink color.

But what about the effects of the schizophrenic blood samples when they were administered to the normal subjects? Possibly Hoffer and his colleagues were so eager to demonstrate their theory that they unwittingly suggested the expected effects to their subjects. Their subjects then displayed the well-known *placebo* effect. That is, even though the chemical was no more potent than tap water, the suggestion that it would make subjects slightly schizophrenic led them to behave in the manner expected of them. Thus, even though there are other lines of evidence that do indeed suggest that biochemistry plays an important role in schizophrenia, these results had a more prosaic explanation.

For every scientific breakthrough there are hundreds of stories like that of the "pink spot" studies. The search for the causes of various forms of abnormal behavior is governed by strict rules of evidence that demand public, repeatable findings and acceptance of findings only when as many alternative explanations as possible have been ruled out. In this chapter we will examine the rules and the research strategies that scientists have used in the study of abnormal behavior.

THINKING ABOUT THE CAUSES OF ABNORMAL BEHAVIOR

Perspectives and Causes

In Chapter 2, you will recall, we discussed different perspectives on abnormal behavior. Each of these perspectives focused on a different aspect of abnormal behavior, and each perspective also thought about the *causes* of abnormal behavior differently. In effect, each viewpoint places different bets about the nature of the cause of abnormal behavior.

The biological viewpoint argues that the causes of abnormal behavior are found in the physiological makeup of the individual. For example, genetic errors may predispose the individual to certain types of psychological disorder or lead directly to faulty development of structures necessary for normal functioning. Another version of the biological perspective suggests the cause can be found in microorganisms or toxic chemicals. In either case, the locus of the cause of abnormal behavior is the physiology of the person.

The dynamic view, on the other hand, locates causes in the psychological dynamics of the person. The major causes of abnormal behavior from the dynamic viewpoint involve intrapsychic conflicts that cannot be resolved. Various defense mechanisms evolve to protect the individual from anxiety generated by the conflicts. The defense mechanisms, in turn, are frequently perceived as abnormal.

The learning perspective suggests that the causes of abnormal behavior are learned and that they may be due either to a failure to learn necessary adaptive behaviors or to the direct learning of maladaptive behaviors. In either case, the abnormal behavior is learned and the causes are presumably located in the stimulus environment of the individual.

The sociological perspective says little about the origins of abnormal behavior but suggests that abnormal behavior is maintained by social processes. In particular, the reactions of other people to the individual labeled as abnormal are thought to have a powerful influence on subsequent behavior.

Finally, the humanistic perspective sees the origins of abnormal behavior as arising from a world too demanding of facades, and surface qualities that too little appreciate qualities like authenticity and openness.

Each of these perspectives suggests a different set of causes for abnormal behavior. A scientist working from the biological perspective will look for causes in quite different places than will a sociologically oriented researcher. In the chapters to follow we will see the influence of different theoretical perspectives on the scientists' choices of variables and definitions of psychological disorder. Perspectives may influence *which* questions are asked, but *how* they are asked is a question of scientific method. How researchers concerned with the causes and treatment of abnormal behavior apply scientific methods to their work is the special focus of this chapter.

Types of Causes

Although scientists frequently ask questions like, "What is *the* cause of abnormal behavior?" it is unlikely that any major disorder is due to any single cause. Instead, scientists tend to think about *classes* of causes. For example, some causal factors are described as *predisposing causal factors*. That is, events or conditions that occur long before any abnormal behavior is observed may predispose the individual to later difficulties. Predisposing causes can be a consequence of previous experiences or some biological condition or both. The important point is that they pave the way for later psychopathology.

A second major type of cause is the *precipitating causal factor*, described as the "trigger" for a disorder. A precipitating life event could be a sudden loss of a loved one, a disaster, a major failure in one's life, or a sudden physiological change.

Finally, a third type of cause is the *maintaining causal factor*. These factors reinforce abnormal behavior and thus maintain it over time.

The phenomenon of child abuse provides an example of all three types of causal factors. Temperamental characteristics of the child such as irritability can influence the mood of the parent, *predisposing* the parent to greater frustration and anger. But by themselves these factors may not be enough to produce an episode of abuse. If the child engages in some transgression, even a minor one, it may *precipitate* or trigger an abusive episode. Furthermore, a number of *maintaining* causal factors may also play a role in continuing abuse. If a parent has no opportunity for relief from the burdens of child care, for

The death of a loved one can be a precipitating factor in the development of psychological distress. (Constantine Manos/Magnum Photos, Inc.)

example, the abusive situation may continue to be maintained.

This example illustrates still another class of causal factors that may be particularly important in understanding the causes of abnormal behavior. Causes may also operate in a *bidirectional* fashion, mutually influencing and reinforcing each other. In the case of child abuse, for example, a child's episodes of crying may evoke physical punishment, which may only increase crying and which, in turn, may evoke still further punishment, and so on.

It may be difficult at times to decide whether a particular event or condition serves as a predisposing event, a precipitating event, or both. The advantage of classifying causal events in this way is that one can construct a *complex model* of the causal process underlying abnormal behavior that is more likely to capture the complexity of the actual causal process.

RESEARCH METHODS

Both scientists and detectives are basically *determinists*. That is, they are both primarily concerned with the causes of events. For a detective the "causal agent" may be a criminal, and for the scientist it may be a chemical in the blood. But in each case the search is for causes. In addition, both detectives and scientists must reconstruct past events. A detective has only the victim and the scene of the crime. A scientist may have only a pattern of symptoms and a sketchy life history to work with.

Both scientists and detectives rely heavily on *observation* to gather evidence in their search for the truth, and both are concerned about the reliability or dependability of their observations. Detectives take photographs, search for fingerprints, and question witnesses independently. Scientists use standardized interviews and tests. Both gather evidence to increase the reliability of their observations.

Detectives and scientists also have hunches or *hypotheses* about the cause of the events, and during their investigations try to rule out less plausible hypotheses. Each draws on a body of knowledge to form hypotheses and to exclude less plausible possibilities. For the detective the body of knowledge may include information about the chemical composition of cigar ashes. For the scientist it may concern a description of the distribution of some disorder across different ages. But in each case prior knowledge is used to test their hunches.

Finally, both scientists and detectives tend to be extremely cautious about the conclusions they draw, and for similar reasons. Their conclusions must withstand critical scrutiny of a jury of critical peers or a court of law.

The analogy between detectives and scientists should not be carried too far. One important difference is that a scientist is concerned with arriving at general statements that allow grouping apparently dissimilar events under a single rule or *generalization*. Detectives, on the other hand, wish to narrow their search to a single person, and are somewhat less interested in the generalizations that might be produced from their work.

Even if an investigator has some hunches or hypotheses about the determinants of abnormal behavior, evidence that supports the hypothesis is required. We will consider some of the most commonly used methods to gather evidence below.

Case Histories

Throughout this book you will find *case histories* describing the development of psychological disorder in particular individuals. In most instances we have provided them to illustrate the clinical features of various disorders. But the life history of a patient can also provide a rich source of information about the patient's difficulty. This information may suggest some unique or unusual feature in the patient's background. This striking feature may then be incorporated into a crude hypothesis such as "Parental permissiveness leads to delinquent behavior," or "Early loss of a loved one leads to later episodes of depression."

In the case history a crude hypothesis can be formed, but very little more can be learned using the case history approach. For example, in the above hypothesis on early loss and depression, we could look at additional case histories of depression and search for instances of loss. But we could not be sure of how representative the case histories were, and therefore the generality of our hypothesis would remain doubtful.

The case history approach would also leave us in doubt about the definition of the key terms in our hypothesis. Are depression and early loss defined in comparable ways in other case histories? If not, we could not be sure that we were looking at the same phenomenon in succeeding cases.

The primary value of the case history approach lies in generating hypotheses or hunches that can then by tested by more rigorous means. The case histories can also provide accounts of unusual or rare clinical phenomena or demonstrate new treatment techniques. This approach is best thought of, however, as a method of hypothesis finding, not hypothesis testing.

Correlational Approaches

If we are on the track of a possible relationship between early life events and depression, we may draw on case history evidence, but, by itself, this evidence would hardly convince skeptical colleagues. Our next step should be an attempt to discover whether a relationship between early loss and depression actually exists.

In order to establish a relationship, we will first have to provide *operational definitions* for key terms in our hypothesis. That is, we will have to develop standard ways of defining depression and early loss. We may use psychological tests, a checklist of behaviors, or a definition that independent observers can use reliably. Whatever our method, we will have provided *public* and *repeatable* operations that other investigators could duplicate.

Our next step should be to try to discover whether there is a statistical relationship between the variables in question. A common method for doing so involves the application of *correlational techniques*. If our hypothesis is viable, there should be more cases of depression that report early loss than those that do not; or the degree of depression should correlate with the extent of early loss. This outcome would be reflected in a *positive correlation* between the two variables. Figure 3–1 shows three possible outcomes of such an investigation. In the first case it appears that individuals who show more signs of depression have also experienced more early loss. In the second there is no relationship, and in the third the opposite of what we expected has occurred and a negative correlation was obtained.

If at this stage of our research we still find positive correlation between early loss and depression, we should find this encouraging but far from conclusive. A number of alternative explanations exist that might "explain away" the relationship and show that it tells us nothing of real importance about the causes of depression. The fact, for example, that early loss and depression seem related to each other may be due to a *third variable* that affects both reports of early loss and depression. A third variable such as

FIGURE 3-1
Three Possible Correlational Relationships between Previous Life Events Reflecting Loss and Rated Current Severity of Depression

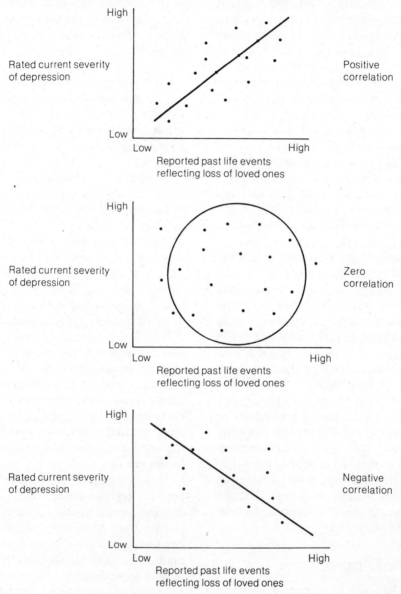

socioeconomic status could affect *both* loss *and* depression and lead us to believe that loss and depression were related when, in fact, both were affected by the experience of poverty. For example, conditions of poverty may be associated with poorer medical care and higher levels of mortality among poor people. At the same time, conditions of poverty might provide feelings of hopelessness and depression. Thus in this example the condition of poverty is the third variable that produces the apparent association between early loss and depression. But the real causal relations are not between early loss and depression; both are actually a result of impoverished life conditions.

Epidemiological Approaches. *Epidemiology* is the study of the frequency and causes of physical and mental disorders. The basic strategy of epidemiologists is to estimate the frequency of disorders in the population to discover if there are fluctuations in the rate of disorder, and to identify groups of people who have especially high rates of the disorder. Originally medical scientists used epidemiological methods to control epidemics of infectious diseases such as typhoid and cholera. More recently epidemiological methods have been used to understand chronic diseases, the distribution of accidents, and other problems in the population (Price & D'Aunno, 1984).

The epidemiological research strategy involves two phases. Determining the frequency of disorders in the population is usually called *descriptive epidemiology,* and attempts to identify variables that contribute to the development of the disorder is called *analytic epidemiology.* Typically, the epidemiological approach involves conducting a survey of individuals in a community—either on a random basis or because those individuals belong to a particular group. The interviewer might ask about the life history of the person, any traumatic events he or she may have encountered, and current life circumstances. At least a portion of the interview might be conducted to identify any indications of psychological disturbance.

Armed with such a set of interviews, the epidemiologist will attempt to identify cases of psychological disorder, and estimate either incidence or prevalence. *Incidence* is the number of new occurrences of a disorder in the population within a specified time interval. *Prevalence* is the total number of cases of the disorder in the population at any given time. Prevalence depends on two factors: the number of new cases that occur in the population during the study period and the number of cases that already exist.

An important epidemiological study of abnormal behavior has recently been conducted called the *Epidemiological Catchment Area Program* (Regier et al., 1984; Robins et al., 1984; Myers et al., 1984). This large-scale study involved the interview of nearly 17,000 community residents in five sites across the country: Baltimore; New Haven; North Carolina; St. Louis; and Los Angeles. The community members were interviewed using the Diagnostic Interview Schedule, which allows interview results to be translated into diagnostic categories.

In addition to estimating the rates of specific disorders, the Epidemiological Catchment Area study provided new information about the rates of specific disorders affecting men and women. For many years it was believed that the rate of psychological disorder was higher among women than men. But most previous surveys concentrated on depression and anxiety disorders, which more commonly affect women than men. The Epidemiological Catchment Area studies have produced a more balanced picture showing that the rates of psychological disorder in men and women are comparable, even though the types of disorders that develop are different. Antisocial personality problems as well as

ECONOMIC CHANGE AND PSYCHOLOGICAL DISTURBANCE: AN EXAMPLE OF CORRELATIONAL RESEARCH

Think for a moment about the possible life changes or coping strategies that might be produced by marked economic change. Perhaps you or your family have experienced some of these changes. Individual stress associated with negative economic changes might include job loss, the necessity of moving from one home to another, the necessity of taking part-time jobs, less leisure time, continued concern and worry about bills and outstanding debts, and increased family conflict over financial matters. Not only do individuals experience additional stresses but entire families may also be made more vulnerable to stress.

One study (Pierce, 1967) examined the relationship between economic change and suicide rates in the United States during the period 1919–1940. Common stock prices were used as the economic change indicator and were examined in relation to the suicide rate. Pierce found that suicide rates increased in relation to economic downturns. How does one explain this relationship? Pierce believes that economic changes reduce social cohesion—and the closeness with which people relate to one another. Like Emile Durkheim (1952), Pierce speculates that this reduction in social cohesion leads to the loss of social support in the face of stress and therefore to an increase in the frequency of suicide.

Perhaps the most detailed and well-known recent study on the relationship between economic instability and abnormal behavior has been done by Harvey Brenner (1973). Brenner has compared changes in employment figures with rates of mental hospitalization over a period of approximately 50 years. His most recent studies show that, throughout the United States, as the rate of employment drops, the rate of hospital admissions increases.

An interesting feature of Brenner's findings is that hospitalization rates do not increase immediately after economic downturns, but that they do so in a systematic way approximately one year later. Perhaps this is because the effects of the stress associated with economic change are not immediate. After a year, however, the impact of economic change is felt strongly enough to increase hospitalization rates.

Who is most severely affected by economic downturns? According to Brenner, the most noticeable effects of a falling economy occur for men from 35 to 54 and for women 25 to 44. Certainly these are periods during which men and women bear a particularly heavy burden of responsibility in providing for their families and, therefore, are more likely to experience stress associated with unemployment.

We should be cautious, however, in interpreting first admissions to mental hospitals as a direct indicator of the rate of mental illness in the country at any given time. Consider for a moment some other possible explanations for changes in the rate of mental hospitalization. One explanation might be that hospital admissions policies change systematically over time. Another possible explanation is

Unemployment during the Great Depression produced massive psychological distress and depression.
(Historical Pictures Service, Inc., Chicago)

that the definition of mental illness could have changed, affecting hospitalization rates. Or perhaps in times of economic stringency the community's tolerance for various forms of abnormal behavior is reduced, thus producing more mental hospitalizations. Although these are all plausible explanations for changes in hospitalization rates, any other explanation must show that it can predict changes in the rates more accurately than economic changes can. So far, no factors have been found that are capable of predicting hospitalization rates as accurately as economic changes.

We should also be clear that it is not correct to suggest that changes in the economy "cause" mental illness in a direct fashion. But certainly any changes in the economy that increase stress for the population are more likely to function as either *predisposing* or *precipitating* *causes.*

The discovery and exploration of a relationship between psychological distress and economic changes suggest opportunities for planning mental health service to respond to increases in the need for psychological support and treatment. In addition, as Dooley and Catalano (1980) note, the one-year lag between economic change and severe psychological disruption suggests that it might be possible to engage in preventive efforts as well. For example, knowing that economic changes may make working-class and poor people even more vulnerable than others suggests that immediately after such economic changes would be an ideal time to provide supportive services. Perhaps preventive efforts are best applied by the federal government itself. Various alternative employment programs, retraining, and income maintenance programs might be developed to buffer the damaging effects of recessions or inflation.

alcohol and drug disorders are more common among men than women, whereas depression and anxiety tend to be more frequent among women.

Epidemiological techniques can also provide information about the likelihood that people in the community with different types of disorders will seek treatment. For example, the ECA study showed that while only 1 percent of the population developed a diagnosable schizophrenic disorder, nearly 50 percent of schizophrenics sought treatment over the six-month period of the study.

An additional important contribution of the epidemiological method is the finding that populations with especially high rates of disorder can be identified. If the circumstances of the population can be modified, this may lead to strategies for preventing disorders from occurring in the first place. In the area of physical health, the Framingham heart study identified the role of cholesterol and obesity as risk factors for cardiovascular disease in just this way.

The task of *analytic* epidemiology is to try to understand the causal role that various life circumstances and risk factors play for populations with especially high rates of disorder. This is scientific detective work at its most sophisticated. Analytical epidemiology frequently involves case control methods in which a group of individuals with a particular disorder are compared with other similar individuals who did not develop the disorder. Factors in the life histories of these persons are compared as part of the search for possible causes. In some instances case and control individuals are followed into the future to distinguish factors that are associated with the development of the disorder and factors that are not.

Experimental Methods

One of the most powerful methods for gathering evidence about the effect of one event or variable on another is the *controlled experiment*. In its most basic form a controlled experiment involves the manipulation of one variable or event while holding constant or controlling all others. If the expected effects occur under these circumstances, then we can be fairly sure it was the event or variable we manipulated rather than something else that had the observed effect.

The classic experimental design involves manipulating the environment of an *experimental group* in some systematic fashion. The experimental group and a *control group* are both measured in one or more ways that presumably will show the effect of the manipulation on the experimental group as compared to the control group. To be sure that the experimental and control groups are comparable in all ways, the subjects are randomly assigned to one group or the other. By allowing chance to dictate group membership, we can be assured that no selective factor will affect group membership or the later comparison of the two groups.

A moment's reflection will indicate that this method in its pure form is of limited use in understanding the causes of abnormal behavior. No one would seriously consider randomly assigning children to experimental and control groups, producing traumatic life circumstances for the experimental group and later comparing the experimental and control groups for differences in the degree and type of abnormal behavior they display.

Experimental Analogues

Researchers have tried to use the power of the experimental method, however, in other ways. One of the common strategies is the use of *experimental analogues*—recreating a particular phenomenon under laboratory conditions with normal people or animals. For example, laboratory animals could be subjected to different experiences of "loss" and observed for later behavioral indications of "depression."

Most people tend to be skeptical about the degree to which animal behavior can be generalized to that of humans. The scientific strategy used in making these generalizations is crucial. The strategy adopted by Harlow and his colleagues at the University of Wisconsin has been to search for important patterns of behavior in human interaction and then to attempt to produce *analogous* behavior in lower species.

Harlow and Suomi have been studying rhesus monkeys for several decades and have become particularly interested in the question of human attachment. After having carefully examined research on attachment carried out with humans, Harlow and his colleagues created several very different rearing situations for infant monkeys. They were able to show that the attraction infant monkeys show to their mothers is not merely

A previously isolated monkey learning contact and play from younger normal "therapist" monkey.
(Courtesy Harry Harlow, Wisconsin Primate Laboratory)

An infant monkey receiving "contact comfort" from surrogate mother. (Courtesy Harry Harlow, Wisconsin Primate Laboratory)

learned by associating the mother's face with hunger satisfaction, as was previously thought, but had a great deal to do with the sheer pleasure of contact with her body, or "contact comfort."

Harlow and his colleagues have studied analogues of human depression by isolating infant monkeys in order to produce pathological behavior patterns such as depression. What is especially interesting about their work is that they have taken their analogue research approach one step further by placing the monkeys reared in total isolation with three-month-old normal monkeys, which they call "therapists." These isolated adult monkeys have no fear of the infant therapists, which then begin to interact with the depressed adults and to rehabilitate them through contact and play.

The potential problem with this use of experimental analogues is fairly evident. The analogy between children and rat pups, for example, may be slight. The laboratory operations used to produce "loss" may not provide a good analogy to the emotional loss suffered in childhood, and the laboratory definitions of depression may be only distantly related to the clinical phenomenon in which we are really interested.

In certain circumstances, especially in biochemical research, experimental analogues can provide useful evidence about the determinants of abnormal behavior. Usually, however, the evidence produced might provide only limited support for the hypothesis in question, rather than definitive evidence.

Single-Subject Experimental Strategies

Just as it is possible to use the principles of experimental design with groups of individuals, it is also possible to apply the same logic to research with a single person. Instead of applying an experimental condition to one group and comparing it with a control group, the single-subject strategy applies an experimental condition to the individual at one point in time and compares the effect to another time period when no experimental condition has been applied.

Consider the example offered by the research of Allen, Hunt, Buell, Harris, and Wolf (1964). Ann, a four-year-old in a preschool setting, was observed by the investigators to have become isolated from other children. The investigators observed her behavior carefully and noticed that she used a variety of strategies for gaining the attention of adults. Since adults did attend to her behavior and since this was incompatible with interacting with her peers, Ann had placed herself in a social situation in which she would become increasingly isolated from her peers.

Allen et al. developed an intervention program in which the reinforcement contingen-

cies were changed so that Ann received reinforcement in the form of adult attention only as a consequence of playing with other children. Figure 3–2 shows the initial *baseline* period in which an estimate of the proportion of time spent with children and adults was obtained. The second period was one in which interaction with other children was reinforced. In this case the portion of time Ann spent with children substantially increased.

Then the investigators used one of the classic strategies of single-subject experimental designs. They *reversed* the condition, thus returning to the original situation. Not surprisingly, Ann reverted to her original behavior pattern and the proportion of time that she spent with adults again increased. Returning again to the original experimental condition, the investigators again reinforced interaction with other children and the rate of interaction with children again increased.

These results provide impressive evidence for the effect of an experimental condition and are very much favored by behaviorally oriented researchers studying abnormal behavior.

Kazdin (1982), who has comprehensively reviewed the many ways that single-case research designs can be used in clinical and applied settings, suggests that response-guided experimentation rather than traditional approaches can be effectively used with single-subject designs. Thus the experimenters' decisions about changes in experimental conditions are guided by the responses of the subject under previous conditions. We will see still other examples of the use of this research strategy in later chapters.

High-Risk Methods

One of the unique difficulties of doing research on the determinants of abnormal behavior is that clinical groups suffering from

FIGURE 3-2
Percent of Time Ann Spent in Social Interaction with Adults and with Peers during Approximately Two Hours of Each Morning Session

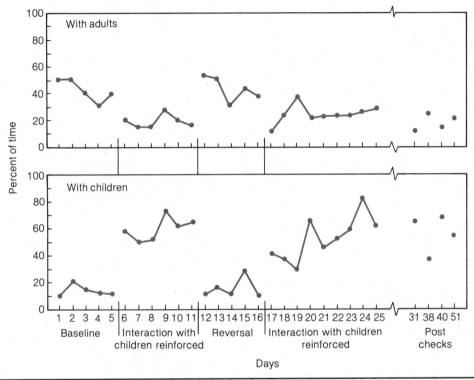

Source: Adapted from Allen, Hart, Buell, Harris & Wolf, "Effects of Social Reinforcement on Isolate Behavior of a Nursery School Child," 1964, *35*, pp. 511–518. © The Society for Research in Child Development, Inc.

a particular disorder are also likely to display other behavior because of associated, but causally unrelated, conditions. Schizophrenic patients, for example, may display behavior patterns resulting from years of hospitalization rather than from the schizophrenia itself. Similarly, family disturbance or the reactions of a family to having a chronically disturbed member of the household could reflect a possible set of causal factors in the schizophrenic. Once the patient has begun to display signs of disturbance, disentangling possible causes from consequences of the disorder is very difficult.

An important approach to studying the development of abnormal behavior is the *high-risk method* (Mednick, 1966). A general design for a high-risk study is shown in Figure 3–3.

You can see that Mednick chose 100 "low-risk" children who have normal mothers and 200 "high-risk" children whose mothers are schizophrenic. The children of schizophrenic mothers are considered to be high-risk cases because it is known that 15 percent of such children will eventually become schizophrenic, and another 35 percent will develop some form of deviant behavior. Thus a longitudinal

FIGURE 3–3
Design for a Study Using High-Risk Samples of 200 Children with Schizophrenic Mothers and 100 Low-Risk Control Subjects

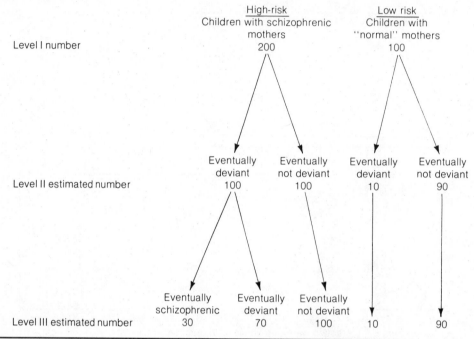

Source: From "Some Premorbid Characteristics Related to Breakdown in Children with Schizophrenic Mothers," by S. A. Mednick and F. Schulsinger, in *The Transmission of Schizophrenia*, ed. D. Rosenthal and S. S. Kety, 1968, Elmsford, NY: Pergamon Press.

sample of children of sufficient size for careful study is assured.

The investigators measure the high-risk and low-risk groups of children on a broadly based battery of physiological and psychological tests at the beginning of the study and periodically in subsequent years. Eventually some of the high-risk children will develop schizophrenic behavior. It will then be possible to compare the results of earlier tests on these children with results for (1) high-risk children who did not develop schizophrenia and (2) low-risk children, to discover differences that are of potential causal significance among the groups.

Despite the great cost and effort involved in conducting high-risk studies, a number of investigators concerned with the causes of schizophrenia have adopted this strategy recently, and we can expect new evidence on the nature of schizophrenia in the near future.

Meta-Analysis: Combining Results

In studying the causes and treatment of abnormal behavior, a single study, no matter how well conceived, is limited in what it can tell us. It would be much preferable if we could combine the results of many studies on a particular question to obtain an overall summary of what has been found. Until recently the techniques for doing so have been unavailable. However, Smith and Glass (1977) have used the technique of *meta-analysis* to answer the question, "Does psychotherapy work?" While there have been literally hundreds of individual studies comparing the effects of therapy for treated and untreated groups, the meta-analysis conducted by Smith and Glass is the first attempt to put all the results of those studies together to produce an overall assessment of the effectiveness of psychotherapy.

In their meta-analysis Smith and Glass carried out an exhaustive search of the literature that turned up no less than 1,000 different evaluations of psychotherapy. Of these, 375 studies were selected for complete statistical analysis. One criterion for inclusion in the analysis was that a study had to compare at least one therapy treatment group to an untreated group or to a different therapy group.

After selecting the studies, Smith and Glass classified the different types of outcomes assessed in the studies. There were 10 categories, including such measures as fear and anxiety reduction, self-esteem, and achievement in school or on the job. Altogether, the 375 studies yielded 833 outcomes. Some studies had more than one outcome because they measured the effect of therapy at more than one time or on more than one type of effect. All these outcomes measures were more or less related to well-being and thus are generally comparable.

Through statistical measurement Smith and Glass then determined the *magnitude of effect* for each therapy outcome. Magnitude of effect, or "effect size," was the mean difference between the treated and control subjects divided by the standard deviation of the control group. The 833 effect-size measures represented about 25,000 subjects in the treatment groups and a similar number in the control groups. According to Smith and Glass, the average client receiving therapy was better off than 75 percent of the untreated members of the control groups (see Figure 3–4). That finding was arrived at by lumping all the 833 effect sizes together.

In view of the continuing controversy over the effectiveness of psychotherapy and of competing types of therapy, the Smith and Glass meta-analysis is a highly significant contribution. It demonstrates a new strategy for summarizing research in a way

FIGURE 3–4
The Results of the Smith and Glass Study of the Effectiveness of Psychotherapy (The average person receiving therapy was better off than 75 percent of the control group.)

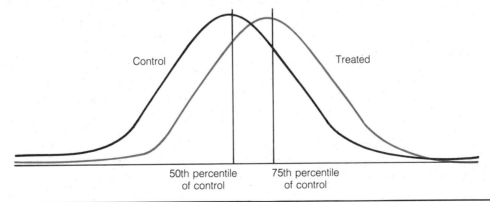

Control   Treated

50th percentile
of control

75th percentile
of control

that allows researchers to draw overall conclusions.

ETHICAL ISSUES IN THE STUDY OF ABNORMAL BEHAVIOR

Imagine, for a moment, that you have carefully developed a procedure for helping people cope effectively with their anxiety. The only way to know whether your new procedure is more effective than other approaches is to test it with individuals suffering from anxiety, in carefully controlled conditions, comparing your treatment with existing treatments. Proper experimental procedure would require that you randomly assign people with severe anxiety problems to your new treatment and to the other treatment approach. How can you know whether your treatment will be as effective as the current treatment? If it is not, then those people assigned to your new treatment might justifiably argue that they were given inferior care. Yet we can never know whether your treatment procedure is superior unless it is subjected to a rigorous experimental test. Thus a dilemma arises between the need for increased knowledge about a promising treatment that ultimately might help thousands of people and the danger of possibly inferior treatment for several dozen patients.

In searching for chemical causes of schizophrenia, or a new drug to relieve anxiety, or a more effective behavioral treatment for depression, scientists must ultimately work with people suffering abnormal behavior. As Henry Beecher has noted, "Man is the final test site." Inevitably, then, scientists studying abnormal behavior will be confronted by ethical dilemmas and concerns. Bernard Barber, a social scientist who has studied medical researchers' attitudes toward ethical issues in research, suggests that the public has recently become much more aware of these issues.

In understanding the ethical issues in human experimentation, two major issues should be considered. The first has to do with the possibility of exposing people to *undue risk*. The second major issue has to do with assuring that people who agree to participate in scientific experiments are able to give *informed consent*. That is, people should ideally agree to participate only if they have a clear understanding of the risks involved. As a student of abnormal behavior, you may find yourself, someday, in the role of subject in a scientific experiment. Or perhaps some years from now you will find yourself in the role of scientist, actually conducting an experiment. In either case, the complex and difficult issues of risk and informed consent need to be considered in detail.

Consider some examples. In the 1930s a group of black subjects with syphilis was kept under observation in an effort to understand the course of the disease. By 1945 penicillin had become available as an effective cure for syphilis. Despite this development, these individuals were not given the cure. Instead, observation of the course of their disease was continued. This is clearly a case in which people were subjected to undue risk. An example of a flagrant violation of informed consent involves two respected cancer investigators who, in the 1960s, injected live cancer cells into a number of geriatric patients without first obtaining the patients' informed consent.

It is difficult to know how common such flagrant violations of codes of ethics are. Barber (1976) has conducted extensive surveys of medical scientists who work with human subjects to discover the scientists' attitudes toward undue risk and informed consent. Barber surveyed scientists across the country and asked them to judge experimental proposals that varied in the amount of risk potential for the subjects involved. In addition, Barber and his colleagues examined the way in which scientists reviewed research proposals that held possible risk for human subjects. In general Barber found that the vast majority of scientists were extremely cautious and concerned about ethical issues in working with human subjects. A consistent minority, however, were likely to approve projects with undue risk or without providing for adequate informed consent.

In the arena of research in abnormal psychology, it will frequently be necessary to work with humans. The conflict between the search for new knowledge and the danger of risk to human subjects will always be present. Increased awareness is, in the long run, our best safeguard.

Ethical Research Principles of Psychologists

As the major national organization of psychologists, the American Psychological Association has been concerned with the ethical practice of psychology and psychological research for many years. The organization has developed an important document entitled *Ethical Principles for Psychologists,* which describes the obligations of psychologists working with human beings in a variety of professional capacities.

Among the main obligations of psychologists working with human subjects are:

- Make a careful evaluation of the study's ethical acceptability.
- Inform the subject of all features of the research that might reasonably be expected to influence willingness to participate.
- When deception is necessary, ensure as soon as possible the subject's understanding of the reasons for this action.

- Respect the individual's freedom to decline to participate in or withdraw from research.
- Protect subjects from physical and mental discomfort, harm, and danger.
- Ensure that information obtained about the individual research participants during the course of the investigation is confidential.
- Use of drugs in research should occur only in such settings as clinics and hospitals.

In the area of research, the principles have been carefully formulated to deal with questions of confidentiality of records, knowing use of procedures that might harm others, disclosure of results, scrutiny of the procedures of any study in which a person participates, and the requirement that an individual give fully informed voluntary consent when participating in any research study.

SUMMARY

In this chapter we have examined a variety of research strategies used in the scientific study of abnormal behavior. We noted that each perspective of abnormal behavior suggests its own set of causes, and that scientists favoring a particular perspective are more likely to look for the causes of behavior in areas suggested by that perspective. We also noted that we may think of several different kinds of causes of abnormal behavior, including predisposing causal factors, precipitating factors, and maintaining causal factors.

The research methods used to understand abnormal behavior are agreed upon procedures that emphasize repeatable observations that constitute evidence about the nature and the causes of abnormal behavior.

Each research method has its own particular strengths in helping us understand the nature and causes of abnormal behavior. Case histories may provide a rich background of detail about a particular phenomenon but do not provide the basis for generalizations to other cases or individuals. Correlational approaches such as epidemiological surveys are particularly useful for identifying potential relationships between variables but can tell us little or nothing about the causal structure of the phenomenon we are investigating.

Experimental methods are the most powerful approach for gaining evidence of the potential causes of behavioral phenomena, but they have had limited use in the study of abnormal behavior. This is because of the ethical and practical constraints associated with subjecting humans to independent variables that we think may be causal factors in the development of abnormal patterns of behavior.

Consequently, a good deal of experimental research in the area of abnormal behavior has been focused on the use of experimental analogues. The analogue may test the effects of a particular independent variable on another species or test the effects of conditions in the laboratory that we think are analogous to those associated with the development of abnormal behavior. In addition, the systematic use of experimental designs with individual subjects has increased substantially, particularly among behaviorally oriented psychologists. We suggested that high-risk methods for studying the development of abnormal behavior promise to uncover important findings about the causes of abnormal behavior.

We also noted that meta-analysis appears to be a promising new strategy for summarizing research. The value of this strategy lies in the researcher's ability to combine the results of many studies on a particular question in drawing overall conclusions.

Finally, we discussed the question of ethical issues in the study of abnormal behavior and noted that the danger of undue risk to experimental subjects and the need to obtain informed consent are two major issues in this field. *Ethical Principles of Psychologists* provides an example of the way in which scientists regulate their own behavior to safeguard the public welfare while pursuing their scientific objectives.

4

Assessment and Diagnosis of Abnormal Behavior

Psychological Assessment
Clinical Interviews
Psychological Tests
Behavioral Observation
Neuropsychological Assessment
Computer-Assisted Assessment

Problems in Assessment
Test Results and Illusory Correlation
Sex-Role Stereotypes
Race Differences

Diagnosis and Classification
Uses of Diagnosis
The *Diagnostic and Statistical Manual*
(DSM III)
Strengths and Weaknesses of the DSM III

Summary

INTRODUCTION

In the description that follows you will hear a clinical psychologist describe his initial assessment interview with a client. As you read, ask yourself about the kind of information the clinician is obtaining and what you think of his interview style.

Ms. Stewart, an attractive 24-year-old woman, was referred to me for counseling by an emergency ward following a suicide attempt. When Ms. Stewart entered the office, I asked her to have a seat. I said that we would talk today mainly about her background. I explained that I needed to know this in order to help her solve her problems. She said that she had just had a meeting with some doctors and nurses who had asked her a lot of ridiculous questions. I asked her what some of the questions were. She listed them off as, "How did I feel when I took the pills?" "Why was I depressed?" "Had I felt that way before?" She did not know how to answer the questions. She did not remember how she had felt when she took the pills. I realized that Ms. Stewart was trying to tell me she wasn't ready to talk about her suicide attempt.

So I changed the subject and asked her to tell me a little about herself, where she was raised, where she went to school, etc. She related that she was born and raised in Connecticut. She has a younger sister who is 21 years old and married. Without further discussion of her family, she said she had been an excellent stu-

dent in high school and had gone on to become a laboratory technician. I asked her if her parents approved. She said it didn't matter much to them but she supposed that they were glad she had a career. I asked her what she had done after she graduated from school. She had worked at a local hospital and then moved to California, where she easily got a job in another hospital.

* * * * *

I then asked her about her social life in high school. She said that she had dated some but did not have a steady boyfriend. I asked her if she would describe her childhood. She related that she was a very friendly child until about age eight, when all of a sudden she became shy. I asked what she meant, and she explained that she stayed home after school and watched TV and ate until she got fat and ugly. I asked her how she felt about that. She said that people made fun of her and she retreated even more. Her family also joked about her and called her names. I asked how she felt about her family calling her names. She said that she did not become bothered by it at first but after a while she felt hurt.

Finally, when she was around 13 she decided to lose weight. I asked why she decided to lose weight then. She was in junior high school and had begun to take an interest in boys and wanted to be more attractive to them. When asked if she dated much, she said no but she did date a little but no one seriously. I asked if she had many friends. She said not many. She did have one special guy she dated in high school but he wasn't a steady boyfriend. Recently she heard that he was killed in an automobile accident. I asked if that upset her. She said it did, especially since she had known him so well.

* * * * *

We then switched to her current situation, and I asked her to tell me more about her taking the pills. She explained that the whole thing started when her boyfriend broke up with her and married someone else. This really upset her. However, she didn't express it by crying. Ms. Stewart said she realizes now that her problem is that she keeps things inside and lets them boil. I asked her what happened then. She decided to leave California and come to Boston, where she easily obtained work at a hospital. She started dating, but after each date she'd return to her apartment and feel depressed. I asked about what. She said she pretended to have fun on dates but she really didn't care about any of the guys. I asked if she ever talked to her friends or family about her depression, and she said no, she just kept it all inside.

I asked her when she took the pills for the first time. She explained that four months ago she took a handful of phenobarbital pills after the man she had been dating told her he didn't want to see her anymore. Her roommate found her and took her to the emergency ward. Things went OK for a while after that until two weeks ago when she again took an overdose of sleeping pills.

Her most recent suicide attempt was explained in some detail. She had been asked to leave her job when a friend with whom she worked falsely accused her of stealing. In dismissing her, her supervisor implied that be-

cause she had had previous psychological problems it would be better if she left work. Again I asked Ms. Stewart if she had talked to anyone about this, and again she said no, she just kept it all inside. She returned to her apartment and again resorted to pills. Ms. Stewart said she knows there is something wrong with her. She didn't really want to die and realizes that she needs help in getting out of her depression. I asked how often she got depressed. She said quite often. She's been depressed since her boyfriend broke up with her. She puts everything into a relationship, and when things go wrong, she takes it as a personal rejection. After a silence, I told Ms. Stewart that she and I would be meeting on a regular basis to discuss her problems. I asked her what day she preferred to come in. She said she wasn't sure which day she'd be able to get a ride to the clinic. I told her I would call her in a few days to discuss an appointment time. She agreed, and we said goodbye (Edinberg, Zinberg, & Kelson, 1975, pp. 102–4).

PSYCHOLOGICAL ASSESSMENT

You may have noticed several things as you read the description of that initial *clinical interview*. First, the clinician was able to obtain a range of brief historical information about the school experiences, work experiences, family life, and personal relationships. Each of these bits of information helps to fill out the clinical picture of the patient. In addition, the psychologist was sensitive to the emotionally laden topic of the patient's previous suicide attempt and allowed Ms. Stewart to discuss the topic only when she appeared ready to do so. Finally, it is interesting to note that this initial assessment interview blended rather naturally into the beginning of a series of counseling sessions. The initial assessment can be thought of as a preliminary psychological intervention as well as an evaluation procedure.

The clinical interview is usually only the first step in a more detailed assessment process that may involve structured interviews, the administration of psychological tests, and the establishment of a psychological diagnosis. Each of these procedures and steps in assessment and diagnosis is designed to help determine the current issues and problems facing the individual, to help in making decisions about the appropriate choice of treatment, and to determine the prognosis or likely outcome for the individual. The assessment of individual characteristics and abilities can provide us with important information to help the individual cope with future life challenges (Sundberg, Snowden, & Reynolds, 1978).

All techniques of psychological assessment attempt to obtain a *sample of behavior* that is assumed to be representative of the behavior displayed by the person in a range of situations, and that will allow us to predict other important outcomes in the individual's life. In what follows we will examine a number of techniques used in psychological assessment of abnormal behavior, including clinical interviews, psychological tests, and observational techniques. We will also discuss a variety of problems that can arise in the process of assessment. Finally, we will consider the process of diagnosis and classification of abnormal behavior. In doing so, we will examine a major classification system currently used in the diagnosis of abnormal behavior, the *Diagnosis and Statistical Manual of Mental Disorders* (DSM III).

Clinical Interview

The clinical interview described at the beginning of this chapter is a fairly typical example of the initial interview used at the beginning of psychological assessment. The interview is one of the most widely used strategies for obtaining psychological information. A skillful interviewer may seem to be carrying on a casual conversation with the person being interviewed, but usually such interviews collect valuable information for the assessment of individual behavior.

The most commonly used interview in assessing abnormal behavior is called the *mental status interview*. Table 4–1 shows the general areas of behavior covered in the mental status interview and also provides an example of a report that might be based on such an interview. The major limitation of the mental status interview is that the interview itself is quite unstructured. Consequently, two different interviewers could obtain quite different results using it.

One solution to this problem is to structure the interview so that the same type of information is obtained in every case. An example of such a structured interview is the

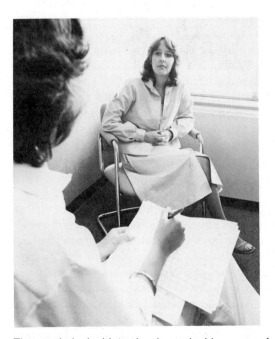

The psychological interview is a valuable source of information for assessment and treatment planning.
(John Thoeming/Dorsey Press)

TABLE 4–1
Excerpts from a Mental Status Interview of a 29-Year-Old Male

Category	Example of Report
General appearance, attitude, and behavior	He is friendly and cooperative. Has made no complaints about ward restrictions. He smiles in a somewhat exaggerated and grotesque manner.
Discourse	He answers in a deep, loud voice, speaking in a slow, precise, and somewhat condescending manner. His responses are relevant but vague.
Mood and affective fluctuations	His facial expressions, although not totally inappropriate, are poorly correlated with subject of discourse or events in his environment.
Sensorium and intellect	The patient's orientation for place, person, and time is normal. His remote and recent memory also are normal. Two brief intelligence measures indicate about average intelligence.
Mental content and specific occupations	He readily discusses what he calls his "nervous trouble." He complains of "bad thoughts" and a "conspiracy." He reports hearing voices saying, "Hello, Bill, you're a dirty dog."
Insight	The patient readily accepts the idea that he should be in the hospital. He feels that hospitalization will help him get rid of these "bad" thoughts. He is not in the least defensive about admitting to auditory and visual hallucinations or to the idea that everyone on earth is his enemy.

Source: Reproduced with permission from B. Kleinmuntz, *Personality Measurement: An Introduction* (Homewood, Ill.: Dorsey, 1967), p. 159.

Psychiatric Evaluation Form developed by Spitzer and Endicott. In Table 4–2 you can see an example of the type of questions asked by the interviewer using the Psychiatric Evaluation Form. An advantage of this method is that the interview results can be translated into ratings that are useful in making decisions about treatment diagnosis and the likely course of the individual's difficulties.

Psychological Tests

Perhaps one of the most important contributions of psychology has been its development of tests to measure and predict behavior. Tests provide a distinct advantage over interviews and observations since they are usually easier to quantify, and therefore it is easier to compare scores among respondents. Psychological tests are designed to sample, in a standardized way, some important aspect of behavior.

Literally thousands of tests have been developed to measure various aspects of per-

sonality and individual abilities. We will consider two examples of psychological tests that have been widely used in assessing abnormal behavior.

The *Minnesota Multiphasic Personality Inventory (MMPI)* (Hathaway & McKinley, 1943) is a self-report inventory consisting of 550 statements to which one can respond "true," "false," or "cannot say." Each statement is included in one or more scales in the MMPI. Table 4–3 describes the different MMPI scales. By looking at the overall pattern of scores on different scales, clinicians are able to develop a personality description of the individual. It is possible for the clinician to use either his or her own experience with these scales or standard personality descriptions to describe particular MMPI profiles.

Marks and Seeman (1963) have developed composite descriptions that fit a particular profile type based on the MMPI. By obtaining an extremely large sample of individuals who have taken the MMPI test and identifying clusters of individuals with similar

TABLE 4-2
Psychiatric Evaluation Form—Diagnostic Version

Interview Guide	Scales

Interview Guide

ORIGINAL COMPLAINT

If a psychiatric patient: Now I would like to hear about your problems or difficulties and how they led to your coming to the (hospital, clinic).

GENERAL CONDITION

Tell me how you have been feeling recently. (Anything else been bothering you?)

PHYSICAL HEALTH

How is your physical condition?
Does any part of your body give you trouble?
Do you worry much about your health?

If necessary, inquire for doctor's opinion about symptoms or illnesses.

When you are upset do you react physically . . . like [stomach trouble, diarrhea, headaches, sick feelings, dizziness]?

APPETITE-SLEEP-FATIGUE

Disturbances in these areas are often associated with depression, anxiety, or somatic concerns.
What about your appetite for food?
Do you have any trouble sleeping or getting to sleep? (Why is that?)
How easily do you get tired?

MOOD

This section covers several moods. The interviewer must determine to what extent the symptoms are associated with either one or the other or several of the dimensions.
What kinds of moods have you been in recently?
What kinds of things do you worry about? (How much do you worry?)
What kinds of fears do you have? (Any situation . . . activities . . . things?)
How often do you feel anxious or tense? (When you are this way, do you react physically . . . like sweating, dizziness, cramps?)

Scales

> The time period for this section is the past month.

PHYSICAL HEALTH

214 **SOMATIC CONCERNS**

Excessive concern with bodily functions; preoccupation with one or more real or imagined physical complaints or disabilities; bizarre or unrealistic feelings or beliefs about his body or parts of body. **Do not include mere dissatisfaction with appearance.**
?   1   2   3   4   5   6

215 **CONVERSION REACTION**

Has a motor or sensory dysfunction which conforms to the lay notion of neurological illness, for which his doctors can find no organic basis (e.g., paralysis or anesthesia)
?   1   2   3   4   5   6

216 **PSYCHOPHYSIOLOGICAL REACTIONS**

Is bothered by one or more psychophysiological reactions to stress. Examples: backache, headaches, hypertension, dizziness, asthma, spastic bowel. **Note: the reaction may or may not involve structural change.**
?   1   2   3   4   5   6

MOOD

217 **ELATED MOOD**

Exhibits or speaks of an elevated mood, exaggerated sense of well being or optimism, of feelings of elation. Examples: Says "everything is great," jokes, witticisms, silly remarks, singing, laughing, or trying to get others to laugh or smile.
?   1   2   3   4   5   6

218 **ANXIETY**

Remarks indicate feelings of apprehension, worry, anxiety, nervousness, tension, fearfulness, or panic. When clearly associated with any of these feelings, consider insomnia, restlessness, physical symptoms (e.g., palpitations, sweating, dizziness, cramps), or difficulty concentrating, etc.
?   1   2   3   4   5   6

Source: From *Psychiatric Evaluation Form* by R. L. Spitzer, J. Endicott, A. M. Mesnikoff, and G. M. Cohen, January 1968, Biometrics Research, New York State Department of Mental Hygiene, Department of Psychiatry, Columbia University.

TABLE 4–3
Personality Characteristics Associated with Elevations on the Basic MMPI Scales

Scale	Characteristics
1 (Hs), Hypochondriasis	High scorers are described as cynical, defeatist, preoccupied with self, complaining, hostile, and presenting numerous physical problems.
2 (D), Depression	High scorers are described as moody, shy, despondent, pessimistic, and distressed. This scale is one of the most frequently elevated in clinical patients.
3 (Hy), Hysteria	High scorers tend to be repressed, dependent, naive, outgoing, and to have multiple physical complaints. Expression of psychological conflict through vague and unbased physical complaints.
4 (Pd), Psychopathic Deviate	High scorers often are rebellious, impulsive, hedonistic, and antisocial. They often have difficulty in marital or family relationships and trouble with the law or authority in general.
5 (MF), Masculinity-Femininity	High-scoring males are described as sensitive, aesthetic, passive, or feminine. High-scoring females are described as aggressive, rebellious, and unrealistic.
6 (Pa), Paranoia	Elevations on this scale are often associated with being suspicious, aloof, shrewd, guarded, worrisome, and overly sensitive. High scorers may project or externalize blame.
7 (Pt), Psychasthenia	High scorers are tense, anxious, ruminative, preoccupied, obsessional, phobic, rigid. They frequently are self-condemning and feel inferior and inadequate.
8 (Sc), Schizophrenia	High scorers are often withdrawn, shy, unusual, or strange and have peculiar thoughts or ideas. They may have poor reality contact and in severe cases bizarre sensory experiences—delusions and hallucinations.
9 (Ma), Mania	High scorers are called sociable, outgoing, impulsive, overly energetic, optimistic, and in some cases amoral, flighty, confused, disoriented.
0 (Si), Social Introversion-Extraversion	High scorers tend to be modest, shy, withdrawn, self-effacing, inhibited. Low scorers are outgoing, spontaneous, sociable, confident.

Source: From *MMPI: Research developments and clinical applications* by J. N. Butcher, 1969, New York: McGraw-Hill.

profiles, they were able to identify typical patterns of characteristics on a variety of other dimensions, including age, sex, personality characteristics, previous educational background, and a variety of other variables. The result is a detailed description of the typical respondent having a particular profile type. Such information can be useful in the assessment of clients since it provides a basis for comparison and suggests avenues for further inquiry.

The MMPI has been used in a variety of research projects focusing on different clinical groups. For example, Kline and Snyder (1985) have used the MMPI to identify different personality types among alcoholic men and women. They found that grouping alcoholics with highly similar MMPI profiles separated them into different personality configurations, which also were associated with different patterns of alcohol use. This type of research is useful both because it helps to illuminate the relationship between personality characteristics and drinking behavior, and because it can provide clues to the motivation and possible treatment for alcoholic patients showing different personality profiles.

Projective Tests. Another form of psychological testing involves the use of *projective tests.* Although there are many types of projective tests, a common feature is that the test material is purposely made ambiguous. The tests are called *projective* because it is assumed that, seeing a relatively ambiguous picture or situation, the person will project his or her own needs, concerns, or values into an interpretation of the picture. Moreover, it is assumed that unconscious as well as conscious concerns are projected onto the ambiguous stimulus. Thus projective tests are designed to tap unconscious processes that underlie the individual's overt behavior. The most famous of all projective tests is the Rorschach Test developed by the Swiss psychiatrist Hermann Rorschach in 1921.

The story of the development of the Rorschach Test is an interesting footnote in the history of psychology. Hermann Rorschach was known to many of his high school friends as "Kleck," a word which means inkblot or painter. This nickname reflected Rorschach's early interest in art and his fascination with creating fancy inkblots, a pursuit then known as klecksography. But long before Rorschach's first dabblings with inkblots, artists and poets had used relatively formless stimuli to enhance their creative imaginings. In the 15th century Leonardo da Vinci was intrigued by the possibility of achieving artistic inspiration by perceiving the forms created by throwing a piece of sponge blotched with colors of paint against a wall. To stimulate the creative process, Kerner, a 19th-century poet, produced inkblots by folding paper over drops of ink. Some of the poems that Kerner wrote and the inkblots that inspired them have been published (Zubin, Eron, & Schumer, 1965). So before Rorschach developed his now-famous inkblot test, there was ample precedent for their use to spark the creative imagination.

Rorschach, however, suggested the use of inkblots to probe the unconscious. After medical training with the eminent psychiatrist Eugen Bleuler, one of Freud's colleagues, Rorschach became a firm believer in the reality of the unconscious. And Rorschach came to believe that a person's personality dynamics could be discerned by examining his or her responses to inkblots. He also believed that associations to such vaguely defined forms were stimulated by unconscious processes characteristic of the individual's personality makeup.

Rorschach conducted experiments with inkblots during his medical school years; after he received his M.D. in 1912, his research with inkblots continued. Nine years later Rorschach published his famous monograph, *Psychodiagnostik*, which described his methods of using inkblots to study personality. In order to get his book published, Rorschach had to agree to omit 5 of the 15 blots used in his research studies. The 10 blots that were finally included were reduced in size and altered in color from the original ones he used. Even the shading of the cards was changed by the printing process used to produce the book. Thus the ultimate product was somewhat different from what Rorschach actually intended. And it is this product that is today known as the Rorschach test (Aronow & Renzikoff, 1976).

The Rorschach is administered and interpreted by an examiner well trained in its use. The examiner shows the subject the cards one at a time and records verbatim the subject's responses and his or her social behavior during the testing.

Beck et al. (1961) recommended giving the following instructions to the subject: "You will be given a series of 10 cards, one by one. The cards have on them designs made up of inkblots. Look at each card and tell the examiner what you see on each card, or anything that might be represented there. Look at each card as long as you like; only be sure to tell the examiner everything that you see on the card as you look at it. When you have finished with a card, give it to the examiner as a sign that you are through with it" (p. 2).

After the subject responds to all 10 cards, the examiner shows each of the cards to the subject a second time. After determining which aspects of the blot prompted the response (color, shading, form, movement, and so forth), and learning which parts of the blot the subject responded to, the examiner is ready to interpret the results.

Clinicians rarely analyze responses in isolation; instead, they are more likely to consider patterns of responses to the inkblots (Aronow & Reznekoff, 1983). Many scoring systems and scales have been devised to measure such personality characteristics as anxiety, hostility, impairment of brain function, and so on. Clinicians who use the Rorschach believe it can provide valuable information regarding the client's capacity for original thinking, empathy, impulsivity and emotional reactivity, and contact with reality.

While experts in the use of projective tests have sometimes achieved impressive results in personality description or the prediction of future behavior, the research indicates that even trained assessors' interpretations of responses to the Rorschach can vary a great deal. Thus the reliability of this technique is frequently quite low.

Zubin (1984) has been particularly critical of the Rorschach as an instrument for psychological assessment and has argued that it is nothing but an unstructured interview procedure. He argues instead in favor of careful experimental testing of responses to

WHAT'S IN AN INKBLOT?

Look at this inkblot. What does it suggest to you? No doubt you will have several impressions. Write them down in the order in which they occur to you. When new concepts no longer emerge read the list to yourself.

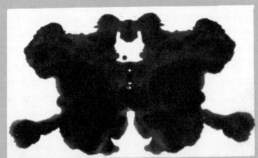

Now compare your impressions with the responses to the same inkblot given by some individual in the course of a diagnostic evaluation.

The center white area near the top reminds me of the heads of two women who are talking.

Near the bottom, the parts sticking out remind me of ice cream cones. They're chocolate, because they're dark. I think I said that because I'm hungry. I have this terrible sweet tooth, you know.

Holding the card upside down, I can see two funny shaped Idaho potatoes.

The lower white area reminds me of the head of a wolf or a coyote.

The whole thing makes me think of a kind of odd butterfly.

The left side of the blot makes me think of a man with a party hat with one of those New Year's favors in his mouth, the kind that shoots out when you blow into them.

Were your responses to this inkblot similar? Were they very different? Even a randomly created inkblot reveals the fact that no two people perceive what we call reality in exactly the same way. The fact that we project our own personality upon our view of the world makes the projective tests a useful assessment tool.

the Rorschach to establish its validity (Zubin, Eron, & Schumer, 1965).

Thematic Apperception Test. Another important projective technique is the *Thematic Apperception Test (TAT)*. Thousands of research studies have been conducted using this technique, which is frequently used to supplement other information in psychological assessment. The TAT is usually administered in an interview format with a single individual. The stimuli are more structured than the Rorschach and consist of pictures, usually of a single individual or people in interaction. Some pictures are administered routinely, such as the first card, which shows a young boy contemplating a violin that rests on a table in front of him.

The psychologist instructs the subject that this is a test of imagination, and that he or she is to make up as dramatic a story for each picture as possible. The subject is asked to tell what event led to the scene in the picture, what is happening at that moment, what the characters are feeling and thinking, and what the outcome might be.

Below are two examples of stories given in response to card number one:

Person A: [A woman, 22 years old] A young boy looking at the violin on the table. His expression is one of tiredness and not much interest. It seems to me that he is too young to be forced to take violin lessons, at an age that he would have no love of the instrument or music. It is possible that his mother either believes that it is *good* to have a child "play something" or has visions of his becoming a great violinist. All of this might lead to the child's dislike of the whole thing.

Person B: [A woman, 33 years old] First impression is the staged effect—child does not look at an unfamiliar object so quiescently. The child's facial expression is one of melancholy. The ap-

pearance is somewhat—the bow is not clear-cut. Emotions as strong as this probably meant to be indicated here, not in the context with quietness of subject—coloring and delineation of individual and violin (Henry, 1956, pp. 140–41).

Obviously, while the length of these two responses is quite similar, they show striking individual differences. The first person gets right to the point of the story, indicates the key issues and motivations, and anticipates the likely outcome. The second person, on the other hand, uses words in an unusual way; reading her story produces a feeling of confusion.

The basic assumption underlying the interpretation of the TAT is that each of the stories told reflects both internal "needs" and perceptions of external demands or "press." The central figure in each picture is assumed to be the person with whom the subject identifies. Overall, the goal of assessment using the TAT is to check hunches or hypotheses about why the person tells the story he or she does, what personality might be revealed in the story, and how the person might cope with different situations or events.

The TAT has not been found to be particularly effective in distinguishing between clinical and nonclinical groups. As Sundberg (1977) observes, projective techniques are not tests but rather techniques for exploring different aspects of personality. To a very large extent it is not possible to separate the characteristics of the interpreter of the TAT story from the results of the assessment. Nevertheless, as exploratory methods to reflect the unique characteristics of each individual, projective techniques have long been regarded as valuable tools in psychological assessment.

The Role of Projective Techniques in Assessment. For a number of years projective techniques have been severely criticized for their lack of reliability and validity. We will discuss this issue in much more detail when we consider the concept of *illusory correlation* later in the chapter. Perhaps the most appropriate question to ask about the Rorschach test, as with any other assessment tool, is, "What is the instrument valid for?" It is impossible for any one test or evaluation instrument to answer every question we might wish to pose about a person. Indeed, the Rorschach surely cannot live up to some early claims that it can provide a mental X ray of the personality. Sundberg et al. (1978) suggest that perhaps the most valid approach to the Rorschach system may be to regard individual responses as a sample of an individual's thinking processes. It is important to conduct additional research to specify the range of personality characteristics that the Rorschach and other personality tests can validly measure.

Since many clinicians do not have complete faith in any one instrument's ability to provide all the information to fully evaluate a client, a *battery* of carefully selected assessment devices often is administered. In order to arrive at a diagnosis of a client, the assessor might interview the person and administer an MMPI, a Rorschach, or any number or combination of other assessment devices. The choice of methods used with a particular individual will probably depend on a number of factors, such as the nature and purpose of the evaluation (is the client a danger to others, suicidal, or schizophrenic?, and what decisions need to be made about the client?, i.e., hospitalization, medication, treatment), the examiner's training and biases, and his or her confidence in a particular test.

Behavioral Observation

Perhaps the most basic way to gather information about a person is to observe him or her in a natural setting. Gerald Patterson and his co-workers at the University of Oregon have developed a system for observing the behavior of young boys in their family context.

Table 4–4 illustrates Patterson's observation system. On the left, a list of some of the behaviors that an observer will look for in observing the home setting is shown. The second column shows how 30 seconds are interpreted using Patterson's behavioral coding system.

If you look closely at this example, you can learn several important things from it. First, Patterson's system, like many behavioral observation systems, is very carefully defined and detailed. It takes the "booming, buzzing confusion" of family life and turns it into a series of coded behaviors that describe the way people are behaving toward each other. It was Patterson's goal to be able to use this information not only to understand the usual patterns of behavior in the home but also to measure progress in treatment. Another thing you can see from this example is that Patterson's system achieves great accuracy at the expense of being very narrow. This system would not work very well in settings other than the home, nor was it designed to do so.

Patterson and his co-workers designed this system so they could discover the *contingencies* that exist in family interactions. Once behavior is coded in six-second segments, systematic relationships between parent and child behavior patterns can be discovered. This information then provides specific ideas for future behavioral intervention in the family interaction to help deal with problematic behavior patterns.

Similar strategies for behavioral observation have been developed for other settings, including the classroom. Behaviorally oriented psychologists argue that such observation techniques allow the possibility of understanding how behavior is reinforced in a

TABLE 4-4
Illustration of the Use of Patterson's (1969) System of Behavioral Observation: Thirty Seconds in the Life of a Boy Named Kevin

Narrative Description of Thirty Seconds in the Life of Kevin	Thirty Seconds in Kevin's Life as a Rater Using Behavioral Observation Might See It
0-6 seconds	
Kevin goes up to father's chair and stands alongside it. Father puts his arms around Kevin's shoulders.	Kevin engages in "normative" behavior (i.e., appropriate behavior not falling under any specific category) and father shows positive physical contact.
7-12 seconds	
Kevin says to mother as Frieda looks at Kevin, "Can I go out and play after supper?" Mother does not reply.	Kevin talks and his mother ignores him.
13-18 seconds	
Kevin raises his voice and repeats the question. Mother says, "You don't have to yell; I can hear you." Father says, "How many times have I told you not to yell at your mother?"	Kevin yells and both mother and father show their disapproval.
19-24 seconds	
Kevin scratches a bruise on his arm while mother tells Frieda to get started on the dishes, which Frieda does.	Kevin is involved in self-stimulation, and Frieda engages in other activities and shows no response.
25-30 seconds	
Kevin continues to rub and scratch his arm while mother and daughter are working at the kitchen sink.	Kevin engages in self-stimulation while mother and Frieda are involved in other activities and show no response.
	[For purposes of scores, Kevin is considered 1; 2 signifies the father; 3 the mother; and 4 the sister.]

Source: Based on G. R. Patterson, R. S. Ray, D. A. Shaw, & J. Cobb, "Manual for Coding of Family Interactions, 1969 ASIS/NAPS c/o Microfische Publications 305 46 St New York NY 10017 Document #01234.

particular situation and lead naturally into a plan for treatment. An example of behavioral observation, you may recall, was given in Chapter 3 in describing single-subject designs for research.

Neuropsychological Assessment

Later, in Chapters 11 and 12, we will discuss disorders of the later years and organic disorders that in many cases involve damage or deterioration to the central nervous system. In recent years medical methods for assessing brain damage have rapidly advanced, providing remarkably accurate visual portrayals of brain structure and abnormalities.

At the same time *neuropsychological assessment* has been developed by clinical and experimental psychologists who wish to understand how damage to the central nervous system can affect behavior. It is this link between brain and behavior that is the central focus of neuropsychological assessment.

Neuropsychologists have developed a number of behavioral tests measuring coordination, visual and auditory perception, speech recognition, and other behavioral functions. They have assessed the performance of various clinical and normal populations on these tests to provide a better understanding of brain-behavior relationships. In addition, the assessment techniques developed by neuropsychologists allow the possibility of identifying neurological problems from tasks testing behavioral performance. Neuropsychological measures are often used to supplement the diagnosis made by a neurologist, who depends more heavily on specialized laboratory techniques including X rays and the electrical recording of brain activity.

A well-known example of a neuropsychological assessment test used to screen individuals for brain damage is the *Bender Visual–Motor Gestalt Test.* This test uses nine geometrical figures that patients are asked to draw. An example of these geometrical figures and the copies made by a brain-damaged individual are shown in Figure 4–1. For most normal people the test takes only 5 to 10 minutes to complete. But for people with visual-motor coordination problems of the kind that often occur in organic disorders, the test may take considerably longer, and the patient may have considerable difficulty duplicating the figures.

One of the best-known batteries of test for organic disorders is the *Halstead-Reitan Neuropsychological Test Battery* (Reitan & Davison, 1974). This procedure involves an extensive series of tasks designed to detect problems in auditory and visual perception, motor performance, and the ability to engage in abstract tasks. For example, one test requires the person to differentiate between rhythmic beats that sometimes are the same and sometimes different. Another test involves tapping speed, and still another asks the blindfolded patient to fit blocks into a formboard by feel alone and then to draw the blocks from memory.

The overall results of the Halstead-Reitan battery can be measured in terms of an impairment index, and extensive research information exists for this battery of tests. For example, recently, Heaton and his colleagues (1985) have shown that victims of multiple sclerosis may actually have significant behavioral impairment, which is detected using the Halstead-Reitan battery but is not identified using standard neurological procedures.

Computer-Assisted Assessment

In our survey of assessment methods we have looked briefly at observation, interview, and psychological tests as clinical assessment tools. Within the last 20 years computers have become part of the psychological assessment process as well (Griest, Klein, Erdman, & Jefferson, 1983).

What can a computer do better than a clinician can? Computers have the advantages of speed, flexibility, and objectivity, and this greatly aids the computer in performing the sensitive and difficult task of psychological assessment. For example, a computer has a "perfect memory." While a clinician may interpret the same psychological test information differently at two different times, the computer's program will always produce the same interpretation of the same test information. The computer is reliable in its responses. In addition, the computer can have a much larger bank of "clinical experience" than can any clinician. It is possible to program a computer with rules for classifying individuals that have been developed on the basis of testing hundreds of thousands of individuals. Furthermore, it is possible to program the computer so that it can efficiently store information to alter its own "memory." Finally, the rules used by a computer to assess an individual's psychological test data and to make predictions about that person are public and explicit. They are part of the computer program itself. The clinician also uses rules to assess psychological test data, but they may be private and intuitive rules that are difficult

FIGURE 4-1
Six of the Bender-Gestalt Figures—Originals and Copies by a 62-Year-Old Brain-Damaged Man

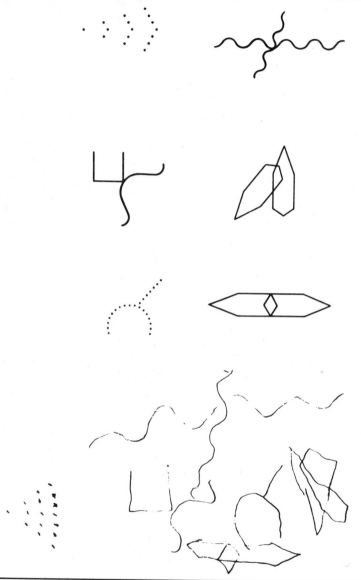

Source: From *The Clinical Use of the Revised Bender-Gestalt Test* (pp. 3 and 170) by M. L. Hutt and G. J. Briskin, 1969, New York, Grune and Stratton (Sundberg, 1977, p. 137).

for the clinician to articulate. With such abilities the computer appears qualified at least to be a partner with the clinician in the task of psychological assessment.

Computers have been used as an aid in psychological assessment in a variety of ways. For example, Spitzer and Endicott (1968) have developed a computer program that is similar to the game of "20 questions." In this system the computer program examines psychological test data for an individual and asks a question of the information that can be answered "true" or "false." Depending on the answer to the question, the computer then rules out one or more possible diagnoses and decides which question to ask next. Just as in 20 questions, the possibilities are finally narrowed down to one or two that are most likely.

How does this system compare to the performance of an expert clinician? When expert clinicians were given the same test data as that presented to the computer, both experts and computer did well. The clear advantage of the computer is that it can do the same job much more rapidly and much more cheaply than the clinician can.

Recently Griest et al. (1983) have observed that computer-assisted assessment can be both an aid to the clinician and a psychological benefit to the client. When computer programs are used to aid a clinician in the interview process, clinicians tend to perform better in conducting the interview because the computer program provides structure and detail often omitted in less structured interview strategies. Interestingly, Griest and his colleagues observe that patient acceptance of being interviewed by a computer program is extremely high, and that in many cases patients would much rather respond to a computer terminal than personally to a clinician, particularly when emotionally sensitive topics are being considered. For example, clients who reported sexual problems were significantly less embarrassed when they were assessed by a computer terminal rather than in person.

Until now the use of computers in assessment and diagnosis has relied on those characteristics of the computer that make them superior to the clinician—its speed and its large and perfect memory. But will the computer ever replace the clinician? It is doubtful that many of the subtleties observed by a clinician in an interview situation can be detected by a computer program, but researchers have not exhausted their ingenuity in developing ways that computers can use information to help the clinician in the task of diagnosis and prediction. It is likely that we will see computers working in still other roles with the clinician in the future.

PROBLEMS IN ASSESSMENT

Does the following personality description fit you? You tend to be critical of yourself and have a strong need to have other people like you. Although you tend to be pretty well controlled on the outside, inside you frequently feel insecure. At times your sexual adjustment has been a problem for you. You like a certain amount of change in your life and become unhappy when you are hemmed in by restrictions and limitations. Sometimes you feel sociable and extroverted, but at other times you feel very reserved and introverted. Overall, you have some personality weaknesses, but you are generally able to compensate for them.

If you felt that that personality description fit you pretty well and described some of your unique individual qualities, you are not alone. You have just experienced what Paul Meehl has called "personality description after the manner of P. T. Barnum." Barnum, the great showman, believed that to succeed you had to have a little something for everybody, and, like Barnum, the personality description that you just read had a little something for everyone—it was composed of *statements that are true about almost every-one.*

Astrologers, handwriting analysts, and fortune-tellers have long known that people who hear very general statements about themselves are likely to feel these statements are accurate descriptions, if they have been told that the description has been prepared especially for them. What is important about this phenomenon from the point of view of psychological assessment is that some test interpretations may contain a great many Barnum statements and therefore appear much more valid than they actually are. Test results that are true of everyone obviously do not allow us to discover the distinguishing characteristics of people. And Barnum statements do not allow psychological assessment to make accurate differential predictions or clinical decisions. Thus it is well to remember that a psychological test instrument that only generates statements that are true of everyone may appear "accurate" but is of no value in the psychological assessment of abnormal behavior.

Just as the Barnum effect shows that apparently meaningful test results can be trivial if they are true of nearly everyone, there are a variety of different sources of bias in the interpretation of psychological tests and assessment strategies. Psychological tests and other assessment approaches have been developed with the goal of providing good descriptions of the characteristics of individuals and accurate predictions about their future behavior. Yet various sources of bias in the use of tests remains. In the following sections we will explore several important problems in assessment.

Test Results and Illusory Correlation

In interpreting the results of projective tests such as the Rorschach, the clinician must interpret the response given to each inkblot. That interpretation provides the clinician

the opportunity to use creative insight, but it also leaves him or her open to making an incorrect interpretation.

Two psychologists at the University of Wisconsin, Loren and Jean Chapman, have done a series of studies to help us understand how clinicians interpret projective tests and make inferences. They have been very interested in a projective test called the Draw-a-Person test (DAP). In using the Draw-a-Person test, the clinician gives an individual a pencil and a blank sheet of paper and requests that a person be drawn on the paper. By examining the way a person is drawn, clinicians believe that they can infer something about the patient's internal conflicts, motivations, and personality. For example, the Chapmans surveyed large numbers of experienced clinicians and asked them about certain characteristics of drawings of people and how they might be related to individual concerns and conflicts. The results they found seem to make "psychological sense." Eighty percent of the clinicians agreed that drawing broad shoulders and a muscular body reflected worries about manliness. Ninety percent of the clinicians agreed that atypical eyes in the drawing indicated suspiciousness of others, and 82 percent of the clinicians agreed that a large or an emphasized head in the drawing indicated that the person worried about intelligence.

These interpretations seem to make good sense, but, as the Chapmans have pointed out, careful research has shown that *none* of these characteristics in drawings predict the symptoms or concerns of the patient as the clinician believed them to be. Chapman and Chapman note that clinicians respond to this finding by saying, "I'll trust my own sense before I'll trust a journal article," and one psychologist said, "I know that paranoids don't seem to draw big eyes in the research labs, but they sure do in my office."

The Chapmans have conducted a series of studies to show that this strong belief in an association between certain aspects of the drawing and certain psychological characteristics are a result of *illusory correlation.* They define illusory correlation as the tendency to see two things as occurring together more often than they actually do. Most of the illusory correlations seen by both experienced clinicians and the undergraduate students they later studied were a result of associations between the test indicator and the interpretation. That is, we tend to associate large eyes and suspiciousness with each other and therefore assume that suspicious clients will draw faces with large eyes. The association makes the test interpreter feel as if the two things "go together," even when they don't actually go together in the real world.

The Chapmans point out that projective tests such as the Rorschach do indeed produce some valid signs that allow clinicians to predict the behavior of the person taking the test. However, the valid signs are seldom intuitively obvious. For example, homosexuality is frequently indicated in people seeing snarling beasts or human-animal crossbreeds in inkblots, but these are not intuitively obvious signs of homosexual behavior. The intuitive signs are almost always a result of illusory correlation.

Is it possible that the theoretical grounding of a clinician's training causes him or her to see certain kinds of behavior patterns as abnormal? Langer and Abelson (1974) assembled two groups of therapists with very different training backgrounds to find out. One group was drawn from a university department that had a very strong learning theory and behavioral bias. The other group was drawn from a training group that had a strong psychodynamic training emphasis. Each of these groups was shown a videotaped interview of a man, but half of the subjects in each group were told that the person was being interviewed as a job applicant. The other half were told that he was a psychiatric patient.

Langer and Abelson found that when the person was described as a job applicant, both the dynamically oriented clinicians and the behavioral clinicians saw the person as fairly well adjusted; but when the interviewee was described as a psychiatric patient, the dynamically trained clinicians saw him as much less well adjusted than did the behaviorally oriented clinicians.

It seems, then, as if prior training can strongly shape the clinician's perceptions when seeing a patient. The study by Langer and Abelson tells us very little about why the behaviorally trained clinicians were relatively immune to the biasing effects of labeling. Perhaps their training led them to respond to the actual behavior of the patient to a greater degree than did that of the dynamically trained clinicians.

Sex-Role Stereotypes

If a person were described to you as independent, objective, active, logical, worldly, direct, adventurous, and self-confident, what sort of judgment would you make about his or her adjustment? If, on the other hand, the person were described as having his or her feelings easily hurt, being more emotional, disliking math and science, and being easily influenced, what would you say about his or her adjustment? These two sets of descriptions conform to conventional sex-role stereotypes that are widely held in our society. Inge Broverman and her colleagues wanted to know whether there was a relationship between sex-role stereotypes and the clinical judgments made by professionals about mental health.

In order to discover whether there was such a relationship, they asked 79 clinically trained mental health workers to respond to a questionnaire that contained a large number of bipolar adjectives like "strong–weak." In each case the mental health professional was asked to choose the adjective descrip-

Sex-role stereotypes can affect clinical judgment.
(Richard Sobol/Stock. Boston Inc.)

tion that best characterized a "male," a "female," and a "mature, healthy adult."

Broverman and her colleagues (Broverman, Broverman, & Clarkson, 1970) found that there existed a great deal of agreement among mental health professionals about the attributes characterizing healthy adult men, healthy women, and healthy adults whose sex was unspecified. This is not so surprising. Most of us can call up images of each of these general stereotypes. What was particularly interesting about these investigators' findings was that clinicians have different concepts of mental health for men and for women, and that these concepts seem to parallel the sex-role stereotypes prevalent in our society. That is, men who are perceived as conforming more closely to the male sex-role stereotype are also judged to be healthier than men who do not. Similarly, women who conform to the female sex-role stereotype are also judged to be healthier than women who do not. This seemingly obvious finding, the authors note, conceals a powerful negative assessment of women. Clinicians are likely to suggest that healthy women are more submissive, more dependent, less

adventurous, more easily influenced, and less objective. They note that this constellation of characteristics seems to be an unusual way to describe a mature, healthy individual.

Broverman and her co-workers also found that the male stereotype more resembled the mental health professional's conception of an "adult, healthy individual" than did the female sex-role stereotype. Thus mental health professionals' concepts of mental health appear to be biased in a male-oriented direction. Furthermore, this was true regardless of whether the mental health professional was a male or a female.

Broverman and her colleagues point out that we should not be so surprised to discover that mental health professionals display this bias. It reflects, they feel, the general acceptance by mental health professionals of an "adjustment" notion of health—the assumption that individuals who conform to sex roles in which they were socialized are healthier than individuals who do not. We should remember, however, that mental health professionals are frequently assumed to have special knowledge about the nature of psychological adjustment. Consequently, when they accept sex-role stereotypes in their judgments of mental health, they may at least implicitly be helping to perpetuate those stereotypes.

Race Differences

We have seen that differences in sex role can produce biases in judgments about abnormality. So far our examples of biasing effects have been due to the "norms" of the clinician, that is, the mental health professional's lack of experience or his or her ingrained beliefs about a particular group of people. But biases can also exist in the norms of a test used as a tool for assessment. For example, if people from a particular ethnic or cultural group are given a psychological test that was originally developed for another group, the test results may erroneously indicate a higher proportion of those people as maladjusted. And if that test is used for job screening or decisions about treatment, systematic biases in the test norms can result in serious discriminatory practices.

Gynther (1972) has reviewed the evidence for test bias in the MMPI when it is given to blacks. After reviewing a number of studies, Gynther concluded that there are differences in the MMPI profiles of black and white individuals and that these differences appear to be due to differences in cultural background. Gynther has examined those items on the MMPI that are answered differently by black and white populations. A common theme that runs through Gynther's results is the marked distrust of society exhibited by blacks and reflected in their test performance. A major finding that emerged from his analysis was that blacks answered many more items reflecting "social cynicism" than did whites. Gynther notes that the dimension of social cynicism is an important and realistic value in black culture.

Interpreting minority group test performance in terms of white normative information can produce misleading interpretations. (John Thoeming/Dorsey Press)

Davis (1975) found no differences in MMPI profiles between races when education and degree of disturbance were held constant. Thus the question of the degree to which the MMPI is appropriate for use with nonwhite populations remains in dispute.

However, a careful methodological review of the literature by Pritchard and Rosenblatt (1980 a, b) has concluded that there are no studies that unequivocally demonstrate social bias in the MMPI. While this issue remains controversial, a study by Bertelson, Marks, & May (1982) suggests that Pritchard's view may be correct. Bertelson and his co-workers matched 231 black and 231 white psychiatric patients on a large number of demographic characteristics and compared their MMPI profiles. They could not identify any systematic differences in MMPI patterns between the groups when demographic factors are controlled (Lanydon, 1984).

A review by Kessler, Price, and Wortman (1985) suggests that much of the distress observed in black populations is associated with differences in socioeconomic status (Kessler & Neighbors, 1983), but there may be counterbalancing forces at work. While blacks may well experience more distress than whites as a result of discrimination and prejudice, they may also experience group solidarity and mutual support (Turner, 1983).

DIAGNOSIS AND CLASSIFICATION

Thus far we have discussed a variety of assessment strategies designed to help understand the circumstances of the client and the nature of the problem the client is experiencing. Frequently another major step in the assessment process is the assignment of a diagnosis to the patient. Diagnosis assumes that patients with the same diagnosis are similar in the problems they experience, the course of their disorder over time, and the potential causes of the disorder. It is also assumed that certain patterns of treatment are more appropriate for some diagnostic groups than for others.

Uses of Diagnosis

There are some important practical reasons for assigning a diagnosis to an individual. Perhaps the most obvious reason is that some diagnostic groups benefit from some treatment approaches more readily than from others. For example, in Chapter 8 we will observe that certain drug therapies are particularly effective for individuals experiencing mood disorders. Thus from the point of view of the practicing clinician, knowledge about diagnosis can have important implications for treatment.

At this point we should also make a distinction between *diagnosis* on the one hand and *classification systems* on the other. Diagnosis is the assignment of an individual diagnostic category to a particular patient. A classification system, on the other hand, consists of all the possible diagnoses available within the system under consideration. Classification systems have a number of important functions in addition to providing the basis for diagnosis. Let us now consider several of these functions suggested by Blashfield and Draguns (1976).

Specialists in nearly every field develop a common language to communicate effectively with one another. Lawyers, plumbers, physicians, used-car sales representatives, and even confidence men have developed their own specialized language to help them discuss the details of the objects and events of their work. One way to view a classification system in the field of abnormal psychology is as a dictionary of terms that allows us to discuss a person or a disorder as a member of a class. In doing so, we are *communicating* information about that individual in a kind of shorthand. When a mental health worker says that an individual is a "reactive depressive," or that the person displays "schizophrenic features," he is using abbreviations to imply a much larger spectrum of features.

The classification of abnormal behavior assumes that the name of a disorder is the *key to scientific information* describing it. By looking at the literature discussing obsessive-compulsive neuroses, we ought to be able to find information on its description, what is known about its causes, and, perhaps, how people have tried to treat it.

Critics of current classification schemes have suggested that we abandon current classifications and start again. But throwing out the current system would bring an enormous loss of information since most of our scientific knowledge about various disorders is catalogued according to this system.

One goal of both clinical practitioners and research scientists is to *describe* the characteristics of the people whose behavior they study. If a classification system categorizes individuals so that the groupings are fairly homogeneous, then the name of a grouping will provide a fairly accurate summary of the important characteristics of the person, at least insofar as abnormal behavior is concerned.

A major purpose of classifying disorders in the field of abnormal psychology is to *predict* certain important characteristics or behaviors of people belonging to each class. Once we have classified a disorder, it should be possible to predict (1) what the causes of the disorder are likely to be, (2) how an individual affected will respond to treatment, and (3) the probable course of the disorder. Indeed, a very large portion of the efforts of scientists in abnormal psychology is devoted to discovering these relationships.

There is a final important way that a classification scheme can be useful. A category in the scheme can become a concept in a theory about abnormal behavior. For example, the classification *schizophrenia* has long served as the reference point for a set of ideas about people who are thought to share characteristics that include social withdrawal and severe disorganization of perception, thought, and emotion. Schizophrenia is an *idea* shared by scientists. It is not a theory, but a *scientific concept* used to summarize a set of characteristics of people's behavior. And like scientific concepts, its usefulness is subject to scientific verification.

The *Diagnostic and Statistical Manual of the American Psychiatric Association:* (DSM III)

Over the years a number of classification schemes have been developed to distinguish various patterns of abnormal behavior from each other. The single most widely used classification scheme has been the *Diagnostic and Statistical Manual of Mental Disorders* published by the American Psychiatric Association. The earlier version of this manual, published in 1968 (DSM II), was developed so that it conformed closely to the international classification of diseases described by the World Health Organization.

Although the second edition of the *Diagnostic and Statistical Manual of Mental Disorders* remained in use for over a decade, it received substantial criticism because of a number of shortcomings. Among them was the fact that within the broad diagnostic classes in the classification system, patterns of behavior included were very heterogeneous.

In addition, the reliability of DSM II was poor, particularly in the broader categories. As we shall see later in this discussion, the ability of two diagnosticians to agree on the diagnosis to be given to a particular individual is critical in the effective use of the system.

The most recent edition of *Diagnostic and Statistical Manual of Mental Disorders* (DSM III) was published in 1980. It represents a radical departure from DSM II and is a clear effort to meet the criticisms leveled at that version. DSM III notes that clear descriptions of diagnostic categories and the provision of diagnostic criteria to produce greater agreement among diagnosticians were the major purposes of the revision.

It is also important to note that DSM III does not attempt to account for how various psychological disturbances come about; it acknowledges a wide variety of theories to account for the development of various disorders. Instead, its primary purpose is an accurate description (Spitzer & Williams, 1983).

The framers of DSM III have attempted to be inclusive rather than exclusive in categorizing various patterns of abnormal behavior. A major criterion for deciding to include a disorder was whether clinicians would be likely to encounter the condition in their clinical work (DSM III, 1980). Thus a variety of relatively mild disorders or problems that may not be in the strictest sense "abnormal" are included in this comprehensive classification system (see Table 4-5). In fact, every disorder receives some sort of classification under this system since one of the categories is "conditions not attributable to a mental disorder."

Multiaxial Classification. DSM III classifies disorders not along one dimension or axis, but five. This has produced a substantial increase in the amount of information a classification will communicate about a disorder. The first axis provides for the classification of a person on the basis of a major pattern of symptoms. The second axis classifies personality disorders. Medical disorders are included on Axis III. The severity of stressors that may have served as precipitating events is rated on Axis IV. Finally, Axis V is

TABLE 4-5
Major Diagnostic Headings in DSM III
(1980, pp. 15-19)

Disorders usually first evident in infancy, childhood or adolescence:
  Mental retardation
  Attention deficit disorder
  Conduct disorder
  Anxiety disorders of childhood or adolescence
  Other disorders of infancy, childhood or adolescence
  Eating disorders
  Stereotyped movement disorders
  Other disorders with physical manifestations
  Pervasive developmental disorders
Organic mental disorders:
  Senile and presenile dementias
  Substance-induced dementias
Substance use disorders
Schizophrenic disorders
Paranoid disorders
Psychotic disorders not elsewhere classified
Affective disorders
Anxiety disorders
Somatoform disorders
Dissociative disorders (or hysterical neuroses, dissociative type)
Psychosexual disorders:
  Gender identity disorders
  Paraphilias
  Psychosexual dysfunctions
Facitious disorders
Disorders of impulse control not elsewhere classified
Adjustment disorders
Psychological factors affecting physical condition
Conditions not attributable to a mental disorder that are a focus of attention or treatment

for an estimate of the highest previous level of functioning of the person. An example of the way in which a particular patient might be classified is shown in the case history on page 106.

The multiaxial classification system is, in effect, five classifications applied simultaneously to a particular individual. Each major classification or category has diagnostic criteria associated with it in DSM III. The importance of these criteria is that they are

an attempt to improve the reliability of DSM III over that of DSM II by providing a checklist of patterns of behavior that are required in order to make the diagnosis. We will discuss many of these criteria when we consider specific patterns of behavior disorders in later chapters.

Strengths and Weaknesses of DSM III

Blashfield (1984) has carefully evaluated the contributions and current problems still to be solved in the use of DSM III. He observes that at least four major innovations can be credited to this latest version of the diagnostic and statistical manual. The first we have already briefly mentioned, the development of *diagnostic criteria* to characterize each of the diagnoses in DSM III. Instead of a general verbal definition of a particular disorder, very detailed lists of symptoms or behaviors are used to characterize each diagnostic classification. Since this strategy reduces the possibility that different clinicians may apply different diagnoses to the same behavior, it should increase reliability of diagnosis. Indeed, Spitzer and Williams (1983) and Spitzer, Forman, and Nee (1979) report improvements in reliability.

However, Blashfield observes that the development of the criteria in this system was not done by studying actual groups of patients. Instead, the criteria were drawn from a committee of clinical experts. This means that while diagnostic criteria will aid clinicians in making more reliable judgments, these diagnostic criteria may not be the best for differentiating among groups of patients. Only studying actual groups of patients to develop diagnostic criteria would allow for this possibility.

The second major innovation noted by Blashfield (1984) has already been described as the development of a *multiaxial diagnostic*

CASE HISTORY DIAGNOSED USING MULTIAXIAL CLASSIFICATION: BEREAVED

"A 17-year-old high-school junior was brought to the emergency room by her distraught mother, who was at a loss to understand her daughter's behavior. Two days earlier the patient's father had been buried. He had died of a sudden myocardial infarction earlier in the week. The patient had become wildly agitated at the cemetery, screaming uncontrollably and needing to be restrained by relatives. She was inconsolable at home, sat rocking in a corner, and talked about a devil that had come to claim her soul. Before her father's death, she was a 'typical teenager,' popular, and a very good student, but sometimes prone to overreacting. There was no previous psychiatric history.

Discussion of Bereaved Case History

Grief is an expected reaction to the loss of a loved one. This young woman's reaction, however, is not only more severe than would be expected (wildly agitated, screaming uncontrollably) but also involves psychotic symptoms (the belief that a devil had come to claim her soul). The sudden onset of a psychotic episode immediately following a marked social stressor, in the absence of increasing psychopathology preceding the stressor, indicates the Axis I diagnosis of Brief Reactive Psychosis. Typically these psychotic symptoms last for more than a few hours but less than two weeks. The diagnosis can be made before the two-week period—the maximum duration of symptoms consistent with this diagnosis—has elapsed. It is anticipated that the symptoms will subside and the patient will return to her usual level of good functioning. If symptoms persist beyond that time, the diagnosis would be changed to another psychotic disorder such as schizophreniform disorder.

Axis II indicates the possibility of a personality disorder with the presence of histrionic traits her mother describes as "overreacting."

Axis III notes the absence of any physical disorder or condition.

Axis IV rates the severity of the father's death as an extreme psychosocial stressor.

Axis V, based on the limited information that she was a typical teenager, popular, and a very good student, rates the highest level of adaptive functioning during the past year as very good.

DSM III Diagnosis:
    Axis I—Brief reactive psychosis.
    Axis II—Histrionic traits.
    Axis III—None.
    Axis IV—Psychosocial stressor: death of father; severity: six—extreme.
    Axis V—Highest level of adaptive functioning past year: two—very good.

Source: From Spitzer, R. L. et al., 1981, pp. 180–81.

system. This system has the advantage of providing considerably more information about the person. Unfortunately, however, the current multiaxial system has the practical drawback of requiring substantial work on the part of the diagnostician that may discourage its complete use. An even more serious problem has to do with the incomplete way in which the last two axes are measured. Each involves only a simple rating scale that is open to substantial subjective distortion on the part of the evaluating clinician.

A third major innovation in DSM III is the substantial *increase in the amount of descriptive information* provided for each diagnostic category. Information is included on essential features of the disorder, characteristic symptoms, age at onset, course, premorbid personality, prevalence, sex ratio, signs for differential diagnosis, and still other characteristics. Thus Blashfield notes DSM III resembles a textbook in abnormal psychology more than the classic diagnostic manuals we have had in the past. Unfortunately, much of this descriptive information is not documented and consequently the accuracy of the information presented in DSM III cannot be checked.

The fourth major innovation associated with DSM III has to do with the substantial *increase in the number of diagnostic categories available* to the diagnostician. Blashfield suggests that DSM II had 182 diagnostic categories while DSM III has expanded to a total of 265 categories. Furthermore, the relationships among these categories have been reorganized in part to reflect new research findings in the field. It remains to be seen if this increase in the number of diagnostic categories actually reflects an improvement in the system (Schact & Nathan, 1977).

Other observers have expressed concern about the DSM III classification of child-

hood disorders. In particular, Rutter and Schaffer (1980) have suggested that there is insufficient evidence for either the reliability or the validity of many of the disorders included in DSM III to identify childhood disorders. Blashfield (1984) notes that at least one subcategory was included simply because of its popularity in contemporary thinking rather than because there was evidence to suggest a discrete syndrome. Although "separation anxiety," a currently popular concept in child psychopathology, may have little clinical or research evidence to support its existence as a distinct entity, it has been included in DSM III.

SUMMARY

In this chapter we have examined a wide range of techniques for psychological assessment and diagnosis. Psychological assessment is the process of identifying individual characteristics that may be important for decisions about treatment or referral. Psychological assessment attempts to obtain a sample of behavior from the person that will allow us to predict other important outcomes in the person's future. Clinical interviews, psychological tests—both objective and projective—and behavioral observations are all used in the process of assessment.

A variety of sources of bias can exist in the assessment process. What at first sounds like an accurate, insightful description of a person may instead be a vague, general statement that applies to most people. For example, concluding that someone has "concerns over sexuality" probably describes most people and so really contributes little to our understanding of the individual. The process of assessment is also biased by illusory correlations made when clinicians interpret a test response on the basis of preconceived ideas rather than on the basis of actual objective criteria. Finally, inadequate normative information about cultural, racial, or gender differences can affect the way psychological tests are interpreted unless careful precautions are taken to avoid potenial biases.

A frequently important end product of psychological assessment is the development of a diagnosis for the individual that aids in making decisions about treatment and making predictions about future outcome. Diagnoses are based on classification systems that can serve a variety of important functions for the scientist and practitioner. Classification systems can enhance communication, provide a key to the scientific literature, and aid in prediction. A category in a classification system also can serve as a scientific building block in the development of theories of abnormal behavior.

The latest version of the *Diagnostic and Statistical Manual of Mental Disorders* (DSM III) provides several innovations in the description of abnormal behavior. DSM III is intended to improve the reliability of diagnosis by specifying more exactly the criteria for membership in a particular diagnostic category. Unlike previous diagnostic systems, DSM III classifies each person not only in terms of the predominant pattern of abnormal behavior but also on the basis of existing personality disorders, medical disorders, the severity of psychosocial stressors, and the highest level of adaptive functioning. Although DSM III is far from proven at this point and soon will be revised to become DSM IV, it represents a substantial change in the direction of both increased specificity and comprehensiveness. In the chapters that follow, a wide variety of different forms of abnormal behavior are described. We will rely heavily on the DSM III system to organize our discussion.

Part Two

Stress, Coping, and Disorders of Adaptation

5

Stress, Adjustment Disorders, and Posttraumatic Stress Disorders

Theoretical Perspectives on Stress, Coping, and Adjustment
Definitions of Stress: Stimulus, Response, Transaction, and Appraisal

Clinical Reactions to Life Stressors
Adjustment Disorders
Posttraumatic Stress Disorder

Factors Affecting Vulnerability to Stress:
Hardiness: Challenge, Commitment, and Control
The Protective Effects of Social Support
Graded Exposure: Natural Healing Process of the Mind

Treatment and Prevention of Stress-Related Disorders
Stress Inoculation Training
Treatment for Rape Victims

Summary

INTRODUCTION

Here is the victim of a devastating flood in Buffalo Creek describing that terrifying day to Kai Erikson (1976):

> I can still see in my mind the houses floating on the water along with the cars and those gas tanks exploding in a big blast of fire. I'll never forget the loud awful sound of the big substation blowing up and shooting up in the air and crumbling down and over. Then the water hit another row of houses in that narrow valley and it started backing up Toney Fork. I felt as though the water was a thing alive and was coming after us to get us all. I still think of it as a living thing (p. 30).

And here are some descriptions of the traumatic effect of the Buffalo Creek disaster, even years later:

> As for myself, every time I go to Buffalo Creek I start to cry because it is like visiting a graveyard. I left there crying after the flood on Sunday and I wake up all through the night crying. I can see the water from the dam destroying my house, clothing, furniture, cars. We lost everything we had saved all our lives in a very few minutes. I can see my friends drowning in the water and asking for help. I will never be the same person again (p. 157).

> Well, you can't think straight. Your mind is muddled and you can't reason things out. People who went through this thing up there are so confused and so frustrated and so torn up that their lives will never be the same again. Nothing will ever be the same again. There is no way to describe the horror of that day (p. 158).

Many of the residents of Buffalo Creek appeared to be experiencing psychological symptoms in response to that traumatic event, even years later. In this chapter we will consider a wide variety of psychological reactions to stress. How people respond to stressors in their lives and how they adjust to stressful events is an important new area of emerging research and treatment in the field of abnormal psychology.

THEORETICAL PERSPECTIVES ON STRESS, COPING, AND ADJUSTMENT

Each of the theoretical perspectives we described in Chapter 2 has been used to explain the effects of stress on behavior. Each emphasized different aspects of stressful experiences and people's response to them. Let us consider each perspective briefly before surveying the range of responses to stressful and traumatic events.

The *dynamic viewpoint* emphasizes the importance of past experience in producing differences in individual vulnerability to stressful events. Freud drastically revised his theory of personality after recording the dreams of soldiers in World War I suffering from "traumatic neuroses." These dreams were repetitive and frightening in nature, and Freud believed that they were attempts to master the terrifying stimulus of combat. This repetition compulsion could be seen in other cases as well, as in the play of children, where mastery seemed to be the goal. Thus for Freud these repetitive, frightening dreams were not merely symptoms of a traumatic combat experience but also active attempts to cope with the fear induced by combat.

Perhaps the single most famous *biological* account of stress is that offered by Hans Selye in his famous book *The Stress of Life* (1956). He argues that stress disorders are really diseases of adaptation. All individuals are, he argues, equipped with a physiology that responds to stressful circumstances by activating the organism. This general pattern of response to stress he calls the general adaptation syndrome.

According to Selye, all stressors of life when prolonged, regardless of whether they are due to conflict or frustration, lead the individual through three stages in the general adaptation syndrome. The first stage, called the alarm reaction, involves excitation of the autonomic nervous system, the discharge of adrenalin, increased heart rate, and gastrointestinal acid secretion. If the organism remains under prolonged stress, it moves to a second stage of resistance. In this stage the organism remains activated but begins to adapt to these physiological changes. However, in the third stage, which Selye calls exhaustion, resistance ultimately breaks down and the organism can no longer sustain high levels of activation. The result is tissue damage in one organ system or another. This account traces the likely developmental course of stress disorders but tells us little about which organ system is likely to be affected.

The *learning perspective* emphasizes the responses to traumatic events through classical conditioning processes. Early in his re-

search Pavlov was working in Leningrad when a great flood occurred. Many of the dogs in his laboratory nearly drowned as water rose in their cages. Pavlov rescued the dogs, but later they showed intense fear at the sight of water. When he tested the dogs to determine the strength of responses conditioned before the flood, Pavlov was surprised to discover that in some cases strongly conditioned responses were much weaker. Furthermore, some previous weakly conditioned responses actually showed a "paradoxical" effect and were much stronger in the traumatized dogs. Pavlov's experiences with traumatic stressors suggested that the fear conditioned by the flood had interfered with learned responses in paradoxical and at times unpredictable ways (Epstein, 1983).

The *sociological perspective* on stress and coping focuses on the relationship between the individual and society. Mechanic (1974) argues that our ability to cope depends on the effectiveness of the solutions that society and culture provide. The skills people develop depend on the adequacy of social institutions such as families and schools that prepare people to deal with the demands of life.

Pearlin and Lieberman (1979) observe that stressful events are of two general types. The first they call normative events. These are major alterations of roles that occur predictably in the course of the unfolding life cycle. Becoming a parent or the change associated with retirement are examples. A second type of event is nonnormative. These events are not easily predictable and are not usually built into the expectations we have about changes in our roles across the life span. Examples include being fired from one's job or being divorced. From the sociological point of view, normative and nonnormative events differ in their predictability and in whether there are social institutions to help individuals cope with the stress of social and personal change.

Existential psychologists, such as Salvatore Maddi, who share the *humanistic perspective* on abnormal behavior believe that a feeling of engagement and control over one's life is essential to mental health. If people can be open to the possibility of change and become genuinely involved in mastering life's problems, and if they feel that they can control events, they will be relatively resistant to the negative effects of stress.

From this point of view, whether life changes are actually stressful and threatening to health and well-being depends heavily on how people experience such events. If the events are seen as challenges and opportunities for growth rather than as uncontrollable, their impact will be much less. Later in this chapter we will consider some research conducted by Maddi and his co-worker, Susan Kobasa, that suggests that individuals experiencing high degrees of stress who are also open to challenge and change are much less vulnerable to the negative effects of stressful experiences.

Definitions of Stress: Stimulus, Response, Transaction, and Appraisal

As these various perspectives suggest, stress has been defined in a number of different ways (Kessler, Price, & Wortman, 1985). Some researchers define stress as a condition of the environment. These *stimulus*-oriented definitions frequently emphasize life events such as war, divorce, or job loss. Other definitions of stress emphasize the *response* aspects of stress. The general adaptation syndrome described by Selye is an example of a response-oriented description.

Still other scientists have argued that stress is best thought of as a *transaction* between the person and the environment (Lazarus & Folkman, 1984; Coyne & Holroyd, 1982). Lazarus and his co-workers have

argued that a critical factor determining whether the event experienced by the person is stressful or not depends on the person's *appraisal* of the event. In this view even the death of a loved one may not be unusually stressful, depending on the meaning of the loss to the bereaved person.

In this chapter we will see that not everyone responds even to the most traumatic events in the same way. Some people are more vulnerable to stressful events than others, and some of the most exciting research in abnormal psychology is aimed at trying to discover what makes some people vulnerable and others relatively immune to stressful experiences.

We will also see the concept of stress play an important role in our discussion of psychophysiological disorders in Chapter 6 and of anxiety in Chapter 7. Let us now examine some of the clinical reactions to life stress in the *adjustment disorders* and *posttraumatic stress disorders*.

CLINICAL REACTIONS TO LIFE STRESSORS

Adjustment Disorders

In the course of our lives, all of us will encounter especially stressful events or circumstances. The stressor may be anticipated, as with getting married, or unanticipated, as is sometimes the case with the death of a parent. Similarly, the stressor may be a discrete event, such as leaving home and starting college, or an event that persists over a period of time, such as prolonged unemployment. Whatever the stressor, the common feature is that the person needs to cope and adjust to his or her changed life circumstances. Although these events will almost certainly cause some difficulties, at times the amount of disruption and disturbance exceeds what is to be normally expected. When the person's reaction to the stressor is excessive and maladaptive, it is diagnosed as an *adjustment disorder*.

The criteria that distinguish an adjustment disorder from normal reactions, on the one hand, and more chronic psychological disturbance, on the other, are spelled out in the DSM III definition of an adjustment disorder:

> The essential feature is a maladaptive reaction to an identifiable psychosocial stressor, that occurs within three months after the onset of the stressor. The maladaptive nature of the reaction is indicated by either impairment in social or occupational functioning or symptoms that are in excess of a normal and expected reaction to the stressor. The disturbance is not merely one instance of a pattern of overreaction to a stressor or an exacerbation of one of the mental disorders previously described. It is assumed that the disturbance will eventually remit after the stressor ceases or, if the stressor persists, when a new level of adaptation is achieved. . . . The severity of the reaction is not completely predictable from the severity of the stressor. Individuals who are particularly vulnerable may have a more severe form of the disorder following only a mild or moderate stressor, whereas others may have only a mild

Robert V. Eckert, Jr./EKM-Nepenthe

form of the disorder in response to a marked and continuing stressor (DSM III, 1980, p. 299).

From this description it is clear that it is not just the severity of the stressor that determines the reaction. Instead, the individual's own vulnerabilities can also play an important part. Moreover, the manner in which the adjustment disorder manifests itself depends on both the person and the stressor. Generally, however, adjustment disorders are characterized by anxiety, depression, antisocial behavior, work inhibition, and/or social withdrawal. In the following pages we will examine some commonly experienced stressors and individual responses to them.

Death and Bereavement.   Few events are so traumatic as the death of a loved one. The initial reaction may be one of shock and disbelief. For many people it is difficult to believe that the person with whom they shared so much will no longer be there for comfort and support. For some, all else fades into the background and they can often only dwell on the person's absence. Sleep often becomes difficult as does facing the reality of the loss. The following passage illustrates the despair and initial denial that follows the death of a spouse:

> Secretly I was really expecting he would come back—I know it couldn't really be true. I would turn to the door each evening, thinking I heard his key. Each time he didn't come in my heart sank—it was eating away at my hope, my belief. Yet I couldn't let go—to accept he was gone for good was somehow disloyal. Occasionally the despair would break over me: for a moment I'd know it was real, he wasn't coming back, he was there in the ground. But most of the time it wasn't like that. In my heart I felt longing for him, and he was so alive there. He just had to come back; he was always such a vital person; he just couldn't be dead. The weeks

went on like that. They all came to offer sympathy, but it was as though I was in another world. He'd been away for weeks before, anyway, and he'd always come back. Then one day I knew it was real, that he wasn't coming back again, and that this was all there was. It wasn't what I wanted, but that's what it was (Raphael, 1983, p. 186).

During the period of mourning, there are a wide range of reactions, many of which would be considered abnormal or symptoms of psychopathology under different circumstances. The most common reaction, of course, is depression. Disturbances of sleep and appetite are common as are feelings of worthlessness and helplessness. The likelihood of suicide increases, especially in the first year after the death. Depression and suicidal thoughts may recur for years afterward on the anniversary of the loss. The depressed mood may mask feelings of anger and resentment. Although normal, these feelings may be denied because they seem unnatural and selfish.

Instead of experiencing his or her grief, the person may try to act it out in various ways. For example, often there is increased drug or alcohol use. This self-medication may reflect either an attempt to block out the pain and grief or a self-destructive reaction to the guilt and conflict aroused by the loss (Raphael, 1983). In the case of the death of a spouse, impulsive sexual acts may also occur. Through sexual acting out, the person may be attempting to cope with the pain of being alone and to regain the physical closeness and affection that has been lost.

Occasionally the bereaved person is unable to mourn at the time of the death. Nearly half a century ago Deutsch (1937) used the term *absent grief* to describe mourning in which there is little or no affect expressed.

Such a reaction is more common in children and may reflect the person's inability to undertake the complex task of mourning. While the absence of affect helps to cope with the pain of the loss, it is only a temporary gain since the necessity to complete the mourning process persists. As long as normal emotions such as sadness, despair, and anger are not experienced and worked through, the attachment to the deceased remains unresolved. Frequently these people will come in for treatment years after the loss, often with a seemingly unrelated complaint. However, their complaint may be just a pretext for seeking help and in the course of the therapy the person may, for the first time, experience the painful affect that has long been repressed or denied.

Unemployment and Adjustment Disorders. Freud once said that psychological well-being is reflected in the capacity to love and to work. Through work we gain a sense of mastery and accomplishment. Our self-esteem is tied up in what we do for a living,

The mourning process often continues long after the death of a loved one. (Robert V. Eckert Jr./EKM-Nepenthe)

and we often define ourselves by our occupational status. Consequently, it is not surprising that the sudden loss of a job may cause great psychological distress for some people.

The immediate reaction to job loss is often one of shock and disbelief. In addition, feelings of shame and inadequacy may emerge as the person feels stigmatized by his or her unemployed status. The longer the period of unemployment, the greater the likelihood of severe psychological disturbance. After four or five months of unemployment the person may experience panic, rage, self-doubt, increased alcohol use, and potentially suicidal depression (Buss & Redburn, 1983).

Interpersonal and marital problems often accompany job loss. The family must not only cope with the frustration and despair of the unemployed member but also with the economic hardships of a much lower family income. There may be a constant preoccupation with financial matters and family conflict over how the money should be allocated. The need to curtail entertainment and recreational activities can further increase the tension within the family. The following account of a 33-year-old steelworker, Percy, and his wife, Rachael, illustrates the impact unemployment can have on the individual and his family:

Sometimes Percy would stumble into the house late at night in a drunken rage, yelling and screaming, waking the children. Rachael said Percy would threaten to carry his loaded "Saturday night special" to work with him the next day; for a while, she feared a telephone call from the police or the morgue. Percy's drinking bouts increased and his bar tabs skyrocketed. Rachael began to scream at the children for the slightest infraction, and she nagged Percy incessantly to quit drinking. The

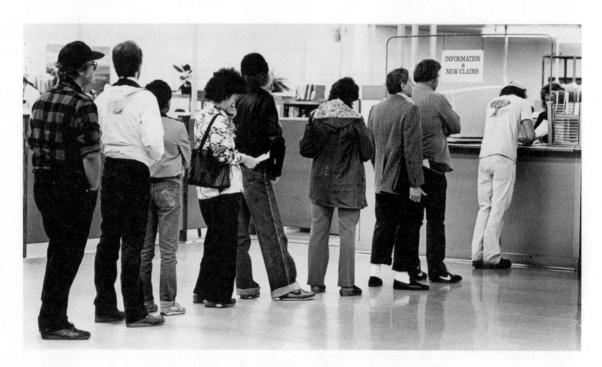

Low self-esteem and depression may result from the experience of unemployment. (Cathy Cheney/EKM-Nepenthe)

couple fought regularly and violently. In desperation, they opted to stay out of each other's way to avoid arguing. Separation was discussed as a realistic option. . . .

Percy spent the Thanksgiving weekend roaming through his home in a drunken rage, screaming, crying, breaking windows and furniture, and sleeping intermittently. When Percy threw the family cat out the front door, Rachael took their children and left. As she later explained, "I didn't know when me or one of the girls might sail down the steps too. . . ." The children seemed to upset him more than in the past. Rachael was frightened at the way Percy yelled at the girls and threatened them with spankings. He occasionally hit them, and this upset Rachael tremendously. Rachael said she, too, became a "screamer"; her own nervous tension stemming from inability to cope with the family's problems. She cried at the least amount of frustration, and after "too many sleepless nights," resorted to "downers" and a little beer in the evenings to help her insomnia (Buss & Redburn, 1983, p. 105–107).

Unfortunately, the shame and stigma that accompanies unemployment keep many who would benefit from community services from seeking them. Moreover, there is increased isolation from social support networks as the person attempts to conceal the extent of his or her problems from others. The loss of these support networks in turn results in increasing feelings of inadequacy and helplessness. Paradoxically, terminated workers may be less likely than nonterminated workers to ask for help. Buss and Redburn (1983) explain this finding in terms of the job loss increasing the desire to be self-reliant and not dependent on others.

Posttraumatic Stress Disorder

When people experience a psychologically traumatic event that is outside the range of usual human experience, such as natural disasters, war, or physical or sexual assault, they may develop a set of symptoms in response to the traumatic event. When the symptomatic responses last longer than six months, the disorder is considered chronic; if they do not occur until at least six months after the trauma, the disorder is considered delayed. DSM III lists *posttraumatic stress disorders* among the anxiety disorders we will discuss in detail in the next chapter. We include the disorder here because of the relatively clear-cut nature of the stressful life event, and the varied patterns of coping and adaptation that follow it.

The symptoms of posttraumatic stress disorder include:

1. Emotional upheaval, feeling ashamed, sad, angry, guilty, irritable, poor self-concept, impaired social relationships, difficulty concentrating and memory lapses.

2. A sense of alienation, isolation, depersonalization, and "psychic numbing," feeling alone, distant and suffering inwardly even while outwardly calm.

3. A reexperiencing of the traumatic event through flashbacks, nightmares, painful moods, and emotional outbursts (DSM III, 1980).

Responses to Combat. Williams (1983) has examined the research documenting posttraumatic stress responses among Vietnam combat veterans. She reports that a considerable body of research now supports the observation that some Vietnam veterans, especially young men involved in heavy combat, are now experiencing delayed psychological difficulties. For example, Fisher (1980) found that 61 percent of 1,168 Vietnam veterans in the study still think about the death and dying that went on in Vietnam, and that 68 percent of combat veterans report frequent nightmares. Egendorf, Remez, and Farley (1981), in a large-scale study of Vietnam veterans, found that those who had served in heavy combat continued to suffer from a variety of stress reaction symptoms, including memory trouble, loss of interest in the external world, thought confusion, nightmares, feelings of loss of control, and panic attacks.

One of the most striking characteristics of posttraumatic stress disorder is the intrusive and recurrent recollection of the traumatic event, including flashbacks or involuntary reenactments of the event, night terrors and nightmares, and thoughts about the event that cannot be dispelled. At times nightmares follow environmental stimuli that remind the veterans of their war experience. Defazio, Rustin, and Diamond (1975) report that seeing a Vietnamese refugee on the street, experiencing a sudden downpour of rain in the summer, or merely having the heat in one's home exceed 80 degrees can be sufficient precipitators. In addition, sometimes violent outbursts will follow these environmental stimuli. Williams (1983) describes one veteran who saw armed guards and thought he was back in Vietnam again.

Posttraumatic stress disorders were a response to combat experiences among some Vietnam veterans.
(Martin Gershen/Photo Researchers, Inc.)

With no weapon to protect himself, he grabbed an innocent passerby for protection and forced the person into his home.

Another characteristic of posttraumatic stress disorder involves intrusive memories that cannot be dispelled. One veteran reports, "Regardless of what I'd like to think about, it comes creeping back in. It's so hard to push back out again. It's old friends, their faces, the ambush, the screams, their faces . . ." (Goodwin, 1980, p. 2).

Williams suggests that while it is conventional to think of these posttraumatic experiences as symptoms, they may also be interpreted as attempts to master and make sense of the traumatic events. She observes that the traumatic experience of war in Vietnam involved trying to make sense of an experience that many people in the veterans' own country considered pointless or wrong. In addition, in many cases veterans had to reconcile their extreme war experiences with their precombat sense of themselves as reasonable and altruistic people.

Thus in the case of Vietnam combat veterans, the trauma of war may have been compounded by the difficulties of reentering a society whose attitudes toward the war were mixed. Making sense of one's experiences in traumatic combat conditions is unlikely to be made easier by returning to a world that is not uniformly sympathetic to that trauma.

Natural Disaster and Collective Trauma. The survivors of the Buffalo Creek flood, whose descriptions of their experiences opened this chapter, displayed many of the symptoms of posttraumatic stress disorder described by Vietnam veterans in the preceding section. However, in the case of natural disasters, such as tornadoes or floods, Erikson (1976) suggests that the individual trauma experienced by survivors is accompanied by a collective trauma he describes as "a blow to the basic tissues of social life that damages the bonds attaching people together

and impairs the prevailing sense of communality" (p. 154).

In the case of the Buffalo Creek flood, the traditional rural coal-mining towns affected by the flood were not only severely damaged but neighbors who had shared a strong sense of community and support for generations were separated. Disaster relief trailers were located in the Buffalo Creek area after the disaster, but not in ways that would facilitate the old community ties. As a consequence, many survivors of the disaster described a variety of patterns of social disintegration that had not been present when the earlier

Victims of floods and other natural disasters often display the symptoms of posttraumatic stress syndrome. (United Press International)

bonds of community provided support of neighbors for each other. Delinquency, alcoholism, street fights, and other forms of conflict emerged in the wake of the flood in ways that had been previously unknown. The interplay of individual distress and community relationships is perhaps nowhere as dramatically portrayed as in the case of a natural disaster (Gleser, Green, & Winget, 1981).

Not all community disasters are as dramatic or clear-cut, however. The community response at Love Canal, a toxic waste dump (Gibbs, 1982), was much more varied. Whether residents were really in danger, and whether their distress might be interpreted as overreaction, made it ambiguous as to whether a crisis was really occurring or not (Heller, Price, Reinharz, Riger, & Wandersman, 1984). Furthermore, in such cases different segments of the community may interpret the crisis differently, depending on their own interests and concerns. What seems to be a threat to health to the mothers of small children living in Love Canal may seem to be quite another kind of crisis to a government official or chemical company official (Levine, 1982).

Sexual Assault and Traumatic Conditioning. Throughout the last decade increasing attention has been focused on the impact of crime victimization. At the same time, growing awareness of the frequency with which women are targets of violence has stimulated research, and the development of services for victims of sexual assault has increased still further.

Kilpatrick, Resick, and Veronen (1981) interviewed a group of adult rape victims and a matched group of nonvictims at one month, six months, and one year after the traumatic rape event. Their findings suggest that victims were significantly more anxious, fearful, suspicious, and confused even a year after the assaults. Nevertheless, there appeared to be significant improvement in the psychological state of victims by approximately six months after the event.

These investigators offer for their findings a social learning theory explanation that views rape as a classical conditioning situation in which the threat of death or physical damage to the victim serves to elicit strong autonomic arousal and fear. The fear is viewed as an unconditioned response, and any stimuli present during the rape such as being alone, the darkness, or seeing a man of a particular appearance can become conditioned stimuli associated with the fear response through the process of classical conditioning. Kilpatrick and her colleagues argue that, to reduce their fear, the victims should engage in a wide range of avoidance behavior, such as avoiding being alone and avoiding interactions with strange men. Unfortunately, this avoidance behavior decreases the likelihood that the conditioned fear reaction will dissipate over time. Thus fear and anxiety may continue for long periods of time, according to the theory of Kilpatrick et al.

This early research has been followed by more detailed studies of the reactions of assault victims, focusing in particular on what factors affect the victims' postassault reactions. Sales, Baum, and Shore (1984) report research that examines a wide range of factors that may affect the response to the assault. These factors include the victims' psychological status before the rape, other life stressors they were experiencing, and the quality of their relationships. The researchers also studied factors associated with the assault itself, including the degree of violence experienced and the relationship between victim and perpetrator. Finally, Sales and her colleagues examined postassault factors, including the way the case was handled by the criminal justice system and the way people in the victim's own social support network responded to the victim upon learning of the assault. These factors are shown in Figure 5-1.

FIGURE 5–1
Model of Factors Relevant to Victim Recovery

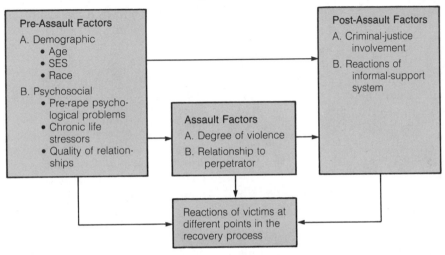

Source: From Sales, Baum, & Shore (1984), p. 121.

Rape victim in police station. (© Sue Markson)

One important finding uncovered by Sales and her colleagues is that there is not a simple reduction in symptoms over time after experiencing a rape. Instead, there appears to be a reactivation of symptoms approximately six months after the event. An additional interesting finding is that while victims' social functioning appeared to improve about six months after the incident, it may have been at the expense of elevation in symptoms. Thus going back out in the world to resume normal social and work relationships may be associated with increased experience of distress.

Different factors appear to play different roles during the period of recovery. The immediate level of symptoms reported by victims seems to be most easily predicted by their psychological status before the rape and the amount of violence in the attack. By the six-month follow-up interviews, however, negative family experiences and whether one had a positive relationship with an intimate other person became more important in recovery.

The importance of this research is that it documents the traumatic distress associated with victimization and begins to help us understand the factors that make people more or less vulnerable to prolonged traumatic distress following an assault. Such knowledge should make us better able to provide responsive supportive service to all crime victims. Nevertheless, we need to focus more attention on the prevention of such assaults rather than only on seeking better ways to treat the victims.

FACTORS AFFECTING VULNERABILITY TO STRESS

Stressful life experiences such as bereavement, unemployment, or a natural disaster can produce clinical reactions in many people. But clinical reactions are not inevitable. Some people survive the loss of loved ones or even the horrors of a concentration camp while others have difficulty coping with everyday problems. One of the most engaging questions in the study of abnormal psychology today is what distinguishes those who stay healthy in the face of severe stress from those who develop psychological or physical disorders. Let us consider some of the promising leads.

Hardiness: Challenge, Commitment, and Control

Researchers at the University of Chicago working in the humanistic tradition (Kobasa, Hiller, & Maddi, 1979) believe that a specific set of attitudes they call *hardiness* is characteristic of stress resistant people. Hardy people view change as a challenge rather than a threat, have a deep sense of commitment to their life and work, and feel as if they can control events. This view is in some ways similar to that of Lazarus and Cohen (1984), who believe that stress is neither something in the environment nor in the person, but that it depends on how the person appraises particular experiences or events.

Kobasa and Maddi have conducted a series of studies to identify the characteristics of the hardy personality. Their first study began with 670 managers at a public utility. These managers were asked to describe stressful experiences in their lives on a checklist. Then Kobasa selected executives who scored high on both stress and illness and another group who scored equally high on stress, but reported below average levels of illness. She then asked both groups to respond to additional personality assessments. Kobasa found that those managers who showed high stress but low levels of illness were more orientated to challenge, higher in their sense of control over events, and felt a deep sense of involvement in their work and social lives.

As we noted in Chapter 3, cross-sectional studies of this kind leave open the question of causal direction. For example, it is possible that illness causes negative attitudes, rather than that positive attitudes of feelings of engagement and control produce resistance to the effects of stress. What was needed was a longitudinal study that allows the examination of changes in health and attitudes over time. Maddi and Kobasa did conduct such a study and the results supported the findings obtained earlier. At the end of two years, people whose attitudes toward life reflected high control, commitment, and challenge remained healthier than others whose attitudes did not. A critical ingredient appears to be the hardy personalities' attitude toward change. When someone loses his or her job, for example, this event can be seen either as a catastrophe or an opportunity to find a new career better suited to one's abilities.

The Protective Effects of Social Support

While openness to change and a sense of engagement in life may be attitudes that help people cope with stressful life change, other evidence is emerging that supportive social relationships can also have a protective effect. Sidney Cobb (1976) defines social support as information leading individuals to feel that they are cared for and loved, that they are esteemed and valued, and that they belong to a personal network of communication and mutual obligation. Supportive and caring relationships among family members, friends, co-workers, neighbors, and others can help people cope with short-term crises and life transitions. These supportive rela-

tionships help people master their emotions and provide information about how to cope with life problems. They can also provide feedback to the persons about how they are coping in stressful circumstances.

But what is the evidence that social support can actually have a protective effect? An important study was conducted by Berkman and Syme (1979). These researchers analyzed data from nearly 5,000 men and women in Alameda County, California, over a 10-year period. They focused on four kinds of social ties: marriage, contact with friends, church membership, and both formal and informal group associations. They then combined all this information about social contacts into a social network index reflecting the number of social connections and social support available to each respondent.

Their findings are shown in Figure 5-2. It is clear that there is a strong relationship between the number of social connections available to each person and that person's likelihood of dying in the 10-year period under study. In every age group those with the fewest social connections had the highest likelihood of dying; the results held true for both men and women. These results and others have led researchers to be particularly interested in the effect of social support on stress and stress-related disorders.

Still other researchers (Gottlieb, 1983) have argued that it should be possible to develop organizations and natural helping groups. Such groups could increase the availability of support to socially isolated individuals who may be particularly vulnerable to change or loss. One example of such a mutual support group is the Widow to Widow program developed by Phyllis Silverman (1974). Recently bereaved widows find much help and support in these groups. In fact, the widows report they also find the experience of helping someone else gives increased meaning and satisfaction to their lives.

FIGURE 5-2
Mortality Varies Not Only with Age But with the Number of Connections in One's Social Network

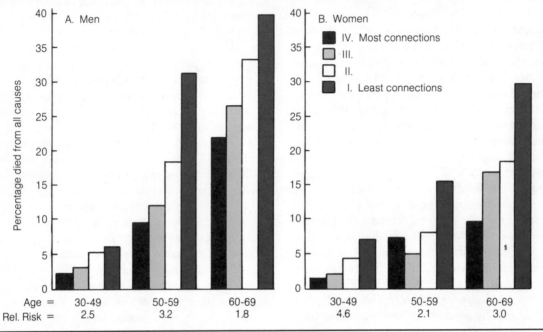

Source: From Berkman & Syme, 1979, Figure 1.

Graded Exposure: Natural Healing Process of the Mind

Imagine yourself standing, gazing out over the countryside from the open doorway of an airplane, wearing a parachute for your first jump. For most people this would clearly be a stressful experience. As Epstein (1983) observes, novice parachutists are almost always extremely fearful before a jump. Often their heart rate rises to double its normal rate. To perform adequately, the parachutists must overcome their fear.

Epstein has used sport parachuting as a natural laboratory for the study of stress for a number of years in order to learn how parachutists learn to cope with their fear as their experience increases over time. Figure 5-3 shows the differences between experienced

and novice parachutists in skin conductance, a measure of autonomic arousal or fear, on the day of the jump. Measurements were taken beginning with arrival at the airport, moving through getting into the aircraft, taking off, leaving the plane, and landing. It is clear that experienced parachutists do display some anxiety as the moment of the jump approaches, but that experience by itself has the capacity to help the parachutist control his or her anxiety.

Epstein believes that graded stress exposure is a highly general principle for the mastery of stress in everyday life and triggers the natural healing processes of the mind. In many cases graded exposure to a feared experience can produce mastery and more effective coping. As research continues in "natural laboratories" like sport parachuting, we

FIGURE 5-3
Tonic Skin Conductance as a Function of Events Leading up to and Following a Jump for Novice and Experienced Parachutists

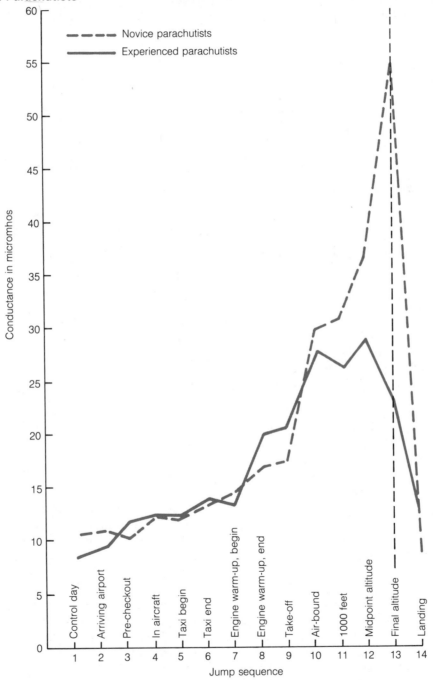

Source: From Fenz & Epstein, 1967.

can expect to learn how people learn to master their fears. Such knowledge can contribute to the development of treatment and therapeutic procedures to cope with stress. We will now turn to consider one such procedure.

TREATMENT AND PREVENTION OF STRESS-RELATED DISORDERS

Most clinical treatment methods are concerned with stress in one way or another. We will discuss a variety of treatment approaches and the perspectives that underlie them in the last four chapters. Here we will focus on therapeutic and preventive procedures aimed at helping people to deal with the effects of stress.

Stress Inoculation Training

Meichenbaum and Cameron (1983) have developed a general paradigm for training coping skills that they call *stress inoculation training*. This approach has been used in helping people cope with stressful medical procedures, the management of clinical pain, and a variety of other stressful experiences.

The basic idea underlying stress inoculation training is to help the person acquire knowledge, self-understanding, and coping skills in order to handle stressful experiences expected in the future. Meichenbaum's program has three basic phases. In the first educational phase, information is provided about how distressing emotions are generated. Particular emphasis is placed on cognitive factors, including statements people make about themselves. In a second rehearsal phase, alternative self statements are provided for the person to use when experiencing emotional distress. These statements help the client to assess the situation and to control unwanted emotions and thoughts and, ultimately, to evaluate his or her own

performance in the stressful situation. In the third application phase, the person tries out what has been learned and practices it.

Here is an example of how the trainer may help the person in stress inoculation training learn specific cognitive strategies for dealing with stress:

We have discussed how your appraisal of your situation, what you think and feel, plays a key role in influencing your stress reaction. (At this point the trainer offers several specific examples from the client's accounts that illustrates the important role of the appraisal process on their stress reactions.)

In fact, the way we think can affect how we feel in a fairly direct intentional fashion. We each influence our thoughts by a sort of *internal monologue*, an ongoing series of *statements to ourselves*, in which we tell ourselves what to think and believe, and even how to act.

You may find that speaking about your thoughts as "self statements" is somewhat unexpected. But there is a good reason for using this phrase. Calling a thought a "statement to yourself" emphasizes the deliberateness of that particular thought, and the fact that it is under your control. Let's consider the kinds of thoughts or self statements and images you had before, during and after your stress reaction (Meichenbaum & Jaremko, 1983, p. 139).

As Meichenbaum and Cameron (1983) note, stress inoculation training can be tailored to a number of specific populations, but at least five common elements exist in the training approach. They are: (1) teaching clients the role that cognition and emotions play in engendering and potentiating stress; (2) training in the self-monitoring of stress-engendering thoughts, images, feelings, and behaviors; (3) training in the fundamentals of problem solving (e.g., problem definition, anticipation of consequences, evaluating feedback); (4) modeling and rehearsal of instrumental and palliative modes of coping (e.g., relaxation, communication skills, use of social supports, attention-focusing skills, and positive self-evaluation); and (5) graded behavioral assignments in actual situations that become increasingly demanding.

Treatment for Rape Victims

Earlier in this chapter we discussed the traumatic impact of rape on the victim. Frequently a rape victim will remain fearful of situations or places previously associated with sexual assault. This fear can be so overwhelming as to constrain the victim's mobility and even the capacity to leave home. Table 5-1 shows the types of fears displayed by treatment candidates and provides a summary of the frequency of fears mentioned by rape victims.

Veronen and Kilpatrick (1983) have described the use of stress inoculation training for rape victims. Training begins by helping the victim to understand how anxieties may be developed as a consequence of the traumatic experience. Veronen and Kilpatrick's use of the learning perspective is evident in this example:

Fear and anxiety following a rape are normal responses. The development of rape related fear can be understood through a process called classical conditioning. Rape is an unconditioned stimulus that brings about the uncon-

ditioned response of pain or fear of being harmed or killed. Persons, situations, or events that are paired with the assault may also bring about fear and anxiety responses. Rape related fears may also generalize; thus persons, situations, or events that are similar to those present at the time of the assault may also bring about fear and anxiety responses. Now, let's look at your target fears and see in what way they are related to the process of classical conditioning (Veronen & Kilpatrick, 1983, p. 359).

Stress inoculation training appears to be most useful for rape victims who remain fearful and anxious, but who have resolved most of the other problems associated with the experience of being rape victims. Other forms of treatment may be needed to deal with the trauma as well.

An advantage of stress inoculation training is that it can be used either as a form of treatment or as a preventive technique to help people deal with anticipated stressful situations they may encounter in the future. For example, stress inoculation training has been used to help people experiencing severe social anxiety (Jaremco, 1983), to help improve the coping skills of military recruits (Novaco, 1983), and to deal with occupational stresses of police officers or air traffic controllers.

TABLE 5-1
Summary of Target Phobias for 25 Treatment Candidates

Being alone/going places alone	80%
Men who look like assailant/strange men	28
Going out	20
Sight of or hearing about violence	16
Darkness*	16

*Darkness or night was mentioned as a component of a target phobia by 72 percent of these candidates.
Source: From Veronen & Kilpatrick, 1983, p. 367.

SUMMARY

In this chapter we have examined various psychological reactions to stress. All of the theoretical perspectives conceptualize the role of stress differently, some focusing on the environment, others on the reaction to the stressor. Stress has been defined as a stimulus, a response, and a transaction between organism and environment. Furthermore, the role of appraisal has recently become of considerable interest in attempting to understand individual differences in response to the same stressful event.

We have divided the psychological disorders resulting from stress into two general categories. The first, the adjustment disorders, reflects an individual's reaction to stressors normally encountered in the life cycle. Although all of us experience difficulties when encountering stress, only when our reaction is excessive and maladaptive is it considered an adjustment disorder. While the pain and distress that accompany the death of a loved one are easily recognized, the loss of one's job is a major stressor that has received less attention. However, job loss can have an impact on both the individual's psychological and social functioning.

A second category of reaction to stressors is the posttraumatic stress disorders. These disorders involve psychologically traumatic events that are beyond the range of normal human experience. We have included in this category people's reactions to natural disasters, war, and physical or sexual assault. Although battle fatigue and shell shock have been recognized for years, only recently have clinicians realized the delayed psychological difficulties that may result from combat experiences. For example, one recent study has found that many Vietnam veterans who served in heavy combat today evidence memory trouble, a loss of interest in the external world, thought confusion, nightmares, panic attacks, and feelings of losing control.

We also considered the role of personality differences in response to stressors. Social support and graded exposure may also be factors that affect vulnerability to stress.

Finally, both prevention and treatment of stress-related disorders are gaining more scientific attention as techniques like stress inoculation training are used for a variety of stressful experiences and occupations.

6

Psychophysiological Disorders and Behavioral Medicine

Behavioral Medicine and Health
    Psychology
Definition of Psychophysiological
    Disorders
Range of Psychophysiological Disorders
Distinguishing Features

Headache
    Tension Headaches
    Migraine Headaches
    Overview of Treatment

Essential Hypertension
    Factors Causing Hypertension
    Overview of Treatment

**Coronary Heart Disease and the Type A
    Behavior**
    The Type A Behavior Pattern
    Overview of Treatment

Asthma
    Overview of Treatment

Ulcers
    Overview of Treatment

Chronic Pain
    Overview of Treatment

Theories of Psychophysiological Disorders
    Psychoanalytic Perspective: The Specific
        Emotion Hypothesis

Learning Perspective: Autonomic
    Learning and the Vicious
    Circle
Stress Perspective

Social Perspective: Stressful Life Events
    and Coping

Summary

INTRODUCTION

In 1962 two Japanese physicians, Ikemi and Nakagawa conducted a fascinating experiment. They demonstrated that hypnotic and direct suggestions given by a prestigious person can produce dramatic skin reactions. Japanese boys highly sensitive to the leaves of a tree that produces skin reactions similar to that of poison ivy were used as subjects. Contact with these leaves produces severe skin reactions that include itching, redness of the skin, swelling of the skin, and small blisters (dermatitis). A group of five boys were exposed to a hypnotic induction that included suggestions for relaxation and drowsiness. Another group of eight boys received no prior hypnotic induction—just waking-state suggestions. All subjects sat with their eyes closed and were not aware of what types of leaves were actually touching them. The highly respected physician then told them they were being touched by leaves of the poison ivy-type tree while actually they were being touched by leaves from a harmless tree. The reactions of these sub-

jects to the suggestion were remarkable. All the hypnotic subjects and all suggestion-alone subjects showed a significant degree of skin disturbance as a result of "thinking" they were touched by the poison ivy-type leaves.

In the second phase of the experiment, the conditions were reversed. Subjects were now told that the leaves of a harmless tree were being applied to their other arm while they were actually exposed to the poison ivy-type leaves. When suggestions led them to believe the leaves were harmless, four of the five hypnotic subjects and seven of the eight suggestion-alone subjects did not show any skin reactions to the leaves. You will recall that these same leaves had consistently caused dermatitis on previous contacts (adapted from Barber, 1983).

This experiment provides a vivid illustration of how psychological or "mental" factors can influence physical processes. Our bodies are, after all, highly complex, finely tuned, adaptive physical mechanisms. Much of what we call a *psychological response* to events in our world manifests itself in the form of physiological reactions that mobilize our bodies to cope with situations. But how does our mind or how do our thoughts create such physical reactions? Is the mind separate from the body? And if so, how do the mind and body interact? These intriguing questions are far from resolved. But they are intimately related to the stress-related psychophysiological disorders we shall consider in this chapter. Indeed, we shall see that many of the psychological theories and treatments for psychophysiological disorders are founded on the premise that the mind and the body are not separate entities.

Today many physicians and psychologists advocate treating the "whole person." There is a growing consensus that illness and one's response to it are determined by multiple factors. According to this emerging *holistic perspective*, understanding and treating an illness require knowledge about relevant psychological, social, and physical factors. As you read about psychophysiological disorders, the artificiality of any distinction between mind and body or psychological and physical components of disorders will become increasingly apparent.

Behavioral Medicine and Health Psychology

Behavioral medicine, an emerging field within psychology and other disciplines (e.g., health education, medical sociology), has contributed a great deal to our understanding of the impact of stress and emotional factors on physical disorders. As its name implies, the field was spawned by an "integration of the behavioral sciences with the practice and science of medicine" (Gatchel & Baum, 1983, p. 9). Behavioral medicine is closely allied to the field of *health psychology*, itself a new member of the family of subspecialties within psychology. Matarazzo (1980) has defined health psychology as "the aggregate of the specific educational, scientific,

and professional contributions of the discipline of psychology to the promotion and maintenance of health, the prevention and treatment of illness, and related dysfunction" (p. 815).

Interventions developed within behavioral medicine and health psychology place primary importance on the prevention of illness and on educating persons about their disorder. Teaching patients more effective coping and problem-solving strategies assists them in reducing stress and maladaptive emotional reactions that may trigger symptoms or make them worse. Increasing compliance with medical regimens and helping patients cope more effectively with chronic conditions such as pain are also important treatment objectives.

In this chapter we will examine the following psychophysiological disorders: headache, essential hypertension, coronary heart disease, asthma, and ulcers. We also will discuss chronic pain, perhaps the most difficult problem treated by physicians today. We will first consider the physiology of each disorder and then present what is known about psychological and social determinants of the illness. We will then present an overview of behavioral medicine and health psychology treatments. At the conclusion of the chapter, we will consider several different theories that try to answer two major questions: Why do some people develop psychophysiological disorders while others do not? And why do those who develop psychophysiological disorders develop one form rather than another?

We now present the case of William L.'s ulcer as an example of a psychophysiological disorder. A brief review of William L.'s difficulties will provide a focus for our discussion on the frequency and defining properties of psychophysiological disorders.

William L. has just taken a job as city editor in a large metropolitan newspaper. To take advantage of this opportunity for advancement in his profession, he has left a comfortable and satisfying editorial job on a small-town newspaper where he worked for over 10 years. His wife and two children were reluctant to make the move from their pleasant life in the country but finally agreed to the change.

Anxious to be a success in his new job, Mr. L. has been working long and irregular hours meeting deadlines for the newspaper. Still he finds himself losing sleep worrying about whether the tasks he has delegated to his staff are being completed properly. William L.'s eating habits have become irregular, and he finds himself drinking large amounts of coffee each day. Occasionally he experiences a burning feeling in the pit of his stomach. But he has ignored it since his digestion has always been rather delicate.

Lately Mr. L. has felt nauseated from time to time and has experienced sharp pains shortly after eating a meal. Still he continues working 16-hour days. Indeed, his efforts are beginning to pay off. He is finding himself more and more effective on the job. At the same time, however, the nausea has gotten worse and once when he actually got sick to his stomach, he noticed blood in his vomit.

Thoroughly frightened, Mr. L. decided to consult a physician. He was told that he had a severe duodenal ulcer and was promptly put on a special diet, given some medication, and told in an offhanded way "to take it easy"—something Mr. L. has never been able to do.

You may say, it is not so surprising that someone like William L. would develop an ulcer. He willingly placed himself under a great deal of stress. But how unusual are the stress-related psychophysiological disorders? Pelletier (1977) notes:

Most standard medical textbooks attribute anywhere from 50 to 80 percent of all disease

to . . . stress-related origins. Even the most conservative sources classify the following illnesses as psychophysiological: peptic ulcer, mucous colitis, ulcerative colitis, bronchial asthma, atopic dermatitis, urticaria and angioneurotic edema, hay fever, arthritis, Raynaud's disease, hypertension, hyperthyroidism, amenorrhea, enuresis, paroxysmal tachycardia, migraine headache, impotence, general sexual dysfunctions, sleep-onset insomnia, alcoholism. . . . An awesome statistic is that 30 million Americans suffer from sleep-onset insomnia. These are the known insomniacs, and practitioners can only estimate how many others there must be who have not sought treatment. Among your friends, how many can you count who have suffered or are suffering from migraine, hypertension, asthma, hay fever, arthritis, peptic ulcer, nervous tension, or alcoholism? If you can answer "None," you have a rare group of friends indeed (p. 7).

Pelletier's remarks highlight the pervasive role of stress and emotional factors in numerous diseases and physical conditions. However, we should remember that certain disorders and conditions, such as syphilis, lead poisoning, and botulism (food poisoning), are purely or mostly organic in nature. Organic disorders are not as common as they once were because medical science has found cures for many of them. However, as we will note in our presentation of the organic disorders in Chapter 13, the physical and psychological consequences of disorders with an organic base can be just as devastating as the repercussions of the psychophysiological disorders.

Definition of Psychophysiological Disorders

Conventionally, the psychophysiological disorders are defined according to several criteria: (1) they are characterized by physical symptoms; (2) they are influenced by

High-stress jobs can lead to a variety of stress-related psychophysiological disorders. (John Thoeming/Dorsey Press)

emotional factors; (3) they involve a single organ system that is usually under autonomic nervous system innervation; (4) the physiological changes are the same as those associated with normally occurring emotional states, but in the psychophysiological disorders the changes are more intense and last for longer periods of time; and (5) the person may not be aware of his or her emotional state.

If you look back over the brief case history, you will see that Mr. L.'s ulcer bears the earmarks of a classic psychophysiological disorder. His ulcer involves a single organ system, the gastrointestinal system, and the emotional factors associated with the physical symptoms are self-evident. If Mr. L. had experienced intense emotional stress over a few days or even a few weeks rather than months, he would probably have experienced only heartburn associated with hyperacidity. But the intense stress of his work

continued over months at a time. He was in a continuous state of high autonomic nervous system activity, and ultimately an organ system began to break down.

If you think about this case for a minute, a number of questions may occur to you. First, why did Mr. L. develop an ulcer rather than a heart attack or migraine headaches, or perhaps asthma? For that matter, why do many other city editors operating under the same deadlines and intense stress seem to avoid ulcers or any other psychosomatic disorder? It is these questions and others like them that researchers try to answer as they study psychophysiological disorders.

Range of Psychophysiological Disorders

When we offered a definition of the psychophysiological disorders, we said that they typically involved a single organ system, usually under autonomic nervous system control. In fact, psychophysiological disorders are likely to occur in association with at least six different organ systems. They are: (1) the gastrointestinal system, involving digestion; (2) the cardiovascular system, involving the distribution and flow of blood throughout the body; (3) the genitourinary system, associated with elimination and sexual functioning; (4) the respiratory system, associated with breathing; (5) the musculoskeletal system, associated with the control of muscles; and (6) the skin, which is an organ system in itself.

Distinguishing Features

As you begin to learn more about the psychophysiological disorders, a number of questions are likely to come to mind. What is it that makes these disorders distinctive? How are they different from a number of other disorders that seem to involve physical complaints? In discussing the somatoform disorders, we will describe conversion reactions and somatization disorders, both of which superficially appear to involve physical complaints. How are psychophysiological disorders different from these patterns of abnormal behavior? On the other hand, you may wonder how psychophysiological disorders differ from other forms of organic disease, since both involve some form of actual tissue damage.

These are important questions. Some key distinguishing features of psychophysiological disorders are shown in Table 6–1. The table shows that the two neurotic disorders, conversion reaction and hypochondriasis, do not result in tissue damage to the affected organ and that physical treatment has little effect. Psychophysiological disorders and organic disorders, on the other hand, have a great deal in common. Both may result in tissue damage and both may respond positively to physical treatment, such as the administration of drugs or surgery.

Psychophysiological disorders are most sharply distinguished from other organic disorders by the degree to which they are likely to involve a psychological component or are stress-related. However, it is likely that all diseases or organic disorders may have some psychological roots. Most of us have recognized the experience of being more susceptible to a cold after a period of prolonged stress has ended. Our resistance to infectious diseases, then, can be substantially affected by stressful psychological experiences.

At this point in our discussion, we should note that DSM III no longer retains a separate category for psychophysiological disorders. Its predecessor, DSM II, contained a specific classification of nine psychophysiological conditions. This implied that only the disorders listed could be influenced by psychological factors. DSM II's classification scheme failed to acknowledge the important role that psychological or emotional factors play in a host of organic illnesses. Recognizing this deficiency, DSM III included a category entitled "Psychological Factors Affecting Physical Condition."

Clinicians are now able to note the contribution of psychological factors to a particular physical condition. The clinician can refer to any physical disorder in which psychological factors are believed to play a significant role, not just the subset of disorders listed in DSM II. Of course, the relative contribution of emotional versus purely organic factors may differ from person to person and from disorder to disorder. Hence, in DSM III the diagnostician can not only indicate whether a physical disease is present but also the degree to which stress and psychological factors are implicated.

Medical treatment, using either drugs or surgery, has long been a standard treatment

TABLE 6–1
Comparison of Organic and Psychophysiological Disorders with Conversion Reactions and Hypochondriasis

	Organic Disease	Psychophysiological Disorders	Conversion Reaction	Hypochondriasis
General definition	Tissue damage resulting from microorganism or physical trauma	Stress-related disorder sometimes resulting in tissue damage	Form of neurosis in which the person suffers a loss of organ function with no organic basis	Irrational or neurotic fear that one is afflicted with a physical disorder
Examples	Appendicitis Common cold Syphilis	Ulcers Migraine headaches Hives Asthma	Hysterical blindness Glove anesthesia Hysterical paralysis Hysterical deafness	Unwarranted belief that one is suffering from cancer Unrealistic fear of germs and infection
Tissue damage	Yes	Often	No	No
Structure involved	Any part of organism	Often involves organ systems stimulated by the autonomic nervous system	Sensory or motor systems	None, but preoccupation with all
Effect of physical treatment	Often positive	Often positive	Usually none	Usually none
Effect of suggestion	Usually none	Usually none	Modifies symptoms	May modify symptoms
Patient attitude toward disorder	Concern	Concern	Labelle indifference	Extreme concern

for psychophysiological disorders. In Table 6–2 you can examine a listing of typical medical treatments used for a number of psychophysiological disorders. However, psychological interventions are increasingly being accepted and utilized in the treatment of such conditions. Let us now turn to the most common of the disorders we shall consider—headache.

HEADACHE

Most people have suffered a severe headache at some time in their lives. In fact, approximately 20 percent of the population suffers from some form of recurrent chronic headache, and millions of dollars are spent each year for drugs to relieve headache symptoms. One survey suggests that people seeking treatment for headache make more than 12 million visits to physicians each year (De Lozier & Gagnon, 1975). About 75 percent of adult headache sufferers are women, whereas more than half of children under the age of 10 who suffer from headaches are male. It appears that the occurrence of headache is not related to social class, intelligence, education, or race (Holroyd & Andrasik, 1982).

TABLE 6-2
Somatic Treatment of Psychophysiological Disorders

Representative Disorder	Somatic Treatment Procedures
Gastrointestinal system	
Peptic ulcer	Rest; typically bland diet involving milk as the basis and several daily feedings of easily digested, palatable, nonirritating foods; multivitamin capsules; medication to minimize hyperacidity and intestinal spasm; blood transfusion for hemorrhage of peptic ulcer; surgical repair of perforation; surgical removal of intractable ulcer (gastrectomy); surgical section of autonomic fibers to gastrointestinal tract (vagotomy).
Ulcerative colitis	Bed rest, liberal fluid intake, nonirritating diet; intramuscular injections of vitamin B-complex; antispasmodics to depress activity of bowel. Medication to thicken bowel discharges as necessary; surgery: ileostomy or colonectomy as indicated for extensive bowel damage.
Cardiovascular system	
Anginal syndrome	Physical rest and avoidance of excitement critical; limited activity and avoidance of overexertion prescribed; low-fat diet may be helpful; smoking is discouraged; drugs to increase coronary blood flow by dilating coronary arteries may be desirable.
Essential hypertension	Administration of hypotensive agents; if obese, weight reduction may be desirable; short-term periods of rest advised; multivitamin tablets; diet with restriction of salt: rice emphasized in a special diet that restricts sodium and protein content; sympathectomy required only in malignant hypertension when less drastic methods have failed.
Headache	Drug treatments include aspirin and acetaminophen for migraine and tension headache, ergotamine for migraine headache, and tricyclic antidepressant medications and muscle relaxants for tension headache.
Respiratory system	
Bronchial asthma	Several drugs may relieve asthma symptoms—theoplylline, ephedrine, epinephrine, aminophylline, cortisone, hydrocortisone, and corticotrophin; certain antihistaminic drugs may be effective in mild asthma.
Skin system	
Urticaria	Antihistaminic drugs, emollient baths, antipruritic lotions and powders; cortisone, hydrocortisone, corticotrophin.
Acne	Keep entire body clean; squeezing, pinching, and picking at lesions must be avoided; steamed towels, antiseptic agents, antiseborrheic lotions; greasy cosmetics to be avoided; deep cysts and abscesses may be opened with thin scalpel; sometimes multivitamin capsules recommended.
Musculoskeletal system	
Rheumatoid arthritis	Cortisone, hydrocortisone, and corticotrophin treatment; rest and avoidance of fatigue; proper posture at rest is stressed; salicylates; transfusion to counteract accompanying anemia; local treatment of joints with heat; certain gold compounds are helpful.

Source: From *Psychosomatic Disorders* (pp. 173–175) by S. J. Lachanan, 1972, New York: John Wiley & Sons.

At least 15 discrete types of headaches have been identified. However, since the overwhelming majority of headaches are diagnosed as either migraine or tension headache (Ad Hoc Committee on Classification of Headache, 1962), they will serve as the focus of our discussion.

Tension Headaches

What is a tension headache like? Tension headache sufferers describe their headache pain as being a persistent, dull ache that occurs on both sides of the head and is accompanied by sensations of tightness and pressure. Their headaches vary in frequency, intensity, and duration, though they are sometimes long-lasting and usually slow in onset and resolution. Tension headaches tend to be more frequent and less severe than migraine headaches.

Tension headache pain is typically attributed to a sustained contraction of the muscles of the scalp and neck, which occurs as a response to stressful events. Feelings of frustration, anger, or anxiety are often accompanied by increases in muscle tension. Similarly, a hard-driving, ambitious person who always seems ready for competition and mobilized for action will often experience chronic muscle tension. But how does muscle tension lead to headache? Tension headache pain is assumed to arise from: (a) the stimulation of pain receptors in contracted muscles; and (b) limited blood supply to the muscles of the neck and scalp resulting from compression of the arteries within the contracted muscles (Holroyd & Andrasik, 1982).

Migraine Headaches

A migraine headache is usually a memorable experience. The pain of migraine can be frightening and result in psychological and physical incapacitation. Consider the following description by a 30-year-old female sufferer of severe and repeated migraine headaches:

> When they were at their worst, I had a headache three to four times a week. The pain was like a gripping vise, always on one side of my head, usually over my left eye. Even the slightest movement would make me dizzy and nauseous. Once I had to be hospitalized and placed in traction. I couldn't move around the house when the headaches were bad, there was no way that I could work, and my marriage suffered, even though my husband tried to be understanding. Sometimes I knew that a headache was coming because I would see flashes of light and feel a lightness and sort of numbness in my hands. I would lie down then, but that didn't seem to work well enough to prevent the headache.

This woman's description conveys many of the commonly reported feelings and symptoms of migraine headache. The typical migraine headache is sudden in onset and is experienced as a severe throbbing pain on only one side of the head. Such pain may last from several hours to a day or two. Loss of appetite, nausea, vomiting, and sensitivity to bright lights often accompany a migraine attack. These symptoms constitute *common* migraine. When the migraine is preceded by sensory or motor disturbances, it is called *classic* migraine. Examples of such disturbances, called *prodromal symptoms*, include blind spots, transient visual images, light flashes, prickling or numbness in the hands and feet, or visual and auditory hallucinations.

Migraine headache symptoms are thought to be primarily vascular in nature. In the first of two phases of a migraine attack, the flow of blood to parts of the head and brain is sharply reduced. This produces a reduction of oxygen available to the brain itself and, as a consequence, certain areas of the brain fail to function effectively. A classic migraine sufferer may experience prodromal symptoms during this first phase; the type of symptoms experienced depend on which area of the brain is affected by the reduced blood flow. For common migraine sufferers the area of the brain receiving reduced blood flow is probably not responsible for sensory or motor functions and thus no prodromal symptoms are experienced. During this first phase the sufferer experiences no pain, but classic migraine sufferers can anticipate it because of the prodromal signs.

The second phase of the migraine headache occurs when a rush of blood to those areas of the brain deprived in the first phase produces a rapid expansion of the arteries in the scalp. This expansion, with the associated stimulation of nerve endings within the blood vessels themselves, produces extreme pain.

What do we know about the determinants of tension and migraine headaches? Nonspecific psychological stress appears to be a major triggering event for headaches. The stress associated with a variety of life changes, such as examinations, increased responsibilities, criticism, and fear of failure have all been associated with the onset of headache. Headaches frequently occur either during or immediately following stressful periods (Bakal, 1982).

There is some evidence that migraine headaches have a genetic component. Migraines are often experienced by immediate family members of migraine sufferers and the few twin studies performed to date have reported much higher concordance rates for identical than for fraternal twins. While there is evidence suggesting a hereditary factor in migraine, the mode of genetic transmission remains unclear. For tension headache sufferers a family history of tension headache is reported less consistently. In any case it is fairly clear that both environ-

mental stresses and constitutional disposition play a role in the etiology of headache.

Efforts to identify personality types associated with migraine and tension headaches have been guided by the notion that a headache arises from intrapsychic conflict or is a result of psychological disturbance (Wolff, 1963). However, because personality characteristics of headache sufferers are assessed only after headache symptom patterns have become well established, such characteristics may be *consequences* of frequent and severe headache pain rather than personality flaws that predispose an individual to headache. Psychological symptoms often observed among headache sufferers include depression, hysteria, and hypochondriasis, with each symptom as likely to be a consequence as it is to be a cause of headache.

Overview of Treatment

The treatment of headache has been approached in three major ways. First, various drugs have been used to treat both migraine and tension headaches. Second, psychotherapy can relieve both kinds of headaches to some extent. Finally, biofeedback and relaxation training methods have become a major approach to the treatment of headache.

Drug therapies have become well established interventions for treating headaches. Drug treatments are intended either to interrupt a headache at its onset, to reduce the pain once a headache has begun, or to prevent a headache from occurring. A wide variety of prescription and nonprescription medications have been used in the treatment of headache with varying success. We all have seen enough commercials touting the advantages of one headache remedy or another to know that over-the-counter medications such as aspirin or acetaminophen are the front-line treatments for headache. These medications can provide relief for

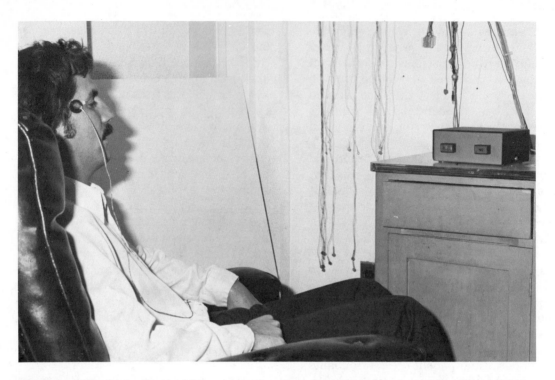

Person receiving biofeedback of the cranial pulse. When the pulse falls below a given rate a light is illuminated giving feedback to the subject. (Courtesy of Ronald Fudge, Ph.D., Lafayette Clinic, Detroit)

many of the milder headaches people experience.

The drugs most often prescribed specifically for migraine are intended to reduce the excessive blood flow through the cranial arteries; medications like *ergotamine* are prescribed for this purpose. For tension headaches the medications prescribed most often are intended either to relax the tense or constricted muscles or to treat depression presumed to underlie the headache. Interestingly, tricyclic antidepressant medications seem to work equally well for treating tension headache whether or not the headache sufferer shows signs of depression. In general, pharmacological treatment can be effective with a majority of headache sufferers.

Another approach to the treatment of headaches associated with stress is psychotherapy.

If psychotherapy leads the headache sufferer to change his or her life situation or the personal attributes that contribute to headaches, it is likely that the headaches will be reduced. Recently, advances have been made in developing cognitive-behavioral techniques for the management of headache. Cognitive-behavior therapy teaches patients to identify and control headache-related stresses and psychological components of headaches (e.g., sensations, feelings, and thoughts).

Cognitive-behavior therapy is conducted in three phases: (*a*) an educational phase in which headache sufferers learn about headaches and headache-related stressful events; (*b*) a self-monitoring phase in which patients are taught to identify events that accompany stressful transactions in their lives, and to identify sensations, thoughts, and feelings associated with their headaches; and (*c*) a problem-solving or coping-skills training phase. By focusing on the way the headache sufferer copes with stress, cognitive-behavior therapy may enable the individual to better manage stress responses that contribute to headaches. In addition, cognitive-behavioral interventions are well suited to dealing with the depression that can be both a cause and a consequence of headache. Cognitive-behavior therapy appears to be a very promising treatment for headache and other psychophysiological disorders (Holroyd & Andrasik, 1982).

Finally, biofeedback and relaxation training constitute a class of self-control training techniques aimed at directly or indirectly altering maladaptive physiological responses that accompany psychophysiological disorders. Relaxation training techniques have been applied to both migraine and tension headaches. In these techniques patients are taught: (*a*) to use self-instructions of feelings of warmth and heaviness; (*b*) to progressively tense and relax selected muscle groups; or (*c*) to engage in passive meditative procedures. It is important to note that clinicians must rule out physiological explanations for headaches, such as tumors, before attempting biofeedback or cognitive-behavior therapies, which are based on the assumption that headaches are stress-related.

Biofeedback techniques have been applied in the treatment of both types of headaches. Neal Miller, one of the scientific pioneers in the psychology of learning and in the study of biofeedback, describes it this way:

> Most people are poor at correctly perceiving their visceral responses, such as blood pressure, and some people with tension or neuromuscular disorders are poor at perceiving feedback from certain skeletal muscles. They are like a blindfolded novice trying to learn to shoot baskets. Modern measuring devices can remove the blindfold by supplying better feedback. Feedback provided by a device that provides prompt measurement of a biological function has been called biofeedback (Miller, 1978, p. 373).

How does biofeedback actually work? Schwartz (1978) has argued that when there is a disregulation in feedback between the brain and an organ system, the organ may suffer tissue damage, or a disease process may result. Biofeedback may be effective because it provides information about the state of the organ or body function in question to the brain. The brain may then use this feedback to engage in regulation of the affected organ system. Thus biofeedback provides the individual with new information about his or her body functions and allows the brain to regulate the system appropriately. The desired goal of biofeedback is to gain a degree of control over the body function being monitored.

For tension headache sufferers, biofeedback helps them learn to reduce the tension of muscles of the forehead and neck. For migraine sufferers, there are two varieties of biofeedback: (*a*) feedback of skin temperature; and (*b*) feedback of the blood flow through cranial blood vessels.

Biofeedback, relaxation training, and combinations of the two have been shown to be equally effective in the treatment of tension headache. Each treatment yields about a 50 percent reduction in headache activity. For migraine, relaxation training and a treatment that combines skin temperature biofeedback with relaxation training are the most effective approaches. They yield reductions in headache activity that average 45 to 55 percent (Holroyd, Penzien, Holm, & Hursey, 1984). Thus self-control training techniques can be effective tools to help people learn to bring their physiological responses under voluntary control and to reduce or perhaps to prevent headache symptoms.

ESSENTIAL HYPERTENSION

Hypertension, or high blood pressure, affects a large proportion of adults in the United States. Estimates of the number of hypertensive persons range from 23 to 60 million (*Report of the Hypertension Task Force*, Vol. 1, 1979). Hypertension is an insidious disease. There are usually no symptoms of hypertension that the individual can detect, and thus hypertension often remains undiagnosed for many years. But the long-term effects of hypertension can be fatal. Without adequate treatment hypertension greatly increases the risk of heart attack, stroke, and kidney failure and contributes to the death of an estimated 250,000 Americans yearly. For 85 to 90 percent of hypertension the cause remains unknown. This type of hypertension is referred to as *primary hypertension* (also *essential* or *idiopathic* hypertension). For the remaining 10 to 15 percent high blood pressure is a symptom of some known cause, such as kidney disease, a tumor of the adrenal gland, or a narrowing of the aorta (Shapiro & Goldstein, 1982). In these cases, when the underlying cause is treated, the blood pressure generally returns to normal levels. Some individuals show an elevation of their blood pressure on an irregular or temporary basis and are referred to as *labile hypertensives*. Increased lability of blood pressure often occurs at the onset of hypertension (Agras & Jacob, 1979).

A *sphygmomanometer* is a device used to measure blood pressure. It can be used to provide two numbers called the systolic and diastolic pressures. The first number, systolic pressure, represents the pressure in the arteries when the heart is actually pumping blood. For adults over the age of 18, the World Health Organization classifies systolic pressures over 160 as elevated, while pressures in the 140 to 159 range are considered borderline. The second number, diastolic pressure, represents the pressure in the arteries when the heart is at rest and filling with blood. Pressures of 90 to 104 are considered mild hypertension, 105 to 114 moderate, and greater than 115 severe hypertension. It should be noted that higher blood pressures are expected for males than for females, and that the level of blood pressure considered normal increases somewhat with age.

Blood pressure at any given moment is multiply determined in a very complex way. Many bodily systems are involved in its regulation. For example, blood pressure is influenced by the heart rate and volume of blood pumped by the heart, by the resistance to blood flow, which is determined in part by the amount of constriction within the blood vessels, and by the total amount of blood within the system, which is determined in part by the renal and endocrine systems. Changing one or any combination of these variables will have an impact on the blood pressure level, and a dysfunction in any of these organs or systems can lead to hypertension.

Blood pressure can normally change on a minute-to-minute basis. Many factors are known to cause temporary changes in blood pressure. Nicotine, alcohol, sodium (salt), caffeine, antihistamines, stimulant drugs, a change in activity level, a change in posture, and a change in stress level all can elevate blood pressure (Chesney, Swan, & Rosenman, 1982). The operation of such factors can make hypertension difficult to diagnose. It is generally recognized that greater risks are associated with greater and more sustained blood pressures.

Factors Causing Hypertension

A number of factors have been identified that dispose an individual toward developing hypertension. Some of these factors, referred to as *risk factors*, are unalterable. One such factor is *age*. An increased risk of hypertension accompanies increased age. People with a *family history of hypertension* also are at an increased risk for developing hypertension. Children of hypertensive parents have twice the risk of becoming hypertensive as children of parents with normal blood pressure (Shapiro & Goldstein, 1982). Though a family history of hypertension undoubtedly influences blood pressure levels through both environmental and genetic factors, twin studies support the existence of genetic involvement (*Report of the Hypertension Task Force*, Vol. 2, 1979). *Racial differences* in the prevalence of hypertension are also known to exist. For instance, the occurrence of high blood pressure among black Americans is almost two times that among white Americans. For blacks, hypertension develops earlier, is more severe, and causes more deaths (*Report of the Hypertension Task Force*, Vol. 1, 1979).

Fortunately, other risk factors have been identified which may be altered. These include: (*a*) *obesity*—people who gain weight later in life are more likely to become hypertensive, while weight reduction reduces blood pressure; (*b*) *physical fitness*—people who are physically inactive show an increased incidence of hypertension; (*c*) *diet*—some evidence suggests that excessive sodium, caffeine, or alcohol consumption may be involved in the development of hypertension, at least for certain people, and can certainly create difficulties for those who are hypertensive, and (*d*) *stress*. There is no solid evidence that stress causes the chronic high blood pressure of hypertension. But stressful events (e.g., natural disasters, prolonged emotional illness, experimentally induced stress) have repeatedly been related to temporary increases in blood pressure (Shapiro & Goldstein, 1982; *Report of the Hypertension Task Force*, Vol. 1, 1979). Thus stress

can most certainly aggravate hypertension and is quite likely to be involved in the development of high blood pressure in some individuals.

The personality or coping style that has long been hypothesized as a risk factor for developing hypertension is the inability to manage anger in a constructive manner. In a review of the research literature Diamond (1982) concluded that at least a subset of hypertensives are hostile, conflicted about expressing anger, and tend to be submissive on the surface while harboring considerable resentment. For example, a number of studies have shown that resentment is associated with higher age-related blood pressures in 10,000 Israeli civil service workers (Kahn, Medalie, Nufield, Reis, & Goldburt, 1972), and in a 20-year prospective study of Harvard graduates (McClelland, 1979). As you might suspect, risk factors such as these that can be modified are primary targets for psychological or behavioral treatments for hypertension.

Overview of Treatment

Because blood pressure is multiply determined, it has been possible to devise a variety of drug therapies that affect different body systems in treating hypertension. The most commonly prescribed medications are diuretic agents like hydrochlorothiazide or chlorthalidone, which serve to lower blood pressure through elimination of sodium and water from the body. If diuretic therapy alone is ineffective, diuretics may be combined with other medications like hydralazine and reserpine, which relax and expand blood vessel walls, or propranolol, which blocks certain actions of the sympathetic nervous system and reduces blood vessel contractions in the heart.

Drugs can be very effective for treating the hypertensive patient. Generally, the higher the blood pressure is before treatment, the greater the benefits from antihypertensive medications. The benefits include reduced occurrences of heart failure, stroke, and kidney malfunction. However, patients with mild hypertension tend to benefit relatively little from the same drug treatments (Agras & Jacob, 1979).

All varieties of antihypertensive medications must be used consistently and continuously to produce good effects. But some estimates suggest that only 50 to 60 percent of hypertensive patients take their medications as instructed (Shapiro & Goldstein, 1982). A number of interventions have been developed to improve patient compliance with medication regimens. These include patient education programs, medication reminders, tailoring drug regimens to simplify schedules and to reduce unpleasant side effects, involvement of significant others to encourage medication compliance, providing patient rewards, and signing patient-clinician contracts (Haynes, Mattson, & Engebretson, 1980). Each intervention has met with some success, even though none is applied routinely in physicians' offices. The lack of compliance continues to plague attempts to treat hypertension with drugs. This problem has, however, encouraged the development of alternative approaches to the treatment of hypertension.

An array of nonpharmacological techniques aimed at reducing blood pressure have been developed in recent years. Hypertensive patients have undergone several types of biofeedback training that can be grouped into two general categories: (*a*) direct feedback of blood pressure or cardiovascular functions; or (*b*) feedback of other responses to reduce blood pressure more indirectly. While many studies have reported initially promising results, a nearly equal number have reported negative results.

Relaxation training methods similar to those we mentioned in our discussion of headache have also been applied to the treatment of hypertension and have met with varying degrees of success (Agras & Jacob, 1979). One such approach was described by Benson (1975) in his book *The Relaxation Response*. Patients set aside time for one or two relaxation breaks during which they practice relaxation for 15-to-30-minute periods. Relaxation is believed to promote physiological regulation and lower levels of arousal. Appel (1984) has observed that relaxation can have psychological as well as physiological benefits. Relaxation training can help people cope effectively and change habitual patterns related to stress. Relaxation not only provides a tension-free interlude from stressful activities but it can also promote calmness, disrupt negative thought patterns by refocusing of attention, and enhance confidence in one's ability to make constructive lifestyle changes. Agras and his colleagues (Agras, Southam, & Taylor, 1983) have reported that blood pressure reductions following relaxation training lasted for 15 months, with gains evident not only in the clinic but the work setting as well. However, patients must actively practice relaxation in order for treatment gains to persist.

Another nonpharmacological approach to treating hypertension is stress management. Stress-management training teaches the hypertensive patient to deal effectively with stressful events that can elevate blood pressure. Stress management uses many of the techniques mentioned in our earlier discussion of cognitive behavior therapy. Studies have been reported that applied stress-management techniques as one segment of a total treatment package. The treatment package also included biofeedback, relaxation, and education about the effects of diet and smoking on blood pressure. In a series of large and well-controlled studies, Chandra Patel has reported substantial reductions in blood pressure and medication use, in addition to reduced blood pressure responses under stressful conditions (Patel, 1977; Patel, Marmot, & Terry, 1981). Despite all of the evidence suggesting that nonpharmacological treatments can be effective, such interventions are still in development and are not yet ready to be applied on a grand scale. Until better methods for regulating blood pressure can be established and successfully applied, hypertension will continue to be a life-threatening disorder for many individuals.

CORONARY HEART DISEASE AND THE TYPE A BEHAVIOR PATTERN

Coronary heart disease (CHD) is the number one cause of death and disability in the United States. It is responsible for about 600,000 deaths annually (Suinn, 1982). The most common form of CHD is atherosclerosis, or the development of a blockage of the coronary arteries. The coronary arteries are blood vessels that encircle the heart and are responsible for providing oxygen to the heart muscle. A partial blockage of the coronary arteries that restricts the flow of blood to the heart muscle can result in extreme pain (called *angina pectoris*) when the heart fails to receive enough oxygen to meet its own needs. A complete blockage of the coronary artery, called a *coronary occlusion*, stops the flow of blood to certain areas of heart muscle which, in turn, causes the death of heart tissue. When heart tissue dies as a result of insufficient blood flow, it is referred to as a *myocardial infarction* (also called a *heart attack* or *coronary*). It leads to permanent damage to the heart and possibly death.

Angina pectoris is a sure indication that a considerable amount of CHD exists, and serves as a warning sign, signaling that the heart muscle is receiving an insufficient blood flow. A variety of medical and surgical approaches are available for treating CHD once it is diagnosed. But advanced stages of the disease may go undiagnosed and remain untreated until after substantial damage to the heart has occurred. Thus massive efforts to develop techniques for the early diagnosis and prevention of CHD have been undertaken in recent years.

Several large-scale studies have been undertaken to provide information about factors that contribute to CHD. The Framingham study (Dawber, Moore, & Mann, 1957) is one such study that continues to examine cardiovascular disease among over 5,000 men and women in Framingham, Massachusetts. As a result of these studies, a number of risk factors for the development of CHD have been identified. These risk factors include: (a) age (being older); (b) sex (overall ratio of males to females is 4:1); (c) diabetes; (d) family history of CHD; (e) hypertension; (f) inadequate exercise; (g) diet (high levels of cholesterol intake); (h) obesity; and (i) smoking. Some of these risk factors cannot be altered, but as you have probably noted, a number of them are related to coping or lifestyle and can be modified.

The Type A Behavior Pattern

A risk factor that is clearly related to lifestyle is the *Type A behavior pattern*. The Type A behavior pattern was identified by two cardiologists, Meyer Friedman and Ray Rosenman (1959), who observed Type A characteristics among their patients. Type A individuals tend to be competitive, impatient, intensely ambitious, involved in multiple activities, preoccupied with a sense of time urgency and deadlines, and often aggressive and hostile. Persons who exhibit a relative absence of these characteristics are referred to as Type B. It is probably best to regard the Type A behavior pattern as a continuum of behaviors that ranges from extreme Type A to extreme Type B rather than to think of Type A and Type B as discrete personality types.

Relative to Type Bs, extreme Type As experience a considerably greater incidence of CHD. Most of the research on the Type A behavior pattern to date has examined the relationship between CHD and Type A behavior in middle-aged white males. Though less well established, the relationship between CHD and the Type A behavior pattern appears to be at least as strong for females as for males (Review Panel on Coronary-Prone Behavior and Coronary Heart Disease, 1981).

The term *Type A behavior pattern* is often used interchangeably with the term *coronary-prone behavior pattern*. However, the Review Panel on Coronary-Prone Behavior and Coronary Heart Disease (1981) has suggested that the terms should not be used synonymously. One of their concerns is that the term *coronary-prone behavior pattern* appears to limit the relationship of the Type A behavior pattern to CHD alone, which may be incorrect. In fact, data from the Framingham study suggest that Type A individuals are at greater risk for accidents, suicide, and homicide (Haynes, Feinleib, Levine, Scotch, & Kannel, 1978).

While there is clearly a high incidence of CHD among extreme Type A individuals, the nature of the relationship between the Type A behavior pattern and CHD is unclear. One model suggests that the Type A behavior pattern leads to CHD primarily through stress-related physiological reactions. Research suggesting that Type As are physiologically more reactive than Type Bs in certain situations supports this model. For example, Type As tend to be more reactive in situations that involve interpersonal confrontations (MacDougall, Dembroski, & Krantz, 1981), threats to self-esteem (Pittner & Houston, 1980), and involvement in competitive tasks while being harrassed (Glass et al., 1980). A second model suggests that

some central aggressive trait (which could be either genetic, learned, or both) independently leads to the occurrence of both the Type A behavior pattern and CHD (Review Panel on Coronary-Prone Behavior and Coronary Heart Disease, 1981). Continued research is necessary to inform us about the accuracy of these models.

Overview of Treatment

Can Type A behavior patterns be modified or are they resistant to change? A few attempts have been made to modify the behavior of extreme Type A individuals with the aim of reducing their risk of developing CHD. Typically, these intervention programs focus on convincing the Type As to behave more like Type Bs through such treatments as brief supportive psychotherapy and stress management training or by directly targeting adoption of non-Type A behaviors (Suinn, 1982). While such attempts have made some impact in promoting changes in Type A behaviors, they have not been entirely successful. For example, while some studies report decreased blood cholesterol levels following Type A intervention programs, other studies report increased cholesterol levels. Indeed, many Type A individuals are quite resistant to changing their Type A ways, even though they may recognize that they are at risk for developing CHD (Levenkron, Cohen, Mueller, & Fisher, 1983). A moment's reflection suggests that one reason why this is so is that there are many societal rewards for engaging in Type A behaviors (e.g., the status and praise earned by accomplishing goals, financial rewards earned by working overtime, and professional advancement earned by being an outstanding worker). In fact, many Type As indicate that they become increasingly anxious about unfinished activities and unmet goals when they try to reduce their hard-driving, rapid-paced lifestyles. While many Type As may work hard to achieve their goals, their impatience and tendency to be overwhelmed may hamper their efficiency and create a negative impression on others. This may result in increased pressure to achieve and master their environment, reinforcing their Type A behavior.

It is not yet established, but it may be the case that Type A individuals who are well adapted to their environment are at lower risk for developing CHD than those Type As whose environments inhibit their Type A behavior. In addition, not all characteristics of the Type A behavior pattern are demonstrated equally by all Type As. Recent research suggests that Type A individuals who exhibit the highest levels of competitive drive, impatience, and hostility are at greatest risk for the development of CHD (Diamond, 1982). Thus interventions for reducing the risk of CHD that target these specific aspects of the Type A behavior pattern for change may be both more efficient and more likely to be adhered to by Type A individuals than interventions attempting a more global change of Type A behavior (Levenkron et al., 1983).

ASTHMA

The following description of an asthma attack was offered by a child who recounted the key elements of the most serious attack he ever suffered:

I got asthma while I was asleep. It was really a bad attack.

I guess that I got out of bed, but I don't remember much about it. I can remember going out into the hall, but that's it. My parents said that my head hit their door when I passed out.

The next thing I remember, we were racing down the street in the car. I can remember seeing some of the lights flashing off the windows of the stores we passed; everything was kinda hazy.

I remember coming to in the emergency room of the hospital. My dad was running around trying to get someone to help me. Then I passed out again.

I remember coming to on the stretcher. The people in the emergency room were taking me down the hall as fast as they could.

They gave me oxygen. It seemed to help a lot. I also got my first IV about then.

It wasn't until I was in a room under an oxygen tent that I really started to see what was happening. My parents and the doctor were there.

My mother was crying, everyone looked scared. It was then that I really got scared (Creer, 1979, p. 178–79).

As we read this dramatic account, a number of questions might come to mind. Just how frequent and severe are asthma attacks? Do fear and agitation invariably accompany an asthma attack? Is asthma a treatable disorder? One of the reasons you might not have a ready answer to such questions is that asthma is a perplexing disorder. Indeed, the general public probably knows less about asthma than about some other psychophysiological disorders such as headaches. References to asthma can be traced to the writings of Hippocrates (460–370 B.C.). However, to this day, arriving at a universally accepted definition of this disorder has proven elusive (Porter & Birch, 1971). As our discussion progresses, it will become increasingly apparent that this lack of agreement stems, in part, from the complex and variable nature of bronchial asthma.

Bronchial asthma is characterized by a narrowing of the airways leading to the lungs, which results in difficulties in breathing (e.g., wheezing, gasping, coughing). One to 4 percent of the population suffer from asthma. Although the onset of the disorder can occur at any age, almost half of all sufferers experience their first attack prior to age 15 (Creer, 1979). Many asthmatics achieve a measure of symptom relief as they grow older, but there are marked differences in the frequency and severity of asthma attacks across the age spectrum (Creer, 1982). Some asthmatics experience a large number of attacks over a short period of time and are then symptom-free for an extended period. For other less fortunate asthmatics, the symptoms are virtually unremitting and occur on a year-round basis.

The severity of asthma attacks varies both among sufferers and within the same person from episode to episode. Creer (1979) has noted that we can think of the severity of a patient's symptoms as ranging on a continuum: at one extreme when asthma attacks occur, they are an uncomfortable nuisance that does not hamper the quality of the patient's life (feeling of tightness in the chest or a slight wheeze); at the other extreme are patients whose lifestyles are centered around coping with persistent and debilitating respiratory problems. Perhaps the most serious asthmatic condition is the potentially fatal *status asthmaticus* in which mucous buildup in the lungs can halt breathing (Renee & Creer, in press).

Despite the potential seriousness of bronchial asthma, Creer (1982) and McFaddon (1980) contend that the hallmark of asthma that distinguishes it from chronic, unremitting conditions such as emphysema is *reversibility*. By this it is meant that the narrowing of the airways of the lungs often reverses spontaneously or after adequate treatment.

The precise physiological, anatomical, and psychological factors associated with asthma attacks are not well understood. One way students of asthma have tried to parcel out the diverse elements that contribute to asthma attacks is to classify bronchial asthma into two major types: extrinsic and intrinsic. In cases of *intrinsic* asthma, a stimulus physiological in nature, such as a viral or bacterial respiratory infection, is the culprit. The *extrinsic* type represents a response to a substance to which the person is allergic. Dust, the chemical composition of some foods, and pollen are common allergens. Between about a third and a half of all cases of asthma are extrinsic (Holman & Muschenheim, 1972).

Unfortunately, in many cases it is impossible to pinpoint the stimulus that triggers an asthma attack. Rackemann's (1928) catch-all category of "mixed type" is still frequently invoked for such ambiguous cases, but this category has not facilitated our understanding of the factors that cause asthma (Creer, 1982). Indeed, classification schemes that define types of asthma on the basis of discrete classes of stimuli may be misleading in that they fail to reflect the fact that asthma attacks frequently have multiple determinants. A rainbow of antecedent factors, such as overexertion, a mild bronchial infection, and crying related to a bout of depression, may combine to trigger an episode of asthma.

The extent to which physical and psychological factors are intertwined has contributed to some of the problems encountered in isolating and mapping the role of psychological factors in asthma. Stress and emotional upheaval have been shown to influence the occurrence and severity of asthma attacks (Creer, 1979; Rees, 1964). But it is unclear exactly how these factors affect the onset and course of asthma. Emotions may not directly "cause" asthma attacks. However, certain *physical responses* to stress or emotional reactions (e.g., crying, laughter, coughing) can trigger attacks in some asthmatic patients (Purcell, 1963). Hence, if an emotional upset results in a burst of tears, there is a greater likelihood that an asthma attack will occur than if the person copes in some other manner that does not have a demonstrable physical link with asthma symptoms.

Some additional complexities in evaluating the role of psychological factors will be evident after we take a close look at a fascinating study conducted by Purcell and his colleagues (Purcell et al., 1969). Purcell was interested in investigating the home environment's role in precipitating and maintaining asthma attacks in some children. Two groups of children were selected. In one group a parent interview suggested that emotional factors were important. In the other group emotional factors seemed unrelated to asthma attacks. Purcell and his co-workers then instituted a dramatic intervention. After selection and careful preparation the children were removed from their homes and a substitute mother lived with the child for a period of two weeks. During the two-week period a number of measures of asthmatic symptoms were taken, including the frequency and intensity of attacks. For the group of children in which emotional factors were thought to be important, there was a definite decrease in the frequency of asthma bouts during separation, but in the group where emotional factors were not thought to be important, very little change in symptoms occurred. When families of the experimental group rejoined their children at home, the asthmatic attacks increased again.

These findings are very interesting because they indicate that, for a subset of children, the family environment can play a significant part in triggering asthma attacks. Perhaps future research will more precisely ascertain the aspects of family environment and the specific psychological changes that mediate symptom improvement. On a rather cautious note, Renne & Creer (in press) have commented that the reduction in asthma symptoms might have had little to do with relatively subtle psychological processes.

Instead, improvement might simply have been a function of the substitute mother's ensuring that the children took their asthma medication on a more regular basis than did the natural parents.

Psychological factors play a prominent role in the sufferer's reaction to the symptoms of asthma. You will recall that the child portrayed in the example at the beginning of our discussion reacted to his symptoms with fear and marked agitation. Not all children react this way. But this way of responding to an asthma attack intensifies the symptoms and can result in an escalating mosaic of anxiety and physical debilitation. In order to treat such patients, it is necessary to help them to learn techniques of relaxation and stress management in order to combat the anxiety that complicates treatment and can have life-threatening consequences. Let us now consider the treatment of the asthma patient in more detail.

Overview of Treatment

The treatment of asthma has ranged widely over the years, from the folk remedies of balancing a penny on the forehead, smelling the aroma of certain woods, and carrying around a small dog, usually a chihuahua, to injecting the patient with sterilized urine he has previously excreted, to truly effective approaches for managing the symptoms of asthma (Renne & Creer, in press). As Creer (1982) has aptly put it, "There simply is no cure for asthma. . . . Asthma can, through proper treatment be controlled" (p. 914).

What steps can be taken to control asthma? Asthma treatment programs often include educational and behavioral training components that teach children to take medication regularly, to participate in appropriate levels of exercise and recreational activities, to avoid specific precipitants of attacks, and to make decisions regarding the treatment of symptoms (Thoresen & Kirmil-Gray, 1983). Drugs like theophylline and epinephrine, a stimulant that expands the air passages and restores free breathing, have proven invaluable in the treatment of asthma, but it is crucial for the symptoms of asthma to be treated early so that a serious attack can be aborted. Often the parents and family members are needed to assist in administering medications and their behavior may also be modified to reduce the possibility that their own responses will contribute to the asthmatic's condition. For example, just as the asthmatic might be trained to react in calm, relaxed manner at the onset of an attack, his or her parents might be trained to respond in a like vein, neither overreacting nor panicking, as in the case presented above.

Holroyd, Appel, & Andrasik (1983) have outlined a four-stage cognitive-behavioral treatment program for asthma sufferers. This paradigm draws heavily upon Creer's (1979) descriptions of self-management techniques in the treatment of asthma. In the first education phase, persons are provided information about the disorder, facilitating their understanding of the precipitants and aggravants of attacks. Procedures and goals are also discussed. In the second phase, persons are trained to self-monitor their asthma attacks by recording information such as the time of occurrence, severity of the attack, and the events or stresses that precipitate them. In the third phase, asthmatics are taught coping and problem-solving skills believed to reduce the frequency and intensity of symptoms experienced. These strategies include relaxation techniques, breathing exercises, and training in problem-solving strategies to better cope with the interpersonal events that often evoke an emotional response that may trigger an asthmatic attack. Since the asthma sufferer is often quite young, other family members may also require training that permits them to assist the asthmatic child in effectively coping with the triggers of the symptoms. The final phase involves an evaluation of the intervention's effectiveness and the revision of previous techniques that have not proven useful in alleviating the frequency or severity of asthmatic symptoms. Behavioral programs such as the one outlined above have proven to be quite effective in the treatment of asthma.

ULCERS

A peptic ulcer is a lesion or inflamed focal area that may occur in the stomach lining or the duodenum. As in the case of William L. presented at the beginning of this chapter, these lesions may produce internal bleeding. In some cases the bleeding may be so severe that it is life-threatening to the individual. Approximately 10 percent of the population will develop a peptic ulcer during their lives. Six thousand to 10,000 deaths in the United States each year can be attributed to peptic ulcers (Pflanz, 1971).

What physiological processes are associated with the development of peptic ulcers? In normal people stomach acid secretion occurs when food enters or is about to enter the stomach, and secretion stops when digestion of the food is completed. However, in people suffering from ulcers, acid secretion may occur when no food is in the stomach. As a result, the stomach acid attacks the tissue of the stomach itself, producing inflammation and the injury we call an ulcer. People suffering from ulcers tend to produce between 4 and 20 times more stomach acid when the stomach is comparatively empty than normal individuals (Maher, 1966). Peptic ulcers can also form when there is insufficient secretion of the mucus that protects the stomach lining. There are two types of peptic ulcers: duodenal ulcers and gastric ulcers.

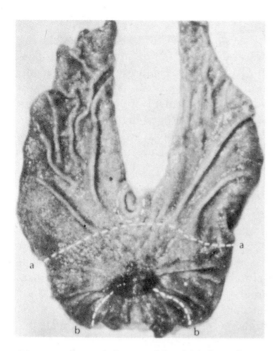

A human stomach (opened) in which there is an ulcer. The esophagus enters at the top center and is seen within the circle of dotted white lines. The point of esophageal entry is surrounded by cells similar to those in the rumen of the rat; the extent of this small region is demarcated by the same dotted circle. Between the two dotted lines, a and b, toward the bottom of the stomach lies the pylorus, and below the lowest dotted line lies the top of the duodenum. The ulcer can be seen at the border of the pylorus and the duodenum. (Source: Reprinted by permission of the publisher from M. Oi, K. Oshida, and A. Sugimuna, 1959, "The Location of Gastric Ulcer." *Gastroenterology, 36,* pp. 45–56. Copyright 1959 by Elsevier North Holland, Inc. Photo courtesy of Williams & Wilkins Company.)

Whitehead and Basmajian (1982) note that persons with duodenal ulcers generally show excess acid secretion, while persons with gastric ulcers do not. Gastric ulcers are thought to be related to insufficient amounts of mucus secretion.

The physiology of ulcers is fairly well understood. But what factors, either psychological or physiological, are associated with the etiology of ulcers? There is no definitive account of the critical factors associated with the development of ulcers. However, the prevailing view is that ulcers are the by-product of biological and psychological factors. It is believed that some persons are predisposed to secrete excessive amounts of gastrointestinal acid. A stressful event that results in sustained emotional arousal may elicit the hypersecretion of acid and an enzyme, pepsin, that stimulates acid production. This oversecretion eventually produces ulcers, and in more severe cases, may actually result in perforations in the wall of the stomach or duodenum.

Many experiments have used animals in an attempt to establish a link between environmental stress and peptic ulcers. However, animal studies have limited relevance for our understanding of ulcers in humans: Animals exposed to stress produce only gastric lesions, whereas 80 percent of peptic ulcers in humans are duodenal ulcers. In addition, experimentally induced stress generally results in the undersecretion of gastric acid, a fact not consistent with the view that peptic ulcers in humans result from excessive secretion of acid and pepsin (Whitehead & Basmajian, 1982).

Animal responses do not apparently mirror accurately human ulcer formation. But evidence for the relationship between chronic stress and the incidence of peptic ulcers in humans is forthcoming from epidemiological studies (Pflanz, 1981). For example, it is well documented that ulcers are more common during wartime and in urban as opposed to rural populations. Furthermore, the incidence of peptic ulcers has been found to be very high in occupations such as air traffic controllers and police officers, two occupations that are considered to be psychologically stressful.

How do we explain the fact that even under stressful environmental conditions some people develop ulcers while others do not? Earlier we noted that some people may be biologically predisposed to secrete excessive amounts of gastric acid. A field study by Weiner, Thaler, Reiser, & Mirsky (1957) provides support for this notion and points to a number of other factors implicated in the development of ulcers. The work of Weiner et al. suggests that there is a relationship between ulcer formation and the amount of pepsinogen in the digestive system of the individual. Pepsinogen is an enzyme that stimulates gastric activity.

Weiner measured the blood level of pepsinogen in over 2,000 draftees before they underwent the stress of basic training in the army. He found that trainees who showed high levels of blood serum pepsinogen developed many more ulcers than those with low levels when exposed to the stress of basic training. Furthermore, he found that among the people who developed ulcers, a particular personality pattern emerged. The group that developed ulcers appeared to be more passive and dependent than those who did not.

Thus we see a complex picture emerging from this study. The results suggest that three factors seem important in the development of ulcers: the presence of stress, a predisposing biological factor, and a pattern of personality characteristics. How these factors combine to produce ulcers, and whether all three are equally important, are still largely unknown. But as is the case with other forms of psychophysiological disorders, biological predisposition, environmental stress, and the person's style in coping with that stress all appear to be critical factors in unlocking the puzzle.

Overview of Treatment

Traditionally, peptic ulcers have been treated with antacid medications that reduce gastrointestinal activity. Bland diets were recommended to patients to reduce the consumption of certain foods thought to stimulate acid secretion. In severe cases surgery is sometimes necessary to repair the perforated lining of the stomach or duodenum. In recent years, however, a new medication, *cimetidine*, has been increasingly used for the treatment of peptic ulcers. This drug, which has proven highly effective in reducing the secretion of gastric acid, leads to the healing of peptic ulcers in most patients within several months (Finkelstein & Isselbacher, 1978).

Psychological treatment of peptic ulcers, especially stress management, also appears promising. Brooks and Richardson (1980), for example, provided ulcer patients with an "emotional skills training program," which combined relaxation techniques with assertiveness training. Patients who received this treatment showed fewer recurrences of ulcer symptoms, consumed less antacid, and experienced less severe symptoms than did patients who did not receive the treatment. Drugs are more cost-effective for the treatment of ulcers in the short run. However, treatment with medication may well lead to a higher recurrence of ulcer symptoms than with behavioral medicine interventions aimed at reducing the stress and emotional reactions that are linked to the development of peptic ulcers (Whitehead & Basmajian, 1982).

CHRONIC PAIN

At one time or another each of us has experienced pain. To know pain is to know that one is alive. But the sensations we label as painful are anything but pleasant reminders of the joys of life. Mercifully, most pain has a sudden onset and is short-lived or acute, like the dull throb of a stubbed toe or the agony of a dentist's drill treading on a nerve. But for millions of Americans, pain is chronic—a daily and unwelcome companion.

Chronic pain typically begins with an acute flare-up but cannot be totally eliminated by medicine or other means. Chronic pain problems account for as many trips to the physician's office as any other medical problem (Nagi, Riley, & Newby, 1973) and disable more individuals than cancer or heart disease. Bresler (1979) has estimated that approximately 80 percent of all patients seeking medical assistance do so for pain-related problems.

Turk et al. (1983) have described three types of chronic pain: chronic, recurrent pain; chronic, intractable, benign pain; and chronic, progressive pain. Let us consider each type in turn. Chronic, recurrent pain is described as those pain conditions in which intense episodes of pain are interspersed with periods when the sufferer experiences no discomfort. Examples of such conditions would include migraine headaches and certain kinds of facial pain.

Chronic, intractable, benign pain is characterized by its continual presence. Although the intensity of pain experienced varies over time, sufferers report that some pain is always present. Such pain patients often develop additional psychological and behavioral complications, such as depression and impairment in many spheres of their life. Many of the more than 70 million sufferers of low back pain would fit this characterization.

Chronic, progressive pain results from certain disorders such as rheumatoid arthritis and, most feared of all, cancer. Cancer is, for most of its 800,000 victims, a particularly frightening disease because of its unpredictable nature and erratic course. The specter of death and feelings of hopelessness frequently compound the pain and distress of cancer.

Patients who endure chronic pain frequently ask themselves questions like, "When will it ever end?" "Will it be worse this time than before?" "How long will it last?" Cancer victims might wonder whether even a slight increase in pain represents a downward, perhaps fatal, turn in the progression of their illness. Each of the three types of pain we have described is frequently associated with anxiety, uncertainty, and feelings of helplessness as well as other negative emotions (Sternbach, 1968). Irritability, anger, and frustration can also be by-products of prolonged periods of pain-related sleeplessness and resulting fatigue (Steger & Fordyce, 1982). Pain patients' anxiety and uncertainty serve only to increase the subjective experience of pain, creating a vicious spiral of escalating pain and anxiety.

The nature and cause of pain have been the subject of speculation for many centuries. However, there is still no universally accepted explanation of how we experience pain. One major theory, termed the *direct transmission model*, conceptualizes pain as the result of direct sensory input. According to this model, the perception of pain occurs when the effects of a pain-producing stimulus are transmitted from pain receptors in free nerve endings directly to the brain. This occurs by way of specific nerve fibers of the peripheral and central nervous system. These impulses are registered as pain, the intensity of which varies as a function of the quality and intensity of the pain-producing stimulus. Many pharmacological and surgical techniques used to control pain are based on the direct transmission model. Many researchers and theorists, however, believe that the direct transmission model is too simplistic.

The experience of pain is determined by an interaction of numerous factors: degree of tissue damage, anxiety or fear level, the perceived consequences of pain, various personality factors, cognitive expectations, and past history of pain experience (Steger & Fordyce, 1982). For example, two women who are apparently experiencing the same kind of pain sensations during childbirth can interpret the sensations very differently. One woman might interpret the sensations as excruciating and unbearable; the other might interpret them as easily tolerable. Furthermore, patients can tolerate more pain when they are convinced they can exercise a measure of control over their pain. Indeed, how patients cope with and adapt to chronic pain is important. If patients are able to effectively distract themselves from pain, reinterpret the sensations as less bothersome, or engage in fewer catastrophic thoughts, they are likely to be able to tolerate greater pain or experience diminished pain (Barber, 1982).

Melzack and Wall (1965, 1970) have advanced a theory of pain known as the *gate-control model*. This theory is gaining in prominence over the direct transmission model. According to the gate-control theory, only a limited amount of sensory input from pain receptors can be processed by the central nervous system at a given point in time. It is believed that a neural mechanism in the dorsal horn of the spinal cord functions as a "gate," controlling the flow of sensory input from peripheral nerve fibers to the central nervous system. If the intensity of a specific sensory input from pain receptors rises above a critical level, or is superseded by some other significant sensory input, the neural mechanism interrupts the flow of pain impulses, acting as a gate. Thus, in theory, pain can be prevented from crossing the gate when there is competition from another sensory input.

The gate-control model of Melzack and Wall provides a more adequate account of how psychological factors mediate our experience of pain than does the direct transmission model. For example, it can account for how our experience of pain varies from situation to situation, depending on our psychological state. All of us have experienced be-

ing so absorbed in an emotional event that we "forgot" the pain we were experiencing from a headache or a trip to the dentist's office. The gate-control model contends that pain was blocked or "gated" from consciousness because of the competing sensory-imaginal stimulation. Turk and his colleagues (1983) indicate that the neural mechanisms underlying this model are speculative. However, the model has received considerable support and has provided the framework for a number of innovative approaches to the treatment of pain. Before we discuss the treatment of chronic pain in some detail, let us consider a therapeutic procedure derived directly from the gate-control theory and known as *transcutaneous nerve stimulation* (TENS).

For many patients who have tried almost every drug, technique, and machine available to treat their pain, TENS can provide at least a brief respite from their discomfort. Patients typically wear a small battery-powered transmitter—about the size of a bar of soap—that sends electrical impulses to block pain sensations. Electrodes that receive the stimulation are placed or implanted at or near the site of the pain, or close to the major nerves serving the area of discomfort. Many physical therapists use TENS to send impulses to compete with the body's pain signals, theoretically closing the "pain gate" and helping to relieve pain in about a third of the patients who undergo this procedure.

Overview of Treatment

Traditional medical treatment of pain has relied on the use of analgesic medications, such as aspirin and narcotics, or surgical techniques that attempt to sever the nerve pathways so that pain impulses are unable to reach the brain. While traditional pharmacological and surgical interventions are usually effective in alleviating acute pain, only 50 percent of those experiencing chronic pain obtain relief from medical interventions (Turk et al., 1983). Melzack and Wall (1983) are quite pessimistic about the adequacy of surgical techniques to control pain, noting that long-term pain control is rarely achieved. In many cases, after a period of relief the pain recurs and is often reported as more severe than before the surgical intervention.

One of the reasons why traditional treatments have failed to achieve sweeping victories in the conquest of pain is that chronic pain is influenced by neurological, psychological, and behavioral factors. Hence, multimodal interventions that incorporate cognitive and behavioral components of treatment have been increasingly utilized to control chronic pain. These procedures are often implemented in conjunction with traditional somatic approaches to pain control.

Behavioral pain control techniques fall within two categories: operant conditioning methods and self-management techniques. Fordyce (1976) has pioneered the development of operant conditioning techniques in the context of comprehensive pain clinics that provide an array of services to pain patients. He has demonstrated that chronic pain patients often show diminished pain and medication intake as well as dramatic increases in physical activity and exercise tolerance if nursing staff and family members are trained to withhold rewards to patients who complain about pain and request others to do things for them because of their pain. Also, attention and praise are provided to the pain patients for "healthful behaviors," such as physical activity and the use of less medication for pain control.

Cognitive pain control techniques teach pain patients cognitive coping skills and strategies to distract their attention or transform the perception of sensations associated with pain. The strategy of imagina-tive inattention involves training patients to generate imagery incompatible with pain. For instance, by vividly imagining relaxing at the beach or enjoying a quiet walk in the country, some patients can distract themselves from the experience of pain. The strategy of imaginative transformation of pain involves teaching patients to reinterpret their experience of pain, transforming it to an experience of numbness, for example. Learning to use such cognitive coping skills can be facilitated by presenting imagery-enhancing suggestions during hypnosis or by providing subjects with instructions to experiment with their abilities to engage in creative imagination. A moment's reflection suggests that the effectiveness of these cognitive maneuvers may be explained by the gate-control model of pain. If pain sufferers attend to other cues or generate internal stimulation via imagery, pain impulses may be blocked by the gating mechanism, thereby reducing their experience of pain. The effectiveness of such techniques may also derive from the pain patient's feeling that he or she has enhanced control over pain.

THEORIES OF PSYCHOPHYSIOLOGICAL DISORDERS

Thus far we have examined some of the defining characteristics of psychophysiological disorders and discussed a number of typical examples. But a number of puzzling questions remain unanswered. Why do some people develop psychophysiological disorders while others seem invulnerable? What is it that triggers the psychophysiological response? Can we identify particular psychological events or genetic predispositions that help answer these questions?

Scientists have sought answers to these questions largely in the context of their own favorite theoretical perspective. Let us

SOME DANGERS OF TRADITIONAL MEDICAL TREATMENT FOR PSYCHOPHYSIOLOGICAL DISORDERS

We have seen that a major treatment approach for psychophysiological disorders involves chemical or surgical intervention with the affected organ system. For headache, drugs may be administered to reduce the pain associated with expanding blood vessels. For ulcers, antacid medications and surgery are often the treatment of choice. For asthma and for hypertension, drugs are routinely administered. But is it possible that using medical interventions of this sort could actually perpetuate psychophysiological disorders rather than relieve them? Schwartz (1977) thinks that this is the case.

You will recall that Schwartz offers the disregulation theory of psychophysiological disorders. In essence the theory argues that the brain maintains the health of various physiological systems by operating as a regulating device, receiving input from various organ systems and altering the level of their functioning. As Schwartz notes, "Because the body, as any complex physical device, can only work effectively within certain tolerances, the brain must continually ascertain that all components are working effectively. If any component begins to break down, the brain must adjust itself to bring the disregulation back into balance" (p. 305).

But when medical interventions are used to treat an affected organ system, *they also have the effect of modifying the feedback from that organ to the brain.* In this case, the brain cannot operate effectively to regulate the organ system.

Schwartz notes that we are no longer constrained to deal with the problem of

physiological disregulation by responding in the natural way. Instead, we would rather change our body chemistry than our style of life by avoiding stressful situations or changing our environment; we choose to operate artificially on those negative feedback systems that generate natural signals of discomfort. The danger, of course, is that when these feedback mechanisms are removed or altered artificially, the brain loses its capacity to regulate the organ system effectively.

Schwartz offers the example of a simple stomach ache. Instead of regulating one's diet or avoiding certain foods, commercials suggest that the appropriate remedy is to dose oneself with antacid drugs. In addition, medicine is developing new and even more complex means of bypassing normal adaptive feedback mechanisms. People can now have a surgical procedure to remove the vagus nerve that provides the neural regulation between stomach and brain. Again, Schwartz notes that "our culture continually reinforces the idea that if the brain and its body cannot cope with the external environment, they will simply have to undergo medical alteration to adjust" (p. 306–307).

The consequences of this approach to dealing with disregulation are, in Schwartz's view, extremely dangerous. He argues that medical procedures should not be the sole approach to treatment. Rather, a thoughtful combination of behavioral strategies, biofeedback, and medical intervention will provide a more adaptive means of coping with the diseases of disregulation—the psychophysiological disorders.

consider some hypotheses regarding the origins of psychophysiological disorders formulated from the psychoanalytic, learning, stress, and social perspectives.

Psychoanalytic Perspective: The Specific Emotion Hypothesis

Psychodynamic theorists suggest that many psychophysiological disorders reflect symbolic expressions of interpersonal or internal conflict. They argue that once the individual gains insight into the nature of these conflicts, the conflict will be lessened and along with it the psychophysiological symptoms.

An example of this hypothesis is offered by Pelletier (1977). Pelletier reports working with a client whose psychophysiological symptom clearly indicated that the condition was symbolic of an underlying psychological problem. Pelletier reports the case of a nurse who came to him for treatment of wry neck, a condition in which the head is turned to face over the patient's right shoulder. The nurse had suffered from this condition for more than five years. In the course of her treatment with Pelletier, she expressed shame about a long-concealed affair with a younger married man. She noted at one point in her treatment, "If my neighbors ever found out, I couldn't look them in the face." Pelletier suggested that her symptom was a symbolic means of preventing her neighbors from looking her straight in the face even if they found out about the affair. He notes that when she began to have insight into the connection between her psychophysiological disorder and her internal psychological conflict about her affair, her condition steadily improved. A number of psychoanalysts, most notably Franz Alexander (1950), argue that *psychophysiological disorders occur when conflicts developed during infancy are repressed but then are stimulated again in adulthood* by some environmental circumstance. Alexander believes that the individual then regresses to this earlier mode of functioning, and that the regression is accompanied by some physiological response that becomes the psychophysiologic symptom.

For example, Alexander attempts to explain the occurrence of stomach ulcers by arguing that infantile cravings to be fed are symbolically equated in childhood with a wish to be loved and feelings of dependency. But as the child grows older, these needs for love and dependency come into conflict with adult standards for independence and self-assertion. When these conflicts are reawakened in adulthood, they activate the gastrointestinal system, which has been previously associated with feeding. The result, according to Alexander, is a peptic ulcer.

This hypothesis, sometimes called Alexander's (1950) *specific emotion hypothesis*, has little controlled experimental evidence to support it. Psychophysiological disorders are often explained *after the fact,* using some version of the specific emotion hypothesis. However, we should remember that it is all too easy to draw selectively on evidence from retrospective clinical reports that is consistent with a psychoanalytic hypothesis while ignoring contrary evidence.

Also, as Maher (1966) notes, it may not be the specific symbolic *content* of the conflict that produces the disorder, but simply the fact that it is a stressor. If this is the case, then focusing on the content of the stressor may lead us to overemphasize its importance while ignoring the more general but important fact that stress may play a role in the development of the disorder.

Learning Perspective: Autonomic Learning and the Vicious Circle

As we might expect, learning theorists have also attempted to offer explanations for the development of psychophysiological disorders. One of the major proponents of this view is Lachman (1972). He argues that most psychophysiological disorders are *learned physiological reactions to stress*. He believes that particular autonomic responses can be learned on the basis of differential reinforcement and that when psychophysiological disorders are rewarded, perhaps by removing the individual from the stressful situation, they are likely to occur again in similar stimulus situations.

Autonomic response learning is another fundamental concept. Not only are autonomic responses learned on the basis of their being conditioned to new stimuli but particular autonomic responses are also selectively learned on the basis of differential reward or reinforcement. A specific rewarded autonomic response tends to be differentiated out of the emotional response constellation and to be selectively strengthened. Thus the individual who is rewarded for his or her expression of gastrointestinal pain by being permitted to stay home from school or from work and who is given special attention, consideration, and love under those circumstances is likely to have strengthened the gastrointestinal reactions that led to the gastrointestinal pain, that is, to have increased gastric acid secretion. This is a statement of the idea that *rewarded autonomic responses may be selectively learned*.

The concept of *vicious-circle effects* is also necessary to understand certain psychosomatic phenomena. Once initiated, a psychosomatic event may produce stimuli that lead to implicit reactions that rearouse or intensify the psy-chosomatic event, and so on. For example, the noxious stimulation from a gastric ulcer may elicit implicit reactions, including facilitated stomach-acid secretion, that will intensify that ulcerous condition. This development will lead to further emotional reaction and further irritation of the ulcer. Theoretically, and perhaps in fact, people may worry themselves to death in such a vicious circle (Lachman, 1972, p. 67–68).

This is an intriguing hypothesis. Certainly it is possible to demonstrate operant learning of specific autonomic responses in the laboratory. For certain disorders, such as asthma, the response of the family to an asthmatic attack in the child may actually reinforce subsequent asthmatic attacks, thus increasing their likelihood.

Furthermore, Lachman's idea that a vicious circle can both maintain and intensify the severity of a psychophysiological disorder is a fruitful one. Thus a person who suffers from cardiac arrhythmia may worry constantly about the possibility of suffering a heart attack. The worry may intensify the psychophysiological reaction and result in even more instances of arrhythmia.

Stress Perspective

In Chapter 5 we discussed Selye's concept of the general adaptation syndrome, the three-stage physiological pattern of response to stress that Selye believed all individuals manifest in reaction to stressful life circumstances. You will recall that according to this

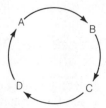

Vicious circle for ulcer development.
A = Noxious stimulation from area of ulcer;
B = Perceptual effect of noxious stimulation;
C = Emotional reaction including gastric gland secretion; and
D = Further inflammation of ulcer.

theory, prolonged stress leads to an alarm re-action, a stage of resistance, and in severe cases an exhaustion in which resistance breaks down and the person can no longer sustain high levels of physiological activation. The culmination of this process is tissue damage to one organ system or another. We also noted that Selye's account traces the likely course of psychophysiological disorders, but is unable to specify which organ system is likely to be affected. However, another hypothesis derived from the stress perspective does suggest a possible answer. Often called the *somatic weakness hypothesis*, it argues that there are large inherited individual differences in physiological reactivity in different organ systems. These inherited differences become particularly important when an individual is subjected to stress. Thus, presumably, some organ systems possess an inherited somatic weakness; with

sufficient stress, it is that organ system that breaks down, resulting in a psychophysiological disorder.

We have already noted that a number of disorders, such as asthma and hypertension, tend to run in families. Twin studies, when they have been conducted, offer at least modest evidence that there is a genetic component in some psychophysiological disorders. In addition, we noted earlier that large individual differences in pepsinogen, an enzyme involved in digestion, exist among ulcer-prone individuals, thus suggesting a possible genetic mechanism.

Certainly the idea of the general adaptation syndrome and the somatic weakness hypothesis are useful parts of the psychophysiological puzzle and help account for some of the observed characteristics of these disorders. But what is the nature of the stressor that Selye talks about? Part of the answer is

Retirement is a life event that can produce stress reactions and may put a person at risk for psychophysiological disorders. (Robert V. Eckert, Jr./EKM-Nepenthe)

to be found in the ideas of researchers who work in the tradition of the social perspective.

Social Perspective: Stressful Life Events and Coping

For the most part we have been referring to stressors in a very general way. But what are these stressors? Can we identify the most common of them? Holmes and his colleagues have conducted numerous studies directed at identifying life events that appear particularly stressful to individuals.

One product of their research is an instrument they call the Social-Readjustment Rating Scale, which lists a large number of potentially stressful life events. Table 6–3 provides us with a list of such stressors. It may be instructive for you to examine this list to see how many of these life events you have recently experienced.

According to this perspective, life events that require major adaptations all have the potential to elicit stress reactions and may place the person at risk for the development of psychophysiological disorders. The more life events experienced by individuals, the more likely they are to become ill from a variety of disorders. For example, Holmes and Masuda (1973) followed the course of 84 resident physicians. Life events rating for a period of 18 months were used as a measure to predict the onset of future illness. Information concerning the incidence of illness was collected for a period of eight months. Resident physicians in both the high- and medium-risk groups reported experiencing significantly greater numbers of physical disorders than did the low-risk group that reported few stressful life events. The study demonstrates that life events requiring major adaptations have the potential to place persons at risk for the development of psychophysiological disorders.

TABLE 6–3
Social-Readjustment Rating Scale

Rank	Life Event	Mean Value
1	Death of spouse	100
2	Divorce	73
3	Marital separation	65
4	Jail term	63
5	Death of close family member	63
6	Personal injury or illness	53
7	Marriage	50
8	Fired at work	47
9	Marital reconciliation	45
10	Retirement	45
11	Change in health of family member	44
12	Pregnancy	40
13	Sex difficulties	39
14	Gain of new family member	39
15	Business readjustment	39
16	Change in financial state	38
17	Death of close friend	37
18	Change to different line of work	36
19	Change in number of arguments with spouse	35
20	Mortgage over $10,000	31
21	Foreclosure of mortgage or loan	30
22	Change in responsibilities at work	29
23	Son or daughter leaving home	29
24	Trouble with in-laws	29
25	Outstanding personal achievement	28
26	Wife begins or stops work	26
27	Begin or end school	26
28	Change in living conditions	25
29	Revision of personal habits	24
30	Trouble with boss	23
31	Change in work hours or conditions	20
32	Change in residence	20
33	Change in schools	20
34	Change in recreation	19
35	Change in church activities	19
36	Change in social activities	18
37	Mortgage or loan less than $10,000	17
38	Change in sleeping habits	16
39	Change in number of family get-togethers	15
40	Change in eating habits	15
41	Vacation	13
42	Christmas	12
43	Minor violations of the law	11

Source: Thomas Holmes and Minoru Masuda, "Psychosomatic Syndromes." Reprinted with permission from *Psychology Today Magazine* © 1972 (American Psychology Association).

A variety of life changes, some of them positive, can also require coping and adaptation from those experiencing them. (Courtesy of Angelo and Gail Lococo)

Stressful life events are far from perfect predictors of future illness. But our ability to predict the impact of life events on the individual can be improved by knowing something about the resources and social support available to the person for coping with environmental change. For example, Spielberger and Jacobs (1979) have noted that anxiety during pregnancy may result in obstetric complications and abnormalities in the neonate. In a study of pregnancy and birth complications conducted by Nuckolls, Cassell, and Kaplan (1972), a relationship emerged between birth complications and coping re-

sources in women with high levels of stressful life events prior to delivery. Women who reported their personal resources were adequate to cope with the pregnancy and delivery had fewer birth complications than women who felt they had less adequate coping resources.

The above discussion suggests that individuals seem to react to stressful events in different ways. If certain behavior patterns (e.g., Type A) increase the likelihood of illness, might personality resources serve as a buffer against the negative effects of stress? One interesting line of research suggests that personality hardiness—commitment, control, and challenge—does in fact decrease the likelihood that stressful life events will produce the symptoms of illness. You will recall that Suzanne Kobasa and her colleagues (Kobasa, Hiller, & Maddi, 1979) hypothesized that the following characteristics describe persons who will remain healthy in the face of considerable stress: (1) a sense of commitment to (rather than alienation from) the various aspects of their lives; (2) a tendency to seek novelty and challenge (rather than familiarity and security); and (3) the belief that one has control over events (rather than the feeling that one is externally controlled). In summarizing the literature on hardiness, Maddi (1985) has noted that its beneficial effects appear to be distinct from the positive effects of exercise, organismic constitution, and social supports. We should also note that hardiness and the Type A behavior pattern appear to tap different personality attributes (Kobasa, Maddi, & Zola, 1983). Future research should help clarify the role of Type A and hardiness in the development of and protection against specific illnesses.

Our discussion suggests that stress may have a great deal to do with transactions with the environment that tax an individual's adaptive resources. A *transactional perspective* implies that stress is a product of the interaction of three factors: life events that require an adaptive response, the individual's response to these events, and, most important, psychological mediating processes (Coyne & Holroyd, 1982; Holroyd, 1979).

We have now surveyed a number of the best-known theories that attempt to account for the development of psychophysiological disorders. It is almost surely the case that stress is an important precipitant of these disorders. And it is likely that there are large individual differences in the degree to which particular organ systems are susceptible to stress as a consequence either of innate genetic disposition or autonomic learning. It is even possible that there are symbolic relationships between the type of psychophysiological disorders developed and current or past conflicts in the individual's life, although evidence for these relationships is less clear. The social and transactional perspectives broaden our conceptualization of stress and suggest that it is important to understand the relationship between the individual's ways of coping with stress, changes in physiology, and disease outcome.

SUMMARY

In this chapter we have examined the stress-related psychophysiological disorders, coronary heart disease, and chronic pain. These disorders are quite common. For example, coronary heart disease is the number one cause of death and disability in the United States; tension and migraine headaches affect about 20 percent of the population; and more than three quarters of all patients seeking medical assistance do so for pain-related problems. In contrast with disorders such as conversion reactions and hypochondriasis, psychophysiological disorders involve some form of actual tissue damage. Most diseases have a psychological or emotional component, but considerable variation can be seen in the proportion of psychological factors that contribute to a particular illness. We noted that stress, predisposing biological factors, and personality or family characteristics all may influence the development and course of psychophysiological disorders. Lifestyle factors were also discussed, including the Type A behavior pattern associated with coronary heart disease and possibly other disorders, and personality hardiness—commitment, control, and challenge—attributes that buffer or protect against the damaging effects of stress.

The emerging fields of behavioral medicine and health psychology have developed and promoted treatments designed to prevent illness and maintain health. When stress is a significant part of the symptom picture, psychological approaches such as cognitive-behavioral therapy, biofeedback, and relaxation techniques are viable psychological interventions that may be used alongside more traditional medical and drug treatments (e.g., tranquilizer drugs, analgesic compounds, surgery, and dietary regulation).

Theories of psychophysiological disorders have attempted to explain their origins from a variety of viewpoints. Psychoanalytic theorists trace the roots of psychophysiological disorders to conflicts developed during infancy that are repressed but then stimulated again by some environmental circumstance. The learning perspective emphasizes the learned nature of physiological reactions to stress. This viewpoint raises the intriguing possibility that particular autonomic responses related to disease may be rewarded, thereby increasing the likelihood that they will occur again. The stress perspective views these disorders as diseases of adaptation. A pattern of response to stress termed the *general adaptation syndrome* has been related to tissue damage and disease. A particular organ system may be affected because of an inherited somatic weakness or vulnerability to stress. The social perspective emphasizes stressful life events in the development of illness. However, resources available to the person for coping with environmental change seem to mediate the stress-illness relationship. A transactional perspective centers around the idea that stress is related to transactions with the environment that tax an individual's abilities to adapt effectively. This model implies that stress is a function of life events requiring an adaptive response, changes in physiology and behavioral response to stressful events, and psychological mediating processes.

7

Anxiety, Somatoform, and Dissociative Disorders

Neurosis and DSM III

Anxiety Disorders
  Phobias
  Anxiety States
  Obsessive-Compulsive Disorders

Somatoform Disorders
  Somatization Disorders
  Conversion Disorders

Dissociative Disorders
  Psychogenic Amnesia
  Fugue
  Multiple Personality

Treatment Strategies
  Psycho-dynamic Approach
  Learning and Behavioral Approaches
  Biological Approaches

Summary

INTRODUCTION

Each of us has specific fears and even moments of panic. But imagine fear as a way of life. How do you live your life when so many things seem terrifying, and when those around you cannot imagine what it is like to experience constant, pervasive fear? The following case involving a lawyer illustrates the debilitating effects of a life ruled by fear:

While defending a client, he experienced a sudden, rapid rise in pulse, with a fear of fainting, and was forced to leave the courtroom and terminate his relationship with the case. Following this incident, he avoided all court appearances. In the above-described episode, the patient thought he was having a heart attack, and for a great many years was obsessionally preoccupied with his cardiac state. In addition to the courtroom phobia, he also had phobias about bridges, enclosed spaces, and tunnels of all sorts. As time went on he developed a speaking phobia whenever he was called upon to give a prepared address. However, if he were called upon unexpectedly, he could function very well and could speak quite persuasively. . . . The fainting attack had occurred when the opposing counsel introduced an argument that the patient had not anticipated, and, therefore, he was taken unaware in a situation in which he felt he was expected to be prepared and thereby in control. He immediately became very tense, excited, and extremely restless. His pulse became very rapid; he felt a sudden pain in his chest and collapsed. It is interesting to note that the argument that caused this reaction was neither significant nor crucial to the ultimate outcome of the case, but since it was unexpected, it could not be dealt with in an ideal and perfect fashion (Salzman, 1982, pp. 32–33).

This is a fairly typical example of a phobic disorder. We will describe this and other anxiety disorders in the following pages. However, first let us step back and describe the historical evolution of this group of disorders.

Neurosis and DSM III

Neurotic is a term familiar to most people whether they have had formal training in the study of abnormal behavior or not. In general, people assume that it refers to a variety of anxiety-ridden, peculiar, self-defeating, but not necessarily bizarre, behavior patterns.

Until recently neurosis was part of the official nomenclature of the *Diagnostic and Statistical Manual of Mental Disorders,* but in DSM III the term was deleted. The behavior patterns previously included under the term *neurosis* are listed separately and emphasize the observed pattern of maladaptive behavior rather than underlying anxiety, as did DSM II.

Over the centuries our ideas about the meaning of neurosis have changed several times. In Chapter 2 we noted that the 19th century was heavily influenced by an *organic orientation* to abnormal behavior. At that time it was believed that neurotic disorders were due to weak or damaged nerves, and that the fatigue and anxiety experienced by neurotic people were a consequence of neurological impairment.

The turn of the century and the emergence of psychoanalysis offered another interpretation of the meaning of neurosis. Instead of focusing on organic causes, Freud and his followers believed that neurotic symptoms, particularly *anxiety* and the *defense mechanisms*, were an expression of underlying id-ego conflicts. In Chapter 3 we discussed the *psychoanalytic perspective* on abnormal behavior in some detail.

Today the controversy about the meaning of neurosis continues. Some researchers are still convinced that there is a biological basis for many neurotic disorders. Other researchers and clinicians believe, as did Freud, that neurosis is best understood in dynamic terms. Still another group of scientists argue that neurotic symptoms are *learned* either through classical or instrumental conditioning. Early pioneers in the field of learning, such as Pavlov and Watson, conducted studies that they believed demonstrated that neurotic symptoms were the product of learning mechanisms. Today this controversy remains unresolved, and the organic, dynamic, and learning explanations each have strong advocates.

Perhaps the most important recent turn in the controversy is reflected in the elimination of the term altogether in DSM III. This decision almost surely reflects a shift in the direction of a more empirical orientation to classifying abnormal behavior and a less inferential approach. In this chapter we will examine three disorders previously described as "neurotic": *anxiety, somatoform,* and *dissociative disorders.*

ANXIETY DISORDERS

Anxiety disorders are among the most common of the psychological disorders. DSM III (1980) estimates that 2 to 4 percent of the general population has at some time experienced an anxiety disorder. However, often these experiences are not diagnosed because people experiencing severe anxiety frequently turn to their family doctor. Between 10 and 15 percent of the cases seen by general medical practitioners involve anxiety problems. Many of these people are given minor tranquilizers such as Valium or Miltown to control their anxiety. DSM III divides anxiety disorders into the separate categories of phobic disorders and anxiety states. We will discuss each of these categories in turn.

Phobias

A phobia is an intense, irrational fear of a specific object or situation. The term derives from the Greek god Phobos, who inspired terror in those who perceived him. People suffering from phobias react to an object or situation with a degree of intensity out of proportion to its actual threat. Phobias may develop in response to a variety of objects and situations, including animals, fire, disease, crowds, darkness, blood, storms, and closed, open, or high places.

It is important for us to distinguish between *anxiety,* which appears to be attached to no specific object, and *phobias* which are always associated with some particular object or situation. Anxiety may be diffuse, but a phobic fear is highly focused and can seldom be explained or reasoned away. Furthermore, the fear is largely beyond voluntary control and typically leads the phobic person to avoid the feared situation.

Acrophobia—fear of heights—is obviously not this man's problem (Robert Houser/Photo Researchers, Inc.)

Although the fears may seem unreasonable to others, they are very intense and real to the people suffering from them and may be endured only at great personal cost. In fact, one of the distinctive features of phobias is that the avoidance of the feared object may lead to a severe *constriction or narrowing in life activities.*

DSM III (1980) distinguishes among three types of phobias: social phobia, simple phobia, and agoraphobia. *Social phobias* refer to persistent irrational fears of situations in which the person may be observed or scrutinized by others. The essence of this type of phobia is a fear of humiliation or embarrassment. Examples of social phobias include the fear of speaking in public, eating in public, and using public bathrooms. Occasionally such persons may be so concerned with not drawing attention to themselves that they are even afraid to breathe or swallow in public.

Simple phobia refers to an irrational fear directed at a specific object or situation other than a fear of humiliation in a social situation. Examples of some simple phobias are given in the box on p. 168. Although simple phobias are relatively common, often instead of seeking treatment the sufferer arranges his or her life so as to eliminate all possible contact with the feared object.

Agoraphobia refers to a generalized fear of open or public places. It is much more common in women, perhaps because of sex-role stereotyping of women as helpless and dependent (Chambless, 1982). Originally agoraphobia meant "fear of the marketplace." Now, as Baumgold (1977) notes, it has come to mean fear of the marketplace of life. Although initially only a specific object or situation may be involved, the number of feared objects may increase so rapidly that there are soon few places where the sufferer feels safe. In fact, cases are recorded of people who were so fearful of the outside world that

VARIETIES OF PHOBIC REACTIONS

Acrophobia: Fear of High Places Such as Cliffs, Roofs, High Windows, Ladders, or Stairwells

Case Example Agnes W., an unmarried woman of 30, had been unable to go higher than the second or third floor of any building for a year. Whenever she tried to overcome her fear of height, she only succeeded in provoking intolerable anxiety. She remembered when it all began. One evening she was working alone at the office when she was suddenly seized with a terror lest she jump or fall out of the open eight-story window. So frightened was Agnes by her impulse that she crouched behind a steel file for some time before she could trust herself to gather up her things and make for the street. She reached the ground level acutely anxious, perspiring freely, her heart pounding, and breathing rapid (Cameron, 1963, p. 282).

Claustrophobia: Fear of Enclosed Places Such as Small Rooms, Closets, Elevators, Alleys, and Subways

Case Example Bert C. entered therapy in part because of his fear of elevators. He walked the four flights to his office whenever possible. If he rode in the elevator, he was terrified over the possibility of being trapped and of being mutilated or killed in trying to escape. He often pictured these possibilities to himself (Cameron, 1963, p. 287).

Zoophobia: Fear of Animals Such as Dogs, Cats, Snakes, Frogs, Bats, Horses, Tigers, and Lions

Case Example Little Hans, a boy of five years old, refused to go into the street because he was afraid of horses. Actually he feared being bitten by them and no amount of rational persuasion could rid him of his fear.

Ocholophobia: Fear of Crowds and Public Gatherings

Case Example M.'s first phobic attack occurred when she was returning home by airplane. It was night and the place was crowded. The people pressed in around her, and M. was seized by an overwhelming feeling of panic that seemed to come "out of the blue." Her stomach turned, she couldn't breathe, she was shaking and sweating and frightened by the very thought of the people pressing around her (Baumgold, 1977).

in 30 years they left their home only a few times (Salholz, 1984). Other agoraphobic persons can leave their homes, engage in a wide range of unrestricted activities, but only when accompanied by a close companion.

The DSM III notes that agoraphobia may at times be associated with panic attacks. Such attacks involve sweating, faintness, choking or smothering sensations, heart palpitations, dizziness, feelings of unreality, and a fear of dying or going crazy.

Chambless (1982) sees the common denominator underlying the agoraphobic person's numerous fears as a fear of any situation where an easy retreat to safety is not possible. This need for an avenue of escape is said to result from the fear of suffering a panic attack in public. Such an experience is so terrifying and humiliating that the person may come to plan his or her life around avoiding such an attack. Chambless argues that the fear of public places is secondary and results from what he calls a *fear of fear*.

Origins of Phobic Behavior. Where do phobias come from? Are they merely the accidental result of some previous traumatic event? Do they serve some purpose in balancing the psychological drives and needs of the individual? Or is there, perhaps, a genetic predisposition to become phobic?

Three major points of view have developed to account for the pattern of specific, irrational fear and avoidance we see in phobic reactions. They are the dynamic explanation, the learning explanation, and the idea of biological preparedness.

Freud was intrigued by phobias and saw them as symbolic of inner psychological conflict. By avoiding the phobic situation a person can avoid the symbolically represented unconscious conflict that is the essence of the phobia (MacKinnon & Michels, 1971). Although Freud saw the phobia as always symbolizing some sexual anxiety, recent dynamic theorists have emphasized that the phobia may symbolize almost any fear (Cameron, 1963). Thus the fear of heights may actually symbolize the fear of falling in the esteem of other people. Similarly, claustrophobia, the fear of closed places, may symbolize the fear of being left alone with one's own dangerous impulses and fantasies.

The psychoanalytic explanation of phobias is illustrated in one of Freud's most famous case histories, that of Little Hans, a five-year-old boy who was terrified that he would be bitten by a horse. This fear was so great that Hans refused to leave the safety of the home. Freud viewed Hans' horse phobia in terms of Oedipal dynamics. Specifically, Hans was said to be struggling with the unconscious wish to kill his father and replace him as his mother's lover. Because Hans was unable to accept this wish into consciousness, he projected it onto his father. Thus Hans' unconscious wish to kill his father was transformed into the belief that his father wanted to kill him. However, as this transformation was still too close to the original wish, it became further transformed into the fear that a horse would bite him. That the horse came to symbolize the father for little Hans was not coincidental. Instead, there were a number of factors involved. Two such factors were that Hans and his father often played "horse," and that Hans had recently been frightened when he saw a carriage horse fall down. Hans was not particularly distressed by his phobia because by avoiding horses he could successfully avoid his unconscious Oedipal conflict.

Although these dynamic speculations are intriguing, advocates of the learning perspective have severely criticized them and argued that *classical conditioning mechanisms* can more simply account for the development of phobic behavior. As Wolpe and Rachman (1960) argue:

In brief, phobias are regarded as conditioned anxiety (fear) reactions. Any neutral stimulus, simple or complex, that happens to make an impact on an individual at about the time that a fear reaction is evoked acquires the ability to evoke fear subsequently. . . . It is our contention that the incident to which Freud refers as merely the exciting cause of Hans' phobia was in fact, the cause of the entire disorder. The evidence obtained in studies on experimental neurosis in animals and on phobias in children indicate that it is quite possible for one experience to induce a phobia (Wolpe & Rachman, 1960, p. 143–44).

Emmelkamp (1982), however, argues that there is little evidence that classical conditioning is involved in the development of clinical phobias. While it may play a minor role in the development of some specific phobias, he does not believe that the available evidence indicates that it plays any important role in the development of agoraphobia.

Why are phobias involving heights, snakes, or spiders relatively common while phobias involving plastics or filing cabinets are almost nonexistent? Phobias do not develop in a random fashion. There is, according to Marks (1977), a very limited range of objects in relation to which phobias typically occur. Fearing snakes, spiders, dogs, and cats makes evolutionary sense. They are fears that, although exaggerated in some people, have clear survival value.

But this does not rule out a learning explanation for the development of phobias. Instead, the idea of biological preparedness suggests that certain objects may, for biological reasons, be *prepotent targets* for phobias. As Marks (1977) puts it, "Preparedness is the lightning rod that conducts associations selectively along certain nervous pathways rather than others" (p. 192). Thus for phobias at least, the laws of learning may make evolutionary sense. Preparedness to make particular associations goes hand-in-hand with the evolutionary history and survival tactics of the organism. If it is true that some objects are prepotent targets for phobic responses, then it should be easier to condition a fear response to some objects than to others.

Anxiety States

DSM III classifies the following three disorders under anxiety states: generalized anxiety disorder, panic disorder, and obsessive-compulsive disorders. *Generalized anxiety disorder* refers to a state of persistent anxiety that is not attached to a specific object or situation. Symptoms include tension, sweating, trembling, rumination, insomnia, and difficulty in concentrating.

Panic disorder refers to acute attacks of anxiety characterized by intense fear and terror. The onset of the attacks is usually unpredictable. Often the attacks lead to a general fear of many situations.

As Sandra Turner describes it to her psychiatrist, the severe anxiety attacks she's been having for the past six months are close to unbearable: "My chest tightens, my palms sweat, I have a sense of dread and it feels like I'm losing control." The attacks seem to arise spontaneously in a variety of situations where ease of exit is difficult—places like supermarket lines, buses, crowded stores, restaurants, and elevators. "I immediately flee," she tells the doctor. "Even if it means that I have to leave a bag of groceries I'm waiting to pay for."

Mrs. Turner, a 30-year-old marketing executive who had no prior history of psychiatric disorder, was bewildered about her symptoms and worried about the way they had begun affecting her job, her marriage, and her life in general. She'd started to shun restaurants and department stores and was avoiding all situations she associated with attacks of anxiety: places where she could not easily make an immediate exit" (Collins, 1983, p. 15).

Panic attacks can happen unpredictably and may involve heart palpitations, a feeling of unreality, sweating, trembling, and dizziness. These attacks can be extremely distressing and may occur as an early stage of agoraphobia.

Typically, panic attacks begin in early adult life or late adolescence but can, in some instances, occur in midlife. In some cases panic attacks may be limited to a single brief period lasting several weeks or months. In other cases the attacks may recur several times or even become chronic. Fishman and Shean (1985) speculate that some panic disorders result when a hormone or neurotransmitter in the brain that normally regulates anxiety is missing or deficient. This explana-

ANXIETY DISORDERS IN WOMEN

Considerable attention has recently been drawn to the fact that the incidence of anxiety disorders is higher in women than in men. A number of biological and social explanations are emerging to account for these differences. For example, culturally determined gender-role expectations may lead some women with traditional role orientations to feel anxious in nontraditional situations outside the home.

In addition, biological factors are being identified that may be of some importance.

One such factor is the identification of mitral valve prolapse, a disorder of the heart valve in some women that leads to heart palpitations and the "fluttering" feeling associated with anxiety (Emmelkamp, 1982). Mitral valve prolapse can be controlled using drug therapy, but it is emerging as yet another biological factor that may underlie some anxiety states.

tion for panic attacks is highly speculative, but research on the biological aspects of panic attacks is increasing rapidly.

Obsessive-Compulsive Disorders

The song that seems to repeat itself again and again in the back of your mind, the frightening thought that recurs even as you try to shut it out, the little superstition that you half believe. . . . If you have experienced any of these thoughts or feelings, even for a moment, you will understand something about the experience of obsessive-compulsive disorders.

Obsessive-compulsive disorders are extremely rare and are estimated to affect only 1 out of every 2,000 people in the general population (Sturgis & Meyer, 1981). The disorder usually occurs early in adulthood, and as a result social behavior can be markedly impaired. The hallmark of obsessive-compulsive disorders is the experience of persistent thoughts, impulses, or actions. Often they are accompanied by a compulsion to engage in the behavior and a conflicting desire to resist it. These impulses or thoughts are usually

frightening and seem irrational or senseless. At times they may involve recurrent impulses to harm someone, or they may involve sexual fantasies. In some cases they may involve exaggerated concerns with neatness or cleanliness. Consider the following example:

A housewife came for consultation because of sudden impulses to destroy objects which did not measure up to her perfectionistic standards. She tore up wallets and clothing which suddenly seemed to displease her because of some imperfection. If she did not give in to her impulses, she became nervous and jittery. It took her many hours to clean the three rooms of her apartment. Everything had to be in exactly the right place, and often she went to the extreme of measuring the distance between objects on the top of her dressing bureau to see that they were systematically arranged. Often, she had an impulse to soil objects after having cleaned them; for example, after having spent a great deal of time cleaning and polishing the surface of a mirror, she would feel compelled to spit on it and then clean it all over again (Bucklew, 1960, p. 82).

Compulsive handwashing can be a distressing affliction for those who suffer from it. (John Thoeming/Dorsey Press)

The dual term *obsessive-compulsive* may be somewhat misleading. Carr, Lafler, and Carter (1974) note that this term has been traditionally used to identify cases in which *both* recurrent thoughts and repeated actions occur. But Carr argues that in all cases the person is disturbed by a *feeling of loss of control* over his or her own behavior. Let us now turn to some current views about the origins of compulsive disorders.

The dynamic interpretation of obsessive-compulsive disorders suggests that the symptomatic behavior is actually an attempt to control dangerous or unwanted impulses. You may recall in Chapter 2 that the psychoanalytic viewpoint sees symptoms as attempts to reduce anxiety associated with id-ego conflicts. Emmelkamp (1982) suggests that compulsive rituals are apparently maintained by anxiety reduction.

In attempting to understand how learning theorists might account for the development of compulsive behavior, a famous experiment by Skinner (1953) is of interest. Skinner placed hungry pigeons in an experimental cage in which food was automatically presented at regular five-second intervals. He observed the birds' behavior closely and discovered that in six out of eight cases the birds developed clearly defined "ritualistic" or "superstitious" behavior.

One bird, Skinner reported, began to turn counterclockwise in the cage, making two or three turns before receiving the food reinforcement. Another repeatedly thrust its head in one of the upper corners of the cage. These ritualistic responses seemed to develop because the bird happened to be executing a particular response as the food reward appeared. The response tended to be repeated and subsequently to be reinforced again. As Skinner notes, "A few accidental connections between a ritual and a favorable consequence sufficed to set up and maintain the behavior, in spite of many unreinforced instances."

Recently Turner, Beidel, and Nathan (1985) have reviewed the biological research on obsessive-compulsive disorders. They report that there is some evidence for genetic factors in the disorder. What may be inherited is the tendency toward chronic elevated arousal or a tendency to respond in an overaroused fashion. They hypothesize that this state of overarousal may lead obsessive-compulsive individuals to adopt their ritual-like behavior as a way of controlling the aroused state.

SOMATOFORM DISORDERS

The essential feature of *somatoform disorders* are *physical symptoms for which there are no demonstrable organic findings* but in which there is some reason to suspect psychological conflicts or problems. An important feature of somatoform disorders is that the symptoms are not under voluntary control. Despite continual complaints or actual loss of physiological function, upon medical examination there is no evidence of actual or chronic damage.

Let us now turn to the first of the somatoform disorders we will discuss—somatization disorders.

Somatization Disorders

John M. was admitted to a psychiatric hospital after a history of job failure and an unstable family background. He made numerous complaints about his physical health. His concerns began when he experienced a swelling of his glands, which led him to seek help from numerous doctors, all of whom gave him treatments, but no treatment yielded relief. Ultimately his physical complaints became so severe that he was unable to work. He is a friendly, pleasant, docile person who expresses deep concern about his physical health. He reports that he believes his sex glands are infected; he has a hernia, suffers from constipation, and has continuous feelings of tightness and pain in his abdomen. In discussing his physical health, he shows deep preoccupation, but later on another topic seems relatively indifferent and even cheerful.

The essential features of this disorder are "recurrent and multiple somatic complaints for which medical attention is sought but that are not apparently due to any physical disorder, beginning before early adulthood (prior to age 25), and having a chronic but fluctuating course" (DSM III, 1980, p. 241).

This disorder has as its most striking clinical feature the fact that the person is continuously preoccupied with fears that he or she is suffering from some physical disease. Such individuals are occupied with their own bodily health and are con-

stantly observing their own bodily functioning with the expectation that a symptom will appear.

It is not uncommon with people suffering from a somatization disorder to go from physician to physician with the conviction that they are suffering from a physical disorder. While most of us would be relieved to hear from a physician that our concerns about the possibility of a physical disease are unfounded, the person with a somatization disorder remains unconvinced and will continue to "shop around" for a physician to confirm his/her suspicion or fear.

It is important to distinguish between somatization disorders and the more bizarre physical complaints sometimes seen in psychotic disorders. Often persons with a somatization disorder will know a fair amount about the physical symptomatology of a particular disease and may even feel that they know more about their disorder than the examining physician.

The life pattern of persons displaying a somatization disorder may reflect not only a continuous preoccupation with physical symptoms but also a continuing pattern of failure in school or work partly attributed to the alleged disease.

In many cases a continued preoccupation with bodily disorders may serve a variety of purposes. It may provide sympathetic attention and an opportunity to avoid life's challenges and to rationalize feelings of inadequacy or failure. Many of us have experienced the temptation to rationalize a loss in an athletic contest on the basis of a pain in our leg or some other physical complaint. In the case of somatization disorders, this motivation is presumably much more pronounced.

Thus in its milder forms this disorder may affect all of us as a part of the "psychopathology of everyday life." It is a form of adaptation to the uncertainties, anxieties, and threats we encounter every day. Our cultural norms excuse people suffering from physical illness from many of the obligations of everyday life. Thus for some people a somatization disorder may serve an important adaptive function.

Conversion Disorders

A second major type of somatoform disorders is the *conversion disorder*. You will recall that the primary focus of somatization disorders is the preoccupation with physical symptoms of disease where no real disability can be found. Conversion disorders, on the other hand, actually involve some form of physical impairment but have no known organic basis. The clinical picture of the client is very different from that of the client suffering somatization disorders. There will be an observed physical disorder such as paralysis, blindness, or deafness, but the person may appear relatively indifferent to it.

Woolsey (1976) has suggested that persons suffering from hysterical disorders tend to show four major psychological characteristics. First, they tend to be extremely *suggestible*. In many cases hysterical symptoms can be made to disappear if the person treating the sufferer is able to provide a convincing treatment. This *placebo effect* may be accomplished by religious faith healing, hypnosis, or the administration of inactive sugar pills.

Second, and perhaps most important, the conversion symptoms, whether they involve paralysis, visual impairment, or loss of feeling in some limb, do not correspond to the pattern of loss one would expect if there were actual organic damage. This is perhaps the single most important distinguishing feature of hysterical disorders.

Third, Woolsey notes that often people suffering from the disorder display what Charcot first termed *la belle indifférence*. That is, they seem totally unworried and indifferent to their physical symptoms. This sometimes occurs in people suffering from a chronic severe disease, however, and is not always a reliable indicator of conversion disorders.

Finally, many people suffering from conversion disorders appear to be obtaining *secondary gains* in the form of sympathy or attention as a result of their symptoms. This characteristic is not unique to hysterical disorders but can often be found in cases of somatization disorder.

Typically, conversion disorders are expressed either through the sensory system or the motor system. Let us examine some of the typical conversion disorders that occur in each of these systems. The three typical forms of sensory conversion disorders are complete loss or partial loss of vision, hearing, or sensation in the skin. It is much less common to observe sensory symptoms involving smell or taste.

In the case of the loss of skin sensation (anesthesia), the person no longer feels pain or perhaps any sensation in the affected part of the body. Often this lack of sensation will be restricted to one part of the body, and these types of anesthesia are typically called *glove anesthesias* or *stocking anesthesias* because they occur in parts of the body that *make psychological sense* rather than *physiological sense*. The patient's idea of nerve supply is what seems to produce the area of insensitivity rather than the actual area of the skin affected by sensory nerves (see Figure 7-1). This clearly shows that the anesthesia is psychological rather than physiological in nature.

Visual conversion symptoms are also sometimes reported. The person will appear to be unable to see certain objects, particularly those of psychological significance. Sometimes only a portion of the visual field will be affected, but this will occur in ways that do not correspond with the neurological

FIGURE 7-1
Example of Glove Anesthesia (a Conversion Disorder) and Pattern of Anesthesia That Would Occur If Actual Neurological Damage Were Involved

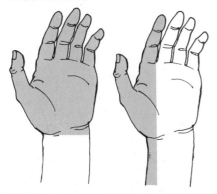

structure of the visual system. In wartime, following the extreme stress of combat, people may suffer from conversion blindness as a way of expressing their refusal to continue to watch the terrifying features of combat.

Hearing may also be affected by conversion symptoms. People appear to listen selectively in any case. Many conversion reactions appear to be exaggerations of this tendency.

The motor system may also be affected in several ways in conversion disorders. Perhaps least serious is a tic. A *tic* is an involuntary twitching or movement of the muscles in some part of the extremities or face or head. A twitching of the corner of the mouth or the winking of an eyelid are fairly common forms of a tic. These movements are automatic and usually occur without the individual being aware of them.

Perhaps the most dramatic form of motor conversion disorder is that of *paralysis*. The onset of conversion paralysis can be sudden and dramatic. The individuals seem literally to be paralyzed—a development that in many cases prevents them from engaging in some frightening or unpleasant task. A form of this disorder is "writer's cramp." In order to avoid confronting the psychological risks associated with writing, some people develop a conversion symptom—a cramp of the hand that makes it impossible to write, thus escaping the threatening task of committing themselves to paper (and perhaps experiencing rejection from an editor).

More severe forms of conversion paralysis may involve the paralysis of both legs or other limbs. The function of hysterical paralysis would appear to be to disengage people from unpleasant tasks or experiences they otherwise would have to confront.

Although we have pointed out that conversion disorders in both the motor and sensory systems do not involve actual organic impairment, there is always the possibility that organic damage may really exist in cases misdiagnosed as conversion disorders. Stefansson et al. (1976) found that, after evaluating the records of several hundreds of people suffering from conversion disorders, most had real physical disorders along with their conversion symptoms. He speculated that real organic disorders can, in some cases, help trigger or suggest additional psychological complaints or pains. Thus we must be careful to distinguish between psychologically induced conversion disorders and organic disorders that appear psychological in nature. It may be that many people who actually have organic or physical problems may have been diagnosed as conversion disorders and therefore have not received proper treatment.

DISSOCIATIVE DISORDERS

According to DSM III, the essential feature of dissociative disorders is *a sudden and usually temporary change in the normal functions of consciousness, identity, or motor behavior.* The person may develop a sudden

DIAGNOSING A CONVERSION DISORDER

Kate Fox, an adolescent of 13 years of age, was admitted to a hospital complaining of extreme nervousness, a partial paralysis of the left leg, and marked loss of appetite. She had had an excellent record of health up to approximately nine months before her admission. At that time her left leg suddenly became paralyzed while Kate was in school, and she felt as if needles were pricking it. She was put to bed, and after a week in a local hospital showed a partial recovery, although she continued to use crutches and lose weight.

Careful clinical examination showed that Kate displayed muscle twitches around her throat and chest but was able to use her left leg when lying down; therefore, organic disease was ruled out as a possible cause of her problem.

When given a psychological interview, Kate described the paralysis, lack of appetite, and other facts of her illness with intelligence and sensitivity, but she was unable to give any explanation for her problem. After considerable probing she told a story of family conflict in which her mother fell in love with a roomer in the home and eloped. Numerous parental conflicts ensued. It was a terrifying experience for Kate. She was particularly terrified by the idea of strife and bitterness in her once happy home.

School was a welcome relief from this strain in her home life, but soon she became fearful in social situations. Her paralysis occurred one day right before recess. Apparently the threat of social interaction and the potential conflict that might ensue led her to develop a paralysis that would allow her to remain in school but avoid the frightening possibility of social interaction.

After long discussions of the meaning of her symptoms, Kate showed a slow but steady recovery from her paralysis and is now functioning normally in her home and school setting (adapted from Pronko, 1963, pp. 169–71).

DSM III lists a number of criteria for distinguishing a conversion disorder from other disorders. Several are listed below. Examine them and decide whether you think Kate Fox was suffering from a conversion disorder or not.

- A loss or alteration of physical functioning, suggesting a physical disorder.
- Psychological factors are judged to be etiologically involved in the symptom, that is, either a temporal relationship between a psychologically meaningful event and the initiation of the symptom or symptoms allows the individual to avoid a noxious activity, or the symptom allows the individual to get support from the environment that otherwise would not be available.
- Symptom is *not* under voluntary control.
- Failure to explain symptom by a known physical disorder after investigation.

inability to recall events or personal information, may engage in unexpected travel and assume a new identity, or may seem to develop two or more distinct personalities. In this section we will consider several types of dissociative disorders and their characteristic features.

Psychogenic Amnesia

Joseph L. woke up one morning in what appeared to be a strange place. He had no memory of who he was or who was lying in the bed next to him. He appeared bewildered and confused. He was suffering from a dissociative disorder, *amnesia.*

A loss of memory with no organic involvement is one of the most common forms of dissociative disorders (DSM III, 1980). Typically the person is unable to recall events or people associated with his or her personal identity. Episodes of amnesia may last a few hours or days, or in some cases weeks or months. When stopped by the police or interviewed by a mental health professional, the person may appear to be dazed and mildly confused.

Victims of dissociative reactions involving amnesia usually are experiencing intense emotional conflict or stress in their social, sexual, or economic life. They literally appear to be escaping from their distressing and conflict-ridden experience by forgetting who they are.

Fugue

Steve had just taken on a challenging new job in a law firm. It had not been going well. One day he disappeared from his apartment and did not report to work. Two weeks later his parents, who had hired a private detective agency, located him working as a dishwasher in a restaurant in a nearby city. He had no recollection of his previous identity and had been drifting from job to job. Steve was suffering from a dissociative disorder known as *fugue.*

In the case of fugue, which may be thought of as a special form of amnesia, victims not only forget their own identity and other significant events in their lives but actually flee their life circumstances. In many cases the person may move to another city some distance from home, and in some cases a secondary personality appears that has little or nothing to do with the person's previous life. The person may change his or her name and carry on an entirely new lifestyle for some time.

In one recorded case (Kisker, 1964), a 22-year-old man disappeared from his fishing boat in Florida and was assumed dead by his family. Six years later he telephoned his brother to say that he had been working in a convalescent home in New Orleans as an orderly and had suddenly remembered his name. He had no memory of what had transpired during the six years since he had left his home in Florida.

Multiple Personality

"Christine is a loving three year old who likes to draw pictures of flowers and butterflies. David is a withdrawn little boy who bangs his head against the wall when upset. Adelena is a young lesbian. These distinct personalities, along with at least seven others, presented a bizarre puzzle in a Columbus, Ohio, courtroom; they all exist within the same individual—William Milligan, 23, who was accused of rape. Last week after a brief trial, the 10 faces of Billy were found not guilty by reason of insanity" *(Newsweek,* December 18, 1978, p. 106). William Milligan is an apparent suffer of a dissociative disorder known as *multiple personality.*

Perhaps the best-known form of dissociative disorder is that of multiple personality. We should note that in popular literature, this disorder is often confused with schizophrenia, but it is a very different disorder. Whereas multiple personality typically involves an alternation between two or more relatively well-defined personalities, schizophrenia refers to a much more severe psychotic disorder in which thought disorder, blunted affect, and severe reality distortion predominate.

The most famous case of multiple personality was documented in Thigpen and Cleckley's book *The Three Faces of Eve* (1954). Thigpen and Cleckley reported different personalities associated with "Eve Black," who typically was flamboyant and uninhibited, and "Eve White," a much more quiet, inhibited, and serious person.

Eve White began to suspect that something was going on when Eve Black would engage in carefree spending, promiscuity, and drinking that later Eve White would have to account for. During her treatment a third personality called "Jane" emerged who was aware of the activities and personality of both Eve White and Eve Black. Finally, a fourth personality developed—one that seemed more stable than either of the three earlier versions.

More recently Jeans (1976) has documented a case of multiple personality in very great detail. Jeans, who had treated this person in therapy for some time, was able to document the strikingly different personalities that emerged as "Gena," "Mary," and "Evelyn." Subsequent to Jeans' discovery and documentation of this case, Osgood, Luria, and Smith (1976) attempted to do a blind analy-

Though extremely rare, cases of multiple personality have been documented in recent years.
(Jean-Claude Lejeune)

sis and interpretation of the strikingly different personalities displayed by Gena, through data collected using the semantic differential.

When Osgood, Luria, and Smith (1976) attempted to do a careful analysis and interpretation of these semantic differential reports collected by Jeans, they found surprising concurrence between Jeans' clinical reports and their own interpretations.

Ludolph's (1982) recent analysis of the multiple personality literature provides some insight into factors associated with the formation of this dissociative disorder. According to her analysis, mothers of multiple personalities tend to be rejecting, unprotective, and depressed while fathers tend to be distant, rigid, alcoholic, and often abusive. In 18 percent of the cases reviewed, the person experienced the death of a parent when the patient was very young. Moreover, many of the other multiple personalities were abandoned or separated from their parents when the patients were young.

Perhaps the most striking finding was the inordinately high rate of early physical and sexual abuse among multiple personalities. Approximately 56 percent of all the reported cases had experienced sexual abuse either at the hands of a relative or a nonrelative. Ludolph notes that this sadistic assault must be experienced by the child as a severe blow to the sense of self. Unable to integrate this experience into his or her self-image, the child may retreat into a dissociative state that allows him or her to deny the traumatic event. The retreat into dissociative functioning may also enable the child to defend against the violence and hatred he or she feels toward the abusive adult.

It is interesting that multiple personality, while still extremely rare, has been diagnosed more frequently in recent years. The reason for this increase is unclear. One possibility is that the overall prevalence has remained constant but that it is observed more because greater attention is being paid to diagnosis. Another possibility is that there actually are more cases of multiple personality as a result of societal changes that foster the formation of multiple identities. A third possibility is that therapists are actually creating the disorder they subsequently diagnose. Ludolph (1982) notes that therapists may foster multiple personality in vulnerable individuals in a number of ways. For example, the therapist might help create multiple personalities by naming various identities of the patient or by suggesting to a hypnotized patient that there are unknown personalities within him or her.

TREATMENT STRATEGIES

The treatment of anxiety, somatoform, and dissociative disorders has been undertaken using a wide variety of methods, including individual and group psychotherapy (Chapters 16 and 18), the prescription of tranquilizing drugs (Chapter 19), and behavioral techniques (Chapter 17).

In our current discussion we will focus on several methods of treating specific anxiety-related complaints, including phobias, obsessions, and compulsions.

Psychodynamic Approach

Because anxiety is seen as a signal of unconscious conflict, treatment of the anxiety reaction in psychodynamic psychotherapy is secondary to uncovering the underlying dynamics. The assumption is that when the deeper cause is uncovered, the anxiety, which is the superficial manifestation of the conflict, will disappear. Moreover, the psychodynamic view argues that treatment of the presenting problem alone, while eliminating the initial complaint, is ultimately unsuccessful. Although its outward manifestation may change, the symptom will continue in altered form because the underlying conflict has been left unresolved.

Treatment of the phobic or anxious patient requires modification in the traditional psychoanalytic techniques. Salzman (1982) argues that instead of being silent and anonymous, the therapist needs to be expressive and participate more actively in the therapy. Otherwise, the patient may gain intellectual but little emotional insight into his or her problems. When an emotional understanding of the underlying conflict is lacking, little real change is possible.

MacKinnon and Michels (1971) maintain that the therapist must facilitate the patient's understanding of his or her anxiety. As often there is a fear of going crazy, initially the therapist is reassuring. In addition, the therapist helps the person recognize his or her emotions and the hypothesized relation between underlying feelings and the presenting symptoms. The phobic person may be reluctant to give up his or her fears because of the secondary gains involved. Thus an important part of the treatment is the exploration of what the person will lose by giving up the phobia. For example, the phobia may allow the gratification of dependency needs, since others may be involved in helping the person avoid certain objects or situations. Because of the secondary gain involved, removal of the presenting symptom is said to result often in depression. Ironically, the appearance of depression in such cases is perceived as an indication of progress.

Learning and Behavioral Approaches

Whereas the psychodynamic approach views anxiety as a symptom of underlying conflict, the behavioral approach maintains that the anxiety itself is the problem. Thus the behavior therapist is concerned primarily with eliminating the presenting symptoms.

The two major behavioral techniques for treating anxiety disorders are *flooding* and *systematic desensitization.* Flooding is a type of anxiety-inducing training that involves exposing the individual to an anxiety-eliciting stimulus while preventing the occurrence of escape or avoidance responses. Continued contact with those situations that evoke discomfort is assumed to bring about relief through the principle of extinction (Rimm & Masters, 1979).

While flooding maximizes the anxiety experienced, systematic desensitization attempts to keep anxiety at a minimum during treatment. This technique involves pairing relaxation with imagined scenes depicting situations that the person has indicated as causing him or her to feel anxious. The idea is to eliminate the anxiety reaction by counterconditioning a response (relaxation) antagonistic to it (Wolpe, 1981).

You will recall from our discussion of phobias earlier in this chapter that Marks described what he called the *evoking stimulus* as the critical factor in identifying the development of phobias. In essence, the principle of exposure in treatment argues that relief from phobias and compulsions occurs when the person suffering from them maintains continued contact with those situations that evoke discomfort until the discomfort subsides (Marks, 1977).

Marks goes on to argue that most behavioral approaches to the treatment of anxiety syndromes employ the principle of exposure in one form or another, regardless of the specific technique. Of course, the exposure principle does not explain why improvement occurs but only indicates the strategy which the therapist may follow.

Emmelkamp (1982) offers a *cognitive-expectancy* model to explain why exposure is an effective treatment for a number of phobias and anxiety disorders. Expectation that therapeutic gain is possible is an important component, but even more important is self-observation of improvement. When the client is exposed to phobic stimuli either in imagination or in an actual situation, observing his or her own improvement has a powerful therapeutic effect in itself.

Biological Approaches

The biological perspective distinguishes between anxiety disorders that involve panic attacks and those that do not. Disorders involving panic respond well to treatment by the antidepressant medication *imipramine*. Investigators hypothesize that the drug works by inhibiting firing action in nerve pathways thought to be the panic center in the brain. The antidepressant presumably makes the person less susceptible to attacks by raising his or her panic threshold (Collins, 1983). Although imipramine does block panic, it does not affect the anticipatory anxiety or avoidance behavior associated with most phobias.

Persons who will benefit from drug treatment are identified by testing their susceptibility to an infusion of sodium lactate. Klein has found that intravenous solutions of sodium lactate will stimulate panic attacks in patients with a history of panic attacks but not controls. Although this effect is not well understood, Klein speculates that the sodium lactate disturbs the body's metabolic homeostasis, or acid-base balance (Weisman, 1983).

Klein believes that panic disorders may be related to the action of a primitive biological separation-anxiety mechanism. Such a mechanism serves an evolutionary function by triggering strong anxiety in young children separated from their mothers. Separation anxiety thus had great survival value because the child's screams would lead to its rescue by the mother. Supporting this view is the fact that many persons who experience panic attacks as adults have experienced acute separation anxiety as children. While proposing a biological predisposition to difficulties in the childhood experience of separation anxiety, Klein also acknowledges that the child's early experiences with separation also play an important role in the development of panic attacks.

SUMMARY

In this chapter we have taken a broad look at psychological disorders characterized by anxiety-specific physical complaints and dissociative disorders. According to DSM III, anxiety disorders can be divided into the separate categories of phobias and anxiety states. Phobias involve intense fears that lead to the avoidance of certain objects or situations. While avoiding the feared object is often successful for specific phobias, this strategy results in a constricted, fearful lifestyle in the case of agoraphobia. For agoraphobic persons so many different situations are feared that without treatment they may eventually reach the point where they cannot leave the safety of their own homes.

The second major category of anxiety disorders is anxiety states. Panic disorders involve acute attacks of extreme, debilitating anxiety while generalized anxiety disorder involves a pervasive, generalized state of anxiety. Obsessive-compulsive disorders, in contrast, are more similar to phobias in that by performing the obsession or compulsion the person is able to avoid feeling anxious. However, while giving in to the obsession or compulsion offers immediate relief from anxiety, the obsessive-compulsive person's life may become more and more routinized and constricted. In fact, the compulsion or obsession may be so compelling and time-consuming that the person may literally spend hours of his or her day engaging in a certain repetitive behavior.

We also discussed the somatoform disorders and noted that they can take two distinctively different forms. On the one hand, continuous preoccupation about physical health can be socially crippling, whereas conversion disorders involve some form of physical impairment such as paralysis or anesthesia but with no known organic cause. The symptoms prominent in conversion disorders may either be sensory, that is, involving a loss of vision or hearing, or motor, that is, involving a loss of movement or the development of paralysis.

Dissociative disorders are characterized by a sudden, and usually temporary, change in the normal functions of consciousness, identity, or motor behavior. Although such problems are technically not adjustment disorders, most authorities agree that the dissociative state results from the person's attempt to cope with a major stressor. Of the dissociative disorders, multiple personality is perhaps the most puzzling. While the exact cause of this disorder is not known, recent research points to the role of early physical or sexual abuse. This finding implies that future research on stress and coping should explore the different effects of stress and trauma at different stages in the life cycle.

Treatment of the anxiety disorders raises important questions. While antidepressant drugs are successful in treating acute anxiety reactions known as panic attacks, they are not effective in dealing with anticipatory anxiety or phobic avoidance behaviors. Instead, most phobic and obsessive-compulsive disorders are treated in psychotherapy. Depending on the orientation of the therapist, treatment may either consist of a short intervention aimed at relieving the presenting problem or of a long psychotherapy aimed at uncovering the unconscious conflicts that underlie the presenting symptoms. Behavioral therapists argue that because anxiety is so painful and debilitating it is unethical not to strive first for symptom relief. Backing their argument is research demonstrating behavioral techniques to be highly successful in treating many phobic disorders. On the other hand, psychodynamic therapists argue that treating the symptoms without resolving the underlying problem is a band-aid approach that will only result in symptom substitution. Thus psychodynamic therapists question the validity of the behaviorist's statistics, claiming that symptom relief is only a temporary solution to long-term conflicts.

Part Three

The Major Disorders: Affective Disorders and Schizophrenia

8

Affective Disorders and Suicide: Description, Research, and Treatment

Depression
Clinical Picture

Manic Episodes
Clinical Picture

Classification of Affective Disorders
Bipolar Disorders
Major Depression

Theories of Depression
Psychoanalytic Theory
Biological Theories
Cognitive Theories
An Interpersonal Perspective

Treatment of Affective Disorders
Biological Treatments
Psychotherapy

Suicide
Factors Associated with Suicide Risk
The Predictors of Suicide
Suicidal Intention and Ideation

Summary

INTRODUCTION

Imagine for a moment that you are a clinical psychologist interviewing someone who has just come to you for help. The young man sitting across from you finds it hard to talk about what is bothering him. At first his conversation was animated, but now as he continues to talk, his voice flattens into a monotone. His face loses its expression and becomes masklike, suggesting the despair below the surface.

As the hour goes on, you begin to get a picture of his life. He maintains a pleasant, active facade only at great personal cost. Even the simplest activities, like dressing or driving to work, have become enormous acts of will. He reports difficulty sleeping, and, unaccountably, he wakes before dawn each day. Frequently at night this man withdraws into his apartment, refusing to answer the telephone. He lies listlessly for hours in front of the television set. Lately, he reports, he has begun to think about suicide.

As you listen to him, you are struck by several things. His mood is obviously downcast and occasionally tears well up in his eyes. His thinking seems pessimistic, and he frequently talks about himself in a disparaging way. The stains on his suit and his rumpled appearance suggest that he no longer cares as much as he once did about his appearance. The bagginess of his suit also suggests that he has lost a fair amount of weight

recently. His world is gray and bleak, not very promising.

As you sit there, listening, you begin to notice your own reactions to this man. First you notice your own mood. The world seems less exciting to you, too, now, and you feel somewhat depressed. As time goes on, you begin to feel some mild irritation with this person. His apparent inability to "shake off" his feeling of sadness and his lack of response to your encouragements are frustrating and vaguely annoying.

You have just interviewed a person suffering from the typical symptoms of a moderately severe depression. Depression has been called the "common cold" of psychological disorders, and over a quarter of a million Americans are hospitalized for the disorder each year. The chances are about one in five that each of us will suffer at least one severe depression during our lifetime. Students, musicians, laborers, physicists, clerks, psychiatrists, and housewives all are subject to depression. Lincoln and Hemingway, F. Scott Fitzgerald and Sylvia Plath all suffered from severe depression.

Return to your clinician's chair again and consider another man. You are jolted by the fact that the person now in your office seems filled with almost boundless energy. He cannot stay in his chair and paces up and down. He is gesturing as he talks about his plans for the future. His speech is rapid and filled with puns and jokes. He winks at you occasionally. This man seems to have no problems at all. On the contrary, he is filled with optimistic plans for the future. As you listen you discover that he is a salesman at a local automobile dealership and has decided to open his own agency. He has simultaneously borrowed money from at least four different banks, has rented a large warehouse, and has hired a number of salespersons for his agency. As you listen, you are astonished to hear that even though this agency is not yet open for business, he is now planning to develop a statewide network of automobile dealerships.

At several points you try to interrupt his seemingly endless flow of speech to ask some questions. But he brushes the questions aside and becomes mildly annoyed when you ask him why he is consulting you. Finally, you discover that his wife, who is very distressed at his current behavior, has convinced him to see a clinician because he has plunged his family deeply into debt. Slowly, as the interview proceeds, you notice that his rapid speech reveals sudden changes in the content of his thoughts. This flight of ideas makes it hard to follow his line of thought, but clearly he sees himself as a perceptive, powerful, and engaging person. His energy seems endless and at the end of 50 minutes you are at a loss as to how to terminate the interview.

Reflecting on your own feelings and reactions to this man, you begin to feel sympathy for his family, who must struggle not to be swept up in his barrage of projects, ideas, schemes, and sudden shifts of interest. You sympathize, too, with his wife's concerns about his apparently thoughtless squandering of their financial resources. His wife reports that he has slept only an hour or two a night for the last 10 days and yet he seems as full of energy as ever.

This person is displaying what is known as a *manic episode*. As we shall see, the ex-

tremely intense level of motor activity, sleeplessness, boundless energy, and grandiose ideas that characterize a manic episode are a second important form of affective disorder.

The two cases seem in some ways to be polar opposites. And yet, as we shall see in this and the next chapter, there may be common threads that bind these two apparently different disorders together. In both instances we will be trying to make sense of behavior that involves the *affect* or emotional tone of the individual.

In this chapter we will consider several approaches to the description, classification, treatment, and theoretical understanding of *affective disorders*. In addition, we will examine the act of suicide,* which is sometimes, but not invariably, associated with affective disturbance.

DEPRESSION

Clinical Picture

The essential feature of depressive episodes is a depressed mood or a generalized feeling of a loss of interest or pleasure in the world. In addition, the person may experience a sleep disturbance involving either an increase or decrease in sleep, feel unable to eat, lose weight, and have a feeling of decreased energy and a subjective sense of worthlessness or guilt. At times some depressed people have thoughts of death or suicide.

Often a person experiencing a depressive episode will begin to withdraw from family and friends and may appear agitated. The person may ceaselessly pace up and down, wring his or her hands, or pull at the skin, hair, or clothing.

The depressed person often reports feeling unable to concentrate; his or her thinking is slowed, and he/she is unable to act decisively.

---

*The authors wish to thank Howard Beazel for providing some of the background research material for the section on suicide.

Depression can be particularly incapacitating for older people. (Romie Flanagan/Image Finders, Chicago)

TABLE 8–1
DSM III Symptom Criteria for a Depressive Episode

A. Loss of interest or pleasure in nearly all activities or past times. Dysphoric mood that is characterized as depressed, sad, blue, hopeless, etc.
Does not include rapid mood shifts and must be prominent in the behavior pattern.

B. At least four of the following symptoms are required for the diagnosis of a depressive symptom:

1. Poor appetite or weight loss or increased appetite or weight gain.
2. Sleeping too much or too little.
3. Feelings of fatigue, tiredness, and loss of energy.
4. Agitation or actual physical slowing down of behavior.
5. Loss of interest or pleasure in usual activity or decrease in sexual motivation.
6. Feelings of inappropriate guilt or self-blame.
7. Complaint of a decreased ability to think or concentrate or other indications of indecisiveness.
8. Recurring thoughts of suicide or death, or any suicidal behavior, including the wish to be dead.

At times even the smallest task may seem difficult or impossible. In severe cases the person will burst into tears without warning, become extremely preoccupied with physical health or his or her financial status.

The DSM III diagnostic criteria for a depressed episode are shown in Table 8–1. Note that the DSM III criteria require that at least one week from the time of the first noticeable change in the person's usual condition occurs before one can diagnose a depressive episode. Moreover, the criteria require that schizophrenic or organic disorders be ruled out.

The symptoms of depression are vividly described in a writer's personal account of the onset of a depressive episode:

Then, inexplicably, I began to witness puzzling changes in myself. I found it harder and harder to concentrate and often struggled at my typewriter for an entire day without finishing a single sentence. Disjointed thoughts darted through my mind like marionettes being jerked across a stage. I'd stand in front of my closet, unable to decide which slacks and sweater to put on. Whereas only months before I'd wandered happily through Casablanca's teeming Kasbah, the thought of a 15-minute bus ride downtown overwhelmed me. "A stranger has invaded my body," I wrote in my journal, on a glorious April morning when the sun flooded the sky with light, giving it the look of polished opal. Usually such a day made me feel exultant, but now it only pointed up an inner darkness. And there were other signs of trouble as well. The very thought of food sickened me.

After having tried for months to lose 5 pounds, 10 suddenly melted off. Always a sound sleeper, my rest became fitful. I tossed for hours, sometimes never closing my eyes. Even when I did eventually fall asleep, I'd wake at four or five in the morning—heart pounding, jaws clenched, eyes frozen open—gripped with a generalized feeling of terror. I was afraid, too, of being alone—me, a person who'd always craved solitude. Though never a moody type, tidal waves of sadness washed over me without warning. I wanted to cry, but no tears came. (Bates, 1983, p. 150).

Depressive disorders can begin at any age, including childhood. The symptoms may develop gradually over days or weeks or be relatively sudden in onset. The degree to which a depressive episode can impair the functioning of the person can be quite variable, but some interference almost always is noted. In the most extreme cases, a person may be unable to feed or cloth himself or herself, function socially, or even take care of personal health needs. As we will see, the most serious complication of depressive episodes is suicide, and the likelihood of serious suicidal attempts increases with age.

Epidemiological studies indicate that 18 to 23 percent of the females in Western countries will experience a depressive episode at some time in their life, whereas approximately 8 to 11 percent of the males will experience such an episode (DSM III, p. 217).

Of course, many individuals who suffer from depression never seek professional help for their difficulties. In fact, one of the most common patterns of behavior for individuals suffering from anxiety and depression is the use of alcohol or other drugs, such as sedatives, to temporarily relieve the insomnia and feelings of depression and helplessness they experience. Since the use of sedatives or alcohol can have the temporary effect of reducing feelings of depression and insomnia,

The use of alcohol frequently occurs as a kind of "self-medication" for depression. (Charles Harbutt/Magnum Photos, Inc.)

they tend to be used increasingly as the symptoms return. Soon a person who was originally experiencing a mild depression may also begin to experience the complications associated with alcoholism or habitual drug abuse. Furthermore, the disorder may be diagnosed as alcoholism when, in fact, the original problem may have been depression.

MANIC EPISODES

Clinical Picture

As we suggested earlier, the essential feature of a manic episode is a distinct period in a patient's life when his or her mood becomes elevated and expansive. Frequently a person

WOMEN'S ROLES AND DEPRESSION

Careful studies of the incidence of depression suggest that women are more prone to depression than men. Let us consider some possible reasons for this finding. One possibility is that women are simply more willing to admit to the experience of depression than men. This would suggest that the differences observed in previous studies have only to do with our willingness to engage in self-disclosure. Involutional melancholia, a depressive disorder that commonly affects women at the age of menopause and is presumed to be, in part, a metabolic disorder, could account for some of the differences, although psychological and physiological changes also occur at the time of the male menopause or climacteric.

But recently social scientists have begun to advance a very different kind of explanation for the higher incidence of depression among women. This explanation is based on the *social role* into which women have traditionally been cast and the role's effects on one's sense of optimism or hopelessness. Jessie Bernard (1976) has suggested that several aspects of the female sex role can lead to depression. Traditionally the woman's subservient role in marriage, lower socioeconomic status, and sense of vulnerability all can predispose her to depression.

Furthermore, in much of our culture, the expectations and perceptions of women's roles are changing. New standards for achievement and independence can clash strikingly with the actual situation in which women, and mothers in particular, may find themselves. This change in social expectations can often intensify women's sense of helplessness.

This way of thinking about the relationship between sex roles and depression implies possible prevention strategies for depression in women. As socialization practices regarding sex roles change, the incidence of depression among women may be reduced.

One of the most interesting lines of research evidence to support these ideas comes from a careful study of depressed women conducted by Weissman and

Increasingly women are engaging in more active work roles. (Ray Ellis/Photo Researchers, Inc.)

Paykel (1974). They found that among women who were clinically depressed, those who worked outside the home were often able to continue in their jobs and showed less impairment than women whose activities were confined to the home. Weissman and Paykel suggest that outside occupation may have a protective effect on people vulnerable to depression. After all, having a job outside the home provides a separate arena in which women can find rewards and cope with their world. If this is true, the "protective effect" of an outside job may also be a contributing factor to the lower incidence of men who seek treatment for depression.

suffering from a manic episode will appear hyperactive and excessively involved in activities, with no apparent concern for the consequences to others. The person will feel euphoric and appear excessively cheerful. This quality can alternate with periods of irritability, particularly when the person's goals are frustrated. Frequently the person will be involved in extensive and sometimes grandiose planning of occupational, sexual, religious, or political activities.

Such persons are often quite sociable and extroverted in their appearance. DSM III suggests:

Almost invariably there is increased sociability such as renewing old acquaintances or calling friends at all hours of the night. The intrusive, domineering, and demanding nature of these interactions is not recognized by the individual. Frequently expansiveness, grandiosity, lack of judgment regarding possible consequences lead to such activities as buying sprees, reckless driving, foolish business investments, and sexual behavior unusual for the individual. Often the activities have a disorganized, flamboyant or bizarre quality; for example, dressing up in strange, colorful garments, wearing excessive or poorly applied makeup, and distributing bread, candy, money, and advice to passing strangers (DSM III, 1980, p. 206).

These behavior patterns are often accompanied by speech that is loud, rapid, and sometimes difficult to interpret. People ex-

periencing manic episodes frequently appear very witty and are fond of puns, jokes, and plays on words. In addition, the manic individual may be easily distracted by irrelevant events in his or her environment. The person will also often display an uncritical self-confidence. Ambitious projects will be taken on, and a person experiencing a manic episode will feel no reluctance to offer advice to anyone who will listen. Sleep disturbances are also a characteristic of manic episodes; during an episode the individual may go for several days without sleep or wake well before the usual time, full of energy.

Fieve (1976), in a recent book on affective disorders, quotes one of his patients, a 45-year-old housewife, as she describes her manic depressive moodswing:

When I start going into a high, I no longer feel like an ordinary housewife. Instead I feel organized and accomplished and I begin to feel I am my most creative self. I can write poetry easily. I can compose melodies without effort. I can paint. My mind feels facile and absorbs everything. I have countless ideas about improving the conditions of mentally retarded children, of how a hospital for these children should be run, what they should have around them to keep them happy and calm and unafraid. I see myself as being able to accomplish a great deal for the good of people. I have countless ideas about how the environment problem could inspire a crusade for the health and betterment of everyone. I feel able to accomplish a great deal for the good of my family and others. I feel pleasure, a sense of euphoria or elation. I want it to last forever. I don't seem to need much sleep. I've lost weight and feel healthy and I like myself. I've just bought six new dresses, in fact, and they look quite good on me. I feel sexy and men stare at me. Maybe I'll have an affair, or perhaps several. I feel capable of speaking and doing good in politics. I would like to help people with problems similar to mine so they won't feel hopeless.

It's wonderful when you feel like this. . . . The feeling of exhilaration—the high mood—makes me feel light and full of the joy of living. However, when I go beyond this stage, I become manic, and the creativeness becomes so magnified I begin to see things in my mind that aren't real. For instance, one night I created an entire movie, complete with cast, that I still think would be terrific. I saw the people as clearly as if watching them in real life. I also experienced complete terror, as if it were actually happening, when I knew that an assassination scene was about to take place. I cowered under the covers and became a complete shaking wreck. As you know, I went into a manic psychosis at that point. My screams awakened my husband, who tried to reassure me that we were in our bedroom and everything was the same. There was nothing to be afraid of. Nevertheless, I was admitted to the hospital the next day (Fieve, 1976, pp. 17–18).

Manic episodes usually begin after age 30—typically with a rapid increase in symptoms over the period of a few days. Some people appear to have episodes separated by many years and then have a cluster or series of episodes, one following rapidly after the other.

A manic episode can produce problems in social and occupational functioning, and substance abuse may accompany a manic episode. Because the individual's judgment is impaired, he or she may also incur financial losses or run into trouble with the law. The proportion of the population experiencing manic disorders is not known. It is a relatively rare phenomenon when occurring without a depressive mood swing following it.

CLASSIFICATION OF AFFECTIVE DISORDERS

DSM III divides the affective disorders into three general groups: (1) major affective disorders, which involve a severe disturbance of mood; (2) other specific affective disorders, which involve a lesser disturbance of mood; and (3) atypical affective disorders, which include affective disorders that do not meet the criteria for either of the above categories. The major affective disorders are further divided into the categories of bipolar disorder and major depression.

Bipolar Disorders

The Bipolar disorders involve either an alteration between manic and depressive mood states at different times or the simultaneous occurrence of both symptom patterns in an intermixed fashion.

Bipolar disorders tend to begin before the age of 30. Typically, in the course of a bipolar affective episode the first episode is usually manic, and both the manic and depressive episodes tend to be more frequent and shorter than those of either the manic or depressive disorders alone. At times there is a normal period in between the two mood swings. In other cases there is no normal period but a rapid cycling from one mood to another.

In general, between .5 percent and 1.2 percent of the adult population are estimated to have experienced bipolar episodes, and bipolar episodes appear to be equally common in men and women.

Joseph Mendels (1970) notes that bipolar cases of affective disorders have been recorded in which the individual alternated between manic and depressive episodes every 24 hours for months on end. This suggests the intriguing possibility that bipolar affective disorders may involve biological rhythms of the individual in ways as yet unclear to us. Although persons suffering from bipolar disorders may report that some environmental stress has triggered their episode, frequently episodes may occur with no obvious precipitating environmental event.

It is tempting to think of mania and depression as merely opposites of one another. Psychoanalytic formulations of depression reinforce this idea by suggesting that mania is best thought of as a "defense against depression." The idea is that depression is such a painful experience that people deny these painful feelings and escape into a manic state.

A very different way of thinking about the relationship between mania and depression is suggested by Mendels (1970). He notes that frequently both manic and depressed symptoms can occur virtually simultaneously in the same patient. Thus a patient in the middle of a manic episode may actually burst into tears. Furthermore, Mendels notes that evidence is emerging to show that the changes in physiological functioning found among manics and depressives may be very similar. If this is so, then it is clearly an oversimplification to think of mania and depression as opposites of one another. The advantage of this way of thinking about affective disorders is that it allows us to include mixed symptom pictures among disorders as well as to include the usual classifications of mania, depression, and bipolar reactions.

Major Depression

DSM III classifies under *major depression* severe depressive episodes in which there is no manifestation of mania. Although DSM distinguishes between single and recurrent episodes, it is estimated that 50 percent of individuals who suffer a single episode of major depression will at some time experience another.

By definition a major depressive episode involves some impairment of social and occupational functioning. In more severe cases the persons may be completely unable to take care of even basic needs, such as feeding or clothing themselves. Also, in more severe episodes delusions or hallucinations may be present. The delusions usually involve feelings of sinfulness and a need to be punished. Major depressive episodes can occur at any age, although with children and adolescents the clinical picture may differ. For example, a major depressive episode in an adolescent may be reflected in school difficulties, restlessness, and antisocial behavior.

THEORIES OF DEPRESSION

In trying to untangle the puzzle of depression, researchers have placed their bets in different places and have pursued their hunches by using different research tactics. In the theory and research we will examine now, you will see some researchers placing their bets heavily on the importance of cognitive events in depression. Others will place their bets on prior learning experiences, while still others believe that it is the biochemistry of depression to which we must attend.

Each of these investigators uses a different strategy to collect evidence. Some draw on their own clinical experience with depressed patients. Others attempt to construct laboratory analogues of the phenomena that they believe are crucial in the development of depression. Still other researchers focus their attention on the metabolism and brain of depressed individuals. And finally, some researchers find it most meaningful to focus on the social field of the depressed person. Their attention is on the

Young adults and children may suffer from depression that goes unrecognized. (Jean-Claude Lejeune)

social interaction of the person suffering from depression.

Psychoanalytic Theory

Of the several well-known theoretical accounts of the development of depression, the psychoanalytic view is unquestionably the most widely quoted. Indeed, some of the earliest thinking in the field of psychoanalysis was devoted to understanding the nature and development of depression. Sigmund Freud wrote his famous paper, "Mourning and Melancholia," in 1917. As we will see, the psychoanalytic approach has been modified in recent years in several important ways. Nevertheless, Freud's early theories of the nature of depression continue to have substantial influence.

Depression as Hostility Turned Inward. Freud viewed depression as the inward turning of aggressive instincts. When we discussed the psychoanalytic perspective in Chapter 3, we noted that the id was described as the source of both sexual and aggressive impulses. Freud believed that the child's early attachment to a loved object, such as a mother, involved both feelings of love and hate. When the child lost the love object or was frustrated in his or her dependency needs, feelings of loss were mingled with feelings of anger. The child could not openly accept feelings of anger toward the love object, however, and therefore turned the hostility inward. The clinical result, Freud argued, was depression. This concept of depression as hostility turned inward suggests that aggression has been *dammed up* and is

THE RIGHT TO FEEL BAD

Obviously all of us prefer feeling happy to feeling depressed. However, our society's emphasis on feeling good has become so strong that to feel bad is considered abnormal and maladaptive. The result is a society wherein antidepressant medication is often prescribed at the first hints of depression.

Psychologist Lesley Hazelton, herself a victim of depression, argues that depression is overpsychologized and overmedicated. While recognizing that many of the clinically diagnosed depressed persons do require medication, she believes that most persons reporting symptoms of depression are feeling normal, appropriate emotions. The problem, she feels, lies with therapists who assume that to feel sad is wrong. Especially among the newer "pop therapies," the emphasis is on self-satisfaction and feeling good at all times. A consequence of these pleasure-oriented approaches is that feeling bad comes to signify failure.

Hazelton is also critical of cognitive theorists, such as Beck, who see depression as a product of misperceptions and faulty logic. In criticizing Beck she writes that his theory "pays no attention at all to the reasons why someone might be depressed. In fact it denies that there is any reason behind distorted perception" (Hazelton, 1984, in *Time*, June 18, 1984). Instead of being maladaptive, Hazelton feels that depression is often a necessary experience that quickly runs its course.

Hazelton is not alone in her criticism of our society's negative attitude toward depression. Wortman and Dintzer (1978) argue that there are many circumstances in which being helpless and depressed is very adaptive. Rather than being dysfunctional, depression at times may provide the motivation for later constructive changes in a patient's life. For example, the authors feel that depression may motivate a person experiencing academic or vocational difficulties to reevaluate his or her goals. Thus, while producing short-term pain and discomfort depression may actually contribute to the long-term adjustment and well-being of the individual.

only capable of being expressed in the form of depression.

A useful question is whether there is any evidence to support this idea. Akiskal and McKinney (1975) indicate that even though the psychoanalytic idea of aggression turned inward is the most widely quoted psychological theory of depression, little systematic evidence substantiates it.

Some research has been reported that tests the idea that if depression represents anger turned inward, then people who are depressed should express considerably less outward anger than would normal nondepressed people. Yet a number of studies conducted by Paykel, Myers, Dienalt, and Weisman (1970, 1973) suggest that it is possible to find substantial numbers of depressed individuals who also express a considerable amount of anger outwardly toward others in the environment.

Depression as a Reaction to Object Loss. Since the early psychoanalytic formulations of depression as hostility turned inward, a second, more important, aspect of the psychodynamics of depression has been emphasized. This second formulation focuses on the idea of *object loss,* the loss of some loved object or individual in the person's life.

The basic idea behind this formulation is that early ungratified dependency needs lead to fixation. Cameron (1963) describes the idea this way:

> The adult who develops a neurotic depression when he regresses is one whose major points of fixation belong to a phase of development when dependency needs were more powerful than needs for self-assertion. We assume that, as a child, such an adult had unusual difficulties in separating himself emotionally from the protective custody of his mother. His need to be taken care of as a baby was either left ungratified or else it was gratified in such a way that only feeble impulses toward mature independence could emerge. What we see in the symptomatology of neurotic depressive adults are derivatives of an early dependent infantile fixation (p. 427).

This idea suggests that hostility turned either inward or outward is not an important cause of depression. It is only a secondary reaction to the fact of the loss of a loved object.

The psychoanalytic perspective on depression focuses on early childhood events and their impact on later behavior. Basically this view maintains that if a child's dependency needs were not fully met early in its development concerns about dependency and loss of love are *fixated* at that time. Later, when the person becomes an adult, the loss of loved objects or even the threat of the loss of love triggers this feeling of vulnerability. The clinical result is depression.

Studies of early attachment and loss are consistent with the revised psychoanalytic version. Much of the research to date has focused on the question of attachment early in life and its implications for later behavior. Perhaps some of the most famous work on early emotional deprivation has been done by Renée Spitz (1946). Spitz reported the reactions of infants separated from their mothers in the second half of their first year of life. The behavior these children displayed has been called *anaclitic depression.* Typically these children displayed continued crying, apprehension, withdrawal, stupor, inability to sleep, loss of weight, and retardation in their growth and development. Similar reactions to separations of children from their mothers have been observed by other investigators.

Perhaps the most famous research on separation was done, not with human beings, but with primates. The work of the Harlows (1969) on the relationship between mother monkeys and their infants has shed considerable light on the importance of attachment and the effects of separation.

The Harlows and others have shown that separating infant rhesus monkeys from their mothers can profoundly affect the infants' behavior. Research with rhesus monkeys on separation has the advantage of allowing the investigators to control carefully extraneous

This infant monkey raised in social isolation shows an exaggerated fear of strangers, apathy, and immobility. (Harry F. Harlow, University of Wisconsin Primate Laboratory)

variables so that the researchers could observe the effect of separation itself. Separation can now be studied as an independent variable; the length, type, and age of separation can be controlled to observe the effects of each. Harlow and his colleagues have shown that separating primate infants from their mothers, once the mother-infant bond has been developed, had clinical effects on the baby very similar to those reported by researchers observing the behavior of human infants following separation. Furthermore, separation from peers (monkeys of the same age) once a bond has been established also produces reactions that look very much like despair and depression.

Research by the Harlow group suggests that separation can indeed play an important role in predisposing rhesus monkeys to later psychopathology. When peers are separated from one another at three to four years of age, they show more abnormal behavior if they have a history of traumatic separation during infancy than if they do not have such a history.

Thus the emphasis on loss of valued relationships in the more recent dynamic formulations is consistent with research conducted in other areas of psychology. The current formulations focus on what appear to be important environmental events in the development of depression.

Biological Theories

Biological explanations for the affective disorders distinguish between exogenous and endogenous depressions. Exogenous depression is a generally less severe form of depression that appears to have environmental causes and precipitants. Endogenous depression, in contrast, occurs without evident external causes, is episodic, is usually more severe, and tends to run in families. It is endogenous depression that most biological theories attempt to explain.

The source of endogenous depression is believed to be found in chemical imbalances in the brain. In our brain the thousands of neurons needed to move a muscle or to perceive an object are not connected directly to one another. Instead, neurons send impulses from one to another by means of chemical substances called *neurotransmitters*. Scientists are discovering more and more about neurotransmitters and how they interact with each other in the brain, but it is already known that these chemicals play a vital role in brain functioning. One group of neurotransmitters is known as the *catecholamines*. There is a whole family of catecholamines, including epinephrine (sometimes called adrenalin), norepinephrine, and dopamine (see Figure 8–1).

For some time scientists have suspected that catecholamines, and norepinephrine in particular, play an important role in depression. Most of the evidence for the role of norepinephrine has been indirect. Schildkraut and Ketty (1967) have suggested that when norepinephrine is depleted in the brain, something resembling depression results. What is the evidence?

One line of evidence has to do with the effects of drugs currently used to treat depression. These drugs, called *monoamine oxidase inhibitors* (MAO inhibitors), have the ability to keep up the level of norepinephrine available in the brain. Thus, scientists reason, it may be the *lack* of norepinephrine in the brain that is associated with depression. Another line of evidence indicates that drugs that increase the level of norepinephrine in the brain tend to produce overactivity and alertness in laboratory animals. Still other evidence suggests that drugs capable of chemically reducing the amount of norepinephrine in the brain tend to produce behavior that looks very much like depression in laboratory animals.

Recent studies have isolated the interactive effects of the neurohormone corticatro-

FIGURE 8-1
Catecholamine Activity in Neurotransmission

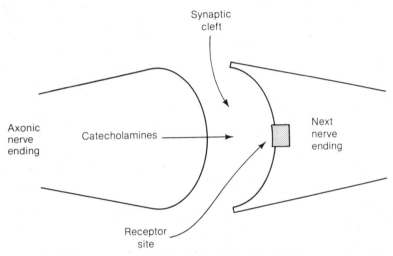

pin releasing factor (CRF) (Asher, 1983). In response to stress, the hypothalamus is believed to secrete CRF, which stimulates the pituitary gland to release the hormone ACTH into the bloodstream. In turn, ACTH causes cortisol to be released by the adrenal glands. Cortisol prepares the person to deal with stress and danger. However, it also inhibits the release of ACTH from the pituitary and so regulates its own levels via a negative feedback.

Research indicates that depressed persons often have unusually high levels of cortisol in their blood. This suggests that depressed persons also experience an excessive amount of CRF secretion. Because CRF activates a portion of the brain important in anxiety and panic states, anxiety is a common feature in depression. Thus depressed persons may actually be in a physiological stage of constant stress. Supporting this hypothesis is evidence that antidepressant drugs may serve as "stress substitutes" and strengthen the brain's ability to adapt.

The CRF theory further hypothesizes that high cortisol levels may result from early

prolonged stress in persons genetically vulnerable to chronically overrelease CRF. Supporting this hypothesis is the fact that many depressed persons have experienced the early stress of separation from a parent or other loved one.

Finally, a number of studies have suggested that there is an important genetic component among the determinants of bipolar affective disorders. Rosenthal (1970) summarized the studies, comparing concordance rates for monozygotic and dizygotic twin pairs. In all the studies examined the concordance rates were much higher for monozygotic than for dizygotic pairs, indicating a genetic component in the disorder.

Does this mean that all affective disorders necessarily have a strong genetic determinant? Not necessarily, according to Winokur and Clayton (1967), who examined the family histories of a sample of persons having affective disorders. These researchers were able to distinguish two groups of individuals. The first group they described as "family history positive" (FH+) cases. These people had a clear history of affective disorder for two generations and were clinically depressed and sometimes manic. The second group, "family history negative" (FH−), had no evidence at all of family histories of affective disturbance and did not display mania, but only depression. This finding suggests that there may be some forms of mood disorders with strong genetic components and others with largely environmental determinants.

Cognitive Theories

The primary emphasis of most theories of depression is on the emotions and mood of the person. This emphasis is not surprising since a depressed mood is the outstanding clinical feature of the disorder. Recently, however, a new emphasis is being placed on *cognitive* events in the psychological life of the depressed person.

Beck's Theory. Beck (1967) believes that the most striking aspect of the depressive's behavior involves the negative expectations and thoughts that are a continuous part of the depressed person's experience. Beck focuses on what he calls the *cognitive triad,* three aspects of negative thinking that characterize depression. The first aspect is *negative conceptions of the self,* the second, *negative interpretations of one's experiences,* and the third, *a negative view of the future.* Note that these are features of the thought patterns of the depressive, rather than qualities of emotional experience. They are essentially "logical errors" to which depressed people tend to be more prone. Depressed people are more likely to accept the blame for negative events in their lives or to interpret negative events as being their responsibility when there is no logical reason for doing so.

Beck believes that a habitual characteristic of depressive thinking involves the use of *schemas* that shape the depressed person's experience. These schemas are habitual

ways of thinking that actually reinforce the negative experiences the depressive typically reports. Among the faulty cognitions that Beck describes as characteristic of depressive thinking are *overgeneralization* and *selective abstraction.*

When people draw an extremely broad conclusion on the basis of some specific fact or minor event, they are engaging in overgeneralization. To conclude that one is worthless and that life is hopeless after merely receiving a parking ticket is an example of overgeneralization. Another example Beck offers involves a man who, when he observed that his children were slow in getting dressed, concluded, "I am a poor father because the children are not better disciplined."

People are engaging in what Beck calls *selective abstraction* when they draw a conclusion on the basis of only a selected aspect of a situation and then engage in self-blame on the basis of this selected event. For example, a person who consistently singles out his or her role in a softball game and accepts the blame for the loss is engaging in selective abstraction.

Recent findings support some aspects of Beck's theory. In one study it was found that overgeneralization was a highly significant predictor of depression among college students (Carver & Ganellen, 1983). Interestingly, not only did women overgeneralize more but the relationship between overgeneralization and depression was far stronger among women than among men. This raises the intriguing possibility that the greater occurrence of depression among women may be due to gender differences in overgeneralization.

The implication of Beck's theory is that the cognitive schema of the person shapes his or her emotional tone rather than the reverse. Although even casual clinical observation suggests that some depressed individuals do indeed display the cognitive distortions Beck describes, whether such distortions are the cause or consequence of depressed affect is unclear. Consequently, Beck's theory has been criticized as a post hoc explanation of depressive symptomatology.

Learned Helplessness. More than 20 years ago a psychologist drowned two rats in the interest of science. He dropped the first rat into a tank of warm water, where it swam for about 60 hours until it finally drowned. The second rat was treated differently. Before being put in the water, the psychologist held the rat in his hand until it stopped struggling. When the rat was finally dropped in the water, it swam around for only a few minutes and then sank to the bottom. The psychologist, Curt Richter (1957, 1958), believes that the second rat had given up hope of escape even before it entered the water. It drowned much sooner because of a sense of helplessness.

Since that first bit of research more than 20 years ago, psychologists have been actively investigating the question of how prior experiences can affect our willingness and ability to cope with loss, change, and stress. In the last few years, the idea that a learned sense of helplessness might be an important component of the phenomenon of depression has gained increasing attention from scientists.

The learned helplessness formulation offered by Seligman (1975) was first introduced as an animal *analogue* of reactive depression. In the original experiments Seligman and his colleagues subjected dogs to a series of inescapable shocks and then placed them in a shuttle box where a warning signal came on before shock occurred. The animals' task was to learn to leap over a hurdle in order to avoid the shock. Animals that had been previously exposed to inescapable shock did not learn to escape when placed in the shuttle

box. Presumably they had learned earlier that nothing they could do would help them escape shock. On the other hand, animals that had not been previously exposed to inescapable shock easily learned the task. Seligman and his colleagues concluded that the inability of the animals that had been exposed to inescapable shock to learn simple escape behavior was an example of learned helplessness.

But what, you may ask, does an experiment on dogs using electric shock in a laboratory have to do with clinical depression? The answer is that Seligman believes there is an important *analogy between learned helplessness and depression.* Recall how in Chapter 4 we noted that *experimental analogues* offer a strategy for conducting research on the problems of abnormal behavior. Experimental analogues allow much more experimental control over the problem of interest and create a set of circumstances that the scientists believe are analogous to those that occur naturally in the social environment.

But for an experimental analogue to be convincing, it is not enough to show a few interesting similarities between the laboratory situation and the clinical phenomenon. It is necessary to spell out the parallels in as much detail as possible. Table 8–2 shows the similarities between the phenomenon of learned helplessness as it is produced in the laboratory and the clinical phenomenon of depression.

However, a number of aspects of depression could not be explained by Seligman's original formulation of the learned helplessness model. For example, the model could not explain why depressed people tend to make internal attributions for failure. In fact, this contradicts the notion that depressed persons feel that events are beyond their control. In addition, the original model could not explain why lowered self-esteem is a symptom of depression nor did it acknowledge that the

TABLE 8-2
Parallels between Learned Helplessness and Depression

Learned Helplessness		Depression
Symptoms	Passivity	Passivity
	Difficulty learning that responses produce relief	Negative cognitive set
	Dissipates in time	Time course
	Lack of aggression	Introjected hostility
	Weight loss, appetite loss, social and sexual deficits	Weight loss, appetite loss, social and sexual deficits
	Norepinephrine depletion and cholinergic activity	Norepinephrine depletion and cholinergic activity
	Ulcers and stress	Ulcers (?) and stress
		Feelings of helplessness
Cause	Learning that responding and reinforcement are independent	Belief that responding is useless
Cure	Directive therapy: forced exposure to responses that produce reinforcement	Recovery of belief that responding produces reinforcement
	Electroconvulsive shock	Electroconvulsive shock
	Time	Time
	Anticholinergics; norepinephrine stimulants (?)	Norepinephrine stimulants; anticholinergics (?)
Prevention	Immunization by mastery over reinforcement	(?)

Source: From *Helplessness: On Depression, Development, and Death* (p. 106) by M. E. P. Seligman, 1975, San Francisco: Freeman.

expectation of uncontrollability per se is not sufficient to produce depression. After all, as Abramson and colleagues note, people do not become sad when each month they receive $1,000 from a trust fund, even though they have no control over the event (Abramson, Seligman, & Teasdale, 1978).

The reformulated learned helplessness model takes into account the attributions people make in attempting to explain and understand the world around them. According to the new model, persons prone to depression attribute negative outcomes to internal as opposed to external factors. Moreover, depression-prone persons are said to be more likely to attribute success to external as opposed to internal factors. For example, such a person might blame a poor test grade on lack of ability and a good score on the ease of the examination. Thus the low self-esteem of depressed persons is thought to be due to their internalization of failure and externalization of success.

The new model maintains that depression-prone persons also make attributions that are global and stable. That is, they tend to see the failures they internalize as fixed and generalized aspects of their personality. The attributions to stable and global factors are said to cause the persistent motivational and performance deficits characteristic of depression (Harvey & Weary, 1984).

Although the language employed differs, the reformulated learned helplessness model is similar to Beck's theory in many ways. For example, where Beck talks of the depressed person's negative interpretations of his or her experiences the reformulated model speaks of internal attributions for failure. Also, what Beck describes as overgeneralization is similar to the new learned helplessness model's description of global and stable attributions. Thus both theories appear to account equally well for the same phenomena. At the same time, however, this similarity means that the reformulated learned helplessness model is subject to the same criticism as is Beck's theory. That is, while internal, global, and stable attributions may indeed be associated with depression, they may be more a consequence than a cause of the syndrome (Harvey & Weary, 1984).

An Interpersonal Perspective

Until now our focus has been largely on the depressed person rather than on the social field that surrounds the person. The cognitive view of depression leaves us with the idea that the depressed person suffers from persistent negative thoughts or misattributions, but this view says little about where these ideas originated.

But what goes on between the depressed person and others in his or her world? Until now the interpersonal phenomena associated with depression have not been well understood, but clearly they deserve careful exploration. In order to avoid *tunnel vision* about the nature of depression, we need to ask some additional questions. For example, how do other people react to the behavior displayed by a depressed person? Is there something unique about the way others react to the depressive? Is it possible that something about the nature of this interactional system affects the persistence of depressive symptoms?

Coyne (1983, 1976) notes that what people think depends more on their external circumstances than either the Beck or learned helplessness model of depression assumes. He argues that there should be a greater focus on the social environment and the role it may play in maintaining depressed behavior. Instead of thinking of depression as something that goes on within individuals, perhaps it is better to think of it as something that goes on between people.

An interpersonal account of depression does not deny the importance of biochemical or genetic factors in the causation of depression. As Price (1974) has argued, even in disorders where the importance of these internal factors has already been established, there are a large number of links in the causal chain between a specific causal factor and the symptoms ultimately displayed by the person. In order to understand the interpersonal view of depression, we need only assume that the individual has begun to display the depressive behavior. The chain of events between the depressed person and others in his or her social environment follows in a straightforward way from this initial display of symptoms.

Coyne (1976a, b) has offered a theoretical description of the nature of transactions between the depressed person and people in the social environment. His description is summarized in Figure 8-2. Coyne views depression as a response to the disruption of a person's social space from which he or she usually obtains support and validation of his or her own experience and identity. This disruption, as we have seen, can take the form of loss of significant relationships, or life changes such as promotion or retirements, or any of a number of other changes in the person's social structure. The symptoms of depression are seen as a set of messages demanding reassurance of the person's place in his or her interactional world. Thus the depressed person's communications of helplessness and hopelessness, his or her slowing and irritability, make others feel obliged to answer the depressed person's request for support and reassurance.

But direct responses and attempts to support and reassure the depressed person often have other messages associated with them as well. Frequently support and reassurance will be given, but the response will be colored by irritation and frustration. Thus the message the depressed person receives is far from an unambiguous support. On the one hand, the depressed person desperately needs support and reassurance that what

FIGURE 8-2
Interactional View of Depression

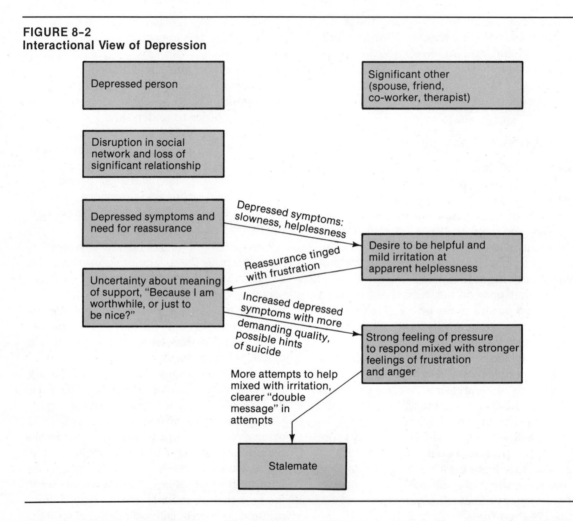

remains of his or her social network is intact. But on the other hand, the messages of support may frequently have a double meaning because the helpers both wish to reassure and feel frustrated with the lack of effect their efforts have.

In addition, by seeking reassurance in this way depressed people have placed themselves in a dilemma from which they cannot easily escape. The dilemma is this: are other people assuring them that they are worthwhile and acceptable because those people really feel that way or only because the pa-

tients have attempted to obtain these responses from them?

Look at Figure 8-2 again. You can see that this interpersonal process will repeat itself, and even subsequent attempts to seek feedback testing the nature of the patient's acceptance by others cannot reduce the uncertainty. Meanwhile, these requests for repeated assurance become increasingly aversive to others in the person's social environment. As Coyne points out, the depressive has reached the first in a number of possible interactive stalemates in which a

The social support of even one close friend can be extremely important in coping with depression. (Tom Ballard/EKM-Nepenthe)

pattern of mutual manipulation has been established. There is a paradoxical character to this stalemate. Requesting information about how people *really* view the depressed person becomes indistinguishable from the depressive's symptoms. Continued requests to ask others how they really feel about that person will probably only produce denial or an angry, defensive response on the part of others.

People who have spent a period of time trying to support, reassure, and be otherwise helpful to a severely depressed person may intuitively agree that they felt compelled to reach out to help and at the same time felt frustrated and perhaps even annoyed when their efforts seemed to have no real effect.

But is there any research that supports this formulation? Coyne (1976a) has conducted an intriguing experiment that has yielded evidence bearing directly on this point. He notes that the behavioral approach suggests that depressed people receive a low rate of positive reinforcement that is contingent on their own behavior. The behavioral view argues that it is the depressed person's lack of social skill that produces this state of affairs. On the other hand, Coyne notes, one could argue that the unwillingness of other people to interact with depressives could explain these findings equally well. More specifically, Coyne argues, the way in which depressed people interact with others may actually induce depression and hostility in those others, and this hostility may in turn lead to social rejection.

In order to test this idea, Coyne selected three groups of *target individuals*. One group consisted of depressed women from a mental health center population; a second comparison group consisted of nondepressed women from the same population; and a third comparison group consisted of normal women drawn from supermarket employees, customers, hospital auxiliary personnel, and neighbors. Coyne then recruited female undergraduates (subjects) to interact with these three groups of target individuals. Each subject was randomly assigned to one target individual and talked with her on the telephone for 20 minutes. Subjects were not aware of which group they were to talk with. Both people involved in the conversation were told that they were engaged in a study of the acquaintance process and that the conversations were taped. In addition, all participants were asked to fill out a questionnaire after the conversation recording their reactions to the other persons.

If Coyne's hypothesis is correct, subjects interacting with the depressed people ought to react very differently from subjects interacting either with nondepressed patients or with normal individuals. Indeed, that is precisely what Coyne found. Subjects who interacted with depressed individuals became more depressed, anxious, and hostile *themselves* following the interactions than did those subjects who interacted with nondepressed patients or with normal controls. Furthermore, subjects were more rejecting of depressed patients and expressed much less willingness to interact with the depressed group again on another occasion.

Analyses of the verbal content of the conversations themselves, however, did not turn up the behavior that led to these strikingly different perceptions.

Thus the depressed patients in this study did produce negative feelings in other people. They were accepted less even though their activity level and rate of positive responses were no lower than those of other people. Coyne argues that the lower activity level of depressed persons is due to the fact that few people are willing to interact with them rather than because, as learning theorists have argued, the rate of behavior of depressed persons is initially lower than that of nondepressed people.

Although Coyne's interpersonal account of depression is promising, a number of factors have been left unexplained. For example, while Coyne provides a sound model for how the depressed state is maintained, he does not explain how the interpersonal cycle of depression first gets started. In addition, his model cannot account for why most depressed persons will experience a spontaneous remission of their depression. Thus Coyne's theory is open to the same criticism as the cognitive theories concerning the nature of causality in depression.

TREATMENT OF AFFECTIVE DISORDERS

In the past severe episodes of depression frequently led to hospitalization. A major reason for the decision to hospitalize a depressed individual often had to do with the danger of suicide attempts. Another major reason for the hospitalization of depressed individuals had to do with the dramatic effect hospitalization often produced. Clinicians have commonly noted that the simple act of hospitalization without any other active treatment often has brought dramatic changes in the individual's depressed mood and behavior. Frequently, of course, these changes were due to the fact that the person was removed from stressful family or work circumstances that had maintained the depressed behavior.

Currently, however, clinicians are much less likely to hospitalize severely depressed patients. There are at least two reasons for this. First, in the last few years there has been an increase in the use of various biological treatments for depression. Both pharmacological and convulsive therapies have yielded some measure of success in reducing depressed behavior. Second, psychological treatments for depression have now gone well beyond the traditional talking cures, and behavioral approaches in particular have been shown to be effective in many cases.

Most often biological and psychological approaches to treatment are used in combination rather than singly. Given our imperfect understanding of the mechanisms involved in depression, it is understandable that the treatment-oriented clinician would wish to use a combination of strategies in the hope that the combination would be more effective than any single approach.

But we should still remain skeptical of the effectiveness of various treatments. There are at least two reasons for this. First, as we noted, many depressed people react strongly to suggestion. Substantial research (Mendels, 1970) shows that a person's expectations about treatment can produce a reduction in depressed behavior. Second, we should recall that depression is frequently a self-limiting disorder. That is, with or without treatment, many depressions will dissipate in six months to a year. With these cautions in mind, let us turn to a brief examination of biological and psychological approaches to the treatment of depression.

Biological Treatments

Drug Treatment. Drugs are usually the treatment of first choice in cases of severe mania or depression. Often the drugs produce dramatic changes in the person's mood so that he or she may be able to continue to function without recourse to hospitalization. The problem is that we do not currently have a sufficient understanding of how the different drugs operate. Consequently, prescribing the proper drug in a given situation can be a hit-or-miss affair. If the drug works, the person is kept on it; if the drug is ineffective, another drug is tried (Waldholz, 1984). Since the drugs require two to three weeks to take effect, the process of finding the proper medication can take months.

One set of compounds commonly used in the treatment of depression are the *tricyclic antidepressants,* such as imipramine. Recent research suggests that antidepressants work by regulating alpha–2 receptors (Hiatt, 1981). When active, alpha–2 receptors inhibit the release of the catecholamine norepinephrine. As previously noted, depressed persons are thought to have low levels of norepinephrine in the brain. Thus, by decreasing the number of alpha–2 receptors, the amount of norepinephrine released is increased.

For certain patients, the monoamine oxidose inhibitors (MAO inhibitors) appear to be most effective. As MAO serves to deactivate catecholamines, MAO inhibitors increase the amount of catecholamines in the body. The MAO inhibitors work best on chronically depressed persons who overeat and oversleep as opposed to exhibiting the usual weight loss and insomnia (Trafford, 1983). However, the evidence for the effectiveness of these drugs is less clear, and they are used much less frequently.

A major problem with both these classes of antidepressant drugs is the troublesome side effects. Included among the possible side effects are constant dryness of the mouth, constipation, weight gain, blurred vision, and sexual problems (Waldholz, 1984). In addition, these drugs are not recommended for the elderly or people with heart conditions. Because such drugs can be lethal when taken in excess, their use must be carefully monitored in the case of suicidal persons. The side effects are especially troublesome because, in episodes of major depression, medication is taken for up to a year and, in cases of recurrent depression, maintenance doses are taken regularly to prevent relapses.

Another important form of pharmacological treatment, described by some writers (Fieve, 1976) as "the third revolution in psychiatry," is the use of *lithium carbonate,* particularly for bipolar affective disorders. Early prescriptions by Greek and Roman physicians of mineral water for affective disorders were probably due to the fact that these waters contained high quantities of lithium. Lithium is not a compound but an element that is one of the lightest of the alkaline metals in the periodic table.

Fieve describes the use of lithium for patients with affective disorders of the "metabolic ward" of the New York State Psychiatric Institute. Patients suffering from mood disorders are brought onto the ward and administered lithium while their behavior and metabolism are monitored. Body chemistry and mood are monitored until the patients' mood stabilizes, at which point they are moved to an outpatient treatment status.

Fieve reports that psychotherapy is of little benefit for these patients. Instead, an outpatient clinic designed to monitor the mood and lithium dosage of the patients is both more effective and considerably less expensive than conventional care. However, most people with a bipolar affective disorder who take lithium continue taking it for the rest of their lives (Trafford, 1983).

Electroconvulsive Therapy. In the 1930s it was often observed that few patients suffering from schizophrenia were also epileptic. Physicians hypothesized that the abnormal electrical activity in the brain of epileptics prevented schizophrenic episodes. As implausible as this hypothesis now seems, physicians developed electroconvulsive therapy (ECT) as a treatment for schizophrenia. The treatment consisted of passing a current of electricity through the brain of the patient until a convulsion occurred.

The results of this treatment for schizophrenic patients was almost uniformly disappointing, but ECT had come into widespread use and soon was being used for the treatment of depression. Interestingly, some severely depressed patients responded extremely well to the administration of electroconvulsive therapy, and it soon became a standard treatment for depression.

Most people find the idea of electroconvulsive therapy frightening and offensive. The idea of placing a patient on a treatment table and passing 70 to 130 volts through the frontal lobes of the brain even for a half second, is a terrifying idea. Typically, today most patients are given an anesthetic and an intravenous injection of a muscle relaxant to prevent injury when the convulsions resulting from the ECT occur.

A typical course of treatment for ECT consists of six to eight treatments given at the rate of three a week. Mendels (1970) notes that more frequent treatment than this is not required since most patients who respond to ECT do so by six or eight treatments.

No one knows why electroconvulsive therapy has its therapeutic effects. The theories offered to explain its effectiveness range from the idea that depressed patients welcome it as an absolution for their guilt feelings to the suggestion that ECT produces biochemical changes in the brain that, in turn, alter the depressed person's mood (Mendels, 1970). One problem with the administration of ECT is that little is known about which patients are benefited by the treatment and which are not. However, some evidence does exist to suggest that endogenous depressions are relatively more benefited by ECT treatments than are exogenous depressions.

A major side effect of electroconvulsive treatment is memory loss. In some individuals the loss can be severe, but for most it is temporary. The memory loss can have a negative effect on the recovery rate of a patient since the loss of memory even for the name of a close friend or relative can produce serious interpersonal complications. However, administering ECT to one side of the brain and monitoring seizure duration (Fink & Johnson, 1982) has greatly reduced this problem.

With the advent of pharmacological and behavioral treatments for depression, electroconvulsive therapy is used much less than in the past. However, research is still needed to identify those patients who may benefit from the treatment.

Psychotherapy

Psychotherapy is used to treat depression both by itself and in conjunction with antidepressant medications. Of the many psychotherapy approaches, the cognitive and behavioral approaches appear the most promising.

Cognitive approach. Beck's cognitive theory of depression has led him to develop a treatment technique that attempts to help depressed individuals recognize and change cognitive habits or schemas typical of depression. Individuals are guided to attempt to change their cognitive habits of arbitrary inference or overgeneralization and therefore alter their depressive schemas. Beck and his co-workers (Beck, Kovacs, & Weissman, 1979) use several strategies to help the depressed individual test the reality of his or her arbitrary inferences or overgeneralizations. For example, depressed clients often feel that accomplishing even the smallest task is almost impossible and tend to conclude erroneously that they can accomplish very little. In Beck's therapeutic approach each task is broken down into relatively small steps, and clients are encouraged to accomplish one at a time. As tasks are accomplished, the clients begin to change their view of themselves while the therapist continues to increase the challenge of the tasks offered.

Beck's therapeutic approach uses still other strategies for helping clients identify cognitive distortions in their thinking. For example, a client who feels worthless will be helped to review past accomplishments and to identify achievements that contradict the presumption of worthlessness. Thus, through a series of concrete attempts to challenge the client's exaggerated or distorted negative cognitions, Beck's therapeutic approach attempts to shift the client's view of self and of his or her accomplishments and to alter the style of depressed cognitions so characteristic of depression.

Beck and his colleagues (Rush, Beck, Kovacs, & Hollon, 1977) have begun to systematically test the effectiveness of Beck's cognitive approach to treating depressives and to compare it with the effectiveness of the antidepressant drug treatment. Two groups of depressed men and women were given either cognitive therapy (as we have just described it) or an antidepressant drug, imipramine. After treatment, changes were observed in the cognitive therapy group, and fewer clients than usual dropped out of this group as well. The real test in such studies is whether the effects remain after a period of time. In this study patients in the cognitive therapy group remained less depressed at a six-month follow-up. Thus it appears that cognitive therapy or some aspects associated with it rival the effects of antidepressant drugs. This is an impressive initial finding supporting the effectiveness of cognitive therapy.

Learned Helplessness Approach. The reformulated learned helplessness theory also provides a model for treating depression. According to this model, there are four strategies for treatment (Abramson, Seligman, & Teasdale, 1978). The first strategy is to alter the environment so that aversive outcomes are less likely and desired outcomes are more likely. Examples of this might include arranging child care, job placement, medical care, or financial assistance. A second strategy is to reduce the aversiveness of highly aversive outcomes and reduce the desirability of highly desired outcomes. The therapist should encourage the patient to adopt more realistic goals and norms and help him or her attain alternatives that are equally desirable. For example, the therapist might encourage a college student unsuccessful in one major to change to a major more in tune with his or her interests and skills. The third strategy is to change the person's feeling of uncontrollability to a feeling of being in control. This may require modifying a person's distorted perception of his or her competence, or it may require teaching skills that were previously lacking. For instance, teaching a child interpersonal skills that he or she lacks may cause the child to feel more in control of how others treat him or her. Finally, the therapist needs to change the person's unrealistic attributions for failure from internal to external factors. As low self-esteem is said to result from internal attributions of failure, a shift in orientation should result in higher self-esteem. At the same time unrealistic attributions for success should be changed from external to internal factors.

The strength of the learned helplessness treatment model lies in its very detailed and systematic treatment strategies. However, more research is needed before the efficacy of this treatment model can be determined.

Behavioral Approaches. A number of psychologists have developed behavioral approaches to the treatment of depression that in some ways parallel the learned helplessness formulation of depression described earlier. Research by Lewinsohn (1974b), for example, assumes that depression involves a *low rate of response contingent positive reinforcement* and that this low rate is a sufficient condition for explaining depression by itself. According to this view, treatment can involve a number of different strategies. One strategy is to increase the individual's activity level, using a graded task assignment procedure that requires the person to gradually increase the number or complexity of tasks he successfully completes. Another behavioral strategy recommended by Lewinsohn involves social skill training that presumably improves the individual's ability to elicit positive reinforcement from the environment. Relaxation training, which promotes relaxation in the face of anxiety-provoking events, is also recommended. Lewinsohn further suggests the use of (1) a three-month time limit for treatment; (2) the use of home observations to examine the social environment of the patient and to gauge progress; and (3) the use of daily mood rating and monitors of the patient's activity level.

A unique concept in the treatment of depression suggested by Lewinsohn (1974) is the use of the *Premack principle*. The Premack principle states that the occurrence of a high-frequency behavior can be used to reinforce a low-frequency behavior. Once the individual emits the low-frequency behavior, the high-frequency behavior is allowed to oc-

cur. Thus the high-frequency behavior can be used as a reinforcer to increase the frequency of the low-frequency behavior. As we have noted, depressives display certain behaviors that occur with very high frequency. Expressed feelings of unhappiness, guilt, self-deprecation, and rejection are examples. Other behaviors that are desirable occur only infrequently, such as self-assertiveness and realistic judgments. Lewinsohn illustrates the use of the Premack principle in the following case:

Mrs. W., who was suffering from depression, displayed an extremely low activity level (low-frequency behavior). In addition, she had many concerns and anxieties and spent a great deal of time telling the therapist about these concerns (high-frequency behavior). The therapist then requested that Mrs. W. increase the proportion of activity she was engaged in if she wished to talk about her complaints. She could talk about her complaints, the therapist explained, when a certain light in the therapy room was turned on. Mrs. W.'s initial reaction to this suggestion was angry indignation. When her verbalization rate for planned activities went up during the subsequent therapy hour, the light was turned on as a signal that she could, if she wished, discuss her complaints and concerns. Lewinsohn reported that her verbalizations in the therapy hour changed dramatically and her activity level subsequently changed as well.

Another illustration of the use of behavioral principles in the treatment of depression is offered by Liberman and Raskin (1971). The patient, a 37-year-old housewife, was severely depressed and had been since the death of her mother. She complained about somatic symptoms, paced, withdrew, and frequently cried. Members of her family responded to these depressed behaviors with helpfulness, sympathy, and concern.

The therapist began rating two classes of behavior for the patient: *coping behavior,* such as cooking, cleaning the house, and tending to her children's needs; and *depressive behavior,* which included crying and complaining. The therapist then joined the patient's entire family and instructed the husband and children to pay instant and frequent attention to her coping behavior and to ignore her depressed behavior. The therapist taught family members to acknowledge her positive actions with approval, interest, and encouragement and to shift their attention from the "sick woman" to the housewife and mother.

Figure 8–3 shows the effect of the treatment. The first seven days of treatment were used to obtain pretreatment baselines for both depressive and coping behavior. You can see that the daily rates of coping behavior in the first week are very low and that the rates of depressive behavior are very high. At the end of the first week, the family was instructed to change its response to the mother's behavior. Dramatic decreases in depressed behavior accompanied by marked increases in coping behavior occurred for the next week.

Recall for a moment that we have said that depressed episodes are frequently

FIGURE 8-3
Modification of Depressive Behavior Using Reinforcement and Extinction Techniques Taught to Family Members

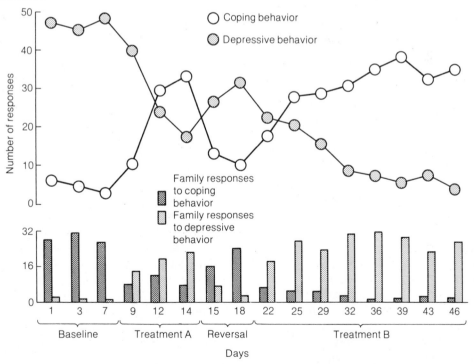

Source: R. P. Liberman and D. E. Raskin, "Depression: A Behavioral Formulation," *Archives of General Psychiatry* 24 (1971), pp. 515–23. Copyright 1971, American Medical Association.

self-limiting. How then are we to know whether the change in the behavior of the family is producing the behavior change in the mother or not? The answer is that these researchers then conducted a *clinical experiment* to demonstrate the causal link between her behavior and the responses generated in her family. On the 14th day the therapist instructed the family to return to its previous behavior. That is, they were again to provide attention and concern for her complaints. Within three days, the investigators note, she was once again showing high levels of depression. The effect can be seen in the "reversal days" of Figure 8–3. After the 18th day the treatment was reinstituted and dramatic improvement again occurred in the behavior of the patient.

This clinical experiment demonstrates the powerful impact the social environment can have on depressed behavior. From our point of view treatment approaches such as these hold great promise in the clinical management of depression.

SUICIDE

In describing depressive affective disorders, we noted that in some cases of severe depression suicide was a potential outcome. It is to this problem that we now turn. Suicide continues to be one of the 10 leading causes of death in the United States. We have chosen to discuss the phenomenon of suicide here not because it is only associated with affective disorders, since it is clearly not, but because both attempts or successful suicides are more frequently associated with depressive affective disorders than with other patterns of abnormal behavior.

Although the act of suicide is not a homogeneous clinical entity, its social importance has led researchers to attempt to understand the phenomenon, its distribution in the population, and its psychological components.

In this section we will examine factors associated with the risk of suicide to provide us with a broad understanding of the phenomenon. We will then turn to the question of the prediction of suicide. As we shall see, the challenge of assessing individuals for suicide risk is especially difficult but must be pursued because of its obvious social importance. Finally, we will consider recent research on the cognitive characteristics of people who have attempted suicide. New research in this area suggests that people who attempt suicide may have certain cognitive patterns in common.

Factors Associated with Suicide Risk

Research over the last 30 years has uncovered a substantial amount of information about how suicide is distributed in the population and other characteristics of the individual who attempts or completes a suicide attempt.

Psychological Disturbance. Depression is by far the most likely pattern of abnormal behavior associated with suicide. According to Choron (1972), only 5 to 15 percent of severely depressed individuals will eventually commit suicide. Schizophrenia and personality disorders are also associated with suicide attempts, as is alcoholism. Approximately 25 percent of successful suicides suffer from chronic alcoholism.

Recently Petrie and Chamberlain (1983) have shown that the relationship between depression and suicide is largely explained by feelings of hopelessness. Individuals who hold a pessimistic view of the future are most likely to kill themselves. The hopelessness of the suicidal individual is captured in the following case:

Carol was referred to a crisis center for help by a physician in the emergency room of a nearby small suburban hospital. The night before, she had attempted suicide by severely slashing her left wrist repeatedly with a large kitchen knife, and she had severed a tendon as a result. When she was first seen by the therapist at the center, her left wrist and arm were heavily bandaged. She appeared tense, disheveled, very pale, and tremulous. She described her symptoms as insomnia, poor appetite, recent inability to concentrate, and overwhelming feelings of hopelessness and helplessness. . . . She told the therapist, "Suddenly I felt empty . . . that everything was over between us. It was just too much for me to handle. He was never going to see me again and was too damned chicken to tell me so to my face! I went numb all over . . . I just wanted to die" Aguilera & Messick, 1978, pp. 117–99).

Previous Suicide Attempts. A persistent myth exists suggesting that if a person has unsuccessfully attempted suicide, he or she is not serious and therefore the likelihood of a subsequent successful suicide attempt is low. This is simply untrue. Studies have consistently shown that in surveys of completed suicides the presence of a previous attempt is a primary factor in predicting the risk of a successful subsequent attempt (Choron, 1972). In addition, the method of the previous attempt is an important predictor of suicide. Previous attempts with highly lethal methods such as guns are much more predictive of later successful suicide than public gestures such as swallowing pills. Still, pills are also a major method in completed suicides, especially among women.

Age Differences. Shneidman and Farberow (1970) indicate that the older the individual, the more likely that a suicide will occur. And indeed, the majority of people who kill themselves are elderly. The peak age for successful suicide is between 55 and 65 years of age. But suicide attempts are much more likely in the 24 to 44 age range. However, recent U.S. census data (1979) indicate that the rela-

tionship between increased age and completed suicides may hold true only for white males.

While the greatest risk for suicide is among certain older age groups, suicide among children and adolescents has attracted considerable attention in recent years. This attention is primarily due to the fact that suicide is the second leading cause of death of people under the age of 20.

It is difficult to determine the reliability of the reported rate of suicide among children. Children are unlikely to leave suicide notes or other evidence of suicide. In addition, many people are likely to assume that the child has met with an accident because the idea of childhood suicide is unthinkable to most of us. Children may not view death as irreversible or suicide as taboo. They may make suicide attempts because of a fear of an impending punishment, a desire to punish others, or in an attempt to join a loved one who has died.

Adolescent suicide ranks as a leading cause of death among the 15–19 age group. Since the 1950s the suicide rate among adolescents has increased by about 300 percent while the rates for other age groups have remained virtually unchanged (Brody, 1984). In fact, more than 10 percent of all suicides are committed by teenagers. This statistic is even more striking when we consider that for every successful suicide, there are estimated to be from 50 to 200 suicide attempts.

Among young people two particular subgroups are apparently at higher risk for suicide. Black males in urban settings constitute one such group. The second group, college students, are twice as likely to commit suicide as their same-age counterparts.

In recent years many colleges and universities have developed hot lines and telephone crisis services to provide an empathic listener to students who feel distressed and hopeless. It is very likely that such a service exists in your own college or university.

Hotlines and other telephone crisis intervention services can be a valuable community resource.
(John Thoeming/Dorsey Press)

Marital Status and Social Support. In general, divorced persons are a higher risk for suicide than either single, widowed, or married individuals, and the lowest suicide rate is found among married people. It is quite likely that the social support associated with the marital relationship is a critical element in preventing suicide.

Sex Differences. In general, approximately, three times as many men as women actually commit suicide, but women are nearly three times as likely to make a suicide attempt (Schneidman, Farberow, & Litman, 1970). Beck (1975) has found that disruption in personal relationships is more likely to precipi-

tate suicides among women than among men. On the other hand, men tend more often to use highly lethal methods of attempting suicides, such as firearms. This may account for the substantial difference in successful suicides among the two groups.

Family History. Suicide is much more likely to occur among individuals with a parent or close relative who has committed suicide. In a recent study Roy (1983) had found that among psychiatric patients with a family history of suicide, almost half had attempted suicide at least once in their lives. Even more dramatic was the effect the child's age at the time of the parent's death had on later suicidal behavior. Of patients in this sample who were less than 11 years old when a parent committed suicide, fully 75 percent had later attempted suicide.

The Predictors of Suicide

The social importance of predicting a possible suicide attempt is obvious on the face of it. As Shneidman et al. (1970) have indicated, most people are acutely suicidal for only a short period of time. Thus intervention during that critical time could be decisive. In light of this fact, the importance of accurately predicting a suicide attempt becomes even more compelling.

Despite its importance, the prediction of suicide presents extremely difficult methodological problems. First of all, suicide is an extremely heterogeneous phenomenon and therefore adequate classification is necessary for accurate prediction (Neuringer, 1974). On the other hand, several critical issues confront the researcher hoping to design an effective prediction method or the clinician hoping to screen clients for the likelihood of suicide.

In order to validate the predictive power of an instrument, the typical procedure is to conduct a *prospective* study. That is, a large number of people are given a test or are screened on variables that are assumed to predict the outcome of the phenomenon under study. In the typical prospective study, events are allowed to run their course and then those factors in the test or a measurement instrument associated with the outcome can be isolated using correlational techniques. However, the ethical constraints against letting someone suspected of attempting suicide complete the act make it obvious that a prospective study would not be ethically feasible.

Another problem confronting the researcher is that the psychological state associated with the likelihood of a suicide attempt may be very brief. Consequently, reliable observations of the state may be difficult to obtain. Furthermore, to be useful, a prediction of suicide must specify the period within which the act may occur, since otherwise the prediction will be of little practical use for the purposes of preventive intervention.

Perhaps the greatest difficulty associated with the prediction of suicide is the relative infrequency (low *base rate*) of the event. Most estimates suggest that approximately 11 out of 100,000 people in the general population successfully complete a suicide attempt. As Goldfried, Stricker, and Weiner (1971) have pointed out, when the occurrence of an event substantially departs from 50 percent in the population, the problems in predicting its occurrence increase. In the case of suicide, it is reasonable to assume that in the general population, only one tenth of 1 percent of the population will actually complete a suicide. Thus, on the basis of the probability alone, you will be correct 99.9 percent of the time if you predict that *no one* will commit suicide. No psychological test administered to the general population can be as accurate. Obviously, whatever satisfaction one might obtain from being correct this often, the social cost of failing to predict a suicide is so great that attempts to devise methods to accurately predict the occurrence of a suicide attempt continue.

Most researchers now try to overcome the base rate problem by identifying population characteristics that substantially increase the likelihood of suicide *in that population*. Then instruments can be developed which can predict suicide attempts within this population having a higher base rate of suicide. Let us now turn to a line of research that

A concerned policeman begins to help his fellow officer who is restraining an elderly woman who is attempting suicide. (United Press International Photo)

may improve our ability to predict the occurrence of suicide attempts.

Suicidal Intention and Ideation

Recently Beck and his colleagues (Beck, Kovacs, & Weissman, 1979) began developing measurement instruments to study suicidal ideation. Suicidal ideation or thought patterns, they believe, may be an important psychological indication of the intent to commit suicide. However, as they point out, intention is only one component of suicide risk. They note:

> Whereas suicidal intent may be regarded as a psychological phenomenon subject to exploration and measurement, suicidal risk is a predictive statement of the probability of a fatal suicide attempt and can be conceived in terms of a complex (although not fully formulated) equation. *Suicidal intention* would represent an important variable in this formula. Other essential components of the suicidal risk formula are factors such as the *lethality* of the method contemplated by the suicidal individual: his or her knowledge of lethal dosages of drugs or skill and familiarity with other forms of self-destruction, and his or her *access to the contemplated lethal method* (such as an adequate number of sleeping pills or firearms or ammunition). Another variable to be factored into the equation is the presence of *environmental resources that would facilitate the detection of suicidal intent* and intervention by another individual who would provide assistance in obtaining immediate and adequate *medical help* following a suicide attempt. Of course, the presence of a viable *social support system* that may diffuse the intensity of the suicidal wish is also an important and tangible factor (p. 345, italics added).

Thus Beck and his colleagues are suggesting that a variety of factors must be taken into

account in the prediction of suicide, but that suicidal ideation, if it can be adequately measured, may be a useful predictor.

In this regard, Beck and his colleagues have developed a scale called the *scale for suicidal ideation*, which is designed to measure the intensity of an individual's conscious suicide intent. This scale is completed by a clinician on the basis of the individual's responses to a structured interview.

A factor analysis of the items in this scale suggests that there are three major components in suicidal thinking: (1) active suicidal desire; (2) preparation; and (3) passive suicidal desire. Future studies will allow further refinement of the scale and examine its usefulness in longitudinal studies.

Another study by Patsiokas, Clum, and Luscomb (1979) attempted to isolate cognitive characteristics that might be important precursors of suicidal acts, using a group of suicide attempters and a group of nonsuicidal controls. They found that suicide attempters tended to be more cognitively rigid. These researchers interpret this rigidity as a low ability to cope with stressful events. However, suicide attempters were found to be no more impulsive or dependent on their external environment than control subjects. Thus we see that a psychological rigidity and inability to see alternative solutions to problems may also be a cognitive component of the disposition to attempt suicide.

SUMMARY

In this chapter we have examined the clinical characteristics of affective disorders and surveyed research and theory on their determinants and treatment. While both mania and depression are classified as affective disorders, depression is far more prevalent. In fact, the relative frequency of depression in the population has led some to call it the "common cold" of psychological disorders. While life events and changes may trigger an affective disorder, research suggests that a variety of social and biological phenomena may predispose certain individuals to depression or manic episodes.

In examining the various theories of depression, we have observed that most of the major perspectives on abnormal behavior are represented. Psychoanalytic views of depression focus on the redirection of hostility or object loss as explanatory factors. Cognitive theories emphasize cognitive styles and distortions of the thought processes of persons with affective disorders. For example, the learned helplessness model focuses on the depressed person's attribution of success to external factors and failure to internal factors. However, biochemical theories and, in particular, the catecholamine hypothesis offer a direct challenge to the cognitive theories as explanations of affective disorders. One final approach examined is the social perspective, which focuses on interpersonal behavior and its role in the development of depression. Thus we see that scientific inquiry into the causes of affective disorders is presenting theoretical challenges to previously established points of view from both biological and social perspectives.

Just as various theories of affective disorders emphasize different potential causal factors, the treatment of affective disorders also reflects a diversity of perspectives. Biological methods, including antidepressant drugs and lithium as well as electroconvulsive therapy, all have shown at least modest success in the treatment of affective disorders. However, psychotherapy and cognitive approaches in particular have developed rapidly and in some studies have been found to be more effective than drug treatment.

Finally, we have also examined the phenomenon of suicide and considered a number of factors associated with increased suicide risk. As important as it is for clinical and humanitarian reasons, the prediction of suicide is difficult because suicide is a statistically infrequent event among the general population and the period of highest risk may be relatively brief. However, recent research on patterns of suicidal cognition may prove helpful in identifying psychological factors that increase suicidal risk.

9

Schizophrenia: Description, Research, and Treatment

Description
    History
    Clinical Description
    Course over Time

Diagnosis and Classification
    DSM III Diagnostic Criteria

Alternative Approaches to Classification
    Experimental Research on Schizophrenic
        Behavior
    Schizophrenics Report on Their Own
        Experiences

Determinants of Schizophrenia
    The Biological Search for Causes
    Family and Society as Contexts for
        Schizophrenia
    An Integration of Perspectives:
        Vulnerability

Treatment
    From Hospital to Community
    Drug Treatment
    Treatment Combinations

Summary

INTRODUCTION

Franz, 23, says he is a riddle of bones. He hears buzzing noises, penetrating squeals, and voices with messages he sometimes understands but cannot remember. He sees flashes of light and shadow in the middle of the room. Strangers, he says, can send their shadow to visit him in bed. He tastes soap in his mouth and absorbs poison from the bed posts. He chews his tie, hoards garbage, sits in a stupor for weeks, and hits his nurses. Occasionally he clowns and walks on his hands (Rodgers, 1983, p. 85).

Franz's behavior reflects many of the striking symptoms of schizophrenia. This major disorder is extremely disabling and most people never fully recover. Indeed, the vast majority of persons requiring long-term care in psychiatric hospitals are diagnosed as schizophrenics. Pictures drawn by schizophrenics as part of their therapy reflect some of their own internal confusion and turmoil.

Approximately 1 percent of the American population will be diagnosed as schizophrenic at some point in their lives. But schizophrenia is a worldwide disorder that affects people of all races, religions, levels of intelligence, and wealth. Recent research done under the sponsorship of the World Health Organization (Tsuang, 1976) examined the incidence of schizophrenia in Nigeria, Colombia, Denmark, Russia, India, and the United

States. In all those countries the incidence of the disorder was about 1 percent. The same study suggested that there seem to be universal signs of schizophrenia. These signs include the belief that one is controlling or is controlled by some external agent, a flatness of emotional tone, hearing voices or other sounds, confusion about location or time, and withdrawal from social contact.

Schizophrenics comprise about half of the patients in mental institutions in the United States. Today many more people experiencing schizophrenic disorders continue to live in society but return periodically to hospital settings for treatment. In general, about one third of the people suffering from schizophrenic disorders improve over time, about a third get worse, and about a third stay the same throughout the course of their lives.

Schizophrenia is a bewildering and terrifying experience. The schizophrenic's thought processes are greatly impaired. The person experiencing a schizophrenic episode may have difficulty understanding what is going on or may develop frightening delusions or hear voices. He or she may frequently feel terrified of others and withdraw, avoiding interpersonal contact as much as possible.

Schizophrenia is one of the most important of the *functional psychoses*. Functional psychoses should be distinguished from organic psychoses. Organic psychoses occur as the consequence of known damage to the brain from, for example, drugs or high fever. Functional psychoses, on the other hand, have no known single cause and remain one of the great puzzles in the study of abnormal psychology.

In fact, learning about schizophrenia is in many ways like a study of abnormal psychology in miniature. Most of the issues and controversies we find across the whole range of abnormal behaviors also occur in the study of schizophrenia. Let us now turn to these issues and controversies. They will serve as our guideposts in this chapter as we learn more about schizophrenic disorders. Despite tens of thousands of scientific studies, schizophrenia remains a puzzle. In fact, we are only now beginning to ask questions that may yield some useful answers. Like much of the study of abnormal behavior, each of these questions has produced controversy. But it is just this controversy that sharpens the issues so that answers can be found. We will focus on three clusters of questions in this and the next chapter.

First, is schizophrenia a single, unitary disorder? Some scientists believe that it is; others argue that it is not a single disorder but a group of similar-looking disorders with different underlying causes. Still others believe that there is no disorder that we can call *schizophrenia* at all. Instead, they argue that schizophrenia is merely a label we use to describe a range of behavior that we do not clearly understand.

Second, how is schizophrenia transmitted? We know that if a child has one parent who is schizophrenic, that child has 10 times greater a chance of developing the disorder than someone selected at random from the general population. If that child has two schizophrenic parents, the risk is 40 times greater. Evidence of this kind cannot be ignored, but its interpretation is far from simple. Does the child inherit some disorder through a genetic mechanism? Or is schizo-phrenia transmitted through social learning in the family context? And what role does society play? We know that the incidence of schizophrenia is much greater among poor people. Does this mean that poverty causes the schizophrenia—or that schizophrenia causes poverty?

While some researchers are attempting to provide us with clearer descriptions of schizophrenia and others are searching for the mechanisms of its transmission, still others are facing the task of offering treatment to people who have already developed the disorder. As we shall see, there have been enormous changes in the treatment of schizophrenia. What treatment lies ahead? Will it be possible for people who have experienced schizophrenic episodes to return to fulfilling lives in society? Research continues to evaluate the effectiveness of various drug treatments. Some scientists claim that large doses of vitamins can have dramatic effects. Still others believe that the treatment of schizophrenia is best accomplished by creating a social environment in the community that allows the schizophrenic an opportunity to recover. In this chapter we will examine all of these issues.

DESCRIPTION

The problem of providing a useful description of the nature of schizophrenia has occupied modern researchers since the 19th century. In Chapter 4 we discussed some of the important purposes of classification. Among them were providing descriptions that would allow decisions about appropriate treatment and provide a common language for behavioral phenomena. The same issues are important to scientists who are trying to provide a description of schizophrenia that has both theoretical and clinical usefulness. Furthermore, in the case of schizophrenia, there is a controversy about whether schizophrenia is a single disorder or a cluster of related disorders with quite different causes. Developing adequate descriptions of the disorder may play a key role in resolving that controversy.

Much of the preoccupation with the description of schizophrenia began in the 19th century. But it is a concern that seems to be reemerging today as our sophistication in developing classification systems and our knowledge about the potential determinants of schizophrenic behavior grow.

History

You will recall that when we discussed the history of abnormal behavior in Chapter 1, we noted that 19th-century Europe was dominated by a concern with organic disorders and pathology. It is not surprising, then, that the early study of behavioral disorders also was affected by this organic preoccupation. The giant of 19th-century German psychiatry, Emil Kraepelin, was particularly concerned with diagnosis and classification. He chose the *outcome* of a disorder as the basis of classification. Those patients who appeared to deteriorate in their functioning over the course of their lives Kraepelin placed in one category, and those who appeared to recover were placed in another. Kraepelin described the deteriorated group as suffering from *dementia praecox*. Essentially this term means psychological deterioration in youth. Among those individuals who seemed to deteriorate fairly early in their lives, Kraepelin discerned three subtypes: *hebephrenic* patients, who acted in an inappropriate, silly fashion; *catatonic* patients, who either became immobilized or were subject to fits of excitement, and *paranoid* patients, who tended to show delusions or mistaken beliefs about their own persecution or delusions of grandeur.

In the history of schizophrenia, perhaps the most important single figure is Eugen

Emil Kraepelin. (National Library of Medicine)

Bleuler. Bleuler was a Swiss psychiatrist who gave us the modern term *schizophrenia*. According to Snyder (1975), one of Bleuler's important contributions was that he recognized that there were patients who were suffering from dementia praecox but who never entered a mental hospital at all. They did not deteriorate in the way that Kraepelin might have expected. Bleuler argued that those people might recover, at least partially, from their symptoms. Thus the clinical picture of schizophrenia, as Bleuler liked to call it, was much more complex than originally imagined.

Perhaps Bleuler's singular genius really lay in his ability to describe the phenomena he observed. He argued that the most important aspect of schizophrenia was not the outcome of the disorder, as Kraepelin has suggested, but that a group of *primary*

Eugen Bleuler. (National Library of Medicine)

behaviors could be identified as the central problems of the schizophrenic. The four types of behavior are commonly referred to in descriptive psychopathology as the *four As*. They are, in order of importance, *associative disturbance, affective disturbance, ambivalence,* and *autism*.

In addition, Bleuler noted symptoms associated with schizophrenia that he called *secondary*. He described them as secondary because they could be observed in other disorders as well and were not unique to schizophrenia. Included among the secondary symptoms were many of the behaviors we associate with severe psychological disturbance, including hallucinations, delusions, withdrawal, and stupor.

Clinical Description

In saying that the four As were unique to schizophrenic behavior, Bleuler was only partly right. These behaviors are indeed critical aspects of schizophrenic disturbance, but every person who is diagnosed as schizophrenic will not necessarily display all four of them at the same time. Let us look at each of these four types of behavior in more detail.

Perhaps the most important is associative disturbance. Associative disturbance is also sometimes called *loose associations* or *thought disorder*. Consider the following example of schizophrenic thought disorder:

> A man of 39, asked whether he felt that people imitated him, replied: "Yes . . . I don't quite gather. I know one right and one left use both hands, but I can't follow the system that's working. The idea is meant in a kind way, but it's not the way I understand life. It seems to be people taking sides, as I understand it. If certain people agree with me they speak to me, and if not they don't. Everybody seems to be the doctor and Mr. H. [his own name] in turn. The superiors here can't do as they like, they can't come up to speak to you as they like, because they have to take their turn of being superior and insuperior. To say things are all wrong means right in turn, but I don't appreciate it that way. If I go into the stores and say 'Are my cigarettes here?' they say 'No.' But if I say 'My cigarettes haven't come' they give them me" (Mayer-Gross, Slater, & Roth, 1969).

You can see that the person's language never seems to be quite on target. It wanders and skips from topic to topic in a vague and disjointed way. Researchers today believe that the peculiar and vague schizophrenic language that one often observes is the result of a fundamental associative disturbance. The usual associations that we make

Union County College
Libraries
Due Dates

User ID: 29354005439458
Library name: ELIZABETH

Date due: 10/10/2016,23:
59
Title: Surviving
schizophrenia : a family
manual
Item ID: 39354001103817

Date due: 10/10/2016,23:
59
Title: Abnormal psychology
Item ID: 39354000911186

Thank you
*

between two words or verbal symbols are considerably weakened or idiosyncratic for the schizophrenic. In mild forms, thought disorder of this sort makes speech vague or difficult to follow. In its more severe forms, such speech is almost impossible to understand.

Another form of associative disturbance in schizophrenia is *blocking*. An interruption in the flow of thinking and speech occurs in blocking, and the individual seems at a loss to explain where a particular train of thought was going. As we will see later, associative disturbance in schizophrenia has been extensively studied in the laboratory by psychologists. Their hope has been to provide a more precise and detailed description of the nature of schizophrenic thought disorder.

While we are still discussing associative disturbances, think to yourself for a moment of what it would be like to have this sort of difficulty in expressing yourself. The frustration and confusion in communication that would result might drive you to withdraw from others. Thus it may be that some primary disturbances in schizophrenia may create problems that the person may attempt to cope with using behavior that still further impairs functioning.

The three other core symptoms described by Bleuler were affective disturbance, ambivalence, and autism. By *affective disturbance* Bleuler meant that many of the individuals he observed seemed to have very little emotional response to situations or stimuli that would elicit joy or sadness in most of us. Another aspect of Bleuler's affective disturbance is inappropriate affect. For example, having been told that a relative or friend had just died, the person might burst into laughter.

Ambivalence is more difficult to describe. In general Bleuler meant to describe the oc-

Schizophrenic behavior is often characterized by inappropriate emotional expression. (Mary Ellen Mark/Magnum Photos, Inc.)

currence of opposing emotions or impulses in the person without their awareness of the contradiction. Frequently schizophrenic individuals report that they simultaneously experience love and hate or depression and excitement in reference to the same person or event.

Finally, Bleuler used the term *autism* to describe the fact that some schizophrenics tend to withdraw from involvement in the external world and become preoccupied by private fantasies. Frequently in these autistic fantasies objective facts become obscured or distorted.

In addition to these core behavior patterns, secondary symptoms of schizophrenia were also described by Bleuler and others. They are thought to be secondary because, although they tend to be very dramatic aspects of schizophrenic disorders, they may be derived as a *response* to the core problems we have just described. And as we noted, these secondary symptoms are not unique to schizophrenia.

The three most important of these secondary symptoms are delusions, hallucinations, and negativism or stupor. By *delusions* we mean strongly held beliefs that are not shared by others in our culture. These beliefs are most characteristic of paranoid schizophrenics and occasionally they are highly systematized.

Hallucinations are sensory experiences without any adequate external stimulus to elicit them. They may be auditory (involving hearing), olfactory (involving smell), tactile (involving the sense of feeling), or visual. As we noted in Chapter 3, the types of hallucinations experienced by schizophrenics are quite different from those experienced by someone who has just taken a psychedelic drug such as LSD. In the case of schizophrenics, hallucinations are almost always auditory. Franz, the patient whose behavior we described at the beginning of this chapter, experienced a wide range of hallucinations, including buzzing noises, squeals, and voices. In some patients the hallucinated voices seem to be expressing disapproval or accusations. In other cases the schizophrenic patient may be unable to discern what the voices are actually saying.

Negativism or stupor refers to behavior displayed by some schizophrenics that tends to make them look paralyzed or immobile. Catatonic schizophrenics, in particular, tend to display this behavior.

It is important for us to remember that not all people classified as schizophrenics will show all these behaviors. In fact, very few people suffering from a schizophrenic disturbance display all the schizophrenic characteristics, primary and secondary, that we have described.

Course over Time

Psychological research and clinical descriptions of schizophrenic behavior help illuminate its possible meaning. But these are only cross-sectional views of the schizophrenia. They give us no idea of the experience and behavior of the schizophrenic over long periods of time. Is it the case that people who display schizophrenic behavior always do so? Or do they have periods of relative normalcy punctuated by bouts of severe symptomatology?

One of the most important contributors to our knowledge about the course of the

A person in a catatonic stupor. (Bill Bridges/Globe Photos, Inc.)

FIGURE 9-1
Course of Disorders over Time

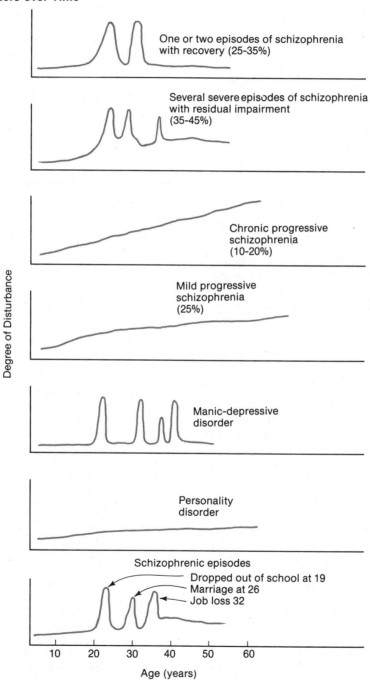

schizophrenic disorder over time is a Swiss researcher named Manfred Bleuler. He is the son of Eugen Bleuler, the 19th-century theorist, whose ideas have been so influential. Manfred Bleuler has devoted his energy to following a large number of schizophrenic individuals over the course of their entire lives. This laborious task has yielded important knowledge of the nature of schizophrenic disorders as they develop over time. Figure 9–1 sketches the course of schizophrenic disorders.

About 25 to 35 percent of M. Bleuler's schizophrenic patients had one or two severe episodes and then recovered after these initial episodes. Another 35 to 45 percent also had episodes of severe schizophrenic disturbance, but between these experiences there was some residual impairment. Still others, about 10 to 20 percent, ran a chronic progressive course that got continuously worse and ended in extremely severe continuous psychosis. Less than 5 percent ran a chronic course ending in chronic but mild disorder.

Contrast these outcomes with those of manic-depressive disorders and personality disorders in Figure 9–1. You can see that manic-depressive disorders tend to be extremely severe, but recovery leaves no residual effect. Personality disorders, on the other hand, develop slowly. There are no marked episodes and no severe deterioration in functioning.

Finally, contrast each of these courses of the disorder with the course of a single person's disorder over time. Although it is difficult to be certain for any single case, it appears that this individual is experiencing an acute onset of schizophrenic disorders with recurrent episodes. These episodes appear in some cases to be triggered by life events and in other cases with no precipitating life events apparent.

Perhaps the most important point to be noted here is that, although schizophrenic

---

TABLE 9–1
DSM III Criteria for the Diagnosis of Schizophrenia

Characteristic Schizophrenic Symptoms

At least one symptom from any of the following 10 symptoms must be present during an active phase of the illness (because a single symptom is given such diagnostic significance, its presence should be clearly established):

Characteristic Delusions

1. Delusions of being controlled: experiences his or her thoughts, actions, or feelings as imposed by some external force.
2. Thought broadcasting: experiences his or her thoughts, as they occur, as being broadcast from his or her head into the external world so that others can hear them.
3. Thought insertion: experiences thoughts, which are not his or her own, being inserted into the individual's mind (other than by God).
4. Thought withdrawal: Believes that thoughts have been removed from his or her head, resulting in a diminished number of thoughts remaining.
5. Other bizarre delusions (patently absurd, fantastic or implausible).
6. Somatic, grandiose, religious, nihilistic, or other delusions without persecutory or jealous content.
7. Delusions of any type if accompanied by hallucinations of any type.

Characteristic Hallucinations

8. Auditory hallucinations in which either a voice keeps up a running commentary on the individual's behaviors or thoughts as they occur, or two or more voices converse with each other.
9. Auditory hallucinations on several occasions with content having no apparent relation to depression or elation, and not limited to one or two words.

Other Characteristic Symptoms

10. Either incoherence, derailment (loosening of associations), marked illogicality, or marked poverty of content of speech—if accompanied by either blunted, flat, or inappropriate affect, delusions or hallucinations, or behavior that is grossly disorganized or catatonic.

behavior at its most severe is extremely dramatic and disabling, it is most often episodic in nature. There are often long periods of time during which the individual is capable of functioning effectively in his or her social world.

DIAGNOSIS AND CLASSIFICATION

DSM III Diagnostic Criteria

Thus far we have described schizophrenic behavior as if it were a relatively homogeneous disorder. In fact, schizophrenia is a relatively heterogeneous group of disorders. Thus decisions about diagnosis have in the past been notably unreliable. However, in keeping with the goal of increasing agreement among clinicians about the diagnosis of various disorders, the DSM III specifies particular symptoms that must be observed in order to make a diagnosis of schizophrenia. These symptoms are shown in Table 9–1.

In addition, these symptoms must be associated with the interference of the ability of the individual to function in life situations. DSM III specifies that this diagnosis should be applied only when the person has displayed the characteristic symptoms for at least six months. The system also makes allowance for examining schizophrenic behavior over time and seeks evidence for a disturbance before the actual onset of symptoms, and/or a "residual" phase following the active phase of the disturbance.

Table 9–2 shows the five main subtypes of schizophrenia listed in DSM III. You will

---

TABLE 9–2
Schizophrenic Subtypes Identified in DSM III

Hebephrenic Type

This psychosis is characterized by disorganized thinking, shallow and inappropriate affect, unpredictable giggling, silly and regressive behavior and mannerisms, and frequent hypochondriacal complaints. Delusions and hallucinations, if present, are transient and not well organized.

Catatonic Type (excited and withdrawn)

It is frequently possible and useful to distinguish two subtypes of catatonic schizophrenia. One is marked by excessive and sometimes violent motor activity and excitement, and the other by generalized inhibition manifested by stupor, mutism, negativism, or waxy flexibility. In time, some cases deteriorate to a vegetative state.

Undifferentiated Type

This category is for patients who show mixed schizophrenic symptoms and who present definite schizophrenic thought, affect, and behavior not classifiable under the other types of schizophrenia. It is distinguished from schizoid personality.

Paranoid Type

This type of schizophrenia is characterized primarily by the presence of persecutory or grandiose delusions, often associated with hallucinations. Excessive religiosity is sometimes seen. The patient's attitude is frequently hostile and aggressive, and his or her behavior tends to be consistent with his or her delusions. In general, the disorder does not manifest the gross personality disorganization of the hebephrenic and catatonic types, perhaps because the patients use the mechanism of projection, which ascribes to others characteristics they cannot accept in themselves. Three subtypes of the disorder may sometimes be differentiated, depending on the predominant symptoms: hostile, grandiose, and hallucinatory.

Residual Type

This category is for patients showing signs of schizophrenia but who, following a psychotic schizophrenic episode, are no longer psychotic.

note that they resemble the traditional Krae-pelinian subtypes with the addition of *undif-ferentiated* and *residual* types to account for cases that do not fall clearly into one of the other subtypes.

The DSM III classification of schizo-phrenic subtypes has not been without criti-cism. Blashfield (1984) observes that the fra-mers of DSM III attempted to narrow the concept of schizophrenia by reducing the number of subtypes. However, they have re-tained three classic subtypes of doubtful reliability and validity plus two "wastebas-ket" categories, residual and undifferentiated. Blashfield (1984) and Carpenter and Ste-phens (1979) both suggest that a classifica-tion system using the course of the disorder and prognosis as key dimensions would more likely be of value than the current sub-types in DSM III.

A review of the research literature on the diagnosis of schizophrenia and affective dis-orders by Pope and Lipinski (1978) calls into question whether or not observing any par-ticular cognitive symptoms of schizophrenia can have value in determining diagnosis or predicting the outcome of the disorder and the response to treatment. They argue that in the United States schizophrenic symp-toms have been relied upon too heavily in di-agnosis, resulting in an overdiagnosis of schizophrenia and an underdiagnosis of af-fective disorders, particularly mania. Spe-cifically they suggest that affective symp-toms do appear to have value in predicting the outcome of psychosis, whereas the schizophrenic symptoms seem to have little value. Furthermore, they maintain that mis-diagnosis of many individuals as schizo-phrenic rather than as affective disorders may expose large numbers of individuals to social stigma and inferior treatment.

In developing DSM III, the category schizoaffective schizophrenic disorder was retained but no diagnostic criteria were pro-vided. This diagnosis was intended to be used only rarely in those instances where a choice between affective disorders and schizophrenia could not be easily made. However, Meltzer (1984) and a number of other researchers have recently explored the question of whether this diagnostic category should be retained. A review of the literature by Harrow and Grossman (1984) suggests that schizoaffective patients tend to fare less well than patients with affective disor-ders over time, but better than schizophrenic patients.

This controversy raises a number of inter-esting questions. Is it possible for a person to simultaneously experience both an affec-tive disorder and schizophrenia? Is there ac-tually a continuum of psychosis ranging from affective psychosis on the one hand to "pure" schizophrenia on the other? This group of patients, who seem to fall between the affective and schizophrenic disorders, raise fundamental questions about the na-ture of psychosis that remain to be resolved.

ALTERNATIVE APPROACHES TO CLASSIFICATION

A number of investigators (Crow, 1980; Seid-man, 1983) have suggested that a distinction between schizophrenic patients based on "positive" and "negative" symptoms may be of considerable value. Positive symptoms are those reflecting delusions, hallucina-tions, and thought disorder whereas nega-tive symptoms involve flattening of affect, poverty of speech, and withdrawal. These two groups of schizophrenic patients may actually have different underlying biochemi-cal and neurological disorders. If so, this dis-tinction will be of considerable value in re-search on the determinants of schizophrenia in the future. The distinction between posi-tive and negative symptoms is closely related to important neurological and biochemical findings that we will discuss later in this chapter.

Some researchers have come to believe that there is little value in attempting to classify schizophrenic patients into various types. They feel it is more appropriate to attempt to arrange people suffering from schizophrenia along a dimension that reflects some important clinical or scientific characteristic.

Perhaps the best-known of these dimensional approaches to describing schizophrenia is the process-reactive dimension. This dimension was orginally designed to help clinicians predict the outcome of schizophrenic disorders. You will remember that Kraepelin was much interested in classifying patients in terms of the outcome of their disorder since no organic pathology could be found that would allow an organic classification system. This concern with *prognosis* (outcome of the disorder) is reflected in the process-reactive distinction originally developed by Kantor, Wallner, & Winder (1953).

Table 9-3 lists the different patterns of behavior thought to exist among process and reactive schizophrenics. One of the most

striking differences between the two ends of the process-reactive continuum has to do with the onset of symptoms. In the case of reactive schizophrenics, symptoms almost always occur as a response to some crisis or stressful life event. In process schizophrenia, on the other hand, the onset of schizophrenic behavior is gradual and begins early in the individual's life. Often process schizophrenia is thought to involve some underlying biological cause, while reactive schizophrenia is thought to be triggered primarily by environmental events.

At least three other attempts to distinguish the ends of a continuum of schizophrenia have been suggested in the literature. *Acute* versus *chronic* schizophrenia involves a distinction developed from medical thinking. Acute schizophrenic disorders are characterized by sudden severe symptoms, but the likelihood of recovery is thought to be good. Chronic schizophrenic disorders are usually thought to be irreversible and not necessarily as dramatic in onset. *Premorbid* adjustment has been suggested by Philips (1953) as an important way of delineating a continuum of schizophrenia. Schizophrenics

TABLE 9-3
Characteristics of Process and Reactive Schizophrenia

	Reactive	Process
Premorbid features	Relatively normal social and intellectual development	Poor early social and sexual adjustment; lower intelligence
Pattern of onset	Occurs later in life; rapid onset in response to life stress	Occurs earlier in life, in childhood or adolescence; onset is slow and gradual; no apparent environmental stress
Pattern of presenting behavior	Depressed or anxious mood; affect preserved disorientation during acute episode	Absence of anxiety or depression; flat affect, bizarre delusions
Course of disorder	Episodic	Continuous
Prognosis	Good	Poor

Source: Based on "Process and Reactive Schizophrenia" by R. E. Kantor et al., 1953, *Journal of Consulting and Clinical Psychology, 17.*

with "good premorbid adjustment" presumably have good social, sexual, and occupational adjustment before the onset of schizophrenia. Patients displaying "poor premorbid adjustment" tend to have poor social, sexual, and occupational adjustment before the onset of the disorder.

A thorough methodological review of the research on premorbid social functioning as a predictor of outcome in schizophrenia (Stoffelmayr, Dillavou, & Hunter, 1983) suggests that when appropriate methodological adjustments are made across various studies, premorbid adjustment is an extremely good predictor of outcome for schizophrenics.

It may be that these various alternative methods of classifying schizophrenia, including the process-reactive dimension, the "positive-negative" distinction, and premorbid adjustment are all closely related to one another. The value of these alternative classifications lies primarily in the fact that they allow more accurate predictions of the symptomatology, course, outcome, and underlying pathology in schizophrenia. This after all is the purpose of diagnosis and classification as we suggested in Chapter 4. We shall return to this topic later in the chapter.

Experimental Research on Schizophrenic Behavior

The descriptions and examples that we have drawn from naturalistic and clinical observations lack the precision and explicitness that more carefully controlled studies might provide us. Psychologists have been concerned, in particular, with providing more precise descriptions of the nature of schizophrenic thought disorder. Such descriptions will give us a clearer understanding of the nature of the disorder and provide us with hints about where to search for its determinants. We will now consider examples of psychological research that attempt to describe the nature of schizophrenic thought disorder in more precise scientific terms.

Thought disorder is a good candidate for psychological study because researchers can apply their knowledge about cognitive processes in normal individuals to understand thought disorder as we observe it in the clinical context. Psychologists have been particularly interested in the mechanism of *attention* and the role it may play in schizophrenic thought disorder (Price, 1968). Schizophrenics often report, "I just can't concentrate," or "I'm so distractable I can't keep my mind on anything." This attentional difficulty can even show up in the middle of a sentence as attention wanders from one topic to another.

Wohlberg and Kornetsky (1973) studied unmedicated discharged schizophrenics and compared them with 20 matched controls using a test of attention called the Continuous Performance Test. Patients were rewarded for correct responses and later tested in a session without distracting stimuli. They could fail to respond to critical stimuli (commit errors of omission) or respond incorrectly to noncritical stimuli (errors of commission). Schizophrenics tended to make more errors of omission, especially when they were distracted, than did the controls. An important aspect of Wohlberg and Kornetsky's findings is that this basic attentional deficit could even be observed in schizophrenics who were not showing severe symptoms and who were not receiving medication. Much of the previous research on the problem of attention in schizophrenia has been complicated by the inability to rule out these factors as important contributors to the experimental performance of the schizophrenic group. This research suggests that the schizophrenic suffers from some fundamental difficulties in attention. But the delusions and hallucinations sometimes reported by schizophrenics are not accounted for with this research.

Delusions and Attention. James Chapman (1966) has argued that delusions may be attempts to make sense out of or cope with the extremely stressful experience of having one's attention and perception so markedly altered. Chapman argues that patients gradually develop less rational and eventually bizarre explanations to account for their altered perceptual experiences. Chapman observed people develop delusions of various kinds as an apparent attempt to cope with the altered experience of a schizophrenic episode. For example, patients' delusions that the CIA is tampering with their minds may reflect their attempts to make sense of their altered experience of the world. Thus delusions may be attempts to understand what is happening to fragmented and altered experience.

This is also suggested in some research on altered perception in schizophrenia conducted by Price (1966). In this research paranoid schizophrenics, nonparanoid schizophrenics, and normal individuals were compared in their ability to make judgments of the size of standard objects when the distance from the viewer was changed. Normals and paranoid schizophrenics both did fairly well at this difficult task. But paranoid schizophrenics also displayed an intriguing characteristic in their performance. When asked to rate their confidence in their own judgments, paranoid schizophrenics reported that they were "extremely confident" in the accuracy of their reports even when their accuracy was poor. Paranoid patients seemed to be compensating for their uncertainty about their own perceptual world. Thus it may be that some schizophrenics attempt to rigidly restructure the meaning of their world in order to cope with an inability to focus attention.

Schizophrenics Report on Their Own Experiences

So far we have examined schizophrenic disorders from the point of view of the clinician who tends to focus on global clinical behaviors, such as ambivalence or delusions, and from the point of view of the psychological researcher whose goal is to provide carefully controlled analytical descriptions and understand their relationship to psychological processes, such as memory or attention. But what about people experiencing schizophrenic disorders? How do they feel about their own schizophrenic experience? Perhaps the reports of people undergoing a schizophrenic experience will give us additional insight into both the experimental research data we have just considered and the clinical behavior of schizophrenics.

As we noted earlier, Chapman (1966) has carefully interviewed schizophrenic patients and asked them to describe the nature of their experience as clearly as they could. Chapman reports that the first signs of an oncoming schizophrenic episode are perceptual. Perceptual distortions can be quite frightening and disorienting. Consider this report: "Last week I was with a girl and she seemed to get bigger and bigger, like a monster coming nearer and nearer. The situations become threatening and I shrink back."

Following these initial perceptual distortions, patients often report that they have extreme difficulty controlling their thoughts. A patient notes:

> I can't control my thoughts. I can't keep thoughts out. It comes on automatically. It happens at most peculiar times—not just when I'm talking, but when I'm listening as well. I lose control at conversation then I sweat and shake all over. . . . I can hear what they are saying all right, it's remembering

what they have said the next second that is difficult. It just goes out of my mind. I'm concentrating so much on little things I have difficulty in finding an answer at the time.

These reports suggest that the person experiencing a schizophrenic episode is having considerable difficulty in focusing attention on external events. It is almost as if a "filter" that we all use to focus our attention in everyday tasks has temporarily ceased to function.

The idea that fundamental attentional problems in the schizophrenic experiences are important in understanding other schizophrenic behavior has been discussed by a number of researchers. For example, Maher (1968) has suggested that the loss of attentional control and the interference of dominant associations are phenomena that can be combined to help us understand the disordered thought and speech of schizophrenics. As Maher cogently puts it, "Uttering a sentence without disruption is an extremely skilled performance, but one that most of us acquire so early in life that we are unaware of this remarkable complexity." He says further, "Our successful sentences come from the successful, sequential inhibition of all interfering associations that individual words in the sentence might generate. Just as successful visual attention involves tuning out irrelevant visual material, so successful utterance may involve tuning out irrelevant verbal static" (p. 30).

The "static" Maher refers to is the inappropriate associations that are so characteristic of schizophrenic speech. Thus it may be that the confused and intriguing patterns of speech are the product of both an inability to focus attention over a sustained period of time on the goal of a particular sentence, and the interference of inappropriate associations that would normally be inhibited.

DETERMINANTS OF SCHIZOPHRENIA

The search for the causes of schizophrenia is one of the most fascinating scientific detective stories in the field of abnormal psychology. The search for causes has ranged broadly; stimulated by a variety of different theoretical perspectives, scientists have examined biochemical, familial, and social phenomena. Perhaps no other major psychological disorder has been examined in such a variety of human contexts. Let us now turn to that search.

At a general level, most scientists will agree that both biological and experiential factors play some role in the development of schizophrenia. But that is where the agreement ends. Researchers tend to look in different places for the causes of schizophrenic behavior. Some scientists believe that the central mechanisms of schizophrenia are genetic. Quite naturally their search is primarily for genetic factors or for biochemical processes. Others believe that extremely powerful socialization forces in the family play a key role in the development of schizophrenia. They conduct their search within the family itself, attempting to isolate developmental experiences that may play a crucial role in the expression of schizophrenia.

Kessler (1969) notes that, "in general, biologically oriented researchers tend to view schizophrenia as a disease resulting from an unidentified organic or hereditary biochemical or neurophysiological defect, whereas psychologically oriented investigators tend to view schizophrenia as a group of disorders resulting from disturbances in sociocultural, familial, and interpersonal processes. After paying homage to the concept of genotype-environment interaction, most investigators, unwittingly or by choice, slip back into more comfortable modes of thought and place their etiological bets on one or the other side" (p. 1341).

Thus, despite the fact that all scientists recognize that social, familial, and biological factors must *interact* to produce the complex behavior we call schizophrenia, even "objective" scientists have difficulty maintaining the neutral stand that such an interactional view would require. Because of their own training or hunches, scientists usually place their bets (and their biases) on either the experiential or the biological side when searching for the causes of schizophrenia.

But whether a researcher's bias is in the direction of biological or psychological causes, there are certain facts that have to be explained. These are the facts that have to do with the *transmission* of schizophrenia. Remember, we said that a child who has one parent that has been diagnosed as

schizophrenic has 10 times greater a chance of developing a schizophrenic disorder than someone who does not have a schizophrenic parent. A child with two such parents has 40 times greater a chance. How do you explain that striking finding?

If you are biologically oriented, the first thing that is likely to occur to you (and to scientists) is that this is evidence of genetic transmission. The child must have inherited something physical or biochemical. But a scientist concerned with the family context would argue that these facts can be just as easily explained by recognizing that the child in a family with one parent who is schizophrenic is more likely to learn schizophrenic behavior—perhaps through modeling. It is equally easy for the experientially oriented scientist to explain the increased risk associated with having two schizophrenic

FIGURE 9–2
Models of Causation in Schizophrenia

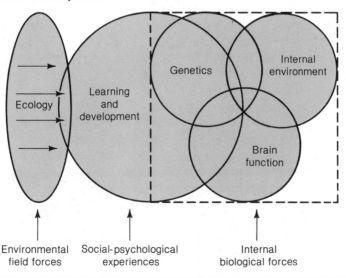

Environmental field forces • Social-psychological experiences • Internal biological forces

parents. Imagine what a child living in such a home must be experiencing. This must be compelling evidence for the power of experience in the causation of schizophrenia.

The important idea to grasp here is that all of these possible causal factors are *correlated* with one another. Each of them looks like a highly likely set of explanations for the development of schizophrenic behavior. Indeed, a look at Figure 9–2 suggests that there are several different "models" of schizophrenic behavior. Now perhaps you can see the puzzle that confronts researchers. Biological, experiential, and social factors all seem to be likely candidates in explaining the causes of schizophrenia. On the surface it seems that each of them by itself could account for the fact of schizophrenic transmission.

In our discussion we will examine the evidence for biological, familial, and social causes in the development of schizophrenia. Having done that, we will examine some of the strategies that scientists are now using to try to untangle the mystery of schizophrenia and we will consider some new views that promise to clear up at least some of the mystery.

The Biological Search for Causes

Scientists concerned with the possible biological causes of schizophrenia have worked simultaneously on two fronts. First, some scientists have been engaged in an attempt to uncover evidence for underlying genetic factors. Second, other scientists, many of whom are already convinced of the importance of genetic factors, have conducted their search for determinants in the biochemistry of the brain. Their working hypothesis is that something about the biochemistry of the schizophrenic brain is disordered, and that finding the nature of this disorder may lead us to understand both the causes of schizophrenic behavior and

possibly also lead us to a biological strategy for prevention or treatment.

Genetic Evidence.   We have already noted that being the offspring of someone diagnosed as schizophrenic greatly increases one's chances of developing the disorder oneself. This is a major finding in *family studies* of schizophrenia. A typical strategy in genetic research is to ask whether a particular disorder runs in families. It if does, then the scientist considers this a clue to the possible genetic causes of the disorder and looks for evidence that will be more convincing.

Perhaps the best-known evidence for a possible genetic contribution to the cause of schizophrenia comes from *twin studies*

Comparison of identical twins reared together and apart form an "experiment in nature" that allows assessment of the genetic contribution to a variety of behavior patterns and traits.
(Susan Richter/Photo Researchers, Inc.)

(Kendler et al., 1981). As you may recall, twin studies help rule out the possibility that it is the experience of living in a family with a schizophrenic member that produces schizophrenia in the offspring rather than genetics. Thus twin studies provide a strategy for obtaining less ambiguous evidence for a genetic component in schizophrenia.

The strategy of twin studies is not hard to understand. We know, of course, that identical twins are *monozygotic;* that is, they develop from the same egg and therefore have identical genetic makeup. Fraternal twins, however, are no more genetically similar than other siblings that have developed from the fertilization of two different eggs. This crucial fact helps us separate the possible effects of environment from those of heredity.

For example, if it is the experience of living in a schizophrenic family that produces schizophrenia, then both members of a pair of identical twins ought to be no more likely to develop schizophrenia than both members of a fraternal twin pair. But now consider the possibility that there is an important hereditary factor in schizophrenia. In this case, if one identical twin is diagnosed as schizophrenic, then the likelihood of the co-twin also being schizophrenic should be greater for identical twins than for fraternal twins.

Table 9–4 illustrates this idea with hypothetical data. In the case illustrating evidence for a possible genetic component, both identical and fraternal twin pairs with one diagnosed schizophrenic member (index case) are compared. In the identical twin group, 90 percent of the co-twins were also diagnosed as schizophrenic, a very high concordance rate. The fraternal co-twins were diagnosed as schizophrenic in only 10 percent of the cases. This would provide strong evidence of a genetic factor. In the other instance no difference in concordance rates are found, suggesting no discernable genetic involvement. Kendler et al. (1981) has reviewed the evidence from twin studies of schizophrenia and finds that while the concordance rates may vary, they still provide strong evidence that genetic factors are important in schizophrenia.

A number of researchers have begun to use a different strategy for separating possible genetic and environmental factors in the development of schizophrenia. The strategy they use has been to take advantage of a natural experiment in nature, that of adoption. Kety, Rosenthal, Wender, and Schulsinger (1968) all have made ingenious use of the fact that some schizophrenics' parents have put up their children for adoption early in the child's life. Furthermore, some nonschizophrenic parents have adopted children born of schizophrenic parents without knowing the identity or diagnosis of the biological parents. Thus adoption provides a situation

TABLE 9–4
Illustration of Possible Outcomes of Twin Studies Indicating Different Degrees of Genetic Involvement in Schizophrenia (Concordance rate—Percent of Twin Pairs Both of Whom Are Diagnosed as Schizophrenic)

	Monozygotic Twins (genetically identical)	Dizygotic Twins (no more genetically similar than siblings)
Evidence for genetic component	90%	10%
No evidence for genetic component	15%	15%

in which entangled effects of heredity and environment can be separated. The trick was to obtain birth records and other information that was detailed enough to allow the researchers to trace adopted children and to discover which of them developed some form of schizophrenic behavior and which did not.

If you think about it for a moment the logic becomes clear. If there is a genetic factor in schizophrenia, then children who were born of a schizophrenic parent but adopted by nonschizophrenic parents will be more likely to develop schizophrenia than will children adopted from nonschizophrenic biological parents and raised by nonschizophrenic adoptive parents.

Rosenthal and his colleagues took advantage of the fact that some countries, such as Denmark, keep extremely detailed birth records so that it is possible to follow individuals throughout the course of their lives. Consequently it was possible for them to begin with a list of all of the children adopted in Denmark over a 23-year period. The study showed that adopted children with one schizophrenic or manic-depressive biological parent are more likely to display schizophrenic spectrum disorders than adopted children whose biological parents had no history of psychological disorder.

A review of the evidence for a genetic predisposition in schizophrenia has recently been conducted by Gottesman and Shields (1982). The results of their survey are seen in Figure 9–2, which shows the relationship between genetic relatedness among individuals and the risk of developing schizophrenia in a lifetime. It is quite clear from this figure that as genetic similarity increases, so does the risk of developing schizophrenia. As Nicol and Gottesman (1983) suggest, an identical twin of a schizophrenic is at least three times as likely as a fraternal twin to develop schizophrenia and 35 to 60 times as likely as an unrelated person from the same general population (see Figure 9–3).

The data strongly suggest that there is a genetic mechanism involved in the development of schizophrenia. However, studies of this sort do not allow us to decide what the *mechanism* of transmission actually is. Researchers have spent considerable time debating whether or not a single gene or many genes are involved in the transmission of the disorder (O'Rourke et al., 1982). Many researchers believe that the available evidence indicates that more than one gene is involved in the development of the disorder and that a polygenetic threshold model is the most appropriate to summarize the multiple risks involved. Figure 9–4 shows the polygenetic threshold model as it is commonly conceptualized. Researchers have proposed this polygenetic threshold model for schizophrenia because it also fits the evidence for a variety of diseases such as diabetes.

It is important to appreciate why researchers build such biological models and pursue data to test them with such vigor. In Chapter 2 we considered the biological perspective with its organic orientation to abnormal behavior. For medical geneticists the idea that schizophrenia is a disease is a highly plausible one. They have successfully pursued other initially puzzling disorders, such as diabetes, to their genetic origins. For them it is no great leap to think about schizophrenia in the same way. If there is an underlying genetic component in schizophrenia, one likely manifestation of such a factor would be the body's biochemistry. Let us now turn to research on the biochemistry of schizophrenia.

Biochemical Research. Scientists have long suspected that the key to unlocking the mystery of schizophrenia lay in the brain biochemistry or the metabolism of the schizophrenic. If only we could understand how the brain chemistry of schizophrenics was different from that of normal people, this would promise both an understanding of the causes of the disorder and the possibility

FIGURE 9–3
Lifetime Risks of Developing Schizophrenia Are Largely a Function of How Closely an Individual Is Genetically Related to a Schizophrenic and Not a Function of How Much Their Environment Is Shared (Data from Gottesman and Shields, 1982)

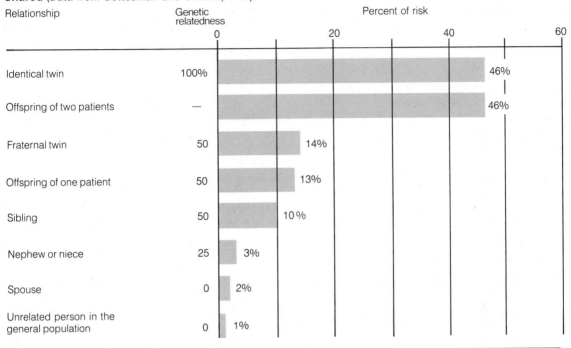

Relationship	Genetic relatedness	Percent of risk
Identical twin	100%	46%
Offspring of two patients	—	46%
Fraternal twin	50	14%
Offspring of one patient	50	13%
Sibling	50	10%
Nephew or niece	25	3%
Spouse	0	2%
Unrelated person in the general population	0	1%

Source: Nicol & Gottesman, 1983, p. 399.

of prevention or cure, perhaps through the regulation of medication.

But the history of the search for the biochemical X factor in schizophrenia has been a discouraging one. The fact that psychologists and psychiatrists have placed their bets so heavily on finding some unique biochemical factor in schizophrenia has led to a long series of premature reports of discoveries of the X factor in schizophrenia (Kety, 1967). These reports were withdrawn with much less fanfare when it was belatedly discovered that something in the diet of the experimental group or some other uncontrolled factor actually was producing the biochemical result. (Think back for a moment to our review in Chapter 3 of the research on the "pink spot" conducted by Hoffer.) The excit-

ing hypothesis that adrenochrome might be the X factor in schizophrenia actually turned out to be a result of poorly controlled laboratory procedures. Blind alleys like this have certainly not discouraged researchers, who continue to seek an understanding of the biochemistry of schizophrenia.

There is, however, an important new set of developments in the biochemistry of schizophrenia that does look promising for the future. This line of research has come to be known as the *dopamine hypothesis* (Keith, Gunderson, Reifman, Buchsbaum, & Mosher, 1976; Nicol & Gottesman, 1983). Snyder (1974) has described the early detective work that led to the implication of dopamine in the biochemistry of schizophrenia. Before we consider that evidence, let us look at Figure

FIGURE 9–4
Polygenic Threshold Model of Schizophrenic Causation

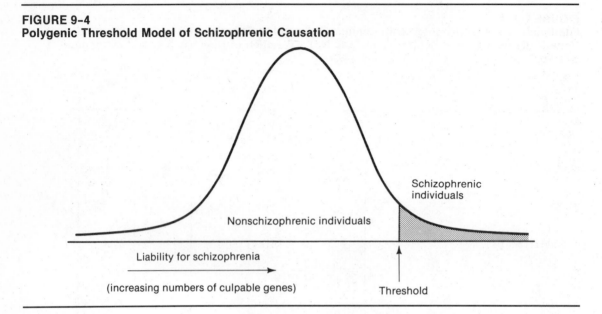

Schizophrenic individuals

Nonschizophrenic individuals

Liability for schizophrenia

(increasing numbers of culpable genes)

Threshold

9–5 to understand the role that dopamine plays in normal brain functioning.

Dopamine is a *neurotransmitter*. Neurotransmitters are chemicals that transmit electrical signals from one neuron in the brain to the next. They are the message carriers that cross the synapse when an electrical impulse must be transmitted from one neuron to the next. Dopamine is one of a whole family of neurotransmitters that occur in various areas of the brain. In Figure 9–5A you can see that dopamine acts as a chemical messenger by leaving the nerve ending and traveling to a receptor site in the succeeding neuron. Once it has sent its message, it is taken up again *(reuptake)* by the original neuron (Seeman, 1980).

The evidence for the involvement of dopamine in schizophrenia is indirect (Figure 9–5B). First, the effect of antischizophrenic drugs such as the phenothiazines is to block the receptor site for dopamine. Thus, to put it crudely, phenothiazines "slow down" the transmission of nerve impulses by partially blocking the dopamine (Haracz, 1982). Second, amphetamine, a central nervous system stimulant, appears to "soup up" the transmission of nerve impulses by blocking reuptake of dopamine, leaving large amounts of it in the synapse. Amphetamine also makes schizophrenic symptoms much worse (Snyder, 1975).

According to Keith el al. (1976), at least three mechanisms for the increase of dopamine could be operating (Figure 9–5C). Increased amounts of dopamine at the nerve terminals could be producing schizophrenic-like behavior. Second, increased sensitivity of dopamine receptors could be producing the effect. Third, the reduction in some antagonistic chemical that normally reduces the amount of dopamine in the synaptic cleft could also be responsible. Obviously there are many potential mechanisms for the increase in dopamine in the synaptic cleft (Meltzer, 1976).

Recent research by Seeman (1980) has identified receptor sites that appear to be

FIGURE 9–5
The Dopamine Hypothesis in Schizophrenia

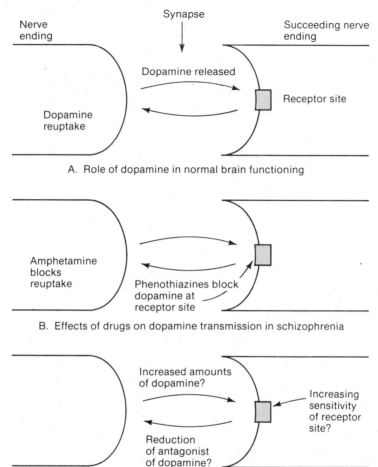

A. Role of dopamine in normal brain functioning

B. Effects of drugs on dopamine transmission in schizophrenia

C. Possible dopamine mechanisms in schizophrenia

highly specific for dopamine transmission. These receptor sites are particularly significant because they respond uniquely to drugs designed to reduce psychotic symptoms. This provides evidence for a direct tie between the dopamine pathways on the one hand and clinical symptomatology of schizophrenia on the other. It appears that this research has identified specific brain receptors implicated in the expresion of schizophrenic symptomatology.

However, this does not necessarily mean that all schizophrenics experience problems with dopamine reception. It is quite possible that this is only one of several mechanisms involved in schizophrenia. Or it may be that only some of the people who experience schizophrenic symptoms do so because of problems in dopamine transmission. It is precisely this idea that is proposed by Haracz (1982) and by Crow (1980). Haracz and Crow both suggest that dopamine transmission may be associated only with those schizophrenics who show strong "positive" or acute signs of schizophrenia, including delusions, hallucinations, and thought disorder. On the other hand, "negative" symptoms such as withdrawal, flattened affect, and poverty of speech may be associated with structural changes in the brain (Seidman, 1983). Thus the dopamine hypothesis is a promising explanation at least for some forms of schizophrenia. We now turn to another line of research examining structual changes in the brain that may account for another large group of schizophrenic disorders.

While considerable interest and energy have been expended on the study of dopamine transmission, other researchers have become interested in the neurotransmitters called *endorphins* we described briefly in Chapter 2. Some research has been conducted that reports an excess of endorphins among schizophrenics while other studies have indicated a deficiency (Shah & Donald, 1982; Ganguli, 1984). Still another line of research has involved hemodialysis of schizophrenics in which their blood is mechanically washed in the same way kidney patients are treated to remove blood impurities. Some researchers have reported finding an abnormal endorphin in the residual material cleaned from the blood of schizophrenics. However, Schulz et al. (1981) have not been able to repeat this finding.

It is important for us to note that the search for dopamine imbalances in the brain of schizophrenics is very different from earlier research in the brain chemistry of schizophrenia. Earlier works attempted to find some X factor unique to schizophrenia. Here, instead, we see attempts to understand imbalances in normally occurring brain chemistry processes rather than some biochemical factor unique to schizophrenia.

Evidence from Brain Research. While biochemical researchers have been making rapid progress, particularly with the dopamine hypothesis, still other research strategies are being used to examine possible biological bases for schizophrenia. The advent of a range of technologies for more precise assessment of brain abnormalities is the primary reason for progress in this field. *Computerized tomography* scanners allow researchers to develop safe, noninvasive composite pictures of the brain that are highly sensitive to cerebral atrophy and other structural abnormalities (Seidman, 1983). A variety of rigorously conducted studies suggest that between 20 and 35 percent of all schizophrenic patients show some brain abnormalities. The most common of these is the enlargement of brain ventricles, suggesting that some of the surrounding brain tissue has been damaged or has died.

A second major development in the field has been *positron emission tomography* or the PET scan. This technique works by placing radioactive tracers in glucose and then giving it to the patient. As the brain cells use the glucose in metabolism, the radioactive material decays and registers on detectors surrounding the patient's head. Thus it is possible to study patterns of metabolism within the brain with great accuracy and to correlate the activity with clinical symptoms. Rodgers (1982) suggests that during hallucinations the speech and hearing centers of the brain burn sugar more rapidly in schizophrenics than in normal individuals.

Recently PET scans were conducted for the Genain quadruplets, all of whom have shown differing amounts of schizophrenic symptomatology. As with identical twins, quadruplets have identical genetic characteristics. Differences in the pattern of brain activity may be associated with clinical symptoms. Bushbaum (1984) also reports that all four quadruplets showed high levels of brain activity in the visual cortex even though the PET scans were given in a dark room. It is possible that the observed brain activity reflects hallucinations experienced by the sisters.

Still another important set of findings is associated with strategies for measuring regional blood flow in the brain. Weinberger (1983) reports that the frontal lobes in the brains of schizophrenic patients respond just the opposite from those of healthy persons when asked to perform a simple card-sorting task. As subjects perform the task, a computerized imaging system determines the rate of blood flow on the basis of how rapidly a radioactive tracer is washed out of the area. Among the schizophrenics studied by Weinberger and his colleagues, the regional blood maps indicated a sharp drop in blood flow to the frontal lobes for approximately half of the schizophrenic patients. Normal control subjects showed increases in blood flow to the region when engaged in the card-sorting task. Thus improvements in scientific technology allowing us to study brain structure and abnormalities and differences in metabolic rates in different portions of the brain have identified important abnormalities among at least some schizophrenic patients.

As we suggested earlier, a number of researchers including Seidman (1983), Haracz (1982) and Crow (1980) suggest that at least two groups of schizophrenics may exist with different types of brain pathology in each group. Schizophrenics with a pattern of acute, positive symptoms are more likely to have impaired dopamine reception while other schizophrenics with a more negative symptom pattern may suffer from a variety of brain abnormalities, including enlarged ventricles. It appears that a new technology for studying brain structure and activity is be-

ginning to reveal important new relationships between the brain and clinical symptoms of schizophrenia.

Family and Society as Contexts for Schizophrenia

The family is both the genetic and experiential context of human development. Both biological influences and social learning intertwine in the family context. For scientists trying to understand the nature of schizophrenia, the family poses an especially important challenge. It is the family that provides a primary context for the transmission of schizophrenia, whether the actual mechanism is biological, environmental, or some interaction of the two.

For most psychologists, however, the family is seen as a place for learning. Their questions about the relationship between families and schizophrenia are most likely to focus on whether and how symptoms are learned through the process of socialization.

Although it is intuitively obvious to look at the family as an arena for the learning of abnormal behavior, there is actually evidence from genetic studies for environmental determinants of schizophrenia. Think back, for a moment, to our examination of twin studies of schizophrenia. These studies clearly indicated that genetic endowment alone could not fully explain the observed incidence of schizophrenia. Concordance rates among identical twins were far from perfect, whereas an exclusively genetic mechanism for the inheritance of schizophrenia would predict perfect concordance among identical twins.

Thus an environmental search for the determinants of schizophrenia can properly begin with a consideration of the family. But as we shall see, the larger society may also play a role. We will consider evidence strongly suggesting a role for societal sources of stress and selection in the development of schizophrenia as well. But in the last analysis we will return to the family, for it is in the family that genetics, learning, and society have their most acute impact on the psychological life of the indivdual.

Family Hypotheses. A common observation of clinicians who treat schizophrenic patients is that much of the content of their preoccupations, fears, delusions, and hallucinations derives from family life. This clinical observation has led a number of different theorists concerned with the causes of schizophrenia to suggest that the family environment operates as an important causal factor in the development of schizophrenia. In fact, their clinical accounts often are very persuasive in suggesting that schizophrenic behavior cannot be understood except in the family context.

But different theorists have different views of *how* the family actually contributes to the development of schizophrenia. The boxed material has a number of different clinically derived hypotheses about the nature of the family of the schizophrenic and its relationship to the development of symptoms.

These hypotheses seem highly plausible and are made more so by the rich clinical detail that is often used to support them. But as important as clinical experience is in *generating* hypotheses, it clearly does not provide an adequate arena for *testing* them.

The reason for this problem is not difficult to grasp. Clinicians are observing families in which a family member has *already developed schizophrenic symptoms.* Thus we are confronted with an unsolvable problem of inference. If we do happen to observe something unique in the patient's family environ-

A number of theorists have argued that the pattern of family interaction is an important determinant of abnormal behavior. (Owen Franken/Stock, Boston, Inc.)

FOUR CLINICALLY DERIVED HYPOTHESES ABOUT THE ROLE OF THE FAMILY IN THE DEVELOPMENT OF SCHIZOPHRENIA

Attachment The difficulties observed in adolescent or adult schizophrenics reflect disruptions in early attachment between the child and caretaker, suggests Otto Will (1970). This disruption in the formation of basic trust results in later fear of loss and separation, withdrawal, panic, odd symbolic communication, and lack of ego development characteristic of schizophrenia.

Schizophrenogenic Mother Mothers who are overprotective, smothering, insensitive, rejecting, seductive, and controlling are capable of eliciting schizophrenic behavior in their offspring, according to Arieti (1959).

Double Bind Certain forms of communication between parent and child are productive of schizophrenic behavior

according to Bateson, Jackson, Haley, and Weaklank (1956). The "binder" communicates to the child in paradoxical fashion, demanding mutually contradictory responses (e.g., "Don't be so obedient"). The dependent child is constrained against pointing out the contradiction and copes in ways that appear schizophrenic, such as withdrawing or searching for hidden meanings in all communications.

Social Learning Ullman and Krasner (1975) suggest differential reinforcement is the key factor in learning schizophrenic behavior in the family. Normal behavior is ignored (extinguished) and bizarre behavior is reinforced through attention. The result is a behavioral repertoire that appears schizophrenic.

ment, we cannot know whether it has played a causal role in the development of those symptoms or whether the unique factor is actually a *response* to the stressful experience of having a severely disturbed person in the family. In short, we cannot know whether the family environment is the *cause* or the *consequence* of schizophrenic behavior.

There is good reason to believe that families who must cope with chronically ill or disabled members show more stress and disturbance than those who do not. Thus the rival hypothesis that family behavior is a consequence rather than a cause of schizophrenia is quite plausible.

There are still other questions about the role of the family that need answers. For ex-

ample, if it is true that the families of schizophrenics do show unusual behavior, then we would want to know whether this behavior is *unique* to families that produce schizophrenic offspring or whether it is typical of families with a deviant member.

On the last question we now have some evidence. A review conducted by Jacob (1975) was unable to uncover any consistent evidence that conflict or positive and negative emotion were uniquely characteristic of families of schizophrenics as opposed to those of various types of control groups. Jacob did find, however, that there appeared to be *less clear communication* in the families of schizophrenics when such families were compared with those of normal controls.

An important controlled study of schizophrenia that throws light on the nature of family interactions in the development of schizophrenic behavior is the *high-risk* study conducted by Mednick (1966) that we described in Chapter 4. Mednick and his colleagues carefully examined a group of 207 children who were at risk for schizophrenia because their mothers had been diagnosed as schizophrenic. These children were compared with 104 low-risk control subjects. As you may recall, some of these high-risk children were expected eventually to develop schizophrenic behavior. Then the data on the schizophrenic children collected *before* they developed schizophrenic symptoms could be compared with the data on the low-risk children to discover what if anything was unique to the schizophrenic group. One set of differences reported by Mednick had to do with the degree to which the autonomic nervous system of high-risk children was able to recover from stimulation. Now a second major set of evidence appears to be emerging. Daughters, but not sons, appear to be affected by the age at which the mother first became seriously disturbed. In families where the mother was younger when she became disturbed, there is more likely to be a damaging disturbance in the daughter. For boys, separation from their mothers seems to be the key factor. The greater the separation from the mother, the more severe the disturbance among high-risk boys who ultimately develop schizophrenic behavior.

Thus it appears from these studies that the *form* and *severity* of schizophrenic behavior may well be crucially affected by the family environment. Let us now turn to evidence that suggests that other social and environmental forces are at work as well.

Social Epidemiology. Epidemiology is the study of the distribution of diseases in society. The distribution may be geographical or it may be in terms of income, jobs, or other demographic dimensions. In the detective work of searching for the causes of disorders, epidemiologists look for the disproportionate numbers of cases in various geographical, ethnic, income, or occupational groups. When an extremely high incidence of a particular disorder is found, say, in a particular occupational group, it may be a clue to the causes of the disorder. The discovery of the cancer-causing properties of certain industrial chemicals was uncovered in just this way. Workers exposed to the chemicals developed more cases of skin cancer.

In a study of schizophrenia, the problems of the mental health epidemiologist are especially acute. To define and diagnose a case of schizophrenia is difficult. Furthermore, schizophrenic disorders are often episodic, making diagnosis even more problematic. Nevertheless, mental health epidemiologists have contributed some important clues to the determinants of schizophrenia.

In 1958 Hollingshead and Redlich published the now classic book, *Social Class and Mental Illness.* They argued that severe mental illness was to be found in disproportionate numbers in the lowest socioeconomic classes of society. Psychotic disorders, and particularly schizophrenia according to their findings, seemed to be much more prevalent in the lower classes while milder psychological disorders, such as the neuroses, were to be found in disproportionately high numbers among middle- and upper-class people. Although other studies (Faris & Dunham, 1939) had suggested similar findings previously, Hollingshead and Redlich's book was a kind of watershed, focusing scientists' attention on the stubborn fact and demanding an explanation.

Mental health epidemiologists found this to be an irresistible problem. At least two major hypotheses could be offered to explain the relationship between socioeconomic status and abnormal behavior. The first of these seems more intuitively plausible as we think about the possible effects of poverty. Recall our discussion of the relationship between economics and abnormal behavior in Chapter 3. There we noted that Brenner (1973) had shown that there was a relationship between mental hospitalization rates and economic change. The idea that poverty produces *social stress* that could be a determinant of schizophrenia seems reasonable to most of us.

The second hypothesis, however, is more subtle. The *social drift* hypothesis argues that people developing schizophrenic symptoms will drift into the lower strata of soci-

ety, primarily because of their reduced ability to cope effectively with the demands inherent in their working life.

The social stress hypothesis takes the clear position that the social stress of poverty is responsible for the higher incidence of schizophrenia in the lower classes. But the drift hypothesis takes a more ambiguous stand. It suggests that the incapacity of schizophrenics is what produces downward mobility, but it does not take a clear position on what causes the schizophrenia in the first place.

The discovery of a relationship between social class and schizophrenia by Hollingshead

The anomic conditions of some urban settings provide little community support for distressed people.
(Ken Firestone)

and Redlich (1958) and Dunham's (1965) description of schizophrenic drift to the central city sets the stage for our discussion. Interestingly we will find that the evidence leads us back to a consideration of the family, but from a new perspective.

Social Class.   Melvin Kohn (1969) has conducted a thorough critical examination of the evidence on the relationship between social class and schizophrenia. Kohn acknowledges the plausibility of the drift hypothesis (schizophrenia leads to lower class status rather than the reverse). The most plausible version of this hypothesis would lead to a genetically susceptible concentration of offspring of schizophrenics in the lowest socioeconomic levels. But the drift hypothesis, says Kohn, cannot by itself account for the incidence of schizophrenia in the lower classes.

Instead, Kohn argues it is something about the conditions of life among poor people in the lowest socioeconomic levels that is responsible for the higher incidence of schizophrenia there. Poor housing, illness, criminal victimization, personal degradation, and the financial hardship of a life of poverty suggest the most obvious determinant: stress. Furthermore, there is evidence that at all class levels, higher levels of stress are associated with higher likelihoods of psychological disorder.

But stress, by itself, does not account for the differences in incidence either. Kohn (1970) argues that the evidence suggests that when people of lower social class are subjected to equal amount of stress as people of higher class levels, the lower-class persons are more vulnerable to the stress and more likely to develop some form of psychological disorder.

Poor people, because of their life conditions, develop a different worldview from that of their more affluent counterparts. The constricting job conditions, limited educational opportunities, and other oppressive conditions experienced in a life of poverty, says Kohn, produce an orientation to the external environment that is more vulnerable to stress and change. It is an orientation of fearfulness, distrust, fatalism, and helplessness.

But how is this worldview born of the oppressive conditions of poverty and social class transmitted? It is the family, says Kohn, that is the most important mode of transmission.

> The family is important for schizophrenia—not because the family experiences of schizophrenics have differed in some presently undisclosed manner from those of normal people of lower social class background, but precisely because they have been similar. If this be the case, there is no reason to restrict our interest to processes that are unique to the family, such as its particular patterns of role allocation. We should emphasize, instead, processes that the family shares with other institutions—notably those that affect [people's] ability to perceive, to assess, and to deal with complexity and stress. The family's importance comes from its being the first and earliest institution to shape orientations to self and society (Kohn, 1970, p. 62).

Thus, Kohn argues, the higher incidence of schizophrenia among lower-class people may be the result of three sources of vulnerability. Genetically vulnerable people, whether disproportionally represented in the lower classes or not, are subjected to the increased stresses of a life of poverty, and because of the effect of those very conditions on the family, an orientation to the external environment develops that makes coping more difficult and gives stressful events even greater impact. People in the lower classes, then, are in triple jeopardy of schizophrenia, says Kohn.

AN INTEGRATION OF PERSPECTIVES: VULNERABILITY

Let us briefly take stock of what we have learned so far about the description and determinants of schizophrenia. It is a heterogeneous disorder or group of disorders. Thought disorder is a primary feature and many sufferers also display hallucinations and delusions. For many it is an episodic disorder, with periods of relatively adequate functioning between episodes.

There is little doubt that the transmission of the disorder is partly genetic. Although almost any single study of genetic similarity and schizophrenia can, by itself, be criticized on methodological grounds, the overall findings are difficult to dispute. No clear answer on the mechanism of transmission is yet available. Whatever is transmitted genetically must have its impact on the biochemistry of the individual. There is promising new evidence that brain chemistry, particularly that involving neurotransmitters like dopamine, may play an important role in the development of schizophrenia. The mechanism is still unclear, although it may be one that involves deviations in some normal regulatory mechanism rather than some biochemical X factor. And even if a neurochemical mechanism is identified, enormous gaps in our knowledge still exist in understanding how the chemical deviation is translated into behavior.

Our survey suggests that family environment and social factors also play a role. The evidence suggests that the social environment has two distinguishably different kinds of impact on the individual. First, it is the source of various learned abilities and skills that may affect the ability to cope with challenge and threats. Second, it is the arena in which stressors or threats are presented. Thus the nature and quantity of stress, and the learned skills available to cope with it,

derive from the family and social environment. The evidence also suggests that both the *form* and the *course* of schizophrenia are affected by the social environment.

Now, at least, we have some of the major pieces in the puzzle. Clearly genetics, biochemistry, and familial and social environments are all involved in the development of schizophrenia, but how? It is not simply a matter of choosing one set of determinants rather than another. We recognize that an acceptable explanation of the causes and development of schizophrenia must take into account all of the available evidence, not merely that which supports our own favorite hypothesis. Furthermore, as we noted at the outset, problems in genetic background, brain chemistry, family environment, and social class all tend to be correlated with each other. It is likely, for example, that the highest incidence of schizophrenia is in poor, genetically vulnerable families with particularly stressful family environments. Thus the causal factors that we have been discussing as if they were separate are actually intertwined with each other.

There are still numerous gaps in any comprehensive account of schizophrenia. Yet are there models that attempt to incorporate what is already known? One such model has been offered by Zubin and Spring (1977). They call it the *vulnerability model* of schizophrenia.

A basic premise of the model is that each of us is endowed with some degree, however small, of vulnerability, and that under the proper circumstances this vulnerability will express itself in an episode of schizophrenia. They argue further that there are both inborn genetic sources of vulnerability and experiential, acquired sources of vulnerability. This, although very general, is certainly consistent with our review of the evidence. Thus an individual's vulnerability is determined by some combination of inborn and acquired factors. But vulnerability, Zubin and Spring argue, is not the same thing as the schizophrenic disorder itself. Whether an individual will actually display schizophrenic behavior depends on the impact of challenging life events.

In Figure 9-6 you can see how Zubin and Spring (1977) think of the relation between vulnerability and challenging life events. An interesting aspect of this formulation is that the actual impact of the same challenging event may be very different depending on the person's vulnerability. An event that most of us with relatively low levels of vulnerability would cope with in a routine fashion might exceed the threshold of a more vulnerable person and precipitate a schizophrenic episode.

This brings us to the last important feature of the vulnerability model. The model argues that vulnerability to schizophrenia is an enduring trait that we all possess to a greater or lesser degree. But vulnerability must be distinguished from *episodes* of schizophrenia, which may or may not appear in a particular person. The authors note that this view helps to account for the episodic nature of the disorder that most other formulations have not fully incorporated into their account.

Like all useful formulations, the vulnerability model raises as many questions as it answers. Are there unique challenging events for schizophrenia? How do the inborn and acquired sources of vulnerability interact? Are the inborn sources of vulnerability specific etiological factors (necessary but not sufficient for schizophrenia to occur), as Meehl (1962) has suggested? Does the view have treatment implications that would not have been perceived without it? It is a beginning, at least.

FIGURE 9-6
Vulnerability Model of Schizophrenia

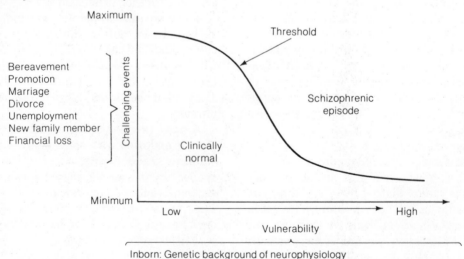

Source: From "Vulnerability: A New View of Schizophrenia" by J. Zubin and B. Spring, 1977, *Journal of Abnormal Psychology, 86,* p. 110. Copyright 1977 by the American Psychological Association. Reprinted by permission.

TREATMENT

A variety of different treatment approaches to schizophrenia have been tried with mixed or only marginal success. More often than not chronic schizophrenics were placed in back wards of state and county mental institutions. There they suffered from the effects of their schizophrenic experience as well as from the effects of an unstimulating, confining life inside the walls of a locked institution.

From Hospital to Community

Today the picture is changing. In order to appreciate how rapidly the treatment of schizophrenia and other severe psychological disorders has changed over the last 20 years or more, let us examine some of the major shifts in treatment. There has been a major shift from inpatient hospital care for severe psychological disorders, especially schizophrenia, to outpatient treatment in the community. This major change is shown in Figure 9–7. It shows clearly that the number of episodes of inpatient care has shifted dramatically from 77 percent of all patient care episodes in inpatient settings in 1955 to only 32 percent in 1973. Further, when severely disturbed people are hospitalized, their hospital stay tends to be much shorter.

Keith et al. (1976) claim that there are at least three major reasons for this shift. First, care in state and county mental hospitals has been reduced from nearly half of all episodes in 1955 to only 12 percent in 1973. A second major force for change in treatment patterns has been the development of community mental health centers. These mental health centers treat patients locally and assist in their care in the community. They have played a major role in transforming the treatment of severe psychological disorders from closed institutions to the community. The third major reason for the change in treatment has been the availability of day hospitals that treat severely disturbed patients during the day and allow them to return home in the evening.

Currently, more schizophrenic individuals than ever before are living outside the walls of institutions. This is a significant change from a number of different points of view, according to Keith et al. (1976). Schizophrenic patients can now, if they wish, retain contact with family friends in their own communities. This may in turn increase the potential for meaningful employment and the feelings of personal dignity and self-esteem that can accompany work. The families of the schizophrenic patient may be less disrupted as a result of this new pattern of care. Since care is given locally, families are less disrupted when a parent, spouse, or child is away for treatment for only brief periods of time. In addition, the community itself may begin to adapt to more first-hand contact with patients experiencing schizophrenic episodes. It even may be that some of the problems of stigma (Price & Denner, 1973) associated with being a mental patient may be reduced as a consequence.

Compared with the closed hospitals of the past, Keith et al. (1976) present an optimistic picture. But think for a moment about our review of the history of treatment in the United States in the 19th century. It may be that this enthusiasm for "community treatment" is no different from the zeal associated with the development of asylums in the Jacksonian era and the enthusiastic reports of "tent therapy" and other innovations of the time. We have little or no reliable information on the quality of life of schizophrenics living in the community. Until data documenting the quality of treatment for released schizophrenics supplements the information we now have on shifting patterns of care, we will have to retain our skepticism. If

FIGURE 9–7
Percent Distributions of Inpatient and Outpatient Care Episodes in Mental Health Facilities, by Type of Facility: United States, 1955 and 1973[1]

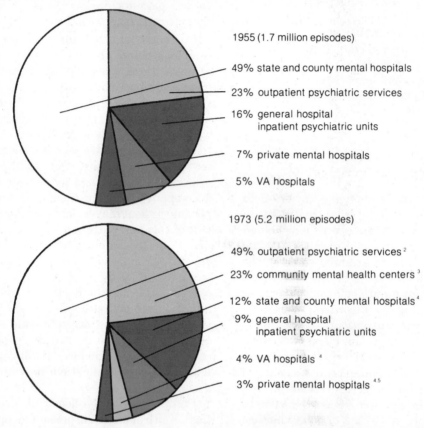

1955 (1.7 million episodes)

49% state and county mental hospitals

23% outpatient psychiatric services

16% general hospital
inpatient psychiatric units

7% private mental hospitals

5% VA hospitals

1973 (5.2 million episodes)

49% outpatient psychiatric services [2]

23% community mental health centers [3]

12% state and county mental hospitals [4]

9% general hospital
inpatient psychiatric units

4% VA hospitals [4]

3% private mental hospitals [4,5]

we do not, we will not have learned the lesson of history (Price & Smith, 1983).

Drug Treatment

The history of the treatment of schizophrenic disorders has been at times more bizarre than the behavior of the sufferers themselves. As Cole (1970) notes, in the recent past patients diagnosed as suffering from schizophrenia have been subjected to brain operations, removal of the colon, years of psychoanalytic therapy, playing with mud,

psychodrama, token economies, induced comas, huge doses of vitamins, family therapy, artifically induced convulsions, prolonged sleep therapy, seclusion rooms, moral treatment, work treatment, group psychotherapy, summer camping, trips to the French Riviera, cold baths, and a wide variety of different psychoactive drugs.

Out of this strange assortment of treatments, one major approach has emerged that has allowed much of the shift in treatment patterns that we described above to occur. It is the development of *neuroleptic*

DEINSTITUTIONALIZATION: LIBERATION OR NEGLECT?

It is tempting to assume that a few isolated but impressive programs for community treatment are typical of the community care given to recently released schizophrenic mental patients. Unfortunately this is not yet the case. It is one thing to close the doors of mental hospitals and quite another to help mental patients make a new life in the community.

The national policy of "deinstitutionalization" that we described earlier has sometimes meant that individuals who have spent 20 years in an institution have abruptly been left to their own devices in the community. The results have often been tragic. Long years of institutionalization cripple an individual's ability to

cope with the demands of the external world. These people may have no place to go once they have been turned out of the hospital. As a consequence, they have been neglected, ignored, or far worse, exploited by unscrupulous individuals who have provided substandard housing and care.

As Cohen and Paul (1976) have noted, extended care treatment has been plagued with bureaucratic problems and inadequate funding. And the results of poorly planned attempts at deinstitutionalization frequently have left mental patients as victims rather than beneficiaries of deinstitutionalization.

Singe-room occupancy hotels in major metropolitan areas have become the only living option available for many newly deinstitutionalized patients.

drugs, especially the phenothiazines, in the treatment of schizophrenia. By 1970 it was very unusual for any patient who had received the diagnosis of schizophrenia not to be treated with one of the major tranquilizers. Today, as Keith et al. (1976) note, many clinicians consider it unethical to fail to use these drugs in the treatment of schizophrenia.

In fact, Synder (1975) has offered evidence to suggest that the drugs usually described as *phenothiazines* have *specific antischizophrenic effects,* rather than merely general tranquilizing properties. Indeed, some researchers have suggested that clinical diagnosis ought to be made on the basis of the way in which patients respond to antischizophrenic drugs because the drugs have been so strikingly effective in treating some forms of schizophrenia.

There is evidence to suggest that drug treatment, especially when combined with other forms of psychological treatment, is especially effective in the treatment of schizophrenia. Table 9–5 shows how the phenothiazines selectively affect the behavior of schizophrenics as opposed to that of people showing other symptoms. We will discuss drug treatment in much more detail in Chapter 18.

Treatment Combinations

Although the phenothiazines appear to selectively affect schizophrenic symptoms, in practice they are seldom the only form of treatment given to schizophrenic patients. Frequently drug treatment is combined with psychotherapy or some other supportive treatment.

Following suit, researchers have also addressed themselves to more complex questions regarding various treatment combinations for schizophrenia. What is the effect of

TABLE 9–5
Analysis of Symptom Sensitivity to Phenothiazines

Bleuler's Classification of Schizophrenic Symptoms	Response to Treatment
Fundamental	
Thought disorder	+ + +
Blunted affect-indifference	+ +
Withdrawal-retardation	+ +
Autistic behavior-mannerisms	+ +
Accessory	
Hallucinations	+ +
Paranoid ideation	+
Grandiosity	+
Hostility-belligerence	+
Resistiveness-uncooperativeness	+
Nonschizophrenic	
Anxiety-tension-agitation	0
Guilt-depression	0
Disorientation	0
Somatization	0

Source: From *Genetic Theory and Abnormal Behavior* by D. Rosenthal. Copyright © 1970 McGraw-Hill. Used with permission of McGraw-Hill Book Company.

these drugs when we compare them directly with other forms of treatment? Are some combinations more effective than others?

A classic study conducted by May (1968) compared improvement in schizophrenic patients who received drug treatment, milieu therapy, drugs plus individual psychotherapy, electroconvulsive therapy, and individual therapy. In this study the drug treatment group tended to have a shorter hospital stay and showed more rapid change in behavior than other experimental groups. At a three-year follow-up the drug-treated group still maintained some advantage.

Hogarty, Goldberg, Schooler, & Ulrich (1974a, 1974b) have studied the effects of psychosocial treatment and the phenothiazines in a large sample of schizophrenics recently discharged from hospitals in Maryland. Hogarty found that 80 percent of the

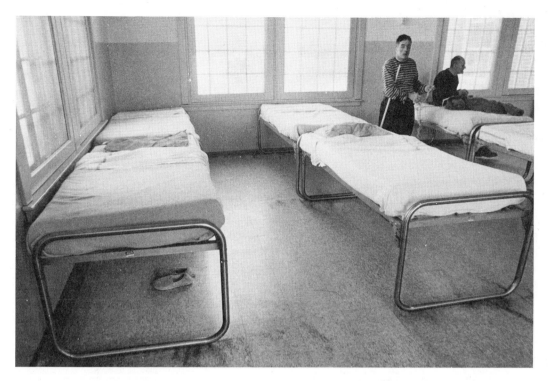

In the past chronic schizophrenics have been placed in back wards of public mental institutions.
(Jeff Albertson/Stock, Boston, Inc.)

placebo-treated patients had serious relapses by 24 months after discharge, whereas
only 48 percent of the drug-treated patients
had similar relapses. These are impressive
results that further demonstrate the effectiveness of the major tranquilizers for
schizophrenia. The results also suggest that,
even with a disorder as severe as schizophrenia, it may be possible to effectively shift
treatment from inpatient settings to the
community.

Another series of studies conducted at the
Institute of Psychiatry in London shows
how the effects of drugs can combine with
other factors in reducing the likelihood of relapse. Early studies at the British research
unit followed schizophrenics after release
from the hospital and found that schizo-

phrenics living alone fared much better than
those who returned from the hospital to a
spouse or parents. Both severity of symptoms and relapse rates were much higher
among patients returning to their families.

These researchers reasoned that something about the atmosphere created by those
living close to the patient was creating the
problem, and they set about trying to discover what it was through detailed interviews. The interviews revealed that the *emotional atmosphere* (particularly emotional
overinvolvement, hostility, and critical comments) was a crucial variable, and the researchers developed a scale to measure this
quality of family life. A subsequent study
(Brown, Birley & Wing, 1972) confirmed
the researchers' hunch. Patients with high

emotional expressiveness in their homes relapsed at a rate of 55 percent while only 16 percent of those in the low expressiveness homes relapsed in the nine months following hospitalization.

But was the high emotional intensity in the homes of the relapsed patients just a reaction to the fact that they were initially more disturbed? Or was emotional atmosphere really causing the relapse? When the severity of disturbance was statistically controlled, the results remained convincing. Emotional expressiveness was indeed a key factor in relapse.

A subsequent series of studies (Vaughn & Leff, 1976; Leff, 1976) has probed the issue still further. The results of these studies are shown in Figure 9–8. You can see that three

FIGURE 9–8
Relapse Rates of Total Group of 128 Schizophrenic Patients after Nine Months with Their Families

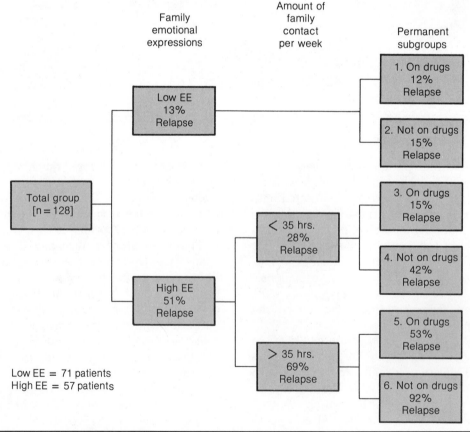

Source: From "The Influence of Family and Social Factors on the Course of Psychiatric Illness" by C. E. Vaughn and J. P. Leff, 1976, *British Journal of Psychiatry, 129*, p. 133.

factors are critical in relapse rates. First, emotional expressiveness of the family environment has a large overall effect. Furthermore, patients who spend more than 35 hours a week in face-to-face contact with relatives suffer higher relapse rates, but *only* if the patients live in a highly emotional family environment. Finally, as one might suspect, drug treatment makes an important difference, but again the difference occurs in the high emotionality families, not in those with low emotional expressiveness.

Leff (1976) suggests that reduced social contact has a protective effect in schizophrenia. In fact, patients may monitor their own emotional sensitivity by using social withdrawal to protect themselves against too much emotional stimulation. Leff notes that patients who enter social gatherings and feel tense will withdraw to reduce the feeling of tension.

In the chapters on treatment that follow we will discuss a variety of approaches to the treatment of schizophrenia and other disorders in more detail.

It seems clear even from our brief review that the severely disabling symptoms of schizophrenia present a considerable challenge to treatment. However, combinations of pharmacological and environmental treatments hold real promise for reducing relapse in the disorder.

SUMMARY

In this chapter we have examined the characteristics of one of the most important of the major psychological disorders, schizophrenia. We have seen that it is both one of the most severe and, from the point of view of social cost, one of the most disabling of the psychological disorders.

Examining the history of attempts to describe schizophrenia, we noted certain key features of the disorder, including autism, associative disturbance, ambivalence, and affective disturbance. We also noted that thought disorder is one of the most salient aspects of schizophrenia. Moreover, problems of attention quite probably underlie a variety of the perceptual and language problems displayed by schizophrenics.

DSM III has identified a number of criteria necessary for the diagnosis of schizophrenia as well as several major subtypes which are in some ways quite similar to the Kraepelinian subtypes we discussed earlier in the chapter. Although the DSM III classification may aid in improving the reliability of diagnosis of the disorder, its usefulness is far from proven. Recent research has suggested that additional emphasis on social competence and affective symptoms may be of more value in predicting the outcome of the disorder.

We have also taken up the question of the etiology of schizophrenia. We examined both biological and environmental hypotheses for the etiology of schizophrenia and saw that relatively strong evidence for a genetic role in the transmission of the disorder is available. However, no clear mechanism for genetic transmission has yet emerged.

In the area of neurochemical research, a variety of neurotransmitters, such as dopamine, may be important factors in the development of schizophrenia. We also noted that new techniques for studying brain structure and function are producing evidence for brain abnormalities in some schizophrenics.

Our examination of family and social environmental evidence suggests that both the form and course of schizophrenia may be affected by social and environmental factors and that a vulnerability model of schizophrenia best fits current evidence. The major advantage of the vulnerability model of schizophrenia is its capacity to incorporate most of the significant observations of other theoretical perspectives in its explanation of the development of schizophrenia. Biological de-terminants as well as social factors play an important role in the model.

Our survey of treatment approaches to schizophrenia ranged from an examination of the recent movement to deinstitutionalize schizophrenic patients on the one hand to the use of phenothiazines that appear to have specific antischizophrenic effects on the other. Combinations of drug and social therapies appear to hold the most promise in the treat-ment of schizophrenia.

Part Four

Abnormal Behavior through the Life Span

10

Disorders of Childhood and Adolescence

Behavioral and Emotional Disorders of Childhood
    Childhood Depression and Suicide
    Childhood Fears and Phobias
    School Phobia/Separation Anxiety
        Disorder

Disorders of Elimination
    Functional Enuresis
    Functional Encopresis

Attention Deficit Disorder
    Developmental Features
    Incidence and Clinical Picture

Child Abuse
    Physical Abuse

Specific Developmental Disorders

Pervasive Developmental Disorders
    Infantile Autism
    Childhood Onset Pervasive
        Developmental Disorder

Disorders of Later Childhood and Adolescence
    Conduct Disorder
    Anorexia Nervosa
    Bulimia

Summary

INTRODUCTION

The following thoughts and feelings, expressed during therapy sessions, describe the world of David, a hyperactive child:

The very first day my teacher says, "Oh, you're David," and right in front of everyone she asks when do I take my pills.

The doctor says I'll be OK when I'm 14. Well, I'm only nine. He acts like 14 is next week.

Medications is like in a big thick space suit with ear muffs, and things get real fuzzylike far off.

Chrissie Wilson had her Reckless Robert Robot in class, and it got started and wouldn't stop, and Randy said, "Man, that robot's hyper like Davey! Give it a pill, Davey," and everyone laughed.

I got no friends 'cos I don't play good, and when they call me Dope Freak and David Dopey, I cry, I just can't help it.

When it's special like a party I have to go to the sitter's—I heard my Mom say, "If only we could send him away to school."

I don't get the pills on the weekends so I can grow, and it's scary because I'm one of the smallest in my class now, and how can I catch up only growing two days a week?

And then Mom gives Dad one of those looks and he like reads it and then he says, "Maybe just your brother and sister should go this time." They think I'm stupid. I know I never get picked to go—every time is this time (adapted from Ross & Ross, 1982).

Children like David are too often stigmatized by their disorder. Their high levels of activity, impulsivity, and attentional difficulties are obvious. Consequently, they are labeled as "different" or "abnormal." However, the fact that David attends school regularly and functions in a relatively normal manner represents enormous progress. Throughout much of history hyperactive children would not have been so fortunate. In ancient times children who were weak or sick or showed some abnormality were abandoned or killed. As late as the 17th century, sexual abuse, beatings, and slavery were common occurrences of childhood. Also, children were expected to mimic acceptable adult behaviors and to labor in the workplace alongside adults. It is only since the beginning of the present century that children have been removed from the labor force and childhood has been recognized as a "special" time of life, full of exciting developmental changes and opportunities. Such modifications in long-standing views of childhood represent a dramatic departure from the past. However, we shall see that some problems such as child abuse have only recently begun to receive scientific and societal attention.

Children change and grow daily. It is often difficult for parents to know if their child's behavior is abnormal. Many parents struggle with questions about whether their child's problem behavior is temporary, or whether it requires professional help. What are the boundaries between highly energetic children and hyperactive children? When does being a "loner" stop and autistic aloneness or schizophrenic withdrawal begin? Is the child's depression a normal function of a series of stressful life events, or does the depressed mood represent a more serious development with long-term implications? Answers to these questions are not always obvious. Even a trained professional may be hesitant in diagnosing a child's problem. However, within the past 40 years, our knowledge of childhood disorders has increased as many major childhood disorders gained increased recognition. Over a recent 12-year period the number of childhood psychological disturbances listed in the diagnostic classification system doubled (DSM II [1968] versus DSM III [1980]). Diagnostic refinements and increased precision have added a degree of specificity and concreteness to the understanding of the dimensions of childhood disorders. In the discussion of childhood disorders that follows, we will closely adhere to the diagnostic scheme elaborated by DSM III.

The seriousness and scope of childhood disorders should not be underestimated. Estimates of the prevalence of moderate to serious disorders range from about 7 percent in very young children to about 20 percent in adolescents (Leslie, 1974; Richman, Stevenson, & Graham, 1975). The greatest number of referrals for professional attention and hospitalization occur during late childhood and adolescence (Taube & Meyer, 1975). There are more boys with childhood disturbance in the diagnostic categories. This trend continues until late adolescence when the sex distribution of abnormal behavior becomes more balanced. For each of the disorders presented, we will cite statistics that pertain to the incidence, sex distribution, and typical age of onset of the disorder. Such information will help you understand and distinguish the disorders from normal, age-appropriate child behaviors.

As you learn more about the disorders of childhood, it will become apparent that children's development and their emerging and vulnerable sense of self are adversely affected. Children and adolescents with "problems" are often acutely aware of their "differentness" and how their distinctive behaviors cause them to be labeled as deviants or outsiders in the eyes of their peers, teachers, and family members. We shall see that even relatively minor psychological disorders have a profound impact on the social and emotional development of children who fail to learn age-appropriate skills and are rejected by their peers. Childhood adjustment is often gauged according to normal social and psychological development. The more serious childhood disorders we shall consider are not only rare but they also involve major distortions in functions and processes typically associated with normal development.

In this chapter we will introduce you to the most important childhood disorders and acquaint you with the most effective approaches to their treatment. The touchstone of our presentation will be the behavioral and emotional disorders of childhood—attachment disorder of infancy, childhood depression and suicide, childhood fears and phobias, attention deficit disorder, and the disorders of elimination, enuresis (bed-wetting), and encopresis (involuntary defecation). The personal and social problem of child abuse will then be discussed. Although abnormal behavior is exhibited in the abuser rather than the victim, abuse may produce psychological disturbances in the child that persist into adult life. We will then outline the frequently occurring specific developmental disorders and discuss the more disabling pervasive developmental disorders. Our presentation will conclude with a discussion of the conduct disorders and the eating disorders, anorexia nervosa and bulimia; these disorders are distinguished from the others by their appearance in later childhood and adolescence.

BEHAVIORAL AND EMOTIONAL DISORDERS OF CHILDHOOD

Reactive Attachment Disorder of Infancy

Ginny was the youngest of 10 children born to Mr. and Mrs. S. Her parents were migrant workers. Despite long hours of hard work, their income was never sufficient to provide adequate clothing and shelter. When Mrs. S. was pregnant with Ginny, it became apparent that it would be best if Ginny were adopted. After her birth Ginny was placed in a large county home. Despite the home's modern facilities, the large staff's frequent turnover and the fact that its members worked on a rotating basis made it impossible for them to meet Ginny's basic emotional needs.

At first Ginny seemed to search the faces of the staff as if trying to find her mother or a familiar face. She cried incessantly, and when approached by a staff member, she frequently moved her hands over her head in a protective fashion. She began sucking her balled-up fist for prolonged periods and often refused to take more than a few swallows of formula. When she drank her formula, she became colicky and vomited. Over the next two months she became less agitated, but seemed withdrawn and unresponsive. Her weight was lower than that of other infants her age. It was clear that her physical growth had nearly ceased.

After three months Ginny was adopted by a young childless couple who were able to devote much time and energy to Ginny's care. Slowly Ginny's withdrawn and apathetic behavior began to change, and she developed an interest in her new environment. By three years of age Ginny was a bright, bubbly little girl who was only slightly behind in physical development. Her physician stated that she would "catch up completely" by the age of five.

As the case of Ginny suggests, psychological disorders may be evident as early as the first year of life. Reneé Spitz was the first to state that these feelings were a form of grief or depression caused by maternal absence. Spitz studied infants in hospitals, orphanages, and foundling homes. He noted that many of the infants shared common characteristics that were never observed in infants whose mothers were present and devoted adequate attention to their emotional needs. The children's apathy, poor muscle tone, immobility, impaired appetite, and excessive sleeping had such a striking resemblance to depression in adults that Spitz called the new syndrome *anaclitic depression*. The terms *failure to thrive* and *hospitalism* have also been applied to this set of symptoms, which are characterized by poor emotional and physical development, the onset of which is prior to eight months of age. The current descriptive term for this syndrome is *reactive attachment disorder of infancy*.

Bowlby (1960) carefully studied institutionalized infants and described three stages that infants experienced as the disorder progressed. During the protest state, the infant exhibits signs of severe distress such as loud crying, shaking the bed, and rejecting substitute caretakers. The withdrawal stage is marked by inactivity, loss of appetite and weight, and lack of responsiveness to contact with others. In the detachment stage, the infant continues to respond to human contact, food, and toys, but seems to lack any real depth of feeling.

Like Spitz, Bowlby believed that maternal absence was responsible for the child's traumatic reaction of withdrawal and detachment. DSM III and current thinking have shifted away from viewing reactive attachment disorder as resulting from maternal absence to viewing inadequate care by the mother or by a substitute caretaker as the cause of reactive attachment disorder. When the disorder is recognized and adequate treatment provided, the prognosis is good. Except in extreme cases the condition can be reversed by the provision of adequate infant care.

Childhood Depression and Suicide

Our discussion suggests that symptoms that resemble depression can appear very early in life. Recently there has been an increasing recognition that depression occurs in children, and that it is a sad and lonely experience that may have tragic results. It may be tempting to analyze a child from an adult perspective and ask, "What's he got to be depressed about? He's just a kid." Such judgments might lead us to ignore the experiential world of the child and preclude adequate treatment. However, between 2 and 10 percent of children suffer from depression (Kashani & Simonds, 1979; McKnew, Cytryn, & Yahraes, 1983). On the basis of these estimates, between 2 and 6 million American children are depressed. Unfortunately, depression often is unrecognized and untreated. Depressed children often are considered the "nicest" and the "best-behaved"; they are frequently the quiet ones who sit in the back rows of the classroom and do not cause trouble (McKnew et al., 1983). While they may appear shy, well-mannered, and helpful, in reality they may be withdrawn and unhappy and have a poor self-image.

Between 2 and 10 percent of children suffer depression. (© Sue Markson)

DSM II and its predecessors did not include a diagnosis for childhood depression. Why was depression in children overlooked? One influential account with roots in the psychoanalytic viewpoint held that depression was a function of the superego, the result of aggression turned against the self. According to this perspective, symptoms of depression would not be manifested until the superego was fully developed during adolescence. Hence, depression in childhood "cannot" exist. However, as other viewpoints arose, and students of child psychology noted similarities between childhood and adult depression, childhood depression gained recognition as a distinct diagnostic entity.

DSM III's inclusion of three diagnoses relating to depressive symptoms in children represents progress in the understanding of childhood depression. While all three diagnoses are listed under the adult disorders, each has a set of criteria for diagnosing the disorder in childhood. The assumption underlying DSM III's classification is that certain parallels can be drawn between adult and childhood depression, although developmental factors must be recognized in understanding the distinctive features of childhood depression. The following DSM III categories are used for diagnosing depression:

1. Major depressive disorder, single episode.
2. Major depressive disorder, recurrent.
3. Dysthymic disorder.

The major depressions covered by the first two categories are quite rare; only about 1 percent of children suffer a major depression. Most depressed children are categorized as dysthymic or neurotic. Such depressions last for more than one year. Symptoms include unhappiness, loss of interest or pleasure in activities, hopelessness, loss of appetite, and sleep disturbance. Other signs include low self-esteem, guilt, anxiety, and suicidal thoughts or actions. These complaints resemble those of depressed adults (Beck, 1967).

Explanations. No single factor has been identified as *the* cause of childhood depression; rather, many factors, either alone or in conjunction with one another, may produce the symptoms of depression. Some of the more prominent causal factors identified with depression are presented below:

1. *Family and social environment.* The family and social environment have a tremendous impact on the developing child. When one or more family members are depressed, particularly the parents, children may be ensnared in an abnormally tight, unhealthy bond that fosters overdependency and depression. Observing a depressed parent may cause the child to identify with and model depressed symptoms. Another situation that predisposes children to depression

occurs when the child's acceptance is predicated on meeting high standards set by the family. The case of Frances exemplifies this point:

> Ten-year-old Frances was a competent swimmer by the age of five. Her parents became increasingly involved in her swimming and hoped and expected her to become a champion. But Frances could not satisfy her family's ambitions. Each time she lost, her family openly expressed disappointment—and, ultimately, disapproval. Frances began to feel guilty for letting her parents down and spoke of herself as a "failure." As Frances's self-esteem plummeted, she became more depressed. She suffered a serious depression that was relieved only after her family received therapy that uncovered the relationship between her parents' behavior and her symptoms of apathy, guilt, and social withdrawal (adapted from McKnew et al., 1983).

A parent's rejection of the child also may result in childhood depression. Such rejection may take the form of blunt statements stressing the child's unworthiness or inadequacy, or it may be expressed more subtly through attitudes or actions that indicate indifference, criticism, and lack of faith in the child's ability.

2. *Separation or the loss of loved persons.* Parental illness or death may lead to the onset of depression in childhood. In cases where the void cannot be filled by a significant other, there is a greater risk that depression will become chronic or recurrent. Although less traumatic than the death of a parent, divorce, remarriage, or even the presence of a new baby in the family may evoke symptoms of depression in children.

3. *Physical and biological factors.* Children who are physically ill or disabled are at greater risk for depression. Those who experience lengthy hospitalization, pain, disfigurement, or chronic illnesses such as kidney disease or severe allergies are more likely to

develop acute or protracted depressive episodes. There is also evidence that suggests a greater risk of depression in children whose families have a history of affective disorder that supports a genetic predisposition toward depression.

Treatment. Both psychotherapy and medication are widely used in the treatment of childhood depression. Studies have shown that antidepressant medication provides symptom relief for depressed children (Frommer, 1967; Gittelman-Klein & Klein, 1971) and that antidepressants are more effective in the treatment of older children and adolescents (Halpern & Kissel, 1976; Cantwell & Carlson, 1979).

Some authorities have advocated a combination of approaches to ease the symptoms of depression. For example, Herzog and Rathburn (1982) have recommended a three-pronged strategy that combines antidepressant drug therapy, psychotherapy, and mobilization techniques. Mobilization techniques use tasks such as school activities, scouting, camp, and sports to help the child experience increased feelings of mastery and self-esteem and to counteract depression. Psychotherapy may take the form of individual or family therapy. Goals often include the establishment of trust and empathy, support and counseling, and the ventilation of negative feelings and conflicts in the safety of a therapeutic setting.

Childhood suicide. It has been established that the incidence of depression and the resulting likelihood of suicide increase during adolescence and continue to rise during young adulthood. Data from the U.S. Office of Vital Statistics reveals that suicide before the age of 10 is extremely rare, but the frequency begins to rise thereafter, increasing sharply after age 14. However, these statistics may represent an underestimation of the actual incidence of childhood suicide. Deaths of children under eight years of age are not recorded by the Division of Vital Statistics as suicide, regardless of the information entered on the death certificate (Cantor, 1983). In addition, the accidental death rate for children under age 14 is extraordinarily high, a fact that has prompted speculation that many of these deaths may be suicides that are not acknowledged as such (Seiden, 1969).

Research reports do, however, suggest that while the rate of childhood suicide is very low, cases of suicide occur even among children younger than five. Bakwin and Bakwin (1972) present the case of a three-year-old child who, along with his 18-month-old sibling, was found in a room with the gas jet turned on. The child reported that he had tried to kill himself because his parents would not take him on a walk that day. An acquaintance of his father's had recently committed suicide by turning on the gas, an incident that was discussed in the child's presence. In general, our culture tends to underestimate the intensity of children's emotions, particularly about suicide.

Childhood Fears and Phobias

Fears are a part of normal childhood development. Most childhood fears are temporary, fairly predictable at certain ages, and they do not interfere with daily functioning. During infancy fears center around environmental events. For example, the startle response, in which the infant shows a "freeze reaction," occurs in response to loud noises or sudden loss of physical support. Later, usually between 5 and 10 months of age, the infant develops a fear of strangers and becomes distressed around unfamiliar people or situations.

Common childhood fears continue to change as children grow older. Among children two to four years old, fear of animals predominates. From the age of four to six these fears are replaced by fears of the dark and of imaginary or supernatural creatures. After the age of 6, few children develop new animal phobias, and by 9 or 10 years of age, they exhibit few fears of animals. However, many children exhibit specific fears of thunder and lightening, cars, strong winds, and trains. Fear of snakes is one of the few fears that are likely to continue into adolescence and adulthood (Marks, 1969).

Morris and Kratochwill (1983) have carefully reviewed the literature on childhood fears and phobias. They concluded that girls have more fears than boys, boys have more fears about the future, and adolescents from high socioeconomic levels have more fears than those from low socioeconomic levels. Figure 10–1 shows the frequency of various fear responses that occur during childhood. Fears should not be ignored, even though many childhood fears appear to emerge suddenly and disappear just as mysteriously (Marks, 1969). But persistent and excessive fears are present in as many as 8 percent of children and merit vigorous treatment (Ollendick, 1979).

FIGURE 10–1
Relative Frequency of Various Fear Responses

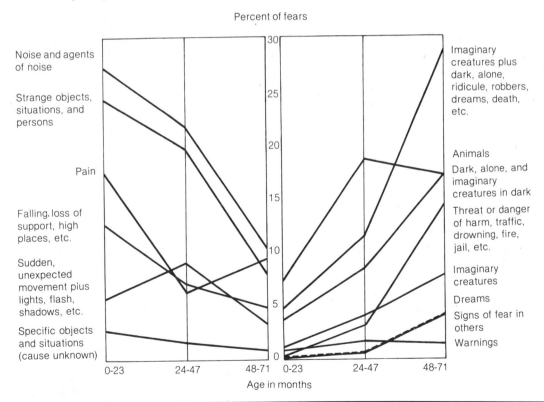

Source: Reprinted by permission of the publisher from Arthur T. Jersild and Frances G. Holmes, *Children's Fears* (New York: Teachers College Press, © 1935).

School Phobia/Separation Anxiety Disorder

The case of Jeannie provides a vivid illustration of "school avoidant" or "school phobic" behavior:

Jeannie is an attractive, petite seven-year-old. She is a "typical" child in many respects. For the past two months, however, Jeannie has attended school only five days. Nearly every day she says that she feels "too bad" to go to school. Usually she complains that she has a headache or a stomachache. When pressured to attend school, Jeannie sometimes develops nausea and vomiting or diarrhea. On weekends, her symptoms improve and she rarely feels sick.

Several significant events occured during the months preceding the onset of her refusal to attend school. First, Jeannie was hospitalized for three weeks with a severe infection; her mother openly voiced her fears that Jeannie might die. During the following month, Jeannie's grandmother died in the hospital after undergoing surgery. Shortly thereafter, Jeannie learned that her tonsils needed to be removed, and that an operation and recuperation time in the hospital would be required. She asked her mother if children die in hospitals. Her parents remarked that Jeannie became reluctant to go places unless they accompanied her.

Jeannie's phobic behavior began one day when her regular teacher was ill and absent from class. Jeannie expressed concern about her. That morning, the substitute teacher yelled at Jeannie for talking, and made her stand in the corner. Jeannie was very upset and humiliated; at lunch she complained of feeling sick and wanted to go home. When her mother could not be reached immediately, Jeannie became upset. The next day she insisted that she felt "too bad" to go to school.

When her complaints of illness continued for several days, her parents took her to the doctor. The doctor was not able to find any physical disorder and recommended that Jeannie consult a child psychologist.

Two diagnoses are recognized by DSM III for school attendance problems: separation anxiety disorder and school phobia. In cases of separation anxiety disorder, school refusal is related to anxiety about separation from people with whom the child has formed a close, emotional bond. In contrast, cases of school phobia are characterized by the child's fear of the school situation, regardless of whether a parent is present. For the purpose of simplifying our discussion, given the overlap of symptoms that describe these disorders, we will consider both types of school avoidant children as "school-phobic."

In the case presented above, Jeannie exhibited many of the problems and concerns that typify children with school phobia. As is the case for many other school-phobic children, Jeannie's complaints revolved around physical symptoms, the most common of which were nausea, headache, diarrhea, and stomachache. Such symptoms are most likely to occur at the beginning of the week and disappear as the weekend approaches. Further, school-phobic children remain at home with the knowledge of their parents; their absences usually last from several days to several weeks. These children often have above-average intelligence. They may behave in a willful and resistant manner at home, particularly in response to parental pleas or demands to return to school; this behavior pattern often is in sharp contrast to their passivity in other settings or situations.

How common is school phobia? Estimates vary, but about 1 to 8 percent of children appear to be school-phobic (Miller, Barrett, &

Hampe, 1974; Kahn & Narstein, 1962). The onset of the symptoms may be sudden or may develop gradually over time. The period of greatest risk of developing school phobia is the elementary school years, with a peak in incidence occurring around age 11 (Chess & Hassibi, 1978). Boys and girls equally show symptoms of school phobia. Factors such as socioeconomic status and birth order do not appear to be associated with the occurrence of school phobia.

Explanations and Treatment. According to the psychoanalytic viewpoint, the roots of school phobia can be traced to the child's tendency to displace anxiety from the parent-child relationship onto the school setting. Psychoanalytic writers have described the mother of the school-phobic child as insecure, with unfulfilled emotional needs that are not gratified appropriately in her marital relationship. This situation results in excessive maternal dependency on the child and the mother's unconscious fostering of dependency on the part of the child. The child's anxiety and fears of separation from the mother are a response to the mother's anxiety. However, the child's anxieties are displaced onto the school setting and result in the symptoms of school phobia that reflect the child's dependency on the mother and related fears of abandonment, separation, and loss (Waldfogel, 1959).

The goal of psychoanalytically oriented treatment is the development of insight and ego strength, with a focus on the underlying problems. The child is helped to resolve dependency and autonomy issues and to gain a firm sense of self and confidence independent of the parents. It is hypothesized that the symptoms seen in the school setting will diminish when the child can recognize the true source of anxiety and achieve control of feelings. While the child may be encouraged to attend school, less importance is placed on the child's quick return to school than with other approaches. Sperling (1974), for example, presents the case of a child who needed two years of analysis before she was able to return to school.

The behavioral approach is an alternative to the psychoanalytic conceptualization and treatment of school phobia. Rather than focusing on underlying conflicts and the development of insight, the behavioral approach views the school phobia as a learned pattern of responses that is maintained by avoidance of the feared situation. School phobia may be the direct result of punishment, embarrassment, and anxiety at school; thus school avoidance is an attempt to avoid anxiety associated with experiences in the school setting. As with other behavior therapy techniques, the emphasis is less on the cause and more on the treatment of the disorder. Returning the child to school is of primary importance.

Using a behavioral approach, Kennedy (1965) developed a rapid procedure for returning children to school. It begins with a distinction between what he believes to be two types of school phobia. These types are shown in Table 10–1. Type I, Kennedy argues, is a "true" phobia and begins with an acute onset. It is much more treatable than Type II phobias, which Kennedy describes as a "way of life."

Kennedy's method for treating Type I school phobias includes (1) establishing an effective relationship with school personnel; (2) avoiding an emphasis on the somatic complaints reported by the child; (3) strong encouragement to attend school from the parents; (4) a training interview with the parents designed to give them the confidence to execute the program of encouraging the child to attend school; (5) a brief interview with the child after school expressing the advantages of facing the fear directly; and (6) a

---

TABLE 10–1
Differential Patterns of School Phobia Symptoms

Type I	Type II
1. The present episode is the first.	1. Second, third, or fourth episode.
2. Monday onset following an illness the previous Thursday or Friday.	2. Monday onset following minor illness not a prevalent antecedent.
3. An acute onset.	3. Incipient onset.
4. Lower grades most prevalent.	4. Upper grades most prevalent.
5. Expressed concern about death.	5. Death theme not present.
6. Mother's physical health in question: actually ill or child thinks so.	6. Mother's health not an issue.
7. Good communication between parents.	7. Poor communication between parents.
8. Parents well adjusted in most areas.	8. Mother shows a neurotic behavior; father, a character disorder.
9. Father competitive with mother in household management.	9. Father shows little interest in household or children.
10. Parents achieve understanding of dynamics easily.	10. Parents very difficult to work with.

Source: Reprinted from "School Phobia; Rapid Treatment of Fifty Cases" by Wallace A. Kennedy, 1965, *Journal of Abnormal Psychology, 70,* p. 286. Copyright 1965 by the American Psychological Association. Reprinted by permission.

---

follow-up interview with the parents to assure academic progress and to check on other fears and issues in the case.

The essence of the treatment program is carried out by the parents. They are cautioned not to discuss the issue of school attendance but to take the child to school and return home. Any attendance at school in the first few days should be praised, there should be no other discussion of school. Each day the child should be taken to school and praised for attendance. Kennedy reports substantial success with this particular treatment method, especially with Type I school phobia. Successful treatment is an important goal. The symptoms of school phobia have been found to precede the development of agoraphobia in adults (Berg, 1976; Ollendick & Mayer, 1983).

DISORDERS OF ELIMINATION

Functional Enuresis

Functional enuresis is a disorder of childhood characterized by persistent, involuntary urination that is not caused by a phys-

ical disorder. Children are diagnosed as enuretic if they involuntarily void urine at least twice a month between the ages of five and six, and at least once a month for older children. DSM III considers enuresis primary when the child has not had at least one year of urinary control or continence, although a six-month period is frequently the interval used in clinical practice (Doleys, 1983). A diagnosis of secondary enuresis is made when the child has shown urinary continence for a specific period.

The most common form of this disorder is nocturnal or nighttime enuresis; it usually occurs in the first few hours of deep sleep and is not related to dream or REM sleep (Pierce, 1963). Nighttime wetting is not considered a disorder in children under five years of age. About 85 percent of nocturnal enuretics have a primary form of the disorder.

It has been estimated that from 10 to 20 percent of five-year-olds are enuretic, although the incidence decreases with age (Lovibond & Coote, 1970). By age 14, only about 2 percent of children are enuretic (Doleys,

1983). Because of this decrease with age, the problem has been ignored or minimized because it was felt that children "outgrow it." However, more recent recognition of the detrimental effects of the embarrassment, punishment, and riducule suffered by many enuretic children has contributed to the development of effective treatment techniques and an appreciation for the value of early intervention.

There is some evidence that children from lower income families are more likely to develop enuresis; this trend continues as the children become older. Therefore a higher proportion of older enuretics are from low-income families (Bloomfield & Douglas, 1956). Overall, enuretic boys outnumber girls by two to one. While enuretic children have been viewed as emotionally disturbed, research findings do not support this contention.

Explanations. Since enuresis was first reported during the 16th century, its cause has been attributed to dreams, laziness, intestinal parasites, weak bladder, acid urine, and allergy (Doleys, Weiler, & Pegram, 1982). At present no definitive cause of enuresis has been identified (Christophersen & Rapoff, 1983). However, some of the major perspectives on abnormal behavior have offered accounts of enuresis.

According to the psychoanalytic viewpoint, the symptoms of enuresis serve multiple needs and drives. These include a substitute form of sexual gratification, an expression of deep-seated anxieties, and hostility toward the parents that the child is unable to express directly. Thus bed-wetting represents both a regression to a more primitive level of the child's expression of feelings and a symptom of underlying conflict or emotional disturbance.

In recent years the hypothesis that genetic factors play a role in the genesis of enuresis has evolved. Support for a genetic contribution to enuresis comes from studies that have reported a higher concordance rate for enuresis among monozygotic than dizygotic twins and from the observation that parents who were enuretic as children have a much higher incidence of the problem among their own children than do parents who were not enuretic during childhood. Further, siblings of enuretic children are more likely to experience this problem than siblings of nonenuretic children. These findings are suggestive but they do not provide direct evidence of a genetic cause (Doleys, 1983).

According to the learning perspective, nighttime wetting is the result of the child's failure to learn to attend to bladder cues that awaken the child or inhibit urination. As we shall see in the next section, techniques that teach the child to attend and respond to cues of bladder fullness have been derived from the behavioral model.

Treatment. Numerous and improbable approaches have been taken to treat enuresis; these include the use of powdered goat claws, roast mouse, hares' testicles in wine, and even clamping of the penis. None of these unappetizing procedures remains popular, and current treatments are far less unpleasant and more effective.

Two of the most widely used treatments are medication and behavior therapy. More traditional psychotherapies are less popular because of the lengthy treatment required, its cost, and limited evidence of its effectiveness (DeLeon & Mandell, 1966; Doleys, 1978). Over the years a number of therapeutic medications have been used. Imiprimine, an antidepressant, has widespread popularity, although the exact mechanisms of its action are not clearly understood. Unfortunately, after initial improvement, prolonged use of antidepressant medication does not seem to be effective. Relapse rates are high, and side effects are often encountered. Because of these problems, many clinicians prefer other treatment methods.

The most widely used and best researched behavioral technique is referred to as the urine alarm or "bell-and-pad" procedure. This method requires that the enuretic child sleep on a device that activates an alarm when minute amounts of urine are sensed. The child is awakened by the alarm, finishes urinating in the bathroom, changes the bed linen, and then returns to bed. Reviewing 15 years of research on the urine-alarm method, Doleys (1977) reported a 75 percent remission rate among children treated with this method. Although the average relapse rate of 41 percent was relatively high, retreatment using the urine-alarm procedure resulted in a return to continence in over two thirds of the cases treated.

Functional Encopresis

DSM III defines *functional encopresis* as the repeated voluntary or involuntary passage of feces in inappropriate places that occurs when the behavior is not the result of a physical disorder. If by age four the child has not developed and maintained normal bowel habits for six months to one year, encopresis is primary. Encopresis is secondary if the problem occurs after the development and maintenance of normal bowel habits. An example of secondary encopresis follows:

When she was first seen in the child therapy clinic, 10-year-old Dee had a four-year history of encopretic behavior. The grandmother, who had raised Dee since her mother abandoned her, reported that she could no longer cope with Dee's encopresis. Dee was successfully toilet-trained by age three and maintained appropriate toileting behaviors for the next three years. When she was six, her mother left the state with a boyfriend, promising to send for Dee as soon as she found a job.

Dee was disturbed by her mother's departure and spent a short time in a foster home before she was placed in her grandmother's care. While in the foster home, Dee began to display mild encopretic behavior. On several occasions her foster parents found that she "soiled" her pants. Upset by her seeming lack of control, her foster parents spanked and scolded her at the time of the initial incident and each time thereafter. In response, Dee would cry and maintain that it was an "accident."

Even when she was placed in her grandmother's custody, Dee continued to soil herself. At first, her grandmother tried lecturing Dee. But when the behavior became more frequent, she spanked, scolded, and sent Dee to bed without supper. Soon the problem transferred to the classroom, and Dee became the butt of children's cruel humor. For days she tried to control her behavior and succeeded in not having any bowel movements. This "retentive" response to her problems only made matters worse. When she had her next bowel movement, it was at a time and a place that proved embarrassing to her. Increasingly she attempted to hide her feces at home, placing them in the heat vents. Her grandmother's frustration reached a breaking point when the heat was turned on in their home. This event precipitated their visit to the child therapy clinic.

Encopresis is estimated to occur in about 1 to 3 percent of children from four to six years of age. The incidence of encopresis decreases with age so that by 16 years of age it rarely occurs (Bellman, 1966). Males are three to six times more likely to develop this disorder than are females (Anthony, 1958; Doleys, 1983). Except for their toileting habits, encopretic children often appear quite normal.

Explanations and Treatment. Biological and behavioral models have addressed the etiology and treatment of encopresis. The biological model focuses on physiological malfunction as the central cause of encopresis and stresses the importance of a thorough physical examination when children show inadequate bowel control. Many cases of encopresis have an organic component. When no physiological malfunction can be identified, the physician or family may treat the problem with purgatives such as laxatives or enemas. Another goal of treatment may be to modify the child's diet to promote "regularity" and increased control. However, in many cases purgatives and diet modification alone are insufficient; they may modify the symptoms, but they do not promote appropriate toileting skills.

Behavioral models view encopresis as the outcome of inadequate or faulty learning experiences. Appropriate toileting is seen as the end product of a chain of behaviors beginning with the child's sensing the need to defecate and ending with appropriate toileting. To further the learning of toileting skills, reinforcement programs that reward appropriate toileting behaviors and ignore or punish undesired behaviors are often employed. A variety of encopretics have been successfully treated by operant procedures that rely on positive reinforcement (Neal, 1963; Balson, 1973).

ATTENTION DEFICIT DISORDER

The signs and symptoms of attention deficit disorder or hyperactivity present a complex picture. Even the best-adjusted children often appear to be overactive, energetic, and restless. Indeed, parents and teachers rate 30 to 50 percent of a normal population of boys as overactive, distractible, or inattentive (Lapouse & Monk, 1958; Werry & Quay, 1971). It is not surprising that the label *hyperactive child* has been misapplied to certain lively youngsters who do not otherwise meet the diagnostic criteria for this syndrome. But truly hyperactive children like David, who was introduced to you at the beginning of the chapter, often behave like caricatures of the well-

adjusted, exuberant, and energetic child. Viewing the disorder from a developmental perspective will bring the chaotic world of the hyperactive child into sharper relief.

Developmental Features

The first signs of hyperactivity may be evident as early as infancy. Parents often report that hyperactive children are colicky, fussy infants who frequently move and shift their position in the crib. By three years of age they are constantly walking or climbing, restless, and more accident-prone than their "normal" peers. But it is not until the elementary school years that the child's behavior patterns are likely to be labeled as "hyperactive" and a treatment referral made. Teachers complain that such children will not remain in their seats, that they do not pay attention, that they will not follow directions, and that they have temper tantrums with little provocation. Lying, destructiveness, and other socially inappropriate behaviors may also be reported. By middle childhood, academic problems and disruptive behavior frequently result from the children's inability to attend and concentrate in the classroom setting. A high level of physical activity may be evident, but it diminishes as the children mature and approach adolescence. By adolescence, overactivity may no longer be a problem; however, impulsiveness, restlessness, inattention, and related academic difficulties comprise a patchwork of adjustment problems. A high level of alcohol abuse is often reported, and hyperactive adolescents are likely to appear in the juvenile courts as a result of running away from home, school truancy, and so forth. It is easy to empathize with the parents of such children; years of attempting to cope with their children's behavior cause anger, frustration, and fatigue.

In the past DSM II used the term *hyperkinetic reaction of childhood* to describe this syndrome. Overactivity and impaired attention were inseparable facets of the total symptom picture. But a different view has evolved as a result of a more complete understanding of the disorder. In DSM III the hyperkinetic diagnostic category was replaced with the category *attention deficit disorder*. Based on the observation that this syndrome is characterized by impaired attention and impulsivity, and may or may not involve hyperactivity, DSM III recognizes two types of attention deficit disorder—one with hyperactivity, and one without. Since much of the important research literature was conducted using the older designation, hyperactivity, we will occasionally refer to that term in our discussion.

Although we have attempted to describe the most prominent and frequently reported features and developmental aspects of hyperactivity, it is important to remember that its course is not fixed and invariable, and that the symptoms of hyperactivity are diverse. For example, many but not all hyperactive children are more aggressive than their nonhyperactive peers. In general, children who are both hyperactive and aggressive tend to be more severely disturbed than children who are exclusively hyperactive.

Incidence and Clinical Picture

It is estimated that between 3 and 5 percent of school-age children satisfy the criteria for attention deficit disorder. Of these, boys outnumber girls by three to one, with some estimates as high as nine to one (Trites, 1979; Werry, 1968). On the basis of these estimates, you would probably find at least one such child in any elementary classroom; that child would probably be a boy. Attention deficit disorder has become one of the most frequent presenting problems in child guidance centers and among children referred to community mental health centers. Parents,

teachers, peers, and others in their environment describe hyperactive children as frustrating and anger-provoking; they seem to test the patience of even the most placid individuals in their social arena.

Explanations. While the exact cause of hyperactivity remains a mystery, numerous explanations have been presented. One of the earliest theories was that hyperactivity resulted from brain damage or injury that occurred at the time of birth. This theory was plausible because children who have brain damage frequently display hyperactive behavior. Hence, when hyperactivity was present, brain damage was inferred, and a diagnosis of minimal brain damage often followed. As it became clear that no evidence of brain damage could be found using the available tests, a newer diagnosis of minimal brain dysfunction became popular. Until recently, the diagnosis of minimal brain dysfunction (MBD) was used interchangeably with the diagnosis of hyperactivity. However, because research evidence has failed to support the equation between hyperactivity and brain dysfunction or damage, these explanations have faded (Ross & Ross, 1982).

During the 1970s, questions about the role of food additives in the development of hyperactivity became prominent. Feingold (1975) reported that the removal of additives such as artificial food coloring and artificial flavors from the diet resulted in significant improvement, particularly with younger hyperactive children. Because subsequent research has produced mixed results, the role of diet in hyperactivity is unresolved (Conners, 1980).

Evidence for a genetic basis for hyperactivity has emerged from diverse family and adoption studies. For example, parents of hyperactive children have exhibited many of the signs of hyperactivity during their own childhoods; full siblings of hyperactive children are more likely than half siblings to show symptoms of hyperactivity; and adoptive parents of hyperactive children show no more psychopathology than control parents. This suggests that the family environment is unlikely to be responsible for the development of hyperactivity (Cantwell, 1975; Morrison & Stewart, 1974). Other research projects have suggested links between hyperactivity in children and hysterical disorders, alcoholism, and antisocial behavior in one of the biological parents of hyperactive children (Cantwell, 1975; Morrison & Stewart, 1974).

Treatment. There is no cure for hyperactivity. Treatment may be medication, behavior therapy, family counseling, individual therapy, or school modification programs.

When medication is prescribed, stimulants are most commonly used. Ritalin (methylphenidate) is the most commonly used drug, then Dexedrine (dextroamphetamine) and Cyclert (pemoline). Stimulants often have a paradoxical effect, since they reduce activity and increase attention span in hyperactive children. However, recent studies suggest that these effects are not limited to hyperactive children; they also occur in normal children (Weingartner et al., 1980). Thus the response of hyperactive children to stimulants is no longer viewed as an unexplained or isolated phenomenon. Between 50 and 75 percent of children treated with stimulants show less distractibility and overactivity, as well as greater concentration. However, a number of side effects such as headaches, stomachaches, decreased appetite, emotionality, and the suppression of normal growth are associated with stimulant treatment, particularly with long-term use (Kerasotes & Walker, 1983). While the growth-retarding effect of stimulants is small, close monitoring by clinicians is strongly recommended (Mattes & Gittelman, 1983).

Behavior therapy techniques are popular and useful in the treatment of hyperactivity. Behavioral approaches involve training the parents to reward appropriate behaviors while ignoring or punishing inappropriate ones. One important goal is to increase the competence and self-confidence of parents in modifying their children's behavior. Guidelines for structuring the home environment and establishing reasonable expectations for the child are often components of a behavioral treatment program. Behavioral techniques have also been applied in school settings to increase desired classroom behaviors such as sitting still and paying attention to relevant aspects of the learning environment (Ayllon & Rosenbaum, 1977). A multimodal approach that combines drug treatment and behavioral techniques may be more useful than any one approach used in isolation.

CHILD ABUSE

Child abuse has many forms—physical, emotional, verbal, sexual—all of which can have profound negative repercussions on a child's life. Although physical abuse often produces clear evidence (e.g., broken bones, bruises, and bleeding), it is difficult to obtain evidence with other forms of abuse. To complicate matters, many professionals disagree on what constitutes abuse, and children often try to protect and cover up for abusive parents. Even after instances of severe abuse, many children will claim that their injury was an accident. Consider the case of Doug:

Doug, age 8, was brought into the emergency room by his father; he had a black eye, a broken jaw, and a mild concussion. Both Doug and his father reported that his injuries were the result of an accidental fall. X rays and hospital records revealed that Doug had been treated for a number of similar injuries in the past year. When questioned by the physician about the extensive history of injuries,

Doug's father stated that Doug was just "accident-prone." Noting that Doug's account of the "accident" did not match his father's story, the physician reported the situation to the authorities.

Questioning revealed that Doug's father had a high-pressure job as a salesman. Doug's parents did not get along well, and his father often drank after he came home from work; he was tired, frustrated, and belligerent. Arguments and fights frequently occurred; Doug often tried to protect his mother from his father's abusive anger. His father admitted beating his son on a number of past occasions. These incidents resulted in a broken nose, broken ribs, and several falls. Doug, however, never admitted that his father had caused any of his injuries.

As was discussed at the beginning of the chapter, the concern for the welfare of children is a relatively recent development. While child abuse was first cited as a problem as early as 1946, little interest and research occurred prior to the 1960s. More recently a plethora of information on the victims of child abuse as well as their abusers has come forth, and a strong child advocacy movement has developed. Current laws mandate that even suspected cases of abuse must be reported to the authorities. Despite these advances, many abusive parents do not realize that they need help or are afraid to admit it; others do not know where or how to obtain help.

Physical Abuse

In 1962 Kempe and his associates (Kempe, Silverman, Steele, Droegemueller, & Silver, 1962) described the physical abuse of children as the *battered child syndrome*, which is characterized by evidence of blows to the head, bone fractures, and soft tissue swelling. Also it includes the regular abuse of children with hot irons, cigarettes, sticks, belts, and other objects. A startling statistic is that each year more than 1,000 of these children die from these injuries. In one year alone more than 160,000 cases involving serious abuse-related injuries are reported in the United States, and indications suggest that the number is rising. Not all abuse, however, results in life-threatening injury. Helfer (1975) has estimated that about 10 percent of all childhood accidents treated in emergency rooms were caused by physical abuse that resulted in relatively minor injury.

What type of child is physically abused? On the basis of studies of emergency room admissions, it appears that about two thirds of abused children are under six years of age (Zuckerman, Ambuel, & Bandman, 1972), and of this number half are less than two years old (Smith & Hanson, 1974). Several factors appear to be related to this finding: (1) young children require more care, attention, and handling, often causing greater frustration to parents; (2) they are unable to defend themselves; and (3) they are more physically fragile than older children. Impaired children who are often viewed as burdensome and unattractive by parents, such as children with physical defects and emotional disorders, also are at high risk for abuse.

It is difficult to understand why a parent would abuse a child. To address this question, research efforts have focused on the environmental situations and personality characteristics of abusive parents. There does not seem to be one cause or one typically abusive personality. Instead, a number of factors interact to increase the probability of abusive behavior. Abusive parents often have histories of physical abuse, rejection, deprivation, and inadequate parenting during their own childhood. As adults, they are likely to have poor impulse control, low self-esteem, unresolved dependency conflicts, and limited social networks; they are more likely to view their child as intentionally annoying them (Bauer & Twentyman, 1985; Salzinger, Kaplan, & Artemyeff, 1983). Women are more likely to be abusive than men because women spend more time with children.

What are the effects of repeated abuse? The answer to this question is critical because nearly half of abused children have histories of prior abuse. It appears that abused children often exhibit diminished intellectual abilities and impaired cognitive functioning. Falls or blows to the head may result in retardation or other neurologic impairments (Friedrich & Einbender, 1983). Repeatedly abused children also have a greater likelihood of developing antisocial behavior and alcoholism in later life.

SPECIFIC DEVELOPMENTAL DISORDERS

During childhood, intellectual, cognitive, and social abilities often develop at an uneven pace. Even normal, well-adjusted youngsters

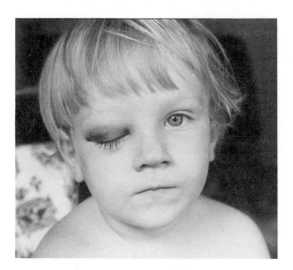

The incidence of child abuse is rising. (James R. Holland/Stock, Boston, Inc.)

SEXUAL ABUSE AND INCEST

Sexual exploitation of children is the involvement of dependent, developmentally immature children and adolescents in sexual activities that they do not fully understand and are unable to give informed consent to. Such activities violate the social taboos of family roles (Schecter & Roberge, 1976). Sex activities are not necessarily limited to intercourse. They can include touching the child's genitals or breasts and inducing the child to touch the genitals of the adult. Adults outside the family may sexually exploit children. The term *incest*, however, usually means sexual behavior between members of the same kinship. Let us examine a number of cases of incest and sexual exploitation of children who were seen at a child-serving mental health facility (Slager-Jorné, 1978):

A 13-year-old girl experienced sexual intercourse at an early age with both her natural father and her stepfather. Presenting problem: evoking seductive responses from strange men.

A 15-year-old girl had sexual relations with her father for several years. The father had sexual relationships with all his sons and daughters. Presenting problem: fainting spells, hysteria.

A four-year-old boy had been sexually abused by his 14-year-old sister. Presenting problem: very aggressive sexually with women and exposing himself.

These brief descriptions raise more questions. How frequently do these kinds of incidents occur? What are the characteristics of individuals who are involved in such activities? What are the consequences of incest and sexual exploitation of children?

Historically the practice of incest has been viewed with disgust, revulsion, and contempt by members of virtually all cultures. Legal and social prohibitions make it unlikely that the act will be reported; the child may fear the consequences of reporting it, and may even be unaware that he or she was sexually abused. Although the actual incidence of incest is not known, it is likely that its true incidence is far greater than the estimates. The occurrence of some form of child sexual exploitation may be as high as 15 percent of all children (Boekelheide, 1978). Many cases of child sexual exploitation occur in the home. About 80 percent of the time the child has some acquaintance with the offender. In approximately 30 percent of the reported cases, the adult is a member of the child's household. Slager-Jorné (1978) reports that about one half of the children are sexually exploited repeatedly and 60 percent of the offenders use some form of threat or force. The offender is most likely a male. In the majority of cases the victim is a girl. About 10 cases of father-daughter incest are reported for each mother-son case. Marital conflict, inadequate supervision of children, financial stress, a parental history of similar abuse, and sexual inferiority and inadequacy are contributing factors.

Although the entire family may be implicated in instances of incest, evidence suggests that the consequences of incest and child sexual exploitation are most severe for the victim. Lukianowicz (1972) concluded that only 23 percent of the females involved in incestuous relationships show no apparent adverse effects. Initially, a child may react with guilt, anxiety, fear, or anger. The closer the relationship between the child and the adult, and the longer the victimization continues, the greater likelihood of psychological problems later in life (Swift, 1978). In many cases negative aftereffects can be attributed to extreme reactions on the part of adults, who communicate to the child that irreparable damage has been done.

may lag in one area of development relative to their peer group. Specific developmental disorders or learning disabilities, as they are sometimes called, are diagnosed when children fail to develop age-appropriate skills and abilities in the areas of language acquisition and expression, speech, reading, and arithmetic abilities.

DSM III defines this group of disorders as those involving specific areas of developmental disturbance that are not due to other disorders. Specific developmental disorders occur with greater frequency than many of the other more serious disorders of childhood. Estimates indicate that as many as 5 to 28 percent of grade-school children experience one or more specific developmental disorders (Wender, 1971; Denckla, 1977).

While children with developmental disorders may have no other abnormal behaviors, they frequently experience secondary adjustment problems. Young children tend to believe that behavior that is "different" from their own is deviant (Dollinger, Thelen, & Walsh, 1980). Older children are more likely to conceive behavior that departs from a social norm as deviant (Ollendick & Hersen, 1984). Children with a developmental disorder are likely to deviate both from social norms and the behavior of their friends and peer group; hence, they are vulnerable to being labeled as deviant and subjected to social ostracism and rejection. For example, a child with a serious reading problem may respond to ridicule from peers by developing a poor self-concept and harboring intense feelings of inferiority. Although such children may have normal or above average intelligence, they often define themselves as less smart than their "normal" peers. While these disorders are usually identified and treated within the educational system rather than the mental health system, they constitute the largest group of referral problems in school-aged children (Knopf, 1984).

Sitting at his desk, Tommy seemed like any other nine-year-old boy. An attractive child of average build, he would flash an engaging smile when talking about his favorite sport, baseball. However, after the clinician looked at Tommy's spelling test or listened to him, it was apparent that Tommy did not have the same skills as other children in his class. While writing, he omitted letters from simple words, and his reading seemed more like that of a first grader than a fourth grader. His peers would sometimes laugh at his pronunciations. In recent months he would not read aloud and would cry at the slightest snicker from a classmate. A recent assessment revealed that while Tommy was of above average intelligence (IQ of 110), he was dyslexic. With 30 other children in the classroom, Tommy's teacher did not have time to give him the special attention he needed to acquire adequate reading and writing skills. Thus Tommy was placed in a special class for several hours each day, where a specially trained professional worked with him to develop better reading, writing, and spelling skills.

Tommy has a *developmental reading disorder*. This disorder involves an impairment in reading skills not caused by social or intellectual factors. It is often called *dyslexia*.

FIGURE 10-2
Writing Sample from Dyslexic Child

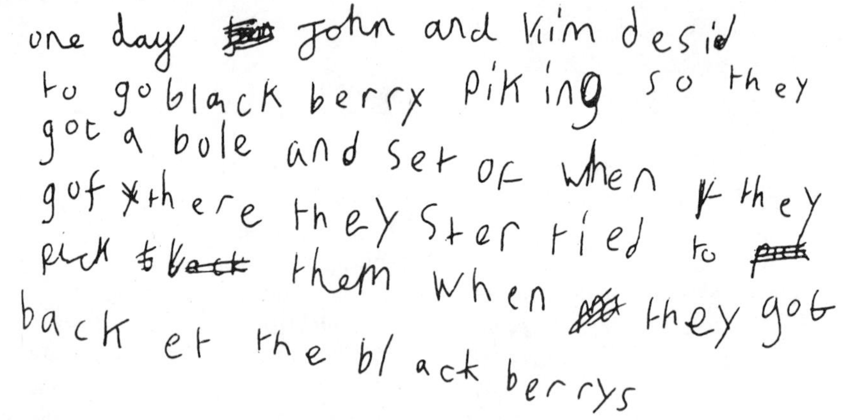

One day John and Kim decided

to go blackberry picking so they

got a bowl and set off, when they

got there they started to

pick them when they got

back (they) ate the blackberries

(Spelling corrected, but not syntax, punctuation, etc.)

Source: From *Reading Disorders: Varieties and Treatments*, by R. W. Malatesha and P. G. Aaron. New York: Academic Press, 1982.

Other terms used to describe it include *congenital word blindness* and *primary reading disability*. Like other dyslexic children, Tommy's oral reading is slow and characterized by the distortion, omission, and alteration of words. Without even realizing it, many dyslexic children start a story in the middle or at the end. Writing and spelling are also affected by this disorder. While dyslexic children will perform well below the level expected on the basis of their intelligence and age, gross neurological deficits are not present. It is not uncommon for dyslexic children to be hyperactive, distractible, poorly coordinated, and also to have poor arithmetic skills. Dyslexic boys outnumber girls by about four to one (Critchley, 1970). Developmental reading disorders have a high incidence of occurrence, with estimates ranging as high as 10 percent of the population. Dyslexic children may come from any socioeconomic level, with a diversity of family attitudes toward school and learning. They usually are referred for evaluation and treatment between the ages of 9 and 11 after consistently failing to acquire age-appropriate reading, writing, and spelling skills in school (Thomson, 1984).

A *developmental arithmetic disorder* involves impairment in the child's arithmetic skills. In such cases the children perform arithmetic tasks at a level significantly below their age or intellectual level. This disorder seems to occur less commonly than most of the other specific developmental disorders.

Developmental language disorders involve the failure to acquire language, delayed acquisition of language, or a language disability that occurs after language has been acquired. Language disability is usually caused by trauma or neurological disorder. Developmental language disorders may be expressive or receptive. Children with expressive difficulties usually have no trouble comprehending what others say to them; rather, they have difficulty articulating words. Their vocabularies are often limited and their speech is below the norm for their age group. Those with a receptive language disorder have a normal articulation of language, but their comprehension of language is impaired.

A developmental articulation disorder involves the mispronunciation of sounds. It has been called *lalling* or *lisping*. The problem may be confined to the mispronouncing of one sound or several. It is interesting that stuttering is not considered a developmental articulation disorder, but is diagnosed separately.

PERVASIVE DEVELOPMENTAL DISORDERS

In this section we will discuss the *pervasive developmental disorders of childhood*. These are called "pervasive" because they are characterized by disruptions of psychological functioning in many areas. Children with these disorders experience many problems in living; consequently, their prognosis is bleaker than children who experience the specific developmental disorders in which normal development is delayed or disturbed in only one area. Both infantile autism and childhood onset pervasive developmental disorder are characterized by the child's failure to develop social skills, language, and reality testing.

Infantile Autism

In 1943 Dr. Leo Kanner reviewed the cases of 11 children who displayed behaviors notably different from other recognized childhood disorders. Kanner called the new syndrome *early infantile autism*, commenting that "the outstanding fundamental disorder is the children's inability to relate themselves in the ordinary way to people and situations from the beginning of life." More recently, Rutter (1978) provided the following summary of the general symptom groups of autism:

1. *From birth extreme aloneness that shuts out normal responses and relationships.* From infancy, autistic children usually do not seek cuddling, kissing, or other forms of attention and affection. In fact, parents often describe them as "happiest when alone," "self-sufficient," and "acting as if people weren't there." Autistic children treat people as objects; they relate to others in a detached way, and then only when it serves their purpose. For example, an autistic child might climb onto an adult's lap in order to reach a preferred toy. However, while doing this, the child totally ignores the adult, using him as one might use a chair or stepladder. Autistic children generally do not participate in normal play activity with other children; instead, they play alone and use toys in a self-stimulatory manner.

2. *Disturbance in language.* The child's failure to develop speech is often the first clear indication that there is a problem. About 50 percent of autistic children never develop functional speech. Many of those who develop speech have abnormal patterns and use speech egocentrically, that is, without effort at meaningful communication. *Echolalia,* or the repetition of words or phrases spoken by others, is common among autistic children. Another characteristic of autistic speech is the reversal of pronouns, particularly *I* and *you.* For example, an

autistic child might say, "You want dessert," meaning "I want dessert."

3. *Demand for sameness in the environment.* The autistic child is intolerant of change. For example, changes in routine or in the arrangement of furniture or toys might result in violent upsets. Consider the following examples that show that autistic children develop strong attachments to objects: Ted, an eight-year-old autistic child, always carried a red rattle. If the rattle was moved or misplaced, he would scream and pound his fists on the floor until it was found. Larry, an autistic boy of five, would not get into bed at night until he had arranged his shoes in a line, patted his pillow twice, and said, "Tick, tock, clock." This ritual lasted two years. Other comon rituals of autistic children revolve around daily activities such as naps, walks, and eating.

Intellectual Functioning. To date, most of the information indicates that the majority of autistic children are mentally retarded. DeMyer and her colleagues (DeMyer, Hingtgen, & Jackson, 1981) reported that approximately 75 percent of autistic children have IQs that place them at the mentally retarded level. But it is generally accepted that in isolated areas some autistic children are capable of exceptional performance. About 10 percent of autistic children, as well as some mentally retarded children who are not autistic, have an outstanding musical, mechanical, or mathematical ability (Restak, 1982). Such children are sometimes called *idiot savants* because of their genius in some areas and their retarded functioning in others. Although she was an autistic child of only three, Nadia showed extraordinary artistic ability. She produced intricate and skillful drawings, but she did not talk (Gardner, 1979). Her sketch of horses is reproduced in Figure 10–3.

Incidence and Explanations. About one out of every 2,500 children is autistic, a ratio that varies little across cultures (Wing, 1976). While males are about four times more likely than females to be autistic, autistic girls generally have more severe cognitive deficits than autistic boys (Lord, Schopler, & Revicki, 1982).

During the past two decades theorizing about autism has gradually shifted away from psychodynamic explanations to organic defects or dysfunctions present from birth. Psychoanalytic theory emphasizes the role of the parents' behavior in the development of autism. Kanner, for example, described the parents of autistic children as obsessive, perfectionistic, humorless, and rigid about rules. Bettelheim (1967) reported that the mothers of autistic children failed to provide the cuddling, rocking, or stroking provided by mothers of nonautistic children. While mothers were described as negative and rejecting of their children, both parents were depicted as cold and aloof. The symptoms of autism were thought to constitute the child's response to the coldness and indifference of the parents.

The popularity of this view has dwindled with the recognition that the parents of autistic children do not display more signs of mental or emotional disorders than the parents of children with organic disorders. The differences noted in the behaviors of parents may be the result rather than the cause of autism. Often it is difficult to sustain warm, caring, and nurturant behaviors toward a child who gives nothing emotionally in return and who may, at the slightest provocation, display violent, angry tantrums.

The failure to find meaningful differences between parents of autistic and nonautistic children has helped to channel interest in biological models of autism. Theories of genetic and specific viral etiologies, as well as traumas to the central nervous system prior to or at the time of birth, have been proposed as explanations for autism. Evidence

FIGURE 10-3
Drawing Sample from Autistic Child, Age Three

Source: From *Nadia: A Case of Extraordinary Drawing Ability in an Autistic Child,* by Lorna Selfe. New York: Academic Press, 1977.

of neurological problems from EEGs and CT scans, and biochemical imbalances found in autistic children are consistent with genetic theories of autism. It has been hypothesized that autism may be tramsmitted directly by a recessive gene.

Treatment.   When the treatment of autism is discussed, it is usually in terms of symptom reduction or improved functioning rather than a cure. Traditional psychotherapies are ineffective with autistic children, and the use of medications remains controversial. Following the successful use of behavioral modification methods with early childhood psychotics by Ferster and DeMyer in 1961, behavioral techniques became widely used in the treatment of autism. Behavioral treatments clearly define problem behaviors and devise corrective strategies (Schreibman & Koegel, 1981). Self-stimulatory behaviors such as babbling or hand flapping occupy the attention of the autistic child to such a degree that appropriate learning is blocked. To reduce such behaviors, a variety of techniques have been used including verbal commands (stop talking) followed by physical gestures (placing a finger across the child's lips), time-out (removing the child from the group and/or withdrawing attention), and reinforcement of behaviors incompatible with self-stimulation (Johnson, Baumeister, Penland, & Inwald, 1982). For self-destructive behaviors such as self-biting or head-banging, spanking and electric shock have been used to reduce the frequency of their occurrence (Chance, 1974; Lovaas, Shaeffer, & Simmons, 1965). However, since techniques based on punishment have proven objectionable to some workers in the field, recent efforts have been geared toward understanding why autistic children engage in self-stimulatory and self-destructive behaviors so that more appropriate behaviors can be substituted (Rincover & Devany, 1982). Using reinforcement

procedures, behaviors such as eye contact, social responsiveness, and imitation have been increased in autistic childred (Hingtgen & Trost, 1966; Blake & Moss, 1967). When motivational or attention deficits are prominent aspects of the symptom picture, reinforcement and "prompts" (extra cues) are also central features of treatment.

While behavioral techniques have proven effective and helpful in changing many problematic behaviors in autistic children, behavioral techniques have been less successful in facilitating language development. As we previously noted, the failure to develop normal communicative speech is one of the classic diagnostic signs of autism. Many autistic children are mute or nearly so, while others exhibit echolalia (pathological repetition of what people say) or use language inappropriately. It has been recognized that modifying these language deficits would facilitate more normal development and adjustment in autistic children; consequently, much effort has been directed toward training language skills. During the past decade sign language programs have been used to develop speech in autistic children. In reviewing 20 studies using sign language or simultaneous sign and speech communication with autistic children, Bonvillian, Nelson, & Rhyne (1981) found that nearly all subjects learned to understand sign language and were able to produce five to 350 signs. Although learning and using sign language did not result in comparable improvements in speech skills, many children acquired a limited spoken vocabulary. More important, these skills generalized to environments other than the training settings.

One of the most innovative programs for working with autistic children is a community-based treatment that uses parents directly to eliminate disruptive behaviors (Schopler, Mesibov, & Baker, 1982). The

Behavior modification techniques are often used with autistic children. (Michael Weisbrat/Stock, Boston Inc.)

TEACCH (Treatment and Education of Autistic and related Communications-handicapped Children) program strives to keep autistic children in special classes in public schools while training parents to act as co-therapists in carrying out a treatment plan. This plan is individually tailored to meet the special needs of their child. A comprehensive evaluation of the program has not yet been done, but preliminary findings are encouraging (Schopler et al., 1982). These findings offer hope to parents of autistic children and point the way to future advances that have the potential to enrich the lives of their children.

Childhood Onset Pervasive Developmental Disorder

DSM III defines the features of childhood onset pervasive developmental disorder as "a profound disturbance in social relations and multiple oddities of behavior." This diagnostic category is new, replacing the category of "childhood schizophrenia" in the latest version of the diagnostic manual (DSM III, 1980). Over the years the terminology and diagnostic criteria relating to serious psychopathology in childhood have changed. Even today, when severely disturbed children are discussed, the terms *schizophrenia, autism, psychosis,* and *pervasive developmental disorder* are often used interchangably. Table 10–2 compares the characteristics of infantile autism and childhood onset pervasive developmental disorder.

Notice that children with a pervasive developmental disorder experience disruptions in intellectual, social, and cognitive functioning. Affective responses and language are also impaired. Many of these children function at retarded levels, and their language is often described as "odd"; they may make up words or give them unusual meanings. Consider the following excerpt from an interview with such a child:

I say, hello, doctor, have you any new toys? Let me open your radiator with this screwdriver. I say let me open it. I say, so what. Can I copy your aminals? I am in a doctor's office. You and I are twins aren't we? I am coloring this camel brown. I said I am coloring it brown. I say, have you a big scissors? Well, here's what I will use. What do you think? It is called a knife. How does my voice sound? What? Judy, what? Is that your name? I'm cutting out this camel. Is it pretty enough to hang on the wall? Can you cut as pretty as this? My sister says camel talk. Isn't that funny? Camel talk. My voice

TABLE 10–2
A Comparison of the Characteristics of Early Infantile Autism with Childhood Onset Pervasive Developmental Disorder

Characteristic	Early Infantile Autism	Childhood Onset Pervasive Developmental Disorder

Diagnostic criteria	Pervasive lack of responsiveness to people
	Gross deficits in language development and use
	Bizarre responses to the environment (resistance to change, peculiar attachment to objects)
		Gross impairment in social relationships
		Three of the following:
		  sudden excessive anxiety
		  inappropriate affect
		  resistance to change
		  oddities of motor movement
		  abnormal speech
		  self-mutilation
		  under- or overresponsiveness to sensory stimuli

Onset	Prior to 30 months of age	After 30 months of age and before 12 years of age
Course	Chronic/over two thirds continue to show retardation and detachment as adults	Chronic/long-term prognosis is usually better than that of infantile autism
Associated features	Peculiar nervous habits (hair pulling), rocking or rhythmic movements, violent mood swings	Bizarre ideas and fantasies, preoccupation with morbid thoughts or interests, pathological attachment to objects
Intellectual functioning	70% are retarded; some exhibit extraordinary feats of memory, musical, or mechanical performance	Usually low IQs but not necessarily retarded; unlikely to have special abilities
Prevalence	Very rare	Very rare
Sex ratio	More common in boys	More common in boys

sounds like up in the library. Can you say li-bra-ri-an? The library is where you get books (adapted from Bender, 1947, pp. 49–50).

Pervasive development disorder is rare, as is the case with childhood schizophrenia. Treffert (1970) reported that only three children in 10,000 met the criteria for a diagnosis of childhood schizophrenia. As with many other childhood disorders, males are more vulnerable, outnumbering females by three to one.

As with infantile autism, the cause of childhood onset pervasive developmental disorder is unclear. Some theorize that it is a result of the child's environment, while others theorize genetic or biological abnormalities. In treating this disorder, it is generally agreed that contact with reality is the first goal (Wolman, 1970). Beyond this initial goal the treatment approaches are diverse and vary according to the theoretical orientation of the therapist.

GROUP PSYCHOTHERAPY FOR CHILDREN

If you were to observe a sample of several psychotherapy groups for children, you would probably witness a variety of dissimilar activities which, taken as a whole, do not resemble psychotherapy. You might see a group of preschoolers talking to each other in chipmunk voices through hand puppets and improvising a dramatic play. You might observe a group of school-age boys wrestling on the floor or building model cars. You might also see a group of adolescent girls sitting in a circle on beanbag chairs discussing the upcoming school dance.

These activities are but a few of those used in group psychotherapy, a preferred intervention for many disorders of childhood. Play is the common element in these diverse activities. As Exline (1969) has noted, play is the child's natural medium of self-expression (as talking is for adults), and for many children group therapy activities include play. Play in a group setting involves interaction between children; and it is this interaction that permits the group to be a curative force in the treatment of psychological disorders.

The most common deficits in children with psychological disorders are in the areas of socialization, communication, and empathy (Shapiro, 1978). Through interaction in the therapy group these deficits can be assessed and improved. The rich interpersonal environment of the therapy group provides an ideal laboratory in which children can learn how they treat others and how they can treat others more effectively and satisfactorily (Lynn & Frauman, 1985). Through feedback from the leader and other group members, children can learn about the impact of their behaviors on others and can accordingly change their behavior.

Many psychotherapy groups for children have five to ten members chosen on the basis of developmental level, sex, and the nature of the disorder. Groups are frequently organized around the naturally occurring events in a child's life (e.g., preschool, kindergarten, latency, early adolescence, late adolescence). This ensures the member's homogeneity with the developmental task that each is facing (Kraft, 1975). Each member will be assisted in working on the specific deficits of his or her disorder as well as the developmental task common to the group. For example, individual work in the early adolescent group should be within the context of helping each member establish a stable and acceptable self-identity. Individual work in the late adolescent group should facilitate each member's budding independence from parental figures.

Males and females may be mixed in preschool and early elementary school groups, but the sexes are usually segregated in latency and adolescent groups. Groups whose members are of the same sex are recommended for adolescents to avoid overwhelming the members with sexual stimulation and to keep them focused on their primary therapy goals. The less serious problems, such as adjustment reactions, parent-child problems, and socialization deficits, can be treated in heterogeneous groups (Ginnott, 1961). However, the more severely impaired, such as psychotics, autistic children, and delinquents, can best be treated in groups homogeneous for each disorder.

Children's groups are often co-led by two leaders, permitting a reexperiencing of the primary family group with two gratifying parental figures. Many problem children have experienced chaotic, threatening, and frustrating relationships with parents. These children may improve significantly when given an opportunity to learn mutually satisfying interactions with adult parent figures.

The numerous literature reports of group therapy for children attest to the popularity and efficacy of this form of treatment (Kraft, 1971; Shapiro, 1978). The unique therapeutic advantages inherent in treating children in groups is an argument for the continued use and refinement of this form of therapy (prepared by David C. Frauman).

DISORDERS OF LATER CHILDHOOD AND ADOLESCENCE

Conduct Disorder

Peter is a 12-year-old boy who recently was involved in a serious theft. He and another boy had stolen a motorcycle, dismantled it, and then hidden the parts. Peter denied his role in the theft until confronted by a witness and police officers. He then admitted his guilt, but expressed no regret. Peter often stayed out late at night, and came home with objects he could not have bought. He admitted getting into fights with other boys at school, and was known to associate with a group of boys who were often in serious trouble.

According to his mother, ever since Peter was two years old it was hard to discipline him and he was unusually aggressive. Even at that age his grandparents and nursery school teachers had difficulty with him, and his parents had used a string of babysitters. He had a violent temper and was extremely irritable. He was self-centered, greedy, and jealous of his sister. Peter's mother was a college graduate and a successful journalist; however, she had run away from home when she was 12 years old, had been involved in shoplifting, and had been placed in a detention house. Her first husband, Peter's father, was a college dropout who was extensively involved in drug abuse. He had a police record and had physically abused Peter (adapted from Stewart, 1977).

One feature of a conduct disorder is a repetitive and persistent pattern of conduct that violates the basic rights of others or the norms or rules of society. It does not include nonserious childhood mischief and pranks. Children and adolescents like Peter who are diagnosed as having a conduct disorder are commonly referred to as "juvenile delinquents." Juvenile delinquency is a legal category used to designate those youngsters who have committed an offense resulting in involvement with the justice system. Although the incidence figures vary, approximately 4 percent of youngsters between ages 10 and 17 appear in the Juvenile Court (U.S. Department of Justice, 1978). Thus, while we may refer to research literature on delinquency, our discussion will pertain to the diagnostic categories of conduct disorder in DSM III.

In 1981 the number of juvenile arrests was about 2 million, accounting for 20 percent of all arrests during that year (Uniform Crime Reports, 1981). This represents a doubling of juvenile arrests since 1973, and the rate appears to be rising. Also, serious juvenile offenses have kept pace with, and in some cases exceeded, the rate of increase of minor juvenile offenses. The rate of recidivism or repeated offenses handled by the courts is high among youngsters. Those who commit more than one offense have an increasingly higher probability of continued offending with each offense (Wolfgang, Figlio, & Sellin, 1972).

Four subtypes of conduct disorder are represented in DSM III. The descriptions of the undersocialized aggressive, undersocialized nonaggressive, socialized aggressive, and socialized nonaggressive subtypes are summarized in Table 10–3. The undersocialized subtypes fail to form a normal degree of affection, empathy, or bond with others. The socialized subtypes show evidence of attachment to a few significant individuals, but may be manipulative and lack guilt concerning their actions toward others. The aggressive subtypes display repeated and persistent patterns of aggressive conduct in which the rights of others are violated. This conduct includes physical violence or thefts involving confrontation with the victim. The nonaggressive subtypes display a repeated pattern of behavior that conflicts with age-appropriate norms. This includes truancy,

substance abuse, vandalism, serious lying, running away from home, and stealing without confronting the victim.

Delinquent youngsters often perform poorly in school; by adolescence, they are likely to become dropouts. Their delinquency rate may be as high as 10 times that of other adolescents (Jeffrey & Jeffrey, 1970). The delinquent child is more likely to be truant, tardy, restless, disinterested, and involved in more conflict with his or her peers than the nondelinquent counterpart. In recent years research has suggested a link between learning disabilities and antisocial behavior (Satterfield, Hoppe, & Schell, 1982).

Causal Factors. A broad array of factors, ranging from television to genetics, have been related to the development of conduct disorders. For example, research has suggested that the presence of an extra Y chromosome in males may be related to criminal behavior (Erickson, 1978). Abnormal EEG patterns have also been reported in children with aggressive conduct disorders. However, because such patterns also occur in normal populations, firm conclusions cannot be drawn (Solomon, 1967). Recently it has also

---

TABLE 10–3
Classifications and Descriptions of Conduct Disorders Based on DSM III Criteria

Socialized Type	Undersocialized Type
Aggressive Type	
Shows evidence of stable social relations with peer-group friends characterized by concern for their welfare, refusal to inform on them, and willingness to help; often part of a gang or group; will use physical violence against persons outside the group or their property.	Fails to establish social attachments with peer-group members; often acts out alone; will use physical violence against persons or property.
Nonaggressive Type	
Shows evidence of stable social relations with peer-group friends characterized by concern for their welfare, refusal to inform on them, and willingness to help; commits persistent nonviolent acts such as stealing, serious lying, running away, substance abuse, and truancy.	Fails to establish social attachments with peer-group members; commits persistent nonviolent acts such as stealing, serious lying, running away, substance abuse, and truancy.

been recognized that many delinquents meet the criteria for an attention deficit disorder.

A number of home and family factors have been linked to delinquent behavior. Delinquent children are more likely to come from single-parent homes in which one parent is absent as a result of divorce, death, or desertion (Jones, Offord, & Abrams, 1980; Hetherington, 1979). Intact homes with high levels of parental conflict also produce a higher incidence of delinquency than homes in which the parental relationship is more stable (Wadsworth, 1979). The form of discipline used by parents has been linked to delinquency; hostile, permissive, erratic, or overly strict parental discipline increases the likelihood of delinquent behavior (Suh & Carlson, 1977; West & Farrington, 1973; McCord & McCord, 1959). Other family characteristics that have been related to a higher risk of delinquency include lower socioeconomic status, poor housing conditions, parental psychopathology, and large families (Robins, 1966; Steward, DeBlois & Cummins, 1979; West & Farrington, 1973).

Several studies have shown a positive relationship between violence seen on TV and aggression, particularly when the violence is easily imitated. Aggression viewed on television at age eight relates to aggression in late adolescence. Follow-up data has provided additional confirmation of this finding (Eron, Husemann, Lefkowitz, & Walder, 1972; Eron, 1980). A direct causal link between television viewing and conduct disorders has not, however, been established.

Treatment. Conduct disorders have been difficult and sometimes intractable disorders to treat. With delinquents, traditional psychotherapy approaches have been slow and costly with little evidence of effectiveness. Institutionalization also has not been effective. Limited funding, poorly conceived and implemented training programs, and in-

adequate staffing have contributed to the findings that only 20 to 30 percent of institutionalized delinquent boys have no subsequent arrests (Gibbons, 1970, Cohen & Filipczak, 1971).

The behavioral approach has become one of the most favored methods of treating conduct disorders (Redner, Snellman, & Davidson, 1983). From a behavioral perspective, undesired behaviors associated with conduct disorders are viewed as current problems. The focus of treatment is on developing and reinforcing appropriate behaviors, while simultaneously extinguishing the undesired behavior. The learning principles involved can be easily applied in a variety of settings, and parents or group home supervisors can be easily trained (Redner, Snellman, & Davidson, 1983). In Chapter 17 we will present a model residential treatment program for treating delinquent and predelinquent youth—Achievement Place.

Anorexia Nervosa

I really want to eat, but I just won't let myself. I find myself thinking, "You don't deserve that dessert, you haven't been good enough." My family is concerned, I can tell. No one says anything, but I know they all watch to see how much I've eaten. The other night when my Mom was clearing the table, she looked at my plate and said, "Well, we've done pretty well tonight." She didn't know that I had most of the food hidden in the napkin in my lap. Later I gave it to the dog.

Tammy, age 13

I know I'm too thin, but you don't know how hard it is to make myself eat. Everybody I know diets—how can I stuff myself when they're not eating? I get so hungry sometimes, but if I let myself go, I'd never stop. Lately, I've been feeling faint sometimes, and once or twice I've noticed my heart fluttering or something. That scared me. If I could get back up to 90 pounds, things would be better, I guess.

Denise, age 20

When I started losing weight all my friends thought it wouldn't last. But I showed them. My first goal was to get from 155 to 135. Then I wouldn't be teased any more. When that was done, I thought, "Why not a little more? Then you'll have a few pounds to play with." So I lost down to 120. I began to realize that I could be as thin as a model if I wanted to. Losing weight meant feeling good, being proud. I always knew that I would look better if I just lost five more pounds. My family had me hospitalized when my weight dropped to 80 pounds.

Maggie, age 16

Such statements are frequently heard by clinicians who work with anorexics. This fascinating and perplexing disorder is rapidly becoming well known to phychologists and physicians who are reporting an increasing number of cases. What is anorexia? Who develops it? What happens to those who do? These are some of the questions we will address in the remainder of the chapter.

Anorexia nervosa is a disorder that usually begins during adolescence. Its characteristics include self-starvation and emaciation, a persistent fear of being fat, a distorted body image, and a relentless pursuit of thinness (Golden & Sacker, 1984). It is only recently that much research and interest have been devoted to anorexia. However, it is not a particularly new disorder. As early as 1869, an English physician, Dr. Richard Morton, described what he termed "nervous consumption," which involved self-starvation due to "an ill and morbid state of the spirits" (Lucas, 1981). In 1873 Gull termed the disorder *anorexia nervosa*, which means a loss of appetite as a result of nervousness. This term

really is a misnomer. Today most individuals diagnosed as anorexic have no loss of appetite. Rather, they report feeling hungry, sometimes quite intensely so, but rigidly deny themselves food. Giving in to the urge to eat, even occasionally, often results in extreme guilt and anxiety, and the anorexic may vomit or abuse laxatives on such occasions to avoid weight gain. In addition to starving themselves, many anorexics exercise vigorously.

Most anorexics are fearful of being fat. In fact, their lives come to revolve around their weight. Along with this "fear of fatness," it has been found that anorexics have a distorted perception of their own body size. Even a very emaciated patient may describe herself as "fat." Others see themselves as "just right" despite a nearly skeletal appearance (Neuman & Halvorson, 1983). Despite the distortion of their own body size, they are usually able to accurately perceive the body size of others. At present this phenomenon is not clearly understood. However, some research suggests that the greater the weight distortion, the worse the prognosis (Slade & Russell, 1973).

According to DSM III, a diagnosis of anorexia nervosa is made when the following five diagnostic criteria are present:

a. Intense fear of becoming obese, which does not diminish as weight loss progresses.

b. Disturbance of body image, e.g., claiming to "feel fat" even when emaciated.

c. Weight loss of at least 25 percent of original body weight or, if under 18 years of age, weight loss from original body weight plus projected weight gain expected from growth charts may be combined to make the 25 percent.

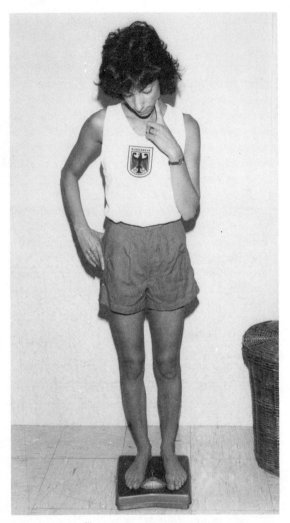

One of the hallmarks of anorexia is an obsessive concern with weight. (© Nancy Bates)

d. Refusal to maintain body weight over a minimal normal weight for age and height.

e. No known physical illness that would account for the weight loss.

Incidence and Clinical Picture. It is currently estimated that about 1 percent of females between the ages of 12 and 18 are anorexic: anorexic females far outnumber anorexic males with estimates varying from 20 to 1 to 7 to 1 (Bemis, 1978). There is some evidence that a milder, subclinical form of anorexia may occur in about 6 percent of the adolescent female population. It has also been suggested that the incidence of anorexia is increasing (Jones, Fox, Babigan, & Hutton, 1980). However, there is controversy as to whether the increase is real or the result of better reporting, a larger population, or less hesitancy to seek help.

There is variability in the personalities of individuals who develop anorexia. However, anorexics often have above average intelligence and usually come from middle and upper socioeconomic levels. One of the parents, often the mother, is likely to be overprotective and controlling, while the other parent is frequently passive or absent. Prior to the onset of the disorder, anorexic females are often described as having been "perfect children"—compliant, academically successful, popular, and even tempered (Golden & Sacker, 1984). Most had a normal weight prior to becoming anorexic. Anorexics often lose between 25 and 50 percent of their normal body weight. This kind of starvation has many more serious ramifications than an emaciated appearance. Eighty to 100 percent of anorexic women experience a cessation of menstruation (Rollins & Piazza, 1978), a fine down called lanugo may appear on the body, and many anorexics lose their hair. With continued low weight, heart problems, including arrhythmias and other EKG abnormalities, may occur (Gottdiener, Gross, Henry, Borer, & Ebert, 1978). Potentially life-threatening electrolyte imbalances also may occur.

Explanations. Early psychoanalytic views of anorexia described it as the result of unconscious conflicts, with fears and fantasies of oral impregnation seen as underlying causes of the food-avoidant behaviors (Lorland, 1943). A more popular psychodynamic theory has been advanced by Bruch (1973).

She views anorexia as a struggle for independence and self-respect. Willful starvation is a central part of this struggle. Bruch contends that the parents of anorexics fail to help them develop a sense of competence and self-value, instead encouraging dependency. Self-control through not eating becomes a way of gaining automony and a sense of personal effectiveness.

Certainly, our culture's current preoccupation with a slender figure makes it an issue for many women. There seems to be an emphasis on appearance, thinness, and diet. A large portion of the books sold in this country are diet and exercise books. In 1978 a Nielsen survey revealed that nearly half of U.S. households have at least one member on a diet during a given year, and that 56 percent of women between the ages of 24 and 54 diet (Schwartz, Thompson, & Johnson, 1982). Among women who diet, over 75 percent do so because of appearance rather than health.

In a study designed to examine changing ideas of feminine beauty during the period 1959 to 1978, Garner and his associates (Garner, Garfinkel, Schwartz, & Thompson, 1980) reviewed data on the Miss America pageant contestants and *Playboy* centerfolds. They reported that over this 29-year period the weight of these women declined even when height and age were controlled. Even more illuminating was the finding that the weight of the average woman increased several pounds over the same period. Thus, while women were becoming slightly heavier, the cultural ideals were becoming thinner. Is it so surprising, then, that more and more women are trying to reduce their weight to fit the ideal—even if it means starvation?

Treatment and Outcome. A variety of treatment approaches have been developed for use with anorexics. The predominant ones include individual or group psychother-apy, family therapy, and in-patient hospitalization. Medication and nutritional counseling are likely to be used in conjunction with any of the above approaches. Often several treatment approaches are used simultaneously, a strategy that some strongly recommend (Goldfried, 1980). Regardless of one's theoretical orientation and choice of treatment strategies, stabilizing the anorexic's physical condition is often a priority. This is always the case when weight loss has reached life-threatening proportions. In such cases immediate hospitalization usually is required, with intravenous or tube feeding, until the anorexic's physical condition has stabilized.

Do anorexics recover? For many anorexics the answer is yes, although there are varying degrees of improvement. Nutritionally speaking, around half of those treated recover completely in two to five years. A majority of this group also regain menstrual functions (Hsu, 1980). However, the outlook is not entirely positive. Relapse frequently occurs, and other psychological problems may be present. Death from this disorder or its complications has been estimated to occur in from 3 to 25 percent of anorexics (Bemis, 1978; Dally, 1967).

Bulimia

Bulimia is an eating disorder characterized by periods of extreme overeating or "binge-eating" followed by purging through self-induced vomiting, laxative abuse, or diuretics. The literal meaning of the term *bulimia* is "ox hunger." It refers to the insatiable hunger experienced by many bulimics. As one bulimic young woman stated, "When I start to binge, I cook and eat all of the food in the apartment. If there doesn't seem to be enough, I go to the grocery store, buy more, and go home and eat it all. My roommate moved out recently because of my binges. I kept eating all of her food and mine too. She would get so angry at me, and I would feel terrible, but I'd still do it again. Now I'm lonely and don't like being by myself all the time, but I can't get another roommate—the same thing would just happen again."

Bulimia is a relatively new clinical entity, emerging over the past 20 years, primarily as a result of the increased research in the areas of anorexia and obesity. It was included in the latest revision of DSM III (1980), reflecting both its recognition and a rapid increase in its incidence. However, despite this new recognition as a disorder, the principles on which it is based have been known. The gorging of food followed by self-induced vomiting dates from the period of the Roman Empire. At that time vomitoria were provided so that feast participants might not be limited by the amounts their stomachs could hold (Chiodo & Latimer, 1983). While other periods in history do not reflect such openness about this practice, its existence seems likely.

Bulimics are aware that their eating habits are abnormal and are embarrassed by them. They try to hide the huge amounts they consume. For example, one young woman ate three separate meals at three different restaurants during a suppertime binge so that no one would notice her actions. A binge often consists of eating huge amounts of "forbidden" foods. Meals may consist of items such as "eight pieces of fried chicken, three helpings of mashed potatoes with gravy, six biscuits, french fries, a chef salad, and an entire freshly baked cake." Bulimics often alternate between periods of going on a binge and rigid dieting. While dieting, they will carefully avoid fattening foods, which are the very things they are most likely to consume during a binge.

The types of food bulimics on a binge eat may vary, although often such meals consist of starches and sugars. One patient reported consuming between 15,000 and 20,000 calories during a single binge (Russell, 1979). Binges usually last one or two hours, and some bulimics go on a binge several times a day. In other cases one binge may last the whole day. Often individuals report five- or six-year histories of such eating habits.

After a binge most bulimics feel guilt, depression, and panic over the loss of control and the likelihood of gaining weight. Like anorexics, they are extremely weight-conscious and fearful of becoming fat. Their image of their own body size may be distorted, and they may see themselves as fat when they are within normal weight ranges. Their answer to the problem is often to purge. This is likely to take the form of self-induced vomiting, if the circumstances allow. If they are in a public place, or perhaps visiting a friend's home, they may feel that it is "too risky" to vomit. On such occasions they may abuse laxatives. It is not uncommon to have a bulimic woman report using a box of 30 over-the-counter laxatives in three days or less. Many even use these two methods of purging in combination to ensure that they do not gain weight.

Incidence and Clinical Picture. The incidence of bulimia is difficult to measure, and estimates vary, ranging from 7 to 20 percent of women (Pope, Hudson, & Yurgelun-Todd, 1984). As is the case with anorexia, a much lower incidence is reported for men. Part of the difficulty in assessing the incidence of this disorder has been the secrecy and embarrassment associated with episodes of binges and purgings. For many bulimics the worst scenario would be to have their family, friends, or acquaintances discover their secret. Such fears and the efforts to hide the problem usually add more stress to an already anxiety-provoking situation, making the secret seem even more "horrible." Another reason for the difficulty in assessing the incidence of bulimia is that, unlike anorexia, its presence is difficult to detect from an individual's physical appearance. Family members often don't know about the disorder because the bulimic is very secretive about her eating, and her physical size remains unchanged. Moreover, in social situations bulimics may eat appropriate amounts (Fairburn & Cooper, 1982). In many cases the bulimia is undetected for years, only surfacing when the bulimic feels out of control and seeks advice or therapy.

Bulimia usually begins in late adolescence, with 18 being the most frequently reported age (Neuman & Halvorson, 1983). Although bulimia occurs in all weight groups, it seems that most bulimics have a history of being moderately overweight or in the upper limit of their normal range. Low self-esteem and feelings of inadequacy are common among bulimics. Interpersonally, they tend to be nonassertive, dependent individuals. Their parents are frequently described as domineering or controlling, and sexual conflicts and fears of rejection by men are also common.

Medical Complications. A number of unpleasant side effects often accompany bulimia. Many are unknown in advance to women with this disorder. Both purging through vomiting and laxative abuse can cause fluid and electrolyte imbalances, resulting in potentially life-threatening situations. Heavy and prolonged laxative abuse can cause permanent damage to the colon. The frequent ingestion of large quantities of sugars and starches as well as the digestive acids present in vomited food can damage the enamel of their teeth. Indeed, it is said that many bulimics are first seen in the dentist's office.

Treatment. While a number of treatment approaches for bulimia have been devised, the two most promising appear to be cognitive behavioral techniques and group therapy approaches. An exemplary cognitive-behavioral program was recently described by Ordman and Kirschenbaum (1985). Their therapy helped 7 of 10 bulimics reduce their chronic cycle of going on a binge and then vomiting to one day per week or less. The treatment program lasted an average of 15 sessions. The participants' gains were more impressive than the minimal gains achieved by another group of 10 women who were simply placed on a waiting list and encouraged to experience the discomfort after eating without purging. In the "full" treatment therapists helped clients to recognize and modify self-defeating thought patterns like the following: "If I gain two pounds, I'll continue to gain weight until I become obese. Vomiting is the only way I can control my weight. Sweets are bad foods and if I eat them I'm a bad person. If I can just lose five pounds, my life will drastically improve. My appearance, especially my weight, is the basis of my self-worth" (p. 307). In order to break the vicious cycle of overeating and reducing anxiety by purging, the clients were prevented from vomiting after eating. Finally, the therapists made explicit contracts with clients (e.g., eating three meals per day) and offered support and encouragement for normal eating. Group therapies share many of the goals of cognitive-behavioral treatments but approach the problem in an interpersonally oriented, group treatment context.

Another treatment approach involves the use of medication, primarily antidepressants. Hospitalization is also sometimes useful in helping to break the binge-purge cycle, particularly in a large medical setting where there is likely to be a unit designed to treat eating disorders with a staff specially trained to deal with problems that may arise.

SUMMARY

In this chapter we have reviewed a number of the major forms of psychopathology that occur during childhood and adolescence. We began with a discussion of some behavioral and emotional disorders of childhood, including childhood depression and suicide, childhood fears and phobias, school phobia, disorders of elimination, reactive attachment disorder of infancy, and attention deficit disorder. Attention deficit disorder, formerly termed *hyperactivity*, is characterized by impaired attention and impulsivity. High levels of motor activity may or may not be present.

Depressive symptoms, as described in the reactive attachment disorder of infancy, may occur very early in life. They result from inadequate care. During childhood, as many as 10 percent of children may experience depressive symptoms. Psychotherapy and medication are both frequently used modalities for treating depression in children. Rates of recorded suicide among young children seem to indicate that it is virtually nonexistent. Some authorities feel that recording procedures as well as societal pressures interact and result in underreporting of childhood suicide.

Many childhood fears and phobias are temporary and present no serious or long-term threat to the child's emotional functioning. However, others such as school phobia, where the child avoids the school situation, have a serious detrimental potential and usually require treatment. The disorders of elimination, enuresis and encopre-sis, are more common among younger children. As the effects of these disorders on personality development have been understood, the value of early intervention has become more accepted.

While child abuse does not represent abnormal behavior on the child's part, it may result in significant and long-lasting psychological disturbance. Cases of both physical and sexual abuse are vastly underreported.

The specific developmental disorders are the most frequently encountered group. Many of them are recognized and treated within the educational system rather than the mental health system. In contrast, the pervasive developmental disorders—infantile autism and childhood onset pervasive developmental disorder—impair every aspect of the child's psychological functioning.

Conduct disorders involve behavior that is often termed *juvenile delinquency*. Included as subtypes of the conduct disorder are socialized and unsocialized types, and aggressive and nonaggressive types. Distinctions between the subtypes are based on the presence or absence of emotional bonds and physical violence. Two other disorders likely to occur during adolescence—anorexia nervosa and bulimia—are increasing in occurrence. Our culture's preoccupation with thinness has frequently been implicated as a causal factor. The side effects of these eating disorders can be unpleasant, and in some cases, life-threatening.

11

Disorders of the Later Years

Sara D.—A Confused Lady

Thoughts about Aging
The Elderly—Our Fastest Growing
Population

Who Is Old?
Concepts of Age
Effects of Senescence versus Effects of
Disease

**Prevalence of Mental Disorders in Older
People**

Areas of Adaptation in Aging

**Frameworks for Understanding Behavioral
Changes with Aging**
A Response-to-Stress Framework
A Learning Framework
A Social-Breakdown Framework

Special Concerns of the Elderly
Retirement
Housing
Family Transitions
Mobility
Health
Sensory Changes
Bereavement

Psychopathological Problems of a Functional Nature
Depression
Pseudodementia
Suicide
Paranoia
Hypochondriasis
Substance Misuse and Abuse
Anxiety
Schizophrenia

Psychological Assessment of the Elderly: Issues and Problems
Cognitive Assessment

Interventions with the Elderly
Psychotherapy with the Elderly
Chemical and Biological Treatments

Summary

Sara D.—A Confused Lady

Sara D., age 71, lives in a long-term care facility (LTCF). For 25 years she was a real-estate agent, living in a home with her husband, who is a retired lawyer. Seven years ago Sara developed pernicious anemia and began to show increased confusion, loss of short-term memory, general discomfort, and substantial weight loss (about 40 pounds). During that time she was also treated for cancer of the right jaw.

Sara began to display increasing irritability and dependency on her family. She had periods of mental wandering, forgetfulness, and depression, although her sleeping, eating, and elimination habits remained good. As she required more care and supervision from her family and a succession of "sitters," her family reluctantly decided to place her in the LTCF. Sara resented this decision and frequently asked to return home.

At the time of this report, Sara has a generalized body tremor, loss of memory for remote as well as recent events, and a shuffling gait with a wide base. Her irregular pulse is believed to be caused by coronary heart disease for which she receives medication (lanoxin, a form of digitalis). She weighs between 80 and 90 pounds. She is anxious and disoriented, feels abandoned and rejected, but is cooperative and makes friends easily.

Sara occasionally plays the piano, likes to attend musical programs and sing-alongs, and enjoys watching soap operas and variety shows on TV. Although very confused and generally disoriented, she does remember her husband. However, her physical and mental conditions are steadily deteriorating.

What has happened to Sara? Are these changes in her personality and her mental controls caused by the inevitable ravages of the aging process? Or are they primarily caused by illness? Has the separation from her husband and family caused her to feel angry, depressed, and abandoned? Or are these feelings caused by her medications?

Certainly Sara's condition reveals how intricate interactions of many influences—environmental, social, and personal—can affect one's mental and physical functioning in the later years. In this chapter we will explore the ways in which illnesses and their treatments, family circumstances, and feelings of hurt and inadequacy can affect the el-

---

FACTS ON AGING QUIZ*

Directions: Circle "T" for True and "F" for False.

1. The majority of old people (past age 65) are senile (i.e., defective memory, disoriented, or demented).   T   F
2. All five senses tend to decline in old age.   T   F
3. At least one tenth of the aged are living in long-stay institutions (i.e., nursing homes, mental hospitals, homes for the aged, etc.).   T   F
4. The majority of old people are seldom bored.   T   F
5. The majority of old people are socially isolated and lonely.   T   F
6. Over 15 percent of the U.S. population are now age 65 or over.   T   F
7. Most medical practitioners tend to give low priority to the aged.   T   F
8. The majority of older people have incomes below the poverty level (as defined by the Federal Government).   T   F

9. The majority of old people are seldom irritated or angry.   T   F
10. More older persons (over 65) have chronic illnesses that limit their activity than younger persons.   T   F
11. Older persons have more acute (short-term) illnesses than persons under 65.   T   F
12. There are two widows for each widower among the aged.   T   F
13. The majority of the aged live alone.   T   F
14. When the last child leaves home, the majority of parents have serious problems adjusting to their "empty nest."   T   F
15. The proportion widowed is decreasing among the aged.   T   F

*(Selected items from Palmore, 1977, 1981.)

Answers:
1. F 2. T 3. F 4. T 5. F 6. T 7. T 8. F
9. T 10. T 11. F 12. F 13. F 14. F 15. T

derly person who may be experiencing the culmination of many social and physical losses simultaneously. We will attempt to understand both adaptive and maladaptive functional changes associated with aging from the frameworks of a learning, a stress, and a sociological model. The functional psychopathologies most commonly experienced by the elderly, as well as problems of medication misuse and abuse, will then be reviewed. A discussion of specific issues in the psychological assessment of the elderly client will follow. Finally we will examine the variety of psychological interventions employed by clinicians in working with elderly people who are in distress.

THOUGHTS ABOUT AGING

What word comes to your mind when you think of yourself as "old"? Do you see yourself as "wrinkled" and "helpless" or as "lonely" and "senile"? Or do you picture yourself as "wise," "respected," "feisty," or "caring"? It might be revealing to consider the reasons for your descriptive terms. Could you be voicing popular misconceptions of aging? Could you be voicing your fear of your own aging? As a colleague said, "I don't fear death so much as how you get there."

What do you know about the elderly? Take the Facts on Aging Quiz to test your knowledge of the elderly and the aging process.

If you answered 10 or more items correctly in the Facts on Aging Quiz, you probably have a realistic understanding of the elderly and their problems. If you answered more than 10 incorrectly, you may believe many of the popular myths that describe the elderly as sick, neglected, poor, mentally unsound, handicapped, and so forth. While some elderly do have these problems, a majority are not seriously incapacitated and lead compara-

tively normal, happy lives. As their population increases, however, the number of those who do have difficulties will also increase.

The Elderly—Our Fastest Growing Population

In recent years there has been an increased concern for the problems of the older adult, particularly those older than 65. Since 1900 the number of people age 60 and over has increased four times as fast as the number under 60. During this period the total population of the United States has doubled, while the number of persons over 65 has increased seven times. Thus a man who is currently 65 years old has a life expectancy of 13 additional years. A 65-year-old woman may live, on the average, 18 additional years. A man age 75 can expect nine more years of life. A 75-year-old woman can expect to live 12 more years. By the year 2030, when the post–World War II babies will be over 65, it is estimated that one out of every five people or 50 million Americans will be older than 65. (See Figure 11–1.)

While the population rose 12.4 percent from 1970 to 1981, the population of people older than 65 increased 31.4 percent in the same time period—from 20 to 26.3 million. Thus about 11.5 percent of the population was older than 65 in 1981 (see Figure 11–2). Overall, by the year 2000 the population of the elderly is expected to be 35 million and to represent 13 percent of the population. The projected percentage of people 65 and over will continue to climb in the 21st century (see Figure 11–2).

A statistic with far-reaching implications is that life expectancy is greater for women than men. At ages 65 and over there are three women for every two men. After age 85 the ratio of women to men is over two to one, as you will note in Figure 11–3.

FIGURE 11-1
Number of Persons Age 65 and Older Compared with Total Population, from 1900
(The Chart Extends to the Year 2030)

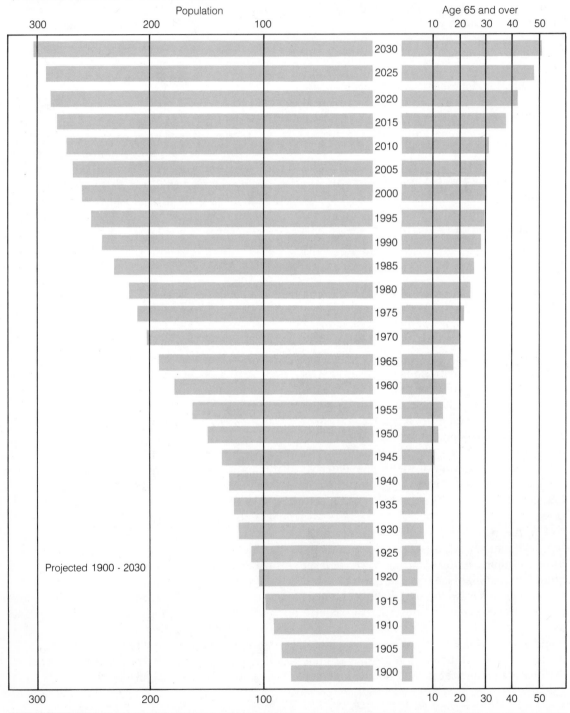

Source: From *Aging and Mental Health* 3d ed. (p. 7) by R. N. Butler and M. I. Lewis, 1982, St. Louis: C. V. Mosby. Data from U.S. Bureau of the Census, 1978.

FIGURE 11-2
Percent of the Total Population in the Older Ages: 1900 to 2040

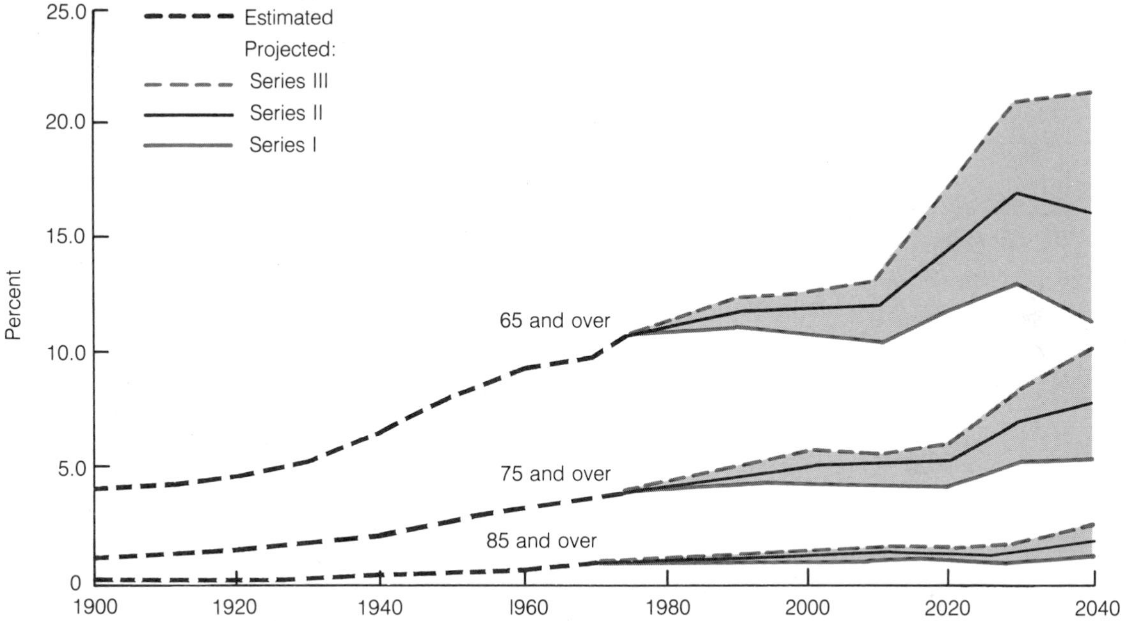

Note: Estimates and projections as of July 1, except for 85 and over, 1900–1930, which relate to April 1. Points are plotted for years ending in zero except for 1975.

Source: From *Demographic Aspects of Aging and the Older Population in the United States* Special Studies Series P-23 no. 59, 2d printing rev. (p. 4) by U.S. Department of Commerce, Bureau of the Census, January 1978, Washington, D.C.: U.S. Government Printing Office.

These statistics have implications for planning services for the elderly, since elderly females use mental health facilities more than elderly males. Furthermore, the elderly have fewer family ties, and many subsist below the poverty level, thus indicating a higher risk for developing mental health problems (Redick & Taube, 1980). In fact, the President's Commission on Mental Health estimated that 15 to 25 percent of older persons have significant mental health problems (Roybal, 1984).

WHO IS OLD?

Concepts of Age

If you were to ask a friend his or her age, the reply would be in terms of calendar years—

21, 35, or 75 years old. Chronological age is a very convenient and straightforward index that conveys a variety of expectations. Age 65, however, is a relatively arbitrary marker for entering old age. In the 1930s Congress set 65 as the legal age at which one becomes eligible for social security benefits.

Chronological age per se does not *explain* any of the behavioral or biological changes that may occur as a person grows old (Birren & Renner, 1977). An analogy is that the iron railing on a house porch does not rust because it has grown old but because of oxidation processes that occur over time.

Birren and Renner (1977) have suggested four other potential indexes of age. One is *biological age*. It refers to the estimate of the person's position on the birth-to-death

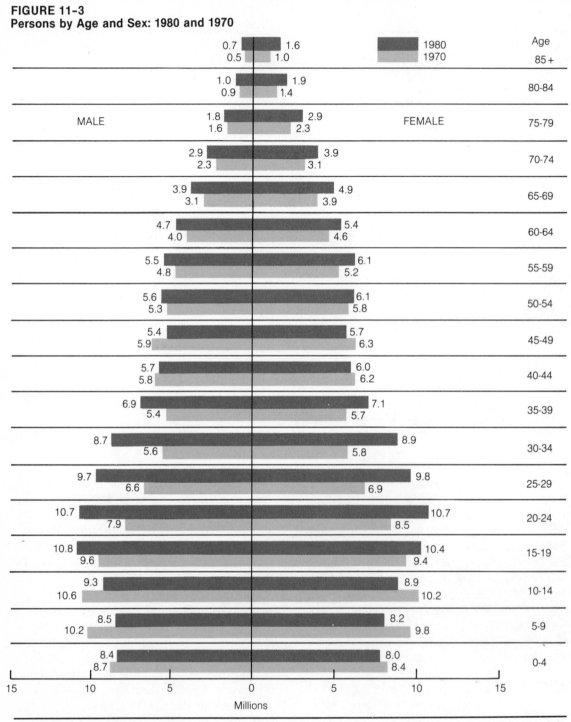

FIGURE 11–3
Persons by Age and Sex: 1980 and 1970

Source: From *General Population Characteristics: Part I United States Summary,* Census of Population, Vol. 1, Chapter B (p. 12) by U.S. Department of Commerce, May 1983, Washington, D.C.: U.S. Government Printing Office.

lifeline in terms of biological functioning. For example, how efficiently are the individual's various organ systems (circulatory, cardiovascular, etc.) functioning, relative to optimal efficiency? Another index is *psychological age,* or a person's capacity to deal with the stresses of an ever changing environment (e.g., the effectiveness of learning, memory, personality processes for adapting to change). *Functional age* is an index of a person's ability to function in given roles in society. Functional age has frequently been suggested as a more appropriate basis for retirement, replacing the arbitrary criterion of the chronological age. Yet another index is *social age.* When we hear that someone dresses "too young for her age," the individual is probably referring to social age, that is, the set of expectations about appropriate social behaviors for a given age.

As you can see, except for its simplicity of measurement, the index of chronological age may have serious shortcomings. Three 75-year-old men, for instance, may vary greatly in their biological, social, functional, and/or psychological ages. Society often seems to lump people into the category of old age. There appears, however, to be greater diversity among older people on almost any physiological or psychological measure than there is among younger age groups (Hoyer, 1974). These broad individual differences among older people must be kept in mind when we consider age-related psychological disorders.

Researchers have made a distinction between the processes of *aging* and the processes of *senescence.* Aging emphasizes the complex interplay of biological, social, and psychological factors; it refers to regular changes that occur as people advance in chronological age. It can include potential *gains* associated with age, such as experience and wisdom, as well as negative changes, such as a decline in visual and mo-

tor abilities (Birren & Renner, 1977). Senescence, more specifically, is that state during which degenerative biological processes overtake regenerative processes, leading to a decrease in the person's powers to adjust and survive (Huyck & Hoyer, 1982). Senescence may contribute to maladjustment in several ways. It reduces the individual's reserves for adaptation and coping with stress. The elderly person may already be operating close to his or her physiological and psychological tolerance levels. In addition, the aging individual's declining ability to ward off disease and chronic illnesses, as well as the slowing up of healing time, may directly or indirectly affect adjustment.

Although there is no agreed upon explanation for the occurrence of senescence, these normal and inevitable processes are considered to be *distinct* from disease processes (Huyck & Hoyer, 1982).

Effects of Senescence versus Effects of Disease

What functional changes can be expected as part of senescence when disease is absent? A much quoted study by Birren, Butler, Greenhouse, Sokoloff, and Yarrow (1963) indicated that many of the decremental changes usually attributed to aging are more appropriately attributed to disease. There do appear to be *some* changes in functioning that occur with age in the absence of disease. These changes, however, produce far less impairment than has been commonly assumed. Let us take a brief look at some of the results of the Birren et al. study.

Birren and his colleagues divided a sample of men 65 and older into two groups. While the men in Group 1 were in optimal health, those in Group 2 were suffering from mild, asymptomatic, or subclinical disease (e.g., arteriosclerosis). The men in Group 1 performed at a higher level on a variety of physiological and psychological measures than those in Group 2. Furthermore, the subjects in Group 1 did not differ significantly from younger men on many of the measures. Both groups, however, had slower electrical brain activity, although those in Group 1 were within the range of younger men. Likewise, both groups had slower psychomotor speed (speed of muscular activity associated with mental processes) than young adults.

The same subjects were reexamined 11 years later (Granick & Patterson, 1971), and the changes noted in them were analyzed. The majority of the subjects in Group 2 had died in the interim, whereas the majority of those in Group 1 were alive. It was found that most of the differences originally noted between the two groups (e.g., performance on intelligence tests, personality adaptation, social losses, and reaction times) were related to survival.

In sum, slower psychomotor speed and electrical brain activity seem to occur as a function of age, regardless of health status. Disease processes, however, can accelerate these changes. It is important to note that even a mild degree of disease appears to have many harmful effects on both physical and behavioral functioning, which often may be inaccurately interpreted as something caused by growing old.

Zarit (1980) cautions against attributing mental changes solely to the aging process. He points out that the status of one's health is a more important determinant of functioning. Brain atrophy can occur before the age of 65, and the symptoms may be very similar to those of senile brain disease. Such similarities are due to a comparable illness, not age. While chronological age and health status are correlated, many exceptions to the pattern would refute generalizations about there being "a stage of old age, in which most persons manifest certain patterns of behav-

ior or other universally shared characteristics" (Zarit, 1980, p. 9).

PREVALENCE OF MENTAL DISORDERS IN OLDER PEOPLE

It is difficult to generalize from studies of the epidemiology of mental illness among the elderly because methods of collecting data and subject populations may not be comparable, or the diagnoses may have low reliability. Blazer (1980) found general agreement, however, that the rate of significant or severe mental impairment among the elderly in the community is from 5 to 10 percent; mild to moderate impairment may affect 10 to 40 percent; while between 50 and 80 percent are not impaired.

Approximately 17 percent of the elderly treated at community outpatient clinics are diagnosed as psychoneurotic (Butler & Lewis, 1982). Butler and Lewis estimated that functional disorders account for 30 to 40 percent of hospitalization of the elderly. The remaining hospitalizations are related to organic problems; 50 percent of these problems may be reversible (e.g., heart conditions, medication complications, infections, or malnutrition). Depression is the most common mental disorder among older people. Suicide rates for persons older than 60 are especially high, accounting for 23 percent of all suicides in the United States—more than for any other age group. It is rare for persons to develop schizophrenia in later life, although many older persons who have developed schizophrenia in earlier years may become "chronic schizophrenics" (Butler & Lewis, 1982).

It has been suggested (Neugarten, 1975) that there are two distinct levels of the elderly: young-old (ages 65–74), and old-old (ages 75 and older). During the young-old years the incidence of functional disorders (mainly depression), while much greater than organic disorders, declines; in the old-old period organic brain disorders become more prevalent.

Let us examine some of the significant areas of adjustment and adaptation associated with the psychological and social functioning of the elderly.

AREAS OF ADAPTATION IN AGING

How the elderly person functions in specific contexts will determine whether the behavior is considered normal and healthy or whether it is seen as pathological and unhealthy. Let us consider positive or negative functioning in three major reference areas: environmental, social, and personal.

1. *Environmental adaptation* is adjustment in impersonal public settings or tasks, such as work, living conditions, financial status, or recreation. Work-related skills, general efficiency, effectiveness, and productivity characterize positive adaptation. A person who effectively works at a job or task shows positive adaptation in the environmental area. A person who shivers in substandard housing has a negative adaptation.

2. *Social adaptation* involves relationships with others, such as family, friends, co-workers, church groups, or neighbors. A man who has lost his spouse or who quarrels with his children may show a negative social adaptation, whereas a woman in a nursing home who has many visitors may have a positive adaptation.

3. *Personal adaptation* is represented by a person's self-attitudes, health, mood, sense of well-being, and the way in which that person feels, reacts, and copes with stress. If a person is depressed or exhibits mental confusion, that would be a sign of a negative personal adaptation, whereas positive functioning might

be shown if the person is competent or optimistic about the outcome of an operation.

The balance between positive and negative functioning in these areas defines the quality of a person's overall adaptation. Depending upon interacting or compensating factors, greater or lesser importance may be assigned by a person to any one event such as retirement. For example, retirement may initially distress a man because it diminishes contact with his friends. However, he may find that the increased leisure permits him to devote more time to his hobbies and, in the balance, to find a positive adaptation in retirement. A woman with a supportive family may be able to endure a physical handicap much better than one who is alone. The meaning, intensity, and balance of positive versus negative functioning in all areas acting in combination—environmental, social, and personal—influence one's adaptation to crises and transitions.

Multiple criteria are therefore needed to describe adaptation: No single criterion can properly account for all conditions or needs. Our discussion suggests that an assessment of the elderly must take into consideration the nature and degree of positive and negative functioning. Treatment of the elderly should be geared to the restoration or improvement of positive functioning as well as to the removal or amelioration of negative functioning. Either increasing positive functioning or decreasing negative functioning, or both, will move the balance of functioning in the direction of healthy adaptation in environmental, social, and personal areas.

FRAMEWORKS FOR UNDERSTANDING BEHAVIORAL CHANGES WITH AGING

Aging is a natural growth process for all living organisms. Inasmuch as many of the difficulties faced by the elderly could be encountered at any age, we must be careful not to consider aging as a "cause" of the elderly's problems. Rather, social and environmental conditions often require unique adaptive behaviors as people grow older.

There are several theoretical positions or models by which we may view adaptive behaviors associated with aging. Models are important because they provide frameworks for understanding behavioral changes and guidelines for intervention approaches and objectives. Although no current model is sufficient for us to fully understand the interaction of all the maturational and environmental processes associated with aging, useful theoretical approaches have interpreted the adaptive behaviors of the elderly in terms of (a) responses to stressors (Renner & Birren, 1980; Schlossberg, 1984); (b) learning principles (Baltes & Barton, 1977); and (c) the social-breakdown syndrome (Kuypers & Bengtson, 1973).

A Response-to-Stress Framework

Many stressful events that require substantial adaptation are likely to occur in later life. Whenever such events occur, they may be termed *transitions*. As defined by Spierer (1977), a transition is any change that has important consequences for human behavior. Social changes, biological conditions, environmental and historical events, or other phenomena may have either immediate and obvious consequences or delayed outcomes that are not always apparent. Some transitions may be sudden, others may be cumulative or insidious.

Adaptation to a transition may be stressful, depending on the nature of the transition and the coping resources the person has in terms of a balance of positive and negative functioning. For some elderly, transitions may be unduly stressful. Having lived longer, residuals of negative functioning acquired

during difficult life events (the death of a spouse or the relocation of housing) or during periods of physical or mental decline (the loss of hearing, high blood pressure, memory losses) have greater impact. At a time when their adaptive functioning capacities are diminishing, the elderly may experience stresses they may not have faced earlier in life.

The diagram in Figure 11–4 illustrates how stressors, such as life events and body changes, may be appraised cognitively by an individual to form the basis for coping strategies and emotional states (Renner & Birren, 1980). A closer look at the resources a person has for appraising and producing coping responses is provided by Schlossberg (1984) in Figure 11–5.

A person's response to stressors may be mediated by (a) the characteristics of the transition, (b) the characteristics of the person, and (c) the nature of the environment. To illustrate, let us consider a problem typical of many elderly:

Abbie, age 61, became depressed and anxious when her husband of 40 years was diagnosed as having cancer and was scheduled for surgery. Subsequently she complained about her loss of memory—she forgot appointments, could not recall where she had placed things, and became upset over keeping track of the family checking account. Very worried about her apparent mental deterioration, she began taking heavy doses of mega-vitamins (smart pills).

To understand Abbie's adaptation style, we might start with the "trigger" event: her husband's illness. In the context of a close, dependent marital relationship, this transition might have a major impact. It would affect her role as a dependent by forcing her to assume financial management and to become his nurse. She was not prepared for either role. Her coping resources would fur-

FIGURE 11–4
Schematic Diagram Illustrating Relationships between Stressors and the Behavioral and Physiological Responses

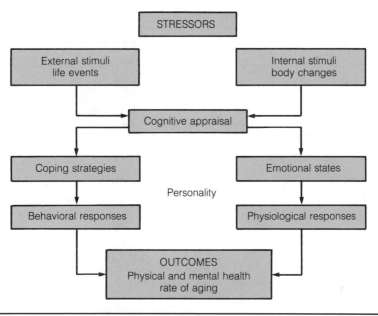

Source: From "Stress: Physiological and Psychological Mechanisms" (p. 311) by V. J. Renner and J. E. Birren in *Handbook of Mental Health and Aging* ed. J. E. Birren and R. B. Sloane, 1980, Englewood Cliffs, NJ: Prentice-Hall.

ther be affected by fears for her own future. As she developed symptoms of memory loss, her emotional controls, which were never strong, became inadequate, resulting in negative functions of anxiety and panic. She did show positive functioning by trying to improve her memory with vitamin pills. Her environment provided few social supports, so she was forced to face her own disability and the prospect of losing her spouse alone. Her anxiety and depressive reactions, perhaps even her memory problems, represent adaptive responses to the stresses of the transition—all these responses result in a negative adaptation.

A Learning Framework

From an operant learning perspective (Baltes & Barton, 1977), age-related behav-

iors, like any behaviors, are acquired, maintained, and modified through environmental contingencies and reinforcements. In other words, barring physical deficiencies that prevent certain behaviors, behavioral decrements of the elderly are *learned;* they are not inevitable aspects of growing old. Being learned, such decrements can be modified or perhaps reversed through the application of learning principles, or even prevented by appropriate environmental contingencies and reinforcements. According to this model, greater understanding of the nature of the elderly's behavior-environment interactions should allow for the design of environments that improve the functioning of older people.

Baltes and Barton suggest a number of aspects of the elderly person's environment that may lead to decrements in behavior. The frequency and number of reinforcing events

FIGURE 11–5
Coping Resources

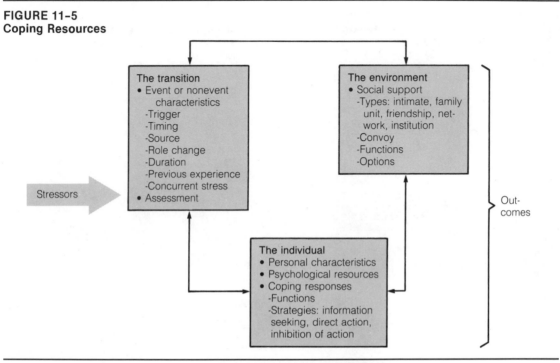

Source: Adapted from *Counseling Adults in Transition* (p. 71) by N. K. Schlossberg, 1984, New York: Springer.

may decline through physical, psychological, and social restrictions on activities and/or capabilities. The elderly person's shrinking social world, as well as physical impairments, may reduce the number of available reinforcers, at the same time that the reinforcement value of those remaining is decreasing. For example, an elderly woman who has a sight impairment, suffers from arthritis, and has no close friend to accompany her may no longer enjoy attending meetings of the garden club. Loss of family members and friends results in fewer reinforcing agents to support the elderly person's endeavors. In turn, the elderly person, as a result of a societal structure which does not esteem old age, may not be sought out because of loss of reinforcing power *to* others. For example, if the opinion of the elderly person is not considered important, the opinion will

not be asked. Furthermore, there may be a loss of discriminative environmental cues, because of changes in work, family, and social settings and because of internal changes such as sensory losses. Lack of cues diminishes the likelihood that behaviors will occur, regardless of potential reinforcers.

In many situations, positive reinforcements for the elderly are made contingent upon their demonstrating maladaptive rather than adaptive behaviors. Consider the following illustration:

Helen, age 81, has lived in a nursing home for the past five years. Following a recent illness during which she was bedridden, she has found it fatiguing to walk and prefers the comfort and security of a wheelchair. She agrees with her physician, however, that she should walk more frequently to maintain her mobility and increase her strength. Close observation of Helen and the nursing staff suggests that she receives more attention and expressions of concern when she is wheeled about in her wheelchair than when she manages to walk alone with her cane.

According to learning principles, Helen is being reinforced for relative immobility, whereas the more positive motor functioning of walking is largely ignored. When environments do not reinforce positive functioning, performance may not only decline in frequency but deteriorate through disuse.

A considerable amount of operant learning research has been conducted to support the contention that intellectual performance, such as speed of responding (Hoyer, Labouvie, & Baltes, 1973), can be improved. Operant conditioning has also increased social interactions and improved self-maintenance behaviors, such as self-feeding, in nursing home and institutionalized elderly people (see Baltes & Barton, 1977, for a review of these studies).

A Social-Breakdown Framework

The social-breakdown syndrome takes a social systems perspective on the problems of growing old. Kuypers and Bengtson (1973) state, "The social-breakdown syndrome suggests that an individual's sense of self, his ability to mediate between self and society, and his orientation to personal mastery are functions of the kinds of social labeling experienced in life" (p. 181). Figure 11–6 gives a representation of the social-breakdown syndrome as applied to old age. As we can see, the system is described as a feedback loop with negative social inputs. Let us examine this loop in greater detail.

Moving into old age, the person is likely to experience the lack of social guidelines for behavior or the *lack of normative guidance* (i.e., there are few clear-cut expectations as to what a person should be doing during old age). At the same time there is a *role loss* through retirement, death of friends, widowhood, and so forth. An additional social change is the *lack of reference groups* (i.e., a lack of defined groups with whom the person can identify and to whom one can look for patterning one's behavior). Such social changes create a vacuum of information for the elderly person concerning who one is in relation to others and how one should act. This produces a *susceptibility* to, and dependence upon, others' evaluations and *external labeling*. Inasmuch as the larger society views the elderly as generally *incompetent* and *obsolete*, elderly people are informed—by direct and indirect cues—of their incompetence, uselessness, and obsolescence as judged by society. Such *negative labeling* produces behaviors in the elderly consistent with this evaluation; it leads to an *atrophy of skills* that are no longer demanded of them. Basic psychological skills previously used for effective adaptation may also decline, leading to a loss of coping mechanisms. The decline of coping skills leads to *self-labeling as incompetent*, whereby the person accepts the negative labeling as true for the self. The loop indicates that negative self-labeling in turn leads to further susceptibility, dependence on social labeling, decline of coping skills, and low self-esteem.

Interventions may interrupt this vicious cycle (Kuypers & Bengtson, 1973). For example, efforts can be made to liberate the elderly person from the viewpoint that self-worth is contingent on "productive" social roles. Efforts can be made to enhance the person's coping capacities by lessening stressful conditions of poverty, poor health, and inadequate housing. Self-esteem can be increased by giving the elderly more control and power over social policies that affect them.

FIGURE 11–6
A Systems Representation of SBS as Applied to Old Age with Negative Inputs from the External Social System

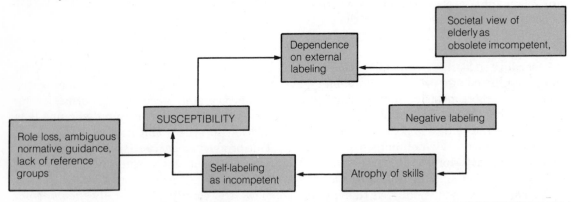

Source: From "Social Breakdown and Competence" by J. A. Kuypers and V. L. Bengtson, 1976, *Human Development, 16*, p. 181–201.

SPECIAL CONCERNS OF THE ELDERLY

Retirement

For the majority of the elderly, retirement is a condition in which an individual is employed less than full-time and income is derived at least in part from a retirement pension earned through prior years of employment (Atchley, 1976). Contrary to popular opinion, the economic position of the elderly in the United States has substantially improved over the past two decades, largely as a result of the liberalization and extension of social security benefits and coverage by pensions. Consequently, the proportion of older persons below the poverty level set by the Social Security Administration dropped from 35 to 14 percent during this period (Clark, 1981).

For many persons, however, the most stressful part of retirement is a reduction in income; a 50 percent decrease is not uncommon. Such financial losses, compounded by a lack of savings, can have a spreading effect upon one's health care, style of living, nutrition, social activities, perhaps even housing and mobility, resulting in negative environmental adaptation.

Retirement also forces many persons who are still able to work to be idle. Loss of work can trigger negative functioning in both social and personal areas of adaptation for the person whose self-esteem or sense of identity

The retirement years can require significant life adaptations. (Frank Siteman/EKM-Nepenthe)

is derived from an occupational role or whose social network is entwined with work roles.

Furthermore, removal of structured daily tasks as a result of retirement, coupled with increased leisure time, may necessitate restructuring one's time. An elderly person may be faced with the alternatives of puttering and watching TV, finding substitutes for work in hobbies, interests, and recreation, or looking for part-time work. Constructive use of leisure may be needed to avoid the sense of loneliness and stagnation that often contributes to alcoholism or suicide.

Housing

Approximately 80 percent of the elderly own mortgage-free homes. However, rising property taxes and increasing costs of maintenance force some people to seek less expensive housing. Older people tend to live in older, less valuable housing; about 30 percent of older Americans live in substandard housing.

A common myth is that most older people live in institutions, such as hospitals or nursing homes. Actually, only about 5 percent are in institutions. Of the remaining, over 70 percent live in households with family members; others may live alone or with friends.

For those who must relocate, there may be serious stresses, especially if the move follows a traumatic episode, such as bereavement, if the elderly have not been prepared for the move, if the move is to a less desirable setting, and if the elderly are already frail (Brody, 1977). Other problems may arise when the elderly move in with their children or relatives because most elderly prefer to be independent.

Family Transitions

One of the most common myths about older people is that they are abandoned or rejected by their families. Eight out of 10 elderly persons have living children or siblings. Shanas (1980) noted that half of all older people with children live in the same household with a child or next door or a few blocks away. "Among those old people who have children and who live alone, half are within 10 minutes distance of a child" (Shanas, 1980, p. 12). Three fourths have family members who live within a half hour's traveling distance, and about three fifths maintain contact with their children. Thus, even those who live alone do have family contacts, if not with their children, then with members of their extended family, such as grandchildren, nieces, nephews, and so forth. As people live longer, it is not unusual for three or four generations of a family to live under the same roof or close by.

Close proximity to one's children or relatives can be a mixed blessing, particularly if the older person requires extensive care or attention. The families of the care givers may be stressed by the situation if extensive physical care or nursing is required, and a decision to institutionalize the older person may have to be made. Contrary to popular opinion, most families delay such decisions until all alternatives have been tried. Most residents of nursing homes have not been abandoned and placed there by uncaring families. Whenever the move to a long-term care facility is made, however, the trauma of relocation can be serious.

Mobility

Many older persons report a lack of adequate transportation as their biggest problem. Problems of retirement and ill health would be easier to accept if they were not compounded by isolation and immobility. For many, private cars are too costly, public transportation too inaccessible or dangerous. Older people, especially those with

The majority of elderly people, even when they live alone, maintain family contacts. (Jill Cannefax/EKM-Nepenthe)

physical or mental limitations, may fear the jostling and crimes associated with public transportation systems or the confusion of schedules. Since much of the coping in environmental and social areas demands mobility for shopping, for visits to the doctor, or for visits to friends and relatives, there is considerable potential for negative functioning.

Health

Chronic diseases are more prevalent among the elderly: 85 percent of those over 65 have at least one chronic ailment, with arthritis, heart conditions, and hypertension leading the list. Older people are not equally im-

paired by these conditions, however. For some, the negative functioning may be slight, since they may customarily refuse to succumb to ailments and may even not consider themselves sick. The danger in refusing to recognize real illness is that a person may not receive timely treatment, thus aggravating the condition. Others, however, may function below their potential because of the care and concern they receive from others. It is not wise to foster older persons' overdependency, hypochondriasis, or their manipulation of care givers.

One might conclude from the prevalence of chronic illnesses among the elderly that they see themselves as ailing and unhealthy. However, 70 percent of the elderly consider themselves in good health when compared with others of their age (USDHEW, 1977). For those who do have chronic illnesses, however, each loss—whether social or physical—has a sense of finality or irreversibility that sometimes precipitates depression or suicide.

Sensory Changes

Loss of communication skills as a result of the impairment of sight, hearing, or speech can be especially handicapping. Of all the areas of psychological investigation, none has produced more clear-cut and consistent age-related findings than sensory changes (Botwinick, 1978). Significant changes in vision with age have been well documented (Botwinick, 1978). Typically, there is a loss in visual sharpness with increasing farsightedness or *presbyopia*. Older people therefore may need bifocals. There are also changes in color vision, marked by a difficulty in discriminating among the blue-greens, blues, and other cooler colors of the spectrum. Older people need greater levels of illumination, yet are also more prone to the effects of glare. Older people do not adapt to the dark as well as younger people. Older people likewise have more difficulty discriminating various brightnesses and contrasts, which may lead to difficulties in getting around their environment. Another visual problem for many older people is cataract, the clouding of the lens of the eye. It has been estimated that 20 to 25 percent of those in their 70s have cataracts (Botwinick, 1978).

Some degree of hearing impairment appears as the individual grows old (Botwinick, 1978). Hearing loss, however, is not equal across all sound frequencies. *Presbycusis,* or age-related loss in audition, is greater for higher-toned pitches. Presbycusis is more pronounced in men than in women. Part of the reason for sex differences may lie in men's greater exposure to noise pollution. Environmental studies have indicated that, when the environment is low in noise, the percentage of poor hearers among elderly people declines (Botwinick, 1978). Related to problems in hearing tones of varying pitch is the decreasing ability among elderly people to discriminate among pitches. Problems in pitch discrimination may affect the older person's speech comprehension, especially in situations where there are competing background noises, such as traffic sounds or the TV (Botwinick, 1978). In turn, impairment in speech comprehension may interfere with effective interpersonal communication.

Data about age-related changes in other sensory modalities (e.g., taste, smell, touch perception, pain perception) are not so well documented (Botwinick, 1978). Overall, Botwinick concludes that, for all the sensory modalities, the age-related pattern may be that of a relatively stable maintenance of function until late middle age, with at least some degree of decline in later life.

Typically, these age-related changes in vision and hearing come about gradually. Older individuals may discover a variety of ways to compensate for such sensory losses. The older person may be coping reasonably well with a sensory impairment. However, such a person might often be judged by others to be inattentive, confused, or intellectually impaired when in truth the individual simply has trouble seeing or hearing clearly. Also, real mental confusion may be compounded by sensory losses.

Bereavement

In this century widowed females have outnumbered widowed males by a ratio of four to one. Widowers tend to remarry, whereas widows may not remarry as often or as rapidly as men (Glick, Weiss, & Parks, 1974). In the first year following the loss of a spouse,

How one copes with the stress of bereavement may be influenced by the significance of the loss and the availability of a support system and viable coping strategies. (Tom Ballard/EKM-Nepenthe)

there is an increased risk of suicide among the elderly. Payne (1975) reports that "for the first four years of widowhood, the number of deaths from suicide exceeds the number of deaths from all other causes" (p. 295). The suicide rate for those living alone is three times higher than for those who live with others.

Clearly, bereavement and grief have profound effects on mental health. Ramsay and Happee (1977) describe seven emotional reactions to grief. These are (a) shock, (b) denial, (c) depression, (d) guilt, (e) anxiety, (f) aggression, and (g) reintegration. Not all grief reactions follow this sequence, however.

Bereavement and its attendant grief and sense of loneliness require extensive social readjustment for the elderly. Patterns of friendship may change since some widows

may not feel welcome in groups of married couples. Therefore, part of their social support system may fall away. One may become dependent on one's family because of ill health or economic losses. The loss of a spouse may affect one's sense of identity. "What good am I? Who cares anymore?" Problems of adjustment to remarriage, if a remarriage occurs, and family reactions to this event may surface. Symptoms such as loss of appetite, disturbed sleep patterns, illnesses, and emotional instability are not uncommon.

PSYCHOPATHOLOGICAL PROBLEMS OF A FUNCTIONAL NATURE

Functional problems refer to the patterns of maladaptive behavior that cause distress and that interfere to a significant degree with the elderly person's day-to-day activities. Significantly, these problems have no identifiable organic or physiological basis; they have primarily a functional or psychological causation (see Chapter 12 for a discussion of the various organic brain syndromes most commonly found in older people).

What constitutes functional psychopathology in the elderly person? It is difficult to define "normal" and "abnormal" behavior in an individual of any age. However, the distinction is especially complex with old people. As we have noted elsewhere, the definition of psychopathology is culturally and socially based. Where stereotypes about aging flourish, the clinician may be biased by expectations as to what constitutes the normal processes of aging. There may be a tendency to view most problems of the older person as due to old age. The misplacing of one's house key, for example, may be attributed, in a younger person, to mere carelessness or to preoccupations with more important matters of a busy day. In an elderly individual, such behavior may raise the question of an initial sign of declining memory or even senility.

The following sections will discuss those patterns of disordered behaviors of a functional nature most frequently seen in clinical work with elderly clients. For communicative purposes, we will use the diagnostic categories that have formed the traditional psychiatric classification scheme.

Depression

It has been estimated that between 2 to 10 percent of elderly people are sufficiently depressed to warrant a diagnosis of depression. When somatic complaints are considered, people over 65 exhibit more symptoms of depression than younger people (Zarit, 1980). The prevalence appears to be even higher in persons with chronic health problems. Depression can also be a significant problem for individuals with senile dementia, especially during the earlier stages of the degenerative disease, when the person is aware of the deterioration. Among hospital admissions, depression appears to be the most frequent diagnosis when considering only geriatric admissions (those over 60 or 65) (Zarit, 1980). Estimates of the prevalence of depression among elderly people, however, have varied considerably. They depend on the criteria and methods used to make comparisons (Gurland, 1976). No matter what criterion is used (e.g., psychiatric diagnosis of community samples, hospital admission rates, etc.), the rate of depression reported among aged people is high (Zarit, 1980).

A particular problem in the recognition of depression in the elderly is that many of the seemingly obvious symptoms may fit stereotypes of the aging process. For example, an elderly client may report loss of appetite, trouble in getting to sleep, and memory problems and, to the clinician, may appear

rather apathetic. Hence, the symptoms may be mislabeled as a natural aspect of growing old, or may be confused with various organic disorders (Epstein, 1976; Zarit, 1980). It is extremely important, however, that depressive symptoms be accurately assessed, as they generally have a favorable prognosis for improvement with appropriate treatment interventions.

With this age group as with younger age groups, symptoms may vary from mild to severe. Older patients, however, most frequently are reported to show dysphoria (a state of general dissatisfaction), loss of interest in their surroundings, fatigue, and occasionally hypochondriacal concerns, agitation, and paranoid ideation (Stenback, 1980). Table 11–1 lists potential signs and symptoms of depression in elderly patients, although not all of these symptoms would necessarily occur in any one individual. For a diagnosis of mild depression, Stenback (1980) contends that both a depressive mood disturbance and reduced activity, usually in the form of apathy, resignation, and passivity, must be evident.

It is not clear what factors precipitate the elderly person's depression. There is some controversy about the role of guilt. Some authors (Busse & Pfeiffer, 1977) believe that guilt is not often associated with depression, especially among the aged. Others (Butler & Lewis, 1982) emphasize that guilt may be an important motivating factor at any time in people's lives "even when they are on a death bed" (p. 72).

Little is known about what happens to middle-aged depressives as they grow older. Furthermore, it is not known whether depressions occurring in late life are specific to old age, or are recurrences of affective disorders that have gone unrecognized in earlier adulthood (Epstein, 1976).

Investigators have hypothesized a variety of causative factors—heredity, personality

TABLE 11–1
Signs and Symptoms of Depression in the Elderly

Dysphoric Mood

Looks sad; mournful or depressed.
Cries easily; eyes moist or tearful.
Reports feeling depressed or blue.
Speaks in a sad, gloomy, or mournful voice.

Suicidal Behavior and Ideation

Reports recurrent thoughts of death, dying, or
suicide.
Expresses wish to be dead.
Says life is not worth living.
Has made suicide attempts.

Pessimism and Inadequacy

Reports future seems bleak, dark, or unbearable.
Reports feeling hopeless.
Is preoccupied with feelings of inadequacy.
Has clinging dependency.
Worries continually about something.
Reports feeling indecisive.

Guilt, Shame, or Worthlessness

Blames self for things done or not done.
Feels worthless and no good to anyone.
Reports feeling inferior to others.
Suffers from troubled conscience.

Anergia or Fatigue

Feels everything is an effort.
Feels tired, worn-out, lacking in energy.
Looks tired and lacking in energy.
Reports waking up feeling tired.
Sits or lies around because of lack of energy.

Apathy and Social Withdrawal

Lacks interest in hobbies previously enjoyed.
Does not enjoy being with others.
Is alone most of the time.
Spends little free time at recreational activities.
Has lost interest in TV or radio.

Retardation in Speech or Behavior

Speaks slowly.
Moves slowly and deliberately.
Subjectively feels slowed down in movements.

Memory

Has trouble remembering recent events.
Has trouble remembering past events such as
those from childhood.
Has good memory one day, bad the next.

Attention or Concentration

Has difficulty in attending or concentrating.
Checks and double-checks every action.

Confusion or Perplexity

Reports feeling confused.
Appears bewildered by events.
Rambles or drifts off topic being discussed.

Sleep Disturbances

See text discussion.

Vegetative Disturbances

Loss of appetite.
Recent weight loss of 10 pounds or more.

Sex Difficulties

No longer shows interest in sex.
Derives little pleasure from sexual activities
previously enjoyed.

Somatic Complaints

Headaches.
Constipation.
Dry mouth.
Pains in stomach.
Pressure in the head.
Nausea or upset stomach.

Source: From "Signs and Symptoms of Psychopathology in the Elderly" (p. 9) by A. Raskin, in *Psychiatric Symptoms and Cognitive Loss in the Elderly*, ed. A. Raskin and L. Jarvik, Washington, DC: Hemisphere.

predisposition, age-related biological changes, and age-related stressful events. Zarit (1980), for example, reports that the risk of incidence of depression in relatives of patients with major depressive disorder may vary somewhat, depending upon the age of the patient at the onset of symptoms. One explanation proposed is that there may be multiple causes of major depression. One type of depression occurring in earlier life has a relatively greater genetic factor. A second type occurring in later life may be less influenced by genetic predeterminants. A second explanation has suggested that genetic factors simply contribute less than other variables when major depression occurs in later life.

Do age-related biological changes predispose the elderly person to a greater probability of developing depression, or do they produce depression directly? There is considerable evidence to suggest that persons with major depressive disorders have biochemical abnormalities, but these abnormalities are not yet clearly understood. Two major theories have involved: (a) hormone imbalance, and (b) neurotransmitter imbalance (see the discussion in Chapter 8 on affective disorders). Some researchers have suggested that the hypothalamus may be a key to depressive disorders. It regulates not only mood but also many other functions typically disrupted by depression. Concerning the influence of age-related hormonal changes, decreased thyroid functioning and decreased responsiveness of the pituitary gland to the hypothalamus as well as alterations in gonadal function could influence the older person's capacity to handle stress (Lipton, 1976). An exclusively biochemical explanation of depression in the aged, however, is probably not adequate.

Life changes may be quite important in bringing on depression among elderly people (Kay, Cooper, Garside, & Roth, 1976; Paykel, 1974; Stenback, 1980; Zarit, 1980). Major life changes such as retirement, loss of friends and relatives, shrinkage of one's social roles, economic hardships, and major illnesses are all potential sources of depression-inducing stress. In addition, living in an environment filled with multiple small losses presumably could trigger a depressive episode in individuals who perceive themselves as unable to cope. Disappointments over the *failure* of desired events to happen, such as the lack of visits from a son or daughter, could also produce considerable distress. Lewinsohn and MacPhillamy (1974) had a sample of adults rate pleasant activities and events for frequency of occurrence during the preceding months and for subjective desirability of those events. They found that both the depressed and the elderly individuals in their samples engaged less frequently in activities judged to be pleasant.

A psychological model for understanding the elderly person's depression is the revised formulation of the learned helplessness model (Abramson, Seligman, & Teasdale, 1978). According to this model, depression depends not only on a belief in the lack of control over reinforcements but also on the attributions or explanations given for this lack of control. People are more likely to become seriously depressed when they attribute lack of control to a cause that is: (a) permanent rather than temporary; (b) internal (some aspect of themselves) rather than external (some aspect of the environment); and (c) generalized (i.e., it applies over many areas of functioning) rather than specific. An elderly person might attribute a distressing event, such as a serious illness, to the aging process. The explanation of old age would appear to fulfill the criteria for depression-inducing attributions that lead to feelings of helplessness and hopelessness and possible depression. Several research studies (Langer & Rodin, 1976; Rodin & Langer, 1977; Schulz, 1976) have demonstrated that when elderly institutionalized people were given responsibility for making decisions about events in their daily lives or for caring for something in their environment (a living plant, as in the Langer and Rodin study), they showed improvement in mental alertness and were rated more active and happier, both by the nursing staff and by themselves.

It may well be that precipitating factors are multiple, however, and that no single or even primary cause will be explanatory. It is generally believed that depressive illness depends on the interaction of the severity and number of stresses, the adaptive capacities (biological and psychological), and particular hereditary predispositions, as well as experiences, of the individual (Jarvik, 1976).

The majority of elderly depressives appear to gain considerable temporary, and sometimes lasting, benefit from appropriate treatment (Epstein, 1976; Steuer et al., 1984). Because depressions are frequently recurring, however, the long-range outlook for the individual may be more guarded. Immediate response to treatment is typically good, especially among persons Neugarten (1975) refers to as "young-old" (i.e., under age 75). Depression among the elderly, as among younger patients, appears to be episodic, and spontaneous recoveries in time can be expected in most episodes. However, the duration of the episode can vary. Especially in older people with already diminished reserves, further deterioration of their physical condition and the social isolation brought about by their depression can be catastrophic to their well-being (Epstein, 1976).

Pseudodementia

The term *pseudodementia* describes a depression primarily characterized by intellectual impairment and confusion. It is easily misdiagnosed as senile dementia or one of the other dementing disorders. Patients are described as showing severe degrees of mental impairment and apathy. These symptoms mimic dementia, but they presumably reflect a depressive episode rather than an underlying basic pathology (McAllister & Price, 1982). Further complicating the distinction is the possibility that a depression can be superimposed upon an underlying dementia. Often cases in which a differential diagnosis is extremely difficult to make will be first treated for depression to see if the symptoms improve. Some of the cases labeled pseudodementia, however, may more

accurately represent acute, confusional states caused by temporary impairment of brain functioning (Zarit, 1980). A variety of factors, such as drug toxicity and vitamin deficiencies, may cause these confusional states, which will clear up when the causes are treated.

Suicide

Suicide is a potentially serious problem among distressed elderly people. Whereas the rate of suicide for the entire U.S. population in 1970 was 11.6 per 100,000, it was 36.9 per 100,000 for persons aged 65 and over (Pfeiffer, 1977).

Such statistics, moreover, do not consider "passive suicides," those cases where self-destruction is carried out by a failure to protect oneself, such as not taking life-sustaining medications. Therefore, the reported rates undoubtedly are an underestimate of the actual incidence among elderly people (Pfeiffer, 1977). Passive suicides may be an especially critical problem among older people who simply wish to end it all without causing distress to their family and friends.

Suicidal ideation in the older person must be taken very seriously. Although a suicide attempt among younger people may often be an expression of hostility, an attempt to manipulate, or a cry for help, these are rarely the motivations in the elderly (Pfeiffer, 1977; Stenback, 1980). According to Pfeiffer (1977), "when an old person attempts suicide, he almost always fully intends to die" (p. 655). Where attempts are unsuccessful, the reasons may be poor planning or an accidental intervention, rather than a gesture about which the person was feeling ambivalent. In elderly people suicide is considered to be more premeditated and deliberate and less impulsive.

Although it has frequently been stated that there is an increasing risk of suicide with age, especially among males, there appears to be no simple relationship between suicide rate and advancing age across nationalities (Stenback, 1980). Rather, there are various age patterns for *both* males and females. Figure 11-7 gives the suicide rates in the United States in relation to age, race, and sex during 1974. As we can see, the older white male is especially at risk as compared with females and nonwhite males. There have been several conjectures as to why there is an increase in suicides among white males with age, a pattern observed in virtually all Western countries. One common explanation is that the white male is more vulnerable to stressful losses of status, especially in terms of income and power, when he retires than is true either of the female or the

nonwhite person. Another conjecture is that males have a stronger disposition to settle problems by forceful actions (Stenback, 1980).

Symptoms that may denote an elderly person "at risk" for suicide (Zarit, 1980) are: (*a*) feelings of hopelessness, which may be expressed through apathy, withdrawal, or somatic complaints, rather than expressed directly; (*b*) alcoholism; (*c*) acute or chronic brain dysfunction, if the person is depressed about his or her condition; (*d*) recent loss of a spouse or other loved one, or other severe losses; (*e*) serious physical illness; and (*f*) low income, possibly with recent economic problems and prior irregular work history. Personality instability and alcoholism are

FIGURE 11-7
Suicide Rates in the United States in Relation to Age and Race (1974)

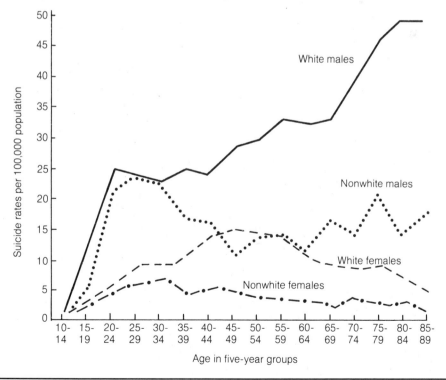

Source: From *Aging in Mass Society* 2d ed. (p. 179) by J. Hendricks and C. D. Hendricks, 1981, Cambridge, MA: Winthrop.

considered less prominent factors in the elderly than in suicides among young people. Suicide sometimes may appear to be a rational decision for the elderly person, whereby he or she avoids suffering a chronic, debilitating illness or becoming what is seen as a burden on loved ones (Butler & Lewis, 1982). When a suicide intent is demonstrated, intervention must be prompt in order to prevent the likelihood of a tragic outcome.

Paranoia

Although believed to be less prevalent than cases of depression, paranoia is a relatively frequent and often quite disturbing disorder among elderly people. Inpatient admission studies have suggested that from 10 to 16 percent of elderly patients admitted for emotional disturbances are diagnosed as paranoid (Zarit, 1980). No estimates are available on the prevalence of paranoid behaviors in outpatient mental health facilities or among community-living older people. Such estimates, however, would probably be an underestimate of the actual prevalence. Paranoids typically do not refer themselves for psychological help and may not cooperate even when referred by family members or community agencies.

According to Tanna (1974), the main features of late-life paranoia are paranoid symptoms that occur for the first time in the fifth or sixth decade of life or later. The clinical picture consists of delusions and possibly hallucinations. The thought disorder, personality deterioration, and loss of reality contact considered typical of schizophrenia are usually absent. Delusions in elderly paranoid people usually lack the bizarre features characteristic of schizophrenia and tend to focus on explanations of rather commonplace, everyday losses and failures (Verwoerdt, 1976). Thus an elderly woman living alone may believe that a neighbor is trying to poison her by injecting poisonous smoke into her house via a backyard barbecue grill. On the other hand, this same individual may show little indication of personality deterioration or thought disorder beyond the specific delusion.

Persons who become paranoid in late life are particularly lonely and insecure. Berger and Zarit (1978) suggest two important factors: social isolation, which perhaps reflects a lifelong pattern of poor social adjustment; and sensory losses, such as loss of hearing or sight. They describe the elderly paranoid as likely to be a woman who has few close contacts with her relatives or children, and who has been living alone for many years before the symptoms appear. A number of authors (Berger & Zarit, 1978; Pfeiffer, 1977) have emphasized the frequency of significant hearing impairment among elderly paranoids. Hearing loss in the elderly may lead to social isolation, decreased reality testing, and consequent attempts to "fill in" stimuli they cannot hear with paranoid ideas. It may be that multiple factors in terms of personality characteristics, coping strategies, and perceived degree of stress interact to produce paranoia. Such interacting factors are illustrated in Brink's (1980) case of an 81-year-old paranoid woman on p. 321.

Paranoid delusions may be triggered by stressful events, such as physical illness or bereavement, over which the person perceives little or no control (Kay et al., 1976; Post, 1966). In chronic illness and organic brain disease, paranoid delusions may serve as compensations for memory loss and other intellectual declines. Conditions such as pernicious anemia and, in a small number of cases, vitamin B-12 deficiency, can also produce paranoid delusions (Berger & Zarit, 1978). Table 11–2 outlines factors in the development of paranoid disorders in later life.

Before making a diagnosis of paranoid behavior, one must first determine if the

TABLE 11–2
Development of Paranoid Disorders in Late Life

Premorbid Factors: An individual with either (a) difficulty with interpersonal relationships, or (b) sensory loss, especially bilateral deafness beginning in the middle years.

Precipitants: An acute stress, usually a loss, that gives the person the feeling of no longer being adequate and in control, or the feeling of a loss of love and attention, to which the person responds with feelings of rage.

Defenses: Use of the strong and high-energy maladaptive defenses of projection or displacement.

Secondary Gains: Positive reinforcements or compensations of symptoms.

Source: From "Late-Life Paranoid States: Assessment and Treatment" by K. S. Berger & S. H. Zarit, 1978, *American Journal of Orthopsychiatry, 48,* no. 3, pp. 528–537 (p. 531).

PARANOIA IN AN 81-YEAR-OLD WOMAN

N, an 81-year-old cantankerous widow, . . . gradually manifested a marked paranoid delusion centering around her neighbors and causing much anguish for them and her family.

N was the middle child in a family of four girls, a baby boy, and two immigrant parents. She had few happy memories of her childhood. She recalls trying to be good but always being picked on by parents and siblings. She claims that she was always sickly from early childhood through middle age, with a tendency toward nausea, vomiting and migraine headaches, culminating in a series of operations during which "everything was taken out." She explains her poor health as being due to her mother's insistence that each child receive a weekly dose of castor oil. She would always vomit and feel horrible afterward, and believes that she is allergic to *all* medicines. During her numerous hospitalizations, she had some severe side effects from antibiotics and analgesics. Her last hospital stay was in 1974 after a heart attack. She became delirious and violent, and refused to speak above a whisper for

fear that her room was bugged. N is convinced that her behavior was caused by the . . . drugs that she received while in the hospital. She recovered rapidly while spending two weeks in her daughter's home and returned to her own residence.

N subsequently underwent two cataract operations and occasionally complains of visual difficulties. She refuses to take any medicines for her hypertension and occasionally suffers "spells" in which she feels weak and "tingly." She also refuses to report for routine medical check-ups. She loves to recount her experiences in the hospital to her acquaintances: how she is allergic to all drugs and how the doctors tried to make her crazy with medicines so that they could put her in a nursing home. She speaks kindly of two physicians, but they apparently agreed with her claims that she could not tolerate the prescribed drugs.

In young adulthood, her views on religion and politics crystallized: both were grand conspiracies devised by lazy but clever men who wanted to dupe and live off ignorant, hardworking people. . . . She has always enjoyed airing her views in a vivid and satirical fashion which has thoroughly entertained her listeners. She became more hostile and outspoken after 1970, when her husband died and she was faced with substantial inheritance taxes. Although she was suspicious of the motives of politicians, priests and physicians, she genuinely enjoyed and trusted most of the people she met. During her 50s she had some problems involving neighbors. Many children from a nearby housing development trespassed in her orchard, committing acts of theft and vandalism. She also caught her husband in an adulterous affair with a neighbor's daughter.

N and her husband decided to sell the orchard and move to a neighborhood inhabited mostly by other retired persons. She seemed to enjoy the company of her neighbors and the opportunity to devote time to gardening. In the past few years, her three adult children have noticed that her behavior has changed for the worse. They report that she seems to get blue and gloomy more often, especially after hearing of the death or illness of a friend, or the worsening of conditions in the world. She says she is ready to die, and wonders why so many young people have to suffer so much. However, the periods of gloominess are brief and seemingly controlled by keeping busy in the garden. She complains of insomnia (a symptom of depression) but denies suicidal ideation. Another change noticed by her family is increased forgetfulness, e.g., forgetting social plans, or getting confused about how to turn the water off. She underwent several tests for senile confusion but scored within the normal ranges on all of them. The memory loss appears to be relatively mild and episodic.

In the last five years she has complained about her neighbors taking her property and replacing it with inferior goods. At first, the complaints were infrequent and somewhat plausible. After her car was serviced she complained that the owner of the garage, a neighbor, had taken her good tires and battery and replaced them with older, used ones. She confronted the owner of the garage, but the charge was denied. Then her next-door neighbor was accused of taking her garbage can and leaving another in its place. In the last two years the frequency and number of her complaints have increased. The next-door neighbor was accused of taking her lawn mower, shears and hose, and leaving his own worn-out equipment in their place. When she sent her television out for repairs, she claimed that the shop sent another one back. When she bought a new carpet and refrigerator, she was certain that the delivered items were not those she had ordered in the showroom. In all these instances, her daughter's observations were to the contrary. Later, N confessed that she might have been mistaken and that her memory might be failing, but she continued to accuse her neighbors of having stolen her property.

Source: From "Geriatric Paranoia: Case Report Illustrating Behavioral Management" by T. L. Brink, 1980, *Journal of the American Geriatrics Society, 28*, no. 11, pp. 519–522 (pp. 520–521).

complaints have a basis in reality. In view of the reduced capacities of many older people to look after their affairs and their potential vulnerability to being victimized, it can never be simply assumed that a complaint *is* delusional. For example, there was an incident in which an elderly woman who was confined to bed in a nursing home complained frequently and bitterly that a nephew was "stealing me blind" by taking possessions from her unoccupied house. Following her death, it was discovered that the nephew, explaining that he assumed his aunt would never be well enough to return home, *had* removed several items, such as a TV set and garden tools, from her home without her permission.

The course of late-life paranoia is unclear (Tanna, 1974; Post, 1966). There are few available studies of prognosis with older people, although such studies suggest that some improvement in symptom reduction is possible. For example, the symptoms may improve notably when sensory impairments contributing to the paranoia are treated. Acknowledging the difficulties of treating an uncooperative, suspicious paranoid person, Berger and Zarit (1978) suggest that there are two goals of psychotherapy with such patients. One is to encourage the person to use medication when appropriate. The second is to establish as supportive and trusting a relationship as possible with the person.

Hypochondriasis

Hypochondriasis, one of the somatoform disorders in the DSM III classification, is commonly reported in geriatric patients. However, its etiology or the criteria for its assessment have not been clearly defined. The peak in incidence is believed to occur within the age range of the sixties, especially among women (Busse, 1976). It is not known whether its prevalence actually increases in late life, as is the case for various genuine chronic diseases and illnesses.

Hypochondriacal symptoms are often a temporary adaptive response to an unfamiliar social stress with which the person feels unable to cope. Social stressors that have been implicated include: (*a*) the partial isolation in which the elderly person may be living; (*b*) a stressful social situation which affects the person's self-esteem but from which

the person perceives little opportunity to escape; and (*c*) a deterioration in the marital relationship because of a prolonged disability of the spouse (Busse, 1976). Hypochondriacal concerns, furthermore, may have important secondary gains for older persons who otherwise may have few interests and social reinforcements in their lives. Among these secondary gains are enhanced feelings of personal importance and esteem from the attention of medical personnel and concerned family and friends; the removal of certain obligations with which the person feels inadequate to cope; a more socially acceptable way of explaining personal failures; and perhaps even a way for socializing with other patients and members of medical staffs.

Hypochondriacal complaints are typically commonplace, such as various aches and pains, especially of the bones and muscles, or symptoms of the gastrointestinal tract (Zarit, 1980). Inasmuch as old age is rarely reached without some realistic health problems, it can be difficult in some cases to judge whether health complaints are realistic or exaggerated. There must be adequate verification, of course, that such complaints are indeed exaggerated. Hypochondriacal individuals, however, do not respond to reassurances about their health status, and they may firmly resist suggestions that they have no physical problems to worry about. They can be extremely frustrating to work with inasmuch as they are often described as "running through physicians" persistently and may keep multiple medical appointments in a day's time.

Recommended treatments have ranged from psychotropic medications and placebos to emotional support offered by the individual's physician. According to Busse and Pfeiffer (1977), patients should not be confronted with the emotional basis of their complaints. Rather, the patient's psychological defenses should be maintained.

Substance Misuse and Abuse

Is an elderly client showing symptoms of psychopathology or symptoms of drug misuse? Frequent medication use makes elderly people at risk to the harmful effects not only of the inappropriate use of drugs but to the interaction effects of taking multiple drugs. Some of these harmful effects may masquerade as symptoms of psychopathological disorders, such as hallucinations or confusion. The term *drug misuse* is applied when the inappropriate use of medications is inadvertent, and neither the elderly patient nor the physician intends for the drugs to be used inappropriately, or is aware of this fact (Glantz, 1983a). The U.S. Public Health Service (cited in Petersen, 1983) estimates that 86 percent of people age 65 and older have one or more chronic illnesses or impairments that extend for three months at a minimum. The Task Force on Prescription Drugs (cited in Petersen, 1983) found that people age 65 and older received one fourth of all prescriptions written in 1967. The typical older person acquired three times as many prescription drugs as those younger than 65. Research suggests that elderly age groups tend to have higher rates of overall drug use than any other age category; they also are more likely to use drugs on a daily basis for extended periods (Petersen, 1983).

Compounding the potential problems of multiple medications is the increased sensitivity of the elderly body to the effects of many drugs. Elderly people have a reduced physiological capacity to handle drugs efficiently. Many drugs may precipitate depression or confusional states (Lamy, 1983). Also, wide individual differences in the rate of both primary aging (senescence) and secondary aging (disease-related physiological changes that accompany aging) may make the effects of a particular drug unpredictable.

Why elderly people misuse drugs is not well understood. At least six potential reasons, however, have been proposed (Whittington, 1983): (a) there may be a communication problem between the older patient and the physician (e.g., the patient may not question the physician's instructions, or the physician may not give clear instructions); (b) the patient may not be competent to self-medicate; (c) there may be inadequate supervision of the person's drug-taking habits, such as continuing a particular dosage past the appropriate duration; (d) there may be economic reasons for the person not to buy the needed medication; (e) the sheer number of medications taken by the typical older person, and often the multiple number of physicians prescribing, may lead to inappropriate prescriptions and/or dosages; (f) the patient, perhaps for a variety of psychological reasons, may be reluctant to use a needed medication. Petersen, Whittington, and Beer (1979) have concluded that, for most elderly misusers, underuse of medication through noncompliance appears to be a bigger problem than overuse or erratic use.

A particular problem of drug misuse, especially psychoactive medications, may occur in nursing homes and other long-term care facilities. Staffs' attempts to control agitated or demanding patients may lead to medications that are inappropriate for the person's actual health status or diagnosis (Whittington, 1983).

The abuse of illegal drugs among elderly people appears to be limited to marijuana and heroin. The number of people who use these drugs is quite low compared to the prevalence among younger people (Petersen et al., 1979). Older people, however, are more likely to use barbiturates and sedatives than younger people.

Petersen et al. (1979) have offered two explanations for the small number of drug addicts over age 40. First, the addiction may cease spontaneously, or "mature out" because of its duration or the addict's age (Glantz, Petersen, & Whittington, 1983). Second, many more older addicts may actually exist but never come to public attention. Capel, Goldsmith, Waddell, and Stewart (1972) concluded that, although some addicts do mature out of their addiction, the majority adapt and conceal their habits by switching to other drugs. They may, for example, substitute more easily obtainable substances such as the barbiturates or alcohol, or simply decrease their daily usage.

The following conclusions concerning drug abuse in the elderly have been made. Only a small proportion of elderly people currently age 65 or older have ever used an illegal drug. Although the extent and magnitude of the problem are unknown, there are many anecdotal reports of older individuals deliberately sharing prescription drugs, obtaining multiple prescriptions, or hoarding drugs for nonprescribed use. There is also evidence that patterns of abuse may begin later in life for more individuals than previously assumed. The consequences of abuse, however, may not be very obvious and may often be mistaken for the consequences of growing old. Finally, it is likely that drug misuse takes place more commonly than abuse (Glantz, 1983a).

Alcohol abuse is a significant problem among the elderly. Although the actual prevalence is not known, estimates of elderly alcoholism based on limited studies range from 2 to 10 percent (Glantz, 1983b). One third of elderly alcoholics are believed to be late-onset problem drinkers. Their drinking is likely to be related to attempts to cope with the stresses and problems of old age rather than to more deeply rooted psychological disorders. Elderly alcohol abusers are likely to drink at least as often, though in smaller quantities, than their younger counterparts. Their alcohol abuse, however, is less likely to have consequences involving severe and obvious social or physical problems. Problems that do result may often be attributed to the normal problems of growing old.

According to Gomberg (cited in Glantz et al., 1983), elderly male alcoholics greatly outnumber female alcoholics. However, the problems and issues facing older women alcoholics have not been studied. Little is known about alcohol problems in the elderly black population.

Gomberg lists three types of elderly alcoholics: (a) the long-term, chronic heavy drinkers; (b) elderly drinkers who have lapsed into and out of alcoholism; and (c) the more reactive drinkers in whom alcoholism appears to have been precipitated by the stresses of the later years. According to Gomberg, the prognosis for the reactive elderly drinker is considered good. Various forms of psychotherapy, including family and group therapy, and Alcoholics Anonymous, seem to be effective in many cases.

The elderly have a decreased tolerance for alcohol, so it is difficult to diagnose alcoholism in the elderly person on the basis of the number of drinks consumed (Wood, 1978). Because of changes in bodily composition, a higher level of alcohol based on body weight is present in the blood of the older person than in that of the younger person when both have drunk equivalent amounts of alcohol. Clinically, excessive consumption of alcohol can result in nutritional deficiencies and pathological changes in various organ systems of the body, thereby exaggerating some of the common physiological changes occurring with aging.

A particular hazard for the elderly drinker is the potentially dangerous effect of medication and alcohol interactions. For example, even mild and intermittent alcohol use may have harmful interaction effects with psychotropic drugs. Both the psychotropics and alcohol are potent central nervous system depressants. Since elderly people exhibit increased sensitivity to both alcohol and psychotropic drugs, excessively confused or altered behaviors may result (Lamy, 1983).

Glantz (1981) suggests that the improvement of the elderly person's social and economic circumstances may be an effective treatment for both alcoholism and drug abuse.

Anxiety

Severe anxiety, unlike severe depression, is relatively infrequent among elderly clients. Milder chronic anxiety, however, is believed to be much more common (Jarvik & Russell, 1979).

Anxiety symptoms in the elderly often differ from those in younger individuals. In the elderly person, agitation and restlessness most often appear in the form of sleeplessness, hypochondriacal concerns about disease and bodily dysfunction, loss of appetite, and in some cases obsessive eating (Raskin, 1979). Phobias and obsessive-compulsive patterns of behavior, on the other hand, have been reported in only a small number of elderly patients. What has been reported about anxiety in elderly people, however, has been based largely on clinical impressions and case histories. There is a scarcity of data from research studies on the prevalence and nature of these symptoms. Therefore, we do not have much evidence regarding which symptoms are so frequently seen in the older population that they cannot be considered psychopathological (Raskin, 1979).

In view of the many stresses assumed to accompany later life and older persons' diminished reserves to recover from stress, we may find it rather surprising that there is not a higher frequency of anxiety symptoms reported among the elderly. Raskin (1979) comments, however, that there appears to be a tendency for the elderly to deny overt feelings of anxiety and tension. Jarvik and Russell (1979) have proposed that elderly people, by dint of their very survival into old age, have developed strategies by which they deal with stresses and thereby ward off anxiety.

Schizophrenia

There is disagreement as to whether schizophrenia can initially occur in old age (Zarit, 1980). Some clinicians consider older clients who show delusional paranoid symptoms as schizophrenic. However, the symptom picture is somewhat different between paranoid patients who show an onset in their younger adult years and those who show an onset in late life. There is generally considered a better prognosis for the latter (see discussion on paranoia on pp. 320–23). Only a few cases of schizophrenia with apparent late-life onset have been reported in the literature when patients who show paranoid symptoms are excluded from consideration (Zarit, 1980).

In terms of geriatric services, the more prevalent problem is the management of the long-term schizophrenic person who has grown old in a mental hospital. In addition to schizophrenic symptoms, the person may show an "institutionalization syndrome" of enhanced social inadequacy and withdrawal caused by many years of hospitalization. Many such long-term schizophrenics have been discharged from mental hospitals in recent years, only to be placed in nursing homes where psychiatric treatment, except for medications, may be even less available (Kahn, 1975).

Schizophrenics who survive into old age appear to become less psychotic. The severity of symptoms may decrease, and the interpersonal adjustment of many schizophrenics may improve. However, studies have indicated that satisfactory overall social adjustment may be achieved by only a relatively small proportion of these patients (see Post, 1980, for a review).

There have been few systematic studies of how schizophrenic symptoms change over the adult years. Likewise, no systematic longitudinal studies are available regarding the effectiveness of phenothiazine medications or other treatment approaches. A program that combines medication and appropriate community supports may be effective in reducing the need for continuing hospitalization of elderly schizophrenics.

PSYCHOLOGICAL ASSESSMENT OF THE ELDERLY: ISSUES AND PROBLEMS

Clinical assessment must often attempt to evaluate accurately the multiple, interlacing concerns of the elderly client, involving a combination of physical, psychological, and social problems. The goals of a complete assessment of an elderly client reflect these interlocking problems (Table 11–3). There are certain difficulties, however, in assessing the older client, above and beyond the issues involved in assessing younger age groups (e.g., Miller, 1980; Schaie & Schaie, 1977). Let us look at a few of the issues with which the clinician must contend in trying to interpret the findings of a psychological assessment battery administered to an elderly client.

One of the major problems is the lack of appropriate age norms. Few of our traditional psychological tests have been standardized on older persons. Without normative data as to how the typical older individual responds, it is difficult to judge whether specific responses are abnormal or normal for a particular age group. Furthermore, the broad individual differences among elderly people caution us to be careful as to what we infer as atypical. For instance, how much of a deficit on a memory test must an older person show

Slower psychomotor speed, fatigue, and visual and hearing problems may lower the older person's performance during a psychological assessment but have little significance in understanding psychopathological behavior. (Tom Ballard/EKM-Nepenthe)

to justify calling the deficit a significant *memory problem?*

Because of age-related differences in educational level, health status, and test-taking attitudes, such as greater cautiousness, the elderly person might not perform as well on a test as the younger client. The difference, however, might be of little or no clinical significance. For example, slower psychomotor speed, fatigue, and possible sensory impairments in sight and hearing may have little psychological significance, yet lower the performance of the older person.

Because many elderly people are already functioning on the edge of their physical and

TABLE 11–3
Goals of Assessment of the Aged

A complete evaluation should include the following classes of information:

1. How well can the person function?

2. Does the person have physical impairments that create service and support needs?

3. Does the person have psychological symptoms that create interpersonal difficulties?

4. What is the person's unique set of needs for socialization, recreation, sex, activity, and work?

5. How well are each person's needs being met?

6. What kinds of placement settings are most relevant to each person?

7. What kinds of living accommodations are most suitable for each person?

8. What kind of housing is productive of maximum satisfactions for which individuals?

9. What are the strengths and weaknesses of residence facilities in relation to the needs of the elderly?

10. What types of psychiatric, medical, drug, psychological, nursing, and rehabilitative treatments work best with the elderly?

Source: From "Conceptual and Practical Issues in the Assessment of the Elderly" by R. Plutchik, in *Psychiatric Symptoms and Cognitive Loss in the Elderly* (p. 22) ed. A. Raskin and L. F. Jarvik, 1979, Washington, DC: Hemisphere Publishing.

psychological reserves, there may be considerable variability in their daily functioning. Often several test samplings should be taken to obtain a more representative picture of the person's functioning. Another issue is whether the behavior of the elderly person on a test in the clinician's office is representative of day-to-day behaviors in the familiar surroundings of the home and neighborhood.

What the clinician considers psychopathological behavior will be influenced by assumptions of what constitutes successful aging, and by personal stereotypes regarding old age. For instance, is it natural for elderly people to withdraw emotional investment in the world around them and "turn inward"? Or should such tendencies be considered undesirable, and questions raised about maladaptive social withdrawal?

Gallagher, Thompson, and Levy (1980) recommend as an ideal assessment model evaluating a number of domains and carefully integrating the findings to obtain a comprehensive picture of functioning. The following points should be considered (Gallagher et al., 1980):

1. An evaluation of physical health status.

2. Assessment of intellectual and memory functioning.

3. An evaluation of the person's emotional status and possible symptoms of psychopathology.

4. A measure of personality.

5. An evaluation of the stressful events confronting the person, along with indications of coping skills and general level of life satisfaction.

6. An assessment of a person's capacity to function, such as handling the activities of daily living, and social and personal adjustment.

Cognitive Assessment

Complaints of memory loss and/or other intellectual problems are frequently expressed by elderly clients or by the people who refer them. When such complaints arise, assessment must determine the following: (*a*) Is there a justifiable basis for the complaint?

(*b*) Is the decline pathological, or consistent with changes which might be expected as a normal aspect of aging? (*c*) If loss is abnormal in degree, does the problem suggest an underlying organic brain pathology (reversible or irreversible) or an affective disorder, such as depression, or possibly both?

To give an illustration of the complexity of assessing cognitive complaints, Gallagher et al. (1980) have described four basic patterns of complaint versus objective functioning, involving memory:

1. The patient may intensely complain about memory functioning and may show an elevated level of depression. However, when memory is objectively tested, the person performs within the normal range. Such a pattern would suggest an affective disorder. In this case, psychotherapy and possibly drug therapy are indicated.

2. The patient may intensely complain about memory problems and give minimal indication of depression. As above, the person tests at a relatively normal level. Neither depression nor significant organic brain impairment appears to be causative. Hence, further evaluation procedures, perhaps with repeated assessments over time, may be indicated to assess possible contributing factors, such as anxiety.

3. Complaints and depression are both high. As assessed on objective tests, memory performance is also poor. The question then is whether the memory problems are due primarily to brain impairment, or to depression, or perhaps to a combination of these factors. A comprehensive assessment involving psychological, neurological, and medical evaluations would be indicated.

4. The person's actual memory functioning is poor. However, complaints about memory are minimal, and depression scores are low. Such a pattern would suggest a serious brain impairment. The patient is not experiencing depression because there is so much cognitive deterioration that the patient is unaware of the degree of the cognitive problem. If the possibility of a pseudodementia exists, treatment for depression may be tried. In any event, additional laboratory tests would be indicated.

A problem in evaluating a client's current level of cognitive functioning is often that of having some reference point indicating previous functioning. Rarely are earlier levels of functioning available to the clinician. Although the client's past history of educational achievement and occupational status is frequently used to estimate earlier intellectual level, there is often a wide range in IQ found among persons in any given occupation or educational level. The greater variability would be among those at the lower levels of formal education engaged in less skilled occupations, where an individual could nevertheless be highly intelligent as measured by a general intelligence test (Miller, 1980).

INTERVENTIONS WITH THE ELDERLY

As we have seen, mental disorders of the elderly have many origins and forms. The aim of intervention is to reduce or eliminate negative functioning and to build in, preserve, or strengthen existing positive functioning. As we direct our attention to one or more target areas, we seek to shift the overall balance of functioning in all areas in a positive direction.

Consider a woman who has recently lost her husband after 45 years of marriage: she feels lonely and depressed. If we believe that loss of social supports through bereavement and her resulting grief and loneliness have contributed to her depression, our approach might include attempts to provide some social supports (environmental resources) by having the person join a self-help support group of widows. With their help the widow might find friendly understanding and emotional protection while working through her grief period so that she can accept her life alone without feeling lonely. Widows who have coped successfully might be able to give practical advice and to serve as role models for the grief-stricken newly widowed person. Positive social functioning in the form of group support has thus been added. As grief is alleviated new coping skills can be developed to promote positive personal functioning that would improve her environmental functioning. Gradually, the balance of functioning moves in a healthy direction, and her depression diminishes. This brief illustration demonstrates that interventions have a point of focus—environmental, social, or personal—and changes in functioning may result in any or all areas of adaptation.

Especially among those in the "old-old" age bracket, psychological interventions tend to be complicated by cognitive and physical impairments of the elderly and by their various medications. Drugs taken to reduce high blood pressure or to relieve congestive heart failure may induce mental confusion and speech disorders. Discomfort due to chronic arthritis or intestinal disorders can affect how one socializes and feels. Careful assessment is needed before any interventions are attempted.

Despite pessimistic views that elderly people are too old or too infirm to benefit from psychological interventions, an increasing number of studies have convincingly demonstrated that many counseling and therapeutic interventions have positive impacts on older clients. In fact, elderly people may make rapid and pronounced positive changes in some areas of functioning with appropriate interventions.

Certain kinds of interventions tend to be favored by those who work with the elderly. Instead of trying to describe all types of interventions, we will examine only those that are more frequently employed.

Psychotherapy with the Elderly

Individual Approaches. Two kinds of individual treatments are typically used: (*a*) *interview methods* that focus on developing an understanding of the origins of problems and providing emotional support while facilitating the growth of emotional and social controls and coping skills; (*b*) *behavioral and cognitive methods* that focus on removing disabling behaviors (regardless of their origin) and building in adaptive functioning by means of selective reinforcements according to principles of learning. In the case of cognitive emphases, such methods focus on changing negative or irrational thoughts and beliefs that may be causing maladaptive behaviors.

Since interview methods assume one has verbal command and adequate cognitive processes, plus a willingness to disclose intimate concerns (all of which may be difficult for elderly people of the present generation, especially if they are mentally impaired), the traditional psychodynamic interview approaches are less likely to be the treatment of choice. Older people do enjoy relating their past experiences, however, so a technique described by Butler and Lewis (1982) as *life review therapy* (see photo) has been found helpful. In this method the older person may produce an extensive autobiography, peruse the family photo album, and search out genealogies in an attempt to evoke crucial memories, responses, and understanding. Coleman (1974) has shown that reminiscence often helps people who have had an unhappy past to come to terms with those events and to become better adjusted.

Behavioral and Cognitive Methods. Traditional behavioral approaches have been found to be valuable in building in competencies with problem-solving techniques and the training of appropriate responses. In ad-

Photo albums may be used in life review therapy to encourage the older client to reflect upon the significance and meaning of one's life. (Robert V. Eckert, Jr./EKM-Nepenthe)

dition to controlling anxiety (Garrison, 1978) and phobias, behavioral methods have been employed for such diverse purposes as relieving depression (Gallagher & Thompson, 1981), developing memory skills (Zarit, 1979), increasing socialization (Toseland & Rose, 1978), and controlling wandering behavior (Hussian, 1981). Behavioral methods have also been used successfully to improve a variety of daily-living skills in residents of long-term care facilities, such as increasing self-feeding, appropriate eating habits, walking, and control of bladder and bowel functioning. Other studies have demonstrated that manipulation of the stimulus field, such as rearranging furniture and systematic prompts and reinforcements, can increase social and leisure activities among institutionalized older people (Patterson & Jackson, 1980).

Beck's (1967) cognitive therapy for depression may also be applicable to elderly clients, if depression in the later years is the result of negative, self-deprecating beliefs and thoughts (Gallagher & Thompson, 1983; Storandt, 1983).

Group Methods. Group therapy often produces positive effects upon older people by promoting their socialization with others and by assisting with personal problem solving (Storandt, 1983). Led by a trained therapist, group members can offer support for each other. Knowing how others are facing similar stressors, the old person can learn from the successes of others.

Certain small group techniques, long popular in mental health institutional settings to help the mentally impaired, have been employed with elderly regressed persons, particularly those affected by dementia who are residing in long-term care facilities. *Reality orientation groups* (Storandt, 1978) aim to help confused and disoriented persons become better oriented with respect to time, place, and person. Great emphasis is placed upon providing information about where they are, who they are, names of people caring for them, dates, special occasions, and so forth, usually in small groups led by institutional personnel. In *remotivation therapy* (Storandt, 1978), the focus of the small group is upon participating in simple, objective aspects of day-to-day living. Topics such as vacations, sports, or gardening are introduced along with various props and pictures, in an effort to engage the person mentally.

Reminiscing groups (Lewis & Butler, 1978) have similar objectives through stimulating memories, thought, and socialization. Indeed, almost any activity that can be performed in a group has been used as therapy with the elderly, such as *music groups* (Eisdorfer & Stotsky, 1977), *art therapy* (Storandt, 1978), *poetry groups* (Hartford, 1980), *bibliotherapy* (reading groups) (Sherman, 1981), *scribotherapy* (writing groups) (Hartford, 1980), and numerous *health-related groups* (Storandt, 1983) that may center interest upon exercise, health lectures, or a specific illness, such as heart disease.

Family Therapy. As the number of mentally impaired elderly persons increases, caregiving responsibilities increasingly fall to their middle-aged children, often provoking serious disruptions in their family life. Herr and Weakland (1979) describe a *family systems approach* to counseling with families of the impaired elderly. Their model is based upon group problem solving led by a family counselor who works with the family to provide specific interventions. Eyde and Rich (1983) recommend a family management system wherein all family members participate under professional guidance as "case managers" to sort out the needs and strengths of the older person, seek services and supports, and carry out evaluations and treatment plans. Family members carry out specific treatments, including such practices as behavioral management, rehabilitation of memory losses, motivation, and remediation of a variety of problems such as depression, alcoholism, and drug abuse.

Chemical and Biological Treatments

Chemotherapy. All of the antipsychotic, antidepressant, and antianxiety drugs used for treating mental disorders described elsewhere in this textbook are used for similar problems with the elderly. Rather than review each, we will only mention that all psychotropic drugs must be administered to older persons with great caution, especially to those over the age of 70. Dosages appropriate for younger people may be excessive for older people who metabolize and excrete drugs less efficiently, thus allowing drugs to remain in their bodily systems longer. Negative side effects of drugs, particularly when taken along with medications for heart or circulatory disorders, can be serious and may even induce confusion, delirium, and cognitive or vision problems (Simonson, 1984).

Biological Treatments. In an attempt to increase blood flow to the brain, and thus to get more oxygen to the brain to prevent ischemic attacks (strokes) believed responsible for some forms of dementia, vasodilators that enlarge the diameter of blood vessels have been used. Hyperbaric oxygen therapy, involving inhalation of pure oxygen at intervals, has been used mainly for multi-infarct (stroke) dementia patients, also to increase oxygen supply to the brain (Raskind & Storrie, 1980).

For persons suffering from dementia due to Alzheimer's disease (see Chapter 12), chemicals designed to stimulate production of acetylcholine (e.g., anticholinesterase, choline, or lecithin), believed to activate neurotransmitters, have been tried. As yet, however, no treatments for Alzheimer's disease have been proven useful or effective (Alexander & Geschwind, 1984). On the whole, chemical and biological treatments for senile dementias are still in an experimental, yet unproven, state of development.

SUMMARY

The remarkable increase in the proportion of elderly people over the age of 65 is expected to continue into the next century. This places at risk increasing numbers of people who are vulnerable to mental disorders related to aging. While most of the elderly are competent in later life, about 20 percent are severely handicapped in their daily functioning, and another 30 percent have significant limitations that require psychological or medical care.

Chronological age is typically the index used to position a person along the life span. However, chronological age *per se* does not explain behavioral or biological changes in functioning. Four other potential age indexes are discussed: biological, psychological, functional, and social. Broad individual differences among older people occur on all these indexes.

Because of society's negative stereotypes about aging, there may be a tendency to see most problems of the elderly as basically due to old age. However, an intricate interaction of many factors—biological, psychological, social, and environmental—is involved in most cases of maladaptive behaviors in the later years.

There is a distinction between *senescence,* the segment of the life span when degenerative biological processes overtake regenerative processes, and *disease* that occurs with aging. Many of the changes in functioning thought to be attributable to senescence appear to be more accurately attributable to disease. Independent of health status, however, a slowing in psychomotor speed and electrical activity of the brain can be anticipated with aging. Moreover, senescence reduces the person's reserves for adaptation and coping with stress.

There are several theoretical models by which adaptive behaviors with aging may be viewed. Although no current model is sufficient for fully understanding the interaction of all the maturational and environmental processes associated with aging, useful theoretical approaches have interpreted the adaptive behaviors of the elderly in terms of (a) responses to stressors, (b) learning principles, and (c) the social-breakdown syndrome.

Adaptation in aging depends upon maintaining a favorable balance of positive to negative functioning in environmental, social, and personal areas. Transitions in one's life may shift the balance of functioning because of characteristics of the transition, of the person, and of his or her environment. Certain transitions are especially stressful for elderly persons. Retirement often entails reduced income, alterations in social roles and social support systems, and a need for constructive management of increased leisure time. Changes in housing, reduced mobility, and chronic illnesses can increase negative functioning, while losses of vision and hearing abilities can compound almost any kind of problem. Families of the elderly are often seriously disrupted by the care of the elderly parents. Bereavement, with its attendant problems of widowhood, constitutes a major transition for the elderly. Healthy adaptation requires a positive balance of functioning in one's coping resources and strategies, plus strength of social and environmental supports, as the elderly person undergoes a transition.

Among syndromes of disordered behavior of a functional nature seen most prevalently in elderly patients, one of the most common disorders is depression. Unfortunately, depressive symptoms in the elderly person may often be overlooked or mislabeled as a "natural" aspect of growing old, or may be confused with various organic disorders. Pseudodementia is a term used to describe a depression in which symptoms are predominately intellectual impairment and confusion. Suicide is a potentially serious problem, especially among distressed older white males. Suicidal ideation must be taken very seriously, since the intent is rarely ambivalent. Paranoia is a frequent and disturbing disorder among elderly patients. Late-life paranoia occurs for the first time in the fifth or sixth decade of life or later, and typically consists of delusions focusing on explanations of commonplace losses and failures, possibly with hallucinations. Social isolation and sensory losses are thought to be especially important etiological factors in late-life paranoia. Hypochondriacal symptoms often appear temporarily as an adaptive response to an unfamiliar social stress with which the person feels unable to cope, but such symptoms may have important secondary gains for the older individual.

An important issue in assessing and treating disordered behaviors in elderly people is the possibility that their symptoms reflect not psychopathological states but the effects of the misuse of medications. Compounding the potentially harmful effects of the interaction of multiple drugs taken at the same time is the increased sensitivity of the elderly body to the effects of many drugs.

The abuse of illegal drugs among elderly people appears quite low when compared with its prevalence among younger age groups. However, alcohol abuse is a significant problem, with one third of elderly alcoholics estimated to be late-onset problem drinkers. Their alcoholism is more likely to be related to attempts to cope with the stresses of old age than to more deeply rooted psychological disorders. A particular hazard for the elderly drinker is the potentially dangerous interaction of alcohol with medications.

Although mild anxiety may be relatively common in elderly people, severe anxiety symptoms, unlike severe depression, appear to be much less frequent. Anxiety may manifest itself somewhat differently in the older person as compared with the younger person. Schizophrenia with late-life onset appears to be rare; a major geriatric concern, however, is the management of the chronic schizophrenic who has grown old in a mental hospital and shows an "institutionalization syndrome" of enhanced social inadequacy in addition to schizophrenic symptoms.

Accurate psychological assessment of the elderly patient can be difficult because of the need to evaluate multiple, interlacing concerns of a physical, psychological, and social nature. Furthermore, assessment with this age group poses certain difficulties typically not encountered with younger patients, such as lack of appropriate test norms, age-related differences in educational level and health status, sensory impairments, and test-taking attitudes. A special diagnostic problem can be the frequent need to differentiate cognitive impairments that may reflect functional disorders, such as depression, from those that may reflect organic brain dysfunction, either reversible or nonreversible.

Interventions for the treatment of mental disorders of the elderly involve the reduction or elimination of negative functioning, plus establishing or strengthening positive functioning in all areas of adaptation: environmental, social, and personal. While most of the traditional individual and group psychotherapies are practiced with the elderly, behavioral methods are finding increasing use for treating specific symptomatic behaviors associated with depression, dementia, and problems of socialization and institutional care. Group work techniques, such as reality orientation, remotivation, reminiscing, and a variety of special interest groups, aim at relieving problems of dementia and socialization. Family therapy seeks to enjoin members of the elder's family as integral workers in a home-based management care system.

While promising leads have opened up in chemical and biological treatments of dementia in the elderly, their effectiveness has yet to be proven.

12

Organic Disorders and Mental Retardation

The Brain
  Disorders Resulting from Trauma
  Dementia
  Cortical Dementing Disorders
  Subcortical Dementing Disorders
  Delirium
  Other Organic Syndromes
  Seizures

Mental Retardation
  A Brief History
  Definition and Classification
  Explanations
  Chromosomal Abnormalities
  Abnormalities of Amino Acid Metabolism
  Infections and Toxic Agents
  Fetal Alcohol Syndrome
  Premature Birth
  Trauma, Injury, and Other Causal Factors
  Environmental and Cultural-Familial
    Retardation
  Approaches to Remediation
  Prevention

Summary

INTRODUCTION

In the late 19th century, shortly after the American Civil War, two baby girls were born in a small town in the Midwest. Beverly and Jane became close friends, attended the same schools, and enjoyed a similar lifestyle. After high school they married two brothers who worked in the family clothing business. Beverly and Jane eventually raised a family of three children each, and remained in the same town for the remainder of their lives.

At about 60 years of age, both Beverly and Jane began to show signs of mental disturbance. Beverly lost her ability to communicate fluidly. She would forget appointments and where she had placed items she had set down just minutes before. She also found it difficult to learn new things, such as how to operate the many "newfangled" household appliances that she received as gifts from her family. Her loss of memory and cognitive abilities progressed until she could no longer manage her household or even remember who her family or friends were. Her condition was a source of sadness and frustration not only for her but also for her loved ones, who felt powerless to reverse her steadily diminishing mental capacity. Her inability to function ultimately led to her admission to the state mental hospital. One ironic fact was noted by family members: despite her inability to provide minimal care for herself, Beverly looked healthier than she had appeared for many years. Her physical alertness, agility, upright posture, and ability to walk without hesitation contradicted family members' impressions of how a person diagnosed as suffering from dementia should appear.

Jane also experienced mental deterioration and difficulties in social functioning that resulted in a diagnosis of dementia. She too could not remember many past and present events; however, when prodded or given a clue, she eventually came up with the right answer. What made her appear quite debilitated was that her activity was greatly slowed down. She walked with a stoop, shuffled her feet along the ground, and her speech was slow and barely above a whisper at times. She spoke less and less as her frustration with her physical condition increased. Jane's inability to initiate activity prevented her from living independently and precipitated her admission to the state mental hospital.

In the hospital Beverly and Jane lived on the same ward and frequently came into contact with one another. Yet during those times not a word was exchanged. Beverly was not aware of who Jane was, and Jane was too apathetic to acknowledge and respond to her old friend Beverly.

The cases of Jane and Beverly raise a number of intriguing questions. What factors account for some of the striking differences in the symptoms they displayed? Why were their conditions not reversible? What is the prognosis for persons like Jane and Beverly? In our overview of organic mental disorders, we will address these and other questions as we acquaint you with the intimate relationship between the brain and the regulation of bodily processes and the expression of human emotions.

The stories of Beverly and Jane underline the devastating social and psychological consequences that can ensue when the brain falls prey to disease or aging processes. According to DSM III, the essential feature of an organic mental disorder is a permanent or temporary dysfunction of the brain that can be attributed to organic factors. The deterioration in mental and social functioning that Beverly and Jane displayed was not the result of psychological trauma or their past learning history. At certain points in their illnesses, however, Beverly's and Jane's symptoms might have been mistaken for depression (diminished capacity to function, slow speech, memory problems), schizophrenia (withdrawal, speech peculiarities), or some other nonorganic condition. Thus in diagnosing organic mental disorders, DSM III stipulates that laboratory evidence (brain X rays, physical examinations, electroencephalograms (EEGs), or a history indicating some organic factor be obtained. This is crucial because psychological and organic factors can produce overlapping symptoms.

The starting point for diagnosing an organic disorder is evidence that an organic factor is responsible for the symptoms or the problem behavior observed. As we have indicated in earlier chapters, scientists have lavished considerable attention on unraveling the organic bases of many psychological disorders. For example, major theoretical accounts of schizophrenia and depression contend that neurochemical imbalances play a prominent role in the development and expression of psychopathology. Neuroscientists will eventually discover many of the brain's secrets. As the development of sensitive techniques of detecting brain function advances our understanding of the brain's intricate properties, it is possible that the physiological basis of many behavioral syndromes will be illuminated. In time, disorders that are now viewed as primarily psychological or functional in nature may come to be seen as organic mental disorders.

In this chapter we will discuss disorders that are characterized by changes in brain function associated with psychological and behavioral problems. A host of factors can produce changes in brain function that affect feelings and behavior—brain injury, infection, a disturbance of the metabolism, the use of an intoxicating substance, brain disease, or even the withdrawal associated with cessation of the intake of alcohol or drugs. Although organic disorders have a variety of different causes, they are physiological in origin and produce either temporary or permanent brain dysfunction. At the end of the chapter we will present an overview of mental retardation. Mental retardation is not defined as an organic disorder in DSM III. However, we will consider this topic within this chapter because organic factors are strongly implicated in the majority of cases in which the cause of mental retardation can be isolated. Before we present the organic disorders and discuss mental retardation, we will provide you with a brief introduction to the structure and working of the human brain. This will help to foster an appreciation for how differences in the location of brain injury or dysfunction and the severity of underlying brain pathology may affect human functioning.

The symptoms of brain disorders are far from uniform. A person's coping abilities and personality may have a bearing on how he or she reacts in the face of the memory problems that are a prominent symptom of dementia. One individual might become very depressed and, as a result, even more forgetful, while another person might make lists and use a variety of strategies to "make the best out of a bad situation." Even well-functioning persons' resources may be taxed by impaired mental and physical functioning. Our discussion suggests that it is often difficult to tease out the exact contribution of brain dysfunction to a particular set of symptoms or behaviors. As we have seen in our overview of the psychological disorders, social, cognitive, and physiological factors interact in a way that often obscures the independent effect of each factor. Certain behavioral dysfunctions, however, have been determined to be caused by brain dysfunction, and it is these disorders that will be the focus of our discussion.

Examine, for a moment, the decision tree for organic syndromes presented in Figure 12-1, which is taken from DSM III. As you read about the different types of organic syndromes, it will become apparent that each consists of a group of psychological or behavioral signs or symptoms. You will note, as well, that no mention is made of the specific cause or etiology of the syndromes. Many different physical disorders or conditions can result in a particular organic brain syndrome. If you carefully review the examples of Beverly and Jane and compare their symptoms with the organic brain syndromes depicted, you will verify that both suffered from dementia.

DSM III makes a distinction between organic brain syndromes and organic mental disorders. An organic brain syndrome can be diagnosed as an *organic mental disorder* when its cause or etiology can be identified. Hence, even though Beverly and Jane displayed the identical organic brain syndrome—dementia—they suffered from dif-

ferent organic mental disorders because the cause or origin of their dementia differed. We will discuss dementia in detail later in the chapter, but let us now turn our attention to that marvelously complex organ—the brain.

THE BRAIN

The brain weighs about 1,300 grams and is bathed in a pool of liquid similar to blood plasma that is called *cerebral spinal fluid*. The brain contains hundreds of billions of nerve cells or neurons, 10 times as many support cells known as *glia*, and an average of 10,000 interconnections between the individual neurons. As you can see in Figure 12–2, these connections or synapses usually never physically touch, as in an electrical circuit. Instead, chemical messages are sent by neurotransmitters that are secreted from the end of the axon of the sending neuron onto the dendrite of the receiving neuron at the synapse. The neurotransmitters are of great importance because, as we have mentioned in regard to depression and schizophrenia, their increase or decrease, relative to normal levels, may play a role in the genesis of abnormal behavior. Furthermore, the majority of the drugs in the psychiatrist's arsenal are used with the goal of restoring neurotransmitter levels to normal balance.

Within the brain, groups of neurons may form a nucleus, and a group of these nuclei may form anatomically distinct areas that are termed *brain regions*. Groups of axons running from one brain area to another form nerve tracts. On the grossest level the vertebrate brain contains a hindbrain, midbrain, and forebrain. From an evolutionary perspective the development of the brain can be compared to first building a small house, then adding a new large wing, and then another large wing. The overall structure, of course, is less unified and perhaps less well

FIGURE 12–1
Decision Tree for Organic Brain Syndromes

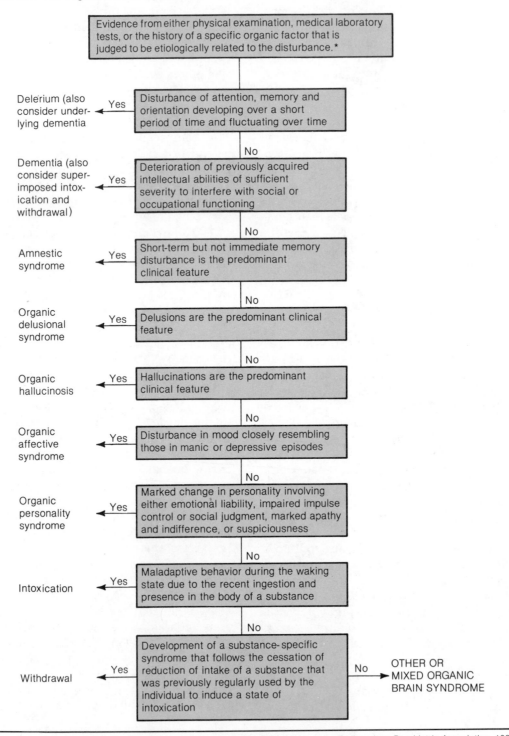

Source: From *Diagnostic and Statistical Manual of Mental Disorders* (DSM III) 3d ed. by the American Psychiatric Association, 1980, Washington, DC: American Psychiatric Association.

FIGURE 12-2
**Chemical Messages Are Sent by Neurotransmitters That Are Secreted from the End of the Axon of
the Sending Neuron onto the Dendrite of the Receiving Neuron at the Synapse**

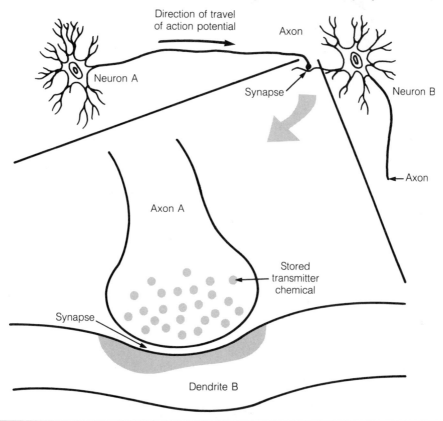

organized than if one had planned the entire structure at once (Kalat, 1984).

Paul MacLean (1967) has described the human brain as consisting of an inner core that he termed the "reptilian brain." This core is composed of those structures that were already well developed in reptiles, and is primarily involved in fixed, stereotyped, ritualistic behaviors necessary for self-preservation and reproduction. These behaviors range from breathing, locomotion, and other simple behaviors to more complex patterns of fighting, mating, securing territory, and communicating. This part of our brain consists of the hindbrain, midbrain,

and a portion of the forebrain. The brains of five animals can be compared by looking at Figure 12-3.

MacLean then described the "old-mammalian brain" (archeocortex) that envelops the reptilian brain and is composed of some forebrain structures that are more or less identical in all mammals. This brain area contributes emotional components such as fear, anger, and love to the functions described above.

The "new-mammalian" brain (neocortex) consists of a multilayered cerebral cortex that surrounds the old-mammalian brain. Although it is completely absent in reptiles,

FIGURE 12-3
Comparison of the Brain Structures of Five Animals

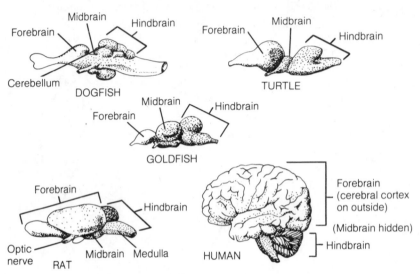

it is at least partially developed in all mammals and is well developed in dolphins, whales, primates, and humans. This part of the brain is responsible for the most advanced processing of sensory information and for motor control. Perhaps most significantly the cerebral cortex controls our rational thinking. As a whole, these three evolutionarily distinct areas of the brain work together. However, since they originated separately, their integration is incomplete (Kalat, 1984). Figure 12-4 illustrates the three layers of the human cerebral cortex.

With the addition of brain areas, there also evolved a greater dependency on the new structures. A lizard, for example, lives its entire life without a cerebral cortex. A rat can still execute some fairly complex behaviors and survive in its environment even after its cortex has been removed. In contrast, a human without a cerebral cortex will quickly lapse into a deep coma. Thus as hu-

mans we have not only evolved to develop a relatively large cerebral cortex, but we are also critically dependent on it (Kalat, 1984). The human neocortex, with brain areas defined, can be seen in Figure 12-5.

Given the many areas, structures, and interconnecting facets of the brain, the study of the brain and brain-behavior relationships is complex. The above discussion implies that one fruitful approach to unlocking the brain's secrets is to adopt a strategy whereby the activity of the brain is broken down into its component parts. Like putting together a jigsaw puzzle, neuroscientists hope that if it is possible to understand the activity of the brain's component parts, it will eventually be possible to discern the workings of the brain as a whole. It could be argued that this approach is, at best, oversimplification. However, this tact has been adopted by many neuroscientists, who largely focus their investigative efforts on separate functions and areas of the brain.

FIGURE 12-4
The Three Layers of the Human Cerebral Cortex Are Evolutionarily Distinct and Incompletely Integrated

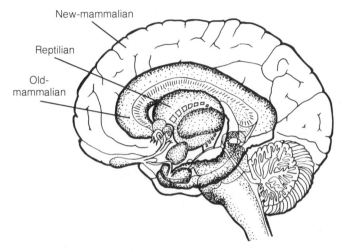

Attempts to relate brain damage in specific locations to behavior and psychological status have helped neuroscientists and physicians to map brain functions. It is well recognized that damage to various brain areas will result in specific behavioral problems. Consider the case of an individual who slips on a wet floor and falls backwards, hitting the back of his head on the floor. Following this accident, he is unable to see. Even before examining the X rays, the neurologist is fairly certain that the problem is localized in the occipital lobe, because this is the cortical area most intimately involved with vision. X rays confirm the presence of a subdural hematoma (a formation of blood under the skull), which is in fact pressing against his occipital lobe. A few days after the physician has drained the hematoma, the accident victim's vision returns. This individual was lucky in that little, if any, permanent damage resulted. However, vision would not have been preserved if the neurons in the area had been destroyed by a gunshot wound, for ex-

ample. The destruction of many neurons would have prevented the brain area from functioning in its normal manner.

While this example highlights the visual area in the occipital lobe, the neocortex is functionally organized into many other specific areas, as presented in Figure 12–5(A). It can be seen that fine control of body movement emanates from an area known as the *motor cortex,* just in front of the central fissure. And just behind this area is a strip of cortex termed the *(somato)sensory cortex,* which is the reception area for sensory information. The *auditory cortex,* located in the temporal lobe, and the *visual cortex,* located in the occipital lobe, receive information from their respective sensory organs. Cortical areas involved in language function are located in different brain sectors, depending on which language function is served. Speech perception, for example, is located towards the occipital lobe, whereas the motor control of speech (talking) is located towards the frontal lobe. However, when we

FIGURE 12–5
The Human Neocortex with Brain Areas Defined

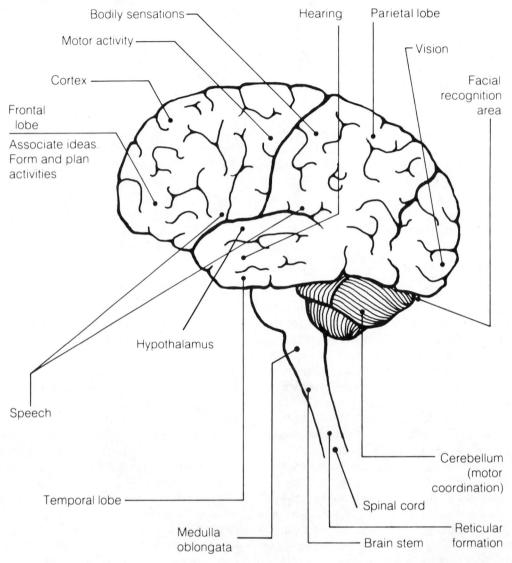

look at Figure 12-5, it is evident that there are many gray colored areas of the cortex that are not labeled as related to a specific function. These areas of the brain are collectively termed the *association cortex* and do not, in fact, subserve a specific function. Rather, the association cortex is presumed to integrate information between various brain areas and the external environment.

Returning once again to the accident described above, the individual could have displayed totally different symptoms depending on which cortical area received the damage. For instance, if the fall would have impacted primarily on the motor cortex, the victim would likely have shown some paralysis, depending on the extent of the damage.

Although we mentioned earlier that permanent destruction of brain tissue known as *lesion* to an area will result in a permanent behavioral disability, this should not be interpreted as a hard and fast rule. In many cases some recovery of function is likely to take place as adjacent brain areas, which are not lesioned, assume some of the functions of the damaged area. In children, there is a great deal of functional recovery after brain damage, since their brains are still plastic enough for other areas to assume some of the lost function. However, as we age, this capacity of the brain diminishes, making it much more difficult for recovery to occur.

The brain is a vulnerable organ in the sense that it and the spinal cord do not have the power to regenerate once they are damaged. Unlike other cells in the body, neurons in the brain and spinal cord do not reproduce. We are born with about as many brain cells as we will ever have, and we lose about 1,000 per day as we grow older. Since the loss accumulates over time, it is not surprising that this is one of the major reasons why older people are at greater risk for organic brain disorders.

In this chapter we will discuss a variety of disorders associated with the destruction of neurons, damage to brain structures, and alterations in the processes that regulate normal brain functioning. We will focus our attention primarily on the disorders associated with aging since they are the most common and representative of the multitude of organic disorders. We will, however, begin our discussion of organic mental disorders with a brief overview of disorders that result from *trauma*. Traumatic brain disorders arise directly from physical injury to the brain. These conditions are not directly related to aging; however, the elderly do seem to have a high proportion of trauma-related disorders due to increased motor incoordination.

Disorders Resulting from Trauma

The following example will illustrate three main types of traumatic conditions. Don and Brett are karate students competing in an important tournament. They are fighting on a matted surface and wearing protective headgear. About halfway through the match, Brett gives Don a hard kick to the head. Don immediately loses consciousness for a short period of time. When he regains consciousness, he experiences a loss of memory for the events that occurred just prior to the kick (*retrograde amnesia*). For a short period of time he is confused and disoriented. However, he feels that he is "not quite himself" for several weeks. Don's physician informs him that he has sustained a *contusion,* which is the mildest form of traumatic injury.

Consider now what would have occurred if Don had not been wearing protective headgear, and Brett's kick had been severe enough to knock the brain against the inside of the skull and bruise the soft brain tissue. Under these circumstances the unfortunate

Don would experience all the symptoms of a contusion, with the addition of dizziness, fatigue, apathy, irritability, and frequent headaches for a period of about six weeks. Intense stimuli such as bright lights or loud noises might also prove bothersome. Upon examination, the neurologist would diagnose Don as having suffered a *concussion*.

A third type of traumatic injury would have even more serious and long-lasting consequences for Don. Consider the possibility that Don and Brett do not take the precaution of wearing headgear and fighting on a matted surface. If Don were to fall and shatter his skull on impact with the unyielding surface of the floor, a skull fragment could pierce his brain, causing grave injuries. Such a *cerebral laceration* might result in injuries so severe that Don could enter a comatose state and possibly never again regain consciousness. A coma is a state of profound unconsciousness from which arousal is usually not possible. During this time bodily processes such as respiration and heartrate also are slowed down. Only after the brain has healed sufficiently will the person recover from the coma. If the injuries were less severe, Don would experience symptoms similar to that of a contusion, but the behavior controlled by the part of the brain that was damaged could possibly never return to normalcy. The nature and degree of impairment sustained would depend on the degree of damage and the location of the part of the brain that was destroyed.

Our example of Don and Brett underscores the point that injuries to the brain can vary from very mild to life-threatening. The skull itself is not invulnerable to injury, and hence may not provide adequate protection to the brain under all circumstances. Although the skull is adequate as a protective cover for most normal situations that we may encounter, it offers the brain virtually no protection against circumstances that were not in our ancestors' environment when the skull was evolving. Evolution failed to anticipate motor vehicles and firearms, which are responsible for many contemporary traumatic brain injuries.

Apart from accidents or intentional injuries, aging and disease processes account for the majority of organic mental disorders. The organic syndromes that these produce are diverse, but DSM III has defined two major syndromes that deserve our careful consideration: dementia and delirium. These syndromes can occur across the age spectrum, but are more commonly observed among the elderly.

Dementia

Perhaps one of the most feared and potentially catastrophic aspects of growing old is that our memory and intellectual capacities deteriorate. It is estimated that more than 5 percent of persons over 65 years of age suffer from severe dementia, while an additional 10 to 15 percent suffer milder but related symptoms (Cummings, 1984). As its name implies, the essential feature of dementia is a deterioration of previously acquired intellectual ability that may interfere with social or occupational functioning. Memory loss invariably accompanies dementia. In addition, difficulties in the areas of inhibiting impulses, exercising sound judgment, and reasoning efficiently often vex the person diagnosed as suffering from dementia.

As the story of Beverly and Jane indicates, the major pattern of deterioration exhibited by persons with dementia is memory loss. A loss of memory for past events as well as the inability to learn new skills are characteristic of dementia. Indeed, the first signs of dementia may be a forgetfulness for telephone numbers and directions that were once familiar. A person may repeatedly leave the water running, or perhaps get lost in his or her own neighborhood. Changes in the individual's personality may be observed—either exaggerations of previous personality attributes or dramatic changes in personality characteristics.

Within the last decade public and scientific interest in dementia has accelerated. The social ramifications of an aging population and recent findings concerning the brain pathology of dementia have become increasingly evident. When persons are able to live semi-independently, cognitive impairment is judged to be mild to moderate. Generally the criterion for severe dementia is considered to be cognitive impairment sufficient to preclude independent living. Dementia is now recognized as the major invaliding problem of individuals who live in this country's 1.2 million nursing-home beds. Caring for these patients consumes 12 billion health-care dollars per year (Cummings, 1984). Although dementia occurs most frequently in the elderly population, it may also occur at any age.

Dementia is associated with numerous brain diseases and pathological conditions. Dementia may be caused by brain tumors, injuries, neurological disease, circulatory problems, intoxication, and infections. As we noted earlier, the many areas of the brain subserve different behavioral functions. The brain damage caused by dementing diseases is likely to be as diverse as the diseases themselves. Many individuals with dementia appear to be similarly impaired on a global level because changes in certain brain structures are necessary in order for the symptoms of dementia to be manifested. It is possible, however, to distinguish various types of dementia on the basis of their underlying neuropathology. Indeed, if we focus carefully on the extent of the loss of behaviors and functions such as movement, language, memory, affect, and visual-spatial abilities, it is often possible to differentially

diagnose the dementias associated with disparate diseases.

We will organize our discussion by categorizing dementing disorders by the areas of the brain that are affected. The two major categories of dementing diseases are those produced by damage to the cortex and those produced by damage to subcortical areas. Let us now consider Alzheimer's and Pick's diseases, two organic mental disorders that arise from damage to the cortical area of the brain.

Cortical Dementing Disorders

Alzheimer's Disease. Alzheimer's disease is the most common cause of dementia, accounting for more than half of the diagnosed cases. There are some problems in arriving at a definitive diagnosis of Alzheimer's disease; it can only be confirmed after a patient has died and the brain is examined. A diagnosis requires the presence of the symptoms of dementia *and* the finding of the typical pathological features: *neurofibrillary tangles* (thickened, twisted, and distorted nerve fibers) and *neuritic plaques* (nerve fiber lesions) in the cerebral cortex. There are a number of physiological abnormalities that can be detected while an Alzheimer's patient is alive. These include an abnormal electroencephalogram (EEG), reduced flow of blood within the brain, and a slower utilization of glucose, the brain's major fuel (Terry & Katzman, 1983). However, other diseases also produce these changes; thus these signs alone can not assist in making a differential diagnosis. At present the clinician, lacking a specific clinical marker for Alzheimer's disease, can only approximate the true diagnosis, on the basis of an overall assessment of the nature and course of the patient's symptoms.

Traditionally, when dementia was diagnosed prior to age 65, it was termed *presenile*

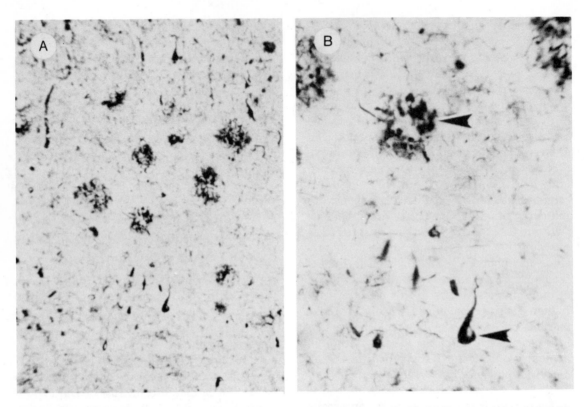

These photomicrographs from the brain of an individual with Alzheimer's disease illustrate at low (A) and high (B) power the neuritic plaques and neurofibrillary tangles that are characteristic features of the disorder. (Johns Hopkins School of Medicine, Dr. Joseph T. Coyle—permission to reproduce from *Science*, p. 1185, March 1983 issue)

dementia, and after that age it was known as *senile dementia of the Alzheimer type.* However, there is an emerging consensus that this distinction is not meaningful or appropriate. After age 50 the proportion of people who acquire this disease is relatively stable across age groups. The existence of two separate statistical distributions with peak incidences before and after age 65 would support the notion that there are indeed two separate disorders. This, however, is not the case. In addition, Alzheimer's patients of late onset (senile patients) may have siblings who develop Alzheimer's early (presenile patients). This, too, is inconsistent with the hypothesis that there are two separate disorders since each disorder would probably be genetically distinct. Therefore, regardless of the age of onset, it is perhaps most legitimate to think of one disorder or syndrome that is collectively known as Alzheimer's disease (Comfort, 1984).

Although there is no reason to think that presenile and senile Alzheimer's disease are two separate diseases, it is important to acknowledge the diversity of the expression of the symptoms of Alzheimer's disease. In this sense the disease may be seen as having many forms, depending on the most prominent symptoms exhibited by the patient. Brain degeneration, for example, does not follow an invariant course across all Alzheimer's patients; nor are other factors that affect mood and behavior, such as the social environment and personality characteristics, constant across Alzheimer's sufferers. Given the manifold factors that influence symptom expression, it is not surprising that the behavioral symptoms of Alzheimer's patients may be quite different from one case to another. For instance, in the early phases of the disease some patients may not show a pronounced memory loss, but instead a delusional syndrome characterized by intense paranoia. For example, a patient may firmly believe that his family and closest friends have turned against him and want to kill him. Such delusional ideas, of course, have no basis in reality. Other sufferers may show classic symptoms of depression, with suicidal ideation and feelings of hopelessness and worthlessness prominent in the overall picture. Still other Alzheimer's patients may seem quite confused and amnestic, recognizing no one. Undoubtedly the abnormal behaviors that characterize an Alzheimer's patient may be quite diverse, especially in the early stages of the disease. However, as the disease progresses and mental functions decline, cognitive impairment and memory loss often become the focal concerns of the patient's family and friends. The course of Alzheimer's disease is about 10 years in younger sufferers and three to five years in the post-65 population, resulting in death in all cases. Another statistic of note is that more women than men develop Alzheimer's disease.

Is Alzheimer's disease inheritable? There is good evidence that some people who develop Alzheimer's disease before age 60 are the most likely to pass on this disorder. In fact, one or more immediate family members of an Alzheimer's patient have a significantly greater than chance likelihood of developing the disease. One not atypical example is that of a 74-year-old man who died after a history of progressive loss of memory, impaired judgment, and other classic symptoms of Alzheimer's that began at age 60. His family history revealed that his father, father's brother, and father's sister had all reportedly suffered from similar symptoms that began at about the same age (Coyle, Price, & De-Long, 1983). Other support for genetic factors in Alzheimer's disease is the finding that if a twin has Alzheimer's disease, there is about a 20 percent chance that the other twin will develop the disease as well. It is also interesting that Down's syndrome (mongolism) in adults is often associated with Alzheimer's changes (Epstein, 1983). Many sufferers of Alzheimer's disease, however, do not have a familial (genetic) form. Nonetheless, recent studies are converging on the conclusion that some people may have an inherited predisposition to Alzheimer's disease.

It is only within the last decade that scientists have begun to penetrate the mysteries of Alzheimer's disease. The recent finding of a specific loss of forebrain neurons that use acetylcholine as their neurotransmitter in Alzheimer's disease has stirred a great deal of excitement in the scientific community. Knowing what brain cells die has important treatment implications and can ultimately lead to more precise understanding of the disease process itself. Various drugs that increase acetylcholine in the brain have been administered to Alzheimer's patients with some success (Thal, Masur, Fuld, Sharpless, & Davies, 1983). Unfortunately, these drugs are not able to reverse or even completely halt the symptoms of dementia. Treatments designed to modify the disease process and arrest its progression await better understanding of the specific factors that contribute to Alzheimer's disease. One promising avenue of inquiry has been initiated by Prusiner and his colleagues (1983), who have recently suggested that a unique and novel class of infectious agents (smaller than a bacteria or virus) called *prions* may be

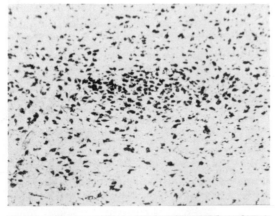

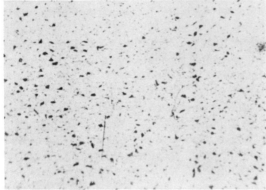

Photomicrographs show nucleus basalis of Meynert in a patient with Alzheimer's disease (top) and in an age-matched control. The number of neurons is diminished in the patient. (Johns Hopkins School of Medicine, Dr. Joseph T. Coyle—permission to reproduce from *Hospital Practice*, p. 62, November 1982 issue)

responsible for the neural degeneration and dementia of Alzheimer's disease. If prions are indeed the culprits, research and treatment efforts could be geared to finding ways to destroy them or to counteract their effects.

Pick's Disease. At 50 Mary was a healthy woman who had successfully raised a family of four children. During her 51st year, however, her actions and emotions became less spontaneous, and she could not remember certain events, such as whether she had eaten lunch earlier in the day. Her symptoms intensified over the next few years. She be-

came confused and disoriented, and her memory loss was profound. Her movements also appeared to be restricted. Her dementia was debilitating, and she lived the remaining two years of her life reduced to a vegetative state. Her physician diagnosed her as having early-onset Alzheimer's disease. However, after she died, examination of her brain failed to reveal the cortical plaques and tangles that signify Alzheimer's disease. Only her frontal and temporal lobes were severely atrophied; the diffuse brain atrophy across the cortex, characteristic of Alzheimer's disease, was absent.

Mary suffered from *Pick's disease*, an extremely rare disorder in which, for some unknown reason, the frontal and temporal lobes of otherwise healthy individuals between the ages of 45 and 60 gradually atrophy over a period of four to seven years, leading to death. In addition, the presence of abnormal inclusions or particles in cortical neurons can be detected (they stain positive for silver). The affected cells are termed *Pick's cells.* The examination of Mary's brain revealed the presence of Pick's cells, confirming the diagnosis.

Mary's example illustrates some of the problems inherent in differentially diagnosing the dementing disorders. The age of onset and the symptoms of diverse disorders overlap to a great extent. Hence, in certain cases a diagnosis can be confirmed only if an autopsy is performed.

Subcortical Dementing Disorders

It is widely believed that almost all progressive mental deterioration or dementia is a direct result of degenerative changes that involve the cortical neurons. In fact, many disorders that produce dementia are the result of lesions primarily affecting subcortical structures. Such disorders are collectively known as *subcortical dementing disorders*

(Benson, 1983). Perhaps the best-known subcortical dementing disorders are Huntington's disease, Parkinson's disease, and Wilson's disease. We will discuss each of these in turn.

Huntington's Disease. Wilkie and Nichols were brothers who lived in a village in Bures, England, and were suspected of practicing witchcraft. They were imprisoned and later accepted banishment from England in order to obtain a release from jail. In 1630 the brothers and their families set sail for America. Both Wilkie and Nichols and half of their offspring developed symptoms of a behavioral disorder characterized by a backward and forward jerking of the head, peculiar grimacing and twitching, weaving motions, puckering of lips, spasmodic movements of the chest and diaphragm, involuntary jerking of the hands, feet, and legs, and severe mental deterioration. People interpreted these "signs" to mean the brothers and their affected children were enduring the suffering of Christ on the cross, and that their affliction was an inherited curse. During the historical period in which they lived, many different or odd persons were thought by the church to be in league with the "Prince of Hell."

Despite their stigmatization, Wilkie and Nichols traveled to America, where they eventually played an important role in a true American tragedy (Vessie, 1974). These brothers were the forefather's of many Americans who suffer from *Huntington's disease*, otherwise known as *Huntington's chorea* or *hereditary chorea*. The word *chorea* stems from the same Greek root as choreography. It refers to the jerky, dancelike movements so prominent in this terrible disorder that afflicts body and mind.

Huntington's disease was described in 1872 by an American physician, George Huntington, as a genetically transmitted disease characterized by chorea and a gradually increasing dementia. The genetic abnormality affects both sexes equally and gives the offspring of an affected individual 50–50 odds of inheriting the disorder (Sanberg & Coyle, 1984). The symptoms usually begin during the fourth or fifth decade of life, although persons as young as 2 or as old as 80 have been known to develop the disease. The life expectancy after the onset of symptoms is on the order of about 10 to 20 years.

Neurologically, Huntington's disease is one of the purest examples of a degenerative process. Neither neurofibrillary tangles nor neuritic plaques (characteristic of Alzheimer's disease) nor other specific changes are seen; the degenerative changes are specific to a loss of brain cells in the forebrain, primarily the brain structure known as the basal ganglia (Sanberg & Coyle, 1984).

Some readers might associate Huntington's disease with Woody Guthrie, the legendary folksinger and songwriter who succumbed to the disorder. Indeed, the popular media frequently refer to Huntington's as *Woody Guthrie's disease*. Guthrie's case illustrates how easy it is to misdiagnose the early symptoms of Huntington's disease. For some time it was thought that Guthrie was an alcoholic because of the uncoordinated movements he exhibited. As his mental functions declined, some believed he was schizophrenic. The course of the disease is not always predictable. In some cases personality and cognitive changes precede the involuntary movements; in other cases the reverse is true. But the end result is invariably death.

Variability in the symptom picture and the overlap of Huntington's symptoms with those of other disorders have significant implications. Indeed, one of the most tragic aspects of Huntington's is that persons who have the disease often do not realize that this is the case until they have children of their own. Not only must they contend with the certainty that they will die from an incurable and debilitating illness but also with the ambiguity of whether their offspring will develop the tragic symptoms later in life. And many of the more than 100,000 children at risk for Huntington's live in terror that they will fall victim to the statistical odds and develop the disease later in life.

Recent discoveries by molecular scientists may lead to advances that will give Huntington's sufferers and their children reason for hope. Gusella and his colleagues (Gusella et al., 1983) studied genetic material (DNA) extracted from the white blood cells of 570 Venezuelans who are part of a group of interrelated families who live near Lake Maracaibo and comprise the largest concentration of Huntington's disease victims in the world. Gusella compared these samples with another set derived from a large American family. In an impressive piece of scientific detective work, using recombinant DNA techniques, Gusella isolated the chromosome within which the abnormal gene responsible for the disease is located. This discovery is tremendously exciting. It may eventually lead to the isolation of the genetic defect of the disease. A treatment for Huntington's disease can be based on knowledge of the exact nature of the genetic defect. Discovering the genetic abnormality also may yield a positive test for detecting future sufferers in the uterus before they are born. Parents can then decide whether they want children carrying the gene; prenatal tests will prove invaluable in detecting whether babies carry the deadly gene.

Scientists are intensely studying Huntington's for another reason. The characteristic subcortical brain damage associated with Huntington's disease has proven to be a valuable tool for studying neurobiological mechanisms of basal ganglia function (Sanberg & Johnston, 1981). In order to examine the role a particular brain area plays in behavior, scientists typically proceed by destroying or creating a lesion in the area and examining the behavioral changes that result. Presumably, behavior that is absent or altered is controlled by the area under consideration. This technique, however, is usually limited to animal research since obvious

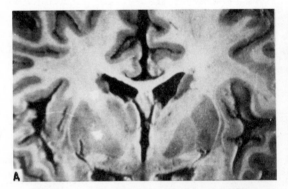 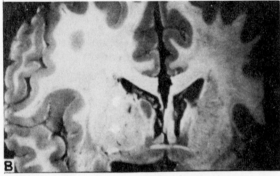

A. Coronal section from the brain of a child (4 years old) who died from leukemia. This slightly skew cut has been made in order to match the section from the patient with Huntington's disease as closely as possible. A small portion of thalamus indents the lateral margin of the left lateral ventricle.

B. Coronal section from the patient. Note the severe atrophy of the caudate and putamen nuclei (arrows) as compared to the control brain. White scars replace the normal appearance of gray matter in these areas. The cortex shows no evidence of significant atrophy. (*Canadian Journal of Neurological Sciences*. Permission to reprint from Vol. 10, No. 3, August 1983 issue) ethical problems surround subjecting humans to such procedures. However, many neurodegenerative diseases such as Huntington's are really "nature's own lesion." Thus, such diseases may facilitate the study of human brain functioning. Traditionally the basal ganglia, which are the largest subcortical area, have been thought to control movement only. However, animal studies in which this area has been lesioned have demonstrated profound changes in affect, learning, and memory (Sanberg & Johnston, 1981). Huntington's disease permits the assessment of the role of the basal ganglia in behavior since it is this area that degenerates, especially in the early stages of the disease. In fact, neuropsychological studies of the dementia of Huntington's disease have supported a role for the basal ganglia in nonmotor functions (Sanberg & Coyle, 1984).

Parkinson's Disease. Parkinson's disease or *paralysis agitans* is another syndrome often associated with dementia and movement disorders. There are three major clinical features of movement abnormalities in Parkinson's disease. The first is *tremor.* This difficulty is apparent mainly when the patient is resting or holding sustained postures. The second feature, *rigidity,* is a manifestation of increased muscle tone. This results in a stooped posture with the slight bending of the knees, hips, neck and elbows that is the characteristic posture of Parkinsonism. *Bradykinesia* is the third feature. This is best described as a disability in initiating and, at times, arresting movement. In fact, it is sometimes typical of a Parkinson's patient to run into a wall or door in order to stop moving. Other symptoms are lack of facial expression, a pervasive feeling of weakness, and a flattened vocal quality (Pincus & Tucker, 1978).

The brain pathology of Parkinson's disease involves a destruction of neurons in the substantia nigra, a structure located in the midbrain. Parkinson's disease is most common in elderly people; it occurs when there is significant damage to cells in the substantia nigra. The cells that die in this region are those that use dopamine as their neurotransmitter and project up to the basal ganglia.

The theory that the substantia nigra and the related loss of dopamine are responsible for the symptoms of Parkinson's disease was recently given dramatic support by an accidental "natural experiment" in northern California. Langston and his colleagues (Langston, Balland, Tetrud, & Irwin, 1983) reported that four persons developed symptoms of Parkinsonism after intravenously using an illicit drug. The users were victims of a mistake made in an illicit laboratory for synthesizing heroinlike drugs for sale on the street. Instead of producing a synthetic heroin drug, a chemical known as MPTP was synthesized that produced the symptoms of severe Parkinsonism in the unsuspecting users. The fact that the drug acts to selectively kill cells in only one area of the brain—the substantia nigra—and produces Parkinson symptoms in animals and humans provided additional support for the link between this brain structure and the disease symptoms.

Scientists are now operating on the premise that a specific neurochemical deficit is involved in Parkinson's disease. This hypothesis suggests that a replacement of the lost dopamine might improve the symptoms of the disease. Unfortunately, simple dopamine replacement is not feasible. When dopamine is directly administered into the body, it does not pass the blood-brain barrier (a barrier that limits what goes into and out of the brain). Given this obstacle, a more indirect approach has been attempted, that of administering L-dopa. L-dopa is an amino acid; for this reason it does cross the blood-brain barrier. In addition, it is the immediate precursor to dopamine and thereby enhances the synthesis of dopamine in the remaining neurons. Although L-dopa has proven effective in improving the quality of life of the

A person with Parkinson's disease before (left) and after (right) treatment with L-dopa. (From *A Psysiological Approach to Clinical Neurology* by J. W. Lance and J. G. McLeod, 1975. Reprinted by permission of Butterworth, Ltd.)

Parkinson's patient, it does not halt the disease process itself.

It is still a mystery why the cells in the substantia nigra die. Naturally occurring or idiopathic Parkinson's disease has been variously thought to be due to an accelerated aging process (McGeer, McGeer, & Suzuki, 1977) or a slow-acting virus. Antipsychotic drugs commonly used to treat schizophrenia and related disorders can produce a syndrome resembling Parkinson's disease that is reversible when the drugs are discontinued. These drugs induce Parkinson's symptoms by interfering with the action of dopamine in the basal ganglia by blocking the receptors that mediate the effects of dopamine. The key to future advances in the treatment of Parkinson's disease will be a better understanding of the disease process itself.

Wilson's Disease. Wilson's disease or *hepatolenticular degeneration*, as it is sometimes termed, is a hereditary disease that produces abnormal movements and dementia. Unlike Huntington's disease, however, Wilson's disease is a multisystem disorder that affects the liver, kidney, and blood, in addition to the brain damage it produces. In addition, its inheritance follows an autosomal recessive pattern in that a parent carrying the abnormal gene need not have the disease.

In Wilson's disease the brain area primarily affected is the basal ganglia. However, damage to the liver rather than the brain ultimately leads to death. The genetic abnormality in Wilson's disease results in an accumulation of copper in the body that leads to tissue destruction. A diagnosis can be made simply by examining the eyes of a patient for a change in the cornea—a brownish green ring on the internal aspect of the cornea—which is caused by copper deposits.

Administration of drugs that remove copper from the body successfully treats Wilson's disease patients. Furthermore, if irreversible brain damage is not already present when the treatment is initiated, the movement abnormalities and dementia will subside. Liver and kidney damage can also be reduced if treatment is started early enough.

Cortical versus Subcortical Demented Disorders. The disorders discussed above represent the major diseases causing dementia that result from cortical or subcortical damage to the brain. You have probably noted that in addition to the cognitive disturbances typical of dementia, subcortical dementing disorders also produce profound changes in movement. In contrast, movement is rarely impaired in the cortical dementing disorders.

Benson (1983) has noted that the behavioral symptoms accompanying dementia may also distinguish the two types of disorders. For example, language disorders occur predominantly in the cortical dementing disorders. Although memory, cognitive, and affective changes occur in all the dementing disorders, the degree of disruption to these processes can vary, depending on the type of disease. In cortical dementing disorders amnesia is usually present, marked by a loss of some past memories and an inability to learn new material. In subcortical dementia the term *forgetfulness* has been suggested (Benson, 1983). Perhaps the best description of this deficit is that the person has difficulty initiating the retrieval of stored memories. Given a hint or prodded to recall, many subcortical dementia patients can retrieve memories previously believed to be lost forever. Similarly, the cognitive loss in subcortical dementia patients is not as severe as in victims of cortical dementia. Cortical dementia patients tend to be unaware of their environment; they may not even know who their closest friends and family are. On the other hand, the subcortical demented individual may actually be aware of his or her environment, but an apparent lack of motivation plus a disinterest in initiating activities is suggestive of the general apathy these patients experience (Benson, 1983).

To help consolidate some of the information we have presented, let us return for a moment to the story of the two girlfriends, Beverly and Jane, which we presented at the beginning of this chapter. Their disparate symptom pictures capture some of the differences between cortical and subcortical dementing disorders. As you will recall, Beverly exhibited significant language impairment and severe memory and cognitive loss. Her movement and speech, however, were spared. Beverly suffered from a cortical dementing disorder, and like many Alzheimer's patients, appeared to be healthy and physically robust. Jane's symptoms were more consistent with those produced by a subcortical dementing disorder such as Parkinson's disease. Her impairment was obvious in her slow, poorly articulated speech and her abnormally slow movement and stooped posture. However, she exhibited no language disorder and her memory was intact, although she did experience some difficulty in retrieving memories. As mentioned previously, both Jane and Beverly were diagnosed as having organic brain syndrome. Yet it is evident that they were victims of different diseases. Many patients in our mental hospitals and nursing homes are routinely diagnosed as having organic brain syndrome; insufficient attention is devoted to ascertaining the exact nature of their disease. Since some diseases are treatable, it is important that all patients be given a thorough diagnostic assessment.

Cardiovascular Dementing Disorders. The brain contributes only 2.5 percent of our total body weight, yet it consumes practically 25 percent of the oxygen we inspire. Because all of our oxygen travels in our cardiovascular system (blood supply), it is no wonder that in just a short period of time a lack of blood to our brain can cause permanent brain damage. The familiar lay term *stroke* is commonly used to denote a sudden neurological affliction resulting from some abnormality in the cerebral blood supply. But the use of this term does little to clarify the exact nature of the disturbance. An abnormality in the blood supply to the brain may be caused by clotting within a blood vessel (thrombosis), obstruction of the vessel by some foreign matter (embolism), or a rupture of the blood vessel walls (hemorrhage). When the blood supply is insufficient to sustain the life of the cells it is servicing, they will undoubtedly die. We term this area of damage an *infarct*. Thus infarcts are lesioned tissues in the brain that are a direct result of a lack of blood supply to the damaged area.

Until the 1970s the most common diagnoses of dementia were *cerebral arteriosclerosis* and *arteriosclerotic dementia.* It was thought that because of aging the walls of our blood vessels thickened and restricted more and more of the blood flowing into our brain, thereby depriving the brain of precious oxygen. However, it is now known that only the most severe degree of arteriosclerotic-induced narrowing of blood vessels will significantly reduce blood flow to the brain. In fact, research has shown little correlation between the thickening of blood vessels in the brain at autopsy, and the severity of dementia (Read & Jarvik, 1984). As mentioned earlier, the majority of patients suffering from dementia have Alzheimer's disease. Nevertheless, dementia due to multiple infarcts is the second major cause, and may play a role in an many as 36 percent of dementia cases (Wells, 1978).

Multiple-infarct dementia (MID) results from a lack of blood supply to various brain areas. If the infarction is limited to brain areas innervated by one artery, this will usually result in a focal syndrome (such as loss of memory, a speech disorder, or some other specific symptom) rather than dementia. Of course, these focal symptoms are related to the fact that separate functions are controlled by different areas of the brain. Dementia, then, is produced only when lesions of multiple brain areas occur as a result of some vascular disorder.

Both cortical and subcortical areas can be involved in MID. This is the case because in both of these areas structures rely on blood from the major vessels. Of course, if there were an abnormality in one of these vessels, all the brain areas that depend on this precious source of blood would be affected. Thus MID patients can show features of the cortical and subcortical dementia disorders.

There are a number of reasons why infarcts occur in the brain. Arteriosclerosis can cause obstructions of arteries, termed *lacunae*, which result in multiple brain lesions. Hypertension (high blood pressure) is the major factor underlying the development of lacunae (St. Clair & Whalley, 1983). *Hypertensive arteriosclerosis* is a progressive increase in the muscle and elastic tissue of the arterial walls as a result of increased blood pressure. Eventually this growth constricts

the opening in the blood vessels, thus restricting the flow of blood. For these reasons it is important to detect blood pressure changes early in order to inhibit the development of cardiovascular abnormalities. Fortunately, antihypertensive drugs are effective in controlling this disorder. It should also be noted that hypotension or low blood pressure can also cause MID because below normal blood flow may damage those parts of the brain that are the farthest away from the main blood supply.

Another major cause of MID are multiple emboli (such as detached blood clots or a mass of bacteria or other foreign bodies) that also can block blood vessels. But direct blood vessel abnormalities are not the only possible triggers of MID. Without any specific infarctions, a heart attack, drowning, or other cause of a lack of oxygen can also produce the patchy neuronal loss that results in dementia.

Because there are so many blood vessels within the brain, no two patients with multiple infarcts will display the identical pathology. Since many different brain areas are vulnerable to damage, the resulting clinical picture of dementia may vary substantially from case to case. Nevertheless, it is important to correctly diagnose the cause of MID. Misdiagnosing a patient who has just begun to display symptoms consistent with dementia could have potentially disasterous consequences. For example, if dementia is caused by a potentially treatable cardiovascular disease, treatment could be initiated to stop the progression of dementia and to permit some recovery of lost function. However, a misdiagnosis of Alzheimer's disease would condemn this person to a relentless mental deterioration and eventual death.

In conclusion, we must stress that despite the current wave of excitement about Alzheimer's disease in the popular press, it is important to avoid labeling all individuals with dementia as Alzheimer's patients. A careful study of each case must be undertaken in order to deter the hazardous consequences of misdiagnosis.

Delirium

Delirium is characterized by a very rapid onset and a clinical picture that includes disturbances of attention, memory, and orientation in time and space. Not only is the onset of delirium rapid but frequently its duration is quite brief—as little as a week and seldom more than a month. There may also be a sleep disturbance so that the person suffering from delirium is unable to sleep or sleeps excessively. As you can see in Table 12–1, the person experiencing an episode of delir-

ium may have perceptual experiences, including hallucinations, delusions, and sometimes disturbed speech.

An important feature of delirium is that symptoms rapidly shift and change and are poorly systematized. Thus the delusions reported by a person suffering from delirium may be only brief and disorganized. Furthermore, dramatic problems of memory and ability to orient oneself are characteristic of delirium. This particular pattern has in the past been called *toxic psychosis, acute brain syndrome,* or *transient cognitive disorder.*

The determinants of delirium are manifold. In people of all ages, delirium can be caused by such diverse influences as infections, metabolic disturbances, the use of alcohol or drugs to excess, or ceasing their use after dependence. Sometimes delirium can occur after a brain injury or after seizures.

Delirium is highly prevalent in the elderly. However, insufficient attention has been paid to this important disorder, relative to other organic disorders such as dementia (Lipowski, 1983). In the elderly patient delirium usually heralds physical illness and hence calls for immediate medical attention.

Other Organic Syndromes

Let us briefly consider the other organic brain syndromes described in DSM III and depicted in the decision tree for organic disorders (Figure 12–1).

Amnestic Syndrome. This pattern of organic brain disorder involves a memory loss that renders the person unable to remember events that occurred as little as 25 minutes earlier. Such a person may be able to repeat a series of half a dozen digits presented one at a time about one second apart but be unable to recall three objects shown to him or her 25 minutes earlier. The most common forms of this disorder are associated with chronic alcohol use or vitamin deficiency. Korsakoff's

---

TABLE 12–1
Diagnostic Criteria for Delirium

A. Disturbance of attention, as manifested by either:
  1. Impairment in ability to sustain attention to environmental stimuli.
  2. Impairment in ability to sustain goal-directed thinking.
  3. Impairment in ability to sustain goal-directed behavior.
B. Disordered memory and orientation, if testing not interfered with by attention disturbance.
C. At least two of the following:
  1. Reduced wakefulness or insomnia.
  2. Perceptual disturbance: simple misinterpretations, illusions or hallucinations.
  3. Increased or decreased psychomotor activity.
D. Clinical features develop over a short period of time and fluctuate rapidly.
E. There is evidence from either physical examination, medical laboratory tests, or the history, of a specific organic factor that is judged to be etiologically related to the disturbance.

Source: American Psychiatric Association, *DSM III* (1980), p. 107.

psychosis and the disease beriberi are both due to a deficiency of vitamin B_1 or thiamine. Korsakoff's psychosis primarily occurs in alcoholics who have poor diets; usually they do not eat balanced meals. This irreversible disorder could be completely prevented if manufacturers of alcoholic beverages would add vitamin B_1 to their products.

Organic Delusional Syndrome. In some cases people suffering from some form of brain impairment develop delusions that may resemble those of schizophrenia. The delusions may be associated with brain tumors or with brain impairment from drug abuse as a result of using amphetamines (see Chapter 14). In differentiating organic delusional syndromes from schizophrenia, the major basis for making distinctions has to do with whether or not there is evidence of the specific organic factor necessary for the development of the delusions.

Organic Hallucinosis. Another organic brain syndrome may produce recurrent and persistent hallucinations in a person who is fully awake and alert. In some cases the person may be aware that the hallucinations are not real; in other cases he or she may be convinced that the hallucinations are real. The hallucinations may be auditory, but any other sensory mode may also be involved. Drug use, particularly of the hallucinogens, most frequently produces visual hallucinations, whereas in the case of alcohol intoxication auditory hallucinations are more likely to occur.

Organic Affective Syndrome. As the name implies, this syndrome involves major disturbances in mood that look a good deal like manic or depressive episodes. Most commonly this particular pattern of behavior is caused by metabolic factors and certain drugs.

Organic Personality Syndrome. In some cases persons experiencing a brain dysfunction may display marked changes in personality. They may become very moody and emotional and lose impulse control or social judgment. Temper outbursts are very common, and at times the organic personality syndrome is reflected in a marked apathy and lack of interest. Most commonly tumors, brain injury, or stroke are the factors associated with personality change.

Intoxication. As the name implies, this is an organic syndrome involving disturbances of perception, wakefulness, thinking, attention, judgment, or emotional control due to the ingestion of some substance into the central nervous system, most commonly, of course, either alcohol or other drugs. DSM III identifies intoxication as a problem only when it is associated with such maladaptive behavior as fighting and impaired judgment or interference with occupational functioning. Thus, presumably, mild social drinking that does not result in maladaptive behavior would not be defined as intoxication.

Withdrawal. If someone has previously used drugs or alcohol habitually to induce a state of intoxication, stopping the use of that substance or reducing it dramatically may produce the organic brain syndrome described as withdrawal. Most commonly withdrawal is characterized by anxiety, restlessness, irritability, insomnia, and impaired attention. Usually this pattern of behavior is self-limiting and occurs over a few days or several weeks at most.

Seizures

Few experiences are as emotionally taxing as observing an epileptic display a generalized convulsive seizure. In fact, the most severe of these has been termed *grand mal*, which in medieval French literally means *great illness*. During a grand mal seizure the person will lose consciousness and fall to the ground. (This has lead to one of the lay names for epilepsy, the *falling sickness*.) Immediately thereafter, breathing stops and the person's body becomes very rigid as the arms become flexed, the legs outstretched, and the fists clench during strong muscular contractions. This is known as the *tonic stage,* which lasts for as long as 60 seconds. This is then followed by a *clonic stage,* which lasts about another minute, in which violent, rapidly repeating muscular jerks occur over the whole body. During this stage the person begins breathing again. As the convulsions cease, the patient remains unconscious for a short time, usually awakening to confusion, exhaustion, headaches, and a pervasive feeling of tiredness.

When the electrical activity of thousands of neurons becomes synchronized, their summated response forms the basis of epileptic activity in the brain. When the electrical activity of the brain is recorded from the scalp by electrodes, epileptic firing of cells in the brain may be seen as an EEG spike. A clinical seizure occurs when these discharging epileptic neurons recruit many additional neighboring neurons.

A person is said to have epilepsy when the seizures are recurrent. There is a great deal of disagreement about the actual incidence of epilepsy. However, a well-designed study by Kurland (1959/1960) suggests that the overall incidence is 3.65 per 1,000 people, excluding children with benign febrile convulsions—an epileptic event occurring with fever. After the fever has been brought under control, the epileptic activity will disappear within one week. Although seizure disorders can occur at any age, the incidence is higher in children and the elderly. Within the elderly population, one of the major causes of seizures is an imbalance in the blood chemistry of glucose, calcium, or sodium (Lubar & Deering, 1981).

Seizures can be classified in a number of ways. If the abnormal discharge remains relatively localized, then the seizure will be partial or focal. But when the abnormal discharge becomes widespread throughout the brain, a generalized seizure like the one described above occurs. There are two general types of generalized seizures: convulsive and nonconvulsive. A convulsion is a violent spasm or series of jerkings of various parts of the body. Nonconvulsive seizures are presumably similar in origin to convulsive seizures; however, there is no involvement of the neurons that control movements (motor neurons), so the patient shows only a loss of consciousness. Actually there are many types of seizures that have quite different clinical signs. Although most seizures can be classified into partial or generalized, Table 12-2 illuminates the variability of seizure disorders.

As you will notice in Table 12-2, there are many seizure types characterized by psychological changes. For example, patients with partial seizures may experience amnesia or hallucinations. In addition, seizures may appear as constant laughing, crying, or speechlessness. Some investigators have argued that some epileptics show personality and behavior changes that persist between seizures. However, the data to support this contention are inconclusive (Hermann & Whitman, 1984). Nevertheless, it is clear that when diagnosing an individual who shows signs of mental changes that are thought to be organic in nature, it is important to evaluate the possibility that an underlying seizure disorder is present.

The causes of various types of seizure disorders are diverse. Practically all the causes of organic brain disorders that we have mentioned can cause seizures as well. In fact, anyone might show epileptic symptoms if his or her threshold for abnormal brain activity were lowered sufficiently by various stresses such as drugs or poisonous foods.

Compared to many other organic brain disorders, the treatment of epilepsy is further

TABLE 12-2
Seizure Classification

International Classification	Synonym	Seizure Signs
I. Partial (focal) seizures		
A. Elementary symptomatology	Focal motor, focal sensory, Jacksonian, adversive	Simple motor or sensory changes
B. Complex symptomatology	Temporal lobe, psychomotor	Impaired consciousness or memory, automatisms, hallucinations
C. Secondarily generalized		Aura prior to loss of consciousness
II. Generalized seizures		
A. Nonconvulsive		
1. Simple absence with "typical" EEG pattern	Petit mal, absence	Impairment of consciousness alone
2. Astatic	Minor motor	Drop attacks
3. Akinetic		Motor arrest
4. Atonic		Sagging
B. Convulsive		
1. Myoclonic		Shocklike movement of large muscle groups
2. Tonic	Grand mal	Sustained flexor or extensor posture
3. Clonic	Grand mal	Alternating contraction of agonists and antagonists
4. Tonic-clonic	Grand mal	
III. Unusual seizure types		
Cursive seizures (running)		
Gelastic seizures (laughing)		
Acquired aphasia		
Headache		
Abdominal pain		
Orgasm		
Reflex epilepsy		
Seizures induced by a variety of sensory stimuli (e.g., light, pattern, reading, writing, music, eating)		

Source: From Lubar & Deering, 1981.

advanced. If the cause of seizures is known, in most cases it is possible to keep the seizures under control or to cure them altogether. For example, if the cause is related to video games, removing this aggravating cause will alleviate the seizures. Even in many instances where no precipitating factor can be discerned, there are a number of different antiepileptic drugs that have rather specific indications for the treatment of seizures. In severe cases that do not respond to antiepileptic drugs, neurosurgery is performed to remove either the epileptic tissue or the connections to and from the epileptic brain areas.

Recently it has been possible for some epileptic patients to use behavioral techniques to control their seizures. Using biofeedback

VIDEO GAMES AND SEIZURES

Perhaps the most bizarre causes of seizures occur in the case of reflex seizures, which are triggered by a variety of sensory stimuli such as music, writing, or various light patterns. Along with the present excitement of video games, which have transformed many a television set into a battleground of alien invasions, have come a number of reports of cases in which seizures were induced by playing video games. Consider the case of a 14-year-old boy whose mother reported that her son experienced a generalized seizure while playing a video game. The patient was such a devoted fan of video games that he "challenged himself" by playing a different game, during which he had another seizure. The second seizure occurred after he was treated with phenobarbital, a barbiturate drug that usually lowers the seizure threshold. Notably, he has stopped playing video games and has not had another seizure (Glista, Frank, & Tracy, 1983).

In another case a 15-year-old boy was playing a video game, after which he felt weak, experienced vision loss, collapsed, and had a generalized seizure. Neurological examinations were normal after the incidents in both cases. It is probable that the flash frequency or the rapid sequencing of various colored lights was responsible for the seizure activity in these individuals. This phenomenon might be similar to the seizures reported in children who have had such episodes after watching television sets that malfunctioned and produced flickering lights. These cases do not suggest that video games are hazardous to healthy, nonseizure prone individuals. They do, however, suggest that persons who have experienced seizures should probably refrain from playing video games.

techniques, epileptics have been trained to recognize epileptic brain wave patterns and suppress them. Consider the 23-year-old white female patient of Sturman and Friar (1972) with a long-term seizure disorder. She had nocturnal generalized seizures, at a rate of once or twice a month, with convulsions and loss of consciousness, even though she was taking anticonvulsant medication. These investigators trained her to produce seizure-suppressing brain wave activity that was recorded with scalp electrodes over the sensorimotor strip of her cortex. This patient showed a rapid decrease in seizures shortly after training was initiated; these benefits persisted for the duration of the study.

From our discussion of the organic mental disorders, it is evident that many of the patterns of behavior associated with brain dysfunction resemble the functional disorders we have described in previous chapters. It is important to keep in mind that the distinguishing feature of the organic brain syndromes is the clear evidence of some underlying brain dysfunction. However, in the broadest sense, most behavior, in one way or another, is mediated by brain function. In the next part of the chapter we will present an overview of mental retardation. We will see that many genetic and organic factors have been implicated in the cognitive impairments reflected in subaverage intelligence.

At the same time we will emphasize the multidimensional features of retardation, the many influences on intellectual functioning, and some of the recent steps that have been taken to prevent and remediate mental retardation.

MENTAL RETARDATION

A Brief History

Perhaps the earliest written reference to mental retardation is the Papyrus of Thebes (1552 B.C.), which includes a discussion of the treatment of individuals with limited intellectual capacities (Repp & Deitz, 1983). In ancient Greece and Rome the mentally retarded were scorned, persecuted, used as slaves, or kept for the amusement of the rich. They were generally viewed as a burden to society, and parents frequently murdered their retarded children. With the advent of Christianity, some efforts were made to provide care for the mentally retarded. During the Middle Ages the retarded were housed in group settings in some societies, while they were abused and shunned in other societies. During this period Henry II of England recorded what is considered the first definition of mental retardation: he described retarded individuals as "natural fools" and made them wards of the king. The 19th century witnessed the first organized efforts to house and educate the mentally retarded. However, until the 20th century, the moralistic idea prevailed that retardation was a punishment from God.

Attitudes toward mental retardation have changed dramatically over the past 25 years. Of particular importance has been the emergence of legal rights for mentally retarded individuals. One of the hallmarks of change was the acknowledgement by President Kennedy that he had a retarded sister; this was followed by the establishment of a presidential panel to make recommendations for improvements in services to the mentally retarded. The recommendations of the panel as well as the efforts of lobbying groups and concerned individuals fostered the passage of laws that established community- and university-affiliated mental retardation research centers. Rehabilitation and education programs for handicapped children also multiplied. Society's positive response to the mentally retarded is reflected in concepts such as normalization and least restrictive environment. These terms and other related concepts are explained in Table 12-3.

Definition and Classification

It is estimated that about 3 percent of the population are mentally retarded (President's Commission on Mental Retardation, 1972). This means that about 7 million persons in the United States would be classified as mentally retarded. DSM III defines mental retardation as follows on the basis of criteria from the American Association on Mental Deficiency: (1) significantly subaverage intellectual functioning; (2) associated impairments in adaptive behavior; and (3) onset before age 18 (American Psychiatric Association, 1980). Significantly subaverage intellectual functioning refers to an IQ below 70 on the basis of an IQ test. Adaptive behavior refers to the effectiveness with which a person meets standards of independence and social responsibility expected of his or her age and cultural group. It is important to note that before a diagnosis of mental retardation can be made, all three of the criteria must be present.

DSM III describes four categories of mental retardation: mild, moderate, severe, and profound. (See Table 12-4.) The borderline category, with IQs between 70 and 84, is no longer considered a category of mental retardation. Mild mental retardation is by far the

TABLE 12-3
New Terms and Concepts in Common Use

Term	Concept	Application
Normalization	Being treated like everyone else.	Home-like environments; same daily activities; little regimentation.
Developmental model	Promote normal development.	Programs foster developmental progress; services facilitate developmental milestones; optimistic view of potential.
Interdisciplinary	Role sharing of professionals.	Collaboration in diagnosis and treatment.
Transdisciplinary	Overlap of disciplinary interests.	Synthesis of professional roles in offering treatment.
Least restrictive environment	Live and receive treatment in normal settings.	Education in public schools in regular classes, if possible; live in community settings.

Source: From "Trends in Service Delivery and Treatment of the Mentally Retarded" by H. J. Cohen, 1982, *Pediatric Annals, 11,* p. 459.

largest category, accounting for more than 80 percent of the retarded population. Children in this group have IQs between 50 and 70. Very few individuals in this category are institutionalized, and these children are termed *educable.* When educable children are identified by the school, they are often placed in classes geared to their special needs. These classes are usually smaller, provide specially trained teachers, and allow the child to learn at his or her own pace.

Mildly retarded children are described as having little motor impairment and in many respects being indistinguishable from normal children until middle childhood or later. Academically, they may be expected to reach about a sixth-grade level. As adults, they are likely to provide at least minimal support for themselves in jobs that are not too complex or intellectually demanding.

Children in the next category, moderate mental retardation, are usually termed *trainable.* They have IQs between 35 and 50. Individuals in this category account for about 12 percent of the mentally retarded population. Thus about 95 percent of retarded individuals fall into either the mild or moderate mental retardation categories. Moderately retarded children may be able to acquire language skills, but they often lack social skills, a deficit that is evident even during the preschool years. Physical deformities may be present. Training is often done in special schools that emphasize practical, simple skills. As adults, moderately retarded individuals are often able to work in sheltered workshop settings and usually require close supervision.

Children considered severely mentally retarded have IQs between 25 and 35. In the past they were often referred to as *imbeciles.* Many of these children suffer genetic abnormalities. DSM III describes severely retarded children as having poor motor development and little or no speech during the preschool years. They may learn to talk during middle childhood. Training usually centers around self-care skills; many severely retarded individuals spend much of their lives in institutions.

Children classified as profoundly retarded have IQs less than 20. Such individuals account for only about 1 percent of the mentally

TABLE 12–4
DSM III Diagnostic Categories of Mental Retardation Based on IQ Score, Parallel Educational Terms, and Expected Level of Intellectual, Vocational, and Social Functioning

IQ	DSM III Diagnosis	Educational Terms	Preschool Age 0–5 Maturation and Development	School Age 6–20 Training and Education
75				
70				
65	Mild retardation	Educable	Able to develop social and communication skills; often not distinguished from normal until later age.	Able to learn academic skills up to about 6th grade level by late teens can be guided toward social conformity.
60				
55				
50				
45	Moderate retardation	Trainable	Can talk or learn to communicate; fair motor development; can be managed with moderate supervision.	Can profit from training in social and occupational skills; unlikely to progress beyond 2nd grade level in academic skills.
40				
35	Severe retardation		Poor motor development; minimal speech; few self-help or communication skills.	Can learn to communicate; can be trained in basic health habits.
30				
25				
Below 25	Profound retardation	Custodial	Minimal capacity for sensorimotor functioning; needs nursing care.	Some motor development present; may acquire minimal self-help skills.

retarded population. During the preschool years these children show minimal sensorimotor functioning. Although further motor development may occur during later childhood, many of these children are unable to learn self-care skills. Serious physical disabilities are common, and the life expectancies of these children are short. For those profoundly retarded who survive into adulthood, institutionalization and extensive care are required.

Explanations

Mental retardation may be caused by a wide range of factors acting alone or in combination with one another. Although as many as 300 known or suspected causes have been identified, these account for only about 25 percent of mental retardation cases (Dunn, 1973; Love, 1973). In the remaining 75 percent of cases, which are termed *cultural-familial retardation,* the causes remain a mystery. We will first discuss some of the more clearly identified genetic and environmental factors that produce mental retardation. We will then discuss those cases of retardation where no etiology can be identified. In conclusion, we will review efforts at prevention and remediation.

Chromosomal Abnormalities

Chromosomal abnormalities that produce retardation can be about equally divided between those that are sex-linked (sex chromosome abnormalities) and those that are not sex-linked (autosomal abnormalities). The abnormality may involve the presence of too many or too few chromosomes, or an abnormal chromosome pattern. About 90 percent of fetuses with chromosomal abnormalities are spontaneously aborted. However, about one in every 20,000 live-born infants has some type of chromosomal abnormality (Holmes et al., 1972).

Perhaps the best known of the autosomal variety of chromosomal disorders that produce mental retardation is *Down's syndrome* or *mongolism.* Most instances of Down's syndrome are attributable to the presence of extra genetic material. Instead of the normal 46 chromosomes in each cell body, a child with Down's syndrome typically has an extra chromosome, creating a total of 47. Since the 21st pair of chromosomes contains the extra or third chromosome, the condition is sometimes called *trisomy 21.*

Among the forms of mental retardation due to known organic causes, Down's syndrome occurs most frequently. Approximately one child in every 640 births has Down's syndrome (Smith & Wilson, 1973). The condition occurs more frequently in boys than in girls, and appears unrelated to race, ethnic background, or socioeconomic class. Women over 35 years of age are at higher risk for having a baby with Down's syndrome (Somasundarum & Papakumari, 1981). While the exact mechanism has not been identified, the chromosomal abnormality is thought to result from faulty intrauterine conditions that occur more frequently in older women. Recent research suggests that the condition does not originate exclusively in the mother; in about 20 to 25 percent of cases, it originates in the father's sperm. Additionally, higher risk of producing a Down's syndrome child occurs for fathers 41 years of age or older (Abroms & Bennett, 1983).

Down's syndrome children are usually mildly to severely retarded, and account for about 15 percent of the institutionally retarded (Love, 1973). Characteristic physical features include obliquely slanted eyes, a broad bridge of the nose, a small mouth, and small, square hands with a single crease running across the palm. Down's syndrome children exhibit both a slower rate of mental and language development and difficulty in learning complex or advanced skills. Life expectancy for those with Down's syndrome is shortened by a variety of physical illnesses and defects. Congenital heart disease, frequently associated with Down's syndrome, represents a clear example of one such factor.

Klinefelter's syndrome is another disorder caused by chromosomal abnormality. This disorder is the result of a sex chromosome abnormality, and occurs only in males. Those with Klinefelter's syndrome have an extra X chromosome, usually of the XXY form, but sometimes of the XXXXXY form in the sex chromosome. About 25 percent of those with Klinefelter's syndrome are mentally retarded. Among these, mild mental retardation usually occurs in XXY males; more severe retardation occurs in males with a higher number of X chromosomes. Characteristics of Klinefelter's syndrome include a tall, rather effeminate body build, sterility, small testes, breast enlargement (after puberty) and reduced facial and body hair.

Turner's syndrome is another sex-linked chromosomal disorder. Although it may occur in males, it is most common in females. Approximately 20 percent of those with Turner's syndrome are mentally retarded. Females with this disorder have only 45 chromosomes instead of the usual 46. Physical characteristics include the absence of secondary sexual development, short stature, webbing of the neck, protuding ears, and a flat nasal bridge.

The *fragile X syndrome* is perhaps the most recent sex-linked abnormality to be associated with mental retardation. Although research on this syndrome is just beginning, retardation is believed to result from a sex-linked recessive gene. The syndrome takes its name from a fragile site that appears as a break on the X chromosome. Mental retardation is produced more frequently in the male members of affected families. Some theorize that the fragile X syndrome may account for the higher incidence of male mental retarda-

tion, and perhaps a substantial proportion of all mental retardation (Lehrke, 1972). Males with fragile X-linked mental retardation are likely to have low IQs (30 to 40), enlarged testicular volumes, repetitive speech patterns, and characteristic facial features that include protuding jaws and large ears (Carpenter, Leichtman, & Burhan, 1982).

Abnormalities of Amino Acid Metabolism

Phenylketonuria (PKU) is a metabolic disorder transmitted by an autosomal recessive gene. The PKU infant lacks a liver enzyme needed to control the build-up of phenylalanine (an amino acid found in protein food). The resulting excess of phenylalanine in the bloodstream causes brain damage and mental retardation. This condition affects about one in 15,000 children in this country.

PKU infants seem normal at first. However, if the disorder is undetected, they develop profound retardation within about six months after birth. In addition to retardation, characteristics of PKU include hyperactivity, bizarre body movements, and severe temper outbursts. Urinalysis and compulsory blood tests at birth have served as screening devices to provide early detection of infants with PKU. Early detection of the condition is extremely important since a diet restricted in foods containing phenylalanine during the first three months of life enhances the likelihood of normal development (Menolascino & Egger, 1978).

Tay-Sachs disease is another metabolic disorder that results from a recessive gene. Children with Tay-Sachs disease are unable to adequately metabolize fatty compounds needed for the development of the central nervous system. Offspring of Eastern European Jewish ancestry account for a high proportion of this disorder, representing 50 to 60 percent of cases (Carter, 1970). Infants with Tay-Sachs disease appear normal during the early months of life. Signs of the disorder appear gradually between 4 and 8 months of age when these infants display sensitivity to noise, tremors, listlessness, and decreased muscle development. Thereafter, deterioration is progressive with death usually occurring between two and four years of age. Blood tests to detect the presence of the recessive gene known to produce Tay-Sach's disease can be performed for prospective parents. If both parents show evidence of the recessive gene, an amniocentesis can be performed to determine if the fetus will have the disorder. Such a procedure involves the insertion of a hollow needle through the abdominal wall and uterus of the expectant mother so that fluid can be withdrawn from the amniotic sac and analyzed. If only one parent carries the recessive gene, the child may also have the recessive gene, but will not develop the disorder.

Infections and Toxic Agents

Some infections contracted by the mother during pregnancy as well as some that the child may contract postnatally are known to cause mental retardation. Rubella or German measles is one of the best known of the prenatal infections that result in mental retardation. The greatest damage from fetal involvement in maternal rubella is likely to occur in the first trimester of pregnancy (Barlow, 1978). Infection occurring later in the pregnancy is likely to result in less serious abnormality. The infection can be prevented entirely by maternal immunization prior to the beginning of pregnancy. No treatment of the active infection is available, and the therapeutic approach often considered most appropriate is termination of the pregnancy (Barlow, 1978).

A mother who has syphilis may also infect the fetus, resulting in mental retardation and a number of other disorders (deafness, blindness) in the newborn. The greatest risk of fetal syphilis infection occurs after the fourth month of pregnancy in mothers who have recently contracted syphilis (Holmes et al., 1972). With the advent of penicillin, the incidence of syphilis declined. Unfortunately, the incidence of syphilis has been increasing in recent years, once more posing a threat to the child.

Postnatal infections such as encephalitis (viral infection of the brain) and meningitis (infection of the membrane covering the brain) may produce mental retardation and brain damage in about 10 to 20 percent of children who experience such infections (Koch, 1971; Telford & Sawrey, 1977). The degree of mental retardation resulting from meningitis may vary from severe retardation to mild changes noticeable only in schoolwork. Encephalitis is the term that covers a number of disorders that produce inflammation of the central nervous system. Mental retardation and personality change are the most common residual effects (Menolascino & Egger, 1978).

A number of toxic substances such as lead, carbon monoxide, cleaning fluid, and so forth, may produce brain damage and retardation. The ingestion of lead by children usually occurs through the eating of old, often flaking paint. The lead interferes with the brain cell metabolism and can produce severe retardation and sometimes death.

Fetal Alcohol Syndrome

Fetal alcohol syndrome is another cause of mental retardation that occurs when the expectant mother abuses alcohol. Research indicates that the higher the alcohol abuse level of the mother, the greater the likelihood that fetal alcohol syndrome will occur, and that it will be severe. Some estimates of the prevalence of fetal alcohol syndrome are as high as

THE CASE OF JERRY

Jerry is an attractive 11-year-old who is ambulatory but nonverbal. He functioned at a normal level for nine months, at which time he drank a considerable amount of cleaning fluid that his mother had left on the kitchen table. This resulted in damage to his central nervous system. Jerry's family kept him at home for several years following the accident but institutionalized him at the age of four. This was necessitated because both parents had to work to support the family, and Jerry required intensive care. In addition, he had developed a number of bizarre behaviors, including a sudden thrusting of the heel of his palm into his mouth while harshly biting into the skin.

Jerry is fortunate in that the institution in which he lives is extremely well run. He resides in a cottage with 60 other clients. Jerry's unit has numerous specially trained personnel, including teachers, nurses, social workers, and physical therapists. He is in programmed instruction or activities from 9 AM to 11:45 AM, 1 PM to 4 PM, and 6:30 PM to 8:30 PM.

About 2 months ago a new program was implemented to decrease Jerry's biting behavior. The program involves the use of punishment and requires Jerry to brush his teeth and gums with Listerine for two minutes immediately following each episode of biting. It also involves rewarding Jerry for periods of no biting. His biting behavior began to decrease within days, and within two weeks it occurred only on an occasional basis. Jerry has not had any biting episodes for the last three weeks. The staff have started working with his parents to maintain his improved behavior at home. If his progress can be transferred to the home environment, they are eager for Jerry to rejoin the family (adapted from Repp & Deitz, p. 117).

three in every 1,000 births. Based on these figures, fetal alcohol syndrome may be the third most commonly recognized cause of mental retardation (Hanson et al., 1978). In addition to mental retardation, maternal alcohol abuse may produce abnormalities such as flattened facial features, decreased growth, and a variety of other physical defects (Clarren and Smith, 1978). The level of mental retardation occurring in fetal alcohol syndrome may range from mild to severe, and is a consequence of central nervous system damage. This syndrome can be prevented through the modification of maternal drinking habits that are compatible with normal prenatal development.

Premature Birth

Premature birth is another factor associated with higher rates of retardation (McDonald, 1964). Both the length of the pregnancy and the weight of the infant are significant factors related to the likelihood of retardation. Infants weighing less than 5 lbs., 8 oz. are termed *low birth weight infants*. The central nervous system of such infants is at greater risk than in normal weight infants. Low birth weight infants often require special postnatal care.

Trauma, Injury, and Other Causal Factors

Other events known to produce mental retardation include prenatal exposure to radiation and X rays, drugs, accidental head injuries, the trauma of birth, and blood incompatibilities. Medical advances have significantly reduced the incidence of birth trauma. However, injuries resulting in intracranial hemorrhage or insufficient oxygen do occasionally occur and may produce brain damage and mental retardation. Blood incompatibilities involve the disease fighting or Rh factors present in an individual's blood. When the mother's Rh factors do not match those of the fetus, brain damage and retardation in the fetus is likely to occur if the condition is untreated.

Environmental and Cultural-Familial Retardation

Environmental and cultural-familial retardation represents that segment of retarded individuals for whom the cause of retardation is unknown. However, individuals in this group share certain characteristics. They are likely to have IQs between 50 and 75. Frequently, there is no evidence of neurological or genetic defects (Hardy, 1965; Kushlick, 1966). It is recognized that a greater proportion of mental retardation occurs among individuals of low socioeconomic status. Children whose parents are very poor may lack adequate nutrition and medical care, and they may be raised in an environment that lacks intellectual stimulation.

Approaches to Remediation

While a few retarded children improve with medication, special diet, or therapy, the main tasks of helping seem to be education to the highest level possible and good care. The type of remedial need a child may have varies with the degree of retardation. In some cases placement in special education classes in school frees the mildly retarded child from the anxiety and pressure of the regular classroom and encourages self-paced learning. In cases of more severe retardation, behavioral techniques may be applied in either the home or an institutional setting to help the child develop self-care skills and to reduce aggressive or self-injurious behaviors such as biting or head banging. Parent training programs are used to help parents understand and use learning principles (Matson, 1983).

In recent years there has been strong trend toward avoiding the institutionalization of the mentally retarded. In the past many large institutions were the scenes of inadequate care and, in a few cases, abuse. Although treatment in large institutions has dramatically improved in the past 25 years, many feel that the mentally retarded function better in smaller, community-based settings (Suran & Rizzo, 1983).

Prevention

While it is unlikely that mental retardation can be eradicated completely, the following steps can be taken to reduce the likelihood of its occurrence and to minimize its severity: improved prenatal care, special care for premature infants, and blood tests to screen for Rh incompatibilities (Crocker, 1982). In addition, genetic counseling should be available to high-risk families, and information regarding alcohol use during pregnancy should be given to prospective mothers. The use of seat belts in cars would also lessen the chances of head injuries resulting in retardation.

Additional prevention strategies stress early identification and treatment of conditions that cause retardation. Such strategies include efforts such as the screening of infants for genetic disorders such as PKU, where the effects can be greatly minimized if the disorder is discovered early in life. Amniocentesis is another prevention strategy that is particularly useful for older mothers who run a greater risk of chromosomal disorders. Crocker suggests that if these approaches were implemented, the incidence of mental retardation could be reduced by 20 to 30 percent.

SUMMARY

The essential feature of an organic mental disorder is a permanent or temporary dysfunction of the brain that can be attributed to organic factors. The brain's inner core, or "reptilian brain," and the next layer, or "old-mammalian brain," provide self-preservation and emotional responses respectively. The "new-mammalian" brain (neocortex) is well-developed in humans. It is responsible for information processing, motor control, and the ability to think rationally.

The destruction of brain tissue, termed a lesion, usually results in behavioral disability. Recovery of function may occur as adjacent brain areas assume the functions of the damaged area. Recovery is greatest in children and diminishes with age. Traumatic brain injuries (falls, motor vehicle accidents, firearms), may produce mild injury such as a contusion, a more serious concussion, or a life-threatening cerebral laceration.

Dementia involves the deterioration of previously acquired intellectual ability and is usually accompanied by memory loss. The cortical dementing disorders may result in Alzheimer's disease or Pick's disease, while the subcortical disorders may result in Huntington's disease, Parkinson's disease, or Wilson's disease. Both cortical and subcortical disorders produce dementia; subcortical dementing disorders also produce changes in movement. Cardiovascular dementing disorders result from infarcts, areas of brain damage due to insufficient blood supply.

Delirium usually has a rapid onset, a brief duration, and may include disturbances of attention, memory, and orientation. Intoxication from the use of drugs or alcohol is considered an organic syndrome, as is withdrawal, a syndrome occurring when an individual stops or dramatically reduces the consumption of drugs or alcohol. Seizures involve the synchronized firing of thousands of neurons in the brain and may be convulsive or nonconvulsive types.

Mental retardation involves significantly subaverage intellectual functioning, associated impairments in adaptive behavior, and onset before age 18. DSM III describes four categories including mild, moderate, severe, and profound retardation. Eighty percent of mentally retarded individuals are "mildly" retarded. During adulthood they may provide minimal support for themselves in jobs that are not too complex or demanding. As intellectual functioning diminishes, language skills, self-care skills, and life expectancy decrease.

Mental retardation may be caused by a wide range of factors, acting alone or in combination. Chromosomal disorders that cause retardation include Down's syndrome, Klinefelter's syndrome, Turner's syndrome, and fragile X syndrome. Metabolic disorders such as phenylketonuria and Tay-Sachs disease, infections and toxic agents, fetal alcohol syndrome, premature birth, and injury also cause retardation. The 75 percent of retardation cases in which the causes remain a mystery are termed *cultural-familial retardation.*

There has been a strong trend toward housing the mentally retarded in small, community based settings rather than the large institutions used in the past. Efforts at prevention of retardation have focused on improved prenatal care, special care for premature infants, blood tests to screen for Rh incompatibilities, genetic counseling, and the use of automobile seatbelts to reduce head injury.

Part Five

Personality Disorders and Social Deviation

13

Personality Disorders

Overview of the Personality Disorders

Compulsive Personality
    Clinical Picture
    Childhood Origins

Histrionic Personality
    Clinical Picture
    Cognitive Style
    Childhood Origins

The Antisocial Personality
    Clinical Picture
    Theory and Research

Narcissistic Personality
    Clinical Picture
    Childhood Origins

Paranoid Personality
    Clinical Picture
    Cognitive Style
    Childhood Origins
    The Paranoid and Society

Borderline Personality
    Clinical Picture
    Childhood Origins
    Diagnostic Utility and Future Trends

Treatment

Summary

OVERVIEW OF THE PERSONALITY DISORDERS

Suppose you accidentally bump into someone while walking down the street, and you knock a package out of the person's hands. Instead of accepting your apology and offer of assistance, the person accuses you of deliberately bumping into him or her and insists that you are trying to steal the package. While it is normal to be somewhat wary when a stranger bumps you on the street, clearly the person's suspicions are exaggerated and inappropriate to the situation. If we found out that this person generally reacted in such an overly suspicious manner, then we would suspect that a *personality disorder* is present.

However, distinguishing between normal variations in personality and personality disorders is not always easy. In fact, of all the psychiatric syndromes personality disorders are historically the least reliably diagnosed. DSM III states that personality disorder should only be diagnosed when personality traits are "inflexible and maladaptive and cause either significant impairment in social or occupational functioning or subjective distress."

This definition of personality disorders suggests that the traits are pervasive in the life experience of the individual. But these traits are not necessarily associated with ineffective social functioning or the experience of distress. In fact, as we shall see, some of these characteristics are highly adaptive in certain settings. For example, in some cases suspiciousness may actually allow the person to be vigilant for a real potential threat, while certain compulsive patterns of behavior may actually be very useful in a setting where order and organization are desirable characteristics. Perhaps more than most patterns of behavior described in this book, whether a person with a personality disorder will be seen as abnormal depends heavily on the context in which the behavior occurs (Price & Bouffard, 1974). Thus the suspiciousness of the paranoid personality may be a liability in a cooperative work group, but a useful trait in a private investigator.

Another important aspect of our understanding of personality disorders is that they need to be distinguished from episodes of behavioral disruption. The diagnosis of personality disorder should be made only when the characteristics are typical of the individual's long-term functioning rather than limited to discrete episodes. Thus the personality disorders are to be distinguished from acute episodes. They are long-standing patterns of behavior that may or may not bring the person into conflict with others or produce distress; depending upon the demands, expectations, and challenges of the person's environment.

Even when persons with a personality disorder experience impairment in their social or occupational functioning, they may feel comfortable with the very patterns of behavior that are causing the difficulties. Acceptance of the exaggerated traits on the part of these persons indicates that they are *ego-syntonic,* that is, such traits are experienced as integral and desirable aspects of the self. In contrast, most other psychological disorders are experienced as *ego-dystonic,* that is, as alien and undesirable. Because a personality disorder is experienced as ego-syntonic, the person is often not motivated to change and does not voluntarily seek treatment.

On the other hand, persons with personality disorders may express distress or dissatisfaction with their lives because of negative reactions their behavior elicits in other people. Thus expressions of anxiety, depression, or moodiness may actually indicate the unhappiness these people feel with others' negative reactions to their behavior. However, instead of accepting responsibility for evoking unfavorable reactions in others, persons with personality disorders are more likely to blame the selfishness and hostility of those around them.

In Table 13–1 the major types of personality disorders described in DSM III are listed. DSM III has grouped these disorders into three clusters—eccentric, erratic, and fearful—to reflect some general similarities that exist among the disorders. However, there is as yet no empirical support for this method of classification. Consequently, in the chapter we will consider each disorder separately. We should also note that very little research is available on many of these disorders. Moreover, recent research confirms that personality disorders are still among the least reliably diagnosed diagnostic categories. DSM III, for example, reports reliability correlations ranging from .56 to .65. In the following pages we will discuss six of these personality disorders in more detail.

TABLE 13–1
The DSM III Classification of Personality Disorders

Eccentric Cluster

Paranoid Personality:
A pervasive and long-standing suspiciousness and mistrust of people in general; individuals with this disorder are hypersensitive and easily slighted; they continually scan the environment for clues that validate their original prejudicial ideas, attitudes, or biases; often their emotional experience is restricted.

Introverted Personality:
A defect in the capacity to form social relationships; introversion and bland or constricted affect.

Schizotypal Personality:
Various oddities of thinking, perception, communication, and behavior; peculiarities in communication with concepts expressed unclearly or oddly.

Erratic Cluster

Histrionic Personality:
Behavior that is overly reactive, intensely expressed, and perceived by others as shallow, superficial, or insincere; often associated with disturbed interpersonal relationships.

Narcissistic Personality:
Grandiose sense of self-importance or uniqueness; preoccupation with fantasies of unlimited success; exhibitionistic needs for constant attention and admiration.

Antisocial Personality:
History of continuous and chronic antisocial behavior in which the rights of others are violated; onset before age 15; failure to sustain good job performance; lying, stealing, fighting, truancy in childhood.

Borderline Personality:
Instability in various areas of life, including interpersonal relationships, behavior, mood, and self-image; interpersonal relationships are often tense and unstable with marked shifts of attitude over time.

Fearful Cluster

Avoidant Personality:
Hypersensitivity to rejection; unwillingness to enter into relationships unless given an unusually strong guarantee of uncritical acceptance; social withdrawal, yet a desire for attention and acceptance.

TABLE 13-1 (*concluded*)

Compulsive Personality:
Restricted ability to express warm and tender emotions; preoccupation with matters of rules, order, organization, efficiency, and detail; excess devotion to work and productivity to the exclusion of pleasure; compulsive personalities are often indecisive.

Passive-Aggressive Personality:
Resistance to demand for adequate activity or performance in both occupational and social areas of functioning; resistance is not expressed directly; as a consequence, pervasive or long-standing social or occupational ineffectiveness often result.

COMPULSIVE PERSONALITY

Clinical Picture

Each of us has known people who organize their world with such meticulous care that the arrangement seemed almost too perfect. For example, these people might carefully map out their day to account for every single minute. Moments of relaxation, instead of being discovered throughout the day, are mechanically structured into the daily schedule. What is striking about such persons is their complete lack of spontaneity. They thrive on order and routine and avoid ambiguity at all costs.

DSM III describes the striving for perfection and preoccupation with organization as primary characteristics of the *compulsive personality*. Other prominent characteristics include a restricted ability to express warm and tender emotions, an excessive devotion to work at the expense of pleasure, and indecisiveness. Compulsive personalities are rigid and inflexible in their approach to life. They prefer facts to emotions and logic to intuition. Moreover, their concern with facts and details often leaves them unable to grasp the larger picture. For example, the compulsive student may be so intent on turning in a perfect paper that he or she misses the deadline. Decisions are a nightmare for such people as

they are desperately afraid of making a mistake and doing the wrong thing.

Not surprisingly, compulsive personalities generally experience difficulties in relations with others. Their rigidity and inflexibility, which to them are a source of great pride, cause others to see them as stubborn and oppositional. Moreover, their discomfort with emotions results in relations that are stiff and superficial.

Compulsive persons often function better in the work environment than in other settings. In fact, the compulsive personality may excel in occupations such as accounting that demand orderliness and attention to detail. Thus the compulsive personality pattern can be a social asset or a major handicap, depending on the situation or task confronting the individual.

Before examining the origins of the compulsive personality it is important to distinguish this disorder from the obsessive-compulsive disorder discussed in Chapter 7. Pollak (1979) notes that in an obsessive-compulsive disorder the person suffers from the persistent intrusion of undesired thoughts and actions. Attempts to stop these intrusions often fail, as they result in great anxiety and distress. The compulsive personality, in contrast, experiences his or her behavior as ego-syntonic. In other words, the compulsive personality regards his or her preoccupation with order and routine as desirable.

Childhood Origins

The determinants of compulsive personality are not yet well understood, but it is believed that family background plays a significant role. Although no evidence for a specific genetic predisposition exists, it may be that a general constitutional predisposition or hypersensitivity creates a vulnerability in the case of compulsive personality. Indeed, Rachman and Hodgson (1980) believe that

The traits of the compulsive personality are highly valued in some settings and illustrate that the "fit" between a personality characteristic and the demands of a setting may be critical in understanding human adaptation. (Ellis Herwig/Stock, Boston, Inc.)

the compulsive personality is a person who is at risk to develop the disorder because of a constitutional predisposition or vulnerability to criticism. If the person has this sensitivity, and if the family environment is pervaded by parental overconcern and overcontrol, two necessary conditions for the development of compulsive personality exist.

If the child is overprotected, he or she may develop a fearfulness about the world and be relatively ineffective at coping. Both through modeling from compulsive parents and through a developing sense of fearfulness, a concern for regularity and order will develop. Similarly, if the parents are overly critical and set extremely high standards, the child will increasingly be concerned about avoiding errors and become overly me-

ticulous in his or her own behavior. Rachman and Hodgson argue that this results in compulsions to check and recheck the details of one's work or life.

Psychodynamic theory views the compulsive personality as continuously involved in a conflict between obedience and defiance (Storr, 1980). The origins of this conflict are traced to the child's early struggles for control with his or her mother. One major battleground is the toilet training of the child. If the mother's training is too rigid and punitive, the child will not develop a sense of mastery or autonomy. Instead, the child learns to forgo his or her desires to avoid parental punishment and disapproval. MacKinnon and Michels (1971) argue that although outwardly obedient to gain parental approval, the child secretly rages at having to relinquish his desires and submit to parental authority. Thus, underlying the compulsive personality's rigid and unemotional exterior are strong feelings of anger and defiance. The hypothesized conflict between obedience and defiance may explain glaring inconsistencies in the behavior of some compulsive personalities. While in most areas of their lives they are preoccupied with order and organization, in some areas they are just the opposite—messy and disorganized. This inconsistency is captured in Rachman and Hodgson's's description of the home environments of some compulsive persons:

After the first dozen or so visits, our capacity for being surprised was greatly reduced. We learned to expect that the homes of compulsive cleaners would contain a bizarre mixture of excessively clean areas and indescribably dirty parts as well. In the same house, the lavatory might be brightly clean and strongly disinfected while parts of the kitchen were caked with month-old food remains. (Incidentally, this particular condition is often encountered in the patients themselves—a compulsive cleaner who washes her hands 200 times per day may leave her legs and feet unwashed for months and wear the same dirty underwear for weeks on end.) (Rachman & Hodgson, 1980, p. 65).

HISTRIONIC PERSONALITY

Histrionic personality is a relatively common personality disorder that is diagnosed far more frequently in women than in men. Until recently it was known as the *hysterical personality*.

Clinical Picture

The essence of the histrionic personality is an overly dramatic and expressive approach to life. Experiences are greatly exaggerated so that minor setbacks become major catastrophes and trivial disagreements become terrible fights. There is a constant drawing of attention to the self as the histrionic personality thrives on others' interest and concern. In addition, such persons are easily bored and constantly crave activity and excitement.

Histrionic personalities often draw attention to themselves through seductive and exhibitionistic behavior. Despite their sexual provocations, these people are often afraid of sexual relations. Initially, others are impressed by their expressivity and liveliness. However, it soon becomes clear that the histrionic personalities are unable to go beyond their superficial presentation and lack insight into their behavior. Thus the histrionic personality has difficulty establishing and maintaining intimate relations. The following case illustrates all of these characteristics:

A 30-year-old cocktail waitress sought treatment after breaking up her relationship with her 50-year-old boyfriend. Although initially she was tearful and suicidal, she brightened up within the first session and became animated and coquettish with the male interviewer. During the intake evaluation interviews she was always attractively and seductively dressed, wore carefully applied facial makeup, and crossed her legs in a revealing fashion. She related her story with dramatic inflections and seemed very concerned with the impression she was making on the interviewer. Although she often cried during sessions, her grief appeared to be without depth and mainly for effect. Several times she asked that the next appointment be changed to accommodate her plans; and when this was not possible, she became furious and talked of how "doctors have no concern for their patients." The patient's history reveals that she is frequently the life of the party and has no problem making friends, although she seems to lose them just as easily and feels lonely most of the time. People apparently accuse her of being selfish, immature, and unreliable. She is often late for appointments; borrows money, which she rarely returns; and breaks dates on impulse or if someone more attractive turns up. She is competitive with and jealous of other women, believes that they are catty and untrustworthy, and is known for being particularly seductive with her friends' boyfriends. (Spitzer, Skodol, Gibbon, & Williams, 1981, p. 265).

This case also illustrates the egocentricism and manipulativeness of the histrionic personality. Suicide gestures or threats are possible as the person attempts to manipulate others into taking care of him or her. Often the person will enact the role of victim and demand repeated assurance of his or her partner's continued love and support.

Although the histrionic personality's emotionality is often described as shallow or without depth, this description is not completely accurate. Instead, it is more accurate to say that the histrionic person's emotions are intense but fleeting. That is, the person's emotional reaction is very intense, but quickly dissipates as the evoking stimulus becomes less salient. For example, the histrionic personality may become extremely angry and upset when receiving criticism, but within a few minutes the event is out of the person's mind.

Cognitive Style

The histrionic person's cognitive style is just the opposite of the compulsive personality's. Whereas the compulsive person is so concerned with facts and details that he or she may miss the broader picture, the histrionic personality is interested only in the global impression and actively dislikes facts and figures. This global cognitive style serves a defensive purpose since it prevents the histrionic person from confronting painful facts or events. Moreover, Baumbacher and Amini (1981) note that the person's exaggeration may enlarge the impact of events to such an absurd degree that they appear unbelievable, and therefore can be discounted.

Shapiro (1965) describes the histrionic's global but relatively diffuse cognition as *impressionistic,* and lists a number of manifestations of this cognitive style. For example, there is a marked lack of concentration. Rather than investing the effort to solve a problem systematically, the histrionic person relies on inspired guesses or hunches. Not surprisingly, the histrionic person shows little intellectual curiosity and instead often settles for the obvious.

A second manifestation of this cognitive style is the histrionic person's impressionability. The histrionic person is highly suggestible and easily influenced by passing trends or fads. Shapiro attributes this quality to the person's relative lack of focused attention leading to distractibility and increased susceptibility to transient influences. Thus histrionic personalities are likely to be overrepresented among adherents to, among other things, revolutionary diets and trendy psychotherapies.

According to Shapiro, a consequence of the histrionic personality's cognitive style is a remarkable deficiency in factual knowledge. Instead of accumulating facts, the histrionic personality accumulates impressions. These impressions have no cognitive focus or anchor; instead, events and memories are associated in a loose, disjointed fashion. The result is a marked lack of knowledge, which results in the histrionic personality's familiar appearance of innocence or naiveté.

Childhood Origins

Social Learning Perspective. The learning perspective focuses on the differential reinforcement histories of boys and girls in our society. Whereas males are generally encouraged to be assertive and independent, females are often rewarded for passive and dependent behavior. Moreover, Halleck (1967) notes that women have been discouraged from directly expressing anger or hostility. Instead of expressing their anger, they learn to gain others' attention and support through the expression of dependent needs. When the expression of these needs is reinforced, the woman learns to exaggerate and dramatize her sense of helplessness and dependency. An image of irresponsibility develops and is maintained by her ability to induce others into taking care of her.

Halleck further notes that sexuality is an accepted means by which women in our society are allowed to initiate and control relationships. At an early age the future histrionic may pick up on and exaggerate these socially reinforced means of control and influence. For example, the future histrionic personality is typified in the little girl who has learned that through coy, often seductive, behavior she can gain favors from her father. We often hear this type of father-daughter relationship called "daddy's little girl" or "daddy's little princess." Note that the reliance on flirtation as a method of influence and control means that men, as the providers of rewards, are valued and sought after, while women are devalued and perceived as rivals. Thus through differential reinforcement women in our society may learn to look to others and not themselves for mastery and rewards. The result may be an interpersonal style characterized by seductiveness, exaggeration, and self-dramatization as the person employs socially sanctioned methods of influencing and controlling others.

Psychodynamic Perspective. According to the psychodynamic view, the histrionic personality is the developmentally most advanced of the various personality disorders. Whereas the other disorders predominantly involve developmentally earlier conflicts and concerns, the histrionic personality reflects fixation at the phallic stage of psychosexual development.

Recall that the Oedipal conflict refers to the child's unconscious wish to murder the same-sexed parent and replace him or her as the lover of the parent of the opposite sex. If the Oedipal crisis is adequately resolved, the child relinquishes his incestuous love for the opposite-sex parent and identifies with the same-sex parent. Difficulties at this phase of psychosexual development mean that the child never completely relinquishes the incestuous object. However, these incestuous desires are too threatening to be retained in consciousness and therefore must be repressed (Baumbacher & Amini, 1981). Moreover, the person's aggressive feelings toward the same-sex parent must also be repressed in order to retain that parent's love. Thus repression is the trademark of the histrionic personality and accounts for the person's impressionistic cognitive style.

The failure to relinquish the incestuous love object and the subsequent repression make adult sexuality threatening to the histrionic personality. Any arousal of sexual feelings is threatening because the repressed incestuous desires are thereby too close to being awakened. Thus, while outwardly seductive, the histrionic personality shies away from actual sexual involvement. In fact, the histrionic's emotional lability and seductiveness, both of which have a childlike quality, serve as defenses against the experiences of true intimacy.

Historical and Cultural Perspective. Krohn (1978) raises the intriguing idea that, while the underlying dynamics remain constant, the overt manifestations of the histrionic personality reflect the dominant themes of a particular culture. Specifically, Krohn argues that the histrionic personality enacts dominant current cultural identities in order to promote a "myth of passivity." By the myth of passivity Krohn is referring to the person's attempt to disown responsibility for his or her thoughts, acts, and impulses.

Krohn hypothesizes that the "possessed" teenage girls at the Salem witch trials who accused others of practicing witchcraft were actually histrionics acting out the acceptable cultural beliefs of the era. In attributing their fits and hallucinations to possessions by the Devil, histrionic persons of the time were able to deny responsibility for their behavior. While denying responsibility for their behavior, the accusers could actually enjoy the power and evil inherent in their involvement with dangerous and sinister forces.

Krohn feels that the histrionic, while remaining within the bounds of convention, is sensitive to new ideas and often in the vanguard of social change. While participating in minor changes, the histrionic does not challenge anything basic to society. In an interesting footnote Krohn argues that the histrionic personality was active in, but ultimately a disaster for, the radical movements of the 1960s. Krohn explains this as follows:

> In the United States in the 1960s political activity was truly fashionable, and the political arena became very attractive to the hysterical personality. Submission to strong, charismatic political leaders and wholesome externalization of guilt onto the society, "the system," ensured a reliable myth of passivity. People who 10 years before would have been found in fraternities or sororities protecting their chastity were now in political movements protecting their goodness, innocence, and righteousness. Movements that considered themselves radical drew many such people, and at rallies radical leaders could get them fired up about revolutionary issues. The leaders came to believe their followers were truly radical and would join in wholesale disruptions of society. When the leaders then tried to spur their followers to revolutionary acts, to their surprise they lost large portions of their following. It is my hunch that among those who fell away were many hysterical personalities. The call to arms of the radical leaders was for them too severe a change, departing too precipitously from what was conventional involving the threat of *active* participation and with it the danger of true responsibility (Krohn, 1978, p. 209).

Thus histrionic personalities may espouse and promote changes so long as their involvement allows them to deny responsibility for their actions by promoting a myth of passivity.

THE ANTISOCIAL PERSONALITY

Considerable empirical research and theoretical work have been devoted to the understanding of this disorder. Previously the antisocial personality has been called the *psychopathic personality,* the *sociopathic personality,* and a variety of other terms as

well. In the present discussion we will use the term *antisocial personality* throughout.

Clinical Picture

According to DSM III, the most marked characteristic of the antisocial personality is a history of continuous and chronic antisocial behavior characterized by the violation of the rights of others, a failure to sustain adequate job performance over several years, lying, stealing, fighting, and truancy in childhood. This particular personality pattern appears to be much more common in males than females, with prevalence usually estimated at 3 percent for American men and approximately 1 percent for women. This behavior pattern is illustrated in the following case:

> A 21 year old male was interviewed by a psychiatrist while he was being detained in jail awaiting trial for attempted robbery. The patient had a history of multiple arrests for drug charges, robbery, and assault and battery. Past history revealed that he had been expelled from junior high school for truancy, fighting, and generally poor performance in school. Following a car theft when he was 14 years old, he was placed in a juvenile detention center. Subsequently he spent brief periods in a variety of institutions, from which he usually ran away. At times his parents attempted to let him live at home, but he was disruptive and threatened them with physical harm. After one such incident during which he threatened them with a knife, he was admitted to a psychiatric hospital; but he signed himself out against medical advice, one day later. The patient has never formed close personal relationships with his parents, his two older brothers, or friends of either sex. He is a loner and a drifter, and has not worked for more than two months at any one job in his life. He was recently terminated, because of fighting and poor attendance, from

a vocational training program in which he had been enrolled for about three weeks (Spitzer, Skodol, Gibbon, & Williams, 1981, p. 34).

The example reported above highlights both the impulsivity and disregard for rules that characterize the antisocial personality. In addition, it illustrates the antisocial personality's inability to engage in close relations with family and friends. The antisocial person is preoccupied with making sure that his or her own immediate needs are met, and demonstrates little concern for the feelings of others. Relations with others are tolerated so long as they continue to satisfy the person's needs.

While DSM III emphasizes the criminal activity of the antisocial personality, others argue such an emphasis overshadows more general traits. Millon (1981) notes that despite their tendency to flout conventional authority and rules, only a small segment of antisocial persons actually experience conflict with the law. Millon explains this as follows:

Many find themselves commended and reinforced in our competitive society, where tough, hard-headed "realism" is admired as an attribute necessary for survival. Most find a socially valued niche for themselves in the rugged side of the business, military or political world. . . . Such behavior is evident also in the machinations of politicians whose facade of good intentions cloaks a lust for power that leads to repressive legislation. Less dramatically, and more frequently, these individuals participate in the ordinary affairs of everyday life: the harshly punitive father; the puritanical, fear-inducing minister, the vengeful dean, and the irritable, guilt-producing mother.

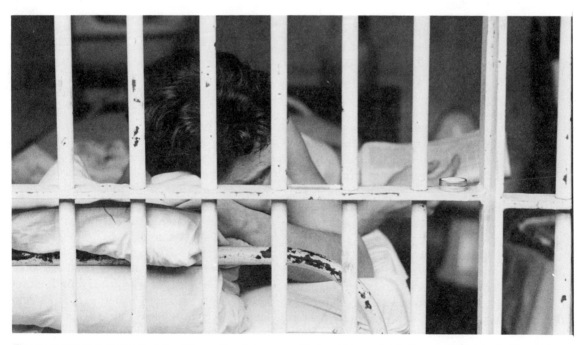

The most marked characteristic of the antisocial personality is a history of violation of the rights of others, lying, stealing, fighting, and truancy in childhood. (Stock Boston/Owen Franken)

According to Millon, the antisocial personality displays "social rebelliousness" and "social vindictiveness." These persons take pleasure in their ability to deceive and humiliate others. They are expert at detecting weaknesses in others and using them for purposes of manipulation. Moreover, they are remarkably adept at coming across as well-meaning and sincere while actually telling blatant lies. Not surprisingly, these persons are often extremely successful swindlers and con artists.

Cleckley (1968, 1976) in his famous book *The Mask of Sanity* offers numerous case descriptions of the disorder. The case histories he offers are not merely of criminals but also of prominent business executives, professionals, and others who fit the antisocial pattern of behavior. The essence of Cleckley's ideas of the antisocial personality is the notion that such people are unable to experience shame or anxiety in response to their social transgressions. He argues that these people are constitutionally unable to experience "normal" guilt in contemplation of their social behavior. As we will see, the absence of guilt figures prominently in the psychoanalytic exploration of the origins of this personality type.

The exact proportion of antisocial personalities among the criminal population depends upon whether one uses the DSM III or Cleckley's criteria. For example, Hare and Schalling (1978) found that by the DSM III criteria 76 percent of prisoners could be classified as antisocial personalities. In contrast, using Cleckley's criteria only 33 percent could be so classified. As actual criminal behavior is a complex phenomenon influenced by various social and psychological variables, it is best to steer away from a definition of the antisocial personality that is so consistent with criminality. Thus the emphasis Cleckley and Millan place on characteristics such as social vindictiveness, lack of responsibility, and the absence of shame seems particularly important in diagnosing this disorder.

Theory and Research

In this section we will consider a variety of theoretical and research approaches to understanding the nature of the antisocial personality. We will consider social learning, psychoanalytic, and biological explanations for the disorder.

The Social Learning Perspective. Learning theorists interested in the possible determinants of antisocial personality have focused heavily on the socialization process during childhood. One such account offered by Maher (1966) focuses on the pattern of reinforcements that occurs when a parent punishes a child for a transgression or some inappropriate behavior. For example, Maher speculates that the child whose parent reduces his or her punishment or who postpones it if the child repents and promises not to repeat the behavior, is actually rewarding repentant behavior. No anxiety will be associated with the actual transgression itself. In effect, the behavior being shaped is an elaborate pattern of repentance and excuse making. The result is that the child becomes adept in developing winning ways and in offering excuses for his or her transgressions. At the same time he or she fails to develop properly socialized behavior.

Another learning theory account of the development of this pattern of behavior has been offered by Ullman and Krasner (1969). The authors argue that antisocial personalities are individuals who from childhood on have not experienced other people as reinforcing. Other people fail to become "acquired reinforcers" to appropriately shape the behavior of the child. In addition, Ullman and Krasner argue that antisocial personalities may also learn undesirable behaviors from their parents through the mechanisms of modeling and observational learning. Many of the distant or cold behaviors or actions exhibited by the parents become acquired by their child in this way. Finally, the social learning account offered by Ullman and Krasner suggests that the parents of the antisocial personality are often inconsistent in the ways in which they reward behavior. This inconsistency produces a situation in which the child learns to avoid punishment and blame for his or her actions but does not necessarily learn consistent standards for appropriate behavior or consistent concepts of right and wrong.

The Psychodynamic Perspective. Psychoanalytic theory focuses on the antisocial personality's limited ability to experience guilt or remorse. According to this theory, the inability to experience such feelings results from an inadequately developed superego (MacKinnon & Michels, 1971). Remember that the superego represents the individual's moral code, his or her sense of what is right and what is wrong. In normal development the superego forms from the resolution of the Oedipal complex. Instead of competing with the same-sex parent, the child identifies with the parent and incorporates his or her standards of behavior. By internalizing the parent's sense of morality the child is able to maintain parental approval and love. Thus through identification with their parents children assimilate the traditional values and ideals of society.

However, if the parent the child identifies with is a pathological model, then the child will incorporate the unsocialized values of this parent. For example, the child who identifies with a parent who lies and deceives will not develop superego prohibitions against these behaviors. Consequently, the child may later engage in these behaviors without experiencing guilt or remorse.

In addition, children who have experienced neglect or abuse at the hands of their caretakers will not develop a sense of basic trust in others. If the ability to trust is not developed at an early age, the child's distrust of others will pervade all future relations. Projection is a common defense mechanism as the antisocial personality perceives in others his or her own indifference and distrust. Thus the motto of the antisocial personality might be: "Do unto others before they do it unto me."

While the preceding explanations suggest that the antisocial personality develops from parental neglect or abuse, this is not necessarily so. MacKinnon and Michels (1971) note that the incorporation of antisocial values can even occur from identification with stable parents who seemingly follow high standards of conduct. Usually in these cases the parents, while overtly conveying one message, unconsciously convey a contradictory message concerning what is right and wrong. The authors give the example of a high-school girl who was arrested for selling narcotics to classmates. Her father was well respected in his community and an elder in his church, but his business success "depended upon selling overpriced merchandise to poor people who did not understand time payment plans." Thus the daughter's delinquent behavior reflected her incorporation of these underlying antisocial parental attitudes.

Biological Explanations. Several things stand out about the behavior of the antisocial personality. First, the person seems remarkably free of anxiety and guilt in instances where most people would react strongly with both emotions. Furthermore, antisocial personalities seem repeatedly to find themselves in the same sorts of problematic situations and appear almost constitutionally unable to learn from past experience. It is not surprising that a number of

David T. Lykken. (Courtesy of David T. Lykken)

researchers have hypothesized that underlying biological deficiencies are major causal factors for this pattern of behavior.

Perhaps the classic study in this field was conducted by Lykken (1957). After noting the striking inability of the antisocial personality to develop feelings of anxiety, Lykken hypothesized that these people were deficient in their ability to develop a conditioned anxiety response. Lykken identified a group of a prisoners who fitted the antisocial personality criteria well, another group of prisoners who displayed the behavior pattern but also showed certain neurotic tendencies, and a group of normal students. The three groups were matched for intelligence and then given a laboratory avoidance learn-

ing task in which they were given 20 trials to learn a "mental maze." When they made an error, they received a shock of moderate intensity.

Lykken assumed that on those trials where subjects received a shock for performing an error, conditioned anxiety responses would develop. If his hypothesis was correct, then the antisocial personalities who were unable to develop a conditioned anxiety response would show higher error scores on trials where errors produced shocks than would the neurotic or normal comparison groups. This is exactly what Lykken found. Furthermore, when Lykken positively reinforced some responses in the task, the groups showed no differences in performance. Thus the failure of the antisocial personality group to avoid shock was assumed by Lykken to reflect a constitutionally based inability to develop avoidance learning responses. These are precisely the responses assumed to be crucial in effective socialization.

In a replication of Lykken's study, Schmauck (1970) clarified the nature of the antisocial personality's avoidance learning deficit. Schmauck found that the antisocial personality's avoidance learning difficulty depends on the type of punishment involved. When either a social reprimand or electric shock was used, the antisocial personality demonstrated the above-cited inability to avoid punishment. However, when the consequence of an error was the loss of money, the antisocial personality performed better than a comparison group. Thus antisocial personalities can learn to avoid punishment, but apparently only those punishments that are relevant to their value system.

Recent studies have examined whether antisocial personalities have specific deficits in cognitive functioning. For example, Hare and McPherson (1984) found that in antisocial personalities the left hemisphere is not as developed for language processing as it is in normal individuals. The authors hypothesize that this deficit may help explain the inconsistent behavior of the antisocial personality. Specifically, they speculate that if the antisocial personality's left hemisphere is not consistently dominant for language, he or she may employ cognitive strategies and overt behaviors that rely less on verbal or logical abilities. Consequently, language might be ineffective as a regulator of the antisocial personality's behavior. This language deficit may help explain the marked inconsistency between what antisocial personalities say and what they actually do.

NARCISSISTIC PERSONALITY

In Greek mythology Narcissus fell in love with his own image reflected in a pool of water. His love for himself was so great that he was unable to leave his reflection and died of disappointment. The term *narcissism* derives from this myth and is commonly used to denote grandiosity or self-love. In recent years characterological narcissism as a personality disorder has received a great deal of attention and has been observed far more frequently. The apparent increase in the prevalence of this disorder may reflect greater interest in a disorder that until now has existed in relative obscurity. However, another explanation is that the increased prevalence of this disorder is the by-product of a society that has become ever more self-oriented. We will address this issue later in our discussion.

Clinical Picture

Narcissistic personalities, as the name implies, are characterized by an inflated sense of personal worth and accomplishment. These people exhibit a haughty grandiosity and strong sense of entitlement. While convinced of their own uniqueness, narcissistic persons characteristically treat others with indifference or contempt and value others only so long as they serve as an admiring audience for the narcissistic personalities' apparent brilliance and genius. As one might expect, their preoccupation with their own needs and interests results in interpersonal relations that are shallow and often short-lived. All these characteristics of the narcissistic personality are evidenced in the following case:

A 25-year-old, single, graduate student complains to his psychoanalyst of difficulty completing his Ph.D. in English Literature and expresses concerns about his relationships with women. He believes that his thesis topic may profoundly increase the level of understanding in his discipline and make him famous, but so far he has not been able to get past the third chapter. His mentor does not seem sufficiently impressed with his ideas, and the patient is furious at him, but also self-doubting and ashamed. He blames his mentor for his lack of progress, and thinks that he deserves more help with his grand idea, that his mentor should help with some of the research. The patient brags about his creativity and complains that other people are "jealous" of his insights. He is very envious of students who are moving along faster than he and regards them as "dull drones and asskissers." He prides himself on the brilliance of his class participation and imagines someday becoming a great professor. He becomes rapidly infatuated with women and has powerful and persistent fantasies about each new woman he meets, but after several experiences of sexual intercourse feels disappointed and finds them dumb, clinging, and physically repugnant. He has many "friends," but they turn over quickly, and no one relationship lasts very long. People get tired of his continual self-promotion and lack of consideration of them. For example, he was lonely at

Christmas and insisted that his best friend stay in town rather than visit his family. The friend refused, criticizing the patient's self-centeredness; and the patient, enraged, decided never to see this friend again (Spitzer et al., 1981, p. 52–53).

This example also clearly displays the interpersonal exploitativeness of the narcissistic personality. Although the person may appear aloof and independent of other's affections, actually he or she is quite dependent on the adulation of other people. Thus the narcissistic person often reacts with anger and rage to the slightest criticism.

Object relations theorists such as Kernberg (1975) and Kohut (1977) are largely responsible for the recent wave of interest in this particular personality disorder. Remember that object relations theory is the branch of psychoanalytic thought that traces character development to the person's early relationship with his or her primary caretaker. These theorists argue that the narcissistic person's grandiosity and sense of entitlement are actually a defense against underlying feelings of inferiority and worthlessness. According to object relations theory, the narcissistic person is unable to maintain a consistent self-image. Instead, the person fluctuates between feelings of emptiness and feelings of omnipotence. Unable to maintain a constant identity on his or her own, the narcissistic person depends on others' attention and interest to achieve a consistent sense of self. Thus others are not perceived as existing independent of the self, but rather as *self-objects*. That is, other people are perceived as objects to be manipulated in ways that will help preserve a positive self-image.

The narcissistic individual's lack of a consistent self-image is illustrated in his or her sexual relations. Often the narcissistic individual is seductive, promiscuous, sexually uninhibited, and given to frequent infatu-ations. Through sexual relations, the narcissistic individual receives the attention and admiration that he or she requires to maintain a positive self-representation. However, the sexual partner is not seen as a separate person but rather as a narcissistic extension of the self. For example, the narcissistic individual is characteristically preoccupied with dating and being seen with the most attractive person of the opposite sex. There is little concern with the partner's personality because he or she is perceived only as a self-object that will elicit feelings of admiration and jealousy in others. Since the narcissistic individual's identity is tied up in the attractive partner, he or she is devastated when the partner breaks off the relationship. Similarly, the narcissistic individual loses all interest in the partner when the partner ceases to make the person feel good. For example, a male narcissistic personality explains divorcing his wife with the comment, "She used to be beautiful but now she is fat." Not surprisingly, the narcissistic individual is unable to remain in love and his or her relationships lack any genuine commitment. We will return to the object relations view of the narcissistic personality when we consider the childhood origins of this disorder.

Childhood Origins

Social Learning Perspective. Millon (1981) speculates that narcissistic personality development can be traced to a family setting in which the child's worth is unrealistically overvalued by the parents. Children in such homes receive tremendous praise and recognition for the most trivial accomplishments. These children soon come to believe that they are at all times lovable and perfect, no matter what they actually say or do. Gradually, future narcissistic personalities learn to think of themselves as special and acquire an exaggerated, unrealistic sense of their own worth.

The parents' undifferentiated praise of all of the child's activities may cause the child to develop a narcissistic belief that his or her very presence brings pleasure to other people. Furthermore, since the parents are repeatedly indulgent and acquiescent, the child learns to expect such treatment from others. In attempting to elicit the accustomed favorable reaction from others, the child employs the same presumptuous and demanding strategies that proved successful in the home environment. Moreover, because the child's image of others is based on the behavior of his or her own parents, others are perceived as weak, manipulatable, and subservient. This attitude fuels the future narcissistic personality's sense of entitlement and increases his or her inclination to manipulate and exploit other people. As others are not considered to be equals, there is little or no sense of interpersonal responsibility.

Unfortunately for the narcissistic individual, not everyone reacts to his or her blusterings as did the parents. Instead, most people react with criticism and disdain to the narcissistic's unrealistic sense of self-importance. The narcissistic individual's grandiosity causes him or her to discount such criticism as reflecting mere ignorance or jealousy. However, in so doing the individual increasingly loses objectivity, and a vicious cycle may soon develop. The narcissistic individual's arrogance results in disparagement by others. Instead of adapting his or her behavior in response to this criticism, the person perceives the criticism as additional evidence of his or her specialness and retreats further into a world of fantasy. This withdrawal elicits greater ridicule and disparagement from others, which in turn results in even less objectivity on the part of the narcissistic individual. Eventually there may be an almost total alienation from others as the narcissistic personality retreats into his or her fantasy world.

Psychodynamic Perspective. Whereas social learning theory argues that narcissistic personality development stems from parental overvaluation of the child, object relations theory maintains that narcissistic development results from inadequate and unempathic caretaking in the first few years of life (Kohut, 1977).

How the young child feels about himself or herself depends on the parents' reaction. For example, when the mother is happy, the child feels lovable and experiences a positive sense of self. However, when the mother is angry or upset, the child feels unlovable and experiences a negative sense of self. In normal development the child eventually succeeds in integrating the positive and negative aspects of himself or herself. When this occurs, the child is able to maintain a constant self-image independent of the mother.

Initially, the young infant is unable to separate his or her own self from that of the parents. Instead, the parents are experienced as *self-objects*. Kohut (1977) identifies two different types of self-object relationships that the young child establishes with his or her parents. These self-object relationships express the child's basic need to both admire and be admired. The first relationship is a *mirroring* one wherein the child experiences the parents as admiring and taking pride in his or her developing abilities. Kohut feels that a mirroring type of self-image is most likely to develop from the relationship with the mother, who is generally the primary caretaker. The second self-object relationship is an *idealizing* one in which the child has a wish to merge with and share the abilities of a parent admired as perfect. This type of self-image is thought by Kohut to develop primarily from the relationship with the father. According to Kohut, the child must develop these self-object relationships with one or both parents in order to attain a stable sense of self and maintain a steady level of self-esteem.

Problems develop when the mother is unempathic and treats the child according to her own needs, ignoring those of the child. Instead of the child being treated as a separate person, he or she is treated more as a narcissistic extension of the parent. As the parent's treatment changes from moment to moment depending on his or her mood, the child will have difficulty establishing a constant sense of self. Moreover, the child will discover that the only way to be loved is to make the mother feel good. From this evolves the belief that the only way to be loved is to be perfect. To be imperfect is to be bad and unlovable. Thus, according to this explanation, there is a splitting between the good, omnipotent self and the bad, worthless self.

Also critical in the psychodynamic view of the development of the narcissistic personality is what Mahler (1967) calls the separation and individuation process. Remember that during this phase of development the child must establish a separate identity independent of the mother. However, if the mother has difficulty allowing the child to separate from her because of her own narcissism, the child will not develop a consistent identity. Unable to maintain a positive sense of self independent of others, the child continues to split his or her good self from the bad self. In order to restore a sense of well-being, the child retreats into developmentally inappropriate feelings of omnipotence and grandiosity. Through formation of what object relations theorists call the *grandiose self,* the child is able to maintain and restore his or her self-esteem.

Kernberg (1975), a noted spokesman for the object relations school, suggests that tremendous rage underlies the narcissistic person's sense of omnipotence. The child experiences this rage in response to repeated frustrations at the hands of a cold, unempathic mother. However, the child recognizes that expressing this rage may cause him or her to lose the mother's love. One way that the child may defend against this rage is to retreat into some aspect of himself or herself that the parent values. For example, the child may take excessive pride in the ability to amuse his or her parents. This ability then becomes exaggerated and an unrealistic self-image or *grandiose self* develops. Meanwhile, the child's unacceptable image of himself or herself as angry and deprived is split off from the grandiose self. This splitting allows the child to avoid underlying feelings of anger and emptiness. In addition, the child's early experiences of deprivation cause him or her to feel that others cannot be depended upon for love and support. Thus, although superficially dependent on those around them for admiration, narcissistic personalities are actually incapable of trusting other people.

PARANOID PERSONALITY
Clinical Picture

Everyone may experience brief moments of distrust and suspiciousness when under stress. For example, imagine that you turn in what you think is a fine paper. Later the paper is returned and you are stunned to receive a very low grade. The thought quickly flashes through your mind that the professor has it in for you. You remember that in class last week you disagreed with the professor about a particular point. Perhaps your instructor dislikes you and has based your current grade on his feelings toward you and not on the quality of the paper. However, as you calm down, you realize that you are being irrational. It is a very large lecture course and the professor probably does not even know who you are. Still you are intrigued by

THE NARCISSISTIC SOCIETY

Some social critics have argued that the prominence of the narcissistic personality can be traced to an increasingly narcissistic society. One of the most outspoken of these critics is Christopher Lasch. In his controversial book *The Culture of Narcissism* (1979), Lasch eloquently denounces a culture that elevates narcissists to positions of eminence and brings out and reinforces narcissistic traits in everyone.

Lasch argues that our preoccupation with the self stems from our denial of the past and concern only with the present. In discounting the past we are left with no standards to judge contemporary attitudes and conditions. According to Lasch, our denial of the past, while superficially progressive and optimistic, actually reflects the despair of a society that cannot face the future. Without a sense of historical continuity, we live for the moment and for ourselves alone.

The search for self-fulfillment, according to Lasch, arises from desperation as we battle subjective experiences of emptiness and isolation and strive to find meaning in our lives. This search for meaning, however, offers only superficial solutions as the trends and institutions we turn to reflect the bankruptcy of our culture. For example, the mass media promote and glorify the cult of the celebrity. We are surrounded by newspapers, magazines, books, and television programs devoted exclusively to keeping us informed of the "glamour" and "excitement" that the stars enjoy. Also, we are bombarded by advertising which is aimed primarily at promoting consumption as a way of life. Advertisers tell us that not only do we "deserve the best," but if we do not buy the best (i.e., the newest) we will soon fall behind the pack in this dog eat dog world. Whereas only five years ago very few families owned a home computer, now we are told that if we do not purchase one we are putting our children at a disadvantage for life.

Lasch feels that our dissatisfaction and boredom with modern life is reflected in the modern-day therapies and consciousness movements. These therapies offer pseudo insight that masquerades for true understanding and emotionality. We learn that mental health means the removal of inhibitions and immediate gratification of every impulse. Love is defined simply as the fulfillment of the person's emotional requirements—there is no reference to the subordination of one's own needs and interests to those of others. We anticipate deception and exploitativeness in interpersonal relations and learn not to take emotional risks. Promiscuity allows an escape from emotional complexity and true intimacy as we attempt to separate the sexual act from the feelings involved. Moreover, Lasch notes that in addressing our own difficulties "instead of drawing on our own experience, we allow experts to define our needs for us and then wonder why those needs never seem to be satisfied" (Lasch, 1979, p. xviii). Thus Lasch suggests that the narcissistic personality may be the outgrowth of a society that itself is increasingly narcissistic.

the ease with which your suspicions accelerated until you were convinced you were being discriminated against.

The example given above illustrates the suspiciousness, distrust, and extreme sensitivity to criticism that characterize the paranoid personality. In this case, however, the person was able to step back and objectively examine the situation once the initial shock had subsided. The paranoid personality, in contrast, does not exhibit this capacity to stand back and objectively check the reality of his or her suspicions. Instead, such people create their own reality and continually scan their environment looking for potential threats and for evidence that will confirm their own ideas and biases.

In addition to the suspiciousness and sensitivity to criticism, DSM III describes the paranoid personality as also characterized by pathological jealousy, secretiveness, and a restricted ability to experience warm emotions. The following case history of a paranoid personality illustrates all of these characteristics.

Paranoid personalities create their own realities and continually scan their environment looking for potential threats and for evidence that will confirm their own ideas and biases. (Stock Boston/K. Rosenthal)

A young male was hospitalized after viciously beating his wife. He had attacked her twice previously, and all three episodes were preceded by his feeling that he could not trust her. Although there was no evidence of infidelity during their 17 years of marriage, he had been persistently jealous and possessive. . . . Their relationship had always been a distant one, which did not seem to bother the patient. He became violent only on those occasions when he felt his wife was changing the equilibrium. This was true when she tried to get closer to him as well as when she withdrew for some reason. . . . He had been a seaman for three years, spending about six months home per year. During this period their marriage was smooth. Difficulties began when he took regular employment with an accounting firm. He became very uncomfortable because other accountants had their desks adjacent to him. He established a job pattern in which he would begin successfully, then gradually become more uncomfortable as his co-workers attempted to become closer. He would then accuse them of being too competitive or taking advantage of his knowledge by asking his advice. He stated that the three things which gave him most comfort were being an accountant, Catholicism, and his wife when she was steady and predictable. He was most relaxed when working with figures since this did not force him into close relationships. He had converted to Catholicism because he felt that the Catholic church "made more sense and had fewer fallacies and loopholes." Again he preferred a structured environment where rules and dogma were relatively constant. He could be close to his wife only when she was predictable; whenever she attempted to lower or raise his emotional barriers, he became very agitated and would insist that she clarify her emotional attitude toward him (Swanson, Bohnert, & Smith, 1970, p. 67).

This example also illustrates the argumentativeness and hostility that characterize the paranoid personality's relations with others. The paranoid person is extremely vigilant to attack and sees deliberate maliciousness in the most trivial slight. Ironically, through a self-fulfilling prophecy the paranoid personality confirms his or her initially unfounded suspicions. That is, the person's suspicious and argumentative manner causes others to react in a similarly suspicious and defensive fashion. Thus the paranoid personality confirms what he or she initially believes and then uses this to justify his or her continued vigilant and defensive stance.

Cognitive Style

The example shown above also illustrates the paranoid personality's search for a constant and predictable environment. Such an environment is created and maintained by interpreting every event in terms of one overall view of life. Shapiro (1965) observes that suspiciousness is, above all else, a way of thinking about the world. Shapiro describes this cognitive style eloquently:

> A suspicious person is a person who has something on his mind. He looks at the world with fixed and occupying expectations and he searches repetitively and only for confirmation of it. He will not be persuaded to abandon his suspicion or some plan of action based on it. On the contrary, he will pay no attention to rational arguments except to find in them some aspect or feature that actually confirms his original view. Anyone who tries to influence or persuade a suspicious person will not only fail, but also, unless he is sensible enough to abandon his efforts early, will, himself, become an object of the original suspicious idea (Shapiro, 1965, p. 56).

Also characteristic of the paranoid personality's cognitive style is the use of projection. By projection we mean the attribution to external figures of motivations, drives, or other tensions that are found to be intolerable and are repudiated or rejected in one's self. Thus impulses or feelings that are unacceptable in oneself are attributed to others.

Before examining the developmental origins of the paranoid personality it is important to distinguish it from the separate disorders of paranoia and paranoid schizophrenia. Although the paranoid personality exhibits delusional thinking, there is less distortion of reality than in paranoia or paranoid schizophrenia. Moreover, there is a greater chance of correcting the distorted beliefs of the paranoid personality. While in both paranoia and paranoid schizophrenia there is significant distortion of reality, the delusions of the paranoid schizophrenic are much more disorganized than the paranoiac. Finally, the behavior of the paranoid schizophrenic is the most disorganized while the paranoid personality functions best and, for example, is more likely to be able to hold down a job.

Childhood Origins

Social Learning Perspective. In speculating on the etiology of the paranoid personality, Millon (1981) differentiates among various subtypes of the disorder. Three of these subtypes are the *paranoid-narcissistic,* the *paranoid-antisocial,* and the *paranoid-compulsive* personalities.

According to Millon, *paranoid-narcissistic* individuals were indulged and overvalued as children. Their special treatment prevented them from learning basic social skills, such as sharing and consideration for the interests of others. Because few limits were imposed, these children developed a strong sense of their own importance. However, once they left the friendly confines of the home and entered school, they experienced interpersonal difficulties. Their selfishness and self-centeredness caused them to be mistreated by their peers. Instead of adapting to the new reality, these children retreated into their world of fantasy. In this world they successfully preserved their sense of importance and entitlement by seeing others as envious of their position. Thus a pattern developed of denying and actually creating a new reality in the face of external threat and criticism.

Millon speculates that *paranoid-antisocial* individuals were physically abused by their parents as children. As a result, these children learned to perceive the world as harsh and cruel. If one wanted to survive, one had to be externally vigilant and not trust or depend on anyone. In the face of repeated attacks, these children isolated themselves and retreated into a world of fantasy, from which delusions of persecution evolved.

Paranoid-compulsive individuals, according to Millon, experienced parental overcontrol through contingent punishment. In order to avoid parental punishment, these children learned to avoid making mistakes and to obey strictly parental authority. Lacking initiative and spontaneity, these individuals were unable to form close interpersonal relations and were terrified of the unknown. Fearing rejection and punishment from others, they too retreated and found comfort in their inner world. However, when attempting to be assertive these individuals feel guilty and fearful. Anticipating punishment for their assertive behavior, they see others as hostile and persecuting.

Psychodynamic Perspective. Freud (1911) felt that unconscious homosexuality was the conflict underlying most paranoid disorders. Unable to accept these threatening impulses, the person defends against them by projecting them onto others. Thus the person's unacceptable homosexual urges are transformed into the irrational belief that someone out there is out to get him or her.

Recent theorists have downplayed the role of unconscious homosexuality in favor of the child's early interactions with his or her mother. MacKinnon and Michels (1971) trace the development of paranoid thinking to difficulties in establishing a warm and trusting relationship with the mother. They argue that often the mother is seductive, arousing sexual feelings in the child while at the same time denying her actions. In addition, the mother may exhibit grandiose features and see herself as always right and the child as always wrong. The child develops intense feelings of hate and anger, which are dealt with by denying them and projecting them onto others. Moreover, MacKinnon and Michels believe that the occasional experiences of intimacy with the mother result in humiliation and rejection. Thus the paranoid develops a marked fear of closeness and intimacy. He or she successfully avoids warm feelings by first denying them and subsequently projecting them onto others. Thus the feeling that "I love him" becomes first "I hate him" and then "he hates me."

The Paranoid and Society

The grandiosity and suspiciousness of paranoid personalities often bring them into conflict with societal rules and regulations. Swanson et al. (1970) note that many unfounded lawsuits are brought by paranoid personalities who imagine persecution or mistreatment where none exists. Moreover, paranoid personalities' rigid adherence to their own tight, systematic construction of reality makes it difficult for them to follow the policy and leadership of others. Instead, these people often become leaders themselves. Moreover, their tight, apparently logical system of beliefs can be very convincing so that they may be very successful in recruiting followers. DSM III notes that the paranoid personality is likely to be overrepresented among leaders of cults, pseudo-scientific, and quasi-political groups. A recent, tragic example of this is the Reverend Jim Jones who led the People's Temple Cult (Osherow, 1981). Jones succeeded in eliciting blind loyalty and obedience from his followers and convincing them that they were the target of a global conspiracy. The result was the mass suicide at Jonestown that left over 900 people dead.

Swanson et al. suggest that the paranoid personality's cognitive style may lend itself even to more mainstream politics. The authors note that the very nature of political strategy encourages a suspicious attitude. The paranoid politician may perceive criticism as a threat and accuse his critics of conspiracy. Often the accusations, coming from a powerful politician, are accepted without question and the original critic becomes an enemy of the system. Swanson et al. warns against this in the following passage:

> Paranoid thinking manifested by a leader easily eludes recognition, couched as it is in terms of political competition, national security, foreign intervention or threatening warfare. The mode of thinking is masked by the thought content and often the opinions of the leader remain unquestioned. Private opinions held by associates which might reveal the distorted thinking are left unsaid. In fact, often no single person has either the stature to question the leader's mental health or the constitutional prerogative to force removal from office and hospitalization. These facts properly arouse concern in the interested citizen who recognizes the destructive potential of a paranoid leader in this part of the twentieth century (Swanson, 1970, p. 383).

While we may assume that our political system is safe from the machinations of individual pathology, the flagrant abuses of power during the McCarthy "red scare" of the 1950s and the more recent Watergate affair suggest that this may not be so safe an assumption.

BORDERLINE PERSONALITY

Borderline personality is a recently formulated diagnosis that has received increasing attention in the last 10 years. Its name derives from the fact that the person appears to be on the "border" between neurotic and psychotic functioning. The borderline diagnosis describes a clinical population that has always been difficult to classify. For example, latent schizophrenia, pseudo-neurotic schizophrenia, psychotic character, ambulatory schizophrenia, and the "as if" personality are just a few of the many labels that have been applied to persons exhibiting borderline features.

The essential features of the borderline personality were recognized in the early years of psychoanalysis when certain patients, believed to be functioning at a neurotic level, literally "fell apart on the couch." Although superficially intact, these patients deteriorated into temporary states of psychosis when faced with the relative deprivation and lack of structure that psychoanalysis entails. The same dynamics are found in the borderline person's performance on psychological tests. For example, on the more structured intelligence tests the borderline may evidence little pathology. However, on the less structured projective tests, especially the Rorschach, the borderline's performance deteriorates and thought disturbance often appears.

Clinical Picture

The borderline personality is the most disorganized of all the personality disorders. Borderline personalities are characterized by extremely unstable, impulsive, and unpredictable behavior. There is a self-destructive quality to this impulsivity as they may engage in potentially harmful acts such as drug abuse, sexual promiscuity, overeating, and even self-mutilation. Often there are suicidal threats or gestures, which are used for purposes of manipulation.

The borderline person's emotions are very unstable and may quickly fluctuate between depression and relative euphoria. All emotions are experienced very intensely, with anger the most prominent. In fact, inappropriate and uncontrolled outbursts of anger are essential features of the borderline personality. This inordinate capacity for anger is illustrated in the following excerpt from a letter written by a borderline personality:

I tried to study my physics tonight and I got more and more tense. I wanted to give up and burn the anger out, and then I started to write you this letter. All at once I struck out at my desk with my fist telling myself that I must not let my hand burn myself. In doing so I cracked my knuckles so hard against the desk that I bruised them. I got scared and was afraid. In trying not to burn myself I succeeded in being destructive to myself. . . . Please forgive me for shrieking out in anger. I have to admit that in seeing the bruise I got even angrier and more tense, seeing what I hadn't planned on happening, and I struck the desk again as if it were my enemy (Hartocollis, 1980, pp. 140–141).

Although borderline personalities may engage in what seems to be appropriate social interaction, on closer inspection their relations are found to lack emotional complexity (Gunderson & Singer, 1975). In everyday interactions borderline persons relate in a transient, superficial manner while in close relations they are intensely dependent and clinging. These dependent relationships are often marked by extreme manipulativeness and constant demands. Moreover, relations with others are characterized by rapid shifts between idealization and devaluation. The same person who is prized and respected one minute may be denigrated and despised the next.

Borderline persons have a great intolerance of being alone. For them, being alone arouses intense feelings of abandonment. In order to protect against these feelings, such persons may rush from one unsuccessful, often self-destructive, relationship to another. Although these relations are ultimately self-destructive, they allow the person to defend temporarily against chronic feelings of boredom and emptiness.

As previously noted, the borderline personality may experience no difficulties in well-structured situations. For example, the person may perform well in certain work or academic settings. However, because they cannot tolerate change or transition they generally function well below their apparent talent or ability. An example of this underachievement is the 35-year-old college graduate who still lives with his or her parents and holds down an unchallenging administrative job. Lacking the ego strengths to handle novel or stressful situations, the person may at times deteriorate into brief episodes of psychosis. The borderline person is also vulnerable to brief psychotic episodes under the influence of certain drugs, such as marijuana, LSD, and mescaline. This capacity for brief psychotic experiences followed by a return to relatively normal functioning is believed by some others to be the distinguishing characteristic of the borderline patient (Gunderson & Singer, 1975).

The following case illustrates many of the dynamics and characteristics of the borderline person:

A 31-year-old musician was referred for psychotherapy by her boyfriend's therapist. She complained of feeling angry a good part of her life and of being in "conflict" with the man with whom she was now involved. He was "an alcoholic" who was possessive, demanding, and physically and verbally abusive. Initially she had hoped to be "the woman he had never had," but more recently she felt in a rage and was provocative and abusive herself. The patient had been been married in her early twenties, but was divorced after three years of bitter fighting. There followed a succession of boyfriends with whom she fell in love but eventually ridiculed and "hated." She was rarely not involved with some man. She said she "panicked" at the thought of being alone. On several occasions when she had been dropped by a boyfriend, she had made a suicidal attempt by an overdose of Valium and alcohol, which she admitted she occasionally took to excess, but she was never admitted to a hospital. Although somewhat accomplished in her art, she frequently felt bored, empty, and as if she had chosen the wrong field. She claimed that she did not know who she really was and said, "I always act the way people expect me to act." She had two brief contacts with psychotherapy before, but both times she dropped out after several sessions that "weren't getting me anywhere" and were "too far to travel to" (Spitzer et al., 1981, pp. 256–57).

The case described above also illustrates what Kernberg (1967, 1975) calls the *identity diffusion* of borderline personalities. That is, borderline personalities lack a clear sense of identity and often hold a vague, contradictory picture of themselves. Lacking an integrated and consistent self-image, these persons often assume the mannerisms of those they encounter. As a result, the borderline person's self-image may dramatically change from one situation to another.

Kernberg traces the borderline personality's identity diffusion to the defense mechanism of *splitting*. Splitting involves the inability to integrate positive and negative images of oneself and others. Because contradictory images are kept separate, there is no integration or synthesis of complex elements of personality. Instead, others are divided into relatively primitive categories of good and bad. Moreover, there is an unreal quality to the borderline person's own identity

because of the existence and alternation of the contradictory self-images. This unreal quality may lead to experiences of depersonalization as the person feels distant from his or her own behavior. In fact, some authors have suggested that multiple personalities are actually a complex subpopulation of borderline personalities. Ludolph (1982), for example, argues that the formation of multiple personalities may represent an extreme form of the child's early splitting of positive and negative self-images. However, it is not known why it is only in the rarest of instances that the splitting of contradictory images results in the formation of multiple identities.

Childhood Origins

The current fascination with the borderline personality is in large part due to recent work by object relation theorists. Presented below are the developmental theories of two such theorists.

Kernberg's Theory. Kernberg (1967, 1973), more than any other contemporary theorist, has brought the borderline personality into the limelight. Ironically, Kernberg does not actually perceive the borderline as a distinct personality disorder but rather as a level of personality organization. However, his theory of borderline organization does coincide with the concept of the borderline personality as used by others.

Kernberg traces borderline functioning to the child's early inability to integrate disparate perceptions of himself or herself and others. This developmental failure results from both a constitutionally based excess of aggressive impulses and intense anger resulting from frustration at the hands of a cold, unempathic mother. The child feels threatened by these hostile impulses because he or she fears they will result in loss of the mother's love. In order to preserve her love, the child uses the primitive defense mechanisms of splitting and projective identification.

Splitting allows both the "good" and "bad" parental images to coexist. Thus, to the child, the mother who frustrates is not the same as the mother who gratifies the child's need. However, splitting also results in an all-or-none quality to the child's experiences with little recognition of ambivalent feelings or emotions. The child sees the mother as either all good or all bad. Because of the failure to integrate contradictory images, the young child does not develop the capacity for "total object relationships." That is, the child never progresses from recognizing partial representations of a person to recognizing a whole representation. For example, there is little tolerance or understanding of shortcomings in others. Instead of developing a complex image of others that allows for such shortcomings, the borderline personality maintains a primitive understanding of people as either good or bad. The "good" represents the kind, rewarding mother while the "bad" represents the cold, depriving mother. This good or bad dichotomy is reflected in the borderline person's rapid shifts between idealizing and devaluing the same person. It is also reflected in his or her failure to achieve a stable identity.

The young child also defends against his or her intense rage through the mechanism of *projective identification*. The child first projects his or her rage onto others and then identifies with the emotion that is projected. Attributing his or her threatening impulses to others enables the young child to maintain a positive self-image. However, in the process the child mistakes the source of his or her feelings. Instead of attributing feelings to his or her own internal state, the child sees them as originating in others. Thus the use of projective identification precludes any true emotional involvement as there is no realistic assessment or empathic understanding of others' true feelings.

Use of this primitive defense mechanism also contributes to the disjointed nature of personal experience as feelings and emotions are not integrated into a consistent identity. Moreover, continued reliance on this defense mechanism can result in faulty differentiation of the self from others. For example, at times borderline persons may be confused about whether the pain or pleasure they experience is their own or actually that of someone close to them. Because self-other boundaries are sometimes blurred, intimacy may cause borderline persons to feel engulfed by or merged with others. This feeling of being engulfed may be particularly intense and frightening when involved in sexual relations. Rather than contributing to the experience, the regression and letting go that sexual activity normally entails may leave borderline personalities feeling out of control and as if they no longer exist separate from the other person.

Masterson's Theory. In contrast to Kernberg, Masterson (1976) traces borderline personality development to failure in the process of separation and individuation from the mother. The borderline patient never achieves a sense of autonomy because separation involves such intense feelings of abandonment that it is experienced as annihilation and death.

According to Masterson, the mother of the borderline personality is usually a borderline person herself. Because she was unable to separate from her mother, she fosters a continued symbiotic union with her child that helps her maintain her own emotional stability. The mother feels threatened when her child seeks greater individuality. Consequently, clinging and dependent behavior is encouraged while attempts at individuation are met by withdrawal. Thus, around 18 to 36 months a conflict develops between the child's own developmental striving for autonomy and his or her fear of loss of the mother's love. As a result, attempts at separation and growth are equated with feelings of abandonment.

Fearful of abandonment, the child allows the mother to perform functions that in normal development the child would perform by him or herself. As the child's needs are merged with those of the mother, he or she experiences difficulties distinguishing between inner and outer stimuli. This difficulty results in deficits such as poor reality perception, low frustration tolerance, and poor impulse control.

The young child also defends against feelings of abandonment via the defense mechanisms of splitting and denial. These mechanisms allow a denial of the separation and promote fantasies of reunion with the mother. Thus a split gradually develops between the child's thoughts and feelings and the reality of his or her functioning.

Masterson notes that the child's developmental failures may not become apparent until later when he or she encounters other separation-individuation tasks. The first of these failures occurs in prepuberty when the child must begin the transition from childhood into adulthood. Whereas in normal development the child masters this transition and exhibits greater autonomy and mastery, the borderline child experiences great conflict as fears of abandonment are reawakened. Consequently, the conflict may precipitate the initial manifestation of the clinical features characteristic of the adult borderline personality.

Masterson's theory maintains that the borderline's early failure to achieve autonomy makes him or her susceptible to regression whenever he or she encounters events in the life cycle that require autonomy or mastery. For example, the last year of high school may precipitate an abandonment depression while the first year of college may precipitate impulsive, acting-out behavior. Moreover, the child's early failure to achieve autonomy results in later difficulties in engaging in intimate relations. Close, intimate relations with others reawaken the borderline person's fears of being engulfed or abandoned. To get too close to another is to feel engulfed while to remain distant is to feel abandoned. Whether the fear of engulfment or abandonment predominates depends on when in the separation-individuation process the child experiences developmental arrest. The earlier the onset of the arrest, the more the fear of engulfment will predominate.

Diagnostic Utility and Future Trends

Although the diagnosis of borderline personality has dramatically increased in recent years, controversy and confusion exist as to how reliable and valid this diagnosis really is. In a review of four sets of borderline diagnostic criteria, Perry and Klerman (1978) found very little overlap between the different diagnostic systems. In fact, of 104 separate criteria, only one was found in all four sets while 55 were present in only one of the four sets. Thus across the different categories almost the entire range of psychopathology of personality is represented.

This wide range of diagnostic criteria calls into question the utility of the borderline diagnosis and suggests there is an overlap with other personality disorders. Support for this position comes from attempts by Pope, Jonas, Hudson, Cohen, & Gunderson (1983) to distinguish borderline patients from patients with other disorders. Although borderline patients were readily distinguished from schizophrenics, they could not be readily distinguished from patients with either histrionic or antisocial personalities.

Currently researchers are attempting to refine the diagnostic criteria for borderline personality. Instead of lumping all the different criteria into one wastebasket category, the emphasis is on identifying various subtypes of the borderline personality. Presumably, each of these subtypes will be described by a slightly different set of criteria. Along these lines recent studies suggest that two different borderline populations can be distinguished on the basis of the presence or absence of depressive symptomatology (Pope et al., 1983). Also encouraging is the development of a research scale, the Diagnostic Interview for Borderlines (DIB), which has gained widespread acceptance.

The DIB is a structured clinical interview that assesses relevant diagnostic criteria such as the person's impulsivity, emotional instability, and quality of interpersonal relations. Recent work with this instrument has demonstrated that borderline persons can be identified with a high degree of reliability (Cornell, Silk, Ludolph, & Lohn, 1983). What remains is to develop a reliable means to distinguish between possible borderline subtypes.

TREATMENT

There is very little research on the treatment of personality disorders. In large part this is because people with personality disorders generally do not seek treatment. As noted earlier in the chapter, such people seek treatment only when their personality traits interfere with their life functioning. For example, a person with a narcissistic personality disorder may enter therapy only when social or occupational pressures threaten his or her sense of importance.

Little is also known about the rate at which people with the different disorders seek treatment. However, it seems likely that the probability of entering therapy varies with the degree of social and occupational disruption associated with each disorder. For example, persons with a compulsive personality disorder can usually find their so-cial or occupational niche and keep conflict at a minimum. In contrast, the unpredictable and impulsive behavior of borderline personalities is likely to get them into frequent trouble.

Specific treatment methods are discussed in later chapters. For now it is important to note that the treatment employed depends on the manner in which the disorder is conceptualized. For example, a social learning approach is consistent with the behavior therapies discussed in Chapter 17. Similarly, a psychodynamic approach is consistent with the insight-oriented therapies discussed in Chapter 16.

SUMMARY

In this chapter we have examined the personality disorders and have observed that, unlike many forms of abnormal behavior, the personality disorders are not necessarily marked by periods of acute distress. Instead, they reflect long-standing personality patterns that the person experiences as ego-syntonic. Whether or not these personality patterns are considered "abnormal" often depends on the context in which they occur. In fact, in some situations these personality patterns may actually be an asset.

Although DSM III lists 11 distinct types of personality disorders, the degree to which they can be reliably distinguished from one another is still unclear and represents an important area of needed research. Moreover, given the fact that several of these disorders may break down along sexual lines, more research into how cultural biases may influence clinical disorders seems appropriate.

We chose to concentrate our attention on six of the most prominent personality disorders. In each case we provided a clinical discription of the disorder and examined its childhood origins.

Both social learning theory and psychodynamic theory offer explanations for the development of the personality disorders. One point of agreement for the two theories is that childhood experience plays an important role in the formation of these disorders. However, the two emphasize separate periods of development. Social learning theory-stresses the cumulative effect of characteristic family socialization practices. Through differential reinforcement and modelling, the distinctive personality disturbances emerge over time.

In contrast, psychodynamic theory stresses the child's early experiences with his or her primary caretaker. According to this theory, personality disorders can be traced to difficulties in the pre-Oedipal period, roughly the first four years of life. The type of disorder depends on the nature and timing of the disturbance in the child's early relationship with the caretaker. Moreover, whereas the social learning model emphasizes the child's overt adjustment to external control, the psychodynamic model stresses the child's unconscious reaction to the early deprivation he or she experiences. Because of its emphasis on unconscious processes the psychodynamic model provides a richer clinical description and accounts for more divergent phenomena. However, this emphasis on unconscious processes ultimately means that many assumptions of the psychodynamic model cannot be subjected to empirical research. Thus, in understanding the personality disorders there is a trade-off between a theory that is empirically verifiable and a theory that is rich in clinical description.

14

Unconventional Sexual Behavior and Dysfunction

Overview

The Gender Identity Disorders and the Paraphilias

Transsexualism: A Gender Identity Disorder
Description
The Etiology of Transsexualism: The Development of Atypical Gender Identity

Unconventional Choice of Sexual Object or Activity: The Paraphilias
Unconventional Choices of Sexual Object
Unconventional Choices of Sexual Activity

Psychoanalytic and Learning Theory Explanations and Treatment Implications
Psychoanalytic Explanations
Learning Theory Explanations

Homosexuality
Is Homosexuality a Psychological Disorder?
The Kinsey Report
The San Francisco Study
Diversity of Experience
Explanations
Treatment of Ego-Dystonic Homosexuality

Psychosexual Dysfunction and its Treatment
The Sexual Response Cycle
Explanations and Assessment

The Psychosexual Dysfunctions
Inhibited Sexual Desire
Inhibited Sexual Excitement
Inhibited Orgasm
Premature Ejaculation
Functional Dyspareunia and Functional
Vaginismus

Direct Therapy for Sexual Dysfunction
Mutual Responsibility
Information and Education

Attitude Change
Eliminating Performance Anxiety
Increasing Communication and
Effectiveness of Sexual Technique
Changing Destructive Lifestyles and Sex
Roles
Prescribing Changes in Behavior

**New Directions and Issues in Sexual
Dysfunctions and Their Treatment**
Diversity of Applications
Sexual Dysfunctions and Homosexuals
The Effectiveness of Sex Therapy

Summary

OVERVIEW

Consider the following scene: An adult man meets a young boy. They are not related. They go off to a private place, probably the man's house. Then with mutual consent, they have sexual relations.

Now stop for a moment and consider carefully your feelings about this scene. Do you feel angry? Disgusted? Shocked? You may be surprised to learn that in Siwan, in northern Africa, the above scene is a normal and accepted part of everyday life. In fact, in Siwan those men who do not engage in such

sexual activities are subject to ridicule by their peers.

Now consider a very different scene: A handsome young man and an attractive young woman are walking in Central Park on a clear spring day. They walk hand in hand gazing into each other's eyes. They pause and touch lips and put their arms around each other. Then they walk on, again holding hands.

Now stop reading for a moment and consider your feelings about this scene. You probably feel considerably more positive about what you have just read. Do you feel sympathy, joy, or approval? As unusual as it may seem, when members of the Thonga tribe first saw Europeans kissing, they probably did not react the way you did. The Thonga tribe members first laughed and then one remarked: "Look at them—they eat each other's saliva and dirt" (Ford & Beach, 1951).

The examples of adult and child homosexuality being accepted in Siwan and kissing not being accepted by the Thonga tribe suggest a most crucial point about human sexual behavior: Our ideas concerning the rights or wrongs of sexual behavior are shaped by the norms, values, and standards of the culture we are a part of. The result is the surprising differences in reactions to the sexual practices mentioned in the two scenes we considered.

In addition to the striking differences from culture to culture you would encounter as you travel around the world, there are some surprises to be discovered when you look at the history of sexual behavior within our own Western culture.

We can trace the roots of our current views of sexual behavior to the beliefs of the ancient Israelis and medieval Christians, who stressed that the natural aim of sex was procreation. By the 13th century, the Christian theologian Thomas Aquinas summarized the thinking of the day by declaring that intercourse was not only reserved for the purpose of procreation but that it was also to be restricted to the right person (i.e., the marriage partner) and in the right way (i.e., coitus).

As the church became less powerful, the psychiatrists became the new authorities about sexual matters and translated the old religious doctrine into medical terminology. However, the old doctrines persisted and what once was sin was now considered to be *sexual psychopathology*. By the 19th century a vast array of sexual "deviations,"

"perversions," and "aberrations" were categorized. People who diverged from the norms of "natural" coitus by choosing the "wrong" sexual object or by choosing the "wrong" sexual activity were believed to suffer from mental disorders (Haberle, 1978). For example, in the sexually repressed Victorian period, people who were known to masturbate were vulnerable to being labeled as having an affliction termed *masturbation insanity*. Frequent intercourse was seen as another cause of mental aberration. Such notions were popularized in the "marriage manuals" that were widely read during the 1830s and gave the stamp of medical authority to prevailing views and taboos. Only when it became clear that nearly everyone engaged in some type of "perverted" behavior did medical authorities begin to acknowledge that many sexual practices considered to be abnormal were in fact exaggerations of normal tendencies. Thus sexual behaviors that were shared by a wide variety of people and that were neither compulsive, destructive, nor personally distressing were no longer regarded as perversions by the medical profession.

Whether you look at the differences in what is acceptable sexual behavior from one culture to another, or whether you look at the differences in what was acceptable in our history compared to today, one thing remains the same. At all times and in all cultures, no matter what the norms, people who conform to the current societal values are seen as "normal," and those who do not are seen as "abnormal" and deviant.

What is considered normal and what is considered abnormal by the mental health practitioners in our culture? Perhaps the clearest statement of current psychiatric thinking about abnormal sexual behavior are the definitions of the psychosexual disorders presented in the DSM III classification.

In this chapter we will acquaint you with the major psychosexual disorders listed in DSM III. Our overview of the psychosexual disorders will begin with a discussion of the gender identity disorders and the paraphilias. These disorders are associated with unconventional sexual activities. More specifically, persons with gender identity disorders manifest their differentness in their feelings of discomfort and inappropriateness about their own anatomic sex, and by acting in ways that we generally associate with the opposite sex. As in previous listings of mental disorders, variations from the norms of conventional choice of sexual objects and choice of sexual activity are considered abnormal. Each of the paraphilias we will describe involves a variation from socially accepted norms and is distinguished by a diminished capacity of the person to engage in close, affectionate sexual relations with another person.

Homosexuality has been deleted from the list of mental disorders in the DSM III classification system. Social deviance is not the sole criterion for classifying a pattern of behavior as a psychological disorder. Homosexuality is one of the most common and therefore least deviant unconventional behaviors. However, the change from the previous classification of homosexuality reflects a growing recognition that homosexual behavior does not necessarily preclude intimate, affectionate, and rewarding relationships. Only when one's homosexuality is unwanted and personally distressing is it listed as the psychosexual disorder *egodystonic homosexuality.*

After we discuss homosexuality, we will conclude with a presentation of the psychosexual dysfunctions. We will see that these disorders are quite common and are characterized by a failure to enjoy and/or achieve accepted sexual behaviors.

THE GENDER IDENTITY DISORDERS AND THE PARAPHILIAS

The gender identity disorders and the paraphilias involve activities that are generally not accepted or viewed with tolerance by the majority of people in our society. Indeed, individuals with these psychosexual disorders often encounter reactions of disgust, surprise, and anger when their "different" behavior becomes known to others. Let us now turn our attention to *transsexualism,* a puzzling yet intriguing gender identity disorder.

TRANSSEXUALISM: A GENDER IDENTITY DISORDER

Description

The patient appears to be a beautiful woman. None of Martha K.'s friends in the fashion world suspect that "she" is actually a biologically normal male. "She" has worked as a highly successful fashion model for many years, unrecognized by anyone in society as not being a normal woman. But as far back as Martha K.'s memory goes, "she" recalls being feminine and wishing "she" were biologically female. "Her" mother confirms this and says that she never saw masculine behavior in her son. She says they were extremely close and loving but that his father was never present. She never dressed the boy in woman's clothing but was surprised and pleased that her son at age two was already dressing up in girls' clothes and putting on makeup. The patient hates "her" male body, wants it changed to female, but does not deny it is male. "She" does not consider "herself" a homosexual but rather a biologically normal male with completely feminine desires. "She" has never had nor even fantasized sexual relations with a woman, getting no excitement from women's bodies but rather feeling the same casualness in regard to them that a heterosexual woman does. Martha K. is very hopeful that the examining psychologists, psychiatrists, and surgeons will grant her request to undergo a sex-change operation (adapted from Stoller, 1971, p. 233).

It is estimated that about 2,500 persons have undergone sex-change operations in order to "make their bodies more like their minds." Benjamin (1966) captures the most characteristic attribute of the male transsexual: "The transsexual feels himself to be a woman trapped in a man's body" (p. 16). This feeling can cause great discomfort and result in severe complications for the transsexual who literally feels like a person of the oppo-

site sex and may attempt to live out that role. As you might imagine, social and occupational problems often result. Severe depression, suicide attempts, and even rare instances of genital mutilation have been reported (DSM III).

Groups of transsexuals have been identified which differ from each other in notable respects. Bentler (1976) has developed a typology of transsexualism that acknowledges the heterogeneous nature of this condition and that has been adopted by the DSM III classification system. Three major groups of transsexuals are distinguished according to sexual preference. They are termed *asexual*, *homosexual*, and *heterosexual*. Asexual transsexuals deny having ever experienced strong sexual feelings. The homosexual

Before sex change, Dr. Richard Raskin felt himself to be a woman trapped in a man's body. (Associated Press)

After sex change, Dr. Renee Richards faced a gradual gender reorientation. (United Press International)

group reports a preference for like-sexed individuals prior to the onset of the full pattern of sexual identification. However, they do not view their behavior as homosexual. This stems from their conviction that they are "really" of the other sex. The heterosexual group reports a history of active heterosexual involvement.

The Etiology of Transsexualism: The Development of Atypical Gender Identity

Martha K.'s experience is typical of transsexuals in that the incongruence between anatomic sex and gender identity (a person's self-concept as a man or woman) begins in early childhood. Richard Green, a researcher whose primary interest is atypical sex-role development in children, has attempted to trace the development of atypical sex-role behavior.

In order to better understand the acquisition of atypical sex-role behavior, Green (1974) has collected detailed information on 50 young boys who show an unusually high degree of feminine behavior but who have a normal male anatomy. These children had begun cross-dressing (dressing in clothes typical of the opposite sex) before their sixth birthday and typically have very poor relationships with other boys, but relate to girls. Frequently in their cross-dressing they improvise dresses and jewelry, and use nail polish or rouge. They are aware that they are males but wish to be females. They hope eventually to become women rather than men and, when given various projective tests, tend to identify feminine objects and themes. If asked to draw a person, these boys will more often draw girls than boys.

Green has studied the case histories of hundreds of these children, and he argues that no simple explanation of their atypical sex-role development is possible. But one can trace a developmental portrait that is typical of these boys.

Usually the mothers of these children believe them to be unusually attractive as infants and devote considerable attention to them. Typically they channel much of their feelings of love and care to the infant. As the child begins to explore his environment he may—as do all children—begin to play with his mother's shoes and cosmetics. Both parents respond positively to the behavior and give him considerable attention for "play acting" of this sort. Often the father perceives the cross-dressing behavior as "cute," but otherwise interacts very little with the child. Later, according to Green, when the father invites the child to play more culturally "masculine" games, the child will display little interest. The father then feels rejected and withdraws still further. By the time the boy starts school, he shows very little assertive behavior, relates poorly to his male schoolmates, and continues to cross-dress at home. The mother continues to regard the behavior as cute, while the father withdraws from the child. By this time the father frequently feels anxious about the child's atypical behavior and apparently feminine attributes. But still, both father and mother tend to regard the behavior as "only a passing phase." Usually by the time the child is seven, his peers have rejected him and the parents become distressed at the child's unhappiness. They may then consult a mental health professional for an opinion of the child's adjustment.

These young children, according to Green, frequently wish to have sex-change operations later in life. They tend to be very unhappy, partly because of the ostracism they feel from their peers and partly because they deeply believe that they are psychologically women, even though anatomically they remain males.

There are many similarities in the backgrounds of male and female transsexuals. In the backgrounds of both groups, early parental reinforcement of opposite-sex appropriate behavior is common, along with few consistent and effective rewards for sex-role stereotyped behavior (Bentler, 1976). As we have seen in the case of male transsexuals, maternal figures actively encourage opposite-sex role behavior, and fathers tend to be nonnurturant, weak, or physically absent from the household. In females, mothers are similarly distant or unavailable and the girl seems to compensate by identifying with her father. Such identification is seen as playing a role in the ultimate adoption of a male gender identity.

The early learning experiences described by Green probably do not account for all transsexual behavior in later life. The life histories of some transsexuals do not seem to fit Green's developmental portrait. Some researchers have wondered whether prenatal exposure of the brain to hormones of the wrong gender may cause transsexualism.

However, at present there is little direct evidence to support this hypothesis.

No one explanation can explain every case of transsexualism. But in both sexes, the complete transsexual pattern usually develops by the middle to late 20s. In adulthood transsexuals are likely to seek employment in jobs that are consistent with their masculine or feminine identification.

One of the puzzles of transsexualism is why there are so many more male than female transsexuals. The rate of males to females requesting sex-change operations varies from 2:1 to 8:1. Green notes that in our culture girls who engage in male sex-role behavior—"tomboys"—are tolerated and even encouraged. Boys who engage in female sex-role behavior, on the contrary, may suffer ridicule and are often rejected by playmates and adults. The greater acceptance of female cross-gender behavior may account, in part, for the greater number of male than female transsexuals.

SEX-CHANGE OPERATION AND THE PSYCHOLOGICAL ADJUSTMENT OF THE TRANSSEXUAL

Since the first sex-change operation was performed more than 30 years ago, hormone therapy and surgical procedures have helped certain transsexuals achieve their goal of "changing their bodies to fit their minds" (Haberle, 1978). The process of *gender reorientation* involves achieving an approximation of the status of the opposite biological sex (Blanchard, 1985). Gender reorientation is gradual and often begins with hormone therapy and getting a job in the opposite-sex role. In males, the hormones stimulate loss of facial hair and growth of breasts; in women, the hormones

encourage the development of masculine characteristics. Clinics and university medical school settings where sexual reassignment surgery is typically performed require that the transsexual successfully live in the role of a member of the opposite sex for six months to one year prior to surgery. To surgically effect a "sex change" in males, the penis and scrotum may be transformed into a vagina, and in women, an artificial phallus may be implanted.

We may think of the desire for a sex-change operation as unusual or even bizarre, but there is little evidence that the majority of transsexuals who apply for sexual reassignment surgery are psychotic or grossly disturbed. A study by Roback, Strassberg, McKee, and Cunningham (1977) found that 16 of 25 anatomical males seeking sexual reassignment surgery did not show signs of severe psychological disturbance on a self-report personality inventory. In a later study, considerable variation in self-concept and personal adjustment were found in a group of 17 female transsexuals applying for sex-change operations. More than half of the persons studied were not seriously disturbed (Strassberg, Roback, Cunningham, & Mckee, 1980). Both of these studies, however, found that the transsexuals who applied for operations were less adjusted than the samples of homosexuals and normals with which they were compared.

The assumption that underlies performing sexual reassignment surgery is that the transsexual will be more content and generally better adjusted following the sex change. Research conducted by Blanchard and his associates (Blanchard & Steiner, 1983; Blanchard, Clemmensen, & Steiner, 1983; Blanchard, Steiner, & Clemmensen, 1985) supports the assumption that gender reorientation is accompanied by diminished emotional distress. In a recent study (Blanchard, Steiner, & Clemmensen, 1985), they evaluated male and female postoperative transsexuals' degree of psychological symptoms and satisfaction with surgery after a period of at least a year. More than 90 percent of those studied indicated that they would repeat the surgery if they had it to do over. None of the subjects answered no to the question, "At the present time, do you feel that you would rather live as (the opposite biological sex)?" The degree of

psychological symptoms reported by the postoperative transsexuals was indistinguishable from that of nonpatient members of the general population. Finally, the majority of transsexuals supported themselves financially without public assistance.

In order to put the meaning of these findings in perspective, it is important to understand that the transsexuals studied were carefully evaluated and had demonstrated a satisfactory adjustment prior to surgery. Indeed, there is reason to believe that not all transsexuals may profit from sexual reassignment surgery. For instance, Beatrice (1985) recently found that transsexuals whose personality functioning is severely impaired may be at risk for further deterioration if they undergo a sex-change operation.

What our discussion suggests is that a thorough evaluation of the appropriateness of sex-change operations for applicants is crucial, along with carefully weighing the pros and cons of alternatives to surgery before irreversible "corrective" surgery is performed. The need for long-term evaluation of the transsexual prior to surgery is underscored by a recent study indicating that nearly half of the transsexuals followed in group therapy for a four-year period decided against surgery as an option (Keller, Althof, & Lothstein, 1982). Additional studies of transsexuals are needed to better predict which individuals are likely to profit from sex-change operations. But until the weight of evidence suggests that many transsexuals are unlikely to benefit from sex-change operations, many transsexuals who desperately seek sex-change operations will continue to find doctors who agree to perform sexual reassignment surgery.

UNCONVENTIONAL CHOICE OF SEXUAL OBJECT OR ACTIVITY: THE PARAPHILIAS

Let us now turn our attention to the paraphilias. DSM III defines the essential features of the paraphilias as involving "persistent and repetitive sexually arousing fantasies, frequently of an unusual nature that are associated with either (1) preference for use of a nonhuman object for sexual arousal, (2) repetitive sexual activity with humans involving real or simulated suffering or humiliation, or (3) repetitive sexual activity with nonconsenting partners" (DSM III, p. 266).

It is clear from the above definition that paraphiliac behavior may be harmful to others, may involve nonconsenting partners, or may include other activities that are at variance with community norms for appropriate behavior. When sexual fantasy and behavior are not only compulsive but lead to brutality and violence, they are particularly likely to be regarded as deviant, to be socially condemned, and to be subject to severe legal punishment. Engaging in sexual relations with children (pedophilia), for example, can be punished as a serious violent crime, whereas exposing one's genitals to a stranger (exhibitionism) is generally regarded as a mere nuisance by legal authorities. Thus the paraphilias are of legal as well as psychological significance. And both social and legal reactions may vary depending upon the nature of the sexual object or the activity involved.

As DSM III points out, many persons with these disorders do not perceive themselves as dangerous or as suffering from a mental disorder. Thus they may only come to the attention of the medical profession and legal authorities when their behavior has brought them into conflict with society. Since the paraphilias may never come to public attention, reliable estimates of their prevalence are difficult to obtain. But it is likely that persons suffering from one or more paraphilias constitute only a tiny fraction of the general population. As in the case of fetishism, which we will next consider, the paraphilias appear to be far rarer in females than in males.

Unconventional Choices of Sexual Object

Fetishism.   Here is a statement by a shoe fetishist:

> I can remember an interest in women's shoes as early as my fourth year. . . . When I was 12 years old I was attracted to my sister's shoes. I used to wait for her to sit at the table. I had a strong urge to get under the table. I would pretend to drop something to get under it. I was interested only in her shoes. . . . At about age 25, when I would sit opposite of a woman I would concentrate on her shoes and legs. In the earlier stages of this practice I would masturbate through my pocket, concealing this by holding a newspaper over my crossed legs. At a later stage . . . the effect of looking at shoes and legs being enough in itself to produce orgasm. . . . I have had only one experience with a girl when the shoe was not needed to make intercourse satisfying (adapted from a case study by Grant, 1958, pp. 142–43).

As can be seen in the case study, fetishism involves the use of an object such as a shoe or an article of clothing to obtain sexual arousal. In partialism, physical attributes or parts of the body assume fetishistic qualities. There are many shades and gradations of fetishistic tendencies. Gebhard (1969) defines a range of fetishistic preferences and behaviors. At one end there exists a mild preference for the fetish. Certain clothes such as high heels, for example, may be especially alluring. A preference for a man with a hairy chest or a woman with large breasts is certainly common and not at all abnormal.

More extreme fetishistic tendencies are evident where Gebhard believes "statistical normalcy ends and fetishism begins." Gebhard illustrates:

> This is nicely exemplified by one man who had his first recognition of his own fetishism when he realized he had ignored a beautiful girl to court a plain girl with a particular hair style. The next stage, that of necessity, would be the case of a man who is impotent unless his partner wears a certain type of shoe. The ultimate stage is the man who habitually dispenses with the female and achieves orgasm with only the shoe (p. 3).

According to DSM III, in true fetishism the fetish is used as the preferred or exclusive means of obtaining sexual arousal. The object may be incorporated in masturbatory fantasies or activities. A boot, for example, may be touched or fondled. The mere sight of the preferred item may be sufficient to produce an orgasm. Fetishism is much rarer in females than males.

Some commonly chosen items include high-heeled shoes and boots, garter belts, black mesh stockings, and corsets. Gebhard reports that when corset fetishism was common, men paid to look through peepholes at customers trying on corsets at certain shops. Fetishists have been known to steal lingerie items from clotheslines. Collecting fetishistic items can be a favored pastime, even a preoccupation, with the fetishist.

For some people with a fetishistic orientation, the material of which the item is made can be a potent source of sexual excitement. For example, the fact that a shoe or glove is

Fetishism involves the use of an object such as a shoe or an article of clothing to obtain sexual arousal.
(Richard Heyza/*The Seattle Times*)

made of leather can be even more important than the form of the object. Rubber, plastic, and fur are other common examples.

We should note that in DSM III fetishism is distinguished from transvestism, where the fetishistic objects are limited to female clothing used in cross-dressing. Prince (1972) found that only 13 percent of 504 transvestites surveyed reported fetishistic excitement.

Pedophilia. Pedophilia, which means literally, love of children, is characterized by a chronic preference for sexual activity with prepubertal children (DSM III). It is important to distinguish the pedophile from a person who engages in isolated instances of child sexual exploitation as a result of intense loneliness, marital conflict, or the recent loss of a loved one. In pedophilia the person *prefers* to have a sexual relationship with a child rather than an adult.

The common stereotype of the pedophile as a "dirty old man" molesting children who are strangers to him after enticing them with candy rarely mirrors reality. Actually, in about 85 percent of the cases, the child is known to the adult, who lives or works in close proximity to the child. Also, the offender is most likely to be married and in the 20 to 40 age range.

Some evidence suggests that pedophiles tend to be religious, moralistic, and socially and sexually immature (Walters, 1975). Presumably they compensate for their feelings of inadequacy by choosing less threatening sexual partners—children. Most often pedophiles look at or touch the genitals of the child; intercourse is rare. The victim is most typically an 8- to 10-year-old girl.

There are both heterosexual and homosexual pedophiles. However, there appear to be about twice as many heterosexual pedophiles. The average homosexual is no more likely to seduce children than the average heterosexual man.

Unconventional Choices of Sexual Activity

Voyeurism. Looking at naked or partially clothed bodies is sexually exciting for many men and women. The commercial success of magazines such as *Playboy* and the popularity of magazines catering to women that feature photographs of nude men attest to the widespread appeal of looking at the naked or partially clothed body. These activities, clearly well within the range of normal sexual interest and activity, can be easily distinguished from those of the voyeur described in the following example.

> Beginning at age 16, the patient went into his neighborhood and looked into windows to observe naked women. At age 20, he married but continued to spend at least one hour a night peering into windows on nights when he didn't have intercourse with his wife. He was primarily interested in seeing women's breasts and occasionally enjoyed watching a woman have intercourse. When he observed these forbidden scenes, he usually masturbated, but sometimes would wait to masturbate, fantasizing about what he had seen. He eventually came to enjoy "peeping" more than sexual relations with his wife. The patient was arrested at age 22 and referred for psychological counseling as a condition of his probation.

The voyeur obtains sexual excitement by looking or "peeping" at unsuspecting women who are either naked, in the act of disrobing, or engaging in sexual activity. He is likely to repeatedly seek out situations where it is possible for him to do this. Like exhibitionism, which we will describe below, these actions are not a prelude for further sexual activity and direct sexual contact is not desired. It is not entirely clear why this behavior is sexually exciting for the voyeur. At least part of the excitement may come from the forbidden and dangerous nature of the activity and the knowledge that the person would be embarrassed or humiliated if she were aware she was observed. Support for this idea comes from the observation that the true voyeur is not stimulated by "peeping" at his own wife or sexual partner. As in the case of the person in our example, masturbation while observing or in response to the memory of the stranger is common. In severe cases the voyeur may prefer peeping to the exclusion of other sexual activities.

The adult voyeur rarely partakes in this activity with another person. He may wait for hours to observe a woman undress and frequently returns to a number of favored places "like an ardent fisherman" (Gebhard, Gagnon, Pomeroy, & Christenson, 1965). He is likely to come to the attention of police when neighbors or passersby report his actions. Occasionally the voyeur may be shot at, mistaken for a burglar, or injure himself falling off a roof or window ledge.

The voyeur is likely to be of normal intelligence, young (average age of first sex offense, 22.5), and neither an alcohol or drug abuser, and the person is unlikely to have serious emotional problems. Gebhard et al.'s study of peepers (1965) showed that although they are not prone to serious antisocial behavior, they are likely to be involved in minor criminality. Only about 20 percent of the offenses involved force, indicating that, as a group, voyeurs are unlikely to be dangerous. Most often, peepers are charged with disorderly conduct. More dangerous voyeurs are likely to enter a building or home in order to observe a woman or draw the attention of the person to the fact that they are watching (Yalom, 1960).

Exhibitionism.   The stereotype of the exhibitionist is that of a lecherous, older man who jumps out of bushes and opens his raincoat to expose himself to a terrified woman. Actually exhibitionists tend to be passive and rather young, ranging in age from about

Societal values differ for male and female bodily exposure. (Jan Lukas/Rapho-Photo Researchers, Inc.)

14 to 38. The onset of exhibitionism occurs most frequently in midpuberty and the early 20s. When their sexual behavior is compared with others in terms of frequency of intercourse, number of sexual partners, and age at first intercourse, exhibitionists fall well below the norm (McWhorter, 1978).

Far from being a dangerous criminal, the typical exhibitionist is likely to more closely resemble a respectable average citizen who may even be married and have children. Characteristics attributed to exhibitionists include compulsive tendencies, sensitivity to criticism, low frustration tolerance, and insecurity in social relations. Marital conflict and poor sexual adjustment also have been reported.

The exhibitionist most notably differs from the average man in the way in which sexual excitement is obtained. For the exhibitionist sexual arousal results directly from exposing his genitals to women or children. Almost invariably, the victim is an unconsenting stranger. Physical contact rarely occurs and conversation is initiated only to attract the victim's attention. Most typically exposure takes place in a public place such as a subway, bus, or a park where the exhibitionist may pretend he is urinating.

The compulsive nature of the exhibitionistic act is underscored by the fact that the exhibitionist risks apprehension by exposing himself in highly public places. The act of exposure is not intended as a prelude to further sexual advances. In fact, the exhibitionist is likely to run away if a female observer responds with interest. Sexual excitement can be immediate or it can occur shortly after the incident.

Depression, anxiety, or stress may trigger an exposure in some exhibitionists. Others report a sudden, irresistible urge to expose themselves with no identifiable precipitants. Some exhibitionists report that they were suffering from temporary amnesia and were curiously detached from their actions at the time of exposure. However, such claims may just as easily be seen as a denial of responsibility for an act that provokes guilt and shame when the person is identified or apprehended.

One thing is clear however: The intent of the exhibitionistic act is to evoke a reaction of surprise, embarrassment, or shock from the victim. The victim's strong reaction may bolster the exhibitor's fragile sense of masculinity. This interpretation is supported by clinical observations that threats to masculine self-esteem often precede exposures. The attention displayed by the victim, the reaction of horror, admiration, or awe may strongly reinforce the deviant behavior, increasing the likelihood of future recurrence.

Even the prospect of apprehension by the police may be exciting and reinforce a sense of power and masculinity for posing such a threat (Mathis, 1969).

Exhibitionism is usually regarded by law enforcement agents as more of a nuisance than a dangerous threat. However, exhibitionism accounts for nearly a third of all arrests for sex-related offenses. In addition, nearly 20 percent of exhibitionists are rearrested, the highest rate for sex offenders. Most offenders receive suspended sentences and are placed on probation and urged to seek counseling.

Cases of adolescents who expose themselves on a dare, adults under considerable stress who expose themselves only on a single occasion, and temporal lobe epileptics whose seizure behavior may be mistaken for exhibitionism should probably be considered separately from the compulsive exhibitionist.

Our society clearly has different values relating to male and female bodily exposure. Women can attract attention and even admiring recognition by wearing revealing clothes. The woman who exposes her body and earns a living by dancing nude on a stage may be considered to be exhibitionistic, but not an exhibitionist. Perhaps there are virtually no reports of compulsive female exhibitionism because society provides women with considerably greater latitude in dress than males.

Our societal attitudes regarding exhibitionistic behavior in men and women are also mirrored in our legal system, which clearly favors the woman. Consider the case in which a man observes a woman undressing in front of an open window. The man is the offender (a voyeur), the woman the victim. However, if the roles are reversed and the woman observes the man undressing, she would again be the victim and the male an exhibitionist.

Transvestism. Here is a description of a transvestite:

The patient, in his 30s, is married, the father of three children, and a precision machine operator. His first experience in dressing in the clothes of the opposite sex is remembered as a tremendously exciting sexual experience in which, as a punishment, an aunt forced him to cross-dress at age 7. While he has no conscious memory of it, however, he has learned that he was first cross-dressed by another aunt at age 4. From puberty on, sexual excitement was invariably and intensely induced by putting on women's shoes. As the years passed, this gradually progressed so that with each episode of cross-dressing he now dresses completely as a woman, and with proper makeup to hide his beard, has passed in society for a few hours at a time. He has never had a homosexual relationship and has sexual interest in female bodies, but though looking excites him, lying next to a woman is more complicated: he can then only maintain full potency either by putting on women's garments or fantasizing that he has them on (adapted from Stoller, 1971, p. 231).

This case provides an excellent illustration of *transvestism*. The transvestite obtains intense sexual arousal by dressing in the clothing of a woman. This pattern of receiving sexual pleasure by cross-dressing may be so habitual and persistent that interference with it can result in intense frustration (DSM II).

The onset is almost invariably in childhood or early adolescence. Perhaps you noticed that the patient in the case history was forced by his aunt to cross-dress as a punishment. Such a humiliating punishment by a maternal figure is common in the backgrounds of transvestites, although it is not clear exactly how this experience contributes to the later development of cross-dressing. As well as representing a source of sexual gratification, cross-dressing may reduce anxiety. Some transvestites tend to cross-dress when they are under stress, and it has

It is important not to confuse homosexuals with transvestites. Some homosexuals cross-dress to attract another male or as a theatrical disguise. Transvestites obtain intense sexual arousal from dressing in the clothing of a woman. (Robert V. Eckert Jr./EKM-Nepenthe)

been hypothesized that this behavior serves as a comforting retreat from the tensions of everyday life. Curiously, there are almost no reports of transvestism in females. While cross-dressing among women is certainly not unknown, it does not appear to be accompanied by sexual arousal.

Although cross-dressing does suggest that the transvestite has a "feminine side" to his personality, he is generally not effeminate. Transvestites firmly identify themselves as males. Like the patient in our example, most transvestites are family men who are married with children and work in traditionally male occupations. When not cross-dressed, the transvestite resembles other men in mannerisms and appearance.

Some reports also suggest that transvestites feel inadequate in heterosexual relationships and fear potential rejection. Some may use marriage as a means of bolstering their masculine self-concept. Marriage, however, is often experienced as stressful and is unsuccessful in eliminating compulsive cross-dressing (Bentler, 1976).

It is very important not to confuse transvestites with homosexuals. Confusion can result because a small number of homosexuals do cross-dress on occasion. The male homosexual's feminine masquerade is designed to attract another male or to disguise himself in a theatrical manner as a woman. However, unlike the transvestite, homosexuals do not experience sexual excitement from wearing female clothing. In addition, the overwhelming majority of transvestites have a clear preference for women over males as sexual partners.

Many transvestites are initially sexually excited by one or a few preferred articles of feminine clothing. Lingerie items such as panties and nightgowns are reported to be especially attractive. Some transvestites begin dressing in complete feminine attire and persist with this pattern throughout their lives. Most commonly, more and more articles of clothing are adopted until a complete feminine costume is preferred.

The power of the woman's garment as a sexual stimulus is underscored by the fact that erectile failure may result when clothing is not worn or fantasized during intercourse by transvestites. About one fifth of the wives of transvestites never learn that their husbands cross-dress. Marital complications such as divorce can arise when the wife is aware of and intolerant of her husband's unusual behavior.

Sadomasochism. The intermingling of sex and aggression is deeply embedded in our culture. A blend of sex and violence is portrayed in movies and artfully packaged in advertisements. Indeed, it is tempting to speculate that the public interest in violence and aggression serves deep-seated sexual needs. Certainly, sexual fantasies that combine sex and aggression are not uncommon. About one in eight females and one in five males studied at the Institute for Sex Research reported being sexually aroused by stories in which the main character either inflicts pain on another or is humiliated and endures personal pain in a sexual context.

Few individuals, however, *prefer* to obtain sexual arousal through giving or receiving physical or psychological pain. The psychosexual patterns in which there is a conjoining of sex, pain, and aggression are termed *sexual sadism* and *sexual masochism*. The consolidated term *sadomasochism* is frequently used since sadism and masochism are often thought of as mirror images of the same phenomenon.

According to DSM III, the central feature of sexual sadism is physical or psychological suffering inflicted on another person. For the sadist, inflicting suffering is necessary to produce sexual excitement. In contrast, the masochist derives sexual pleasure from experiencing suffering. Some masochists find pleasure in being humiliated, bound, beaten, or placed in elaborate restraints. The sadist may enjoy the reverse role: humiliating, degrading, or injuring another as a preferred way of achieving sexual excitement.

Unless they are acted out, sadistic or masochistic fantasies are not sufficient for diagnosing sexual sadism or masochism. In fact, the overwhelming majority of people with sadomasochistic tendencies never act out their fantasies. One important outlet for sadomasochistic impulses is reading "trade magazines" that feature pictures of women dressed in leather and high-heeled shoes who dominate, restrain, and torture their "victims" with whips, chains, gags, and ropes.

Sadomasochistic behaviors vary in their degree and intensity. The mildest forms that may accompany intercourse probably should not be regarded as truly sadomasochistic (Levitt, 1971). In fact, in some societies aggressive behavior and inflicting pain on one's partner are part of normal love play. Women on the island of Truk customarily poke a finger into the man's ear when they are sexually excited. Charotic tribe women spit into their partner's face during intercourse, and the Arpinage tribe woman may bite off her lover's eyebrows and noisily spit them to one side (Ford & Beach, 1951).

Surprisingly few sadomasochists actively seek situations in which extreme pain is involved. The situational context in which the sadomasochistic drama is enacted is perhaps more important than the pain itself. The sadomasochistic session usually follows a "script." The masochist must have transgressed or done something worthy of punishment; threats and suspense precede the punishment. The sadist must be sensitive to the amount of pain that the masochist desires and can tolerate or risk losing a partner. Intermixing love and tenderness with pain and punishment seems to add to the sexual tension and the power of the ritual. The script may be somewhat altered for masochists who prefer bondage. Here, stimulation is derived not from pain but from a sense of helplessness, constraint, and discomfort. Fetishistic paraphernalia such as leather clothing, whips, black stockings, garter belts, and restraining devices may be part of the drama and heighten sexual arousal. Pain, punishment, or bondage may be experienced before, during, or after a sexual act (Gebhard, 1969).

A study by Spengler (1976) provides us with a closer look at the characteristics and experiences of the heterosexual and homosexual sadomasochist. Answering contact ads in "trade" magazines and partly with the help of sadomasochistic clubs, Spengler was able to survey 245 German males. Although the sample represented only sadomasochists who were searching for a partner through use of the communications media, the results were of some interest. Spengler found that few men were exclusively sadistic or masochistic. Most sadomasochists enacted both roles in order to accommodate to different partners. Since sadists are far rarer than masochists, role trading is a virtual necessity.

When two masochists meet, necessity dictates that they take turns at the sadist's role. Spengler also found that nearly half of the men surveyed achieved sexual satisfaction without sadomasochistic experiences. In fact, only about 15 percent experienced sexual excitement exclusively in connection with sadomasochistic activities.

A high level of adjustment and self-acceptance was expressed by the majority of the respondents. Only 10 percent of those surveyed required professional help with regard to their sadomasochistic orientation. Very few reported a past suicide attempt. Most of the participants expressed positive attitudes toward their sexual orientation, with only 20 percent preferring to have "no sadomasochistic desires." These results may present an unusually favorable picture of the sadomasochist because the respondents tended to be males who were well educated, held responsible jobs, and enjoyed high social status.

PSYCHOANALYTIC AND LEARNING THEORY EXPLANATIONS AND TREATMENT IMPLICATIONS

Psychoanalytic Explanations

At the heart of the numerous psychoanalytically oriented explanations of the paraphilias are conflicts and fears having their origins in the earliest years of life. For example, in psychoanalytic thinking voyeurism is viewed as related to the primal scene: the child observing the parents having intercourse. Observing individuals making love is interpreted as an attempt to return to the primal scene and gain mastery over it. It has also been suggested that in fetishism the fetish represents, on a symbolic level, a loved or sexually desired person. Unrewarding relationships that are perceived as threatening may also contribute to reliance on objects as a primary source of sexual gratification.

A variety of paraphilias have been conceptualized as symptoms of deep-seated Oedipal conflicts and castration fears. This is consistent with the psychoanalytic perspective's assumption that childhood developmental difficulties and problems in later life are linked. The pedophile is seen as driven by powerful yet forbidden desires for his mother. To reduce Oedipal anxiety and fears of retaliation by his father (castration), he avoids mature sexual relationships with adults and instead seeks immature sexual relationships with children. These fears operate at an unconscious level but nonetheless exert a potent influence on behavior.

The sadist copes with feelings of inferiority and fears of castration by adopting a controlling, domineering stance in sexual relations. Both the role that the sadist assumes and the victim's suffering reassure the sadist that he is more powerful than his partner and neutralize any threat she could pose. At the same time as the sadist's actions say, "I am in charge here," his acts of cruelty convey the message, "You deserve to be punished for having sexual thoughts and taking part in sex." By associating sex with power, subjugation, and violence, instead of with conventional sensuality, the sadist may sidestep guilt feelings related to childhood prohibitions against sexual expression. The masochist, on the other hand, forestalls guilt and allays his fear of punishment by experiencing himself as the passive victim of aggression (Reik, 1941; Shapiro, 1981).

Earlier we made note of the reinforcing aspects of the victim's startled reaction in cases of exhibitionism. Analytic thinkers would contend that the woman's shock, horror, or awe bolster not only the sense of power the man seeks over women but also the man's feelings of masculinity and his denial of castration fears (Tollison & Adams, 1979).

The explanations given above came about by applying psychoanalytic concepts and terminology to frequently observed characteristics of paraphiliacs: atypical sexual behavior, poor social skills, fears of rejection, and insecurity in social relationships. These characteristics have also been the wellspring of behavioral models of the genesis and treatment of paraphilias. Psychodynamic psychologists think about and treat the paraphilias by way of promoting insight into past-related conflicts and fears. In contrast, behavioral psychologists stress the assessment and modification of present behaviors, thoughts, and feelings. Behavior therapists invoke the concepts and principles of learning to understand the paraphilias.

Learning Theory Explanations

A learning theory explanation of the development of exhibitionism and other paraphilias underscores the importance of sexual fantasies. McGuire, Carlisle, and Young (1965) noted that more than three quarters of a sample of patients with various paraphilias reported the use of a "deviant" fantasy while masturbating. They reasoned that exhibitionistic behavior and other unconventional sexual activities might be reinforced through masturbatory activity. An initial exhibitionistic act may supply the person with a fantasy that may be used during masturbation. Using the fantasy repeatedly during masturbation may reinforce the fantasy *and* the exhibitionistic behavior as a source of sexual arousal. Maletsky (1974) used a foul-smelling substance, which was presented to the client as exhibitionistic images were imagined, to reduce exhibitionistic behavior. The fact that "deviant" fantasies may be initially tied to unconventional sexual behavior may account, in part, for the success of using such fantasies as the target of behavioral treatments like those just described.

A TREATMENT PROGRAM FOR PARAPHILIAS

Schwartz and Masters (1983) have recently described a still experimental behaviorally oriented treatment program for the paraphilias. Their therapeutic model conceptualizes the paraphilia as an interpersonal relationship disorder. All paraphiliacs, they feel, share a common feature: the inability to cope with the intimacy of close relationships without withdrawing into a secret, comfortable world of fantasy. Paraphiliacs experience discomfort and stress in adult erotic relationships and resort to deviant fantasies and behavior in order to reduce anxiety. This anxiety reduction has powerful reinforcing properties and enhances the "hold" the disorder has on the person. In order to counteract the power of deviant sexual fantasies and associated activities, Schwartz and Johnson believe it is necessary to neutralize the roadblocks to achieving appropriate expressions of sexuality and intimacy. This is accomplished in a two-phase treatment program. In the pretreatment counseling phase, which is also termed Phase One, male patients attend 14 three-hour group sessions once a week. The group therapy format is used to teach dating and social/assertiveness skills, reduce misconceptions about sexuality, enhance self-confidence, and help patients find potential female partners for the second treatment phase. Men who have adequate social skills and are able to establish a relationship are not required to complete Phase One. Behavioral techniques to change erotic imagery may also be used in this and the second phase of treatment.

In Phase Two the man and his partner live in social isolation for two weeks and come to the clinic on a daily basis. While they live together 24 hours a day, the destructive patterns that interfere with the development of a truly satisfactory intimate relationship come to the forefront and become the target for therapeutic interventions. Fears of closeness are likely to surface in the bedroom when the couple engages in sexual activity. A graded series of structured touching exercises helps the couple to experience sexual relationships in an atmosphere that is nonthreatening and nondemanding. These sensate focus exercises will be discussed in some detail in the section on sexual dysfunctions. Communication and assertiveness skills are also reinforced in this stage of treatment: self-assertion, self-responsibility, intimacy, and self-esteem issues are tackled in a direct manner. Suggestions are made on how to behave and interact differently in order to better cope with stress and to relate in a nondestructive manner. After the two-week, intensive treatment period, supportive follow-up is available for another two years.

The cornerstone of the treatment philosophy is the hypothesis that "when all is well in the love relationship, the paraphiliac's desire to act out usually is markedly diminished or completely alleviated" (Schwartz & Johnson, 1983, p. 14). This hypothesis has great appeal. Indeed, psychoanalytic and behavioral thinkers both stress the disruption in the ability of the paraphiliac to achieve intimacy. However, as Schwartz and Johnson are careful to note, until long-term follow-up data on the success of the program are available, their hypothesis must remain tentative. Given the long-standing and tenacious character of the paraphilias, outcome data on this treatment program will prove to be of great interest to the scientific community.

In early life behaviors may be reinforced that are associated with the later development of unusual sexual behaviors. For example, observations of transvestites and their families suggest that parents, particularly mothers, may actively encourage and praise the child for dressing in his mother's clothes. In later life reliance on such activities for sexual gratification may lead to self-hatred and social withdrawal and isolation. Furthermore, persons who develop deviant sexual practices may do so, in part, because they are shy, socially unskilled, and unable to establish rewarding relationships with appropriate, suitable partners. In addition to altering fantasy patterns, behavior therapists are likely to modify the behavior of the paraphiliac in order to increase the likelihood that mature, socially and sexually rewarding relationships can be established. A recent trend in behavioral treatment programs is to include the following components for normalizing relationships and sexual practices: dating practice, sexual education, communication skills, training in making appropriate assertive responses, and encouraging social risk taking.

HOMOSEXUALITY

I dare to speak out as a mother—as an American—as a Christian, I urgently need you to join with me and my family in a national crusade against this attack on God and His laws. It's really God's battle, not mine (Anita Bryant, speaking about homosexuality, quoted by McNaught, 1977, p. 34).

Since I've joined the Gay Liberation Movement . . . I've come to an unshakable conclusion: The illness theory of homosexuality is a pack of lies concocted out of the fundamentalist myths of a patriarchial society for the *political* purpose of perpetuating the current societal ethic. Psychiatry, dedicated to making sick people well, is the cornerstone of a system of oppression that makes people sick (Ronald Gold, Chairman, News and Media Committee of the Gay Activities Alliance of New York, in a speech to the American Psychiatric Association, 1973, p. 1).

The issue has to be decided on the basis of solid clinical and scientific evidence. The overwhelming bulk of data on hand, both clinical and scientific, show that homosexuality is the result of certain pathological patterns. This is not something to decide by popular vote (Dr. Harold Voth, comments after the American Psychiatric Association decision to remove homosexuality from its list of mental disorders, 1974).

Is Homosexuality a Psychological Disorder?

Homosexuality is a topic that behavioral scientists are struggling to understand. Considerable disagreement persists about its fundamental nature and cause. Whether or not homosexuality should be considered a mental disorder has been the subject of much controversy. In April 1974 in a history-making decision, the American Psychiatric Association supported a motion to remove homosexuality from its list of mental disorders. The decision was accompanied by the creation of a new category in the APA's *Diagnostic and Statistical Manual of Mental Diseases* (DSM II) termed *Sexual Orientation Disturbance.* The term applied only to those who were distressed or in conflict with their sexual orientation. Although it did not go so far as to say homosexuality was "normal," homosexuality by itself would no longer be viewed as a mental illness unless accompanied by internal conflict or social dysfunction.

This classification represents a more tolerant approach than previous attempts to categorize homosexuality. In 1952 DSM I listed homosexuality as a subcategory of sociopathic personality along with antisocial personality, alcoholism, and drug addiction. In 1968 the revised edition, DSM II, no longer

Many homosexuals are not only satisfied with their sexual orientation but are also psychologically and socially adjusted. (Rick Grosse/EKM-Nepenthe)

In order to better appreciate the wisdom of the decision to reclassify homosexuality, we will survey a number of ground-breaking studies that have helped to dispel stereotypes and misconceptions about homosexuality.

The Kinsey Report

Public furor followed Kinsey's startling revelation that homosexuality was far more widespread than previously believed. Perhaps the most surprising finding was that 37 percent of white American males had at least

listed homosexuality as a separate category of sexual deviation. Thus homosexuality was included among "sexual perversions" such as sadism, masochism, fetishism, and voyeurism.

In the most recent revision, DSM III, homosexuality per se is not included. A new category was created, *ego-dystonic homosexuality.* This is characterized by a desire to acquire or increase heterosexual arousal so that heterosexual relationships can be initiated or maintained. In addition, there is a sustained pattern of overt homosexual arousal that the individual explicitly complains is unwanted and is a source of distress. It is obvious that this represents a dramatic change from previous classifications that emphasized the pathological nature of homosexuality.

Dr. Alfred O. Kinsey, the famed and controversial sex researcher who founded the Institute for Sex Research. (Associated Press)

one homosexual experience leading to orgasm between adolescence and old age. Half of all males reported a homosexual encounter by age 55. Since many of the contacts reported were limited to sporadic experiences in adolescence, a more relevant, yet equally unexpected finding was that 10 percent of the sample was almost exclusively homosexual for at least three years between 16 and 55. In addition, about 4 percent of males reported exclusive homosexuality.

The incidence of homosexuality appeared to be considerably lower in females. Estimates vary, but percentages of males reporting homosexual behavior are consistently twice that of females (Cory & LeRoy, 1961; Kinsey, Pomeroy, Martin, & Gebhard, 1953). Some researchers have suggested, however, that there may be as many female as male homosexuals, but that women may be better able to conceal their homosexuality.

After Kinsey's monumental work, scientists could no longer ignore the fact of homosexuality. Kinsey's efforts were also important because he helped to clarify and sharpen our thinking about homosexuality. Before the first Kinsey report, it was common practice to think of people as either homosexual or heterosexual. Kinsey discovered that people reported widely different amounts of homosexual experience. Some individuals appeared to be exclusively homosexual, while others experienced only a single homosexual contact in early adolescence. Kinsey contended, "It would encourage clearer thinking on these matters if persons were not categorized as heterosexual or homosexual, but as individuals who have had certain amounts of heterosexual experience and certain amounts of homosexual experience" (quoted by Haberle, 1978, p. 230). Indeed, if we were to categorize as homosexual all persons with one homosexual experience, a sizable number of males would fall into this category.

In keeping with his view that homosexual and heterosexual behavior ranged along a continuum, Kinsey and his associates (1953) devised a seven-point scale that measured the balance of heterosexual and homosexual psychological reactions and overt experiences. This scale is illustrated in Figure 14–1.

A person's place on this continuum may change as a result of age and life circumstances (Bell, 1973). People differ not only in terms of the extensiveness of their homosexual experience but also in the way they think and feel about their homosexuality. There may be a disparity in one's behavior rating and the ratings of homosexual feelings on the Kinsey scale. Many people who engage in sporadic homosexual activities do not think of themselves as homosexuals. Men with no prior homosexual experience when imprisoned may engage in homosexual activities, yet later return to an exclusively heterosexual lifestyle. Some male prostitutes who cater to a homosexual clientele consider themselves to be heterosexual. When not earning their living as a prostitute, they are exclusively heterosexual (Reiss, 1961). Humphreys (1970) studied men who occasionally partake in anonymous homosexual activities in public restrooms ("tearooms"). He found that many of the men were heterosexually married and clearly identified themselves as heterosexual. Perhaps the most clear-cut and defensible way of classifying homosexual orientation is preference for same-sex romantic and sexual partners (Schwartz & Masters, 1984).

The San Francisco Study

Now that we have a clearer understanding of the complexities involved in defining and assessing homosexuality, let us turn our attention to a pioneering study conducted by Alan Bell and Martin Weinberg, also of the Kinsey Institute of Sex Research. The way in which the so-called San Francisco study was conducted is perhaps as fascinating as

FIGURE 14–1
Heterosexual-Homosexual Rating Scale

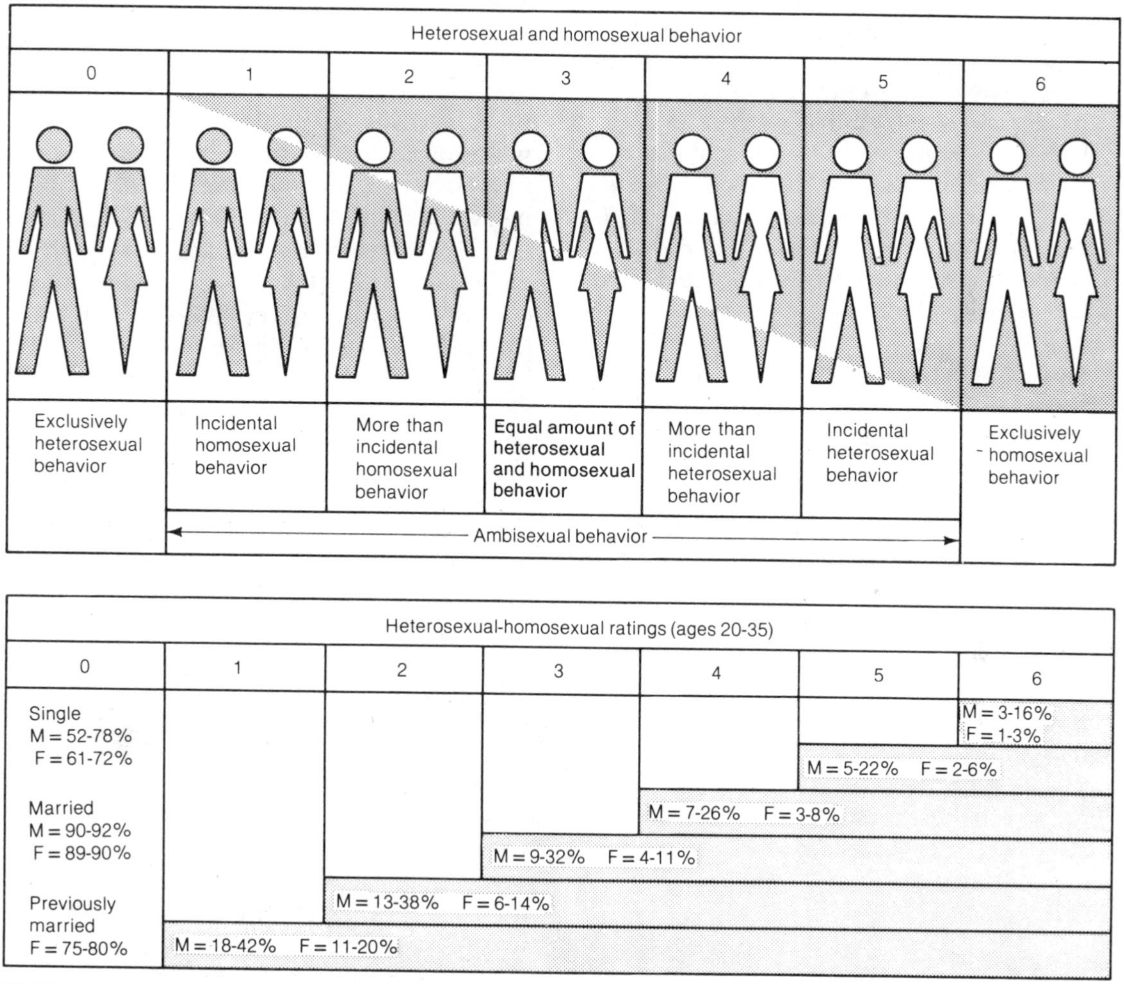

	Heterosexual and homosexual behavior					
0	1	2	3	4	5	6
Exclusively heterosexual behavior	Incidental homosexual behavior	More than incidental homosexual behavior	Equal amount of heterosexual and homosexual behavior	More than incidental heterosexual behavior	Incidental heterosexual behavior	Exclusively homosexual behavior

←———————— Ambisexual behavior ————————→

	Heterosexual-homosexual ratings (ages 20–35)					
0	1	2	3	4	5	6
Single M = 52-78% F = 61-72%						M = 3-16% F = 1-3%
					M = 5-22% F = 2-6%	
Married M = 90-92% F = 89-90%				M = 7-26% F = 3-8%		
			M = 9-32% F = 4-11%			
Previously married F = 75-80%		M = 13-38% F = 6-14%				
	M = 18-42% F = 11-20%					

Note: Scale and figures adapted from Kinsey's data for males (M) and females (F) published in 1953. The ranges of percentages result from different ratios in various subgroups within the seven categories. These categories themselves are somewhat arbitrary, and the whole scale should therefore be read as a continuum.

Source: Adapted from Kinsey et al., "Sexual Behavior in the Human Female," from *The Sex Atlas* by Erwin J. Haberle. Used by permission of The Continuum Publishing Corporation, New York.

the data itself. Bell (1973) summarizes the mechanics involved:

We recruited subjects from all kinds of sources: through public advertising of various kinds, in public and private bars and restaurants where approximately 1,000 hours were spent recruiting potential subjects, at small gatherings in private homes or through contacts made on a one-to-one basis in an effort to get at the most covert individuals; we sent information about the study to almost 6,000 individuals, using the mailing lists of various homophile organizations, bars, and bookstores.

We recruited in eight different steam baths, at the meetings and social activities of 23 different homophile organizations in the Bay Area, in men's rooms, theater lobbies and balconies, parks and beaches, the streets and public squares. Needless to say, it would have been much easier to rely entirely on the bars or the homophile organizations for our subjects, but we wanted to make sure that we included as many different kinds of homosexuals as possible in our samples. Otherwise, the incredible range of homosexual experience would have been missing (p. 6).

Ultimately 979 homosexual men and women were interviewed in 1970. In addition, 477 heterosexuals drawn from a random sample of San Francisco area residents were questioned. Males, females, blacks, and whites participated in a three- to four-hour face-to-face interview. The study, based as it was in an area well known for its tolerance of gay individuals, may present a somewhat unrealistically favorable picture of homosexual adjustment. However, it represents the first time that a truly diverse sample of homosexuals have been studied, that homosexuals have been compared with one another, and that types of homosexuals have been compared with heterosexuals. Thus while the findings may not be representative of all homosexuals, the results are based on substantial numbers of all types of homosexuals. Previous studies have tended to focus

A TYPOLOGY OF HOMOSEXUALITIES

One of the overriding goals of Bell and Weinberg's research was to map the diversity of homosexual lifestyles. In keeping with this goal, they defined an inclusive typology of homosexuals. The categories they present suggest that important differences in adjustment among homosexuals can be identified and parallels between homosexuals and heterosexuals can be discerned as well. Homosexuals were categorized into the five distinct groups presented below:

1. The *close coupleds* resembled "happily married" heterosexual couples in many ways. They lived in quasi-marriages, which tended to be long-standing. Such relationships were characterized by emotional commitment, fidelity, and a sharing of household responsibilities. Close coupleds expressed few regrets about their lifestyles, claimed to have few sexual

problems, and appeared to be relatively content and self-accepting. In terms of psychological adjustment, they could not be distinguished from the heterosexuals and actually scored higher on happiness measures. When compared with the other groups of homosexuals, they were the best adjusted. They were more self-accepting, happier, and less lonely and depressed.

2. *Open coupleds* also lived as partners but engaged in substantial sexual activity apart from their primary relationships. This type of independent, nonattached relationship was most common among males. Open coupled women experienced such a relationship as more difficult than men. Males tended to be more self-accepting and less lonely than women in this type of relationship. With respect to psychological adjustment, open coupleds tended to resemble the average homosexual respondent.

3. The *functional* homosexuals were highly active sexually and freewheeling, comparable in behavior to "swinging singles" among heterosexuals. Sexual experiences played an especially important role in their lives. They reported the greatest number of sexual partners, the fewest sexual problems, and expressed the least regret about their homosexuality. Of all groups, they were most involved in the homosexual community. They *cruised* frequently for partners, attended gay bars, and were most likely to come in contact with the police on account of their homosexuality. Their psychological adjustment was relatively good, but they were more tense, unhappy, and lonely than the close coupleds.

4. At the less positive end are the *dysfunctional* homosexuals. Bell and Weinberg state, "The dysfunctionals are the group in our sample which most closely accords with the stereotype of the tormented homosexual. They are troubled people whose lives offer them little gratification, and in fact, they seem to have a great deal of difficulty managing their existence. Sexually, socially, and psychologically, whenever they could be distinguished from homosexual respondents as a whole, the dysfunctionals displayed poorer adjustment. If we had numbered only dysfunctionals among our respondents, we very likely would have had to conclude that homosexuals in general are conflict-ridden social misfits" (pp. 225–26).

As a group, the males were more lonely, worrisome, paranoid, depressed, tense, and unhappy than other homosexual respondents. They reported more job difficulties, robberies, assaults, and extortion on account of their being gay. Furthermore, the dysfunctionals were most likely to have had some contact with the police regardless of the reason. They reported more sexual problems and expressed the most regrets about being homosexual.

5. Finally, Bell and Weinberg identified *asexuals,* who were the most secretive and withdrawn, the least sexually active, and less exclusively homosexual. The asexual lesbians expressed the highest incidence of suicidal thoughts. Together with the dysfunctionals, asexuals reported less self-acceptance and more loneliness than other homosexuals and than heterosexuals.

on special groups of homosexuals, such as those undergoing psychotherapy, men in prisons, and members of homophile organizations (Brody, 1978).

Diversity of Experience

The San Francisco study highlights the great diversity of the homosexual experience. With respect to the level of sexual interest and activity reported, little evidence was obtained to support the stereotype that homosexuals are sexually hyperactive or inactive. Thirteen percent of the white male sample asserted that sex was relatively unimportant in their lives. The majority of homosexuals engaged in sexual relations only two or three times a week. Women reported they had sexual relations an average of only once a week. Men tended to cruise for sexual partners in gay bars, but 40 percent did so as infrequently as once a month or not at all. Women seldom or never cruised. Furthermore, the majority of men and women had been involved in stable, relatively monogamous relationships lasting one to three years. Most lesbian women had fewer than 10 sexual partners. More than three fourths of the women were involved in a stable relationship with another woman. The majority of homosexual men denied they ever had sexual relations with minors or prostitutes. Bell and Weinberg note that heterosexuals are far more likely than homosexuals to seduce minors and make objectionable advances.

Great diversity was also found in the degree of acceptance of one's homosexuality and in the relative overtness of homosexuality. Only one fourth of male homosexuals tended to regret being homosexual, seriously considered stopping their homosexuality, and wished they had been entirely heterosexual from birth. Homosexual women tended to express less difficulty accepting their homosexuality.

Since homosexuals are a distinct minority in the population and often the target of prejudice and discrimination, it is not surprising that some go to great lengths to conceal their homosexual lifestyles. Only about one fourth of males surveyed indicated their employers and most of their fellow workers knew they were gay. The lesbian women were less likely to report their colleagues or employers were aware of their homosexuality. Some homosexuals whose families knew they were gay were still "in the closet" in their work situation. In the family context, mothers were most likely to know that their sons were homosexual, whereas fathers were reportedly least likely to be aware of their sons' homosexuality.

The findings of the Bell and Weinberg study can be seen as congruent with the rationale given by the American Psychiatric Association for excluding homosexuality from the new classification system:

A significant proportion of homosexuals are apparently satisfied with their sexual orientation, show no signs of significant manifest psychopathology (unless homosexuality, by itself, is considered psychopathology), and are able to function quite effectively, with no impairment in the capacity to love or work. These individuals may never come to treatment, or they may be seen by a mental health professional because of external pressure or other problems requiring psychiatric help (e.g., depression) (DSM III, draft, 1978, L. 33).

Explanations

The Psychoanalytic Perspective. Since for many years homosexuality has been viewed as a pathological condition, it is not surprising that scientists have searched for clues to the etiology of homosexuality. Psychoanalytically oriented etiological explanations emphasize the role of early family relationships in the later development of homosexual behavior. Oedipal conflicts that emerge from the family context and disrupt normal heterosexual development are seen as a prime motivating factor. Freud believed that anxiety resulted from deep-seated incestuous desires for the seductive mother and the fear of castration as a retaliation by the father. Women come to be feared because the sight of female genitals evokes childhood-based anxiety associated with castration fears. Others have viewed homosexuality as the product of feminine identification stemming from identification with a dominant, attentive mother. Still another view links lack of heterosexual involvement with fears of being psychologically engulfed by women, who are equated on an unconscious level with the smothering, overly intimate mother.

Bieber and his colleagues (1962) discovered a pattern of family relationships consistent with the analytic view that adverse family relationships predispose one to later homosexuality. In a study of 106 male homosexual patients and 100 heterosexual patients, the family constellation most reliably associated with homosexuality was a seductive, overly intimate, and protective mother and a detached and/or hostile father. Critics, however, point out that the pattern of intense maternal involvement together with an indifferent or poor relationship with the father is not always evident in the backgrounds of homosexuals. Some homosexuals come from homes with idealized fathers, while others report an intensely ambivalent relationship with an older sibling or an absent mother (Marmor, 1971).

The Learning Perspective. Behaviorists, emphasizing explanations based on learning theory, assume that pleasurable and painful experiences shape sexual orientation. Kinsey et al. (1948), for example, contended that early pleasurable homosexual contacts increased the likelihood of ultimately adopting a homosexual orientation. Early pleasant childhood and adolescent sexual and romantic fantasies with homoerotic themes may play a similar role in shaping homosexuality (Saghir & Robins, 1973). On the other hand, sexual experiences perceived as negative or traumatic may inhibit approaching the opposite sex to obtain sexual and interpersonal reinforcement.

A Biological View. Biological theories represent a departure from both learning theory and family-oriented etiological explanations. Researchers are currently looking for genetic, chromosomal, and hormonal differences between heterosexuals and homosexuals. Kallman (1952) reported an impressive 100 percent concordance rate in overt homosexual behavior in 40 pairs of monozygotic twins. A similar relationship was not found in the degree of concordance for fraternal twins. Such findings are entirely consistent with a genetic explanation. However, other studies have failed to replicate these findings. For example, in one study of seven monozygotic twin pairs only one of the siblings in each pair was homosexual (Kolb, 1963). Nevertheless, researchers encouraged by findings that concordance rates are generally higher in monozygotic than dizygotic twins suggest that evidence for a genetic predisposition toward homosexuality will eventually be forthcoming.

Little evidence has been obtained to suggest that chromosomes are significantly different in homosexual and heterosexual males.

Researchers, however, have found some intriguing hormonal differences between homosexuals and heterosexuals. Several studies suggest that levels of testosterone and its breakdown products are lower in homosexuals than heterosexuals (Loraine, Ismael, Adamopoulous, and Dove, 1970; Margolese, 1973). This finding must be interpreted with caution, however. Other factors such as diet, stress, and general health may account for such results and must be ruled out as causative agents before more firm conclusions can be made. Even if a genetic or constitutional predisposition toward homosexuality were identified, social learning would play an important role in determining whether homosexual behavior and feelings are expressed.

Each of the theories we have considered has emphasized a single set of etiological factors. Bell (1973) cautions against accepting a unitary etiological explanation:

> Just as there is such a diversity of adult homosexuality, so there are multiple routes into this orientation, routes which may well account for differences in the way a particular person experiences and expresses his or her homosexuality as well as the nature of his psychological makeup and of his social adjustment. For some, certain kinds of parental relationships and identifications may loom large. For others, negative same-sex peer relationships may be paramount. For still others, early satisfactions associated with homosexual behavior may stand out or negative heterosexual experience during adolescence may be dominant (pp. 16–17).

Treatment of Ego-Dystonic Homosexuality

Masters and Johnson and their colleagues (Masters & Johnson, 1979; Schwartz & Johnson, 1984) have recently shown that it is possible to treat certain homosexuals who are dissatisfied with their sexual orientation and desire to change. Using direct sexual therapy procedures and psychotherapy to hurdle obstacles to achieving interpersonal intimacy, Masters and Johnson treated 54 ego-dystonic homosexual males and 13 lesbian women who first had to prove their motivation to change their sexual orientation. The majority of homosexuals who were treated were married and accompanied by their opposite-sexed partners. A sizable minority of homosexuals came with the heterosexual partners they hoped to marry; the remaining homosexuals came with more casual partners who were committed enough to the patients to engage in the demanding, intensive therapy. The failure rate, gauged in terms of establishing a heterosexual lifestyle, was 21 percent immediately after treatment. After 5 years' follow-up, it was 28 percent (Schwartz & Masters, 1984).

Despite the apparent success of the program, sharp divisions of opinion and criticisms of Masters and Johnson's work have surfaced. Questions such as the following ones have been raised: Is the successful application of the therapy limited to only highly motivated homosexuals who enter treatment with partners committed to helping them achieve "reorientation"? Does the therapy simply effect a change in homosexual *behavior* and not a parallel change in feeling and thinking about oneself? Would the therapy be equally effective with individuals with varying degrees of heterosexual/homosexual experience and committment to a gay lifestyle? Will sexual reorientation therapies be able to effect permanent changes, or will they be relatively short-lived? Answers to such questions are critical to our understanding of the limits and potential of treatments designed to reorient dissatisfied homosexuals.

As social and professional attitudes become more tolerant of homosexuality, treatment programs will probably be developed

The husband-wife research team of William Masters and Virginia Johnson. (Howard Earl Day/Wide World)

to help clients surmount difficulties in accepting their homosexuality. If the trend toward liberalization of attitudes continues in the future, the number of homosexuals who seek reorientation therapy may decline.

PSYCHOSEXUAL DYSFUNCTION AND ITS TREATMENT

In about 50 percent of American marriages, some type of sexual dysfunction affects the marital unit (Masters & Johnson, 1970). Indeed, clinical experience suggests that men commonly seek help for premature ejaculation and failure to attain or maintain an erection (impotence). Women may be concerned with a lack of sexual desire or an absence of excitement during sexual relations (frigidity and difficulty in reaching orgasm). Pain during intercourse and delay or absence of orgasm in males are less frequently expressed concerns.

The Sexual Response Cycle

Until recently many misconceptions about sexual functioning created barriers to successful treatment of sexual problems. Little information about how the human body responds to sexual stimulation was available.

Consequently therapeutic approaches tended to be largely ineffective. The pioneering research of Masters and Johnson (1966) yielded basic data on normal and dysfunctional sexual responses that proved to be invaluable to clinicians concerned with helping persons with sexual difficulties. In addition, their findings paved the way for their later developing a remarkably successful therapy program for sexual problems.

In 1954 Masters and Johnson launched an innovative research program to study males and females sexually stimulated in the laboratory. At the Reproductive Biology Research Foundation in St. Louis, Masters and Johnson collected information on over 10,000 male and female sexual response cycles. Kaplan describes their wide-ranging efforts:

> Their observations included a wide spectrum of sexual behaviors under every imaginable condition. They studied coitus in many positions, between strangers, between happily married couples, between couples who had various sexual and interpersonal difficulties. Different techniques of erotic stimulation were explored, as were various types of self-stimulation. The sexual behaviors of men and women of a wide range of ages was studied. Sex was observed during menstruation. The sexual responses of men who are circumcised were compared with those who are not circumcised. The effects of various contraceptive devices on sexual behavior were studied. In addition, sexual responses were investigated in the presence of various pathological conditions, including the artificial vagina, etc. (Kaplan, 1974, pp. 3–4).

At first Masters and Johnson interviewed male and female prostitutes. While they furnished much valuable information, particularly about sexual techniques, Masters decided not to use them as subjects because they tended to move about the country too much and because the women often suffered from a chronic pelvic congestion that affected their sexual response. The volunteers chosen tended to be quite ordinary people: patients and students whose participation was motivated largely by curiosity and the desire to contribute to the understanding of sexual functioning.

In order to be accepted into the program, it was essential that the volunteers be able to achieve orgasm in the laboratory. The laboratory was equipped with a bed, monitoring equipment to measure physiological changes, cameras, and a specially constructed transparent penis-shaped probe that contained a camera to record changes in the vagina during sexual intercourse. People accommodated to the laboratory with surprising ease; there were remarkably few instances of failure to reach orgasm.

In their first book, *The Human Sexual Response* (1966), Masters and Johnson reported on their findings of the sexual response cycle as males and females attained orgasm. Surprisingly, they found that the basic sexual arousal cycle was the same for both men and women. They defined four phases in this cycle: excitement, plateau, orgasmic, and resolution.

> The excitement phase is initiated by whatever is sexually stimulating for a particular individual. If stimulation is strong enough, excitement builds quickly, but if it is interrupted or if it becomes objectionable, this phase becomes extended or the cycle may be stopped. If effective sexual stimulation is continued, it produces increased levels of sexual tension that lead ultimately to orgasm. This increased tension is called the plateau phase. If the individual's drive for sexual release in this phase is not strong enough, or if stimulation ceases to be effective or is withdrawn, a man or woman will not experience orgasm, but will enter a prolonged period of gradually decreasing sexual tension. The climacteric or orgasmic phase,

FIGURE 14-2
The Human Sexual Response

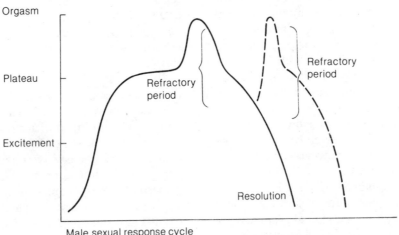

Male sexual response cycle

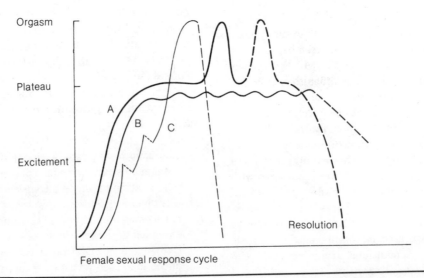

Female sexual response cycle

Source: From *Human Sexual Response* by M. H. Masters and V. E. Johnson, 1966, Boston: Little, Brown.

a totally involuntary response, consists of those few seconds when the body changes resulting from stimulation reach their maximum intensity. During the resolution phase, after orgasm, there is a lessening of sexual tensions as the person returns to the unstimulated state. Women are capable of having another orgasm if there is effective stimulation during this phase. The resolution period in the male includes a time, which varies among individuals, when restimulation is impossible. This is called the refractory period.

In both sexes, the basic responses of the body to sexual stimulation are myotonia (increased muscle tension) and vasocongestion (filling of the blood vessels with fluid) especially in the genital organs, causing swelling. Of course, these basic physiologic sexual responses remain the same regardless of the stimulation—coital, manipulation, or fantasy. However, intensity and duration of responses vary with the method of stimulation used. Masturbation produced the most intense experiences observed in the laboratory, partner manipulation the next, and intercourse the least (Belliveau & Richter, 1970, pp. 33–34).

DSM III retains much of the basic scheme advanced by Masters and Johnson but includes a number of modifications. According to DSM III, the first phase is termed *appetitive* and consists of the sexual fantasies and interest and desire to engage in sexual activity which initiate the sexual response cycle. The second phase, described by the new classification system as *excitement,* essentially condenses much of what Masters and Johnson term *excitement* and *plateau* into one phase. This simplification is appealing since the plateau phase can be seen as a more advanced state of sexual excitement that occurs just before orgasm (Kaplan, 1974). As in the Masters and Johnson scheme, *orgasm* and *resolution* are the final phases of the sexual response cycle.

Explanations and Assessment

Sexual disorders can be associated with each of the three primary components of the sexual response—appetitive or desire, excitement, and orgasm—since each is vulnerable to disruption by emotional responses such as anxiety. Indeed, a diagnosis of psychosexual dysfunction is not made when the difficulty is primarily the result of organic rather than psychological factors.

Kaplan (1977) implicates anxiety as one of the basic causes of sexual dysfunctions. She states:

> Sexually disruptive anxiety does not seem to arise from one specific base; rather it appears to originate in a wide spectrum of causes. It ranges from the anxiety produced by ignorance, unrealistic expectations about sexual functioning, and performance anxiety through the more profound fears of rejection and fears of intimacy and commitment to unconscious guilt derived from childhood and the fear of sex with the opposite gender, which originated in childhood pathological family interactions (p. 8).

Since many diverse etiological factors may have an impact on sexual dysfunctions, it is important to determine their nature and role in any sexual problem. This is often accomplished in the initial evaluation of the dysfunctional sexual behavior. Hogan (1978) describes the following factors that can result in sexual dysfunctions: (1) early environmental problems, for example, problems in the parents' relationship, rape, incest, traumatic experiences with prostitutes, religious orthodoxy, and homosexuality; (2) misconceptions and lack of knowledge about sex; (3) lack of a skilled sexual partner; (4) psychological factors such as anxiety, guilt, fear, depression, and fear of losing control; (5) relationship problems, including hostility, marital conflicts, lack of communication, and lack of attraction toward one's partner; (6) other sexual problems; (7) physical and physiological factors such as illness, surgery, irritation from contraceptive materials, and medication.

A complete assessment should also include a determination of the exact nature of the problem, its frequency and severity, its effect on the individuals involved, whether it is generalized or limited to specific situations or partners, and whether it has been present throughout life or developed after a period of relatively normal functioning. Sexual disorders are termed *primary* when the sexual history suggests that the person has never functioned normally. They are termed *secondary* if the person reports at least one instance of normal sexual functioning with respect to the disorder being evaluated. Secondary sexual dysfunctions tend to have a better therapeutic prognosis than primary dysfunctions.

THE PSYCHOSEXUAL DYSFUNCTIONS

Inhibited Sexual Desire

As we stated previously, sexual dysfunctions are associated with each of the major phases of the sexual response cycle. The disorder associated with the desire, or appetitive, phase is inhibited sexual desire. Since there are no established criteria for "normal" sexual desire, the diagnosis is usually made when lack of desire is problematic either to the individual or to his or her partner.

The independence of the components of the sexual response is reflected in the ability of some people with inhibited desire to experience sexual excitement and even orgasm. Their sexual activity, however, is not motivated by desire but perhaps by a wish to please their partner. In other cases low sexual desire can inhibit other phases of the sexual response.

Inhibited Sexual Excitement

Sexual dysfunctions with inhibited sexual excitement include what have commonly been termed impotence in the male and frigidity in the female. Since both of these terms have negative connotations and have been used to describe a number of different sexual difficulties, it is necessary to clarify their meaning in this context. DSM III considers the male dysfunction with inhibited sexual excitement (impotence) to be reflected in "partial or complete failure to attain or maintain erection until completion of the sexual act." Its counterpart in the woman (frigidity) involves "partial or complete failure to attain or maintain the lubrication-swelling response of sexual excitement until completion of the sexual act" (p. 279). Some women with this disorder consider the sexual experience to be an unpleasant ordeal or endure sexual relations only to preserve their marriage. Others may enjoy touching or physical closeness, yet not experience erotic feelings (Kaplan, 1974).

Occasional failure to achieve or to maintain an erection are not uncommon. Emotional stress, fatigue, and alcohol excess may produce transient episodes of impotence. Since nearly half of all men experience such difficulties at one time or another, a diagnosis of secondary impotence is warranted only when a man fails to achieve an erection in 25 percent of his attempts (Masters & Johnson, 1970).

The incidence of impotence appears to gradually rise with age, particularly after age 45. Before age 35, impotence is relatively rare. By age 70 about 27 percent of males in the Kinsey study reported erectile failure and by 80, 75 percent reported impotence. Many men, however, have no erectile problems well into their eighth and ninth decade of life.

Inhibited Orgasm

Sexual disorders associated with the orgasm component of the sexual response include persistent and repeated delay or absence of orgasm. Failure to reach orgasm can occur in

TABLE 14-1
Overall Results of the Masters and Johnson Treatment Program (1970)

Type of Sexual Problem	Numbers of Couples Treated	Percentage Success at the End of Therapy	Percentage Success at Two-Year Follow-up
Primary impotence	32	59.4	59.4
Secondary impotence	213	73.8	69.1
Premature ejaculation	186	97.8	97.3
Ejaculatory incompetence	17	82.4	82.4
Male totals	448	83.1	80.6
Primary orgasmic dysfunction	193	83.4	82.4
Situational orgasmic dysfunction	149	77.2	75.2
Female totals	342	80.7	79.2
Male and female totals	790	81.1	80.0

Source: From *Principles of Behavior Therapy*, p. 156, by G. T. Wilson and D. K. O'Leary, 1980, Englewood Cliffs, NJ: Prentice-Hall.

males and females who are responsive to erotic stimuli and experience a normal sexual excitement phase. This disorder is much more common in females than in males. Kinsey, Pomeroy, Martin, and Gebhard (1953) reported that up to 15 percent of women never reached orgasm even after 20 years of marriage. Failure to ejaculate and experience orgasm is rare and probably affects fewer than 1 in 700 men of all ages (Katchadourian & Lunde, 1972).

Premature Ejaculation

Another disorder associated with the orgasm phase is premature ejaculation. DSM III defines it rather flexibly as ejaculation that "occurs before the individual wishes it, because of recurrent and persistent absence of reasonable voluntary control of ejaculation and orgasm during sexual activity" (p. 280). It is the most common presenting problem of males seeking sex therapy (Kaplan, 1974). Premature orgasm in the female is not considered a sexual dysfunction since women are responsive to sexual stimulation shortly after orgasm and some regularly attain multiple orgasm.

Functional Dyspareunia and Functional Vaginismus

Vaginismus and dyspareunia can drastically interfere with sexual relations. Dyspareunia refers to painful intercourse not caused exclusively by organic factors. It may be associated with, but is distinct from, vaginismus, which is an involuntary spasm of the muscles of the lower third of the vagina. This condition can make intercourse difficult, if not impossible. Dyspareunia can occur in both sexes, but vaginismus is, of course, limited to the female. Vaginismus and dyspareunia are probably the least common of the sexual dysfunctions.

DIRECT THERAPY FOR SEXUAL DYSFUNCTION

Beginning in the late 1950s, Masters and Johnson began to develop a brief, direct treatment program for sexual dysfunctions. The publication of *Human Sexual Inadequacy*

(1970) described their research findings and treatment approach and sparked considerable optimism that sexual difficulties could be treated with a high degree of success. Indeed, Masters and Johnson reported an overall success rate of 81 percent for sexual dysfunctions. Their impressive results encouraged others to develop a wide variety of behaviorally oriented programs based on the notion that dysfunctional sexual behavior could be treated directly without emphasizing in-depth personality change. Such approaches have come to be called *direct sexual therapies*. They have proved to be more effective than traditional psychotherapies such as psychoanalysis, which stress insight and extensive personality change. As Gagnon (1977) states, " For many people, particularly those with sexual difficulties in their day to day living, talking about the past can be extremely frustrating, since the problems may continue to occur 4 or 5 times a week. . . . After many treatment sessions many patients are still suffering from the presenting problem and have only an apparent understanding of Mom and Dad" (p. 369).

Lo Piccolo and Friedman (1985) have defined a number of basic principles used by Masters and Johnson as well as by other clinicians who follow a direct, behavioral treatment approach.

Mutual Responsibility

In direct therapies sexual dysfunctions are conceptualized as *shared disorders*. Masters and Johnson (1970) emphasize that "there is no such thing as an uninvolved partner in any marriage in which there is some form of sexual inadequacy." Sexual problems are often a source of distress to both partners and can be symptomatic of problems that exist in the relationship. Lo Piccolo (1978) states that "the husband of an inorgasmic woman is partially responsible for creating or main-

taining a sexual dysfunction, and he is also a patient in need of help" (p. 3). The couple rather than the individual are the treatment focus since their attitudes, communication patterns, and sexual interactions are important targets for modification in therapy. In order to minimize one partner's blaming the other for the dysfunctional behavior and to further involvement in the therapeutic enterprise, shared responsibility for the sexual problem is stressed by the therapist. In addition, Masters and Johnson as well as many other direct therapists use a male-female, cotherapy team to provide each person a therapist to identify with.

Information and Education

Since sexual dysfunctions often involve lack of information, and not uncommonly misinformation, providing information and reeducation are major components of direct therapy. Masters and Johnson treated couples in a two-week, intensive program in which educational presentations, therapy sessions, and sexual exercises were individually tailored to meet the unique needs of the dysfunctional couple. When round table discussions revealed an area where additional information was necessary, it was provided to both partners. For example, the notion that sexual intercourse necessarily involves pain could be easily corrected in this context. Discussions, educational reading materials, and educational films have been used to correct misconceptions and instruct couples in effective sexual technique.

Attitude Change

Direct therapy attempts to modify negative attitudes toward sexual behaviors that result in anxiety and, in some cases, in disgust in sexual encounters. Some procedures used include providing positive reading materials on sexuality, discussions with sympathetic clergy in the case of religiously based negtive attitudes, instructing the husband to express to his wife that he will respect her more, not less, if she becomes more sexual, and encouraging patients to attend workshops and lectures on sexuality and sexual values (Lo Piccolo & Friedman, 1985).

Eliminating Performance Anxiety

Anxiety and concern about performance interfere with the spontaneous expression of sensuality and inhibit sexual responsiveness. Performance anxiety almost invariably results in the patient assuming the role of spectator instead of an involved participant. Performance anxiety can be minimized by reducing the demands to perform in sexual situations. Patients are instructed to involve themselves in and enjoy the *process* of lovemaking instead of keeping score and striving for results. The therapist may give the woman permission to enjoy intercourse without striving for orgasm on every occasion. In cases of impotence, the therapist may direct the man to engage in sexual foreplay and to deliberately avoid sexual intercourse, thereby reducing concerns about whether an erection sufficient for orgasm will occur (Lo Piccolo & Friedman, 1985).

Increasing Communication and Effectiveness of Sexual Technique

Sexual problems often revolve around patterns of negative interactions and expectations. Sensitivity to criticism about sexual performance and pessimistic attitudes about the problem inhibit clear communication and experimentation with new, possibly more satisfying sexual techniques. Direct therapy encourages the sharing of sexual likes and dislikes, sexual experimentation, and furnishing feedback about sexual technique and response. Helping the couple to communicate more effectively during love-

making may be supplemented with other procedures. These include suggesting that the partners share erotic fantasies, read explicit erotic literature, and view explicit sexual movies to learn new sexual techniques (Lo Piccolo & Friedman, 1985).

Changing Destructive Lifestyles and Sex Roles

Where patients' lifestyles permit little time for relaxed, tension-free interactions, resolving sexual difficulties may be particularly problematic. Sex-role separation, where there are no mutual responsibilities for household tasks, diminishes the likelihood that sexual relations will be experienced in a close, sharing manner. Direct therapists assume a very active role in such cases and suggest that the patients arrange "dates" with each other for relaxing times together (Annon, 1974). The therapist may also suggest that the husband assume greater household responsibilities in the evenings so that his wife may enjoy less pressured, shared time to get "in touch with her sex drive and her sexual responsiveness" (Lo Piccolo & Friedman, 1985).

Prescribing Changes in Behavior

Lo Piccolo and Lo Piccolo (1978) suggest that "if there is any one procedure that is the hallmark of direct treatment of sexual dysfunctions, it is the prescription by the therapist of a series of gradual steps of specific sexual behaviors to be performed by the patients in their own home. These behaviors are often described as 'sensate focus' or 'pleasuring exercies' " (p. 6). Sadock and Sadock (1976) describe this approach:

> Beginning exercises usually focus on heightening sensory awareness to touch, sight, sound, and smell. Initially, intercourse is interdicted, and couples learn to give and receive bodily

pleasure without the pressure of performance. They are simultaneously learning that sexual foreplay is as important as intercourse and orgasm. Genital stimulation is eventually added to general body stimulation. The couple are instructed sequentially to try various positions for intercourse, without necessarily completing the union, and to use varieties of stimulating techniques before they are instructed to proceed with intercourse (p. 465).

In our discussion of psychosexual dysfunctions we have emphasized the multiplicity of causes of sexual problems, the need for a careful evaluation of a person's sexual difficulties, and the innovative treatment approaches of direct sexual therapies that have proven effective in treating psychosexual disorders.

NEW DIRECTIONS AND ISSUES IN SEXUAL DYSFUNCTIONS AND THEIR TREATMENT

Diversity of Applications

In recent years sex therapists have moved toward treating the sexual dysfunction in the context of the whole person. There is a growing recognition that sexuality cannot be divorced from how people create relationships—how they seek or avoid intimacy and express a gamut of positive and negative emotions. Sex therapists acknowledge that it makes little sense to compartmentalize their clients' personalities into "sexual" and "nonsexual" aspects. Marital and intensive individual therapy are increasingly incorporated into treatment programs that tackle personal and relationship issues interwoven with the sexual problems that initially bring people to treatment. Also, the presence of significant psychopathology is less likely to deter the sex therapist from initiating treatment than was the case in the past. Even psychotic clients and those with major personality disorders, such as an antisocial personality, are now the recipients of direct sex therapy (Kolodny, Masters, & Johnson, 1979; Lo Piccolo & Friedman, 1985).

Diverse populations are availing themselves of the benefits of sex therapy. Handicapped, physically ill, and aged persons are more and more realizing their sexual potential as myths and stereotypes about these populations give way to new knowledge and a recognition of the special needs of these groups. George and Weiler (1981), for example, have recently demonstrated that sexual decline with aging is not necessarily inevitable. The aging process itself is not always responsible for the sexual dysfunctions seen in the elderly. Changes in sexual drive and performance may be misattributed to the aging process instead of to the detrimental effects of medications, for example.

Sexual Dysfunctions and Homosexuals

In their book *Homosexuality in Perspective*, Masters and Johnson (1979) reported the findings of more than 15 years of accumulated research evidence that incisively challenges the myth that there are tremendous differences between homosexuals and heterosexuals in sexual functioning. Their research also suggests that it is possible to treat homosexuals' sexual dysfunctions with the same direct therapy techniques that have been successfully applied with heterosexual persons.

Masters and Johnson's research spans the period from 1964 to 1977. This first study examined the physiological sexual responses of sexually functional homosexual subjects in a laboratory setting. The research project involved 94 male and 82 female homosexuals who ranged in age from 21 to 54. Their sexual responses and activities were compared with 687 heterosexual male and female volunteers, the majority of whom participated in the study of the sexual response cycle described earlier in this chapter.

Let us now consider some interesting highlights of the project. The capacity of heterosexuals and homosexuals to respond to effective sexual stimulation was indistinguishable. There were no differences between homosexuals and heterosexuals in the physical processes of lubrication, erection, ejaculation, and orgasm. Homosexuals communicated their feelings about sexual wants and needs more freely than their heterosexual counterparts; they also tended to "take turns" achieving orgasms, allowing them to concentrate more fully on their own pleasure rather than focusing on "distracting" concerns about their partners' pleasure. Furthermore, homosexuals occasionally fantasized about heterosexual loveplay, just as many heterosexuals occasionally have homosexual fantasies.

The results of this project prompted Masters and Johnson to consider treating homosexuals' sexual dysfunctions. Thus in their second research program they treated homosexuals with a variety of sexual dysfunctions by using the techniques of direct sexual therapy they had pioneered with heterosexual clients. Fifty-six male and 25 female couples were treated during a nine-year period beginning in 1968. The treatment included a five-year follow-up to evaluate the long-term success of the therapy. The major presenting complaint of males was impotence; the major presenting complaint for females was inhibited orgasm. For all homosexuals during that period the treatment failure rate was less than 12 percent at the five-year follow-up.

The Effectiveness of Sex Therapy

In a critique of Masters and Johnson's research methods Zilbergeld and Evans (1980) unleashed a storm of controversy concern-ing the effectiveness of direct sex therapies. In a *Psychology Today* article they questioned the validity of the data presented by Masters and Johnson in support of their treatment methods. Zilbergeld and Evans criticized the lack of specificity of Masters and Johnson's outcome measures, their reliance on therapists' subjective ratings to classify treatment successes and failures, and their use of a telephone call by the therapist five years after treatment to judge the long-term stability of treatment gains.

Masters and Johnson (1983) have since clarified the outcome criteria issue and other sources of ambiguity in their research, while others have risen to their defense (e.g., Kolodny, 1981; Heiman & LoPiccolo, 1983; LoPiccolo & Friedman, 1985). In answer to the question, "Is direct therapy effective?", most students of the area would answer yes, with little hesitation. Indeed, the majority of reviews (e.g., Hogan, 1978; Kilmann & Auerback, 1979) support this conclusion. Even when objective outcome measures of sexual and marital satisfaction are utilized, a wide variety of individuals appear to benefit from direct sex therapy (Heiman & LoPiccolo, 1983). Zilbergeld and Evan's critique is valuable in that it cautions us about uncritically embracing a new and promising treatment before it has been subjected to rigorous standards of scientific evaluation. However, as Heiman and LoPiccolo (1983) conclude, "While the effectiveness of sex therapy may not live up to the early reports of guaranteed cures for all patients . . . the procedures are remarkably effective in rapidly alleviating sexual and marital dissatisfaction for many couples."

SUMMARY

In this chapter we have reviewed the major psychosexual disorders listed in the DSM classification system. We began our overview with an examination of the gender identity disorders, which are characterized by identification of the self as a member of the opposite sex, and of the paraphilias, which involve unconventional sexual behaviors and are characterized by a diminished capacity to engage in close, affectionate sexual relations with another person. The paraphilias that involve an unconventional choice of sexual object are fetishism and pedophilia. Unconventional choices of sexual activity are reflected in cases of voyeurism, exhibitionism, transvestism, and sadomasochism.

We also noted that changes in our thinking about sexual behavior are reflected in the deletion of homosexuality from the list of mental disorders in DSM III. A preference for sexual relations with members of the same sex is now listed as a psychosexual disorder only when it is unwanted and personally distressing (ego-dystonic homosexuality).

We reviewed a number of recent studies that challenge widely held stereotypes of homosexuality. These studies suggest that homosexuality does not preclude intimate, affectionate relationships; that the experience of homosexuals is incredibly diverse; that homosexuals do not differ from heterosexuals in significant ways; that sexual dysfunctions can be treated as effectively with homosexuals as with heterosexuals; and that it is possible to "reorient" certain homosexuals who are dissatisfied with their sexual orientation and desire to change. Although a number of theories have been advanced to explain the development of homosexuality, at the present time no etiological explanation appears to be entirely satisfactory.

The gender identity disorders and paraphilias were contrasted with the much more common psychosexual dysfunctions. The latter are frequently encountered disorders characterized by a failure to enjoy and/or achieve accepted sexual behaviors. The following psychosexual dysfunctions were described: inhibited sexual desire, inhibited sexual excitement, inhibited orgasm, premature ejaculation, functional dyspareunia, and functional vaginismus. We discussed the characteristics of these disorders, their etiology and assessment, and available treatments. We devoted considerable attention to the techniques of "direct" sexual therapies based on the research program of Masters and Johnson. Direct therapy programs are aimed at reducing performance anxiety, alleviating shame and guilt through education and attitude change, helping the couple to develop a sense of mutual responsibility for the problem and the treatment outcome, and resolving interpersonal conflict and increasing communication in the context of the sexual relationship. In conclusion, we highlighted the need to consider sexual disorders in the context of understanding and treating the whole person, the recent extension of sex therapy to diverse populations, (including the elderly and individuals with psychopathology), and, finally, the issue of whether sex therapy is effective.

15

Substance Use Disorders

Overview
    Common Factors in Drug Use
    Substance Abuse and Dependence

The "Social Drugs"
    Alcohol
    Treatment
    Tobacco

The Illegal Drugs
    Marijuana
    Short-Term Effects of Marijuana
    Some Consequences of Marijuana Use
    LSD
    The Opiate Narcotics: Heroin
    Cocaine

The Prescription Drugs
    Amphetamine
    The Sedative-Hypnotics: Barbiturates

Explanations of Drug Use
    The Psychodynamic Perspective
    A Sociocultural View
    The Learning Perspective
    Genetic and Biological Evidence

Summary

OVERVIEW

Allen H.'s father is a successful business-man who frequently works overtime to maintain their luxurious suburban home. His wife and 18-year-old Allan scarcely see him. Frequently the father feels tired and overwrought, but two martinis at lunch and another drink when he finally gets home help him to calm his nerves.

Allan's mother feels lonely, bored, and neglected. In attempts to overcome her resentment and depression, she often reaches for a sedative, tranquilizer, or barbiturate. Recently she has made increasing demands on Allan to fill the emotional vacuum in her life. Suddenly the H.s are communicating. They are both deeply involved with the "Allan problem." It appears that Allan has been missing school, and his grades have markedly dropped. In a recent conference with the school counselor, Allan confided that he has been taking barbiturates from the family medicine cabinet and also buying them from a friend at school. For over a month he has made futile attempts to discontinue this practice. He is deeply unhappy. Allan's mother now recalls that recently he has appeared drowsy and "not himself."

It was an hour before the Alcoholics Anonymous meeting. Jeffrey W. was silently rehearsing the speech he would give when it was his turn to stand up, to tell his story, and to testify, "I am an alcoholic." Since it was his first meeting, he was nervous, but he found that he was repeating to himself, "I have to do this! I have to take the Big Step!" Jeffrey W. made mental notes: "I must not forget to tell the group how I just couldn't seem to quit on my own; how I had to drink more and more just to feel OK. I have to confess all the problems and embarrassment I brought to my family: the drinking sprees, the blackouts. I have to tell how I lost the best job I ever had; how I felt on the trip to the hospital emergency room and the horror of the withdrawal symptoms, the DTs. It's time to go now." Jeffrey resolutely walked to the meeting.

Drug use has a far-reaching history. Weil (1972) has observed that the use of drugs reflects an innate need for altered states of consciousness, that it "has been a feature of all human life in all places on the earth and in all ages of history." Some might question whether drug use represents a basic human appetite, as Weil suggests, but few would argue that drugs play a prominent role in contemporary life. Indeed, ours is a drug-consuming culture. Allan H. in his first exploration of the family medicine chest probably had a wide choice of drugs. According to a report by the American Pharmaceutical Association (1977), the public spends

TABLE 15-1
Lifetime Prevalence and Recency of Use, by Age, in Percent

	Youth (Age 12–17)		Young Adults (18–25)		Older Adults (26 +)	
	Ever Used	Used Past Month	Ever Used	Used Past Month	Ever Used	Used Past Month
Marijuana and/or hashish	26.7	11.5	64.1	27.4	23.0	6.6
Hallucinogens†	5.2	1.4	21.1	1.7	6.4	*
Cocaine	6.5	1.6	28.3	6.8	8.5	1.2
Heroin	*	*	1.2	*	1.1	*
Nonmedical uses of:						
Stimulants	6.7	2.6	18.0	4.7	6.2	.6
Sedatives	5.8	1.3	18.7	2.6	4.8	*
Tranquilizers	4.9	.9	15.1	1.6	3.6	*
Analgesics	4.2	.7	12.1	1.0	3.2	*
Any nonmedical use	10.3	3.8	28.4	7.0	8.8	1.2
Alcohol	65.2	26.9	94.6	67.9	88.2	56.7
Cigarettes	49.5	14.7	76.9	39.5	78.7	34.6
Number of persons	1,581	1,581	1,283	1,283	2,760	2,760

*Less than .5%.
†LSD & other hallucinogens, such as PCP or Phencyclidine, Mescaline, Peyote, Psilocybin, and DMT.
Source: Miller, J. A. et al., *National Survey on Drug Abuse: Main Findings 1982.* U.S. Department of Health and Human Services publication no. (ADM) 83–1263.

between $4 and $8 billion per year on self-prescribed and self-administered drugs for self-diagnosed illnesses. Given the ubiquity of drugs, it is not surprising that their misuse is a serious problem. Yet it is only within the past few decades that the abuse of legal and illegal drugs has moved to the center stage of attention as a social problem.

A glance at Table 15-1 reveals what most readers already know: The use of drugs cuts across the age spectrum of the population. Note that a greater percentage of individuals have used alcohol and tobacco than the other drugs cited in the table. But the impact of the so-called social drugs can easily be underestimated. Although society sanctions the use of alcohol and tobacco, we will see that a flood of personal, medical, and social problems emanates from their use. Drugs differ in the way they are perceived by society, in the personal, social, and legal costs associated with their use. In the course of our survey of the major drugs abused, we will examine the personal, physiological, and social factors that influence drug use in the human context.

We will begin our overview of drug use by highlighting some factors common to the use of diverse substances frequently abused in our culture. Our discussion of specific drugs will begin with the "social drugs," alcohol and tobacco. We will then consider drugs that can only be obtained through illegal means (heroin, LSD, marijuana, cocaine, and PCP). These drugs are generally not well accepted or tolerated by society. Yet if we consider the total number of all nonmedical drugs used that are more potent than marijuana, it is apparent that between a half and a third of young adults have used one or more of them (Miller et al., 1983). Following our overview of the use of illegal drugs, our attention will turn to drugs that can be used legally when prescribed by a physician. As we will note, persons who misuse the barbiturates or amphetamines either do not use them as prescribed by a physician or obtain them illegally.

Common Factors in Drug Use

One of the most recent trends in the study of addictive behaviors is to identify commonalities in the abuse of diverse substances such as alcohol, heroin, and tobacco (Lang, 1983; Levison, Gerstein, & Maloff, 1983; Marlatt, 1980; Miller, 1980). Within the past decade parallels have been drawn not only between the use of different substances but also between drug addiction and other behavior patterns that have "addictive" qualities, such as overeating and pathological gambling (e.g., Donegan, Rodin, O'Brien, & Solomon, 1983; Peele & Brodsky, 1976). Regardless of whether the individual develops a strong dependency on food or on a powerful mind-altering substance such as LSD, the initial or short-term gratifications derived may be supplanted by long-term adverse consequences that affect health, the capacity for productive work, *and* social relations.

The case of Jeffrey W. exemplifies this point. He had never expected to become an alcoholic. He never even considered alcohol or tobacco, for that matter, as dangerous drugs. In his circle of friends, serving alcohol was an approved method of greeting a guest, and Jeffrey had long ago been conditioned by movies and advertisements to believe that this was an acceptable way to relax, to be sociable, and to "be with it." The use of alcohol constituted a coping mechanism for Jeffrey, a problem-solving technique of sorts. He kept resisting the growing awareness that as time went on, he had to keep increasing the number of drinks needed to feel "really good." In time, Jeffrey W. felt unable to deal with his needs and cope with the demands of life without using alcohol as a prop. Jeffrey W. fell prey to a spiral of increasing

dependence on alcohol. As alcohol became the focal point of his life, other interests and sources of gratification receded into the background, further increasing his dependence on alcohol and intensifying his problems. Eventually Jeffrey W. had to confront the fact that a substance that has the potential to give pleasure may also hold the potential for harm. Stanton Peele (1980) has argued that this pattern characterizes not only alcohol but any drug or activity that is a candidate for abuse and dependence.

Chemical substances are used not only to "feel good," but also to regulate moods and transactions with others. For some persons like Jeffrey W., drug use clearly serves an adjustive function. It provides a means of coping with the stresses and strains of daily living. Many persons who do not wish to repeatedly visit a physician's office, or who have a tendency to deny the psychological basis of their problems in living, may use over-the-counter medications or illegal drugs for self-treatment.

A pattern can be identified in the relationship between the use of diverse illegal drugs and age. Illegal drug use typically begins in early adolescence, peaks in early adulthood, and declines sharply thereafter (Kandel & Maloff, 1983). Frequently young adults seeking their own identity may find in drug use a source of multiple gratifications of their emerging needs. They may turn to drugs for novel experience, a way of rebelling against parental authority, and a way of gaining approval from peers. Indeed, the characteristics of impulsivity, sensation seeking, difficulty in tolerance of delaying gratification, and an antisocial personality style seem to predispose some individuals to the use of drugs (Lang, 1983). However, no single personality "type" or constellation of traits has been shown to lead to substance use independently of other factors that contribute to drug-related problems. For example, research

Some people are able to enjoy alcohol without abusing it. (Richard Phelps/Rapho-Photo Researchers, Inc.)

has clearly documented that peer pressure can exert a potent effect on adolescent drinking (Jessor & Jessor, 1977), and that favorable attitudes about marijuana and its use by friends are strongly predictive of marijuana use (Smart, Gray, & Bennett, 1978). Later in life, social and personal pressures to secure and maintain stable employment and to establish a family tend to contradict some of the earlier pressures and attitudes associated with drug use.

Another widespread aspect of addictive behavior patterns is *transferability of indulgences*—the tendency of persons who have difficulty controlling the use of one substance to have problems controlling the use of other substances (Lang, 1983). This can be seen in polydrug abuse, the simultaneous or consecutive use of different drugs and alcohol. This pattern of usage is now thought to be the norm (Kaufman, 1982). Drug users frequently indulge in multiple drug use or "trade down" to another drug when their

drug of choice is not readily available. Alcoholics, for example, may use narcotics or barbiturates when they are available because they share with alcohol certain psychological and physiological effects. But drugs that have opposite effects on the nervous system such as amphetamines (stimulants) and alcohol (a depressant) are not infrequently used together (Jaffe, 1970). Substances that have a high potential for addiction share the property of inducing alterations in subjective experience. "Upper" and "downer" drugs may be used by the same individual because changes in consciousness may be a more desired goal than specific changes in the direction of subjective experience (Mello, 1977). However, as we shall see, the combined and heavy use of certain drugs may pose special risks for the user, including overdose, coma, and death.

Drug use is not randomly determined. An individual tends to begin drug use when the drug becomes easily available, when it is approved by his or her particular culture or subculture, and when, at least initially, serious consequences of drug use are not anticipated. The effects of drug use vary with the nature of the drug and the habits of drug usage an individual adopts. When drug usage is limited to occasional experimental use and is motivated by curiosity and the desire to share an experience with friends, the risk of serious, long-term ill effects is relatively low. Drugs may also be used on a sporadic or circumstantial basis for specific purposes, such as an aid in cramming for exams or in improving athletic performance. However, when drug use becomes more frequent and regular, and involves the use of one or multiple substances over an extended period of time, the dangers of serious consequences may increase, particularly with drugs more potent than marijuana. Even more serious than experimental, recreational, circumstantial, and intensified drug use is the pattern termed *compulsive use* (National Commission on Marijuana and Drug Abuse, 1973). Users who manifest this pattern exhibit increasing physical and psychological dependence on the drug. Physical discomfort and psychological distress, often reflected in the disruption of personal and social functioning, motivate frequent drug taking and compulsive attempts to obtain the drug. In many instances, however, a fine line divides recreational use of drugs and what may be considered drug abuse.

The DSM III classification system provides some useful guidelines for clarifying the various dimensions and consequences of drug usage.

Substance Abuse and Dependence

Let us now reconsider the cases of Allan H. and Jeffrey W., looking at them in the light of the DSM III classification system, which clarifies the distinction between substance abuse and substance dependence. The following are DSM III criteria for diagnosing substance abuse disorder: *duration* (at least one month); *a pattern of pathological use* (e.g., inability to cut down or stop, need for daily use for adequate functioning, intoxication throughout the day, repeated efforts to control use); and *social or occupational complications* (e.g., family problems, legal difficulties, accidents, erratic and impulsive behavior, and inappropriate expressions of feelings such as anger).

The case of Allan H. appears to meet the criteria for the classification of *substance abuse* for the following reasons:

1. He had been taking the drug for a sufficiently long period (more than one month).

2. His pattern of drug usage was pathological. He had used the drug every day for over a month. He also manifested psychological dependence; that is, he experienced a compelling desire to continue using the drug, and he had for some time unsuccessfully tried to curtail his use of barbiturates.

3. He suffered social complications: He missed school, his school performance deteriorated, and his mother noticed that he was "not himself."

Let us now examine the case of Jeffrey W., which illustrates the more severe disorder termed *substance dependence*. A number of years ago the term *addiction* would have been used to describe Jeffrey W.'s condition. But at present the preferred term is *drug* or *substance dependence*. This diagnosis is applicable if the user exhibits either *tolerance* or *withdrawal* symptoms in addition to the criteria mentioned under the substance abuse classification.

1. *Tolerance.* As Jeffrey W. continued to drink, he found that he needed increasing amounts of alcohol to obtain the same effect. Thus he acquired a tolerance to the effects of alcohol. A moment's reflection suggests that acquiring tolerance to a drug can have the effect of increasing the financial costs associated with its use, especially if the substance is a controlled, illicit drug. This added financial burden may increase the stress experienced by the user and therefore enhance the attractiveness of a substance that serves to reduce stress (Donegan, Rodin, O'Brien, & Solomon, 1983).

2. *Withdrawal.* Prolonged and excessive consumption of alcohol results in an altered physiological state that demands its continued ingestion. When Jeffrey W. stopped drinking, he no longer satisfied this demand, and his body responded to this sudden deprivation with painful and frightening symptoms termed *withdrawal.* The exact nature of the withdrawal or abstinence syndrome will vary with the drug taken and the duration and intensity of prior drug use.

Jeffrey W., like other users of drugs that lead to an abstinence syndrome, tended to avoid the withdrawal symptoms by consuming even more of the drug. Thus Jeffrey's alcohol consumption was not only reinforced by the pleasurable drinking experience but also by the avoidance of unpleasant withdrawal symptoms (e.g., morning "shakes" and malaise).

DSM III provides substantial refinements over DSM II. First, DSM III has removed alcohol and drug abuse from their former grouping with personality disorders and created separate categories for drugs of abuse. Second, the DSM III diagnostic system provides clear and specific criteria that can help distinguish recreational use of drugs from more destructive patterns of misuse. The criteria reflect the diversity of signs, symptoms, and behaviors associated with maladaptive patterns of drug use. But it is important to remember that drug-related social and occupational problems as well as medical complications and symptoms of physical dependence (tolerance/withdrawal) exist in various degrees and may also be thought of as ranging on a continuum (Lang, 1983; Miller, 1983; Skinner & Allen, 1982). Third, it is now possible for the clinician to specify whether drug use is best characterized as episodic, continuous, or in remission. Finally, DSM III provides categories that associate specific drugs with organic brain disorders. A further refinement permits ascribing the origin of the organic problem to intoxication or withdrawal and noting whether additional problems such as hallucinations and affective disorders are associated with it.

Substance abuse and dependence are multifaceted problems. In addition to the pharmacological effects of a substance, psychological and social factors combine to produce the powerful "hold" that certain drugs have on certain people. The subjective effects of a drug, for example, are determined by a complex interaction of factors: the dosage of the drug; the social setting or the psychological and social environment; the personality of the user; and the "set" or the user's expectations of the drug's effects and his attitudes about taking the drug (Zetner, 1976). There is a growing concensus in the field of substance abuse that a truly comprehensive theory of drug use must encompass diverse contributing factors such as genetic predispositions, learning and cognitive processes, sociocultural influences, and the biological and physiological mechanisms related to addiction (Miller, 1980). We will present models based on these etiological factors in our discussion of the drugs that have a high potential for abuse and dependence as defined by DSM III. But an integrative theory that provides a satisfactory account for the varieties of substance abuse disorders has yet to be articulated. Let us now turn our attention to alcohol, which is commonly referred to as a "social drug," but which is no less dangerous than other drugs of abuse despite this label.

THE "SOCIAL DRUGS"

Alcohol

The subjective effects of alcohol have long been known to man. From the time that fermented honey was made into the drink mead more than 8,000 years ago, alcohol has played an important role in social, religious, and medical contexts. Yet throughout history it has been recognized that the misuse of alcohol can contribute to human misery and suffering. Almost 2,000 years ago the Roman philosopher Seneca commented, "Drunkenness is nothing but a condition of insanity purposely assumed," while others have observed that alcohol is a "curse second only to war."

The history of the term *alcoholism* dates back to the 19th century, at which time it was synonomous with *dypsomania*, a disease-like condition of irresistible craving for alcohol (Miller, 1983). This view implies that alcoholics and nonalcoholics are qualitatively

(© William S. Nawrocki)

(© 1978, Rafael Macia)

(© Jan Halaska)

different. The question of whether alcoholism is a disease has persisted and is still the subject of controversy (see Marlatt, 1983; Miller, 1983). We will probe this question later when we discuss the equally controversial issue of *controlled drinking*.

In the 1950s the World Health Organization (WHO, 1952) formulated a broad definition of alcoholism to include problems in living or health problems related to the use of alcohol. Implicit in this definition is the notion that alcohol-related problems can be regarded as existing on a continuum of personal and public health consequences that range in severity from mild to severe.

The task of defining terms that refer to alcohol users is complicated by the wide range of drinking patterns and characteristics of persons who drink excessively. We shall use the generic term *problem drinker* to refer to the entire spectrum of individuals who experience personal or social problems because of alcohol abuse (Cahalan, 1970). When we use the more narrow term *alcoholic*, we refer to problem drinkers who fall on the severely impaired end of the continuum of alcohol-related social/occupational problems and who manifest signs of physical dependence or organic disorders linked with excessive drinking (Miller & Caddy, 1977). Such terms will be used for the sake of convenience, and with the recognition that such distinctions are somewhat arbitrary and fuzzy at times (Miller, 1980). Indeed, it is necessary to go beyond simply labeling an individual *alcoholic* or *problem drinker* to carefully evaluate the consequences of alcohol consumption on a continuum of drug-related disabilities and dependence.

Personal, Social, and Health-Related Consequences of Alcohol Abuse. The recreational use of alcohol is so common that it is easy to forget that alcohol is a potent and potentially dangerous psychoactive drug. Indeed, the majority of the nearly 100 million Americans who drink are able to enjoy its ef-

Two men socialize over drinks at open house.
(Cathy Cheney/EKM-Nepenthe)

fects without becoming enslaved by it. However, for the 10 million Americans who are dependent on alcohol, excessive drinking can be not only a serious personal problem but a source of more problems for family, friends, employers, and the police than any other drug in America (Mayer, 1983).

Alcohol abuse affects a wide spectrum of the population. Perhaps less than 5 percent of persons with serious alcohol problems conform to the stereotype of the Bowery bum alcoholic. In a classic study nearly two thirds of persons with alcohol problems were employed, married, living with their families, and overrepresented in high-status positions (Straus & Bacon, 1951). However, being unmarried or divorced does seem to be a risk factor, as does living in a large city (National Institute on Alcohol Abuse and Alcoholism, 1975).

A recent national survey (Zucker & Hartford, 1983) suggests that sizable numbers of young people are frequent and heavy consumers of alcohol. By the age of 13, 30 percent of boys and 22 percent of girls drink at least once a month. By the age of 18, 20 percent of boys and 6 percent of girls drink heavily, that is, at least once a week, typically consuming large amounts per occasion. Although the majority of young and older alcoholics manage to keep their alcoholism hidden from others, the flagrant personal and dollar costs of alcoholism are more difficult to conceal. Consider the following statistics:

- Of the nearly $50 billion in economic costs of alcohol abuse in the United States, approximately $13 billion will be spent on health care costs (Mayer, 1983).
- Alcoholics' life expectancy is shortened by 10 to 12 years; alcohol-related deaths may constitute as high as 11 percent of all deaths each year (DeLuca, 1981).
- According to statistics compiled by the Office of Technology Assessment (1983), as many as 58 percent of successful suicides are persons who were alcoholic; alcohol abuse is a factor in nearly 55 percent of all automobile accidents, and alcohol abuse is estimated to be a factor in up to 40 percent of all problems brought to family courts.
- In as many as 50 percent of all homicides, either the victim or the assailant or both had been drinking (Kinney & Leaton, 1982).
- Infants born with alcohol-related birth defects during a single year will cost the state of New York's economy approximately $155 million in lifetime care (Blume, 1981).

Alcohol is a powerful drug that poses a substantial threat to health and well-being. Alcohol use constitutes the third leading cause of death in the United States, after heart disease and cancer. Nearly 90,000 deaths per year can be attributed to its use.

Alcohol affects many organ systems. Cirrhosis, a disease that results in degeneration of the liver tissue, is the cause of most alcohol-related deaths. Cirrhosis is the seventh most common cause of death in this country, and estimates of alcohol involvement in its etiology range from about 40 percent to more than 90 percent (Eckardt et al., 1981). Excessive, long-term drinking has also been linked with an increased risk of developing other medical problems that include certain cancers, damage to the heart muscle, sexual impotence, and malnutrition.

During the past decade the health hazard known as *fetal alcohol syndrome* has received attention in the media and scientific circles. As the pregnant drinker increases her alcohol consumption, the risk of bearing an infant who suffers from one or more of the cluster of problems that comprise this syndrome increases (e.g., heart defects, poor coordination, growth deficiencies, hyperactivity, mental retardation, small head, joint and limb abnormalities). The overall risk of fetal alcohol syndrome is low (DeLuca, 1981). But as little as two drinks per day on a twice-weekly basis have been tied to both increases in spontaneous abortions and lower birth rates when drinking continues through pregnancy (Little, 1979). At present it is unclear whether there is a level of drinking during pregnancy that poses no risks to the unborn. Caution, then, would argue against drinking during pregnancy.

One of the first adverse consequences of chronic heavy drinking that typically appears long before liver damage is evident is mental impairment and brain damage. About 60 percent of alcoholics show evidence of cognitive impairment (e.g., ranging from minor memory or spatial and visual-perceptual problems to dementia and brain atrophy). Fortunately, many of the deficits associated with alcohol abuse can be reversed rather quickly after drinking ceases, but more permanent disabilities are especially likely to occur in persons who have been drinking heavily for 10 years or longer (Goldman, 1983). How frequently a person drinks appears to be a less adequate predictor of cognitive impairment than how much a person drinks per occasion (Miller & Saucedo, 1983). But evidence is accumulating to suggest that even social drinkers show signs of premature mental blunting induced by alcohol (Marlatt & Gordon, in press).

We have seen that alcohol-related problems can have devastating personal and societal consequences. It should be evident that the adverse effects of alcohol and other drugs are not confined to a single age group, work setting, or social class. You have no doubt observed that drinking does not inevitably lead to serious problems with alcohol; all persons who drink do not become alcoholics, but some persons undeniably do. You may wonder, however, whether alcoholism is irreversible or permanent. Evidence exists to the contrary. Some persons seem to "mature out" of serious drinking patterns (Hyman, 1976); others fluctuate between periods of abuse and nonabuse (Polich, Armor, & Braiker, 1981); and as many as a fifth of persons with drinking problems may recover "spontaneously" in the absence of treatment (Imber, Schultz, Funderburk, Allen, & Flamer, 1976). For some drinkers, alcohol abuse appears to be progressive, but for other very heavy drinkers it is not invariably progressive (Valiant & Milofsky, 1982). These findings should not be taken to mean that alcoholics should not be treated intensively—they should. These studies do, however, underline the existence of divergent patterns and consequences of alcohol consumption and the variability of the course of alcohol abuse and dependency.

Subjective, Behavioral, and Physiological Effects of Alcohol. What are the effects of alcohol? The short-term effects of intoxication are directly related to the concentration of alcohol in the blood. The feeling of intoxication is largely dependent on the rate of absorption of alcohol by the bloodstream, mostly through the stomach and intestine. This rate is affected not only by the concentration of alcohol in the drink and the rate of drinking but also by the amount of food in the body. The more food in the stomach, the less quickly alcohol is absorbed. Certain sex differences are notable. In comparison to men, women have more body fat (alcohol is not fat-soluble) and less water in which to dilute their alcohol. Hence, a woman whose weight is equal to that of a man, and who has consumed the same amount of alcohol, will have a higher blood alcohol level than the man (Kinney & Leaton, 1983). Figure 15–1 shows the relationship between certain effects of alcohol and the amounts of beverage and alcohol concentration in the blood. These effects will vary, from person to person, because of the factors we have noted that affect rate of absorption of alcohol by the bloodstream.

Alcohol is a central nervous system depressant. Its action, however, has been termed biphasic. At relatively low doses alcohol depresses those areas of the brain that inhibit emotion and behavior, thereby releasing them from inhibitory control and serving as a physiological (Pohorecky, 1977) and emotional (Tucker, Vucinich, & Sobell, 1982) stimulant. Alcohol can promote feelings of relaxation, act as a mood elevator, increase psychomotor activity, lower inhibitions, and impair judgment. But at higher doses, when the blood alcohol content reaches .05 to .10, the sedating and depressant effects of alcohol become more apparent as the motor centers of the brain are depressed, impairing walking and muscular coordination. The effects of alcohol have been found to be more pronounced when the blood alcohol is rising rather than falling (Jones & Parsons, 1975).

FIGURE 15–1

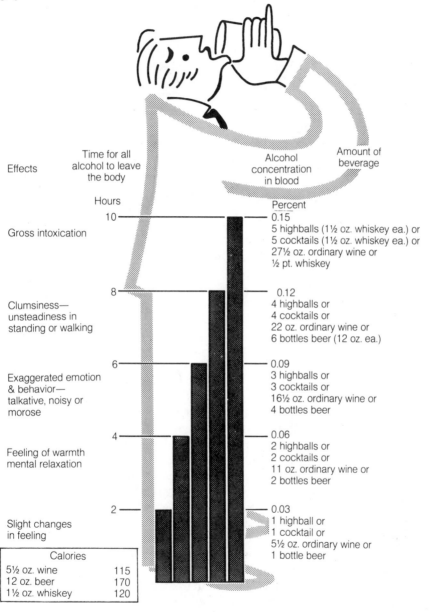

Effects	Time for all alcohol to leave the body		Alcohol concentration in blood	Amount of beverage
	Hours		Percent	
Gross intoxication	10		0.15	5 highballs (1½ oz. whiskey ea.) or 5 cocktails (1½ oz. whiskey ea.) or 27½ oz. ordinary wine or ½ pt. whiskey
Clumsiness—unsteadiness in standing or walking	8		0.12	4 highballs or 4 cocktails or 22 oz. ordinary wine or 6 bottles beer (12 oz. ea.)
Exaggerated emotion & behavior—talkative, noisy or morose	6		0.09	3 highballs or 3 cocktails or 16½ oz. ordinary wine or 4 bottles beer
Feeling of warmth mental relaxation	4		0.06	2 highballs or 2 cocktails or 11 oz. ordinary wine or 2 bottles beer
Slight changes in feeling	2		0.03	1 highball or 1 cocktail or 5½ oz. ordinary wine or 1 bottle beer

Calories	
5½ oz. wine	115
12 oz. beer	170
1½ oz. whiskey	120

Source: Reprinted by permission from *Time*, The Weekly News Magazine; Copyright Time Inc. 1974.

In most states .10 blood alcohol content is the cutoff for legal intoxication; at this point the operation of an automobile is clearly hazardous. As the blood alcohol content rises, impairment increases to the point where strong sedation occurs in the range of .20 to .30 and unconsciousness occurs at levels of .40 to .50. Blood alcohol levels of .50 to .60 may prove fatal (Schlaadt & Shannon, 1982). Alcohol (ethanol) is metabolized by the body at the rate of about one-half ounce per hour (the equivalent of about an ounce of whiskey).

Earlier in our discussion we noted that the effects of drugs may be determined, in part, by the expectancies of the users. At low alcohol dose levels, culturally learned expectancies play an important role in influencing complex social behaviors and perceptions of the effects of alcohol. Indeed, research suggests that expectancies are more important than the physiological effects of alcohol in influencing social behaviors such as aggression (Lans, Goeckner, Adesso, & Marlatt, 1975). Expectancies may override the pharmacological effects of alcohol in facilitating humor, anxiety reduction, and sexual responsivity in males. In contrast, nonsocial behaviors, such as reaction time and motor coordination, are more influenced by alcohol than by expectancies (see Marlatt & Rohsenow, 1980).

Toxic Effects: Organic Mental Disorders.

Alcohol Withdrawal Syndrome. The toxic effects of alcohol on the central nervous system are reflected in a number of organic mental disorders. The most common is the unpleasant symptoms of the alcohol withdrawal syndrome that may begin after several days of heavy drinking. Shortly after the person stops drinking or reduces the intake of alcohol, the hands, eyelids, and tongue may show a coarse tremor. One or more of the following symptoms may also be prominent during the two to seven days that the withdrawal syndrome persists: sleep disorders, nausea and vomiting, anxiety, depression, irritability, grand mal seizures, weakness, and elevated heart rate and blood pressure.

Idiosyncratic Intoxication. For a small fraction of people who drink even small quantities of alcohol, insufficient to produce intoxification in most people, dramatic behavioral changes occur that are atypical of the person when not drinking. In what is termed *idiosyncratic intoxication*, a shy, retiring person may undergo a "personality change" in an almost Jekyll-Hyde fashion and become aggressive, boisterous, and assaultive. Curiously, the person may seem out of contact with others during the episode and have no memory for the period of intoxication. This condition may be related to a brain abnormality in which massive disruptions in EEG patterns occur when alcohol is consumed.

Alcohol Withdrawal Delirium (Delirium Tremens). Delirium tremens, a disorder you may know as the DTs, is the most severe withdrawal phenomenon. In fact, it can constitute a serious medical emergency; prior to the advent of proper medical treatment now available, it had a mortality rate as high as 15 percent (Moore, 1977). DTs are much less common than alcohol withdrawal and can be clearly distinguished from this syndrome by the clear presence of delirium—disorientation, confusion, hallucinations, and memory problems. Agitation, sleep problems, tremor, and autonomic hyperactivity almost always accompany the delirium. The symptoms usually begin within two or three days after continuous drinking and abate within a week after the first signs of DTs are noticed.

Alcohol Hallucinosis. This rare withdrawal disorder occurs most frequently about 24 to 48 hours after an extended period of intoxication in persons who are physically dependent on alcohol. Auditory hallucinations that are sometimes accompanied by delusions are the hallmark of this condition. Alcohol hallucinosis may require hospitalization because of the terrifying and threatening nature of the hallucinations and an accompanying mood of fear, anger, and depression.

Treatment

A wide variety of methods have been employed in the treatment of alcohol abuse, including detoxification, medications, hypnosis, psychotherapy, family therapy, videotape feedback, relaxation training, and for a period in the late 50s and 60s, treatment with LSD. Reviews of treatment outcomes indicate that no single approach has proven superior in achieving a goal of abstinence, and some,

such as traditional insight-oriented psychotherapy and treatment with LSD, have not proven as effective as the rest of the pack (Miller & Hester, 1980). Let us first consider some of the more traditional approaches to the treatment of alcohol misuse.

Alcoholics Anonymous. Alcoholics Anonymous is a fellowship of men and women who share their experience, strength, and hope with each other so that they may solve their common problems and help others to recover from alcoholism.

The only requirement for membership is a desire to stop drinking. There are no dues or fees for A.A. membership; they are self-supporting through their own contributions.

A.A. is not allied with any sect, denomination, politics, organization, or institution; it does not wish to engage in any controversy; neither does it endorse or oppose any causes.

A.A. meeting. (Courtesy Alcoholics Anonymous)

THE TWELVE STEPS OF ALCOHOLICS ANONYMOUS

1. We admitted we were powerless over alcohol—that our lives had become unmanageable.
2. Came to believe that a Power greater than ourselves could restore us to sanity.
3. Made a decision to turn our will and our lives over to the care of God as we understood Him.
4. Made a searching and fearless moral inventory of ourselves.
5. Admitted to God, to ourselves and to another human being the exact nature of our wrongs.
6. Were entirely ready to have God remove all these defects of character.
7. Humbly asked Him to remove our shortcomings.
8. Made a list of all persons we had harmed, and became willing to make amends to them.
9. Made direct amends to such people wherever possible, except when to do so would injure them or others.
10. Continued to take personal inventory and when we were wrong, promptly admitted to it.
11. Sought through prayer and meditation to improve our conscious contact with God as we understood Him, praying only for knowledge of His will for us and the power to carry that out.
12. Having had a spiritual awakening as the result of these steps, we tried to carry this message to alcoholics and practice these principles in all our affairs.

From Alcoholics Anonymous copyright © 1939, by Alcoholics Anonymous World Services, Inc. Reprinted by permission of Alcoholics Anonymous World Services, Inc.

According to an A.A. statement, "Our primary purpose is to stay sober and help other alcoholics to achieve sobriety" (pamphlet, Alcoholics Anonymous World Services, 1978).

The beginnings of Alcoholics Anonymous can be traced to a meeting that took place over 30 years ago between two men who were struggling to control their drinking. Through their acquaintance, Bill W. a stockbroker and Bob S. a surgeon, made an important discovery: They could help each other stay sober through mutual support. Inspired by their discovery that alcoholics could successfully help each other, they shared the story of their recoveries with other alcoholics. And within a few years, small groups of alcoholics began to meet regularly to share their drinking backgrounds, offer support, hope, and encouragement to one another, and testify that they were victims of a habit they were powerless to control.

Alcoholics Anonymous is now the largest worldwide organization for treating alcoholics, with over 22,000 chapters and an estimated 650,000 members (Valiant & Milofsky, 1982). Today, as in early days, there is an evangelic atmosphere in many A.A. meetings. A number of the twelve steps toward sobriety around which the program is loosely organized exhort the member to entrust his difficulties to a higher power—"God as we understand Him." The twelve steps seem to have an interdenominational appeal, and many believe the program facilitates the attainment of renewed self-respect, diminishes unproductive guilt feelings, and promotes behaviors that are a substitute for drinking behavior. In addition to establishing norms that foster a less stressful lifestyle, A.A. encourages positive relationships among its members and furnishes a viable social support network that probably serves to reduce the risk of relapse (Alford, 1980, Moos & Finney, 1983; Valiant & Milofsky, 1982a).

Many hospitals and clinics have incorporated A.A. meetings in their programs to treat alcoholics. Upon release, continued care is available through attending A.A. meetings in the community. Alcoholics Anonymous has inspired the creation of Al-anon and Alateen, groups that help the spouses and children of alcoholics cope with alcohol abuse.

Many of the extravagent claims that have been made about the success of A.A. are not supported by scientific data. Studies that have not employed control groups have yielded success rates for A.A. (between 26 and 50 percent) that are comparable to the rates achieved by other forms of therapy for alcoholics (Miller & Hester, 1980). An extensive and controlled investigation of A.A. (Brandsma, Maultsby, & Welsh, 1980) failed to demonstrate superiority of A.A. over alternative approaches. A.A. has undoubtedly had a positive impact on the lives of many alcoholics, but research is needed to evaluate its effectiveness relative to other approaches and to clarify which alcoholics may best be served by its program (Valiant, 1983).

Biological Treatment. Detoxification is the medical process of taking a substance-dependent person safely through withdrawal. Alone, detoxification is not a sufficient treatment for alcoholics, but for those pharmacologically addicted to alcohol, detoxification is quite often a necessary precursor of other treatment.

The use of the drug disulfiram, or antabuse, has been described as an "insurance policy against impulsive drinking for those who sincerely wish to abstain from alcohol" (Weinberg, 1977, p. 256). This description has a sound basis: When ingested with alcohol, antabuse causes a potent reaction that includes nausea, vomiting, racing heart, and flushing. With even small quantities of alcohol, like the amount present in cough syrup, antabuse can trigger unpleasant effects for two to three days. The effects of antabuse are the result of interference with the metabolism of alcohol and the resultant accumulation of acetaldehyde, a toxic breakdown product of alcohol.

Antabuse alone cannot cure alcohol abuse since, at best, it can only postpone drinking. Antabuse is most frequently used as an adjunct to treatment in outpatient programs that encourage or require their patients to take it regularly. The rationale is that it can provide a period of abstinence during which a patient can learn and implement new coping skills. However, serious questions have been raised about whether elevated improvement rates with antabuse are the result of the specific effects of the drug or are the byproduct of placebo effects (Becker, 1979). Furthermore, the use of antabuse is contraindicated in persons who suffer from certain physical disorders, and research now points to dangers inherent in the use of antabuse, including carcinogenic (cancer-causing) properties and nervous system toxicity. Finally, a clear limitation of antabuse is that persons who are not sufficiently motivated may simply not take their "regular dose" of antabuse.

Behavioral Treatments. One of the best known behavioral treatments is aversive conditioning. In aversion therapy, drinking alcohol is associated with unpleasant consequences, making the experience of drinking itself unpleasant. We will now describe a chemical aversion procedure used with alcoholics at Schick and Raleigh Hills hospitals. Patients in the treatment program are first escorted to the "tavern," a room decorated like a neighborhood bar and stocked with an ample and varied supply of liquor. Treatment takes place in a "real life" situation to promote transfer of the aversion to alcohol to the real drinking environment. The patient is then injected with the chemical emetine and given his or her favorite alcoholic beverage by the "bartender." The patient is instructed to savor the aroma and take a sip, but not swallow the alcohol. The timing of the procedure is arranged so that just after the patient sips the drink, the emetine produces nausea and prolonged vomiting. After three to six days of treatments, the alcoholic presumably associates nausea and alcohol.

Electrical aversion treatments follow a similar procedure. Instead of emetine the patient receives painful, yet tolerable electric shocks every time he or she attempts to take a drink. After the patient spits the drink out, the shock is terminated.

Cautela (1966; 1970) has devised an aversive conditioning approach called *covert sensitization* that utilizes unpleasant images in place of electric shocks or chemicals. In a typical treatment session patients are instructed to close their eyes and imagine that they are about to drink their favorite alcoholic beverage. When they report that the image is clear and vivid, the therapist then suggests that the patients are experiencing sensations of nausea and vomiting. The therapist repeatedly suggests the unpleasant graphic imagery to the patients until presumably a conditioned aversion is established to the sight, smell, and taste of alcohol.

Of the three treatments, therapy outcome studies favor chemical aversion as the most successful in facilitating long-term abstinence. Nausea may be the most effective aversive agent because it is more central to the drinking sequence than shock and more immediate than imagery.

A common criticism of aversion therapy is that it is a simplistic and naive approach to a complex clinical problem. It is argued that if treatment ignores the determinants of drinking behavior in the patient's living situation, therapy gains are likely to be short-lived. In their comprehensive behavioral self-control training (BSCT) program, Miller and his colleagues (e.g., Miller, 1977, 1978a,b) train problem drinkers to self-monitor and set appropriate limits for alcohol consumption, to control the rate of their drinking, and to self-reinforce progress. The program also teaches problem drinkers coping skills that are applicable in situations where alcohol was previously used as a coping mechanism (Miller & Mastria, 1977). Many studies that sample a broad spectrum of patients have shown this program to be effective (Miller & Hester, 1980). Because the focus of this treatment is on moderation of drinking, it is contraindicated in cases in which total abstinence is the foremost treatment goal.

Complementing the BSCT strategy, Marlatt and his associates (Cummings, Gordon, & Marlatt, 1980; Marlatt & Gordon, 1980) have proposed focusing prevention efforts on helping problem drinkers to cope effectively with high risk for relapse situations as well as the initial signs of situations that culminate in high-risk situations. Problem drinkers are more at risk to deviate from their treatment goal (either abstinence or moderation) when experiencing negative emotional states, interpersonal conflict, or social pressure (Marlatt & Gordon, 1979, 1980; Moos et al., 1981). The premise is that if the problem drinker is prepared for these situations, relapse is less likely. In addition to the components that risk prevention shares with BSCT (such as self-monitoring blood alcohol level and modifying drinking behavior—sipping, not gulping, spacing drinks, interspersing nonalcoholic drinks—risk prevention involves setting guidelines for when drinking is appropriate and planning what will be consumed and how much will be consumed on a given occasion. The ultimate goal—self-control of alcohol consumption—is accomplished by teaching social, personal, and cognitive skills to combat relapse. In summary, behavioral treatment programs emphasize self-monitoring and assessment to gauge the nature and dimensions of alcohol use, flexibility, and individually tailored treatment procedures that take into consideration specific client needs (Marlatt, 1983).

Controlled Drinking. As you probably noted, behavioral treatments assume that a viable treatment goal for some alcohol abusers is moderation of drinking rather than abstinence. The controversial question of whether controlled drinking is an appropriate goal has been vigorously debated. The traditional viewpoint, long espoused by Alcoholics Anonymous and shared by many professionals, is that lifelong abstinence is the only acceptable goal for alcoholics. Alcoholism is viewed as a progressive biomedical disease which is incurable but which can be arrested by unyielding abstinence. The A.A. position is expressed in the following quote from the book *Alcoholics Anonymous* (1939):

> But there is a man who at 55 years found he was just where he left off at 30 (the man having taken his first drink in 25 years.) We have seen the truth demonstrated again and again: "once an alcoholic, always an alcoholic." Commencing to drink after a period of sobriety, we are in short time as bad as ever (p. 44).

In contrast to this position, the behavioral viewpoint is founded on the assumption that excessive drinking is a learned, habitual behavior problem that is maintained by a variety of social and physical reinforcers (Marlatt, 1984). It is held that like other behaviors, alcohol use can be modified and, in some individuals, subject to satisfactory self-control short of total abstinence.

In a review of studies relevant to the issue of controlled drinking, Miller (1983) maintains that the following conclusions are justified by the research evidence: (1) at follow-ups as long as one to three years, controlled-drinking treatments are at least as successful as approaches with the goal of abstinence; (2) no differences in relapse rates or improvement in other life problem areas are evident when controlled drinking methods and abstinence approaches are compared; (3) on the average, about two thirds of patients trained in drinking in moderation maintain successful outcomes a year after treatment; (4) controlled drinking methods are most likely to be effective with younger, less dependent problem drinkers and least likely to be effective with older, more advanced patients with symptoms of alcohol dependence.

The implications of the last statement—that some alcohol abusers may potentially benefit from controlled drinking treatment while others may not—are weighty. Negative social and physical consequences are possible outcomes when addicted alcoholics fail to achieve abstinence (Pendery, Maltzman, & West, 1982). This awareness has prompted caution on the part of many behavioral clinicians as well as more traditional therapists. Indeed, in cases where serious physical or mental problems would be exacerbated by drinking alcohol, no responsible clinician would recommend any treatment goal other than abstinence. Hence, as Nathan (1984) has commented, "Few clinicians nowadays would recommend a controlled-drinking goal for an alcoholic" (p. 101).

If controlled drinking is not for all alcohol abusers, it may nonetheless be appropriate for some alcohol users. Thus moderation approaches may have a place in treatment programs that offer a range of options for problem drinkers. Among behavior therapists, at least, considerable consensus exists that controlled drinking treatments may be useful for problem drinkers who resist seeking therapy because they do not desire total abstinence. The availability of therapies with a controlled drinking goal may help problem drinkers seek help earlier than if abstinence were the only alternative. Controlled drinking may also be worth attempting with patients who have repeatedly failed to achieve abstinence in programs that emphasize this goal. Controlled drinking remains so controversial, however, that it is unlikely that the near future will witness the widespread use of controlled drinking treatments by the majority of professionals engaged in the treatment of alcohol abuse.

Tobacco

Consider the following statements that highlight some of the health hazards associated with smoking tobacco:

- A pack-a-day smoker takes more than 40,000 puffs per year, and each puff delivers nicotine and perhaps 3,000 other toxic chemicals into the bloodstream. Nicotine, the most active agent in tobacco, is a poisonous alkaloid more toxic than heroin and is sometimes used as an insecticide. The carbon monoxide content of cigarette smoke is considerably higher than Los Angeles smog on the worst day (Jarvik, 1977; Schlaadt & Shannon, 1982).

- "Last year, smoking was a major factor in 220,000 deaths from heart disease, 78,000 lung cancer deaths, and 22,000 deaths from other cancers. These facts mean that people who smoke are committing slow-motion suicide." Statement by former Secretary of Health, Education, and Welfare James Califano (Lyons, 1978).

- It can now be unequivocally stated that cigarette smoking affects the developing fetus. Cigarettes increase the rate of spontaneous abortion, stillbirth, and early postpartum deaths of children (Julien, 1981).

- One in three smokers will die as a result of smoking and it has been estimated that one's life is shortened 14 minutes for every cigarette smoked. A 30- to 40-year-old male cigarette smoker who smokes two packs of cigarettes per day loses about eight years of his life (Julien, 1981).

As you read these statements you may have asked yourself questions like the ones that follow: If smoking tobacco is so dangerous—and, indeed, surveys suggest that 90 percent of the public believe it to be harmful to health (Surgeon General's Report, 1979)—what accounts for the fact that 54 million Americans smoke? Why is the habit so tenacious that nearly two out of three smokers say they would like to quit, yet continue to smoke despite having tried to quit at least once? Before we address these questions, let us first examine some of the physiological effects of nicotine.

Effects of Nicotine. Nicotine is a powerful drug. Its effects register on the brain, spinal cord, the peripheral nervous system, the heart, and other bodily organs. Nicotine is a stimulant drug, one that revs up the central nervous system by stimulating receptors sensitive to the neurotransmitter acetylcholine (Volle & Kohle, 1975). This stimulation effect increases epinephrine (adrenaline), heart rate, blood pressure, and gastrointestinal activity. Smokers often report feelings of stimulation as well as tranquility, relaxation, and alertness. As we will see below, nicotine may play its most prominent role in maintaining smoking behavior.

The Multidimensional Nature of Smoking Behavior. Some people are drawn to smoking not only because of the physiological effects of nicotine but also because of the psychological effects of smoking and what cigarettes come to represent. In this section we will illustrate the multidimensional nature of smoking behavior and, by extension, other drug-taking behavior as well. The question of why people smoke has eluded a simple, unitary answer. However, it is apparent that the variables associated with the onset of smoking may be very different from those related to the maintenance of smoking behavior.

Leventhal and Cleary (1980) have observed that smoking begins long before a child experiments with the first cigarette. Positive attitudes and images associated with smoking enhance the appeal of cigarettes for some young people. One important early function of smoking relates to what Coan (1973) has termed its *adjustive value*— smoking serves particular needs such as reducing tension or anxiety, enhancing self-esteem, and providing pleasure and enjoyment. Initial experimentation appears to be crucial. One noteworthy statistic is that 85 to 90 percent of those who smoke four cigarettes become regular smokers (Salber, Freeman, & Abelin, 1968). As smoking becomes more habitual, it also tends to become automatic. Tolerance to the effects of smoking develops slowly, usually over a period of two years or longer.

Nicotine and Smoking Maintenance. Some researchers believe that nicotine is the major culprit in *maintaining* smoking behavior. The primary psychological effects of nicotine consist of mild to moderate stimulation of the central nervous system (Julien, 1978). It has been hypothesized that smokers regulate their smoking in order to maintain some desirable level of nicotine, and that withdrawal symptoms appear when an optimum level of nicotine cannot be maintained (Sherman, Presson, Chassin, & Olshavsky, 1979). But the evidence for this viewpoint is inconsistent and, therefore, not totally convincing. Some, but not all, studies show that smokers given low tar and nicotine cigarettes will smoke more cigarettes to equal the level of nicotine they were accustomed to. Schachter speculated that the failure to consistently find evidence for precise nicotine regulation may lie in the fact that not all smokers are addicted. Schachter (1977) found that while long-term heavy smokers showed nicotine regulation, long-term light smokers did not. Schachter concluded that long-term heavy smokers behave as if they were addicted, while long-term light smokers are either not addicted or manage to keep their habit under tight psychological control.

Schachter and his associates have conducted a series of studies designed to better understand the relationship between smoking and nicotine regulation. One of the hypotheses they tested was that the acidity of the urine may mediate nicotine regulation, and that when the urine is acidified, more nicotine is flushed out of the body. Schachter and his group reasoned that if smoking serves to regulate nicotine, smokers would be expected to smoke more when the urine is acid, in order to compensate for the greater amounts of nicotine excreted. This is precisely what they found when they manipulated the acidity of the urine by the use of acidifying or alkalizing agents. There was a marked decrease in smoking when smokers were given bicarbonate to make the urine less acidic, and a dramatic increase in smoking when vitamin C was administered to acidify the urine.

Subsequent studies have demonstrated that stress and party going, events commonly associated with heavy smoking, lead to increased acidification of the urine and increased smoking (Silverstein, Kozlowski, & Schachter, 1977). In the final study of the series it was found that when the urine is experimentally maintained at alkaline levels, stress had no effect on smoking. These findings not only appeared to support the general hypothesis that heavy smokers smoke for nicotine but also that the acidity of the urine is the crucial biochemical link between stress and smoking.

But nicotine regulation does not provide a totally satisfactory explanation for the maintenance of smoking behavior. Not all smokers who cease smoking experience withdrawal symptoms. While some persons experience severe symptoms, including gastric disorders, dry mouth, irritability, sleeplessness, headaches, and impaired concentration, others report no symptoms.

When the main need satisfied by smoking is merely the need for another cigarette, smoking can truly be said to be maladjustive—an unpleasant habit accompanied by an unwelcome craving for cigarettes (Coan, 1973). Leventhal and Cleary believe it may be said an individual is truly a "smoker" when smoking is an integral part of one's self-definition—"I am a smoker"—and smoking is used to enhance positive reactions and to minimize negative emotional reactions in a variety of situations. Thus smoking plays an important role in regulating emotions, including the distress experienced when the nicotine level drops. But much remains to be learned abut the mixture of social, psycho-logical, and pharmacological factors that accounts for the power of cigarettes to produce dependence in the user (Leventhal & Cleary, 1980).

Treatment. Despite governmental anti-smoking efforts over the past 20 years that have had a significant impact on reducing smoking behavior, cigarettes continue to exert a stranglehold on many users. Although a wide range of techniques have been tried, including hypnosis, nicotine chewing gum, tranquilizers, group pressure, and behavior modification, no one technique has proven to be clearly superior or very effective. Less than one in four smokers is successful in permanently quitting before the age of sixty (Russell, 1977) and the dropout rate of smokers in treatment programs approaches 50 percent (Leventhal & Cleary, 1980). Smoking withdrawal and therapy clinics have successfully treated only about 20 percent of smokers after a one year follow-up (Hunt, Barrett, & Branch, 1971). It is, however, preferable to treat smoking rather than to ignore it and minimize the risks it poses to health. In addition, therapies that bolster motivation and teach effective coping skills have some advantage over other methods, but this advantage is not impressive (Leventhal & Cleary, 1980).

THE ILLEGAL DRUGS

Marijuana

Let us now consider marijuana, a drug that some would argue has achieved the status of a social drug much like alcohol and tobacco. As its public acceptance has grown, certain groups have made concerted efforts to legalize marijuana. Penalties for its use have decreased or have not been rigorously enforced, as more and more people of different walks of life have tried it. It remains, however, an illegal and controlled drug, and there are growing indications that the public's reluctance to fully accept marijuana is justified on medical grounds. Indeed, concerns about health are apparently associated with the downward trend in the use of marijuana among high-school seniors. About 60 percent of more than 17,000 students surveyed in 1982 attributed "great risk" to regular marijuana use, compared to about a third of a comparable sample of students in 1978. During that period reports of current use dropped from 37 percent to 29 percent (Johnston, Bachman, & O'Malley, 1982).

Despite this trend, marijuana is still the frontrunner as the most popular illicit drug in the United States, with nearly two thirds

More and more people from different walks of life have tried marijuana. (© Sue Markson)

of young adults (64 percent) aged 22 to 25 years nationwide having used marijuana in 1982 (Kandel, 1984). As you might imagine, the widespread use of marijuana has stimulated a great deal of interest in better understanding its effects and the social and medical consequences of its use and abuse. Before we address key questions about the long-term effects of marijuana use, let us first turn our attention to the subjective effects and short-term physiological effects of marijuana.

Short-Term Effects of Marijuana

Users of marijuana report that the short-term subjective effects of marijuana include a sense of well-being and a tendency to talk and laugh more than usual. Later the user may become more quiet, introspective, and sleepy. Mood changes are not uncommon. Other effects have been reported that may be particularly prominent at higher dosages include distortion of the sense of time, spatial and perceptual changes, and an altered sense of self. At very high doses, there have been rare reports of extreme anxiety and panic and even rarer reports of psychotic episodes. Pharmacologically, marijuana is usually classified as a mild hallucinogen (drugs whose trademark is producing alterations of perception, mood, and thought) but it also may have sedative or hypnotic (sleep-inducing) qualities. Marijuana does not produce a physical dependence at normal doses, but tolerance to its effects has been verified by research.

The subjective effects of marijuana are caused by the primary ingredient in the marijuana plant (cannabis sativa), THC (tetrahydrocannabinol). Hashish is more potent than marijuana because it contains greater concentrations of THC.

When marijuana is smoked or administered orally, the most obvious physiological changes result from alternations in the functioning of the cardiovascular system and the central nervous system. The most prominent physiological changes are an increase in heart rate, reddening of the eyes, and dryness of the mouth.

Some Consequences of Marijuana Use

Marijuana, Criminal Activity, and Driving. Some definitive conclusions can be drawn with respect to the relationship between marijuana and criminality. Evidence reviewed by the National Commission on Marijuana and Drug Abuse in 1972 suggests that there is no evidence to substantiate the association between marijuana and criminal, violent, aggressive, or delinquent behavior. In fact, marijuana users are less likely to commit violent or nonviolent crimes of a sexual or nonsexual nature than are nonusers.

There is also little question that marijuana, like alcohol, appears to increase the likelihood of an accident when "mixed" with driving. A study of highway accidents in the Boston area found that marijuana smokers were overrepresented in traffic fatalities (Sterlins-Smith, 1976). A relationship between marijuana intoxication and impaired driving performance has been documented in studies of driving-related perceptual skills, driver simulation and actual driving performance, and users' own evaluations of their driving skills while high (Peterson, 1977).

The "Amotivational Syndrome." In 1974 Senator James Eastland cautioned that "if the cannabis epidemic continues . . . we may find ourselves saddled with a large population of semi-zombies—of young people acutely afflicted by the amotivational syndrome" (Ray, 1978). Concerns like those expressed by Senator Eastland are reminiscent of earlier claims that marijuana led to

personality destruction and degeneration. Indeed, the belief is still prevalent that the regular use of marijuana leads to passivity, unproductivity, and a loss of motivation to pursue goals valued by society. However, we shall see that a causal link between marijuana use and the so-called amotivational syndrome has yet to be established.

Let us examine the findings of a study that is now frequently referred to as the Jamaican Study. Anthropologists Vera Rubin and Lambros Comitas studied 2,000 working-class Jamaican males who, like the majority of workers in Jamaica, smoke a potent variety of marijuana called ganga as they are engaged in their everyday labors. The workers smoked an average number of about seven marijuana cigarettes each day, each of which is about 2 to 20 times as strong as marijuana smoked in the United States.

Rubin and Comitas' research provides another illustration of the manner in which expectancies may interact with drug use. Over the more than 100-year history of marijuana use in Jamaica, the average user has come to view the consequences of smoking ganga as harmless, if not beneficial. Far from being seen as a substance that dampens motivation, marijuana is most often smoked at work and is even given to school-age children to improve their classroom performance. In the work context improved concentration and work capacity are attributed to marijuana use.

When Rubin and Comitas analyzed workers' thoughts before and after smoking ganga, they found that after smoking workers indicated that they spent more time thinking about their work than they did before taking the drug. Rubin notes that among the Jamaicans, marijuana is "not taken to drop out but to hold on, to eke out a precarious living" (*APA Monitor*, 1976, p. 5). Relatedly, a study of chronic heavy marijuana smokers in Costa Rica revealed that the heaviest users were found to have the highest incomes and the most stable job history of those studied. In addition, they reported that their favorite activity while smoking is to work (Coggins, 1976).

The Jamaican and Costa Rican studies suggest that motivation may be dependent on cultural expectations associated with marijuana use. However, observations from other areas of the world (e.g., Nepal), where marijuana is also readily available, report *decreased* initiative and work output among chronic marijuana users (Sharm, 1975). Further, the small number of persons evaluated in such studies makes it difficult to draw generalizations that can be applied with confidence to the whole culture (HEW report, 1979). We must be especially cautious about directly translating these results to our more urbanized, industrial American society. The findings may have little relevance to American adolescents at an earlier stage in development and under different social conditions (HEW report, 1976). What is needed is research that addresses the link between marijuana and motivation in our culture.

Marijuana and "Harder" Drugs. Does marijuana serve as a stepping stone to more dangerous drugs, as the antimarijuana sensationalism of the 1920s and 1930s would lead us to believe? A study by Gould and his colleagues (Gould, Berberian, Kasl, Thompson, & Kleber, 1977) addresses the question of whether college-age drug users tend to take drugs in some kind of stepwise, orderly sequence. The study examined the patterns of multiple drug use reported by a random sample of 1,094 high-school students living in Connecticut. They found that respondents who used more than one drug tended to first use alcohol, next marijuana, and then hashish. But the patterns of drug use are not consistent thereafter. Those who progressed beyond hashish were about equally likely to

progress next to amphetamines, LSD, barbiturates, or mescaline. Only a small minority of students' drug experience extended beyond these four drugs. For example, over one half of the students had tried marijuana, but only 2 percent of the students had used heroin. Thus, although using marijuana tends to precede the use of heroin, the great majority of users never try heroin. The findings show that the use of marijuana, at least in the population studied, is not causally linked to the use of heroin in a simple, straightforward fashion.

Marijuana and Health. Because the adverse effects of cigarette smoking have received so much attention, it is not surprising that considerable concern has been expressed about the hazards posed by smoking marijuana. Recent reports suggest that long-term exposure to marijuana smoke produces cellular changes in lung tissue as well as an impairment of many of the lung's defense mechanisms. Marijuana smokers often develop bronchitis, asthmalike conditions, and bronchial cough (Jones, 1980).

Consuming marijuana may be hazardous for persons with cardiac abnormalities. Since marijuana increases heart rate and may also temporarily weaken the muscle contractions of the heart, persons with heart problems who smoke marijuana are exposing themselves to unnecessary risks.

There is considerably less agreement about heavy marijuana use as regards chromosome damage, brain damage, suppression of the body's disease-fighting mechanism, and reduced levels of male sex hormones. The bulk of research studies indicate that physiological changes produced by marijuana tend to remain within normal limits. However, there are inconsistent and contradictory findings in each of the above areas of medical concern. Much more research is needed to evaluate the possibility of medical complications.

LSD

Subjective Effects of LSD. LSD is an incredibly powerful drug. Profound changes in consciousness can result from taking small amounts of LSD. The amount contained in pills about the size of two aspirins would provide more than 6,000 doses. One of the most interesting and distinctive characteristics of LSD and other drugs termed *hallucinogens* or *psychedelics* (e.g., mescaline, psilocybin, and peyote) is the wide variety of subjective effects they facilitate. You will recall reading in Chapter 3 a number of personal accounts of the effects of ingesting hallucinogenic drugs on mood, perception, and thought. Like other drug experiences, the effects of LSD are affected by the dosage, purity, setting, personality, and expectations of the user.

Proponents of hallucinogens like Timothy Leary have emphasized the more positive types of experiences that users report. Experiences of this variety include astonishingly lucid thought, fascinating changes in sensations and perceptions, synesthesia (the blending of senses—the "smelling of noises," for example), the dramatic emergence into consciousness of material that has previously been unconscious or preconscious, and finally, peak, cosmic, or transcendental experiences characterized by a sense of unity or oneness with everything, transcendence of time and space, and a sense of reverence and wonder that is difficult to communicate (Pahnke, Kurland, Unger, Savage, & Grof, 1970). In contrast, those who have cautioned about the dangers of hallucinogens have emphasized their potential to produce intense, negative experiences. Experiences of this type include fear to the point of panic, paranoid delusions of suspicion or grandeur, toxic confusion, depression, feelings of isolation, and bodily discomfort. In actuality many "LSD trips" are a blend of different experiences, although intensely positive or negative experiences may predominate.

Barber (1970) notes that whether or not a person becomes suspicious, hostile, and paranoid during an LSD session appears to be functionally related to his or her predrug personality. Linton and Langs (1964) conducted an experiment in which 30 subjects ingested small doses of LSD after completing a battery of personality tests. Individuals who were judged as guarded and undefended on the basis of the personality measures showed the greatest number of bodily effects and the greatest degree of anxiety during the LSD session. Paranoid tendencies revealed by the tests were openly expressed by subjects after ingesting LSD.

The richness, intensity, and range of LSD's subjective effects proved so fascinating to the Central Intelligence Agency (CIA) that in 1953 a program of research was initiated (called MKULTRA) that was designed to explore LSD's potential as a mind-control drug. This secret program of operations involved administering LSD to unsuspecting individuals, including a group of army scientists. After one of the scientists experienced a psychotic reaction and jumped to his death from a hotel window, the CIA turned to testing the effects of LSD on drug-dependent persons and prostitutes. The full scope of this covert operation has only recently come to light and received public exposure in the media. LSD was not found to be a promising mind-control agent because, as we have noted, the subjective effects of the hallucinogens are determined by a fairly complex interaction of factors that result in large individual differences in responding.

The inability to predict and control a person's reaction to LSD has limited its therapeutic potential. Beginning in the 1960s, LSD was used in psychotherapy for personal problem solving, treating alcoholics, and for helping terminally ill patients come to terms with death. Overall, the therapeutic outcomes achieved with LSD have not been impressive, and the drug has been abandoned as an adjunct to psychotherapy.

Physiological Effects. Despite the profound psychological alterations facilitated by LSD, the associated bodily changes are rather subtle. LSD stimulates the sympathetic nervous system to augment sensitivity to environmental stimuli: It dilates the pupils and produces slight increases in body temperature, heart rate, and blood pressure (Schlaadt & Shannon, 1982). The psychedelic effect of LSD may stem from its interference with the action of the neurotransmitter serotonin at the synapse where it is released.

The hallucinogens to do not produce physical dependence and withdrawal symptoms when their use is discontinued. A tolerance to the effects of most psychedelics develops rapidly, but it is quickly reversed, usually within two days. Users rarely develop a tolerance because the effects of the hallucinogens are so intense that few people take them more than once a week.

Use of LSD. The "psychedelic age" was ushered in by the sensationalistic news coverage of Drs. Timothy Leary's and Richard Alpert's experiments with psilocybin with friends and students at Harvard. Their frank advocacy of psychedelics as well as their forced withdrawal from Harvard in 1963 catapulted the hallucinogens into a prominent place among drugs of potential abuse. By the mid-to-late 1960s LSD reached its peak in popularity. In 1965 the federal government restricted the use and manufacture of hallucinogens. Since 1968 the use of LSD has declined sharply. Nonetheless, as of 1982, it was estimated that 21 percent of Americans age 18 to 25 have tried some form of hallucinogenic drug.

Dangers and Adverse Reactions. During the 1960s much concern was expressed about LDS's effect on the brain and its al-

leged potential to damage chromosomes. Research suggests that such concerns are, for the most part, unjustified. For example, there is little evidence that LSD damages chromosomes to any greater extent than other drugs and activities like taking aspirin, drinking coffee, and watching color TV. Also, the use of psychedelic drugs has not been related to a higher incidence of birth defects. However, LSD does cross the placental barrier and it may have yet undetermined effects on the developing fetus. Infrequent and low-dosage use of LSD seems to pose little or no threat of damage to the brain. Though there is no firm evidence that long-term use of larger doses of LSD results in detectable brain damage, some subtle form of impaired brain function cannot as yet be ruled out.

Psychotic reactions are occasionally reported to persist long after the end of a psychedelic experience. They appear to occur most often in cases where there is a history of mental problems. But the intensity of negative reactions which a psychedelic experience is capable of eliciting can cause temporary psychosis in seemingly well-integrated individuals.

Flashbacks refer to the reinstatement of a psychedelic experience long after the drug has been ingested and eliminated from the body. Curiously, there is no known pharmacological basis for their occurrence. Flashbacks are apparently rare occurrences. One explanation of flashbacks is that they are triggered by something in the environment or an emotional state that the user associates with a past psychedelic experience.

The Opiate Narcotics: Heroin

Effects of Heroin.

Heroin is the king of drugs. Heroin is king because it leaves you floating on a calm sea where nothing seems to matter and everything is

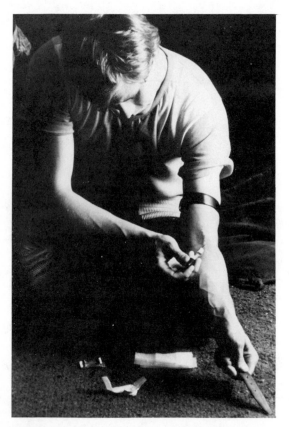

Intravenous heroin use. (Dan McCoy/Black Star)

okay. It is the beatific world of peaceful fantasy where your mind swims in the warm, comfortable, somatic sensation of being held, without pain, and protected from the concerns and worries that make up your life. Suddenly the emptiness disappears. The great gaping hole that hurts, which you had to hide from everyone is gone; the terrible growing inadequacy has vanished. And in its place is the power and comfort that's called confidence. No one can get to you when you keep nodding (Rosenberg, 1973, pp. 25–26).

Rosenberg's description conveys a sense of the euphoria, anxiety reduction, and dissipation of inferiority feelings that the user of heroin may experience. The pleasurable ef-

fects of injecting heroin intravenously may be so powerful and reinforcing that an overwhelming need to try it again is created. Indeed, a strong psychological dependence can develop as early as the first injection. If a person takes a moderate daily dose of heroin over a two-week period, he becomes physically dependent on the drug (Witters & Witters, 1975).

But there is one fact which every heroin addict knows: The pleasurable effects of heroin are limited to the three or four hours that the usual dose lasts. If another dose is not taken within four to six hours, abstinence results in the painful symptoms of the heroin withdrawal syndrome: abdominal cramps, vomiting, craving for the drug, running nose, sweating, chills, and yawning. Mild symptoms resemble the discomfort of influenza, but in persons who have developed a high tolerance for the drug, the symptoms can be quite severe.

With continued use of heroin, the euphoric effect of the drug becomes gradually less intense. The addict may continue using heroin as much to avoid withdrawal symptoms as to reexperience the euphoria of the first few injections (Julien, 1981).

Heroin and other drugs in the opiate family are often called *narcotics* because of their ability to relieve pain and to induce sleep. The sleep-inducing properties of heroin derive largely from its depressant effect on the central nervous system: drowsiness follows injection, breathing and pulse rate are slowed, and the pupils constrict. With high doses coma and death may ensue. The opiate drugs include not only heroin but drugs like morphine and codeine derived from the opium poppy, a plant found in abundance in Asia. Morphine is the major ingredient in opium. The action of heroin is virtually identical to that of morphine, but heroin is about three times as potent. Heroin now accounts for 90 percent of opiate abuse. Medically, narcotic drugs are used to relieve acute and chronic pain, to curb diarrhea, and to depress coughing.

Social and Personal Complications of Heroin Dependence. One of the common misconceptions of heroin use is that it is confined to urban areas. Although heroin is most prominent in large, inner-city poverty areas, it can also be found in suburban areas and small towns. Since heroin is illegal and must be purchased on the illicit market, the cost of a heroin habit can easily be as much as $100 to $200 a day. Because of the high cost, many addicts are driven to criminal activities, including theft, drug sales, robbery, forgery, pimping, and assault. In a study of the 11-year criminal history of male opiate addicts, Ball, Rosen, Flueck, and Nurco (1982) found that the 243 addicts in their sample had been responsible for more than 473,000 crimes. Ball and his associates estimate that the 450,000 addicts in the United States commit a staggering 50 million crimes per year.

Medical complications are frequently associated with the use of heroin. These can arise from using unsterilized and shared needles, contamination of the drug with other substances, and inadequate medical care. The unsterile conditions in which heroin is commonly taken can cause serum hepatitus, pneumonia, skin abscesses, and inflammation of the veins. Obstetric complications may result in regular users of heroin who are pregnant.

Addicts have a considerably higher death rate than nonusers in the general population. A disproportionately high number of addicts die from violent causes such as murder, suicide, and various accidents as well as from various illnesses and infections (DuPont, 1976). Accidental overdose can be fatal. Most heroin is cut or diluted with milk or sugar to give it bulk. Addicts may regularly use heroin that is only 3 to 5 percent pure. If an addict purchases an unusually potent bag of heroin, he or she may die shortly after injecting it. This occurs because of a lack of tolerance to the unusually high dose. Heroin-related deaths may also be caused by the drugs used to dilute it in the street market (Robins, 1979).

Treatment Approaches.

Biological Approaches. Before the 1960s, heroin addiction was commonly thought to be a chronic disease and the pessimistic view prevailed: "Once an addict, always an addict." Treatment programs tended to emphasize a drug-free approach and addicts were often taken off heroin abruptly. The disappointingly high relapse rates reported by

Methadone can be dispensed on an outpatient basis to stabilize narcotic addicts. (Leo Choplin/Black Star)

such programs only served to reinforce an already existing climate of negative thinking about the treatment of addiction.

But in 1964 Vincent Dole, a researcher at Rockefeller University, and Marie Nyswander, a psychiatrist with an interest in treating heroin addiction, made a discovery that had tremendous implications for the rehabilitation of heroin addicts. As part of a metabolic study of addiction, they maintained two addicts on morphine while metabolic tests were conducted. They then transferred the addicts to high doses of methadone—a synthetic opiate—in preparation for detoxification. Detoxification involved administering decreasing amounts of an opiate in order to reduce the severity of withdrawal symptoms.

The administration of methadone had some unanticipated but beneficial effects on their patients. The addicts stabilized physically and emotionally and their social functioning improved. The addicts no longer experienced a narcotics "craving," and methadone prevented the occurrence of withdrawal symptoms. Maintained on daily doses of methadone, the patients were no longer preoccupied with acquiring heroin through illicit sources. After the addicts were stabilized on methadone in the hospital setting, they were released and treated on an outpatient basis. They returned to the hospital for daily doses of methadone and continued to show improvement in their daily functioning (DeLong, 1975).

In an expanded treatment program, Dole and Nyswander were able to demonstrate that methadone could be effective in the long-term treatment and rehabilitation of addicts for another reason: While on maintenance doses of methadone, the addict experiences neither the euphoric effects of heroin nor the lethargy that usually follows the "high." The effects of methadone last consid-erably longer than heroin (24–36 hours), and it can be conveniently administered in pill form. Unlike heroin, which requires an intravenous injection four or five times a day, an addict can be stabilized on a single daily dose of methadone that he or she receives at the treatment center. Though participants in methadone programs continue to be addicted to an opiate, studies have shown that the criminality of methadone users is substantially reduced (McGlothlin, Witt, Anglin, & Wilson, 1978).

As of 1978, there were approximately 75,000 former addicts receiving methadone in drug rehabilitation programs approved by the federal government. Treatment programs that use methadone may differ from one another in significant ways. Some restrict the use of methadone to treating withdrawal symptoms (detoxification), after which the use of methadone is discontinued. But most programs stabilize users on methadone and place varying degrees of emphasis on therapy and vocational training and counseling. Methadone has become the most widely used mode of treating heroin addiction.

Methadone is far from an ideal treatment for addiction. People are maintained on methadone but rarely become totally independent of synthetic opiates because withdrawal from methadone seems to be about as difficult as withdrawal from heroin (Etzioni, 1973). Even advocates of methadone maintenance admit that a drug-free state is still an unreachable goal for many addicts (Senay, 1982).

Methadone is now available on the illicit market, and overdose poses a significant risk of death. Critics of methadone programs legitimately argue that the programs addict the patient to yet another drug and are responsible for leaking methadone to street users. But methadone programs at least offer an alternative to the many addicts who find abstinence from opiates difficult, if not impossible.

Narcotic antagonist and agonist programs are among the newest entries into the treatment scene. Narcotic *antagonists* such as naltrexone block the effects of narcotics. After an addict is detoxified, the narcotic antagonist is administered orally, once a day. Even if environmental and social cues lead to the addict using heroin, the drug will no longer have a reinforcing effect. Other narcotic antagonists such as naloxone have been used to test whether applicants for methadone programs are physically dependent on heroin or are chronic users. If withdrawal symptoms are precipitated by naloxone, it signifies dependence on heroin and the potential viability of methadone treatment. But if the naloxone test fails to confirm that candidates are truly dependent on heroin, drug-free treatment is indicated in order to minimize the risk of addiction to methadone (Judson & Goldstein, 1983). Clonidine, a narcotic *agonist*, has gained recognition as being useful in detoxification from opiates. This drug appears to alleviate symptoms of opiate withdrawal in methadone and heroin addicts, but it too appears to have potential for abuse and has already appeared in the street scene (Ginzburg, 1983).

A Social Perspective: Therapeutic Communities. Advocates of therapeutic communities are perhaps the most vocal critics of programs that encourgae reliance on drugs as a means of treating addiction. Synanon, the prototypic therapeutic community, was founded in 1958 by Charles (Chuck) Dederich, a recovered alcoholic. Dederich believed that by living in a drug-free community staffed by former addicts, the "junkie" could learn to modify destructive behavior patterns and thereby achieve abstinence from drugs. Addicts who enter the Synanon program are first helped through "cold turkey" or drug-free withdrawal. They are then given a job and encouraged to develop a strong and self-reliant character by participating in small group "games"; the aggressive, direct, and confrontational encounters are known as Synanon.

Synanon's no-holds-barred approach to self-understanding has generated much controversy and criticism. Some professionals argue that the group leaders and members may tear down the defenses of some of the ex-addicts and leave them with little foundation on which to build a well-adjusted personality. Yalom and Lieberman's (1971) study of encounter group "casualties" indicated that aggressive group leaders, as well as attack and rejection by other members of the group, were the major causes of "casualties." Of the five aggressive leaders in their study, two were Synanon leaders. Clearly, the aggressive approach of some therapeutic communities is not without risk. Indeed, addicts' negative feelings about the "games" may at least partly account for the fact that about half of the addicts leave Synanon without completing the therapy.

Another controversial aspect of Synanon is the belief that an addict can never be cured. According to this line of thought, the addict can never by completely independent of Synanon and successfully reenter the community without remaining affiliated to and active in the Synanon program. Many have challenged this belief and some have questioned whether the coercive pressures of the Synanon program are moral or ethical (Ray, 1978). Indeed, over a 10-year period (1958–68), an average of no more than 20 persons per year have returned to the community drug-free (Murray & Trotter, 1973). Other programs modeled after Synanon, such as Daytop Village and Phoenix House, encourage participants to become involved in activities in the comunity and to leave the program after a period of time.

Cocaine

Effects of Cocaine. Cocaine is obtained from the leaves of a shrub, erythoxylin cocoa, which grows in abundance in the mountainous region of South America. Cocaine is known colloquially as coke, happy dust, flake, heaven, girl, Bernice, toot, nose candy, gold dust, C, snow, and so forth. Cocaine is the most potent natural stimulant drug. Acting directly on the central nervous system, cocaine induces increased heart rate, respiration rate, and blood pressure. It is pharmacologically similar to the amphetamines, which we will discuss later, and produces similar effects, although the effects of cocaine are shorter acting and dissipate within a half hour. Users commonly report experiencing euphoria, enhanced mental and physical capacity, stimulation, a decrease in hunger, indifference to pain, and a sense of well-being accompanied by diminished fatigue.

Cocaine is also one of the most powerful pharmacological reinforcers. When conditioned to self-inject cocaine, rhesus monkeys will remain intoxicated for long periods of time. They may "dose themselves to death" when unlimited quantities of cocaine are available (Johanson, Balster, & Bonese, 1976). Rats trained to press a bar to obtain a drug would press it 10,000 times to obtain cocaine, compared to 4,000 times to obtain heroin, and 250 times to obtain caffeine. Heavy use of cocaine by humans also produces an intense compulsion to continue to use the drug (Spotts & Shontz, 1976, 1983), but the possibility of physical dependence is in question. Although withdrawal effects are less severe than is the case with heroin or

Cocaine is most commonly "snorted" to produce a euphoric high. (Charles Gatewood/Stock, Boston, Inc.)

barbiturates, depression may occur after taking cocaine.

Chronic use of cocaine can result in loss of weight, insomnia, depression, digestive disorders, paranoid psychosis sufficiently debilitating to require hospitalization (Noya, 1978; Spotts & Shontz, 1980), chronic nasal problems, and hallucinations of bugs crawling under the skin, as has been reported by amphetamine users. In contrast with the widespread "street" belief that cocaine is not a dangerous drug, deaths due to cocaine, while uncommon, have been reported (Finkle & McClosky, 1977; Welti & Wright, 1979).

Modes of Administration. Cocaine can be injected intravenously, but more commonly it is inhaled or "snorted" through the nose, where it is absorbed through the nasal mucous membranes. *Free-basing* refers to smoking a highly concentrated dose of cocaine that is produced by dissolving cocaine in an alkaline (basic) solution and then boiling it until a whitish lump, or free-base remains. There has been a sharp increase in the popularity of this mode of administering cocaine that is probably attributable to the intense euphoria it produces. But the "high" is short-lasting. Free-basers often report that euphoria is followed by negative, dysphoric feelings that contribute to smoking large quantities of cocaine—not infrequently until whatever cocaine available is consumed (Gottheil & Weinstein, 1983). Heavy cocaine users may also use large amounts of alcohol and are at risk for becoming dependent on alcohol. The alcohol, a central nervous system depressant, is said by cocaine users to reduce the anxiety and depression that often accompany cessation of heavy cocaine use.

Changing Patterns of Use. Cocaine has a long and interesting history. About 30 years after it was extracted from cocoa leaves, its anesthetic properties were discovered. By the late 1800s cocaine was hailed as a cure-all by doctors, who prescribed it for a wide range of maladies. Around the turn of the century, patent medicines, wines, and alcoholic tonics containing cocaine and cocoa extracts were quite popular. Until 1903 cocaine was an ingredient in Coca-Cola, which was advertised to "cure your headache and relieve fatigue for only 5 cents."

Even Freud advocated the use of cocaine to treat morphine addiction and used cocaine himself to improve his mood. Freud's early fascination with cocaine is captured in the following quote that conveys his personal impressions of the effects of cocaine use:

Long-lasting, intensive mental or physical work can be performed without fatigue; it is as though the need for food and sleep, which otherwise makes itself felt peremptorily at certain times of the day, were completely banished. While the effects of cocaine last one can, if urged to do so, eat copiously and without revulsion; but one has the clear feeling that the meal was superfluous. Similarly, as the effect of cocoa declines it is possible to sleep on going to bed, but sleep can just as easily be omitted with no unpleasant consequences. During the first hours of the cocoa effect one cannot sleep, but this sleeplessness is in no way distressing (Freud, 1884, in Byck, 1974, p. 60).

Freud reversed his position on cocaine and came out strongly against its use after dependence problems began to surface shortly after the drug became popular. In 1906 cocaine came under strict control, and it is today legally classified as a narcotic drug.

Over the past 20 years cocaine has steadily gained in popularity and acceptance, to the point that it has become a fashionable drug—perhaps *the* status drug—because of its very high price and the exotic properties attributed to its use. Gottheil and Weinstein (1983) observed that 20 years ago there were about 10,000 users in the United States, 10 years ago there were 10 times that number, and at the beginning of the 1980s it is estimated that 10 million persons use cocaine and another 5 million persons have experimented with it. Young people's use of cocaine increased dramatically in the 1970s until it leveled off between 1979 and 1981. In 1982 reports of annual use among high-school seniors fell from 12.4 percent to 11.5 percent (Johnston, Bachman, & O'Malley, 1984). This slight downward trend parallels a diminished use of other drugs, including marijuana, stimulants, sedatives, and hallucinogens in the same period. The decline of cocaine use may be attributable, in part, to a heightened awareness of the dangers associated with its use as well as its high price ($100 to $150 per gram) and somewhat limited availability. Persons most at risk for heavy, chronic use have been described as strong, resourceful persons who are typically white, aged 20 to 44, and well-educated (Spotts & Shontz, 1983), but cocaine abuse cuts across all age and socioeconomic groups.

It seems appropriate to conclude this section with the following observations by Gottheil and Weinstein (1983) that contrast

PCP: THE "TERROR" DRUG

PCP, or phencyclidine, is a recent entry into the illicit drug scene. First used as an anesthetic for veterinary purposes, it was legitimately available from Parke, Davis & Co. under the brand name Sernyl. PCP made an unheralded appearance in San Francisco under the street name Peace Pill, but it was not long before its unpleasant and sometimes debilitating effects on humans received much notoriety. Indeed, adverse effects of PCP use prompted *Time* magazine to call it the "terror drug." Negative publicity about PCP has undoubtedly contributed to the recent decline in its use. Because of its abuse potential, all legal manufacturing of PCP ceased in 1979. Let us now examine some of the effects of PCP and the reasons why more and more students appear to be turning away from this drug.

PCP belongs to a class of substances (arylcyclohexylanines) that are chemically distinct from the other drugs we have surveyed. Depending on the dosage, type of administration, and circumstances of use, PCP can act as a depressant, stimulant, or hallucinogen (Davis, 1982). It is thought that the drugs acts to "scramble" internal stimuli and to affect perceptual functioning by acting on the sensory cortex and other brain structures (thalmus, midbrain) (National Institute on Drug Abuse, 1978). The neurochemical action of the drug may mimic processes thought to be associated with the biochemical etiology of schizophrenia. Specifically, PCP appears to increase the release of dopamine and inhibit its reuptake by brain cells. Garey (1979) has argued that schizophrenia and the acute psychotic episodes experienced by some PCP users may share a common neurochemical basis.

The common pattern of subjective effects described by users includes an "ozone stage" that occurs 5 to 15 minutes after smoking PCP. In the ozone state, which usually lasts from two to six hours, a person usually has a difficult time talking and walking, becomes confused, demonstrates repetitive behavior, and has a lack of attention. Things seem to slow down for a person on PCP. As one user described the drug, "It makes me not feel; I can put my mind in a box. It's not like getting high" (Jacob, Marshman, & Carlen, 1976). Even at low doses some users may experience numerous negative reactions. These include irritability, depression, paranoia, bodily and perceptual distortions, a feeling of disturbing detachment, and frightening hallucinations. Higher doses produce sedation, catalepsy, general anesthesia, and convulsions. A sense of impending death is a frequently reported negative experience associated with PCP use.

Reading such negatively toned descriptions, it is not easy to understand the drug's appeal. However, a closer look at the phenomenology of the PCP user suggests that the "worst" experiences may also be the "best" in certain respects. For instance, Feldman (1979) has reported that users experienced their "confrontations with death" as exciting, at least in retrospect. Death survival experiences perhaps contributed to users' feeling more alive and daring after the ordeal and also provided a good story to share with others. Thus an analysis of the PCP experience suggests a crucial point about drug experiences more generally: in order to understand why people use drugs, it is essential for us to attempt to understand drug effects from the vantage point of the unique perspective of each user (Davis, 1982).

As we mentioned above, PCP has the potential to produce schizophreniclike symptoms and to exaggerate pathology already present in the individual. Luisada (1977) reports that from 1974 to 1977 one third of the inpatient admissions at a large psychiatric facility in Washington, D.C., were related to PCP poisoning. In addition to PCP-related psychoses, chronic PCP use may induce severe depression. PCP-induced depression does appear to respond to conventional antidepressant drugs (Caracci, Migone, & Mukherjee, 1983).

The long-term effects of chronic use are in need of further study. Reports of brain damage with repeated use of PCP need to be replicated (Cohen, 1977). The effects of the use of PCP along with other drugs such as alcohol also need to be determined before the social costs of PCP use can be accurately assessed. But given what we already know, the costs are likely to be great.

sharply with cocaine's image in some circles as a "glamour drug":

> We do know that cocaine can all too readily be abused. It has the ability to cause the dissipation of fortunes; the destruction of families; and the reduction of intelligent, highly functional human beings to obsessed, burned-out shells of themselves; and it can kill. Much, much more, needs to be learned about this drug (p. 213).

THE PRESCRIPTION DRUGS

Amphetamine

Edward K., a truck driver, has just taken a dose of a drug powerful enough to enable him to make a round trip from New York to Los Angeles without resting. Truckers have termed the dose of this drug necessary to accomplish this feat the *L.A. turnaround.*

In 1969 Astronaut Gordon Cooper took a drug to increase his alertness just before he manually controlled the reentry of his Apollo space capsule.

In 1964 an Olympic athlete, a gold medal hopeful competing in the 100-meter dash event, took a drug which he believed would improve his performance. Four years later the Medical Commission of the International Olympic Organization ruled that athletes who have taken this drug must forfeit any medals they won in Olympic competition.

In 1934 a group of psychology students at the University of Minnesota took a drug in order to improve their attitude toward their work, diminish fatigue, and improve concentration while they studied for an exam. Reports suggest that this is the first use of this drug for "cramming."

As you may already have guessed, the drug taken in each of these examples was an amphetamine, one of the most widely used and misused stimulants. Stimulants are drugs that increase alertness, activity, and excitement. Amphetamines, as well as other stimulants such as coffee, cocaine, and nicotine, speed up bodily processes through their action on the central nervous system. Some of the better-known drugs in the amphetamine family are amphetamine itself (e.g., Benzedrine), dextroamphetamine (e.g., Dexedrine), methamphetamine (e.g., Methedrine), and methylphenidate (e.g., Ritalin).

The therapeutic potential of the amphetamines was first recognized by Gordon Allen in 1827. His research led to the use of the drug in the Benzedrine inhaler to aid in dilating the bronchial passages. Amphetamines have been used in the treatment of obesity, narcolepsy (uncontrolled fits of sleep), and hyperkinetic behavior. Since amphetamines have serious abuse potential and their contribution to the effectiveness of weight reduction programs is questionable, physicians are increasingly hesitant to prescribe them for the treatment of obesity.

The nonmedical use of stimulants ranks second only to marijuana among young adults. As of 1982, 28 percent of high-school seniors surveyed had tried amphetamines (Johnston, Bachman, & O'Malley, 1982). This survey also indicated that nonprescription, over-the-counter diet pills are far more popular than was previously acknowledged. Forty percent of the female high-school seniors polled had used over-the-counter diet pills, and one in seven had used them in the past month. Most of these pills contain phenylpropanolamine, a mild stimulant drug. Because a substantial percentage of young women are using these drugs in their formative years, future research should address the question of whether these drugs are being abused and whether they are truly as safe as their manufacturers claim they are.

Effects and Patterns of Amphetamine Use. As we indicated at the beginning of this chapter, the pattern of drug use that is adopted is an important determinant of the drug experience and the potential consequences of abuse. We will illustrate this point by describing a number of patterns of amphetamine use that have been identified (Amphetamine, U.S. Department of HEW report, 1975):

1. *Intermittent low-dose use.* The first pattern involves occasional use of small doses of oral amphetamines to postpone fatigue, elevate mood while doing an unpleasant task, help recover from a hangover, "cram for a test," or to "experience a feeling of well-being and euphoria." Amphetamine use is not a part of the user's lifestyle. The most common source of pills is a friend who has received a legitimate prescription.

2. *Sustained low-dose use.* In this pattern, amphetamines are obtained from a doctor for weight reduction but are used on a regular daily basis for stimulant and euphoria-producing effects. A potent psychological dependence may occur that is followed by withdrawal depression if regular use is interrupted. Dependence is reinforced by renewed use of amphetamines to alleviate withdrawal distress. Increased doses may be taken to counteract tolerance to some of the desired drug-related effects. If intake of amphetamines gradually increases, insomnia may result and be countered by alcohol or sleeping pills. This eventuates in an "upper-downer" cycle that increases the likelihood of overdose.

3. *High-dose intravenous use.* This pattern corresponds to the behaviors associated with the "speed-freak"—the street user who injects large doses of amphetamines intravenously in order to achieve the "flash" or "rush" of pleasure immediately following the injection. The "speed cycle" has been described by David Smith (1969) in terms of an "action-reaction" phenomenon (see Figure 15–2).

The "action-phase" marks the onset of the drug effect. Euphoria, restlessness, talkativeness, and excitement are part of the action phase. The individual may shoot speed repeatedly to prolong the euphoria. Inability to sleep and loss of appetite also characterize the so-called speed-binge. The user may become increasingly suspicious and even develop a paranoid psychosis, similar to paranoid schizophrenia, as increasing amounts of

FIGURE 15-2
The Speed Cycle

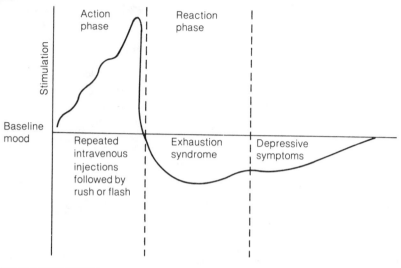

Source; Reprinted from D. E. Smith, "The Characteristics of Dependence in High Dose Amphetamine Use," *International Journal of the Addiction,* 4 Marcel Dekker, Inc., N.Y. (1969), pp. 453–59, by courtesy of Marcel Dekker, Inc.

amphetamine are accumulated within the body. Some users may begin to do peculiar things over and over, without apparent reason. And many users may become aggressive and hostile, perhaps as an expression of their paranoid feelings.

The reaction phase begins when the injecting of amphetamines is interrupted for reasons that include fatigue, paranoia, or lack of the drug. As drug effects diminish, the user may experience exhaustion and sleep continuously for up to two days. Following exhaustion, severe depressive symptoms may emerge, which may last for as long as several weeks. The paranoid symptoms associated with amphetamine psychosis will also usually disappear within a few days or weeks after the drug use is stopped. But in some cases symptoms of depression, hallucinations, anxiety, and paranoia may persist for a prolonged period after use of the drug has been discontinued.

The Sedative-Hypnotics: Barbiturates

Effects of Barbiturates. When people have problems falling asleep or when they experience the unpleasant symptoms of anxiety, they may consult a physician and obtain a sedative-hypnotic drug. The name *sedative-hypnotic* derives from the fact that at low doses these drugs reduce anxiety (sedative effect), while at moderate doses they induce sleep (hypnotic effect). Since the sedative-hypnotic drugs have a depressant effect on the central nervous system, they can be extremely dangerous drugs at high dosages and produce unconsciousness, coma, and death.

The sedative hypnotics are usually grouped under three classifications: barbiturates, nonbarbiturates, and benzodiazepines. Valium, one of the benzodiazepines, is the most widely prescribed drug in the United

States. It is commonly used to relieve anxiety. Nonbarbiturates that are most frequently abused include methaqualone (Sopor, Quaalude) and meprobanate (Miltown). Methaqualone is one of the major drugs abused among teenagers. The most frequently abused barbiturates are secobarbitol (Seconal, or reds), pentobarbital (Nembutal), and Tuinal. Because of their abuse potential, the often fatal consequences of overdose, and the life-threatening consequences of withdrawal from barbiturates, they will serve as the focus for our discussion.

Patterns of Abuse. Physicians are the major source of barbiturates as well as of other sedative-hypnotic drugs. Many people who overuse barbiturates are introduced to the drug by a physician. Indeed, the ready availability of the barbiturates is one reason why they are so widely abused. In 1976 over 18 million prescriptions were written for barbiturates (Cooper, 1977). The family medicine cabinet may be one source of barbiturates, but there also exists a black market by which access to the drugs can be obtained. In young people the pattern of abuse tends to be episodic in contrast to the pattern of chronic abuse more commonly found in adult abusers. Barbiturates produce a state of intoxication very similar to the effects of alcohol. Younger users may take the drug with friends in a group context to get "high," or they may use the drug on an individual basis to relieve tension or to reduce sexuality (Blum & Associates, 1969). Stimulant users occasionally take barbiturates to counteract the effects of amphetamines (Jaffe, 1970). Heroin users are known to use barbiturates when heroin is not readily available or to supplement their habit.

Long-Term and Adverse Effects of Barbiturates. Of all the psychoactive drugs we have considered, the physical dependence that develops in response to the barbiturates is potentially the most dangerous.

The ready availability of drugs in our society contributes to problems of abuse. (Tom Ballard/EKM-Nepenthe)

Even withdrawal from heroin does not usually pose a life-threatening risk. But sudden withdrawal from barbiturates can lead to convulsions, coma, and death. Withdrawal is usually managed by a gradual tapering off process in which the maintenance dose is reduced by about 10 percent every day or two. Most frequently this occurs in a hospital setting.

As tolerance to barbiturates develops, the danger of an overdose or suicide increases. Reported estimates of drug-related deaths attributable to barbiturates range from 17 to 39 percent (Cooper, 1977). Barbiturates can be especially lethal because unlike heroin, cocaine, and amphetamines, the lethal dose of a barbiturate does not increase with development of tolerance to the drug's effects. With barbiturates, as the dose necessary to achieve a desired effect increases, the lethal dose remains about the same. Thus, as the barbiturate abuser increases the dose in order to promote a restful sleep, to relieve anxiety, or to "get down," he or she approaches a dose that may have fatal consequences. Since barbiturates have a very narrow range of safe doses, they are particularly dangerous in this regard. If it takes 1 pill to induce sleep, it may take 5 pills to induce a coma, and only 10 pills to cause a fatal overdose (Sikorski & Nash, 1979).

When alcohol is taken in combination with a barbiturate, it greatly increases the risk of overdose. Since both are central nervous system depressants, they multiply each others' effects.

EXPLANATIONS OF DRUG USE

The Psychodynamic Perspective

According to psychodynamic thinking, drug abuse is related to unfulfilled needs and ways of achieving gratification that have their roots in the early years of life. One psychodynamic explanation traces the origins of alcoholism, and "cravings" for other drugs, back to the oral stage of psychosexual development. During this stage discomfort is reduced and pleasure is obtained through oral pleasures such as sucking and nursing. In times of stress, the alcoholic, for example, is believed to resort to "oral" behaviors which at one time provided security but which in adult life are no longer functional. According to this viewpoint, alcohol may serve as a pacifier for the easily frustrated, dependent, and demanding "oral character" who has never truly matured beyond the oral stage of development. Thus alcohol, like the oral gratifications so comforting in earlier

years, may help the adult alcoholic reduce discomfort and cope with the tension and stresses of everyday life. The fact that alcoholics tend to be heavier smokers than nonalcoholics may reflect the strong oral needs of the alcoholic (Maletzky & Klotter, 1974).

More recent object relations views of drug abuse place less emphasis on understanding the parallels between phases of childhood development and drug use and more emphasis on understanding the role of drugs in gratifying present-day needs and coping with conflicts, interpersonal relations, and stressors in the environment. Severe ego impairments involving difficulties with basic drives such as aggression and dependencies are considered etiological factors in drug dependence. For example, Khantzian (1983) contends that heroin is the drug preferred by persons whose ego mechanisms of defense are inadequate to ward off anxiety and depression resulting from the need to counteract overwhelming feelings of anger and rage. According to this viewpoint, heroin not only replaces the negative feelings with more euphoric feelings but it also contains anger and aggressive impulses, protecting the ego from being overwhelmed. Relatedly, Hendlin (1980) found that users of psychedelic drugs seemed to wish to "fragment themselves" as a way of avoiding the feeling of being "trapped" by their family relationships and as a way of managing their frustration and anger with their families.

Object relations explanations view dependency on a particular drug as arising from the interaction between specific drugs' effects and an individual's personality organization that, together, predispose the user to drug dependency. Some recent evidence supports the hypothesis that the risk of alcoholism may be associated with certain personality characteristics. Sher and Levinson (1982) found that the stress-dampening effect of drinking alcohol was particularly great for individuals who were outgoing and impulsive, and who showed evidence of antisocial personality tendencies. The authors noted that individuals with these characteristics might find consuming alcohol particularly reinforcing, thereby increasing the risk of addiction. Other evidence, however, suggests that personality characteristics such as those associated with the antisocial personality may often be the result rather than the cause of drug dependence (Valiant & Milofsky, 1982).

At the beginning of the chapter we noted that no single personality type invariably leads to drug use. Indeed, researchers have failed to identify a single "addictive personality" type that is a necessary or sufficient condition for substance use (Lang, 1983). Further, little empirical support exists for the notion that childhood variables play a significant role in later drug use (Valiant & Milofsky, 1982). However, contemporary object relations theorists appear to be increasingly willing to admit that many factors can influence substance abuse. This recognition is in keeping with a growing consensus in the substance abuse field that multicausal models most adequately reflect the multiple and complex determinants of drug abuse.

A Sociocultural View

The sociocultural explanation stresses the importance of social and cultural determinants of drug consumption. We earlier noted that peer pressure can exert a strong influence on the use of a variety of drugs. Contact with other users appears to play a pivotal role in experimenting with marijuana (Kandel, 1984). Kandel and Maloff (1983) describe a process wherein novice drug users are initiated into the world of drugs by more experienced teachers (friends, family members, popular folk heroes), who present positive images of the substance and transmit the how, when, and where of the use of a particular drug.

The sociocultural view's emphasis on the importance of a social network and cultural climate that facilitates drug use can be seen in the four cultural orientations that Kinney and Leaton (1982) have identified as influential in determining societal rates of alcoholism.

Where an attitude of *total abstinence* is dominant, drinking is strictly prohibited and very low rates of alcoholism are evident, as with the Moslems or Mormons. Somewhat higher alcoholism rates are found in groups that condone *ritual use* and *convivial use*. Where ritual use is acceptable, drinking is limited to religious practice, ceremonies, and special occasions. But in other contexts drinking is frowned upon. A pattern of convivial use describes groups in which drinking is tied to social occasions, with the emphasis on social solidarity and comraderie. Italian Americans and Jewish Americans, both from cultures in which drinking centers around the family or religious occasions, drink moderately but have low rates of alcoholism (Calahan, Cisin, & Crossley, 1969). Finally, in societies that condone *utilitarian use*, there are virtually no controls or sanctions against drinking. In France, which has the highest rate of alcoholism in the world (an estimated 10 to 12 percent of the population, including some children), drinking alcohol is seen as a healthy, useful part of daily life. Valiant and Milofsky (1982) recently found that men of Irish extraction were seven times more likely to manifest alcohol dependence than men of Jewish, Italian, Syrian, Greek, or Portugese extraction. The researchers believe that this difference may be accounted for by differences in attitudes toward alcohol and its abuse.

Sociocultural factors do not, however, account for individual variations within a particular culture. Alcoholics are not at all uncommon in groups with strong sanctions against drinking, and many nonalcoholics live in societies with a high prevalence of alcohol dependence.

The Learning Perspective

According to the learning perspective, addictive behaviors are learned habits that are acquired and maintained by a variety of sociological, psychological, and physiological factors (Miller, 1980; Miller & Eisler, 1977). As we mentioned earlier in our discussion of cocaine, a drug's powerful reinforcing effects are evident when animals self-administer the drugs if given an opportunity to do so. Such demonstrations suggest that opiates and stimulants may act directly on the brain to produce positive emotional states that serve to reinforce and maintain drug use (Stewart, DeWit, & Eikelboom, 1984). However, the applicability of such findings to humans has been challenged by observations that when volunteers are tested under controlled conditions, the majority of subjects react to heroin with either dislike or indifference (Alexander & Hadaway, 1982; Beecher, 1959; Smith & Beecher, 1962). Although most addicts experience euphoria on their first exposure, volunteers given repeated doses of heroin do not necessarily experience euphoria (Oswald, 1969). As we have noted elsewhere, social and psychological factors, including subjects' attitudes and expectancies about drug use in general and about specific substances in particular, moderate the pharmacological effects of a drug. A drug's chemical structure alone does not predict whether it will be addictive to a particular individual (Peele, 1980).

According to the *tension reduction* hypothesis, drug-taking serves to reduce tension, thereby reinforcing drug use and increasing the probability of continued usage. Drinking alcohol, for example, can be re-warding for a variety of reasons, which include decreasing anxiety, tension, depression, and work-related pressures. However, Marlatt (1976) suggests that drinking will be a response to stress only in those situations the drinker defines as stressful and in which he or she believes that alcohol will be an adequate response to the stressful situation. Thus alcohol and other drugs probably have few inherent stress-reducing properties, independent of the user's expectancies, needs, and personality characteristics.

However, once dependence on a drug develops, if access to the drug is denied, the discomfort of withdrawal symptoms can motivate drug-seeking behavior and continued use. The *opponent-process* theory of acquired motivation (Solomon, 1980) attempts to explain both the withdrawal symptoms of heroin addiction and why the euphoric effect of heroin gradually diminishes with continued use. It maintains that any intensely pleasurable stimulus involves opponent processes or aftereffects that are unpleasant, negative states of being that oppose the positive, euphoric effects of a drug such as heroin. These opponent aftereffects, known as *B states*, bring the heroin user to a physical/emotional state below his or her neutral or baseline state, and it takes some time for the individual to regain the original neutral feeling. It is argued that the cravings and withdrawal experience of heroin abusers are a direct result of these B states or opponent aftereffects. These aftereffects have a long latency and are strengthened with use, more fully opposing the euphoric effects of the drug over time. This process may explain why heroin abusers need larger doses to maintain their normal or baseline state and why drug use is readily conditioned or associated with withdrawal symptoms. This theory is promising and worthy of attention; however, as we mentioned above, the effects of heroin are not always pleasant, as this model assumes, and research to date has not demonstrated that the B states are sufficiently long-lasting to account for heroin cravings that sometimes recur after months or even years of abstinence (Alexander & Hadaway, 1982).

Advocates of conditioning theories of substance dependence have drawn attention to the role of the environmental stimuli present when the drug was initially taken. They note that animals prefer places, objects, and events associated with stimulant and opiate drugs; this association is believed to occur through conditioning processes (Siegel, 1977). These conditioned drug effects are believed to mimic the actual effects of the drug, serving to maintain drug-taking behavior.

In certain instances situational factors appear to mediate or interact with physical dependence. For example, when Robins (1974) studied returned Vietnam veteran drug users, he discovered a surprisingly high remission rate for heroin addiction without benefit of treatment, after the drug users left the environment and the stimuli associated with drug dependence. Similarly, hospital patients receiving regular doses of a narcotic at higher than street-level concentrations rarely have difficulty with withdrawal symptoms upon returning home. There are, however, limitations in interpreting these findings as the result of straightforward conditioning processes. Addicts who returned from Vietnam, for example, may have not resorted to drug use upon return home because they no longer experienced the high levels of stress that perhaps maintained their drug habit. Further, it should be noted that many addicts do not improve upon relocating, while other addicts improve without relocating (Waldorf & Biernacki, 1981).

While no single learning theory-based explanation may provide a totally adequate account of all facets or cases of drug abuse, learning may nonetheless play an important part in the acquisition and maintenance of drug-taking behavior. Comprehensive social learning models of drug abuse acknowledge the contribution of psychological, physical, and social learning factors: positive consequences of drug taking, situational determinants, the avoidance of withdrawal symptoms, and cognitive factors that include attitudes and expectancies that moderate drug effects. Learning occurs through divergent channels—modeling peers, social reinforcement for drug taking, and the drug's stress-regulating adjustive function—all of which can contribute to drug-related problems in living. Finally, social learning theorists contend that the effects of classical and operant conditioning on drug consumption are modulated by the user's genetic endowment, which either predisposes or restrains the development of substance abuse (Nathan, 1980). In the final section, we will consider biological and genetic perspectives on drug abuse.

Genetic and Biological Evidence

Recent studies of hereditary factors and alcoholism suggest that there may indeed be support for a concept of *familial alcoholism*. Cotton (1979) has surveyed studies conducted over the last four decades and concluded that, on the average, almost one third of any sample of alcoholics will have had at least one parent who was an alcoholic. But as researchers in this area are quick to point out, just because alcoholism runs in families does not imply that genetic, rather than social factors, are responsible for such findings. Speaking Swahili runs in families, but not because of genetic transmission.

Evidence for the role of hereditary factors in alcoholism has come from twin studies that point to genetic control of drinking behavior. That is, identical twins tend to be more concordant for alcoholism than fraternal twins (Goodwin, 1979). Adoption studies have also provided strong support for a genetic hypothesis. Goodwin compared Danish boys and girls born of alcoholic parents who were adopted and raised by nonalcoholic parents with a similar sample of children raised by their alcoholic biological parents. Goodwin found that children of alcoholics are more likely to become alcoholics whether raised by their alcoholic parents or by nonalcoholic foster parents. Thus alcoholism cannot simply be attributed to being reared in the same household with an alcoholic parent.

Goodwin contends that separating alcoholics into familial versus nonfamilial types may be a useful distinction. Cases of alcoholism that are likely to have a hereditary component include the following features: (1) a family history of alcoholism; (2) early onset of alcoholism, usually by age 30; (3) severe symptoms requiring treatment at an early age; and (4) absence of other conspicuous pathology.

Although some cases of alcohol abuse may be linked with possible genetic mechanisms, a large percentage of alcoholics—ranging from 47 to 82 percent—do not come from families in which one or both parents were alcoholics (Cotton, 1979). Also, while some data suggest that the offspring of alcoholics metabolize alcohol differently from the offspring of nonalcoholics (Shuckit & Rayses, 1979), differences in the rate of alcohol metabolism, the route of metabolism, and the site of metabolism of alcohol have not been detected (Nathan, 1980).

One of the most fascinating developments on the frontier of investigation of substance abuse is the discovery of the brain's natural opiatelike chemicals, enkephalin and beta endorphin, which we referred to in Chapter 2. The study of these substances may shed light on the biochemical mechanisms involved in the processes of drug tolerance and physical dependence. For example, Goldstein (1976) has hypothesized that tolerance to opiates may develop when, after opiate use, enkephalin levels fall after first being overstimulated by opiates; increasing amounts of opiates must then be administered in order to achieve the same effect. Enkephalin eventually ceases to be released with continued opiate use. However, if opiate use ceases as well, neither the opiate nor enkephalins are present at the receptor sites where these chemicals are active, and withdrawal symptoms appear (Julien, 1981). Withdrawal symptoms end when enkephalins are gradually reintroduced and return to normal activity. The desire to use opiates after withdrawal has been explained by a failure of enkephalins or the level of their release to return to normal levels before dependency problems existed; this physical condition creates a lingering predisposition to use opiates (Schlaadt & Shannon, 1982).

Although much remains to be learned about the biochemical processes associated with substance dependence, the next decade holds a great deal of promise for exciting discoveries in this area. It is important to recognize that even if genetic and biological factors are found to increase vulnerability to drug abuse, social, psychological, and environmental variables play no less of a role in substance abuse.

SUMMARY

We began our overview of the major drugs of abuse by highlighting some factors that cut across the use of these substances. Regardless of the drug abused, the initial or short-term gratifications derived may be supplanted by long-term adverse consequences that affect health, the capacity for productive work, and social relations. A common pattern associated with drug abuse is that it typically begins in early adolescence, peaks in early adulthood, and declines sharply thereafter. It also appears to be the case that persons who have difficulty controlling the use of one substance, tend to have problems controlling the use of other substances. Different patterns of drug use have been identified that range in the degree of negative consequences from recreational use to the far more detrimental pattern termed *compulsive use*. The DSM III classification scheme categorizes drug misuse in terms of substance abuse (duration of one month, a pattern of pathological use, and social or occupational complications) and the more severe disorder, substance dependence, in which the user develops tolerance to the drug's effects or a withdrawal syndrome when use is discontinued. We noted that the subjective effects of drugs are determined by a complex interaction of four factors: the dosage of the drug; the setting or psychological and social environment; the personality of the user; and the set, or the user's expectations of the drug's effects and attitudes about taking the drug.

Although alcohol and tobacco are the most widely and frequently abused substances, their costs to the individual and society are often underestimated. Alcohol and tobacco pose considerable threats to health and well-being. Idiosyncratic intoxication, the alcohol withdrawal syndrome, alcohol withdrawal delirium (DTs), and alcohol hallucinosis, are the result of the toxic effects of alcohol. At low doses, culturally learned expectancies may play an important role in influencing complex social behavior such as aggression. In our discussion of smoking, we emphasized the complex, multidimensional nature of substance abuse. The variables associated with the initiation of substance abuse may be different from those related to the maintenance of the habit. For example, at first, smoking cigarettes may have an "adjustive value," but after it becomes habitual and automatic, nicotine regulation

and physical dependence can maintain the maladaptive behavior. No one treatment for either alcohol abuse or cigarette smoking has been demonstrated to be extremely effective or superior to other treatments. However, approaches that teach effective coping skills and bolster motivation appear to be promising.

We next discussed the illegal drugs, marijuana, LSD, opiate narcotics (heroin), cocaine, and PCP (phencyclidine). Many questions about these drugs are unresolved. For example, marijuana has not been causally linked with the diminished motivation in cross-cultural studies, but its effects on youths in our culture begs further study. The medical risks of the illegal drugs also are in need of investigation. However, the following complications and risks are among those that have been well documented: damage to lung tissue (marijuana), cardiac complications in persons with heart problems (marijuana), obstetric complications (heroin), chronic nasal problems (cocaine), and convulsions (PCP). Long-term psychological effects of patterns of abuse of cocaine (anxiety, depression) and PCP (schizophreniclike psychotic breaks, depression) have received recent attention. Of all these drugs, the use of heroin probably meets with the most negative societal reaction. Recent treatment approaches to heroin dependence, such as methadone maintenance and the more recent experimentation with the use of narcotic antagonists (e.g., naltrexone) and agonists (e.g., clonidine), appear promising but are nonetheless controversial.

We next discussed the amphetamines and the sedative-hypnotic drugs that can be used legally when prescribed by a physician. Abusers of amphetamines may develop paranoid symptoms associated with amphetamine psychosis. As tolerance to barbiturates develops, the danger of an overdose or suicide increases. When alcohol is taken in combination with a barbiturate, it greatly increases the risk of overdose.

Finally, we presented a number of explanations of substance abuse. According to the psychodynamic perspective, drug problems are related to unfulfilled needs and ways of achieving gratification that have their roots in the early years of life. Object relations theory emphasizes more contemporary needs, conflicts, and ego impairments in the genesis of substance abuse. The sociocultural explanation stresses the importance of social and cultural determinants of drug consumption. According to the learning perspective, addictive behaviors are learned habits that are acquired and maintained by a variety of sociological, psychological, and physiological factors. We also discussed the possible role that genetic and biochemical factors might play in substance abuse, including the intriguing possibility that the brain's natural opiatelike chemicals, enkephalin and beta endorphin, may be involved in opiate tolerance and withdrawal reactions. A consensus in the substance abuse field is emerging that a truly comprehensive theory of drug use must encompass diverse contributing factors such as genetic predispositions, learning and cognitive processes, personality factors, sociocultural influences, and the physiological mechanisms related to substance abuse and dependence.

Part Six

Treatment

16

The Insight Therapies

Overview
  The Client
  The Therapist
  The Therapeutic Relationship

Insight Therapies
  Dynamic Psychotherapy
  Psychoanalysis

Developments in Psychoanalysis
  The Neo-Freudian Tradition
  Ego-Analytic Psychotherapy

Humanistic-Existential Psychotherapy
  Rogers' Client-Centered Therapy
  Gestalt Therapy
  Logotherapy

Similarities and Differences

Is Psychotherapy Effective?

Summary

OVERVIEW

At those scared and lonely moments Jim worried about his therapist's opinion of him. The dependency that had developed frightened him. He was afraid that she would reject and abandon him. When he felt this way about people he cared for, he would "stuff" with food. Despite the countless calories Jim consumed at a sitting, he rarely felt filled, truly satisfied, worthwhile, and whole. He often thought of himself as a "nothing," a "big fat zero." Despite his huge girth, he sometimes felt that there was no one "inside," nothing of substance for him or others to care about. With therapy, however, that was beginning to change. When his therapist listened to him, he felt that she cared. When she accurately reflected his feelings, he felt that she understood, and when she stated her personal reactions to him with candor, he felt that he could trust her. Slowly, almost imperceptibly, Jim was developing a sense of self-worth. He was beginning to connect with his feelings and share them with others. Jim was starting to learn that those he cared about would be there for him, even when they were not physically present. But he still experienced scared, lonely moments of self-doubt.

Leslie vowed that she would never again let herself be devastated by a casual remark that she knew was meant only as a joke. It had always been this way, at least as far back as she could remember. She was the most sensitive of the children in her family; she recalls being painfully aware of subtle shifts in her parents' mood and reactions to her. She would cry at night, thinking she had failed them and wondering how to please them—especially her father. Night after night the fantasy recurred; she would be "perfect," beyond reproach. Over the past few months, Leslie has begun to make some crucial connections between her past and her current hypersensitivity to criticism and tendency to please others at the expense of her own needs and feelings. She became increasingly aware of how important it was for her to please her analyst, whom she sometimes saw as a demanding and critical figure. At first she had stubbornly resisted the interpretation by her analyst that her feelings about her father and her analyst might be related. However, as she came to accept the interpretation that she had transferred her feelings about her father onto her therapist, Leslie came to experience her analyst as more warm, caring, and supportive than before. Leslie has learned that conflict and pain sometimes herald the most valuable insights. Yet Leslie has a keen awareness that the seemingly endless hours of sharing dreams, verbalizing whatever comes to mind, and taking "calculated risks" outside of therapy, have been of immense benefit (Lynn & Garske, 1985).

When we read case histories like the ones presented above, it is evident that the context is psychotherapy and that something therapeutic is occurring. Each of us has some implicit and explicit notions of what psychotherapy is, and yet it eludes simple description.

What actually is psychotherapy? Who are the people who seek psychological treatment? Who provides it? How are people helped? Does it really help? We will begin to answer these questions with a brief overview of the field. We will characterize the domain of psychotherapy and identify elements that unite diverse psychotherapeutic approaches. We will look at the people who undertake therapy and at the people who practice it. We will illustrate how therapy is practiced in two systems that rely on the attainment of insight as the crucial factor in psychotherapy: the psychodynamic and the humanistic. In later chapters we will consider behavior therapy, group therapy, family therapy, biological treatments, and community-based treatment approaches.

Let us now return to the case histories you encountered at the beginning of the chapter. In each case help was sought for problems of a psychological nature. Jim and Leslie were motivated to seek treatment because they were dissatisfied and uncomfortable with their thoughts, feelings, and behaviors. They consulted a person they believed had the ability to help and who was in a position to help by virtue of his or her professional role.

A series of interactions occurred in the context of a psychotherapy relationship. One person was defined as a therapist and the other as a client. Jim and Leslie's therapists carried out interventions defined as *therapeutic*, which were intended to relieve

suffering, alter maladaptive thinking, and facilitate behavior change. Despite differences in the therapists' tactics, they attempted to create a warm, relaxed, confidential, and uncritical emotional atmosphere in which trust and hope could thrive. A therapeutic alliance was forged to foster a positive attitude toward treatment. This attitude catalyzed Jim's and Leslie's motivation to risk the experience of novel thoughts, feelings, and behaviors. In both cases, the therapist's personality played a role in the process and the eventual outcome of therapy. Finally, each of the interventions was grounded in a conceptual model that associates positive therapeutic outcomes with certain principles of behavior or personality change. Thus we can see that vastly different psychotherapies resemble each other with regard to the definition of roles of helper and help seeker, the structure of therapy, and the crucial presence of a guiding model and related methods of therapy (Lynn & Garske, 1985).

Despite the existence of a common ground among therapies, there are a host of modern-day treatment approaches with different aims, underlying assumptions, and methods for measuring and attaining desired outcomes. Since Freud's discoveries ushered in the age of modern psychotherapy, the field has expanded tremendously. Dr. Sigmund Freud of Vienna would indeed be amazed to see some of the changes that the scope of psychotherapy has undergone in recent years. Today there are more than 200 different systems of psychotherapy. Which model is most effective, efficient, and conceptually elegant is open to vigorous debate. All models have made positive claims regarding their viability and success. As Garfield (1981) observed, "No therapy has claimed to be less successful than its rivals" (p. 180).

Psychotherapy has expanded not only the range of its theoretical and technical perspectives but also the diversity of individuals treated. We have seen that therapists work with children, drug addicts, delinquents, the very old, and chronic pain sufferers. Even people who function quite well are seeking expanded awareness, better ways of relating to others, and new, more meaningful ways of living.

The number and heterogeneity of individuals practicing some form of therapy or counseling has also vastly increased. Psychiatrists, clinical psychologists, counselors, and psychiatric social workers are still the mainstays of the mental health profession. However, a great number of other individuals concerned with problems in living and mental distress have entered the field. Among these other professional helpers are pastoral, marital, vocational, and rehabilitation counselors.

Entrée to the mental health field is not exclusively limited to helpers trained in a professional context. Volunteers and so-called paraprofessionals provide much-needed psychological services in settings such as crisis intervention centers and other social service agencies. Such individuals vary in their educational background and the nature and extent of their training in formal psychotherapeutic methods. The provision of such services has helped compensate for the sizable gap between the high demand for and the meager supply of professional practitioners. What all of these divergent therapists have in common is the conviction that human beings can change and can learn to harness their abilities, assets, and personal resources in order to grow and overcome their difficulties in living.

The Client

Who seeks psychotherapy? As you have gathered from the material presented in earlier chapters, the experience of impaired psychological functioning is evident in almost infinite variety. Along with specific presenting problems, several common themes are often apparent: helplessness, social isolation, and a sense of failure or lack of worth (Garfield, 1978). Clients often feel that they are in the grip of forces they cannot control—prevented somehow from being the person they want to be and achieving what they want to achieve. There is a prevailing feeling of being excluded from the general stream of life, discouraged, anxious, and generally unhappy. One patient described herself as follows: anxious about sex; feeling inadequate because her breasts are too small; feeling "left out" by her friends; worried about school performance; unable to concentrate; and hopeless about any favorable changes in her life. Another patient spoke about being "unable" to work all day without experiencing tension. He also complained about difficulties in family relationships and sexual problems.

For many people the decision to enter therapy is painful and difficult. Strupp, Fox, and Lessler (1969) in extensive studies of patients' experiences found that over half of the subjects were aware of their problems long before they decided to act on their need for help. Many waited for over two years.

Therapy is undertaken on the basis of widely differing expectations. Some patients believe that the therapist will help them attain all they have wished for. Some dream the therapist will enlighten them and give them peace of mind, purpose, a meaningful life. Some hope to find in the therapist the loving, protective, problem-solving parent they have been seeking since childhood. Those who are more realistic anticipate that the therapist will relieve them of painful psychological states, phobias, or inhibitions. Strupp notes, "The more the client is troubled, the greater is his or her tendency to imbue the therapist with superior powers" (1978, p. 6).

Variables summarized by Phares (1979) as conducive to success in psychotherapy are the following: high ego strength, a moderate degree of psychological disturbance, high motivation, relative youth, intelligence, verbal ability, and likeability.

The Therapist

Despite many different theoretical orientations, despite the diversity of the therapist training programs, despite the broad spectrum of individual differences among therapists, many therapists share common goals and attitudes:

1. Therapists strive to create a "therapeutic" atmosphere and relationship.

2. Therapists cultivate an objective attitude toward the client so that their emotional reactions will not interfere with their therapeutic efforts.

3. Therapists explore the historical origins and/or present determinants of psychological problems.

4. Therapists provide a framework that casts the client's difficulties in terms that are understandable within the client's frame of reference. This framework provides a plausible rationale for understanding the therapist's interventions, and generates expectations of hope and treatment gain (Cornsweet, 1983; Frank, 1973).

5. On the basis of their model of therapy, psychotherapists devise strategies for redirecting maladaptive behavior patterns, irrational beliefs, negative emotions, or self-defeating ways of relating to others.

6. Therapists foster the transfer of insights and/or new behaviors acquired in therapy to everyday life.

7. Therapists provide a model of healthy attitudes and functioning.

A client and a therapist interact during an individual psychotherapy session. (Menninger Foundation Photo)

The Therapeutic Relationship

We will now consider the therapeutic relationship in which patient variables, therapist variables, and technique variables all interact to form the unique experience that each therapy situation creates. Attempts to define the therapeutic relationship vary with the theoretical orientation of the therapist.

Freud's concept of the therapist-patient relationship was clearly medical. The actual analysis was conducted by the therapist, and the patient was the passive recipient of the therapist's (doctor's) effort to cure him or her.

The neo-Freudians expanded the therapeutic relationship to one of mutual responsibility for the course of treatment. For example, Whitehorn (1951) perceived psychotherapy as a cooperative enterprise, in which the patient is the most active agent, and the therapist is an "expert assistant."

The shift toward stronger emphasis upon the patient's responsibility for successful treatment and upon the therapeutic relationship as the curative instrument found its ultimate expression in Rogerian, humanistic-existential therapy. "It has become increasingly evident that the probability of therapeutic movement in a particular case depends primarily not upon the counselor's personality, nor upon his techniques, nor even upon his attitudes, but upon the way all these are *experienced by the client in the relationship* "(Rogers, 1951). (Italics mine.)

In sharp contrast to conceptions of the relationship as a valuable or major component of therapy, we have the point of view of some behavior therapists. Behavior therapists tend to agree that positive feelings between patient and therapist may motivate the patient to cooperate in their technical procedures. But many minimize the significance of the relationship per se as crucial to behavior change (Parloff, Waskow & Wolfe, 1978). This, of course, does not imply that behavior therapists lack the positive attributes of other therapists such as warmth, empathic understanding, and sensitivity. It merely reflects their difference in emphasis on the importance of the many factors involved in psychotherapy.

All of the above views of the therapeutic relationship have been formulated by therapists. We will now look at the relationship from the patient's point of view. Strupp et al. (1969) wrote:

> Psychotherapy was seen by our respondents as an intensely personal experience. Most important, the therapist's warmth, his respect and interest, and his perceived competence and activity emerged as important ingredients in the amount of change reported by the patients (p. 77).

The composite view of the "good" therapist was that of a human expert. The patients experienced themselves to be in a real relationship with him or her. From the patient's point of view, confidence in the integrity of the therapist appeared to be the major component of an effective relationship. Gurman's (1977) review of client's perceptions of the therapeutic relationship concludes that perceptions of the quality of the therapeutic relationship are closely tied to the outcome of psychotherapy.

INSIGHT THERAPIES

We will now attempt to answer the question: How is insight therapy actually practiced? We will introduce you to some of the more prominent therapeutic approaches and briefly explain their methods. We will begin with an overview of some of the beliefs shared by psychodynamic therapists. We will describe Freud's psychotherapeutic techniques and the modifications in his basic therapeutic approaches developed by the neo-Freudians (Jung, Sullivan). We will then describe some of the humanistic-existential therapies. Expanded awareness (Freud's insight) still remains the goal of such therapies. But the orientation of the therapist and the techniques used to reach this goal depart widely from the psychodynamic approaches.

Dynamic Psychotherapy

Dynamic psychotherapists share the following beliefs:

1. Much of human behavior is motivated by unconscious needs and conflicts.

2. Manifestations of abnormal behavior that appear irrational do not occur by chance; they have a cause and are meaningful.

3. The patient's present difficulties have their roots in childhood experience. Therefore, a thorough knowledge of the patient's life history is essential to treatment.

4. The patient's relationship with the therapist is an essential aspect of therapy.

5. Emotional expression and the opportunity to reexperience emotionally significant past events are important aspects of therapy.

6. When the patient achieves intellectual and emotional insight into previously

unconscious material, the causes and the significance of symptoms become apparent and the symptoms may disappear.

With these assumptions in mind, we will now attempt to give you a glimpse of some of the therapeutic techniques utilized by Sigmund Freud, Carl G. Jung, and Harry Stack Sullivan.

Psychoanalysis

Freud defined the goal of psychoanalytic therapy as that of making the unconscious conscious. More specifically, this means that Freudian analysts work with their patients to overcome unconscious blocks that interfere with the patient's capacity to "work well and love well."

Freud realized that his "talking cure" was not universally applicable. He clearly described the kind of patient who could benefit from it. He envisioned his ideal patient as follows. He or she is young, not over 50 years of age, fairly well educated, of good character, sufficiently motivated to seek therapy of his or her own volition, and neither psychotic, confused, or deeply depressed.

Freud limited the characteristics of the ideal psychoanalyst to two requirements: He must be a man of irreproachable character and "he must have overcome in his own mind that mixture of lewdness and prudery with which . . . many people consider sexual problems" (Freud, 1904, p. 262). This last qualification was important since Freud was convinced that sexual repression was basic to most neurotic problems.

You may wonder what occurs when the young, educated patient of reliable character has taken his or her place upon the couch, and the analyst of irreproachable character has been seated behind the patient with "evenly hovering attention." It is at this

point that psychoanalysis actually begins. It continues on an hourly, five or six day a week basis for three or more years.

Let us now consider the major procedures utilized in psychoanalytic therapy.

Free Association. As the patient lies on the couch in a comfortable, relaxed position, the analyst instructs him or her to say whatever comes to mind no matter how silly, embarrassing, or illogical. The patient must express every thought without selection or censorship of any kind. This is the famous *fundamental rule of psychoanalysis*. The unique atmosphere of the analytic situation, with the analyst sitting out of sight and the absence of all distractions, is designed to weaken the patient's defenses and encourage the emergence of unconscious material.

The analyst gradually begins to note the connections between the client's communications and inadvertently expressed unconscious impulses and wishes. In session after session, as the patient relates whatever enters his or her stream of consciousness, the analyst gathers data and forms hypotheses regarding the origin and nature of the patient's difficulties. The analyst begins to interpret such data to the patient as rapport becomes fully established and his or her own understandings of the client's psychodynamics are clarified. Eventually the patient begins to discover for himself or herself the interrelationships and implications of the material the free association process has elicited.

Dream Analysis. Dream analysis is a complex, multifaceted procedure. Each dream has both manifest and latent contents. The dream, as it is recalled, represents its manifest content. The latent content of a dream represents the emergence of repressed material in disguised form. For example, the real meaning of the dream may be expressed in distorted or symbolic form. Thus the appearance of an ogre in a dream may represent a

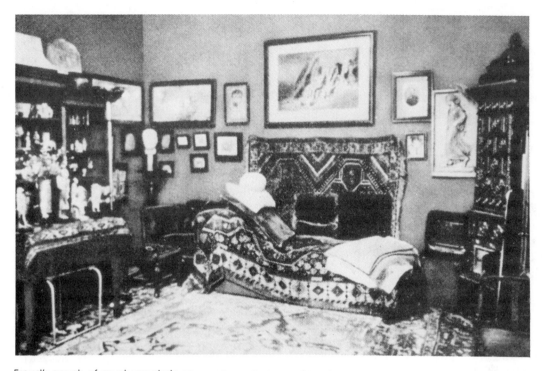

Freud's couch of psychoanalysis. (Historical Pictures Service, Inc., Chicago)

hated and feared parent. The disguise of the latent dream material is the work of *dream censorship*. The latter operates to reduce the anxiety the dreamer would experience if he or she were to encounter the repressed material directly.

In attempting to understand a dream, the analyst will view it in terms of the patient's personality. Furthermore, he will consider the relation of the dream to the patient's daytime experience and the dream's symbolic significance. Above all, the analyst will be guided by the patient's free associations to various aspects of the dream because the analyst views the dream as a logical expression of unconscious elements that strongly influence the patient's conscious life. If clearly understood, dreams contain "the psychology of the neurosis in a nutshell" (Freud in a letter to Fleiss, 1897, that appears in Jones, 1953, p. 355).

Interpretation. Interpretation is the ultimate tool of psychoanalysis. Analytic interpretation usually takes the form of a statement formulated to help the patient understand the unconscious basis of his or her behavior. The analyst may also point out the disguised expression of a repressed idea, impulse, or wish. Let us consider some examples: (1) pointing out the unconscious basis of a symptom: "Having these repeated accidents perhaps assured you of getting the attention you felt you could not get otherwise"; (2) pointing out a repressed impulse: "Could it be that your present effeminate behavior is a defense against the aggressive masculinity your mother punished when you were little?"

The analyst attempts interpretation only when he has a reasonably clear picture of the patient's personality dynamics and the historic source of his difficulties. He also must time the interpretations carefully or risk arousing anxiety and resistance if they are offered too soon. But interpretations presented when the patient is ready for them may elicit a flow of new, meaningful associations and lead to real movement in therapy.

Resistance. As treatment progresses and the patient becomes painfully aware of some previously unconscious aspects of his or her personality, the patient begins to resist further confrontation. This helps him or her evade the anxiety that recognition of previously repressed material evokes.

The task of the therapist in overcoming resistance is perhaps the most important aspect of analysis. And it proceeds as follows: (1) the patient must be made aware of the fact that he or she is unconsciously resisting therapeutic efforts; (2) in each new expression of resistance, the analyst makes clear to the patient exactly *how* he or she is resisting the elimination of the repressions; (3) the analyst must point out to the patient just *what* it is he or she is avoiding (Reich, 1949).

Transference. As analysis continues, the patient begins to express toward the analyst intense, unrealistic feelings and expectations that Freud labeled *transference.* The unseen vague figure of the analyst becomes the focus of emotions once directed at the significant persons of the patient's childhood.

As the analysis progresses, the patient's view of the therapist becomes increasingly distorted by unconscious needs and wishes. The patient may project upon the analysis a gamut of unrealistic feelings. The patient may feel that the analyst is indifferent, that he is attempting to manipulate him or her, to hurt the patient's feelings, and so on. Early ungratified strivings for love are also reactivated and the patient may begin to act seductively toward the analyst, bring presents, and spend hours rehearsing what he or she will say in the next session. This, of course, interferes with therapy.

The analyst, instead of responding warmly to the patient's advances, proceeds to interpret the fact that this behavior is inappropriate and that the patient is actually resisting therapy. When this occurs, the patient may begin to experience the frustration he or she knew in childhood and the violent anger once felt toward frustrating, disapproving parental figures. At this point transference often becomes negative, and the "loved" analyst may become the target for hate with all of its irrational childish intensity. Monroe (1958, p. 522) gives a dramatic example of this phenomenon:

> I admire the *sang-froid* of the analyst who looked into a gun (pointed at him) and said calmly, "This is what I meant about your murderous feelings toward your father (Laugh). Do you see it now?" According to the analyst, the patient laughed also, albeit a bit hysterically, and lay down on the couch—in such a position that the analyst could now unobtrusively wipe the sweat off his brow.

The analyst, in the example above, interpreted to the patient that his violent anger was really directed at his father and not at his doctor. The fact that this potentially dangerous situation was controlled and the patient was able to laugh about it is evidence that the interpretation was effective in reorienting the patient toward reality. Skillful use of interpretation makes the transference situation a truly therapeutic instrument.

Since the patient is emotionally reliving the painful aspects of his childhood, he is giving the analyst the opportunity to observe and interpret the unconscious factors that have been operating all his life to distort his perception of events and relationships. Analysis of the transference behavior permits the patient to better understand the irrational expectations and demands he brings not only to the analyst, but to people in his real-life situation.

Working Through. Even when analysis seems to be successfully completed, difficulties recur. As new experiences in the patient's life threaten a new and fragile adjustment, the patient begins to reinstate neurotic responses that had long been interpreted as such and apparently understood and accepted as such. Resistance once more strongly operates and "it often appears as if the patient had never heard the analyst's previous interpretation" (Menninger, 1958, p. 138). Interpretations must be repeated anew in many forms and once more related to the patient's past and present functioning.

DEVELOPMENTS IN PSYCHOANALYSIS

The psychoanalytic perspective has immense historical and contemporary significance. Freud's observations and theories gave birth to the field of psychotherapy and have continued to exert a major influence a century after his first discoveries. Although all systems of psychotherapy may be considered to have been drawn from the well of psychoanalysis, the reactions to Freud's ideas have resulted in entirely new schools and traditions within the family of psychoanalysis (Baker, 1985).

The Neo-Freudian Tradition

The neo-Freudians are a group of therapists who, although influenced by Freud and his writings, discarded certain aspects of his model and devised distinctive and unique therapeutic approaches. An important development within this tradition has been concern with the conscious aspects of the client's functioning. Besides the Freudian emphasis on sexuality and unconscious psychological conflict, the neo-Freudians recognize the impact of other powerful needs as well as cultural and interpersonal influences on behavior and development across the lifespan. Thus they may explore with the client her or his need for love, dependence, power, status, and so on. Significant attention is also devoted to the processes that describe normal, healthy psychological development, including creativity and the capacity for love and social consciousness (Adler, 1938). Neo-Freudians have been quite critical of Freud's view of the Oedipal conflict and his portrayal of women as psychologically inferior (Baker, 1985). Some contributions of the prominent neo-Freudians Jung and Sullivan will be examined below.

Jung's Analytic Psychology. Carl Jung's knowledge of mythology, alchemy, and religion imparted depth and color to his thinking and writing. His brilliance impressed Freud to the degree that he told Jung he was adopting him as "an eldest son, anointing him as successor and crown prince" (Jung,

Carl Jung. (National Library of Medicine)

1961, p. 316). Unfortunately the close relationship between Freud and Jung could not withstand their increasingly divergent views. Freud reacted to Jung's involvement in parapsychology and belief in precognition as "sheer nonsense." Jung had exactly the same reaction to Freud's pervasive emphasis on sexuality. They eventually parted, bitterly disappointed in one another, their growing theoretical differences creating an ever-widening gulf between them.

Unlike the Freudian analyst, the Jungian therapist is less formal, more open and accepting. He or she meets a patient in face-to-face sessions, is willing to discuss present-day problems, and freely gives advice and suggestions. Jungian analysis is concerned not only with the patient's past, but also with his or her aspirations and goals for the future.

To Freud's concept of the personal unconscious, Jung added his conception of the *collective unconscious.* The latter is his term for the memory traces he believed are shared by the whole human race, regardless of when we lived or will live. In Jung's view the answer to patients' problems will be found in their recognition and acceptance of the roles that both their personal and collective unconscious play in influencing present behavior and efforts toward the achievement of future goals.

Neither the personal unconscious nor the collective unconscious can be contacted directly, but Jung developed a number of methods that tap what he believed to be rich sources of potential for growth. Among the techniques Jungians use to elicit unconscious material are the following: drawing, writing and reading poetry, modeling in clay, discussing day dreams and fantasies, "ideas out of the blue," and most important, nocturnal dreams.

Dream Analysis. Dream analysis is the principal technique of Jungian therapists.

By examining Jungian dream analysis, we can better understand some of the differences between the Jungian and Freudian approaches. In Freudian dream analysis, free association created a chain of thoughts that eventually led to emotion-laden unconscious material. Jung believed his method, which he called *amplification,* to be a far broader and richer process. In Jungian dream analysis associations are not "free" but focused upon the dream material. Furthermore, such associations are given by the analyst as well as the patient. The analyst brings to dream analysis his or her knowledge of material found in fairy tales, myths, and legends. According to Jung, such analyses will clarify the dream content. They will direct the interpretation process toward the nucleus of the dream and the message from the unconscious the dream conveys. Jungians believe that in many cases a single dream is difficult to interpret accurately. Therefore a whole series of dreams may be considered as one unit with a single message. The example presented below shows how the analyst may use dream interpretation to help a patient achieve insight:

An unmarried woman patient dreamed that *someone gave her a wonderful, richly ornamented, antique sword dug up out of a tumulus.*
Associations:
Her *father's* dagger, which he once flashed in the sun in front of her. It made a great impression on her. Her father was in every respect an energetic, strong-willed man, with an impetuous temperament, and adventurous in love affairs. A *Celtic* bronze sword: Patient is proud of her Celtic ancestry. The Celts are full of temperament, impetuous, passionate. The ornamentation has mysterious look about it, ancient tradition, runes, signs of ancient wisdom, ancient civilizations, heritage of mankind, brought to light again out of the grave.

Interpretation:

It is as if the patient needed such a weapon. Her father had the weapon. He was energetic, lived accordingly, and also took upon himself the difficulties inherent in his temperament. Therefore, though living a passionate exciting life, he was not neurotic. This weapon is a very ancient heritage of mankind, which lay buried in the patient and was brought to light through excavation (analysis). The weapon has to do with insight, with wisdom. It is a means of attack and defense. Her father's weapon was a passionate unbending will, with which he made his way through life. Up until now the patient has been the opposite in every respect. She is just on the point of realizing that a person can also will something and need not merely be driven, as she had always believed. The will based on a knowledge of life and on insight is an ancient heritage of the human race, which also is in her, but till now laid buried, for in this respect, too, she is her father's daughter. But she had not appreciated this till now, because her character had been that of a perpetually whining, pampered spoilt child. She was extremely passive and completely given to sexual fantasies (Campbell, 1971, pp. 281–82).

Another helpful attribute of the dream is the *regulative activity* of the unconscious upon the conscious mind. Dreams express attitudes, impulses, thoughts, and feelings that are the opposite of conscious attitudes. Dreams influence the total psychic reality of the individual in the direction of balance and harmony.

The following example of a "compensatory" dream is given by Jacobi (1973, pp. 77–78).

Someone dreams that it is spring but that his favorite tree in the garden has only dry branches. This year it bears no leaves or blossoms. What the dream is trying to communicate is this: Can you see yourself in this tree? This is how you are, although you don't want to recognize it. Your nature has dried up, no tree grows within you. Such dreams are a lesson to persons whose consciousness has become autonomous and overemphasized. Of course the dream of an unusually unconscious person, living entirely by his instincts, would correspondingly emphasize his "other side." Irresponsible scoundrels often have moralizing dreams while paragons of virtue frequently have immoral dream images.

Prognostic Dreams. In the Jungian view, dreams may also warn the dreamer of danger. Jung gives the following example:

I remember the case of a man who was inextricably involved in a number of shady affairs. He developed an almost morbid passion for dangerous mountain climbing, as a sort of compensation. He was seeking to "get above himself." In a dream one night, he saw himself stepping off the summit of a high mountain into empty space. When he told me his dream, I instantly saw his danger and tried to emphasize the warning and persuade him to restrain himself. I even told him that the dream forshadowed his death in a mountain accident. It was in vain. Six months later he "stepped off into space." A mountain guide watched him and a friend letting themselves down on a rope in a difficult place. The friend had found a temporary foothold on a ledge, and the dreamer was following him down. Suddenly he let go of the rope, according to the guide, "as if he were jumping into the air." He fell upon his friend, and both went down and were killed (Jung, 1964, p. 50).

The ultimate goal of Jungian analysis is the integration of various, often opposing, aspects of the patient's personality into a harmonious "whole." Jung calls this process *individuation* and the harmonious whole, the *self*. Individuation is never complete; it is a lifelong endeavor.

Sullivan's Interpersonal Psychotherapy.
Sullivan's methods are basically psychoanalytic, but they are far more flexible than Freud's, and his view of the patient is far more hopeful and optimistic. In fact, he believes that the analyst does not "cure." The analyst merely helps the patient to become aware of the ways in which he or she hampers progress toward successful living and gratifying relationships. When this is accomplished, the patient "cures" himself or herself (Sullivan, 1954). Thus, for Sullivan therapy is a collaborative undertaking, and the analyst's role in it is that of a *participant observer.*

It is through his observation of the patient as the two of them interact that the analyst begins to discover and communicate to the patient the self-defeating and unrealistic aspects of his or her attitudes and behavior. Such unrealistic attitudes are termed *parataxic distortions.* Sullivan believes that the continuous analysis of such distortions strengthens the patient's capacity for reality testing and reduce the patient's dependence on the analyst.

The emphasis on interpersonal relationships is the hallmark of Sullivan's psychotherapy. And it is this emphasis that most clearly distinguishes Sullivan from his predecessors, Freud and Jung. For Sullivan the processes that constitute therapy take place neither in the client nor in the therapist, but in the situation created through the relationship.

Sullivan believed that therapy was an intensely personal and human enterprise. He brought his wry sense of humor and his profound compassion into the therapy situation where he directly faced his patient. He could, as the situation demanded, be "mildly amused," sarcastic, or profoundly supportive. He could act bored or irritated when he felt such an attitude would speed up therapy, or he could be warm and accepting when the patient revealed facts that were experienced as painful or "bad." Occasionally he used loaded questions, related anecdotes that helped him to accent a point he was making, or used deliberate silence to elicit communication from the patient.

The following is an example of Sullivan's insight and sensitivity in his interaction with patients. Note Sullivan's spontaneity, directness, and focus on the interpersonal relationship.

Sullivan is commenting on the progress of a young schizophrenic who is delusional and uncommunicative. This boy has had a love affair that ended when the girl married someone else. Whenever the boy mentions this girl, he stresses the fact that the affair with her is of no importance to him. Sullivan states:

Harry Stack Sullivan. (Courtesy of the William Alanson White Psychiatric Foundation, Inc.)

There is a marvelous chance to get at a very severe disappointment of this patient if one uses as a cue these little remarks that the girl is "of the past" or she is "out of my mind," or that she was something of "no importance." If the psychiatrist swiftly comes back with something like "Nonsense, you were happy with her," he may have opened the patient's mind. It is the very speed and directness of a completely unsuspected comment like that which sometimes fixes vividly the involuntary attention of the patient. And if the psychiatrist can then move a few steps further, after he has caught the attention of the patient, he may actually reopen an issue that has in truth been treated rather as this patient's remarks suggest—namely, the experience has been abandoned because it is a source of too great regret and grief. In a situation of this kind, once I have startled the patient into any alertness by some variant of "Nonsense, you liked her," I continue the attack by some such remark as, "And there's no reason on earth why the pleasure you had in her company should be thrown away just because the relationship didn't last forever." And if the patient is still in touch with me, I can then become a bit philosophical and say that in my experience any pleasure one has with anybody, even if it is only for a day, is something that it is good to *treasure*. There will be plenty of pain anyway. And if there was some pleasure before the pain—isn't that something to have had?

What I am really doing here is something of much theoretic complexity. Insofar as he was happy with this girl, he has proved that he can be human and enjoy life. Now that is far too important for me to leave it alone, no matter how ghastly the finish of his relationship was. It indicates that the patient has some asset which can then be extrapolated into the future—that he might again be happy with someone, even if again the relationship might end badly. This is immeasurably better than being haunted by obscure, practically transcenden-

tal horrors which probably are the most vivid experience that the patient has now (Sullivan, 1956, pp. 376–78).

How does all this help to transform the patient? Sullivan answers this question:

The magic occurs in interpersonal relations and the real magic is done by the patient, not by the therapist. The therapist's skill and art lie in keeping things simple enough so that something can happen; in other words, he clears the field for favorable change, and then tries to avoid getting in the way of its development (Sullivan, 1954, p. 227).

Ego-Analytic Psychotherapy

We have seen that psychoanalytically oriented therapists who do not practice classical psychoanalysis are much more flexible than Freudian analysts. The client may be seen frequently for short intervals of time or seen less frequently over a longer period. There may also be interruptions of treatment for a specific purpose. The analyst strives to attain a therapeutic balance between the need to maintain an objective attitude and the need to provide emotional support for the client's efforts to overcome his or her conflicts. The therapist may give advice, make suggestions, or use humor to make a point. The client's attention may be drawn to what is nonverbally communicated by the body—a clenched fist, a yawn, a sigh, or averted eyes may speak more clearly than words. Occasionally, with the client's permission, the analyst may meet with other family members on his or her behalf and engage in environmental manipulation to make the patient's home situation less stressful.

The ego-analytic tradition includes the contributions of ego-psychology and object relations theory. Theorists and practitioners have highlighted the importance of the ego

BRIEF PSYCHODYNAMIC PSYCHOTHERAPY

The length of psychoanalytic therapy has increased immensely since the technique was first developed. Freud initially treated successfully many psychological problems, such as Gustave Mahler's impotence, with a few sessions of the "talking cure." A famous early case, Katharina, was helped by Freud on an Alpine mountaintop in but a single session (Breuer & Freud, 1985).

As the theory and practice of psychoanalysis evolved, the idea of brevity waned. Neurotic problems came to be viewed as so complex and resistant to change that only a gargantuan effort by therapist and patient would suffice. The result has been that psychoanalysis now typically requires 855 sessions or more (cf., Kernberg et al., 1972).

The trend in the health care sector is clearly toward efficiency. Psychotherapeutic services, like other medical services, are being closely scrutinized by consumers, policymakers, and insurance companies. The result has been the emergence of psychotherapies that are brief and increasingly more efficient than their long-term counterparts.

Brief psychodynamic psychotherapy is a short-term, efficient treatment based on psychoanalytic principles and techniques. While there are many versions of this approach, they share several common features (Garske & Molteni, 1985):

1. Brief psychodynamic psychotherapy is geared at the change of a focal problem. Unlike psychoanalysis, which is an open forum through free association for anything and everything that might be troubling a patient, the brief dynamic approach is restricted. A focal problem is comprised of a symptom *and* a hypothesized psychodynamic component, such as an unresolved Oedipal conflict or a psychosexual fixation. The psychodynamic hypothesis highlights a recurrent pattern in the patient's behaviors with origins early in psychological development.

2. From the beginning of treatment, the duration of brief psychodynamic psychotherapy is planned to be short. This is usually accomplished through the use of time limits. After the focal problem has been formulated (usually in the first hour or two), the patient is told that the therapy will last for a fixed number of sessions. Typical patients seeking psychotherapy are usually limited to 12 hours (cf., Mann, 1973). More severe problems might require extended limits while less severe problems, such as students at a university counseling center, respond well to five-hour limits (Molteni, Garske, & Stedman, 1984).

3. The focal nature and limited duration of brief psychodynamic psychotherapy prescribe behaviors for the patient and therapist. The patient is highly motivated to explore the focal problem and experiment with new behaviors since he or she knows the therapy will end soon. It is not timeless and seemingly interminable like psychoanalysis. Transference reactions develop quickly and issues regarding termination (loss, separation, individuation, etc.) are immediately catalyzed. While the therapist interprets resistances, defenses, and transference reactions like a psychoanalyst, his or her interventions are more active and limited to the focal problem. The actions are powerful and

often anxiety-provoking (Sifneos, 1979). For both parties the adherence to a therapeutic focus and a time limit intensifies the psychoanalytic process, condensing the events and changes that usually take place over many hours into a few.

Brief psychodynamic psychotherapy is not for everyone. Severely disturbed patients (e.g., psychotics), those in emergency situations and crises (e.g., those troubled by thoughts of suicide and adverse drug reactions), and those with substantial character deficits (e.g., borderline cases) are usually excluded. For patients with a high motivation to change and good ego strength, the brief psychodynamic approach not only relieves symptoms but also produces the psychodynamic changes previously thought to be limited to long-term psychoanalytic procedures.

Prepared by John P. Garske.

as a separate entity, able to function independently of the sexual or aggressive drives of the id (A. Freud, 1962; Erickson, 1950; Hartmann, 1950; Winnicott, 1958). They have emphasized interpersonal experiences termed *object relations,* and have tended to describe significant aspects of the client's difficulties in terms of basic problems with trust, attachment, separation, identity formation, and individuation (Baker, 1985). Ego-analytic therapists such as Kernberg (1975) and Kohut (1971) have modified psychoanalytic techniques to treat clients with narcissistic and borderline personality disorders. The treatment of seriously disturbed clients extends the reach of analytic techniques beyond the neurotic populations that are the focus of classical psychoanalysis.

HUMANISTIC-EXISTENTIAL PSYCHOTHERAPY

Under the heading of humanistic-existential psychotherapy, we find a number of different approaches. We will look at three very different systems of humanistic-existential psychotherapy that have become perhaps the most prominent and widely used: Rogers' client-centered therapy, Perls' Gestalt therapy, and Frankl's logotherapy. The theoretical underpinnings of these therapies are rooted in the humanistic perspective you encountered in Chapter 2. There is a commitment in this orientation to the development of human potential and faith in humanity's basic goodness. There is a sincere desire to help people overcome the sense of alienation so prevalent in our culture; to develop sensory, intellectual, and emotional awareness; to express their creativity and to become fully alive, loving, responsible, and authentic beings.

Humanistic-existential therapists reject the interpretive techniques of psychoanalysis. Such techniques are perceived as manipulative and ineffective. Humanistic-existentialist therapists regard people as having the potential to develop the freedom and capacity to choose their own goals, to make the kind of choices that are self-enhancing, and to move toward becoming the kind of person they want to become. The therapist attempts to relate to the client by assuming his or her frame of reference and to understand the inner world of the client through empathy and intuition. The approach to the client is *phenomenological.* This means that the therapist encounters the client as he/she is at this moment.

Humanistic-existential techniques are highly divergent. It has been said that there are as many techniques as there are humanistic-existential therapists. But techniques are considered secondary to *presence:* the being together of therapist and patient in a profound, emotionally involved, authentic relationship.

We will now turn our attention to Carl Rogers' client-centered therapy.

Rogers' Client-Centered Therapy

The therapy Carl Rogers developed clearly exemplifies the humanistic principles we have presented. Rogers' therapy is *client-centered* because progress in therapy is directed toward the attainment of the client's own goals for himself rather than the goals the therapist may believe to be appropriate and worthy. Rogerian therapy is also *nondirective*. This means that therapists do not define the clients' problems or tell them how to solve them. The therapists do not make suggestions or plans for the clients to follow. They let the clients conduct the therapy session, and permit clients to use the therapeutic hour as they choose.

Rogers firmly believed that the innate, universal human tendency is to maintain and enhance one's self. Thus one drive, the drive for self-actualization, motivates behavior.

In order to be therapeutic, the therapist-client relationship must satisfy three conditions:

1. The therapist must be genuine. He or she must be a truly authentic person who wears no mask of any kind and plays no particular role. The therapist presents to the clients exactly what he or she is.

2. The therapist must express unconditional positive regard. The therapist listens to the clients' communications with an unjudgmental attitude that permits unconditional acceptance of all feelings. An emotional climate is

Carl Rogers. (Courtesy of Carl Rogers, photo by Nozizwe S.)

established where permission is given to the clients to be truly themselves without the threat that unless they feel, think, or behave in ways others have defined as "good," they are not worthy persons. The therapist is never morally outraged; and he or she can accept hostility as well as warm, positive feelings. Rogers is convinced that unconditional positive regard elicits a more positive self-concept.

3. The therapist must relate to the clients with empathic understanding. Empathy is the capacity to feel what the client is feeling. "To sense the client's world as if it were your own,

but without ever losing the 'as if' quality. This is empathy" (Rogers, 1957, p. 98). Here is an example of Rogers' (1951) empathic response to a client's expression of feelings about him:

Client: *[Begins to talk in a hard, flat voice, quite unlike her usual tone. Doesn't look at counselor. There was much repetition, but the following excerpts give the major thoughts.]* You feel I want to come, but I don't! I'm not coming any more. It doesn't do any good. I don't like you. I hate you! I wish you never were born.

Rogers: You just hate me very bitterly.*

Client: I think I'll throw you in the lake! I'll cut you up! You think people like you, but they don't. . . . You think you can attract women but you can't. . . . I wish you were dead!

Rogers: You detest me and you'd really like to get rid of me.*

Rogers also commented on the critical necessity for the clients to feel, at least to some degree, the therapist's acceptance and the understanding that the therapist relate to them.

Since Rogers specified the "core conditions" of psychotherapy, debate has flourished regarding their status as necessary *and* sufficient factors in effective psychotherapy. Such debate has fueled research investigations that have failed to yield firm support for the specific effects of the change mechanisms hypothesized by Rogers. While empathy, unconditional positive regard, and genuineness may not be *sufficient* to pro-

duce treatment gains, they may, nevertheless, be important ingredients of effective psychotherapy (Garske, 1982; Parloff, 1978).

The Therapy Process. Rogers defines therapy as the "releasing of an already existent capacity in a potentially competent individual, not the expert manipulation of a more or less passive personality" (Rogers, 1957, p. 221). Therapists make no attempt to diagnose a client's pathology or point out to him or her the self-defeating aspects of his/her personality or behavior. They are convinced that explanations or interpretations, no matter how accurate, have no enduring beneficial effects. Nor is effort expended to explore the patient's past and trace the origins of difficulties. Rogers believes that significant emotional patterns will be revealed equally clearly in the client's present functioning (Rogers, 1942).

The principle techniques of Rogerian therapy are reflection of feelings, clarification of feelings, and expression of the therapist's feelings.

Reflection. The therapist accepts the client's feelings and communicates his or her understanding of them by restating them in words that attempt to mirror the very essence of what the client is trying to communicate:

Client: I was small and I envied people who were large. I was—well, I took beatings by boys and I couldn't strike back. . . .

Therapist: You've had plenty of experience in being the underdog (Rogers, 1942, p. 145–46).

Clarification of Feelings. As the client progresses in search of himself or herself, the client's thinking and the expression of his or her feelings may become confused and incoherent. The demand on the therapists is for total attention and sensitivity so that they may understand what the client is attempting

---

*Just as it is impossible to convey on paper the venom and hatred in the client's voice, so it is utterly impossible to convey the depth of empathy in the counselor's (Rogers') responses. The counselor states, "I tried to enter into and to express in my voice the full degree of the soul-consuming anger which she was pouring out. The written words look incredibly pale, but in the situation they were full of the same feelings she was so coldly and deeply expressing" (Rogers, 1951, pp. 211–12).

to share and help the client to express his or her feelings clearly.

After a very complicated and somewhat incoherent statement by a husband, I respond, "And so, little by little, you have come to hold back things that previously you would have communicated to your wife? Is that it?"

Client: Yes (Rogers, 1970, p. 51).

Expression of the Therapist's Feelings. Rogers has concluded that to be genuine, therapists should reveal their own reactions to what the client is communicating when they feel this is appropriate.

Client: I think I'm beyond help.

Therapist: Huh? Feel as though you're beyond help. I know. You feel just completely hopeless about yourself. I can understand that. I don't feel hopeless, but I realize you do" (Meador & Rogers, 1979, p. 157).

These techniques defuse the threat inherent in the therapy situation. And in time the clients begin to look at themselves less de-

---

"WHAT IS THE THERAPIST SELLING?" A PERSONAL STATEMENT BY A HUMANISTIC PSYCHOTHERAPIST

What I offer in the therapeutic encounter changes, not only from patient to patient and from hour to hour, but, with an individual patient, from moment to moment. As we proceed, the person across the desk from me may change from patient to friend, from dependent to teacher. . . .

I hold out the hope that if we can continue our dialogue, if he will permit himself to borrow some of my strength, the heaviness may lift. I argue that he *will* be able to expose to light the contents of his private Pandora's box and that he can endure the painful process of dissolution and reorganization of his personal structure—that he can find a niche to live in that has both color and tone. I promise that he and I together will do something about the message that his pain is communicating to him. I make clear that physical or psychological death is not the only solution.

There are alternatives. He *can* acquire a sense of joyousnesss

I believe the construct of joy is central in what I have to offer. The patient can learn that there is joy in risking, joy in the creation of meaning, joy in experiencing—even though the experiencing be painful at times. There is joy in our dialogue. To feel, to sense one's aliveness is a joyous thing. . . .

I also see pain—the ability to experience it and to incorporate it—as an essential ingredient of living. Only as you learn that to be in pain is not to die—only then can you know freedom from fear and freedom to live. Similarly, when you learn that to fail is not to die, you are free to act without constraint. This, too, I sell in my office.

Source: From *Voices: The Art and Science of Psychotherapy* (vol. 6, pp. 40–42) by S. Lipkin, American Academy of Psychotherapists, 1970, Emerson, NJ: Emerson Quality Press.

fensively. Feelings that were previously denied become apparent and the clients begin to accept them as the therapists accept them. Because the responsibility for making connections and drawing conclusions about themselves is clearly the clients', they explore themselves further. As the clients become less defensive and feelings are admitted that were previously threatening, less reliance is placed on conforming to the values of others in order to gain a feeling of security. As therapy progresses, clients learn to trust their bodily feelings and tendencies toward action as reliable cues as to their true selves.

The crystallization of a healthy self-concept occurs as the clients gain insight. Insight achieved by the clients is evident in such statements as: "I think I always saw people as being critical toward me because to make myself feel better about myself, I kept criticizing other people." Even self-destructive tendencies are now less confusing. "I kept on failing in school and losing job after job because I was sure I couldn't get anyone's approval no matter how hard I tried. (*Crying softly*.) I tried so hard to get my father to love me, but I couldn't ever live up to his expectations."

With increased awareness, a reorganization of the self on a new, more realistic level occurs. Behavior changes along with this reorganization. It becomes more adaptive, less anxious, and more effective. The force that motivates the client to achieve this is the "basic tendency": *self-actualization* (Rogers, 1961).

Gestalt Therapy

Of Fritz Perls, founder of Gestalt therapy, it has been said, "He was the most exciting therapist who ever lived. His was the unique ability to pierce down into a person and grasp what was most basically awry, where

grief, fury, death lay deeply hidden; . . . the struggle achingly agonizing, sometimes seeming to last for centuries, sometimes finished with breathtaking rapidity. . . . The surrender to life, to wholeness, to forgiveness, release, tenderness, joy, beauty. . . . Faces now transformed, movement fluid, existence radiant and open" (Fagan, 1971, p. 16).

Some of the concepts and terminology of Gestalt therapy are borrowed directly from Gestalt psychology, a theory of perception developed in Germany by Max Wertheimer and Wolfgang Kohler. The most widely used concepts will be explained below.

Gestalt. The word *gestalt* (configuration) represents an organized whole. It is the organization of various aspects of its parts that gives it meaning. In gestalt therapy, each individual is viewed as an organized whole—a more or less complete gestalt. The striving for wholeness is here equated with the striving for self-actualization. This urge is believed to be innate and present in everyone. You probably recall that you met this concept in Jungian and Rogerian therapy. Neurotic individuals represent incomplete gestalts because they tend to exclude experiences from their awareness that trigger pain and anxiety. They also disown aspects of their personality that they find unacceptable.

Figure and Ground. An aspect of a gestalt is that of *figure and ground*. Figure is anything on which the individual's attention is focused at this moment. Ground is everything that recedes into the background but is still somehow relevant. Picture a writer in the throes of creation. At this moment his book occupies his attention. It is the figure and everything else recedes and becomes the ground. But right now, if someone yells "Fire!" suddenly the fire and the need to escape from its threat become the figure and the book has become the ground.

The blocked individual is "stuck." Psychological health requires the ability to be

For many years Fritz Perls was a resident at the Esalen Institute, a human growth center located in Big Sur, California. In the many workshops he conducted, Perls worked with as many as 20 to 30 people at a time who came up one by one to relate dreams or gain insight into their problems in the "hot seat." Here an Esalen staff member tells of a dream in which he was first a Rube Goldberg cartoon figure and then a bottle of Fresca. (© 1968 Michael Alexander)

flexible, to be able to recognize the pattern in figure and ground. For individuals considered to be neurotic, this is difficult. They live with a rigid orientation to experience. Some examples of this are phobias, obsessions, and compulsions. The inability to form new figures is another serious block to the utilization of the individual's capacity for growth. It limits behavior that leads to new experience, the acquisition of new skills, new interests, and new relationships.

Closure. Gestalt psychologists assert that mental activity occurs in coherent wholes. When such wholeness is incomplete, there is a strong urge to complete it and create closure by finishing "unfinished business." This represents a painful or traumatic experience in the client's past that still interferes with functioning. Unfinished business is *finished* by being brought into clear awareness, reexperienced and reformulated into a new gestalt. The new gestalt is no longer a source of pain, fear, or guilt. It is no longer a block to growth. With closure, the painful experience ceases to be a figure and fades into the ground, leaving the individual free to permit new figures to emerge. The individual is no longer "stuck."

Gestalt therapy also shows the influence of both existential and psychoanalytic concepts. As in existential analysis the approach to the client is *phenomenological.* Like Rogers, the therapist attempts to understand the client's unique worldview through empathy and intuition. The concept of personal responsibility for what one does and what one becomes in the course of living is also existential. The therapist assumes that each individual is a process, always becoming and changing. The client can *choose* to remain a dependent child, spending his or her life in pursuit of environmental support, or the client can choose to become an aware, independent, and creative self, actively working to achieve actualization.

From psychoanalysis come the belief that expanded awareness or insight is the key to personality change, the emphasis on dream analysis, and the conviction that therapy must be an emotional experience.

Gestalt therapy is actually an expression of the humanistic-existential philosophy of life. It is transmitted to the client not by explanation but by the therapeutic process itself. Gestalt therapy is confrontational. It places a premium on clients' reflecting on what they are doing and thinking, even though temporary pain and uneasiness may be by-products of self-knowledge (Maddi, 1985).

Therapeutic Procedures. The "rules" of Gestalt therapy as formulated by Levitsky and Perls (1970) are the following:

1. Communicate in the present tense. Don't dwell on the past or anticipate the future. The only way to integrate the past is to bring it into the present.

2. Do not talk *at* people, talk *with* them. This may be especially relevant when gestalt therapy is practiced in a group context.

3. Use "I" language rather than "it" language. For example: Therapist: "What is your hand doing?" Client: "It is trembling." Therapist: "Say, 'I am trembling.' " By using the "I" language, the client takes responsibility for his behavior and feelings.

4. Focus on immediate experience. The therapist may repeatedly ask what the client is feeling "at this moment."

5. Do not gossip. Don't talk about someone, talk directly to him or her.

6. Don't ask questions. Instead, make a statement because the question often represents a disguised and manipulative way of stating opinions.

Levitsky and Perls also describe some of the "games" that gestalt therapists often use to increase the client's awareness. Let us now consider several such "games."

1. *Games of dialogue.* The client is asked to have a dialogue with two conflicting aspects of his or her personality. The *two-chair technique* is frequently used in such games. Here, the therapist asks the client to create a dialogue between two opposing forces in himself or herself and, using two empty chairs alternately, to give both feelings full expression as if an argument were going on between them. The "good boy" versus the "spoiled brat" may be a "split" in the client's personality and serve as the focal point for a two-chair dialogue. Often, when this procedure is followed, a synthesis or gestalt of the two opposing sides occurs. For example, the overcontrolled good boy, always anxious to please others, may learn from an interchange with the spoiled brat that it is acceptable to be assertive and even demanding in certain instances. Thus the "good brat" may be more effective and authentic than either the good boy or the spoiled brat. A variation of this technique is for the client to occupy one chair and pretend that a significant person who is absent or dead is occupying the other one. The client addresses the absent person, expressing feelings he or she had never dared to vocalize before. The client then pretends that the imaginary person in the other chair answers, and a dialog follows. Such interaction often leads to closure because an intrapersonal conflict may be resolved, or an interpersonal situation may be clarified.

2. *"I take responsibility."* In this game the client is asked to make a statement about himself or herself that is true and to end it with the phrase, "and I take responsibility for it." For example, "I feel depressed, and I take responsibility for it."

3. *Reversals.* A client who claims that she or he is shy and timid may be asked to play the role of a loud, extroverted character.

Dream Analysis. Gestalt therapy utilizes dreams by having the client act out every part or selected parts of the dream. In the following example the client is a 26-year-old male attorney who describes himself as follows: "I am very good-looking, successful, and smart. I don't know why I am depressed most of the time." This client related the following dream: "I see the alley behind the apartment where I live, but the alley is tilted up at a 45 degree angle. I am in a trash can rolling down this alley. A huge monster is chasing me. I have a feeling of fear and impending doom."

Therapist: Let yourself feel the fear and doom. How do you experience it?

Client: My chest has a tight band around it. My throat is dry and I feel constricted.

Therapist: Exaggerate these symptoms. And now let yourself become the alley. Start a sentence with "I am the alley" and tell me how you feel, and what is happening to you.

Client: I am the alley. People ride their cars over me. It is dirty.

Therapist: There is no "it." Say, "I am dirty."

Client: I am dirty. People store their garbage on me.

Therapist: How does it feel to be tilted at a 45 degree angle?

Client: I feel uncomfortable, unnatural, cramped, and not the way I should.

Therapist: Become the trash can.

Client: If I were the trash can.

Therapist: You *are* the trash can.

Client: I am dirty, rusty. I get tossed around by garbage collectors with dirty hands. Kids kick me. [*Starts crying*]

Therapist: Stay with this feeling. Don't interrupt your experience." [*Client sobs*]

Client: I don't think much of myself, do I?

Therapist: How do you *really* feel?

Client: I hate myself.

Therapist: Again, louder!

Client: I HATE myself! HATE! HATE! And I'm the monster, too, who is terrifying me! Destroying me! I know it now! [*Sobs*]

The client has come in contact with feelings he had previously been avoiding. When a breakthrough of strong negative feelings occurs, the therapist responds with empathy and warmth.

Gestalt therapy is directed toward the achievement of self-knowledge and self-realization, with the therapist acting as facilitator. Perls warns that this is not an "instant cure" form of therapy. Many successive exercises involving serious emotional investment on the client's part are necessary. Equally important is creative, sensitive, and empathic behavior on the therapist's part. The message the gestalt therapist conveys to the client is: Live in the here and now! Don't try to live up to the standards, values, and expectations of others. Listen to yourself and take responsibility for yourself. Use your eyes, ears, nose, sex organs, feelings, and thoughts to contact the world and be fully alive in it. Become what you are capable of becoming.

Logotherapy

Victor Frankl's psychotherapeutic orientation was influenced by his experiences in the dehumanizing environment of four Nazi concentration camps where he lost his parents, his brother, and his wife. Out of the suffering he experienced and witnessed, Frankl came to believe that human beings can preserve spiritual freedom and independence of mind even under conditions of enormous psychological and physical stress (Frankl, 1965). It is this freedom of which no one can deprive the individual that permits one to retain dignity even in a concentration camp. It is this freedom that makes life meaningful under *any* condition and lends meaning to suffering and to our inescapable eventual confrontation with death. When no other freedom remains, one can still choose one's own attitude toward pain or despair.

Frankl's writings embody the existentialist view that human beings construct meaning for themselves and have the power to make decisions that affirm the full unfolding of experience and the realization of possibility (Maddi, 1985). Like other existentialists, Frankl stresses responsibility and the need to rise to life's challenges. Examining thoughts and feelings regarding responsibility, isolation, and death can be painful and, in the short run, can upset one's sense of security. However, each of these topics is believed to be of universal relevance; confronting them can lead to broadened awareness, self-acceptance, and an enhanced sense of control over one's life.

Frankl defines logotherapy as the treatment of the patient's *attitude* toward his or her existence. Frankl found attitudinal treatment effective in his work with prison inmates facing the gas chamber and with terminal cancer patients (Frankl, 1965). However, even under normal conditions of life, Frankl found that often patients complain of feeling "empty" and seeing their life as meaningless. He found that such patients can be helped to overcome the "existential vacuum" and find the meaning of their lives in encounters with a therapist.

What the therapist offers is empathy, wisdom, and a "reaching beyond himself" to the patient. The therapist discourages patients from blaming past circumstances, other people, and adverse situations for their difficulties.

Frankl has contributed two techniques to the repertoire of the therapist:

1. *Paradoxical intention.* Here the patient is asked to do that which he or she fears most (i.e., the symptom). Consider the following example: A woman who was afraid to go shopping because she was certain she would faint, was told to enter a store and tell herself: "I am going to faint! I'll show everyone how well I can faint. I'll force myself to faint all over the place!" According to Frankl, the change in attitude from one of fearful avoidance to one of direct and humorous confrontation is a curative factor. Also, acceptance of what can not initially be controlled aids in controlling it. As Maddi (1985) has noted, "the first order of business for an existential psychotherapist confronted with psychopathological symptoms is to help the client gain control over his or her life" (p. 207).

2. *Dereflection.* Many people observe and analyze themselves to a degree that interferes with their capacity to live spontaneously and happily. For existential therapists, fulfillment lies not in self-preoccupation or dwelling in the past, but in fully encountering the present. Here is an example of how the technique of dereflection might be used. A person who thinks her traumatic past must limit her present life *will* actually limit and restrict her life. Such patients are told to stop thinking about their past, ignore their symptoms, and attend to their everyday tasks, concerns, and relationships. In such cases a change in attitude releases the patient's capacity for living.

SIMILARITIES AND DIFFERENCES

As we have proceded in our consideration of the psychodynamic and humanistic-existential therapies, you have no doubt noted some similarities and differences in these approaches. The approaches differ in the favored therapeutic techniques and in their concepts of psychopathology and their views of the essential nature of humanity.

Maddi (1985) has provided a useful distinction between humanistic and existential psychotherapies. He notes that humanistic therapists view self-actualization as an essentially automatic process unless it is hampered by developmental roadblocks, while existential therapists contend that the path to human fulfillment is not trodden without struggle, pain, and self-discipline. Despite these points of contrast, Maddi contends that existential therapy can be regarded as a humanistic approach in its "emphasis upon consciousness as an accurate guide in the process of living, decision making as that which constructs meaning, and the importance of development through the life-cycle" (p. 217).

Humanistic therapists take issue with the psychodynamic concept of psychological disturbance as some diagnosable condition to be labeled by the therapist as psychosis, phobia, and so on. They contend that neither psychological "sickness" nor health are absolute states. In all people we can find gradations of psychological disturbances that are revealed in various ways, to varying degrees, and over varying periods of time. As we have seen in the chapter on sexual disorders, judgments about what is "normal" are often culturally biased and relative, and depend on the degree to which a person's behavior is perceived by others to depart from social expectations.

Humanistic therapists have argued that analysts see their patients as machines—as complex energy systems composed of conflicting intrapsychic forces. In the humanistic-existential view human beings are not machines to be repaired. They are, it is believed, a valued and respected "being-in-the-process-of-becoming" (Allport, 1968).

Humanistic-existentialist therapists also oppose the pessimism of the analytic view of humanity. Rogers wrote: "I have little sympathy with the rather prevalent concept that man is basically irrational and that his impulses, if not controlled, will lead to destruc-tion of others and self. Man's behavior is exquisitely rational, moving with subtle and ordered complexity toward the goals his organism is endeavoring to achieve" (Rogers, 1961, pp. 194–95). Recent years have seen more of a meeting of the humanistic-existential and psychoanalytic therapies. A convergence can be seen in ego-analytic therapy's emphasis on conscious, goal-directed mental processes, development across the life span, and needs other than sexual and aggressive needs as motivators of human behavior.

Another criticism of psychodynamic therapy frequently voiced by those of the humanistic-existential persuasion is that its emphasis on the past provides patients with excuses for irresponsible behavior. They contend that the patient is encouraged to blame his or her parents or unconscious for difficulties encountered: "It wasn't I who did it, it was my compulsion" or "My childhood trauma is responsible" (Perls, 1971). In contrast, humanistic-existential psychotherapists stress the critical importance of assuming responsibility for decisions and living fully in the present.

The neo-Freudian response to such criticism is that to ignore the patient's history and unconscious motivation is to approach him or her on a very shallow basis. The crux of psychodynamic therapy is to help patients understand the unconscious meaning and sources of their symptoms. Without such understanding, they believe, no genuine personality restructuring can occur.

Despite the points of contrast mentioned above, psychodynamic and humanistic-existential therapists share the commitment to self-knowledge as a curative agent in pschotherapy. Although the language of the humanistic perspective stresses personal growth and self-actualization, psychodynamic therapists are equally committed to helping their patients enrich their lives in meaningful ways.

IS PSYCHOTHERAPY EFFECTIVE?

For more than 25 years, psychologists have debated whether psychotherapy with neurotics is any more helpful than no therapy at all. The controversy about the effectiveness of psychotherapy can be traced to the publication of Hans Eysenck's review of studies of traditional therapeutic approaches to the treatment of neurosis (1952). Eysenck made the startling claim that patients who did not receive psychotherapy improved to the same extent as subjects who participated in the process. Eysenck's conclusion that traditional therapy was ineffective was based on his findings that 72 percent of patients appeared to improve without any special treatment ("spontaneous remission") after a two-year period, compared to a recovery rate of only 44 percent of patients in psychoanalysis and 66 percent of patients who participated in "eclectic" therapy. In later reviews Eysenck argued forcefully against the notion that traditional therapy is effective and claimed that "uniformly negative" results extended to disorders other than neurotic conditions.

Eysenck's pessimism about the effectiveness of psychotherapy stimulated ardent defenses of its value. His conclusions were vigorously challenged. His reviews were criticized on both conceptual and statistical grounds. Furthermore, his opponents claim that he had selected therapy studies and criteria of improvement that were biased against finding positive gains for traditional psychotherapy. It has also been argued that nontreated patients in control groups actually do receive support and advice (therapy) from friends, relatives, members of the clergy, and physicians. The qualities of effective psychotherapists may not be limited to licensed professionals. Individuals in the natural social environment may serve a therapeutic function for persons with neurotic disorders. Such spontaneous, unprogrammed therapy may account for some of the spontaneous remissions in nontreated individuals who seek and obtain therapeutic help from nontherapists. Thus the recovery rates of nontreated individuals may have been inflated because neurotic persons may have received therapeutic aid in the natural environment (Bergin & Lambert, 1978).

Bergin and Lambert (1978) have argued that the rate of spontaneous remission is actually much lower than the statistic reported by Eysenck. On the basis of recomputations of the data Eysenck drew from, Bergin concluded that a spontaneous remission rate of 43 percent may be more representative than the two thirds estimate originally reported by Eysenck. Even if Eysenck's higher spontaneous remission rate were an accurate measure of improvement for nontreated neurotics, Bergin notes that the practice of psychotherapy would still be supported because patients in therapy improve in a much shorter time.

A number of more recent reviews support the conclusion that therapy is indeed effective. Mary Smith and Gene Glass (1977) at the University of Colorado in Boulder analyzed the results of 375 controlled studies that reported the therapy outcomes of nearly 25,000 men and women. Smith and Glass found that regardless of the type of therapy they examined, psychotherapy always had some beneficial effect. On the basis of the studies they surveyed, they determined that the typical client who received treatment was better off in some way than three quarters of those who were untreated. Patients with symptoms of fear and anxiety showed even more impressive treatment gains over untreated control patients. These patients appeared to be more improved than 83 percent of the patients who did not receive psychotherapy.

The studies summarized by Smith and Glass involved many different types of subjects, ranging from college students to traditional psychiatric patients. Andrews and Harvey (1981) examined the set of data used by Smith and Glass' research but tabulated only the studies that considered more typical therapy clients—those who had sought treatment for depressions, phobias, neuroses, and psychophysiological disorders. The general conclusion that psychotherapy "works" was strongly supported: After treatment the condition of the typical patient was better than that of 77 percent of untreated controls measured at the same time.

Garske and Lynn (1985) contend that the state of the science in psychotherapy research permits a two-tiered conclusion. First, many types and forms of psychotherapy are modestly effective. Second, in terms of degree and breadth of effectiveness, psychotherapies appear to be more alike than different. Garske and Lynn suggest that since choices among therapies cannot be made strictly on the basis of effectiveness, other factors should be considered such as the client's preference for a particular therapeutic approach and cost-effectiveness (Zilbergeld, 1983).

SUMMARY

In this chapter we have presented an overview of the rapidly expanding field of psychotherapy, with special emphasis on the insight therapies. Despite their differences regarding theoretical emphases and technical procedures, therapists share many common attitudes and goals. They attempt to create a therapeutic climate in which trust and hope can grow; they explore the origins or determinants of the client's difficulties and devise strategies for cognitive, emotional, and behavioral change; they attempt to produce lasting changes that transfer to real-life situations; and they serve as models of

healthy attitudes and functioning in the context of a professional relationship with a client seeking help. Furthermore, vastly different psychotherapies resemble each other with regard to the definition of the roles of helper and help seeker, the structure of therapy, and the crucial presence of a guiding model of therapy.

To understand the process of psychotherapy, it is necessary to take note of therapist, patient, and relationship variables. The therapeutic relationship is considered to be important by therapists of all persuasions, but behavior therapists see it as less crucial than psychodynamic and humanistic therapists.

The attainment of insight is a common therapeutic goal of both psychodynamic and humanistic-existential therapists. Psychodynamic therapists are united in the belief that much of human behavior is motivated by unconscious needs and conflicts. However, the neo-Freudians (Jung and Sullivan) depart from Freud in their theoretical emphases, their views of the therapist-patient relationship, and some technical modifications and innovations. They tend to be more flexible in their use of therapeutic techniques, more concerned with conscious aspects of functioning, and more present-centered than their psychoanalytic colleagues. The ego-analytic tradition includes the contributions of ego-psychology and object relations theory, which describes client's difficulties in terms of basic problems with trust, attachment, separation, and identity formation. Psychoanalytic or psychodynamic psychotherapy applies supportive and educational techniques to treat persons not necessarily in need of extensive personality "reconstruction."

The humanistic perspective on behavior provides the theoretical basis for the humanistic-existential therapies of Carl Rogers, Fritz Perls, and Victor Frankl. These therapies capture humanistic-existential psychology's emphasis on the unfolding of human potential, its view of humanity as rational, and its commitment to a phenomenological approach. Humanistic-existential therapists differ in the techniques utilized to help the client attain enhanced self-awareness. But all consider the therapist and client in an emotionally involved, authentic relationship of prime importance.

In conclusion, it was noted that many types of psychotherapy are modestly effective and that, in terms of degree and breadth of effectiveness; psychotherapies appear to be more alike than different.

17

The Behavior and Cognitive Behavioral Therapies

Overview

Techniques of Behavior Therapies
    Systematic Desensitization
    Confrontation Procedures
    Modeling
    Assertion Training
    The Token Economy: Achievement
        Place—A Treatment Program for
        Delinquent Adolescents
    Aversion Therapies
    Self-Control Procedures
    Cognitive-Behavioral Therapies

Issues in Contemporary Psychotherapy
    Insight versus Behavior Therapy: The
        Issue of Outcome
    Common Factors in Psychotherapy
    The Trend toward Eclecticism and
        Integration

Summary

OVERVIEW

How is behavior therapy different from traditional insight therapy. What are some general considerations that guide behavior therapists in approaching their clients? Are behavior therapies more effective than insight therapies? These are some of the questions we will address in this chapter. We will also acquaint you with some of the most prominent and widely practiced techniques of behavior therapy.

The following examples represent only a few of the many types of clients and problem behaviors treated with behavior therapy:

David F. is a writer. Each day he spends what seems like interminable hours staring at a blank piece of paper in his typewriter. Unable to accomplish anything, he finds that his frustration mounts as he feels increasingly helpless. He wonders whether he will ever be able to finish his novel.

Seven-year-old Frank L. wets his bed each night. When other children invite him to stay overnight, Frank refuses, goes home, and cries bitterly. More and more of Frank's friends seem to avoid him now and he asks himself: "Do they know?"

Jennifer L. finds sweets irresistible. She alternates between periods of severe self-denial in attempts to control her weight, and eating binges in which she secretly consumes two pounds of chocolate or a whole whip cream pie. She feels frustrated and embarrassed every time that she inadvertently glances at herself in the mirror. "Do I look that bad to other people?" she asks herself.

Richard M. is a 16-year-old boy who despite his parents' best efforts to "correct" his behavior continues to engage in petty thievery, come home after the curfew, and perform below his ability level at school.

Herman L. constantly checks the windows, doors, and stove in his house. It takes a lot of his time and energy, but he insists that "one can never be too careful."

The scope and range of application of behavior therapy techniques has expanded enormously over the past few decades. And the special needs of groups of persons like the aged and the retarded have been addressed with behavioral techniques.

The ultimate goal of all therapy is to help the client eliminate behavior patterns that are maladaptive and self-defeating. Behavior therapists take a direct path toward this goal. Unlike the psychodynamic therapists, they make no attempt to help the client understand the unconscious bases of his or her difficulties. Unlike the humanistic-existentialist therapists they do not attempt to show the client how "unfinished business" from the past and failure to assume responsibility for feelings block the expression of the potential for self-actualization. Instead, the behavior therapist concentrates on the specific difficulty that has led the client to undertake psychotherapy. The therapeutic interventions of behavior therapists flow from the assumption that most psychological disorders are acquired through life experiences or are responsive to environmental manipulation.

As we noted in Chapter 2, the theoretical basis of behavior therapy differs from other therapeutic approaches. Its roots are in learning theory, which grew out of experimental investigations of learning processes in animals. However, therapists of this orientation are not limited to a perception of behavior change as resulting from operant or classical conditioning. Recently there has been a trend to recognize the influence of social, cognitive, and emotional factors on behavior. Later in our discussion we will note how this trend is reflected in techniques based on modeling and on cognitive-behavioral approaches that directly change the client's maladaptive beliefs. Behavior therapists believe that many behaviors society labels *abnormal* result from inadequate learning of more effective responses to events and other people. Therefore they see their therapeutic effort as educative—as a training program in effective and productive behavior. All behavior therapists share the assumption that psychology is a scientific approach to behavior; that behavior change, whether in the clinic, school, or animal laboratory results from the operation of scientific principles. Behavior therapy is the deliberate application of such principles to remediate maladaptive behavior. The results are subject to verification, with success defined as observable and measurable improvement in target behaviors. Objective, empirical tests of the effectiveness of methods are a hallmark of behavior therapy.

Like their psychodynamic and humanistic colleagues, the behavior therapists bring to their clients genuine interest, warmth, and understanding. A study by Sloane and his colleagues at Temple University (Sloane, Staples, Cristol, Yorkston, & Whipple, 1975) found that experienced behavior therapists were rated by their clients as equally warm, empathetic, and concrete as experienced nonbehavioral therapists. On one measure, genuineness, behavior therapists received even higher ratings than their nonbehavioral colleagues! Findings like these have helped challenge the belief that behavior therapists present themselves to their clients as cold and mechanical technicians.

Although behavior therapists do not stress the therapeutic relationship as an important aspect of therapy, they utilize their initial sessions with their clients to establish rapport and to learn the nature of the client's specific difficulties. They attempt to learn the environmental aspects of the client's experience, the nature, the degree, and the duration of the problem(s), and the client's attitudes toward them and motivation for change.

A wide variety of *behavioral assessment* techniques are used to clarify environmental determinants of the client's problem, establish specific and measurable treatment goals, and devise appropriate therapeutic procedures. For example, verbal description of the nature and dimensions of the problem, scores on paper and pencil inventories, and measures of physiological processes may all be used to determine whether and how to treat the person. Systematic evaluation of the client's progress continues throughout the course of therapy. Behavior therapists are flexible in using alternative techniques and assessment strategies with the same client when this appears useful.

The five phases of most behavior therapy efforts are nicely summarized by McNamara (1978, p. 4): (1) identification of the problem(s), (2) establishment of behavioral objectives, (3) design of a behavior change strategy,

(4) program implementation, and (5) systematic evaluation of the modification effort, with feedback relating outcome data to successful intervention or the need for program modification. The client will also be encouraged to apply his or her newly acquired coping skills to everyday life situations. Behavior therapists recognize the importance of including specific procedures to help clients learn strategies and ways of behaving that will increase the likelihood of gains made in the clinic persisting in the real world.

Let us now turn our attention to some of the most prominent and widely used techniques of behavior therapy.

TECHNIQUES OF BEHAVIOR THERAPIES

Systematic Desensitization

> We will begin treatment by helping you to become really relaxed. Then you are going to imagine scenes related to your fear, starting with ones that are only slightly frightening. Because I will be introducing the scenes in a gradual way, and because you will be relaxed when you imagine them, before long you will be able to imagine situations related to your fear of heights and actually feel comfortable at the same time. And if you can imagine flying in an airplane or looking down from a high place and still feel calm, then when you are in such a situation out there in the real world, you will find you are not afraid anymore (adapted from Rimm & Masters, 1979).

What you have just read is a therapeutic rationale that might be presented to a client about to participate in systematic desensitization to help him or her overcome a fear of heights. Systematic desensitization is a widely used behavior therapy procedure that was developed by Joseph Wolpe in 1958 to help clients manage maladaptive, unrealistic anxiety. The technique has proven to be

Joseph Wolpe. (Courtesy of Joseph Wolpe.)

extremely effective with clients suffering from a wide range of phobic disorders. Systematic desensitization has also been successfully applied to other disorders, including insomnia (Steinmark & Borkovec, 1974), speech disorders (Walton & Mather, 1963), and asthmatic attacks (Moore, 1965).

Wolpe's techniques are based on the reciprocal inhibition principle that clients cannot experience two conflicting responses simultaneously. Therefore, they cannot feel anxiety while they are also deeply relaxed. The relaxation response inhibits the anxiety response. And this serves to desensitize the clients to the anxiety provoking aspects of the stimulus.

Let us now consider how a therapist might actually proceed in treating a client with a fear of heights. With the assistance of the therapist, the client first learns deep muscular relaxation. Various approaches to inducing relaxation have been utilized, including imagining pleasant relaxing scenes, focusing on breathing and maintaining a slow breathing rate, and hypnotic suggestion. Many therapists, however, favor a technique based on progressive relaxation developed by Edmund Jacobson (1938). Jacobson's technique involves alternately tensing and relaxing various muscle groups in a predetermined order. This procedure helps the clients to tell when they are tense and when they are relaxed. Discriminating tension from relaxing presumably helps clients to attain a more profound state of relaxation. After two to six sessions most clients are able to experience deep muscular relaxation.

Before the desensitization session can begin, the clients construct an anxiety hierarchy with the assistance of the therapist. The hierarchy is a series of situations or scenes that are arranged in order from the least to most anxiety evoking. Let us consider a hierarchy used by Rimm in the treatment of a 40-year-old man who developed a fear of heights after discharge from the Air Force during World War II:

1. You are beginning to climb the ladder leaning against the side of your house. You plan to work on the roof. Your hands are on the ladder and your feet are on the first rung.

2. You are halfway up the ladder, and you happen to look down. You see the lawn below you and a walkway.

3. As you are driving with the family, the road begins to climb.

4. You are driving with the family on a California coastal highway with drop-off to the right.

5. You are on a California seashore cliff, approximately six feet from the edge.

6. You are driving with the family, approaching a mountain summit.

7. You are in a commercial airliner at the time of takeoff.

8. You are in an airliner at an altitude of 30,000.

9. You are in an airliner at an altitude of 30,000 with considerable turbulence.

10. You are on a California seaside cliff, approximately two feet (judged to be a safe distance) from the edge and looking down.

11. You are climbing the water tower to assist in painting, about 10 feet from the ground.

12. Same as above, but you are about 20 feet from the ground.

13. You are on the catwalk around the water tank, painting the tank (Rimm & Masters, 1979, p. 48).

After the client has learned relaxation and the anxiety hierarchy is prepared, he is ready to begin the desensitization session. Below is an example of a desensitization session that would take place after a client is deeply relaxed:

Therapist: Fine. Soon I shall ask you to imagine a scene. After you hear a description of the situation, please imagine it as vividly as you can, through your own eyes, as if you were actually there. Try to include all the details in the scene. While you're visualizing the situation, you may continue feeling as relaxed as you are now. If so, that's good. After 5, 10, or 15 seconds, I'll ask you to stop imagining the scene and return to your pleasant image and to just relax. But if you begin to feel even the slightest increase in anxiety or tension, please signal this to me by raising your left forefinger.

When you do this, I'll step in and ask you to stop imagining the situation and then will help you get relaxed once more. It's important that you indicate tension to me in this way, as we want to maximize your being exposed to fearful situations without feeling anxious (Goldfried & Davison, 1976, pp. 124–125).

If the client reports anxiety at any point in the process, the procedure is interrupted. The client is asked to completely relax and return to the fantasy of the scene that preceded the one that evoked fear. When relaxation is once more completely achieved, the anxiety-provoking scene is reintroduced. In successive therapy sessions this process is continued until even the most frightening scenes in the hierarchy may be confronted without anxiety. Wolpe (1958) reported that the median number of sessions to complete a desensitization hierarchy is eight.

Systematic desensitization is demonstrably more effective than both no treatment and many forms of psychotherapy with which it has been compared (Leitenberg, 1976). A recent trend in anxiety-reduction methods has been the move toward training clients to self-administer desensitization and other relaxation and anxiety management procedures (Deffenbacher & Suinn, 1982; Goldfried, 1971). In *self-control desensitization*, for example, clients are encouraged to practice relaxation at home and are given homework assignments designed to get them to participate in the feared activity that is the focus of treatment. As in traditional desensitization, the situations are imagined or experienced while the clients are in a relaxed physical and mental state. In *cue-controlled relaxation* (Cautela, 1966), clients associate a cue word or phrase such as "relax," "calm," or "calm control" with the experience of deep relaxation. When clients experience tension or anxiety outside the

DISMANTLING DESENSITIZATION

Just as behavior therapists have voiced skepticism about the value of insight in psychotherapy, they have also questioned Wolpe's reciprocal inhibition explanation of desensitization. For more than a decade behavior therapists have searched for an answer to the question: "Why does desensitization work?" They have carefully evaluated desensitization to learn more about the mechanisms that account for the treatment's undisputed success.

One way in which a therapeutic procedure like desensitization can be evaluated is by isolating what appear to be specific components of the technique and

comparing their effects with the full treatment package (Wilson & O'Leary, 1980). This enables the researcher to better understand which aspects of the treatment are essential or contribute maximally to its effectiveness. Lang (1969) has termed this method of evaluating specific techniques a *dismantling* strategy. How might this strategy be applied to desensitization? To determine whether relaxation is a necessary ingredient in desensitization, the effects of a procedure in which relaxation is omitted might be compared with a "complete" desensitization treatment. If we find that the two treatments are equally effective in reducing phobic anxiety, we might then conclude that relaxation is not an essential aspect of desensitization.

Researchers have subjected various components of desensitization to just this type of analysis. Numerous studies have cast doubt on whether any one component of desensitization (i.e., relaxation, imagery, a graduated hierarchy, low-anxiety levels) is essential (Murray & Jacobson, 1978). This has opened the door to diverse interpretations about the processes involved in the successful desensitization of phobic anxiety. Let us examine a number of accounts that have been proposed to explain the positive results produced by desensitization.

One intriguing possibility is that expectancies and cognitive factors aroused by the desensitization procedure reduce phobic anxiety. The impressive, highly credible treatment package, the optimistic treatment rationale and the scientific, yet relaxed treatment atmosphere all combine to foster positive expectancies in the client. After undergoing desensitization, the client may be convinced that he or she can overcome or better cope with troubling, yet unrealistic fears. Indeed, a number of outcome studies have shown that desensitization fares no better than a placebo control procedure specifically designed to arouse the same degree of positive expectancies as the desensitization treatment (e.g., Lick, 1975). There is little in the desensitization literature to contradict the idea that expectancies may be potent determinants of treatment gains (Kazdin & Wilcoxin, 1976).

Other cognitive views suggest that clients may come to see their attitudes toward the phobic situation as irrational or they may learn to focus their attention on less threatening aspects of the object they once feared after experiencing desensitization

(Wilkins, 1971). Such adaptive changes in attitudes may promote contact with the phobic object or situation. Since phobias are actually unrealistic fears, successfully approaching the phobic object may further reinforce the belief that the fear associated with it has no objective basis.

A popular noncognitive account of desensitization's success is based on the learning theory concept of extinction. In our discussion of neurosis in Chapter 7, we saw that Marks (1978) makes the strong argument that relief from phobias occurs when the person suffering from them is able to make sustained contact with those situations that evoke discomfort until the discomfort subsides. The fear response is extinguished by repeated contact with the feared stimulus in the absence of negative consequences. According to this view, we might expect that desensitization would be successful to the degree that it facilitates contact with the phobic object or situation.

In a recent formulation of what occurs as a result of desensitization, Wilson and O'Leary (1980) combine a number of ideas. They contend that clients undergoing desensitization "(a) perceive that they are no longer upset by previously feared situations; (b) they acquire a coping skill for managing anxiety (relaxation); and (c) they rehearse in imagination the successful performance of previously feared actions" (p. 164).

The question "Why does desensitization work?" is as yet unresolved and remains the subject of much controversy. But our brief overview reflects the active and thought-provoking efforts of contemporary behavior therapists to understand exactly why their techniques work. Much to their credit, behavior therapists subject techniques with proven value, like desensitization, to the same critical scrutiny as less well-established procedures.

therapy session, they are instructed to present the cue to themselves to "short-circuit" the anxiety response. Deffenbacher and Suinn (1982) report that both of these procedures have been shown to be effective in reducing targeted anxieties.

Confrontation Procedures

Implosive therapy and flooding are fear-reducing techniques that require the client to confront the aversive situation either imaginarily or in the real world or both until the anxiety subsides. Hence, they can be considered *confrontation procedures.* In the following example, the implosive therapist begins with a scene that is the most frightening event the client can imagine and embellishes it to prolong the anxiety at an intense level. The scene is quite typical of one that might be presented to a client to visualize at the beginning of the implosive treatment for a fear of heights.

Implosive Therapy. You are at the top of a tall building, looking down at the street below. Your feet are on a narrow walkway and your hands are gripping a guard rail. As you look down, you notice how small things appear and you feel a mounting sense of terror washing over you. You notice how fast your heart is beating; how your breath comes in short gasps, and yes, how you can't catch your breath. And as you think of how cold and sweaty your hands feel, you begin to feel yourself lose your grip. The slight sense of dizziness you felt as you walked up the steps to the top of the building is much greater now and everything begins to swirl around you, faster and faster, faster and faster. As you wonder whether you can hold on, your feet begin to slip, first one, then the other. Your feet slip off and your hold on the guard rail breaks. Now you're falling. You feel the wind on your face. Your thoughts quickly flash on how you will look to others lying on the concrete when they find you. Down,

down you go, watching the windows go by as you fall. You know your body will hit the hard pavement in the next instant. And you imagine it all as if you're watching a slow-motion film. Your feet strike the ground first, but they can't prevent your body and head from being crushed by the hardness of the concrete. Hear your bones snap, crack, and break apart. Your guts are pouring out of the holes in your body. Look at the horrified stares of the onlookers. Shortly, they will walk away, uncaring for your lifeless body.

This way of helping clients conquer their fear of heights contrasts sharply with the gradual, relaxation-oriented approach taken by a practitioner of systematic desensitization. An implosive therapist might ask clients to vividly imagine the anxiety-producing scene or story for as long as an hour and a half. Implosive therapy most frequently involves the exclusive use of imagery.

Perhaps the most distinctive aspect of implosive therapy is the therapist's use of imagery presumed to be related to conflicts of a psychodynamic nature. It is assumed that in addition to being associated with conscious cues, anxiety is also conditioned to unconscious cues that reflect repressed thoughts, feelings, and impulses (Stampfl & Levis, 1967). Areas of conflict and themes that might be touched on are aggression, conflict, death, and sexual problems. Session after session, the story or a variation of it designed to elicit anxiety will be repeated until the client no longer reports fear in reaction to the suggested scenes.

According to the extinction theory that underlies implosive therapy, height phobics, for example, never learn that the disasterous consequences they fear will not occur. This is because they continually avoid the phobic situation—high places. By repeatedly eliciting anxiety in the absence of any actual negative consequences, the clients' fear of heights will eventually dissipate and cease to be anticipated and experienced in real-life situations.

Flooding. Flooding is most frequently conducted in the real world, with real, not imaginary stimuli (Wilson & O'Leary, 1980; Rimm & Cunningham, 1985). Flooding involves the client's actually confronting a situation that maximizes anxiety. Unlike implosive therapy, flooding does not involve the presentation of psychodynamic cues or themes (e.g., aggression, sex). Flooding has been used with success in treating numerous disorders, including obsessive-compulsive behaviors and agoraphobia.

Response Prevention. One important component of flooding procedures is *response prevention*, which involves preventing clients from performing their typical avoidance behaviors (Spiegler, 1983). Response prevention is nicely illustrated in the following case of the use of flooding in the treatment of a hand-washing compulsion (reported by Myers, Robertson, & Tatlon, 1975).

The client felt compelled to wash her hands and change her clothes whenever she encountered anything even remotely associated with death. After it was determined that her greatest fear involved dead bodies, she and her therapist visited a hospital mortuary, where they both handled a dead body. During the treatment the therapist prevented the woman from engaging in compulsive rituals that previously had brought her some relief from anxiety. For example, hand washing was not permitted. The woman was made to confront other sources of anxiety, such as touching the picture of a man who had been shot to death in the street. The treatment, which lasted for less than two weeks, was judged to be successful over an eight-month follow-up period. The compulsion to cleanse herself when confronted with death-related stimuli was successfully eliminated by the treatment. Another indication of the treatment's success was that the woman married a man who had previously been a source of anxiety to her because his ex-wife had died before the client and the man met.

In Vivo Exposure. *In vivo exposure* is a simple, yet powerful tool to undercut long-standing habit patterns of avoidance. The essence of the message that the therapist gives the client is: "If you're afraid to do it, do it! (Chambless & Goldstein, 1980). The technique is a member of the family of flooding procedures—exposure or contact with the feared situation continues until anxiety dissipates. In in vivo exposure the client is exposed to the feared situation on a graduated, step-wise basis, in contrast to flooding in which the client is exposed to the most fearful situation from the beginning of treatment. In vivo exposure differs from systematic desensitization in that the tasks chosen evoke considerable anxiety. As Wilson & Lazarus (1983) have noted, the rationale is that the unrealistic fear response will eventually be extinguished as a result of repeated exposure to fear-producing cues. Let us now consider a case in which in vivo exposure was used in the treatment of agoraphobia.

Only a few months ago Mike accepted the fact that he was an agoraphobic. After Mike lost his job, he developed vague fears about straying far from the security of his home. Over a period of six months, his fears escalated in intensity and generalized to so many situations that he was unable to leave his home without experiencing paralyzing anxiety. When Mike became anxious, he developed a heightened sensitivity to his heartbeat, felt that his heart would stop beating, and feared that he would die. His behavior therapist targeted an ultimate goal of leaving home and traveling unescorted. The strategy, however, was to proceed in a step-wise fashion. Mike exposed himself to a series of anxiety-provoking situations until the anxiety diminished to tolerable levels. Some situations Mike encountered and eventually mastered were the following: stepping outside, walking 200 feet, walking around the block, going shopping. Therapy moved as fast as Mike was capable of progressing. His therapist urged Mike to tackle steps that were about as frightening as he could tolerate. Mike remained in each of the target situations until his anxiety subsided. Initially his therapist accompanied him. For each milestone Mike successfully passed, his therapist lavished support and encouragement on him. Later, however, Mike executed each step on his own and then with family members. As Mike carried out his homework assignments of venturing outside to a wide variety of locations, his bodily symptoms and preoccupations diminished. Mike now considers himself "cured." Three months after therapy began, he is no longer "homebound" and panicky to the extent that his fears interfere with his life.

A recent trend in behavior therapy is to experiment with the combination of fear-reduction techniques and drug approaches (Rimm & Cunningham, 1985). Sheehan (1982), for example, has suggested that the treatment effects of flooding procedures for agoraphobics may be enhanced by the addition of drug therapy. Sheehan recommends treating agoraphobia first with drugs, such as MAO inhibitors or tricyclic antidepressant drugs, and then introducing in vivo exposure or other behavioral procedures.

After reviewing the research on the effectiveness of implosive therapy and flooding, Rimm and Masters (1979) concluded that there is evidence for their usefulness. Flooding, however, is generally found to be more effective than implosive therapy. Flooding and desensitization may produce comparable outcomes, but confrontation procedures involve considerable discomfort and may be less practical in this respect: Clients may fail to return to treatment because the procedures are so aversive. Many behavior therapists follow the general rule that confrontation procedures should be implemented only after less negative and more conservative forms of therapy, such as systematic desensitization, have proven ineffective (Spiegler, 1983). Flooding procedures, however, have been found to be more effective than desensitization in the treatment of obsessive-compulsive disorders (Rachman & Hodgson, 1980) and are increasingly considered the treatment of choice in cases of agoraphobia.

Modeling

From the therapist's notebook:

> Aside from the changes this client has manifested that I have previously noted, there appears to be a new tendency that is becoming increasingly evident. Looking at Ellen as she walks into my office, I am beginning to feel that I am looking at a mirror image of myself. Her new clothes are almost exact copies of mine. Her manner of speaking has changed. She is apparently imitating my way of talking, and this includes my tendency to hesitate before making a statement. I have recently noticed that Ellen no longer complains endlessly in the whiney, irritating, childlike voice that used to be so characteristic of her.

In all the therapeutic approaches you have encountered in your reading thus far, clients tend to use their therapists as models in various ways. This trend often operates to help the client learn new, more adaptive ways of behaving and interacting with others. When you read about assertion training in the next section, you will note that modeling is an important aspect of treatment.

Modeling used to be called imitation but now is most frequently referred to as *observational learning*. For more than two decades Bandura and his colleagues have researched the applications of modeling

By observing a model, children can learn to overcome their fears of petting and playing with a dog.
(Source: Albert Bandura and Frances L. Menlove, "Factors Determining Vicarious Extinction of Avoidance Behavior through Symbolic Modeling," *Journal of Personality and Social Psychology,* 1968, *8,* 99–108. Copyright 1968 by the American Psychological Association. Reprinted by permission.)

procedures to the treatment of phobias. More recently, Bandura (1971; 1977) has been an especially strong advocate of *participant modeling,* a technique that involves modeled demonstration along with client participation. Offering a great deal of support, praise, and reassurance, the therapist guides the client through the same steps previously modeled by the therapist. As the client develops increasing confidence, the therapist's support is gradually withdrawn until the client can cope effectively unassisted.

Bandura, Blanchard, and Ritter (1969) compared the effectiveness of participant modeling in the treatment of snake phobias with two other treatments and a no treatment control group. As Figure 17–1 shows, participant modeling was found to be superior to systematic desensitization and symbolic modeling in which subjects watched a film

rather than a live model interacting with a snake. Subjects who received one of the three types of treatment showed much greater fear reduction than subjects who were untreated.

Assertion Training

Consider the following statements made by clients to therapists:

Don G: I feel like a worm. I don't stand up for myself. If I'm not for me, who will be for me, right? Just last night Maxine and I were in a restaurant and the meat we ordered was cold. I know I could have asked the waiter to take it back, but I was afraid that I'd hurt his feelings.

John G: Whenever I ask a pretty girl out, I can't believe what happens. My face

FIGURE 17-1
Mean Number of Snake-Approach Responses Performed by Subjects before and after Receiving Different Treatments

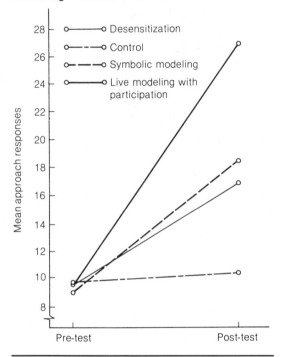

Source: A. Bandura, E. B. Blanchard, and B. Ritter, "The Relative Efficacy of Desensitization and Modeling Approaches for Inducing Behavioral, Affective, and Cognitive Changes," *Journal of Personality and Social Psychology* 13 (1969), pp. 173–99. Copyright 1969 by the American Psychological Association. Reprinted by permission.

anxieties and inhibitions related to social interactions. The primary goals of assertion training are: (1) to facilitate the honest and straightforward expression of thoughts and feelings in a socially appropriate manner; and (2) to ensure that one is not taken advantage of, bullied, ignored, or denied one's legitimate rights capriciously or callously.

How might behavior therapists help a client to achieve these goals? Perhaps the most commonly used assertion training technique is behavioral rehearsal or role playing (Rimm & Masters, 1979). Behavioral rehearsal involves role playing to help the client rehearse assertive responses in a particular situation. The therapist plays the role of relevant person in the interaction such as a spouse, parent, or employer. The client then reacts to the character enacted by the therapist. The therapist provides coaching and immediate feedback about the adequacy of the client's verbal and nonverbal responses. To give the client an opportunity to model assertive behavior, the therapist and client may reverse roles, with the therapist playing the client's role.

turns red, I almost lose my voice, and a couple of times I almost fainted. Maybe it's because I think she won't go out with me, but I just get tongue-tied and feel like a fool.

Judy R: I know the boss likes my work; he even told me so. But I just don't seem to be able to ask him for a raise. The funny part is, I know I deserve it.

Each of these clients might benefit from assertion training. The techniques of assertion training are used to help clients with

Perhaps the most commonly used assertion training technique is behavioral rehearsal or role playing.
(© Sue Markson)

THE INTERPERSONAL CONSEQUENCES OF ASSERTION

Assertion training programs help clients to accomplish immediate goals in interpersonal situations. The guiding assumption of such programs is that behaving assertively is generally preferable to behaving in either a nonassertive or an aggressive way. However, a study by Deborah Hull and Harold Schroeder (1979) suggests that while assertive behavior may help the client to attain immediate goals, the reactions of others to such behaviors may not be uniformly positive.

To study the interpersonal consequences of assertive behavior, the researchers looked at the responses of 42 male and 42 female college students to a partner who behaved either nonassertively, assertively, or aggressively. The subject's partner was actually a confederate whose behavior was modeled after descriptions based on clinical judgments commonly used in assertion training programs.

The subjects and their partners interacted in role-played situations that involved refusals and requests for behavior change. In both types of situations, the desires of the confederate and the subject were in conflict. In each role-played situation, the subject read a script to initiate the interaction. The partner then responded in a nonassertive, assertive, or aggressive way. The subject was then given a chance to respond spontaneously.

Hull and Schroeder discovered some interesting differences in the way subjects responded to their partners enacting different behaviors. Both assertive and aggressive behaviors were more effective in accomplishing immediate goals than nonassertive behaviors. But subjects rated nonassertive behavior more positively on some dimensions than both assertive and aggressive behavior. The nonassertive partners were seen as more sympathetic, friendly, and nonrevengeful than the assertive and aggressive partners. The aggressive partners were rated most negatively, but assertive partners were seen as dominant, unsympathetic and aggressive.

Hull and Schroeder note that the results of their study may have important implications for assertion training programs. If assertive responses are negatively evaluated, the relationship with the person asserted against may suffer. This suggests the importance of teaching clients to evaluate the likely responses of another person to assertion. Assertion training programs need to be concerned with more than training clients to accomplish their immediate goals. Indeed, assertion training programs might do well to help the client learn to "accommodate the needs and desires of both people involved" and to recognize the importance of achieving compromises in interpersonal situations.

"Has it ever occurred to you, Leland, that maybe you're too candid?" (From *The Wall Street Journal*, with permission of Cartoon Features Syndicate.)

Rimm and Masters (1979) offer the following examples of behavioral rehearsal with a college student who had difficulty making dates with girls.

Client: By the way [*pause*] I don't suppose you want to go out Saturday night?

Therapist: Up to actually asking for the date you were very good. However, if I were the girl, I think I might have been a bit offended when you said, "By the way." It's like your asking her out is pretty casual. Also, the way you phrased the question, you were kind of suggesting to her that she doesn't want to go out with you. Pretend for the moment I'm you. Now, how does this sound: "There is a movie at the Varsity Theater this Saturday that I want to see. If you don't have other plans, I'd very much like to take you."

Client: That sounded good. Like you were sure of yourself and liked the girl too.

Therapist: Why don't you try it?

Client: You know the movie at the Varsity? Well, I'd like to go, and I'd like to take you Saturday, if you don't have anything better to do.

Therapist: Well, that certainly was better. Your tone of voice was especially good. But the last line, "if you don't have anything better to do," sounds like you don't think you have too much to offer. Why not run through it one more time?

Client: I'd like to see the show at the Varsity, Saturday, and if you haven't made other plans, I'd like to take you.

Therapist: Much better. Excellent in fact. You were confident, forceful, and sincere.

Since different assertive responses are required in different situations, the therapist and client usually work with one situation at a time. As in systematic desensitization, the client "moves up" a hierarchy of increasingly anxiety-arousing situations. The client's practice of increasingly complex and difficult assertive responses promotes self-confidence in interpersonal situations that formerly aroused intense anxiety. Confronting situations that were previously avoided, the client learns that many of his or her fears were unrealistic. In order to facilitate the generalization of responses learned in the clinic to everyday life, the client is required to practice and master the newly acquired assertive responses in real-life situations.

The Token Economy: Achievement Place—A Treatment Program for Delinquent Adolescents

The *token economy* is an excellent example of how the principles of operant conditioning can be applied in treatment programs in institutional and residential settings. You probably recall that the highly effective social learning program for chronically institutionalized schizophrenics developed by Paul and Lentz (1978) involved a token economy system. One of the essential features of token reinforcement systems is that certain behaviors are consistently rewarded with tokens that can be exchanged for other, more tangible rewards, while other behaviors are ignored or not reinforced. Thus token economy programs shape new behaviors and facilitate learning new skills by the consistent and systematic application of reinforcement principles. Rimm and Masters (1979) have specified three basic considerations involved in developing a token system: (1) identifying target behaviors; (2) defining the currency; and (3) devising an exchange system.

At this point an example will help clarify how each of these considerations may come into play in implementing a token system.

The program we have selected for our example is Achievement Place, a community-based treatment program for delinquent and predelinquent youth. Achievement Place is a home-style facility located in Lawrence, Kansas, for 12- to 16-year-old youths who are typically referred by the courts after getting in trouble with the law. Since many of the young people who participate in the program are three to four years behind academically, the focus of treatment includes improving academic performance as well as eliminating antisocial behaviors and increasing self-care and interpersonal skills. Specific target behaviors that have been identified and increased include studying school assignments, conversing, accepting criticism without aggressing, room cleaning, and saving money. Behaviors that have been decreased include the use of poor grammar, aggressive statements, tardiness in returning home to the facility, and going to bed late (Kazdin, 1978).

Modification of target behaviors is accomplished by participation in the token system and through the instructional efforts of parent-teachers who provide the youth with specific feedback about the adequacy of his task performance, specific instructions for improvement, and verbal reinforcement and encouragement. The "currency" in the token economy is simply points the boys receive each time they complete a task or behavior appropriately. The exchange system involves trading the points earned for privileges and/or desirable objects. An examination of Table 17–1 will inform you of the relationship between various target behaviors and the points that can be earned or lost.

Each boy is responsible for recording points earned on an index card. The total number of points earned are traded each day for privileges that can be used the following day if a minimum number of points are accumulated on that day. Boys who perform adequately all of the target behaviors listed on the home bulletin and who incur few "costs" are entitled to all of the privileges. There are seven different kinds of privileges a youth can earn: (1) basic, including use of the telephone, tools, radio, record player, and recreation room; (2) snacks after school and before bedtime; (3) television time; (4) home time, which permits the youths to go home on weekends or to go downtown; (5) allowances of from one to five dollars a week; (6) bonds, which the youths can accumulate to buy clothes or other items they need; and (7) special privileges, which include any other privileges the youths may want. Fines have also been used to modify behavior at Achievement Place.

One problem Kazdin (1979) emphasizes is that, more often than not, behaviors that are learned in token economy programs are not maintained after the contingencies are withdrawn and the person confronts the "real world" where "privileges" are not exchanged for "points." How does Achievement Place deal with the potential problem of the failure to transfer what is learned in the program to everyday life situations outside the home? As soon as a boy consistently demonstrates appropriate behavior patterns, the point system is phased out and replaced by a merit system in which all privileges are free and no points are given or taken away. Before careful plans are initiated to return the boy to his own home he must demonstrate that he can behave appropriately without relying on the token program. Careful follow-up after the boy returns home helps to ensure that continued contact with the staff is available if problems recur. Indeed, if severe problems arise, the youth may return to the program for a short period of time to resolve the difficulties with the staff's support.

Is the Achievement Place program effective in maintaining treatment gains beyond the youth's period of residence in the home?

TABLE 17–1
Behaviors and the Number of Points They Earn or Lose

Behaviors Earning Points	Points
1. Watching news on TV or reading the newspaper.	300 per day
2. Cleaning and maintaining neatness in one's room.	500 per day
3. Keeping one's person neat and clean.	500 per day
4. Reading books.	5–10 per page
5. Aiding house parents in various household tasks.	20–1000 per task
6. Doing dishes.	500–1000 per meal
7. Being well dressed for an evening meal.	100–500 per meal
8. Performing homework.	500 per day
9. Obtaining desirable grades on school report cards.	500–1000 per grade
10. Turning out lights when not in use.	25 per light

Behaviors Losing Points	
1. Failing grades on the report card.	500–1000 per grade
2. Speaking aggressively.	20–50 per response
3. Forgetting to wash hands before meals.	100–300 per meal
4. Arguing.	300 per response
5. Disobeying.	100–1000 per response
6. Being late.	10 per minute
7. Displaying poor manners.	50–100 per response
8. Engaging in poor posture.	50–100 per response
9. Using poor grammar.	20–50 per response
10. Stealing, lying, or cheating.	10,000 per response

Source: Reprinted from E. L. Phillips, "Achievement Place: Token Reinforcement Procedures in a Home-Style Setting for Pre-delinquent Boys," *Journal of Applied Behavior Analysis* 1 (1968), p. 215. Copyright 1968 by the Society for the Experimental Analysis of Behavior, Inc.

More specifically, is it effective in reducing or eliminating antisocial behaviors and contacts with the courts? The answers to both of these questions is an unqualified yes. Kazdin (1979) notes that "up to two years after individuals graduated from Achievement Place, these youths showed fewer contacts with police and the courts, committed fewer acts which resulted in readjudication, and had slightly higher grades than individuals who had attended traditional institutional treatment or originally had been placed on probation" (from Fixsen, Phillips, Phillips, & Wolf, 1976).

Aversion Therapies

For more than six months the symptoms had persisted. Just about every 40 seconds she sneezed in a vigorous manner. Doctors had examined her and could not determine any physical cause for her debilitating symptom. The following behavior therapy procedure was implemented: A microphone was placed around her neck; it was connected to a voice key that tripped a relay which delivered a shock to her fingertips every time she sneezed. After just four hours of this treatment, she stopped sneezing. She was symptom-free after a follow-up 13 months later (Kushner, 1968).

He was a married, 32-year-old police officer who made up to 20 obscene telephone calls a week to young women in his community. During the calls he would masturbate. He would continue masturbating to orgasm if the woman hung up before he reached orgasm. He ultimately was arrested because he telephoned a woman he knew. She recognized his voice and alerted the sheriff's office. After the details of his behavior surfaced, he lost his job but was permitted to seek psychiatric help in lieu of criminal charges being filed against him. Because he experienced considerable guilt and shame after he made the calls, the following procedure was felt to have a reasonable probability of success. Therapy consisted of the client making an obscene call to a female listener in another office who was instructed to listen and answer questions in a passive but noncomplying manner. Two young, attractive women listeners were part of the treatment; they were instructed not to hang up first. After each telephone contact, the client and listener shared their feelings. This evoked a great deal of anxiety, shame, and embarrassment on the part of the client. The therapist also was present at each of the meetings. Under these circumstances the client experienced the telephone calls as extremely unpleasant. These feelings apparently generalized to the client's real-life situation. For nine months after the brief three-week treatment, the client reported no strong urges to make an obscene call and the authorities in the community were not notified of any such calls (adapted from Boudewyns, Tanna, & Fleischman, 1975).

Since she was 12 years old Laura had struggled with recurrent urges and thoughts about setting fires. Laura's "dangerous" thoughts most reliably occurred after she was angry. They served to divert her anger from the actual object of her wrath and provide her with a release of tension of sorts. On two occasions that she now dearly regrets, Laura yielded to temptation. In both instances Laura set fires after she was angry and felt "out of control." Fortunately, no one was injured, but substantial property damage was incurred. Prior to her sentencing,

Laura participated in a multifaceted treatment program that included anger management, assertion, and relaxation training components. However, the most novel aspect of her treatment required that, when she first became aware of thoughts of fire setting, Laura should imagine herself being confronted by the police, arrested, and taken to jail. The therapists even played a tape recording of a loud police siren during periods when she was instructed to initiate a fantasy about fire setting (Wilson & O'Leary, 1980). Laura was urged to incorporate the siren into her own fantasies to help counteract the "dangerous" thoughts. The treatment package was successful in reducing thoughts and impulses related to fire setting. Her therapists made a convincing argument to the judge to place her on two-year probation, the terms of which included follow-up "booster" therapy sessions rather than the much feared alternative of incarceration.

The above case histories illustrate *aversion therapy* procedures. Perhaps as you read the cases, you connected these examples with some others you had encountered earlier in your reading. You may recall that the tactic of pairing an unpleasant stimulus with a behavior that was the target of change was also used in the treatment of alcohol and exhibitionism. As we noted, quite promising results in reducing problem behaviors associated with both disorders have been obtained with aversion methods.

Aversion therapy is aptly named. To achieve their ends, therapists use a wide range of events that are painful, distasteful, unpleasant, or revolting to the client. Electric shocks, shame, humiliating feelings and unpleasant thoughts, hot air, and smoke are just a few of the stimuli or events that have been used to bring forth a negative reaction in the client and to reduce the frequency of a problem behavior.

Because many clients have qualms about subjecting themselves to aversion procedures, behavior therapists frequently prefer to use *covert sensitization techniques* in which the client only imagines the aversive event (Cautela, 1966; 1970). We illustrated the symbolic or imaginal presentation of aversive stimuli in the above-presented case of Laura. Covert sensitization may not only be less repugnant to the client, but may have other advantages as well. For example, the client can self-administer covert sensitization imagery in situations outside the therapy office, in the very situations in which the undesirable behavior or thoughts are likely to occur. Indeed, treatment gains are likely to persist to the extent that the client acquires a useful strategy or way of coping with the problem behavior in everyday life. As we indicated in Chapter 14, aversive imagery has been shown to be quite effective in certain cases of sexual deviance; however, covert sensitization has not been demonstrated to be comparably effective in treating disorders such as obesity, substance abuse (including alcoholism), and cigarette smoking. Evidence is accumulating to suggest that aversion techniques may be most effective when used in conjunction with other behavioral and psychotherapeutic approaches (Cannon, Baker, & Wehl, 1981).

The client's welfare and clear-cut, defensible treatment objectives should motivate the decision to use any form of aversion therapy. As we suggested in our discussion of confrontation methods, lowest risk or minimally distasteful techniques are first-line treatments that are generally attempted before more risky or unpleasant measures are undertaken. A decision to implement aversion methods should be made in concert with the client, after carefully weighing the costs and benefits of aversion therapy relative to alternative approaches. For example, a client may choose to endure the discomfort of aversion procedures when they are judged to involve negligible "costs" (short-term pain, shame, etc.) compared to the negative consequences of continuing to display the maladaptive behavior (arrest, public humiliation, etc.). Studies that compare aversion therapies with less noxious forms of therapy are needed. Such research could help establish guidelines for the use of aversion procedures.

Self-Control Procedures

Reflect for a moment on the cases of Jennifer L. and David F. presented at the beginning of the chapter. You probably recall that Jennifer's erratic eating patterns embarrassed and frustrated her. Her repeated attempts to decrease her food intake only reinforced her sense that she lacked control over her behavior. David's frustration increased every time he sat down at his typewriter to work on his novel. Since he was unable to accomplish what he set out to do, his self-concept plummeted as his exasperation and feelings of helplessness increased. Despite their best intentions, both Jennifer and David seem unable to control their behavior to suit their needs and wishes.

One way to increase desired behaviors (like David's time spent working productively) and to decrease undesired behaviors (like Jennifer's overeating) is with operant procedures. Institutional based operant procedures such as the token economy require considerable environmental control over the individual. Jennifer and David's behavior could conceivably be modified in an institutional setting with operant procedures. But a moment's reflection suggests that this would be a drastic, restrictive, and costly course of action for their problems.

One of the more recent innovations in behavior therapy is the use of *self-control techniques* to modify behavior. Instead of relying on external controls, clients like Jennifer and David can be taught to self-administer behavior change techniques in the natural environment where their problems typically occur. Like the token economy, many self-control techniques involve contingency management. Contingency management approaches modify behavior by controlling its consequences. But in the case of self-control procedures, the person arranges the reinforcement contingencies, instead of some external agent. The goal of self-control techniques is to provide the person with "active coping strategies for dealing with problem situations" (Rimm & Masters, 1979, p. 421).

In self-control programs the therapist assumes the role of a consultant. Clients are instructed in self-control techniques, their progress is monitored, and the therapist offers suggestions, where appropriate. Ideally the clients reach the point where they can become their own therapists.

Watson and Tharp (1972) have outlined the basic steps that are carried out in an operant-oriented self-control program:

1. The basic idea in self-modification is to arrange situations so that desirable behavior is positively reinforced and unwanted behavior is not reinforced.

2. Reinforcement is made contingent, which means that is is gained only if some particular behavior (the target) is performed.

3. The steps in self-modification are:
   a. Specifying the target in terms of behavior in a specific situation.
   b. Making observations on how often the target behavior occurs, the antecedents that precede it, and the consequences that follow it.
   c. Forming a plan to intervene by contingently reinforcing some desirable behavior and by arranging situations to increase the chances of performing that behavior.

   d. Maintaining, adjusting, and terminating the intervention program (p. 48).

This program, like many other self-control programs, involves three stages: self-monitoring or observation; self-evaluation to determine whether there is a match between what one is doing and what one wishes to do; and the administration of self-reinforcement (Kanfer, 1975).

Let us now consider a weight reduction program developed by Richard Stuart (1967) that combines a number of self-control techniques to successfully treat obesity. Self-reward for appropriate changes in eating behavior seems to play an especially important role in weight reduction programs like Stuart's (Mahoney, Moura, & Wade, 1973). But we selected Stuart's program as an example because it relies heavily on *stimulus control* procedures. Stimulus control techniques modify behavior by rearranging environmental cues (Wilson & O'Leary, 1980). In Stuart's treatment, these techniques were initiated after subjects were first trained in self-monitoring their daily weight, the time and circumstances of eating, and their food intake. Stimulus control procedures were used to reduce the number of stimuli cueing or eliciting eating behavior. Subjects were told to eat meals only in the kitchen and to engage in no other activities while eating such as watching television or reading. The goal was to make eating a "pure" experience restricted to only one specific setting, the kitchen. To cut down on impulsive eating, subjects were asked to eat slowly and to eat only foods which require preparation.

Stuart's treatment program was conducted over a 12-month period, with each of the self-control techniques gradually added in a stepwise fashion. An inspection of Figure 17–2 reveals that the results of Stuart's program were indeed impressive. The four women

FIGURE 17–2
Weight Profile of Four Women Undergoing Behavior Therapy for Overeating

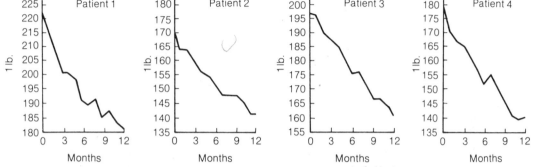

Source: Adapted with permission from Richard B. Stuart, "Behavioral Control of Overeating," *Behavior Research and Therapy* 5, 1967, pp. 357–64. Copyright 1967, Pergamon Press, Ltd.

who participated lost an average of 37.8 pounds over the course of treatment.

Self-control procedures have been successfully applied to problems like smoking (Nolan, 1968; Tooley & Pratt, 1967), poor study habits (Watson & Tharp, 1972), and insomnia (Bootzin, 1972). In Chapter 6 we noted the recent surge of interest in biofeedback. Biofeedback qualifies as a self-control procedure because the client ultimately learns strategies to control a physiological response in the absence of feedback. A variety of other self-control procedures have been devised, too numerous to detail here, but they all have a common goal: fostering adaptive behavior and competencies in the absence of external control to increase the client's ability to function independently of the continued support of a therapist or a restrictive environment.

Cognitive Behavioral Therapies

The principles of cognitive behavioral therapy are compatible with some of the basic tenets of social learning theory (Bandura, 1974; 1977; 1981) summarized by Meichenbaum (1985):

1. A large portion of human learning is cognitively mediated.

2. Rather than responding to environmental consequences, humans respond primarily to cognitive representations of environmental events (i.e., the individual selectively attends and interprets events).

3. Thoughts, feelings, behaviors, and their consequences are causally interrelated.

4. Individuals not only react to environmental events but actively create such events.

This scheme suggests that cognitive behavioral therapists believe that conscious thoughts play a major role in determining the way a person feels and behaves. Since it is assumed that maladaptive thoughts play a part in the genesis of psychological disorders, the major task of treatment is to alter or "restructure" the faulty cognitions (Rachman & Wilson, 1980).

Albert Ellis has long been one of the most forceful advocates of the cognitive behavioral approach. Since the mid-1950s Ellis has been an exponent of Rational Emotive Therapy (RET). Ellis' RET vigorously attacks the client's irrational beliefs and stimulates an adaptive, rational approach to living.

In 1976 Garfield and Kurtz observed that RET is more widely practiced than client-centered therapy. RET is just one of a number of *cognitive-restructuring therapies* that incorporate behavioral methods to spur behavioral as well as cognitive change. In Chapter 8 we described Beck's conceptualization and treatment of depression, which emphasizes cognitive factors. Meichenbaum's stress inoculation training, which we described in Chapter 6, is another cognitive behavioral approach. When Smith (1982) gauged trends in counseling and psychotherapy, he found that cognitive behavioral options represent one of the strongest, if not *the* strongest, theoretical emphases today. The mushrooming popularity of cognitively oriented approaches bolsters Garske and Lynn's (1985) contention that cognitive psychology might very well emerge as the "fourth force" in contemporary psychology, following to the forefront of prominence psychoanalysis, humanistic psychology, and behaviorism.

Since RET is the oldest and most popular of the cognitive behavioral approaches, we will begin our discussion of these methods by describing Albert Ellis' *A-B-C theory* of psychological dysfunction. This theory specifies one of the pivotal assumptions of cognitive-restructuring approaches: Psychological disturbances are not *caused* directly by events or life circumstances but arise from the way the person interprets or evaluates them.

Consider the following example that illustrates Ellis' A-B-C theory. Ted and Sally are two competent and skilled workers who have been fired from their jobs. Ted reacts to the loss of his job with anxiety, despair, and depression. He tells his wife that he has "given

up" and that he has lost all motivation to find another job. Sally, on the other hand, reacts with disappointment but retains her sense of self-worth and actively searches for appropriate employment. Sally and Ted are responding to the identical event (called an activating event, or A). But as you can see, the consequences of getting fired from their jobs are very different for these two individuals.

Learning something about Ted and Sally's beliefs about getting fired (B) will help you to better understand what prompted their reactions. When Ted lost his job, he said something like the following to himself: "Well, that's the end of the line for me. I must be incompetent. What will people think! No one will ever hire me again. I must have this job to go on; it's a total wipeout. I'll never get it together." Now consider what Sally said to herself: "Boy, it's really too bad that I lost my job, what a drag! But life will go on. It's going to be tough, but I know I can handle this. It may be some rough going, but I'll find another job, I'm sure I will."

In considering this example, we can see that the differences in the way Ted and Sally feel and behave are mediated by the views and beliefs they hold about losing their jobs. In RET language, A (activating event) does not directly cause C (emotional and behavioral consequences); B (one's beliefs about A) does (Ellis, 1977).

According to RET, the first task confronting the therapist is to identify the activating events and irrational beliefs that interfere with the client's confronting life's challenges in an adaptive manner. Ellis has identified 12 irrational ideas (presented below) that he believes are quite common in our culture. You might find it interesting to see which of these beliefs you have entertained at one time or another in your life. Since such ideas are so much a part of many people's thinking, it would not be at all unusual to agree with a number of the beliefs listed below:

1. The idea that you must, yes, *must* have sincere love and approval almost all the time from all the people you find significant.

2. The idea that you must prove yourself thoroughly competent, adequate, and achieving; or that you must at least have real competence or talent at something important.

3. The idea that people who harm you or commit misdeeds rate as generally bad, wicked, or villainous individuals, and that you should severely blame, damn, and punish them for their sins.

4. The idea that life proves awful, terrible, horrible, or catastrophic when things do not go the way you would like them to go.

5. The idea that emotional misery comes from external pressures and that you have little ability to control your feelings or rid yourself of depression and hostility.

6. The idea that if something seems dangerous or fearsome, you must become terribly occupied with and upset about it.

7. The idea that you will find it easier to avoid facing many of life's difficulties and self-responsibilities than to undertake some rewarding forms of self-discipline.

8. The idea that your past remains all-important and that, because something once strongly influenced your life, it has to keep determining your feelings and behavior today.

9. The idea that people and things should turn out better than they do;

and that you have to view it as awful and horrible if you do not quickly find good solutions to life's hassles.

10. The idea that you can achieve happiness by inertia and inaction or by passively and uncommitedly "enjoying yourself."

11. The idea that you must have a high degree of order or certainty to feel comfortable; or that you need some supernatural power on which to rely.

12. The idea that you give yourself a global rating as a human and that your general worth and self-acceptance depends on the goodness of your performance and the degree that people approve of you (Ellis, 1977, p. 10).

To modify the client's irrational beliefs, the therapist assumes the role of an active, directive teacher. The client may be persuaded, encouraged, and cajoled into rethinking the assumptions, conclusions, and personal philosophy that underlie the psychological disturbance. The therapist may assign "homework" to ensure that the client engages in behaviors that are consistent with an increasingly rational philosophy of life. For example, shy clients may be given an assignment to talk to an attractive man or woman who might previously have been avoided, or a person who is anxious when speaking in groups may be encouraged to inject comments in various group situations.

Ellis, along with therapists of other persuasions, is careful to point out that successful treatment involves not only change in the way people think about their problems but also the way they behave. There are differences, however, in the extent to which behavioral methods are explicitly incorporated in the so-called cognitive behavioral approaches. For example, in Meichenbaum's method of stress inoculation, clients are routinely exposed to behavioral procedures that include modeling, assertion and social skill training, and graded task assignments to enhance treatment effects. Beck's cognitive therapy also places greater weight on behavioral procedures than Ellis' RET, which places great emphasis on teaching logical thinking and changing the client's worldview.

Other differences between cognitive behavioral approaches are worthy of note. In Meichenbaum's method of stress inoculation, there is an emphasis on examining individual differences in coping with stressful events, instead of focusing attention on specific irrational beliefs, as Ellis does. Unlike Ellis, who directly attacks the client's irrational assumptions, Beck fosters a Socratic dialogue with the client to stimulate self-discovery of distorted thoughts related to undesirable moods and behaviors (Wilson & O'Leary, 1980). Although cognitive behavior therapists may differ in the specific procedures they employ, they tend to agree that changing maladaptive thought patterns is a central therapeutic goal (Mahoney & Arnkoff, 1978).

Cognitive behavioral methods have been used with considerable success in treating numerous problems and disorders, including test anxiety (Holroyd, 1976), assertiveness problems (Craighead, 1979), phobias (Odom, Nelson, & Wein, 1978), institutionalized schizophrenics (Meichenbaum & Cameron, 1976), and chronic anger (Novoco, 1976). Cognitive therapies have been found to be quite effective in treating depression (e.g, Beck, Rush, Shaw, & Emery, 1979; Kolata, 1981), and as we shall document in the final chapter, they appear to be at least as effective as drug therapies.

Meichenbaum (1985) has indicated that comprehensive reviews of cognitive behavioral therapy support the following conclusions about its effectiveness: (1) it is more effective than no treatment or placebo treatment; (2) it is equally effective as other forms of treatment (e.g., certain forms of behavior therapy); (3) it can be combined effectively with other forms of treatment such as drug therapy and marital counseling; and (4) there are not enough studies to compare different cognitive behavioral approaches. These conclusions can be supplemented by a recent review of 48 cognitive behavior therapy outcome studies (Miller & Berman, 1983), which noted that firm evidence was lacking to support the superiority of cognitive behavioral therapies over other established psychotherapies such as systematic desensitization.

ISSUES IN CONTEMPORARY PSYCHOTHERAPY

Insight versus Behavior Therapy: The Issue of Outcome

Behavior therapists have devised numerous techniques specifically designed to treat a multitude of problems in living. Our brief review of some of the most prominent techniques reveals that behavioral approaches should perhaps be considered the treatment of choice in treating phobias, obsessive-compulsive disorders, and agoraphobia. In this and other chapters we have seen that behavior therapy has been successfully applied to sexual problems, assertion difficulties, substance abuse disorders, and a host of other difficulties. Behavior therapy has made inroads in helping groups of persons, such as mentally retarded and autistic children who usually are neglected by other forms of therapy.

Behavior therapists have been sharply critical of both psychodynamic and humanistic psychotherapy. They have, for example, questioned the economics and effectiveness of insight therapies. Behavior therapists have argued that insight therapies are best suited to verbal, intelligent, introspective, wealthy, and relatively well-functioning individuals. The time-consuming, intellectual, and expensive insight therapies are seen as having little value to vast numbers of people, including the lower class, children, the elderly, and psychotics.

Behavior therapists also contend that well-controlled studies are lacking to support the superiority of insight therapies over less costly and time-consuming approaches. Advocates of behavior therapy have argued that behavioral approaches have proven to be at least as effective as comparison treatments and often more effective.

Behavior therapists feel that these considerations give their approach the edge over insight therapies. However, the superiority of behavioral methods over traditional psychotherapy has yet to be conclusively demonstrated. Studies that have used experienced therapists who practiced behavioral, psychodynamic, and client-centered approaches have found that all were more successful in helping clients than no treatment at all (DiLoretto, 1971; Sloane, Staples, Cristol, Yorkston, & Whipple, 1975). Large-scale reviews of hundreds of therapy outcome studies, like that of Smith and Glass (1977) mentioned in the previous chapter, have been able to demonstrate that certain therapies are apparently superior to others only when some research studies are not included in the analysis (Garske & Lynn, 1985). Kazdin (1979) has noted that much more research is needed to show that gains derived from behavior therapy persist over long intervals. Whether behavior therapy fosters long-term gains to a greater degree than insight therapy has yet to be ascertained.

According to Kazdin and Wilson (1978), statements about the relative effectiveness of behavioral and traditional approaches are premature because the two approaches have not been compared on a number of important criteria. They argue that the criteria used in most therapy outcome studies to gauge the success of treatment are too narrowly defined. That is, the value of a particular technique can be judged on criteria other than the average number of clients who "improve" at the end of treatment, as is most often the case. For example, Kazdin and Wilson suggest that the importance of the changes, the breadth of the changes, and the durability of the changes attributed to therapy are relevant criteria that are often ignored. Other important criteria that could be considered are the cost effectiveness of the technique, the ease of administration, the appeal of the procedure to the client, and the time required to treat the client with a particular treatment mode. Behavioral and insight-oriented techniques may fare differently across various measures of treatment outcome.

The use of multiple criteria would help us to better understand the complex ways in which different treatments affect clients. Using a broader range of outcome measures, we may learn more about the impact of different therapeutic techniques and which ones are most suited to the individual client's problem. In some cases behavioral techniques may be better suited to the specific problems, needs, and desires of a client, whereas in other cases insight therapy may be the treatment of choice. Perhaps the question therapy outcome researchers should address is not simply: "Is behavior therapy more effective than insight therapy?" Instead, it might be more productive to ask: "What is the potential value of a treatment in relation to specific therapeutic and social goals?" Given the state of the art of psychotherapy outcome research, we are a long way from answering this complex question.

Common Factors in Psychotherapy

The conclusion that psychotherapies appear to be comparable in terms of their effectiveness poses a challenge to psychotherapists who place great stock in their preferred theoretical orientation and argue that their approach surpasses its rivals. But if psychotherapies are indeed comparable in terms of their effects, how might one explain the process of change? One hypothesis that has stimulated a great deal of interest is that all effective psychotherapies share active ingredients—common factors—that are instrumental in behavior change. We might ask, then, what features, goals, and processes are common to both traditional and behavioral therapies?

Jerome Frank (1973; 1981) and Murray and Jacobson (1978) have made important contributions to our understanding of the common factors that unite diverse approaches to helping. The first basic process common to different therapies is the expectation of help instilled in clients. The promise of help offered to the demoralized clients who seek therapy serves to boost morale. The social setting of psychotherapy—the trappings of the therapist's office, for example—also promote expectancies that help and change will be forthcoming (Frank, 1976; Goldfried, 1980; Prochaska, 1984). Divergent technical procedures may produce positive treatment effects because they provide clients with success experiences and mobilize expectancies of improvement and treatment gain.

Bandura's (1977; 1981) social learning theory maintains that clients who acquire expectancies that they can successfully perform new behaviors may be more likely to engage in the behaviors (both within and outside therapy) than clients who do not develop such expectancies. Bandura believes that any successful therapy program serves to enhance the clients' self-efficacy. However, the most convincing source of information about the ability of people to successfully perform a task derives from their success in actually performing the task. Techniques like participant modeling, then, would be expected to be highly effective because they enhance the client's self-efficacy expectations. And as we have noted, participant modeling is more effective than modeling and systematic desensitization in reducing certain fears. Efficacy expectancies may stimulate efforts to change and, in turn, be generated by such changes, bolstering treatment effects and enhancing the therapist's credibility (Lynn & Garske, 1985).

Many effective psychotherapeutic outcomes are the product of a learning experience—the assimilation and integration of meaningful emotional, behavioral, and cognitive learnings into the client's life (e.g., Alexander & French, 1946; Goldfried, 1980; Strupp, 1982). Successful learning experiences often involve the neutralization of irrational fears and the acquisition of new behavior patterns by confronting thoughts, feelings, and actions that were previously experienced as threatening and were avoided. For example, the process of interpretation in psychoanalysis and ascending a fear hierarchy during systematic desensitization may be effective because both of them expose a client to an anxiety-evoking thought that he or she was avoiding and result in a meaningful learning experience.

Murray and Jacobson (1978) believe that successful psychotherapy often involves correcting maladaptive beliefs about the self and the world. The therapist's model or theory of psychotherapy may be absorbed by the client and may furnish a way of understanding the self, psychological problems, and human relationships (Cornsweet, 1983). The psychodynamic therapist's permissive attitude may encourage the client to rethink views about sexual behavior, for example. Cognitive behavioral therapists deal in a direct fashion with beliefs about the self and the world. Modeling and operant procedures may inform the client about real-world reinforcement contingencies.

Therapists of all persuasions strive to convey an unconditional acceptance of the person. Humanistic-existential therapists are the most explicit about the importance of the relationship as a vehicle for enhanced self-esteem. However, Murray and Jacobson note that behavior therapists also communicate a basic acceptance by their efforts to positively change socially undesirable behavior.

Virtually all therapies help the client develop competencies in social living. In behavioral and insight therapies, the therapist models socially appropriate behavior. Gestalt and client-centered therapists reflect feelings and thoughts, and provide feedback about social relationships. Assertion training deals in a most direct way with developing social competencies.

Specific factors are, undoubtedly, associated with different therapeutic approaches. However, it is possible that such factors do not enhance treatment effectiveness beyond those that are held in common with other approaches. According to the *common factors* hypothesis, specific factors give a therapy character and definition while common factors give a therapy clout (Garske & Lynn, 1985). Perhaps the greatest challenge facing psychotherapy researchers is to discover the variables most reliably associated with positive therapeutic outcomes (Goldfried, 1980).

Our discussion suggests that although the techniques and guiding models of behavioral and insight therapies are very different (Messer & Winokour, 1980), the similarities between these two approaches may outweigh the differences (Farkas, 1980; McNamara, 1980). The most notable difference between behavior therapies and insight therapies is the commitment of the behavior therapies to the assumption that psychology is a scientific enterprise.

The Trend toward Eclecticism and Integration

There are important differences between schools of therapy in their philosophical perspectives and assumptions regarding human behavior and change. However, one of the current trends in psychotherapy is the move toward pluralism, eclecticism, and the integration of theories and techniques. This trend is evident in recent surveys (e.g., Garfield & Kurz, 1976; Norcross & Prochaska, 1983) suggesting that the popularity of narrow schools of psychotherapy is waning. Increasing numbers of clinicians favor the use of a pragmatic combination of viewpoints and techniques tailored to the needs of particular clients (Garske, 1982).

How might such an eclectic system of psychotherapy operate? For purposes of illustration, let us briefly consider one such approach—*multimodal therapy*—devised by Arnold Lazarus. Lazarus notes that the central question of interest to the multimodal therapist is, "Who or what is best for this particular individual" (Lazarus, 1981, p. 4). The therapist is empirical and pragmatic. By assessing seven different modes of behavior and experience, multimodal therapists search for optimal treatment methods tailored to the unique characteristics and circumstances of an individual.

The acronym BASIC I.D. provides a memory device for remembering the seven modes that clinicians who adopt this method assess: B = Behavior, A = Affect, S = Sensation, I = Imagery, C = Cognition, I = Interpersonal, and D = Drugs. Wilson and Lazarus (1983) offer the following case example. The person treated states that his image of his late mother's funeral "makes me feel sad and sorry for myself, as I keep thinking that I am to blame for her premature death, which, in turn, makes me feel tense all over." The interventions that a multimodal behavior therapist would pursue include the following:

Behavior: Increase the number of positive-reinforcing activities in which the patient participates.

Affect: Teach the patient to express anger in an assertive manner instead of lapsing into self-pity.

Sensation: Use deep muscle relaxation to overcome generalized tension.

Imagery: Show the patient how to dwell on pleasant memories instead of focusing on negative elements.

Cognition: Try to alter negative self-talk by disputing internalized guilt-inducing sentences.

Interpersonal: Be sure that friends and family members are not reinforcing the self-denigrating behaviors by inappropriately offering sympathy and warmth.

Drugs: If sadness or depression persists or becomes more intense, medication may be indicated. (p. 124–25)

Theorists and researchers identified with very different treatment approaches have joined hands in acknowledging that the cross-fertilization of rival models has the potential to enrich the field of psychotherapy. As Garske and Lynn (1985) have noted, a softening of theoretical rigidities makes accessible the scientific and clinical advances of diverse schools of psychotherapy.

Cognitive and social learning theory concepts make them viable candidates to stimulate attempts to develop integrative theories and models of psychotherapy. The future will probably witness the elaboration of theories with increasing breadth and diversification. Current trends also suggest a search for robust techniques and clinical strategies that result in potent treatment effects (Goldfried, 1980).

Psychotherapists are not, however, about to abandon their theoretical orientation. This is also true for therapists with an eclectic orientation. Perhaps Frank (1981) is correct that the choice of a theoretical orientation is best guided by the therapist's personal preference. However, "if a therapist's orientation is an open rather than a closed system, there is reason to believe that it will be mutually beneficial for the therapist and the client" (Gerske & Lynn, 1985).

SUMMARY

Behavior therapy has contributed numerous techniques that have been applied to many different problems and populations. The roots of behavior therapy are in the learning perspective, but we noted that behavior therapists are not limited to a narrow view of behavior change as resulting only from operant or classical conditioning. As the learning perspective has expanded to encompass social learning and cognitive views, behavior therapy has developed techniques that reflect recent developments in the learning field. Behavior therapists proceed by conducting a careful behavioral assessment of the client's specific difficulties, establishing specific treatment objectives, designing a behavior change program that can be effectively implemented, and systematically evaluating and monitoring their efforts to determine whether modifications are necessary to maximize treatment gains.

We discussed in some detail a number of the most prominent and widely used behavior therapy techniques. Systematic desensitization was developed by Wolpe to help clients cope with maladaptive, unrealistic anxiety. It is based on the reciprocal inhibition principle that clients cannot experience anxiety while they are deeply relaxed. In recent years this explanation has been challenged by alternate accounts of its effectiveness that rely on cognitive factors and extinction models among others. Why desensitization works is still an unresolved question, but its effectiveness is virtually undisputed.

Implosive therapy and flooding confront the client with the most feared stimuli to elicit maximal anxiety so that it can eventually be extinguished with repeated and prolonged exposure. Flooding has been shown to be effective with obsessive-compulsive disorders and agoraphobia. However, both flooding and implosive therapy may be less desirable than other techniques that clients might find less aversive.

In many treatments clients model themselves after their therapists. Bandura and his colleagues have developed specific modeling procedures that have proven quite effective in treating phobias. Participant modeling, which involves modeled demonstration along with client participation, may be especially effective.

Assertion training procedures seem to be helpful with anxieties and inhibitions related to social interactions. Behavioral rehearsal or role playing is perhaps the most central technique in assertion training.

Operant procedures like the token economy have been used extensively in institutional settings with diverse populations. Achievement Place, a community-based treatment program for delinquent and predelinquent youth, has reduced or eliminated antisocial behaviors in this population. Many self-control procedures also utilize contingency management, but the person self-administers these techniques in the absence of external controls to effect desired behavior changes.

Cognitive behavioral approaches are among the most popular recent innovations in behavior therapy. We described Albert Ellis' approach in some detail, but numerous other cognitive behavioral treatments have been developed in recent years. While specific techniques may differ, cognitive behavior therapists are united in their belief that maladaptive thinking patterns are important targets of treatment efforts.

We noted that although the techniques of behavior and insight therapies are very different, the similarities between these two approaches may outweigh the differences. Behavior therapy has a proven effectiveness with certain disorders, but it is probably premature to conclude that behavior therapy is generally superior to more traditional approaches.

18

Group, Family, and Community-Based Treatment

Overview of Group Therapy
Curative Factors in Group Therapy
Psychodrama
T–Groups
Encounter Groups
Marathon Groups
Evaluation of Group Therapy

Family Therapy
Satir's Conjoint Family Therapy
Structured Family Therapy
Evaluation of Family Therapy

New Ways of Helping: Mental Health and the Community
Community Mental Health Today
From Mental Hospital to Community
Crisis Intervention
The Promise of Prevention

Legal and Ethical Issues in the Treatment of Abnormal Behavior
Ethical Problems in Identifying High-Risk Cases
Ethics and Psychotherapy
Involuntary Commitment
Patients' Rights and Informed Consent
The Insanity Defense

Summary

OVERVIEW OF GROUP THERAPY

About nine people file into a room slowly, tentatively. Each has seen only one other person in the room—the therapist—a week earlier in a diagnostic interview. Some appear reluctant, some enthusiastic, but all have come to this first meeting with at least the willingness to go along with the therapist's belief that the group could be useful to them. They sit in a circle, quiet and expectant. Their posture reveals a bit of anxiety. What will go on here? What can go on here? What will the therapist do? Several in the group have had previous psychotherapy. One woman begins the interaction by describing her current predicament and the disappointments she experienced in previous treatments. Others chime in. Sympathetic offerings of similar tales of woe are heard from various people in the room. From time to time the therapist comments, pointing out the expectations of the various group members. People are beginning to get to know one another. Each of the people is attending for a different reason, but they all share some similar concerns. Will the group members accept me? Are there other people in this room with similar problems and concerns? Will I be really understood? Can I take risks with these people? After the first session all of the group members have had an opportunity to express why they came and what their expectations are for future meetings. This is but one of many different types of groups. But for this group, for these people, group therapy begins (adapted from Lieberman, 1975).

What does group treatment have to offer? How are groups conducted? Is group therapy effective? These are some of the important questions and issues we will address in our overview of group treatment methods. As you are no doubt aware, group treatment methods utilize the skills of a helping person with two or more persons at a time. In this section we will consider a number of group treatment approaches. We will also take a close look at family therapy—a form of group therapy conducted with members of the same family. But first let us take note of the dramatic increase in the popularity of group approaches to treatment.

The popularity of group approaches has paralleled the increased demand for psychological services in the general population—a trend that became especially apparent in the years following World War II. Today there seems to be a group experience tailored to suit the interests and meet the needs of virtually anyone who seeks psychotherapy, personal growth, or simply support and companionship from others. Most of you have probably participated in or know of someone who has been involved in one of the myriad forms of group experience available today. If you have not had direct or indirect contact with a group like Alcoholics Anonymous, a consciousness-raising group, a religious inspirational group, an encounter group, or a weight control group, you may be in the minority of your peers. As this brief listing suggests, the diversity of group approaches is impressive. Approaches range from self-help groups like Alcoholics Anonymous to groups that adapt psychoanalytic principles and techniques to the group setting. In recent years the encounter group has become very popular. There seems to be a move towards using group methods to promote personal growth in individuals with no serious psychological disturbances. Lieberman has noted that by 1975 more than 5 million Americans had participated in encounter groups aimed at personal growth and change.

The popularity of groups can also be seen in their extension to numerous settings. Groups conducted in homes, hospitals, businesses, weekend retreats, community agencies, and professional offices reach people of all races, ages, economic levels, and so on.

Recent years have also witnessed the expansion of group therapy to encompass an ever widening range of applications. Lynn and Frauman (1985) have recently surveyed the broad terrain covered by group methods. Special populations such as the blind, divorced persons, gender identity patients, and children in inpatient settings are receiving increasing attention. Clients who are generally thought to be difficult to treat are being reached by way of groups specifically oriented to their unique characteristics. Borderline and narcissistic clients, substance abusers, and severely disturbed medical outpatients have all been the recipients of group therapy. Furthermore, the special problems of women and the elderly have recently been addressed by group methods. But apart from their popularity and the real human needs that group methods address, their place in the spectrum of therapeutic methods is assured for another reason: group

methods are efficient, time-saving, and less costly than individual treatment methods. Levine (1979) has commented that "group therapy can help with most anything that individual therapy can, providing an appropriate group is available and the individual will accept the group as the mode of treatment" (p. 11). The virtues of group therapy have been recognized by therapists of every major theoretical orientation, although different therapists may work very differently within a group framework.

Some therapists, for example, adopt psychoanalytic principles by encouraging free associations of group members and interpreting transference reactions between the therapist and individual patients. Other therapists administer behavior therapy procedures such as systematic desensitization and assertiveness training. Such therapists are likely to play a very active, directive role in the groups they conduct. Still other therapists focus on communication and styles of relating among group members, emphasizing interpersonal relationships as a key vehicle for change and growth. But despite differences in therapist style and approach to group treatment, there are some common elements in diverse groups that contribute to their effectiveness.

Curative Factors in Group Therapy

Yalom (1975) has contributed to our understanding of the usefulness of group methods by specifying curative factors believed to be common to diverse group approaches. A consideration of the following list of curative factors in group therapy will help us to answer one of the questions we posed earlier: What do group treatments have to offer?

1. Imparting information. In every therapy group there is ample access to information provided by the therapist

and other group members. Group members, then, have an opportunity to receive suggestions, advice, or direct guidance from the group. Didactic instructions may be formally incorporated into the group, or may arise from the dynamics of group life as the members interact and share experiences that are relevant to commonly held problems or concerns.

2. Instilling hope. Hope is an essential ingredient of any successful therapeutic approach. If there is no hope of a favorable treatment outcome, it is unlikely that maximum benefit will be derived from therapy. Observing other group members who have coped successfully with similar problems or di-

lemmas may be a potent source of inspiration. Contact with persons who have improved is especially important in groups like Alcoholics Anonymous that rely heavily on personal testimonials and the exemplary activity of members.

3. Universality. As group members share initimate feelings and disclosures, it may be comforting to learn that others share similar fears and concerns, have endured equally difficult situations, and have surmounted hurdles in life that some of the group members are only beginning to confront. The very knowledge that one is not alone in one's suffering and in one's struggles to cope effectively

Group therapy is often conducted in a relatively relaxed atmosphere. (© Sue Markson)

with life's challenges may be a source of relief as well as an impetus for change and growth.

4. Altruism. Clients often enter group treatment demoralized, unsure of themselves, and lacking in self-esteem. But over the course of the group experience, members can learn a valuable lesson: that they can be of help and value to others. The contribution to the personal growth of other group members can lead to a greater sense of self-worth and a heightened awareness of personal resources.

5. Interpersonal learning. The complex interplay of relationships and personalities that fashion the shape of the group affords an excellent context for learning about interpersonal relationships, social skills, sensitivity to others, and conflict resolution.

6. Imitative behavior. Group members may acquire new behaviors by modeling desired and effective behaviors. Group members can learn from one another as well as from the individual designated as the therapist.

7. Corrective recapitulation of the primary family. The group experience may offer the client a unique opportunity to explore and resolve conflicts and problems related to family members that continue to be expressed in relationships outside the family context. Insight into the way one reenacts past family dramas and scripts for behaving that stem from the primary family may be an important first step in breaking free from the hold of the past. Behaviors that may have been rewarded and even functional in the family of origin may come to be viewed as maladaptive and inappropriate in the context of the treatment group.

8. Catharsis. The open expression of feelings toward others is an essential part of the group process. Learning how to express feelings in an open, honest, and straightforward way may lead to closer bonds among group members and a greater sense of mutual trust and understanding.

9. Group cohesiveness. Group cohesiveness is one of the primary curative factors. It is the sense of "groupness" that binds individuals together, serving much the same function as the relationship in individual therapy. In a tightly knit group where members feel close to one another and a sense of trust exists, members may more freely take risks, accept feedback from one another, and experience a sense of self-esteem that derives from acceptance by the group. There is likely to be the free flow of feeling and interpersonal exchange that is so essential to the emergence of the other curative factors we have mentioned.

A moment's reflection on the curative factors Yalom describes suggests that groups provide a rich context for change and growth. You probably noted that the group experience may help foster a sense of personal validation and self-worth. It may provide the impetus for interpersonal learning and the opportunity to profit from the experiences of others, and it may offer the group member an opportunity to help others in their quest for change and growth.

Let us now turn to another question: How is group therapy conducted? Actually no *one* answer applies to all types of groups. But we hope that an inspection of several very different types of groups will give you a sense of the interplay of curative factors in group treatments and the range of techniques employed by group therapists.

The roots of group therapy as practiced today are often traced back to the efforts of Joseph Pratt, a Boston internist, who worked with groups of tubercular patients in the early 1900s. Meeting with his patients in a class format, Pratt described his work in this way: "The class meeting is a pleasant social hour for members . . . made up as a membership of widely different races and sexes, they have a common bond in a common disease. A fine spirit of camaraderie has developed. They never discuss their symptoms and are almost invariably in good spirits . . ." (1907). The inspiration of hope, the identification with other patients experiencing a similar plight, and the camaraderie, mutual support, and group cohesiveness all seem to be important "therapeutic ingredients" in Pratt's early groups. Groups like Alcoholics Anonymous, Weight Watchers, and Synanon have an inspirational quality reminiscent of Pratt's classes.

Like Pratt's groups, self-help groups like Alcoholics Anonymous tend to be composed of people who share a similar problem. However, self-help groups are not led by professionals and draw their "therapists," or leaders, from their own ranks.

Psychodrama

Jacob Moreno, a psychiatrist who first used the term *group therapy,* developed a group treatment knows as *psychodrama* in the early 1920s in Vienna. Psychodrama uses techniques of dramatic play and unrehearsed acting to stimulate the spontaneous expression of feeling. The dramatic techniques utilized tend to obscure the distinction between fantasy and reality and seem to provide a sense of security because new behaviors and attitudes can be explored in the safety of a play-acting situation. J. M. Sacks (in Rabin & Rosenbaum, 1976) provides us with a concise description of a psychodrama session:

The psychodrama group meets in a small theater-like room. The therapist, called the director, begins with a "warm up" or a structuring of the session to prepare the members for action. In the second phase of the session, the dramatic production, a protagonist is selected who enacts relevant scenes from his past, present, or future. He may take his own role or roles of other people. "Auxiliary egos" play the complementary roles and may either be group members or trained professionals. They may play roles opposite the protagonist or accompany him as his extension or "double." In the "mirror" technique the protagonist watches the auxiliaries play out scenes from his life. The director frequently calls for a "role reversal" in which the protagonist and antagonist change their positions to experience the scene from the other's point of view. During the third and final phase a general discussion is held in the "light of the drama" (p. 60).

Through role reversal and role-playing techniques, the group member, or protagonist, as he or she is called, may gain greater self-awareness, explore previously hidden conflicts, and engage in new and experimental behaviors under the guidance of the "director." The audience, in turn, may furnish valuable feedback and make observations regarding the "performance" that may add to the impact of the "production."

Mintz (1970) offers the following example of an "alter ego" technique as might be used in a psychodrama group:

Susan, a young woman married to Don, a medical student, wishes him to accept her father's help during their financially difficult years. They discuss the problem, reverse roles, then interact with another participant who impersonates the father and expresses feelings of hatred and rejection. After the situation has been played out on a realistic level, several group members volunteer to function as what Moreno has termed "alter egos," speaking for the secret thoughts and feelings of one of the participants as they guess them to be. The role playing proceeds:

Susan: Why shouldn't I have a comfortable way to live? Daddy wants to help us and he certainly can afford it.

Susan's alter ego (standing behind her): You're just angry because daddy's rich and can afford to give me the things you can't. Why I believe you're jealous.

Don: You're my wife and I want to support you. It wouldn't hurt for you to live economically for a few years.

Don's alter ego (standing behind him): I feel castrated by you and your father.

Father: It hurts my feelings you won't let me help you.

Father's alter ego: I want to prove I'm a better man than that young fellow who's my son-in-law!

The alter ego technique, as used in this episode, brought into the open what Don and Susan believed to be one another's underlying attitudes and Don's suspicions about the concealed attitude of his father-in-law. It is impossible to see the consequences of an alter ego psychodrama. In this case, once Don's anxiety and suspicions had been ventilated, he decided that they were not justified, and a compromise was reached which satisfied both wife and husband (p. 63–64).

Psychodrama continues to be practiced by therapists in the United States and abroad, but the techniques of role playing and role reversal have been more widely adopted by behavior therapists in assertiveness training and by gestalt therapists and leaders of encounter groups who stress emotional expressiveness as a pathway to personal growth. Psychodrama rarely makes use of the group as a whole. Instead, it focuses attention on the drama centering around an individual, thereby deemphasizing interpersonal interactions within the group.

T-Groups

A more contemporary development in group methods is the T-group (T stands for training). T-groups were stimulated by the efforts of Kurt Lewin, a scientist who believed that human behavior could be changed by working with individuals in groups to improve problem-solving skills and the quality of interpersonal relationships. At the request of the Connecticut Interracial Commission, Lewin and his colleagues, Leland Bradford, Kenneth Benne, and Ronald Lippit, conducted a workshop to reduce racial tensions. The workshop stressed group training in human relations and was viewed by the participants as an extremely positive experience. Impressed by the success of group methods in reducing intergroup tensions, Lewin's colleagues established the National Training Laboratores (NTL) after his death in 1946. NTL became a center for human relations training. The T-group developed as an outgrowth of research in group dynamics at NTL and soon became an accepted instrument for teaching interpersonal interaction skills. Within several years hundreds of people received human relations training through workshops conducted by NTL staff and T-groups began to be conducted in industry and in the community. Executives received training in social skills, businesspeople were trained in leadership and decision-making skills, and workers in industry and in the community were urged to discuss problems encountered in their work, explore possible alternatives, and ponder the consequences of the alternatives presented.

Buchanan (1964) describes the T-group as follows:

Training approaches meriting the name laboratory (or T-group) utilize: (1) face-to-face, largely unstructured groups as a primary vehicle for learning; (2) planned activities involving interaction between individuals and/or between groups; (3) systematic and frequent feedback and analysis of information regarding what happened in the here and now and what effect it had; (4) dilemmas or problems for which "odd ways" of behaving for most of the participants do not provide effective courses of action (and thus for which innovative or "search" behavior is required); and (5) generalization, or reformulation of concepts and values based upon the analysis of direct experience (p. 216).

The group usually consists of 8 to 16 members and a leader or trainer. The participants meet for varying time periods in the "laboratory," at each others' homes, or at a resort; the important aspect of the environment is that it is away from their workday world and everyday stresses. The interaction process in each group is varied with its purpose; the emotional depths probed range in a continuum that extends from the problem-solving executive group in the shallow end to the intensive, highly charged groups usually referred to as *encounter groups*, which we will discuss next.

Encounter Groups

The encounter group emerged from attempts to expand the range of the T–group's functions and goals to include increasing the individual's capacity for enriched experience and personal improvement. Stoller has noted that the goals of encounter groups are "growth and change, new behavioral directions, the realization of potential, heightened self-awareness, and a richer perception of one's circumstances as well as the circumstances of others" (p. 3). Thus in encounter groups, the emphasis is shifted away from learning about social behavior in groups to learning about oneself (Korchin, 1976). Encounter groups are seen by their proponents as having universal applicability. Unlike traditional group psychotherapy, which implies psychological disturbance and patient status, encounter groups are considered by many to be relevant to normal personalities who want to "grow, change, and develop" (Lieberman, 1975, p. 440).

Encounter groups tend to stress emotional aspects of individual functioning and utilize techniques to amplify feelings. A gamut of techniques, including body awareness, fantasy, dream analysis, and psychodrama, may be used. Nonetheless, the relationships that develop in the group and cognitive learning are also essential to self-exploration and change.

"In the city this would be called a group therapy session and it would be costing us fifteen bucks apiece." (From *The Wall Street Journal,* with permission of Cartoon Features Syndicate.)

SOME ENCOUNTER GROUP EXERCISES

Many encounter groups use structured group exercises, especially in the early stages of the group. Structured exercises may be used to ease the entry of individuals into the group, to facilitate communication, to increase feedback among group members, and to amplify and intensify feelings. It is important to emphasize that structured group exercises are not really an end in themselves. This point is nicely illustrated by what Jerrold Shapiro has called *the golden rule of structured experiences:* "It is far less important to complete the exercise than to deal with whatever behaviors and feelings are generated by the exercise or the suggestion of the exercise" (1978, p. 193). Thus structured exercises are perhaps best thought of as catalysts that help to initiate the processes considered to be of great importance in encounter groups. Here are a number of structured group exercises which, Shapiro suggests, are appropriate for encounter-type groups.

1. Introductory Exercises
   a. Leader: Let's start by giving our names and saying briefly why we're here. Please share, if you'd like, what you hope to get out of this group and what you fear from this group.
   b. Leader: Please choose a name you'd like to be called during this group. It can be a real name or something you've always wanted to be called. Don't tell why you've chosen this name or whether it's your real name or not. Write the name on a 4 by 6 card and put the card in front of you.
   c. Each person gives a first name and a personality descriptive adjective or adverb beginning with the same letter, such as "Sexy Sadie," or "Angry Arnie." Each person will then say the names and adjectives of each preceding individual, in reverse order. For example, "I'm 'Good Guy,' and this is 'Sexy Sadie,' and this is 'Horrible Harmon,' and so on," Introductions end when the first person gives the names of all others.
   d. Leader: Since it's easier to begin talking to one person than a group of people, please choose one partner. Somebody here you don't know or someone you would like to get to know better. (*When everyone has paired off, the leader continues.*) Okay, now decide who will talk first and who will talk second. The person who will talk second is to interview, try to get to know the person in a personal way, not just status or occupation but values, attitudes, feelings, likes, dislikes, and so on. When this is done, you'll be asked to introduce your partner to the group.
2. A Trust Exercise: The blind walk
   Leader: This exercise is called a blind walk. Each person should choose a partner. After you have chosen a partner, you will be blindfolded. Place

the blindfold across the eyes of one person. From now on there should be no verbal communication until the exercise is completed. Your task is to lead the blindfolded person around, giving him as full a sensory experience as you can, safely. Each person will lead for 20 minutes. Everyone should be back in this room in 40 minutes and we'll discuss this experience.

3. Exchanging Feedback: The truth pillow
Leader: As a way of increasing our communication I'd like to recommend this exercise (*picking up a pillow.*) This pillow will have special qualities for awhile. If someone throws this pillow to you, you're required to give that person positive and negative feedback. Say something you like and something you don't like about that person in this group. For example, if I were to throw this to Tom, he would give me feedback. Then Tom could throw it to whomever he wanted to receive feedback from. Okay, let's begin (*throwing it to a member*) (adapted from Shapiro, 1978, p. 196–205).

Carl Rogers (1970) acknowledges the great diversity in encounter groups yet speculates that certain "practical hypotheses" tend to be shared by groups with widely divergent activities and emphases. Here is Rogers' attempt to formulate one such set of "practical hypotheses" that account for basic aspects of group experience:

1. A facilitator can develop, in a group which meets intensively, a psychological climate of safety in which freedom of expression and reduction of defensiveness gradually occur.

2. In such a psychological climate many of the immediate feeling reactions of each member toward others, and of each member toward himself, tend to be expressed.

3. A climate of mutual trust develops out of this mutual freedom to express real feelings, positive and negative. Each member moves toward greater acceptance of his total being—emotional, intellectual, and physical—as it *is,* including its potential.

4. With individuals less inhibited by defensive rigidity, the possibility of change in personal attitudes and behavior, in professional methods, in administrative procedures and relationships, becomes less threatening.

5. With the reduction of defensive rigidity, individuals can hear each other, can learn from each other, to a greater extent.

6. There is a development of feedback from one person to another, such that each individual learns how he appears to others and what impact he has in interpersonal relationships.

7. With this greater freedom and improved communication, new ideas, new concepts, new directions emerge. Innovation can become a desirable rather than a threatening possibility.

8. These learnings in the group experience tend to carry over, temporarily or more permanently, into the relationships with spouse, children, students, subordinates, peers, and even superiors following the group experience.

Rogers' description conveys the optimism of the human potential movement regarding the ability of the group member to exchange authentic responses for more rigid, stereo-typed behavior, given the appropriate facilitative conditions. In addition, we can clearly see the dynamic interplay of the curative factors Yalom believes are operative in all groups. Perhaps you noted that the high level of cohesiveness that can be achieved in encounter groups seems to promote a sense of universality and hope, and it stimulates interpersonal learning, catharsis, and exchange of information.

Marathon Groups

The marathon group is a kind of extended one-session, encounter-type group developed by H. Stoller and George Bach. Stoller experimented with marathon groups for the first time in 1963 with a group of seriously disturbed, psychotic patients. Since then, the technique has been used with individuals of varying degrees of adjustment, including "normals." The group is planned to continue for 24 to 30 hours, or longer. It assumes that participants are capable of tolerating undiluted intense experience and do not require carefully measured exposure to psychotherapy. Virtually no limits are placed on the intensity of emotional experience in such groups.

In a marathon group, the 10 to 15 participants are requested to react to each other immediately and spontaneously at all times. Feedback from others informs the person of the nature of the impact he or she has on the group. Labels such as doctor or lawyer are avoided, so that individuals may not fall back on a particular role for security, and are forced to build their security from their participation in the group. The group is instructed to remain together for the duration of the session, and psychological jargon is not permitted. The goal of interactions is not to be understood but to be reacted to.

Schwartz & Schwartz (1969) believe that the marathon group offers a uniquely effective emotional experience for the following reasons: (1) there is intensity of participation as each individual reveals his or her own life drama and, in the presence of the group, gives up long-held defenses. Tolerance for anxiety increases with the mounting cumulative emotionality expressed in the group and eventually permits the expression of intense feelings such as love, grief, and despair; (2) deprived of their usual environment where roles and lifestyles are fixed, the participants are less apt to rely upon stereotyped reactions and habitual defenses. Thus their behavior becomes more flexible and open to change; (3) fatigue, constantly growing toward the end of the marathon period, becomes a disinhibitory factor, breaking down resistance and leading to authentic, spontaneous responses; and (4) toward the end of the marathon, with the knowledge that this experience will soon be terminated, there is an urgency to "get from the marathon what the participants came for" and a "release of emotion seldom seen in any other setting."

Evaluation of Group Therapy

After surveying a number of divergent group approaches, we now come to the final question posed at the beginning of the chapter: Does group therapy work? Recent reviews of the group therapy literature (Bednar & Kaul, 1978; Coché & Dies, 1982; Dies, 1979) suggest that the answer to this question is a qualified yes. The most general conclusion that can be distilled from the literature is that group therapy seems to help people to attain more positive and perhaps healthier evaluations of themselves and others than no treatment or placebo treatments. The importance of this potential treatment gain should not be underestimated: Much human suffering is associated with an overly punitive view of oneself and a negative perception of others. In some circumstances group therapies have been found to be more effective than other psychological treatments with which they have been compared.

It is premature, however, to conclude that group therapy is generally superior to individual therapy. Much more research is needed to determine the extent to which self-reported positive changes in self-concept and personality are reflected in actual behavioral changes outside the group setting. Coché and Dies (1982) have recently drawn attention to the pressing need for well-designed studies conducted in clinical settings with ongoing groups. More research is also needed to evaluate the relationship between the various curative factors we have discussed and the outcome of various group treatments.

Bednar and Kaul (1978) caution against accepting the conclusion that group therapy "works" without also heeding the following qualification: Not all groups have uniformly positive and beneficial results. This observation appears to be warranted. Data provided by Lieberman, Yalom, and Miles (1973) regarding the experiences of over 200 Stanford University students who participated in 10 different types of group therapy (psychodrama; gestalt therapy, NTL–T–group, psychoanalytically oriented groups, etc.) suggests that very disparate reactions may be elicited by group therapy. At least in terms of the subjects' self-report of attitudes, self-concepts, and social values, a high degree of gains were experienced by a third of the group participants.

But just as groups apparently stimulated positive changes in some individuals, in others, negative, and even harmful effects were experienced as a result of their group participation. Eight percent of the participants

were considered to be "psychiatric casualties." Their very negative reactions ranged from psychotic episodes to experiences of great discomfort and distress. Clearly negative but less serious problems and experiences were reported by another 11 percent of the sample studied. Thus participants in group therapy do not uniformly experience positive benefits from their group experience.

Lieberman and his colleagues completed a more fine-grained analysis of the experiences of group members and discovered that the style of the group leader and the group atmosphere he or she created were related to the experience of the group members. Casualties tended to occur in groups where leaders displayed an attacking, confronting, "energizing" style in which strong pressures were exerted on members to express emotions and to make intimate, highly personal self-disclosures. The leaders who were most successful rewarded caring in the group and provided students with a cognitive framework for change, often translating feelings and experiences into ideas for the members of the group. Thus Lieberman and his colleagues found that it was not the type of group so much as the leadership style that accounted for differences in outcome.

Research like that of Lieberman and his colleagues emphasizes the need for an even greater understanding of the processes that lead to constructive change in group therapy. We are only beginning to learn about what types of people are likely to make gains in divergent groups and much more research is needed to answer this important question. Prescreening of participants for serious disturbances seems to be indicated before vulnerable personalities are exposed to excessively stressful interpersonal situations. But with an adequately screened clientele and with trained and competent leaders, groups may be a remarkably effective means of maximizing services to a wide variety of people in need of help.

FAMILY THERAPY

Consider for a moment, Block and LaPerrière's (1973) definition of family therapy as

> Face to face psychotherapy of a natural system, natural in contrast to a group formed specifically for the purposes of therapy. The therapist or a team of therapists, directly engages the family, or some substantial elements of the family, of the index patient. . . . What unites all family therapists is the view that change, which is significant to the psychotherapeutic endeavor, takes place in the family system. With this unifying thread, they may vary considerably as to the size of the elements of the family they engage, the techniques they employ, and the theory to which they adhere (p. 1).

As you may have noted, unlike practitioners of group psychotherapy, family therapists strive to change problem behavior in the system in which it "naturally" occurs—the family system. Since family therapists see most problems as having their roots in a dysfunctional family system, it is not surprising that they believe that treatment must focus on the family context out of which the problems arise. Thus in family therapy, the patient—the focus of treatment—is the family unit itself. In order to create change in the family system and thereby in the individual, family therapists often focus on communication and patterns of interaction among family members.

There are, however, numerous theoretical and clinical approaches to family therapy. Some family practitioners adapt psychoanalytic or object relations theories (e.g., Bowlby, 1969; Guntrip. 1969) to understanding and treating family dysfunction. Robin Skynner (1981), for example, believes that

Family therapy can be an opportunity for new openness among family members. (Tom Ballard/EKM-Nepenthe)

parents' unresolved conflicts in their own development may create stress and tension in a family. Such conflicts may be reflected in symptoms expressed by a family member. For example, consider the case of a father who, as a child, unsuccessfully tried to live up to the impossibly high standards of his harsh, demanding, and hypercritical father. Still intent on "proving himself" in adulthood, he assumes a hard-driving, success-oriented, and competitive stance to life. Unconsciously perceiving his own son as an extension of himself, he attempts to drive and push him to excel (just as his father did). As a way of carving out his own identity, the son begins to rebel and gains a reputation at school as a "classic underachiever." The son's behavior, in turn, rekindles the conflicts his father experienced as a child; the father pushes even harder, further inflaming the situation and eventually embroiling the entire family in conflict.

Behavioral approaches have also been used with whole families. When they are, the approach is very different from the one described above. They focus less on the childhood origins of family conflict and the transmission of conflicts across generations than on the assessment and treatment of carefully defined, specific problems. Many behavior family therapists gear their efforts toward teaching parents effective child-management techniques (Patterson, 1971) or training marital partners in more productive communication strategies (Gottman, 1979) to benefit the family as a whole. Behavioral family therapists, then, are more likely to work with the marital unit than are therapists from other schools of family therapy.

Behavior therapists carefully assess the marital relationship or family system, tailor their treatment programs to alleviate concrete problems or negative relationship patterns, strive to develop ways of increasing positive behaviors, and teach and supervise interaction skills. Therapy frequently involves ongoing monitoring of behaviors that are the target of change and contingency contracting in which one spouse agrees to do something depending on the behavior of the other spouse. An example might be, "I will stay with our daughter tonight if you will go shopping tomorrow" (Foster & Gurman, 1985).

In the next section we will present a very popular and mainstream treatment approach termed *conjoint family therapy*, which was developed by Virginia Satir (1964). Satir's approach emphasizes modifying communication and interaction patterns within the family to bring about change. We have chosen to present Satir's approach because we believe that it has been more influential than any other in the burgeoning field of family therapy.

Satir's Conjoint Family Therapy

Before therapy is initiated, the conjoint family therapist needs to know something about the family members' experience of the problem and who feels hurt or threatened on account of the problem. The therapist will learn something about the family's expectations about therapy and will share with the family his or her guiding belief: The problems or symptoms of any family members involve and concern the whole family (Sorrells & Ford, 1969).

Therapy usually begins with an evaluation of the communication patterns and interactions among family members. The therapist might be interested in such things as how messages are given, received, and verified; how direct, specific, and clear the family communications are; and finally, how feedback is given and received by different family members. The therapist might also learn something about the self-concepts of the family members by observing the way in which the family makes decisions and resolves or fails to resolve differences, as well as by the way members of the family express their uniqueness. One way in which the therapist develops hypotheses regarding communication processes and the family rules governing interactions is through the use of a structured interview.

The structured interview consists of a set of tasks that provide an opportunity for the therapist to learn more about how the family displays many of its rules and communication patterns. Sorrells and Ford (1969) provide the following example of a structured interview utilized by Virginia Satir.

1. "What is the main problem in your family at this point in time?" This question is asked to each family member individually and is then posed as a matter for family discussion.

2. "Plan something that you could do together," This task is given to the whole family and to various segments of the family, such as parents alone, children alone, males, etc.

3. The marital couple is asked, "How did you two, out of all the people in the world, get together?"

4. The parents are given the proverb, "A rolling stone gathers no moss." They are asked to discuss the proverb, to come to some conclusion about its meaning, and then to teach the proverb to the children.

5. Main fault, main asset. Each person in the family is asked to write on a card the main fault, as he sees it, of the person on his left. The members are arranged in the order of husband, wife, and then children in descending chronological order. The therapist then reads the cards, changing the wording to preserve anonymity. Each person is asked to vote for whom he or she thinks each item applies to most in the family. Each member is then asked to specify what he or she thinks is his or her own main fault.

6. Each person is asked, "Who's in charge of this family?"

7. Similarities and differences.
   a. Each parent is asked which child he thinks is most like himself or herself and which child is most like the spouse.
   b. Each child is asked which parent he perceives himself or herself as being most like. After making this choice, the child is then asked how he or she is like the other parent and how he or she is different from the parent chosen.
   c. Both spouses are asked how they are alike and how they are different (from each other).

8. A relatively unstructured overview of the meeting completes the format.

Most therapists are interested in finding out how the interview was experienced by all the family members. In addition, the therapist may wish to draw attention to parts of the interview that seemed significant for future work and to ensure that each member leaves the interview with a feeling of "completed transactions" (i.e., that the therapist heard and understood what was said).

Although one family member may be singled out as the "identified patient" with *the* problem, the real source of difficulties lies in the dysfunctional ways in which family members communicate and relate to one another. The goals of family therapy, then, relate to removing the barriers to effective, meaningful communication among family members. Sorrells and Ford (1969) have specified the following goals of family therapy that are closely aligned with Satir's therapeutic approach:

1. That the family be able to communicate with clarity, specificity, directness, and congruence.

2. That the family adopt and manifest the value of completed transactions so that each member is always sure that he or she is heard, seen, and understood.

3. That each member be able to give feedback to other family members and accept feedback about himself or herself without distortion, denial, or disqualification.

4. That the family value the unique contribution of each individual member.

5. That the family strive to make decisions that provide for the needs and wants of each individual affected.

6. That the family use the ways in which individuals differ as a means for growth rather than as a barrier to understanding.

These goals are accomplished by first creating a "safe" therapeutic atmosphere in which each person is willing to take risks and share intimate feelings. The therapist models and encourages appropriate communication in his or her own interactions with family members. In each session an effort is made to help each family member to feel included and valued. The therapist stresses the value of feedback and teaches clients that feedback can be given or received as a "gift" rather than as an assault. Clients are discouraged from assigning blame to others, and family members are asked to avoid use of words like *always* or *never*. Each family member may be asked to make a commitment to believing in the possibility of change on the part of the whole family or any individual member (Sorrells & Ford, 1969).

When family members are secure about not being judged negatively by others in the group, the therapist attempts to foster insight into the patterns of words and actions that tend to inhibit communication and problem resolution. Once the patterns are made clear, the therapist and family members must arrive at some agreements about how family members would prefer to be dealt with, how problem solving might take place with minimum conflict, and how family members will continue to practice any new behaviors or alternatives that have been defined in the family itself (McPeak, 1979).

Structured Family Therapy

Before we leave the topic of family therapy, let us briefly consider another treatment approach: *structured family therapy* (Minuchin, 1974). In their efforts to help a troubled family, structured family therapists alter the way in which relationships and interactions among family members are structured and organized. In contrast with the less active, communications-oriented conjoint family therapist, the structured family therapist actively immerses himself in the everyday activities of the family to make planned changes in the way family members interact with each other. Rossman, Minuchin, and Liebman (1975) provide an example:

> Eating lunch with the family provides exceptional opportunities to observe family members' transactions around eating and to make on-the-spot interventions to change the patterning of these interactions. This session also serves broader diagnostic purposes, since structural and dysfunctional characteristics of the family are more readily apparent in this context (p. 846).

The structured family therapy approach is further illustrated by Aponte and Hoffman's (1973) successful treatment of a 14-year-old girl who refused to eat. The therapists first carefully observed the relationships and communications patterns of the family. They noted that the girl, Laura, was able to successfully compete for her father's attention by refusing to eat. By not eating, Laura was able to exercise considerable power in the family. The goal of the therapists was to help Laura and the rest of the family members to express their needs and wants in a straightforward manner. And eventually Laura was able to express in words the message that her refusal to eat conveyed indirectly. When Laura was better able to verbalize her wants and needs directly, she no longer resorted to refusing to eat to attain the affection she desired.

Evaluation of Family Therapy

As our brief presentation of family therapy suggests, there is no "one" family therapy. If the present status of family therapy is any indication of what is to come, then there is reason for optimism. Foster and Gurman (1985) have recently summarized what is known about the effectiveness of family therapy. First, family therapy has generally been demonstrated to be more effective than no treatment. Second, for problems clearly associated with dysfunctional interactions, family therapy is generally more effective than individual (child or adult) treatment. Third, it seems to make little difference whether family therapy is relatively brief (up to 20 sessions) or long-term. Fourth, outcome appears to be enhanced by including the father and other family members in the treatment. And finally, the therapist's relationship skills: warmth, use of humor, and the ability to see connections between the family's feelings and behavior are linked with successful treatment. These positively toned conclusions are consistent with the findings of an earlier review: "Family therapy appears to be at least as effective and possibly more effective than individual therapy for a wide variety of problems, both with apparent 'individual' difficulties and more obvious family conflicts" (p. 883).

One of the challenges of the future will be to not only further document the effectiveness of family therapy but also to understand why family therapy works. In order to meet this challenge, it will be important to learn more about the interaction among personal, interpersonal, and family system aspects of family interaction and relate these factors to treatment outcome. The future of family therapy will likely witness the increasing integration and refinement of different theories and clinical practices (Foster & Gurman, 1985).

NEW WAYS OF HELPING: MENTAL HEALTH AND THE COMMUNITY

If you were to imagine the treatment of an emotionally disturbed person, you would most likely think of a person talking with a mental health professional. We all have a culturally determined image of how abnormal behavior should be treated. Perhaps, if you know a bit more than the average person, you are likely also to think that treatment may include the administration of tranquilizers or that it may also occur in group psychotherapy or in some other setting. It has certainly not always been this way.

Think back for a moment to our discussion of the history of abnormal behavior in Chapter 1. There we related how people displaying odd or disturbed behavior were once treated as witches or common criminals and often unceremoniously thrown into dungeons. Many people mark the beginning of the "first revolution in mental health" from the time in 1792 when Pinel broke the chains on the inmates in the Paris hospital called the Bicêtre as a symbolic act of humanitarian reform.

Certainly the development of the psychological point of view by Sigmund Freud, at the turn of this century and throughout the beginning of the 20th century, marks a "second revolution" in the field of mental health. Freud's brilliant insights into the nature of psychological dynamics and his development of a treatment technology, psychoanalysis, truly revolutionized our thinking about the nature and treatment of abnormal behavior.

In fact, we are still living, to some degree at least, with the remants of that second revolution in the field of mental health. Most people still think that individual problems in living and various forms of abnormal behavior are best dealt with over long periods of time in intensive individual psychological treatment. The analyst's couch has replaced the mental hospital in the public mind as the most appropriate way of dealing with abnormal behavior. Freud's views have dominated during most of the 20th century. Still, treatment for human distress on the analyst's couch has been only available for those with the economic means to buy it. There has been no real way for the poor or for minority groups to receive the benefits of the second mental health revolution.

But in 1946 the National Institute of Mental Health was formed and the Public Mental Health Act was instituted. This signified the beginning of an effort in the United States to serve every citizen. Also, by the middle of the 1950s, the major tranquilizers had come into use and mental hsopitals had begun to change as a result. It was then possible to reduce the size of the staff and to bring psychotic symptoms under control. Soon patients began to be released more quickly from the hospital and a "revolving door" phenomenon began to develop. People leaving the mental hospital, with their symptoms under temporary control, soon found themselves back in a community that was not necessarily ready to receive them. So new crises would ensue and many of these people found themselves reentering the mental hospital. By 1961 a Joint Commission on Mental Health and Mental Illness was instituted to investigate these problems and to think systematically about how we could produce a third revolution in mental health in this country.

A ground-breaking book by Gurin, Veroff, and Feld entitled *Americans View Their Mental Health* (1960) documented for the first time the degree to which most of us in this country saw persons suffering from mental illness as stigmatized people. The knowledge that someone was suffering from psychological problems was often hidden, an embarrassment to the sufferer. Gurin, Veroff, and Feld's results showed us that there existed natural helpers in the community, people who were able, through their individual skills and dedication, to help others even though they did not possess conventional psychiatric degrees. These helpers were the clergy, bartenders, and even hairdressers. They were people who, through their day-to-day sympathetic contacts with others, often provided help for those who were not financially privileged enough or inclined to hire a therapist.

The results of the studies of the Joint Commission on Mental Illness and Mental Health included recommendations for (1) increased emergency care for people suffering from psychological crises, (2) improved care for chronic mental patients, (3) expanded care in the community for people who had been discharged from mental hospitals, and (4) mental health education for the public so that people who were suffering from psychological difficulties would be better understood. Then in 1963 President John F. Kennedy instituted the Community Mental Health Center Act, a bold new approach to the development of community mental centers throughout the country.

These developments have been called the third revolution in mental health. But as we pointed out earlier, history can be written in such a way as to lead us to believe that every new development is a victory in the march of progress. A more judicious and thoughtful view of the recent history of mental health care is one that recognizes the third revolution as a real change in our orientation to treatment, but whether it reflects progress only time and careful research will tell (Price & Smith, 1983).

Community Mental Health Today

In the remainder of this chapter we will discuss some of the innovative treatment practices associated with community mental health today. For the moment, however, we will discuss some of the major dimensions of the third revolution in mental health. Bloom (1977) suggests a number of characteristics of the community health movement. Let us consider some of them briefly.

First, community mental health today emphasizes practice in the community. The underlying premise is that the community itself should be responsible for the mental health of its own citizens. One consequence of this goal has been a movement toward deinstitutionalization. As we will see, attempts are being made to provide a new life in the community for patients who have spent many years in public mental hospitals. These programs raise a variety of complex and difficult questions. How would you yourself feel living next to a person who had just been discharged from a mental hospital? Would you be willing to volunteer to help provide community-based programs for such people?

A second emphasis of the community mental health movement is a focus on *total populations* rather than individuals. Thus the "client," as Denner and Price (1973) note, is no longer the individual, or even a family unit, but entire communities and populations of people. This is an entirely new way for individually oriented psychologists to think about their work and it will be many years before this becomes a natural part of our thinking.

Another important characteristic of community mental health today is an emphasis on prevention rather than treatment. The goal is to reduce the incidence of disturbed behavior rather than merely to treat new cases. Some innovative programs are already under way to help populations who are at risk for the development of a variety of psychological disorders. Widows suffering from depression are being helped by other widows. Programs to teach children interpersonal problem-solving skills are being developed in school systems. We will return to discuss prevention later in this chapter.

Yet another important characteristic of the community mental health movement is an emphasis on *indirect rather than direct services*. Many mental health professionals have knowledge that they can provide to other community helpers, including teachers, members of the clergy, public health nurses, and others. These people see far more of the public than do most psychologists or psychiatrists. They can then use the mental health knowledge and skills provided by the mental health professional to enhance their own effectiveness. Thus by "helping the helpers" the mental health professional can produce a "multiplier effect" and expand his or her own impact. For example, members of the police who often find themselves in the middle of psychological emergencies when they intervene in a family crisis can be trained to intervene more effectively in family disputes. It has already been shown that such training programs delivered by mental health professionals to the police can reduce the risk of injury to the police and improve the quality of service to disturbed families (Bard, 1970).

Community mental health also seeks to develop innovative clinical strategies. Rather than thinking about long-term psychotherapy as the single method of choice, crisis intervention services can be developed, and hot lines, call-in services, and suicide prevention lines are being offered to whole new populations within a community.

Finding new sources of person power to deliver mental health services is another goal. As Albee (1968) has noted, there will never be enough professionals trained to meet the mental health needs of people in the community. As our population continues to increase, the number of mental problems will certainly increase as well. We must begin to think about new populations of people who are able to deliver mental health services.

This suicide prevention center is providing a training seminar to teach volunteers to evaluate the nature of callers' problems, to assess the seriousness of a suicide threat, and to develop a plan of action while still on the phone with the caller. Such efforts are part of the community mental health movement's attempt to find new sources of nonprofessional help in the community. (Courtesy of San Francisco Suicide Prevention, Inc.)

They may be housewives who, in many cases, can work effectively in the delivery of certain kinds of treatment. They may be volunteers who work in community mental health centers. They may be college students serving as peer counselors to other students, in their own university, who are finding it difficult to adjust to the demands of university life.

Finally, community mental health research is oriented to identifying sources of stress within the community. Unemployment, for example, can be a source of stress with major mental health implications. The community mental health movement is oriented to identifying these sources of stress and developing methods of helping people cope with them.

This is a new way to think about mental health in the community. As an approach to the provision of mental health services, it deserves our serious and thoughtful examination. We will consider some examples in more detail in the remainder of this chapter. And we will also consider evidence for the effectiveness of these new approaches. Innovations should always be looked at with a critical eye. The innovations of yesterday, such as the mental hospital, quickly become the institution that we wish to reform tomorrow.

From Mental Hospital to Community

You will recall that in the middle of the 19th century asylums began to be built all over the United States. As Rothman (1971) observed, these new asylums were viewed as sanctuaries from the chaos and uncertainty of a social environment that was assumed to be the major cause of pyschological difficulties.

The first asylums were relatively orderly and supportive institutions in which care for the severely disturbed could be obtained. But by the end of the 19th century, mental hospitals began to take on a new function. People who were socially or intellectually disabled for a wide variety of reasons began to be placed in mental hospitals. The hospitals became crowded and the quality of care deteriorated. Thus by the beginning of the 20th century, the well-ordered asylum of the Jacksonian era had become an institution in which conditions of crowding, poor treatment, and even maltreatment predominated. Most large public mental hospitals had few rehabilitative programs and little resembled the early asylums of the Jacksonian era.

In fact, during this period, as Price and Denner (1973) have noted, people were often removed from their community for various forms of odd behavior and committed to mental institutions where they received little help. If, indeed, they were released, they often found themselves rejected and stigmatized in the community. Mental hospitals began to receive substantial criticism at this time and studies by the Joint Commission on Mental Illness and Mental Health (1961) reinforced the public concern about the quality of care in mental institutions.

Experiments in Community Living. Concern with the quality of treatment in hospitals and a strong national policy shift toward "deinstitutionalization" has, in recent years, led to increased efforts to return residents of mental hospitals to the community.

Earlier, in discussing the treatment of schizophrenia, we described an important demonstration project conducted by Paul and his colleagues (Paul & Lentz, 1978). Paul's behaviorally oriented program was explicitly designed to help chronic schizophrenic patients learn living skills that would allow them to function relatively independently in the community.

Another important innovation that demonstrated that mental patients can be taught to live effectively in the community is that of Fairweather and his colleagues (Fairweather, 1964; Fairweather, Sanders, Maynard, & Cressler, 1969). These researchers conducted a series of carefully designed field experiments in which they hoped to demonstrate that small groups of severely disturbed mental paitents could live in the community in small communal living situations. Fairweather later called these houses *lodges*. Hospitalized patients were first taught skills in group decision making and problem solving. When Fairweather compared the group that received this training with groups that were treated in more conventional ways, it was shown that Fairweather's groups could be discharged more readily from the hospital with their newly found social skills. Fairweather then moved his experimental group to a lodge within the community, where group members began to cope with their new community role. They received training in jobs as gardeners and janitors and became relatively self-sufficient.

One of the outstanding qualities of Fairweather's innovation is that it is far more than a demonstration project. Throughout the development of Fairweather's program, he carefully compared the lodge innovation with appropriate control groups so that the relative effectiveness of the lodge could actually be compared with more conventional approaches to treatment. Fairweather did not feel that placement in the community was necessarily a "good in itself." Results had to be demonstrated.

In this initial set of studies, Fairweather was able to demonstrate that the lodge group's ability to avoid rehospitalization was substantially greater than that of a control group. The control group used outpatient clinics and other typically available community resources.

The lodge group's time spent in the community rather than back in the hospital over a 40-month period was between 80 percent and 100 percent, whereas the control group's median time in the community was only 20 percent. Similarly, the lodge group members were employed for much larger proportions of the time than were the control group.

Since these early demonstrations by Fairweather and his colleagues, Fairweather has attempted to disseminate his lodge model throughout the country as a supplement to public mental hospital treatment. Although a relatively small proportion of public mental hospitals have been receptive to the development of Fairweather's lodges, those that have been receptive have shown relatively good success in maintaining patients in the community.

Another similar demonstration project is called Training in Community Living (Stein & Test, 1985; Fields, 1978), a program developed by the Mendota Mental Health Institute in Madison, Wisconsin, The orientation of the staff in the Training in Community Living Program is to help patients "make it" in the community. Staff go grocery shopping with patients, teach them how to cook or do laundry, find them a place to live, and talk to clerks, landlords, employers, and police to prepare the way for a community living situation for people who have been hospitalized sometimes for as much as 20 to 30 years. The program includes the opportunity for patients to return to the hospital if it is needed.

In the past, research has shown that community treatment for patients has produced an extremely high drop-out rate (Fields, 1978). This so-called "revolving door" phenomenon was a major concern in the late 60s and early 70s when more and more patients were moved into the community. However, an active support system for patients in the community of the sort developed by the Training in Community Living Program can make a substantial difference.

Research on this program began with a random sample of patients from Mendota State Hospital who, although they were seen as needing hospital care, were placed directly in the community. Staff worked with these patients developing their coping skills and supported them. At the end of the five months the patients were much more successful in the community than a comparable control group that did not receive the skill training and support. However, once the support program was withdrawn, many of these patients returned to the hospital. Continuing support in the community is necessary for many of these patients. The results of a second larger study in which community support was sustained for 14 months and in which patients were carefully linked with community agencies, produced several important findings. At the end of a year the TCL group had spent very little time in institutions as compared with control groups, and they were significantly better adjusted to their homes in the community. In terms of employment and social relationships, they also experienced greater satisfaction with their lives than did the control group. In addition, when one compares the TCL project with that of the hospitalized group, there is little difference in cost of care.

As Fields (1978) notes, the Training in Community Living project is really a "floating hospital ward." In the project, staff are highly motivated to work hard to retain patients in the community. But as with all demonstration projects designed to show that such services actually can be provided, we must ask whether enough commitment and skill and resources can be brought to bear to repeat the Training in Community Living Program on a large scale throughout the country.

Two Images of Deinstitutionalization: "Dumping" or Community Support? Studies like those of Fairweather (1964) and the TCL project clearly indicate that with enough resources and effort even chronically institutionalized mental patients can be supported in the community. From examining these studies alone we might be inclined to conclude that our efforts at deinstitutionalization have been a success. But how widespread are the sorts of projects that we just described?

Another, much less optimistic perspective has been offered by Koenig (1978). He notes that nearly 40,000 poor chronic mental patients have been "dumped" in New York City alone. Patients who have been dependent on life in a mental hospital for as much as 20 years have been placed in single-room occupancy hotels, where they receive little or no care, live on public assistance funds, and

Social workers do their best to help deinstitutionalized patients with their problems in living, but sometimes there's not enough help to go around. (© Bob Adelman)

only occasionally receive the support of one overworked social worker (Bassuk 1984).

Which image is true? It is fair to say that so far projects like the Training in Community Living project are the exception rather than the rule. The fact is that most patients discharged from mental hospitals will not find themselves with a rich array of community supports (Price & Smith, 1983).

In fact, Scull (1977) argues that the "decarceration" of dependent individuals from institutional settings does not have the quality of benevolent reform that some would claim. Instead, Scull argues that decarceration is actually supported because it is more inexpensive to return mental patients to the community than it is to provide them with institutional care.

Whether Scull is correct or not, there is little question that our efforts to develop an effective community support program for hospitalized patients to replace the mental hospital are only beginning. The National Institute of Mental Health's development of a community support program (Turner and Ten Hoor, 1978) suggests that a national

This 35-year-old mental outpatient, like many others, drifts from single room occupancy to single room occupancy. After a few months at the Continental, he recently moved to a hotel in Harlem. (From *New York Times Magazine*, May 21, 1978, p. 16.)

program is now getting underway. Such a program will have to contend with the extensive needs of chronically hospitalized patients as well as with communities who may resist the placement of ex-mental patients in their neighborhoods. There is little question that we are in the midst of a major experiment in social change in the field of community mental health. And the outcome is still uncertain.

Crisis Intervention

Caplan (1970) has suggested that we all experience at least two kinds of crises in our normal life development. The first of these are *developmental crises* that occur at predictable times in our life cycle. Examples of such developmental crises might include the birth of a child, entry into school, leaving school to take one's first job, and so on. The second type of crisis can be thought of as an *accidental crisis*. These are unpredictable and can occur in a variety of different forms. The death of a loved one, the onset of a severe physical illness, the loss of a job are all examples of accidental crises.

Earlier we noted that many times in the face of a psychological emergency or crisis, people have had nowhere to turn. Only a few years ago psychological help in the face of a personal crisis was often unavailable to the average person. Long waiting lists for conventional psychotherapy were commonplace. Admission to a psychiatric hospital did not necessarily mean that constructive help with a personal crisis would be available. Today, suicide prevention services, hot lines, and crisis intervention services are much more readily available than they were even 10 years ago.

But what are the elements of a successful crisis intervention? Rappaport (1977) and McGee (1974) suggest that successful crisis intervention services typically use nonprofessional personnel, with professional mental health workers acting as consultants. They are embedded in a network of agencies, and are committed to evaluating their own effectiveness.

Let us consider an example. McGee's own work, as exemplified by the Suicide and Crisis Intervention Service in Gainesville, Florida, began with the assumption that immediate face-to-face contact between trained volunteers and people who were in crisis was a crucial ingredient in the service itself. They were oriented to "respond to every request to participate in the solution of any human problem whenever and wherever it occurs" (McGee, 1974, p. 181).

McGee's crisis intervention team often acted as *advocates* on the behalf of people in crisis. They played a variety of helping roles

This crisis intervention worker is talking with a young woman who has found herself confused and upset in a strange town. The police had called in the crisis intervention team. (Courtesy of Alachua County Crisis Center, photo by Nancy Blackmon)

that were considerably more diverse than that of a conventional therapist. They might, as Rappaport (1977) suggests, go to court to tell a judge that they are trying to help the person in crisis find a job, or they might attempt to reestablish contact between a young person and his or her parents. They might intervene in family disputes, or, in some cases, help with direct human needs such as the provision of clothing and shelter.

When the crisis intervention team opened a case, their first goal was to establish communication with the person in crisis and to develop an action plan. During early intervention the team tries to establish a close working relationship with the persons in crisis, determine if they are suicidal, and assess their resources in the community. Once the crisis intervention team has moved into action, it attempts to establish realistic mutual goals between the person and the worker with whom the person will continue to communicate.

A key aspect of this sort of crisis intervention work is that the crisis intervention worker attempts to find whatever other sorts of resources exist for the person in the community and to mobilize those resources to help the person. Thus, rather than a lonely and private relationship, as in psychotherapy, crisis intervention involves a broad range of collaborative efforts designed to help clients overcome their crisis situation.

Typical problems found in crisis intervention centers, hot lines, and suicide prevention centers include marital and family problems, alcoholism and drug abuse, juvenile problems, vocational and school adjustment problems, homosexual problems, loneliness, alienation, and other problems.

The important point here is that significant psychological help can be provided for a wide variety of emergency or crisis situations. In most cases, that help can be provided by trained volunteers. In fact, McGee notes that almost 80 percent of the personnel surveyed in over 200 crisis intervention centers across the country were nonprofessional volunteers. Thus on a number of dimensions, crisis intervention is sharply contrasted with our conventional image of long-term psychotherapy.

The Promise of Prevention

Unquestionably our greatest victories over disease and suffering have been those involving prevention rather than treatment. In fact, many of these victories occurred long before we had sophisticated laboratories and biochemical knowledge of disease (Caplan, 1964). Consider the following examples:

The British Admiralty was impressed by reports that sailors on ships that were well stocked with citrus fruits and vegetables did not suffer from scurvy. They ordered that fruits and vegetables be included in the diets of sailors and scurvy virtually disappeared.

A London physician in the 19th century named Snow suspected that the water supply might have something to do with the epidemic of cholera raging in the city at the time. He noted from the addresses of the people developing cholera that they all drew water from the Broad Street pump. Furthermore, he noticed that people who drew their water from other sources did not contract the disease. His prevention strategy was as simple as it was effective. He simply removed the handle from the pump! The cholera epidemic was brought under control and new cases of the disease were prevented from occurring.

One of the most difficult challenges in the field of mental health is in finding methods for preventing the development of abnormal behavior. It remains to be seen whether we will be able to find the handle to our own Broad Street pump. In this section we will examine some of the key concepts emerging in the field of prevention of abnormal behavior as well as some examples of prevention programs. Finally, we will consider research strategies that hold promise in discovering new ways of preventing abnormal behavior.

Many fundamental concepts in the field of prevention have been derived from the fields of public health and community mental health. They are based on the premise that our efforts need to focus not on individuals who have already developed a disorder but on groups or populations of people who are *at risk* for disorder. Goldenberg (1977) notes:

> Prevention programs are based upon: (1) a commitment to a public health model with its focus on whole community *populations* rather than individuals; (2) a concern with *reducing the incidence* (number of new cases) and prevalence (total number of existing cases) of psychological disorders in the community; and (3) an effort to locate particularly *vulnerable individuals* who, because of genetic background, unique personal experiences or exposure to excessive environmental stresses, are thought to

have especially high potential for developing abnormal behavior (p. 36, emphasis added).

This seems reasonable enough, but how might we actually create programs that accomplish these goals? The strategies of individual treatment are familiar enough, but the strategies of prevention may be less so.

Bloom (1980) distinguishes between three different types of preventive efforts. The first involves communitywide efforts where all residents in a community are exposed to the program. In the field of public health it is easy to identify such *communitywide* preventive efforts. Heller (1984) points out that water purification to eliminate typhoid fever or the supervision of food and water processing are public health measures that provide communitywide prevention programs. Psychologically oriented communitywide prevention programs might involve newspaper or television public information programs to educate people in more effective parenting skills or to eliminate corporal punishment in the schools.

A second type of prevention program is called a *milestone program*. As Heller and Monahan (1977) note, in the milestone approach citizens are exposed to the program at specified intervals in their lives and "residents of a specified area march, as it were, past the program, prior to reaching it they are not protected" (Bloom, 1971, p. 118). An example of a milestone prevention program in public health might be smallpox vaccination required upon admission to school. Psychological milestones, suggested Heller (1984), might include critical developmental periods in a person's life, such as the birth of a sibling, school entry, the first year of a marriage, or the birth of one's first child. The stresses of these critical periods of social development could be reduced by helping people to gain skills that would help them cope with the life transition (as in the case of marriage or parenthood) or by changing the social environment associated with the transition, as in the case of school entry.

The third type of prevention strategy is called the *high-risk* program. It focuses on populations of people who are, for genetic or environmental reasons, vulnerable to specific disorders. An example offered by Heller and Monahan is that of a program in a school system that provides special support to children who are beginning to show signs of emotional disorders. Other high-risk populations might be the children of mental patients, children who experience the death of a parent at an early age, or the survivors of natural disasters such as earthquakes, floods, or plane crashes.

In Table 18–1, Bowers (1963) provides us with a variety of examples of "normal emotional hazards" encountered throughout life that might suggest appropriate high-risk or milestone-oriented preventive interventions.

The idea that mental health professionals could actually develop programs that would prevent rather than merely treat psychological disorder is an extremely appealing one. Indeed, the President's Commission on Mental Health (1978) argues that such programs can be developed, but that they must be based on a strong research base. Prevention remains a goal and few convincing demonstrations are yet available. Nevertheless, the demonstrations that we do have are instructive. Let us consider several examples of attempts to prevent rather than merely treat psychological disorders.

Anticipatory Coping. Unavoidable surgical procedures, especially for young children, can produce a genuinely stressful emotional hazard, and programs focused on helping the child anticipate and cope with the stress may prevent later severe emotional reactions.

A study by Cassel (1965) focused on children between the ages of 3 and 11 who were about to undergo a serious diagnostic experience called *cardiac catheterization*. The experience of being in a strange operating room and having this procedure carried out can be stressful indeed. Cassel rehearsed the operating room procedure with the child by acting it out in a puppet play. The puppet was actually dressed in a hospital gown, had electrodes attached to it, and went through the steps involved in administering anesthetic. After the child watched this procedure, the roles were reversed and the child played the part of the doctor with the therapist acting the role of the frightened child and asking reassurance from the child who was now playing the doctor.

Compared with a control group that did not receive this experience, the children who received anticipatory guidance showed much less emotional upset during the procedure itself and were more willing to return to the hospital for further treatment. But, interestingly, as Heller and Monahan (1977) note, the intervention effect was no different when the children in the two groups were compared at home or later in the hospital. Thus, many intervention effects may be highly specific in their impact. Careful research on the actual impact of such efforts is needed if we are to succeed in achieving prevention goals.

Skill Training. An example of a different sort of prevention program is offered by the work of Spivak and Shure (1974). The rationale for their research was that it should be possible to provide children with interpersonal and cognitive problem-solving skills early in their school development. These skills included the ability to sense problems, to identify feelings, and to look for alternative solutions. Spivak and Shure reasoned that training of this kind should help children to cope with interpersonal problems effectively in the future and therefore reduce a child's vulnerability to later psychological distress. The investigators provided chil-

TABLE 18–1
Suggestions for Possible Primary Prevention Programs Applicable to Various Institutions and Agencies

Institutions and Agencies	Normal Emotional Hazard	Possibilities for Preventive Action
1. Family	Loss of father through death, divorce, or desertion	Reinforcement of childcare services for working mothers
	Loss of mother	Reinforcement of fosterhome services
	Adolescence	Increase in staff and professionalization of high school counselors, deans, and vice principals
	Birth of sibling	Pediatric or well-baby clinic counseling
	Death	Management of grief—religious or community agency worker
2. Public health	Phenylketonuria (a form of mental retardation)	Detection and diet
	Childhood illnesses	Vaccination, immunization
	Stress caused by children—economic, housing, etc.	Reinforcement of well-baby clinic through mental health consultation to staff
	Pregnancy	Adequate prenatal care for mothers of lower socioeconomic status
3. School	Birth of sibling	Recognition of event by school and appropriate intervention
	School entrance of child	Screening vulnerable children
	Intellectual retardation	Special classes and assistance
	Teacher concern and anxiety about a child's behavior	Consultation by mental health specialists
	School failure	Early identification and prevention through appropriate school program
4. Religion	Marriage	Counseling by clergy
5. Job or profession	Promotion or demotion	Opportunity to define role through services of a mental health counselor
6. Recreation	Appropriate and rewarding use of leisure time	Active community and city recreational programs
7. Housing	Lack of space, need for privacy	Working with architects and housing developers

Source: Reprinted with permission from E. M. Bower, "Primary Prevention of Mental and Emotional Disorders: A Conceptual Framework and Action Possibilities," *American Journal of Orthopsychiatry* 33(5) (October 1963), pp. 832–48. Copyright 1963 by the American Orthopsychiatric Association, Inc.

dren four years of age with 46 such lessons over a 10-week period. The children did appear to acquire the key skills and their behavioral adjustment was also shown to improve. A year later, when these children were followed in new class settings, program improvements were maintained over time (Spivak & Shure, 1975).

Early Identification. Still another strategy for prevention is to identify children with early signs of emotional disorder and to intervene to reduce the possibility of the disorder becoming more severe. Technically this type of effort is "secondary prevention" (Caplan, 1964) since its goal is to reduce the *duration* of psychological problems rather than to reduce the incidence of new cases.

As part of the Primary Mental Health Project, Cowen and his colleagues have conducted a series of studies (Cowen et al., 1963; 1966; 1975) that identify children who show signs of disorder as judged by their peers and their mothers and other observers. The children's case folders were "red tagged" and singled out for special help and companionship by teacher's aides and other paraprofessional helpers.

Cowen et al. (1975) have reported what they believe is a reduction in the rate of worsening among red-tagged children, although as Heller and Monahan (1977) point out, several interpretations of these findings are possible. Nevertheless, the Primary Mental Health Project (PMHP) represents an important effort in using community volunteers to prevent the worsening of incipient psychological disorder (Cowen et al., 1980). This and future efforts of the PMHP are likely to tell us a great deal about our potential for preventing emotional distress in the developing lives of children.

Research for Prevention. Despite the ethical problems reviewed in the featured article and our relative lack of knowledge, the goal of primary prevention is a worthy one. The question, however, of turning the goal into operational programs with demonstrated effectiveness is far from solved. In reviewing the strategies for doing research on prevention, the President's Commission on Mental Health suggests that five questions should be answered by research to help us in our pursuit of valid and effective prevention programs. They are: (1) What groups of people are at high risk for the disorder? (2) What is the relative importance of specific risk factors? (3) Can we effectively reduce or eliminate the most important risk factors? (4) Does eliminating these risk factors effectively lower the rate of disorder? and (5) If the disorder can be prevented, are the costs of the

intervention justified by the degree of prevention obtained (p. 1818)?

But where are we to begin? Heller, Price, and Sher (1980) suggest three "boot-strapping" strategies for evaluating the effects of primary prevention programs. The first of these strategies is to identify clearly an end state for which prevention efforts are justified. In the field of public health these are fairly easy to identify: brain damage as a result of being poisoned by lead-based paints, infection associated with syphilis, or the consequences of certain genetic diseases. Other end states may be defined by a changed social status rather than by a disease. Examples of these would be school failure or delinquency. In the end state approach, an operational definition of the end state itself must be developed. Following this, a method for identifying cases at risk must be provided, and an intervention strategy then mounted to prevent the end state, followed by rigorous evaluation of the effect of the intervention.

A second strategy is to attempt to identify a group that appears to be at risk for one or several negative outcomes. Such high-risk groups might include single parents, widows, children entering the hospital for a surgical procedure, or children experiencing divorce in their family. Beginning with such a potential high-risk group, the second step is to discover what the risk factors actually are. A program must then be mounted to reduce these risks and finally an evaluation of the program must be developed.

A third strategy involves beginning with a program that demonstrates the potential for building competence or effectiveness. Many such educational programs already exist. The question, then, becomes what effects the program actually has. Even if positive effects occur, we should still ask if any negative outcomes are actually prevented. These are research strategies that will require large amounts of time and human effort to implement, and yet they are critical in deciding about the relative effectiveness of any prevention strategy.

LEGAL AND ETHICAL ISSUES IN THE TREATMENT OF ABNORMAL BEHAVIOR

While we have made considerable progress in the treatment of abnormal behavior, there are a number of legal and ethical issues that remain controversial. In fact, it may be that the development of new treatments will raise still more ethical and legal dilemmas as these treatments become more widely used. In the treatment of abnormal behavior, ethical issues may arise that force us to question the nature of the relationship between therapist and client and between professional and community member. These are issues that you need to consider as an informed consumer of psychological services.

There are also occasions when the needs and well-being of a distressed individual come into conflict with the needs and well-being of the community at large. In some instances these conflicts are decided in favor of the community, and legal statutes and procedures are developed that may restrict individual freedom or involve involuntary treatment. As we shall see, these legal issues raise important questions about the rights of the individual versus those of society.

Ethical Problems in Identifying High-Risk Cases

Heller and Monahan (1977) have argued that prevention efforts often require us to identify cases that are at risk for the development of some psychological disorder. But we know that our ability to predict who will and who won't develop a disorder is far from perfect. Are there psychological costs in being identified as being "at risk?" In the example of Cowen's Primary Mental Health Program,

children's case folders were "red-tagged" as being vulnerable to future problems and singled out for special attention. Is it possible that being singled out this way might actually lead teachers or others to see the child as a problem and reject the child still further?

Heller and Monahan suggest a series of steps to be followed to avoid these problems. They state:

We would suggest that prevention programs based on the early identification of problem cases should pass through four stages of evaluation.

Stage one: The precise "end-state" that one wishes to prevent must be defined. What cannot be defined cannot be predicted.

Stage two: The reliability of case identification and the validity of the predictive scheme being used must be assessed. Can different people agree that this is a potential problem case? If they can agree, does their common prediction have any basis in fact (i.e., without intervention, will the "early-identified" case turn into a "full-fledged" case later)?

Stage three: Is an effective intervention program available for those people correctly predicted to be problem cases? Do those people who receive the prevention program in fact have lower rates of the problem during their lives than people who do not participate in the program?

Stage four: What effect does the prevention program (or merely the screening process) have on those people incorrectly identified as future problem cases?

Only when the issues raised in these four stages are answered can one begin the complex ethical weighing that leads to a decision as to whether to undertake a secondary prevention program (p. 140).

Ethics and Psychotherapy

With the practice of psychotherapy comes the professional responsibility to be sensitive to the needs and the best interests of the client. Attention to ethical concerns is of crucial importance because therapists who are insensitive, who misapply procedures, or who abuse their role and power as helpers, have the potential to harm rather than help their clients. The list below summarizes some critical ethical issues, framed in questions, which are crucial to any therapeutic endeavor.*

Have the goals of treatment been adequately considered?

- Have the therapist and client agreed on the goals of therapy?
- Will serving the client's interests be contrary to the interests of other persons?

Has the choice of treatment methods been adequately considered?

- Does the published literature show the procedure to be the best one available for that problem?
- Has the client been told of alternative procedures that might be preferred by the client?

Is the client's participation voluntary?

- Have possible sources of coercion on the client's participation been considered?
- If treatment is legally mandated, has the available range of treatments and therapists been offered?

When another person or an agency is empowered to arrange for therapy, have the interests of the subordinated client been sufficiently considered?

- Has the subordinated client been informed of the treatment objectives and participated in the choice of treatment procedures?
- Where the subordinated client's competence to decide is limited, have the client as well as the guardian participated in the treatment discussions to the extent that the client's abilities permit?

Has the adequacy of treatment been evaluated?

- Have quantitative measures of the problem and its progress been obtained?
- Have the measures of the problem and its progress been made available to the client during treatment?

Has the confidentiality of the treatment relationship been protected?

- Has the client been told who has access to the records?
- Are records available only to authorized persons?

Does the therapist refer the clients to other therapists when necessary?

- If treatment is unsuccessful, is the client referred to other therapists?
- Has the client been told that if dissatisfied with the treatment, referral will be made?

Is the therapist qualified to provide treatment?

- Has the therapist had training or experience in treating problems like those of the client?
- If the therapist is not adequately qualified, is the client referred to other

---

*Reprinted from *Behavior Therapy* 8 (1977), v–vi.

therapists, or has supervision by a qualified therapist been arranged?

This series of questions summarizes many of the critical issues to be considered by professional therapists in the conduct of their work. But such questions can be viewed in another way. Answers to these questions could help you as a consumer draw conclusions about the therapy or therapist you may be considering for yourself or may recommend to a friend.

To Treat or Not to Treat, That Is the Question. Is it advisable to treat schizophrenics without antipsychotic medication? Should chronic schizophrenics be graduallly withdrawn from their medication? These are some of the questions that Marian MacDonald and her colleagues (MacDonald, Lidsky, & Kern, 1979) have addressed in a recent paper that crtically examines the value of antipsychotic medication with schizophrenics.

MacDonald's group came to the following conclusions based on their interpretation of the literature on the effects of antipsychotic medication with schizophrenics: (1) the severity of side effects resulting from antipsychotic medications does not justify prolonged maintenance for a significant proportion of schizophrenic patients; (2) a significant proportion of schizophrenics might not be worse off if their medications were withdrawn, especially if active treatment efforts accompany gradual withdrawal; and (3) the physiological and psychological effects of antipsychotic medication may reduce the effectiveness of learning-based therapeutic programs.

On the basis of these conclusions, MacDonald and her colleagues have argued that patients should receive antipsychotic medication only when they are a clear and present danger to themselves and/or others. For first-admission psychotic patients, they advocate crisis intervention in a setting that emphasizes community return, in place of drug treatment. They contend that schizophrenic patients who are receiving maintenance doses of antipsychotics should be exposed to therapeutic learning experiences as they are gradually withdrawn from their medication. For more chronic schizophrenics, they recommend learning-based, drug-free programs to prepare them for independent community life. As you can see, these authors express a clear preference for learning-based programs over chemotherapy for schizophrenic patients.

MacDonald and her colleagues' recommendations are indeed thought-provoking. But is their position realistic or overoptimistic? Only carefully conducted studies that compare how medicated versus drug-free patients who participate in therapeutic programs fare in the community will help to answer this question.

Involuntary Commitment

There are times when people are hospitalized for treatment without their consent. When the state through its legal authority hospitalizes people without their consent or even despite their protests, the procedure is called *involuntary commitment*. In most cases mental health professionals recommend involuntary commitment when they believe people are a danger to themselves or others. There are additional requirements in many states before commitment proceedings can be undertaken (Price & Denner, 1973). At least three criteria are used in most states to determine whether someone should undergo involuntary commitment. They are: (1) dangerousness to self, (2) dangerousness to others, and (3) psychological disability.

In general, suicide attempts or gestures represent one indication of potential dangerousness to oneself. But the range of criteria is extremely broad and ambiguous and considerable professional judgment is involved in concluding that people are dangerous to themselves (Stone, 1975).

A second major criterion for involuntary hospitalization is that a mental health professional believes a person is dangerous to others. While it would seem that this criterion should be fairly clear-cut, careful research by Monahan (1976) suggests that psychologists, psychiatrists, and psychological tests are unable to predict dangerousness with acceptable levels of accuracy. This leaves the mental health professional with a painful dilemma. To conclude that people are dangerous when they are not is to deprive them of their individual freedom through commitment. On the other hand, to conclude that they are not dangerous when in fact they are, is to place the community in jeopardy.

The third criterion for commitment, psychological disability, is at least in some cases also difficult to determine. In many cases, even schizophrenic individuals with delusions or hallucinations are not necessarily so disabled that they cannot live in a community.

Thus the criteria for involuntary commitment, while seemingly reasonable at first glance, have a troublesome ambiguity about them that leaves mental health professionals and the community with a difficult dilemma to resolve.

Patients' Rights and Informed Consent*

Protecting the rights of patients in the mental health setting is an important but difficult task. Critics of our mental health system, such as psychiatrist Thomas Szasz (1970), have claimed that the system robs

---

*Prepared by Errol Liebowitz.

people of their freedom of choice by subjecting them, without their consent, to the effects of mind-controlling drugs and other treatments. They argue that patients should have the freedom to decide whether or not they should receive treatment.

Because the disorders patients suffer from can be considered mind-controlling in their own right, the issue of when a patient's rights are being protected becomes very complicated. Take, for example, the case of a schizophrenic patient whom we shall call Brad. Brad was hospitalized following a suicide attempt. When interviewed, he reported that he had tried to kill himself in an attempt to silence voices inside himself that were constantly tormenting him. Brad was afraid to accept treatment because of what the voices would do to him and consequently refused all attempts to help him. Brad's psychiatrist implemented antipsychotic drug treatment over the patient's objections. As a result of this treatment, the voices disappeared and with them Brad's desire to commit suicide.

Was the psychiatrist correct in treating Brad without his consent? In this case apparently yes. The problem is, we are making this decision knowing the results of treatment. The psychiatrist treating Brad believed treatment would help, but he could not be sure. Brad could have gotten worse, he could have developed severe reactions to the drugs or any of a number of other possibilities. Would we still judge the psychiatrist's decision as correct under different circumstances?

A number of legal and ethical guidelines have been established to help decide when a psychiatrist can administer treatment over a patient's objections. The most frequently used criterion is that of dangerousness to one's self or others. This is the criterion that was used in Brad's case. Another criterion is that of rationality. That is, for a patient's refusal to be considered valid, the patient's reason for refusal must be logical and based on an understanding of the likely results of accepting or not accepting treatment. However, the rationality criterion is not always accepted by the law. For example, in one case (*Rogers* v. *Okin*, 1979) patients sued their psychiatrists for the right to refuse medication. The judge ruled that patients could refuse drugs as long as they were not a threat to themselves or others. Even patients who were "irrational" or who would remain ill without drugs could refuse medication.

Guidelines have also been established for psychiatrists to follow in informing patients about treatment. Before psychiatrists ask a patient to accept treatment, they are required to give patients information about the risks and benefits of the proposed treatment, what the alternatives are, and what is likely to happen if the patients decide to refuse all treatment. When a patient is not capable of understanding the information for whatever reason, the psychiatrist is supposed to inform a relative or other guardian, who then decides about treatment for the patient.

How do psychiatrists feel about these guidelines? There is considerable controversy within the psychiatric community concerning what treatments patients' rights guidelines should cover and with what patients. A study by Liebowitz and McNamara (1980) examined the circumstances under which psychiatrists favored providing information and accepting refusal of medication by schizophrenic patients. They found several factors related to psychiatrists' beliefs. One factor was the impact psychiatrists believed such information would have on patients. When they believed that patients would understand the information and that it would help treatment, they reported being more willing to inform patients than when they thought information would create fear and

anxiety in the patients. Another factor was the psychiatrists' beliefs about the risks and benefits of antipsychotic drugs. Psychiatrists were most partial to treatment refusal when they believed there was risk associated with the use of medication. When they believed drug treatment was safe and routine, they appeared to be less likely to allow treatment refusal. A third factor was whether psychiatrists believed other treatments also worked. When this was the case, they were also more likely to accept treatment refusal.

In general, it appears that psychiatrists believe their primary responsibility is to heal the patient. They are in favor of permitting treatment refusal if it does not result in significant conflict with this responsibility. The question is, Do psychiatrists, as a group, underestimate the importance of the individual to choose his or her own fate? There are many who believe so.

The Right to Treatment. Do patients have a right to adequate treatment? A landmark case addressing this question is that of *O'Connor* v. *Donaldson* (1975):

Kenneth Donaldson was committed to the Florida State Hospital by his aging parents when he was 48 years old. He had been previously hospitalized for a short time and appeared to have some minor psychiatric symptoms. On the other hand, he did not appear to be dangerous to himself or others. The judge committed Donaldson and he remained in the Florida State Hospital with virtually no treatment being administered for the next 14 1/2 years. Donaldson wrote letters requesting that he be released, but many of them were intercepted by the hospital staff. Finally, an advocacy group, the Mental Health Law Project, sued for his release. The suit ultimately went to the Supreme Court, which ruled that people who were not dangerous and who were capable of remaining in the community could not be confined in a psychiatric hospital. This ruling is important since it will sharpen the criteria by which judgments of the appropriateness of involuntary commitment are made. Furthermore, it helps ensure that people who are hospitalized will have a right to treatment, not just incarceration.

The Insanity Defense

There are occasions when people who have been arrested for a criminal act may be judged guilty of the crime, but not responsible for their actions because they are judged to be legally "insane." The concept of insanity is a legal concept rather than a psychological one, and has been defined using legal rather than psychological criteria. In general, the basis of the insanity defense has been that such persons are not legally responsible for the crime because they lack *mens rea*, which means a "guilty mind."

The history of the insanity defense is a fascinating one. In modern times it begins in 1843 when Daniel M'Naughten murdered the secretary of the British prime minister. M'Naughten actually had intended to kill the prime minister himself, but said that he had been told to kill the prime minister by a voice from God. In M'Naughten's defense it was argued that he was clearly suffering from a defective reasoning and was unable to tell right from wrong.

This defense was later modified by the Durham rule (1954) in which it was decided the insanity defense could be raised if the unlawful act appeared to be the product of "mental disease or mental defect." This rule has not been widely adopted and more recent judicial decisions, such as the *United States v. Brawner* (1972), set out several criteria: (1) the act was a result of mental disease or defect; (2) the person is unable to appreciate the wrongfulness or criminality of his or her conduct; and (3) the person is unable to engage in conduct that fits the requirements of law.

The insanity defense is interesting because of the underlying assumption that each person is responsible for his or her own behavior—not because it is used very often in criminal proceedings. In some sense, as Stone (1975) observes, the insanity defense is the exception that proves the rule. The general assumption is that we are all responsible for our behavior, and the insanity defense enforces that rule by making an exception.

Competence to Stand Trial. The insanity defense is seldom used, and when employed, seldom successful (Lunde, 1975). But there are many people whose case is never even tried in a courtroom because they have been judged as not competent to stand trial. If people are judged to be incompetent to stand trial, they are hospitalized and will remain in a hospital until they recover enough to appreciate the meaning of the trial proceedings. Unfortunately, being hospitalized often actually amounts to a long incarceration. In some instances people have remained incarcerated longer than the criminal penalty would have been for the crime committed.

The underlying rationale for the competence-to-stand-trial proceeding is that such a person lacks the capacity to understand the proceedings against him or herself and to assist in his or her own defense. In *Jackson* v. *Indiana* (1972) the court ruled that a person who will never be competent to stand trial could not be retained indefinitely in a hospital for the criminally insane. Jackson in this case was a mentally retarded deaf-mute and therefore was unlikely to ever be able to assist in his own defense and understand the proceedings against him. However important this case is, it does not spell out in detail how long people can be held and under what circumstances, once they are judged incompetent to stand trial.

SUMMARY

We have seen that the group therapies offer psychological help in a wide variety of settings for a number of different types of psychological and interpersonal problems. Despite their diversity, the group therapies offer a set of common characteristics that include practical information, hope, a context for learning from others, and a sense of belonging. The special advantages of group therapy go beyond the fact that a number of people can be simultaneously helped by a single professional. The social learning and modeling processes that are critical ingredients of the group process offer an added dimension to the therapeutic process.

Family therapy provides still another context for helping. It occurs in a natural system, the family, which may contain some of the roots of disturbance as well as an arena for the development of new adaptive behavior. Family therapies usually focus upon communication and interaction patterns within the family and, in some cases, can be structured to alter the way in which relationships and interactions among family members are organized.

An examination of research on the effectiveness of group therapy suggests that group-oriented approaches to treatment can indeed produce beneficial effects, although it is currently unclear whether they are actually superior to individual approaches. But like all interventions into the life of a person, group approaches can produce casualties as well. The style of the group leader as well as characteristics of people who fail to benefit or experience harmful effects are likely to be important factors in the degree of benefit derived from group-oriented treatment.

Over the past three decades, our perspective on the ways in which people may receive psychological help has been considerably broadened. The community mental health movement has opened up new possibilities for helping in a variety of community contexts that go beyond the traditional view of individual psychotherapy. Rather than replacing individual treatment, however, the community mental health approach has emphasized (1) an orientation to larger populations and groups rather than individuals, (2) short-term emergency-oriented crisis treatment, and (3) pioneering experiments in community living for many hospital paitents who previously had been thought to be treatable only in institutional settings.

The research on the effectiveness of these new approaches is only now beginning to yield a substantial body of scientific literature. In addition, efforts to deinstitutionalize mental patients have not always produced humane community treatment; such efforts require careful preparations for community support and community living. Nevertheless, the community mental health approach to coping with psychological problems offers new strategies for treatment that promise to reach a wider range of people suffering from psychological distress.

The community mental health approach also suggests that prevention programs may provide still other avenues for reducing the incidence of psychological distress. These innovative programs are directed at people who are judged to be vulnerable to psychological distress. We have seen that such programs are being developed and evaluated for children, people experiencing major life transitions, and other vulnerable groups. Solid experimental research on preventive approaches is badly needed and represents one of the major challenges facing researchers concerned with alleviating human misery and reducing psychological distress in our communities.

Legal and ethical issues have been raised with respect to the treatment of abnormal behavior. There is still much debate about the methods of properly identifying high-risk cases in prevention efforts. Likewise, there is some question about the side effects of certain treatments that may prove harmful to patients. Even though involuntary commitment has been instituted to protect society as well as persons who may harm themselves, questions exist about such issues as the rights of patients, including their right to receive treatment. When a crime has been committed by someone suffering from a psychological disorder, should such a person be subject to the usual criminal sanctions for his or her actions? The fact that the insanity defense has been accepted in some cases suggests that bringing such patients to trial is not the proper procedure. Perhaps even more problematic an issue is the fact that many persons suffering from a psychological disorder have been judged incompetent to stand trial and, as a result, have been subjected to long periods of involuntary hospitalization without being able to have recourse to a criminal trial.

19

The Biological Treatments

Antipsychotic Drugs
   Side Effects and Complications of
      Antipsychotic Drugs
   Prescribing Antipsychotic Medication:
      Treatment Considerations

Antidepressant Drugs

Lithium

Antianxiety Drugs

**Some Concluding Comments on
   Chemotherapy**

Electroconvulsive Therapy

Psychosurgery

Summary

INTRODUCTION

Strapped to a stretcher, you are wheeled into the ECT room. The electroshock machine is in clear view. It is a solemn occasion; there is little talk. The nurse, the attendant, and the anesthetist go about their preparation methodically. Your psychiatrist enters. He seems quite matter-of-fact, businesslike—perhaps a bit rushed. "Everything is going to be just fine. I have given hundreds of these treatments. No one has ever died." You flinch inside. Why did he say that? But there is no time to dwell on it. They are ready. The electrodes are in place. The long clear plastic tube running from the bottle above ends with a needle in your vein. An injection is given. Suddenly—terrifyingly—you can no longer breathe; and then. . . . You awaken in your hospital bed. There is a soreness in your legs and a bruise on your arm you can't explain. You are confused to find it so difficult to recover memories. Finally you stop struggling in the realization that you have no memory for what has transpired. You were scheduled to have ECT, but something must have happened. Perhaps it was postponed. But the nurse keeps coming over to you and asking, "How are you feeling?" You think to yourself: "It must have been given"; but you can't remember. Confused and uncomfortable, you begin the dread return to the ECT room. You have forgotten, but something about it remains. You are frightened (Taylor, 1975).

In this dramatic case history Taylor (1975) depicts one patient's reaction to a powerful biological treatment—electroconvulsive therapy (ECT). Just how accurate is this portrayal? Many helping persons concerned with treating severely depressed individuals would contend that it paints an unjustly negative picture of ECT. Witness: In 1978, a task force organized by the American Psychiatric Association surveyed 4,013 randomly selected members. Among the more than three quarters of the members who responded, a full 72 per cent agreed with the statement, "There are many patients for whom ECT, either alone or in combination with other measures, is the safest, least expensive, and most effective form of treatment." Only 20 percent disagreed (Fink, 1978).

What are the risks of ECT? What are its benefits? Who might profit from ECT? These are questions that merit our most serious consideration. Indeed, over the past two decades searching questions with far-reaching implications have been raised concerning the appropriate use as well as the potential for abuse of biological treatments. ECT, psychosurgery, and drug treatments for mental disorders have been the subject of vigorous debate. Why has a cloud of controversy surrounded their use? Perhaps part of the reason is that these potent and dramatic interventions directly alter the physiology of the patient in order to effect cognitive, emotional, or behavioral change.

In this chapter we will carefully evaluate each of the major biological treatments in use today. When used judiciously, biological treatments can be cost-effective and efficient treatments for very serious mental disorders. While the psychotherapies have proven helpful with neurotic disorders and sexual and substance abuse disorders, the biological treatments appear to be powerful therapeutic agents in the treatment of the psychoses and severe affective disorders. Psychotherapy, however, can be quite helpful when used in conjunction with biological treatments. Let us now turn to a description of the antipsychotic drugs that have revolutionized the treatment of schizophrenia.

The demonstration of the effectiveness of chlorpromazine in the treatment of schizophrenia brought new hope for treating seriously disturbed mental patients. (© Sue Markson)

ANTIPSYCHOTIC DRUGS

The l950s were years of tremendous excitement for physicians practicing psychiatry with seriously disturbed mental patients. Before that decade, many of the more than 560,000 patients confined in hospitals had little hope of leaving that setting and returning to the community. Medical treatments for schizophrenia and severe depression consisted of little more than palliative measures to sedate and calm agitated, disorganized, and assaultive patients. Smoking and drinking alcohol were sometimes employed to calm the more aggressive and assaultive patients. Mania was treated with hot packs, restraints, needle showers, and hydrotherapy. Amphetamines were the only pharmaceuticals used in the treatment of depression. Agitated schizophrenic patients often required the not so gentle restraint of the straitjacket. Liberal doses of barbiturates merely served to temporarily suppress the behavior of patients who were incapable of responding to the reasoned logic of the hospital staff. And more often than not, when

the restraints were removed or the effect of the drug wore off, another cycle of disruptive behavior and unsuccessful, frustrating attempts to treat it would begin. Psychoanalysis and other forms of psychotherapy proved to be equally ineffective with the majority of seriously disturbed patients (Hackett, 1979).

But with the demonstration of the effectiveness of chlorpromazine in the treatment of schizophrenia by Delay, Deniker, and Harl, in 1952, came new hope for treating seriously disturbed mental patients. Chlorpromazine (Thorazine) calmed agitated schizophrenics and eased symptoms such as delusions, hallucinations, disordered thinking, and social withdrawal. Sensing the promise of antipsychotic medications, pharmaceutical companies were quick to synthesize other drugs in the phenothiazine family, such as trifluoperazine (Stelazine), thoridazine (Mellaril), fluopenazine (Prolixin), and prochlorperazine (Compazine). Potent medications that altered mood and combated anxiety were synthesized only a few years after the value of chlorpromazine in treating schizophrenia was recognized. These developments ushered in the "pharmacological revolution"in the treatment of serious mental disorders. For the first time physicians could choose from a variety of medications to treat a variety of mental disorders. Chemical treatments came to enjoy widespread appeal and application. And the search for different and more potent medications continues. For example, a recently developed drug, haloperidol (Haldol) is quite effective in treating acute psychotic episodes.

Today the antipsychotics, or major tranquilizers as they are sometimes called, are the primary form of treatment for persons diagnosed as psychotic. MacDonald and Tobias (1976) have estimated that 87 percent of all psychiatric inpatients are maintained on psychotropic drugs. One measure of the impact of antipsychotic medications is the fact that at the beginning of the 1980s, there were nearly 300,000 fewer mental patients residing in mental institutions than in the early 1950s. (See Figure 19–1.)

Despite the dramatic changes in the treatment of seriously disturbed patients over the past 30 years, antipsychotic medications have not provided the long sought after "cure" for schizophrenia. Although many patients are able to leave the hospital, they are not entirely symptom-free when they return to the community. Symptoms tend to persist but in milder form, leaving the patient with some difficulties in speech and cognition and with social liabilities (Klerman & Izen, 1978). In order to help prevent a relapse, about 80 percent of psychiatric outpatients receive some form of maintenance drug therapy (Gunderson & Mosher, 1975). But some patients seem to deteriorate even with continued drug therapy and must return to the hospital. Hogarty (1977) has cited a relapse rate of 37 percent for patients receiving maintenance doses of antipsychotic medication. About one fifth of patients diagnosed as schizophrenic do not seem to be helped at

FIGURE 19–1
Number of Psychiatric Patients in VA Hospitals
(Based on Data from the Veterans Administration)

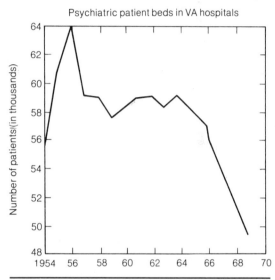

Psychiatric patient beds in VA hospitals

Source: Reprinted with permission of Macmillan Publishing Co., Inc., from W. L. Witters, and P. Jones-Witters, *Drugs and Sex*, (New York: Macmillan, 1975), p. 209. Copyright © 1975 by Weldon L. Witters.

all by drug treatment. In addition, serious side effects and complications of antipsychotic drug treatment can be harmful to certain patients. But even with the limitations we have mentioned, the efficiency of antipsychotic medication relative to alternative approaches has great appeal. Before we turn our attention to how a physician might go about prescribing medication to a schizophrenic patient, let us consider the important issue of the side effects of antipsychotic drugs.

Side Effects and Complications of Antipsychotic Drugs

A number of side effects that are usually temporary and reversible occur within the first month or so of treatment with drugs, if not sooner. These include feelings of muscle weakness and fatigue, slow initiation of movements, soft monotonous speech, muscle contractions and abnormal posturing, difficulties in sleeping, and extreme restlessness. Even if untreated, these symptoms will usually disappear and, if they do not, drug treatments are available to counter these unpleasant side effects. The broad spectrum of antipsychotic side effects can be seen in Table 19–1.

A far more serious side effect of major tranquilizers is *tardive dyskinesia*, a neurological disorder. The symptoms include grotesque involuntary movements of the facial muscles and mouth, and twitching of the neck, arms, and legs. Most often the disorder begins after several years of high-dosage treatment, but it has occasionally been observed after only a few months of therapy at low dosages (Simpson & Kline, 1976). It is clear that significant proportions of schizophrenics, especially older and more long-term patients, develop tardive dyskinesia. Kane and Smith (1982) examined the findings of 56 surveys of schizophrenics treated with antipsychotic medication. The surveys were conducted between 1959 and 1979 and sampled more than 34,000 patients. Twenty percent of the patients developed symptoms of TD (tardive dyskinesia) as compared to 5 percent of persons who developed TD spontaneously in 19 samples of persons who were not treated with antipsychotic medication. Two factors associated with increased risk of developing TD were advancing age and female sex.

Because the symptoms of tardive dyskinesia are often noticed when dosages are reduced or the drug is withdrawn, many experts argue that it is essential to take patients off antipsychotic medication periodically to check for early signs of tardive dyskinesia (Crane, 1973; Gardos & Cole, 1976; Prien & Caffey, 1975). Early detection is very important because the symptoms

TABLE 19–1
The Spectrum of Antipsychotic Side Effects

Behavioral
  Fatigue
  Lethargy
  Weakness
  Psychomotor retardation
  Insomnia
  Nightmares
  Confusion
  Delirium

Neuromuscular
  Tardive dyskinesia
  Reduced seizure threshold
  Akinesia
  Akathesia

Parkinsonian Reactions
  Reduced arm accessory movements
  Mask-like faces
  Resting tremor
  Shuffling gait
  Rigidity
  Excessive salivation

Other Bodily Reactions
  Blurred vision
  Other visual problems
  Changes in cardiac rhythms
  Dizziness, postural hypotension
  Itching
  Eczema
  Pallor
  Flushing
  Photosensitivity
  Urticaria
  Dryness of mouth
  Decreased sweating
  Urinary retention
  Difficulty in voiding urine
  Difficulty with erection
  Delayed ejaculation
  Constipation
  Liver problems
  Blood changes
  Weight gain
  Irregular menstruation
  Breast enlargement
  Decreased sex drive

Source: Adapted from "Prescribing Antipsychotics" by J. G. Bernstein, *Drug Therapy, 9,* p. 79.

may otherwise become long-term or irreversible (Quitkin, Rifkin, & Gochfeld, 1977). Our discussion of the complications of antipsychotic drug treatment suggests that patients treated by short-term drug treatment are likely to experience fewer risks than those on long-term maintenance therapy. This points to the need for careful monitoring of the patient's condition and an accurate assessment by the physician of the risk factors involved in treating the patient. Let us now examine some of the considerations a physician might have in prescribing antipsychotic medication.

Prescribing Antipsychotic Medication: Treatment Considerations

Denber (1979) has described a number of "general rules" for prescribing medication for patients with mental disorders such as schizophrenia. Denber emphasizes the importance of a treatment plan in the pharmacological treatment of schizophrenia. It is essential that the treatment plan be tailored to the patient.

The first step in developing a treatment strategy is to conduct a thorough evaluation of the patient and to establish an accurate diagnosis. The physician collects information about the patient's past history, prior drug usage, and response to chemotherapy. The probable course of the psychological problem and the response to drug therapy are also assessed. The evaluation guides the physician in the development of the treatment plan. The plan includes the appropriate medication and dosage level, alternate drug treatments if the initial medication proves ineffective, a determination of the drug's possible side effects, and plans for integrating psychotherapy, family therapy, and other therapeutic interventions into the treatment plan. If the patient is hospitalized, the staff are informed of the details of the plan; in all cases the patient and the family are informed about what to anticipate and how to recognize side effects of treatment.

Antipsychotic drug therapy can be thought of as consisting of three phases (Bernstein, 1979). In the initial phase of treatment, the dosage is increased over the first week to bring psychotic symptoms, such as hallucinations, delusions, and disordered thinking, under control. This phase of treatment is called *pharmacolysis* of psychosis because its goal is to relieve psychotic symptoms pharmacologically. As we noted in Chapter 9, one possible mechanism by which the major tranquilizers reduce psychotic symptoms is by blocking dopamine activity within the central nervous system. Thus it has been hypothesized that when drug levels reach a high enough concentration, psychotic symptoms will diminish.

During the next phase of treatment, termed *stabilization*, the physician gradually reduces the dosage of the medication after the acute symptoms of psychosis begin to disappear. The goal of this phase is to begin to gain enduring control of the psychotic symptoms.

The third and final phase is termed *maintenance*. The goal of this phase of treatment is to maintain the patient free of psychotic symptoms with the minimal dosage of antipsychotic medication. Ideally the patient can be "weaned" from the drug by gradually decreasing the dosage until there is no longer a need for continued medication. But many patients, as we have indicated, may need long-term, perhaps indefinite, chemotherapy. It is very important to establish an effective, yet minimal dosage level, since the risk of harmful side effects is greater with high dosage, long-term treatment. Some schizophrenics treated on an outpatient basis respond quite favorably to substantial dosage reductions and show few early signs of TD (Kane, 1983).

ANTIDEPRESSANT DRUGS

Since the antidepressant drugs were introduced in the early 1950s, they have enjoyed widespread acceptance and use. Blaine, Prien, and Levine (1983) observe that over 15 million prescriptions were filled for antidepressant drugs during 1980. According to a National Survey of Psychotherapeutic Drug Use, more than 2 percent of noninstitutionalized adults used medically prescribed antidepressants in 1979.

In Chapter 8 you were introduced to the two main classes of antidepressant drugs: the tricyclic compounds and the monoamine oxidase inhibitors (MAOI). (See Table 19–2.) Studies have not, however, conclusively demonstrated superiority of one of the marketed antidepressant drugs over another (Blaine et al., 1983; Klein, Gittleman, Quitkin, & Rifkin, 1980). In addition, no one antidepressant drug has sufficient freedom from side effects to suggest that compliance could be improved to an extent that would justify its routine use as a first-choice drug. Tricyclic antidepressants, however, are the most widely preferred drugs, largely because they are most familiar to prescribing physicians (Blackwell, 1982).

Since the antidepressant drugs were developed, knowledge has been gained regarding which symptoms are most likely to respond positively to medication. Table 19–3 presents the factors associated with the likelihood of response to tricyclic antidepressants. This pattern of symptoms has been identified with the so-called endogenous

TABLE 19–2

Generic Name	Brand Name
Tricyclic agents:	
Amitriptyline	Amitid, Amitril, Elavil, Endep, SK-Amitriptyline
Desipramine	Norpramin, Pertofrane
Doxepin	Adapin, Sinequan
Imipramine	Antipress, Imavate, Janimine, Presamine, SK-Pramine, Tofranil
Nortriptyline	Aventyl, Pamelor
Protriptyline	Vivactil
MAO inhibitors:	
Isocarboxazid	Marplan
Phenelzine	Nardil
Tranylcypromine	Parnate
*Combination agents**	
Amitriptyline and chlordiazepoxide	Limbitrol
Amitriptyline and perphenazine	Etrafon, Triavil

*These agents include tranquilizers in addition to the antidepressant.
Source: From "Treating Depression" by A. J. Gelenberg, 1979, *Drug Therapy, 9*(11), p. 113.

TABLE 19–3
Factors Correlating with Likelihood of Response to Tricyclic Antidepressants

Positive Correlation

Consistent sadness and depression
Feelings of hopelessness, helplessness, worthlessness
Feelings of guilt
Sleep disturbance, particularly with early morning awakening
Depression worse in the mornings
Loss of appetite
Weight loss
Diminished libido
Change from normal personality
Depressions present over a period of weeks

Negative Correlation

Histrionics
Feelings of anger and resentment
Self-pity
Longstanding character pattern of unhappiness
Emotional lability
Manipulativeness

No Correlation

Presence or absence of precipitating event

Source: From "Prescribing Antidepressants" by A. J. Gelenberg, 1979, *Drug Therapy, 9*(11), p. 96.

THE ANTIDEPRESSANTS: WORDS FROM A PHYSICIAN

In order to gain a better sense of what it might be like to be treated with an antidepressant drug, consider the following statements about tricyclic drug therapy which a physician might relate to a patient experiencing depression:

The drug which you are being treated with is a tricyclic antidepressant drug. It is called a tricyclic because of the three-ring chemical structure of the compound. The drug will not relieve your depression overnight. It's going to take time—anywhere from two to four weeks. In the beginning the drug may help you sleep, but you may feel the side effects before you start feeling better. Even then, the first signs of improvement are likely to be short-lived or limited to one or two symptoms. Because the results of antidepressant therapy are not going to be apparent immediately, it is all too easy to become discouraged. However, only by persisting with the treatment regimen prescribed for you, will it ultimately be successful. Never increase or decrease the dosage or stop taking the drug on your own. If you have any problems or feel uncomfortable, be sure to let me know about it. Once this initial stage is over, overall progress will probably become much more obvious.

During the first week of therapy, I will be gradually increasing the dose to build up your tolerance to the drug's side effects. Side effects are common adverse reactions to the presence of a foreign chemical substance in your body. Although mildly uncomfortable, these reactions will let you know that the drug is in your system and working.

What sort of effects can you expect? Most people being treated with the drug I have prescribed experience one or more of the following: drowsiness, dryness of the mouth, constipation, morning "hangover," dizziness, blurred vision, difficulty in urinating. As a rule, these symptoms will diminish or disappear as you continue to take the drug at the prescribed dosage. If you find these effects particularly unpleasant or disabling, don't hesitate to call me.

As I mentioned earlier, the first signs of improvement should begin to appear two to four weeks after you start therapy, although a close friend or family member may notice the improvement a few days or a week before you do. Initially, you may notice that you sleep better, are able to concentrate more, have more energy, or your appetite has increased and you are beginning to gain weight. With time, the sadness, helplessness, and emptiness you have been feeling will also diminish. To be sure, this will not happen all at once, and good periods may sometimes be followed by a return of depressive symptoms. But once you have begun to improve, the odds are that you will continue to get better (adapted from Gelenberg, 1979).

type of depression. The MAOIs are used most often in patients who do not respond favorably to treatment with tricyclics. There are indications that the MAO inhibitors may be the treatment of choice with a subtype of depressive patients suffering from *atypical depression*. In contrast with the patient who responds favorably to tricyclic medication, the patient with atypical depression is likely to have difficulty falling asleep, to overeat as a way of coping with depression, and to feel more depressed in the evening than in the morning.

The fact that the tricyclics may not begin to reach their peak effectiveness for upwards of two weeks can be a drawback in the treatment of patients who are seriously depressed and where there is a risk of suicide. With such patients electroconvulsive therapy might be utilized because it can produce quicker results and diminish the likelihood of a suicide. But with most patients suffering from depression, a trial of antidepressant medication is prescribed before electroconvulsive therapy is considered.

Antidepressant drugs have been found to be effective in treating depression. Overall, the antidepressant drugs appear to benefit about 70 percent of the patients treated (Morris & Beck, 1974). Compliance with antidepressant medications may be a problem because of specific side effects and/or general attitudes toward treatment. About 50 percent of depressed patients who take medications drop out of treatment, and about a fifth of depressed patients refuse antidepressant medications (Blackwell, 1983).

If a sizable percentage of patients cannot tolerate or do not desire drug treatment, is psychotherapy an effective treatment alternative? The answer appears to be yes. A recent meta-analytic review of 56 outcome studies considered the relative effectiveness of drug therapy and psychotherapy (Steinbrueck, Maxwell, & Howard, 1983). Psycho-therapy was found to be somewhat more effective than drug therapy in the treatment of major depression in adults. If we look at studies that directly pit cognitive therapy against drug therapy for depression, the majority of them find that the two treatments are equally effective in moderately to severely depressed outpatients (Murphy, Simons, Wetzel, & Lustman, 1984). Furthermore, the two treatments do not have an additive effect. It is still unclear which patients profit the most from psychotherapy versus drug treatment. Future research will clarify the precise nature of the changes that result from both types of therapy and how long treatment gains persist.

Before we conclude this section, it is important to point out that antidepressant drugs are not indicated in treating mild episodes of sad or depressed feelings and brief depressions related to situational stresses. Although a trial of antidepressant medication may be considered in these cases, brief supportive psychotherapy or a change in the patient's living situation may be more helpful.

LITHIUM

In a fascinating study Dawson, Moore, and McGanitz (1970) found an intriguing relationship between concentrations of lithium in drinking water and the number of mental hospital admissions in Texas. They discovered an inverse relationship between amounts of lithium in residential drinking water and the incidence of admissions and readmissions to state mental hospitals.

In Chapter 8 we noted that lithium, an element present in trace amounts in water throughout the world, has important and widespread applications. Patients with mood disorders can be treated with lithium while their behavior and metabolism are carefully monitored. Manic episodes and bipolar affective disorders are especially susceptible to treatment with lithium.

A manic episode, you will recall, can produce severe problems in social and occupational functioning. Acutely manic patients may require hospitalization before their mood can be stabilized with lithium and maintenance treatment in the community is feasible. But after about two weeks of lithium treatment, 70 to 80 percent of even acutely agitated patients seem to improve (Baldessarini, 1977). Normal functioning can be restored in many patients who, before taking lithium, were severely disturbed and distressed.

Lithium can also have a "protective" effect. The results presented in Table 19–4 show that lithium can prevent relapses of both manic and depressive episodes in bipolar disorders. Mood swings tend to occur less often and, if they do occur, are less debilitating (Van Praag, 1978).

Despite the remarkable personality and mood changes that often accompany treatment with lithium, some physicians are reluctant to prescribe it. Managing patients on

---

TABLE 19–4
Rate of Recurrence of Mania or Depression in Bipolar Manic-Depressives with Lithium or Placebo

Treatment	Percent of Relapses*	
	Manic (120)	Depressive (63)
Lithium	29.2	36.5
Placebo	70.8	63.5
"Protection Ratio" (Placebo:Lithium)	2.4	1.7

*Data are mean percent of patients relapsing in the manic or depressive phases of bipolar affective illnesses during treatment with lithium or placebo. The results are derived from the only two controlled studies that provided sufficient data to evaluate the differential effects of the treatment on the two phases of the illness. Lithium appears to produce a protective effect against both types of relapse, but the results are too few to permit statistical analysis. It is interesting to note that about two thirds of all 183 relapses were manic in type regardless of the treatment.
Source: From *Chemotherapy in Psychiatry* (p. 63) by R. J. Baldessarini, 1977, Cambridge: Harvard University Press.

---

a lithium regimen can prove difficult. The levels of lithium in the blood must be monitored and carefully regulated. Recall that in Fieve's "metabolic ward," which you read about in Chapter 8, bodily functions were closely monitored so that dosages could be adjusted on an individual basis. Lithium is a drug with a very narrow "safe" range. If the dose is not properly adjusted, it can act as a toxic agent, impairing various bodily processes. Overdosage can produce quite serious complications, and very depressed, suicidal patients can take a lethal dose of lithium.

Over the years, however, the popularity of lithium has increased, and more and more physicians feel comfortable prescribing it to patients they believe will benefit from its use. Lithium's range of effectiveness may be even broader than was previously believed. It is making inroads into the treatment of certain schizophrenic patients. Although lithium is not useful in cases of chronic schizophrenia, when added to an antipsychotic agent, lithium may benefit roughly half of patients who meet DSM III criteria for schizophrenia (Donaldson, Gelenberg, & Baldessarini, 1983). Even schizophrenic patients who show no signs of having an affective disorder may respond positively (Biederman, Lerner, & Belmaker, 1979; Braden, Fink, Qualls, Ho, & Samuels, 1982).

Lithium may also prove useful when patients are unresponsive to antidepressant drugs such as tricyclics. In a recent series of studies, when lithium was added to antidepressant therapy, the majority of patients' depressive mood lifted in a time span ranging from 24 to 48 hours (De Montigny, Cournoyer, Morissette, Langlois, & Caille, 1983) to 8 days later (Henninger, Charney, & Sternberg, 1983).

Despite these promising findings that supplement a broad consensus that lithium is effective, many more patients than the number currently taking lithium could benefit from it (Donaldson et al., 1983). Yet few psychiatrists would take serious issue with the observation that lithium treatment is one of the "great success stories of modern psychiatry" (*Newsweek*, 1979, p. 100).

ANTIANXIETY DRUGS

There is perhaps no greater testimony to the wide-ranging impact of the "drug revolution" than the prescription of antianxiety medications to millions of Americans each year. Primary care physicians routinely prescribe medication when anxiety, irritability, and agitation become severe enough to interfere with their patients' daily functioning. Antianxiety drugs are the most widely prescribed drugs in medical history (Mielke & Winstead, 1981). Over the past two decades the prescriptions written worldwide for these drugs number in the billions.

The most frequently prescribed antianxiety agents are the *benzodiazepines*, or anxiolytics, as they are sometimes called. This family of drugs includes the most commonly prescribed drug Valium along with a number of other frequently prescribed drugs such as Librium and Serax. The meprobamate drug group (Miltown, Equanil) and the barbiturates (phenobarbital) are less routinely used, and their effectiveness in treating anxiety is less well established than the benzodiazepines.

Whatever drug the physician prescribes, it is likely that it will be suggested only after other approaches like support, reassurance, and advice fail to help the patient. The use of anxiolytics is most common among persons between 30 and 50 years of age—about twice as many women as men are users (Mielke & Winstead, 1981).

Unlike antipsychotic medication, anxiolytics medication is most likely to be prescribed on a time-limited basis. Treatment with these drugs is usually limited to periods of stress that produce noticeable discomfort in the patient.

Because of the potential for abuse and dependence, the prescribing physician should carefully monitor and adjust the dosage in response to changing levels of stress and tension. Where it is clear that the drugs have little impact on the individual's level of anxiety, their use should be reevaluated. Psychotherapy or alteration of the patient's lifestyle and environment may be indicated rather than continued drug treatment.

Indeed, in many instances psychotherapy may be more appropriate than drug treatment for anxiety. The real source of the person's anxiety may be masked by the calming effects of the medication. Patients whose treatment is limited to drug therapy may never get in touch with the causes of their anxiety. Thus they may be deprived of an opportunity to learn how to better manage internal conflicts or stressful situations. On the other hand, when anxiety seriously disrupts the patient's ability to function, anxiolytic medication may be a valuable adjunct to psychotherapy and an effective treatment in its own right.

SOME CONCLUDING COMMENTS ON CHEMOTHERAPY

As chemotherapy has gained increasing acceptance, thought-provoking questions about the proper use, effectiveness, and limitations of drug treatments have been raised. One frequently voiced criticism of chemotherapy is the overuse of medication. Even advocates of drug treatment acknowledge that medications sometimes are prescribed with "excessive zeal" (Baldessarini, 1977). Consider Baldessarini's (1977) comments on this point:

In busy clinics or office practice, it is particularly tempting to allow the "ritualization" of

PSYCHOLOGICAL COMPLICATIONS OF DRUG TREATMENT

Before the Food and Drug Administration (FDA) will grant approval for the marketing of a new drug, it first must undergo extensive clinical tests to insure its clinical value and safety. Even after a drug has met the rigorous licensing standards of the FDA, it still may produce side effects in certain patients. We have noted many of the physical side effects that are produced by drugs used to treat a variety of psychological disorders. But many of these drugs also induce psychological side effects that may change or compound the patient's symptoms. Such side effects are easily neglected or overlooked in a psychiatric population. A worsening of the patient's condition may be attributed to the "natural course" of the disorder instead of to drug-related complications.

Flaherty (1979) has summarized the psychological side effects of the antipsychotics, the antianxiety agents, and the antidepressant drugs. Let us now consider some of the major complications that can be induced by drugs in each of these classes.

Psychological side effects of drugs can be serious and easily neglected or overlooked in a psychiatric population. (John Thoeming/Dorsey Press)

Antipsychotic Drugs

The major groups of antipsychotics are all capable of worsening the symptoms of psychosis by producing visual hallucinations, disorientation, and autonomic symptoms. In some cases antipsychotic medications can induce a fairly serious depression with insomnia, suicidal thoughts, and slowed motor activity. Reducing the dosage or substituting another drug may be helpful when such side effects are detected.

Antianxiety Agents

Antianxiety drugs can heighten anxiety in patients with agitated depressions and increase the severity of depressed symptoms in patients who are depressed as well as anxious. Antianxiety drugs like the barbiturates have a fairly high abuse potential. If their use is abruptly discontinued for some reason in an addicted patient, a dangerous withdrawal syndrome may develop that requires prompt medical attention and treatment.

Antidepressant Drugs

Tricyclic antidepressants can, in some patients, increase irritability. An acute manic episode may be triggered in patients with a history of mania. Schizophrenic symptoms may increase in severity if they are present during the course of administration of antidepressants (Flaherty, 1979).

These examples suggest that drug treatment for psychological disorders is not as straightforward as many people think. The very drugs that are used to treat a particular disorder may actually make the condition worse or create other problems for the patient. Over the entire course of treatment, careful monitoring of the psychological as well as the physical condition of the patient appears to be an absolute necessity.

chemotherapy to displace sensitive and honest attention to painful and difficult psychological and social issues, needs, and wishes of the patient (p. 153).

Such "ritualization" of practice arises, in part, from the fact that drugs are easy to administer, nondemanding of the physician's time, and generally effective. Unfortunately, routine reissuing of prescriptions may substitute for regular evaluation of the patient's condition and thoughtful consideration of alternate treatments.

The physician's enthusiastic promotion of chemotherapy may foster an unhealthy dependence on medication. Patients may attribute positive changes to the medications they are taking. They may come to invest drugs with almost magical powers, overvaluing their effects. The patient's belief in a drug's curative powers may reinforce the physician's tendency to prescribe drugs on a routine basis.

The overvaluation of medication may affect the patient in other ways. Treatment gains may be more long-lasting when people believe that their own efforts, rather than a chemical agent, are responsible for positive changes (MacDonald, Lidsky, & Kern, 1979). This suggests that by encouraging patients to attribute gains to themselves, physicians may promote more enduring positive changes.

Critics of chemotherapy have pointed out that drug treatments are of little value in helping the patient to learn social skills, to modify self-defeating behaviors, or to cope more adaptively with conflict-producing situations. Psychotherapy, vocational counseling, and learning-based social skills programs all may promote adjustment in the community when combined with drug treatments. Falloon & Lieberman (1983) demonstrated the potential of family therapy to reduce the relapse rates of schizophrenics who received optimal doses of antipsychotic medication. After a two-year follow-up patients treated with family therapy still showed improved social adjustment and family functioning relative to patients treated with drug treatment alone. Karon & Vandenbos (1981) have shown that unmedicated schizophrenic patients can profit from psychoanalytic psychotherapy, as measured by decreased thought disorder, improved overall adjustment, and shortened hospitalization. Psychotherapy can yield substantial economic savings as well. The costs of hospitalization were greater for medicated patients who did not receive psychotherapy than for unmedicated psychotherapy patients. Unless patients learn effective coping skills or are able to change their environment in beneficial ways, they may be no better off after drug treatment than they were before it was started.

But just as drugs have their limitations, psychotherapeutic approaches are not without their own shortcomings. Indeed, in the areas where chemotherapy appears to be most effective, psychotherapy seems to have the least proven value. Michel Hersen (1979), a well-known behavior therapist, notes that many psychologists and behavior therapists have strong, preconceived biases against the use of drugs with very disturbed patients. Hence they are inclined to minimize the very real contributions of drugs to the treatment of certain disorders. For example, the treatment of choice in bipolar affective disorders appears to be lithium car-

bonate. Severe depressions may be more effectively treated with tricyclic antidepressants than with behavioral or other psychotherapeutic approaches. And schizophrenic symptoms seem most amenable to treatment with the antipsychotic agents. Smith and Glass's (1977) meta-analytic study suggests that drug therapy may be more effective than psychotherapy in the treatment of many disorders.

Hersen also points out that drugs may be used to bring symptoms under control so that psychotherapeutic procedures may be more readily applied. Schizophrenic patients, for example, may be distracted by hallucinations and delusions that minimize their potential to learn new behaviors. Hersen has found that unless the dosage of antipsychotic medication is finely adjusted, schizophrenics do not seem to derive benefit from a social skills training program.

The value of drugs can also be seen in their ability to enhance certain therapeutic techniques like systematic desensitization (Liberman & Davis, 1975) and flooding (Marks, Viswanathan, Lipsedge & Gardiner, 1972). There is still much to be learned about how various drugs and therapeutic approaches can be combined to maximize treatment effects. And we can expect new and exciting innovations in this area. It is likely that chemotherapy will continue to have both ardent defenders and detractors, but drug therapy's contribution to the treatment of serious psychological disorders seems difficult to dispute.

ELECTROCONVULSIVE THERAPY

Electroconvulsive therapy is used more frequently than is generally believed. It has been estimated that ECT is administered about 10,000 times a day in the United States (Pitts, 1972). In our earlier discussion of depression in Chapter 8, we noted that no one knows exactly why ECT has its therapeutic effects. Some evidence does exist to suggest that endogenous depressions benefit more from ECT treatments than other forms of depression. We also noted that memory loss, a side effect of electroconvulsive therapy, can have a negative effect on the recovery of certain patients.

But a review of 60 studies comparing ECT with control procedures or alternative treatments suggests that ECT may be more effective for certain patients than was previously believed. For example, Scovern and Kilmann (1980) note that ECT appears to be markedly superior to drug treatments with patients who suffer from endogenous depressions and additionally are severely disturbed or deluded. Involutional and manic-depressive patients also appear to respond quite favorably to ECT treatments. The fast action of ECT can make it a lifesaving treatment for depressed patients at serious risk for suicide. ECT may be the treatment of choice in such cases because, as you recall, antidepressant medication may not be maximally effective for upwards of two weeks after treatment is initiated.

ECT is not as effective with other disorders. The treatment appears to be of little value in relieving the symptoms of the less severe or "neurotic" depressions. While ECT may help certain schizophrenics, in that it may aid the depressive symptoms that may complicate the symptom picture, it does not appear to alter the primary symptoms of thought disorder. Scovern and Kilmann's review also suggests that the value of ECT in the treatment of depression may be limited to altering the patient's subjective experience of depression. Although patients tend to report feeling better after ECT treatments, parallel changes in intellectual, perceptual, and motoric retardation are typically not observed. Further research is needed to determine which symptoms are most affected by electroconvulsive therapy.

In prescribing electroconvulsive therapy for any patient, the task challenging the physician is to determine whether the potential therapeutic gains outweigh the potential costs associated with the treatment. As we mentioned earlier, ECT can adversely affect memory. In his review of the literature, Fink (1977) was unable to disconfirm the belief that ECT can cause permanent brain damage. Thus, given what is known about ECT, the physician is probably wise to prescribe ECT "only with utmost care" (Scovern & Kilmann, 1980, p. 299).

Yudofsky (1982) has cautioned that when ECT is adopted, it is vitally important for the patient and his or her family to understand the procedure, risks, and potential benefits of the treatment. After ECT, frank discussion about having been depressed and having received ECT should be encouraged. It is possible to mistakenly attribute the "normal," occasional forgetting of a name to the detrimental side effects of ECT. What is actually a common occurrence that is unrelated to ECT treatments may become a frightening symbol of depression and ECT. ECT should always be used in the context of a carefully devised treatment plan that incorporates psychotherapy, when appropriate.

PSYCHOSURGERY

There is little doubt that psychosurgery is the most dramatic biological treatment for psychological disorders. As you might imagine, the "therapeutic" destruction of brain tissue to control behavior and emotion has been the focus of much controversy. Critics of psychosurgery have raised questions about the effectiveness of the treatment, the use of psychosurgery for social control, and the fundamental values underlying behavioral control. Psychosurgical procedures are usually regarded as a treatment of the "last resort" for disorders seemingly untreatable by other methods. Schizophrenia, depres-

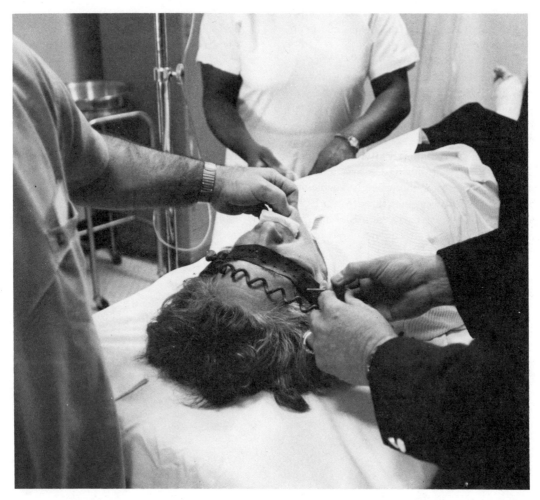

Electroconvulsive therapy should be cautiously prescribed, but its results can be impressive with severely depressed patients. (Paul Fusco/Magnum Photos, Inc.)

sion, and severe obsessive-compulsive neuroses are some of the disorders that have been treated with psychosurgery.

The results of psychosurgery are not always predictable. Consider the following two cases of patients who received psychosurgical operations:

L.W. is an obese, 32-year-old unmarried and unemployed woman, inarticulate to the point of near muteness, with a history of over 10 years of intermittent hospitalizations for what

has been described as both "chronic schizophrenia" and "depression." When she was in her early 20s, L.W. began to have episodes of destructive rage and irrational speech and became unable to care for herself. She had three psychosurgical operations without apparent success. Her parents indicate some moderate improvement after the first operation, but it was short-lived. There was no improvement after either of the subsequent operations. The patient is profoundly hypokinetic, cannot give any history, cannot be tested except with operant methods. She has had an undetermined number of shock treatments and is on many different drugs.

T.M. is a married woman of 37, also overweight (220 lbs.), with a similar diagnostic history of schizophrenia and depressive hallucinations. Her first psychotic episode occurred when she was in her early 20s.

T.M. was married shortly afterwards, at age 22. Soon after that, during her first and only pregnancy, she grew increasingly suspicious and agitated. She was given three to four ECTs and hospitalized for two years. She had her first psychosurgery (a cingulotomy) at age 30—because of suicidal tendencies—and reportedly felt tremendous relief. She was still suspicious, but no longer felt "as if encased in a plastic cube." There were no side effects, she insists, except perhaps for weight gain (80 pounds in the first six months after the operation).

T.M. says she functioned fairly well for five years as a schoolteacher, but then got worse again and began drinking heavily in the latter part of 1974. She and her husband made a trip West to seek the help of a neurosurgeon in California from whom she received a psychosurgical operation. This was in January 1975. Immediately afterwards, the patient reported

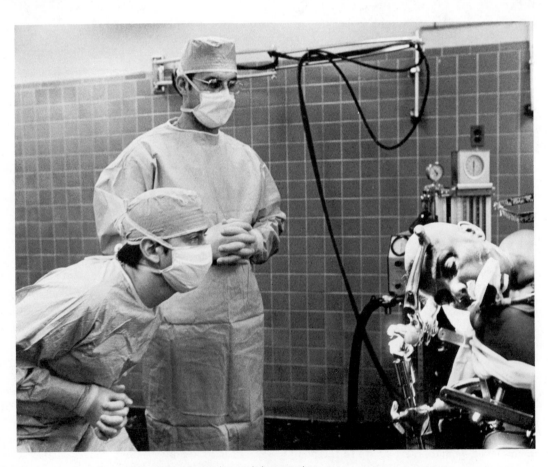

Psychosurgery is a dramatic and highly controversial procedure. (©Mitchell Payne/Jeroboam, Inc.)

that she was no longer suspicious, but still felt fearful. . . . She went back to her psychiatrist in the East, who suggested one more operation. She received this third psychosurgical operation the following August, after which, except for one six-week regression, she reports being entirely well.

Previously, this patient had received 27 ECTs and 60 insulin coma treatments. Asked for her views of psychosurgery and whether she would recommend it to others, she says emphatically, "I would tell them to snap it up as quick as they could. It's a godsend, it is. I cannot say enough about them (the operations). I don't know why they work or how they work, but they are a true godsend. They gave me back my life" (adapted from the *APA Monitor*, 1978).

In examining these two cases, it is apparent that the treatment outcomes are very different. Negative views of psychosurgery arise, in part, from a lack of data about which patients respond most favorably to treatment. Concerns about harmful side effects have also contributed to skepticism about the safe and effective use of psychosurgical procedures. It is often unclear when the benefits of psychosurgery outweigh the risks of impairing memory, blunting the personality, diminishing emotion and creativity, and the ordinary dangers of brain surgery (Neville, 1976).

But as is often the case with new treatments, when psychosurgery was first introduced, it was hailed as a promising innovation. Indeed, Egas Moniz, the Portuguese neurologist who developed psychosurgery techniques in the early 1930s, won a Nobel Prize for his surgical operations and studies of the brain. Freeman and Watts introduced psychosurgery in this country and published highly favorable reports about their successful treatment of thousands of patients.

The early psychosurgical operations were termed *lobotomies*. The technique consisted of severing the fibers between the frontal lobes and the lower portions of the brain. Valenstein (1973) notes that the pressing need to treat psychiatrically disturbed veterans during and after World War II played a significant role in the widespread adoption of psychosurgical procedures. Psychosurgery remained a popular technique until the mid-1950s, after which time "the tide receded in the face of a strong reaction against psychosurgery precipitated by reports of 'dehumanized zombies,' the overuse of the surgical approach, and the availability of psychoactive drugs as an alternative to surgery"(p. 269).

In the 1960s a new form of psychosurgery came into prominence. The procedure involves creating small lesions in the amygdala or in the other parts of the limbic system of the brain, which is thought to control emotions. Primitive surgical procedures have been replaced by ultrasound, electricity, freezing of tissues, and implants of radioactive materials. New automated surgical devices have added precision to delicate brain surgery.

Despite certain advances in psychosurgery, it still remains an experimental technique with potential for misuse. Critics of psychosurgery note that the motives for conducting such operations may not always be benign. Indeed, in the past, it has been used with violent sexual criminals and homosexual child abusers, and in prisons to control violent inmates whose behavior was judged irrational. Punitive and therapeutic motives may, in some instances, be difficult to separate. This raises the possibility that social goals (the control of behavior) may be confused with therapeutic goals that best serve the interests of the patient.

Questions also have been raised about when to perform psychosurgery. As we have indicated, psychosurgery is performed as a treatment of "last resort." But it is not always clear when alternative, less drastic treatment procedures have been exhausted. Recognizing the need to protect the interests of the patient, the federal government has recommended establishing institutional review boards in hospitals where psychosurgery is performed. Valenstein (1973) has argued that in submitting recommendations to such review boards, "the burden of proof that alternative treatments have been adequately explored should always be on those recommending psychosurgery" (p. 339). Institutional review boards would help insure that there is a clear rationale for the operation, that the patient has received an appropriate preoperative and postoperative evaluation, that the patient has been informed about the surgery and has consented to the operation, and that the operating physician is competent to conduct the surgical procedures.

It is important to keep in mind the fact that psychosurgery is still an experimental procedure. It is not a treatment for any specific psychological disorder (Kalinowsky, 1975). Careful evaluations of psychosurgery, it is hoped, will guide future decisions about where its use may help alleviate psychic pain and where its use represents an unacceptable risk to the patient.

SUMMARY

Over the past three decades biological treatments have made great contributions to the treatment of severely disturbed patients. Since the introduction of antipsychotic drugs, many patients have been able to leave the hospital and live relatively normal lives in the community. The antipsychotics are the primary form of treatment for persons diagnosed as schizophrenic. Although many patients who take antipsychotic drugs improve enough to leave the hospital, their symptoms tend to persist, but in milder form. Antipsychotic drugs also have rather serious side effects that need to be taken into consideration when prescribing these potent medications. The most serious side effect is tardive dyskinesia, a neurological disorder. Estimates of patients with tardive dyskinesia vary, but it is clear that significant proportions of schizophrenics, especially older, long-term, female patients develop it.

Denber (1979) has described three phases of treatment with antipsychotic medication. In the first phase, pharmacolysis, the goal is to relieve psychotic symptoms within about the first week by gradually increasing the dosage. During stabilization, dosage is regulated to gain enduring control of the psychotic symptoms. In the third phase, maintenance, a minimal dosage of the drug is administered to maintain the patient free of psychotic symptoms.

The tricyclic antidepressant drugs are more widely prescribed than the MAOIs, but the tricyclic's superiority or relative freedom from side effects has not been conclusively demonstrated. Antidepressant medication is usually prescribed for serious depressions, but not for mild or brief depressive episodes. Lithium may not only be effective in treating manic and depressive episodes in bipolar disorders but it also may be useful in treating patients who are unresponsive to antidepressanat drugs, such as the tricyclics, as well as certain schizophrenic patients.

Antianxiety drugs are the most widely prescribed drugs in medical history. However, their use is best limited to conditions where other supportive measures fail to help the patient. Dependence on antianxiety agents may be a greater risk than the potential benefit of such drugs.

Electroconvulsive therapy is a widely practiced, yet still controversial treatment. It is especially effective with endogenous depressions, where evidence suggests that it may be superior to drug treatment. Given the potential side effects and risks associated with ECT administration, its use is warranted only after carefully weighing the risks and benefits.

Psychosurgical procedures are the most dramatic and controversial of the biological treatments. Generally they are regarded as a treatment of "last resort," with its use indicated only for disorders seemingly untreatable by other methods. Its effects are quite unpredictable, but new surgical procedures have increased its credibility to some degree. Despite certain advances in technical procedures, it still remains an experimental technique with potential for misuse. Careful evaluation of psychosurgery may guide future decisions regarding cases in which its use might be maximally beneficial.

GLOSSARY

Abnormal behavior: Behavior that is disturbing to others, subjectively distressing, or psychologically handicapping to the person displaying it.

Abreaction: Expression of pent-up emotions.

Acetylcholine: A neurotransmitter used by parasympathetic nerves at neuromuscular junctions and in many brain areas. Specific degeneration of acetylcholine-containing neurons in the forebrain has been linked to Alzheimer's disease.

Acquired reinforcers: Stimuli that through a learning process come to reinforce certain behaviors.

Acrophobia: Fear of high places.

Acute: Describes a disorder of sudden onset and relatively short duration.

Acutely suicidal: Sudden onset of self-destructive thoughts and behavior.

Adjustment disorders: Psychological disturbance, such as depression, brought on by a stressful event.

Adoptive studies: Genetic studies in which environmental and genetic effects are separated by examining persons with the genetic factor but in a new adoptive home environment.

Affect: The emotional aspect or correlate of a mental state or idea. In general, a mood, feeling, emotion, or emotional response.

Affective disorders: Mood disturbances in which feelings of sadness or elation become intense and unrealistic.

Agoraphobia: Fear of open places.

Alcohol hallucinosis: Severe and distressing hallucinations, usually auditory, occurring about two weeks after abrupt cessation of alcohol use.

Alcohol withdrawal: Pattern of physiological responses to abrupt cessation of alcohol use, usually following a period of chronic use. Symptoms can be severe and life-threatening.

Alcoholics Anonymous: A self-help organization to rehabilitate alcoholics.

Alcoholism: Excessive use of alcohol, usually associated with psychological and physical dependency, which impairs ability to function in several areas of life.

Ambivalence: Existence of simultaneous contradictory emotional attitudes toward the same person or object, for example, love and hate.

Amino acids: NH_2-containing organic compounds that are essential to human metabolism. They are the building blocks of proteins.

Amnesia: The partial or total loss of memory for past experiences. May be associated with either organic brain disorders or dissociative reaction.

Amotivational syndrome: Apathy and lack of life goal purported to be related to use of marijuana.

Amphetamine: Drug that produces a physiologically and psychologically stimulating effect.

Amphetamine psychosis: A usually temporary, psychoticlike reaction to high levels of amphetamine in the blood stream. Paranoid ideation is prominent.

Amplification: In Jungian analysis, a technique of dream interpretation in which the analyst and the patient provide associations that are focused on the dream material, as opposed to the "free" association technique used by Freud.

Anaclitic depression: Profound depression in an infant when separated from its primary caretaker for a prolonged period.

Analytic epidemiology: The second phase of an epidemiological research strategy that is concerned with the identification of variables that contribute to the development of disorders.

Anesthesia: Loss of sense of touch or numbness in part of the body surface.

Angina pectoris: A severe pain that is the result of a lack of oxygen to meet the heart's needs. The condition is usually the result of restriction of blood flow to the heart because of a partial or complete blockage of the coronary arteries.

Anginal syndrome: Chest pain sometimes associated with cardiac insufficiency.

Animal magnetism: Belief that people have magnetic fluids within them and psychological problems can be treated by redistributing these fluids.

Anorexia nervosa: Loss of appetite, probably of psychological origin.

Antabuse: A drug which, when present in the blood stream, causes severe body distress when the individual ingests alcohol.

Anticipatory coping: Helping people to prepare for predictable life change or crisis through provision of information and social support.

Antidepressant drugs: Drugs that elevate mood and relieve depression.

Antihypertensive drugs: Substances that are intended to relieve hypertension or high blood pressure.

Antisocial personality: Classification applied to people who display repeated conflicts with society, do not experience guilt, and are incapable of loyalty to others (synonymous with *sociopath* and *psychopath*).

Anxiety: State of increased arousal and generalized feelings of fear and apprehension usually without a specific object of fear.

Anxiety disorders: Disorders listed in DSM III, in which anxiety plays an important role. Examples include phobic disorders, anxiety states, and obsessive compulsive disorders.

Arousal: Either behavioral or physiological state of activation.

Asexual homosexuals: According to Bell and Weinberg's typology, homosexuals who are secretive and withdrawn, who are not highly sexually active, and who may not be exclusively homosexual or well adjusted.

Assertiveness training: A therapeutic technique, usually involving behavior rehearsal, in which persons learn to assert themselves appropriately.

Associative disturbance: Disturbance in the association of ideas that is often reflected in unusual speech patterns or patterns of logic. Characteristic of schizophrenic disorders.

Asthma: A respiratory disorder.

Atrophy: A failure to develop or a wasting away of cells, tissues, and organs or of whole areas of the body.

Attachment behavior: Behavior reflecting strong emotional bond between infant and his/her caretaker.

Attention deficit disorder: A developmental disorder of childhood marked by impaired attention and impulsivity. Hyperactivity may or may not also be present.

Autism: See Infantile autism.

Auxillary egos: Members of a psychodrama group or trained professionals who enact the role of the protagonist or interact in an opposite role.

Barbiturates: Sedatives used to induce sleep or relaxation.

"Barnum effect": The impression of accuracy produced by a test or other assessment method because the traits used to describe the person are characteristic of most people in the population and are therefore trivially accurate.

Basal ganglia: Usually refers to three subcortical nuclear masses: the putamen, globus pallidus, and caudate. Sometimes the amygdaloid complex and/or the thalamus are also included. Degeneration of neurons in the basal ganglia has been associated with Huntington's disease.

Base rate: The prevailing proportion of an event or object in the total population.

Battered child syndrome: The term applied to the repetitive physical injury inflicted on a child by a parent or caregiver.

Behavior observation: A method of gathering information about a person that involves observing behavior in a natural setting.

Behavior therapy: A method of psychotherapy that uses learning principles such as reinforcement, extinction, and modeling to change behavior.

Behavioral medicine: An emerging transdisciplinary field (e.g., health education, medicine, medical sociology, psychology) that represents an integration of the behavioral sciences with the practice and science of medicine.

Bender-Gestalt Visual-Motor Test: A neuropsychological assessment instrument that involves the drawing of nine geometrical figures.

Bidirectional factors: Causes of abnormal behavior that mutually influence and reinforce each other.

Biochemical research: The search for the cause of a disorder in the biochemistry of the brain.

Biofeedback: A technique by which individuals can monitor their own physiological processes such as pulse, blood pressure, and brain waves with mechanical aid.

Biological perspective: A view that assumes abnormal behavior is a result of biological abnormalities that either affect behavior directly or do so in combination with stressful environmental influences.

Biological preparedness: The idea that certain objects may for biological reasons be prepotent targets for phobias.

Biological treatments: Treatments of psychological disorders that focus on evoking physiological changes, such as through the administration of drugs.

Bipolar episode: An affective disorder involving both depressive and manic episodes.

Blood alcohol levels: A measure of the amount of alcohol in the blood stream.

Bodily humors: The theory formulated by Hippocrates that inbalances in four body fluids (blood, black bile, yellow bile, and phlegm) cause depression and other mood changes.

Borderline personality: A personality disorder characterized by extremely unstable, impulsive, unpredictable, and often self-destructive behavior.

Booster treatments: Additional treatment sessions administered during a follow-up period to bolster treatment gains.

Bulimia: An eating disorder characterized by periods of extreme overeating (bingeing), followed by purging through vomiting or use of laxatives and diuretics.

Career: The sequence of movements from one position to another in a social or occupational system.

Case history: The collection of historical or biographical information on a single person for the purpose of discovering or illustrating psychological principles.

Catatonic schizophrenia: Form of schizophrenia characterized by a disturbance in motor behavior, often with alternating periods of immobility and extreme agitation.

Catecholamines: The neurotransmitters, together as a class.

Catharsis: Similar to abreaction; refers to expression of pent-up emotion.

Cathartic method: Discharge of emotional tension associated with repressed material by talking it out.

Childhood onset pervasive developmental disorder: A disorder of childhood characterized by a profound disturbance in social relations and multiple oddities of behavior, accompanied by disruption of intellectual, social, and cognitive functioning.

Childhood schizophrenia: Childhood disorder that occurs after a period of normal development. The child shows disturbances in social adjustment and in reality contact.

Chronic: Describes a disorder of lengthy duration, often irreversible.

Classic migraine headache: A migraine headache that is preceded by sensory and motor prodromal symptoms.

Classical conditioning: A form of learning in which a neutral stimulus (conditioned stimulus) is associated with an unconditioned stimulus to bring about a conditioned response.

Classification systems: The set of all possible diagnoses available within a diagnostic system. The system helps scientists describe and predict varieties of abnormal behavior.

Client-centered therapy: A therapy approach developed chiefly by Carl Rogers that is directed toward the attainment of the client's own goals in an accepting, empathic, and warm therapeutic atmosphere.

Clinical experiment: Experiments conducted to illuminate the nature of acquisition, maintenance, and change of abnormal behavior.

Clinical interview: An interview conducted by a mental health professional that is concerned with collecting important diagnostic information about a person.

Clinical observation: Noting and recording abnormal behavior as it occurs.

Close coupled homosexuals: According to Bell and Weinberg's typology, homosexuals who live in quasi marriages and tend to be well adjusted.

CNS (central nervous system) depressants: Drugs that have a sedative or hypnotic (sleep-inducing) effect on an organism. Overdose leads to anesthesia, coma, and, finally, death.

Cocaine: A stimulant made from the coca plant that produces feelings of euphoria.

Cognitive behavior therapy: A recent variation of behavior therapy based on the assumption that changing an individual's thoughts will result in changes in feelings and behavior.

Cognitive social learning theory: Social learning perspective that emphasizes that a person's thoughts or beliefs about a situation influence his or her subsequent performance.

"Cold turkey" withdrawal: Usually refers to quitting heroin use abruptly, without support of other medication.

Collective unconscious: A term coined by Carl Jung to refer to the inherited memory traces that are part of the unconscious and that are shared by the whole human race.

Common migraine headache: Migraine headache not necessarily accompanied by prodromal symptoms. Typical symptoms include pain limited to one side of the head, loss of appetite, vomiting, and sensitivity to bright lights.

Complex model: A model that takes into account the complexity and bidirectionality of the causal process underlying abnormal behavior.

Compulsion: Irrational and repetitive impulse to perform some act or behavior.

Compulsive personality: A personality disorder characterized by preoccupation with matters of rules, order, organization, efficiency, detail, indecision, and restricted ability to express warm and tender emotions.

Computerized tomography: Process in which scanners allow researchers to develop safe, noninvasive composite pictures of the brain that are highly sensitive to structural abnormalities.

Concordance: In genetic research, the occurrence of the same disorder or behavior in two subjects.

Conditioned response: A simple response to a neutral stimulus that is the result of repeatedly pairing the neutral stimulus with another nonneutral stimulus that would have naturally elicited the response.

Conditioned stimulus: The neutral stimulus that elicits a particular response as a result of repeated pairings with a nonneutral or unconditioned stimulus that naturally elicits that response.

Conditions of worth: A person's view of his or her own experiences as being more or less worthy of respect. In the humanistic perspective, a predisposing factor in the development of abnormal behavior.

Conduct disorder: A persistent pattern of conduct that violates the basic rights of others or social rules or norms occurring during childhood and adolescence.

Conflict: Simultaneous arousal of opposing impulses, desires, or motives.

Conjoint family therapy: Therapeutic intervention with the entire family to alter family dynamics viewed as a total system.

Control group: Those subjects in an experiment who are not exposed to whatever experimental conditions are being studied and who serve as a comparison to assess the effects of the experimental manipulations.

Controlled drinking: An approach to alcoholism treatment that sanctions ingestion of small amounts of alcohol recreationally. This is in contrast to the more traditional abstinence approach.

Controlled drug: Substance defined as illegal to possess without medical prescription.

Controlled experiment: An experiment in which one variable is manipulated while all others are held constant.

Conversion reaction: A reaction involving bodily symptoms, usually of the skeletal musculature and sensory functions with no detectable tissue damage.

Coronary heart disease: This term most commonly refers to disease or blockage of the coronary arteries, the blood vessels that encircle the heart and provide the heart muscle with oxygen.

Coronary occlusion: A total blockage of the coronary artery, the possible precipitant of a myocardial infarction or heart attack.

Correlation of causal factors: The degree to which factors occur together.

Correlational approach: Research in which the relationships between two or more variables are examined but no manipulations of the variables are used.

Co-twin: Term used in genetic research to refer to the twin of the index case.

Countertransference: Arousal of feelings of transference on the part of the analyst during the course of psychoanalytic therapy in response to behavior or characteristics of the client.

Coverage: Degree to which a classification or diagnosis is capable of identifying a significant segment of the population in question.

Covert sensitization: A behavioral technique in which the client imagines repulsive, aversive associations to eliminate a target behavior.

Crisis intervention: Methods for rendering immediate therapeutic assistance to people in acute distress.

Cross-fostering: An experimental procedure in which observations are made on normal children who are raised by disordered adopting parents.

Defense mechanism: In psychoanalysis, behavior that protects the person from anxiety provoked by sexual and aggressive impulses.

Deinstitutionalization: The policy of removing patients from hospitals and transferring their care to the community. In part, this treatment policy stems from a recognition of the debilitating effects of long-term hospitalization and the negative effects of the patient role.

Delirium: State of mental confusion characterized by confusion, disorientation, restlessness, excitement, and at times hallucinations.

Delirium tremens: Delirium associated with prolonged alcoholism and characterized by anxiety, hallucinations, and tremors.

Delusion: A usually persistent belief that is contrary to the consensus of other people.

Dementia: Severe mental disorder involving impairment of mental ability, including memory and reasoning ability.

Dementia praecox: A term used by Emil Kraepelin to refer to a form of psychotic behavior now called *schizophrenia*.

Depression: A disorder characterized by apathy, dejection, sadness, and self-blame.

Dereflection: A therapeutic technique devised by Victor Frankl in which the person's capacity to live spontaneously is enhanced by instructions to ignore symptoms, focus on the present, and attend to everyday concerns and relationships.

Descriptive epidemiology: An initial research strategy concerned with determining the frequency of disorders within a population.

Detoxification: Treatment for alcoholism consisting of removing alcohol from the patient's system.

Diagnosis: The process or act of determining or identifying the nature of a disease by considering the patient's symptoms.

Diagnostic and Statistical Manual of Mental Disorders (DSM III): The single most widely used classification system. Published by the American Psychiatric Association, it strives to provide clear descriptions of diagnostic categories and outline diagnostic criteria.

Diagnostic criteria: A list of symptoms or behaviors necessary to diagnose a given psychological disorder.

Diathesis-stress: A hypothesis that asserts that individuals predisposed toward a particular psychological disorder will be affected by stress and will then manifest abnormal behavior.

Direct therapy: Behaviorally oriented sex therapy programs based on the idea that sexual dysfunctions can be treated directly without focusing on in-depth personality changes.

Direct transmission model: A model of pain that views pain as the result of direct sensory input arising from pain receptors in free nerve endings.

Displacement: Defense mechanism in which an emotional attitude or symbolic meaning is transferred from one object or concept to another.

Disregulation: Hypothesis that psychophysiological disorders are the result of disruption in the brain's regulatory feedback system with various other organ systems.

Dissociative disorders: Psychological disorders resulting from the apparent splitting off of some psychological function from the rest of conscious thought.

Dizygotic twins (DZ twins, fraternal twins): Twins who develop from two eggs fertilized by two different sperm and who have only approximately 50 percent of their genes in common, as do other sibling pairs.

Dopamine: A neurotransmitter found in high concentrations in the basal ganglia and substantia nigra. Specific degeneration of dopamine-containing neurons in the substantia nigra has been linked to Parkinsonism.

Dopamine hypothesis: A theory that schizophrenia is caused by an increased level of the brain neurotransmitter, dopamine.

Double bind: An interpersonal relationship in which the person is confronted by mutually inconsistent messages to which he or she must respond.

Draw-a-person test: Projective test requiring that a picture of a person be drawn; inferences regarding the characteristics of the subject are then drawn.

Dream analysis: The interpretation of the patient's dreams in psychotherapy.

Dream censorship: In psychoanalytic theory, the process or manner in which the latent dream material is disguised to reduce the anxiety of the dream and permit undisturbed sleep.

Drift hypothesis: Hypothesis that psychologically disabled people, especially schizophrenics, "drift" to a lower social status rather than that the lower social status plays a direct causal role in the development of the disorder.

Drive: Internal conditions directing an organism toward a specific goal, usually involving biological rather than psychological motives.

Drug addiction: Reliance on a drug developed through continual use; characterized by increased tolerance and withdrawal symptoms and physiological dependence.

Drug combination (interaction): The way in which two or more drugs affect the individual when the drugs are taken concurrently.

Drug detoxification: Usually refers to the process of medical and psychological support necessary after initial cessation of drug use.

Drug-induced euphoria: Intense feeling of pleasure and power produced following ingestion of drug.

DSM III: *Diagnostic and Statistical Manual of Mental Disorders,* published by the American Psychiatric Association. The official list of diagnostic terms and definitions.

Dualistic position: The philosophical doctrine attributed to Descartes that contends that the mind and body are separate entities, the body being material and the mind immaterial.

Dynamic unconscious: In psychoanalytic theory, the notion that thoughts and behavior are determined by unconscious processes.

Dynamic viewpoint: The view of abnormal behavior in which intrapsychic conflicts are thought to be the cause.

Dysfunctional homosexuals: According to Bell and Weinberg's typology, homosexuals who are poorly adjusted sexually, socially, and psychologically.

Dyslexia: The term for a developmental reading disorder characterized by distortion, omission, and alteration of words when reading.

Early infantile autism: A severe childhood disorder with an onset prior to 30 months of age, characterized by the child's inability to relate in ordinary ways to people and situations.

Eccentric personality disorders: One of the clusters of personality disorders listed in DSM III that include paranoid, introverted, and schizotypal personality disorders.

Echolalia: The repetition of words or phrases spoken by others often in a chanting fashion without effort at communication. This pattern of behavior is usually seen with psychotically disturbed children and adults.

Ecology: The study of the relation or interaction between organisms and their physical or behavioral environment.

Ego: That part of the psychological structure that is usually described as the "self." It is the aspect of the personality that mediates between the needs of the id and reality.

Ego ideal: The person or "self" the individual thinks he or she could and should be.

Ego-dystonic: Thoughts or behavior that a person experiences as alien and undesirable.

Ego-dystonic homosexuality: A recent addition to the list of psychosexual disorders (indexed in DSM III). It involves homosexual thoughts and/or feelings that are personally distressing and unwanted.

Ego-syntonic: Personality characteristics that a person values and experiences as desirable.

Electroencephalogram (EEG): The recorded tracing of changes in electric activity from different parts of the brain (usually the cerebral cortices), obtained by means of electrodes attached to the scalp. It is often used as an aid in diagnosing degenerative brain states, tumors, trauma, epilepsy, and drug-induced abnormalities.

Electroshock (EST) or electroconvulsive therapy (ECT): Use of the electric shock to the brain as treatment, usually for depression.

Empathy: The ability to appreciate and share the emotional or mental state of mind of another person.

Encopresis: The repeated inappropriate defecation or withholding of feces by a child over three years of age and not due to a physical disorder.

Encounter group: Group including features of the T-group and the sensitivity group; emphasizes personal growth.

Endogenous: Resulting from or referring to internal causes.

Endogenous depression: Depression attributable to internal rather than external causes. No reasonable precipitating external cause can be found.

Endorphins: Neurotransmitters in the brain that may influence the development of schizophrenia.

"Entrance" life events: Life events that involve moving into the social field (e.g. engagement, marriage, birth). Depressives and normals have the same number of entrance life events.

Enuresis: Persistent, involuntary urination in children past the age of four or five, not caused by a physical disorder.

Epidemiological: The study of the distribution of illnesses in populations or geographic areas.

Epidemiological catchment area program: A large-scale epidemiological study of abnormal behavior involving interviews of nearly 17,000 persons in five different sites across the country.

Epinephrine: Hormone secreted by the adrenal glands that acts as a stimulant. It is released when the body experiences stress.

Ergot: A poisonous fungus that may cause convulsions and abnormal behavior.

Erratic personality disorders: One of the clusters of personality disorders listed in DSM III. It includes histrionic, narcissistic, antisocial, and borderline personality disorders.

Essential or primary hypertension: The 85 to 90 percent of cases of high blood pressure for which the cause is unknown.

Ethnocentrism: Belief that one's own country, culture, and race are superior to other countries, cultures, and races.

Etiology: Cause or determinant.

Evoking stimuli (ES): In Mark's (1977) terminology, the stimuli that trigger a phobic response.

Exhibitionism: Displaying one's genitals to an involuntary observer for the purpose of sexual arousal.

Existential therapy: Therapy based on existential concepts, emphasizing the development of a sense of self-direction and meaning in one's existence.

"Exit" life events: Life events that involve some removal from the social field (e.g., death, divorce, or family member leaving home).

Exogenous: Resulting from or referring to external causes.

Exogenous depression: Depression attributable to external causes (death in family, separation from loved one).

Exorcism: Techniques practiced in medieval times for casting "evil spirits" out of the possessed or afflicted.

Experimental analogue: Experimental study of a phenomenon different from but analogous to the actual interests of the investigator.

Experimental group: In research, the group on which the manipulation of interest is performed.

Experimental neurosis: Maladaptive behavior produced in animals in the laboratory by inescapable conflicts and other types of stress.

Extinction: Gradual disappearance of a conditioned response when it is no longer reinforced.

Failure to thrive: A condition of infancy characterized by failure to grow, gain weight, and develop at a normal rate, with no underlying physical disorder.

Family hypothesis: The idea that schizophrenia is caused by dysfunctional family functioning.

Family sacrifice: The idea that schizophrenia in a child is caused by rejection by his/her family.

Fearful personality disorder: One of the clusters of personality disorders listed in DSM III. It includes avoidant, compulsive, and passive-aggressive personality disorders.

Fetishism: Use of an object or nongenital body part for sexual arousal and satisfaction.

Fixation: In psychoanalysis, developmental arrest at a childhood level of psychosexual development.

Flashback: Usually disturbing, brief, vivid, and intense reliving of a drug experience days, weeks, or months after the actual drug ingestion.

Flight of ideas: Characteristic of manic disorders. Rapid and irrational series of thoughts and/or images.

Flooding: Therapeutic technique in which the person is made to confront the stimuli that arouse anxiety until the anxiety extinguishes.

Follow-up study: Research procedure in which individuals are studied over a period of time or are recontacted at a later time after initial study.

Free association: Psychoanalytic technique in which the analysand is instructed to say whatever comes to mind, without selection or censorship of any kind; the goal is to examine and clarify the implication of the material elicited.

Fugue: A type of dissociative reaction in which the person moves to a new locale, begins a new life, and is amnesic of his or her previous life.

Functional analysis: An analysis of the frequency of particular behaviors, the situations in which they occur, and their consequences. Used by behaviorally oriented clinicians and researchers.

Functional dyspareunia: Painful intercourse not caused exclusively by organic factors.

Functional homosexuals: According to Bell and Weinberg's typology, highly sexually active "swinging" homosexuals who tend to have a good psychological adjustment.

Functional psychosis: Severe disturbance in thought, behavior, and emotional behavior without known damage to the brain or other organ systems.

Gate control model: A model of pain that postulates a gating mechanism in the dorsal horn of the spinal cord that controls the flow in sensory impulses from nerve fibers to the central nervous system. Competition from other sensory input can diminish pain because it activates the "gate" interrupting the flow of pain impulses.

Gender identity disorders: Psychological disorders in which discomfort and inappropriateness about the person's anatomic sex are expressed and in which the behavior is generally congruent with that of the "opposite" sex.

General adaptation syndrome: A pattern of reaction to excessive stress; consists of the alarm reaction, the stage of resistance, and the stage of exhaustion.

General sexual dysfunction: The absence or weakness of the physiological changes in women that normally accompany the excitement phase of sexual response.

Generalized other: A concept developed by Mead (1934) that is used to summarize the way each person develops an idea of how other people will react to his or her behavior.

Genetic factors: Inherited genetic material that causes disorder.

Genetic heterogeneity: The theory that specific genes in specific combinations cause disorder.

Genetic marker: A known genetic characteristic that allows prediction of risk for a disorder.

Genetics: Scientific study of heredity.

Gestalt therapy: An approach to psychotherapy emphasizing the integration of thought, feeling, and action.

Glove anesthesia: A form of dissociative reaction in which the person reports a numbness in his or her hand from the tips of the fingers to a clear cut-off point at the wrist; this numbness does not conform to the neurological pattern to be expected if nerve damage were the cause.

Grandiose ideas: Exaggerated expression of self-importance and/or power.

Grandiose self: In object relations theory, the child's development of inappropriate feelings of omnipotence in order to maintain self-esteem.

Group therapy: Treating psychological disorders by having several persons seen simultaneously by a single therapist. Group interaction is an important therapeutic agent.

Hallucination: Perception in any sensory modality (but particularly auditory, visual, and tactile) without adequate external stimuli.

Hallucinogenic: Capable of producing hallucinations.

Halstead-Reitan Neuropsychological Test Battery: A battery of tests for assessing organic disorders. The procedure involves tasks designed to detect problems in auditory and visual perception, motor performance, and the ability to engage in abstract tasks.

Health psychology: A newcomer to the area of psychology, this field stresses the contributions of a psychological nature to the promotion and maintenance of health.

Hebephrenic schizophrenia: Schizophrenic pattern characterized by severe personality disintegration, confusion, and giggling.

Hidden observer: A part of consciousness, described by Hilgard, that continues to monitor external circumstances even though a person remains deeply hypnotized.

High-risk method: Research following persons believed to be at risk for developing a disorder over time, usually in comparison to a low-risk group for the purpose of identifying characteristics of the high-risk group that may play a causal role in the disorder.

High-risk strategy: A means of studying a disorder in which children judged at risk for the disorder are observed prospectively. Events that precede the disorder can hopefully be examined.

Histrionic personality: A personality disorder characterized by an overly dramatic, impressionistic, and exhibitionistic approach to life.

Hives: Skin condition characterized by itching patches. Often considered a stress-related disorder.

Holistic perspective: This viewpoint or position holds that understanding and treating a physical disorder require an appreciation for the "whole" person, the psychological, social, and physical factors associated with illness and health.

Homeostasis: The process whereby equilibrium or balance is maintained in a dynamic system such as the organism.

Homosexuality: Sexual attraction toward one's own sex.

Hot line: Telephone service where people in trouble can call and receive immediate attention and advice from trained volunteers.

Humanistic perspective: A view of abnormal behavior that emphasizes personal growth and emphasis on the whole person. Includes self-theories, some elements of existentialism, and some elements of phenomenology.

Hyperactivity: A developmental condition marked by extreme overactivity and distractibility, which often improves by late adolescence.

Hypertension: A chronic elevation of blood pressure due to constriction of the arteries. Often a stress-related physical disorder.

Hypnosis: Trancelike state resembling sleep, characterized by increased suggestibility.

Hypochondriasis: A psychological disorder in which an individual converts anxiety into a preoccupation with bodily functioning.

Hypothesis: Proposition tested in an experiment. May be denied or supported by empirical results but never proved conclusively.

Hysteria: A physical disability (paralysis or sensory loss) for which no organic causes can be found.

Id: The reservoir of instinctual drives in the psychological structure of the individual. It is the most primitive and most inaccessible structure of the personality.

Identity diffusion: A feature of borderline personality; it describes a distorted, inconsistent, and vague sense of self.

Idiosyncratic intoxification: A radical and abrupt personality shift in an individual following substantial ingestion of alcohol.

Illness perspective: A view of abnormal behavior in which the language and concepts of physical medicine are used as a model to describe deviant behavior.

Imipramine: An antidepressant medication that successfully treats the anxiety associated with panic attacks.

Implosion therapy: A technique for reducing fears; the client is induced to imagine himself/herself in the most frightening situations and to visualize bizarre images.

Implosive therapy: Form of flooding therapy.

Impotence: Absence or weakness of the physiological changes that produce an erection.

Incest: Sexual relations between close relatives.

Incidence: The rate at which new cases occur in a given place at a given time.

Incongruence: A discrepancy or conflict that the organism experiences. The discrepancy is between the self as the individual perceives it and the actual experience of the organism. For example, one may perceive oneself as having one set of characteristics, but an accurate symbolization of one's experience would indicate a different set of characteristics. A state of incongruence in the organism may be characterized as internal confusion or tension.

Index case (proband case): In genetic research, the individual in the family who has the diagnosed case of the disorder.

Infantile autism: A disorder in children in which the primary symptom, from infancy onward, seems to be the inability to relate to others. Also, speech disturbances and stereotyped behaviors are apparent.

Informed consent: Procedure for obtaining permission of research subjects to participate in an experiment after assuring that the subject is aware of the demands and risks of participating.

Inhibited orgasm: According to DSM III, the sexual disorders defined by persistent and repeated delay or absence of orgasm in males and females who are responsive to sexual stimuli and capable of experiencing a normal sexual excitement phase.

Inhibited sexual excitement: According to DSM III, a sexual disorder characterized by failure to attain or maintain sexual excitement until the sexual act is completed; commonly termed *impotence* in the male, and *frigidity* in the female.

Innervation: The nerve supply to an area or organ of the body.

Instrumental conditioning: Process of development of behavior in which the organism must emit the response before reinforcement can occur. Therefore, the response is instrumental in receiving reinforcement.

Interpretation: Statement made by an analyst to help patients understand the unconscious basis of their behavior, which repression and resistance have kept them from perceiving.

Interrater reliability: The extent to which independent observers can agree on ratings or other scores for a set of observations.

Interview: A psychological method of assessment involving a face-to-face conversation between subject and interviewer.

La belle indifférence: Lack of concern and indifference about a physical symptom, often displayed by persons suffering from conversion disorders.

Labile hypertensive: A person with high blood pressure who shows abnormal elevations on a temporary or irregular basis.

Latent content: In psychoanalytic theory, the unconscious or "real" meaning of a dream, which is expressed in disguised, distorted, or symbolic form.

Learned helplessness: A concept referring to passive acceptance of discomfort and lack of responsiveness after responses do not provide a means of escape or alter the situation.

Learning disabilities: The failure to develop age-appropriate skills in areas of language, speech, reading, and/or arithmetic.

Learning perspective: A view of abnormal behavior that describes both a formulation of abnormal behavior as well as a relatively well-defined program of treatment based on the principles of learning theory.

Lesbianism: Female homosexuality.

Lethal dose: A dose or amount of a drug that will result in death when ingested.

Lethality: The likelihood of fatal outcome for particular methods of suicide.

Life events: Common problems that temporarily engender stress and sadness in most individuals but that do not usually result in serious psychological disturbance.

Lithium carbonate: A drug shown to be useful in treating affective disorders.

Logotherapy: Viktor Frankl's existential therapy that involves helping the patient to assume responsibility for his or her life and his or her attitudes for it and to find personal meaning and value in everyday life.

Longitudinal study: A type of study that involves observations of a sample population at regular time intervals over an extended period of time.

Low rate of response: In the learning theory of depression the depressed person is not receiving reinforcement for the behaviors he or she emits. This results in an impoverishment of responses to the environment.

Lysergic acid diethylamide–25 (LSD): A potent hallucinogen.

Machiavellianism: As defined by Christie and Geis (1970), a personality trait characterized by manipulating others, lack of concern with conventional morality, lack of gross pathology, and low ideological commitment.

Magnetic fluids: Invisible energy Anton Mesmer hypothesized was the reason some of his patients were cured.

Magnitude of effect: The mean difference between treated and control subjects divided by the standard deviation of the control group.

Maintaining factors: Factors that reinforce abnormal behavior and thus maintain it over time.

Major depression: Severe depressive episodes involving some impairment of social and occupational functioning.

Malleus Maleficarum: *The Witch's Hammer*, a book written by two friars during the Middle Ages. Although the book purported to identify witches, it resulted in the persecution of poor people who happened to behave in a peculiar manner.

Mania: A form of psychosis involving extreme euphoria, hyperactivity, grandiose thinking, and sleep disturbances.

Manic episode: A period during which the person experiences euphoria, along with associated characteristics of mania. This period usually lasts more than one week.

Manifest content: In psychoanalytic theory, the content of the dream as recalled by the patient.

Marathon group: A form of group therapy run for long periods of time, the assumption being that defenses can be worn down by the fatigue produced through intensive and continuous group interaction.

March of progress school of history: A view of history that stresses breakthroughs and famous persons in each century.

Marijuana: Drug derived from the plant *Cannabis sativa*, often used in cigarettes.

Marital schism: Marriage relationship characterized by conflict and discord that threatens continuation of marital relationship.

Marital skew: Marriage maintained at expense of distorted relationship in favor of one of the partners.

Masochism: Sexual deviation in which an individual obtains sexual gratification from having pain inflicted upon him/her.

Medical view: View that mental illness is attributable to organic or mental disease of some sort.

Mental status interview: An unstructured clinical interview concerned with assessing the degree of emotional and cognitive disturbance.

Mesmerism: Theory of hypnosis invoking "animal magnetism" advanced by Anton Mesmer.

Meta-analysis: A research strategy involving the collection of hundreds of individual studies for one exhaustive, overall statistical analysis.

Methadone: A synthetic addictive narcotic used for treating heroin addicts; acts as a substitute for heroin.

Method lethality: The probability of death connected with a specific means of self-destruction.

Migraine headache: A form of headache associated with contractions of the cranial arteries and dilation of blood vessels in the brain.

Milieu therapy: Therapy in which disturbed patients live together in an atmosphere designed to maximize their sense of independence, their activity level, and their sense of dignity and participation.

Minnesota Multiphasic Personality Inventory (MMPI): A self-report inventory composed of 550 true-false statements. The test yields a personality profile on which the person can be compared to norms for different psychological disorders.

Mobilization techniques: Methods of getting a person involved in tasks that are likely to increase feelings of mastery and self-esteem and counteract depression.

Model: An analogy that helps scientists order their findings and see important relationships among them.

Model psychosis: Psychotic symptoms induced by drugs that are thought to provide a model for the study of the disorder itself.

Modeling: Behavior learned through imitation.

Monoamine oxidase inhibitors (MAOI): Antidepressant drugs that prevent the enzyme monoamine oxidase from deactivating neurotransmitters of the brain and central nervous system.

Monogenic theory: Hypothesis that a disorder is transmitted by a single gene at one location on a chromosome.

Monozygotic twins (MZ twins): Twins who develop from a single fertilized egg and have exactly the same genotype.

Moral anxiety: In Freudian theory, the result of conflict between the id impulses and the superego. A person feeling moral anxiety will often feel intense shame or guilt.

Moral treatment: The treatment of the American asylum movement in the 19th century. It was assumed that the peace and serenity of the country and removal from the rapid pace of the city was essential to cure. The heart of moral treatment was disciplined routine.

Motor symptoms: In neurotic disorders, apparent loss of motor function with no apparent tissue damage (e.g., paralysis).

Multiaxial classification: Classification of disorders on multiple dimensions or aspects of behavior; the method employed by DSM III.

Multiple personality: Dissociative reaction characterized by the development of two or more relatively independent personalities in the same individual.

Myocardial infarction: This term is also known as a *heart attack,* the destruction of tissue due to insufficient blood flow.

Narcissistic personality: A personality disorder characterized by strong dependence on the admiration of others and fluctuation between feelings of superiority and feelings of worthlessness.

Narcotic antagonists: A group of drugs that block and reverse the effects of opiates.

Narcotic drugs: Drugs such as morphine which may lead to physiological dependence and increased tolerance.

Need: Biological or psychological condition whose gratification is necessary for the maintenance of homeostasis or for self-actualization.

Neuroleptic drugs: Tranquilizing drugs used in the treatment of schizophrenia.

Neurology: Field concerned with the study of the brain and nervous system.

Neuropsychological assessment: The evaluation of the link between damage to the central nervous system and behavior. The evaluation may consist of a battery of behavioral tests measuring coordination, visual and auditory perception, and speech recognition.

Neuroscience: A branch of science concerned with the study of the nervous system.

Neuroses: Term previously used to denote conditions in which maladaptive behaviors serve as a protection against sources of unconscious anxiety.

Neurotransmitter: A chemical that transmits electrical signals between brain cells.

Nicotine: A mild stimulant found in tobacco.

Nondirective therapy: An approach to the client (usually associated with Rogerian therapy), in which the therapist does not define the client's problems or tell him or her how they might be solved.

Norepinephrine (noradrenaline): A hormone or biogenic amine that plays a role in transmitting neural impulses in many parts of the body, including the brain.

Norepinephrine depletion: A theory of depression held by Weiss, which states that depression is a result of lowered levels of the neurotransmitter norepinephrine.

Object relations theory: A recent movement in psychoanalytic thinking that traces abnormal behavior to disruptions in the child's early relationship with his or her mother.

Obsession: Recurrent idea or thought that intrudes and seems uncontrollable to the person experiencing it.

Obsessive-compulsive disorder: Preoccupation with unwelcome thoughts (obsession) and/or stereotyped, involuntary repetition of an unnecessary action (compulsion).

Oedipus complex: In psychoanalytic theory, belief that boys desire sexual relations with their mothers.

Open-coupled homosexuals: According to Bell and Weinberg's typology, independent, nonattached homosexual couples.

Operant conditioning: Form of learning in which the correct response is rewarded and then becomes more likely to occur.

Operational definition: Defining a concept on the basis of the set of operations that are used to measure and observe it.

Opiates: Drugs derived from opium, including heroin, morphine, and codeine.

Opium: Chemical substance derived from the opium poppy; one of the narcotic drugs.

Oral character: A personality type purportedly fixated at an early stage of psychosexual development (oral). Such persons are purported to be prone to develop alcoholism.

Organic brain syndrome: Psychological, behavioral, and physical disturbances caused by some known physical disease or injury.

Organic psychosis: A disorder in which intellectual or emotional functioning are impaired due to dysfunction resulting from physical disease or injury.

Overgeneralization: A characteristic of depressive thought where a person draws an extremely broad conclusion based on some specific fact.

Panic disorder: Acute attacks of anxiety that are characterized by intense fear and terror.

Paradigm: A basic conceptual framework specifying concepts considered legitimate and procedures to be used in the collection and interpretation of data.

Paradigm clash: The conflict or clash between the prevailing view of normal science and a new, emerging conceptual scheme. Often the new paradigm produces a shift in the problems available for scientific investigation and transforms the ways in which the scientist sees the world.

Paradoxical intention: One of Viktor Frankl's techniques in which the patient is asked what he or she fears most and to exaggerate the fear or symptoms to gain a sense of mastery or control over the symptom.

Paranoid personality disorder: A personality disorder defined by suspiciousness and mistrust.

Paranoid schizophrenia: A type of schizophrenia characterized by delusions, hallucinations, and some personality disorganization.

Paraphilias: Psychosexual disorders included in DSM III that involve variations from the norms of conventional choice of sexual objects and choice of sexual activity in which the person is hindered in his or her capacity to engage in close, affectionate sexual relations.

Parataxic distortion: Unrealistic attitude or misperceptions of reality, with roots in childhood and carried over into adult relationships. The term was coined by H. S. Sullivan.

Partial penetrance: Theory that a known genotype does not always manifest itself phenotypically.

Participant observer: The collaborative role the therapist assumes in treatment in Sullivan's interpersonal psychotherapy.

Pathology: The functional and structural abnormalities associated with a disease state; any deviation from normal physical and mental functioning.

Pedophilia: Preference for obtaining sexual gratification through contact with children.

Penetrance: Percent of cases who manifest the trait in question.

Performance anxiety: Anxiety and concern about performance that contribute to sexual dysfunctions.

Personality disorder: An inflexible pattern of behavior that may cause impairment in social or occupational functioning, presumably developed at an early age and of long duration.

Perspective: A theoretical point of view organized around a central conception that provides a framework for understanding phenomena.

Phenomenological: Referring to the immediate experience of the individual.

Phenothiazines: A class of drug found effective in the treatment of schizophrenia.

Phenotype: The observable characteristics that result from the combination of a person's genotype with environmental influences.

Phobia: Irrational fear, often associated with avoidance of specific objects and situations, such as crowds or heights.

Physical monist position: In contrast to Cartesian dualism, this doctrine contends that the mind and body are not separate but are one entity; all activities attributed to the mind can be reduced to the physical activity of the brain.

Placebo effect: Any behavioral or psychological effect caused by creating a belief or expectancy that a change will occur.

Plastic: Refers to the capacity to be molded or to undergo change. Infants, for example have a "plastic" brain, in that it has the capability of regenerating injured neurons and changing the function of specific brain areas.

Pleasure principle: In psychoanalytic theory, the desire or instinctual need to be immediately gratified regardless of reality constraints.

Polygene threshold model: Theory that genes causing a disorder exert a cumulative effect. However, only when a threshold number of genes is reached will the disorder occur.

Polygenic theory: Hypothesis that a disorder is transmitted by two or more genes on a chromosome.

Position emission tomography: A technique for scanning patterns of metabolism in the brain. It involves placing traces of radioactive material in glucose, a substance brain cells use in metabolism.

Possession (spirit): Belief that people who behaved in a particular manner were inhabited by evil spirits.

Posthypnotic suggestion: Suggestion given during the hypnotic trance to be carried out by the person after he is brought out of the trance.

Posttraumatic stress disorders: Delayed psychological distress resulting from an earlier traumatic event. Symptoms include flashbacks, nightmares, anger, difficulty concentrating, and feelings of depersonalization.

Precipitating environmental events: External stresses or events that are thought to act as a catalyst in causing disorders.

Preconscious: In Freudian theory the second level of consciousness that consists of contents the person can recall without great difficulty.

Predictive validity: Degree to which a test or measure is capable of predicting some future state or status of an individual.

Predisposing factor: Factor that lowers the individual's stress tolerance and paves the way for the appearance of a disorder.

Premack Principle: The Premack Principle states that the occurrence of a high-frequency behavior can be used to reinforce a low- frequency behavior.

Premature ejaculation: According to DSM III, the absence of voluntary control of ejaculation and orgasm during sexual activity, so that ejaculation occurs before it is desired.

Premorbid: Usually refers to adjustment of persons before they develop behavior problems.

Prevalence: In epidemiological studies of a disorder, the proportion of a population that has the disorder at a given time.

Primary prevention: Establishing environmental conditions designed to prevent occurrence of mental disorders.

Primary process: Usually refers to modes of thinking that are primitive, illogical, and perceptually vivid. Primary process may also refer to drive energy that is mobile and can be displaced onto other objects.

Primary sexual disorders: The term for sexual disorders in which a sexual history suggests that the person has never functioned normally with respect to the disorder being evaluated.

Process-reactive dimension: Classification of schizophrenics according to whether the onset of the disorder is gradual (process) or sudden and precipitated by some traumatic event (reactive).

Prodromal symptoms: The sensory and motor symptoms that precede a classic migraine headache; these include blind spots, brief visual images, light flashes, visual and auditory hallucinations, and numbness in the hands and feet.

Prognosis: In diagnosis, a prediction of the future course and outcome of the patient's problem.

Prognostic dreams: According to Carl Jung, dreams that foretell a future event or warn the dreamer.

Projection: A defense mechanism in which the person disowns some impulse and attributes it to another person or object.

Projective identification: A feature of the borderline personality: it reflects the person's attribution of threatening thoughts or emotions to others followed by the subsequent identification with these same emotions.

Projective test: Psychological tests using unstructured stimuli like ink blots or figures.

Prospective research: A method of research in which data are gathered before the phenomenon under study has occurred.

Protagonist: A member of a psychodrama group who enacts relevant scenes from his/her past, present, or future, playing the role of himself or herself or of other people.

Psychedelic drugs: Mind-expanding or altering drugs, such as LSD, that may result in hallucinations.

Psychiatrist: A physician who specializes in the treatment of psychological disorders.

Psychoactive drug: Substance that affects the person's behavior or subjective experience.

Psychoanalysis: Theoretical model of psychological functioning and therapy technique developed by Sigmund Freud.

Psychoanalyst: Person who has received specialized training at a psychoanalytic institute.

Psychodrama: A group treatment developed by Jacob Moreno that uses techniques of dramatic play and unrehearsed acting to stimulate the spontaneous expression of feeling.

Psychodynamic: Any theory that views abnormal behavior as the result of intrapsychic conflict.

Psychological approach: An approach to abnormal behavior that de-emphasizes physicalistic explanations. Events in the person's life and intrapsychic interpretations of these events are viewed as important.

Psychological assessment: A detailed evaluation of an individual's functioning concerned with establishing a psychological diagnosis. Clinical interviews, structured interviews, and psychological tests are all part of the assessment process.

Psychological test: An assessment technique in which the subject is presented with a series of stimuli to which he or she is asked to respond.

Psychomimetic: Resembling psychosis.

Psychosexual dysfunctions: Psychological disorders characterized by a failure to enjoy and/or achieve accepted sexual behaviors.

Psychosurgery: Brain surgery used to treat psychological disorders.

Psychotherapy: As defined by Strupp (1970), an interpersonal process designed to bring about changes of feelings, cognitions, attitudes, and behavior that have proven troublesome to the person seeking help from a trained professional.

Psychotomimetic: A drug that can induce a psychotic-like state, i.e., mimic psychosis (e.g., LSD and other hallucinogens).

Rape: To force sexual relations upon another person.

Rapid cycling of mood: Short-lived alternations between euphoria and depression.

Rapport: Relationship characterized by an attitude of cooperation, confidence, and harmony.

Rational-emotive therapy: Therapeutic approach developed by Albert Ellis that emphasizes cognitive-change techniques and change in irrational beliefs.

Reaction formation: According to dynamic theory, a state in which a person represses feelings that arouse anxiety and then professes the exact opposite of these feelings.

Reactive attachment disorder of infancy: A disorder of infancy with onset prior to eight months of age, characterized by poor physical and emotional development occurring because of a lack of adequate caretaking.

Reality anxiety: A state in which a person is threatened by something actual in the outside world.

Reality principle: Awareness of the demands of the environment and adjustment of behavior to meet these demands.

Recessive gene: Gene that has effect when it is paired with an identical gene.

Recreational use: Occasional use of alcohol or other drugs without pathology or serious disruption of life experiences.

Reform movement: Humanitarian spirit arising from the American and French revolutions that resulted in kinder treatment and improved living conditions for mental patients.

Regulative activity: In Jungian thinking, the unconscious, through activities like dreams, works toward achieving psychic harmony and balance.

Reinforcement: The process by which response strength (i.e., the probability of a response) is changed as a result of either classical conditioning or operant conditioning.

Reliability: The extent to which a test or observation method is consistent in measuring whatever it does measure.

Repression: Defense mechanism in which impulses threatening to the ego are pushed out of awareness and into the unconscious.

Resistance: In psychoanalytic thinking, the tendency to resist treatment to avoid the anxiety which recognition of previously repressed material evokes.

Risk factors: Factors that dispose an individual to develop an illness or stress-related disorder. These can include psychological as well as physical factors.

Ritalin (methylphenidate): A stimulant drug often prescribed for hyperactivity and attention deficit disorders.

Role theory (antisocial personality): An account offered by Gough that argues that the antisocial personality is undersocialized, lacking in empathy, and unable to evaluate behavior from the point of view of another.

Rorschach: A projective personality and diagnostic test making use of ink blots.

Sadism: Sexual deviation in which sexual gratification is obtained by inflicting pain upon others.

Sample of behavior: A major goal of a psychological assessment. Behavior assumed to be representative of the person's behavior in a range of situations is gathered to help predict other important outcomes.

Satir's structured interview: An interview format developed by Virginia Satir that is used in family therapy; it consists of a set of tasks that enable the therapist to learn about the family's rules and communication problems.

Scapegoat: Person or groups blamed for the misfortune of others.

Schemas: In depression theory, schemas are habitual ways of thinking that actually reinforce the negative experiences the depressive typically reports.

Schizomimetic conditions: Conditions that produce behavior that is similar to schizophrenia.

Schizophrenia: A group of psychoses marked by severe disorganization of thought, distortion of perception and of affect, by bizarre behavior, and frequently by social withdrawal.

Schizophrenogenic mother: A mother who is capable of causing schizophrenia in an offspring.

School phobia: A childhood disorder characterized by avoidance of school usually through the presence of physical symptoms. The child is fearful of the school situation itself and not separation from the parents, as in the case of a separation anxiety disorder.

Secondary pain: Indirect benefit from symptoms.

Secondary prevention: Efforts to reduce the severity or rate of an existing disorder.

Secondary process: In Freudian thinking, usually refers to thinking that is logical or rational. It is also used to refer to drive or drive energy bound to specific objects or ideas.

Secondary sexual disorders: The term for sexual disorders in which a sexual history suggests that the person has functioned normally in the past with respect to the disorder being evaluated.

Selective abstraction: A characteristic of depressive thought where a person draws a conclusion based on a selected aspect of a situation and then engages in self-blame.

Self: In Jungian terminology, the "ultimate individuation"—the psychological organization that embodies all of the different and sometimes opposing elements of the psyche.

Self-actualization: Important theme of the humanistic movement. A process described by Maslow and others in which one develops the ability to perceive reality efficiently, be detached and objective, be interested in one's fellow human beings, and discriminate between means and ends. Self-actualized people are creative, have a sense of humor, and are able to resist the forces of the culture in which they live.

Self-esteem: A sense of personal worth.

Self-objects: In object relations theory, the experiencing of others as not existing independent from the self but rather as objects to be manipulated in order to help preserve a positive self-image.

Semantic differential: A rating scale with contrasting adjectives at each end of the scale.

Sensate focus: A series of gradual steps of specific sexual behaviors that are used in direct sex therapy programs to increase sexual pleasure and reduce performance demands and anxiety.

Sensory symptoms: In neurotic disorders, apparent loss of sensory function with no apparent tissue damage (i.e., apparent blindness, deafness, numbness).

Separation anxiety: Anxiety that may be intensely experienced; related to separation from a parent, caretaker, or significant other.

Separation and individuation: The ongoing developmental process where young children begin to distinguish themselves from their mothers and establish a separate, independent identity.

Separation anxiety disorder: Refusal to go to school often with the presence of physical symptoms, and related to a child's anxiety about separation from people with whom the child has a close emotional bond.

Sex-role stereotype: Fixed conception of the behavior patterns and role characteristics of men or women.

Sexual inadequacy: Impaired ability to experience or give sexual gratification.

Sexual response cycle: The phases of physiological responses manifested by males and females to sexual stimulation as orgasm is approached and attained.

Sick role: Role provided by society for individual suffering from physical or mental disorder.

Simple phobia: An irrational fear that is directed at a specific object or situation.

Single-subject experiments: Experiments conducted with a single individual, often using instrumental conditioning methods.

Situational reaction: Maladaptive response to newly experienced life situations that are especially difficult or trying.

Social drift hypothesis: A theory used to explain the relationship between socioeconomic class and schizophrenia; schizophrenics naturally drift into a low socioeconomic class because of their reduced abilities to function effectively.

Social norms: Group or societal standards concerning behaviors viewed as appropriate or inappropriate.

Social perspective: A view of abnormal behavior that emphasizes the role of society in judging whether mental illness exists. This perspective looks to context and social reactions rather that to symptoms in isolation.

Social phobia: Persistent irrational fears of situations in which the person may be observed or scrutinized by others.

Social role: Pattern of behavior expected of individual occupying a given position in group.

Social stress hypothesis: A theory used to explain the relationship between socioeconomic class and schizophrenia. Lower social class and poverty create stress that creates schizophrenia.

Social support system: The available resources a person may turn to during times of stress. These resources may include family, friends, clubs, or community agencies.

Socialization: The process by which individuals adapt to and learn to cope with the demands of society over the course of the life span.

Sodomy: Sexual intercourse via the anus.

Somatic: Referring to the body.

Somatic weakness hypothesis: Beliefs that a particular organ is vulnerable to psychological stress, thus producing a particular psychophysiological disorder.

Somatization disorder: "Neurotic" disorder in which physical complaints are prominent.

Somatoform: A "neurotic" disorder characterized by physical symptoms.

Somnambulism: Sleepwalking.

Specific developmental disorders: The failure to develop age-appropriate skills in areas of language, speech, reading, and/or arithmetic.

Specific emotion hypothesis: The hypothesis that specific attitudes or feeling states are associated with a particular psychophysiological disorder.

Specific etiology: The causal condition that is necessary but not sufficient for an illness to occur, it does not by itself produce the illness.

Speed freak: A person who abuses or is dependent on amphetamines or other stimulants.

Sphygmomanometer: A device used to measure systolic (pressure when the heart is pumping) and diastolic (pressure in the arteries when the heart is at rest) blood pressure.

Splitting: A feature of borderline personality; it reflects the inability to integrate positive and negative images of oneself and others. Instead, the self and others are alternately experienced as good or bad.

Spontaneous remission (recovery): Recovery of a person with a psychological disorder in the absence of therapy or with minimal treatment.

Status asthmaticus: A potentially fatal asthmatic condition in which mucus build-up in the lungs can halt breathing.

Stimulants: Drugs that increase alertness and reduce fatigue.

Stimulus generalization: Tendency to respond to similar stimuli other than the original stimuli to which one has learned to respond.

Stress: Any adjustive demand that requires coping behavior on part of individual or group.

Stress inoculation training: A preventive technique designed to help people cope with future stressful events through facilitating self-understanding, coping skills, and knowledge of the anticipated stressor.

Stressful "triggering" effects (depression): Events associated with employment, health-related events, and marital events that are related to depression.

Structured family therapy: A method of family therapy devised by Salvador Minuchin in which the therapist alters the way relationships and interactions between family members are structured and organized.

Stupor: State of unresponsiveness, with partial or complete unconsciousness.

Substance abuse: Nonpathological use of a substance; episodes of intoxication without definite patterns of pathological use.

Substance dependence: Use of substance in a pattern that impairs social or occupational functioning. Usually tolerance or withdrawal effects are evident.

Substantia nigra: The largest nuclear structure of the midbrain. It is darkly pigmented, hence the name "black substance," and contains high concentrations of dopamine neurons. For the most part it is involved in coordinating motor movement. Parkinsonism is associated with the degeneration of this structure.

Suicidal ideation: Persistent thoughts or desires to kill oneself.

Suicidal risk: The probability that a person will commit suicide on the basis of observed predictors.

Suicide: Intentionally taking one's own life.

Superego: That structure of the personality concerned with ethical and moral feelings and attitudes. The superego is usually identified with the conscience.

Symptom: A sign or manifestation of a physical or psychological disorder.

Synapse: The gap between two neurons where the nerve impulse passes.

Syndrome: Patterns or constellations of symptoms that are typical of a disorder.

Systematic desensitization: A behavioral technique for eliminating anxiety responses to particular situations or stimuli.

T-group: Training group in which participants learn about the dynamics of effective group functioning and apply the principles to their own interactional patterns.

Tardive dyskinesia: A neuromuscular disorder caused by the antipsychotic drugs, the phenothiazines.

Test-retest reliability: The degree to which test or measure is consistent in its measurement over repeated occasions.

THC (tetrahydrocannabinol): The chemical many chemists feel is the active ingredient in marijuana.

Thematic Apperception Test (TAT): A projective test involving the administration of different cards with pictures of people on them. The person being tested is asked to make up a dramatic story for each of the pictures. These stories are assumed to reveal information concerning the person's personality and internal conflicts.

Thought disorder: Synonym for schizophrenia.

Token economy: A behavioral treatment of hospitalized patients in which desired behaviors are rewarded by tokens; the tokens can then be exchanged for a range of rewards from which the patients can choose.

Tolerance (to drugs): A condition in which the continued use of some drugs results in the need for larger and larger doses to produce the same effect.

Tranquilizers: Drugs used for reduction of anxiety and tension or to reduce psychotic symptoms.

Transactional perspective of stress: Stress is viewed as the product of psychological mediating factors and an individual's response to events that require adaptation and changes in physiology.

Transference: The analysand's feelings, attitudes, and expectations which are projected onto the analyst and which were once directed at significant persons in the patient's past.

Transmission of schizophrenia: The passing of schizophrenia from parent to child.

Transsexualism: Gender identification with the opposite sex or belief that one is of the opposite sex.

Transvestism: The practice of dressing in the clothing of the opposite sex, usually for the purpose of sexual stimulation.

Trephining: A practice of the Stone Age, in which a hole was cut in the skull of a person who was behaving strangely to allow the escape of evil spirits.

Tricyclic antidepressants: A class of antidepressant medication that works by increasing the amount of norepinephrine the brain releases.

Twin studies: An experimental procedure in which twins, judged at risk for a disorder, are observed as sharing or not sharing the disorder.

Type A behavior pattern: A lifestyle-related risk factor associated with the development of coronary heart disease that is characterized by competitiveness, intense ambition, time urgency, involvement in multiple activities, hostility, and aggressiveness.

Ulcer: An open sore or lesion in the wall of the stomach or in a portion of the small intestine produced by abnormal high levels of gastric activity.

Unconditional positive regard: Positive regard experienced toward an individual irrespective of that individual's values or behavior. As Rogers (1959) puts it: "If self-experiences of another are perceived by me in such a way that no self-experience can be discriminated as more or less worthy of positive regard than any other, then I am experiencing unconditional positive regard for this individual" (p. 208).

Unconditioned response: A natural, unlearned response to a stimulus.

Unconditioned stimulus: A stimulus that elicits a natural or unconditioned response.

Unconscious: The portion of the psychological structure of the individual where repressed or forgotten memories or desires reside. These memories or desires are not directly available to consciousness but can be made available through psychoanalysis or hypnosis.

Undue risk: Exposure of experimental subjects to unethical dangers or risks.

Upper-downer cycle: A pattern of drug use in which the person uses depressants to get to sleep, then uses stimulants to overcome depressant hangover; more depressants are then needed to sleep.

Urinary continency: Effective voluntary control over urination.

Validity: The degree to which a test is consistent with other sources of information about the same attributes or characteristics.

Variable: A measure of a characteristic that may take on one of a set of different qualities.

Vascular: Pertaining to the blood vessels or blood supply.

Vicarious conditioning: Learning by observing the reactions of others to stimuli or events.

Victorian morality: Pervasive social norms of the 19th century in western Europe that stressed work, diligence, and achievement and discouraged outward expression of sexuality.

Voyeurism: Achievement of sexual pleasure through "peeping"; usually watching other persons disrobe and/or engage in sexual activities.

Vulnerability model: The idea that susceptibility to schizophrenia is determined by genetic and acquired factors but triggered by life events.

Well-ordered asylum: Because early 19th-century American society viewed mental illness as stemming from social pressures and environmental tensions, institutions in America emphasized orderly, regular, and disciplined routine.

Withdrawal syndrome: Result of physical dependency on drugs in which an intense physical reaction occurs when the drug is discontinued.

Working through: In psychoanalytic therapy, the term refers to the need to confront resistance until satisfactory adjustment is achieved.

X-factor: An unknown chemical that is thought to cause schizophrenia.

Zone of transition: The slum area of a city heavily populated by schizophrenics.

REFERENCES

Abelson, H. I., Fishburne, P. M., & Cisin, I. H. (1977). *National survey on drug abuse, 1977: A nationwide study—youth, young adults, and older adults.* Princeton, NJ: Response Analysis Corporation.

Abramson, L. Y., Seligman, M. E. P., & Teasdale, J. D. (1978). Learned helplessness in humans: Critique and reformulation. *Journal of Abnormal Psychology, 87,* 49–74.

Abroms, I. I., & Bennett, J. S. (1983). Current findings in Down's syndrome. *Exceptional Children, 49,* 449–450.

Ad Hoc Committee of Classification of Headache. (1962). Classification of headache. *Journal of American Medical Association, 179,* 717–718.

Adler, A. (1938). *Social interest: A challenge of mankind.* London: Faber & Faber.

Agras, S., & Jacob, R. (1979). Hypertension. In D. F. Pomerleau & J. P. Brady (Eds.), *Behavoral medicine: Theory and practice.* Baltimore: Williams and Wilkins.

Agras, W. S. (1982). Behavioral medicine in the 1980s: Nonrandom connections. *Journal of Consulting and Clinical Psychology, 30,* 797–803.

Aguilera, D., & Messick, J. M. (1978). *Crisis Intervention,* 3d ed. St. Louis: C. V. Mosby.

Akhtar, S., & Thomson, J. A. (1982). Overview: Narcissistic personality disorder. *American Journal of Psychiatry, 139,* 12–20.

Akiskal, H. S., & McKinney, W. T. (1975). Overview of recent research in depression. *Archives of General Psychiatry, 32,* 285–305.

Albee, G. W. (1968). Conceptual models and manpower requirements in psychology. *American Psychologist, 23,* 317–320.

Alcoholics Anonymous World Service. (1978). *Alcoholics Anonymous:* Alcoholics Anonymous World Service.

Alcoholism: New victims, new treatment. (1974, April 22). *Time,* pp. 75–81.

Alexander, B. K., & Hadaway, P. F. (1982). Opiate addiction: The case for an adaptive orientation. *Psychological Bulletin, 92,* 367–381.

Alexander, F. (1950). *Psychosomatic medicine: Its principles and applications.* New York: W. W. Norton.

Alexander, F., & French, T. (1946). *Psychoanalytic theory: Principle and application.* New York: Ronald Press.

Alexander, M. P., & Geschwind, N. (1984). Dementia in the elderly. In M. L. Albert (Ed.), *Clinical neurology of aging* (pp. 254–276). New York: Oxford University Press.

Alford, G. S. (1980). Alcoholics Anonymous: An empirical outcome study. *Addictive Behaviors, 5,* 359–370.

Allen, K. E., Hart, B., Buell, J. S., Harris, F. R., & Wolf, M. M. (1964). Effects of social reinforcement on isolate behavior of a nursery school child. *Child Development, 35,* 511–518.

Allport, G. (1968). *The search for self.* New York: Norton.

American Medical Association. (1971). Failure to diagnose barbiturate intoxication. *The Citation, 24,* 22–23.

American Pharmaceutical Association. (1977). *Handbook of nonprescription drugs.* (5th ed.). American Pharmaceutical Association.

American Psychiatric Association, Task Force on Nomenclature and Statistics. (1980). *Diagnostic and statistical manual of mental disorders* (DSM III). Washington, DC: Author.

Andrasik, F., & Holroyd, K. (1978, November). *A test of the specific effects in the treatment of tension headache.* Paper presented at the Association for the Advancement of Behavior Therapy Convention, Chicago.

Annon, J. S. (1974). *The behavioral treatment of sexual problems.* Honolulu: Kapiolani Health Services.

Anonymous. (1939). *Alcoholics Anonymous.* New York: Works Publishing, 1939.

Anthony, E. J. (1958). An experimental approach to the psychopathology of childhood encopresis. *British Journal of Medical Psychology, 30,* 146–175.

APA Monitor. (1976). Here to stay? Marijuana. *APA Monitor, 5,* 10.

Aponte, H., & Hoffman, L. (1973). The open door: A structural approach to a family with an anorectic child. *Family Process, 12,* 1–44.

Appel, M. A. (1984). The usefulness of stress reduction methods in psychological practice. In J. R. McNamara (Ed.), *Critical issues, developments, and trends in professional psychology* (Vol. 2, pp. 108–154). New York: Praeger.

Applebaum, S. (1978). Pathways to change in psychoanalytic therapy. *Bulletin of the Menninger Clinic, 42,* 239–251.

Arieti, S. (1959). Manic-depressive psychosis. In S. Arieti (Ed.), *American handbook of psychiatry.* New York: Basic Books.

Arnow, E., & Reznikoff, M. (1983). *A Rorschach introduction: Content and perceptual approaches.* New York: Grune & Stratton.

Aronow, E., & Reznikoff, M. (1976). *Rorschach content interpretation.* New York: Grune & Stratton.

Asher, J. (1983). Hormone studies spark theory linking stress and depression. *ADAMHA NEWS, 9,* 4–5.

Atchley, R. C. (1976) (1977). *The sociology of retirement.* New York: John Wiley & Sons.

Athanasiou, R., Shaver, P., & Tarvis, C. (1970, April). Sex. *Psychology Today,* pp. 37–52.

Axline, V. M. (1969). *Play therapy.* New York: Ballantine Books.

Ayllon, T., & Rosenbaum, M. (1977). The behavioral treatment of disruption and hyperactivity in school settings. In B. Lahey & A. Kazdin (Eds.), *Advances in clinical child psychology* (Vol. 1). New York: Plenum Press.

Bachman, J., & Johnston, L. (1983). Teenage drug use. (Institute for Social Research Newsletter). Ann Arbor, MI: University of Michigan.

Bakal, D. (1975). Headache: A biopsychological perspective. *Psychological Bulletin, 82,* 369–382.

Bakal, D. A. (1982). *The psychobiology of chronic headache.* New York: Springer Publishing.

Baker, E. (1985). Psychoanalysis and psychoanalytic psychotherapy. In S. J. Lynn, & J. P. Garske (Eds.), *Contemporary psychotherapies: Models and methods.* Columbus: Merrill.

Bakwin, H., & Bakwin, R. M. (1972). *Behavior disorders in children.* Philadelphia: W. B. Saunders.

Baldessarini, R. J. (1977). *Chemotherapy in psychiatry.* Cambridge, MA: Harvard University Press.

Ball, J. C., Rosen, L., Flueck, J. A., & Nurco, D. N. (1982). Lifetime criminality of heroin users in the United States. *Journal of Drug Issues,* 225–239.

Ball, J. C., Smith, J. P., & Graff, H. (Eds.). (1977). International survey. *Addictive Diseases, 3,* 1–138.

Balson, P. M. (1973). Case study: Encopresis: A case with symptom substitution? *Behavior Therapy, 4,* 134–136.

Baltes, M. M., & Barton, E. M. (1977). New approaches toward aging: A case for the operant model. *Educational Gerontology, 2,* 383–405.

Bandura, A. (1968). A social learning interpretation of psychological dysfunctions. In Perry Landon and David Rosenhan (Eds.), *Foundations of Abnormal Psychology.* New York: Holt, Rinehart & Winston.

Bandura, A. (1971). Psychotherapy based on modeling principles. In A. E. Bergin & S. L. Garfield (Eds.), *Handbook of psychotherapy and behavior change.* New York: Wiley.

Bandura, A. (1974). Behavior theory and models of man. *American Psychologist, 29,* 859–869.

Bandura, A. (1976). Social learning analysis of aggression. In E. Ribes-Inesta (Ed.), *Analysis of delinquency and aggression.* Hillsdale, N.J.: Erlbaum.

Bandura, A. (1977). Self-efficacy: Toward a unifying theory of behavioral change. *Psychological Review, 84,* 191–215.

Bandura, A. (1981). In search of pure unidirectional determinants. *Behavior Therapy, 12,* 30–40.

Bandura, A., Blanchard, E. B., & Ritter, B. (1969). The relative efficacy of desensitization and modeling approaches for inducing behavioral, affective, and cognitive changes. *Journal of Personality and Social Psychology, 13,* 173–199. Copyright 1969 by the American Psychological Association.

Bandura, A., Grusec, J. E., & Menlove, F. L. (1967). Vicarious extinction of avoidance behavior. *Journal of Personality and Social Psychology, 5,* 16–23.

Bandura, A., & Rosenthal, T. L. (1963). Vicarious classical conditioning as a function of arousal level. *Journal of Personality and Social Psychology, 3,* 54–62.

Barber, B. (1976). The ethics of human experimentation with human subjects. *Scientific American, 234,* 25–31.

Barber, T. X. (1970). *LSD, marijuana, yoga, and hypnosis.* Chicago: Aldine.

Barber, T. X. (1982). Hypnosuggestive procedures in the treatment of clinical pain: Implications for theories of hypnosis and suggestive therapy. In T. Millon, C. Green, & R. Meagher (Eds.), *Handbook of clinical health psychology.* New York: Plenum Press.

Barber, T. X. (1983). Changing "unchangeable" bodily processes by (hypnotic) suggestions: A new look at hypnosis, cognitions, imaging, and the mind-body problem. In A. A. Sheikh (Ed.), *Imagination and Healing.* Farmingdale, NY: Baywood Publishing.

Bard, M. (1970). *Training police as specialists in family crisis intervention.* Washington, DC: U.S. Government Printing Office.

Bard, M., & Berkowitz, B. (1967). Training police as specialists in family crisis intervention: A community psychology action program. *Community Mental Health Journal, 3,* 315–317.

Barlow, C. F. (1978). *Mental retardation and related disorders.* Philadelphia: F. M. Davis.

Basch, N. F. (1981). Dynamic psychotherapy and its frustrations. In P. L. Wachtel (Ed.) *Resistance.* New York: Plenum.

Bassuk, E. L. (1984). The homelessness problem. *Scientific American, 251(1),* 40–45.

Bates, L. O. (1983, January 24). What I didn't know about depression almost killed me. *U.S. News & World Report,* pp. 150–56.

Bateson, G., Jackson, D. D., Haley, J., & Weakland, J. (1956). Toward a theory of schizophrenia. *Behavioral Science, 1,* 251–264.

Baumbacher, G., and Amini, F. (1981). The hysterical personality disorder: A proposed clarification of a diagnostic dilemma. *International Journal of Psychoanalytic Psychotherapy, 8,* 501–532.

Baumgold, J. (1977, December 4). Agoraphobia: Life ruled by panic. *New York Times Magazine,* p. 46. © 1977 by The New York Times Company. Material reprinted by permission.

Beatrice, J. (1985). A psychological comparison of heterosexuals, transvestites, preoperative transsexuals, and postoperative transsexuals. *Journal of Nervous and Mental Disease, 173,* 358–365.

Beck, A. T. (1967). *Depression: Clinical, experimental, and theoretical aspects.* New York: Hoeber (Harper & Row).

Beck, A. T. (1970). Cognitive therapy: Nature and relation to behavior therapy. *Behavior Therapy, 1,* 184–200.

Beck, A. T. (1971). Cognition, affect, and psychopathology. *Archives of General Psychiatry, 24,* 495–500.

Beck, A. T., Beck, R., & Kovacs, M. (1975). Classification of suicidal behaviors: 1. Quantifying intent and medical lethality. *American Journal of Psychiatry, 132,* 285–287.

Beck, A. T., Kovacs, M., & Weissman, A. (1979). Assessment of suicidal intention: The scale for suicide ideation. *Journal of Clinical and Consultant Psychology, 47,* 243–252.

Beck, A. T., Resnik, H. L. P., & Lettieri, D. J. (Eds.). (1974). *The prediction of suicide.* Bowie, MD.: Charles Press.

Beck, A. T., Rush, A. J., Shaw, B. F., & Emery, G. (1979). *Cognitive therapy of depression.* New York: Guilford Press.

Beck, S. J., Beck, A. L., Levitt, E. E., & Molish, H. B. (1961). *Rorschach's test 1. Basic processes* (3rd ed.). New York: Grune & Stratton.

Becker, C. E. (1979). Pharmacotherapy in the treatment of alcoholism. In J. H. Mendelson & N. K. Mello (Eds.), *The diagnosis and treatment of alcoholism.* New York: McGraw-Hill.

Becker, H. S. (1953). Becoming a marijuana user. *American Journal of Sociology, 59,* 235–242.

Bednar, R. L., & Kaul, T. J. (1978). Experiential group research: Current perspectives. In S. L. Garfield & A. E. Bergin (Eds.), *Handbook of psychotherapy and behavior change* (2d ed.). New York: John Wiley.

Beecher, H. K. (1959). *Measurement of subjective responses: Quantitative effects of drugs.* New York: Oxford University Press.

Bell, A. (1973, July 13). *Homosexuality.* Lecture delivered at the Institute for Sex Research Summer Program, Bloomington, IN.

Bell, A. P., & Weinberg, M. S. (1978). *Homosexualities: A study of diversity among men and women.* New York: Simon & Schuster. Copyright © 1978 by Alan P. Bell and Martin S. Weinberg. Material reprinted by permission of Simon & Schuster, a Division of Gulf & Western Corporation.

Belliveau, F., & Richter, L. (1970). *Understanding human sexual inadequacy.* New York: Bantam (Books). Copyright © 1970 by Fred Belliveau and Lin Richter.

Bellman, M. (1966). Studies on encopresis. *Acta Paediatrica Scandinavia,* Suppl. 170.

Bemis, K. (1978). Current approaches to the etiology and treatment of anorexia nervosa as a disease. *Psychological Bulletin, 85,* 593–617.

Bender, L. (1947). Childhood schizophrenia. *American Journal of Orthopsychiatry, 17,* 40–56.

Benjamin, H. (1966). *The transsexual phenomenon.* New York: Julien Press.

Benson, D. F. (1983). Subcortical dementia: a clinical approach. In R. Mayeux & W. G. Rosen (Eds.), *The Dementias* (pp. 185–194): New York: Rauen Press.

Benson, H. (1975). *The relaxation response.* New York: Morrow.

Bentler, P. (1976). A typology of transsexualism: Gender identity theory and data. *Archives of Sexual Behavior, 5,* 567–584.

Berg, I. (1976). School phobia in the children of agoraphobic women. *British Journal of Psychiatry, 128,* 86–89.

Berger, K. S., & Zarit, S. H. (1978). Late-life paranoid states: Assessment and treatment. *American Journal of Orthopsychiatry, 48,* 528–537.

Bergin, A. E., & Lambert, M. J. (1978). The evaluation of therapeutic outcomes. In S. L. Garfield & A. E. Bergin (Eds.), *Handbook of psychotherapy and behavior change* (2nd ed.). New York: John Wiley.

Berkman, L. F., & Syme, S. L. (1979). Social networks, host resistance, and mortality: A nine year follow-up study of Alameda County, residents. *American Journal of Epidemiology, 109(2),* 186–204.

Bernard, J. (1976). Kurt Lewin memorial address. *American Psychological Association.*

Bernstein, J. G. (1979). Prescribing antipsychotics. *Drug Therapy for the Family Physician, 9,* 71–88.

Bertelson, A. D., Marks, P. A., May, G. D. (1982). MMPI and race: A controlled study. *Journal of Consulting Clinical Psychology, 50,* 316–318.

Bettelheim, B. (1943). Individuals and mass behavior in extreme situations. *Journal of Abnormal and Social Psychology, 38,* 417–452.

Bettelheim, B. (1960). *The informed heart.* New York: Free Press.

Bettelheim, B. (1967). *The empty fortress.* New York: Free Press.

Bieber, I., Dain, H. J., Dince, O. R., Drelich, M. G., Grand, H. G., Grundlack, R. H., Kremer, M. W., Rifkin, A. H., Wilbur, C. B., & Bieber, T. B. (1962). *Homosexuality: A psychoanalytic study.* New York: Basic Books.

Biederman, J., Lerner, Y., & Belmaker, R. H. (1979). Combination of lithium carbonate in schizoaffective disorder. *Archives of General Psychiatry, 36,* 327–333.

Birren, J. E., Butler, R. N., Greenhouse, S. W., Sokoloff, L., & Yarrow, M. R. (Eds.). (1963). *Human aging: A biological and behavioral study* (Publication No. HSM 71–9051). Washington, DC: U.S. Government Printing Office.

Birren, J. E., & Renner, V. J. (1977). Research on the psychology of aging: Principles and experimentation. In J. E. Birren & K. W. Schaie (Eds.), *Handbook of the psychology of aging* (pp. 3–38). New York: Van Nostrand Reinhold.

Blackwell, B. (1982). Antidepressant drugs: Side effects and compliance. *Journal of Clinical Psychiatry, 43,* 14–18.

Blaine, J. D., Prien, R. F. (1983). The role of antidepressants in the treatment of affective disorders. *American Journal of Psychotherapy, 37,* 502–520.

Blake, P., & Moss, T. (1967). The development of socialization skills in an electively mute child, *Behavior Research and Therapy, 5,* 349–356.

Blanchard, R. (1985). Gender dysphoria and gender disorientation. In B. W. Steiner (Ed.), *Gender dysphoria: Development, research, management* (pp. 365–392). New York: Plenum Press.

Blanchard, R., Clemmensen, L. H., & Steiner, B. W. (1983). Gender reorientation and psychosocial adjustment in male-to-female transsexuals. *Archives of Sexual Behavior, 12,* 503–509.

Blanchard, R., Steiner, B. W., & Clemmensen, L. H. (1985). Gender dysphoria, gender reorientation, and the clinical management of transsexualism. *Journal of Consulting and Clinical Psychology, 53,* 295–304.

Blanck, G., & Blanck, R. (1974). *Ego psychology: Theory and practice.* New York: Columbia University Press.

Blashfield, R. K., & Draguns, J. G. (1976). Evaluative criteria for psychiatric classification. *Journal of Abnormal Psychology, 85,* 140–150.

Blazer, D. (1980). The epidemiology of mental illness in last life. In E. W. Busse & D. G. Blazer (Eds.), *Handbook of geriatric psychiatry* (pp. 249–271). New York: Van Nostrand Reinhold.

Bleuler, E. (1950). *Dementia praecox, or the group of schizophrenias.* J. Zinkin (Trans.). New York: International Universities Press. (Originally published in 1911.)

Block, D., & LaPerriere, K. (1973). Techniques of family therapy: A conceptual frame. In D. Block (Ed.), *Techniques of family psychotherapy: A primer.* New York: Grune & Stratton.

Bloom, B. (1977). *Community Mental Health.* Monterey, CA: Brooks-Cole.

Bloom, B. L. (1971). Strategies for the prevention of mental disorders. In Division 27, American Psychological Association, Task Force on Community Mental Health, *Issues in community psychology and preventive mental health.* New York: Behavioral Publications.

Bloom, B. L. (1980). *Social and community interventions. Annual Review of Psychology, 31,* 111–142.

Bloomfield, J. M., & Douglas, J. W. B. (1956). Bedwetting prevalence among children aged 4–7 years. *The Lancet, 1,* 850–852.

Blum, R., (1964). *Utopiates.* New York: Atherton.

Blum, R. H., & Associates. (1969). *Students and drugs* (Vol. 2). San Francisco: Jossey Bass.

Boekelheide, P. D. (1978). Incest and the family physician. *Journal of Family Practice, 6,* 87–90.

Bonvillian, J., Nelson, E. E., & Rhyne, M. J. (1981). Sign language and autism. *Journal of Autism and Developmental Disorders, 11,* 125–137.

Bootzin, R. (1972). A stimulus control treatment for insomnia. Proceedings of the American Psychological Association, *1,* 395–396.

Borman, L. D., Borck, L. E., Hess, R., & Pasquale, F. L. (1982). *Helping people to help themselves: Self help and prevention.* New York: Haworth Press.

Botwinick, J. (1978). *Aging and behavior* (2d ed.). New York: Springer Publishing.

Boudewyns, P. A., Tanna, V. L., & Fleischman, D. J. A. (1975). A modified shame aversion therapy for compulsive obscene telephone calling. *Behavior Therapy, 6,* 704–707.

Bower, E. M., (1963). Primary prevention of mental and emotional disorders: A conceptual framework and active possibilities. *American Journal of Orthopsy-*

chiatry, 33, 832–848. Copyright 1963 by the American Orthopsychiatric Association, Inc.

Bowers, K. S. (1976). *Hypnosis for the seriously curious.* Monterey, CA: Brooks-Cole.

Bowlby, J. (1960). Grief and mourning in infancy and early childhood. *Psychoanalytic Study of the Child, 15,* 9–52.

Bowlby, J. (1969). *Attachment.* New York: Basic Books.

Bowlby, J. (1973). *Attachment and loss: Separation, anxiety and anger* (Vol. 2). New York: Basic Books.

Braden, W., Fink, E. B., Qualls, C. B., Ho, C. K., & Samuels, W. O. (1982). Lithium and chlorpromazine in psychotic inpatients. *Psychiatry Research, 7,* 69–81.

Brady, J. V. (1958, October). Ulcers in "executive" monkeys. *Scientific American,* pp. 95–100.

Brandsma, J. M., Maultsby, M. C., & Welsh, R. J. (1980). *The outpatient treatment of alcoholism: A review and comparative study.* Baltimore, MD: University Park Press.

Brenner, M. H. (1973). *Mental illness and the economy.* Cambridge, MA: Harvard University Press.

Bresler, D. E. (1979). *Free yourself from pain.* New York: Simon & Schuster.

Breuer, & Freud, S. (1955). *Studies on hysteria.* In standard edition, vol. 2. London: Hogarth Press. (First German Edition, 1895).

Bridell, D. W., & Wilson, G. T. (1976). The effects of alcohol and expectancy set on male sexual arousal. *Journal of Abnormal Psychology, 85,* 225–234.

Brink, T. L. (1980). Geriatric paranoia: Case report illustrating behavioral management. *Journal of the American Geriatrics Society, 28,* (11), 519–522.

Brody, E. M. (1977). *Long-term care of older people.* New York: Human Sciences Press.

Brody, J. E. (1978, July 9). Study finds some homosexuals are happier than heterosexuals. *New York Times.*

Brody, J. E. (1984, March 4). The haunting specter of teen-age suicide. *New York Times,* p. 8E.

Brooks, G. R., & Richardson, F. C. (1976). Emotional skills training: A treatment program for peptic ulcers. *Biofeedback and Self-Regulation, 1,* 323–324.

Broverman, I. K., Broverman, D. M., & Clarkson, F. E. (1970). Sex-role stereotypes and clinical judgments of mental health. *Journal of Consulting and Clinical Psychology, 34,* 1–7.

Brown, G. W., Birley, J. L. T., & Wing, J. K. (1972). Influence of family on the course of schizophrenic disorders: A replication. *British Journal of Psychiatry, 121,* 241–258.

Bruch, H. (1973). *Eating disorders.* New York: Basic Books.

Bruch, H. (1978). *The golden cage: The enigma of anorexia nervosa.* Cambridge, MA: Harvard University Press.

Buchanan, P. C. (1964). Innovative organizations: A study in organizational development. In *Applying behavioral science research in industry.* New York: Industrial Relations Counselor, 1964.

Buchwald, A. M., & Young, R. D. (1969). Some comments on the foundations of behavior therapy. In C. M. Franks (Ed.), *Behavior therapy: appraisal and status.* New York: McGraw-Hill.

Buck, J. A., & Graham, J. R. (1978). The 4-3 MMPI profile type: A failure to replicate. *Journal of Consulting and Clinical Psychology, 46,* 344.

Bucklew, J. (1960). *Paradigms for psychopathology: A contribution to case history analysis.* Philadelphia: J. B. Lippincott.

Burns, R. S., & Lerner, S. E. (1976). Perspectives: Acute phencyclidine intoxication. *Clinical Toxicology, 4,* 14–18.

Buss, A. H. (1966). *Psychopathology.* New York: John Wiley.

Buss, T. F., & Redburn, F. S. (1983). *Mass unemployment: Plant closing and community mental health.* Beverly Hills, CA: Sage Publications.

Busse, E. W. (1976). Hypochondriasis in the elderly: A reaction to social stress. *Journal of the American Geriatrics Society, 24,* 145–149.

Busse, E. W., & Pfeiffer, E. (1977). *Behavior and adaptation in late life* (2d ed.). Boston: Little, Brown.

Butler, R. N., & Lewis, M. I. (1982). *Aging and mental health* (3d ed.). St. Louis: C. V. Mosby.

Byck, R. (1983). *Cocaine papers by Sigmund Freud.* New York: Stonehill.

Cadoret, R. J. (1978). Psychopathology in adopted away offspring of biologic parents with antisocial behavior. *Archives of General Psychiatry, 35,* 176–184.

Calahan, D. (1970). *Problem drinkers: A national survey.* San Francisco: Jossey-Bass.

Calahan, D., Cisin, I. H., & Crossley, H. M. (1969). *American drinking practices: A national study of drinking behaviors and attitudes.* New Brunswick, NJ: Rutgers Center of Alcohol Studies.

Cameron, N. (1963). *Personality development and psychopathology: A dynamic approach.* Boston: Houghton Mifflin, 1963. Copyright © 1963 by Houghton Mifflin Company. Material reprinted by permission of the publishers.

Campbell, J. (Ed.). (1971). *The portable Jung.* New York: Viking Press.

Cannon, D. S., Baker, T. B., & Wehl, C. K. (1981). Emetic and electric shock alcohol aversion therapy: Six and twelve-month followup. *Journal of Consulting and Clinical Psychology, 49(3),* 360–368.

Cannon, W. B. (1929). *Bodily changes in pain, hunger, fear, and rage* (2d ed.). New York: Appleton-Century-Crofts.

Cannon, W. B. (1936). The role of emotion in disease. *Annals of Internal Medicine, 9,* 1453–1456.

Cannon, W. B. (1939). *The wisdom of the body.* New York: W. W. Norton.

Cantor, P. (1983). Depression and suicide in children. In C. E. Walker and M. C. Roberts (Eds.)., *Handbook of clinical child psychology.* New York: John Wiley & Sons.

Cantwell, D. P. (1975). Genetics of hyperactivity. *Journal of Child Psychology and Psychiatry, 16,* 261–264.

Cantwell, D. P., & Carlson, G. A. (1979). Problems and prospects in the study of childhood depression. *Journal of Nervous and Mental Disease, 167,* 522–529.

Capel, W. C., Goldsmith, B. M., Waddell, K. J., & Stewart, G. T. (1972). The aging narcotic addict: An increasing problem for the next decades. *Journal of Gerontology, 27,* 102–106.

Caplan, G. (1964). *Principles of preventive psychiatry.* New York: Basic Books.

Caplan, G. (1970). *The theory and practice of mental health consultation.* New York: Basic Books.

Caplan, R. B. (1969). *Psychiatry and the community in nineteenth century America.* New York: Basic Books.

Caporael, L. R. (1976). *Science, 192,* 21.

Caprio, F. S. (1973). Fetishism. In A. Ellis & A. Abarbanel (Eds.), *Encyclopedia of sexual behavior.* New York: Jason Aronson, 1973.

Caracci, G., Migone, P., & Mukherjee, S. (1983). Phencyclidine abuse and depression. *Psychosomatics, 24,* 932–933.

Carpenter, N. J., Leichtman, L. G., & Burhan, S. (1982). Fragile X-linked mental retardation. *American Journal of Disturbances of Childhood, 136,* 392–398.

Carr, A. T. (1974). Compulsive neurosis: A review of the literature. *Psychological Bulletin, 81,* 311–318.

Carter, C. H. (1970). *Handbook of mental retardation syndromes.* Springfield, IL: Charles C Thomas.

Carver, C. S., & Ganellen, R. J. (1983). Depression and components of self-primitiveness: High standards, self-criticism, and overgeneralization. *Journal of Abnormal Psychology, 42,* 330–337.

Casey, R. L., Masuda, M., & Holmes, I. H. (1967). Quantitative study of recall of life events. *Journal of Psychosomatic Research, 11,* 239–247.

Cass, L. K., & Thomas, C. B. (1979). *Childhood pathology and later adjustment: The question of prediction.* New York: John Wiley. Copyright 1979 John Wiley & Sons, Inc.

Cassell, S. (1965). Effect of brief puppet therapy upon the emotional responses of children undergoing cardiac catheterization. *Journal of Consulting Psychology, 29,* 1–8.

Cautela, J. R. (1966). A behavior therapy treatment of pervasive anxiety. *Behavior Research and Therapy, 4,* 99–109.

Cautela, J. R. (1966). Treatment of compulsive behavior by covert sensitization. *Psychological Record, 16,* 33–41.

Cautela, J. R. (1970). The treatment of alcoholism by covert sensitization. *Psychotherapy: Theory, Research, and Practice, 7,* 86–90.

Cautela, J. R. (1971) Covert conditioning. In A. Jaacobs & L. B. Sachs (Eds.), *The psychology of private events: Perspectives on covert response systems.* New York: Academic Press.

Chambless, D. (1982). Characteristics of agoraphobics. In *Agoraphobia: Multiple perspectives on theory and treatment.* Chambless, D., and Goldstein, A. (Eds.). New York: John Wiley & Sons.

Chambless, D., & Goldstein, A. (1980). The treatment of agoraphobia. In A. Goldstein, & E. B. Foa (Eds.), *Handbook of behavioral interventions.* New York: John Wiley & Sons.

Chambless, O. L., & Goldstein, A. J. (1979). Behavioral psychotherapy. In R. J. Corsini (Ed.), *Current psychotherapies.* Itasca, IL: F. E. Peacock.

Chance, P. (1974). A conversation with Ivar Lovaas. *Psychology Today, 7,* 76–84.

Chapman, J. (1966). The early symptoms of schizophrenia. *British Journal of Psychiatry, 112,* 225–251.

Chesney, M. A., Swan, G. E., & Rosenman, R. H. (1982). Assessment of hypertension. In F. J. Keefe & J. A. Blumenthal (Eds.), *Assessment Strategies in Behavioral Medicine.* New York: Grune and Stratton.

Chess, S., & Hassibi, M. (1978). *Principles and practices of child psychiatry.* New York: Plenum Press.

Chiodo, J., & Latimer, P. R. (1983). Vomiting as a learned weight-control technique in bulimia. *Journal of Behavior Therapy & Experimental Psychiatry, 14,* 131–135.

Choron, J. (1972). *Suicide.* New York: Charles Scribner's Sons.

Christie, R., & Geis, F. (1970). *Studies in Machiavellianism.* New York: Academic Press.

Christophersen, E. R., & Rapoff, M. A. (1983). Toileting problems of children. In C. E. Walker and M. C. Roberts (Eds.), *Handbook of clinical child psychology.* New York: John Wiley & Sons.

Churchill, D. W. (1978). Language: The problem beyond conditioning. In M. Rutter and E. Schopler (Eds.), *Autism: A reappraisal of concepts and treatment.* New York: Plenum Press.

Clark, R. L. (1981). Aging, retirement, and the economic security of the elderly: An economic review. In C.

Eisdorfer (Ed.), *Annual review of gerontology and geriatrics: Vol. 2* (pp. 299–319). New York: Springer.

Clarren, S. K., & Smith, D. W. (1978). The fetal alcohol syndrome. *New England Journal of Medicine, 298,* 1060–1067.

Clayton, P., Halikas, J., & Maurice, W. (1972). The depression of widowhood. *British Journal of Psychiatry, 120,* 71–77.

Cleckley, H. (1968). Psychopathic personality. In O. L. Sills (Ed.), *International encyclopedia of the social sciences* (Vol. 13). New York: Macmillan.

Cleckley, H. (1976). *The mask of sanity* (5th ed.). St. Louis: C. V. Mosby.

Coan, R. W. (1973). Personality variables associated with cigarette smoking. *Journal of Personality and Social Psychology, 26,* 86–104.

Cobb, S. (1976). Social support as a moderator of life stress. *Psychosomatic Medicine, 38*(5), 300–314.

Coche, E. B., & Dies, R. R. (1981). Integrating research findings into the practice of group psychotherapy. *Psychotherapy: Theory, Research, and Practice,* (Winter), *18,* 410–415.

Coggins, W. J. (1976). Costa Rica cannabis project: An interim report on the medical aspects. In M. C. Braude & S. Szarn (Eds.), *Pharmocology of marijuana.* New York: Raven Press.

Cohen, H. L., & Filipczak, J. (1971). *A new learning environment.* San Francisco: Jossey-Bass.

Cohen, S. (1977). Angel dust. *Journal of the American Medical Association, 238,* 515–516.

Cohen, W., & Paul, G. L. (1976). Current trends and recommended changes in extended-care placement of mental patients: The Illinois system as a case in point. *Schizophrenia Bulletin.*

Cole, J. O. (1970). Schizophrenia: The therapies, a broad perspective. In J. D. Cole & L. E. Hollister (Eds.), *Schizophrenia.* MEDCOM.

Coleman, P. G. (1974). Measuring reminiscence characteristics from conversation as adaptive features of old age. *International Journal of Aging and Human Development, 5,* 281–294.

Collins, G. (1983, January 24). A new look at anxiety's many faces. *New York Times,* p. 15.

Comfort, A. (1984). Alzheimer's disease or "Alzheimerism"? *Psychiatric Annals, 14,* 130–132.

Connors, C. K. (1980). *Food additives and hyperactive children.* New York: Plenum Press.

Cooper, J. R. (Ed.). (1977). *Sedative-hypnotic drugs: Risks and benefits.* U.S. Department of Health, Education, and Welfare, DHEW Publication No. (ADM) 78–92. Washington, DC: U.S. Government Printing Office.

Copp, L. A. (1974). The spectrum of suffering. *American Journal of Nursing, 74,* 490–495.

Cornell, D. G., Silk, K. R., Ludolph, P. S., and Lohr, N. E. (1983). Test-retest reliability of the Diagnostic Interview for Borderlines. *Archives of General Psychiatry, 40,* 1307–1310.

Cornsweet, C. (1983). Nonspecific factors and theoretical choice. *Psychotherapy: Theory, Research and Practice, 200,* 306–313.

Cory, D. W., & LeRoy, J. P. (1964). *The homosexual and his society: A view from within.* New York: Citadel.

Cotton, N. S. (1979). The familial incidence of alcoholism: A review. *Journal of Studies on Alcohol, 40,* 89–116.

Cowen, E. L., Gesten, R. L., & Weissberg, R. P. (1980). An integrated network of preventively oriented school-based mental health approaches. In R. H. Price and P. E. Politser (Eds.), *Evaluation and action in the social environment.* New York: Academic Press.

Cowen, E. L., Izzo, L. D., Miles, H., Telschow, E. F., Trost, M. A., & Zax, M. (1963). A preventive mental health problem in the school setting: Description and evaluation. *Journal of Psychology, 56,* 307–356.

Cowen, E. L., Trost, M. A., Lorion, R. P., Dorr, D., Izzo, L. D., & Isaacson, R. V. (1975). *New ways in school mental health: Early detection and prevention of school maladaption.* New York: Human Sciences.

Cowen, E. L., Zax, M., Izzo, L. D., & Trost, M. A. (1966). Prevention of emotional disorders in the school setting: A further investigation. *Journal of Consulting Psychology, 30,* 381–387.

Cox, A., et al. (1975). A comparative study of infantile autism and specific developmental receptive language disorder: II. Parental characteristics. *British Journal of Psychiatry, 126,* 146.

Coyne, J. C. (1976). Depression and the response of others. *Journal of Abnormal Psychology, 85,* 186–193.

Coyne, J. C. (1976). Toward an interactional description of depression. *Psychiatry, 39,* 14–27.

Coyne, J. C., & Gotlib, I. H. (1983). The role of cognition in depression: A critical appraisal. *Psychological Bulletin, 94,* 472–505.

Coyne, J. C., & Holroyd, K., (1982). Stress coping and illness: A transactional perspective. In T. Millon, C. Green, & R. Meagher (Eds.), *Handbook of clinical health psychology.* New York: Plenum Press.

Coyle, J. T., Price, D. L. and DeLong, M. R. (1983). Alzheimer's disease: A disorder of cortical cholinergic innervation. *Science* 219, 1184–1190.

Craighead, L. W. (1979). Self-instructional training for assertive-refusal behavior. *Behavior Therapy, 10,* 529–542.

Crane, G. E. (1971). Persistence of neurological symptoms due to neuroleptic drugs. *American Journal of Psychiatry, 127,* 1407–1410.

Crane, G. E. (1973). Persistent dyskinesia. *British Journal of Psychiatry, 122,* 395–405.

Creer, T. L. (1979). *Asthma therapy: A behavioral health care system for respiratory disorders.* New York: Springer.

Creer, T. L. (1982). Asthma. *Journal of Consulting and Clinical Psychology, 50,* 912–921.

Critchley, M. (1970). *The dyslexic child.* London: William Heinemann.

Crocker, A. C. (1982). Current strategies in prevention of mental retardation. *Pediatric Annals, 11,* 450–457.

Cummings, C., Gordon, J. R., & Marlatt, G. A. Relapse: Prevention and prediction. In W. R. Miller (Ed.). (1980). *The addictive behaviors.* Oxford, England: Pergamon Press.

Cummings, J. L. (1984). Dementia: definition, classification, and differential diagnosis. *Psychiatric Annals, 14,* 85–89.

Dabrowski, K. (1964). In J. Aronson (Ed.), *Positive disintegration.* Boston: Little, Brown.

Da Fonseca, A. F. (1959). *Analise heredo-clinica des perturbacoes affectivas* (Doctoral dissertation, Universidade do Porto, Portugal.)

Davis, B. L. (1982). The PCP epidemic: A critical review. *The International Journal of the Addictions, 17,* 1137–1155.

Davis, J. M. (1976). Overview: Maintenance therapy in psychiatry: II. Affective disorders. *American Journal of Psychiatry, 133,* 1–13.

Davis, W. E. (1975). Race and the differential power of the MMPI. *Journal of Personality Assessment, 39,* 138–40.

Dawber, T. R., Moore, F. E., & Mann, G. L. (1957). Coronary heart disease in the Framingham study. *American Journal of Public Health, 47,* 4–23.

Dawson, E. B., Moore, T. D., & McGanity, W. J. (1970). The mathematical relationship of drinking water, lithium, and rainfall to mental hospital admissions. *Diseases of the Nervous System, 31,* 811–820.

Defazio, V., Rustin, S., & Diamond, A. (1975). Symptom development in Viet Nam era veterans. *American Journal of Orthopsychiatry, 45,* 158–163.

Deffenbacher, J. L., & Suinn, R. M. (1982). The self-control of anxiety. In P. Karoly, & F. H. Kanfer (Eds.), *Self-management and behavior change: From theory to practice.* New York: Pergamon.

Delay, J., Deniker, P., & Harl, J. (1952). Utilization thérapeutique psychiatrique d'une phénothiazine d'action centrale élective (4560 RP). *Annals of Medical Psychology, 110,* 112–117.

DeLeon, G., & Mandell, W. (1966). A comparison of conditioning and psychotherapy in the treatment of functional enuresis. *Journal of Clinical Psychology, 22,* 326–330.

DeLong, J. V. (1975, March 16). The methadone habit. *New York Times Magazine,* pp. 16, 78, 80, 86, 90, 91, 93.

De Lozier, J. E., & Gagnon, R. O. (1975). *National ambulatory medical care survey: 1973 summary, United States,* May 73–April 74. (DHEW Publications No. HRA 76–1772). Washington, DC: U.S. Government Printing Office.

DeLuca, J. R. (Ed.). (1980, January). *Fourth special report to the U.S. Congress on alcohol and health.* U.S. Department of Health, Education and Welfare.

deMontigny, C., Cournoyer, G., Morissette, R., Langlois, R., & Caille, G. (1983). Lithium carbonate addition in tricyclic antidepressant-resistant unipolar depression. *Archives of General Psychiatry, 40,* 1327–1334.

DeMyer, M. K., et al. (1972). Parental practices and innate activity in normal, autistic, and brain-damaged infants. *Journal of Autism and Childhood Schizophrenia, 2,* 49.

DeMyer, M. K., Hingten, J. N., & Jackson, R. K. (1981). Infantile autism reviewed: A decade of research. *Schizophrenia Bulletin, 7,* 388–451.

Denber, H. C. B. (1979). *Textbook of clinical psychopharmacology.* New York: Stratton Intercontinental Medical Book Corporation.

Denckla, M. B. (1977). Minimal brain dysfunction and dyslexia: Beyond diagnosis by exclusion. In M. E. Blaw, I. Rapin, and M. Kinsbourne (Eds.), *Topics in child neurology.* New York: Spectrum.

Denner, B., & Price, R. H. (Eds.). (1973). *Community mental health: Social action and community reaction.* New York: Holt, Rinehart & Winston.

Densen-Gerber, J., & Benward, J. (1975). Incest is a causative factor in antisocial behavior: An exploratory study. *Contemporary Drug Problems, 4,* 323–340.

DePiano, F. A., & Salzberg, H. C. (1979). Clinical applications of hypnosis to three psychosomatic disorders. *Psychological Bulletin, 86,* 1223–1235.

Deutsch, H. (1937). The absence of grief. *Psychoanalytic Quarterly, 6,* 12–22.

Diamond, E. L. (1982). The role of anger and hostility in essential hypertension and coronary heart disease. *Psychological Bulletin, 92,* 410–433.

Dies, R. R. (1979). Group psychotherapy: Reflections on three decades of research. *Journal of Applied Behavioral Sciences, 15,* 361–374.

DiLoreto, A. O. (1971). *Comparative psychotherapy: An experimental analysis.* Chicago: Aldine-Atherton.

Dohrenwend, B. S., Dohrenwend, B. P., Dobson, M., and Shrout, P. E. (1984). Symptoms, hassles, social supports, and life events: Problems of confounding measures. *Journal of Abnormal Psychology, 93*:222–30.

Doleys, D. M. (1977). Behavioral treatments for nocturnal enuresis in children: A review of the recent literature. *Psychological Bulletin, 84*, 30–54.

Doleys, D. M. (1978). Assessment and treatment of enuresis and encopresis in children. In M. Hersen, R. Eisler, & P. Miller, (Eds.), *Progress in behavior modification*. New York: Academic Press.

Doleys, D. M. (1983). Enuresis and encopresis. In T. H. Ollendick and M. Hersen (Eds.), *Handbook of child psychopathology*. New York: Plenum Press.

Doleys, D. M., Weiler, D., & Pegram, V. (1982). Special disorders of childhood: Enuresis, encopresis and sleep disorders. In J. R. Lachenmeyer and M. S. Gibbs (Eds.), *Psychopathology in childhood*. New York: Gardner Press.

Dollard, J., & Miller, N. E. (1950). *Personality and psychotherapy*. New York: McGraw-Hill.

Dollinger, S. J., Thelen, M. H., & Walsh, M. L. Children's conceptions of psychological problems. *Journal of Clinical Child Psychology, 9*, 191–194.

Donaldson, D. (1976). *Insanity inside out*. New York: Crown.

Donaldson, S. R., Gelenberg, A. J., & Baldessarini, R. J. (1983). The pharmacologic treatment of schizophrenia: A progress report. *Schizophrenia Bulletin, 9*, 504–527.

Donegan, N. H., Rodin, J., O'Brien, C. P., & Solomon, R. L. (1983). A learning-theory approach to commonalities. In P. Levison, D. R. Gerstein, & D. R. Maloff (Eds.), *Commonalities in substance abuse and habitual behavior*. Lexington, MA: Lexington Books.

Dooley, D., & Catalano, R. (1980). Economic change as a cause of behavior disorder. *Psychological Bulletin, 87*, 450–468.

Drugs and psychiatry: A new era. (1979, November 12). *Newsweek*, pp. 98–106.

Dunham, H. W. (1965). *Community and schizophrenia: An epidemiolcgical analysis*. Detroit: Wayne State University Press.

Dunn, L. M. (1973). Children with moderate and severe general learning disabilities. In L. M. Dunn (Ed.), *Exceptional children in the schools: Special education in transition* (2d ed.). New York: Holt, Rinehart & Winston.

DuPont, R. L. (1976, May 10–14). *Current national heroin use trends*. Paper presented at the Scientific Program of the Annual Meeting, American Psychiatric Association, Miami.

Dupont, R. I., Goldstein, A., & O'Donnell, J. (1979). Treatment modalities for narcotics addicts. In R. Dupont, A. Goldstein, & J. O'Donnell (Eds.), *Hand-book on drug abuse*. Washington, DC: National Institute on Drug Abuse, U.S. Government Printing Office.

Durham v. *United States, 214* F. 2d 862 (DC Cir., 1954).

Durkheim, E. (1952). *Suicide* (J. A. Spaulding & G. Simpson, Trans.). London: Routledge & Kegan Paul.

Eastman, C. (1976). Behavioral formulations of depression. *Psychological Review 83*, 277–291.

Eckardt, M. J., Harford, T. C., Kaelber, C. T., Parker, E. S., Rosenthal, L. S., Ryback, R. S., Salmoiraghi, G. C., Vanderveen, E., & Warren, K. R. (1981). Health hazards associated with alcohol consumption. *Journal of the American Medical Association, 246*, 648–666.

Edinburg, G., Zinberg, N., & Kelson, W. (1975). *Clinical interviewing and counseling: Principles and techniques*. New York: Appleton-Century-Crofts.

Egendorf, A., Remez, A., & Farley, J. (1981). Dealing with the war: A view based on the individual lives of Viet Nam Veterans. In A. Egendorf et al. (Eds.), *Legacies of Viet Nam: Comparative adjustment of veterans and their peers* (Vol. 5). Washington, DC: U.S. Government Printing Office.

Eisdorfer, C., & Stotsky, B. A. (1977). Intervention, treatment, and rehabilitation of psychiatric disorders. In J. E. Birren & K. W. Schaie (Eds.), *Handbook of the psychology of aging* (pp. 724–748). New York: Van Nostrand Reinhold.

Eisenberg, L. (1956). The autistic child in adolescence. *American Journal of Psychiatry, 112*, 607.

Eisenberg, L. (1958). School phobia: A study in the communication of anxieties. *American Journal of Psychiatry, 114*, 712–718.

Ellis, A. (1976). Rational emotive therapy. In V. Binder, A. Binder, & B. Rimland (Eds.), *Modern therapies*. Englewood Cliffs, NJ: Prentice-Hall.

Ellis, A. (1977). The basic clinical theory of rational-emotive therapy. In A. Ellis & R. Grieger (Eds.), *Handbook of rational-emotive therapy*. New York: Springer Publishing Co., Copyright © 1977 by Springer Publishing Company, Inc. Material used by permission.

Emmelkamp, P. M. G. (1982). *Phobic and obsessive-compulsive disorders: Theory, research, and practice*. New York: Plenum Press.

Emrick, C. D. (1975). A review of psychologically oriented treatment of alcoholism: II. The relative effectiveness of different treatment approaches and the effectiveness of treatment vs. no treatment. *Journal of Studies on Alcohol, 36*, 88–108.

Engel, B. P. (1973). Clinical applications of operant conditioning techniques in the control of cardiac arrhythmias. *Seminars in Psychiatry, 5*, 433–438.

Epstein, C. J. (1983). Down's syndrome and Alzheimer's disease: implications and approaches. In *Biological aspects of Alzheimer's disease,* Branbury Report 15, Cold Spring Laboratory, pp. 169–182.

Epstein, L. J. (1976). Depression in the elderly. *Journal of Gerontology, 31,* 278–282.

Epstein, S. (1983). Natural healing processes of the mind: Graded stress inoculation as an inherent coping mechanism. In D. Meichenbaum & M. E. Jaremko (Eds.), *Stress reduction and prevention* (pps. 39–66). New York: Plenum Press.

Erickson, E. (1950). *Childhood and society.* New York: Norton.

Erikson, K. T. (1976). *Everything in its path: Destruction of community in the Buffalo Creek flood.* New York: Simon & Schuster.

Erickson, M. T. (1978). *Child psychopathology: Assessment, etiology, and treatment.* Englewood Cliffs, NJ: Prentice-Hall.

Eron, L. D. (1980). Prescription for reduction of aggression. *American Psychologist, 35,* 244–252.

Eron, L. D. Husemann, L. R. Lefkowitz, M. M., & Walder, L. O. (1972). Does television violence cause aggression? *American Psychologist, 27,* 253–263.

Ethical issues for human services. (1977). *Behavior Therapy, 8,* V–VI.

Etzioni, A. (1973, April). Methadone: Best hope for now. *Smithsonian Magazine, 48,* 67–74.

Eyde, D. R., & Rich, J. A. (1983). *Psychological distress in aging.* Rockville, MD: Aspen Systems Corporation.

Eysenck, H. J. (1952). The effects of psychotherapy: An evaluation. *Journal of Consulting Psychology, 16,* 319–324.

Fagen, J. (1971, Spring). The importance of Fritz Perls having been. *Voices, 7,* 16–20.

Fairbairn, R. (1946). Endopsychic structure considered in terms of object relationships. *Psychoanalytic Quarterly, 5,* 54–69.

Fairburn, C. G., & Cooper, P. J. (1982). Self-induced vomiting and bulimia nervosa: An undetected problem. *British Medical Journal, 284,* 1153–1155.

Fairweather, G. W. (Ed.) (1964). *Social psychology in treating mental illness: An experimental approach.* New York: John Wiley & Sons.

Fairweather, G. W., Sanders, D. H., Cressler, D. L., & Maynard, H. (1969). *Community life for the mentally ill: An alternative to institutional care.* Chicago: Aldine.

Falloon, I. R. H., & Liberman, R. P. (1983). Interactions between drug and psychosocial therapy in schizophrenia. *Schizophrenia Bulletin, 9,* 543–554.

Faris, R. E. L., & Dunham, H. W. (1939). Mental disorders in urban areas: An ecological study of schizophrenia and other psychoses. Chicago: University of Chicago Press.

Farkas, G. M. (1980). An ontological analysis of behavior therapy. *American Psychologist, 35,* 364–374.

Farkas, G. M., & Rosen, R. C. (1976). The effect of alcohol on elicited male sexual response. *Journal of Studies on Alcohol, 37,* 265–272.

Federal Bureau of Investigation (1981). *Crime in the United States: Uniform Crime Reports.* Washington, DC: U.S. Government Printing Office.

Federal Commission OK's psychosurgery. (1976, November). *APA Monitor,* 4–5.

Feingold, B. (1975). *Why your child is hyperactive.* New York: Random House.

Feldman, H. W. PCP use in four cities: An overview. (1979). In H. W. Feldman, M. H. Agar, & G. M. Beschner (Eds.), *Angel dust.* Lexington, MA: D. C. Heath.

Fenichel, O. (1945). *The psychoanalytic theory of neurosis.* New York: Norton.

Ferster, C. B. (1973). A functional analysis of devression. *American Psychologist, 28,* 857–870.

Ferster, C. B., & DeMyer, M. K. (1961). The development of performances in autistic children in an automatically controlled environment. *Journal of Chronic Diseases, 13,* 312–345.

Fields, S. (1976). Folk healing for the wounded spirit. *Innovations, 3,* 3–18.

Fields, S. (1978, Spring). Support and succor for the "walking wounded." *Innovations, 5*(1), 2–15.

Fieve, R. R. (1975). *Moodswing: The third revolution in psychiatry.* New York: Bantam. Copyright © 1975 by Ronald R. Fieve. Material reprinted by permission of William Morrow & Company.

Fink, M. (1977). Myths of "Shock Therapy." *American Journal of Psychiatry, 134,* 991–996.

Fink, M. (1978). Efficacy and safety of induced seizures (EST) in man. *Comprehensive Psychiatry, 19,* 1.

Fink, M. & Johnson, L. (1982, October). Monitoring the duration of electroconvulsive therapy seizures: Cuff and EEG methods compared. *Archives of General Psychiatry, 39*(10), 1189–1191.

Finkelstein, W., & Isselbacher, K. J. (1978). Cimetidine. *New England Journal of Medicine, 299,* 992, 996.

Finkle, B. S., & McClosky, K. L. (1977). The forensic toxicology of cocaine. In R. Petersen, & R. Stillman (Eds.), *Cocaine: 1977* (NIDA Research Monograph, No. 13, DHEW Publication No. ADM 77–432). Washington, DC: U.S. Government Printing Office.

Fisher, V. (1980). Myths and realities: A study of attitudes toward Viet Nam veterans. Washington, DC: U.S. Government Printing Office.

Fixsen, D. L., Phillips, E. L., Phillips, E. A., & Wolf, M. M. (1976). The teaching-family model of group home treatment. In W. E. Craighead, A. Kazdin, & M. J. Mahoney (Eds.), *Behavior modification*. Boston: Houghton Mifflin.

Flaherty, J. A. (1979). Psychiatric complications of medical drugs. *The Journal of Family Practice, 9,* 243–254.

Folstein, S., & Rutter, M. (1977). Genetic influences and infantile autism. *Nature, 265,* 726.

Foltz, E. L., & Millett, F. E. (1964). Experimental psychosomatic disease states in monkeys: I. Peptic ulcer-executive monkeys. *Journal of Surgical Research, 4,* 445–453.

Footlick, J. K., & Lowell, J. (1978, December 18). The ten phases of Billy. *Newsweek,* p. 106.

Ford, C. S., & Beach, F. A. (1952). *Patterns of sexual behavior.* New York: Harper & Row.

Fordyce, W. E. (1976). *Behavioral methods for chronic pain and illness.* St. Louis: C. V. Mosby.

Foster, S. W., & Gurman, A. S. (1982). On talking systems and treating people. In L. R. Wolberg & M. L. Aronson (Eds.), *Group and family therapy 1982.* New York: Brunner/Mazel.

Foucault, M. (1965). *Madness and civilization* (R. Howard, Trans.). New York: Random House.

Frank, J. D. (1973). Persuasion and Healing, 2d ed. Baltimore: Johns Hopkins University Press.

Frank, J. D. (1976). Restoration of morale and behavior change. In A. Burton (Ed.), *What makes behavior change possible?* New York: Bruner/Mazel.

Frank, J. D. (1981). Therapeutic components shared by all psychotherapies. In J. H. Harvey, & M. M. Parks (Eds.), *Psychotherapy research and behavior change.* Washington, D.C.: American Psychological Association.

Frankl, V. E. (1965). *The doctor and the soul: From psychotherapy to logotherapy.* New York: Alfred Knopf.

Frankl, V. E. (1970). *The will to meaning.* New York: New American Library.

Frankl, V. E. (1971). *Man's search for meaning: An introduction to logotherapy.* New York: Washington Square Press.

Freidrich, W. N., & Einbender, A. J. (1983). The abused child: A psychological review. *Journal of Child Psychology, 12,* 244–256.

Freud, A. (1962). *The ego and the mechanisms of defense.* New York: McKay.

Freud, S. (1911). Psychoanalytic notes upon an autobiographical account of a case of paranoia. In P. Rieff (Ed.), *Three Case Histories.* New York: Macmillan.

Freud, S. (1933). *New introductory lectures on psychoanalysis.* New York: Norton.

Freud, S. (1951). Letter to an American mother. *American Journal of Psychiatry, 102,* 786.

Freud in a letter to Fleiss, 1897. (1953). In E. Jones, *The life and works of Sigmund Freud* (Vol. 1). New York: Basic Books.

Freud, S. (1959). On psychotherapy. In E. Jones (Ed.), *Sigmund Freud Collected Papers.* (Vol. 1). New York: Basic Books, Hogarth Press. (Originally published, 1904.)

Friar, L. R., & Beatty, J. (1976). Migraine: Management by trained control of vasoconstriction. *Journal of Consulting and Clinical Psychology, 44,* 46–53.

Friedman, M., & Rosenman, R. H. (1959). Association of specific overt behavior pattern with blood and cardiovascular findings—blood cholesterol level, blood clotting time, incidence of arcur senilis, and clinical coronary artery disease. *Journal of the American Medical Association, 169,* 1286–1296.

Fromm, E. (1947). *Man for himself.* New York: Holt, Rinehart, and Winston.

Frommer, E. H. (1967). Treatment of childhood depression with antidepressant drugs. *British Medical Journal, 1,* 729.

Fromm-Reichman, F. (1950). *Principles of intensive psychotherapy.* Chicago: University of Chicago Press.

Gagnon, J. H. (1977). *Human sexualities.* Glenview, IL: Scott Foresman.

Gallagher, D., & Thompson, L. W. (1981). *Depression in the elderly: A behavioral treatment manual.* Los Angeles, CA: Ethel Percy Andrus Gerontology Center.

Gallagher, D., & Thompson, L. W. (1983). Cognitive therapy for depression in the elderly: A promising model for treatment and research. In L. D. Breslau & M. R. Haug (Eds.), *Depression and aging: Causes, care, and consequences* (pp. 168–192). New York: Springer.

Gallagher, D., Thompson, L. W., & Levy, S. M. (1980). Clinical psychological assessment of older adults. In L. W. Poon (Ed.), *Aging in the 1980s* (pp. 19–40). Washington, DC: American Psychological Association.

Gallup, G. (1977, July). *Three part series on the homosexual in U.S. society.* Unpublished paper, Princeton, NJ.

Gardner, H. (1979). Children's art: Nadia's challenge. *Psychology Today, 13,* 18.

Gardos, G., & Cole, J. O. (1976). Maintenance antipsychotic therapy: Is the cure worse than the disease? *American Journal of Psychiatry, 133,* 323–336.

Garey, R. E. (1979). PCP (phencyclidine): An update. *Journal of Psychedelic Drugs, 11,* 265–275.

Garfield, S. L. (1978). Research on client variables. In S. Garfield & A. Bergin (Eds.), *Handbook of psycho-*

therapy and behavior change. New York: John Wiley & Sons.

Garfield, S. L. (1981). Psychotherapy: A 40-year appraisal. *American Psychologist, 31,* 174–183.

Garfield, S. L., & Kurtz, R. (1976). Clinical psychologists in the 1970s. *American Psychologist, 31,* 1–9.

Garner, D. M., Garfinkel, P. E., Schwartz, D., & Thompson, M. (1980). The cultural expectations of thinness in women. *Psychological Reports, 47,* 483–491.

Garrison, J. E. (1978). Stress management training for the elderly: A psychoeducational approach. *Journal of the American Geriatrics Society, 26,* 397–403.

Garske, J. P. (1982). Issues regarding effective psychotherapy: A research perspective. In J. McNamara, & A. Barclay (Eds.), *Critical issues, developments, and trends in professional psychology.* New York: Praeger.

Garske, J. P., & Lynn, S. J. (1985). Toward a general scheme for psychotherapy. In S. J. Lynn, & J. P. Garske (Eds.), *Contemporary psychotherapies: Models and methods.* Columbus: Merrill Press.

Gebhard, P. H. (1969). Fetishism and sadomasochism. *Science and Psychoanalysis, 15,* 71–80.

Gebhard, P. H., Gagnon, J. H., Pomeroy, W. B., & Christenson, C. V. (1965). *Sex Offenders.* New York: Harper & Row.

Gelenberg, A. J. (1979). Prescribing antidepressants. *Drug Therapy, 9,* 95–112.

George, L. K., & Weiler, S. J. (1981). Sexuality in middle and late life: The effects of age, education, and gender. *Archives of General Psychiatry, 38,* 919–923.

George, W. H., & Marlatt, G. A. (in press). Problem drinking: Biomedical consequences and self-management strategies. In K. Holroyd, & T. Creer (Eds.), *Self-management in health psychology and behavioral medicine.*

Gibbs, L. M. (1982). *Love canal: My story.* Albany, NY: State University of New York Press.

Gibbons, D. C. (1970). *Delinquent behavior.* Englewood Cliffs, NJ: Prentice-Hall.

Gill, M. (1954). Psychoanalysis and exploratory psychotherapy. *Journal of the American Psychoanalytic Association, 2,* 771–797.

Ginott, H. G. (1961). *Group psychotherapy with children.* New York: McGraw Hill.

Ginzburg, H. M. (1983). Use of clonidine or lofexidine to detoxify from methadone maintenance or other opioid dependencies. In J. R. Cooper, R. Altman, B. S. Brown, & D. Czechowicz (Eds.), *Research in the treatment of narcotic addiction: State of the art.* (DDHS Publication No. ADM 83–1281), Washington, DC.: U.S. Government Printing Office.

Gittelman-Klein, R., & Klein, D. F. (1971). Controlled imipramine treatment of school phobia. *Archives of General Psychiatry, 25,* 204.

Glantz, M. (1981). Predictions of elderly drug abuse. *Journal of Psychoactive Drugs, 13(2),* 117–126.

Glantz, M. D. (1983a). Drugs and the elderly adult: An overview. In M. D. Glantz, D. M. Petersen, & F. J. Whittington (Eds.), *Drugs and the elderly adult* (DHHS Publication No. ADM 83–1269, pp. 1–3). Washington, DC: U.S. Government Printing Office.

Glantz, M. D. (1983b). Alcohol use and abuse. In M. D. Glantz, D. M. Petersen, & F. J. Whittington (Eds.). *Drugs and the elderly adult* (DHHS Publication No. ADM 83–1269, pp. 151–153). Washington, DC: U.S. Government Printing Office.

Glantz, M. D., Petersen, D. M., & Whittington, F. J. (1983). *Drugs and the elderly adult* (DHHS Publication No. ADM 83–1269). Washington, DC: U.S. Government Printing Office.

Glass, C. R., Gottman, J. M., & Shmurak, S. H. (1976) Response acquisition and cognitive self-statement modification approaches to dating skills training. *Journal of Counseling Psychology, 23,* 520–526.

Glass, D., Krakoff, L. R., Contrada, R., Hilton, W. F., Kehoe, K., Manucci, E. G., Collins, C., Snow, B., & Elting, E. (1980). Effect of harrassment and competition upon cardiovascular and catecholamine responses in Type A and Type B individuals. *Psychophysiology, 17,* 453–463.

Gleser, G. C., Green, B. L., & Winget, C. (1981). *Prolonged psychosocial effects of a disaster: A study of Buffalo Creek.* New York: Academic Press.

Glick, I. O., Weiss, R. S., & Parks, M. C. (1974). *The first year of bereavement.* New York: John Wiley & Sons.

Glista, G. G., Frank, H. G., Tracy, F. W. (1983). Video games and seizures. *Archives of Neurology 40,* 588.

Goffman, E. (1961). *Asylums: Essays on the social situation of mental patients and other inmates.* Garden City, NY: Anchor, 1961.

Gold, R. (1973, May 9). Stop it, you're making me sick. Paper (expanded version) presented at the American Psychiatric Association, Honolulu, HI.

Goldberg, S., & Lewis, M. (1969). Play behavior in the year-old infant: Early sex differences. *Child development, 40,* 21–31.

Golden, N., & Sacker, I. M. (1984). An overview of the etiology, diagnosis, and management of anorexia nervosa. *Clinical Pediatrics, 23,* 209–214.

Goldenberg, H. (1977). *Abnormal psychology: A social/community approach.* Monterey, CA: Brooks-Cole.

Goldfried, M. R. (1971). Systematic desensitization as training in self-control. *Journal of Consulting and Clinical Psychology, 27,* 228–234.

Goldfried, M. R. (1980). Toward the delineation of therapeutic change principles. *American Psychologist, 35,* 991-999.

Goldfried, M. R., & Davisco, G. C. (1976). *Clinical behavior therapy.* New York: Holt, Rinehart & Winston.

Goldfried, M. R., & Sprafkin, J. N. (1974). *Behavioral personality assessment.* Morristown, NJ: General Learning Press. © 1974 General Learning Corporation. Material reprinted by permission of Silver Burdett Company.

Goldfried, M. R., Stricker, G., & Weiner, I. B. (1971). *Rorschach handbook of clinical and research applications.* Englewood Cliffs, NJ: Prentice-Hall.

Goldman, M. (1983). Cognitive impairment in chronic alcoholics: Some cause for optimism. *American Psychologist, 38,* 1045-1054.

Goodwin, D. W. (1979). Alcoholism and heredity. *Archives of General Psychiatry, 36,* 57-64. Copyright 1979, American Medical Association.

Goodwin, J. (1980). The etiology of combat-related post-traumatic stress disorders. In T. Williams (Ed.), *Post-traumatic stress disorders of the Viet Nam veteran.* Cincinnati, OH: Disabled American Veterans National Headquarters.

Gordon, J. S. (1971, January). Who is mad? Who is sane? H. D. Laing: In search of a new psychiatry. *The Altantic,* pp. 50-66.

Gottdiener, J. S., Green, H. A., Henry, W. L., Borer, J. S., & Ebert, M. H. (1978). Effects of self-induced starvation on cardiac size and function in anorexia nervosa. *Circulation, 58,* 425-433.

Gottesman, I. I., & Shields, J. (1967). A polygenic theory of schizophrenia. *Proceedings of the National Academy of Sciences, 58,* 199-205.

Gottheil, E., & Weinstein, S. O. (1983). Cocaine: An emerging problem. In S. Akhtar (Ed.), *New psychiatric syndromes: DSM III and beyond.* New York: Jason Aronson.

Gottlieb, B. H. (1978). The development and application of a classification scheme of informal helping behaviours. *Canadian Journal of Science/Rev. Canad. Sci. Comp., 10*(2), 105-115.

Gottlieb, B. H. (1983). *Social Support Strategies.*

Gottman, J. M. (1979). *Marital interaction: Experimental investigations.* New York: Academic Press.

Gottman, J., & Markman, H. (1978). Experimental designs in psychotherapy research. In S. L. Garfield & A. E. Bergin (Eds.), *Handbook of psychotherapy and behavior change* (2d ed.). New York: John Wiley & Sons.

Gough, H. G. (1948). A sociological theory of psychopathy. *American Journal of Sociology, 53,* 359-366.

Gould, L. C. Berberian, R. M., Kasi, S. V., Thompson, W. D., & Kleber, H. D. (1977). Sequential patterns of multiple-drug use among high school students. *Archives of General Psychiatry, 34,* 216-222.

Gove, W. R. (Ed.) (1975). *The labeling of deviance: Evaluating a perspective.* Beverly Hills, CA: Sage Publications.

Grace, W. J., & Graham, D. T. (1952). Relationship of specific attitudes and emotions to certain bodily diseases. *Psychosomatic Medicine, 14,* 243-251.

Graham, D. T., Kabler, J. D., & Graham, F. K. (1962). Physiological response to the suggestion of attitudes specific for hives and hypertension. *Psychosomatic Medicine, 24,* 159-169.

Graham, D. T., Stern, J. A., & Winokur, G. (1958). Experimental investigation of the specificity of attitude hypothesis in psychosomatic diseases. *Psychosomatic Medicine, 1958, 20,* 446-447.

Granick, S., & Patterson, R. D. (1971). *Human aging, II: An eleven-year follow-up biomedical and behavioral study.* Publication No. (HSM) 71-9037. Washington, DC: U.S. Government Printing Office.

Grant, V. W. (1958). A case study of fetishism. *Journal of Abnormal and Social Psychology, 48,* 142-149. Copyright 1953 by the American Psychological Association. Excerpt in text reprinted by permission.

Green, A. H. (1976). A psychodynamic approach to the study and treatment of child abusing parents. *Journal of the American Academy of Child Psychiatry, 15,* 414-429.

Green, H. (1974). *Sexual identity conflict in children and adults.* Baltimore: Penguin Books.

Greenson, R. (1967). *The technique and practice of psychoanalysis.* New York: International Universities Press.

Griest, J. H., Klein, M. H., Erdman, H. P., & Jefferson, J. W. (1983). Computers and psychiatric diagnosis. *Psychiatric Annals, 13*(10).

Grimshaw, L. (1964). Obsessional disorder and neurological illness. *Journal of Neurology, Neurosurgery and Psychiatry, 27,* 229-231.

Gunderson, J. G., & Mosher, L. R. (1975). The cost of schizophrenia. *Archives of General Psychiatry, 132,* 901-906.

Gunderson, J. G., and Singer, M. T. (1975). Defining borderline patients: An overview. *The American Journal of Psychiatry, 132,* 1-10.

Guntrip, H. (1969). *Schizoid phenomena, object relations and the self.* New York: International Universities Press.

Gurin, G., Veroff, J., & Feld, S. (1960). *Americans view their mental health.* New York: Basic Books.

Gurland, B. J. (1976). The comparative frequency of depression in various adult age groups. *Journal of Gerontology, 31*, 283–292.

Gurman, A. S. (1977). The patient's perception of the therapeutic relationship. In A. S. Gurman, & A. M. Razin (Eds.), *Effective psychotherapy: A handbook on research.* New York: Pergamon.

Gurman, A. S., & Kniskern, D. P. (1978). Research on marital and family therapy: Progress, perspective, and prospect. In S. L. Garfield & A. E. Bergin (Eds.), *Handbook of psychotherapy and behavior change* (2d ed.). New York: John Wiley & Sons.

Gusella, J. F., Wexler, N. S., Conneally, P. M., Naylor, S. L., Anderson, M. A., Tanzi, R. E., Watkins, P. C., Ottina, K., Wallace, M. R., Sakaguchi, A. Y., Young, A. B., Shoulson, I., Bonilla, E. and Martin, J. B. (1983). A polymorphic DNA marker genetically linked to Huntington's disease. *Nature 306*, 234–238.

Gutheil, T. G., & Avery, G. (1977). Multiple overt incest as family defense against loss. *Family Process, 16*, 105–116.

Gynther, M. D. (1972). White norms and black MMPI's: A prescription for discrimination? *Psychological Bulletin, 78*, 386–402.

Gynther, M. D. (1981). Is the MMPI an appropriate assessment device for blacks? *Journal of Black Psychology, 7*, 67–75.

Gynther, M. D., & Green, S. B. (1980). Accuracy may make a difference, but does a difference make for accuracy? A response to Pritchard and Rosenblatt. *Journal of Consulting Clinical Psychology, 48*, 267–272.

Hackett, T. P. (1979). Editorial: The rational use of psychotropic drugs. *Drug Therapy for the Family Physician, 9*, 39–40.

Haeberle, E. J. (1978). *The sex atlas.* New York: Seabury Press. Material used by permission of The Continuum Publishing Corporation, New York.

Halleck, S. L. (1967). Hysterical personality traits. *Archives of General Psychiatry, 16*, 750–757.

Halpern, W. I., & Kissel, S. (1976). *Human resources for troubled children.* New York: John Wiley & Sons.

Hanson, J. W., Streissguth, A. P., & Smith, D. W. (1978). The effects of moderate alcohol consumption during pregnancy on fetal growth and morphogenesis. *Journal of Pediatrics, 92*, 457–460.

Hardy, J. B. (1965). Perinatal factors and intelligence. In S. F. Osler and R. E. Cooke (Eds.), *The biosocial basis of mental retardation.* Baltimore, MD: Johns Hopkins University Press.

Hare, E. H. (1956). Mental illness and social conditions in Bristol. *Journal of Mental Science, 102*, 349–357.

Hare, R. D. (1985). Comparison of procedures for the assessment of psychopathology. *Journal of Consulting and Clinical Psychology, 53*(1), 7–16.

Hare, R. D., and McPherson, L. M. (1984). Psychopathy and perceptual asymmetry during verbal dichotic listening. *Journal of Abnormal Psychology, 93*, 141–149.

Hare, R. D., & Schalling, D. (1978). *Psychopathic behavior: Approaches to research.* New York: John Wiley & Sons.

Harlow, H. F., & Harlow, M. K. (1969). Effects of various mother-infant relationships on rhesus monkey behaviors. In B. M. Foss (Ed.), *Determinants of infant behavior IV.* London: Methuen.

Hartford, M. E. (1980). The use of group methods for work with the aged. In J. E. Birren & R. B. Sloane (Eds.), *Handbook of mental health and aging* (pp. 806–826). Englewood Cliffs, NJ: Prentice-Hall.

Hartmann, H. (1950). Comment on the psychoanalytic theory of the ego. *The Psychoanalytic Study of the Child, 5*, 74–96.

Hartocollis, P. (1980). Affective disturbance in borderline and narcissistic patients. *Bulletin of the Menninger Clinic, 44*, 135–146.

Harvey, J. H. & Weary, G. (1984). Current issues in attribution theory and research. *Annual Review of Psychology* Vol. 35, 427–459.

Hathaway, S. R., & McKinley, J. C. (1943). *Minnesota multiphasic personality inventory: Manual.* New York: Psychological Corporation.

Haughton, E., & Ayllon, T. (1965). Production and elimination of symptomatic behavior. In L. Ullmann & L. Krasner (Eds.), *Case studies in behavior modification.* New York: Holt, Rinehart & Winston, pp. 94–98.

Hauser, S. L., DeLong, G. K., & Rosman, N. P. (1975). Pneumographic findings in the infantile autism syndrome. *Brain, 98*, 667.

Haynes, R. B., Mattson, M. E., & Engebretson, T. O. (1980). *Patient compliance to prescribed antihypertensive medication regimens: A report to the National Heart, Lung, and Blood Institute.* (NIH Publication No. 81-2102). Washington, DC: U.S. Government Printing Office.

Haynes, S. N., Feinlieb, M., Levine, S., Scotch, N., & Kannel, W. B. (1978). The relationship of psychosocial factors to coronary heart disease in the Framingham study, II: Prevalence of coronary heart disease. *American Journal of Epidemiology, 107*, 384–402.

Heaton, R. K., Nelson, L. M., Thompson, D. S., Burks, J. S., & Franklin, G. M. (1985). Neuropsychological findings in relapsing-remitting and chronic-progressive multiple sclerosis. *Journal of Consulting and Clinical Psychology, 53*(1), 103–110.

Heiman, J. R., & LoPiccolo, J. (1983). Clinical outcome of sex therapy. *Archives of General Psychiatry, 40*, 443–449.

Helfer, R. E. (1975). *The diagnostic process and treatment programs.* DHEW publication (OHD 75-69).

Washington, D.C.: U.S. Department of Health, Education, & Welfare, National Center for Child Abuse and Neglect.

Heilbrun, A. B., Jr. (1979). Psychopathy and violent crime. *Journal of Consulting and Clinical Psychology, 47,* 517–524.

Heller, K. (1984). Prevention and health promotion. In *Psychology and community change: Challenges of the future* (2d ed.) (pps. 172–226). Homewood, IL: Dorsey Press.

Heller, K., & Monahan, J. (1977). *Psychology and community change.* Homewood, IL: Dorsey Press.

Heller, K., Price, R. H., & Sher, K. J. (1980). Research and evaluation in primary prevention. In R. H. Price, R. F. Ketterer, B. C. Bader, & J. Monahan (Eds.), *Prevention in mental health.* Beverly Hills, CA and London: Russell Sage Foundation.

Heller, K., Price, R. H., Reinharz, S., Riger, S., Wandersman, A., & D'Aunno, T. (1984). *Psychology and community change: Challenges of the future* (2d ed.). Homewood, IL: Dorsey Press.

Hendlin, H. (1980). Psychosocial theory of drug abuse: A psychodynamic approach. In D. J. Lettieri, M. Sayers, & H. W. Pearson (Eds.), *Theories on drug abuse: Selected contemporary perspectives.* (NIDA Research Monograph No. 30, DHEW. Rockville, MD: National Institute in Drug Abuse.)

Hendricks, J., & Hendricks, C. D. (1981). *Aging in mass society* (2d ed.). Cambridge, MA: Winthrop.

Henninger, G. R., Charney, D. S., & Sternberg, D. E. (1983). Lithium carbonate augmentation of antidepressant treatment. *Archives of General Psychiatry, 40,* 1335–1442.

Henry, W. (1956). *Analysis of Fantasy* (pp. 140–141).

Hermann, B. P., & Whitman, S. (1984). Behavioral and personality correlates of epilepsy: A review, methodological critique, and conceptual model. *Psychological Bulletin 95,* 451–497.

Herr, J. J., & Weakland, J. H. (1979). *Counseling elders and their families.* New York: Springer.

Hersen, M. (1979). Limitations and problems in the clinical application of behavioral techniques in psychiatric settings. *Behavior Therapy, 10,* 65–80.

Hersov, L. A. (1960). Persistent non-attendance at school. *Journal of Child Psychology and Psychiatry, 1,* 130–136.

Herzog, D. B., & Rathburn, J. M. (1982). Childhood depression. *American Journal of Disturbances of Childhood, 136,* 115–120.

Hetherington, E. M. (1979). Divorce—A child's perspective. *American Psychologist, 34,* 851–858.

Hiatt, B. (1981). Depression: Clinical Studies Unit, Clinical Psychobiology Program. *Research News. 32,* 3–15.

Higgins, R. L., & Marlatt, G. A. (1973). Effects of anxiety arousal on the consumption of alcohol by alcoholics and social drinkers. *Journal of Consulting and Clinical Psychology, 41,* 426–433.

Higgins, R. L., & Marlatt, G. A. (1975). Fear of interpersonal evaluation as a determinant of alcohol consumption in male social drinkers. *Journal of Abnormal Psychology, 84,* 644–651.

Hilgard, E. R. (1962). *Introduction to Psychology* (3d ed). New York: Harcourt Brace Jovanovitch.

Hilgard, E. R. (1977). *Divided consciousness: Multiple controls in human thought and action.* New York: John Wiley & Sons.

Hingtgen, J. N., & Trost, F. C., Jr. (1966). Shaping cooperative responses in early childhood schizophrenics: II. Reinforcement of mutual contact and vocal responses. In R. Ulrich, T. Statchnick, & J. Mabry (Eds.), *Control of human behavior* (Vol. 1). Glenview, IL: Scott, Foresman.

Hogan, D. R. (1978). The effectiveness of sex therapy: A review of the literature. In J. LoPiccolo and L. LoPiccolo (Eds.), *Handbook of sex therapy.* New York: Plenum Press, 1978.

Hogan, R. A. (1968). The implosive technique. *Behavior Research and Therapy, 6,* 423–432.

Hogarty, G. E. (1977). Treatment and the course of schizophrenia. *Schizophrenia Bulletin, 3,* 587–599.

Hogarty, G. E., Goldberg, S. C., Schooler, N. R., & Ulrich, R. F., & the Collaborative Study Group. (1974a). Drug and sociotherapy in the aftercare of schizophrenic patients: II. Two year relapse rates. *Archives of General Psychiatry, 31,* 603–608 (a).

Hogarty, G. E., Goldberg, S. C., Schooler, N. R., Ulrich, R. F., & the Collaborative Study Group. (1974b). Drug and sociotherapy in the aftercare of schizophrenic patients: III. Adjustment of nonrelapsed patients. *Archives of General Psychiatry, 31,* 609–618 (b).

Hollingshead, A. B., & Redlich, F. C. (1958). *Social class and mental illness.* New York: John Wiley & Sons.

Holmes, L. B., Moser, H. W., Halldorsson, S., Mack, C., Pant, S. S., & Matzilevich, B. (1972). *Mental retardation: An atlas of diseases with associated physical abnormalities.* New York: Macmillan.

Holmes, T. H., & Masuda, M. (1972, April). Psychosomatic syndromes. *Psychology Today,* pp. 71–106.

Holmes, T. H., & Masuda, M. (1973). Life change and illness susceptibility, separation, and depression. *American Association for the Advancement of Science,* 161–186.

Holmes, T. H., & Rahe, R. H. (1967). The social adjustment rating scale. *Journal of Psychosomatic Research, 11,* 213–218.

Holroyd, K. A. (1976). Cognition and desensitization in the group treatment of test anxiety. *Journal of Consulting and Clinical Psychology, 44,* 991–1001.

Holroyd, K. A. (1978). Effects of social anxiety and social evaluation on beer consumption and social interaction. *Journal of Studies on Alcohol, 39*, 737–744.

Holroyd, K. A. (1979). Stress, coping and the treatment of stress related illness. In J. R. McNamara (Ed.), *Behavioral approaches in medicine: Application and analysis.* New York: Plenum Press.

Holroyd, K. A., & Andrasik, F. (1982). A cognitive-behavioral approach to recurrent tension and migraine headache. In P. C. Kendall (Ed.), *Advances in Cognitive-Behavioral Research and Therapy.* New York: Academic Press.

Holroyd, K., Andrasik, F., & Westbrook, K. (1977). Cognitive control of tension headache. *Cognitive therapy and research, 1*, 121–133.

Holroyd, K. A., Appel, M. A., & Andrasik, F. (1983). A cognitive-behavioral approach to psychophysiological disorders. In D. Meichenbaum & M. Taremka (Eds.) *Stress prevention and management: A cognitive-behavioral perspective.* New York: Plenum Press.

Holroyd, K. A., Penzien, D. B., Holm, J. E., & Hursey, K. G. (1984, June). *Behavioral Treatment of Tension and Migraine Headache: What does the Literature Say?* Paper presented at the meeting of the American Association for the Study of Headache, San Francisco.

Holzman, P. S. (1970). *Psychoanalysis and psychopathology.* New York: McGraw-Hill.

Hook, S. (1959). Science and mythology in psychoanalysis. In S. Hook (Ed.), *Psychoanalysis, scientific method, and philosophy.* New York: New York University Press.

Horowitz, M. J. (1976). *Stress response syndromes.* New York: Jason Aronson.

Hoyer, W. J. (1974). Aging as intraindividual change. *Developmental Psychology, 10*, 821–826.

Hoyer, W. J., Labouvie, G. V., & Baltes, P. B. (1973). Modification of response speed deficits and intellectual performance in the elderly. *Human Development, 16*, 233–242.

Hsu, L. (1980). Outcome of anorexia nervosa: A review of the literature (1954–1978). *Archives of General Psychiatry, 37*, 1041–1046.

Hull, D. B., & Schroeder, H. E. (1979). Some interpersonal effects of assertion, nonassertion, and aggression. *Behavior Therapy, 10*, 14–19.

Humphreys, L. (1970). *Tearoom trade: Impersonal sex in public places.* Chicago: Aldine-Atherton.

Hunt, W. A., Barnett, J., & Branch, L. G. (1971). Relapse rates in addiction programs. *Journal of Clinical Psychology, 27*, 455–456.

Huntington, G. (1972). On chorea. *Medical Surgery Reporter (Philadelphia) 26*, 317–321.

Hussian, R. A. (1981). *Geriatric psychology: A behavioral perspective.* New York: Van Nostrand Reinhold.

Huyck, M. H., & Hoyer, W. J. (1982). *Adult development and aging.* Belmont, CA: Wadsworth.

Hyman, M. M. (1977). Alcoholics 15 years later. *Annals of the New York Academy of Sciences, 273*, 613–623.

Ikemi, Y., & Nakagawa, S. (1962). A psychosomatic study of contagious dermatitis. *Kyushu Journal of Medical Science, 13*, 335–350.

Imber, S., Schultz, E., Funderburk, F., Allen, R., & Flamer, R. (1976). The fate of the untreated alcoholic. *Journal of Nervous and Mental Disease, 168*, 238–247.

Jackson v. *Indiana*, 406 U.S. 715 (1972).

Jacob, M. S., Marshman, J. A., & Carlen, P. L. (1976). *Clinical toxicology of phencyclidine.* Toronto, Ontario: Addiction Research Foundation.

Jacob, T. (1975). Family interaction in disturbed and normal families: A methodological and substantive review. *Psychological Bulletin, 82*, 33–65.

Jacobi, J. (1973). *The psychology of C. G. Jung.* New Haven, CT: Yale University Press.

Jacobson, E. (1938). *Progressive relaxation.* Chicago: University of Chicago Press.

Jaffe, J. H. (1970). Drug addiction and drug abuse. In L. S. Goodman & A. Gilman (Eds.), *The pharmacological basis of therapeutics* (4th ed.). New York: Macmillan.

Janeway, E. (1975,). Witches and witch hunts. *The Atlantic*, pp. 80–84. Copyright © 1975, by The Atlantic Monthly Company, Boston. Material reprinted with permission.

Jarvik, L. F. (1976). Aging and depression: Some unanswered questions. *Journal of Gerontology, 31*, 324–326.

Jarvik, L. F., & Russell, D. (1979). Anxiety, aging, and the third emergency reaction. *Journal of Gerontology, 34*, 197–200.

Jarvik, M. (1970). The role of nicotine in the smoking habit. In W. Hunt (Ed.), *Learning mechanisms in smoking.* Chicago: Aldine.

Jarvik, M. E. (1977). Biological factors underlying the smoking habit. In *Research on smoking behavior* (NIDA Research monograph series: 17) U.S. Department of Health, Education, and Welfare. Washington, DC: U.S. Government Printing Office.

Jeans, R. F. I. (1976). An independently validated case of multiple personality. *Journal of Abnormal Psychology, 85*, 249–255.

Jeffrey, C. R., & Jeffrey, I. A. (1970). Delinquents and dropouts. An experimental program in behavior change. *Canadian Journal of Corrections, 12*, 47–58.

Jellinek, E. M. (1960). *The disease concept of alcoholism.* New Haven, CT: College and University Press and Hillhouse Press, New Brunswick, NJ.

Jersild, A. T., & Holmes, F. B. (1935). Children's fears. *Child Development Monographs*, No. 20.

Jessor, R. (1979). Marijuana: A review of recent psychosocial research. In R. I. Dupont, A. Goldstein, & J. O'Donnell (Eds.), *Handbook on drug abuse*. Washington, D.C.: National Institute on Drug Abuse, U.S. Government Printing Office.

Jessor, R., & Jessor, S. L. (1977). *Problem behavior and psychosocial development*. New York: Academic Press.

Johanson, C. C., Balster, R. L., & Bonse, K. (1976). Self-administration of psychomotor stimulant drugs: The effects of unlimited access. *Pharmacology, Biochemistry, and Behavior, 4*, 45–51.

Johnson, L. D., Bachman, J. G., & O'Malley, P. M. (1975–1982). *Student drug use, attitudes, and beliefs*. Washington, DC: National Institute on Drug Abuse.

Johnson, W. L., Baumeister, A. A., Penland, M. J., & Inwald, C. (1982). Experimental analysis of self-injurious, stereotypic, and collateral behavior of retarded persons: Effects of overcorrection and reinforcement of alternative responding. *Analysis and Intervention in Developmental Disabilities, 2*, 41–66.

Joint Commission on Mental Health and Illness. *Action for mental health*. New York: John Wiley.

Jones, B. M., & Parsons, O. (1975, August). Alcohol and consciousness: Getting high, coming down. *Psychology Today, 8*, 53–60.

Jones, D. J., Fox, M. M., Babigan, H. M., & Hutton, H. E. (1980). Epidemiology of anorexia nervosa in Monroe County, New York: 1960–1976. *Psychosomatic Medicine, 42*, 551–558.

Jones, M. (1975). Community care for chronic mental patients: The need for a reassessment. *Journal of Hospital and Community Psychiatry, 26*, 94–98.

Jones, M. B., Offord, D. R., & Abrams, N. (1980). Brothers, sisters, and antisocial behavior. *British Journal of Psychiatry, 136*, 139–145.

Jones, R. T. (1980). Human effects: An overview. In R. C. Petersen (Ed.), *Marijuana Research Findings: 1980*. (NIDA Research Monograph No. 31) Washington: DC: U.S. Government Printing Office.

Judson, B. A., & Goldstein, A. (1983). Uses of naloxone in the diagnosis and treatment of heroin addiction. In J. R. Cooper, F. Altman, B. S. Brown, & D. Czechowicz (Eds.), *Research in the treatment of narcotic addiction: State of the art*. (DDHS publication No. (ADM) 83–1281. Washington: DC: U.S. Government Printing Office.)

Julien, R. M. (1981). *A primer of drug action* (3d ed.). San Francisco, CA: W. H. Freeman.

Jung, C. G. (1909/1961). *Memories, dreams, and reflections*. New York: Random House.

Jung, C. G. (1964). Approaching the unconscious. In C. G. Jung et al. (Eds.), *Man and his symbols*. London: Aldus Books. Copyright 1964, Aldus Books Limited.

Jung, C. G. (1964). The state of psychotherapy today. *Collected works, Vol. 10: Civilization in transition*. Princeton, NJ: Princeton University Press. Copyright © 1960, 1969 by Princeton University Press. Excerpts reprinted by permission.

Jung, C. G. (1971). The transcendent function. In J. Campbell (Ed.), *The portable Jung*. New York: Penguin.

Jus, A., Pineau, R., Lachance, R., Pelchat, G., Jus, K., Pires, P., & Villeneuve, R. (1976). Epidemiology of tardive dyskinesia, I. *Diseases of the Nervous System, 37*, 310–314.

Kahn, H. A., Medalie, J. H., Neufield, H. M., Riss, E., & Goldbourt, U. (1972). The incidence of hypertension and associated factors: The Israeli ischemic heart disease study. *American Heart Journal, 84*, 171–182.

Kahn, J. H., & Narsten, J. P. (1962). School refusal: A comprehensive view of school phobia and other failures of school attendance. *American Journal of Orthopsychiatry, 32*, 707–718.

Kahn, R. B. (1982). *Work and health*. New York: John Wiley & Sons.

Kahn, R. L. (1975). The mental health system and the future aged. *The Gerontologist, 15* (1, Part 2), 24–31.

Kalat, J. W. (1984). *Biological Psychology* (2d. ed.). Belmont, CA: Wadsworth.

Kalin, R., McClelland, D. C., & Kahn, M. (1964). The effects of male social drinking on fantasy. *Journal of Personality and Social Psychology, 4*, 441–452.

Kalinowsky, L. (1975). Psychosurgery. In A. Freedman, H. Kaplan, & B. Saddock (Eds.), *Comprehensive textbook of psychiatry* (Vol. 2). Baltimore: Williams & Wilkins.

Kallmann, F. J. (1952). A comparative twin study on the genetic aspects of male homosexuality. *Journal of Nervous and Mental Diseases, 115*, 283–298.

Kandel, D. B. (1984). Marijuana users in young adulthood. *Archives of General Psychiatry, 41*, 200–209.

Kandel, D. B., & Maloff, D. (1983). Commonalities in drug use: A sociological perspective. In P. Levison, D. R. Gerstein, & D. R. Maloff (Eds.), *Commonalities in substance abuse and habitual behavior*. Lexington, MA: Lexington Books.

Kane, J. M. (1983). Low-dose medication strategies in the treatment of schizophrenia. *Schizophrenia Bulletin, 9*, 528–531.

Kane, J. M., & Smith, J. M. (1982). Tardive dyskinesia: Prevalence and risk factors, 1959 to 1979. *Archives of General Psychiatry, 39*, 473–481.

Kanfer, F. H. (1975). Self-management methods. In F. H. Kanfer, & A. P. Goldstein (Ed.), *Helping people change*. New York: Pergamon Press.

Kanner, L. (1942). Autistic disturbances of affective contact. *Nervous Child, 2*, 217.

Kantor, R. E., Wallner, J. M., & Winder, C. L. (1953). Process and reactive schizophrenia. *Journal of Consulting and Clinical Psychology, 17*, 157–162.

Kaplan H. S. (1974). *The new sex therapy: Active treatment of sexual dysfunctions.* New York: Quadrangle.

Kaplan, H. S. (1977, Spring). Hypoactive sexual desire. *Journal of Sex and Marital Therapy*, 1–11. Copyright 1977, Human Sciences Press.

Kaplan, M. (1983). A woman's view of DSM III. *American Psychologist, 38*, 786–792.

Kaplan, N. M. (1974). *Your blood pressure—The most deadly high: A physician's guide to controlling your hypertension.* New York: MEDCOM.

Kashani, J., & Simonds, J. F. (1979). The incidence of depression in children. *American Journal of Psychiatry, 136*, 1203–1205.

Katchadourian, H. A., & Lunde, D. T. (1972). *Fundamentals of human sexuality.* New York: Holt, Rinehart & Winston.

Kaufman, E. (1982). The relationship of alcoholism and alcohol abuse to the abuse of other drugs. *American Journal of Drug and Alcohol Abuse, 9*, 1–17.

Kaufman, I., Peck, A. L., & Taguiri, C. K. (1954). The family constellation and overt incestuous relations between father and daughter. *American Journal of Orthopsychiatry, 24*, 266–277.

Kay, D. W. K., Cooper, A. F., Garside, R. F., & Roth, M. (1976). The differentiation of paranoid from affective psychoses by patients' premorbid characteristics. *British Journal of Psychiatry, 129*, 207–215.

Kazdin, A. E. (1978). The application of operant techniques in treatment, rehabilitation, and education. In S. L. Garfield & A. E. Bergin (Eds.), *Handbook of psychotherapy and behavior change* (2d ed.). New York: John Wiley & Sons.

Kazdin, A. E. (1979). Fictions, factions, and functions of behavior therapy. *Behavior Therapy, 10*, 629–654.

Kazdin, A. E. (1982). *Single-case research designs: Methods for clinical and applied settings.* New York: Oxford University Press.

Kazdin, A. E., & Wilcoxin, L. A. (1976). Systematic desensitization and nonspecific treatment effects: A methodological evaluation. *Psychological Bulletin, 83*, 729–758.

Kazdin, A. E., & Wilson, T. W. (1978). Criteria for evaluating psychotherapy. *Archives of General Psychiatry, 35*, 407–416.

Keefe, F. J. (1982). Behavioral assessment and treatment of chronic pain: Current status and future directions. *Journal of Consulting and Clinical Psychology, 50*, 896–911.

Keith, S. J., Gunderson, J. G., Reifman, A., Buchsbaum, S., & Mosher, L. R. (1976). Special report: Schizophrenia, 1976. *Schizophrenia Bulletin, 2*, 510–565.

Keller, A. C., Althof, S. E., & Lothstein, L. M. (1982). Group therapy with gender-identity patients—A four year study. *American Journal of Psychotherapy, 2*, 223–228.

Kempe, C. H., Silverman, F., Steele, B., Droegemueller, W., & Silver, H. (1962). The battered child syndrome. *Journal of the American Medical Association, 181*, 17–24.

Kendell, R. E. (1969). The classification of depressive illness: The uses and limitation of multivariate analysis. *Psychiatria, Neurologia and Neurochirurgia, 72*, 207–216.

Kennedy, W. A. (1965). School phobia: Rapid treatment of 50 cases. *Journal of Abnormal Psychology, 70*, 285–289.

Kerasotes, D., & Walker, C. E. (1983). Hyperactive behavior in children. In C. E. Walker and M. C. Roberts (Eds.), *Handbook of clinical child psychology.* New York: John Wiley & Sons.

Kernberg, O. (1967). Borderline personality organization. *Journal of the American Psychoanalytic Association, 15*, 641–685.

Kernberg, O. (1975). *Borderline conditions and pathological narcissism.* New York: Jason Aronson.

Kessler, R. C., & Neighbors, H. W. (1983). *Special issues related to racial and ethnic minorities in the United States.* Unpublished paper, Institute for Social Research, University of Michigan.

Kessler, R. C., Price, R. H., & Wortman, C. B. (in press). Psychopathology: Social approaches. *Annual Review of Psychology.*

Kessler, R., Price, R. H., & Wortman, C. (1985). Psychopathology: Social factors. *Annual Review of Psychology.*

Kessler, S. (1969, September 26). The etiological question in mental illness. *Science*, 1341–1342.

Kety, S. S. (1967). Current biochemical approaches to schizophrenia. *New England Journal of Medicine, 276*, 325–331.

Kety, S. S., Rosenthal, D., Wender, P. H., & Schulsinger, F. (1968). The types and prevalence of mental illness in the biological and adoptive families of adopted schizophrenics. In D. Rosenthal, & S. S. Kety, (Eds.), *The transmission of schizophrenia* (pp. 345–362). Oxford: Pergamon Press.

Khantzian, E. J. (1983). *An ego/self theory of substance dependence: A contemporary psychoanalytic perspective.* In D. J. Lettieri, M. Sayers, & H. W. Pearson (Eds.), *Theories on Drug Abuse* (NIDA Research Monograph No. 30). Washington, DC: U.S. Government Printing Office.

Kidd, K. K., & Cavalli-Sforza, L. L. (1973). An analysis of the genetics of schizophrenia. *Social Biology, 20*, 254–265.

Kilmann, P. R., & Auerbach, R. R. (1979). Treatments of premature ejaculation and psychogenic impotence:

A critical review of the literature. *Archives of Sexual Behavior, 8,* 81–100.

Kilpatrick, D. G., Resick, P. A., & Veronen, L. J. (1981). Effects of a rape experience: A longitudinal study. *Journal of Social Issues, 37*(4), 105–122.

Kinney, J., & Leaton, G. (3d ed 1982). *Loosening the grip: A handbook of alcohol information.* St. Louis: C. V. Mosby.

Kinsey, A. C., Pomeroy, W. B., & Martin, C. E. (1948). *Sexual behavior in the human male.* Philadelphia: W. B. Saunders.

Kinsey, A. C., Pomeroy, W. B., Martin, C. E., & Gebhard, P. H. (1953). *Sexual behavior in the human female.* Philadelphia: Saunders.

Kisker, G. W. (1964). *The disorganized personality.* McGraw-Hill. Copyright © 1964 by McGraw-Hill. Excerpt in text used with the permission of McGraw-Hill Book Company.

Klein, D. F., Gittelman, R., Quitkin, F., & Rifkin, A. (1980). *Diagnosis and drug treatment of psychiatric disorders: Adults and children.* Baltimore: Williams & Wilkins.

Klein, M. (1932). *The psychoanalysis of children.* London: Hogarth Press.

Klein, M. (1948). *Contributions to psychoanalysis.* London: Hogarth Press, (originally published 1921–1945).

Klerman, G. L., & Izen, J. E. (1978). Psychopharmacology. In W. T. Reich (Ed.), *Encyclopedia of bioethics* (Vol. 3). New York: Free Press.

Kline, R. B., Snyder, D. K. (1985). Replicated MMPI subtypes for alcoholic men and women: Relationship to self-reported drinking behaviors. *Journal of Consulting and Clinical Psychology, 53(1),* 70–79.

Knight, R. A., Roff, J. D., Barnett, J., & Moss, J. L. (1979). Concurrent and predictive validity of thought disorder affectivity: A 22-year follow-up of acute schizophrenics. *Journal of Abnormal Psychology, 88,* 1–13.

Knopf, I. J. (1984). *Childhood psychopathology: A developmental approach.* Englewood Cliffs, NJ: Prentice-Hall.

Kobasa, S. C. (1979). Stressful life events, personality and health: An inquiry into hardiness. *Journal of Personality and Social Psychology, 37,* 1–11.

Kobasa, S. C., Hiller, R. R. J., & Maddi, S. R. (1979). Who stays healthy under stress? *Journal of Occupational Medicine, 21,* 595–598.

Kobasa, S. C., Maddi, S. R., & Kahn, S. (1982). Hardiness and health: A prospective study. *Journal of Personality and Social Psychology, 42,* 168–177.

Kobasa, S. C., Maddi, S. R., & Zola, M. A. (1983). Type A and hardiness. *Journal of Behavioral Medicine, 6,* 41–51.

Koch, R. (1971). Postnatal factors in causation. In R. Koch and J. C. Dobson (Eds.), *The mentally retarded child and his family: A multi-disciplinary handbook.* New York: Brunner/Mazel.

Koenig, P. (1978, May 21). The problem that can't be tranquilized. *New York Time Magazine,* pp. 14–16.

Kohn, M. L. (1969). *Class and conformity: A study in values.* Homewood, IL: Dorsey Press.

Kohut, H. (1971). *The analysis of the self.* New York: International Universities Press.

Kohut, H. (1977). *The Restoration of the self.* New York: International Universities Press.

Kolata, G. B. (1981). Clinical trial of psychotherapies is under way. *Science, 212,* 432–433.

Kolb, L. S. (1963). Therapy of homosexuality. In J. Mosserman (Ed.), *Current psychiatric therapies* (Vol. 3). New York: Grune & Stratton.

Kolodny, R. C. (1981). Evaluating sex therapy: Process and outcome at the Masters & Johnson Institute. *The Journal of Sex Research, 4,* 301–318.

Kolodny, R. C., Masters, W. H., & Johnson, V. E. *Textbook of sexual medicine.* Boston: Little, Brown, 1979.

Kolvin, et al. (1971). Studies in the childhood psychoses: I–VI. *British Journal of Psychiatry, 118,* 381.

Korchin, S. K. (1976). *Modern clinical psychology.* New York: Basic Books.

Kraft, I. A. (1971). Child and adolescent group psychotherapy. In H. I. Kaplan, & B. J. Sadock (Eds.), *Comprehensive group psychotherapy.* Baltimore: Williams & Wilkins.

Krasher, L. (1962). The therapist as a social reinforcement machine. In H. H. Strupp & L. Luborsky (Eds.), *Research in psychotherapy* (Vol. 2). Washington, DC: American Psychological Association.

Kroger, W. S. (1977). *Clinical and experimental hypnosis* (2d ed.). Philadelphia: J. B. Lippincott.

Krohn, A. (1978). *Hysteria: The elusive neurosis.* New York: International Universities Press.

Kuhn, T. S. (1962). *The structure of scientific revolutions.* Chicago: University of Chicago Press.

Kurland, L. (1959/1960). The incidence and prevalence of convulsive disorders in a small urban community. *Epilepsia 1,* 143–161.

Kushlick, A. (1966). Assessing the size of the problem of subnormality. In J. E. Meade and A. S. Parkes (Eds.), *Genetic and environmental factors in human ability.* (A symposium held by the Eugenics Society in September-October 1965). New York: Plenum Press.

Kushner, M. (1968). The operant control of intractible sneezing. In C. D. Spielberger, R. Fox, & B. Masterson (Eds.), *Contributions to general psychology.* New York: Roland Press.

Kuypers, J. A., & Bengtson, V. L. (1973). Social breakdown and competence. *Human Development, 16,* 181–201.

Lachman, S. J. (1972). *Psychosomatic disorders: A behavioristic interpretation.* New York: John Wiley & Sons.

Laing, R. D. (1959). *The divided self.* London: Tavistock.

Laing, R. D. (1967). *The politics of experience.* New York: Ballantine.

Laing, R. D., & Esterson, A. (1971). *Sanity, madness, and the family.* New York: Basic Books.

Lamy, P. P. (1983). Pharmacology and therapeutics. In M. D. Glantz, D. M. Petersen, & F. J. Whittington (Eds.). *Drugs and the elderly adult* (DHHS Publication No. ADM 83-1269, pp. 121-129). Washington, DC: U.S. Government Printing Office.

Lang, A. R. (1983). Addictive personality: A viable construct? In P. Levinson, D. R. Gerstein, & D. R. Maloff (Eds.), *Commonalities in substance abuse and habitual behavior.* Lexington, MA: Lexington Books.

Lang, A. R., Goeckner, D. J., Adesso, V. J., & Marlatt, G. A. (1975). Effects of alcohol on aggression in male social drinkers. *Journal of Abnormal Psychology, 84,* 508-518. Copyright 1975 by the American Psychological Association. Text quote reprinted by permission.

Lang, P. E. (1969). The mechanics of desensitization and the laboratory study of fear. In C. M. Franks (Ed.), *Behavior therapy: Appraisal and status.* New York: McGraw-Hill.

Langer, E. J., Abelson, R. P. (1974). A patient by any other name . . . : Clinician group difference in labeling bias. *Journal of Consulting and Clinical Psychology, 42,* 4-9.

Langer, E. J., & Rodin, J. (1976). The effects of choice and enhanced personal responsibility for the aged: A field experiment in an institutionalized setting. *Journal of Personality and Social Psychology, 34,* 191-198.

Langston, J. W., Ballard, P., Tetrud, J. W. & Irwin, I. (1983). Chronic Parkinsonism in humans due to a product of meperidine-analog synthesis. *Science 219,* 979-980.

Lanydon, R. I. (1984). Personality Assessment. In M. R. Rosenzweig & L. W. Porter (Eds.), *Annual Review of Psychology, 35,* 667-701.

Lapouse, R., & Monk, M. A. (1958). An epidemiological study of behavior characteristics in children. *American Journal of Public Health, 48,* 1134-1144.

Larsen, S. R. (1965). *Strategies for reducing phobic behavior* (Doctoral dissertation, Stanford University)

Lasch, C. (1978). *The culture of narcissism.* New York: W. W. Norton.

Laughlin, H. P. (1965). *The neuroses in clinical practice.* Philadelphia: W. B. Saunders.

Lazarus, A. (1980). Toward delineating some causes of change in psychotherapy. *Professional Psychology, 11,* 863-870.

Lazarus, A. A. (1971). *Behavior therapy and beyond.* New York: McGraw-Hill.

Lazarus, A. A. (1976). *Multimodal behavior therapy.* New York: Springer.

Lazarus, A. A. (1981). *The practice of multimodal therapy.* New York: McGraw-Hill.

Lazarus, R. S. and Cohen, J. B. (1977). Environmental stress. In I. Altman & J. F. Wohlwill (Eds.), *Human Behavior and the Environment: Current Theory and Research.* New York: Plenum Press.

Lazarus, R. S. & Folkman, S. (1984). *Stress, appraisal, and coping.* New York: Singer Press.

Lechtenberg, R. (1982). *The psychiatrist's guide to diseases of the nervous system.* New York: John Wiley & Sons.

Leff, J. P. (1976). Schizophrenia and sensitivity to the family environment. *Schizophrenia Bulletin,* 566-574.

Lehrke, R. (1972). A theory of X-linkage of major intellectual traits. *American Journal of Mental Deficiency, 76,* 611-619.

Leighton, D. C., Harding, J. S., Macklin, D. B., Hughes, C. C., & Leighton, A. H. (1963). Psychiatric findings of the Sterling County study. *American Journal of Psychiatry, 119,* 1021-1026.

Leitenberg, H. (1976). *Handbook of behavior modification and behavior therapy.* Englewood Cliffs, NJ: Prentice-Hall.

Leo, J. (1984, June 18). Learning to live with the blues. *Time,* p. 91.

Lerner, H. E. (1974). The hysterical personality: A "woman's disease." *Comprehensive Psychiatry, 15,* 157-164.

Leslie, S. A. (1974). Psychiatric disorder in the young adolescents of an industrial town. *British Journal of Psychiatry, 125,* 113-124.

Levenkron, J. C., Cohen, J. D., Mueller, H. S., & Fisher, E. B. (1976). Modifying the Type A coronary-prone behavior pattern. *Journal of Consulting and Clinical Psychology, 51,* 192-204.

Leventhal, H., & Cleary, P. D. (1980). The smoking problem: A review of the research and theory in behavioral risk modification. *Psychological Bulletin, 88,* 370-405.

Levine, A. G. (1982). *Love Canal: Science, politics, and people.* Lexington. MA: D. C. Heath.

Levine, B. (1979). *Group psychotherapy: Practice and development.* Englewood Cliffs, NJ: Prentice-Hall.

Levinson, D. R., Gerstein, & Maloff, D. R. (Eds.). (1983). *Commonalities in substance abuse and habitual behavior.* Lexington, MA: Lexington Books.

Levitsky, F., & Perls, F. S. (1970). The rules and games of gestalt therapy. In J. Fagan & I. L. Sheperd (Eds.), *Gestalt therapy now: Therapy, techniques, application.* Palo Alto, CA: Science and Behavior Books.

Levitt, E. E. (1971). Sadomasochism. *Sexual Behavior, 1,* 68–80.

Levitt, E. E., & Lubin, B. (1975). *Depression: Concepts, controversies and some new facts.* New York: Springer.

Lewinsohn, P. M. (1974a). A behavioral approach to depression. In R. J. Friedman & M. M. Katz (Eds.), *The psychology of depression: Contemporary theory and research.* Washington, D.C.: V. H. Winston.

Lewinsohn, P. M. (1974b). Clinical and theoretical aspects of depression. In K. S. Calhoun, H. E. Adams, & K. M. Mitchell (Eds.), *Innovative treatment methods in psychopathology.* New York: John Wiley & Sons.

Lewinsohn, P. M., & MacPhillamy, D. J. (1974). The relationship between age and engagement in pleasant activities. *Journal of Gerontology, 29,* 290–294.

Lewis, M., & Ban, P. (1971, October). *Stability of attachment behavior: A transformational analysis.* Paper presented at the Society for Research in Child Development, Minneapolis.

Lewis, M., & Butler, R. (1978). Life review therapy: Putting memories to work in individual and group psychotherapy. In S. Steury & M. Blank (Eds.), *Readings in psychotherapy with older people* (pp. 199–205). Rockville, MD: U.S. Government Printing Office.

Lewis, M. L., & Sorrel, P. M. (1969). Some psychological aspects of seduction, incest, and rape in childhood. *Journal of the American Academy of Child Psychiatry, 8,* 606.

Liberman, R. P., & Davis, J. (1975). Drugs and behavior analysis. In M. Hersen, R. M. Eisler, & P. M. Miller (Eds.), *Progress in behavior modification* (Vol 1). New York: Academic Press.

Liberman, R. P., & Raskin, D. E. (1971). Depression: A behavioral formulation. *Archives of General Psychiatry, 24,* 515–523. Copyright 1971, American Medical Association.

Lick, J. (1975). Expectancy, false galvanic skin response feedback, and systematic desensitization in the modification of phobic behavior. *Journal of Consulting and Clinical Psychology, 43,* 557–567.

Lidz, T., Fleck, S., & Cornelison, A. (1965). *Schizophrenia and the family.* New York: International Universities Press.

Lieberman, M. A. (1975). Group methods. In F. H. Kanfer & A. P. Goldstein (Eds.), *Helping people change.* New York: Pergamon Press.

Lieberman, M. A., Yalom, I. D., & Miles, M. B. (1973). *Encounter groups: First facts.* New York: Basic Books.

Liebowitz, E., & McNamara, J. R. (1980). *Neuroleptics and the need for informed consent with schizophrenic patients.* (Preliminary report to the Ohio Department of Mental Health, Office of Program Evaluation and Research).

Linton, H. B., & Langs, R. J. (1964). Subjective reactions to lysergic acid diethylamide (LSD-25) measured by a questionnaire. *Archives of General Psychiatry, 10,* 469–485.

Lipowski, Z. J. (1983). Transient cognitive disorders (delirium, acute confusional states) in the elderly. *American Journal of Psychiatry 140,* 1426–1436.

Lipton, M. A. (1976). Age differentiation in depression: Biochemical aspects. *Journal of Gerontology, 31,* 293–299.

Little, R. E. (1979). Drinking during pregnancy: Implications for public health. *Alcohol Health and Research World, 4,* 36–42.

LoPiccolo, J., & Friedman, J. (1985). Sex therapy: An integrative model. In S. J. Lynn, & J. P. Garske (Eds.), *Contemporary psychotherapies: Models and methods:* Columbus, Merrill Press.

LoPiccolo, J., Heiman, J. R., Hogan, D. R., & Roberts, C. W. (1985). Effectiveness of single therapists versus cotherapy teams in sex therapy. *Journal of Consulting and Clinical Psychology, 53,* 287–294.

LoPiccolo, J., & LoPiccolo, L. (Eds.). (1978). *Handbook of sex therapy.* New York: Plenum Press.

Loraine, J. A., Ismael, A. A., Adamopoulous, P. A., & Dove, G. A. (1970). Endocrine functions in male and female homosexuals. *British Medical Journal, 4,* 406.

Lord, C., Schopler, E., & Revicki, D. (1982). Sex differences in autism. *Journal of Autism and Developmental Disorders, 12,* 317–329.

Lorland, S. (1943). Anorexia nervosa: Report on a case. *Psychosomatic Medicine, 5,* 282–292.

Lotter, V. (1966). Epidemiology of autistic conditions in young children. *Social Psychiatry, 1,* 124 and 163.

Lovass, I. O. (1977). *The autistic child.* New York: Irvington Publishers.

Lovass, I. O., Schaeffer, B., & Simmons, J. Q. (1965). Building social behavior in autistic children by the use of electric shock. *Journal of Experimental Research and Personality, 1,* 99–109.

Love, H. D. (1973). *The mentally retarded child and his family.* Springfield, IL: Charles C Thomas.

Lovibond, S. H., & Caddy, G. R. (1970). Discriminated aversive control in the moderation of alcoholics' drinking behavior. *Behavior Therapy, 1,* 437–444.

Lovibond, S. H., & Coote, M. A. (1970). Enuresis. In C. G. Costello, *Symptoms of psychopathology: A handbook.* New York: John Wiley & Sons.

Lubar, J. E. and Deering, W. M. (1981). *Behavioral Approaches to Neurology.* New York: Academic Press.

Lucas, A. R. (1981). Toward the understanding of anorexia nervosa as a disease entity. *Mayo Clinic Proceedings, 56,* 254–264.

Ludolph, P. (1982). *A reanalysis of the literature on multiple personality.* Paper presented at the American

Psychological Association Annual Meeting, Washington, DC.

Lunde, D. (1975). *Murder and madness*. Stanford, CA: Stanford Alumni Association.

Luisada, P. V. (1977, August). *The PCP psychosis: A hidden epidemic*. Paper presented at the VI World Congress of Psychiatry, Honolulu, HI.

Lukianowicz, N. (1972). Incest. *British Journal of Psychiatry, 120*, 301–313.

Lykken, D. T. (1955). A study of anxiety in the sociopathic personality. (Doctoral dissertation, University of Minnesota, 1955). *University Microfilm No. 55-944*.

Lykken, D. T. (1957). A study of anxiety in the sociopathic personality. *Journal of Abnormal and Social Psychology, 55*, 6–10.

Lynn, S. J., & Frauman, D. C. (1985). Group psychotherapy. In S. J. Lynn & J. P. Garske (Eds.), *Contemporary psychotherapies: Models and methods*. Columbus: Merrill Press.

Lynn, S. J., & Freedman, R. R. (1979). Transfer and evaluation of biofeedback treatment. In A. P. Goldstein and F. Kanfer (Eds.), *Maximizing treatment gains: Transfer enhancement in psychotherapy*. New York: Academic Press.

Lyons, R. D. (1978, January 12). Califano in drive to end smoking; calls habit "slow motion suicide." *New York Times*, p. 14A.

MacDonald, M. L., Lidsky, T. I., & Kern, J. M. (1979). Drug instigated effects. In A. P. Goldstein & F. Kanfer (Eds.), *Maximizing treatment gains: Transfer enhancement in psychotherapy*. New York: Academic Press.

MacDonald, M. L., & Tobias, L. L. (1976). Withdrawal causes relapse? Our response. *Psychological Bulletin, 83*, 448–451.

MacDougall, J., Dembroski, T., & Krantz, D. (1981). Effects of types of challenge on pressor and heart rate responses in Type A and B women. *Psychophysiology, 18*, 1–9.

MacKinnon, R. A., and Michels, R. (1971). *The psychiatric interview in clinical practice*. Philadelphia: W. B. Saunders.

MacLean, P. D. (1967). The brain in relation to empathy and medical education. *Journal of Nervous and Mental Disease 144*, 374–382.

McAllister, T. W., & Price, T. R. P. (1982). Severe depressive pseudodementia with and without dementia. *American Journal of Psychiatry, 139*(5), 626–629.

McArthur, C., Waldron, E., & Dickinson, J. (1958). The psychology of smoking. *Journal of Abnormal and Social Psychology, 56*, 267–275.

McClelland, D. C. (1973). Testing for competence rather than "intelligence." *American Psychologist, 28*, 1–14.

McClellend, D. C. (1979). Inhibited power motivation and high blood pressure in men. *Journal of Abnormal Psychology, 88*, 182–190.

McCord, W., & McCord, J. (1959). *Origins of crime. A new evaluation of the Cambridge-Somerville Youth Study*. New York: Columbia University Press.

McDonald, A. D. (1964). Intelligence in children of very low birth weight. *British Journal of Preventative Social Medicine, 18*, 59–74.

McFadden, E. R., Jr. (1980). Asthma: Airway reactivity and pathogenesis. *Seminars in Respiratory Medicine, 1*, 287–296.

McFadden, E. R., Jr. (1980). Asthma: Pathophysiology. *Seminars in Respiratory Medicine, 1*, 297–303 (a).

McGee, R. K. (1974). *Crisis intervention in the community*. Baltimore: University Park Press.

McGeer, P. L., McGeer, E. G., and Suzuki, J. S. (1977). Aging and extrapyramidal function. *Archives of Neurology 34*, 33–35.

McGlothlin, Witt., Anglin, M. D., & Wilson, B. D. (1978). Narcotic addiction and crime. *Criminology*.

McGuire, R., Carlisle, J. M., & Young, B. G. (1965). Sexual deviation as conditioned behavior: A hypothesis. *Behavior Research and Therapy, 2*, 185–190.

McKnew, D. H., Cytryn, L., & Yahraes, H. (1983). *Why isn't Johnny crying?* New York: W. W. Norton.

McNamara, J. R. (1978). Socioethical considerations in behavior therapy research and practice. *Behavior Modification, 2*, 3–24.

McNamara, J. R. (1980). Behavior therapy in the seventies: Some changes and current issues. *Psychotherapy: Theory, Research, and Practice, 17*, 2–9.

McNaught, B. (1977). A response to Anita Bryant . . . why bother with gay rights? *Humanist, 37*, 34–36.

McPeak, W. R. (1979). Family therapies. In A. P. Goldstein & F. H. Kanfer (Eds.), *Maximizing treatment gains: Transfer enhancement in psychotherapy*. New York: Academic Press.

McWhorter, W. L. (1976). *The naked man in open raincoat: A sociological perspective of exhibitionism*. Unpublished manuscript, Virginia Polytechnic Institute and State University, Blacksburg, VA.

Maddi, S. R. Existential psychotherapy. (1985). In S. J. Lynn, & J. P. Garske (Eds.), *Contemporary psychotherapies: Models and methods*. Columbus, OH: Charles E. Merrill.

Maher, B. (1968, June). The chattered language of schizophrenia. *Psychology Today, 2*, pp. 30–64.

Maher, B. A. (1966). *Principles of psychopathology*. New York: McGraw-Hill.

Maher, B. A., McKean, K., & McLaughlin, B. (1966). Studies in psychotic language. In P. Stone (Ed.), *The general inquirer: A computer approach to content analysis*. Cambridge, MA: Massachusetts Institute of Technology.

Mahler, M., Pine, F., & Bergmann, A. (1975). The psychological birth of the human infant: Symbiosis and individuation.

Mahler, M. S. (1967). On human symbiosis and the vicissitudes of individuation. *Journal of the American Psychoanalytic Association, 15,* 740–763.

Mahoney, M. J. (1981). Psychotherapy and human change processes. In J. H. Harvey & M. Parks (Eds.), *Psychotherapy research and behavior change.* Washington, D.C.; American Psychological Association.

Mahoney, M. J., & Arnkoff, D. (1978). Cognitive and self-control therapies. In S. L. Garfield & A. E. Bergin (Eds.), *Handbook of psychotherapy and behavior change* (2d ed.). New York: John Wiley.

Mahoney, M. J., Moura, N. G., & Wade, T. C. (1973). Relative efficiency of self-reward, self-punishment, and self-monitoring techniques for weight loss. *Journal of Consulting and Clinical Psychology, 40,* 404–407.

Maletzky, B. M., & Klotter, J. (1974). Smoking and alcoholism. *American Journal of Psychiatry, 131,* 445–447.

Margolese, M. (1973). Androsterone/etiochalanolone ratios in male homosexuals. *British Medical Journal, 3,* 207–210.

Marks, I. (1978). Behavioral psychotherapy of adult neurosis. In S. L. Garfield and A. E. Bergin (Eds.), *Handbook of psychotherapy and behavior change: An empirical analysis* (2d. ed.). New York: John Wiley & Sons.

Marks, I. M. (1969). *Fears and phobias.* New York: Academic Press.

Marks, I. M. (1977). Phobias and obsessions. In J. Maser & M. Seligman (Eds.), *Experimental psychopathology.* New York: John Wiley & Sons.

Marks, I.M., Viswanathan, R., Lipsedge, M. S., & Gardiner, R. (1972). Enhanced relief of phobias by flooding during waning diazepam effect. *British Journal of Psychiatry, 121,* 493–505.

Marks, P. A., & Seeman, W. (1963). *Actuarial description of abnormal personality.* Baltimore: Williams & Wilkins.

Marlatt, A. (1983). The controlled-drinking controversy: A commentary. *American Psychologist, 10,* 1097–1110.

Marlatt, G. A. (1976). Alcohol, stress, and cognitive control. In C. D. Spielberger & G. Sarason (Eds.), *Stress and anxiety* (Vol. 3). Washington, DC: Hemisphere Publishing.

Marlatt, G. A., & Gordon, J. R. (1980). Determinants of relapse: Implications for the maintenance of behavior change. In P. O. Davidson & S. M. Davidson (Eds.), *Behavioral medicine: Changing health lifestyles.* New York: Brunner/Mazel.

Marlatt, G. A., Kosturn, C. F., & Lang, A. R. (1975). Provocation to anger and opportunity for retaliation

as determinants of alcohol consumption in social drinkers. *Journal of Abnormal Psychology, 84,* 652–659.

Marlatt, G. A., & Rohsenow, D. J. (1980). Cognitive processes in alcohol use: Expectancy and the balanced placebo design. In N. K. Mello (Ed.), *Advances in substance abuse: Behavioral and biological research.* Greenwich, CT: JAI Press.

Marmor, J. (1971). Homosexuality in males. *Psychiatric Annals, 4,* 45–59.

Marx, A. J., Test, M. A., & Stein, L. I. (1973). Extrahospital management of severe mental illness. *Archives of General Psychiatry, 29,* 505–511.

Maslow, A. (1967, Spring). Synanon eupsychia. *Journal of Humanistic Psychology,* 28–35.

Maslow, A. H. (1954). *Motivation and personality.* New York: Harper & Row.

Masters, W. H., & Johnson, V. E. (1966). *Human sexual response.* Boston: Little, Brown.

Masters, W. H., & Johnson, V. E. (1970). *Human sexual inadequacy.* Boston: Little, Brown.

Masters, W. H., & Johnson, V. E. (1979). *Homosexuality in perspective.* Boston: Little, Brown.

Masterson, J. F. (1976). *Psychotherapy of the borderline adult.* New York: Brunner/Mazel.

Matarazzo, J. D. (1980). Behavioral health and behavioral medicine: Frontiers for a new health psychology. *American Psychologist, 35,* 807–817.

Mathis, J. L. (1969, June). The exhibitionist. *Medical Aspects of Human Sexuality,* 89–101.

Matson, J. L. (1983). Mentally retarded children. In R. J. Morris and T. R. Kratochwill (Eds.), *The practice of child therapy.* New York: Pergamon Press.

Mattes, J. A., & Gittelman, R. (1983). Growth of hyperactive children on maintenance regimen of methylphenidate. *Archives of General Psychiatry, 40,* 317–321.

Matthews, K. A., Glass, D. C., Rosenman, R. H., & Bortner, R. W. (1977). Competitive drive, pattern A, and coronary heart disease: A further analysis of some data from the Western Collaborative Group Study. *Journal of Chronic Diseases, 30,* 489–498.

May, P. R. A. (1968). *Treatment of schizophrenia: A comparative study of five treatment methods.* New York: Science House.

Mayer, W. (1983). Alcohol abuse and alcoholism: The psychologist's role in prevention, research, and treatment. *American Psychologist, 38,* 1116–1121.

Mayer-Gross, W., Slater, E., & Roth, M. (1969). *Clinical psychiatry,* 3d ed. Baltimore: Williams & Wilkens. Revised and reprinted 1977, Baillière, Tindall, London.

Mead, G. H. (1934). *Mind, self, and society* (C. W. Morris, Ed.). Chicago: University of Chicago Press.

Meador, B. D., & Rogers, C. R. (1979). Person centered therapy. In J. R. Corsini (Ed.), *Current psychotherapies*. Itasca, IL: F. E. Peacock Publishers.

Mechanic, D. (1974). Social structure and personal adaptation: Some neglected dimensions. In G. V. Coelho, D. A. Hamburg, & J. E. Adams (Eds.), *Coping and adaptation*. New York: Basic Books.

Mednick, S. A. (1966). A longitudinal study of children with high risk for schizophrenia. *Mental Hygiene, 50*, 522–535. Material reprinted by permission of The National Mental Health Association.

Meehl, P. E. (1962). Schizotypy, schizophrenia. *American Psychologist, 17*, 827–838.

Meichenbaum, D. (1977). *Cognitive-behavior modification*. New York: Plenum Press.

Meichenbaum, D. (1985). Cognitive- behavior therapies. In S. J. Lynn, & J. P. Garske (Eds.), *Contemporary psychotherapies: Models and methods*. Columbus: Merrill.

Meichenbaum, D. H., & Cameron, R. (1973). Training schizophrenics to talk to themselves: A means of developing attentional controls. *Behavior Therapy, 4*, 515–534.

Meichenbaum, D., & Cameron, R. (1983). Stress inoculation training: Toward a general paradigm for training coping skills. In D. Meichenbaum and M. E. Jaremko (Eds.), *Stress reduction and prevention* (pp. 115–154). New York: Plenum Press.

Meichenbaum, D., & Jaremko, M. E. (1983). *Stress reduction and prevention*. New York: Plenum Press.

Mello, N. (1977). Stimulus self-administration: Some implications for the prediction of drug use liability. In P. Thompson & K. Unna (Eds.), *Predicting dependence liability of stimulant and depressant drugs*. Baltimore: University Park Press.

Meltzoff, J., & Kornreich, M. (1970). *Research in psychotherapy*. New York: Atherton.

Melzack, R. & Wall, P. (1965). Pain mechanisms: A new theory. *Science, 50*, 971–979.

Melzack, R. & Wall, P. (1970). Psychophysiology of pain. *International Anesthesiology Clinic, 8*, 3–34.

Melzack R., & Wall, P. (1983). *The challenge of pain*. New York: Basic Books.

Mendels, J. (1970). *Concepts of depression*. New York: John Wiley.

Menninger, K. (1958). *Theory of psychoanalytic technique*. New York: Basic Books.

Menolascino, F. J., & Egger, M. L. (1978). *Medical dimentions of mental retardation*. Lincoln, NE: University of Nebraska Press.

Mercer, J. R., & Lewis, J. (1977). *System of multi-cultural pluralistic assessment*. New York: Psychological Corporation.

Messer, S. B., & Winokur, M. (1980). Some limits to the integration of psychoanalytic and behavior therapy. *American Psychologist, 35*, 818–827.

Metrakos, K. and Metrakos, J. (1974) Genetics of epilepsy. In P. Vinken and G. Bruyn (Eds.), *Handbook of Clinical Neurology* (Vol. 15): *The Epilepsies*. New York: American Elsevier.

Meyer, J. K., & Reter, D. J. (1979). Sex reassignment. *Archives of General Psychiatry, 36*, 1010–1015.

Meyer, V., Robertson, J., & Tallon, A. (1975). Home treatment of an obsessive-compulsive disorder by response prevention. *Journal of Behavior Therapy and Experimental Psychiatry, 6*, 37–38.

Mielke, D., & Winstead, D. K. (1981). The problem of drug dependence. *Psychiatric Annals, 11*, 15–17.

Miller, C. R., & Berman, J. S. (1983). The efficacy of cognitive behavior therapies: A quantitative review of the research evidence. *Psychological Bulletin, 94*, 39–53.

Miller, E. (1980). Cognitive assessment of the older adult. In J. E. Birren & R. B. Sloane (Eds.), *Handbook of mental health and aging* (pp. 520–536). Englewood Cliffs, NJ: Prentice-Hall.

Miller, I. W., & Norman, W. H. (1979). Learned helplessness in humans: A review and attribution theory model. *Psychology Bulletin, 86*, 93–118.

Miller, J. A., Cisin, I. H., Gardner-Keaton, A., Wirtz, P. W., Abelson, H. I., & Fishburne, P. M. (1983). *National survey on drug abuse: Major findings 1982*. (Department of Health and Human Services Publication No. (ADM) 83–1263).

Miller, L. C., Barrett, C. L., & Hampe, E. (1974). Phobias of childhood in a prescientific era. In A. Davids (Ed.), *Child personality and psychopathology: Current topic* (Vol. 1). New York: John Wiley and Sons.

Miller, N. E. (1978). Biofeedback and visceral learning. In *Annual Review of Psychology* (Vol. 29). Palo Alto, CA: Annual Reviews.

Miller, P. M. (1980). Theoretical and practical issues in substance abuse assessment and treatment. In W. R. Miller (Ed.), *The addictive behaviors*. Oxford, England: Pergamon Press.

Miller, P. M., & Eisler, R. M. (1977). Alcohol and drug abuse. In W. E. Craighead, A. E. Kazdin, & M. J. Mahoney (Eds.), *Behavior modification principles, issues, and applications*. Boston: Houghton Mifflin.

Miller, P. M., & Maistra, M. A. (1977). *Alternatives to alcohol abuse*. Champaign, IL: Research Press.

Miller, P. M., Stanford, A. G., & Hemphill, D. P. (1978). A comprehensive social learning approach to alcoholism treatment. *Social Casework, 59*, 240–251.

Miller, W. R. (1977). Behavioral self-control training in the treatment of problem drinkers. In R. B. Stuart

(Ed.) *Behavioral self-management: Strategies, techniques and outcomes.* New York: Brunner/Mazel.

Miller, W. R. (1978). Behavioral treatment of problem drinkers: A comparative outcome study of three controlled drinking therapies. *Journal of Consulting and Clinical Psychology, 46,* 74–86.

Miller, W. R. (Ed.) (1980). *The addictive behaviors.* Oxford, England: Pergamon Press.

Miller, W. R. (1983). Controlled drinking: A history and a critical review. *Journal of Studies on Alcohol, 44,* 68–83.

Miller, W. R., & Caddy, G. R. (1977). Abstinence and controlled drinking in the treatment of problem drinkers. *Journal of Studies on Alcohol, 38,* 986–1003.

Miller, W. R., & Hester, R. K. (1980). Treating the problem drinker: Modern approaches. In W. R. Miller (Ed.). *The addictive behaviors.* Oxford, England: Pergamon Press.

Miller, W. R., & Joyce, M. A. (1977). Prediction of abstinence, controlled drinking, and heavy drinking outcomes following behavioral self-control training. *Journal of Consulting and Clinical Psychology, 47,* 773–775.

Miller, W. R., & Saucedo, C. R. (1983). Neuropsychological impairment and brain damage in problem drinkers: A critical review. In C. J. Golden (Ed.), *Behavioral effects of neurological disorders.* New York: Grune & Stratton.

Millon, T. (1981). *Disorders of personality.* New York: John Wiley & Sons.

Mintz, E. (1971). *Marathon groups: Reality and symbol.* New York: Appleton-Century-Crofts.

Minuchin, S. (1974). *Families and family therapy.* Cambridge, MA: Harvard University Press.

Mischel, W. (1969). Continuity and change in personality. *American Psychologist, 24,* 1012–1018.

Mohr, J. W., & Turner, R. E. (1967). Sexual deviations part IV—pedophilia. *Applied Therapeutics, 9,* 362–365.

Molteni, A. L., Garske, J. P., & Stedman, J. L. (1984). *Effects of explicit time-limits on psychotherapy outcome.* Unpublished manuscript, Ohio University.

Monahan, J. (1976). *Community mental health and the criminal justice system.* Elmsford, NY: Pergamon Press.

Monroe, R. (1955). *Schools of psychoanalytic thought.* New York: Dryden.

Moore, N. (1969). Behavior therapy in bronchial asthma. *Journal of Psychosomatic Research, 9,* 257–276.

Moore, R. (1977). Dependence on alcohol. In S. N. Pradhan & S. N. Dutta (Eds.), *Drug abuse: Clinical and basic aspects.* St. Louis: C. V. Mosby.

Moos, R. H., & Finney, J. W. (1983). The expanding scope of alcoholism treatment evaluation. *American Psychologist, 38,* 1036–1044.

Morris, J. (1974). *Conundrum.* New York: Harcourt Brace Jovanovich.

Morris, J. B., & Beck, A. T. (1974). The efficacy of antipsychotic drugs. *Archives of General Psychiatry, 30,* 667–671.

Morris, R. J., & Kratochwill, T. R. (1983). Childhood fears and phobias. In R. J. Morris and T. R. Kratochwill (Eds.), *The practice of child therapy.* New York: Pergamon Press.

Morrison, J. R., & Steward, M. A. (1974). Bilateral inheritance as evidence for polygenicity in the hyperactive child syndrome. *Journal of Nervous and Mental Diseases, 158,* 226–228.

Murphy, G. E., Simons, A. D., Wetzel, R. D., & Lustman, P. J. (1984). Cognitive therapy and pharmacotherapy. *Archives of General Psychiatry, 41,* 33–41.

Murray, E. J., & Jacobson, L. I. (1978). Cognition and learning in traditional and behavioral therapy. In S. L. Garfield & A. E. Bergin (Eds.), *Handbook of psychotherapy and behavior change* (2d ed.). New York: John Wiley & Sons.

Murray, J. J., & Trotter, A. B. (1973). Treatment in drug abuse: Counseling approaches and special programs. In R. E. Hardy & J. G. Cull (Eds.), *Drug dependence and rehabilitation approaches.* Springfield, IL: Charles C Thomas.

Myers, J. K., Weissman, M. M., Tischler, G. L., Holzer, C. E., III, Leaf, P. J., Orvaschel, H., Anthony, J. C., Boyd, J. H., Burke, J. D. Jr., Kramer, M., & Stoltzman, R. (1984). Six month prevalence of psychiatric disorders in three communities. *Archives of General Psychiatry, 41*(10), 959–967.

Nagi, S. Z., Riley, L. E., & Newby, L. G. (1973). A social epidemiology of back pain in a general population. *Journal of Chronic Disease, 26,* 769–779.

Nash, M. R., Johnson, L. S., & Tipton, R. D. (1979). Hypnotic age regression and the occurrence of transitional object relationships. *Journal of Abnormal Psychology, 88,* 547–554.

Nathan, P. (1984). The length and breadth of alcoholism. *Contemporary Psychology, 29,* 101–103.

Nathan, P. E. (1976). Alcoholism. In H. Leitenberg (Ed.), *Handbook of behavior modification.* New York: Appleton-Century-Crofts.

Nathan, P. E. (1980). Etiology and process in the addictive behaviors. In W. R. Miller (Ed.), *The addictive behaviors.* Oxford, England: Pergamon Press.

Nathan, P. E., & O'Brien, J. S. (1971). An experimental analysis of the behavior of alcoholics and nonalcoholics during prolonged experimental drinking. *Behavior Therapy, 2,* 455–476.

National Cancer Institute. (1975). *Cigarette smoking among teenagers and young women.* U.S. Department of Health, Education, and Welfare, Public Health Service.

National Clearinghouse for Drug Abuse Information. *Narcotic antagonists* (Report Series 26). Washington, DC: U.S. Government Printing Office.

National Commission on Marijuana and Drug Abuse. (1973). *Drug use in America: Problem in perspective. Second report of the National Commission on Marijuana and drug abuse.* Washington D.C.: U.S. Government Printing Office.

National Institute on Alcohol Abuse and Alcoholism (NIAAA). (1975). *Alcohol and health: 2d special report to the U.S. Congress, new knowledge.* U.S. Department of Health, Education and Welfare (DHEW Publication No. (ADM) 75–212). Washington, DC: U.S. Government Printing Office.

National Institute on Drug Abuse. (1976). *Marijuana Research Findings.* Washington, DC: U.S. Department of Health, Education, and Welfare, Research Monograph, No. 14.

National Institute on Drug Abuse. (1979). *Diagnosis and treatment of phencyclidine (PCP) toxicity.* (NIDA drug abuse clinical notes, October, 1979). Washington, DC: U.S. Government Printing Office.

National Prescription Audit, 1976. (1976). Ambler, PA: IMS America.

Neal, D. H. (1963). Behavior therapy and encopresis in children. *Behaviour Research and Therapy, 1,* 139–150.

Neisworth, J. T., & Moore, F. (1972). Operant treatment of asthmatic responding with the patient as therapist. *Behavior Therapy, 3,* 95–99.

Nelson, K. and Ellenberg, J. (1978) Prognosis in children with febrile seizures. *Pediatrics 61,* 720–727.

Neugarten, B. L. (1975). The future and the young-old. *The Gerontologist, 15*(1, Pt.2), 4–9.

Nielsen, A. C. (1979). *Who's dieting and why?* Chicago: Research Department. A. C. Nielsen.

Neuman, P. A., & Halvorson, P. A. (1983). *Anorexia nervosa and bulimia.* New York: Van Nostrand Reinhold.

Neuringer, C. (1974). Rorschach ink blot test assessment of suicidal risk. In C. Neuringer (Ed.), *Psychological assessment of suicidal risk.* Springfield, IL: Charles C Thomas.

Neville, R. (1978). Psychosurgery. In W. Reich (Ed.), *Encyclopedia of bioethics, Vol. 3.* New York: Free Press.

Nolan, J. D. (1968). Self-control procedure in the modification of smoking behavior. *Journal of Consulting and Clinical Psychology, 32,* 92–93.

Norcross, J. C., & Prochaska, J. O. (1983). Psychotherapists in independent practice: Some findings and issues. *Professional Psychology: Research and Practice, 14,* 869–881.

Norcross, J. C., & Wogan, M. (1983). American psychotherapists of diverse persuasions: characteristics, theories, practices, and clients. *Professional Psychology: Research and Practice, 14,* 529–539.

Novoco, R. W. (1976). Treatment of chronic anger through cognitive and relaxation controls. *Journal of Consulting and Clinical Psychology, 44,* 681.

Noya, N. D. Coca and cocaine: A perspective from Bolivia. In R. C. Petersen (Ed.), *The international challenge of drug abuse* (NIDA Research Monograph No. 19 DHEW Publication No. (ADM) 78–654). Washington, DC: U.S. Government Printing Office, 1978.

Nuckolls, C. B., Cassell, J., & Kaplan, B. H. (1972). Psycho-social assets, life crises and the prognosis of pregnancy. *American Journal of Epidemiology, 95,* 431–441.

Nurco, D. N. (1971). A choice of treatments. In C. C. Brown & C. Savage (Eds.), *The drug abuse controversy.* Baltimore: National Educational Consultant.

Nurco, D. N. (1979). Etiological aspect of drug abuse. In R. I. Dupont, A. Goldstein, & J. O'Donnell (Eds.), *Handbook on drug abuse.* Washington, DC: National Institute on Drug Abuse, U.S. Government Printing Office.

Odom, J. V., Nelson, R. O., & Wein, K. S. (1978). The differential effectiveness of five treatment procedures on three response systems in a snake phobia analog study. *Behavior Therapy, 9,* 936–942.

Ohman, A., Eriksson, A., Fredriksson, N., Hugdahl, K., & Oloffson, C. (1974). Habituation of the electrodermal at orienting reaction to potentially phobic and supposedly neutral stimuli in normal human subjects. *Biological Psychology, 2,* 85–92.

Oi, M., Oshida, K., & Sugimura, A. (1959). The location of gastric ulcer. *Gastroenterology, 36,* 45–56.

Ollendick, T. H. (1979). Fear reduction techniques with children. In M. Hersen, R. M. Eisler, & P. M. Miller (Eds.), *Progress in behavior modification* (Vol. 8). New York: Academic Press.

Ollendick, T. H., & Hersen, M. (1984). *Child behavioral assessment: Principles and procedures.* New York: Pergamon Press.

Ollendick, T. H., & Mayer, J. (1983). School phobia. In S. M. Turner (Ed.), *Behavioral treatment of anxiety disorders.* New York: Plenum Press.

Oppenheim, R. C. (1974). *Effective teaching methods for autistic children.* Springfield, IL: Charles C Thomas.

Ordman, A. M., & Kirschenbaum, D. S. (1985). Cognitive-behavioral therapy for bulimia: An initial outcome study. *Journal of Consulting and Clinical Psychology, 53*, 305–313.

Osgood, C. E., Luria, Z., & Smith, S. W., II. (1976). A blind analysis of another case of multiple personality using the semantic personality technique. *Journal of Abnormal Psychology, 85*, 256–270.

Osherow, N. (1981). Making sense of the nonsensical: An analysis of Jamestown. In E. Anonson (Ed.), *Readings about the social animal*. San Francisco: W. H. Freeman.

Oswald, I. (1969). Personal view. *British Medical Journal, 3*, 438.

Pahnke, W. N., Kurland, A. A., Unger, S., Savage, C., & Grof, S. (1970). The experimental use of psychedelic (LSD) psychotherapy. In J. R. Gamage & E. L. Zerkin (Eds.), *Hallucinogenic drug research: Impact on science & society*. Beloit, WI: Stash Press.

Palmore, E. (1977). Facts on aging: A short quiz. *The Gerontologist, 17*(4), 315–320.

Palmore, E. B. (1981). The facts on aging quiz: Part two. *The Gerontologist, 21*(4), 431–437.

Parloff, M. B., Waskow, I. E., & Wolfe, B. E. (1978). Research on therapist variables in relation to process and outcome. In S. L. Garfield, & A. E. Bergin (Eds.), *Handbook of psychotherapy and behavior change: An empirical analysis* (2d ed.). New York: John Wiley & Sons.

Patel, C. H. (1977). Biofeedback-aided relaxation in the management of hypertension. *Biofeedback and Self-Regulation, 2*, 1–141.

Patel, C. H., Marmot, M. G., & Terry, D. J. (1981). Controlled trial of biofeedback-aided behavioural methods in reducing mild hypertension. *British Medical Journal, 6281*, 2005–2008.

Patsiokas, A. J., Clum, G. A., & Luscomb, R. L. (1979). Cognitive characteristics of suicide attempts. *Journal of Consulting and Clinical Psychology, 47*, 478–484.

Patterson, G. R. (1971). Behavioral intervention procedures in the classroom and in the home. In A. E. Bergin & S. L. Garfield (Eds.), *Handbook of psychotherapy and behavior change*. New York: John Wiley & Sons.

Patterson, R. L., & Jackson, G. M. (1980). Behavior modification with the elderly. In M. Hersen, R. M. Eisler, & P. M. Miller (Eds.), *Progress in behavior modification: Vol. 9* (pp. 205–239). New York: Academic Press.

Pattison, E. M., Sobell, M. B., & Sobell, L. C. (1977). *Emerging concepts of alcohol dependence*. New York: Springer Publishing.

Paul, G. L., & Lentz, R. J. (1978). *Psychosocial treatment of chronic mental patients; Milieu vs. social learning programs*. Cambridge, MA: Harvard University Press.

Paykel, E., Myers, J., Dienalt, M., et al. (1980). Life events and depression. *Archives of General Psychiatry, 21*, 753–760.

Paykel, E. S. (1974). Recent life events and clinical depression. In E. K. E. Gunderson & R. H. Rahe (Eds.), *Life stress and illness* (pp. 134–163). Springfield, IL: Charles C Thomas.

Paykel, E. S., & Weisman, M. M. (1973). Social adjustment and depression. *Archives of General Psychiatry, 28*, 659–663.

Payne, E. C. (1975). Depression and suicide. In J. G. Howells (Ed.), *Modern perspectives in the psychiatry of old age* (pp. 290–312). New York: Brunner/Mazel.

PCP: "A terror of a drug." (1977, December 19). *Time*, p. 53.

Pearlin, L. I., & Lieberman, M. A. (1979). Social sources of emotional distress. In J. Simmons (Ed.), *Research in community and mental health*. Greenwich, CT: JAI Press.

Peele, S. *Addiction to an experience: A social-psychological-pharmacological theory of addiction*. In D. J. Lettieri, M. Sayers, & H. W. Pearson (Eds.), *Theories on Drug Abuse* (NIDA Research Monograph No. 30). Washington, DC: U.S. Government Printing Office.

Peele, S., & Brodsky, A. (1976). *Love and addiction*. New York: Signet.

Pelletier, K. R. (1977). *Mind as healer, mind as slayer*. New York: Dell Publishing.

Pendery, M. L., Maltzman, I. M., & West, L. J. (1982). Controlled drinking by alcoholics: New findings and a reevaluation of a major affirmative study. *Science, 217*, 169–174.

Perls, F. S. (1971). *Gestalt therapy verbatim*. New York: Bantam Books.

Perls, F. S. (1976). *The gestalt approach and eye witness to therapy*. New York: Bantam Books.

Perry, J. C., and Klerman, G. L. (1978). The borderline patient: A comparative analysis of four sets of diagnostic criteria. *Archives of General Psychiatry, 35*, 141–150.

Perry, J. W. (1962). Reconstitutive process in the psychopathology of the self. *Annals of the New York Academy of Sciences, 96*, 853–876.

Petersen, D. M. (1983). Epidemiology of drug use. In M. D. Glantz, D. M. Petersen, & F. J. Whittington (Eds.), *Drugs and the elderly adult* (DHHS Publication No. ADM 83-1269, pp. 13–16). Washington, DC: U.S. Government Printing Office.

Petersen, D. M., Whittington, F. J., & Beer, E. T. (1979). Drug use and misuse among the elderly. *Journal of Drug Issues, 9*(1), 5–26.

Peterson, R. C. (1977). Cocaine: An overview. In R. C. Peterson & R. C. Stillman (Eds.), *Cocaine 1977.*

Washington, DC: U.S. Government Printing Office.

Petrie, K., & Chamberlain, K. (1983). Hopelessness and social desirability as moderation variables in predicting suicidal behavior. *Journal of Consulting and Clinical Psychology, 51,* 485–487.

Pfeiffer, E. (1977). Psychopathology and social pathology. In J. E. Birren & K. W. Schaie (Eds.), *Handbook of the psychology of aging* (pp. 650–671). New York: Van Nostrand Reinhold.

Pflanz, M. (1971). Epidemiological and sociocultural factors in the etiology of duodenal ulcer. *Advances in Psychosomatic Medicine, 6,* 121–151.

Phares, E. J. (1979). *Clinical psychology.* Homewood, IL: Dorsey Press.

Philips, L. (1953). Case history data and prognosis in schizophrenia. *Journal of Nervous and Mental Disease, 117,* 515–525.

Phillips, E. L. (1968). Achievement place: Token reinforcement procedures in a home-style rehabilitation setting for "predelinquent" boys. *Journal of Applied Behavior Analysis, 1,* 213–223.

Pierce, A. (1967). The economic cycle and the social suicide rate. *American Sociological Review, 32,* 457–462.

Pierce, C. M. (1963). Dream studies in enuresis research. *Canadian Psychiatric Association Journal, 8,* 415–419.

Pincus, J. H. & Tucker, G. J. (1978). *Behavioral Neurology,* New York: Oxford University Press.

Pittner, N., & Houston, B. (1980). Response to stress, cognitive coping strategies, and the Type A behavior pattern. *Journal of Personality and Social Psychology, 39,* 147–157.

Pitts, F. N. (1972). Medical aspects of ECT. *Seminars in Psychiatry, 4,* 27–32.

Plutchik, R. (1979). Conceptual and practical issues in the assessment of the elderly. In A. Raskin & L. F. Jarvik (Eds.), *Psychiatric symptoms and cognitive loss in the elderly* (pp. 19–38). New York: Hemisphere Publishing.

Pohorecky, L. (1977). Biphasic action of ethanol. *Biobehavioral Review, 1,* 231–240.

Polich, J. M., Armor, D. J., & Braiker, H. B. (1981). *The course of alcoholism: Four years after treatment.* New York: John Wiley & Sons.

Pollak, J. M. (1979). Obsessive-compulsive personality: A review. *Psychological Bulletin, 86,* 225–241.

Pollit, J. (1957). Natural history of obsessional states. *British Medical Journal, 1,* 195–198.

Pope, H. G., Hudson, J. I., & Yurgelun-Todd, D. (1984). Anorexia nervosa and bulimia among 300 suburban women shoppers. *American Journal of Psychiatry, 141,* 292–294.

Pope, H. G., Jonas, J. M., Hudson, J. I., Cohen, B. M., and Gunderson, J. G. (1983). The validity of DSM III borderline personality disorder. *Archives of General Psychiatry, 40,* 23–30.

Pope, H. G., & Lipinski, J. F. (1978). Diagnosis in schizophrenia and manic-depressive illness. *Archives of General Psychiatry, 35,* 811–828.

Porter, R., & Birch, J. (Eds.). (1971). Report of the working group on the definition of asthma. *Identification of asthma.* London: Churchill Livingston.

Post, F. (1966). *Persistent persecutory states of the elderly.* Elmsford, NY: Pergamon Press.

Post, F. (1980). Paranoid, schizophrenia-like, and schizophrenic states in the aged. In J. E. Birren & R. B. Sloane (Eds.), *Handbook of mental health and aging* (pp. 591–615). Englewood Cliffs, NJ: Prentice-Hall.

Pratt, J. H. (1907). The class method of treating consumption in the homes of the poor. *Journal of the American Medical Association, 49,* 755–759.

President's Commission on Mental Health. (1978). *Report to the President, Vol I.* Washington, DC: U.S. Government Printing Office.

President's Commission on Mental Retardation. (1972). *MR 71: Entering the era of human ecology (No. 5).* Department of Health, Education, & Welfare: Washington, DC.

Price, R. H. (1966). Signal detection methods in personality and perception. *Psychological Bulletin, 66,* 55–62.

Price, R. H. (1968). Analysis of task requirements in schizophrenic concept identification performance. *Journal of Abnormal Psychology, 73,* 285–293.

Price, R. H. (1974). Etiology, the social environment, and the prevention of psychological dysfunction. In P. Insel & R. H. Moos (Eds.), *Health and the social environment.* Lexington, MA: D. C. Heath.

Price, R. H. (1978). *Abnormal behavior: Perspectives in conflict* (2d ed.). New York: Holt, Rinehart & Winston.

Price, R. H., & Bouffard, D. L. (1974). Behavioral appropriateness and situational constraint as dimensions of social behavior. *Journal of Personality and Social Psychology, 30,* 579–586.

Price, R. H., & D'Aunno, T. (1984). The context and objectives of community research. *Psychology and Community Change* (2d ed.) (pp. 51–67). Homewood, IL: Dorsey Press.

Price, R. H., & Denner, B. (Eds.). (1973). *The making of a mental patient.* New York: Holt, Rinehart & Winston.

Price, R. H., & Eriksen, D. W. (1966). Size constancy in schizophrenia: A reanalysis. *Journal of Abnormal Psychology, 71,* 155–160.

Price, R. H., & Moos, R. H. (1975). Toward a taxonomy of inpatient treatment environments. *Journal of Abnormal Psychology, 84,* 181–188.

Price, R. H., and Smith, S. S. (1983). Two decades of reform in the mental health system (1963–1983). In E. Seidman (Ed.), *Handbook of social intervention.* Beverly Hills, CA: Sage Publications.

Prien, R., & Caffey, E. (1975). Guidelines for antipsychotic drug use. *Resident and Staff Physician, 9,* 165–172.

Prince, C. (1972). A survey of 504 cases of transvestism. *Psychological Reports, 31,* 903–917.

Prince, M. (1906). *The dissociation of a personality.* New York and London: Longmans Green.

Pritchard, D. A., & Rosenblatt, A. (1980a). Racial bias in the MMPI: A methodological review. *Journal of Consulting and Clinical Psychology, 48,* 263–267.

Pritchard, D. A., & Rosenblatt, A. (1980b). Reply to Gythner and Green. *Journal of Consulting and Clinical Psychology, 48,* 273–274.

Prochaska, J. O. (1984). *Systems of psychotherapy: A transtheoretical analysis* (Rev. ed.), Homewood, IL: Dorsey.

Pronko, N. H. (1963). *Abnormal psychology.* Baltimore: Williams & Wilkens.

Prusiner, S. B., Bolton, D. C., Bowman, K. A., Groth, D. F., Cochran, S. P., and McKinley, M. P. (1983). Prions and dementia. In *Biological Aspects of Alzheimer's Disease* (Branbury Report No. 15, Cold Spring Harbor Laboratory, 373–386).

Purcell, K. (1963). Distinctions between subgroups of asthmatic children: Children's perceptions of events associated with asthma. *Pediatrics, 31,* 486–494.

Purcell, K., Brady, K., Chai, H., Muser, J., Molk, L., Gordon, N., & Means, J. (1969). The effect on asthma in children of experimental separation from the family. *Psychosomatic Medicine, 31,* 144–164.

Quitkin, F., Rifkin, A., & Gochfeld, L. (1977). Tardive dyskinesia: Are first signs reversible? *American Journal of Psychiatry, 134,* 84–86.

Rabin, H. M., & Rosenbaum, M. (1976). *How to begin a psychotherapy group: Six approaches.* New York: Gordon and Breash Science Publishers.

Rabkin, J. G., & Struening, E. L. (1976). Life events, stress, and illness, *Science, 194,* 1013–1020.

Rachman, S. J., & Hodgson, R. J. (1980). *Obsessions and compulsions.* Englewood Cliffs, NJ: Prentice-Hall, © 1980. Material reprinted by permission.

Rachman, S., & Wilson, G. T. (1980). *The effects of psychological therapy.* Oxford: Pergamon.

Rackemann, F. M. (1928). Studies in asthma—Analysis of 213 cases in which patients were relieved for more than 2 years. *Archives of Internal Medicine, 41,* 346–355.

Ramsay, R. W., & Happee, J. A. (1977). The stress of bereavement: Components and treatments. In C. Spielberger & I. Sarason (Eds.), *Stress and anxiety, Vol. 4.* London: John Wiley.

Rank, O. (1929). *The trauma of birth.* New York: Harcourt.

Raphael, B. (1983). *The anatomy of bereavement.* New York: Basic Books.

Rapaport, D. (1967). *Collected papers.* New York: Basic Books.

Rapaport, D., & Gill, M. M. (1967). The points of view and assumptions of metapsychology. In Merton M. Gill (Ed.), *Collected papers of David Rapaport.* New York: Basic Books.

Rappaport, J. (1977). *Community psychology: Values research and action.* New York: Holt, Rinehart & Winston.

Raskin, A. (1979). Signs and symptoms of psychopathology in the elderly. In A. Raskin & L. F. Jarvik (Eds.), *Psychiatric symptoms and cognitive loss in the elderly* (pp. 3–18). New York: Hemisphere Publishing.

Raskin, M., Johnson, G., & Rodestvedt, J. W. (1973). Chronic anxiety treated by feedback induced muscle relaxation. *Archives of General Psychiatry, 23,* 263–267.

Raskin, N. H., & Appenzeller, D. (1980). *Headache.* Philadelphia: W. B. Saunders.

Raskind, M. A., & Storrie, M. C. (1980). The organic mental disorders. In E. W. Busse and D. G. Blazer (Eds.), *Handbook of geriatric psychiatry* (pp. 305–328). New York: Van Nostrand Reinhold.

Ray, O. S. (1978). *Drugs, society, and human behavior.* (2d ed.) St. Louis: Mosby.

Read, S. L. & Jarvik, L. F. (1984). Cerebrovascular disease in the differential diagnosis of dementia. *Psychiatric Annals 14,* 100–108.

Redick, R. W., & Taube, C. A. (1980). Demography and mental health care of the aged. In J. E. Birren & R. B. Sloane (Eds.), *Handbook of mental health and aging* (pp. 57–71). Englewood Cliffs, NJ: Prentice-Hall.

Redlich, F. C., & Freedman, D. X. (1966). *The theory and practice of psychiatry.* New York: Basic Books.

Redner, R., Snellman, L., & Davidson, W. S. (1983). Juvenile delinquency. In R. J. Morris & T. R. Kratochwill (Eds.), *The practice of child therapy.* New York: Pergamon Press.

Rees, L. (1964). The importance of psychological, allergic, and infective factors in childhood asthma. *Journal of Psychosomatic Research, 7,* 253–262.

Regier, D. A., Goldberg, I. E., & Taube, C. A. (1978). The defacto mental health services system. *Archives of General Psychiatry, 35,* 685–693.

Regier, D. A., Myers, J. K., Kramer, M., Robins, L. N., Blazer, D. G., Hough, R. L., Eaton, W. W., & Locke, B. Z. (1984). The NIMH epidemiologic catchment area program. *Archives of General Psychiatry, 41*(10), 934–941.

Reich, W. (1949). *Character analysis.* New York: Orgone Institute Press.

Reik, T. (1941). *Masochism in modern man.* New York: Farrar & Straus.

Reiss, A. J. (1961). The social integration of queers and peers. *Social Problems* (Fall), *9,* 102–120.

Reitan, R. M., & Davison, L. (1974). *Clinical neuropsychology: Current status and applications.* Washington, D.C.: V. H. Winston.

Renner, V. J., & Birren, J. E. (1980). Stress: Physiological and psychological mechanisms. In J. E. Birren & R. B. Sloane (Eds.), *Handbook of mental health and aging* (pp. 310–336). Englewood Cliffs, NJ: Prentice-Hall.

Report of the Hypertension Task Force: Volume One—General Summary and Recommendations. (1979). (NIH Publication No. 79-1623). Washington, DC: U.S. Government Printing Office.

Report of the Hypertension Task Force: Volume Two—Scientific Summary and Recommendations. (1979). (NIH Publication No. 79-1624). Washington, DC: U.S. Government Printing Office.

Repp, A. C., & Dietz, D. E. D. (1983). Mental retardation. In T. H. Ollendick and M. Hersen (Eds.), *Handbook of child psychopathology.* New York: Plenum Press.

Restak, R. (1982). Islands of genius. *Science,* 62–67.

Review Panel on Coronary-Prone Behavior and Coronary Heart Disease. (1981). Coronary-prone behavior and coronary heart disease: A critical review. *Circulation, 63,* 1199–1215.

Reyher, J. (1967). Hypnosis in research on psychopathology. In J. E. Gordon (Ed.), *Handbook of clinical and experimental hypnosis.* New York: Macmillan.

Rice, D. P., Feldman, J. J., and White, K. L. (1977). *The current burden of illness in the United States.* Washington, DC: National Academy of Sciences.

Richman, N., Stevenson, J. E., & Graham, P. J. (1975). Prevalence of behavior problems in 3-year-old children: An epidemiological study in a London borough. *Journal of Child Psychology and Psychiatry, 16,* 277.

Richter, C. P. (1957). On the phenomenon of sudden death in animals and man. *Psychosomatic Medicine, 19,* 191–198.

Richter, C. P. (1958). The phenomenon of unexplained sudden death in animals and man. In. W. H. Gant (Ed.), *Physiological basis of psychiatry.* Springfield, IL: Charles C Thomas, 148–171.

Rickers-Ovsiankina, M. A. (Ed.). (1960). *Rorschach psychology.* New York: John Wiley & Sons.

Riegel, K. F. (1972). Influence of economic and political ideologies on the development of developmental psychology. *Psychological Bulletin, 78,* 129–141.

Rimm, D., & Cunningham, M. (1985). The behavior therapies. In S. J. Lynn, & J. P. Garske (Eds.), *Contemporary psychotherapies: Models and methods.* Columbus: Merrill.

Rimm, D. C., & Masters, J. C. (1979). *Behavior therapy: Techniques and empirical findings* (2d ed.). New York: Academic Press.

Rincover, A., & Devany, J. (1982). The application of sensory extinction procedures to self-injury. *Analysis and Intervention in Developmental Disabilities, 2,* 67–81.

Roback, H. B., Strassberg, D. S., McKee, E., & Cunningham, J. (1977). Self-concept and psychological adjustment differences between self-identified male transsexuals and male homosexuals. *Journal of Homosexuality, 3,* 15–19.

Robins, L. N. (1979). Addict Careers. In R. I. Dupont, A. Goldstein, & J. O'Donnell (Eds.), *Handbook on drug abuse.* Washington, D.C.: National Institute on Drug Abuse, U.S. Government Printing Office.

Robins, L. N., Davis, D. H., & Nurco, D. N. (1974). How permanent was Viet Nam drug addiction? In M. H. Greene & R. L. DuPont (Eds.), *The epidemiology of drug abuse* (NIDA Journal Supplement, Part 2, Vol. 54). Washington, D.C.: U.S. Government Printing Office.

Robins, L. N., Helzer, J. E., Weissman, M. M., Orvaschel, H., Gruenberg, E., Burke, J. D., & Reiger, D. A. (1984). Lifetime prevalence of specific psychiatric disorders in three sites. *Archives of General Psychiatry, 41*(10), 949–958.

Robins, N. L. (1966). *Deviant children grown up.* Baltimore: Williams & Wilkins.

Rodin, J., & Langer, E. J. (1977). Long-term effects of a control-relevant intervention with the institutionalized aged. *Journal of Personality and Social Psychology. 35,* 897–902.

Rogers, C. R. (1942). *Counseling and psychotherapy.* New York: Houghton Mifflin.

Rogers, C. R. (1951). *Client-centered therapy.* Boston: Houghton Mifflin, 1951. Copyright © 1951, renewed 1978, Houghton Mifflin Company. Material reprinted by permission of the publishers.

Rogers, C. R. (1957). The necessary and sufficient conditions of therapeutic personality change. *Journal of Consulting Psychology, 21,* 95–103.

Rogers, C. R. (1959). A theory of therapy, personality, and interpersonal relationships as developed in client-centered framework. In S. Koch (Ed.), *Psychology: A study of a science (Vol. 3) Formulation of the person in the social context.* New York: McGraw-Hill.

Rogers, C. R. (1961). *On becoming a person.* Boston: Houghton Mifflin, 1961. Copyright © 1961 by Houghton Mifflin Company. Material reprinted by permission of the publishers.

Rogers, C. R. (1970). *On encounter groups.* New York: Harper & Row, 1970. Copyright © 1970 by Carl R. Rogers. Excerpt in text reprinted by permission of Harper & Row, Publishers, Inc.

Rogers v. *Okin.* (1979, October 29). Civil Action 75–1610–T. (OC Mass.).

Rollins, N., & Piazza, E. (1978). Diagnosis of anorexia nervosa. *Journal of the American Academy of Child Psychiatry, 11,* 114–131.

Roney, J. G., & Nall, M. L. (1966). *Medication practices in a community: An exploratory study, research report.* Menlo Park, CA: Stanford Research Institute.

Rosen, G. (1968). *Madness in society.* New York: Harper & Row.

Rosenberg, P. (1973). The effects of mood altering drugs: Pleasures and pitfalls. In R. E. Hardy & J. G. Cull (Eds.), *Drug dependence and rehabilitation approaches.* Springfield, IL: Charles C Thomas. Material reprinted courtesy of Charles C Thomas, Publisher.

Rosenhan, D. L. (1973). On being sane in insane places. *Science, 179,* 250–258. Copyright 1973 by the American Society for the Advancement of Science.

Rosenthal, D. (1970). *Genetic theory and abnormal behavior.* New York: McGraw-Hill. Copyright © 1970 McGraw-Hill. Excerpt in text used with permission of McGraw-Hill Book Company.

Rosenthal, D. (1973, August). Evidence for a spectrum of schizophrenic disorders. Pager presented at the annual meeting of the American Psychological Association, Montreal, Canada.

Ross, D. M., & Ross, S. A. (1982). *Hyperactivity.* New York: John Wiley.

Rossman, B., Minuchin, S., & Liebman, R. (1975). Family lunch session: An introduction to family therapy in anorexia nervosa. *American Journal of Orthopsychiatry, 45,* 846–853.

Rothman, D. (1971). *The discovery of the asylum.* Boston: Little, Brown.

Roy. A. (1983). Family history of suicide. *Archives of General Psychiatry, 40,* 971–974.

Roybal, E. R. (1984). Federal involvement in mental health care for the aged. *American Psychologist, 39*(2), 163–166.

Rush, A. J., Beck, A. T., Kovacs, M., & Hollon, S. (1977). Comparative efficacy of cognitive therapy and pharmacotherapy in the treatment of depressed outpatients. *Cognitive Therapy and Research, 1,* 17–37.

Russell, G. (1979). Bulimia nervosa: An ominous variant of anorexia nervosa. *Psychological Medicine, 9,* 429–448.

Russell, M. A. H. (1977). Smoking problems: An overview. In *Research on smoking behavior* (NIDA Research Monograph Series: 17). Washington, DC: Department of Health, Education, and Welfare, U.S. Government Printing Office.

Rutter, M. (1978). Diagnosis and definition of childhood autism. *Journal of Autism and Childhood Schizophrenia, 8,* 139–161.

Rutter, M., Greenfeld, D., & Lockyer, L. (1967). A five to fifteen year follow-up study of infantile psychosis: II. Social and behavioural outcome. *British Journal of Psychiatry, 113,* 1183.

Rutter, M., & Lockyer, L. (1967). A five to fifteen year follow-up study of infantile psychosis: I. Description of sample. *British Journal of Psychiatry, 113,* 1169.

Sadock, V. A., & Sadock, B. J. (1976). Dual sex therapy. In B. J. Sadock, H. I. Kaplan & A. M. Freedman (Eds.), *The sexual experience.* Baltimore: Williams & Wilkins.

Saghir, M. T. & Robins, E. (1973). *Male and female homosexuality.* Baltimore: Williams & Wilkins.

Salber, E. J., Freeman, H. E., & Abelin, T. (1968). Needed research on smoking: Lessons from the Newton study. In E. F. Borgatta & R. R. Evans (Eds.), *Smoking, health and behavior.* Chicago: Aldine.

Sales, E., Baum, M., & Shore, B. (1984). Victim readjustment following assault. *Journal of Social Issues, 40*(1), 117–136.

Salholz, E. (1984, April 23). The fight to conquer fear. *Newsweek.*

Salzinger, K. (1975). Behavioral Analysis. In M. R. Rosenzweig & L. W. Porter (Eds.), *Annual Review of Psychology, 26,* 623–629.

Salzinger, S., Kaplan, S., & Artemyeff, C. (1983). Mothers' personal social networks and child maltreatment. *Journal of Abnormal Psychology, 92,* 68–76.

Salzman, S. (1982). Obsessions and agoraphobia. In D. Chambless, & A. Goldstein (Eds.), *Agoraphobia: Multiple perspectives on theory and treatment.* New York: John Wiley & Sons.

Sanberg, P. R., & Coyle, J. T. (1984). Scientific approaches to Huntington's disease. *CRC Critical Reviews in Clinical Neurobiology 1.*

Sanberg, P. R., & Johnston, G. A. (1981). Glutamate and Huntington's disease. *Medical Journal of Australia 2,* 460–465.

Sandler, J., & Hazari, A. (1960). The "Obsessional": On the psychological classification of obsessional character traits and symptoms. *British Journal of Medical Psychology, 33,* 113–122.

Sarbin, R. R., & Nucci, L. P. (1973). Self-reconstitution processes: A proposal for reorganizing the conduct of confirmed smokers. *Journal of Abnormal Psychology, 81,* 182–195.

Sarbin, T. R. (1972, June). Schizophrenia is a myth born of metaphor, meaningless. *Psychology Today*, pp. 18–27.

Satir, V. (1964). *Conjoint family therapy: A guide to therapy and technique.* Palo Alto, CA: Science and Behavior Books.

Satterfield, J. H., Hoppe, C. M., & Schell, A. M. (1982). A prospective study of delinquency in 110 adolescent boys with attention deficit disorder and 88 normal adolescent boys. *American Journal of Psychiatry, 139,* 795–798.

Schachter, S. (1971). *Emotion, obesity and crime.* New York: Academic Press.

Schachter, S. (1977). Nicotine regulation in heavy and light smokers. *Journal of Experimental Psychology (General), 106,* 5–12.

Schachter, S., Silverstein, B., Kozlowski, L. T., Herman, C. P., & Liebling, B. (1977). Effects of stress of cigarette smoking and urinary ph. *Journal of Experimental Psychology (General), 106,* 24–30.

Schact, T., & Nathan, P. E. (1977). But is it good for psychologists? Appraisal and status of DSM III. *American Psychologist, 32,* 1017–1025.

Schaie, K. W., & Schaie, J. P. (1977). Clinical assessment and aging. In J. E. Birren & K. W. Schaie (Eds.), *Handbook of the psychology of aging* (pp. 692–723). New York: Van Nostrand Reinhold.

Schechter, M., & Roberge, L. (1976). Sexual exploitation. In R. E. Helfer & H. Kempe (Eds.), *Child abuse and neglect, the family and community.* Houston: Houston Law Review.

Scheff, T. J. (1966). *Being mentally ill: A sociological theory.* Chicago: Aldine.

Scheff, T. J. (Ed.). (1975). *Labeling madness.* Englewood Cliffs, NJ: Prentice-Hall.

Schildkraut, J. J., & Ketty, S. S. (1967). Biogenic amines and emotion. *Science, 156,* 21–30.

Schlaadt, R. G., & Shannon, P. T. (1982). *Drugs of choice.* Englewood Cliffs, NJ: Prentice-Hall.

Schlossberg, N. K. (1984). *Counseling adults in transition.* New York: Springer Publishing.

Schmauk, F. J. (1970). Punishment, arousal, and avoidance learning in sociopaths. *Journal of Abnormal Psychology, 76,* 443–453.

Schneidman, E. S., & Farberow, N. L. (1970b). A psychological approach to the study of suicide notes. In E. S. Schneidman, N. L. Farberow, & R. E. Litman (Eds.), *The psychology of suicide.* New York: Jason Aronson.

Schneidman, E. S., Farberow, N. L., & Litman, R. E. (Eds.) (1970a). *The psychology of suicide.* New York: Jason Aronson.

Schopler, E., Mesibov, G., & Baker, A. (1982). Evaluation of treatment for autistic children and their parents. *Journal of the American Academy of Child Psychiatry, 21,* 262–267.

Schov, M. (1976). Current status of lithium therapy in affective disorders and other diseases. In A. Villeneuve (Ed.), *Lithium in psychiatry, a synopsis.* Quebec: Les Presses de l'Univérsité Laval.

Schreibman, L., & Koegel, R. L. (1981). A guideline for planning behavior modification programs for autistic children. In S. Turner, K. Calhoun, and A. Adams (Eds.), *Handbook of clinical behavior therapy.* New York: John Wiley & Sons.

Schuckit, M. A., & Haglund, R. M. J. (1977). An overview of the etiological theories of alcoholism. In N. J. Estes & M. E. Heinman (Eds.), *Alcoholism: Development, consequences, and interventions.* St. Louis: C. V. Mosby.

Schuckit, M. A., & Rayses, V. (1979). Differences in acetaldehyde levels in relatives of alcoholics and controls. *Science, 203,* 79–87.

Schulz, R. (1976). Effects of control and predictability on the physical and psychological well-being of the institutionalized aged. *Journal of Personality and Social Psychology, 33,* 563–573.

Schwartz, D. M., Thompson, M. G., & Johnson, C. (1982). Anorexia nervosa and bulimia: The sociocultural context. *International Journal of Eating Disorders, 1,* 23–25.

Schwartz, G. (1978). Psychobiological foundations of psychotherapy and behavior change. In S. Garfield & A. E. Bergin (Eds.), *Handbook of psychotherapy and behavior change (2d edition).* New York: John Wiley & Sons.

Schwartz, G. E. (1972). Voluntary control of human cardiovascular integration and differentiation through feedback and reward. *Science, 175,* 90–93.

Schwartz, G. E. (1973). Biofeedback as therapy: Some theoretical and practical issues. *American Psychologist, 28,* 666–673.

Schwartz, G. E. (1977). Psychosomatic disorders and biofeedback: A psychobiological model of disregulation. In J. D. Maser and M. E. P. Seligman (Eds.), *Psychopathology: Experimental models.* San Francisco: W. H. Freeman.

Schwartz, J. J., & Schwartz, R. (1969, Fall-Winter). Growth encounters. *Voices, 5,* 7–16.

Schwartz, M. F., & Masters, W. H. (1983). Conceptual factors in the treatment of paraphilias: A preliminary report. *Journal of Sex & Marital Therapy, 9,* 3–18.

Schwartz, M. F., & Masters, W. H. (1984). The Masters and Johnson treatment program for dissatisfied homosexual men. *American Journal of Psychiatry, 141,* 173–181.

Scovern, A. W., & Kilmann, P. R. (1980). Status of electroconvulsive therapy: Review of the outcome literature. *Psychological Bulletin, 87,* 260–303.

Scull, A. T. (1977). Community treatment and the deviant: A radical view. *Decarceration.* Englewood Cliffs, NJ: Prentice-Hall.

Seiden, R. H. (1969). Suicide among youth. *Bulletin of Suicidology, 6,* (Suppl.).

Seligman, M. E. P. (1975). *Helplessness: On depression, development and death.* San Francisco: W. H. Freeman.

Selling, L. S. (1940). *Men against madness.* New York: Greenberg.

Selye, H. (1956). *The stress of life.* New York: McGraw-Hill.

Selye, H. (1978, March). On the real benefits of eustress. *Psychology Today,* pp. 60–63; 69–70.

Shanas, E. (1980). Older people and their families: The new pioneers. *Journal of Marriage and the Family, 42*(1), 12.

Shapiro, A. P., Schwartz, G., Ferguson, D., Kedmand, D., and Weiss, S. M. (1977). Behavioral approaches to the treatment of hypertension: Clinical status. *Annals of Internal Medicine, 86,* 626–636.

Shapiro, D. (1965). *Neurotic styles.* New York: Basic Books.

Shapiro, D. (1981). *Autonomy and rigid character.* New York: Basic Books.

Shapiro, D., & Goldstein, I. B. (1982). Biobehavioral perspectives on hypertension. *Journal of Consulting and Clinical Psychology, 50,* 841–858.

Shapiro, D. A., & Shapiro, D. (1982). Meta-analysis of comparative therapy outcome studies: A replication and refinement. *Psychological Bulletin, 92,* 581–604.

Shapiro, J. L. (1978). *Methods of group psychotherapy and encounter: A tradition of innovation.* Itasca, IL: F. E. Peacock Publishers.

Sharm, B. P. (1972). Cannabis and its users in Nepal. *British Journal of Psychology, 127,* 550–555.

Sheehan, D. V. (1982). Panic attacks and phobias. *New England Journal of Medicine, 307,* 156–158.

Sher, K., & Levenson, R. (1982). Risk for alcoholism and individual differences in the stress-response-dampening effect of alcohol. *Journal of Abnormal Psychology, 91,* 350–367.

Sherman, E. A. (1981). *Counseling the aging.* New York: Free Press.

Sherman, S. J. Presson, C., Chassin, L., & Olshavsky, R. (1979). *Social psychological factors in adolescent smoking.* Grant application, submitted to the U.S. Department of Health, Education, and Welfare.

Shuckit, M. A., & Rayses, V. (1979). Differences in acetaldehyde levels in relatives of alcoholics and controls. *Science, 203,* 54–55.

Siegel, S. Learning and psychopharmacology. (1977). In M. E. Jarvik (Ed.), *Psychopharmacology in the practice of medicine.* New York: Appleton-Century-Crofts.

Sikorski, K., & Nash, M. *Substance abuse: Training tapes and manual.* Columbia, MO: Everyday People.

Silverman, L. H. (1976, September). Psychoanalytic theory: The reports of my death are greatly exaggerated. *American Psychologist, 31*(9), 621. Copyright 1976 by the American Psychological Association. Text quotation reprinted by permission.

Silverstein, B., Kozlowski, L. T., & Schachter, S. (1977). Social life, cigarette smoking, and urinary ph. *Journal of Experimental Psychology (General), 106,* 20–23.

Simonson, W. (1984). *Medications and the elderly: A guide for promoting proper use.* Rockville, MD: Aspen Systems Corporation.

Simpson, G. M., & Kline, N. S. (1976). Tardive dyskinesia: Manifestations, etiology, and treatment. In M. D. Yahr (Ed.), *The basal ganglia.* New York: Raven Press.

Sinclair-Gieben, A. H. C., & Chambers, C. (1959). Evaluation of treatment of warts by hypnosis. *Lancet, 2,* 480–482.

Skinner, B. F. (1953). *Science and Human Behavior.* New York: Macmillan.

Skinner, B. F. (1971). *Beyond freedom and dignity.* New York: Knopf, 1971. Copyright © 1971 by B. F. Skinner. Material reprinted by permission of Alfred A. Knopf, Inc.

Skinner, H. A., & Allen, B. A. (1982). Alcohol dependence syndrome: Measurement and validation. *Journal of Abnormal Psychology, 91,* 199–209.

Skynner, A. C. R. (1981). An open-systems, group-analytic approach to family therapy. In A. S. Gurman, & D. P. Kniskern (Eds.), *Handbook of family therapy.* New York: Brunner/Mazel.

Slade, P. D., & Russell, G. F. M. (1973). Awareness of body dimensions in anorexia nervosa: Cross-sectional and longitudinal studies. *Psychological Medicine, 3,* 188–189.

Slager-Jorné, P. (1978). Counseling sexually abused children. *Personnel and Guidance Journal, 12,* 103–105.

Slater, E. (1953). *Psychotic and neurotic illnesses in twins.* London: Her Majesty's Stationary Office.

Slater, E. (1965). Clinical aspects of genetic mental disorders. In J. N. Cummings & M. Kremer (Eds.), *Biochemical aspects of neurological disorders* (2d Series). Oxford: Blackwell Scientific Publications.

Slater, E., & Glithero, E. (1965). A follow-up of patients diagnosed as suffering from hysteria. *Journal of Psychosomatic Research, 9,* 9–13.

Sloane, R. B., Staples, F. R., Cristol, A. H., Yorkston, N., & Whipple, K. (1975). *Psychotherapy versus behavior therapy.* Cambridge, MA: Harvard University Press.

Smart, R. G., Gray, G., & Bennett, C. (1973). Predictors of drinking and signs of heavy drinking among high school students. *International Journal of the Addictions, 13*, 1385–1394.

Smith, D. (1982). Trends in counseling and psychotherapy. *American Psychologist, 37*, 802–809.

Smith, D. E., Wesson, D. R., & Lannon, R. A. (1970). New development in barbiturate abuse. *Clinical Toxicology, 3*, 57–65.

Smith, D. W., & Wilson, A. A. (1973). *The child with Down's syndrome (mongolism)*. Philadelphia: W. B. Saunders.

Smith, E. (1969). The characteristics of dependence in high dose amphetamine abuse. *International Journal of the Addiction, 4*, 453–459.

Smith, G. M., & Beecher, H. K. (1962). Subjective effects of heroin and morphine in normal subjects. *Journal of Pharmacology and Experimental Therapeutics, 136*, 47–52.

Smith, M. L., & Glass, G. V. (1977). Meta-analysis of psychotherapy outcome studies. *American Psychologist, 32*, 752–760.

Smith, R. J. (1978). *The psychopath in society*. New York: Academic Press.

Smith, S. M., & Hanson, R. (1974). 134 battered children: A medical and psychological study. *British Medical Journal, 3*, 666–670.

Snyder, S. H. (1975). *Madness and the brain*. New York: McGraw-Hill.

Solomon, R. L. (1980). The opponent-process theory of acquired motivation: The costs of pleasure and the benefits of pain. *American Psychologist, 35*, 691–712.

Solomon, S. (1967). The neurological evaluation. In A. M. Freedman and H. I. Kaplan (Eds.), *Comprehensive textbook of psychiatry*. Baltimore: Williams & Wilkins.

Somasundarum, O., & Papakumari, M. (1981). A study on Down's anomaly. *Child Psychiatry Quarterly, 14*, 85–94.

Sorrells, J. M., & Ford, F. (1969). Toward an integrated theory of families and family therapy. *Psychotherapy: Theory, research, and practice, 9*, 150–161.

Spanos, N. P. (1982). Hypnotic behavior: A cognitive, social, psychological perspective. *Research Communications in Psychology, Psychiatry, and Behavior, 7*, 199–213.

Spanos, N. P. (1984). *Multiple personality: A social psychological perspective*. Unpublished manuscript, Carleton University, Ottawa, Ontario.

Spanos, N. P., & Gottlieb, J. (1976). Ergotism and the Salem village witch trials. *Science, 194*, 1390–1394.

Spengler, A. (1976, August 24). *Sadomasochists and their subculture: Results of an empirical study*. Paper presented at the annual meeting, International Academy of Sex Research, Hamburg, Germany.

Sperling, M. (1974). *The major neuroses and behavior disorders in children*. New York: Jason Aronson.

Spiegler, M. (1983). *Contemporary behavioral therapy*. Palo Alto, CA: Mayfield.

Spielberg, C. D. & Jacobs, G. A. (1979). Maternal emotions, life stress and obstetric complications. In L. Zichella, P. Pancheri (Eds.), *Psychoneuroendocrinology in Reproduction*. North-Holland Biomedical Press: Elsevier.

Spierer, H. (1977). *Major transitions in the human life cycle*. New York: Academy for Educational Development. Cited in N. K. Schlossberg, *Counseling adults in transition*. New York: Springer Publishing, 1984.

Spitz, R. A. (1946). Hospitalism: A follow-up report. *Psychoanalytic study of the child* (Vol. 2). New York: International Universities Press.

Spitzer, R. L., & Endicott, J. (1968). Diagno: A computer program for psychiatric diagnosis utilizing the differential diagnosis procedure. *Archives of General Psychiatry, 28*, 746–756.

Spitzer, R. L., Endicott, J., & Robins, E. (1975). Clinical criteria for psychiatric diagnosis and DSM III. *American Journal of Psychiatry, 132*, 1187–1192.

Spitzer, R. L., Endicott, J., & Robins, E. (1975). *Research diagnostic criteria*, New York: Biometrics Research.

Spitzer, R. L., Forman, J. B. W., & Nee, J. (1979). DSM III field trials: Initial interrater diagnostic reliability. *American Journal of Psychiatry, 136*, 815–817.

Spitzer, R. L., Skodol, A. E., Gibbon, M., & Williams, J. B. W. (1981). *DSM casebooks*, 1st ed., American Psychiatric Association.

Spitzer, R. L., & Williams, J. B. W. (1983, October). The revision of DSM III. *Psychiatric Annals, 13*(10), 808–811.

Spivack, G., & Shure, M. B. (1974). *Social adjustment of young children: A cognitive approach to solving real life problems*. San Francisco, CA: Jossey-Bass.

Spotts, J. V., & Shontz, F. C. (1976). *The lifestyles of nine American cocaine users: Trips to the land of cockaiqne*. (Alcohol, Drug Abuse, and Mental Health Administration, NIDA Issue No. 16) Washington, DC: Department of Health, Education, and Welfare, PHS; U.S. Government Printing Office.

Spotts, J. V., & Shontz, F. C. (1983). Drug-induced ego states. 1. *The International Journal of the Addictions, 18*, 119–151.

Srole, L., Langner, T. S., Michael, S. H., Opler, M. K., & Rennie, T. A. C. (1962). *Mental health in the metropolis: The midtown Manhattan study*. New York: McGraw-Hill.

St. Clair, D. and Whalley, L. J. (1983). Hypertension, multi-infarct dementia and Alzheimer's disease. *British Journal of Psychiatry, 143*, 274–276.

Stampfl, T. G., & Levis, D. J. (1967). Essentials of implosive therapy: A learning theory-based psychodynamic behavioral therapy. *Journal of Abnormal Psychology, 72,* 496–503.

Stefansson, J. G., et al. (1976). Hysterical neurosis, conversion type. *Acta Psychiatrica Scandinavia, 53,* 119–138.

Steger, J., & Fordyce, W. E. (1982). Behavioral health care in the management of chronic pain. In T. Millon, C. Green, & R. Meagher (Eds.), *Handbook of clinical health psychology.* New York: Plenum Press.

Stein, L. I., & Test, M. A. (1985). *The training in community living model: A decade of experience.* San Francisco: Jossey-Bass.

Steinbrueck, S. M., Maxwell, S. E., & Howard, G. S. (1983). A meta-analysis of psychotherapy and drug therapy in the treatment of unipolar depression with adults. *Journal of Consulting and Clinical Psychology, 51,* 856–863.

Steinmark, W. W., & Borkovec, T. D. (1974). Active and placebo treatment effects on moderate insomnia under counterdemand and positive demand instructions. *Journal of Abnormal Psychology, 83,* 157–163.

Stenback, A. (1980). Depression and suicidal behavior in old age. In J. E. Birren & R. B. Sloane (Eds.), *Handbook of mental health and aging* (pp. 616–652). Englewood Cliffs, NJ: Prentice-Hall.

Sterling-Smith, R. S. (1976, April). *A special study of drivers most responsible in fatal accidents.* (Summary for Management Report, Contract No. DOTHS 310-3-595).

Sternbach, R. (1968). *Pain: A psychosocial analysis.* New York: Academic Press.

Steuer, J. L., Mintz, J., Hammen, C. L., Hill, M. A., Jarvik, L. F., McCarley, T., Motoike, P., & Rosen, R. (1984). Cognitive-behavioral and psychodynamic group psychotherapy in treatment of geriatric depression. *Journal of Consulting and Clinical Psychology, 52,* 180–189.

Stewart, J., DeWit, H., & Eikelboom, R. (1984). Role of unconditioned and conditioned drug effects in the self-administration of opiates and stimulants. *Psychological Review, 91,* 251–268.

Stewart, M. A., DeBlois, C. S., & Cummings, C. (1979). Psychiatric disorder in the parents of hyperactive boys and those with conduct disorder. *Journal of Child Psychology and Psychiatry, 21,* 283–292.

Stewart, M. A., & Gath, A. (1978). *Psychological disorders of children: A handbook for primary care physicians.* Baltimore: Williams & Wilkins.

Stoller, F. H. (1970). A stage for trust. In A. Burton (Ed.), *Encounter.* San Francisco, CA: Jossey-Bass.

Stoller, R. J. (1971). The term "transvestism." *Archives of General Psychiatry, 24,* 230–237. Copyright 1971, American Medical Association.

Stone, A. A. (1975). *Mental health and law: A system in transition.* Rockville, MD: National Institute of Mental Health, Center for Studies of Crime and Delinquency.

Storandt, M. (1978). Other approaches to therapy. In M. Storandt, I. C. Siegler, & M. F. Elias (Eds.), *The clinical psychology of aging* (pp. 277–293). New York: Plenum Press.

Storandt, M. (1983). *Counseling and therapy with older adults.* Boston: Little, Brown.

Storr, A. (1980). *The art of psychotherapy.* New York: Methuen.

Strassberg, D., Roback, H., Cunningham, J., & McKee, E. (1980). TSCS-indicated psychopathology in self-identified female transsexuals, homosexuals, and heterosexuals. *Archives of Sexual Behavior.*

Strauss, J. S. (1979). Social and cultural influences on psychopathology. *Annual Review of Psychology, 30,* 397–415.

Strupp, H. H. (1978). Psychotherapy research and practice. In S. Garfield & A. Bergin (Eds.), *Handbook of psychotherapy and behavior change.* New York: John Wiley & Sons.

Strupp, H. H. (1982). Foreword to Goldfried, M. *Converging themes in psychotherapy.* New York: Springer.

Strupp, H. H., Fox, R. E., & Lessler, K. (1969). *Patients view their therapy.* Baltimore: Johns Hopkins University Press.

Stuart, R. B. (1967). Behavioral control of overeating. *Behavior Research and Therapy, 5,* 357–365.

Study finds drinking—often to excess—now starts at earlier age. (1977, March 27). *New York Times,* p. 38.

Sturgis, E. T. & Meyer, V. (1981). Obsessive-compulsive disorders. In S. M. Turner, K. S. Calhoun & H. E. Adams (Eds.) *Handbook of clinical behavior therapy* (pps. 68–102). New York: John Wiley.

Sturman, M. B., & Friar, L. (1972) Suppression of seizures in an epileptic following sensorimotor EEG feedback training. *Electroencephalography and Clinical Neurophysiology 33,* 89–95.

Suh, M., & Carlson, R. (1977). Childhood behavior disorder . . . A family typology: An epidemiological study to determine correlation between childrearing methods and behavior disorder in children. *Psychiatric Journal of the University of Ottawa, 2,* 84–88.

Suinn, R. M. (1982). Intervention with Type A behaviors. *Journal of Consulting and Clinical Psychology, 50,* 933–949.

Sullivan, H. S. (1954). *The psychiatric interview.* New York: W. W. Norton. Copyright, The William Alonson White Psychiatric Foundation.

Sullivan, H. S. (1956). *Clinical studies in psychiatry* (Part II). In H. S. Perry, & M. C. Gaywell (Eds.), *The collected works of Harry Stack Sullivan.* New York: W. W. Norton. Copyright by the William Alanson White Psychiatric Foundation.

Sundberg, N. (1977). *Assessment of persons.* Englewood Cliffs, NJ: Prentice-Hall.

Sundberg, N. D., Snowden, L. R., & Reynolds, W. M. (1978). Toward assessment of personal competence and incompetence in life situations. *Annual Review of Psychology, 29,* 179–221.

Sundel, M., & Schanie, C. F. (1978). Community mental health and mass media preventive education: The alternatives project. *Social Services Review, 52,* 297–306.

Suran, B. G., & Rizzo, J. V. (1983). *Special children: An integrative approach* (2d ed.). Glenview, IL: Scott, Foresman.

Swanson, D. W., Bohnert, P. J., & Smith, J. A. (1970). *The paranoid.* Boston: Little, Brown.

Swift, C. (1978, January 11). *Sexual assault of children and adolescents.* Paper presented to the Domestic and International Scientific Planning, Analysis, and Cooperation Subcommittee of the Committee of Science and Technology of the U.S. House of Representatives, New York.

Szasz, T. (1970). *The manufacture of madness.* New York: Harper & Row.

Szasz, T. S. (1967). *The myth of mental illness.* New York: Dell Publishing.

Szasz, T. S. (1976). *Schizophrenia: The sacred symbol of psychiatry.* New York: Basic Books.

Tanna, V. L. (1974). Paranoid states: A selected review. *Comprehensive Psychiatry, 15*(6), 453–470.

Taube, C. A., & Meyer, N. G. (1975). Children and state mental hospitals. (DHEW Statistical Note 115. Publication No. (ADM) 75-158). Rockville, MD: U.S. Department of Health, Education and Welfare.

Taylor, R. (1975, May/June). Electroconvulsive treatment (ECT): The control of therapeutic power. *Exchange,* 32–37.

Teen smoking rate dips. (1979, April 26). *Columbus Dispatch,* p. A-5.

Telford, C. W., & Sawrey, J. M. (1977). *The exceptional individual* (3d ed.). Englewood Cliffs, NJ: Prentice-Hall.

Terry, R. D., & Katzman, R. (1983). Senile dementia of the Alzheimer's type. *Annals of Neurology 14,* 497–506.

Thal, L. J., Masur, D. M., Fuld, P. A., Sharpless, N. S., & Davies, P. (1983). *Memory improvement with oral physostigmine and lecithin in Alzheimer's disease.* (In "Biological Aspects of Alzheimer's disease", Branbury Report No. 15, Cold Spring Harbor Laboratory, 461–469).

Thigpen, Z. H., & Cleckley, H. (1954). *The three faces of Eve.* New York: McGraw-Hill.

Thomson, M. (1984). *Developmental dyslexia: Its nature, assessment and remediation.* London: Edward Arnold.

Tollison, D. C., & Adams, H. E. (1979). *Sexual disorders.* New York: Gardner Press.

Tooley, J. T., & Pratt, S. (1967). An experimental procedure for the extinction of smoking behavior. *Psychological Record, 17,* 209–218.

Torrey, E. F. *The death of psychiatry.* New York: Penguin Books, 1975.

Torrey, E. F., Hersh, S. P., & McCabe, K. D. (1975). Early childhood psychosis and bleeding during pregnancy: A prospective study of gravid women and their offspring. *Journal of Autism and Childhood Schizophrenia, 5,* 287.

Toseland, R., & Rose, S. D. (1978). A social skills training program for older adults: Evaluation of three group approaches. *Social Work Research Abstracts, 14,* 13.

Trafford, A. (1983, January 24). New hope for the depressed. *U.S. News & World Report.*

Treffert, D. A. (1970). Epidemiology of infantile autism. *Archives of General Psychiatry, 22,* 431–438.

Trites, R. L. (1979). Prevalence of hyperactivity in Ottawa, Canada. In R. L. Trites (Ed.), *Hyperactivity in children. Etiology, measurement, and treatment implications.* Baltimore: University Park Press.

Tsuang, M. (1976). Schizophrenia around the world. *Comparative Psychiatry, 17,* 477–481.

Tucker, J., Vucinich, R., & Sobell, M. (1982). Alcohol's effects on human emotions. *International Journal of the Addictions, 17,* 155–180.

Turner, J., & Ten Hoor, W. (1978). The NIMH community support program pilot approach to a needed social reform. *Schizophrenia Bulletin, 4,* 319–344.

Turner, R. J. (1983). Direct, indirect, and moderating effects of social support on psychological distress and associated conditions. In H. B. Kaplan (Ed.), *Psychosocial stress: Trends in theory and research.* New York: Academic Press.

Turner, S. M., Beidel, D. C., & Nathan, R. S. (1985). Biological factors in obsessive-compulsive disorders. *Psychological Bulletin, 97*(3), 430–450.

Uhlenhuth, E. H., Balter, M. B., & Lipman, R. S. (1978). Minor tranquilizers: Clinical correlates of use in an urban population. *Archives of General Psychiatry, 35,* 650–655.

Ullmann, L. P., & Krasner, L. (1969). *A psychological approach to abnormal behavior.* Englewood Cliffs, NJ: Prentice-Hall.

Unger, S. M. (1963). Mescaline, L.S.D., psilocybin, and personality change. *Psychiatry, 26,* 111–125.

United States v. *Brawner,* 471 F. 2d 969 (D.C. Dir., 1972).

U.S. Department of Commerce, Bureau of the Census. (1978). *Demographic aspects of aging and the older population in the United States* (Special Studies Series P-23, No. 59, 2d printing). Washington, DC: U.S. Government Printing Office.

U.S. Department of Commerce, Bureau of the Census. (1983). *General population characteristics. Part 1: United States Summary* (1980 Census of Population). Washington, DC: U.S. Government Printing Office.

U.S. Department of Health, Education and Welfare. (1975). Amphetamine. (DHEW Publication No. ADM 75-52, Maryland).

U.S. Department of Health, Education and Welfare. (1976). *Adult use of tobacco—1975*. Public Health Service, Center for Disease Control, National Clearinghouse for Smoking and Health.

U.S. Department of Health, Education and Welfare. (1977). *Health United States, 1976-77*. Washington, DC: Public Health Service.

U.S. Department of Health, Education and Welfare. (1978). *Juvenile Court Statistical Series*. Washington, DC: U.S. Government Printing Office.

U.S. Department of Health, Education and Welfare. (1979). *Marijuana and Health*. (Report to the U.S. Congress by the Secretary of Health, Education and Welfare). Washington, DC: U.S. Government Printing Office.

U.S. News & World Report, 85(1), July 10, 1978.

Valenstein, E. S. (1973). *Brain control*. New York: John Wiley & Sons.

Valentine, C. W. (1930). The innate bases of fear. *Journal of Genetic Psychology, 37*, 394-419.

Valiant, G. E., & Milofsky, E. S. (1982a). The etiology of alcoholism: A prospective viewpoint. *American Psychologist, 37*, 494-503.

Valiant, G. E., & Milofsky, E. S. (1982b). Natural history of male alcoholism IV. Paths to recovery. *Archives of General Psychiatry, 39*, 127-133.

Van Praag, H. M. (1978). *Psychotropic drugs: A guide for practitioners*. New York: Brunner/Mazel.

Vaughn, C. E., & Leff, J. P. (1976). The influence of family and social factors on the course of psychiatric illness: A comparison of schizophrenic and depressive-neurotic patients. *British Journal of Psychiatry, 129*, 127-137.

Veronen, L. J., & Kilpatrick, D. G. (1983). Stress management for rape victims. In D. Meichenbaum & M. E. Jeremko (Eds.), *Stress reduction and prevention* (pps. 341-374). New York: Plenum Press.

Verwoerdt, A. (1976). *Clinical geropsychiatry*. Baltimore: Williams & Wilkins.

Vessie, P. R. (1974). History of the Bures family group. *Journal of Nervous and Mental Diseases 76*, 553-573.

Videka-Sherman, Lynn. Effects of participation in a self help group for bereaved parents: Compassionate Friends. In *Helping people to help themselves: Self-help and prevention*. New York: Haworth Press.

Volle, R. L., & Koelle, G. B. (1975). Ganglionic stimulating and blocking agents. In L. S. Goodman & A. Gilman (Eds.), *Pharmacological basis of therapeutics. (5th ed.)*. New York: Macmillan.

Wachtel, P. (1977). *Psychoanalysis and behavior therapy: Toward an integration*. New York: Basic Books.

Wachtel, P. (1982). What can dynamic therapies contribute to behavior therapy? *Behavior Therapy, 13*, 594-609.

Wachtel, P. (1985). Integrative psychodynamic psychotherapy. In S. J. Lynn, & J. P. Garske (Eds.), *Contemporary psychotherapies: Models and methods*. Columbus: Merrill.

Wadsworth, M. (1979). *Roots of delinquency: Infancy, adolescence and crime*. New York: Barnes & Noble Books.

Waldfogel, S. (1959). Emotional crisis in a child. In A. Burton (Ed.), *Case studies in counseling and psychotherapy*. Englewood Cliffs, NJ: Prentice-Hall.

Waldholz, M. (1984). *The Wall Street Journal*.

Waldorf, D., & Biernacki, P. (1979). The natural recovery from opiate addiction: Some preliminary findings. *Journal of Drug Issues, 9*, 281-289.

Wallace, A. F. C. (1972). Mental illness, biology and culture. In Frances, L. K. Hsu (Ed.), *Psychological anthropology*. Cambridge, MA: Schenkman Publishing.

Wallace, J. (1977). Alcoholism from the inside out: A phenomenological analysis. In N. J. Estes & M. E. Heinman (Eds.), *Alcoholism: Development, consequences and interventions*. St. Louis: C. V. Mosby.

Wallerstein, R. (1966). The current state of psychotherapy: Theory, practice, research. *Journal of the American Psychoanalytic Association, 14*, 183-225.

Walters, D. (1975). *Physical and sexual abuse of children: Causes and treatment*. Bloomington, IN: Indiana University Press.

Walton, D., & Mather, M. D. (1963). The relevance of generalization techniques to the treatment of stammering and phobic symptoms. *Behavior Research and Therapy, 1*, 121-125.

Waring, M., & Ricks, D. (1965). Family patterns of children who become adult schizophrenics. *Journal of Nervous and Mental Disease, 140*, 351-364.

Waters, W. E. (1971). Migraine: Intelligence, social class and familial prevalence. *British Medical Journal, 2*, 77-78.

Watson, D. L., & Tharp, R. G. (1972). Self-directed behavior: Self-modification for personal adjustment. Monterey, CA: Brooks/Cole. Copyright © 1972 by Wadsworth, Inc. Material reprinted by permission of the publisher.

Watson, J. B., & Rayner, R. (1920). Conditioned emotional reactions. *Journal of Experimental Psychology, 3*, 1-14.

Weil, A. (1972). *The natural mind.* New York: Houghton Mifflin.

Weinberg, J. R. (1977). Counseling the person with alcohol problems. In N. J. Estes & M. E. Heinman (Eds.), *Alcoholism: Development, consequences and interventions.* St. Louis: C. V. Mosby.

Weinberg, S. K. (1955). *Incest behavior.* New York: Citadel Press.

Weiner, H., Thaler, M., Reiser, M. F., & Mirsky, J. A. (1957). Etiology of duodenal ulcer. *Psychosomatic Medicine, 19,* 1–10.

Weingartner, H., Rapoport, J. L., Buchsbaum, M. S., Bunney, W. E., Ebert, M. H., Mikkelson, E. J., & Caine, D. E. (1980). Cognitive processes in normal and hyperactive children and their response to amphetamine treatment. *Journal of Abnormal Psychology, 89,* 25–37.

Weisman, R. (1983, July 8). A perspective on panic: The research of Donald Klein. *NIMH Science Reporter,* pp. 5–8.

Weiss, J. M. (1971). Effects of coping behavior in different warning signal conditions on stress pathology in rats. *Journal of Comparative and Physiological Psychology, 77,* 1–13(a).

Weiss, J. M. (1971). Effects of coping behavior with and without a feedback signal on stress pathology in rats. *Journal of Comparative and Physiological Psychology, 77,* 22–30(b).

Weiss, J. M. (1971). Effects of punishing the coping response (conflict) on stress pathology in rats. *Journal of Comparative and Physiological Psychology, 77,* 14–21(c).

Weiss, J. M., Glazer, H. I., & Pohorecky, L. A. (1976). Coping behavior and neurochemical changes: An alternative explanation for the original "learned helplessness" experiments. In G. Serban and A. Kling (Eds.), *Relevance of the animal model to the human.* New York: Plenum Press, pp. 141–173.

Weiss, J. M., Stone, E. A., & Harrell, N. (1970). Coping behavior and brain norepinephrine level in rats. *Journal of Comparative and Physiological Psychology, 72*(1), 153–160.

Weissman, M. M., & Paykel, S. (1974). *The depressed women: A study of social relationships.* Chicago: University of Chicago Press.

Wells, C. E. (1978). Role of stroke in dementia. *Stroke, 9,* 1–3.

Welti, C. V., & Wright, R. K. (1979). Deaths caused by recreational cocaine use. *Journal of the American Medical Association, 241,* 2519–2522.

Wender, P. H. (1971). *Minimal brain dysfunction in children.* New York: John Wiley & Sons.

Wender, P. H., Rosenthal, D., Kety, S. S., Schulsinger, F., & Weiner, J. (1973). Social class and psychopathology in adoptees: A natural experimental method for separating the roles of genetic and experiential factors. *Archives of General Psychiatry, 28,* 318–325.

Wender, P. H., Rosenthal, D., Kety, S. S., Schulsinger, F., & Weiner, J. (1974). Crossfostering: A research strategy for clarifying the role of genetic and experiential factors in the etiology of schizophrenia. *Archives of General Psychiatry, 30,* 121–128.

Werry, J. S. (1968). Studies on the hyperactive child IV: An empirical analysis of the minimal brain dysfunction syndrome. *Archives of General Psychiatry, 19,* 9–16.

Werry, J. S., & Quay, H. (1971). The prevalence of behavior symptoms in younger elementary school children. *American Journal of Orthopsychiatry, 41,* 136–143.

West, D. J., & Farrington, D. P. (1973). *Who becomes delinquent?* London: Heinemann.

Whitehead, W. E., & Bosmajian, L. S. (1982). Behavioral medicine approaches to gastrointestinal disorders. *Journal of Consulting and Clinical Psychology, 50,* 972–983.

Whitehead, W. E., & Schuster, M. M. (1982). The treatment of functional gastrointestinal disorders. In R. L. Gallon (Ed.), *The psychosomatic approach to illness.* New York: Elsevier Biomedical.

Whitehorn, J. C. (1951). *Psychodynamic considerations in the treatment of psychotic patients.* London, Ontario: University of Western Ontario Press.

Whittington, F. J. (1983). Misuse of legal drugs and compliance with prescription directions. In M. D. Glantz, D. M. Petersen, & F. J. Whittington (Eds.), *Drugs and the elderly adult* (DHHS Publication No. ADM 83-1269, pp. 63–69). Washington, DC: U.S. Government Printing Office.

Wilkins, W. (1971). Desensitization: Social and cognitive factors underlying the effectiveness of Wolpe's procedure. *Psychological Bulletin, 76,* 311–317.

Will, O. A. (1970). Analytic etiology: A primer. In J. O. Cole & L. E. Hollister (Eds.), *Schizophrenia.* New York: MEDCOM.

Williams, C. C. (1983). The mental foxhole: The Viet Nam veterans' search for meaning. *American Journal of Orthopsychiatry, 53*(1), 4–17.

Wilson, G. T. (1977). Alcohol and human sexual behavior. *Behaviour Research and Therapy, 15,* 239–252.

Wilson, G. T. (1980). Toward specifying the "nonspecific" factors in behavior therapy: A social learning analysis. In M. J. Mahoney (Ed.), *Psychotherapy Process.* New York: Plenum.

Wilson, G. T., & Evans, I. M. (1978). The therapist-client relationship in behavior therapy. In A. S. Gurman & A. M. Razin (Eds.), *Effective psychotherapy:*

A handbook of research. New York: Pergamon Press.

Wilson, G. T., & Lawson, D. M. (1976). Expectancies, alcohol and sexual arousal in male social drinkers. *Journal of Abnormal Psychology, 85,* 587–594.

Wilson, G. T., & Lawson, D. M. (1978). Expectancies, alcohol, and sexual arousal in women. *Journal of Abnormal Psychology, 87,* 358–367.

Wilson, G. T., & Lazarus, A. A. (1983). Behavior modification and therapy. In B. Wolman (Ed.), *The therapist's handbook.* New York: Van Nostrand.

Wilson, G. T., & O'Leary, K. D. (1980). *Principles of behavior therapy.* Englewood Cliffs, NJ: Prentice-Hall.

Wing, L. (1976). Epidemiology and theories of aetiology. In L. Wing (Ed.), *Early childhood autism (2d ed.).* New York: Pergamon Press.

Winnicott, D. (1958). *Collected papers—Through pediatrics to psycho-analysis.* New York: Basic Books.

Winokur, G. (1973). Genetic aspects of depression. In J. P. Scott and E. C. Senay (Eds.), *Separation and depression: Clinical and research aspects.* Washington, D.C.: American Association for the Advancement of Science.

Winokur, G., & Clayton, P. (1967). Family history studies: I. Two types of affective disorders separated according to genetic and clinical factors. In *Recent Advances in Biological Psychiatry, 9.* New York: Plenum Press.

Witters, W. L., & Jones-Witters, P. (1975). *Drugs & sex.* New York: Macmillan.

Wohlberg, G. W., & Kornetsky, C. (1973). Sustained attention in remitted schizophrenics. *Archives of General Psychiatry, 28,* 533–537.

Wolff, H. G. (1963). *Headache and other head pain.* New York: Oxford University Press.

Wolff, S., & Chess, S. (1973). An analysis of the language of fourteen schizophrenic children. *Journal of Child Psychology and Psychiatry, 6,* 29.

Wolfgang, M. E., Figlio, R. M., & Sellin, T. (1972). *Delinquency in a birth cohort.* Chicago: University of Chicago Press.

Wolman, B. B. (1970). *Children without childhood.* New York: Grune & Stratton.

Wolpe, J. (1958). *Psychotherapy by reciprocal inhibition.* Stanford, CA: Stanford University Press.

Wolpe, J. (1981). Reciprocal inhibition and therapeutic change. *Journal of Behavior Therapy and Experimental Psychiatry, 12.*

Wolpe, J., & Rachman, S. (1960). Psychoanalytic "evidence": A critique based on Freud's case of Little Hans. *Journal of Nervous and Mental Diseases, 130,* 135–148.

Wood, W. G. (1978). The elderly alcoholic: Some diagnostic problems and considerations. In M. Storandt, I. C. Siegler, & M. F. Elias (Eds.), *The clinical psychology of aging* (pp. 97–113). New York: Plenum Press.

Woolsey, R. M. (1976). Hysteria: 1875 to 1975. *Diseases of the Nervous System, 37,* 379–386.

World Health Organization. (1952). *Expert Committee on Mental Health. Alcoholism Subcommittee: second report.* (WHO Tech. Rep. Ser., No. 48.) Geneva, 1952. (No. 5543).

Wortman, C. B. & Dintzer, L. (1978). Is an attributional analysis of the learned helplessness phenomenon viable?: A criticque of the Abramson-Seligman-Teasdale reformulation. *Journal of Abnormal Psychology, 87,* 75–90.

Wynne, L. C. (1970). Communication disorders and the quest for relatedness in families of schizophrenics. *American Journal of Psychoanalysis. 30,* 100–114.

Yalom, D. (1960). Aggression and forbiddenness in voyeurism. *Archives of General Psychiatry, 3,* 305–319.

Yalom, I. (1975). *The theory and practice of group psychotherapy.* New York: Basic Books.

Yalom, I. D., & Lieberman, M. A. (1971). A study of encounter group casualties. *Archives of General Psychiatry, 25,* 16–30.

Yates, A. J. (1970). *Behavior therapy.* New York: John Wiley & Sons.

Yudofsky, S. C. (1982). Electroconvulsive therapy in the eighties: Technique and technologies. *American Journal of Psychotherapy, 36,* 391–398.

Zarit, S. H. (1979). Helping an aging patient to cope with memory problems. *Geriatrics, 34*(4), 82–90.

Zarit, S. H. (1980). *Aging and mental disorders.* New York: Free Press.

Zax, M., & Cowen, L. (1972). *Abnormal Psychology: Changing conceptions* (2d ed.). New York: Holt, Rinehart & Winston.

Zetner, J. L. (1976). The recreational use of LSD-25 and drug prohibition. *Journal of Psychedelic Drugs, 8,* 299–305.

Zigler, E., & Phillips, L. (1961). Psychiatric diagnosis and symptomatology. *Journal of Abnormal and Social Psychology, 63,* 69–75.

Zilbergeld, B., & Evans, M. (1980). The inadequacy of Masters and Johnson. *Psychology Today, 14,* 29–43.

Zubin, J. (1984). Ink blots do not a test make. *Contemporary Psychology, 29*(2), 153–154.

Zubin, J., Eron, L. D., & Schumer, F. (1965). *An experimental approach to projective techniques.* New York: John Wiley & Sons.

Zubin, J., Salzinger, K., Fleiss, J. L., Gurland, B., Spitzer, R. L., Endicott, J., & Sutton, S. (1975). Biometric approach to psychopathology: Abnormal and clinical psychology—statistical, epidemiological, and diagnostic approaches. In M. R. Rosenzweig and L. W. Porter (Eds.), *Annual Review of Psychology*, 647.

Zubin, J., & Spring, B. (1977). Vulnerability: A new view of schizophrenia. *Journal of Abnormal Psychology*, 103–126.

Zuckerman, K., Ambuel, J., & Bandman, R. (1972). Child neglect and abuse: A study of cases evaluated at Children's Hospital in 1968–1969. *Ohio State Medical Journal, 68*, 629–632.

Name Index

Abelson, R. P., 100
Abrams, N., 288
Abramson, L. Y., 200, 207-8
Adamapoulous, P. A., 427
Adams, H. E., 418
Adesso, V. J., 452
Adler, A., 495
Agras, S., 144
Aguilera, D., 210-11
Akiskal, H. S., 194
Albee, G. W., 560
Albelin,. T., 459
Alexander, B. K., 479, 480
Alexander, F., 157, 538
Alford, G. S., 455
Allen, B. A., 446
Allen, K. E., 76
Allen, R., 450
Allport, G., 510
Althof, S. E., 409
Ambuel, J., 275
Andrasik, F., 136, 138, 141, 150
Andrews, 512
Anglin, M. D., 468
Annon, J. S., 435
Anthony, E. J., 270
Appel, M. A., 144, 150
Arieti, S., 243
Armor, D. J., 450
Arnkoff, D., 536
Aronow, E., 91, 92
Artemyeff, C., 275
Asher, J., 196-97
Auerback, R. R., 437
Ayllon, T., 48, 273

Babigan, H. M., 290
Bachman, J. G., 461, 471, 474
Bacon, 448
Bakal, D. A., 139
Baker, A., 282-83
Baker, E., 495, 501
Baker, T. B., 531
Bakwin, H., 264
Bakwin, R. M., 264
Baldessarini, R. J., 589, 590-92
Ball, J. C., 467
Balson, P. M., 271

Balster, R. L., 470
Bandman, R., 275
Bandura, A., 50-51, 523-24, 533, 538
Barber, B., 80-81
Barber, T. X., 131, 154, 464
Bard, M., 560
Barrett, C. L., 266-67
Barrett, J., 460
Basmajian, L. S., 151, 152
Bassuk, E. L., 564
Bates, L. O., 187-88
Bateson, G., 243
Bauer, 275
Baum, 132
Baum, M., 120
Baumeister, A. A., 282
Baumgold, J., 167, 169
Beach, F. A., 404, 417
Beatrice, J., 409
Beck, A. T., 194, 198-201, 207-8, 212,
    215, 534, 536, 588
Beck, S. J., 91
Becker, C. E., 455
Bednar, R. L., 552, 553
Beecher, M. K., 479
Beidel, D. C., 172
Bell, A., 422-25, 427
Belliveau, F., 431
Bellman, M., 270
Belmaker, R. H., 589
Bemis, K., 290, 291
Bender, L., 283-84
Benjamin, H., 406
Bennett, C., 444
Benson, H., 144
Bentler, P., 406, 408, 415
Berberian, R. M., 463
Berg, I., 268
Bergin, A. E., 511
Bergmann, A., 45
Berkman, L. M., 123
Berman, J. S., 536
Bernard, J., 189
Bernstein, J. G., 585
Bertelson, A. D., 102
Bettelheim, B., 50, 280
Bieber, I., 426
Biederman, J., 589
Biernacki, P., 480
Birch, J., 147

Birley, J. L. T., 253-54
Blackwell, B., 586, 588
Blaine, J. D., 586
Blake, P., 282
Blanchard, E. B., 524
Blanchard, R., 408, 409
Blashfield, R. K., 103, l05-7, 228
Block, D., 554
Bloom, B., 559-60
Bloom, B. L., 567
Bloomfield, J. M., 269
Blum & Associates, 476
Blume, 449
Boch, G., 552
Boekelheide, P. D., 276
Bonse, K., 470
Bonvillian, J., 282
Bootzin, R., 533
Borer, J. S., 290
Borkovec, T. D., 517
Boudewyns, P. A., 530
Bower, E. M., 568
Bowers, K. S., 29
Bowlby, J., 261-62, 554
Braden, W., 589
Braiker, H. B., 450
Branch, L. G., 460
Brandsma, J. M., 455
Brenner, M. H., 72, 245
Bressler, D. E., 153
Breuer, J., 500
Brodsky, A., 443
Brody, J. E., 211, 424
Brooks, G. R., 152
Broverman, D. M., 101
Broverman, I. K., 101
Brown, G. W., 253-54
Bruch, H., 3, 290-91
Buchanan, P. C., 548-49
Buchsbaum, S., 237, 238, 252
Buchwald, A. M., 53
Bucklew, J., 171
Buell, J. S., 76
Bushbaum, 241
Buss, T. F., 116

Caddy, G. R., 448
Caffey, E., 584

Cahalan, D., 448, 478
Caille, G., 589
Cameron, N., 168, 195
Cameron, R., 126, 536
Campbell, J., 496–97
Cannon, D. S., 531
Cantor, P., 264
Cantwell, D. P., 264, 273
Caplan, G., 565, 566, 569–70
Caplan, R., 22
Caporael, L. R., 15
Carlen, P. L., 472
Carlisle, J. M., 418
Carlson, G. A., 264
Carlson, R., 288
Carpenter, N. J., 228
Carr, A. T., 172
Carraci, G., 473
Carter, C. H., 172
Carver, C. S., 198
Cassel, S., 568
Cassell, J., 161
Catalano, R., 73
Cautela, J. R., 456, 519, 531
Chamberlain, K., 210
Chambers, C., 29
Chambless, D., 51–52, 167–69, 522
Chance, P., 282
Chapman, J., 99–100, 231–32
Chapman, L., 99–100
Charney, D. S., 589
Chassin, L., 459
Chesney, M. A., 142
Chess, S., 267
Chiodo, J., 292
Choron, J., 210, 211
Christenson, C. V., 412, 413
Christophersen, E. R., 269
Cisin, I. H., 478
Clarkson, F. E., 101
Clayton, P., 197–98
Cleary, P. JD., 458, 459
Cleckley, H., 178
Clemmensen, L. H., 409
Clum, G. A., 215
Coan, R. W., 459, 460
Cobb, S., 123
Coché, E. B., 552, 553
Coggins, W. J., 462–63
Cohen, H. L., 288
Cohen, J. B., 122
Cohen, J. D., 146, 147
Cohen, W., 251
Cole, J. O., 250, 584
Collins, G., 181
Comitas, L., 462
Connors, C. K., 272
Cooper, J. R., 476
Cooper, P. J., 293
Coote, M. A., 268
Cornsweet, C., 490, 538
Cory, D. W., 422
Cotton, N. S., 480, 481
Cournoyer, G., 589
Cowen, E. L., 570, 571
Cowen, I., 11, 24
Coyne, J. C., 113, 162, 201–4

Craighead, L. W., 536
Crane, G. E., 584
Creer, T. L., 147–50
Cressler, D. L., 562–63
Cristol, A. H., 516, 537
Critchley, M., 278
Crossley, H. M., 478
Crow, 228, 240, 241
Cummings, C., 456–57
Cummins, C., 288
Cunningham, J., 409
Cunningham, M., 522, 523
Cytryn, L., 262, 263

Dally, 291
D'Aunno, T., 71
Davidson, W. S., 288
Davis, B. L., 472–73
Davis, J., 593
Davis, W. E., 102
Davisco, G. C., 518–19
Davison, L., 96
Dawber, T. R., 145
Dawson, E. B., 588
DeBlois, C. S., 288
Defazio, V., 118
Deffenbacher, J. L., 519, 521
DeLeon, G., 269
DeLozier, J. E., 136
DeLuca, J. R., 449
Dembroski, T., 146
De Montigny, C., 589
DeMyer, M. K., 280
Denber, H. C. B., 585, 598
Denckle, M. B., 277
Denner, B., 560, 562, 573
Denner, D. W., 249
DePiano, F. A., 29
Deutsch, H., 115
Devany, J., 282
DeWit, H., 479
Diamond, A., 118
Diamond, E. L., 143, 147
Dienalt, M., 194
Dies, R. R., 552, 553
Dilavou, 230
DiLoretto, A. O., 537
Dole, V., 468
Doleys, D. M., 268–70
Dollinger, S. J., 277
Donald, 240
Donaldson, S. R., 589–90
Donegan, N. H., 443, 446
Dooley, D., 73
Douglas, J. W. B., 269
Dove, G. A., 427
Draguns, J. G., 103
Droegenmueller, W., 274
Dunham, H. JW., 244–46
DuPont, R. L., 467

Ebert, M. H., 290
Eckardt, M. J., 449
Edinberg, G., 86

Egendorf, A., 118
Eikelbloom, R., 479
Einbender, 275
Eisler, R. M., 479
Ellis, A., 533–36
Emery, G., 536
Emmelkamp, P. M. G., 169–72, 180–81
Endicott, J., 87–89, 98
Engebretson, T. O., 144
Epstein, C. J., 124–25
Epstein, S., 112
Erdman, H. P., 96, 98
Erickson, E., 501
Erickson, M. T., 287
Erikson, K. T., 111, 119
Eron, L. D., 91–93, 288
Etzione, A., 468
Evans, M., 437
Exline, 285
Eysenck, H. J., 511

Fagen, J., 505
Fairburn, C. G., 293
Fairweather, G. W., 562–64
Falloon, I. R. H., 593
Farberow, N. L., 212, 213
Faris, R. E. L., 244
Farkas, G. M., 539
Farley, J., 118
Farrington, D. P., 288
Feingold, B., 272
Feinleib, M., 146
Feldman, H. W., 472
Feldman, J. J., 8
Fields, S., 563, 564
Fieve, R. R., 190–91, 205, 589
Figlio, R. M., 287
Filipczak, J., 288
Fink, E. B., 589
Fink, M., 206, 581, 594
Finkelstein, W., 152
Finkle, B. S., 470
Finney, J. W., 455
Fisher, E. B., 146, 147
Fisher, V., 117–18
Fishman, 170–71
Fixsen, D. L., 529
Flaherty, J. A., 591
Flamer, R., 450
Fled, S. C., 559
Fleischman, D. J. A., 530
Flueck, J. A., 467
Folkman, 113
Ford, C. S., 404, 417
Ford, F., 555–57
Fordyce, W. E., 153
Forman, J. B. W., 105
Foster, S. W., 555, 557–58
Foucault, M., 18
Fox, M. M., 290
Fox, R. E., 489, 491
Frank, J. D., 490, 538, 540
Frankl, V. E., 501, 508–9
Frauman, D. C., 285, 544
French, T., 538

Freud, A., 501
Freud, S., 18, 29–31, 39–46, 91, 111–12, 115, 166, 169, 193–94, 426, 471, 488, 490–96, 498, 500, 558
Friedman, J., 434
Friedman, M., 145
Friedrich, 275
Frommer, E. H., 264
Funderburk, F., 450

Gagnon, J. H., 412, 413, 434
Gagnon, R. O., 136
Ganellen, R. J., 198
Ganguli, 240
Gardiner, R., 593
Gardos, G., 584
Garey, R. E., 472
Garfield, S. L., 488, 489, 534, 539
Garfinkel, 291
Garner, 291
Garske, J. P., 487–88, 500, 512, 503, 534, 537–40
Gatchel, 132
Gebhard, P. H., 410–13, 417, 422, 427, 433
Gelenberg, A. J., 587
George, L. K., 436
Gerstein, 443
Gibbons, D. C., 288
Gibbs, L. M., 120
Gill, M. M., 41
Ginnott, H. G., 285
Ginzburg, H. M., 469
Gittelman, R., 273
Gittelman-Klein, R., 264
Gittleman, R., 586
Glass, D., 146
Glass, G. V., 78–80, 511–12, 537, 593
Gleser, G. C., 120
Gochfeld, L., 585–85
Goeckner, 452
Goffman, E., 53–54
Goldberg, S. C., 252–53
Goldbourt, U., 143
Golden, N., 289, 290
Goldenberg, H., 567
Goldfried, M. R., 213, 291, 518–19, 538, 540
Goldman, M., 449–50
Goldstein, 481
Goldstein, A., 51–52, 469, 522
Goldstein, J. B., 142–44
Goodwin, D. W., 119, 480–81
Gordon, J. R., 450, 456–57
Gottdiener, J. S., 290
Gottesman, I. I., 236, 237
Gottheil, E., 471–73
Gottlieb, B. H., 123
Gottlieb, J., 15
Gottman, J. M., 555
Gould, L. C., 463
Gove, W. R., 57
Graham, P. J., 260
Grant, V. W., 410
Gray, G., 444

Green, B. L., 120
Green, H., 407–8
Griest, J. H., 96, 98
Grof, S., 464
Gross, H. A., 290
Grossman, 228
Gunderson, A., 237, 238, 252
Gunderson, J. G., 583
Guntrip, H., 554
Gurin, G., 559
Gurman, A. S., 491, 555, 557–58
Gynther, M. D., 102

Hackett, T. P., 582, 582
Hadaway, 479, 480
Haberle, E. J., 404, 408, 422
Haley, J., 243
Halpern, W., 264
Halvorson, P. A., 289, 293
Hampe, E., 266–67
Hanson, R., 275
Haracz, 238
Harlow, H. F., 75, 195–96
Harlow, M. K., 195–96
Harris, F. R., 76
Harrow, 228
Hartford, 448–49
Hartmann, H., 501
Harvey, 512
Harvey, J. H., 200–201
Hassibi, M., 267
Hathaway, S. R., 88
Haughton, E., 48
Haynes, R. B., 144
Haynes, S. N., 146
Hazelton, L., 194
Heaton, R. K., 96
Heiman, J. R., 437
Helfer, R. E., 275
Heller, K., 567, 568, 570, 571
Hendin, H., 477
Henninger, G. R., 589
Henry, W., 93
Henry, W. L., 290
Hersen, M., 277, 593
Herzog, D. B., 264
Hester, R. K., 453, 455, 456
Hiatt, B., 205
Hilgard, E. R., 25–27
Hiller, R. R. J., 122, 161
Hingtgen, J. N., 280, 282
Ho, C., 589
Hodgson, R. J., 523
Hogan, D. R., 431, 437
Hogarty, G. E., 252–53, 583
Hollingshead, A. B., 244–46
Hollman, 148
Hollon, 207
Holm, J. E., 141
Holmes, T. H., 160
Holroyd, K., 113, 162
Holroyd, K. A., 136, 138, 141, 150, 536
Holzman, P. S., 40–41
Hook, S., 46
Hoppe, C. M., 287

Houston, B., 146
Howard, G. S., 588
Hsu, L., 291
Hudson, J. I., 292
Hull, D. B., 527
Humphreys, L., 422
Hunt, B., 76
Hunt, W. A., 460
Hunter, 230
Hursey, K. G., 141
Husemann, L. R., 288
Hutton, H. E., 290
Hyman, M. M., 450

Inber, S., 450
Inwald, C., 282
Ismael, A. A., 427
Isselbacher, K. J., 152
Izen, J. E., 583

Jackson, D. D., 243
Jackson, R. K., 280
Jacob, M. S., 472
Jacob, R., 144
Jacob, T., 243
Jacobi, J., 497
Jacobs, G. A., 161
Jacobson, E., 518
Jacobson, L. I., 520
Jaffe, J. H., 444, 476
Janeway, E., 14, 16
Jaremko, 126, 127
Jarvik, M. E., 458
Jeans, R. F. I., 178–79
Jefferson, J. W., 96, 98
Jeffrey, C. R., 287
Jeffrey, I. A., 287
Jessor, R., 444
Jessor, S. L., 444
Johanson, C. C., 470
Johnson, 427–28
Johnson, C., 291
Johnson, L., 206
Johnson, L. S., 28
Johnson, V. E., 427–34, 436–37
Johnson, W. L., 282
Johnston, L. D., 461, 471, 474
Jones, B. M., 450
Jones, D. J., 290
Jones, E., 493
Jones, M. B., 288
Jones, R. T., 463
Judson, B. A., 469
Julien, R. M., 458, 459, 466, 481
Jung, C. G., 492, 495–98

Kahn, H. A., 143
Kahn, J. H., 266–67
Kahn, S., 161
Kalinowsky, L., 598
Kallman, F. J., 427

Kandel, D. B., 443, 461, 478
Kane, J. M., 584, 585–86
Kanfer, F. H., 532
Kannel, W. B., 146
Kanner, L., 279, 281
Kantor, R. E., 229
Kaplan, B. H., 161
Kaplan, H. S., 429, 431–33
Kaplan, S., 275
Karon, 593
Kashani, J., 262
Kasi, S. V., 463
Katchadourian, H. A., 433
Kaufman, E., 444
Kaul, T. J., 552, 553
Kazdin, A. E., 76, 520, 528, 529, 537
Keith, S. J., 237, 238, 252
Keller, A. C., 409
Kelson, W., 86
Kempe, C. H., 274
Kendler, 234–35
Kennedy, W. A., 267–68
Kern, J. M., 573, 592
Kernberg, 500
Kernberg, O., 501
Kerosotes, D., 273
Kessler, R., 113
Kessler, R. C., 102
Kessler, S., 232–33
Ketty, S. S., 196
Kety, S. S., 237
Keyt, S. S., 235–36
Khantzian, E. J., 477
Kilmann, P. R., 437, 594
Kilpatrick, D. G., 120, 127
Kinney, J., 449, 450, 478
Kinsey, A. C., 421–22, 427, 433
Kirmil-Gray, 149–50
Kirschenbaum, D. S., 293
Kisker, G. W., 177
Kissel, S., 264
Kleber, H. D., 463
Klein, D. F., 264, 586
Klein, M., 181
Klerman, G. L., 583
Kline, N. S., 584
Kline, R. B., 90
Klotter, J., 477
Knopf, I. J., 277
Kobasa, S. C., 113, 122, 161
Koegel, R. L., 282
Koelle, G. B., 458–59
Koenig, P., 564
Kohn, M. L., 246
Kohut, H., 501
Kolata, G. B., 536
Kolb, L. S., 427
Kolodny, R. C., 436, 437
Korchin, S. K., 549
Kornetsky, C., 230
Kovacs, M., 207, 215
Kozlowski, L. T., 460
Kraft, I. A., 285, 286
Krasner, L., 243
Kratochwill, T. R., 265
Kroger, W. S., 28–29
Kuhn, T. S., 34

Kurland, A. A., 464
Kurtz, J. P., 539
Kurtz, R., 534
Kushner, M., 529

Lachmann, S. J., 158
Lafler, 172
Lambert, M. J., 511
Lang, A. R., 443, 444, 446, 446, 478
Lang, P. E., 519
Langer, E. J., 100
Langlois, R., 589
Langs, R. J., 464
Lans, 452
LaPerière, K., 554
Lapouse, R., 271
Latimer, P. R., 292
Lazarus, 113
Lazarus, A. A., 28, 522, 539
Lazarus, R. S., 122
Leaton, G., 449, 450, 478
Leff, J. P., 254–55
Lefkowitz, M. M., 288
Leitenberg, H., 519
LeLong, 468
Lentz, 526
Lentz, R. J., 562
Lerner, Y., 589
LeRoy, J. P., 422
Leslie, S. A., 260
Lesser, K., 489, 491
Levenkron, J. C., 146, 147
Leventhal, H., 459, 560
Levine, 586
Levine, A. G., 120
Levine, B., 544
Levine, S., 146
Levinson, R., 477–78
Levis, D. J., 521
Levison, D. R., 443
Levitsky, F., 507
Levitt, E. E., 416
Lewin, K., 548
Lewiwnsohn, P. M., 208
Liberman, R. P., 208–10, 593
Lick, J., 520
Lidsky, T. I., 573, 592
Lieberman, M. A., 112, 469, 543, 544, 549, 553
Lieberman, R. P., 593
Liebman, R., 557
Liebowitz, E., 575
Linton, H. B., 464
Lipinski, J. F., 228
Lipsedge, M. S., 593
Litman, R. E., 212, 213
Little, R. E., 449
LoPiccolo, J., 434, 435, 437
Loraine, J. A., 427
Lord, C., 280
Lothstein, L. M., 409
Lovass, O. I., 282
Lovibond, S. H., 268
Lucas, A. R., 289
Ludolph, P., 179

Luisada, P. V., 473
Lukianowicz, N., 276
Lunde, D., 576
Lunde, D. T., 433
Luria, Z., 178–79
Luscomb, R. L., 215
Lustman, P. J., 588
Lynn, S. J., 285, 487–88, 512, 537–40, 544
Lyons, R. D., 458

McClelland, D. C., 143
McClosky, K. L., 470
McCord, J., 288
McCord, W., 288
MacDonald, M. L., 573, 583, 592
MacDougall, J., 146
McFaddon, E. R., Jr., 148
McGanity, W. J., 588
McGee, R. K., 565–66
McGlothlin, 468
McGuire, R., 418
McKee, E., 409
McKinley, J. C., 88
McKinney, W. T., 194
MacKinnon, C. A., 169, 180
McKnew, D. H., 262, 263
McNamara, J. R., 516–17, 539, 575
McNaught, B., 420
McPeak, W. R., 557
McWhorter, W. L., 413
Maddi, S. R., 113, 122, 161, 507, 509–10
Maher, B., 157, 232
Maher, B. A., 150
Mahler, M., 45
Mahoney, M. J., 532, 536
Maistra, M. A., 456
Maletsky, B. M., 418, 477
Maloff, D., 443, 478
Maloff, D. R., 443
Maltsman, I. M., 457
Mandell, W., 269
Mandels, J., 191–92
Mann, 500
Mann, G. L., 145
Margolese, M., 427
Marks, I., 520
Marks, I. M., 170, 180, 265, 593
Marks, P. A., 88–90, 102
Marlatt, G. A., 450, 452, 456–57, 479
Marmor, J., 426–27
Marmot, M. G., 144–45, 144–45
Marshman, J. A., 472
Martin, C. E., 422, 427, 433
Maslow, A. H., 58–61
Masters, J. C., 180, 517, 518, 523, 525–27, 532
Masters, W. H., 419, 422, 427–34, 436–37
Masuda, M., 160
Mathis, J. L., 414
Mattes, J. A., 273
Mattson, M. E., 144
Maultsby, M. C., 455
Maxwell, S. E., 588

May, G. D., 102
May, P. R. A., 252
Mayer, J., 268
Mayer, W., 448, 449
Mayer-Gross, W., 222
Maynard, H., 562-63
Meador, B. D., 504
Mechanic, D., 112
Medalie, J. H., 143
Mednick, S. A., 77-78, 244
Meehl, P. E., 248
Meichenbaum, D., 51-52, 126, 533-36
Mello, N., 444
Meltzer, 228, 238
Melzack, R., 154, 155
Mendels, J., 204
Menninger, K., 495
Mesibov, G., 282-83
Messer, S. B., 539
Messick, J. M., 210-11
Meyer, N. G., 260
Meyer, V., 171
Meyers, J. K., 8, 71
Michels, R., 169, 180
Mielke, D., 590
Migone, P., 473
Miles, M. B., 553
Miller, 442
Miller, C. R., 536
Miller, E., 479
Miller, J. L., 446
Miller, L. C., 266-67
Miller, N. E., 141
Miller, P. M., 456, 479
Miller, W. R., 446, 448, 450, 453, 455-57
Milofsky, 450, 454, 455, 478
Mintz, E., 547-48
Minuchin, S., 557
Mirsky, J. A., 152
Molteni, A. L., 500
Monahan, J., 567, 568, 570, 571, 574
Monk, M. A., 271
Monroe, 494
Moore, F. E., 145
Moore, R., 452
Moore, T. D., 588
Moos, 456
Moos, R. H., 455
Morissette, R., 589
Morris, J. B., 588
Morris, R. J., 265
Morrison, J. R., 273
Mosher, L. R., 237, 238, 252, 583
Moss, T., 282
Moura, N. G., 532
Mueller, H. S., 146, 147
Mukherjee, S., 473
Murphy, G. E., 588
Murray, E. J., 520, 538, 539
Murray, J. J., 469
Muschenheim, 148
Myers, 522
Myers, J., 194

Nagi, S. Z., 153
Narstein, J. P., 266-67

Nash, M., 477
Nash, M. R., 28
Nathan, P., 457-58
Nathan, P. E., 107, 480, 481
Nathan, R. S., 172
Neal, D. H., 271
Nee, J., 105
Neighbors, H. W., 102
Nelson, E. E., 282
Nelson, R. O., 536
Neuman, P. A., 289, 293
Neville, R., 597
Newby, L. J., 153
Nicol, 236, 237
Nolan, J. D., 533
Norcross, J. C., 539
Novaco, 127
Novaco, R. W., 536
Noya, N. D., 470
Nuckolls, C. B., 161
Nufield, H. M., 143
Nurco, D. N., 467
Nyswander, M., 468

O'Brien, C. F., 442, 446
Odom, J. Y., 536
Offord, D. R., 288
O'Leary, K. D., 519, 520, 530, 532, 536
Ollendick, T. H., 265, 268, 277
Olshavsky, R., 459
O'Malley, P. M., 461, 471, 474
Ordman, A. M., 293
O'Rourke, 236
Osgood, C. E., 178-79
Oswald, I., 479

Pahnke, W. N., 464
Papakumari, M., 365
Parloff, M. B., 491, 503
Parsons, O., 450
Patel, C. H., 144-45
Patsiokas, A. J., 215
Patterson, G. R., 94-95, 555
Paul, G. L., 251, 562
Paykel, E., 194
Paykel, S., 189-90
Pearlin, L. I., 112
Peele, S., 443, 479
Pegram, Y., 269
Pelletier, K. R., 133, 157
Pendery, M. L., 457
Penland, M. J., 282
Penzien, D. B., 141
Perls, F. S., 501, 505-8, 510
Peterson, R. C., 462
Petrie, K., 210
Pflanz, M., 150, 151
Phares, E. J., 490
Phillips, E. A., 529
Phillips, E. J., 529
Phillips, L., 229
Piazza, N., 290
Pierce, A., 72
Pierce, C. M., 268

Pines, F., 45
Pittner, N., 146
Pitts, F. N., 593
Pohorecky, L., 450
Polich, J. M., 450
Pomeroy, W. B., 412, 413, 422, 427, 433
Pope, H. B., 292
Pope, H. G., 228
Porter, R., 147
Pratt, S., 533
Presson, C., 459
Price, R. H., 7, 23, 34, 71, 102, 113, 120, 201, 230, 231, 249-50, 559, 560, 562, 570, 573
Prien, R., 584
Prien, R. F., 586
Prince, C., 411
Prince, M., 29
Pritchard, D. A., 102
Prochaska, J. O., 538, 539
Pronko, N. H., 176
Purcell, K., 149

Qualls, C. B., 589
Quay, H., 271
Quitkin, F., 584-85, 586

Rabin, H. M., 547
Rachman, S., 169, 533
Rachman, S. J., 523
Rackemann, F. M., 148
Rapaport, D., 41
Raphael, B., 115
Rapoff, M. A., 269
Rappaport, J., 565, 566
Raskin, D. E., 208-10
Rathburn, J. M., 264
Ray, O. S., 462, 469
Rayner, R., 47-48
Rayses, V., 481
Redburn, F. S., 116
Redlich, F. C., 244-46
Redner, R., 288
Regier, D. A., 8, 71
Reich, W., 494
Reifman, A., 237, 238, 252
Reik, T., 418
Reinharz, S., 120
Reiser, M. F., 152
Reiss, A. J., 422
Reitan, R. M., 96
Remey, A., 118
Renee, 148
Renne, 149
Resick, P. A., 120
Revicki, D., 280
Reynolds, W. M., 87
Reznekoff, 91, 92
Rhyne, M. J., 282
Rice, D. P., 8
Richardson, F. C., 152
Richman, N., 260
Richter, C. P., 199
Richter, L., 431

Riegel, K. F., 10
Rifkin, A., 584–85, 586
Riger, S., 120
Riley, L. E., 153
Rimm, D., 522, 523
Rimm, D. C., 180, 517, 518, 523, 525–27, 532
Rincover, A., 282
Riss, E., 143
Ritter, B., 524
Roback, H. B., 409
Roberge, L., 276
Robertson, 522
Robins, 480
Robins, E., 427
Robins, L. N., 8, 71, 288, 467
Rodgers, 219, 240
Rodin, J., 443, 446
Rogers, C. R., 57–61, 490–91, 501–5, 510, 551–52
Rohsenow, D. J., 452
Rollins, N., 290
Rose, S., 38
Rosen, L., 467
Rosenbaum, M., 273, 547
Rosenberg, P., 465–66
Rosenblatt, A., 102
Rosenhan, D. L., 54–56
Rosenman, R. H., 142, 145
Rosenthal, D., 36
Rosenthal, S., 235–36
Rosenthal, T. L., 50
Ross, D. M., 259, 272
Ross, S. A., 259, 272
Rossman, B., 557
Roth, M., 222
Rothman, D., 19–20, 562
Roy, A., 212–13
Rubin, V., 462
Rush, A. J., 207, 536
Russell, G., 292
Russell, G. F. M., 289
Russell, M. A. H., 460
Rustin, S., 118
Rutter, 107

Sacker, I. M., 289, 290
Sacks, J. M., 547
Sadock, B. J., 435–36
Sadock, V. A., 435–36
Saghir, M. T., 427
Salber, E. J., 459
Sales, E., 120
Salholz, E., 167–68
Salsinger, S., 275
Salzberg, H. C., 29
Salzman, S., 165, 180
Samuels, W. O., 589
Sanders, D. H., 562–63
Satir, V., 555–57
Satterfield, J. H., 287
Saucedo, C. R., 450
Savage, C., 464
Schacht, T., 107
Schachter, S., 459–60
Schaeffer, B., 282

Schaffer, 107
Schechter, M., 276
Scheff, T. J., 53–56
Schell, A. M., 287
Schildkraut, J. J., 196
Schlaadt, R. G., 452, 458, 465, 481
Schneidman, E. S., 212, 213
Schooler, N. R., 252–53
Schopler, E., 280, 282–83
Schreibman, L., 282
Schroeder, H. E., 527
Schulsinger, F., 235–36
Schultz, E., 450
Schulz, 240
Schumer, F., 91–93
Schwartz, D. M., 291
Schwartz, G. E., 156
Schwartz, J. J., 552
Schwartz, M. F., 419, 422
Schwartz, R., 552
Scotch, N., 146
Scovern, A. W., 594
Scull, A. T., 564
Scwartz, G., 141, 156
Seeman, 238
Seeman, W., 88–90
Seiden, R. H., 265
Seidman, 228
Seligman, M. E. P., 48–50, 199–201, 207–8
Sellin, T., 287
Selling, L. S., 11
Selye, H., 112, 113, 158–59
Senay, 468
Shah, 240
Shannon, P. T., 452, 458, 465, 481
Shapiro, D., 142–44, 418
Shapiro, J. L., 285, 286, 550–51
Sharm, B. P., 463
Shaw, B. F., 536
Shean, 170–71
Sheehan, D. V., 523
Sher, K., 477–78
Sher, K. J., 570
Sherman, S. J., 459
Shields, J., 236
Shontz, F. C., 470
Shore, B., 120
Shuckit, M. A., 481
Shure, M. B., 568–69
Siedman, 240, 241
Siegel, S., 480
Sifneos, 500–501
Sikorski, K., 477
Silver, H., 274
Silverman, F., 274
Silverman, P., 123
Silverstein, B., 460
Simmons, J. Q., 282
Simonds, J. F., 262
Simons, A. D., 588
Simpson, G. M., 584
Sinclair-Giebin, A. H. C., 29
Skinner, B. F., 46, 48, 49, 52–53, 172
Skinner, H. A., 446
Skynner, A. C. C. R., 554
Slade, P. D., 289
Slager-Jorné, P., 276

Slater, E., 222
Sloan, R. B., 516
Sloane, R. B., 537
Smart, R. G., 444
Smith, D., 474, 534
Smith, G. M., 479
Smith, J. M., 584
Smith, M. L., 78–80, 511–12, 537, 593
Smith, S. M., 275
Smith, S. S., 23, 249–50, 559
Smith, S. W., II, 178–79
Snellman, L., 288
Snowden, L. R., 87
Snyder, D. K., 90
Snyder, S. H., 337, 65, 221, 237, 238, 252
Sobell, M., 450
Solomon, R. L., 443, 446, 479
Solomon, S., 287–88
Somasundarum, O., 365
Sorrells, J. M., 555–57
Southam, 144
Spanos, N. P., 15
Spengler, A., 417
Sperling, M., 267
Spiegler, M., 522, 523
Spielberg, C. D., 161
Spitz, R. A., 195, 261, 262
Spitzer, R. L., 7, 87–89, 98, 104, 105
Spivak, G., 568–69
Spotts, J. V., 470
Spring, B., 247–48
Stampfl, T. G., 521
Staples, F. R., 516, 537
Stedman, J. L., 500
Steele, B., 274
Stefanson, J. G., 175
Steger, J., 153
Stein, L. I., 563–64
Steinbrueck, S. M., 588
Steiner, B. W., 409
Steinmark, W. W., 517
Stephens, 228
Sterling-Smith, R. S., 462
Sternbach, R., 153
Sternberg, D. E., 589
Stevenson, J. E., 260
Stewart, 286
Stewart, J., 479
Stewart, M. A., 273, 288
Stoffelmayr, 230
Stoller, H., 549, 552
Stoller, R. J., 406, 414–15
Stone, A. A., 573–74, 576
Strassberg, D. S., 409
Straus, 448
Strauss, J. S., 6
Stricker, G., 213
Strupp, H. H., 489, 491, 538
Stuart, R. B., 532–33
Sturgis, E. T., 171
Suh, M., 288
Suinn, R. M., 145, 146, 519, 521
Sullivan, H. S., 492, 498–99
Sundberg, N., 93, 94
Sundbeerg, N. D., 87
Suomi, 75
Swan, G. E., 142

Swift, C., 277
Syme, S. L., 123
Szasz, T. S., 39, 574

Tanna, V. L., 530
Tatlon, 522
Taubee, C. A., 260
Taylor, 144
Taylor, R., 581
Teasdale, J. D., 200, 207-8
Ten Hoor, W., 564-65
Terry, D. J., 144-45, 144-45
Test, M. A., 563-64
Thaler, M., 152
Tharp, R. G., 532, 533
Thelen, M. H., 277
Thigpen, Z. H., 178
Thompson, M. G., 291
Thompson, W. D., 463
Thoreson, 149-50
Tipton, R. D., 28
Tobias, L. L., 583
Tollison, D. C., 418
Tooley, J. T., 533
Trafford, A., 205-6
Treffert, D. A., 284
Trites, R. L., 272
Trost, F. C., 282
Trotter, A. B., 469
Tsuang, M., 219
Tucker, J., 450
Turk, 153-55
Turner, J., 564-65
Turner, R. J., 102
Turner, S. M., 172
Twentyman, 275

Ullman, L. P., 243
Ulrich, R. F., 252-53
Unger, S., 464

Valenstein, E. S., 38, 597, 598
Van Praag, H. M., 589
Vandenbos, 593
Vaughn, C. E., 254-55
Veroff, J., 559
Veronen, L. J., 120, 127
Viswanathan, R., 593

Volle, R. L., 458-59
Vucinich, R., 450

Wade, T. C., 532
Wadsworth, M., 288
Walder, L. O., 288
Waldfogel, S., 267
Waldholz, M., 205
Waldorf, D., 480
Walker, C. E., 273
Wall, P., 154, 155
Wallace, A. F. C., 6
Wallner, J. M., 229
Walsh, M. L., 277
Walters, 51
Walters, D., 412
Wandersman, A., 120
Waskow, I. E., 491
Watson, D. L., 532, 533
Watson, J. B., 47-48
Weakland, J., 243
Weary, G., 200-201
Wehl, C. K., 531
Weil, A., 441
Weiler, D., 269
Weiler, S. J., 436
Wein, K. S., 536
Weinberg, J. R., 455
Weinberg, M. S., 422-25
Weinberger, 241
Weiner, H., 152
Weiner, J. B., 213
Weinstein, S. O., 471-73
Weisman, M. M., 194
Weisman, R., 181
Weissman, A., 207, 215
Weissman, M. M., 189-90
Welsh, R. J., 455
Welti, C. V., 470
Wender, P. H., 235-36, 277
Werry, J. S., 271, 272
West, D. J., 288
West, L. J., 457
Wetzel, R. D., 588
Whipple, K., 516, 537
White, K. L., 8
Whitehead, W. E., 151, 152
Whitehorn, J. C., 490
Wilcoxin, L. A., 520
Wilkins, W., 520

Will, O., 243
Williams, C. C., 117-18
Williams, J. B. W., 7, 104
Wilson, B. D., 468
Wilson, G. T., 519, 520, 522, 530, 532, 533, 536
Wilson, T. W., 537
Winder, C. L., 229
Wing, 280
Wing, J. K., 253-54
Winget, C., 120
Winnicott, D., 501
Winokour, M., 539
Winokur, G., 197-98
Winstead, D. K., 590
Witt, 468
Witters, 466
Witters, W. L., 466
Wohlberg, G. W., 230
Wolf, M. M., 76, 529
Wolfe, B. E., 491
Wolff, H. G., 139
Wolfgang, M. E., 287
Wolman, B. B., 284
Wolpe, J., 169, 180, 517, 519
Woolsey, R. M., 174
Wortman, C., 113
Wortman, C. B., 102
Wright, R. K., 470

Yahraes, H., 262, 263
Yaliant, 450, 454, 455, 478
Yalom, I., 413, 544-46, 552
Yalom, I. D., 469, 553
Yorkston, N., 516, 537
Young, B. G., 418
Young, R. D., 53
Yudofsky, S. C., 594
Yurgelun-Todd, D., 292

Zax, M., 11, 24
Zetner, J. L., 446
Zilbergeld, 512
Zilbergeld, B., 437
Zinberg, N., 86
Zola, M. A., 161
Zubin, J., 91-93, 247-48
Zucker, 448-49
Zuckerman, K., 275

Subject Index

A-B-C theory, 534
Abnormal behavior
  defining and explaining, 4–8
  in history, 9–31
  as human problem, 8–9
  perspectives on, 34–35
Absent grief, 115
Accidental crises, 565
Acetylcholine, 349
Achievement Place, 528–29
Acne, 137
Acrophobia, 168, 169
ACTH, 197
Acute brain syndrome, 357
Acute schizophrenia, 229
Ad Hoc Committee on Classification of
  Headache, 138
Addiction; See Substance abuse
Adjustive value, 459
Adjustment disorders, 113–17
Adolescents, 260
  anorexia nervosa in, 288–91
  attention deficit disorder in, 271
  bulimia in, 291–93
  conduct disorder in, 286–88
  homosexual experiences of, 421–22
  suicide by, 211, 264
Adoption studies, 235–36, 481
Adrenalin; See Epinephrine
Adrenochrome, 65–66, 237
Affective disorders, 186; See also
  Depression
  classification of, 191–92
  and schizophrenia, 228
  treatment of, 204–10
  types of, 186–91
Affective disturbance, 222, 223
Age
  of parents, and Down's syndrome, 365
  and suicide, 211
Aggression
  and depression, 193–94
  and sadomasochism, 416
Aging; See Elderly
Agoraphobia, 167–68, 170, 522–23
Al-anon, 455
Alarm reaction, 112, 158–59
Alateen, 455
Alcohol abuse, 442, 447–48
  and controlled drinking, 457–58

Alcohol abuse—Cont.
  and depression, 188
  with drug abuse, 471, 477
  effects of, 448–53
  explanation of, 477–81
  and fetal alcohol syndrome, 367–68,
    449
  and organic brain syndromes, 357–58
  and personality type, 90
  and suicide, 210
  treatment for, 453–57
Alcohol hallucinosis, 452–53
Alcoholics Anonymous (A.A.), 453–55,
  457, 543–45, 547
Alcoholism; See Alcohol abuse
Allen, Gordon, 473–74
Alpert, Richard, 465
Alter-ego technique, 547–48
Alzheimer's disease, 332–33, 347–50,
  355–57
Ambivalence, 222
American Association on Mental
  Deficiency, 362
American Pharmaceutical Association,
  441–42
American Psychiatric Association, 581;
  See also Diagnostic and Statistical
  Manual of the American Psychiatric
  Association (DSM III)
American Psychological Association, 81
Americans View Their Mental Health
  (Gurin, Veroff, and Feld), 559
Amino acid metabolism abnormalities,
  366–67
Amnesia, 177
  and aging, 328–29
  and dementia, 346, 349, 354–55
  and ECT, 38, 206, 594
  hypnotic treatment of, 29
Amnestic syndrome, 357–58
Amniocentesis, 367, 370
Amotivational syndrome, 462
Amphetamines, 238, 463, 470, 473–75,
  582
Amplification, 496
Anaclitic depression, 195, 261
Analytic epidemiology, 71, 74
Anger
  and borderline personality, 396
  and depression, 193–94

Angina pectoris, 144
Anginal syndrome, 137
Animal magnetism, 25–27
Anorexia nervosa, 4, 288–91
Antabuse, 455
Antianxiety drugs, 590, 592
Antidepressant drugs, 586–89
  and anxiety disorders, 181
  and bulimia, 293
  and depression, 194, 196, 205, 207, 264,
    588
  and elderly, 332
  and functional enuresis, 269
  and headache, 140
  side effects of, 587, 588, 592
Antipsychotic drugs, 582–83
  and elderly, 332
  and schizophrenia, 250–53, 582–83,
    593
  side effects of, 354, 573, 583–85, 592
  treatment considerations for, 585–86
Antisocial personality, 376, 382–87, 477–
  78
Anxiety; See also Stress
  and antisocial personality, 366
  and assertion training, 524–26
  and chronic pain, 153
  and depression, 197
  in elderly, 326
  Freud on, 43
  hierarchy of, 518, 538
  phobia versus, 166
  during pregnancy, 161
  separation, 45, 107, 181, 266–68
  and sexual dysfunction, 431, 435
Anxiety disorders
  treatment of, 179–81
  types of, 166–72
Anxiety states, 170–72
Anxiolytics; See Benzodiazepines
APA Monitor, 462, 596–97
Appetitive phase, 431
Aquinas, Thomas, 404
Archeocortex, 341, 343
Arithmetic, and developmental disorder,
  278
Art therapy, 332
Arteriosclerosis
  cerebral, 355–56
  hypertensive, 356

Arteriosclerotic dementia, 355–56
Articulation, and developmental
  disorder, 279
Asclepiades, 12–13
Assertion training, 524–27, 539, 548
Association cortex, 345
Associative disturbance, 222–23, 230,
  240
Asthma, 147–48
  causes of, 148–49, 158, 159
  treatment of, 137, 149–50
Asylums, growth of, 19–23, 562
Atherosclerosis, 145
Attention, and schizophrenia, 230–32
Attention deficit disorder, 259, 271–73,
  288
Atypical depression, 588
Auditory cortex, 343
Autism
  infantile, 279–84
  in schizophrenia, 222–24
Autonomic response learning, 158
Aversion therapy, 455–56, 529–31
Avoidant personality, 376

B states, 479–80
Barbiturates, 463, 475–77, 582, 590, 592
Barnum, P. T., 98–99
Basal ganglia, 351–54
BASIC I.D., 539–40
Battered child syndrome, 274–75
Beecher, Henry, 80
Behavior rehearsal; See Role playing
Behavior therapy, 491, 515–17; See also
    Cognitive behavior therapy;
    Learning perspective
  and alcoholism, 455–58
  with elderly, 330–31
  in family therapy, 554–55
  in group therapy, 544
  and hypnosis, 28
  insight therapies versus, 536–39
  and integrative approach, 539–40
  and mental retardation, 369
  and paraphilia, 418–20
  and seizures, 360–61
  techniques of, 517–36
Behavioral medicine, 132–33
Behavioral observation, 76, 94–95
Bell, Sir Charles, 25
Bell-and-pad procedure, 270
Bender Visual-Motor Gestalt Test, 96, 97
Benzedrine, 473
Benzodiazepines, 475–76, 590
Bereavement, 114–15, 313–14
Beriberi, 357–58
Beta endorphins, 37, 481
Beyond Freedom and Dignity (Skinner),
  52–53
Bibliotherapy, 332
Biofeedback, 139, 141, 144, 533
Biological age, 301–3
Biological perspective, 35–39, 60–62; See
  also Drugs; Electroconvulsive
  therapy (ECT); Psychosurgery

Biological perspective—Cont.
  and alcoholism, 480
  and antisocial personality, 385–87
  and anxiety-related disorders, 181
  and causes of abnormal behavior, 66
  and depression, 196–98, 204–6
  and homosexuality, 427
  and neuroses, 166
  and schizophrenia, 236–41
  and stress reactions, 112
Biological preparedness, 169, 170
Bipolar disorders, 191–92, 205–6, 588–
  89, 593
Blacks
  and hypertension, 143
  and suicide, 211
  and test bias, 102
Bleuler, Eugen, 91, 221–24
Bleuler, Manfred, 224–26
Blocking, 223
Borderline personality, 376, 395–400
Bradykinesia, 353
Brain, 339
  and aging, 329
  and alcohol, 449, 450
  and biofeedback, 141
  and biological research/treatment, 37–
  38
  and depression, 196–97, 205, 206
  and drug tolerance/dependance, 481
  and ECT, 594
  and mental retardation, 367, 369
  and migraine headaches, 138–39
  minimal dysfunction of, 272
  neuropsychological assessments of
    damage to, 95–96
  and organic mental disorders, 345–61
  and organic psychoses, 219–20
  and psychosurgery, 594–97
  regions of, 339–45
  and schizophrenia, 236–41, 247
Breuer, Joseph, 29
Brief dynamic psychotherapy, 500–
  501
Broca, Paul, 35
Buffalo Creek flood, 111, 119–20
Bulimia, 43, 291–93

Cancer, 153
Cardiovascular system, 135, 137, 145
Case histories, 68–69
Catatonic schizophrenia, 221, 224, 227
Catecholamines, 196
Cathartic method, 29–30
Causes
  and perspectives, relationship
    between, 66–67
  types of, 67–68
Central Intelligence Agency (CIA), 464
Cerebral arteriosclerosis, 355–56
Cerebral cortex, 341–45, 347–50, 354–55
Cerebral laceration, 346
Cerebral spinal fluid, 339
Charcot, Jean, 29, 174
Chemotherapy; See Drugs

Child abuse, 259, 273
  causal factors in, 67–68
  physical, 273–75
  sexual, 276–77
Children, 259–61; See also Adolescents;
    Infancy
  attention deficit disorder in, 271–73
  brain injuries in, 345
  depression in, 262–64
  developmental disorders of, 275–84
  elimination disorders of, 268–71
  fears/phobias of, 264–67
  and mental retardation, 362–70
  older, disorders of, 286–93
  prevention programs for, 568–70
  seizures in, 359
  suicide by, 211, 264
Chlorpromazine, 582
Chlorthalidone, 143
Chorea; See Huntington's disease
Chromosomal abnormalities
  and homosexuality, 427
  and mental retardation, 365–66
Chronic schizophrenia, 229
Cimetidine, 152
Cirrhosis, 449
Clarification of feelings, 503–4
Classical conditioning, 47–48, 112, 120,
  169–70
Classification system(s), 103–4
  of DSM III, 104–7
Claustrophobia, 168, 169
Cleomenes, 12
Client-centered therapy, 501–5, 534, 539
Clinical interview, 86–88
Clonic stage, 359
Clonidine, 469
Closure, 506
Cocaine, 470–73
Codeine, 466
Cognitive behavior therapy, 51–52, 533–
  36
  effectiveness of, 538
  with elderly, 331
  for headache treatment, 140–41
  and integrative psychotherapy, 540
Cognitive social learning theory, 51
Cognitive theory of depression, 198–201,
  203–4, 206–7
Cognitive-expectancy model, 180–81
Collective unconscious, 496
College students, and suicide, 211
Coma, 346
Combat, stress reactions to, 117–19
Community, and mental health, 558–71
Community Mental Health Center Act,
  559
Compazine, 582
Competence to stand trial, 576
Comprehensive behavioral self-control
    training program (BSCT), 456–57
Compulsive personality, 377–79, 400
Computer-assisted assessment, 96–98
Computerized tomography, 240
Concussion, 346
Conditioning
  classical, 47–48, 112, 120, 169–70

Conditioning—*Cont.*
  instrumental, 48–50, 53
  operant, 155, 526, 531
  vicarious, 50–51
Conditions of worth, 57–58
Conduct disorder, 286–88
Confrontation procedures, 521–23
Congenital word blindness; *See* Dyslexia
Conjoint family therapy, 555–57
Conscience, 42
Conscious processes, 40
Contingency management, 532
Continuous Performance Test, 230
Control groups, 74
Controlled experiment, 74
Contusion, 345–46
Conversion disorders, 135; 136, 174–76
Convulsions, 359
Coronary heart disease (CHD), 145–47, 158
Coronary occlusion, 145
Coronary-prone behavior pattern, 146
Correlational techniques, 69
Corticatropin releasing factor (CRF), 196–97
Cortisol, 197
Covert sensitization, 456, 531
Criminality
  and antisocial personality, 382–84
  and drugs, 462, 467
  and voyeurism, 413
Crisis intervention, 565–66, 573
Cue-controlled relaxation, 519–21
Cultural relativism, 6
Cultural-familial retardation, 365
Culture
  and abnormality, 5–7
  and sexuality, 404–5
  and substance abuse, 478–79
Culture of Narcissism, The (Lasch), 391
Cyclert, 273

Dangerousness, of patient, 573–74
Death
  and bereavement, 114–15
  drug-related, 467, 470, 476–77
  likelihood of, and social support, 123–24
  smoking-related, 458
Dederich, Charles, 469
Defense mechanisms, 43–44, 46
Defensive behavior, Rogers on, 57–58
Deinstitutionalization, 251, 562–65
Delirium, 357
Delirium tremens (DTs), 452
Delusions
  and Alzheimer's disease, 349
  and delirium, 357
  and depression, 192
  and late-life paranoia, 320
  and organic delusional syndrome, 358
  and schizophrenia, 222–28, 231, 240
Dementia, 346–47
  presenile, 347–48
  pseudo-, 318, 329
  senile, 315, 318

Dementia praecox, 220
Dementing disorders
  cardiovascular, 355–57
  cortical, 347–50, 354–55
  subcortical, 350–55
Depressants, 38, 450, 466
Depression, 185
  and Alzheimer's disease, 349
  and amphetamines, 474–75
  anaclitic, 195, 261
  atypical, 588
  in bereavement, 115
  biological basis of, 37–38
  childhood, 262–64
  and chronic pain, 153
  diagnostic criteria for, 186–88
  in elderly, 304–5, 315–18, 324, 329, 331
  Harlow study of, 75
  and headaches, 139–41
  as learned helplessness, 48–50
  major, 191, 192, 263
  and suicide, 188, 204, 210
  theories of, 192–204
  treatment of, 204–10, 536, 582, 586–90, 593–96
  and women's roles, 189
Dereflection, 509
Descriptive epidemiology, 71–74
Detoxification, defined, 455
Developmental crises, 565
Developmental disorders, 275–77
  arithmetic, 278
  articulation, 279
  childhood onset pervasive, 283–84
  language, 279
  pervasive, 279–83
  reading, 277–78
Dexedrine, 273, 473
Dextroamphetamine, 273, 473
Diagnosis, 102–3
  and DSM III, 104–7
  uses of, 103–4
Diagnostic and Statistical Manual of the American Psychiatric Association (DSM III), 7, 104–7
  on abnormal sexual behavior, 404–6, 410, 411, 415, 416
  on adjustment disorders, 114
  affective disorders classification of, 191
  on anorexia nervosa, 289–90
  on anxiety disorders, 166, 168, 170
  on attention deficit disorder, 271–72
  on bulimia, 292
  childhood disorders classification of, 260
  on conduct disorders, 287
  on depression, 187, 188, 192, 262–63
  on developmental disorders, 277, 283
  on dissociative disorders, 175, 177
  on elimination disorders, 268, 270
  on homosexuality, 405, 420–21, 426
  on intoxication, 358
  on manic episodes, 190
  on mental retardation, 362–63
  and neuroses, 165, 166

Diagnostic and Statistical Manual of the American Psychiatric Association (DSM III)—*Cont.*
  on organic mental disorders, 338–39, 346
  on personality disorders, 375–77, 382–84, 392, 394
  on posttraumatic stress disorders, 117
  and psychophysiological disorders, 135
  on schizophrenia, 227–28
  on school phobia/separation anxiety disorder, 266
  on sexual function/dysfunction, 430, 432, 433
  on somatization disorders, 173
  on substance abuse, 445–46
Diagnostic Interview for Borderlines (DIB), 400
Diagnostic Interview Schedule, 71
Diet, 6, 143, 272
Direct sexual therapies, 434–36
Direct transmission model of pain, 153, 154
Disease; *See also* Psychophysiological disorders
  and aging, 303–4, 312–13
  and hypnosis, 29
  and stress, 122–33, 133
  and substance abuse, 449–50, 458, 463, 465, 467, 470
Displacement, 44
Disregulation theory, 141, 156
Dissociative disorders
  treatment of, 179–81
  types of, 175–79
Disulfiram, 455
Divorce, 263
Dix, Dorothea, 20
Dopamine, 37, 196, 237–41, 247, 353–54, 585
Down's syndrome, 349, 365
Draw-a-Person test (DAP), 99
Dreams
  analysis of, 492–93, 496–97, 507–8
  and stress, 111–12
Driving, and marijuana use, 462
Drug abuse; *See* Substance abuse
Drugs; *See also* Antidepressant drugs; Antipsychotic drugs
  antianxiety, 590, 592
  antiepileptic, 360
  for asthma treatment, 150
  for elderly, 332
  ethics of administering, 573
  with fear-reduction techniques, 523
  for headache treatment, 139–40
  and hyperactivity, 273
  for hypertension treatment, 143–44, 350
  illegal, 460–73
  prescription, 473–77
  social, 442, 447–60
  for ulcer treatment, 152
  value/limitations of, as treatment, 590–93

DSM III; *See Diagnostic and Statistical Manual of the American Psychiatric Association* (DSM III)
Duodenal ulcers; *See* Ulcers
Durham rule, 576
Dynamic perspective, 35, 39–46, 60–62, 192–96; *See also* Psychoanalysis
  and anxiety-related disorders, 169, 179–80
  and causes of abnormal behavior, 66
  and childhood disorders, 267, 269, 280, 290–91
  and homosexuality, 426–27
  and neuroses, 166
  and paraphilia, 417–18
  and personality disorders, 378, 381, 385, 389–90, 394
  and psychophysiological disorders, 157
  and stress reactions, 111–12
  and substance abuse, 477–78
Dynamic unconscious, 45; *See also* Unconscious
Dypsomania, 447
Dyslexia, 277–78
Dyspareunia, 433

Early infantile autism, 279
Eastland, James, 462
Echolalia, 279, 282
Economic change, and psychological disturbance, 72–73
ECT; *See* Electroconvulsive therapy (ECT)
Effect size, 79
Ego, 41–43
Ego defense mechanisms, 43
Ego ideal, 42
Ego-analytic psychotherapy, 499–501, 510
Ego-dystonic, 376
Ego-dystonic homosexuality, 405, 420–21, 427–28
Ego-psychology, 499–501
Ego-syntonic, 376
Elderly, 297–99
  areas of adaptation by, 305
  concepts of, 301–4
  concerns of, 310–14
  delirium in, 357
  dementia in, 346–50, 353–54
  depression in, 304–5, 315–18, 324, 329, 331
  frameworks for understanding behavior changes in, 305–9
  mental disorder prevalence in, 304–5
  organic brain disorders in, 345
  psychological assessment of, 327–29
  psychopathology in, 314–27
  seizures in, 359
  sexual dysfunction in, 436
  statistics on, 299–301
  suicide in, 211, 304, 314, 318–20
  treatment of, 329–33
Electroconvulsive therapy (ECT), 38, 206, 252, 581, 588, 593–94

Elimination disorders, 268–70
Embolism, 355, 356
Emetine, 456
Emotional atmosphere, and schizophrenia, 253–55
Empathy, 502–3
Encephalitis, 367
Encopresis, functional, 270–71
Encounter groups, 544, 549–52
Endogenous depression, 196, 206, 594
Endorphins, 37, 240
Enkephalins, 37, 481
Enuresis, functional, 268–70
Epidemiological Catchment Area Program, 71–74
Epidemiology, 71–74, 244
Epilepsy, 12, 358–60
Epinephrine, 150, 196
Equanil, 590
Ergotamine, 140
Essential hypertension; *See* Hypertension
Ethical issues, 80–81, 571–76
Ethical Principles for Psychologists, 81
Ethnocentrism, 5
Evoking stimulus, 180
Excitement phase, 429–31
Exhaustion stage, 112, 158–59
Exhibitionism, 410, 413–14, 418
Existential psychotherapy; *See* Humanistic-existential psychotherapy
Exogenous depression, 196, 206
Exorcism, 11, 25–27
Experimental analogues, 74–76, 199
Experimental groups, 74
Experimental methods
  with groups, 74–76
  with single subjects, 76
Experimental neurosis, 46

Facts on Aging Quiz, 298, 299
Failure to thrive; *See* Reactive attachment disorder of infancy
Falsifiability, 46
Familial alcoholism, 480–81
Family; *See also* Family therapy; Mother; Parents
  and childhood depression, 263
  and delinquency, 288
  and elderly, 311
  and group therapy, 546
  and homosexuality, 426–27
  and schizophrenia, 220, 233–34, 241–47, 253–55
Family therapy, 554–55
  conjoint, 555–57
  drug treatment versus, 593
  with elderly, 332
  evaluation of, 557–58
  structured, 557
Fears, childhood, 264–65; *See also* Phobias
Feelings, reflection, clarification, and expression of, 503–5
Fetal alcohol syndrome, 367–68, 449

Fetishism, 410–11, 417
Figure and ground, 505–6
Fixation, 41, 195
Flashbacks, and LSD, 465
Flooding, 180, 521–23
Fluopenazine, 582
Food and Drug Administration (FDA), 591
Forgetfulness, 355
Four As, 221–22
Fragile X syndrome, 366
Framingham study, 145, 146
Free association, 492, 496
Free-basing, 470–71
Frigidity, 428, 432
Fugue, 177
Functional age, 303
Functional psychoses, 219–20

Galen, 13
Gassner, Johann Joseph, 25–27
Gastric ulcers; *See* Ulcers
Gastrointestinal system, 134, 135, 137, 157
Gate-control model of pain, 154, 155
Genain quadruplets, 240–41
Gender identity disorders, 405–9
Gender reorientation, 408, 409
General adaptation syndrome, 112, 113, 158–59
Generalizations, 68
Generalized anxiety disorders, 170
Genetics; *See* Heredity
Genito-urinary system, 135
Genuineness, 502, 503
German measles, 367
Gestalt therapy, 501, 505–8, 539
Glia, 339
Glove anesthesia, 174–75
Graded exposure to stressor, 124–26
Grand mal seizures; *See* Seizures
Grandiose self, 390
Greece, ancient, 10–13, 18, 25, 362
Greisinger, William, 24
Group therapy, 543–44; *See also* Family therapy
  with children, 285–86
  curative factors in, 544–46
  with elderly, 331–32
  evaluation of, 552–54
  types of, 547–52
Guthrie, Woody, 351

Halidol, 583
Hallucinations
  and alcohol hallucinosis, 452–53
  and cocaine, 470
  and depression, 192
  and late-life paranoia, 320
  and organic hallucinosis, 358
  and schizophrenia, 222–28, 231, 240
  and seizures, 359
Hallucinogens, 65, 464, 477
Haloperidol, 583

Halstead-Reitan Neuropsychological Test Battery, 96
Hardiness, 122–23, 161
Hashish, 461, 463
Headache, 136–38
  migraine, 138–39, 141, 153
  tension, 138–41
  treatment of, 137, 139–42
Health psychology, 132–33
Health-related groups, 332
Hearing
  and aging, 313, 320
  and conversion disorders, 175
Heart attack, 145
Heart disease; *See* Coronary heart disease (CHD)
Hebephrenic schizophrenia, 221, 227
Hemorrhage, 355
Henry II of England, 362
Hepatolenticular degeneration, 354
Heredity
  and alcoholism, 480–81
  and Alzheimer's disease, 349
  and depression, 197–98, 315–17
  and elimination disorders, 269, 272–73
  and homosexuality, 427
  and Huntington's disease, 351–52
  and hypertension, 143
  and infantile autism, 282
  and migraine headaches, 139
  and schizophrenia transmission, 220, 232–36, 241, 247
Heresy, 14
Herodotus, 12
Heroin, 443
  effects of, 465–67, 479–80
  and treatment, 467–70
  and use of other drugs, 463, 476
High blood pressure; *See* Hypertension
High-risk methods, 76–78, 244
Hippocrates, 12, 147
Histrionic personality, 376, 379–82
Hoffer, Dr. Abraham, 65–66
Holistic perspective, 132
Homosexuality, 100
  causes of, 426–27
  as deviant behavior, 404, 405, 420–21
  ego-dystonic, 405, 420–21, 427–28
  and pedophilia, 412
  and sexual dysfunction, 436–37
  studies of, 421–26
  and transsexualism, 406–7
  and transvestism, 415–16
  unconscious, and paranoid personality, 394
Homosexuality in Perspective (Masters and Johnson), 436–37
Hospitalism; *See* Reactive attachment disorder of infancy
Hospitalization
  and bulimia, 293
  cost of, and medication use, 593
  deinstitutionalization versus, 562–65
  and economic change, 72–73
  of elderly, 304, 311, 315, 326
  involuntary, 573–74
  and lithium in drinking water, 588

Hospitalization—*Cont.*
  of mentally ill, early, 16–23, 562
  for schizophrenia, 219, 249–51
Hot lines, 565, 566
Housing, of elderly, 311
Human Sexual Inadequacy (Masters and Johnson), 433–34
Human Sexual Response, The (Masters and Johnson), 429
Humanistic perspective, 35, 57–62, 501
  on causes of abnormal behavior, 67
  and stress reactions, 113
Humanistic-existential psychotherapy, 490
  approaches to, 501–9
  effectiveness of, 536–39
  outlook in, 509–10
Huntington, George, 351
Huntington's disease, 351–53
Hydralazine, 143
Hydrochlorothiazide, 143
Hyperactivity; *See* Attention deficit disorder
Hyperbaric oxygen therapy, 332
Hypertension, 142
  causes of, 142–43, 159
  treatment of, 137, 143–45
Hypertensive arteriosclerosis, 356
Hypnosis, 25–30
Hypochondriasis, 135, 136, 139, 323
Hypotension, 356
Hypothalamus, 37, 197, 317
Hypotheses, 68, 69
Hysteria, 12, 29–30, 139; *See also* Conversion disorders
Hysterical personality. *See* Histrionic personality

Id, 41–43, 193
Identity diffusion, 397; *See also* Self-image
Idiopathic hypertension; *See* Hypertension
Idiosyncratic intoxication, 452
Idiot savants, 280
Illness; *See* Disease
Illusory correlation, 94, 99–100
Imaginative inattention, 155
Imbeciles, 363
Imipramine, 181, 205, 269
Implosive therapy, 521–23
Impotence, 428, 432
In vivo exposure, 522–23
Incidence, 71
Individuation, 497
Industrial Revolution, 16–18, 23–24
Infancy
  and infantile autism, 279–83
  reactive attachment disorder of, 261–62
Infarcts, 355–56
Infections, and mental retardation, 367
Informed consent, 80–81, 574–75
Innocent VIII, Pope, 14
Inquisition, 14–16
Insanity defense, 576

Insight therapies; *See* Humanistic-existential psychotherapy; Psychoanalysis
Insomnia, 133, 188, 190
Institute of Psychiatry, 253
Instrumental conditioning, 48–50, 53
Intelligence quotient (IQ)
  and mental retardation, 362–63, 366, 369
  and occupation, 329
Interpersonal psychotherapy, 498–99
Interpretation, psychoanalytic, 493
Interview methods, with elderly, 330
Intoxication, 358
  alcoholic, 450–52
  barbiturates, 476
Introverted personality, 376
Involuntary commitment, 573–74
Involutional melancholia, 189

Jackson v. *Indiana*, 576
Jamaican Study, 462–63
Janet, Pierre, 29
Jarvis, Edward, 19–20
Joint Commission on Mental Health and Mental Illness, 559, 562
Jones, Reverend Jim, 394–95
Juvenile delinquency, 286–88, 526–28

Kennedy, John F., 362, 559
Kerner, Justinus, 91
Klinefelter's syndrome, 366
Koro, 6
Korsakoff's psychosis, 357–58
Kraepelin, Emil, 25, 35, 221–22, 227–29

Labile hypertensives, 142
Lalling, 279
Language
  and autism, 279–80, 282
  and brain, 343, 354
  development of, in antisocial personality, 386–87
  developmental disorders of, 279
L-dopa, 353–54
Learned helplessness, 48–50, 199–201, 207–8, 317
Learning perspective, 35, 46–53, 60–62; *See also* Behavior therapy; Conditioning
  and aging, 307–9
  and anxiety-related disorders, 169–70, 180–81
  and causes of abnormal behavior, 66
  and childhood disorders, 267–73, 282, 288, 293
  and depression, 198–200, 203–4, 208
  and homosexuality, 427
  and neuroses, 166
  and paraphilia, 418–20
  and personality disorders, 380–81, 384–85, 388–89
  and psychophysiological disorders, 157–58

Learning perspective—*Cont.*
 and stress reactions, 112, 127
 and substance abuse, 479–80
Leary, Timothy, 464, 465
Legal issues, 571–76
Lesions, brain, 345
Librium, 590
Life review therapy, 330, 332
Lisping, 279
Lithium carbonate, 205–6, 588–90, 593
Little Hans, case of, 169
Lobotomies, 597
Lodges, 562–63
Logotherapy, 501, 508–9
Loose associations; *See* Associative
 disturbance
Love Canal, 120
LSD, 65, 66, 224, 443, 453, 463–65

Magnitude of effect, 79
Maintaining causal factors, 67
Maintenance phase, 585
Major tranquilizers; *See* Antipsychotic
 drugs
Malleus Maleficarum, 14–16
Manic episodes, 185–86, 188–91, 588–89;
 See also Bipolar disorders
Manic-depressive disorders, 226
MAOI; *See* Monoamine oxidase (MAO)
 inhibitors
Marathon groups, 552
Marijuana, 460–63
Marital status, and suicide, 212
Mask of Sanity, The (Cleckley), 384
Masochism; *See* Sadomasochism
Masserman, Jules, 46
Masturbation, 404, 411, 412, 418
Medical students' syndrome, 9
Meehl, Paul, 98
Melaril, 582
Memory loss; *See* Amnesia
Mendota Mental Health Institute, 563–64
Meningitis, 367
Mental health centers, 249
Mental hospital admissions; *See*
 Hospitalization
Mental illness; *See also* Abnormal
 behavior
 as myth, 38–39
 sociological perspective on, 53–57
Mental retardation
 and autism, 280
 causes of, 365–69
 definition and classification of, 362–65
 history of, 362
 prevention of, 369–70
 and remediation, 369
Mental status interview, 87–88
Meprobamates, 476, 590
Mescaline, 463, 464
Mesmer, Anton, 25–28
Meta-analysis, 78–80
Methadone treatment, 468–69
Methamphetamine, 473

Methaqualone, 476
Methedrine, 473
Methylphenidate, 473
Middle Ages, 13–16, 18, 25, 362
Migraine headaches, 138–39, 141, 153
Milestone program, 567–68
Milligan, William, 177
Miltown, 476, 590
Minimal brain dysfunction (MBD), 272
*Minnesota Multiphasic Personality
 Inventory* (MMPI), 88–90, 94, 102
Mitral valve prolapse, 171
M'Naughten, Daniel, 576
Mobility, of elderly, 311–12
Modeling, 50–52, 523–25, 538
Mongolism; *See* Down's syndrome
Moniz, Egas, 597
Monoamine oxidase (MAO) inhibitors,
 196, 205, 586, 589
Moral anxiety, 43
Moral treatment, 20–23
Moreno, Jacob, 547
Morphine, 466
Morton, Dr. Richard, 289
Mother; *See also* Family; Parents
 in object relations theory, 44–45
 and personality disorders, 389–90,
 394, 397–99
 schizophrenogenic, 243
 and school phobia, 267
 separation from, 181, 195–96
Motor cortex, 343, 345
"Mourning and Melancholia" (Freud),
 193
Multimodal therapy, 539–40
Multiple personality, 29, 177–79, 397
Multiple-infarct dementia (MID), 356
Multiaxial diagnostic system, 104–6
Musculo-skeletal system, 135, 137
Music groups, 332
Myocardial infarction, 145

Naloxone, 469
Naltrexone, 469
Narcissistic personality, 45, 376, 387–91,
 400
Narcotics, 466–67, 471
National Commission on Marijuana and
 Drug Abuse, 445, 462
National Institute of Mental Health,
 564–65
National Institute on Alcohol Abuse and
 Alcoholism, 448
National Institute on Drug Abuse, 472
National Training Laboratories (NTL),
 548
Natural disaster, and collective trauma,
 119–20
Needs, Maslow's hierarchy of, 58
Negativism, 222, 224
Nembutal, 476
Neocortex, 341–43
Neo-Freudian tradition, 490, 495–99, 510
Neuroleptic drugs, 250–52
Neurology, 24–25

Neurons, 339, 359
Neuropeptides, 37
Neuropsychological assessment, 95–96
Neuroses, 165–66, 244
 effectiveness of therapy in treating,
 511
 and Gestalt therapy, 505–6
Neurotic anxiety, 43
Neurotransmitters, 37, 196, 238, 339
New-mammalian brain; *See* Neocortex
Newsweek, 177, 590
Nicotine, 458–60
Nonbarbiturates, 475–76
Nonnormative events, 112
Norepinephrine, 196, 205
Normal science, 34
Normative events, 112
Nursing homes, 311, 324, 326

Obesity, 143
Object loss, 194–96
Object relations theory, 44–45, 499–501
 and borderline personality, 397–99
 and narcissistic personality, 388, 390
Observation, 68
Observational learning; *See* Modeling
Obsessive-compulsive disorders, 170–72,
 180, 377, 594–95
Ocholophobia, 168
O'Connor v. Donaldson, 575–76
Oedipal conflict, 169, 381, 385, 417–18,
 426, 495
Office of Technology Assessment, 449
Old mammalian brain, 341, 343
Operant conditioning, 155, 526, 531
Operational definitions, 69
Opium, 466
Opponent-process theory, 479–80
Oral stage, 477
Organic affective syndrome, 358
Organic brain syndromes, 339, 357–58
Organic delusional syndrome, 358
Organic hallucinosis, 358
Organic mental disorders
 definition and diagnosis of, 338–39
 types of, 345–61
Organic personality syndrome, 358
Organic psychoses, 219–20
Orgasm
 inhibited, 432–33
 phase of, 429–31
Overgeneralization, 198, 200

Pain
 chronic, 152–55
 control of, 28
Panic disorders, 170, 181
Paradigm clash, 34
Paradoxical intention, 509
Paralysis, conversion, 175
Paralysis agitans; *See* Parkinson's
 disease

Paranoia
  and Alzheimer's disease, 349
  in elderly, 320–23, 326
  paranoid personality versus, 393
Paranoid personality, 375, 376, 390–95
Paranoid schizophrenia, 221, 227, 231,
  393
Paranoid-antisocial personality, 394
Paranoid-compulsive personality, 394
Paranoid-narcissistic personality, 393–94
Paraphilias, 405, 410–19
Parataxic distortions, 498
Parents; *See also* Family; Mother
  abusive, 275
  and anorexia nervosa, 290–91
  and autism, 280, 282–83
  and personality disorders, 179, 378,
    384–85, 388–90, 393–94
  and schizophrenia transmission, 220,
    233–34
  and transsexualism, 407
Parkinson's disease, 353–55
Participant modeling, 524–25, 538
Passive-aggressive personality, 377
Pasteur, Louis, 35
Patienthood, 53–57
Pavlov, Ivan, 46, 47, 112, 166
Pedophilia, 411–12, 417–18
Pellagra, 39
Pemoline, 273
Pentobarbitol, 476
Pepsinogen, 152, 159
Peptic ulcers; *See* Ulcers
Personality; *See also* Personality
    disorders
  antisocial, 376, 382–87
  avoidant, 376
  borderline, 376, 395–400
  compulsive, 377–79, 400
  hardiness in, 161
  histrionic, 376, 379–82
  and hypertension, 143
  introverted, 376
  and migraine headaches, 139
  multiple, 29, 177–79, 397
  narcissistic, 45, 376, 378–91, 400
  and organic personality syndrome, 358
  paranoid, 375, 376, 390–95
  passive-aggressive, 377
  projective tests of, 88–94
  schizotypal, 376
  and substance abuse, 443–44, 477–78
  Type A/Type B, 145–47, 161
  and ulcers, 152
Personality disorders, 45
  definition and classification of, 375–
    400
  and schizophrenia compared, 226
  treatment of, 400
PET scan, 240–41
Peyote, 464
Pharmacolysis, 585
Phenobarbital, 590
Phenomenological approach, 501, 506
Phenothiazines, 238, 250–52, 327
Phenylketonuria (PKU), 366, 370

Phobias, 166–70, 180–81
  and behavior therapy, 517–24, 536
  childhood, 264–65
  school, 266–68
Physical fitness, and hypertension, 143
Pibloktoq, 6
Pick's disease, 347, 350
Pinel, Philippe, 18–19, 23, 25, 559
Placebo effect, 66, 174
Plateau phase, 429–31
Pleasure principle, 42
Pleasuring exercises, 435–36
Poetry groups, 332
Politics, 382, 395
Polygenetic threshold model, 236, 238
Positron emission tomography, 240–41
Posttraumatic stress disorders, 117–22
Poverty, and schizophrenia, 244–46
Pratt, Joseph, 547
Precipitating causal factors, 67
Preconscious processes, 40
Predisposing causal factors, 67
Pregnancy, anxiety during, 161
Premack principle, 208–10
Premature birth, 368–69
Premature ejaculation, 428, 433
Premorbid adjustment, 229–30
Presbycusis, 313
Presbyopia, 313
President's Commission on Mental
    Health, 568, 570
Prevalence, 71
Prevention, 566–71
Primary hypertension; *See* Hypertension
Primary Mental Health Project, 570, 571
Primary reading disability; *See* Dyslexia
Prisons, 349–50
Problem drinkers, 448
Process schizophrenia, 229
Prochlorperazine, 582
Prodromal symptoms, 138–39
Prognosis, 229
Progressive relaxation, 518
Projection, 44, 385, 393, 394, 398
Projective identification, 398
Projective tests
  interpreting, 99–102
  types of, 90–94
Prolixin, 582
Propranodol, 143
Pseudodementia, 318, 329
Psilocybin, 464, 465
Psychedelics; *See* Hallucinogens
Psychiatric Evaluation Form, 87–89
Psychiatry, development of, 25, 29–31
Psychoactive drugs, 38
Psychoanalysis, 18, 30, 40–46, 166; *See
    also* Dynamic perspective; Object
    relations theory
  contemporary developments in, 44–46,
    495–501
  criticisms of, 501, 510
  effectiveness of, 511, 536–39
  in family therapy, 554
  Freudian, 40–44, 492–95
  fundamental rule of, 492

Psychoanalysis—*Cont.*
  in group therapy, 544
  and neuroses, 166
Psychodiagnostik (Rorschach), 91
Psychodrama, 547–48
Psychodynamic perspective; *See*
    Dynamic perspective
Psychological age, 303
Psychological assessment, 86–87
  diagnosis as part of, 102–7
  of elderly, 327–29
  problems in, 98–102
  procedures in, 87–98
Psychological disability, 5
Psychological tests
  interpreting, 99–102
  types of, 88–94
Psychological view of abnormal
    behavior, 18, 25–31
Psychology Today, 437
Psychopathic personality; *See* Antisocial
    personality
Psychophysiological disorders, 133–34
  common types of, 136–55
  distinguishing features of, 135–36
  range of, 134–35
  theories of, 155–62
Psychoses
  and borderline personality, 395, 396
  epidemiology of, 244
  functional, 219–20
  organic, 219–20
Psychosexual dysfunctions, 428
  explanations/assessments of, 431–32
  and sexual response cycle, 428–31
  treatment of, 433–37
  types of, 432–33
Psychosexual stages, 41
Psychosurgery, 38, 594–98
Psychotherapy, 487–89; *See also specific
    therapies*
  and biological treatments, 582, 588,
    590, 593
  client-therapist relationship in, 489–
    91
  common factors in, 537–39
  and depression, 205–10, 264
  dynamic, 491–501
  eclectic system of, 539–40
  effectiveness of, 78–80, 511–12
  for elderly, 325, 329–32
  ethical issues in, 571–76
  for headache treatment, 139–41
  for hypertension, 144
  insight versus behavioral approaches
    to, 536–37
  LSD in, 464–65
  and schizophrenia, 252–53
  and school phobia, 267–68
  sexual, 433–37
  for Type A behavior pattern
    modification, 146
  for ulcer treatment, 152
Psychotomimetic drugs, 65
Psychotropic drugs, 325–26
Public Mental Health Act, 559

Quaalude, 476

Rape; *See* Sexual assault
Rational Emotive Therapy (RET), 533–36
Rationalization, 43–44
Reaction formation, 44
Reactive attachment disorder of infancy, 261–62
Reactive schizophrenia, 229
Reading, developmental disorder in, 277–78
Reality anxiety, 43
Reality orientation groups, 332
Reality principle, 42
Reds, 476
Reflection of feelings, 503
Reform movement, 18–23
Refractory period, 430
Reinforcements, 48
Relaxation Response, The (Benson), 144
Relaxation training, 139, 141, 144, 208
Remarriage, 263
Reminiscing groups, 332
Remotivation therapy, 332
Renaissance, 16, 17
Report of the Hypertension Task Force, 142, 143
Repression, 43, 381, 492–94
Reptilian brain, 341, 343
Research methods
    and ethical issues, 80–81
    meta-analysis of results of, 78–80
    types of, 68–78
Reserpine, 143
Resistance
    in psychoanalysis, 494–95
    as stress reaction stage, 112, 158–59
Resolution phase, 429–31
Respiratory system, 135, 137
Response prevention, 522
Retirement, 305, 310–11, 317
Retrograde amnesia, 345
Review Panel on Coronary-Prone Behavior and Coronary Heart Disease, 146
Rh factors, and mental retardation, 369
Rheumatoid arthritis, 137, 153
Right to treatment, 575–76
Risk, undue, 80–81
Ritalin, 273
Rogers v. *Okin*, 575
Role playing, 525–27, 547–48
Role reversal, 547–48
Rome, ancient, 11–13, 18, 362
Rorschach, Hermann, 91
Rorschach Test, 91, 94, 99, 100, 395
Rubella, 367

Sadism; *See* Sadomasochism
Sadomasochism, 416–18
Salem witch trials, 15, 381
San Francisco Study, 422–26
Scale for suicidal ideation, 215

Scapegoating, 14–16
Schemas, 198–99, 206–7
Schizoaffective schizophrenia, 228
Schizophrenia, 219–20
    biological basis of, 36–37, 39, 60, 65–66, 232–41
    childhood, 283, 284
    as classification, 104, 227–32
    description of, 220–27
    in elderly, 304, 326–27
    ethics in treating, 573
    family/society as contexts for, 241–46
    high-risk method in studying, 77–78
    as label, 54–55
    multiple personality versus, 178
    organic delusional syndrome versus, 358
    and suicide, 210
    treatment of, 206, 249–55, 582–86, 589, 593–96
    vulnerability model of, 247–48
Schizotypal personality, 376
School phobia, 266–68
Science, 56
Science and Human Behavior (Skinner), 46
Scientific concept, 104
Scribotherapy, 332
Secobarbitol, 476
Seconal, 476
Sedative-hypnotics, 475–77
Seizures, 358–61
Selective abstraction, 198
Self
    grandiose, 390
    Jungian, 497
Self-actualization
    Maslow on, 58
    Rogers on, 57–59, 505, 510
Self-control desensitization, 519
Self-control techniques, 531–33
Self-esteem
    and depression, 198–200, 207
    in elderly, 309–11
    and group therapy, 546
Self-image
    in borderline personality, 397–99
    in narcissistic personality, 388–90
Self-objects, 388–90
Seneca, 447
Senescence, 303–4
Senile dementia, 315, 318; *See also* Alzheimer's disease
Sensate focus, 435–36
Sensory cortex, 343
Separation anxiety; *See also* Object loss
    as childhood disorder, 107, 266–68
    and panic disorders, 181
    as phase, 45
Serax, 590
Sex change operations, 406–9
Sex differences
    and aging, 313
    and alcohol use, 325, 448, 450
    and anxiety disorders, 170
    and child abuse, 275, 276

Sex differences—*Cont.*
    and childhood disorders, 260, 265, 270, 272, 278, 284, 290, 292
    and depression, 188–90, 198
    and life expectancy, 299, 313
    and personality disorders, 380–82
    and psychological disorders, 71–74
    and sexual behavior, 408, 414, 415, 422
    and suicide, 212, 319
Sex-role stereotypes, 100–101
Sexual abuse
    of children, 276–77
    and multiple personality, 179
Sexual assault, 120–22, 127
Sexuality; *See also* Homosexuality; Psychosexual dysfunctions
    and culture, 404–5
    and gender disorders, 405–9
    and histrionic personality, 379–80
    and narcissistic personality, 388
    and paraphilias, 405, 410–19
    and psychoanalysis, 492, 495, 496
    response cycle in, 428–31
Simple phobia, 167
Skin
    and glove anesthesia, 174
    and hypnotic suggestion, 29
    and psychophysiological disorders, 135
Social age, 303
Social class
    and mental retardation, 369
    and schizophrenia, 244–46
Social Class and Mental Illness (Hollingshead and Redlich), 244
Social disability, 5
Social drift hypothesis, 245–46
Social learning theory, 50–52, 533, 538, 540
Social perspective; *See* Sociological perspective
Social phobia, 167
Social Readjustment Rating Scale, 160
Social roles, of women, 189
Social support
    and stress, 123–24
    and suicide, 212, 215
Social-breakdown syndrome, 309
Sociological perspective, 35, 53–57, 60–62
    and aging, 309
    and causes of abnormal behavior, 67
    and stress reactions, 112, 160–62
    and substance abuse, 478–79
Sociopathic personality; *See* Antisocial personality
Sodium lactate, 181
Somatic weakness hypothesis, 159
Somatization disorders, 173–74
Somatoform disorders
    treatment of, 179–81
    types of, 172–75
Sopor, 476
Sour grapes rationalization, 43–44
Specific emotion hypothesis, 157
Speed cycle, 474–75

Sphygmomanometer, 142
Splitting, 397–99
Stabilization phase, 585
Status asthmaticus, 148
Stelazine, 582
Stimulants
  examples of, 458–59, 470, 473–75
  and hyperactivity, 273
  and reinforcement, 479
Stocking anesthesia, 174–75
Stress
  and adjustment disorders, 113–17
  aging and adaptation to, 306–7
  and alcoholism, 479
  and asthma, 148
  definitions of, 113
  and depression, 197
  and headaches, 139
  and hypertension, 143
  perspectives on, 111–13
  and posttraumatic disorders, 117–22
  and psychophysiological disorders,
    132–35, 158–62
  social, and schizophrenia, 245–46
  and ulcers, 133, 151–52
  vulnerability to, 122–26
Stress inoculation training, 126–27, 534–
  36
Stress management training, 144–46
Stress of Life, The (Selye), 112
Strokes, 355
Structured family therapy, 557
Stupor, 222, 224
Subcortical dementing disorders, 350–56
Subjective distress, 4–5
Substance abuse, 441–42; *See also*
  Alcohol abuse
  common factors in, 443–45
  and depression, 188
  in elderly, 324–25
  explanations of, 477–81
  substance dependance versus, 445–46
  types of, 447–77
  and withdrawal, 358
Substantia nigra, 353–54
Suicide
  and bereavement, 115
  childhood and adolescent, 264
  and depression, 188, 204, 210, 588, 594
  and economic change, 72
  in elderly, 211, 304, 314, 318–20
  and involuntary commitment, 573
  predictors of, 213–15
  risk of, 210–13
  and suicidal ideation, 215
Suicide prevention services, 565, 566
Superego, 41–43, 262, 385
Surgery, for pain control, 154–55; *See*
  also Psychosurgery
Susto, 6
Sweet lemon rationalization, 43–44
Symptoms
  and Freud, 40
  instrumental conditioning of, 48

Synanon, 469–70, 547
Syphilis, 367
Systematic desensitization, 28, 180,
  517–21, 523, 528, 593

Tardive dyskinesia, 584
Tay-Sachs disease, 366–67
Tension headaches, 138–41
T-groups, 548–49
Thematic Apperception Test (TAT), 93–
  94
Theophylline, 150
Therapeutic communities, 469–70
Third variable, 69–71
Thorazine, 582
Thoridazine, 582
Thought disorders; *See* Associative
  disturbance
Three Faces of Eve, The (Thigpen and
  Cleckley), 178
Thrombosis, 355
Tics, 175
Tobacco, 443, 458–60
Toilet training, 378
Token economy, 527–29, 531, 532
Tolerance
  drug, 446
  smoking, 459
Tonic stage, 359
Toxic agents, and mental retardation,
  367
Toxic psychosis, 357
Training in Community Living, 563–64
Tranquilizers, major; *See* Antipsychotic
  drugs
Transactional perspective, 162
Transcutaneous nerve stimulation
  (TENS), 154
Transferability of indulgences, 444
Transference, 494
Transient cognitive disorder, 357
Transitions, 306
Transsexualism, 405–9
Transvestism, 411, 414–16, 418
Trauma
  brain disorders from, 345–46
  mental retardation from, 369
Treatment and Education of Autistic
  and related Communications-
  handicapped Children (TEACCH),
  282–83
Trephining, 10–11
Tricyclic antidepressants, 205, 586–88,
  592, 593
Trifluoperazine, 582
Tuinal, 476
Tuke, William, 19, 25
Turner's syndrome, 366
Twin studies; *See also* Heredity
  and alcoholism, 480–81
  and homosexuality, 427
  and psychophysiological disorders, 159
  and schizophrenia, 36, 234–36, 241

Two-chair technique, 507
Type A behavior pattern, 145–47,
  161

Ulcerative colitis, 137
Ulcers, 133, 134, 150
  causes of, 150–52, 157–59
  treatment of, 137, 152
Unconditional positive regard, 502, 503
Unconscious
  collective, 496
  and Freudian psychoanalysis, 30, 40–
    41, 45, 491–95
  and implosive therapy, 521
  regulative activity of, 497
Unemployment, 115–17, 561
Uniform Crime Reports, 286
United States v. *Brawner*, 576
Urine alarm, 270
Urticaria, 137
U.S. Department of Health, Education,
  and Welfare, 463, 474
U.S. Department of Justice, 286
U.S. Office of Vital Statistics, 264
U.S. Public Health Service, 324

Vaginismus, 433
Valium, 475–76, 590
Vicarious conditioning, 50–51
Vicious-circle effects, 158
Victorian Age, 16–18, 30–31
Video games, and seizures, 360, 361
Vietnam combat veterans, studies of,
  117–19, 480
Vinci, Leonardo da, 91
Violation of accepted social rules/norms,
  5
Vision
  and aging, 313
  and conversion disorders, 174–75
Visual cortex, 343
Voyeurism, 412–13, 417

Weight Watchers, 547
Weight-reduction program, 532–33
Widow to Widow program, 123
Widowhood, 123, 313–14, 329–30
Wilson's disease, 354
Witch Hammer, The, 14–16
Witch hunts, 14–16
Withdrawal, 358, 445, 446
  alcohol, 452
  drug, 466, 470, 474, 476, 479, 481
  tobacco, 459, 460
Women; *See* Sex differences
Woodward, Samuel, 23
World Health Organization, 104, 142,
  219, 448
Writer's cramp, 175

Zoophobia, 168

About the Authors

Richard H. Price is a professor of psychology and chairs the Community Psychology Program at The University of Michigan. He graduated from Lawrence College in 1962 and earned his M.A. and Ph.D. from the University of Illinois in 1965 and 1966, respectively. He is Director of the Michigan Prevention Research Center and a faculty associate with the Social Environment and Health Program, both at The University of Michigan. Dr. Price has written or coauthored ten books, including *Psychology and Community Change, Principles of Psychology,* and *Prevention in Community Health: Research, Policy, and Practice.* He is active in the American Psychological Association and has served as a consulting editor for the *Journal of Abnormal Psychology, American Journal of Community Psychology,* and *Journal of Applied Developmental Psychology.*

Steven Jay Lynn is associate professor of psychology at The Ohio University. He received his B.A. from The University of Michigan in 1967 and his Ph.D. from Indiana University in 1976. He completed an NIMH post-doctoral clinical fellowship at Lafayette Clinic in Detroit. Dr. Lynn has published a total of over three dozen articles and book chapters on psychotherapy, depression, behavior medicine, and hypnosis. He is coeditor, with John P. Garske, of *Contemporary Psychotherapies: Models and Methods.* Beyond his academic commitments, Dr. Lynn is a consultant with the American Lung Association, is active in the American Psychological Association, and is a consulting clinical psychologist and clinical practitioner.

A NOTE ON THE TYPE

The text of this book was set in a film version of 10 point Century Schoolbook. Century Schoolbook is based on Century Expanded, a variation of the original face in the family Century Roman, which was drawn in 1894 by Lynn B. Benton and Theodore De Vinne for *The Century* magazine. Wider, with less variation between thicks and thins than Century Expanded, Century Schoolbook is classified a "Modern" typeface because of its symmetry, vertical stress, and sharply bracketed serifs. All these traits combine to make Century Schoolbook a bold, readable typeface.

Composed by Carlisle Graphics, Dubuque, Iowa.

Printed and bound by The Maple Press Company, York, Pennsylvania.